WHO'S WHO IN
BRITISH HISTORY

BEGINNINGS TO 1901

VOLUME 2

WHO'S WHO IN
BRITISH HISTORY

BEGINNINGS TO 1901

VOLUME 2
I-Z

General Editor
Geoffrey Treasure

Authors and Contributors
Ian Dawson • Roger Ellis
Richard Fletcher • Michael Hicks
Peter Hill • Peter Holmes
C. R. N. Routh • Geoffrey Treasure
Christopher Tyerman • Stephen Wright

FITZROY DEARBORN PUBLISHERS
LONDON • CHICAGO

This library edition published in 1998 by Fitzroy Dearborn Publishers
by arrangement with Shepheard-Walwyn (Publishers), London

Most of the entries in this edition were first published by
Shepheard-Walwyn (Publishers), London, between 1988 and 1997,
in eight volumes, chronologically arranged from Roman to Victorian times.

FITZROY DEARBORN PUBLISHERS
70 East Walton Street
Chicago, Illinois 60611
USA

or

11 Rathbone Place
London W1P 1DE
England

British Library Cataloguing in Publication Data
Who's who in British history
   1. British – Biography   2. Great Britain – Biography
   3. Great Britain – History
   I. Treasure, G. R. R. (Geoffrey Russell Richards)
   941'.0099

   ISBN 1-884964-90-7

Library of Congress Cataloging in Publication Data is available

First published in the USA and UK 1998

Front cover image:
Parliament in the Reign of Elizabeth I

Typeset by Alacrity, Banwell Castle, Weston-super-Mare, UK
Printed in the USA by Braun-Brumfield, Inc, Ann Arbor, Michigan

CONTENTS

ALPHABETICAL LIST OF ENTRIES

Dugdale, Sir William 1605-1686
Dunbar, William 1460(*c.*)-1513(*c.*)
Duncan I 1010(*c.*)-1040
Duncan, Adam (Viscount Duncan of Camperdown) 1731-1804
Dundas, Henry (Lord Melville) 1742-1811
Dunning, John (1st Baron Ashburton) 1731-1783
Dunstan, St 910(*c.*)-988
du Puiset, Hugh 1120/25(*c.*)-1195
Duras, Louis (2nd Earl of Feversham) 1640?-1719

Eadbert 768(*d.*)
Eadmer 1125(*d.c.*)
Eadred 924(*c.*)-955
Eadric Streona 1017(*d.*)
Eadwig or Edwy 940(*c.*)-959
Ealdred 1069(*d.*)
Easton, Adam 1325(*c.*)-1397
Eastry, Henry 1331(*d.*)
Ecgfrith 645-685
Edgar 943-975
Edgar Atheling 1057(*c.*)-1125(*c.*)
Edgeworth, Maria 1767-1849
Edington, William 1310(*c.*)-1366
Edmund 921-946
Edmund, St 870(*d.*)
Edmund Crouchback (Earl of Lancaster and Leicester) 1245-1296
Edmund Ironside 1016(*d.*)
Edward I 1239-1307
Edward II 1284-1327
Edward III 1312-1377
Edward IV 1442-1483
Edward V 1470-1483
Edward VI 1537-1553
Edward the Black Prince or Edward of Woodstock 1330-1376
Edward the Confessor, St 1005?-1066
Edward the Elder 872(*c.*)-924
Edward the Martyr, St 963(*c.*)-978
Edwards, Thomas 1599-1647
Edwin 585-633
Egbert 766(*d.*)
Egbert 839(*d.*)
Egbert of Iona 639-729
Egerton, Francis (3rd Duke of Bridgewater) 1736-1803
Eleanor of Aquitaine 1122(*c.*)-1204
Eleanor of Provence 1291(*d.*)
Elias of Dereham 1188-1245(*fl.*)

Eliot, George 1819-1880
Eliot, Sir John 1592-1632
Eliott, George Augustus (1st Baron Heathfield) 1717-1790
Elizabeth I 1533-1603
Elizabeth (Princess) 1596-1662
Elizabeth of York 1465-1503
Elphinstone, Mountstuart 1779-1859
Elstob, Elizabeth 1683-1756
Emma 1052(*d.*)
Empson, Sir Richard 1450(*c.*)-1510
Erasmus, Desiderius 1466?-1536
Eric Bloodaxe 954(*d.*)
Ernest Augustus (Duke of Cumberland and Teviotdale, King of Hanover) 1771-1851
Erskine, John (11th Earl of Mar) 1675-1732
Erskine, Thomas (1st Baron Erskine) 1750-1823
Espec, Walter 1153/58(*d.*)
Ethelbald 757(*d.*)
Ethelbert 616(*d.*)
Ethelflaed 918(*d.*)
Ethelfrith 616(*d.*)
Ethelred 911(*d.*)
Ethelred II 966(*c.*)-1016
Ethelweard 999(*d.c.*)
Ethelwold, St 910(*c.*)-984
Ethelwulf 858(*d.*)
Evelyn, John 1620-1706

Fairfax, Sir Thomas (later 3rd Baron Fairfax) 1612-1671
Faraday, Michael 1791-1867
Fastolf, Sir John 1378(*c.*)-1459
Fawcett, Dame Millicent 1847-1929
Fawkes, Guy 1570-1605
Fell, John 1625-1686
Fell, Margaret 1614-1702
Felton, John 1595?-1628
Fenner, George 1618(*d.*)
Fenton, Edward 1603(*d.*)
Fenwick, Sir John 1645?-1697
Ferguson, Robert 1714(*d.*)
Ferrar, Nicholas 1592-1637
Ferrar, Robert 1504(*c.*)-1555
Fielding, Henry 1707-1754
Fiennes, Celia 1662-1741
Finch, Daniel (2nd Earl of Nottingham) 1647-1730
Fisher, John 1469-1535
Fitch, Ralph 1550?-1611
FitzCount, Brian 1147/49(*d.*)
FitzGerald, Lord Edward 1763-1798

FitzHerbert, William 1154(*d.*)
FitzNeal (or FitzNigel), Richard 1130(*c.*)-1198
FitzOsbern, William 1071(*d.*)
FitzOsbert, William 1196(*d.*)
FitzPeter, Geoffrey 1213(*d.*)
FitzRalph, Richard 1300(*c.*)-1360
Fitzroy, Augustus Henry (3rd Duke of Grafton) 1735-1811
FitzRoy, Geoffrey 1151/53-1212
Fitzroy, Henry (Duke of Richmond) 1519-1536
Fitzroy Somerset, Lord (1st Baron Raglan) 1788-1855
FitzWalter, Robert 1170?(*c.*)-1235
Flaxman, John 1755-1826
Fleetwood, Charles 1618-1692
Fletcher, John William 1729-1785
Foliot, Gilbert 1105/10-1188
Forbes, Duncan 1685-1747
Forest, John 1470/74-1538
Forster, William 1818-1886
Fortescue, Sir John 1390(*c.*)-1476
Forz, Isabella (Countess of Devon and Aumale) 1236(*c.*)-1293
Fox, Charles James 1749-1806
Fox, Richard 1447?-1528
Fox Talbot, W. H. 1800-1877
Foxe (or Fox), John 1517-1587
Francis, Sir Philip 1740-1818
Fraser, Simon (12th Baron Lovat) 1667?-1747
Frederick Augustus (Duke of York) 1763-1827
Free, John, alias Phreas 1430(*c.*)-1465
Frere, Sir H. Bartle 1815-1884
Frideswide, St 7th-8th century?
Frith, John 1503-1533
Frith, William Powell 1819-1909
Frobisher, Sir Martin 1539-1594
Froissart, Jean 1334(*c.*)-1405
Fry, Elizabeth 1780-1845
Fuller, Thomas 1608-1661
Fursa, St or Fursey 620-645(*fl.c.*)

Gainsborough, Thomas 1727-1788
Gardiner, Allen Francis 1794-1852

Gardiner, Stephen 1497?-1555
Garrick, David 1717-1779
Gascoigne, Dr Thomas 1403(*c.*)-1458
Gascoyne-Cecil, Robert (3rd Marquis of Salisbury) 1830-1903
Gaskell, Elizabeth 1810-1865
Gaunt, Elizabeth 1685(*d.*)
Gaveston, Piers (Earl of Cornwall) 1312(*d.*)
Gay, John 1685-1732
Geoffrey of Brittany 1158-1186
Geoffrey of Coutances 1093(*d.*)
Geoffrey of Monmouth 1154/55(*d.*)
George I 1660-1727
George II 1683-1760
George III 1738-1820
George IV 1762-1830
George (Duke of Clarence) 1449-1478
George of Denmark (Prince) 1653-1708
Gerald of Wales 1146-1223
Gerard, Father John 1564-1637
Germanus, St 375(*c.*)-437
Gibbon, Edward 1737-1794
Gibbons, Orlando 1538-1625
Gibbs, James 1682-1754
Gibson, Edmund 1669-1748
Gideon, Sampson 1699-1762
Gilbert of Sempringham 1083/89-1189
Gilbert, Sir Humphrey 1539?-1583
Gilbert, Thomas 1720-1798
Gilbert, Sir William Schwenck 1836-1911
Gildas 490-520?(*fl.c.*)
Gillray, James 1756-1815
Girtin, Thomas 1775-1802
Gladstone, William Ewart 1809-1898
Glanvill, Ranulf 1120/30-1190
Goddard, Jonathan 1617?-1675
Godfrey, Sir Edmund Berry 1621-1678
Godiva, Lady, properly Godgifu 11th century
Godolphin, Sidney (1st Earl of Godolphin) 1645-1712
Godric of Finchale 1170(*d.*)
Godwin 1053(*d.*)
Godwin, William 1756-1836
Goldsmith, Oliver 1728-1774
Gordon, Charles George 1833-1885
Gordon, Lord George 1751-1793

CHRONOLOGICAL LIST OF ENTRIES

BC310(*fl.c.*)	Pytheas of Marseilles
BC102-44	Caesar, Gaius Julius
BC54(*fl.c.*)	Cassivellaunus
BC10-AD54	Claudius, properly Tiberius Claudius Drusus Nero Germanicus
AD5-41(*fl.c.*)	Cunobelin
40-52(*fl.*)	Caratacus
61(*d.*)	Boadicea
43-85(*fl.c.*)	Cogidubnus, Tiberius Claudius
40-93	Agricola, Gnaeus Julius
76-138	Hadrianus, Publius Aelius
3rd century?	St Alban
211(*d.*)	Severus, Lucius Septimius
293(*d.*)	Carausius, Marcus Aurelius Mausaeus
275(*c.*)-337	Constantinus, Flavius Valerius
388(*d.*)	Maximus, Magnus Clemens
411(*d.*)	Constantine III
4th-5th century?	Cunedda
380-420(*fl.c.*)	Pelagius
375(*c.*)-437	St Germanus
384-423	Honorius, Flavius Augustus
5th century?	Arthur
5th century?	Aurelianus, Ambrosius
5th century?	St Ninian or Nynia
425-455?(*fl.c.*)	Vortigern
415?(*c.*) 493?	St Patrick
450?(*fl.c.*)	Hengist
480?(*fl.c.*)	Aelle
490-530?(*fl.c.*)	Cerdic
490-520?(*fl.c.*)	Gildas
6th century	St Illtud
540/550(*d.c.*)	Gwrthefyr (Vortiporix)
549(*d.c.*)	Maelgwyn Gwynedd
560(*d.c.*)	Ida
588?(*d.*)	Aelle
593(*d.*)	Ceawlin
522(*c.*)-597	St Columba or Columcille
530(*c.*)-590(*c.*)	St David
540(*c.*)-604	St Gregory the Great
585-633	Edwin
7th-8th century?	St Frideswide
604/609(*d.*)	St Augustine
616(*d.*)	Ethelbert
616(*d.*)	Ethelfrith
627?(*d.*)	Redwald
602?-690	St Theodore of Tarsus
620-645(*fl.c.*)	St Fursa or Fursey
627(*fl.c.*)	Coifi
614-680	St Hilda
642(*d.*)	St Oswald
644(*d.*)	Paulinus
648(*d.c.*)	St Birinus
651(*d.*)	St Aidan
655(*d.*)	Penda
664(*d.*)	St Cedd
670(*d.*)	Oswy
672(*d.*)	St Chad or Ceadda
675?(*d.c.*)	Agilbert
628?-689	Biscop, Benedict
634-709	St Wilfrid
634(*c.*)-687	St Cuthbert
639-729	Egbert of Iona
660-680(*fl.c.*)	Caedmon
642-716	Ceolfrith
645-685	Ecgfrith
658-739	St Willibrord
659(*c.*)-689	Cadwalla
705(*d.*)	Aldfrith
709/710(*d.*)	St Aldhelm
709/710(*d.*)	Hadrian
725(*d.*)	Wihtred
726(*d.*after)	Ine
732?(*d.*)	Albinus
673(*c.*)-735	St Bede
739(*d.*)	Nothelm
740(*d.*)	Acca
745(*d.*)	Daniel
675(*c.*) 754	St Boniface
675(*c.*)-714	St Guthlac
757(*d.*)	Ethelbald
758(*d.*)	Cuthbert
764(*d.*)	Ceolwulf
766(*d.*)	Egbert
768(*d.*)	Eadbert
780(*d.*)	Albert
780(*d.c.*)	St Leoba
718-764(*fl.c.*)	Cuthbert
700(*c.*)-786	St Willibald
786(*d.*)	St Lullus or Lul
789(*d.*)	St Willehad
796(*d.*)	Offa
Early 9th century?	Nennius
9th century?	Cynewulf
804(*d.*)	Alcuin
812(*d.c.*)	St Cynehelm or Kenelm
839(*d.*)	Egbert
849(*d.*)	St Wigstan or Wystan
852/856?(*d.*)	Ragnar Lothbrok
858(*d.*)	Ethelwulf
858(*d.*)	Kenneth I (MacAlpin)

1376(*c.*)-1447	Beaufort, Henry
1378(*c.*)-1459	Fastolf, Sir John
1378(*c.*)-1449	Hungerford, Lord Walter
1378(*c.*)-1417	Oldcastle, Sir John (Lord Cobham)
1380(*c.*)-1455	Payne, Master Peter
1380(*c.*)-1460	Savernake, William
1382-1439	Beauchamp, Richard (Earl of Warwick)
1387-1422	Henry V
1387(*c.*)-1453	Talbot, John (Earl of Shrewsbury and Waterford)
1388-1428	Montagu, Thomas (Earl of Salisbury)
1389-1435	John (Duke of Bedford)
1390-1447	Humphrey (Duke of Gloucester)
1390(*c.*)-1476	Fortescue, Sir John
1390(*c.*)-1460	Pecock, Reginald
1390(*c.*)-1465	Whetehamstede, John
1394-1437	James I (King of Scots)
1394(*c.*)-1456	Cromwell, Ralph (3rd Lord Cromwell)
1394(*c.*)-1486	Wayneflete, William
1428(*fl.*)	Baxter, Margery
1395(*c.*)-1455(*c.*)	Somerset, Master John
1396-1450	de la Pole, William
1450(*d.*)	Cade, Jack
1400(*c.*)-1454	Cobham, Eleanor (Duchess of Gloucester)
1400(*c.*)-1450	Moleyns, Adam
1400(*c.*)-1460	Neville, Richard (Earl of Salisbury)
1402-1474	Canynges, William
1402-1460	Stafford, Humphrey (Duke of Buckingham)
1403(*c.*)-1458	Gascoigne, Dr Thomas
1459(*d.*)	Soper, William
1406(*c.*)-1455	Beaufort, Edmund (Duke of Somerset)
1407(*c.*)-1478	Hopton, John
1408?(*b.*)	Blacman, Master John
1469(*d.*)	Herbert, William (Earl of Pembroke)
1471(*d.*)	Malory, Sir Thomas
1410(*c.*)-1468	Brome, John
1410(*c.*)-1478	Cook, Sir Thomas
1410(*c.*)-1469	Wydeville, Richard (Earl Rivers)
1411-1460	Richard (Duke of York)
1411(*c.*)-1491	Rous, John
1478(*d.*)	Margaret, Lady Hungerford
1415-1495	Neville, Cecily (Duchess of York)
1415-1483(*c.*)	Worcester, William, alias Botoner
1415(*c.*)-1491	Caxton, William
1420(*c.*)-1461	Butler, James (Earl of Wiltshire and Ormond)
1420(*c.*)-1490	Clervaux, Sir Richard
1420(*c.*)-1479	Hall, John
1420(*c.*)-1482	Paston, Margaret
1420?-1500	Morton, John
1421-1471	Henry VI
1421-1466	Paston, John
1427(*c.*)-1470	Tiptoft, John (Earl of Worcester)
1428-1471	Neville, Richard (Earl of Warwick and Salisbury)
1430-1460	James II (King of Scots)
1430-1482	Margaret of Anjou
1430(*c.*)-1465	Free, John, alias Phreas
1431(*c.*)-1483	Hastings, Lord William
1431(*c.*)-1495	Tudor, Jasper (Duke of Bedford and Earl of Pembroke)
1432(*c.*)-1476	Neville, George
1435?(*c.*)-1505(*c.*)	Henryson, Robert
1436-1464	Beaufort, Henry (Duke of Somerset)

1439(*c.*)-1500	Kebell, Thomas
15th century	Cabot, John
1440(*c.*)-1498	Ambrose, Christopher
1440(*c.*)-1483	Catesby, William
1440(*c.*)-1492	Wydeville, Elizabeth
1442-1483	Edward IV
1442(*c.*)-1483	Wydeville, Anthony
1443-1509	Beaufort, Margaret
1443-1524	Howard, Thomas (Earl of Surrey, 2nd Duke of Norfolk)
1443(*c.*)-1513	Vere, John (Earl of Oxford)
1445-1502	Tyrell, Sir James
1514(*d.*)	Hunne, Richard
1447?-1528	Fox, Richard
1449-1478	George (Duke of Clarence)
1449(*c.*)-1489	Percy, Henry (4th Earl of Northumberland)
1449(*c.*)-1494	Stonor, Sir William
1450(*c.*)-1510	Empson, Sir Richard
1450?-1532	Warham, William
1485(*d.*)	Howard, John
1451-1488	James III (King of Scots)
1452-1485	Richard III
1457-1509	Henry VII
1457(*c.*)-1483	Stafford, Henry (Duke of Buckingham)
1458(*c.*)-1489	Cely, George
1460(*c.*)-1513(*c.*)	Dunbar, William
1460?-1524	Linacre, Thomas
1462?-1510	Dudley, Edmund
1465-1503	Elizabeth of York
1535(*d.*)	Standish, Henry
1466/67-1519	Colet, John
1466?-1536	Erasmus, Desiderius
1467-1537	Darcy, Lord Thomas
1538(*d.*)	Lambert, John
1469-1535	Fisher, John
1470-1483	Edward V
1470(*c.*)-1555	Vergil, Polydore
1470/74-1538	Forest, John
1473-1513	James IV (King of Scots)
1473(*c.*)-1530	Wolsey, Thomas
1474-1559	Tunstal, Cuthbert
1474(*c.*)-1499	Warbeck, Perkin
1475?-1525	Simnel, Lambert
1478-1535	More, Sir Thomas
1484?-1557	Cabot, Sebastian
1485-1536	Catherine of Aragon
1485?-1540	Cromwell, Thomas
1485?-1555	Latimer, Hugh
1486-1502	Arthur (Prince of Wales)
1488?-1568	Coverdale, Miles
1489-1556	Cranmer, Thomas
1489-1541	Margaret Tudor
1491-1547	Henry VIII
1491/95(*c.*)-1536	Tyndale, William
1495-1540	Barnes, Robert
1495?-1531	Bilney, Thomas
1496-1533	Mary Tudor
1497-1543	Holbein (the Younger), Hans
1497?-1555	Gardiner, Stephen
1537(*d.*)	Aske, Robert
1499?-1562?	Cavendish, George
1500-1558	Pole, Reginald
1500(*c.*)-1555	Rogers, John
1500?-1569	Bonner, Edmund
1501-1581	Davies, Richard

WHO'S WHO IN
BRITISH HISTORY

BEGINNINGS TO 1901

VOLUME 2

I

IDA (*d.c.*560) was the first recorded King of Bernicia, the northern half of the Anglo-Saxon kingdom of Northumbria. Bede states that he ruled from 547 for twelve years. Northern annalists add that his power was based at Bamburgh on the coast of Northumberland. Traditions preserved by Nennius of fighting between the sons of Ida and the northern Britons in the late sixth century also suggest that at that date Bernician rule did not extend far inland. The extreme scarcity of archaeological finds of Anglian type and sixth-century date from inland sites is consistent with this. It was Ethelfrith, grandson of Ida, who first significantly extended Bernician power westwards to the hinterland.

ILLTUD, ST (6th century?) was one of the most celebrated amongst the early Welsh saints. Our knowledge of his life depends on a biography, written in Brittany *c.*610, of a student at Illtud's foundation of Llantwit. The *Life of St Samson*, however, is a source which, like others of these early times, cannot be regarded as factually reliable. Nevertheless, it is clear that Illtud was an abbot rather than a bishop; reportedly of noble Breton descent, he embraced the monastic life under St Cadoc and is said to have been a student of St Germanus of Auxerre. His original foundation may have been on Caldy Island, off the coast of south Dyfed, but it was Illtud's great abbey of Llan-Illtut, or Llandtwit, which was his enduring achievement. The foundation was only ten miles from Dinas Powys, probable later seat of the Kings of Glywysing. This area of south Wales was no isolated backwater: it was the centre of the vibrant Celtic churches and French, Greek and Egyptian pottery of the time has been found at Dinas Powys. Although the monasticism of this period was ascetic in style, Illtud was reported a scholar 'learned in the teachings of the church, in the culture of the Latins and in the traditions of his own people'.

IMPEY, SIR ELIJAH (1732-1809) became Chief Justice of Bengal in 1774, earned the threat of impeachment from his association with Warren Hastings and the celebrated verdict of Macaulay: 'rich, quiet and infamous'. He was born in London, the son of a merchant from Hammersmith, and educated at Westminster, where he was elected into college at the same time as Hastings. He went to Trinity College, Cambridge, and became a Fellow of the College in 1757. When he was made head of the Supreme Court set up by North the year before, he had a solid reputation amongst lawyers, and a large family. His friends included Dunning and Thurlow, but his appointment was earned by merit rather than by jobbery. He was knighted and thus placed in a strong position in his dealings with the Council of Bengal, where he ranked second in authority to Hastings himself; but the functions of his court of four were not clearly defined. Was every servant of the company, whatever his race, to be accounted a British subject? Were all revenue cases within the Supreme Court's jurisdiction? What then of the quasi-judicial functions of the Governor's council? Those questions might have led to paralysing disputes between Hastings and Impey had not Hastings, who was interested in native law, found Impey sympathetic and ready to co-operate.

By 1781 the Supreme Court had given up its claim to decide upon revenue cases and Impey agreed to link the two systems of law by serving in person on Hasting's civil courts for Indians, but the conflict of authority had already been troublesome: for instance, a rajah had been ordered to pay by the Supreme Court – and not to pay by the Supreme Council. Cases like this made rich material for critics of Hastings's régime and Impey was represented at home, notably by Francis, as the tool of Hastings. The alacrity with which Impey and his fellow judges were able to find Nand Kumar, the central figure in Francis's attack upon Hastings, guilty of forgery was also held against him. With more justice he could be accused of jobbery. 'Pulbundi' he was called after he had got the 'pulbundi' – upkeep of roads and embankments – of Burdwan, worth £15,000 a year, for an impoverished cousin. So he came home in 1783 to find a menacing temper among the Whigs. In 1788 he was impeached and sat under a remarkable display of oratory by Elliot, who moved himself and others to tears with his elegiac upon 'the murdered rajah'. Impey lacked a winning personality. 'If you are in the hanging mood', said Cornwallis, who expressed sympathy for Hastings, 'you may tuck up Sir Elijah Impey without giving anybody the smallest concern'. Burke put the Whig view with a crude disregard for the conventions: 'He (Hastings) murdered Nand Kumar by the hand of Elijah Impey'. But Impey defended himself with skill and Pitt and his legal advisers declared their disbelief in the existence of a conspiracy between Hastings and the Chief Justice. The impeachment was not pressed and he was acquitted honourably. However, he discovered that the popular view did not die so easily, when he stood for parliament at Stafford in 1790. He chose his opponent unwisely. The followers of Sheridan paraded about the streets with the effigy of a black man hanging from a gibbet, and Impey had to go elsewhere to find himself a seat.

Further Reading
Sir J. Stephen, *The Story of Nuncomar and the Impeachment of Sir Elijah Impey*, 2 vols, 1905.

INE (*d*.after 726) was King of Wessex from 688 to 726. His long reign is illuminated for us by a larger and more diverse body of evidence than can be brought to bear upon the reign of any earlier English king. In particular a code of laws and a number of charters – the formal written record of grants of land – issued by Ine have survived. Historians are duly grateful for this, but their gratitude should be tinged with awareness of certain hazards. Not only does the new evidence present knotty technical problems of interpretation; there is the more insidious danger that its very existence may affect the way we look at King Ine. It is tempting to draw a contrast between the barbaric Cadwalla and the statesman-like Ine who succeeded him. But Ine's reign may have been quite as violent as Cadwalla's. Bede tells us that he ruled Sussex just as oppressively. He laid Kent under massive tribute. We hear of dynastic conflict within Wessex, of civil strife, of the banishment and slaying of a rival. Above all, Ine was active against the still independent British kingdom of Dumnonia in the south-west.

Ine's father had been a sub-king in Wessex, possibly in Dorset. It is likely that Ine came from rather further west than Cadwalla, and this might explain his preoccupation with western affairs. During the seventh century, and especially in the reigns of Cenwalh (643-74) and Centwine (676-85), the kingdom of Wessex had been expanding westwards at the expense of the Britons of Dumnonia. Although the process cannot be traced in confident detail it is likely that by about 700 much of Devon was under West Saxon domination. We hear of wars between Ine and the Britons in 710 and 722, and there may have been more fighting of which we know nothing. At one stage of his reign Ine was able to dispose of land to the west of the river Tamar, in Cornwall.

Although he did not do away with the kingdom of Dumnonia – which seems to have lingered on until the last quarter of the ninth century – Ine consolidated the West Saxon presence in Devon and perhaps to some degree in eastern Cornwall. A glance at a map will show that English place-names predominate in Devon and eastern Cornwall, Celtic ones further west.

In 705 the vast West Saxon bishopric of Winchester – for the see established by Birinus at Dorchester had lapsed at some point in the second half of the seventh century – was divided. A new bishopric was set up at Sherborne under Aldhelm with ecclesiastical responsibilities for the new western districts. There is some likelihood that a community of British clergy already existed at Sherborne. It is probable that there were other communities of monastic or quasi-monastic type which experienced similar continuity; for instance, at Stoke, near Hartland in Devon. The most abundantly documented of them is Glastonbury, where it is almost certain that there was a British monastery before the arrival of the West Saxons. Ine was a generous benefactor to Glastonbury, as he also was of monasteries established further east such as Malmesbury and Abingdon.

This willingness to integrate British communities into the West Saxon establishment is also displayed in Ine's code of laws, the earliest such code issued by a ruler of Wessex, promulgated in about 694. Ine's laws also show the king throwing the weight of his authority behind the church. For example, he enforced the payment of the tax known as church-scot, an annual payment in kind, probably quite a heavy one, rendered by all free men to the church. Ine's ability to enforce the church's claim to tax is indicative of a degree of ordered power at his disposal. This is borne out by other clauses in his laws. We can dimly make out an apparatus of government for the peaceful administration of justice and the economic support of the royal establishment, operating upon a diverse and not uncomplicated society. It is likely, for example, that already in Ine's day the West Saxon kingdom was divided for administrative purposes into shires, each of them centred upon an important royal estate and presided over by an ealdorman who was in some sense the king's deputy in his shire.

Ine's laws have something in addition to tell us of the economic activity which underpinned this institutional superstructure. They suggest a wealthy economy, predominantly agrarian yet one accustomed to the use of coin, in which trading and merchants were sufficiently important to be the subject of legislation. Recent archaeological discoveries have fleshed out the skeleton revealed by the written sources. At *Hamwih*, the ancestor of the modern Southampton, excavation has shown the remains of a big and prosperous trading settlement which was active during this period. Ine may have been instrumental in developing the port. The tolls that he could levy there were probably an important source of royal revenue. It is significant that by the year 755 (at latest) the place-name *Hamtun*, the royal estate immediately adjacent to *Hamwih*, had given its name to one of the administrative divisions of Wessex: *Hamtun-scir*, Hampshire.

Ine was the most formidable king of his day in northern Europe. In 726 he resigned his throne, like Cadwalla before him, and went on pilgrimage to Rome, there to end his days at some date unknown. Even the Romans he impressed: after his death they regarded him as a saint.

Further Reading
R. Hodges, *Dark Age Economics*, 1982, is stimulating on towns and trade but needs to be used with caution.
S. M. Pearce, *The Kingdom of Dumnonia*, 1978, is useful on the south-west.

INGIMUND (*fl*.902-7) was the leader of a Viking invasion and settlement of the north-western regions of England. He was a member of the Norwegian colony in Dublin. Expelled from Ireland in 902, Ingimund attempted to settle in north Wales but was driven off. Pushing further east he managed to settle his followers in the Wirral peninsula of north Cheshire. It is not impossible that this was a peaceful settlement made under treaty with the English authorities, Ealdorman Ethelred of Mercia and his wife Ethelflaed – akin to the settlement of Scandinavians in Normandy in 911, though on a smaller scale. Whether or not the initial settlement was peaceful, hostilities soon broke out between the new arrivals and the indigenous population. At some point the Norse attempted to seize Chester: this incident may lie behind the reference in the *Anglo-Saxon Chronicle* to the 'restoration' of Chester in 907. The slightly later construction of English fortresses in north-west Mercia – Eddisbury (914), Runcorn (915), Thelwall (919) and *Cledemutha* (probably Rhuddlan, 921) – is best interpreted as a successful attempt to contain Norse expansion from the Wirral.

Ingimund is a very shadowy figure, but he serves to symbolize the Norwegian contribution to the Scandinavian settlement of England. West of the Pennines from the Wirral to the Solway and in much of south-western Scotland there is plentiful evidence for a Norse presence in the tenth and eleventh centuries. This evidence consists principally of place-names formed from Old Norse, such as Thingwall, Amounderness, Wasdale or Beckermet. There is a little archaeological evidence as well. To call these settlers 'Norse' is to oversimplify. They probably came for the most part from Viking settlements, themselves not exclusively Norse in origin, of quite long standing in Ireland, the Isle of Man and the Western Isles of Scotland, where mixture with the indigenous Gaelic-speaking populations had taken place. Not surprisingly, therefore, there is evidence of Hibernian, Manx or Scottish elements among the new settlers. In Cumberland, for instance, the place-name Ireby is marked by the suffix -*by* as a name of Scandinavian type, but the first element *Ire*- points elsewhere: the name means 'settlement of the Irish'. Or again, Irish as well as Scandinavian and Old English names occur among the moneyers who operated the mint at Chester in the later tenth century. This mingling of cultures in the regions washed by the Irish Sea could give rise to some spectacular works of art: the Gosforth cross is one of the grandest monuments of the Viking age.

Further Reading
R. N. Bailey, *Viking Age Sculpture in Northern England*, 1980, is a fine treatment of the surviving stone monuments.
F. T. Wainwright, *Scandinavian England*, 1975, contains much material on the Norse settlements.

INGRAM, SIR ARTHUR (1565-1642) was a company promoter and moneylender whose career throws light on the management of public finance in the reigns of the first two Stuarts. The son of a Yorkshireman well established as a London merchant in the later years of Elizabeth's reign, he took over from his father about 1600. He moved rapidly into the customs service, with its opportunities of pickings and certainty of patronage, and soon became a controller of the Port of London. Thereafter his enterprises were manifold – including the management of customs farms, the sale of prize goods, of licences, and of Crown lands, monopolies of dyewoods and of starch-making – and to all of them he brought acumen, unscrupulousness, a ruthless appetite for profit and a staggering self-righteousness. He benefited substantially from a long partnership with Cranfield, yet avoided serious damage when the latter fell. To courtiers he became invaluable both as a 'contact man' and a source of ready cash, and in 1615 he was asked to produce a memorandum on fiscal policy for the government. He seems to have been extraordinarily unpopular, and his unsuccessful attempt to secure the office of Cofferer of the Royal Household provoked an uproar throughout the department. Before this he had bought the post of Secretary to the Council of the North, and although his devotion to its duties was little more than minimal, he spent much of the later part of his life in Yorkshire. Here he invested his profits in land and built houses for himself and his sons, in York, at Sheriff Hutton and, most notably, at Temple Newsam. In the 1630s he was the leading citizen of York, founding Bootham Hospital. His business activities at this stage included the organization of the production of alum (in which he lost substantially), the farming of recusancy fines, and the management of various financial enterprises for his fellow Yorkshireman Thomas Wentworth with whom, scarcely surprisingly, he eventually quarrelled. He sat in a succession of parliaments from 1610 onwards; somewhat Puritan in his religious outlook, he had by the time of his death in 1642 moved cautiously but clearly to the side of the opposition in the Commons.

Further Reading
A. F. Upton, *Sir Arthur Ingram*, 1961.

IRETON, HENRY (1611-51), was born at Attenborough in Nottinghamshire. His parents were Puritan gentry; two years earlier his mother had been presented to the archdeacon's court for refusing to be churched according to the rites of the Church of England. All the evidence we have of Henry Ireton throughout his life underlines the descriptions of him by Lucy Hutchinson (his cousin's wife) as 'a grave, serious, religious person', and by Bulstrode Whitelocke as 'a Person very active, industrious and stiff in his ways and purposes'. He went to Trinity College, Oxford, in 1626 and to the Middle Temple in 1629. Ireton can have had no difficulty in deciding where his sympathies and duty lay as the Civil War drew near and in 1642 he led a troop of horse to join the parliamentarians under Essex before Edgehill. He met Cromwell for the first time in the fighting in the east Midlands in 1643, and henceforward Ireton's fortunes were closely linked with the career of Oliver. In 1644, after fighting at Marston Moor, he was a prominent critic of the cautious generalship of Manchester. He commanded the left wing at Naseby (1645), was present at the surrender of Bristol, accompanied Fairfax in the western campaign of 1645-6, and was one of the commissioners for the surrender of Oxford in June 1646, the month in which he married Cromwell's daughter Bridget, then aged twenty-two.

Ireton was a brave soldier, but he seems to have been a competent rather than a distinguished commander. At Naseby, where he 'fought like a lion', he was routed by Rupert's cavalry. His importance for the history of his time rests not upon his military achievements but upon his part in the political manoeuvres of the period between Naseby and the execution of the king. For Ireton, although scarcely an original thinker, had a very sharp intellect. He combined a taste for constitutional law with an eye for political reality in a manner rare among the officers of the New Model; he was an effective, though perhaps long-winded, debater, and had a real aptitude for what Whitelocke called 'the business of the Pen'. His influence on the slower and far less clear mind of Cromwell was considerable; whether it was as great or as sinister as contemporaries, both royalists and left-wingers like Wildman and Lilburne, alleged, is hard to assess. Throughout 1647 Ireton played a prominent part, sometimes the leading role, in the complicated negotiations which the army leaders were conducting simultaneously with the king, with the Presbyterian majority in the Commons, and with the 'Agitators' who represented the rank and file. His aim at this time, like that of his military superiors Cromwell and Fairfax, was to obtain a settlement which guaranteed peace and order, secured wide religious toleration, and gave reasonable terms of disbandment to the soldiers. In the summer of 1647 he was the principal architect of what must be regarded as the wisest settlement offered to Charles I, the Heads of the Proposals. These provided for biennial parliaments meeting for 120 days, a revision of county representation in proportion to taxation, parliamentary control of the militia for ten years, a Council of State appointed for a maximum of seven years, and the exclusion of leading royalists from office and from parliament for five years; there was to be religious toleration for all except papists, neither the Book of Common Prayer nor the Covenant was to be compulsory, and the bishops were to lose their coercive powers. Such terms were quite unacceptable to Charles, yet he temporized, and in the autumn Ireton, Cromwell and Fairfax were in frequent negotiation with him at Hampton Court. Against this background, an effective setting for mistrust of the generals, the Agitators of the regiments put forward in *The Case of the Army duly Stated* and *The Agreement of the People* demands for more radical constitutional change, including complete parliamentary sovereignty and suffrage for all free-born men over the age of twenty-one. These were discussed at length in the Putney Debates (October-November 1647); and here Ireton was the most outspoken and forceful champion of political and social conservatism. To the Leveller doctrine of equality of rights he replied that 'no person hath a right to an interest or share in the disposing of the affairs of the kingdom … that hath not a permanent fixed interest in the kingdom'. 'All the main thing that I speak for is because I would have an eye to property.' Here was a clear statement of the limitations which the leaders of the English Revolution succeeded in imposing upon it.

In November 1647 Charles escaped from Hampton Court to Carisbrooke in the Isle of Wight; from this time Ireton and, more slowly, Cromwell lost what trust they still had in him. During the Second Civil War, Ireton – like the army as a whole – showed a harshening of spirit towards the royalists; this was evident at Colchester in his implacable condemnation of Sir Charles Lucas and Sir George Lisle to the firing-squad on the grounds that they were traitors to parliament and entitled to no quarter. In November 1648 he wrote *The Remonstrance of the Army*, a pamphlet bitterly attacking the king and demanding his trial. Ireton was responsible for the decisive intervention of the army, culminating in Pride's Purge. His name followed those of Bradshaw, Fairfax and Cromwell at the head of the list of commissioners for the trial, and he was not one of those who withdrew.

In the early months of the Commonwealth, Ireton was busy on committees – although he failed to win election to the Council of State. Later in 1649 he was appointed as Cromwell's second-in-command in the Irish campaign, and when Oliver returned home in 1650 Ireton became Lord Deputy. Waterford surrendered to him in that year; Limerick, after a long siege, in 1651. A month later Ireton, weakened by incessant work, died of fever. He was given a state funeral in Westminster Abbey, whence his remains were dug up to be gibbeted at the Restoration. Stern, strict, honest, never sparing himself, Ireton scarcely deserved John Lilburne's description of him as 'the cunningest of Machiavalians'; keener yet far narrower in range of mind than Cromwell, he was the subordinate whom Oliver could least afford to lose.

Further Reading
Howard Shaw, 'Henry Ireton', *History Today*, April 1970.
Maurice Ashley, *Cromwell's Generals*, 1954, pp.65-82.
R. W. Ramsey, *Henry Ireton*, 1949.

IRVING, SIR HENRY (1838-1905), actor-manager, was born at the right time. During the second half of the nineteenth century English theatre experienced an exciting renaissance. The proscenium stage, gas lighting and elaborate scenery all helped to create a more powerful sense of illusion: the railway and the omnibus turned the middle classes into theatre-goers: Queen Victoria made the stage respectable by starting Windsor theatricals and building a stage in her drawing room. Between 1851 and 1899 forty-two theatres were built in London and its suburbs, and many more in the provinces.

But there was no silver spoon in young Irving's mouth. The son of a poor village shopkeeper who moved from Somerset to London to earn his living, Henry, then called Brodribb, learnt his trade by taking elocution, fencing and dancing courses and by closely studying plays, while working as a solicitor's clerk. His powerful mother thought actors disreputable, and when he did make the plunge and join a company in Sunderland, it took fourteen years and nearly 600 parts before he had his first big success. Though tall and handsome, he had a flat voice and distorted vowels, and dragged his leg slightly as part of his mannered style. But his commitment to the theatre was total. He thought deeply about the parts he played, and won over many initially hostile audiences by his courage, perseverance and compelling personality. Melodramatic villains were his forte, and it was in 1871 in *The Bells*, as Mathias, a conscience-stricken murderer, that he became famous. The play required an actor of genius to enable the audience to suspend disbelief, as Mathias was gripped by the nightmare of the sleigh bells of his victim's sledge ringing in his ear. Irving built up layer on layer of horror until people fainted. It was a performance he was to repeat 800 times in the next thirty-four years.

Once established, he set up his own company in the Lyceum, which he took over from the widow of 'Colonel' Bateman, the American impresario who had put on *The Bells*. He inculcated a close company spirit as they toured the provinces, and he took everyone with him, stage hands and all, on his seven American tours. He had an eye for talent; Frank Benson, John Martin Harvey, and most famously, Ellen Terry, who acted opposite him until 1901. He played most of the big Shakespearian tragic heroes. Hamlet was his most successful, the 1874 production running for 200 nights at a time when long runs did not happen. He developed the portrait of a young man, psychologically disturbed by his intolerable situation, to the climax of his scene with Ophelia, when a hurricane of applause shook the benches. Other renowned successes were his Benedick opposite Ellen Terry's Beatrice, Mephistopheles in *Faust* (375 performances in a sixteen-month run), and the eponymous hero in Tennyson's play, *Becket*, which he performed to Queen Victoria at Windsor. She knighted him in 1895, the first actor to be thus honoured.

Throughout his career Irving was strongly criticized. He had his failures. He lacked the voice to play an effective Othello or Macbeth, and his rather aged Romeo was an embarrassment. As they drove away from the party celebrating the triumph of *The Bells* his wife asked him how long he was going to go on making a fool of himself – whereupon he stopped the carriage, climbed out and never returned home to her again. Henry James wrote: 'That an actor so handicapped by nature and culture should have enjoyed so much prosperity is striking proof ... of the chaotic condition of taste.' Shaw led the anti-Irving critics. Irving believed that the way to act was to take a character and turn him into yourself. This he often did so powerfully that he commanded hushed audiences and explosions of applause. Under his influence the Victorian theatre was an actor's theatre. Shaw wanted it to be a playwright's theatre and his was the rising star. By the start of the new century, Irving was on his way out. The heavy costs of his extravagant productions, with paintings by Burne-Jones or Alma-Tadema and music by Sir Edward German, followed by a fire which destroyed its magnificent collection of scenery, crippled the company, and the Lyceum had to be sold to a music hall developer. His health gave way. Trouper that he was, he died on the job, in a Bradford hotel after a performance of *Becket*. He had transformed the public's view of the theatre and the status of his profession, and was appropriately buried in Westminster Abbey.

Further Reading
L. H. F. Irving, *Henry Irving, the actor and his world*, 1951.

ISABELLA OF ANGOULÊME (*c.*1188-1246) was the daughter and heiress of Aymer (*d.*1213), Count of Angoulême, a strategically important county in southwest France. Although betrothed to Hugh IX, Count of Lusignan, Isabella was married to King John in 1200. Whether diplomacy or an allegedly uncontrollable passion for the twelve-year-old were uppermost in John's motives, it proved an expensive move. His subsequent hostility to Hugh led to the count's appeal to the King of France which was the pretext for the formal confiscation of John's French lands in 1202. From 1213, when she inherited Angoulême, Isabella attracted rumours about her infidelity. John may have believed them, as there is a story he placed her under house arrest at Gloucester in December 1214. After John's death, and the establishment of a stable regency for her son Henry III in 1217, she returned to her county. In 1220 she married Hugh X of Lusignan, the son of her suitor of 1200. For the rest of her life she was perched precariously between the interests of her two families. Her Poitevin sons may have sought their fortunes at Henry III's court, to that king's ultimate detriment, but Hugh betrayed him at Taillebourg in 1240. She died and was buried at Fontevrault in 1246, beside Henry II, Eleanor of Aquitaine and Richard I. From her perspective, the collapse of the Angevin empire was not a defining moment of national history, but one episode in French comital relations in which her role was that of territorial pawn. At least until the 1250s, it was a perspective shared by her sons in England.

ISABELLA OF FRANCE (*c*.1296-1358), consort of Edward II, is normally remembered as the 'She-Wolf of France', who ruled corruptly and tyrannically between 1326 and 1330. This was an uncharacteristic phase in the life of an otherwise conventional queen-consort and queen-dowager. The daughter of Philip IV of France (1285-1314), she was the child-bride of a diplomatic match, which nevertheless seems to have made a successful marriage. Apparently very beautiful, she bore four children, and 'confined herself to being a devoted wife and a loyal queen, a mere spectator of the successive crises her husband had to face both within France and England'. After 1330 she lived in luxurious leisure, principally but not only at Castle Rising, patronized the Franciscans and joined their third order. Only during her son's minority did she defy convention and expose talents and defects otherwise concealed.

Edward II's male favourites twice caused Isabella problems. The king was forced to marry her because of prior diplomatic commitments, not from choice, and spitefully honoured Gaveston rather than her. As Isabella was only twelve, she cannot have been effective politically, but her father was, joining the magnates and compelling Gaveston's exile and respect for the queen. Thereafter Edward was acutely conscious of Isabella's French connections, exploiting them in diplomacy with her father and three brothers, successive Kings of France. Such ties enabled the Despensers to disgrace her during the St Sardos war in 1324: her lands and debts were seized, her household purged of Frenchmen, her children were removed, and her household was closely supervised. Again sent to treat with France, she was followed by Prince Edward, and tried to make a bargaining counter of their return:

I protest that I will not return until this intruder is removed, but, discarding my marriage garment, shall assume the robes of widowhood until I am avenged of this pharisee (Despenser).

When Edward refused, Isabella and Mortimer, from 1325 her lover, used control of the young Edward, whom they betrothed to Philippa of Hainault, to plot an invasion, at which her husband's régime collapsed.

Isabella took over government on her return. She plundered the royal treasury, made massive grants to herself and Mortimer, appointed docile ministers, and then pushed her husband's deposition and Edward III's succession through parliament in as constitutionally regular a manner as possible. Mortimer remained her lover. Parliament also set up a council of regency headed by the Earl of Lancaster, but Isabella circumvented it. 'Edward's youthful loyalty to Isabella was the real mainstay of her rule and no council of magnates could ever equal the influence exerted by the queen on her son.' Parliament was used to rubber-stamp decisions made elsewhere. Naked self-aggrandizement distinguished her régime, like that of the Despensers, whose methods she adopted, and 'subordinated national interests to her own self-seeking'. She lacked policies, concentrating like Edward's favourites on remaining in power, and her treaties with Scotland and France, however desirable, were mere pusillanimous expedients. She relied increasingly on Mortimer to crush opposition. She had not planned what to do on the king's majority, resting content with an ephemeral and adulterous tyranny.

Further Reading

P. C. Doherty, 'Isabella, Queen of England, 1296-1330', Oxford DPhil thesis, 1977.
P. Doherty, 'The Date of Birth of Isabella, Queen of England (1308-58)', *Bulletin of the Institute of Historical Research* xlviii, 1975.
H. Johnstone, 'Isabella, "She-Wolf of France"', *History* xxi, 1936.

J

JACKSON, JOHN (1769-1845), boxer, lifted the sport above its level of lethal, bare-fisted combats in makeshift rings, before seedy, raucous crowds, behind 'The Fancy', whose entry qualification was willingness to bet huge sums. Jack Broughton, heavyweight champion from 1734 to 1750, had introduced some rules under which – if they were enforced – it was forbidden to hit an opponent who was down or to grasp him below the waist. After him, Daniel Mendoza was held to be the first boxer to be scientific in his approach, with emphasis on footwork. Gloves would not be worn till later in the century, but in 1839 the London Prize Ring rules defined the size of the ring and extended the list of fouls to include butting and biting. But Jackson's influence extended beyond science and rules. The sport already had its fashionable spectators. Hazlitt's memorable essay conveys something of the thrill of a great fight as he goes post-haste to Newbury to see Tom Hickman the Gas Man fight Jem Belcher the Game Chicken. Through 'Gentleman' Jackson it came to be more of a sport for the amateurs for whom the 'Queensbury Rules' would eventually obtain. Patronized by 'The First Gentleman', the Prince of Wales, he ran a boxing academy in London. Byron was one of his pupils and rewarded Jackson with a line in *Don Juan*. Jackson was renowned for feats of strength: he could lift ten hundredweight and a quarter. With his teaching, and some notable victories came wealth and position as a respectable member of society.

JAMES I (1394-1437) of Scotland was the third son of Robert III and Queen Annabella Drummond. The queen supervised James's early education, probably at his birthplace of Dunfermline, until her death in 1401, when the child was placed in the charge of Henry Wardlaw, soon to be consecrated Bishop of St Andrews. The death of his elder brother David, Duke of Rothesay meant that only James stood between his uncle, the Duke of Albany, and the throne, a circumstance deemed hazardous to the boy's health. After a delay of many months, Robert III arranged for James to be sent to France. But in March 1606 he was captured by English pirates off Flamborough Head, taken to London and imprisoned in the Tower. He was twelve years old. A few days later Robert died, but James remained in England, a king without a crown, who had not sworn a coronation oath, and whose legal status in Scotland was therefore uncertain. When the Exchequer rolls of 1409 referred to 'the prince, son of the king, now in England', this was not merely a matter of the ambition of the Governor Albany who ruled in his absence.

In England James was taken to various places of captivity, including Nottingham Castle and Evesham. Among the more notable of his fellow political prisoners were Griffin, the son of the Welsh prince, Owain Glendower, and Murdoch, Earl of Fife, son of Governor Albany, captive since the battle of Homildon Hill in 1402. Soon after the accession of Henry V in 1413 all three were recommitted first to the Tower and from there, in August, to Windsor Castle; here they were joined in 1415 by Charles of Orleans, though all these prisoners were probably kept apart. In 1416, however, Murdoch was ransomed by his father and returned to Scotland. James's captivity may therefore have seemed doubly irksome, but a complaint about his gaolers' failure to change bed-linen may suggest that, by fifteenth-century standards, his quarters were relatively comfortable. James was educated from 1417 by Sir John Pelham and lived mainly at Windsor. In 1419 an expedition of Scots under the Earl of Buchan arrived in France. As a result, James was forced to accompany Henry V at the sieges of Melun and Meaux, and (unavailingly) to command their Scottish defenders to cease fighting alongside the French.

Events in Scotland and France were working in James's favour. In November 1412, he had written to the powerful Douglases to enlist their support against Albany's foot-dragging. (These finely written letters are the earliest to survive of any Scottish monarch.) His appeal had been unsuccessful and had perhaps even hardened Albany's resolve. But following the death in 1420 of the first Duke of Albany, sections of the nobility grew disenchanted with the rule of the second duke, Murdoch, and his brood of lawless sons. As confidence in the governor collapsed, the Earl of Douglas began to work for James's return. Meanwhile, following the death of Henry V in 1422, the regency English government, short of money and worried by French resistance, began to consider the wisdom of freeing James as a means to detach Scotland from its ally.

It was as these conditions were maturing, in May 1623, that by happy chance the king met Joan Beaufort, daughter of the Earl of Somerset. In the only poem certainly attributable to him, 'The Kingis Quair', James recalled with feeling how he fell instantly in love with the lady glimpsed 'walking under the toure' of Windsor. So it may safely be left to case-hardened cynics to draw attention to Joan's rather large dowry, and a relationship (cousin) to Henry VI which certainly cannot have harmed the prospects of her suitor's release. The marriage took place at the church of St Mary Overy (later Southwark Cathedral), on 13 February 1424. The Scots had already agreed in December to pay 60,000 merks ransom, thinly disguised as 'compensation' for James's upkeep. 10,000 merks were remitted as the dowry of Joan Beaufort. Hostages were provided for the ransom, and the Scots agreed not to send more troops to France. James arrived back in Scotland in early April and was crowned at Scone on 2 May 1424.

The inauguration of the new régime and the new French policy led to a confrontation with the sons of Murdoch, Duke of Albany. The eldest, Walter, was keeper of the important fortress at Dumbarton, a port often used by voyagers between Scotland and France. He had been actively involved in the patriotic struggle of the Franco-Scottish alliance against the English enemy, and in the slightly less patriotic business of abstracting moneys from the customs. Walter's record also revealed a deep disinclination to obey lawful authority, and James very quickly had him arrested, probably reasoning that continuing the dispatch of men and material to France would undermine the truce. In 1425 came the decisive rift between King James and Murdoch's family and friends, whose immediate causes are not certainly known, and which has been variously attributed to their disloyalty and his greed. Albany himself, his sons Alexander and Walter, and his father-in-law Duncan, Earl of Lennox, were brought before a parliamentary assize in May, convicted on charges unknown, and beheaded at Stirling, reportedly to the delight of its inhabitants. Their fate may have been brought about by Murdoch's younger son James, who, having burned Dumbarton and murdered Sir John Stewart (Walter's replacement as keeper of its castle), made his escape to Ireland.

Whatever the reasons for all the bloodletting, the effect was enormously to strengthen the Crown, which acquired the chief estates of the Albany connection – the earldoms of Lennox, Fife and Menteith. Later, James acquired the earldoms of Buchan and Mar on the death of their holders, handing over the poorly endowed estate of Buchan as compensation to the heirs of March, whom he had excluded in 1434 under the flimsiest of legal pretexts. James found other means of improving the financial position of the Crown. Income was increased by the use of fines and forfeitures, and officials of James's household leaned heavily upon the sheriffs to deliver the revenue. The scale of grants and pensions from customs and taxes was drastically pruned, and revenues increased substantially as venality tapered off. The parliament of 1424 granted a twentieth on goods and land-rents, though it was collected with difficulty.

Parliament met with greater regularity than previously, not primarily for financial reasons, but as part of James's effort to impose central authority through statute law. This was not just a matter of passing acts. The statute of 1426, which enacted that only the king's laws should govern all his subjects, was itself practical recognition that this had not, in fact, been the case; the statute laid down the means of its own enforcement, and that of other laws, which devolved essentially on the sheriffs and other royal officials. The practical supremacy of the king's law also required the supersession of private armies complained of in other acts, and the subordination of other jurisdictions (such as those of the church and the barons) to that of parliament, which was inundated with the legal business of aggrieved parties. James made an important start in initiating a new court of selected Members of Parliament which could adjudicate in certain civil cases, which is known to have been active throughout the reign, and which, in the next, came to be known the Session. The enhanced importance of parliament itself was reflected in new arrangements for the management of its business, including the creation of the Lords of the Articles, a body which drafted or amended proposed legislation, so that parliament received it in a coherent form which reflected the wishes of the interest groups involved; this body in later years proved a powerful means of royal control over parliament.

The statutes relating to parliament itself and its organization have aroused considerable controversy among historians. There was legislation which sought to ensure an enhanced institutional status for the burghs and more regular attendance of lesser barons and freeholders. These were probably stimulated primarily by the king's need for money, rather than as an attempt to counterbalance the power of the great barons. And yet the act of 1428 does seem to embody a response to such tendencies: the provision for the attendance of shire members by a method of election (at the sheriff court) can be understood as helping to ensure baronial domination of a 'commons' chamber in an incipient bicameral system which might otherwise fall under the influence of burgess much more dependent on the king. However that may be, the act was not implemented and the system remained unicameral, though there was a continuing gradual evolution of the distinction between barons and lords of parliament (who attended as a matter of course) and lesser landowners who came if invited by the king.

In general, the king was less disposed than for many years to be indulgent to the great lords, and energetically sought to build up the power of the Crown, as a 'private' landowner and as the central authority of the state, against them. James sought to enhance the role of parliament, not only because he needed grants of money from it, but as a unifying agency in the state, so that laws once enacted with its active consent could be made binding on all. But this carried the danger that a baronial solidarity might develop against an assertive king not overly sensitive to their interests. In 1428, in a bid to establish royal authority (and tax-raising capability) in the north-west, James summoned a parliament to Inverness, and unscrupulously arrested the forty chiefs who responded to the call, executing three of them. Alexander Macdonald, Lord of the Isles (the son of Donald defeated at Harlaw in the days of Albany), who was almost a king in that region, was arrested. Released upon promise of good behaviour, he was so resentful of his humiliation that he burnt Inverness. In June 1429, James defeated Alexander in Lochaber and enforced his appearance, unarmed, at Holyrood Abbey, and imprisoned him at Tantallon Castle.

The following year, James ventured to imprison an even more powerful baron, none other than Archibald, fifth Earl of Douglas, probably on suspicion of negotiating with the English at Berwick for the release of a hostage, Malise Graham. James was looking to improve relations with France, but here he may have been aroused by more than the dangers of freelance foreign policy-making. Graham was a representative of the line of Robert II and his second wife, Euphemia Ross, which could claim better title to the throne than that of the king himself, whose descent was from Robert's canonically unsound first marriage to Elizabeth Mure. Earl Douglas is very unlikely to have been backing a dynastic challenge to the throne, but it is possible that the king had suspected as much; Douglas may also have been seeking to obstruct the king's tax-raising efforts. At any rate, it soon became clear that James had overreached himself. In the Highlands, Alexander Macdonald's devotion to the king had not been strengthened by his confinement, for in 1431, his kinsman Donald Balloch raised the standard of rebellion and defeated government forces under the Earls of Mar and Caithness at Inverlochy. In October, parliament compelled James to release both Douglas and Alexander, for although it was prepared to grant the taxes necessary to finance an army, it placed strict controls on their collection and disbursement, which James was not prepared to accept. The result was to strengthen the power of the Macdonald Lords of the Isles in the western Highlands; after the death of the Earl of Mar in 1435, they also dominated his earldom of Ross.

James's early foreign policy initiatives included a commercial treaty with the Duke of Burgundy, and a renewed alliance with Denmark which resolved the dispute over payments for the Hebrides, both in 1426. But England and France remained the chief foci of Scottish diplomacy. James had begun his reign by ending military assistance to France in the interests of his own release and of a truce with England. By 1428, however, the French were in desperate straits; final defeat would release the forces of England for other projects, from which, history suggested, activity north of the Tweed could not be excluded. In July 1428, a treaty was signed between James and Charles VII providing for the dispatch of 6,000 troops and for the marriage of the Princess Margaret, aged two, and Louis the Dauphin. With the relief of Orleans and further victories, under the inspired leadership of Joan of Arc, the French recovered, and James was able to renew his truce with England.

James did not lack piety, or at least, due respect for the reputation of the church. He restored the estates of St Andrews, and founded a Carthusian monastery at Perth. In lending the secular arm to the pursuit of heretics, James may have learned something from the Lancastrian example; anyway, it won him the approval of the bishops. In 1433, Paul Crawar, a Hussite missionary, was burnt at St Andrews, and James rewarded inquisitor Fogo with the abbacy of Melrose. He had also returned Scotland (the last state to adhere to Avignon) to the obedience of Rome. But despite all this, relations with the papacy were tempestuous, since James, like other royal centralizers, found that his secular ambitions impinged on terrain held to be sacred. Most literally, of course, this applied to the right of sanctuary, but the conflict was implicit in every claim of the church or its clergy to exercise privileges not available to other subjects, and in their role in upholding ecclesiastical laws, courts, and a political superstructure, which were not the king's. James tried to stop clergymen from going abroad, and took other measures to stem the outflow of money used to purchase benefices and sees, or to pursue suits at Rome. The papacy responded by twice sending William Croyser, Archdeacon of Teviotdale, as a nuncio to summon to Rome the man held responsible, John Cameron, Bishop of Glasgow. On the second occasion, in 1433, Croyser was hauled before the Scottish parliament and stripped of his benefices in Scotland; that year too, James supported the conciliarists' assembly at Basle. In 1435 Pope Eugenius issued a bull restoring Croyser; discussions were started the following year, but were interrupted by the king's death.

The backdrop to that event was an abrupt shift in the foreign policy landscape; possibly because of the collapse of the Anglo-Burgundian alliance, which further weakened the English position, James moved towards a more aggressive posture probably designed to extract a peace from them. A failed English attempt to capture Margaret, en route for her marriage to the Dauphin may have acted to harden his resolve. However, for reasons which are unclear, but which may possibly have involved the resentment of barons including the Earl of Douglas, his siege of Roxburgh was ingloriously abandoned. James proceeded to the Dominican friary at Perth, at which city he is reported to have played chess with a knight who recounted a prophecy of the death of a king that year. On 20 February 1437, in the middle of the night, James's chamberlain, Sir Robert Stewart, admitted to the building Sir Robert Graham of Kincardine and his men. Thrusting aside the queen's maid, Catherine Douglas, who barred the way, they burst into the king's quarters. James had heard the commotion, pulled up some floor-boards, and hidden himself in a vault under the floor, but he was soon discovered and murdered with many sword cuts.

The reasons for the assassination have been endlessly debated. James's high handed, and high spending ways, his abandonment of hostages provided against an unpaid ransom, and his sometimes capricious tendency to arrest prominent persons have all been canvassed as the basis for baronial revolt, and the opposition of the parliament to James's war surely reflected widespread dissatisfaction among the barons with the king's 'tyrannical' style of government and his extravagance. Complex dynastic conspiracies used to be suggested as a contributing or alternative explanation. True, Stewart was the grandson of the Earl of Atholl and might have seen himself as heir in the line of Euphemia, and in parliament in 1436, he opposed the granting of taxes for the English war. It is certain that Graham had two reasons to bear a personal grudge against James. He had been imprisoned at the start of the reign during the drive against the Albany family, and he had also been the uncle and tutor of Malise, whose succession to the earldom of Strathearn had been forbidden by James, and who had died while a hostage in England. Expert logicians may contend that James's own love of tennis ranks high among the causes of his tragedy, since the tendency of balls to be trapped at the exit from his underground hiding place had led him to have it blocked off. But what did motivate the killers? Perhaps Robert Stewart thought merely to become guardian of the king's elder son James, born in October 1430. It is now thought that Stewart, probably in association with Atholl, misinterpreted the general dissatisfaction with policy and with the war, and the leading role accorded to him by parliament, as implying licence for a putsch. But the universal support of the young James among the barons argues against the idea that there was any widespread support for an attempt to oust the dynasty. At any rate, the leading perpetrators

were found, tortured with great barbarity for three days, and executed. James was buried in the Church of the Charterhouse at Perth.

Further Reading
Michael Brown, *James I*, 1994.

JAMES II (1430-60) of Scotland was born one of twins (the other, named Alexander, died young) on 16 October 1430. Following the murder of his father at Perth, he was crowned at Holyrood on 25 March 1437. James and his sisters remained in the care of Queen Joan. Nothing is known about the new king's education. His appearance was disfigured by an extraordinary purple birthmark, covering the whole left side of his face and giving rise to the nickname 'James of the fiery face'. The first twelve years of his reign were marked by baronial coups and countercoups and at times by the virtual collapse of central authority.

Archibald, the fifth Earl of Douglas, had become regent or lieutenant, and Cameron, Bishop of Glasgow, continued as chancellor. Douglas was a very powerful magnate who could also claim to be the next male heir to the throne. But many were not prepared to respect his authority, even when backed by parliament, and barons began to brawl in contempt of official efforts to restrain them. At the top there unfolded a struggle, of unstable alliances and sudden betrayals, for control of the state. After the death from the plague of the fifth Earl Douglas in June 1439, this contest became tangled up with attempts to control all or part of the sprawling Douglas empire. Two of the principal actors in this complex and sanguinary struggle were the former ministers of James I, Sir William Crichton, also keeper of Edinburgh castle, and Sir Alexander Livingston.

Custody of James had from the start been fiercely contested. The queen did not trust Crichton, and smuggled the boy out of Edinburgh (in a trunk, according to a later tradition). Alexander Livingston was now able to execute a tortuous series of unprincipled manoeuvres which almost gained him the ascendancy. First, he used the queen's distrust of Crichton to acquire official recognition as her protector at Stirling. Having connived at the displacement of Chancellor Cameron by Crichton, he joined with him to undermine the rule of the nominal regent, Douglas. When the frightened Joan married James Stewart, 'The Black Knight of Lorne', Livingston arrested her on the pretence that the union threatened the dynasty, and was able thus to grab custody of James and the dowry of his mother. This in turn disrupted the bloc with Crichton, who in August 1439 kidnapped and imprisoned James, now aged nine, releasing the boy from Edinburgh castle only on the threat of war.

It was at this point that the regent, Earl Archibald Douglas, died, to be succeeded by the sixth earl, William. Both Livingston and Crichton rightly saw in the ambitious young man a potential challenger in the state, and in November 1440 they combined to lure him to visit the king at Edinburgh castle. Here at the 'Black Dinner', William and his brother and heir David, having been perfunctorily 'tried' for treason, were taken out and executed over the anguished protests of the young James. The killers may very well have acted with the connivance of another Douglas, James 'the Gross', Earl of Avondale, who succeeded to the Douglas earldom as a result of the crime. For the next three years, there seems to have been something of a balance between the three accomplices. This may have owed something to the lethargy of James the Gross, who is said to have carried around 'four stones of tallow', and who may have wanted no more than to digest peacefully the large estates which had just come his way. These however, did not amount to the whole Douglas empire. The title, and the estates inherited by James the Gross, on the deaths without issue of Earl William and David at the Black Dinner, had reverted to him by entail, as the brother of the fourth earl. Much property, however, passed to the youths' nine-year-old sister, Margaret 'the fair maid of Galloway'. Annandale, as a male fief, reverted to the Crown, and title to other lands was disputed, not least by Margaret's mother who had remarried – a Livingston. When James the Gross died in 1443, his son William became the eighth Earl Douglas; William made haste to marry his cousin, Margaret 'the fair maid of Galloway', and took what he claimed was legal control of the reunited Douglas lands.

The young man began in high royal favour, and was received as chief companion to the king. William was more politically active than his father, favouring the Livingstons in order to detach them from the Crichtons. On 4 November 1443, for the first time, James presided at a council general at Stirling, which took action favourable to the Douglas-Livingston combination, depriving the two Crichton brothers of their offices and installing Livingstons as Justiciar, Chamberlain and Comptroller and as keepers of several castles. The effect was a renewed destabilization, in which the Crichtons, backed by the Bishop of St Andrews, were just able to hang on against the weight of Douglas, the Livingstons and the Earl of Crawford. Central authority wilted whilst the contending coalitions battled it out, ravaging each other's property, whilst lesser barons, Lindsays, Ogilvies, Hepburns, Ruthvens and Stewarts, also took the opportunity to pursue their several internecine feuds by the traditional means of burning and looting. In the borders, baronial enterprise gave rise to violence and destruction on both sides of the Tweed which threatened a more general conflagration, until a new truce was signed at the end of 1449.

Meanwhile, on 3 July that year, James, now almost nineteen years old, was married to Mary of Gueldres,

niece of the Duke of Burgundy. It was at this point that James began to take over the reins of government. Perhaps remembering their earlier maltreatment of his mother and her second husband, and perhaps partly because he suspected them of embezzling Crown revenue, James arrested the Livingstons. In January 1450, two were executed and several others imprisoned, including Sir Alexander, though his eldest son James escaped to the Highlands. The family were abandoned by their former ally, Earl Douglas; their estates were made forfeit, and the earl was rewarded with a generous share of the booty. Attempts were now made to reimpose peace by the symbolic re-enactment of statutes of James I's reign against baronial and official lawlessness, though these were not effective. In the government, Crichton had been able to return as chancellor, and Bishop Kennedy was influential, but in 1450 the leading figure was still certainly Douglas.

In November 1450, however, when Earl William was absent in Rome, James, apparently alarmed at the bankruptcy of the state treasury, invaded Douglas territories in Galloway and Selkirk, areas which the earl claimed through the right of his new wife, in a bid to assert Crown control, through escheat, or by legal challenge based on grants of James I. But on Douglas's return, the king was forced by the Parliament of Edinburgh in June 1451 to restore all the confiscated lands. Douglas, rather than resting content at the restoration of his estates, seems to have been unsettled by the king's attempt on them, and made what was probably a defensive alliance with the Earl of Crawford and with John Macdonald, Lord of the Isles and Earl of Ross, latest in a dynasty traditionally willing to deal with the English. James chose to treat this as disloyalty. He invited William to visit Stirling, under a royal safe-conduct, and there, on 22 February 1652, demanded that he disown his alliance or 'band'; the earl's refusal led to angry exchanges in which the king stabbed him to death.

In March James, Bishop of Aberdeen, the ninth Earl Douglas, and his dead predecessor's younger brother, paraded in strength through Stirling with the worthless safe-conduct tied to a horse's tail, and shouting his defiance of authority, looted and burnt the town. His ally, the Earl Crawford, raised a rebellion in the north, but was defeated by Huntly, at Brechin in May. On 12 June 1452 at Edinburgh, parliament found that James had not committed murder, because the earl's alliances had been treasonable. In the south, the king's army of 30,000 ravaged the Douglas lands; in August 1452, the earl was forced to capitulate and to promise not to carry forward any blood feud, or to band against James. Briefly, peace returned. James was probably aware of baronial alarm at the humiliation of the largest of their number, and their fear of further royal depradations, and he acted with some restraint. Papal dispensation was obtained for the new earl's marriage to the wife of his dead brother, Margaret, Maid of Galloway, which offered reassurance that no further attempt was intended on properties which William had claimed through her right.

The respite was short-lived. In London as head of an embassy to discuss a possible truce with England, now launched upon the troubles of Henry VI's reign, Earl Douglas made the error of arranging for the release of Malise Graham, a potential pretender to the throne, and there were rumours of deals with the Yorkists at court. If the earl's initiatives were intended, like the 'band' of his predecessor, as an insurance against royal attempts to seize his estates, they backfired spectacularly. James grasped his chance to present the expropriation of the Douglases as essential to the security of the state. He mobilized a massive campaign, defeating the earl, his brothers and their several allies including the Earls of Ormonde, Crawford and Moray, Lord Balvenie and Lord Hamilton, in engagements of which the battle of Arkinholm was the most important. Finally, Threave castle in Galloway, the principal seat of the Douglases, was pounded by imported Flemish heavy cannon, which gave the king an advantage against even the best fortified baronial strongholds. James made it his business to attend its surrender in person, but the ninth earl himself escaped to England. The Douglas estates were made forfeit during the parliaments of June and August 1455, together with the Crawford lordship of Brechin.

Parliament acquiesced in these and other annexations, however, because, irrespective of the justice or legality of such actions, it explicitly recognized that the Crown's relative poverty was damaging to its authority and to internal and external security. This was of the more concern since relations with England were rapidly worsening. It was therefore reaffirmed that the Crown should normally finance itself not through taxation or expensive borrowing, but through customs and through its own land-revenues. A century earlier, parliament had sought unsuccessfully to restrain David II from alienating Crown lands; it now renewed its effort, by using the novel tactic of treating the lands recently annexed as essentially national assets, which James must swear not to alienate, but leaving disposal or not of his 'own' possessions to his discretion. This has convincingly been interpreted as a significant move by parliament towards exerting control of the 'purse strings' and as a quid pro quo for acquiescence in the expropriation of the Douglas estates. This reflected a general dislike of taxation, but it was not anti-monarchical, except in the sense that it prevented the monarchy undermining its own authority for short term reasons; in a similar vein, the grant of regalities without parliamentary consent was prohibited. These measures, which sought to strengthen the central institutions of state, were not successfully implemented. But there was continuing pressure towards carrying their

essentially declaratory principles into action: measures of 1458 gave more formal shape to the Session court instituted in the previous reign, and provided for the suppression of the abuse of existing regalities by their lords. Such measures as these helped to gain for James something of his father's reputation of reformer.

From autumn 1455 Scotland was at war with the English, relations having further deteriorated partly because of the reception of Douglas by Henry VI's protector, the Duke of York, who had responded contemptuously to James's protests. In autumn 1456 James personally led a Scottish raid deep into Northumberland. With the ousting of the duke the following year, a truce was signed, but in 1460, as the conflict in England grew, James prepared a new invasion. When Henry was captured at Northampton in July 1460, his wife and son fled north. James, posing as the champion of the legitimate King of England, launched his forces upon the stronghold of Roxburgh, held by the Yorkists. On 3 August he was killed by one of his own cannon, when its barrel exploded. Shortly afterwards, on 8 August, the town fell. James was taken back to Edinburgh and buried in Holyrood Abbey. His son, James III, was crowned in the abbey of Kelso on 10 August.

Further Reading
C. McGladdery, *James II*, 1990.

JAMES III (1451-88) of Scotland succeeded to the throne on the death of his father, and was crowned in Kelso Abbey on 10 August 1460. Aged nine years, James continued what had already become a Stewart tradition of royal minorities, in which government was unstable and authority was restored when the king came of age. The reign of James III diverged from this pattern in that his mature rule was as chaotic as that of his minority.

In the first phase, the queen mother, Mary of Gueldres, and Bishop Kennedy of St Andrews were the chief directors of government. Two opportunities to change the face of England and Scotland were missed in the first three years of the reign. Queen Margaret of Anjou (wife of Henry VI) had sheltered in Scotland during his troubles. Her partly Scottish army defeated the Yorkists at St Albans, but failed to press home the advantage. Yorkist forces occupied London, Edward IV was crowned and in 1461 Henry, Queen Margaret and their son fled to Scotland. Edward now made a pact with James, the forfeited ninth Earl of Douglas, and John Macdonald, Lord of the Isles and Earl of Ross, in which they pledged to partition Scotland between them and to hold it as his vassals. Ross was able to behave with even greater impunity than normal in the far north, but neither he nor Douglas made military progress. Meanwhile, following the defeat of the Lancastrian forces, a new policy of *rapprochement* with England, later taken up by James, was initiated by Queen Mary, though she was at first opposed by Bishop

Kennedy. In June 1464, Edward IV agreed a fifteen-year truce, abandoning his Scottish malcontents, and Ross finally capitulated at Inverness. Queen Mary died on 16 November 1463, and Bishop Kennedy in May 1465.

In July the following year, the young king, now aged fourteen, was seized at Linlithgow by a group led by Lord Boyd of Kilmarnock and his brother Sir Alexander Boyd, keeper of Edinburgh castle, with the help of Lord Kennedy, brother of the deceased bishop and the king's uncle. At Edinburgh, in October, a parliament was held in James's name, at which he was induced to grant to the Boyds custody of three of his brothers and of the royal castles. Sir Alexander Boyd's son Thomas was created Earl of Arran and married to the Lady Mary, James's sister. Arran and Lord Boyd were instrumental in arranging James's own marriage to Margaret, daughter of Christian of Denmark, at Holyrood in July 1469. The Danes agreed that the yearly payments of 100 merks in respect of the Hebrides, agreed long ago in 1263, should be discontinued; Christian also handed over as pledges for Margaret's dowry his lands and rights in Orkney and Shetland, which were not redeemed. (Later, in 1472, the islands were united to the Scottish Crown, the Earl of Orkney having been compensated for his lost rights there.)

From the time of his marriage, James III took over the government. This turned out badly for the Boyds. Arran had been sent to Denmark to escort James's future bride to Scotland, while his father, Lord Boyd, was in England on an embassy. In their absence, others were able to influence the king, whose earlier abduction was suddenly discovered to have been treasonous. The earl was warned by his wife of the impending catastrophe while still aboard the ship which had just brought Princess Margaret to Leith. Dumping its royal cargo, the vessel turned round smartly and headed back across the North Sea. At Bruges, Arran encountered his father, who had heard the news while still in London. In November 1469 the Boyds were forfeited, their lands, including Arran, Bute, and estates in Ayrshire, were annexed to the Crown, and Sir Alexander Boyd was beheaded.

By this time there was already concern about the king's conduct of the government, and of justice. Parliament repeatedly complained that James was inactive in providing the firm and even-handed action which could compose magnate quarrels, especially in remoter parts. Here, the noble subjects of the Crown were apt to pursue their feuds in contempt of it, visiting violence and destruction upon the tenants and property of their opponents. James, it is clear, failed to uphold the law determinedly, preferring to pardon the leading miscreants rather than give them cause to dislike him. In 1475, a serial offender of this ilk, John, Lord of the Isles and Earl of Ross, having ignored many summonses, was finally visited with punitive raids and forfeited for treason. He

appeared before James III in July 1476 and surrendered his estates, but the king magnanimously restored all but the earldom of Ross. Unhappily, the main effect of this royal gesture was to preserve the region for anarchy, of which John and his bastard son Angus were for years the most incorrigible perpetrators.

One reason for James's behaviour may have been that his interests and attitudes were out of step with those of most of his lords. The king does not seem to have had much time for martial pastimes. He was deeply interested in architecture and employed his confidant Robert Cochrane to restore the Great Hall of Stirling Castle. He collected manuscripts, enjoyed contemporary poetry, and is said to have enjoyed singing and playing musical instruments. James's love of the choir of the Chapel Royal was to help in a small way to bring about his downfall. It is unlikely that many of James's lords counted such activities in their daily routine. But many kings, before and since, took pleasure in music and poetry. If James III had treated matters of state in the serious manner which loyal nobles expected of their kings, they would have forgiven him not only his own pleasures but his lack of pleasure in theirs. As it was, his indifference to the enthusiasms of what might be called the hunting and hawking fraternity did not endear him to the baronial mind. Perhaps James was aware of this, and sought to win the approval of his chief subjects by treating leniently such time-honoured lordly pursuits as feuding with the neighbours.

There was growing evidence that while the king treated errant barons mildly, he lacked the judgement to tell apart real and imaginary threats to his position, and thus came to initiate capricious and vengeful acts against (probably) innocent parties. There was the arbitrary cutting down of the Boyds – and its bizarre sequel. In 1471, in defiance of James, the Boyds' ally Patrick Graham, who had replaced Kennedy as Bishop of St Andrews during their ascendancy, travelled to Rome to be consecrated. He returned in 1473 with a prize which obviated the need for such journeys, an age-old dream of Scottish bishops and kings: St Andrews was raised to the status of archdiocese (and himself to the dignity of primate). James was evidently unimpressed by Graham's initiative. The new archbishop was charged with heresy, perhaps at the instigation of William Scheves, the king's confidant and physician, and expelled from the university. The Vatican was forced to send a commission of investigation, at which point Graham seems to have lost his head entirely, claiming that he himself was the real pope, so that the commission found that he was not heretical but insane, and deposed him from the primacy. Heavy royal pressure was involved in the decision to appoint William Scheves as Graham's successor at St Andrews.

In 1479-80 James arrested two of his brothers,

Alexander Duke of Albany and the Earl of Mar, for reasons which will never be certainly known, but which may have included jealousy of their public popularity. Mar was never charged with any offence. He met his end in prison, probably of natural causes, but in such circumstances as to arouse deep, widespread, and understandable suspicion. Albany was arrested, but had escaped to France, before the charges against him were even framed. These centred on the suspicion that as March Warden, his (necessary) dealings with the English kings had been treasonable. There is no convincing evidence for this, and Albany may well have fled in the belief that his arbitrary imprisonment without charge signalled that he would be unjustly dealt with. Parliament repeatedly postponed considering the charges against Albany, and it seems likely that members feared being forced to condemn him in his absence.

Albany had certainly been one of a number of political opponents of the king's English policy. In 1474, a promising start had been made in improving relations. A truce of forty-five years was signed, and it was agreed that James's son (James, later James IV, born in March 1473) should marry Edward IV's daughter Cecilia for a dowry of 20,000 merks. James proposed other marriages with prominent English nobles for his sisters, but these fell through. In 1475, Edward IV withdrew his invasion force from France in exchange for a pension from Louis XI, and when he also defaulted on his dowry payments, James's English alignment began to look out of date. Although the truce held up there were reasons enough in the late 1470s to think it had run its course politically. This was the situation when Albany reached France in spring 1479.

He arrived, of course, not as an ambassador but as a fugitive, bent upon exculpation, probably revenge, and possibly usurpation. But Louis XI was seeking a *rapprochement* with the Scottish government (which James was foolish enough to reject). So Albany sailed to England. Edward IV made him welcome; he had already embarked on an aggressive anti-Scottish policy, renewing his pact with those tireless veterans, the former Earl Douglas and the Lord of the Isles. In June 1482, Albany agreed formally that once enthroned, he would acknowledge Edward as overlord, and cede to him Berwick and large tracts of the borders. English forces under Gloucester and Albany closed on Berwick, while at Edinburgh, James assembled 50,000 troops, and marched south, encamping at Lauder. It was at this point that mutiny broke out in the Scottish army, led by Earls Angus, Buchan, Huntly, Crawford and Lennox. They hanged Cochrane, Preston and perhaps others among James's circle, at the bridge of Lauder, and imprisoned the king in Edinburgh castle.

There is now considerable scepticism among historians about the role of the king's 'low-born favourites' in alienating noble support for James III. Recruitment of officials and advisers from outside the aristocracy was not invented by him, and most new faces were not nearly as plebeian as sixteenth-century chroniclers made out. Sir William Knollis, who was to be treasurer under James IV, is dubbed 'Torpichen', James III's 'fencing master'. Imputations of homosexuality once sustained colourful analogies with Edward II of England. But, as the career of James VI and I indicates, kings could raise the most intimate favourites to the highest rank, and still escape destruction. James III's barons may well have wanted to place themselves in his counsels, but their desperate throw at Lauder surely also reflects exasperation at the crisis to which Scotland had been brought. The apparently blameless career and suspicious death of Mar may have helped to convince them that it was James's caprice and not Albany's treachery which had brought them to the brink of catastrophe. Robert Cochrane had been given Mar's earldom, and perhaps this was a reason for his fate. But the central political purpose of the barons was to compel James to deal justly with his brother; they settled down in Edinburgh to await the arrival of Albany and Gloucester, accepting the (final) loss of Berwick, in August 1482, as the unavoidable cost.

It was with this intention, and not to make him king, that the barons met with Albany; he made no attempt to implement by force his agreement with Edward made at Fotheringay, and persuaded Gloucester to withdraw the English forces. In parliament, he was restored to his properties and titles and pardoned for the treaty with Edward. In December 1482, parliament appointed him lieutenant-general, but in February he was in touch with Edward IV, who renewed his promise to help him gain the Crown. When this news emerged, James III issued a new pardon, but Albany fortified Dunbar and continued his intrigues until the death of Edward IV in April. By this time it was too late. In Scotland, Albany was at last forfeited in June 1483, along with some of the earls who had supported him. In England, Richard III was in a shaky position, and quickly signed a truce (James renewed it with Henry VII). Albany's only remaining recourse was a joint expedition with the indefatigable Douglas, but this was a failure. Douglas was pardoned and pensioned by James; Albany escaped to France and was killed in a tournament there in 1485.

Whether or not Albany seriously aimed to supplant the king in 1479, it seems that this became ever more tempting and, if only because of James's responses to the challenge, ever more realistic. For these tests served to focus the unending complaints at James's inability to uphold justice and the laws, and further undermined confidence in the king among sections of the nobility. The final blow came in 1488. James had persuaded the pope to suppress the priory of Coldingham with a view to transferring its revenues to his beloved choir of the Royal Chapel. Unhappily, these had been grasped by the powerful Homes, and there was a sudden and violent clamour against the attempt to dispossess them, particularly among the barons of the south and east. At the parliament in Edinburgh in January 1488, James sought to arrest his opponents, but failed and was forced to cross the Forth. Most of the northern earls remained loyal, and James rallied an army of 30,000 men. The king's opponents found a focus in his son and heir apparent, James, Duke of Rothesay, aged fifteen, who escaped from Stirling Castle in February, possibly provoked by moves which promised his disinheritance.

Several barons came over to him, including the Earl of Angus, the Bishop of Glasgow, and Lords Gray, Home and Lyle (who had been loyal in 1482) and they too were able to raise substantial forces. A temporary pact at Blackness on the Forth merely put off the day of reckoning, and both sides prepared for it. The king appealed to Henry VII to send an army, a move which bore no fruit but the desertion of the Earl of Argyll. The two sides met at Sauchieburn, near the field of Bannockburn, on 11 June 1488; however, the issue was decided not by a great and decisive battle, but in a bathetic scene which somehow typifies the reign. James left the field and, having revealed his identity, was killed at Bannockburn mill, by an unknown person. The tradition that the assassin posed as a priest is almost certainly apocryphal. James III was buried at Cambuskenneth.

Further Reading
N. Macdougall, *James III*, 1982.

JAMES IV (1473-1513) of Scotland was born on 17 March 1473, the eldest son of James III and Margaret, daughter of Christian of Denmark. The boy was chiefly resident at Stirling. Little is known of his education, but he certainly acquired an intelligent interest in the arts and sciences, and in the mid-1490s Ayala, the Spanish ambassador, reported that he spoke Latin, French, German, Flemish, Italian, Spanish and 'the language of the savages who live in some parts of Scotland and of the Islands', i.e. Gaelic.

James IV came to the throne as a result of his attempt to usurp his father, James III. In January 1488, James III, abandoned by most of the southern nobility, went north to raise troops, leaving his son, James, Duke of Rothesay, at Stirling. But the king evidently did not trust the duke (one judgement in which he was probably not mistaken). Having already initiated moves towards arranging a royal marriage for his younger son (also James), on 29 January he made him Duke of Ross. All this strongly suggested that Rothesay was to be displaced as heir, and it may very well be that this provoked his bid for power. On 2 February, the fifteen-year-old James placed himself at the head of the rebels and left

Stirling castle. Bewailing the effects of incompetent advice upon his unhappy father, he spread slanders about those responsible and offered his own services as counsellor. James IV has sometimes, unconvincingly, been portrayed as an innocent tool of unscrupulous barons. But even before his accession, he showed political acumen and ruthlessness.

James was in command of the troops at the battle of Sauchieburn, and ordered that the king should not be harmed; his father's death at Bannockburn mill is said to have weighed heavily on the conscience of the new monarch, who wore a heavy iron chain in penance for it. He was crowned at Scone on 26 June 1488. Leading supporters were well rewarded. The Earl of Argyll became chancellor, and there were powerful positions for the Earl of Angus, Lord Home and Lord Hailes, who was created Earl of Bothwell in place of John Ramsay, the confidant of James III, now degraded. Others among the late king's most prominent supporters were forfeited, but the heirs of those killed at Sauchieburn were allowed to succeed and the Earls of Buchan and Crawford were pardoned. In 1489 Earls Lennox and Huntly and Lords Forbes and Lyle, raised rebellion in the north and west, but even though forfeited, they were soon restored and their allies and supporters pardoned. James sought to build ecclesiastical support, marginalizing William Scheles, whom James III had promoted, and favouring the ambitions of Robert Blacadder. He ill-advisedly sought to pursue this, however, by obtaining for Blacadder the dignity of Archbishop of Glasgow, for the creation of two Scottish archiepiscopates gave rise to endless friction.

The parliament of April 1491 passed a measure providing for 'wapenschaws' or musters in the shires, and James himself travelled around the kingdom to preside over criminal proceedings known as the 'Justice Ayres'. James revived 'the Session', a civil court founded by James I, which had fallen into disuse, and which now emerged in a new form. The court comprised mainly of king's councillors rather than Members of Parliament, and began to meet regularly in Edinburgh. The city was increasingly recognized, in practice as well as formally, as the kingdom's capital, a trend encouraged by James's construction of Holyroodhouse next to the palace, to serve as a new residence. The king used the policy of temporary imprisonment for his barons, but dealt ruthlessly with less prominent miscreants. He is said to have demonstrated his concern for the tranquillity of his kingdom by riding alone from Stirling to Elgin and to have emerged unscathed.

It may be doubted whether he would have progressed safely far into Ross. In his reign (as in almost every other) the problem of establishing and enforcing a uniform system of law and government was posed most acutely in the north and west, and especially in the Isles, whose skies were traditionally lit by the constellation of the clan Macdonald. Among its brightest orbs was Angus, bastard son of John of the Isles, who had enjoyed himself for many uninterrupted years, feuding with his father and ignoring James III. But when Angus was murdered by the Irish chief Diarmaid O'Cairbre, there appeared a new star in the north, Alexander of Lochalsh, nephew of John. Alexander recapitulated the careers of many of his forefathers, establishing his dominance in Lochaber, capturing the unfortunate town of Inverness, being defeated by royal or local forces (in this case the Mackenzies of Kintail), retreating temporarily to the Isles, invading the mainland again (1497), and suffering defeat and death in battle (1498), to be replaced by a new aspirant. James repeatedly visited the far north and the far west, forfeiting John of the Isles in 1493, but the use of field armies to overawe such regions had only a temporary effect.

Even royal expeditions were by no means always triumphal progresses. In 1494, having just set sail, James watched impotently as his castle of Dunaverty was overrun, and its keeper executed, by John of Islay. The stronghold was recovered for the Crown, Islay and his four sons were executed, and James received the submissions of many island chiefs at Mingary castle, Ardnamurchan in 1495. In between these dramatic military sweeps, James relied on magnates such as the Gordons of Huntly and the Campbells of Argyll, men with private interests which were not necessarily those of the Crown. It cannot be said that James's best efforts were sufficient to solve the stubborn problem of the far north and west, and dealing with his southern neighbour was just as challenging.

Henry VII greeted James with suspicion. The new king's chief supporters had generally shared a scepticism of the Anglophile policies of his predecessor and had now successfully got rid of him. In 1489, there was a series of incidents at sea, in one of which a London merchant, Stephen Bull, acting with royal approval, sought to avenge the capture by Scots of five English privateers and was himself recaptured in the Forth. James IV encouraged the building of merchant and war ships, but his position in Scotland was not yet secure. Anxious to avoid war, the king released Bull and returned him to England. But relations remained strained. Henry financed a plot by discontented Scots, including John Ramsey (the degraded Earl of Boswell) and the Earl of Buchan, to kidnap James and his young brother the Duke of Ross, and the Earl of Angus seems to have offered to hand over Hermitage castle to him in the event of war. When James discovered this he imprisoned Angus, but once more as a warning; Angus was soon released, and though he was not allowed repossession of Hermitage, he was compensated with less strategically placed property. Henry seems to have come

to the conclusion that attempts to destabilize or harrass James's government were not likely to bear fruit, and a truce for five years was signed in 1491.

In November 1495 at Stirling James, now on bad terms with Henry VII received Perkin Warbeck, who claimed to be Richard, Duke of York, younger brother and heir of Edward V. It is now reasonably certain that the princes had been murdered in the Tower, probably at the instigation of their uncle Richard III, but the evidence of their demise was not available to James in 1495. Convinced partly by the backing of Margaret of Burgundy that Warbeck was the genuine article, James allowed him £1,200 a year and in January 1496 married him to Huntly's daughter, Katherine Gordon. But James's policy depended for success not just on Warbeck being who he said he was, but on his being accepted and enthroned in England. In the meantime it did nothing but anger Henry VII, who was not mollified by the efforts of the Spanish monarchs to act as peacemakers. Ferdinand and Isabella wished a Tudor land for their daughter, Catherine of Aragon, and her future husband Arthur, Henry's son, but they were anxious also to befriend the Scots, and thus detach them from the embrace of France. James's invasions of England in 1496-7 found no enthusiasm for the putative king, and he must have been relieved when Warbeck decided to leave Scotland in July. (Warbeck, after a brief and abortive attempt to raise support in Cornwall, was arrested, confessed his true identity and was finally executed in 1499.) This opened the way for a truce, signed in September 1497, and relations improved.

In 1495 Henry VII's had offered James the hand of his daughter Margaret, but James was too preoccupied with Warbeck; now, in 1498, Henry renewed the offer. James had by now reached the age of twenty-five; there had been several proposals for his marriage, beginning with his betrothal in 1474 to Princess Cecilia, daughter of Edward IV; in 1484 a proposed marriage to Ann de la Pole had come to nothing. In the parliament of April 1491 there was much concern about the king's marriage, and search parties were sent out to scour Europe for suitable candidates, to no avail. In the meantime, the king made do with a number of extra-marital liaisons. An early partner was Marion Boyd of Bonshaw, who gave the king a son, Alexander. Marion was superseded in James's affections by Janet, the daughter of Lord Kennedy, who gave birth to James, created Earl of Moray in June 1501. Then came Margaret, daughter of Lord Drummond, by whom James had Lady Margaret Stewart, born in 1497. From May 1496, Margaret Drummond was the king's chief mistress, and he seems to have developed great affection for her. It may be that this was the reason why James responded coolly to Henry VII's offer. But things turned out well, for everyone but Margaret and her sisters, for in 1500 they all died of poison, perhaps deliberately administered, as it was rumoured, by vindictive relations of the displaced Janet Kennedy. This left James free to marry Margaret Tudor, a union celebrated, at vast expense to the Scottish treasury, at Holyrood Abbey on 8 August 1503, and recorded in 'The Thrissil and the Rois' by William Dunbar, whose evocation of the queen ('young tender plant of pulchritude') seems to have strained somewhat the concept of poetic licence.

James patronized Dunbar generously, and did not lack interest in education and science. In 1494, with Bishop William Elphinstone, he played a role in the foundation of Aberdeen University, the third in Scotland. In 1496, he initiated legislation requiring men of substance to send their sons to school at the age of eight or nine, until they had learned their Latin; the objective seems to have been mainly to encourage the study of law, though we do not know how effective the measure was. James cultivated an interest in science, including surgery and dentistry, and encouraged the studies in alchemy of Damian, Abbot of Tongland, in Galloway. Damian also tried to fly; in 1507, having fashioned a pair of wings, he launched himself from the ramparts of Stirling castle, and seems to have survived the resultant crash. It was also that year that the king licensed the first known Scottish printing press, of Walter Chepman and Andrew Myllar, in Edinburgh, which printed chiefly devotional material.

The king, indeed, seems to have taken religion seriously. His struggle to establish state power in remoter regions broadly corresponded with the task of implementing orthodoxy, both against paganism, and new and rarer beliefs. In about July 1494 he and his council interviewed the Lollards of Kyle at Glasgow at the insistence of Robert Blacadder, Archbishop of Glasgow, which corresponded with the effort to impose royal control in Kintyre. James may have been pious, but he was certainly not other-worldly or dominated by a fascination with learning. His son Alexander Stewart studied at Siena and Rome under Erasmus, but James did not scruple to appoint him as Archbishop of St Andrews at the age of eleven. He controlled other benefices in the financial interests of the Crown, notably using the ecclesiastical revenues to support his brother, the Duke of Ross, while appropriating the secular revenues of Ross for the state!

However, James seems to have been genuinely enthusiastic for joint action with other Christian monarchs against the Ottoman empire, now moving towards the greatest extent of its expansion in south-eastern and central Europe. His ardour, however, was not shared by Pope Julius II, who instead built a bloc with Louis XII and the Emperor Maximilian against Venice, known as the League of Cambrai (1508). Venice was then a strong maritime republic and a bulwark against the Turks, but it

also stood in the way of Julius's objective of building his own state in central Italy. Scotland, he thought, would be useful if England decided to attack his French allies, but James, though still bound by his treaty with France, refused to be drawn further in. France, meanwhile, showed its reverence for papal realpolitik by following up the defeat of Venice with an occupation of much of northern Italy. The pope, recognizing the dangers posed in the east by the obliteration of Venice, formed a 'Holy League' against the French in 1511. The danger to France was also a danger to Scotland, especially given that the young Henry VIII had acceded (1509), and the historic general peace between England and the Scots (the first for almost two centuries) was a casualty of these circumstances.

Henry's aggressive policy, as at the start of James's reign, was fuelled by a series of clashes at sea and by repeated English claims to be acting as allies of the pope and therefore of religion. The impounding by the English of the *Lion* and the *Jenny Pirwin* led James to appeal to the pope to restrain Henry, but Julius threatened James with excommunication if he should declare war on England. By the end of 1511, this was becoming ever more likely, as the beleagured Louis XII looked to turn the traditional Scottish alliance (formally renewed in 1492) into material assistance. In 1512, James, acutely aware of the likely consequences for Scotland should France be overwhelmed, agreed to help Louis in the event of an English invasion, though he tried hard to slow down the drive to war, appealing both to the pope and Ferdinand to reduce tension by diplomacy. The election of a new pope, Leo X, promised to improve matters but did not. In April 1513, Henry made agreements with Maximillian and Ferdinand for war against France.

In August 1513, James invaded England with an army of about 20,000, destroying three Northumbrian castles and provoking the English under Earl Surrey to follow him northwards. Surrey, who commanded a force about the same size as James's, caught up with the Scots at Flodden Edge, and battle was joined on 9 September. An abortive naval expedition had sailed to France under the direction of the Earl of Arran; much of James's skilled artillery-men had been committed to this enterprise, and were sorely missed. The English also made devastating use of their bills (a long pole with a scythe-like blade attached, topped off with a spike), slashing through the shafts of the Scottish spears. The king seems to have died in an early charge with his spearmen. His death proves the truth of Ayala's report, twenty years earlier, remarking upon James's eagerness to 'undertake the most dangerous things. On such occasions he does not take the least care of himself', and was 'courageous, more than a king should be'. This aptly described not only the manner of James's death at Flodden field, but the fact that he was there at all. For Ayala's remark reflected a new consciousness that the appearance of kings, as medieval knights on the battleground, was a foolhardy courage. Nine earls and thirteen lords were lost, and the English estimate of 10,000 men may well not be fanciful. Hall's comment upon James's bravery 'to fight in battle as a mean soldier' was mere romanticism. James's body was not found. John Stowe later claimed that it had been taken to Skene monastery in Surrey, that the head had then been hacked off and, later still, taken, complete with red beard, by the Elizabethan Launcelot Young to Wood Street, there to be buried in the church. James IV's son James was the only one of his six legitimate children to survive, and became James V aged only one.

Further Reading
N. Macdougall, *James IV*, 1989.
R. Nicolson, *Scotland: the Later Middle Ages*, 1974.
R. L. Mackie, *King James IV of Scotland*, 1958.

JAMES V (1512-42) of Scotland was born in April 1512 and came to the throne in 1513 after the death of his father James IV at Flodden. As usual during Stewart regencies there was a protracted series of factional struggles for custody of the king and for the political power which this conferred. But throughout the long period between James's accession and his coming of age, politics was largely fought out between proponents of *rapprochement* with England and those who favoured the 'auld alliance' with France. Such a persistent political (rather than sectional) division, was novel and reflected new realities in Europe.

Not surprisingly, James's mother, Queen Margaret, who had been named as regent in the will of James IV, favoured a policy of friendship with her brother Henry VIII (who might be expected to favour her, in the hope of exerting influence through her on Scotland). In 1514, the queen married Archibald, the 'Red' Douglas, sixth Earl of Angus. Douglas himself was chiefly concerned with his own advancement and that of his family, but their hostility to the Stewarts had generally aligned them with the anglophile opposition. Margaret's remarriage technically disqualified her from retaining custody of James, and it also prompted a group of nobles alarmed by the prospect of subordinacy to England following the debacle at Flodden, to send to France for the young king's uncle and heir presumptive, John Stewart, the Duke of Albany (the son of Duke Alexander, who had done so much to ensure the dispossession of James III).

Albany arrived in 1515 and removed by force the three-year-old James from the charge of his mother, entrusting him to the care of Lord Erskine, the keeper of Stirling castle. Though at the time he was rumoured to have been responsible for the death of James's young brother, Alexander, Albany ensured that James was well looked after. The boy listened to stories from Sir David Lindsay, who seems to have shown him as much

affection as anyone, in what was in reality an orphan's childhood. He received formal tuition from Gavin Dunbar, later Archbishop of Glasgow, learning Latin, French and developing an affection for music; however, on his mother's return from England in 1524, James's education was neglected.

Albany generally pursued a francophile policy, though the French were by no means necessarily hostile to England. Scottish relations with these countries depended to a large extent in this period upon its dealings with the Habsburgs and with the papacy. Spain had only recently been unified, but had won great possessions and treasure in the New World, and from 1519, it became part of a huge territorial complex, joined with the Empire, the Low Countries and southern Italy, through the person of Charles V. Encircled France was at times tempted towards trying to make friends with Henry VIII rather than the more distant and weaker Scots. Thus, to the extent that Albany's 'pro-French' policy was 'anti-English' it was sometimes opposed by France: whilst on embassy there in 1517, he was detained for four years! When Anglo-French relations soured, Albany returned, but his efforts in 1522 and 1524 to mobilize the nobles for war against England were resisted by a strong faction who saw him as a tool of the French.

Albany's failure and departure for France in 1524 threw James, now aged twelve, and the government, back into the hands of the pro-English faction, in the persons of the queen and the Earl of Arran, and Archbishop James Beaton. In July 1524, the boy was publicly invested with the crown and sceptre, but there were still powerful voices opposing their policy and internal feuding with Douglas (who Margaret divorced in 1525), which was temporarily resolved by inventing a three month rota for the custody of James. At the end of his stint, in September 1526, Douglas simply refused to hand over the boy, and imprisoned him at Edinburgh. During the period of his captivity, James's academic education was neglected, though he learned much of martial arts, and (towards the time of his release) young women were found for him. James was given large sums of money, and (to the later misfortune of his subjects) allowed to cultivate expensive tastes. Whether all this was just what the Douglases thought appropriate for a young adolescent or whether it amounted to a Machiavellian ploy to distract him from serious matters is unknown. If so it failed, and in his enforced isolation James cultivated both self-centred ruthlessness and a deal of resentment against his gaolers.

A rescue plot by Queen Margaret and the Earl of Lennox was foiled, and Lennox was murdered in the attempt, but eventually, in the spring of 1528, the king was able to escape. Douglas's friends and relations, who had been packed into the leading state offices, and had survived so long only because of fear that they might murder their young charge, were overwhelmed and forfeited, the earl fleeing to England. The period of weakened state authority had depleted revenues and there remained debts left by James IV; Crown finances were in a very poor state. But there were opportunities, in these tense times when everyone was searching for alliances, to secure a large dowry through the international dynastic marriage market. While James was searching he conducted a string of affairs, with Elizabeth Shaw, Margaret daughter of Lord Erskine, Euphemia Elphinstone, Elizabeth Carmichael, Elizabeth Stewart and Elizabeth Beaton, and had by them several children. With commendable candour, James wrote to Albany explaining that he favoured an early marriage, among other reasons, in order 'to avoid the procreation of bastards'. Despite extensive discussions, James was not yet able to secure a bride. But monetary relief was at hand from the fate of another marriage.

By this time, all Scotland's diplomatic relations, including and especially those with the Habsburgs and the papacy, had become entangled with Henry VIII's celebrated divorce from Catherine of Aragon (daughter of Ferdinand and Isabella) and with the consequent breach with Rome. The reformation was in full swing in Germany, and there were political reasons why, there and elsewhere, princes and nobles might find reasons to support it; reasons too, why senior churchmen such as James Beaton and his nephew David, successive Archbishops of St Andrews, might strive to maintain the status quo. Already by the late 1520s, reformed (Lutheran) literature was circulating in burghs such as Aberdeen and St Andrews, and in 1528 Protestantism claimed its first martyr, Patrick Hamilton. As the 1530s wore on, Protestant sentiment grew in the burghs and even among some sections of the magnates, and these provided a permanent support for a foreign alignment with reforming England; conservatives, by contrast tended to rally to the pro-French stance favoured by Albany and the king.

Yet irrespective of Scottish religious sentiment, and despite James's own conservatism in such matters, Henry's defiance and European dissent put the pope in an extraordinarily weak position in Scotland. This provided James with the perfect conditions for extracting the money he needed from the Scottish church. In 1531, he reminded the pope that the Crown of Scotland, in order to hold the City of God against the barbarian hordes of heresy which surged around it, needed funds; £10,000 a year in perpetuity, thought James, would do nicely. After several months of negotiation, a compromise was worked out in which the bishops agreed to provide £72,000 over four years and benefices were assigned to provide £1,400 per year for the foundation of a College of Justice. Only the name was new, and James was thus enabled to pay the fourteen judges allocated to the already existing civil Court of Session.

Scotland did not follow Henry out of the Roman obedience, despite arm-twisting by the English king. James might be thought to have done rather well on his uncle's coat tails; he obtained access to substantial church resources without the risk of opprobrium of Henry's breach with Rome, or his violent assault upon the monasteries. Appearing before the pope, and the powerful French and Hapsburg monarchs alike as a loyal catholic, he was also in the happy position of being courted by Henry as a potential ally.

James became one of Europe's most eligible bachelors. The French suggested Mary of Bourbon, and the king took a veritable armada across the channel to pay court, only to find that Mary's looks disappointed him. Other agents were indefatigable in ferreting out brides (Danish, Hungarian and Portuguese princesses were offered), and there had also been talk, up to 1534, of a marriage with Henry's daughter, Mary Tudor. But on New Year's Day 1537, at Notre Dame in Paris, James married Madeleine, the daughter Francis I, in belated accordance with the Treaty of Rouen, signed by Albany twenty years earlier. His wife brought a dowry of 100,000 livres, but survived less than two months in Scotland. In June 1538, James married Mary of Guise, who brought him a dowry of 150,000 livres; in 1540-1 she gave birth to two sons, but both died within months.

French marriages were complemented by growing fashions at court for French architecture, art and decoration which flourished under the powerful monarchy of Francis I. James added a new tower to his father's palace of Holyrood, developed the residence at Linlithgow, and employed French architects to build new palaces at Stirling and Falkland. It has been suggested that his building work may have cost in the region of £50,000, an enormous sum in those days, and the whole enterprise reflects the king's desire to parade himself as a European sovereign in the era when unified states like France and England, and the huge transnational empire of the Habsburgs, were generating resources for display on a grand scale. Only part of James's windfalls from the bishops was spent on the renamed Court of Session, but it was not all squandered either; the Crown's finances were much improved during his majority, some spent to good effect.

The king also made some progress in reducing the lawlessness of remoter parts. This was no thanks to the Earls of Argyll and Moray, who had abused their trust as royal lieutenants to advance their private interests. Partly through the good offices of the Macdonalds of Islay, other continuingly turbulent western clans were bridled. Further north, a royal fleet enforced a higher degree of compliance with the law and the collection of revenue after 1540. In the Borders, there was more serious trouble, which included not only general lawlessness but also continuing disaffection of some of the Marcher lords, first made evident in their refusal to serve against England under Albany, and now resurrected in the form of underhand political dealings with the English. In 1530 James took an army to the Borders and hanged one John Armstrong and forty of his followers. This may have served well as a demonstration of royal power, but it did not solve the political problem of the growing resentment (particularly in the south), issuing from a range of different motives, at the pro-French drift of government policy. During the late 1530s, James adopted an increasingly intimidatory posture to nobles who opposed or otherwise inconvenienced him, especially the Douglases; there were brutal executions for treason, based on flimsy evidence, and part of the king's new prosperity was based on unscrupulous forfeits. James seems not to have realized the importance of persuasion in dealing with powerful men, relying increasingly upon the support of the chief prelates, especially David Beaton (Cardinal Beaton from 1538) who supported his conservative francophile alignment.

James's relations with England were unstable. Henry VIII, in his isolation, looked anxiously at the Roman Catholic power north of the Tweed. Twice he moved from anxious attempts at persuading James of the need for reform, to outright military aggression. Henry encouraged the Scottish internal opposition, and there were cross-border forays between 1532 and May 1534, when a truce was signed. Henry's international situation was such that, while he must have been alarmed at James's French marriage, he was in no position to attempt any large scale action against the Scots. Later in his reign, Henry urged a meeting with his Scottish counterpart at York, hoping to convince him of the need for religious change. James agreed but, his advisers fearing kidnap (which could by no means be ruled out) and his clergy fearing reform, he did not appear there, while Henry fumed for twelve days. The English king was no longer isolated in Europe, taking the emperor's side in his renewed rivalry with France, and he was angry enough with James to sanction official hostilities. These, however, were inconclusive, Sir Robert Bowes's defeat by Huntly being balanced by the Duke of Norfolk's burning of Roxburgh and Kelso.

It was the Scottish response which was of more significance. James could not persuade many of his nobles that their interests lay in war on behalf of the old alliance with France. Many refused even to muster at Fala Muir, and far fewer were prepared to cross the border, where their opponents were encamped. It was this which provided the background to the disaster at Solway Moss on 24 November 1542, in which a small English army overwhelmed and humiliated a much larger but ill-led and ill-motivated Scottish force. There now existed an important segment of Scottish opinion which resented the depradations of their king and had no confidence in

his policy. Recognizing the need for religious reform, many saw English pressure as a means to bring it about. Little (in military terms) lay between Henry and the Scottish capital.

The debacle seems to have cast James into a deep depression, from which the birth to Queen Mary on 8 December of a child Mary, later Mary, Queen of Scots, failed (if the traditional story is to be believed) to rouse him; it 'came with a lass and it will gang with a lass' was the king's lugubrious response to the joyous news of an heir (the Stewart dynasty was descended from Marjorie Bruce), and he died six days later.

JAMES VI and I (1566-1625) was crowned King of Scotland on 29 July 1567. The ceremony was novel in several respects. It was held in a parish church, of Holy Rude, Stirling. The king was annointed by a bishop ordained before the reformation but now a reformer (Adam Bothwell of Orkney), and the sermon was given by none other than John Knox. James's coronation was the result of the ousting of the Roman Catholic Mary, Queen of Scots, whose policy of toleration had won her many minds, but whose behaviour in the connected affairs of Darnley, Riccio and Earl Bothwell had lost her many more hearts. Still, Mary's party remained strong among the lords, and the fight for her return was not stilled until, in summer 1574, the Hamiltons deserted the cause, and the diehards in Edinburgh castle surrendered in the face of English bombardment. By this time, a succession of regents, the Earls of Moray, Lennox and Mar, had come and gone, and government was in the charge of James Douglas, fourth Earl of Morton. Morton continued the general policy of seeking accommodation with England, and was able to bring some measure of stability to the kingdom. The young James remained in the care of Lady Mar, fearful and untrusting of the aloof and intimidating figure of the regent; his portrait depicts a sad little boy, prematurely aged.

One of James's tutors (from the age of four) was the Calvinist George Buchanan. James learned Latin and French, and Buchanan did his very best to convince the boy of the vileness of his mother, Mary, and of the rightness of resistance to ungodly rulers such as herself. Unlike the English, the Scots had eventually accomplished independence from Rome despite the religion of their monarch, James's mother. The Scottish reformed church was able, in the circumstances of its birth, to acquire and develop from the new European sources the latest religious ideas (and some radical political ones). Doctrines of resistance to the unjust and ungodly magistrates were taken up by Knox and Buchanan, 'the most radical of all the Calvinist revolutionaries', which fuelled the engines of struggle against magistrates in several countries. In Scotland, as in Holland, the search for godly instruments had led to the mobilization of the urban middle classes and even the poor. James later recalled his well-learned lesson, that in the Scottish reformation 'many things were inordinately done by a popular tumult and rebellion ... and not proceeding from the Princes order' as they had in England, Denmark and parts of Germany.

The disintegration of Mary's party in 1574 corresponded with the return to Scotland from Geneva of the Presbyterian Andrew Melville. For Melville and his supporters, the appropriation by Morton of much of the revenues of the archbishopric of St Andrews typified the corrupt and unreformed state of Scotland's church. They were aghast at the effects of recent compromises upon the ideals which they cherished. Melville built on Knox and Buchanan, aiming to carry forward the unfinished business of the Scottish reformation, to dispatch episcopacy, to establish kirk discipline through a hierarchy of courts and to establish clerical supremacy over the lay element in the Scottish system. Gradually they made progress through the General Assembly of the Kirk, pressing forward with further reformation under the general protection of the state. Meanwhile, after vicious internal plotting in the councils of state, those many persons who temporarily ousted Morton in 1578 were routed, and Morton moved to dispossess the Hamiltons. This in turn led Esmé Stuart, heir to the house of the Lennox Stuarts (which had stood next to the Hamiltons in the succession to the throne, and which now stood first) to visit Scotland from his native France. James became infatuated with Esmé, who provided something of the affection and attention lacking in the young boy's life. Esmé was instrumental in Morton's fall and execution in 1581 (the charge was the murder of James's father, Darnley); he was given the title Earl of Lennox and became effectively regent. These developments alarmed the Protestant party which did not trust the genuineness of Lennox's recent conversion and suspected him of having dealings with Mary and/or Spain. The result was the capture and imprisonment of James by Protestant lords led by William Ruthven, Earl of Gowrie, in 1582; the expulsion of Lennox; and the ratification of these proceedings by the General Assembly of the Kirk under the influence of the Melvillians. James never forgot the bitter experience of being parted from his new friend and adviser and imprisoned by the agents of the kirk's most fanatical party.

In contrast to the kirk, the Scottish parliament was usually much less truculent, and James now deliberately invoked its authority as a buttress for his own. The Scottish parliament was, even more than the English, dominated by the nobles, and later James was able to control its agenda through the Lords of the Articles. In 1584, parliament was persuaded to pass the Black Acts designed to reverse the progress towards Presbyterian structures which the kirk had made, and it specifically named for suppression *De Jure Regno apud Scotos* and the *History of Scotland*, by James's old tutor, Buchanan.

However the Black Acts, though much complained of by the Protestant party, had little permanent effect. The kirk was a powerful force which no monarch whose main aim was the establishment of central authority could afford to ignore, even though he might find many of its doctrines and ambitions repugnant. Until Mary's execution in 1587 there were powerful and disaffected Catholic lords, especially in the north, who still hankered after her return and, led by Huntly, intrigued with Spain to bring it about. From 1586, the Scottish régime was underwritten by a formal accord with England, which though its brand of reform was rather distinctive, was equally a Protestant power in counter-reformation Europe. His chancellor, John Maitland of Thirlstane, persuaded James to make a series of concessions to Melville's supporters, while refusing demands to initiate an anti-Catholic crusade in the wake of Huntly's rebellion and the murder of Moray in 1592, which had given the Presbyterian cause great impetus by linking it with patriotic sentiment. Up to the mid-1590s, James maintained the alliance, but after Maitland's death, the success of his punitive expedition against Boswell and the Catholic earls' departure from Scotland, his enthusiasm for the struggle against them waned, and his attitude to the kirk became sharper. Melville and his friends were at first able to carry the rest of the kirk in their outrage at James's leniency to the Catholic earls. In 1596, Melville contemptuously labelled the king 'God's silly vassall', but a riot at Edinburgh was used to strengthen the moderate party and ensure his defeat; later the Gowrie plot was used to further intimidate the ministers. This weakened the kirk's intransigence, but its position remained deeply entrenched; gradually however, James was able to isolate his opponents, using the more conservative instincts of the northern clergy as a counterweight to the enthusiasts of the south. By means including bribery and intimidation, as well as the power of ecclesiological disputation, he was able to impose an episcopal top layer upon the kirk, and to neuter the power of its General Assembly.

It was perhaps James's greatest achievement in Scotland to bring a degree of peace not only to the conservative north, but to the turbulent border regions, in both of which feuding was endemic, by the ruthless use of such men as Argyll. In the Borders, he was much helped by the peace with the English, who co-operated in the kind of police measures necessary. James, as great-grandson of Margaret Tudor, sister of Henry VIII, was ambitious to succeed to the English throne now that it was clear that Elizabeth would remain childless (to which end he had made only a formal protest at his mother's execution), and he was enabled to achieve his ambition not least through the patient and subtle work of Robert Cecil.

Elizabeth died on 24 March 1603 and when the news reached James he set off without delay to claim his inheritance. He was enthusiastically welcomed. Nobles, officials and office-seekers, courtiers and flatterers sped northwards to escort their new king to London; great crowds of the common people blocked the country roads and pressed upon the royal cavalcade. For all the devotion to Gloriana, it was good to have a king again. Popular relief at the peacefulness of his accession, after a generation of apprehension about what would happen when Elizabeth died, redounded to James's credit; and he made a good first impression on nobles and courtiers.

His popularity did not last. James I is difficult to assess; perhaps more than many characters of the past, he is a victim of the historian's knowledge of later events, for we tend to see his reign as a prologue to the catastrophe of Charles I. Nor can we easily expect normality of him. As has been explained, before he was a year old, his father had been murdered, his mother had married the murderer, and he had seen her for the last time; his boyhood was a weird blend of flattery and Presbyterian sermons, self-indulgence and the terror of being kidnapped or assassinated. He was a precocious and intelligent child, apt at languages, with a retentive memory; he became a learned man, shrewd and pedantic rather than original, yet certainly the most learned of kings. His writings were prolific, the most interesting being *The Trew Law of Free Monarchies* (1598) which expounded his ideas on kingship and the duty of subjects; *Basilikon Doron* (1599), a book of instruction for his son, Henry; and some short treatises such as *Daemonologie* (1597), dealing with witchcraft, and his vigorous *Counterblaste to Tobacco* (1604). He came to the English throne a man of thirty-six, 'an old, experienced king, needing no lessons', as he told the Commons; and the flattery he received in his first months in England (as Bishop Montague put it, 'God hath given us a Solomon') blinded him to the truth about himself and about his new country.

Physically unprepossessing, with spindly legs and a tongue over-big for his mouth, which made him an undignified eater; a heavy drinker, who tended to get drunk more often as he grew older; dirty in habits (he washed rarely) and slovenly in dress; uncouth in speech, often to English ears unintelligible in his broad Scots; fond of bawdy jokes even beyond the generous taste of his age; frequently homely, to say the least, in his language (as soon after his accession, when, his courtiers having told him the crowds came of love to see him, he cried 'God's wounds! I will pull down my breeches and they shall also see my arse', or at Hampton Court Conference in 1604, when he 'wished those who would take away the surplice might want linen for their own breeches'); terrified of assassination and wearing dagger-proof doublets – he was neither superficially attractive nor dignified.

But these were relatively small things, though much magnified by the contrast with James's high opinion of himself. There were more serious defects, pointed out by his mother's envoy, Fontenoy, in 1584, who observed, 'he does estimate correctly his poverty and insignificance but is over-confident of his strength and scornful of other princes; his love for favourites is indiscreet and wilful and takes no account of the wishes of his people; he is too lazy and indifferent about affairs, too given to pleasure, allowing all business to be conducted by others. Such things are excusable at his age [James was then eighteen], yet I fear they may become habitual'. The next forty years proved the accuracy of this analysis. James's laziness was demonstrated in a lifelong passion for hunting, for which he was ready to set aside all affairs of state and which led to a roaming, restless life for the court and to inefficient 'government by correspondence'. He relished being a king but neglected the business of governing. His love for favourites led to his pathetic and drooling affection first for Robert Carr, and then for George Villiers, Duke of Buckingham. The use Buckingham made of the power which James's passion gave him did great harm to the realm and exacerbated relations between Crown and parliament. Above all, there was his colossal vanity. Fed by the extravagant flattery characteristic of the age, it made him regard the welcome he received in 1603 as a tribute to his own wisdom and goodness. The Hampton Court Conference (1604) was an opportunity to display his theological expertise. The House of Commons was a body to be lectured on the art of government, the European world a stage on which he would demonstrate his power as a peacemaker. The most obvious outlet for his vanity came in his interpretation of the doctrine of the Divine Right of Kings. In his words, 'Kings are not only God's lieutenants upon earth and sit upon God's throne, but even by God himself they are called gods'. Perhaps his most outrageous expression of it was his defence to the Council in 1617 of his relations with Buckingham, when he said, 'I wish to speak in my own behalf and not to have it to be thought a defect, for Jesus Christ did the same and therefore I cannot be blamed. Christ had his John, and I have my George.'

James had been an effective King of Scotland, the most successful of all its Stuart rulers. (By 1603 the royal house of Stewart was usually known as Stuart, commonly thought to be due to French influence.) Perhaps this very success unfitted him for the different problems he met in England. On some of these his judgement was badly wrong. The poverty of Scotland prepared him to believe England and the English Crown far richer than they were, and the hectoring manners of the Scottish

Presbyterian clergy made him suspicious of the real moderation of English Puritans early in his reign. He could not see why so many Englishmen regarded his foreign policy as pro-Spanish rather than enlightened. From the start he misunderstood the function of the Commons and misjudged the temper of its members. Yet in some ways the first decade of his reign did not go ill. He crossed the Commons over several matters, and relations were bad when he dissolved his first parliament in 1611; but on the most immediately important problem, the right to levy extra-parliamentary taxes by 'Impositions', the judges had decided in his favour. His chief and wisest minister, Robert Cecil, Earl of Salisbury, had managed by 1610 to get the Crown's debts down to the figure at which Elizabeth had left them. James had made peace with Spain in 1604; and whatever the long-term consequences of the Hampton Court Conference, the canons of that same year were an effective damper on clerical puritanism for the time being. A generation later English churchmen would look back on James I's time as a period of scholarship and moderation, free from violent dispute and symbolized by the Authorized Version of the Bible (1611).

The middle years of the reign brought a deterioration in the king's relations with the 'political nation', illustrated by the futility of the Addled Parliament (1614). In part this was the result of factors outside James's control, like the deaths in 1612 of Salisbury and of the heir to the throne, Prince Henry, and the outbreak in Germany in 1618 of the Thirty Years' War. These too were the years of the favourites, of Somerset to 1615 and of Buckingham thereafter; of the influence of Gondomar, Spanish ambassador from 1613; and of the execution of Sir Walter Ralegh in 1618. The king himself was in physical decline by the time he was fifty (1616), with recurrent arthritis and gout; after the queen's death in 1619 he was desperately ill with nephritis. He grew even less willing to deal with the routine of government, and fell into what was occasionally maudlin dependence on Buckingham, upon whom he showered titles, offices, wealth, opportunities of patronage, and political responsibility.

Yet both his physical decline and its effects upon policy – particularly upon foreign policy – can be exaggerated. Thus from 1618 to 1624 James resisted pressure for war against Spain on behalf of his son-in-law Frederick of the Palatinate; when the parliament of 1621 demanded war, he dissolved it and tore out of the Commons Journal the page recording their protestation. Although after the foolhardy and futile journey of 'his two sweet boys' to woo the Infanta in Madrid in 1623 he changed his policy, he made it plain that he was ready to send troops to the Low Countries to restore the Palatinate but not to fight Spain at sea.

When James I died in 1625 he left to his son a legacy whose most obviously dangerous element was an arrogant and hated favourite. The old king had fallen out with parliaments, had mismanaged his finances, and had disappointed those who wanted him to lead a Protestant crusade in Europe. Yet he 'was still ruling over a united country'.* External peace, a working union with Scotland, a national church which enjoyed the confidence of the vast majority of his English subjects – all these must be set to his credit. The crisis which developed in the next reign – and within its first five years – reflected the policies of a new and more active king, and the changing response of a Commons at once more fearful and bolder. They must not distort our assessment of James VI and I.

Further Reading
Jenny Wormald, 'James VI and I: Two Kings or One?', History, June 1983.
S. J. Houston, James I, 1973.
R. Ashton, James I by his contemporaries, 1959.
D. H. Willson, King James VI and I, 1956.

JAMES II (1633-1701), second son and third child of Charles I and Henrietta Maria, was born at St James's Palace and was given the title of Duke of York. His childhood was clouded, and his political opinions fixed for life, by the Civil Wars. Nearly captured at Edgehill, he was taken prisoner when Oxford fell in 1646, but in 1648 he escaped to Holland. Notably loyal to his brother Charles in the years of exile, he was nevertheless much influenced by Henrietta who was far less of a realist than her eldest son. From 1652 to 1655 James served in the French army under Turenne and earned a reputation as a brave cavalry commander. When the exiles were driven out of France by Mazarin's agreement with Cromwell, he took service with Spain, and in 1658 commanded the right wing against the New Model at the Battle of the Dunes.

He returned to England at the Restoration, and in several ways was a prominent figure throughout his brother's reign. Having got Clarendon's daughter, Anne Hyde, with child, he married her (1660) at Charles's orders. His mistresses were numerous, if fewer than those of Charles; they were also uglier, and Charles, whose taste was more discriminating, once said he believed his brother had his mistresses given him by his priests for penance. Until 1673 he was Lord High Admiral (an office to which he had been first appointed at the age of four-and-a-half). He had a genuine love of the sea and an aptitude for naval command, as he showed during the Dutch Wars, in the English victory off Lowestoft in 1665 (where he had Sir William Penn as his adviser) and in the drawn battle of Southwold Bay in 1672, and he cannot be blamed for the financial stringency which led to the Dutch raid up the Medway in 1667. His main

*Conrad Russell, Parliament and English Politics, 1621-1629, 1979, p.420.

contribution to the navy lay in his readiness to support reforms like those of Pepys, and he improved the system whereby officers were trained as well as the organization of discipline.

Sometime in the 1660s James was converted to Roman Catholicism; his admission to the Roman communion seems to have become known after about 1668, and in the last fifteen years of the reign he represented the threat of popery. What made his position peculiarly significant was the infertility of Queen Catherine. James was the heir to the kingdom. Moreover, although Anne Hyde's two surviving children, Mary and Anne, were brought up as Protestants, James's second wife, Mary of Modena, the girl of fifteen whom he married in 1672, was a Catholic. Conversion made James more moral, in quantitative terms; he was content with a single mistress thereafter. It also made him even more reactionary in outlook. All he had learned from the Civil Wars was that it was disastrous to yield to opposition, and basically he was in political outlook an extreme royalist of 1642. As F. C. Turner has said, 'in none of his letters and in none of his reported words can there be found a hint of a liberal aim', and this attitude was fortified by conversion in the era when the champion alike of despotism and of Catholicism was his cousin Louis XIV. In the 'Grand Design' which emerged in the Treaty of Dover of 1670 it was James who wanted to use force to compel the nation to Rome.

His influence upon his far more intelligent brother was surprisingly great, although we must be careful not to exaggerate his power. Charles treated James with an odd mixture of contempt and respect: contempt for his stupidity ('*la sottise de mon frère*'), his lack of humour, his tiresome ardour for his faith, respect for his loyalty, his courage, above all for his readiness to work while the king idled. The Test Act of 1673 meant that James resigned the offices of state which he held, but not that his influence upon policy disappeared. This influence was probably greater in foreign policy than in domestic affairs; James's acceptance of the marriage of his elder daughter Mary to William of Orange in 1677 and the part he played in the Anglo-Dutch agreement against France in 1678 antagonized Louis XIV. When the Exclusion Crisis of 1678-81 developed, Charles fought tenaciously and subtly for his brother's right to succeed, yet he welcomed his exile first to Brussels and then to Scotland. With the reaction of the last four years of the reign (1681-5) English opinion, apart from that of the discredited Whigs, swung round violently in James's favour, and he was ruler of Scotland and the dominant figure in England. It was characteristic of his vindictiveness that he employed the medieval procedure of *Scandalum Magnatum* to secure damages against those who had spoken freely against him in the years of 'Exclusion'.

In 1685 he succeeded to the throne in a glow of popularity, with the Whigs broken, the Tory Anglicans vowing non-resistance, London tamed and the countryside enthusiastic. Monmouth's unsuccessful rising strengthened his position, increasing national loyalty and providing cogent reasons for a larger army. Within three years he had thrown away all these advantages and by the end of 1688 he was in exile in France. The reasons for this extraordinary downfall are to be found almost entirely in his own character. The Glorious Revolution would never have occurred or succeeded had James not displayed an incredible degree of folly, blindness and mismanagement. He had always been obstinate, a bad judge of men, incapable of appreciating other men's sincerely-held beliefs. Converted to a faith that most Englishmen thought wicked, he had learned nothing from his unpopularity at the time of Exclusion except the false lesson that English resistance would yield. Now, at his accession, there were signs of mental decline, of a form of paranoia which increasingly led him to ignore the general effects of his policies, and to regard criticism, or even moderation, as disloyalty. His first aim was to improve the lot of his fellow Catholics. This in itself, in the light of the last century of English history and of Louis XIV's persecution of the Huguenots by the Revocation of the Edict of Nantes at this very time, was scarcely prudent. What made it disastrous was the evidence which James seemed to provide that this first aim was merely a preliminary to the reconversion of England to Romanism. In the process he appeared to threaten the entire constitution of the country.

Parliament, which met in 1685 both before and after Monmouth's rising, was extravagantly loyal and liberal with supply. But the Commons presented an address against the illegal employment of Catholic officers in the army, and the Lords made plain the weight of opinion against any measures which seemed likely to threaten Protestantism. James truculently prorogued parliament: it was not dissolved until 1687, but it never met again in James's reign. He built up a standing army of some 16,000 men on Hounslow Heath to overawe London, and ignored the protests against Catholic officers. The decision of the court in the collusive action of *Godden v. Hales* (1686) legalized the use of the dispensing power to give Catholics military and civil office – and demonstrated the royal control of the Bench, aided by dismissals of judges. Ministers critical of his policy were also relieved of their posts, notably Halifax who ceased to be Lord President of the Council after he had shown himself unwilling to support the repeal of the Test Act and Habeas Corpus. He was replaced by the able and pliable Sunderland who may be regarded as the king's principal minister, even though much of his advice consisted of waiting to hear what James intended to do and then approving of it. The brutal Jeffreys became Lord Chancellor; the Jesuit Father Petre was in the inmost ring of the king's advisers; the navy was put under the command of a Catholic. The evidences of Romanism began to spread. Catholic chapels, schools and friaries appeared in London. There was a handful of conversions among men in high place. Recusancy fines ceased to be collected. The king opposed anti-Catholic preaching – and also did his best to limit the help given to French Huguenot refugees. In 1686 he began a direct attack on the Church of England itself by instituting a body of Ecclesiastical Commissioners, headed by Jeffreys, to bring it to heel. He extended his attack to the universities, the seedground of Anglicanism, and in 1687 turned Magdalen College, Oxford, into a Catholic seminary when the Fellows refused to accept his Catholic nominee as their President. In the same year he issued his first Declaration of Indulgence as an attempt to win the support of Protestant Nonconformists, while he also began a remodelling of local government in order to secure the election at a later date of a parliament which would do his will. Town corporations were made less Anglican. The lists of Lords Lieutenant and JPs were revised, and many were dismissed. Then James through the Lords Lieutenant put to the JPs – the leading representatives of the class from which MPs came – three questions which in effect asked their approval of a policy of repealing the tests and the penal laws against recusants. The answers were so hostile that James abandoned for the moment any plan of recalling parliament.

In his foreign policy James pursued a line which, despite a creditable element of independence, was eventually fatal to him. He was on good terms with William of Orange at the time of Monmouth's rising, but their relations deteriorated, partly over the question of the English regiments in the service of the States-General, partly over William's refusal to lend his support to the programme of a repeal of the tests. Towards Louis XIV, James was non-committal although he asked for cash at the start of his reign, and he paid surprisingly little heed to the advice and information which came to him from France, even in the critical summer of 1688.

The series of events leading to James's fall began with the second Declaration of Indulgence (May 1688). To put on trial for seditious libel the Seven Bishops who petitioned against its reading was perhaps the most stupid of all the king's actions, for it brought the full weight of the Church of England against him, and provided an issue round which public resistance could swiftly crystallize; the cheers which greeted their acquittal (June) heralded the failure of James's entire régime. The birth earlier in the same month of a Prince of Wales stimulated into action the growing conspiracy against James, and in July the famous invitation, signed by seven leading Englishmen, reached William of Orange. Yet not until September was James sufficiently

convinced of his peril to make concessions, such as the abolition of the Ecclesiastical Commission and the restoration of the ejected Fellows of Magdalen, and then they were too late, too obviously inspired by fear, and indeed too limited, to recover the loyalty he had lost. And he rejected French help until the help was no longer available; Louis had insufficient ships at Brest to stop William in the Channel, and in September he committed his land forces to an attack in the Rhineland.

William landed in Torbay on 15 November.* The events which followed found James a man who had lost his nerve, frequently changing his mind, broken by the desertions of his peers and generals and of his daughter Anne. He joined his army at Salisbury on 29 November, and set out back to London on 4 December; opened negotiations with William, and then decided to send his queen and the infant prince to France and to flee his country. His failure to do even this successfully – for he was captured by Kentish fishermen as his ship was waiting for the tide off the Isle of Sheppey – was ironically characteristic of James at this stage. His second and successful departure was by compulsive courtesy of William, whose Dutch guards even guarded James for a night in his own palace. With the Duke of Berwick and a handful of servants he landed at Ambleteuse at Christmastide 1688.

James II lived on until 1701, vigorous in physical energy, senile in mind. His one considerable effort to regain his throne failed at the battle of the Boyne in Ireland (1690), whence he bolted back to France in undignified haste. Apathetic yet oddly contented, never ceasing to believe that the people of England were ready to receive him back, detached from his own troubles, the symbol of Jacobitism contributed in the last ten years of his life nothing to his cause save his mere existence. His days were spent in hunting and, increasingly, in devotional exercises. He died at St Germain in 1701, charging his thirteen-year-old son James Edward to die rather than abandon his Roman faith. A pathetic rather than a tragic figure, James II by his follies had created the problem of Jacobitism and done no service to his fellow Catholics; and by this final legacy to the Old Pretender he ensured that Jacobitism would remain a lost cause.

Further Reading
John Miller, *James II: A Study in Kingship*, 1991.
J. P. Kenyon, *The Stuarts*, 1958, pp.158-81.
F. C. Turner, *James II*, 1948.

JAMES, DUKE OF BERWICK (1670-1734), Marshal of France, was the natural son of James II and Arabella Churchill, the elder sister of John Churchill, later Duke

---

*New style; 5th old style, and so the anniversary of the Gunpowder Plot.

of Marlborough. He appears to have inherited Churchill rather than Stuart qualities, for he became a distinguished soldier and a shrewd judge of political reality. Born and brought up in France as a Roman Catholic, he was given the title of Duke of Berwick in 1687. As a soldier he fought against the Turks in Hungary and against William III in Ireland and in Flanders, before taking command in 1705 of the French army in Spain. In 1706 he recaptured Madrid for King Philip, and in 1707 won at Almanza the decisive battle of the Spanish campaign, the victory which determined the ultimate failure of the British cause in the peninsula. The High Tories toasted him as 'the brave English general who had defeated the French' – for the 'British' commander in the battle was the French Huguenot Ruvigny, Earl of Galway. His other campaigns for Louis XIV included the reduction of the Camisard rebels of the Cévennes and the capture of Nice in 1705, and the subjugation of Barcelona and its Catalan defenders in 1714. In the later years of Anne's reign Berwick was deeply involved in the Jacobite plans for the succession, and his letters show a sense of the possible unusual among the Jacobites. Berwick was also one of the channels through which Marlborough maintained his Jacobite links, and he grew rather contemptuous of his uncle's attention to political insurance. After the deaths of Anne in 1714 and Louis XIV in 1715 he was a supporter of the Anglo-French *rapprochement* pursued by Orleans. He was killed in battle at Philipsbourg in 1734.

Further Reading

Sir C. Petrie, *The Marshal Duke of Berwick*, 1953.

JAMES, DUKE OF MONMOUTH (1649-85), claimant to the throne, was the eldest son of Charles II. The child of Charles's Welsh mistress Lucy Walter, he was born at The Hague and spent his childhood in exile. Until her death in 1658 his mother embarrassed Charles by claiming to be his lawful wife. Monmouth grew to manhood in the Restoration court as the spoiled favourite of Charles. At nineteen he was made Captain of the King's Life Guard and at twenty-one Captain-General of the army; in 1672-3 he served against the Dutch, and in 1678 he commanded the expeditionary force sent to Ostend against the French. Good-looking, athletic, dashing and brainless, he was a considerable libertine and popular with the London mob. Popularity stimulated his vanity, as did his victory at Bothwell Brig in 1679, when he led the force sent against the covenanting rebels and showed unusual clemency to the defeated; and it was vanity that set him at this time on the course which brought him to the scaffold six years later. A Protestant, easily led, with a claim to the throne strong enough to win support yet weak enough to compel him to be a constitutional rather than a despotic ruler, Monmouth seemed the ideal tool for Shaftesbury and the Whig extremists in the succession crisis which followed the Popish Plot revelations.

Yet his own conduct in the Exclusion campaign was certainly one of the factors which turned moderate men against his cause, for he showed himself to be indiscreet, self-willed, and politically inept. Banished in the autumn of 1679, he returned without permission almost at once. Deprived of all his offices and ordered abroad again, he refused to go. Instead he went on a series of progresses (1680-82) round England, conducting himself in half-royal state, and spreading the tale of the 'Black Box' which was alleged to contain Lucy Walter's marriage lines. Charles was sufficiently moved to sign before the Privy Council a formal statement of Monmouth's illegitimacy, and in 1682 to arrest his son for a short spell. By this time the attempt to gain exclusion by parliamentary means was over, and some of the Whigs were turning to plans of insurrection. Monmouth's role in the so-called Rye House Plot was equivocal. He was the only member of the Whig Council of Six to escape arrest, but in 1683 he was banished from court, and after a short-lived reconciliation with his father he fled to Holland.

He came back to England for the last time in the summer of 1685, landing at Lyme Regis to claim the throne from his uncle James II. Monmouth's Rebellion was doomed before it began, as much for his own deficiencies as for the general readiness to trust James in 1685. After he was crowned at Taunton there came the decisive moment at Keynsham, when he turned away from an attack on Bristol. As he retired westwards his numbers fell away. His attempt at a surprise attack by night at Sedgemoor failed, and he fled the battlefield, leaving his wretched peasant followers to be butchered. Captured in a ditch in the New Forest, he was executed on Tower Hill after his pitiful pleas to James for mercy had failed. James had always been jealous of him, yet he can scarcely be blamed for refusing pardon – although the effect of his decision was to clear the way for a far more dangerous claimant, William of Orange. Monmouth was a shallow lightweight, absurdly unfit for the responsibilities which chance brought upon him. The cause for which he claimed to stand, Protestantism and constitutional monarchy, was that of the future, but his death was more advantageous to it than his life. David Ogg has somewhat generously observed that Monmouth 'was the only Stuart who understood the common man'.* The real tragedy in his career was that of the hundreds of common men whom he led to death or exile in 1685.

Further Reading

Ivan Roots, ed., *The Monmouth Rising*, 1986.
Robin Clifton, *The Last Popular Rebellion: the Western Rising of 1685*, 1984.
Elizabeth d'Oyley, *James, Duke of Monmouth*, 1938.

---

*D. Ogg, *England in the Reigns of James II and William III*, 1955, p.148.

JAMES, 1st EARL STANHOPE (1673-1721), states-man, was one of the most talented statesmen of the early Georgian period. He came late to the centre of politics after a strenuous career in the army. In seven years he made his mark, vigorous in foreign policy, liberal and imaginative at home. He died at the height of his powers in the middle of a political scandal for which he was in no way to blame.

His father was a diplomat and he was born in Paris. He spent much of his early life abroad, but he was sent to school at Eton, where he became an accomplished classic. An impatient, active man, he was also scholarly in his tastes, and a bibliophile who left a fine library behind him. Dubois called him *'un philosophe'* and Speaker Onslow once referred to him as 'the best scholar perhaps of any gentleman of his time'. After a spell at Trinity College, Oxford, he served as a volunteer in Flanders. At the start of the Spanish Succession War he was a colonel in the Guards. In these days he was 'a young man that did not mind anything divine or human when it came into competition with his own humour'. He was a heavy drinker and a boon companion, amongst others, of Henry St John, later his political foe. He saw his principal service in Spain where he was second in command under the eccentric Peterborough, who captured Barcelona in 1705 and Madrid in 1706. He was not present at the battle of Almanza in 1707, but was sent home soon afterwards to represent the view of the Archduke Charles that the war should be pursued to the bitter end. Unfortunately the English and Austrian troops found themselves confronted by a patriotic movement in favour of the Bourbon Philip V; he was sent back by the government with orders to 'enlarge the bounds' of the operations, but with so small a force that he could only play a minor role. With the imperial general Stahrenberg, he was unable to regain the initiative. In July 1710, however, he distinguished himself in the small action of Almenara, meeting and killing the enemy cavalry commander. The general advance on Madrid that followed represented his policy of offensive action at all costs, but the skilful generalship of Vendôme, divisions between him and Stahrenberg, and his own rashness brought disaster. At Brihuega, in December, with an army of 4,000, he was trapped, battered and forced to surrender. By then the Whig government had been ousted and with it their policy of 'no peace without Spain'. The Tories were in no hurry to effect Stanhope's release; he came home only to face indict-ment, in the House of Lords, at the hands of his old commander, Peterborough, and his successor in Spain, Argyll.

Stanhope had good cause to be an ardent Whig. First elected in 1701, he had been defeated, in his absence in Spain, in a raucous Westminster contest, by the Tory general Webb. Like Marlborough, he was now hounded by Tory politicians and pamphleteers. The peace of Utrecht, repudiating Whig commitments to the Arch-duke Charles, touched him personally. He disapproved too of the Tory religious policy, their Occasional Conformity and Schism Acts. His energy, honesty and tolerance won the respect of the Whig leaders. In the last days of Queen Anne, when Bolingbroke was trying to engineer a Jacobite succession, Stanhope directed the tactics of his party. At the fateful dinner party, assembled by Bolingbroke on 28 July to test Whig views, it was he who delivered the ultimatum to the Tory leader: 'Harry, you have only two ways of escaping the gallows. The first is to join the honest party of the Whigs; the other to give yourself up entirely to the French king and seek his help for the Pretender'. George I succeeded without trouble, and Stanhope received his reward, on the prompting, perhaps, of his friend, George's secretary, Robethon, in the shape of the office of Secretary of State.

It was his object to restore the prestige which he considered England to have lost by the Treaty of Utrecht. He was one of the few ministers who could approach George I in his grasp of European affairs, and he was often by his side in his stays in Germany. This separation of the ministers, as much as differences of personality and policy, was responsible for the Whig schism when Walpole and Townshend left the ministry. Along with Sunderland, Stanhope, who became First Lord of the Treasury in 1717, Secretary of State again in 1718, enjoyed until his death the confidence of the king. He brought England into the centre of a European coalition designed to thwart the ambitious plans of Elizabeth Far-nese, wife of Philip of Spain, and her minister Alberoni. The base of his system was the alliance with France, made possible by the treaty of Utrecht and the moder-ation of the Regent Orleans. Round this novel entente were grouped, by the Triple and Quadruple Alliances of 1717 and 1718, Holland and the Empire. In 1718 the British fleet was used to crush the pretensions of Spain when Byng won the battle of Cape Passaro. Alberoni's Northern Alliance dissolved when Charles XII of Swe-den died, in the same year. Stanhope had been prepared to wage war on him too, when he was discovered to be involved in a plot to restore the Pretender and the English Baltic fleet was given orders to 'burn, sink and destroy' Swedish men-of-war. Stanhope was not afraid to be belligerent, but he could also be constructive, even tactful. Working through his ambassador, Carteret, he patched up the differences between Hanover and Prussia which touched England closely in the person of her Hanoverian king. He was less successful in his attempts to buttress Sweden against the demands of Russia, and the Northern War ended with the peace of Nystadt giving control of the Baltic to Russia. It is surprising to find that Stanhope was ready, on one occasion, to cede

Gibraltar to Spain, and was only prevented from doing so by parliamentary outcry. His judgement was not infallible, his actions like his temper sometimes rash, and his policies involved expensive subsidies; on balance, however, he left England stronger and more respected than in 1714.

At home his record is chequered. Secure in the king's support, he trod somewhat heavily through the political maze, more interested in the uses of power than in the means by which it was got. His realistic appraisal of the cause of recent political turbulence led him and his colleagues to pass the Septennial Act (1716) which doubled the life of parliament and the value of patronage, and did more than anything else to secure the Whig supremacy. His religious liberalism was reflected in the repeal of the Schism and Occasional Conformity Acts. He wished to do the same with the Corporation Act and Test Act, to restore civil rights to dissenters and ease the position of the Catholics, but was thwarted by the opposition of the church, led by Archbishop Wake. His impetuosity, too, disturbed some of his supporters who feared that violent change might bring violent reaction. Walpole was his constant critic and led the opposition which killed Stanhope's ill-conceived project, the Peerage Bill (1719), to restrict the king's prerogative of creating new peers. He himself had been created viscount in 1717, earl in 1718.

The government's scheme to liquidate the National Debt that led to the speculative mania of the South Sea Bubble was not Stanhope's work, but Sunderland's. Nor was Stanhope involved financially, as were several of the ministers. But it was while defending the government's policy in the House of Lords, in February 1721, that he suffered a stroke and died. None of the odium for the financial debacle clung to him. In his lifetime he was respected for his integrity. After his death, during the long peace of Walpole's ministry, his countrymen reaped the benefit of his diplomatic efforts. He had made England, for a few years, the arbiter of Europe.

Further Reading

Paul Langford, *Modern British Foreign Policy. The Eighteenth Century*, 1976.
J. J. Murray, *George I, the Baltic and the Whig Split of 1717*, 1969.
Basil Williams, *Stanhope*, 1932.

JAMESON, SIR LEANDER STARR (1853-1917), the eponymous villain (hero to many) of the Jameson Raid, was an Edinburgh doctor, who went out to the Kimberley diamond mine in 1878, and became Rhodes's closest friend. This eager and impulsive man, 'a Scottish terrier waiting to pounce' as one of his officers described him, was a 'natural' amongst the settlers, with his casual dress and infectious sense of fun. He explored a potential railway route from Fort Salisbury (Harare) to the sea, and led the expedition in 1893, which defeated King Lobengula and took over Matabeleland, the area around modern Bulawayo.

But the Boer Republic of Transvaal lay between South Africa and the new Rhodesia. Its reoccupation was essential to the fulfilment of Rhodes's imperial vision, and the opportunity arose through the uitlanders, gold miners from all over the world who had flocked to Johannesburg and were resentful of the restrictive rule of Kruger's Boer government. Rhodes encouraged them to rise, and promised support from company troops. To provide this Jameson went to the frontier of Transvaal in December 1895, ostensibly to protect the new railway there. He armed himself with a letter of invitation from leading uitlanders, and was poised to move. But the uitlanders were no revolutionaries, and were unsure whether they wanted to emerge as a separate republic or a British colony. They postponed their summons for help. Jameson, who had told a friend that anyone could take the Transvaal with half a dozen revolvers, decided not to wait. He rode hard for Johannesburg, his men armed with one day's rations and 120 rounds of ammunition. He never arrived there. The uitlanders did not move, and the Boers cornered his 350 troopers and forced them to surrender. Rhodes had to resign as prime minister of the Cape. Jameson was tried in England and sent to prison for fifteen months.

Yet such was his personality that he emerged to become prime minister of the Cape Colony after the Boer War. He worked with Botha to prepare the way for the South Africa Act of 1909, which completed the formal reconciliation between Boer and Briton. His purpose was to make reparation for the war he had helped to provoke, for his remorse went deep. Kipling saw him as the man who could 'meet with triumph and disaster, and treat those two imposters just the same'. He is buried alongside Rhodes in the Matopos Hills.

JEFFREY, LORD FRANCIS (1773-1850), lawyer and critic, was the son of George Jeffrey, depute clerk of the Court of Session, and of Henrietta Louden. He was educated at Edinburgh High School along with Brougham, Horner and Cockburn. He was at Glasgow University and, for a year, at Queen's College, Oxford, which he did not enjoy. He was admitted to the Scottish bar in 1794 but secured few briefs. He was a Whig and the Tories then held the establishment, legal as well as political, in a firm grip. Literature offered brighter prospects.

With the enterprising and generous Constable as publisher, together with Sidney Smith, the original projector, Brougham and Horner, fellow luminaries of the Speculative Society, Jeffrey started the *Edinburgh Review*. 'Every Tory principle being absorbed in the horror of innovation', Whiggery appealed to intelligent men who were prepared to postpone professional advancement in return for the luxury of free expression of ideas. At first, however, the *Edinburgh* was not entirely partisan. Tories like Scott approved. After the notorious Cevallos article (number 26) which Jeffrey wrote with Brougham, it became more decidedly Whig in tone. In 1809 the *Quarterly Review* was started by Lockhart and Tory friends. The two papers had much in common: serious but biased analysis of political issues, and literary criticism in a classical and conservative manner. Dogmatic and ruthless in matters of taste, Jeffrey pounded romanticism in the person of Wordsworth. In political questions the papers adopted predictable lines, the one broadly reflecting Fox-Grey Whiggery with a strong admixture of the more radical Brougham, the other being Pittite and clerical, with a flavour of Southey-type paternalism.

As the Whigs came more into their own, Jeffrey's practice at the bar grew steadily, though he was never one of the great advocates. In 1820 he became Lord Rector of Glasgow University: a mark of recognition. He became dean of the faculty in 1829 and retired from the editorship of the *Edinburgh* in that year. 1830 saw a Whig government at Westminster and Jeffrey Lord Advocate, with a seat in parliament successively for Malton and Edinburgh, and responsibility, in his official capacity, for the Reform Bill for Scotland. In 1834 he reached his summit as a judge in the Court of Session. At the time of the disruption he gave a momentous decision for the free church. He was lucky in his biographer: that doughty Whig and entertaining raconteur, Lord Cockburn, who became Solicitor-General in 1830, wrote eulogistically about his friend. We learn of his high moral character, his gaiety, industry and courage. His writing presents several of the more obnoxious features of Whiggery: the *Edinburgh* was notably arrogant and obtuse in its condemnations of the British performance in the Napoleonic wars. But Jeffrey must be judged by the standards of his day. Canning and Cobbett were his contemporaries, Brougham his colleague, Lockhart his rival: was he less fair in controversy than any of these?

All Jeffrey's best work was done for the *Edinburgh*, anonymously and hurriedly. He was aggressive but bore no malice. In 1806 he accepted a challenge from Tom Moore as a result of an article in the *Edinburgh*. Fortunately they were arrested in time to prevent their doing each other – or more likely themselves – any injury. They afterwards became great friends. Tories said of Jeffrey that he 'left a small library and a large, well-stocked cellar'. Cockburn more pleasantly recalls the hospitality of Craigbrook, where Jeffrey went to live in 1815. 'No unofficial house in Scotland has had a greater influence on literary or political opinion … The Craigbrook Saturdays during the summer session! Escape from the court and the town, scenery, evergreens, bowls, talk, mirth, friendship and wine …'

Further Reading
Henry Cockburn, *Life of Jeffrey*, 1852.

JEFFREYS, GEORGE, 1st BARON JEFFREYS OF WEM (1648-89), the most brutal of James II's agents, was born at Acton, near Wrexham, member of a gentry family of some distinction. Educated at Shrewsbury, St Paul's Westminster (under Busby), Trinity College, Cambridge, and the Inner Temple, he was called to the bar in 1668. He had a strong voice, great assurance, a clear mind and a ready wit, a flair for savage cross-examination, a taste for low company, and considerable capacity for dissipation; he employed all these qualities in his swift rise to high legal rank, yet he owed most to his introduction, by Chiffinch and the back stairs, to James, Duke of York, who made him his Solicitor-General in 1677. Next year he was appointed Recorder of the City of London. Both in that capacity, as Judge at the Old Bailey, and as Counsel for the prosecution before the King's Bench, he enjoyed the Popish Plot trials, showing himself mocking and vindictive. As Roger North put it, 'he loved to insult, and was bold without check; but that only when his place was uppermost'. Among those he prosecuted were Archbishop Plunket and the London joiner, College, and also Russell after the Rye House Plot.

In 1683 Charles II appointed Jeffreys as Lord Chief Justice. His faults – his savage and coarse language, his bad temper, his bullying and scoffing, his ruthless contempt for evidence – were patent, and his knowledge of the law was limited. The price of so disgraceful an appointment was paid by Algernon Sidney, condemned on the flimsiest of evidence after the Rye House Plot; by Titus Oates, upon whom Jeffreys gleefully imposed a sentence which began with a whipping from Aldgate to Newgate followed after two days by another from Newgate to Tyburn, and was completed by life imprisonment with periodic exhibition in the pillory; by Richard Baxter, whose trial Jeffreys began by denouncing him as 'an old rogue, a schismatical knave, a hypocritical villain' and by singing through his nose in imitation of Puritan prayers; and by the victims of the 'Bloody Assizes', which Jeffreys held in 1685 in the west of England after Monmouth's rebellion. He began at Winchester by sentencing Lady Alice Lisle, who was over seventy, to death by burning for harbouring rebels, after some outrageous directions both on fact and on law to the jury. It is uncertain how many rebels were put to death by the 'Bloody Assizes'; perhaps 300, perhaps 120. Jeffreys made a lot of money out of selling pardons, and also out of the traffic in those sentenced to transportation. What is certain is the spirit of cruel jocularity with which he conducted the business, and the vile name he left behind him.

James II, characteristically, rewarded him. Jeffreys became Lord Chancellor and in that role defended the king's use of the dispensing power and undertook the congenial work of purging municipal charters. He was the dominant figure on the notorious Ecclesiastical Commission: not only was he its chairman, it could not meet at all without him. So he presided over the suspension of Compton and the invasion of the privileges of the universities. Nevertheless, Jeffreys was shrewd enough to sense the need for concession before the end of 1687 – and to obtain a pardon in full and legal form for himself the month before William landed in 1688. When the royal cause collapsed Jeffreys handed over the Great Seal to James and took refuge in Wapping disguised as a seaman, but he was recognized in the *Red Cow* in Anchor and Hope Alley by a scrivener whom he had once bullied in court, and removed to the Tower, where he died in 1689. In some sense of course Jeffreys was the mirror of his age: there were other brutal prosecutors and judges in the late seventeenth century, and the rules of courts were looser and their conventions harsher than they later became. In civil matters, it must be said, he delivered quotable judgements which have found their way into the books. Moreover, he suffered greatly from the stone, and he drank a great deal of brandy. Yet when every sort of allowance is made he stands out in his own age as a man who committed many inexcusable actions and said many foul and merciless words, treating people and principles alike with contempt; and on a longer view as the most scandalous criminal judge who has ever disgraced the English Bench.

Further Reading

E. W. Keeton, *Lord Chancellor Jeffreys and the Stuart Cause*, 1965.

H. Montgomery Hyde, *Judge Jeffreys*, 1940.

JENKINSON, ANTHONY (*d.*1611), merchant, traveller and navigator: the date of his birth is unknown; he died in 1611. Practically nothing at all is known of his early life. It was the custom in his day for a boy who wanted to follow a career in trade to be sent to the Levant, and Jenkinson seems to have left England for the east in 1546. According to his own account, he travelled through Flanders, Germany, over the Alps into Italy, through Piedmont into France; he visited Spain and Portugal, and travelled thence to the Levant via all the principal islands: Malta, Sicily, Candia, Rhodes and Syria; he went all over the Holy Land; he was also in north Africa; and all this he accomplished between 1546 and 1553. (The list of his travels is printed in Delmar Morgan's *Early Voyages and Travels to Russia and Persia*, Hakluyt Society, vol. ii, pp.341-3.)

In 1553 Jenkinson was in Aleppo, where he witnessed the entry of Suleiman the Magnificent on 4 November. He was granted an interview with that monarch and obtained from him a safe-conduct, which was in reality a guarantee of free trade in all Turkish ports. It is not known for certain what purpose Jenkinson was pursuing, but almost certainly the merchants in England were preparing a plan for developing trade between England and the Levant in order to secure a regular supply of spices. Nor is it known whether Jenkinson followed up the privileges he had obtained from the Sultan. If he did, he gave up the hope of cashing in on eastern trade by this method and turned his attention to developing the promising results which flowed from Chancellor's contacts with Moscow.

The first journey, 1557. In 1557 Jenkinson was admitted a member of the Mercers' Company, the same year in which the Russian ambassador, Nepeja, arrived in London after his shipwreck in Scotland. In April 1557 the Muscovy Company fitted out a fleet of four vessels to trade with Russia and explore the possibilities of reaching Cathay by land and it appointed Jenkinson – 'a man well travelled whom we mind to use in further travelling' – as Captain-General of the fleet and as the Company's agent at a salary of £40 a year for three years. The appointment was made because Jenkinson was a skilful navigator who understood surveying as far as the science was known in the sixteenth century. His observations for latitude showed wide errors, but they were wonderfully accurate if we consider how crude were the instruments available to him.

The ships set sail from Gravesend on 12 May 1557, and Nepeja sailed with Jenkinson in the flagship, *Noble Primrose*. The Lofoten Islands were reached on 27 June, the north Cape on 2 July; the fleet then passed what Jenkinson called Lappia (Lapland) and Sviatoi Ness, named by Borough Cape Gallant. It entered the White Sea and anchored safely at St Nicholas Road on 12 July having covered 2,250 miles from London. Jenkinson and Nepeja then landed, went by boat up the Dwina river as far as Kholmogori and Vologhda and thence by land to Moscow, where they arrived on 6 December.

They were kindly received by the tsar, Ivan the Terrible, with whom they dined on Christmas Day. They spent nearly five months at Moscow, and it was not until 23 April 1558 that the next stage of the journey was begun.

On that day Jenkinson, with letters of recommendation from the tsar, set out from Moscow for Cathay, taking with him Richard and Robert Johnson – Richard had been with Chancellor on the 1553 voyage and with Borough in the *Serchthrift* in 1556 – and an interpreter. Their first objective was down the Volga to Astrakhan at the head of the Caspian Sea, the farthest outpost of the Russian domains. They found the city in a ghastly condition, for after it had suffered from famine the plague attacked it, so that the Englishmen were met with thousands of corpses lying about in the streets (14 July). Jenkinson here picked up what he called a 'wench' named Aura Soltana, whom he sent to England as a present to the new queen, Elizabeth I. Jenkinson now bought a boat and set sail from Astrakhan, the first

Englishman to enter and navigate the Caspian Sea (10 August 1558). He explored the delta of the Volga and the north coast of the Caspian, and charted the northern shores. (His map of these parts was published in 1562.) During this time Jenkinson was exceedingly ill, and he and his party were all but captured by robbers, who boarded the boat under the pretence of searching for infidels. Only hard swearing by the interpreter saved the four Englishmen. On 3 September they reached the Mangishlak peninsula, where they landed, and set out on the 14th overland for Vezir.

Jenkinson now found himself in a land infested with robbers and marauders, wild tribesmen with whom it was impossible to have any dealings. In the end Jenkinson was glad to pay their many exactions and to be rid of them. The caravan with which he was travelling numbered 1,000 camels. After five days' travelling, they reached the domains of Timur Sultan, brother of Hakjim, the Khan of Khiva. His subjects stopped and plundered the caravan, but Jenkinson rode off to Timur and made his complaints so forcibly that he was given a horse worth half the value of the stolen goods and excellent entertainment. He stayed in Vezir until 14 October, when he moved on to Urgendj. Here he spent six weeks, but he found that it was impossible to trade owing to the wild marauders of those parts; therefore he set out for Bokhara, which he reached on 23 December, having had to repel an attack on the way.

At Bokhara Jenkinson was well received and on the 26th he was granted an interview with Abdullah Khan, to whom he presented the letters he had brought from the Tsar of Russia. Abdullah was much interested in the arquebuses which the Englishmen carried, and 'did himself practise the use thereof'. He also bought some of the travellers' goods, but before he had paid for them he set out on a military expedition and his servants refused to honour his debts, so that Jenkinson had to take what he could get.

So great was the anarchy and confusion of the country that it soon became clear to Jenkinson that it was impossible to pass from Bokhara to Cathay, which put an end to establishing trade with Cathay by this route. Nor did the inhabitants of Bokhara want the English exports. The only thing to do was to go back by the way he had come. On 8 March 1559 Jenkinson left Bokhara with a caravan of 600 camels for the Caspian, where he arrived on 23 April. He found his ship, but it was now without anchor, cable or sail. The travellers set about spinning a cable out of hemp and making a sail out of some cloth, and they were preparing to manufacture an anchor out of a wooden cartwheel, when a barque from Astrakhan arrived with a spare anchor. The three Englishmen, together with six ambassadors who were bound for Russia and twenty-five liberated Russian slaves, set sail and arrived at Astrakhan on 28 May. To his great

disappointment, Jenkinson had learned that English cloth could not compete with a similar article imported via the Levant and Syria: he had also discovered that the Caspian area was unsuited to trade owing to its few harbours, its shortage of ships, the frequent ice, and the poverty of the people. Therefore on 10 June he left Astrakhan, went up the Volga for six weeks to Kazan, which he left on 7 August and arrived at Moscow on 2 September, having been on his travels for one year, five months and nine days since he last left that city. He stayed in Moscow until 17 February 1560, when he set out for home via the White Sea, arriving in London probably some time in the autumn, after 'a journey so miserable, dangerous and chargeable with losses, charges and expenses as my pen is not able to express the same'.

It had been and still remains a memorable journey. In spite of the robbers and their exactions, the voyage showed a satisfactory financial profit. Jenkinson had proved conclusively that further attempts to trade in Central Asia would be a waste of time and money, a verdict 'which was accepted as final and centuries passed before Bokhara saw another English visitor' (Foster, *England's Quest of Eastern Trade*, p.22). But there seemed to be a chance that trade might be built up by exploiting the hatred which existed between the Persian Shiah Mohammedans and the Turkish Sunni Mohammedans, who were frequently at war. English goods might be injected through the north. It might also be possible to persuade the Asian merchants to carry their goods for Syria and Europe to the Persian markets and there to exchange them for English goods: or the Russia Company might secure privileges to pass through Persia and seek the Asian goods themselves. It was Jenkinson who persuaded the company to send a second expedition to explore these possibilities. Hence the second journey, 1561.

The second journey, 1561. The instructions given to Jenkinson by the company were to obtain from the tsar leave to carry its trade through Russia into Persia, for which it was prepared to pay a reasonable tariff. He was then to go on to Persia and there to ask of the Shah – the Great Sophi, as he was known in England – permission to trade freely in Persia, and also for a guarantee 'for free passage also for us at all times to pass, as often as we will, with our goods and merchandise into any part of India, or other countries thereunto adjoining, and in like manner to return through his dominions into Russia or elsewhere'(Delmar Morgan, ib., i, p.117). Jenkinson was also to carry letters from Queen Elizabeth to the tsar and to the shah.

Jenkinson sailed from Gravesend in the *Swallow* on 14 May and he arrived at Kholmogori on 26 July. From there he went overland to Moscow, where he arrived on 20 August, having taken only thirteen days over a journey which usually took five weeks by water. He found the tsar was celebrating his second marriage, and there was considerable delay before an interview could be arranged. So little success did he achieve when at last he met the tsar that he made up his mind to return to England. He sold the company's cloth and other goods, received his passport and paid for the post-horses for the return journey; he was on the point of leaving when Nepeja called on him and persuaded him to cancel his arrangements and wait for a time further. Within three days Jenkinson received the permission to travel through Russia into Persia: he was promised letters of recommendation to the foreign princes through whose countries he would have to pass; he was also entrusted by the tsar with some secret and very important political commissions; and the tsar, to show his gratitude, gave to the company wider privileges than it had ever had before. On 15 March Jenkinson dined with the tsar and also with the Persian ambassador, who travelled with him when he left Moscow on 27 April 1562.

Astrakhan was reached on 10 June. The Persian ambassador here parted from Jenkinson, who remained in the city until 15 July, when he sailed into the Caspian. The voyage was beset with dangers from pirates and in one specially severe storm Jenkinson lost an anchor and his ship became very leaky, but he survived these perils and arrived at Derbend on 1 August. Derbend belonged to Persia and Jenkinson was the first Englishman to visit it. From Derbend he moved on to Shabran in the province of Shirvan under the rule of Abdullah Khan. Jenkinson set out to interview Abdullah at Shemakha and he was there entertained at a gigantic feast, 'with divers kinds of meats to the number of 140', which were followed by 'a banquet of fruits of sundry kinds with other banquetting meats to the number of 150 dishes'. Abdullah promised him a bodyguard to carry him safely to the Shah at Kazvin and early in October Jenkinson started for the Persian capital.

The ruling Shah was Shah Tahmasp (Jenkinson calls him Shaw Thamas) with whom Jenkinson had an interview on 20 November, when he presented 'the Queen's Majesty's letters' and also the presents which he had brought for the Great Sophi. The Shah asked in what language the letters were written: 'I answered in the Latin, Italian and Hebrew; well, said he, we have none within our realm that understand those tongues.' The Shah asked whether Jenkinson was a '*Gower*, that is to say an unbeliever, or a Muslim, that is of Mahomet's law'. Jenkinson answered that he was a Christian. 'What is that said he unto the King of the Georgians' son (who being a Christian was fled unto the said Sophi) and he answered that a Christian was he that believeth in *Jesus Christus*, affirming him to be the Son of God and the greatest prophet: Doest thou believe so said the Sophi unto me: Yea, that I do, said I: Oh, thou unbeliever, said

he, we have no need to have friendship with the unbelievers, and so willed me to depart.' Jenkinson took his leave, but he was followed by a man with a basin full of sand which he 'sifted all the way that I had gone within the said palace, even from the said Sophi's sight unto the court gate'. At one moment it looked as if the Shah would put Jenkinson to death, but Abdullah Khan intervened on his behalf and 'the said Sophi changed his determined purpose and on the 20th day of March 1562 he sent me a rich garment of cloth of gold and so dismissed me without any harm'.

While he was at Kazvin, Jenkinson got into touch with some Indian merchants and arranged with them that, if he succeeded in establishing a permanent trade in Persia, they would supply him with as much spice as he was ready to take. On his way home he called again on Abdullah Khan, who gave him most valuable concessions to buy and sell freely in Shirvan exempt from all customs dues.

Meantime the King of Georgia was being attacked by both Turks and Persians and he sent to Jenkinson to ask him to arrange with the tsar to send him help. Jenkinson urged the king to send an embassy to the tsar to make his request in person. He also sent one of his companions, Edward Clarke, to try to penetrate into Georgia from Arrash, the centre of the silk industry, and to get permission from the Georgian king for the company to trade freely in his kingdom, but Clarke found that this was impossible without jeopardizing the good relations with Abdullah Khan. This was a striking example of the way in which Jenkinson lost no opportunity of furthering the trading interests of the company.

On his arrival at Moscow Jenkinson had another interview with the tsar who gave him even more valuable privileges for the company than he had before, in return for the commissions which Jenkinson had carried out for the tsar in buying for him jewels and silks and fulfilling the secret political negotiations which he had entrusted to him (August 1563).

Jenkinson spent the winter in Moscow (1563/4) and he organized a second expedition to Persia on which Cheinie and Alcock set out probably in May 1564. On 9 July 1564 Jenkinson embarked for England in the *Swallow* and he arrived in London on 28 September, after an absence of over three years. His second journey is no less remarkable than the first and was of great value to the company, for he had for the first time opened up the possibilities of trade with Persia. He had also established a reputation as a trustworthy and successful political agent.

Jenkinson, as a result of his own wide experience, was now convinced that it would prove perfectly possible to navigate the Polar sea and open the passage from west to east, provided that the right time of year was chosen and proper planning preceded the expedition. In May 1565 he wrote a petition to the queen, urging her to finance such an exploit and offering himself to lead the expedition. The thrifty Elizabeth was not prepared to risk money on such a scheme and nothing came of Jenkinson's proposal.

In the autumn of 1565 Jenkinson was despatched by the government on a highly responsible mission. The English Channel at this time swarmed with English adventurers who were indistinguishable from mere pirates. They attacked Spanish and French ships, and the complaints of these foreign governments at last alarmed Elizabeth to such an extent that she made up her mind to put an end to their depredations. On 17 September 1565 Jenkinson sailed from Queensborough in command of the *Ayde*, 200 tons, with the queen's commission to stop the pirates. But he had also a more serious order: he was to prevent Bothwell, husband of Mary, Queen of Scots, and other Scottish lords from landing in Scotland: therefore he at once sailed for the Firth of Forth. Arriving at Berwick, he heard that Bothwell had already landed; therefore Jenkinson turned his attention to the pirates. A certain Charles Wilson had been employed by the governor of Berwick to watch out for Bothwell, but he missed him. Wilson was in reality a pirate, and although he held Bedford's licence, Jenkinson captured him. Thereupon Bedford wrote furiously to the Privy Council, describing Jenkinson as 'that vile man' and asserting that 'never was any so abused by a villain as (Wilson) had been by Jenkinson'. There is no record of how the episode ended (1565).

The third journey, 1566. A few months later the Russia Company sent Jenkinson on a mission to Russia to safeguard its interests against an Italian merchant, Barberini, who had extracted from the queen letters of recommendation to the tsar and who, in the opinion of the company, was infringing its rights granted by the tsar. Jenkinson sailed from London on 4 May 1566 in the *Harry*, and he arrived at Moscow on 23 August: he had an audience with the tsar on 1 September, when he delivered the queen's letters and the normal presents. He was wholly successful in securing a complete monopoly of trade for his company (1567) (Delmar Morgan, ib., i, 48 seqq.).

The fourth journey, 1571-2. The tsar seems to have been a mercurial creature. In 1571, in a temper against Elizabeth, he annulled the privileges he had granted to the company: at once the company sent Jenkinson to Russia to deal with the crisis; so in the summer of 1571 Jenkinson was again in Russia. He arrived at St Nicholas on 26 July to hear that the tsar was furious with him and was threatening to cut off his head. With immense bravery Jenkinson set out for Moscow. He reached Kholmogori (1 August 1571), where he found the plague raging. A messenger of his was all but burnt for trying to force the cordon drawn round the city. He remained at Kholmogori until 18 January, ignored by the tsar, destitute of money and ill-treated by the inhabitants. But at last the plague ended and Jenkinson was ordered to go to Moscow, where he arrived on 3 February. It was not until 23 March that the tsar admitted him to an interview and explained the reasons for his discontent. Jenkinson attributed everything to the incompetence of the Russian ambassador in England and to the bad behaviour of the company's agents in Russia. On 13 May 1572 Jenkinson saw the tsar again and was well received. The tsar went out of his way to compliment Jenkinson and he then restored the privileges to the company. Jenkinson left Russia on 23 July and arrived in England on 10 September. This was the last journey that Jenkinson undertook. For fifteen years he had devoted himself to fostering good relations between England and Russia and he had been entirely successful. 'And thus, being weary and growing old, I am content to take my rest in mine own house, chiefly comforting myself in that my service hath been honourably accepted and rewarded of her Majesty and the rest by whom I have been employed.'

Between 1572 and 1578 Jenkinson moved from London to live at Sywell in Northamptonshire. He was married probably in 1568 and he had twin daughters who died in infancy. A son who was born in 1580 also died as a baby, but there was another son who survived and gave to Jenkinson three grandchildren. He took much interest in the voyages of Frobisher. In 1577 he was sent on a mission to treat with the King of Denmark on the right of the English to navigate the northern seas. He sat on the commission which reported on the ore brought back by Frobisher in 1578. About 1600 he moved to Ashton in Northamptonshire and he died at Tighe in Rutland in 1611. From Anthony Jenkinson was descended Robert Jenkinson, second Lord Liverpool, who was prime minister in 1812 to 1827.

If Jenkinson is to be remembered as a traveller and trader and a diplomat, he ought not to be forgotten as a geographer. The vaguest and most inaccurate ideas prevailed in England and Europe about the east. The early voyages of Englishmen to the White Sea dispelled some of the erroneous notions; Jenkinson's travels greatly extended western European geographical knowledge. He was the first man to describe from personal observation the eastern parts of Russia, the first to descend the Volga since it had become a Russian river, the first to navigate the Caspian Sea and to realize that it was a landlocked sea, the first to describe accurately the countries which lay along its coasts. Some of his descriptions of lands farther afield, especially of the rivers, were far wide of the mark, as when he tried to explain what he took to be the underground flow of the Oxus. His influence on geography was not always beneficial: his vivid descriptions were published in all the best collections of travels and his map was included by

Ortelius in his famous atlas: thus Jenkinson's errors were perpetuated. All the same, he bridges the gap between Marco Polo in the thirteenth century and the English and Russian travellers of the eighteenth century. Jenkinson's map, which was published in 1562, has been attributed to William Borough, but there are good grounds for thinking that it was chiefly the work of Jenkinson. Borough may have done the drawing.

Further Reading

W. Foster, *England's Quest of Eastern Trade*, 1933.
Delmar Morgan, *Early Voyages and Travels to Russia and Persia*, 1886.

JENKINSON, CHARLES, 1st EARL OF LIVERPOOL

(1727-1808), who played a large and controversial role in politics under George III, was a descendant of Anthony Jenkinson, the Elizabethan explorer who penetrated into Muscovy and Central Asia. Succeeding generations had been less bold and the family had settled into the life of Oxfordshire gentry. They provided successive generations of baronets and parliamentary members and had Jacobite sympathies. Charles came from a younger and relatively poor branch of the family. His father commanded the Blues at Dettingen. He was educated at the grammar school at Burford and at Charterhouse; then at University College, Oxford. In the hotly contested Oxfordshire election of 1760 a lively election song which he composed was believed to have carried the day for the wealthy court candidate, Sir Edward Turner. Jenkinson's earlier more serious poetic efforts had found few readers, but he was recommended to the notice of the Earl of Bute, who made him a private secretary and became his close friend. In 1761 he was made an Under-Secretary of State and became an MP for the borough of Cockermouth.

Under Bute and Grenville, Jenkinson managed much of the electoral work on which the ministries depended for support. With the more frequent changes of minister in the first years of George III's reign, the individual ministers did not always have time to build up large connections in the constituencies where their government departments had posts to offer. In these circumstances the Treasury became more important in keeping in touch with local election agents. Jenkinson, who was made a Secretary at the Treasury, kept up a large correspondence with agents and voters throughout the country. In 1765 when Lord Rockingham's party came to power and interrupted his political ascent, he was given a post in the household of George III's mother, the Dowager Princess of Wales, and George himself came to rely heavily upon him for advice, especially after Bute's retirement from politics. He was referred to as the leader of the king's supporters in the House of Commons and he enjoyed many high positions. In 1766 he was made a Lord of the Admiralty (and was shown the door by Grenville's

servants, since this post meant a break with one of his old patrons). In 1767 he became a Lord of the Treasury; under Lord North Vice-Treasurer for Ireland and a Privy Councillor. In 1775 he secured from Fox a lucrative sinecure, the Clerkships of the Pells, and soon afterwards became Master of the Mint. In 1778, while the conflict with the American colonies was in progress, he rose to be Secretary at War and, though he thought North 'a weak mind' incapable of facing the dangers that clustered around him, he showed his loyalty to George by defending North's dwindling majorities. He was frequently named by the enemies of the king as one of the secret advisers at court and he was believed to have immense influence.

Accounts of his fawning manner and gestures of humility suggest Uriah Heep. 'For God's sake, Mr Jenkinson,' Lady Bute cried out, 'do not make those motions.' His eyelids twitched and fluttered and his whole appearance lent colour to the idea that he was an arch-intriguer. He was methodical and pernickety: the thermometer at his house always stood at 60°. Careful compilations of statistics and notes made him a valuable assistant to senior ministers, while his treatise on *Coins of the Realm* was authoritative enough to be reprinted by the Bank of England as late as 1880. 'A bureaucrat rather than a politician' (Gash), sometimes his talents were employed in politics, drawing up lists of junior officials who might suffer from a change of power higher up, or calculating the possible votes in a local election or a parliamentary debate. On the fall of North's administration he retired temporarily from the government and made a collection of treaties although he still conducted negotiations for the king.

When George again had a minister to his taste, the Younger Pitt, 'Jenky' returned, as Lord Hawkesbury, at the head of the Board of Trade, which Burke had abolished but Pitt revived. Pitt was warned that his inclusion in the government would imply too much royal influence, but 'Jenky' remained in the background and dealt principally with economic affairs; he supported the policy of 'defence' against that of 'opulence'. In July 1789, when his cousin, Sir Banks Jenkinson, the sixth baronet, died, he succeeded to the family estates. The extent of his influence is shown by the fact that he was able to procure the position of Collector of the Customs Inward, one of the lucrative places which Pitt had declared his intention of abolishing. In 1796 he became Earl of Liverpool and was allowed to quarter the arms of the city with those of his family. The mark of favour was specially requested by the citizens of Liverpool because of his vigorous defence of the slave trade which brought in such a large fortune to the port. His last parliamentary speech was in 1800 on the subject of Ireland and, as one might expect, he took his cue from George III rather than Pitt in the dispute between king and minister. From 1800 onwards he suffered from a debility in the knees which prevented him from standing, and the last years of his life were devoted to safeguarding the interests of his son. 'Young Jenky' was later to be the prime minister of England during some of the most eventful years in its history.

Further Reading
N. S. Tucker, ed., *The Jenkinson Papers, 1760-1766*, 1949.

JENKINSON, ROBERT BANKS, 2nd LORD LIVERPOOL (1770-1828) was First Lord of the Treasury and head of a Tory administration for fifteen years, from 1812 to 1827. To Disraeli he was the 'Arch-Mediocrity', but Gladstone believed that 'England was never better governed than between the years 1822 and 1830', and in the words of his biographer, Yonge, he was 'the very last who, in the strict sense of the word, can be said to have governed England'. His accomplishments were solid rather than exciting. In a period of menace and novelty he preserved a calm and fortitude that evoke respect. In a fluid political situation he maintained a coherence in government that witnessed to his political skill and personal integrity. His ministry contained at different times six future prime ministers: Canning, Goderich, Wellington, Peel, Aberdeen and Palmerston besides the talented Huskisson and Castlereagh, who did not become prime ministers. Essentially a manager in outlook and method, Liverpool showed little inclination to lift his eyes above the details or to examine the principles upon which policy rested. From the beginning he showed that mistrust of general ideas which is characteristic of a certain type of Tory. He may be remembered as the prime minister of the Six Acts. But he was also the man who encouraged the liberal measures of Canning, Huskisson and Peel.

Liverpool's father, one of a line of Oxfordshire baronets who had been rustic and obscure since Anthony Jenkinson, the explorer of Queen Elizabeth's reign, became a specialist in patronage. Without rising in office beyond the Board of Trade he acquired a fortune and an earldom. He meant his son to be a paragon and watched closely every stage of his development. Robert Jenkinson's career was grafted on to his father's solid stock. It was later said of him that 'he always quoted his father'. At Charterhouse and Christ Church he was solemn and consequential; good nature and a sharp intellect were not always proof against envy and ridicule. Long-necked, heavy-looking, in manner he was awkward rather than absurd. His great friend at Oxford was the brilliant and caustic Canning, storm petrel of Tory politics throughout Liverpool's political career. Canning's barbs were to fly more venomously after 1801 when he resigned with Pitt, and Liverpool went on to serve under Addington. Eventually, however, Liverpool was to be instrumental in bringing Canning back into government.

After Oxford Jenkinson travelled abroad. The grand tour could translate an academic acquaintance with the classics into a living experience of the continuity of European culture. He was present at the taking of the Bastille, which only confirmed his suspicion of the French. While he was abroad he had been returned for Sir John Lowther's borough of Appleby, though still under age (1790). In 1791 he made his maiden speech, on the Russian question, and earned Pitt's compliments: it was a speech, said Pitt, 'so full of philosophy and science, strong and perspicuous language, that it would have done credit to the most practised debater and most experienced statesman that ever existed'. Pitt could recognize an old head on young shoulders. He rarely rose to this level again, but he remained a cogent parliamentary speaker; for many years he bore the main burden of debate for the government in the Lords. In 1793 he secured a seat on the India Board. In the same year he changed Appleby for Rye and freed himself of patronage. He became colonel in the Kentish militia. He was serious about his soldiering and equally so in his approach to marriage. Despite his father's pompous opposition he married Lady Louisa Hervey, daughter of the Earl of Bristol, a steady girl who made him an admirable wife. He was happy, but his friends found her dull.

After Pitt's resignation upon the Catholic emancipation issue he became Foreign Secretary under Addington. A strong anti-Catholic himself, he felt no need to go out with his chief. He devoted himself nonetheless to reconciling Pitt and the Canningites to Addington. He supported the war with the optimism of a man who did not believe that revolutionaries could win wars. 'Jenky's march', the march on Paris which he had predicted in 1794, was later held against him. He was associated with the intransigents, anti-Jacobin, anti-French. A cartoon of Gillray in 1796 showed him tied with Canning to the *lanterne* by the Whigs of Brooks's. As prime minister in the year of Waterloo he may be said to have answered his critics! His conduct of affairs was always marked more by realism and courage than by imagination.

He was properly sceptical of Napoleon's intentions in the Amiens peace negotiations and insisted on holding on to the island of Malta. When Pitt returned in 1804, he became Home Secretary. Since 1802 he had sat in the House of Lords, with the title of Lord Hawkesbury. George III thought better of him. On Pitt's death he sent for Hawkesbury, who advised him to bury the hatchet and summon Fox: public-spirited but perhaps also calculating advice. Fox was ailing and Hawkesbury only thirty-five: the Whigs had belatedly accepted the war – let them now try to run it. The field was left to 'the talents' but Hawkesbury was given the valuable wardenship of the Cinque Ports which had been Pitt's. Next he served under Portland in an administration which was virtually a committee of four: Castlereagh, Canning, Spencer Perceval and himself. The quarrel between Castlereagh and Canning brought Portland down; and ensured that future Tory administrations would be weakened by the absence of one or the other. The Whigs behaved impossibly, at least from the point of view of the prince regent, their former patron. Defeatist about the war, they were stiff in their political demands: they would come in as a party or not at all. So Spencer Perceval grasped the reins: an untried leader, at a dark moment when victory seemed to be remote, with a makeshift administration. He had established himself by energy and pluck when he was assassinated in May 1812.

Under Perceval, Liverpool (he had inherited the earldom in the previous year) became Secretary for War and the Colonies. Austria was at last subservient to France, the continental system was being tightened by the co-operation of Russia and Sweden and English mercantile interests were suffering accordingly; with the opposition seeming to consult Whig traditions rather than the nation's interests, with ministers united only by their own unpopularity, the situation called for strong nerves and good planning. Wellington had some harsh criticisms to make of the government, but to Liverpool he owed support through all parliamentary storms, unfailing supplies – and a free hand. When Liverpool became prime minister the Peninsula policy had been vindicated and Wellington was on the high road to victory. Napoleon was bound for Moscow and a calamity which was to do more than all Wellington's victories to destroy him. But the nation was in the throes of an economic crisis for which war with America and the Orders in Council, the government's retaliation to Napoleon's economic warfare, were held responsible.

The prince regent preferred a coalition but without Whig co-operation he had to accept Liverpool. The latter wooed the Canningites with the promise that the Catholic question would remain 'open' – without success. The new government began with a vote of no confidence in the Commons and resigned. Wellesley and Moira tried in turn to form governments. Moira seemed to have succeeded but either lost his nerve or yielded to the pressure of the regent, his friend, to stand down for Liverpool. In June 1812 Liverpool resumed, second-best for all but his closest colleagues. He had wide experience in the great offices of government. He was transparently honest. He would work in the spirit of his family motto 'Palma non sine pulvere'. In practical terms of government he was the indispensable co-ordinator of men and measures – though few can have guessed in 1812 that he would still be thought so ten years later.

To see the war through, to hold a firm course in the depressed commercial climate of the post-war years, to encourage and help to steer the liberal and reforming measures which seemed desirable in the twenties – these were to be his tasks. At first Liverpool was assisted by the diplomatic ability of Castlereagh and the unique authority of the victor of Waterloo. In the second phase he had Huskisson in the key post of President of the Board of Trade, and Peel, high Tory with a taste for pragmatic reform, as Home Secretary. Canning returned in 1822, the year of Castlereagh's suicide and Sidmouth's resignation from the home secretaryship; and this year has been seen as the dividing line between the two phases of Liverpool's premiership. The obituarist of the *Annual Register* reminds us, however, of the importance of continuity in these years. 'Himself immoveable in his hostility to the demands of the Catholics, it was still he who had introduced into office Mr Canning … The alterations in the Silk Trade, the Navigation Laws, the Corn Laws, in the whole system in short, of the duties and prohibitions, had taken place under Lord Liverpool's authority and with his approval. His character at the same time was to the public a sufficient pledge that love of novelty and theory would not be allowed to run into extravagance.'

The legislative record was not so barren before 1822 – nor so fertile after 1822 – as to justify a firm distinction between the two periods. Canning and Robinson were brought into the Cabinet in 1816 and 1812 respectively. Huskisson had Liverpool's ear from 1814. He supported the Corn Law of 1815. Canning, like Wilberforce, supported the Six Acts, in 1819. In 1812 protestant dissenters had been freed from the relics of penal legislation. In 1814 a generous peace was made with the United States. In 1819 final steps were taken towards resumption of cash payments. In the same year the Factory Acts gave some protection to children in cotton mills; in 1820 the first Truck Act was passed. Economic revival contributed as much as new ministers to the reforms of subsequent years (though Peel's reforms as Home Secretary are largely an exception). It is true that the government in the immediate post-war years sometimes appeared to be timidly repressive. Disraeli's charge, that Liverpool 'was peremptory in little questions, and great ones he left open', is not unfounded.

Ministers had recourse to what they called strong measures. Two of the Six Acts have passed into permanent law. In view of the turbulence of the new towns and old cities like London and Bristol; the Cato Street conspiracy whose object was to murder the whole Cabinet; machine-breaking; above all a lack of civil police which compelled the use of troops in affairs like that of St Peter's Fields – those much abused Acts may seem more like reasonable precautions than instruments of bigoted repression. Despite clamorous appeals for extraordinary government action, even for the formation of 'armed associations of the well-disposed' – a sure way of fomenting civil war – Liverpool held calmly to a middle course, equally resolute against agitators of the left and worried magistrates and mill-owners of the right.

For a successful politician Liverpool was unusually sensitive; he seemed to be genuinely upset by criticisms. 'Blinkinson', as Canning called him, was notorious for the twitches and fidgets which betrayed the strains he underwent. Periods of depression were more likely to be caused by friction in Cabinet than by public upsets and problems. But colleagues admired him, even warmed to him. The opinion of an opponent is worth quoting. Lord Dacre, who presented Queen Caroline's petition in the Lords, said that Liverpool, who had the embarrassing task of defending the interests of George IV in this matter, was 'very able and the honestest man that could be dealt with. You may always trust him … and, though he may be going to answer you, after a speech you may go out and leave your words in his hands and he will never mis-represent you'. Like Baldwin in the abdication crisis of 1936, Liverpool was at his best in a messy case like this, when the issues were not clear-cut, when public personalities were cruelly exposed. His essential respectability was reassuring. He stood above scandal or suspicion of personal gain. Canning realized the extent to which ministry, king and country depended on Liverpool at this time. 'Nothing but plain management, or rather absence of all management, will suit the crisis; and happily Liverpool stands in a situation in which *his own* word will carry him through.' Pitt and Peel were greater men than Liverpool; neither did more than he to reconcile the English of the important, soon to be enfranchised, middle classes, to the politician. The elder Pitt had thought it worth while to parade his honesty as a political virtue; a hundred years later it was taken for granted.

Liverpool 'had no habits of any but official employment'. He could be benign, even unreserved with close friends, but when he unbent it was usually with an effort. He lacked spontaneity in company and when he tried to be jolly he risked being ridiculous. Princess Lieven, the wife of the Russian ambassador, made a conquest of him or so she boasted. One evening 'after a long and solemn dinner, he amused us by the odd fancy of jumping over the back of a big sofa, on which I was seated, and establishing himself on a little footstool in front of me. The great Liverpool hovered and then settled on the ground, looking very comic.' Canning encountered him at Bath in 'a huge pair of jack-boots, of the size and colour of fire buckets'. The laughter was rarely malicious, and he continued to be respected. There was sufficient thought behind his actions to set him apart from the mere technicians of politics. To read him, for instance, on the subject of the old representative system is to discover a conservatism that was not blind but deep, even wise. We learn that 'the landed interest is the stamina of the country'. He held that the House of Commons was

primarily a deliberative assembly. 'If public opinion is necessarily to affect their decisions on every occasion, it will cease to be a deliberative assembly … Public opinion ought never to have so great a weight as to prevent their exercising their deliberative functions.'

In 1821 he intervened to prevent the members of the disenfranchised borough of Grampound being given to Leeds, and to give them to the county of Yorkshire instead: to confer upon the 'populous manufacturing towns' the right of election 'would subject the population to a perpetual factious canvass, which would divert more or less the people from their industrious habits, and keep alive a permanent spirit of turbulence and disaffection amongst them … I do not wish to see more of such boroughs as Westminster, Southwark and Nottingham. I believe them to be more corrupt than any other places when seriously contested … and the persons who find their way into parliament from such places are generally those … who are least likely to be attached to the good order of society.' The principles of representation mattered less to him than the end product. In the boroughs he was concerned about violence and corruption, in parliament about the sort of man who arrived to debate and vote. Parliament – and this was the classic Tory defence – represented interests rather than numbers. In giving due weight to the landed gentry, the church, the universities, Liverpool did not neglect the interests of finance, commerce and manufacturing. In the unreformed parliament there were at least a hundred who came into one of the latter categories.

Liverpool's part in the evolution of economic policy was no small one. In 1812 he said: 'When it was asked what should be done to make commerce prosper, the answer was laissez faire.' In 1820 he told a free trade deputation that the principle of agricultural protection was wrong: 'Some believe that we have risen because of that system. Others, of whom I am one, believe that we have risen in spite of that system.' He was for 'leaving capitalists to find out the way in which their capital could best be employed' and held that 'on all commercial subjects the fewer laws the better'. At the same time he understood that it was important to preserve the balance of economic interests in the country. To his credit he defended the bill of 1818 to regulate the hours of children in cotton factories, pointing out that 'to have free labour there must be free agents'; children were not free agents and they were undoubtedly harmed by excessive labour.

Under Liverpool the duties of the First Lord of the Treasury were not nominal. The Chancellor of the Exchequer was still regarded as his assistant. Liverpool guided, even if he did not dictate, post-war fiscal policy, and after Robinson succeeded Vansittart in 1823 his direction became if anything firmer. He also acted as a link between the fiscal and commercial policies of the nation. Huskisson had been an intimate since 1814, and the introduction of free trade measures into Robinson's budgets reflects not only the influence of Huskisson over Robinson, but also Liverpool's personal interest.

In matters of foreign policy Liverpool was lucky to be served by Castlereagh and then by Canning. He was responsible, however, for bringing Canning back into government; indeed he would have preferred Canning, of the two, in 1812. He had little sympathy with Castlereagh's European outlook, or his close association with Metternich, though he supported him loyally; after 1822 he identified himself closely with Canning's liberalism. The majority of the Cabinet had been in sympathy with Castlereagh. Canning was inevitably regarded with suspicion, though more because of the tone of his pronouncements than what he actually did. Liverpool had therefore to come out as a partisan, in open support. His nerves were frayed by the furious exchanges in Cabinet between Wellington and Canning. He knew that England's interests required that Canning should remain foreign minister; but that effective government relied upon the support of the 'ultras'. Liverpool's success in reconciling the factions; in creating, if not a lasting harmony, at least a situation in which positive measures of government could receive general consent, is emphasized by the course of events after his retirement. 'Ours is not, nor ever has been, a controversial Cabinet upon any subject', said Wellington in 1821. This was hardly true after 1822. Yet the crucial policy statement, 'that it is the opinion of the Cabinet that any further step to be taken towards the South American states should be decided without reference to the opinions and wishes of the continental allied powers', was taken with only one dissenting voice. Liverpool tackled the formidable Wellington on the South American issue with courage and tact. After the government decision of December 1824, to recommend that the king recognize the South American republics, Canning acknowledged what he owed to Liverpool: 'Spanish America is free and, if we do not mismanage our affairs sadly, she is English and *Novus saeclorum nascitur ordo*. You will see how nobly Liverpool fought with me on this occasion.'

It is only rarely that we find measures which were Liverpool's alone and reflect his special interests. One such was the grant of a million pounds in 1818 for the building of new churches; another half-million was allocated for this purpose from the repayment of the Austrian loan in 1824. From the same source came £60,000 towards the purchase of pictures from the Angerstein collection for a National Gallery. It is appropriate that Lawrence's portrait of Liverpool should show him holding the charter of the National Gallery. Earnest in a mildly evangelical way, civilized as well as learned, Liverpool may not have acted decisively enough to leave the idea of a great man, with contemporaries or in the history books. By any standards, however, he was a good man, and a sound prime minister. After his stroke on 17 February 1827, he lingered for nearly two years in semi-consciousness. He died in December 1828. By then Canning too had died. Robinson, now Lord Goderich, had tried, and failed, to govern. The Duke of Wellington, prime minister, and Peel had already decided that Catholic emancipation must be granted. Predictably this split the Tories, already weakened by the departure of Huskisson from the Cabinet and the loss, therefore, of Canningite support. It is hard to resist the conclusion that the death of Liverpool was also the death of old Toryism. Fortunately for his country, Liverpool had done enough to ensure that some of its best features survived, to reappear in later governments, notably those of Peel and Disraeli. The strength of English Conservatism has ever been to adapt to circumstances while standing firm on essential principles. Of this Conservatism Liverpool was a strong representative.

Further Reading
N. Gash, *Lord Liverpool*, 1984.
W. R. Brock, *Lord Liverpool and Liberal Toryism, 1820-27*, 1941.

JENNER, EDWARD (1749-1823), physician, saved countless lives by his demonstration that immunity from smallpox could be obtained by vaccination with the virus of the milder cow-pox or vaccinia. The son of a Gloucestershire clergyman, apprenticed to a surgeon of Sodbury, he later studied medicine under John Hunter, who became his life-long friend and taught him that the study of medicine could be transformed by a methodical and broad scientific approach. Today, when specialization in depth and on the narrowest of fronts is leading advances in medical science, it is remarkable to think of Jenner pursuing at once the study of botany, zoology and geology. He began to practise at his native town of Berkeley in 1773 and became a Fellow of the Royal Society in 1788.

Inoculation with the virus of smallpox itself as a preventive had been pioneered by Lady Mary Wortley Montague early in the century and was not uncommon. But it was hazardous and suspect on religious as well as on clinical grounds. Jenner made a study of the incidence of cow-pox and examined the tradition that dairy-maids and others employed with cows did not take the smallpox. He experimented exhaustively with inoculations with cow-pox and then smallpox; the latter did not develop and his theory was proved. In a series of publications, culminating in 1800 with *A Complete Statement of Facts and Observations*, he stated the case for vaccination. He established an institute for the supply of cow-lymph and secured grants from parliament in 1802 and 1806 amounting to £30,000 for the spread of the practice. Soon opposition died away and he became celebrated and admired. Seventy leading physicians signed a declaration affirming their confidence in the vaccine. In 1814 he was interviewed by the tsar and the King of Prussia. He received many gifts from grateful people, but he made no attempt to make money from his discovery or to exploit fashionable interest. After a brief stay in London he returned to Gloucestershire and busied himself with the propagation of his treatment.

After the example set by the Scandinavian and several German states, vaccination was made compulsory in England in 1853 and the disease which had been so dreaded and dangerous became virtually extinct. The work of Louis Pasteur and others upon immunology in other diseases was directly inspired by Jenner. All who have bared their arms to the doctor's needle should bless the name of Jenner, whose statue in Gloucester Cathedral records a generous, warm-hearted and supremely useful life.

JEWEL, JOHN (1522-71), Bishop of Salisbury, was one of a family of ten, the children of John Jewel of Berrynarbor in north Devon. His education began at Barnstaple School, whence he went in 1535 to Merton College, Oxford. His tutor was Parkhurst, later Bishop of Norwich, who recommended him after four years to migrate to Corpus Christi College. He took his BA degree in 1540 and soon became a Fellow of his new college. In 1547 Peter Martyr, a Florentine reformer who became Regius Professor of Divinity at Oxford, arrived in Oxford and Jewel came much under his Protestant influence. In 1552 Jewel took the degree of BD and became Public Orator just in time to have to make the oration congratulating Queen Mary on her accession. Weakly he subscribed to religious doctrines which he did not believe, gave up his Protestantism, and then fled abroad to Frankfurt (1555), where he acknowledged his weakness and recanted his recantation. He moved about among the Protestant exiles in Frankfurt, Strasbourg and Zurich, then toured Italy and spent a short time at Padua.

On the death of Mary, Jewel returned to England (1559) and was consecrated Bishop of Salisbury. By nature and instinct, by upbringing and education, Jewel was sympathetic towards the Puritans. He had a supreme contempt for what he called 'the scenic apparatus of divine worship'. Vestments he labelled 'theatrical habits' and 'ridiculous trifles': the cope was a 'comical dress', the linen surplice 'a vestige of error'. This 'rubbish' and these 'fooleries' he wished to see done away with, because they could only disturb 'weak minds'. But what makes Jewel a notable figure in the history of his own times is that he was capable of seeing these 'trifles', not merely as trifles and therefore to be abolished, but also as trifles which mattered nothing in comparison with the vital necessity of preaching the gospel and the Word of Life. Therefore he put up with these 'fooleries', because

he recognized that 'the doctrine (of the Anglican church) is everywhere most pure' and must be maintained against the Romish errors. To this work the rest of his life was dedicated. Even so, he felt so strongly that everything must be done in a decent and orderly way that he was prepared to enforce things which in his heart he disliked against the Puritans, with whom he had much in common.

To the defence of the established church Jewel brought the help of his profound learning, his deep piety and his unselfish sense of service. He set great store by education and he tried by incessant preaching throughout his diocese to raise the standard of his clergy. His most important piece of writing was his *Apologia Ecclesiae Anglicanae* (written in Latin in 1562 and translated into English in 1564 by Ann Bacon, mother of Francis Bacon), in which he justified the position of the Anglican church and transferred the accusation of innovations to the Church of Rome. The *Apology* did not define Anglican beliefs: that explanation had to wait for Hooker. Jewel was a gentle, kindly, hospitable man, generous and courteous, yet he was ungenerously discourteous to the Roman church, whose clergy he assailed in vulgar terms and whose pope he denounced as the 'hangman of the church'.

Jewel was a great patron of friendless and needy scholars, and he kept a kind of school in his palace at Salisbury where he trained poor boys of intellectual promise: it was here that Richard Hooker found the encouragement and often the financial aid which enabled him to stay at Oxford. In appearance Jewel was worn and emaciated, and in his later years he seemed a living skeleton. He wore himself out by going round his diocese preaching, maintaining that a bishop 'should die in his pulpit'. Being booked to preach at Laycock, although too ill to keep his appointment, he insisted on doing so. When the service was ended he rode to Monckton Farleigh, where he went to bed and died, 23 September 1571.

Further Reading

J. E. Booty, *John Jewel as Apologist of the Church of England*, 1963.

F. O. White, *Lives of the Elizabethan Bishops*, 1898.

JOAN OF KENT (*c.*1328-85), 'Fair Maid of Kent' and Princess of Wales, was renowned for her beauty, love affairs, and as mother of King Richard II. Froissart described her as 'this young lady of Kent [who] was the most beautiful and most amorous lady in the whole kingdom of her time'. The younger daughter of Edmund of Woodstock, Earl of Kent and youngest son of Edward I, Joan was still only an infant at her father's execution in 1330 and was brought up by the Earl and Countess of Salisbury, who doubtless intended her for their own son. Although of the blood royal, she only became an heiress in 1352 on the death of her brothers and sister, at which point her husband Sir Thomas Holland became recognized as Earl of Kent in her right.

A genuine love affair may therefore lie behind the twelve-year-old Joan's exchange of vows before witnesses with Holland and sexual intercourse with him in May 1340. Such a contract, though clandestine and involving no religious ceremony, constituted a valid marriage in the eyes of the church. Initially it was kept secret and in 1340-1, during Holland's absence in Prussia, Joan – still only thirteen – was married publicly to William Montagu, the future second Earl of Salisbury, who presumably knew nothing of her earlier marriage. They lived together as man and wife until 1347 when Holland commenced a suit of nullity, which Montagu resisted – he appears to have been genuinely fond of Joan – but which Holland successfully concluded with Joan's support in 1349. Following his death in 1360, she remarried to Edward of Woodstock, the Black Prince, eldest son of Edward III. He was the third distinguished soldier and Knight of the Garter to become her husband. That he was still unmarried at thirty has been taken as evidence of a prior attachment: was he waiting for Joan? That this union too was clandestine and indeed invalid without a dispensation indicates that it too was a love match and opposed by the king, although Edward III acted vigorously to secure its validity once it had been contracted. That a lady of such high birth could marry irregularly twice suggests that the formality of the arranged marriage may often conceal romantic attachments and shows how ladies could decisively influence their careers in practice, as dowagers indeed customarily did.

Once married, however, Joan almost disappears from the historical record, except for the monotony of childbirth: three sons and three daughters to Holland, two sons to the Black Prince. She accompanied the Black Prince to Aquitaine, her two children being born at Angoulême and Bordeaux. To praise her as 'a devoted wife to the Black Prince and in no sense a political intriguer' (McKisack) is to make a positive statement from the absence of evidence about her activities. With the death of the Black Prince in 1376, Joan again became a dowager, and with the succession of her son Richard next year whilst still under age she became an important independent element on the political scene. Initially, indeed, she continued to care for her young son and was able to contribute to the maintenance of domestic peace: notably in 1377, when she reconciled John of Gaunt and the citizens of London, and in 1378, when she intervened on behalf of John Wyclif. In 1381 she was molested by rebellious peasants in the Tower. Thereafter Richard acted more independently and his declared intention of punishing his brother John Holland, Earl of Huntingdon for murder of another nobleman is said to have contributed to the demise of their mother, still only fifty-seven. Presumably she had deliberately decided against any further marriages.

Further Reading
K. P. Wentersdorf, 'The Clandestine Marriages of the Fair Maid of Kent', *Journal of Medieval History* v, 1979.

JOCELIN OF BRAKELOND (*fl.*1180s-after1200) became a monk at Bury St Edmunds in Suffolk in 1173. Shortly after 1202 he completed a *Chronicle* of events in the abbey from 1180 to 1202, effectively a biography of Abbot Samson (abbot 1182-1211), who had been Jocelin's novice master in the 1170s. Jocelin was ideally placed for his work, as he had been Samson's chaplain and secretary (1182-7). At the time of writing, Jocelin was the abbey's guestmaster. Adequately trained in the Latin classics (Virgil, Horace, Ovid etc.), Jocelin kept abreast of contemporary historical writing, quoting Ralph Diceto's *Ymagines Historiarum* (finished by 1200), and included considerable information about the customs, administration and tenants of the abbey. His account of Samson is tinged with hagiography, although, when considering the events after he had ceased to be the abbot's secretary, Jocelin allows a more objective, occasionally critical tone to intrude. Most striking, however, is the vivid description of Samson's physique and personality which, unlike most monastic chroniclers, is convincingly drawn from life, not from an honoured exemplar. The accounts of the internal factions; the struggles over Samson's administrative and financial reforms; and the tensions between young and old in the monastery are sharply observed, conveying a sense of reality. Jocelin's purpose may have been to praise Samson and, ultimately, the patronal saint, Edmund, but in the process he left the clearest and most lively description of the life and aspirations within a community of monks written in the medieval England. Jocelin also wrote a now lost *Life of St Robert*, a boy supposedly killed by Jews in Bury in 1181. Jocelin and his *Chronicle* were popularized by Thomas Carlyle's *Past and Present* (1843) as evidence of the virtues of a pre-industrial society run by heroic individuals, a sentimental view wholly of the nineteenth not the thirteenth century.

Further Reading
The Chronicle of Jocelin de Brakelond, ed. and trans. H. E. Butler, 1949.

JOHN (1167-1216; King of England 1199-1216) is the most notorious English king, one of the most unfairly maligned but also one of the least successful. The legend of his awfulness as a person as well as a ruler dates from his own lifetime. Even now, when his positive qualities as a conscientious judge, a careful administrator, a man of culture and a ruler of energy are widely recognized, his personality and style leave a nasty taste in the mouth. 'Foul as it is … Hell itself is defiled by the fouler presence of King John'. This verdict of Matthew Paris of St Albans in the thirteenth and J. R. Green in the nineteenth century sums up the 'Bad King John' theory, investigated with more pathos and psychological sympathy by A. A. Milne in his wistful poem 'King John's Christmas' where the monster is reduced to loneliness, self-knowledge and child-like yearning. Other opinion portrays John as able but flawed, 'the ablest and most ruthless of the Angevins' (J. R. Green again) with, in the words of a post-war biographer, W. L. Warren, 'the mental abilities of a great king, but the inclinations of a petty tyrant'. This interpretation too has a long pedigree. In the 1220s, the annalist of Barnwell Priory near Cambridge, commented 'he was a great prince certainly but hardly a happy one'. For Shakespeare in the 1590s, John was the unprincely prince, the schemer whose schemes all came unstuck, whose outward show of regality and power concealed a character unstable and deceitful but not monstrous.

More recently, the arguments have moved away from John's character – more or less irrecoverable – to his rule. Thus John's arbitrary government has been studied by J. A. Jolliffe without going down the cul-de-sac of moral judgement. Rehabilitation has come with scrutiny of offical records, from which John appears hard-working and competent. J. C. Holt has even compared John's administrative achievement with that of Henry II or Edward I. This has drawn the retort from J. Gillingham that 'John is the most overrated king in English history', only the accident of record-keeping making him seem busier and more industrious than his predecessors. After all, the contemporary Ralph, Abbot of Coggeshall, awarded only faint praise: John governed 'satis laboriose', with enough effort. The problem with assessing King John is that he presents an image of contradictions: energetic and slothful; judicious and corrupt; sensitive and myopic; intelligent and brutish; cultured and violent. Such, to the confusion of contemporaries and historians, was the sum of John's humanity.

Critics and apologists are faced with one supreme fact. Tactically successful – in gaining the throne, defeating his rival Arthur of Brittany, exploiting the fiscal potential of England, gathering a coalition against France, supervising English administration, recruiting vital political and material aid from the pope when he needed it most – as a whole John's reign was a disaster. Having lost much of his continental inheritance by 1204, by his death he had forfeited the loyalty of most of the English baronage and was facing civil war and a foreign invasion. He left his dynasty's future in the hazard, its survival dependent on the repudiation of John and his style of rule. Even King Stephen had retained more support than John. His responsibility for this is related to

why his personality inspired such a loathsome reputation. The vilification of John is comparable in English history only to the Protestant slander of Mary I. Other kings had angered the church by their policies, yet clerical and monastic chroniclers reacted much more violently to John and the Interdict than to Henry II and Becket's murder. Why did the normally sober William of Newburgh call John 'nature's enemy'?

John was born in 1167, like his brother Richard at Oxford, the last child of Henry II and Eleanor of Aquitaine, who was forty-seven at the time of John's birth. Significantly younger than his brothers, John was excluded from the dynastic settlement of 1169, but in the 1170s various schemes for John's endowment were proposed. Interestingly, with four healthy sons, Henry II ignored the option of directing any of them to the church. A plan for John to marry the heiress to the county of Maurienne, which controlled the western Alpine passes vital for access to Rome and the Mediterranean, came to nothing. (Both John's sons, Henry III and Richard of Cornwall, actually did marry into the family which controlled this strategically important region.) In 1177, John was created Lord of Ireland, an empty title carrying opportunity and risk rather than authority or profit. This was especially true after John's unsuccessful visit in 1185 designed to establish his position. With hindsight, chroniclers saw a pattern in John's political adventures. In Ireland, he frittered away the money his father had provided and indulged with his young friends in luxurious living and mockery of the locals: ridicule of the hairy Irish; disdain for the Anglo-Norman settlers. John was not the last insensitive and futile English pro-consul in Ireland. But a reputation for failure clings.

The Irish fiasco of 1185 did not prompt Henry to moderate his devotion to his youngest child. There were rumours – which the future Richard I believed – that Henry was contemplating making John his heir. None of this prevented John from deserting his father at the last, a betrayal that caught the disgust of contemporaries. Small wonder the well-informed Richard of Devizes thought him flighty, an habitual traitor. On his accession in 1189, Richard I provided John with an heiress to marry – Isabella of Gloucester – and vast estates in England, the honour of Lancaster and the counties of Nottingham, Derby, Dorset, Somerset, Devon and Cornwall; in Normandy the county of Mortain which the young Henry I had held. There was no doubt that John was then regarded as Richard's heir. In the king's absence on crusade, he set about reinforcing his position. Almost in defiance of the regency government under Longchamp, John established his own court complete with justiciar, chancellor, etc. Nobles earlier in the century had had their own Exchequers, but John's establishment had the air of a rival government. Perhaps resentful at not being given the regency himself, John led opposition which forced Longchamp's removal in 1191. Continued exclusion from power thereafter, combined with his brother's designation at the treaty of Messina (1191) of their nephew Arthur of Brittany as his heir, drove John to take advantage of the king's captivity in Germany (1193-4) to ally with Philip II in dismembering Richard's continental lands. This second betrayal, especially of a crusader, did little to enhance John's reputation: nor did his subsequent volte-face. In 1194, John had been given Evreux by Philip; after submitting to a remarkably forgiving Richard, he returned to Evreux and massacred his French garrison. Henry II had been a notorious liar and cheat, and yet earned grudging respect. The same traits in John just made him appear shifty.

Richard I's sudden death in April 1199 propelled John to his inheritance. In a possibly apocryphal story circulating twenty years later, William Marshal and Hubert Walter, Archbishop of Canterbury, debated whether to support Arthur of Brittany or John as King of England. William persuaded Hubert that legally and politically John should be preferred, but the archbishop warned: 'So be it … but mark my words, Marshal, you will never regret anything in your life as much as this'. Yet the early signs must have encouraged both. After a vigorous diplomatic and military campaign, by September John had been accepted by all the Angevin provinces in France and had been crowned King of England; Arthur of Brittany and his mother Constance had submitted; and Philip of France had agreed to parley. At the treaty of Le Goulet (May 1200) Philip recognized John as rightful heir to all Richard's lands in return for a relief (payment to a lord by a vassal entering into possession of an inherited fief) of 20,000 marks. The fact of acknowledging Capetian overlordship was neither novel nor degrading. Henry II and Richard I had openly acknowledged it, as had, tacitly, Henry I. What the Capetians made of their recognized suzerainty depended less on them than their vassals, Angevin, Burgundian, Flemish or Champagnois. Here lay the difference between John and his predecessors: they coped with Capetian overlordship; John did not. The relief, however, was new, and an added drain on John's finances. There is little evidence that John's, or Richard's, demands exhausted Angevin territories. However, whereas Richard's demands led to results that were popular – the crusade; the king's release; the counterattack in France – John's exactions, heavy from the start of his reign, produced no such positive results. Furthermore, where Richard could persuade English nobles to support his continental wars, John had much greater difficulty. The elusive element of personality was central. The task of a medieval monarch was to convince a few hundred men, and a few women, to follow his lead. Richard could do it; John could not.

John's reign had three distinct phases. During the policing and ultimate loss of Normandy and Anjou, to 1204, John was as absent from England as much as any of his predecessors. Between 1204 and 1214 most of his energies went in amassing the funds to recapture his continental lands, his presence in England presenting novel circumstances for a political nation used to an absentee overlord. The failure of the reconquest led directly to the final challenge to his authority, the civil war and French invasion 1215-16. It is largely a consequence of the clerical monopoly on chronicles and later attempts to place John's resistance to the papacy in a suitably Anglican light that have exaggerated the importance of the papal Interdict (1208-13), making John a monster of godless depravity or, as in *The troublesome reign of King John* (1591), a flawed Protestant champion. In fact, as far as John's control over the church and his nobility, the Interdict made little difference; its resolution if anything strengthening John's position by gaining a useful ally against enemies both foreign and domestic.

Throughout his reign, John showed vigour and intelligence comparable to his father and brother. His hurried divorce and subsequent marriage to the twelve-year-old Isabella of Angoulême in 1200 secured a strategically important alliance in Aquitaine. In 1202, decisive military action and a forced march of eighty miles in less than two days out-manoeuvred his enemies at Mirebeau, where Arthur of Brittany was captured. Angevin control of Poitou was consolidated by the limited expedition of 1206. Careful naval preparations were rewarded by the first major English victory at sea at the battle of Damme in 1213. During the dark days of civil war in the winter of 1215-16, John wrong-footed the rebels with a lightning three-month campaign through their territory, his march from Winchester to Berwick taking less than five weeks. This was coercive warfare in the best style of Henry II. Elsewhere in the British Isles, with only the threat of force, John imposed a harsh treaty on the inveterate troublemaker, William the Lion, King of Scots, in 1209. In 1210, a brief expedition to Ireland established royal authority over the Anglo-Irish barons in the east. In 1211, Llywelyn, Prince of North Wales was subdued so that, in the words of the Barnwell chronicler, 'now no-one in Ireland, Scotland or Wales … did not bow to his nod'. From such successes, John derived not only political clout but substantial booty.

John was no slouch as an administrator. He personally supervised the work of the Exchequer. He was an assiduous judge: in 1209-12, the central judicial bench which customarily sat at Westminster was suspended, the justices following the king around the country. During the reign there were significant developments in bureaucracy: household offices became increasingly specialized; systematic collection of administrative and judicial records was instituted; a royal privy seal was employed to expedite business; the distinction was established between the civil (Common Pleas) and criminal (King's Bench) jurisdiction of the Westminster judges. John presided over the creation of a national customs system based upon standardized weights and measures and the organization of a royally funded and built navy. The tone of John's government is captured in his instructions to agents in Southampton in 1206 to carry out his orders with 'immediate haste', whether 'night or day' 'as you love us, our honour, the peace of our kingdom, and regard your own safety and welfare'. All the ingredients of Angevin success and failure are present: urgency; attention to detail; authority; menace.

Yet John was no bureaucrat. His close involvement in the government of England was largely enforced by the loss of Normandy and Anjou. Thereafter, John, whose restlessness was notorious (only once in his reign staying more than a month in any one place), travelled incessantly in his kingdom, as some saw it meddling in his subjects' affairs. In areas such as the north, rarely visited by kings since the tenth century (indeed even Henry III only went north three times in fifty-six years), the presence of an inquisitive and acquisitive monarch on the doorstep came as a rude shock. It was no accident that the rebellion of 1215 was initiated by a group known as 'the Northerners'. The impression of John's conscientiousness, no less than that of a more specialized household, may simply reflect the creation of new ways of recording business which coincided with John's reign. Consequently, by accident, John can be studied in far greater detail than any of his predecessors. The administrative initiatives probably owe more to John's civil servants than to the king. Under John England was run by veterans of Angevin service who had been ruling the kingdom for years before 1199, such as the justiciar, Geoffrey FitzPeter, and the chancellor, Hubert Walter. It was for political rather than bureaucratic reasons that John introduced his own men into English government, such as the Tourainers Peter des Roches (Bishop of Winchester from 1205; justiciar 1213-15), Peter de Mauley, Engelardde Cigogné and Gerard d'Athée and the Norman Falkes de Bréauté.

Whatever his achievements, John consistently undermined them. The nickname 'Softsword' stuck because of a willingness to give up a cause before decisive action. John left Normandy in December 1203, six months before the fall of Rouen, and three before the fall of Château Gaillard. The month before Rouen capitulated in June 1204, the archives of Norman government were shipped to England and taken to London in carts provided by the king, hardly an encouraging sign to those still at their posts in the duchy. In 1214, on the news of the defeat of his allies at Bouvines, John withdrew. Eighteen months later, instead of combating the invasion of Prince Louis of France, John allowed him to land without resistance. With the exception of the Welsh campaign of 1211, John, in marked contrast to his father and brother, lacked tenacity in adversity. On each occasion, however, he feared treachery and would not expose himself to the risk of battle or campaigns against the odds.

Suspicion ate at the heart of John's personality and rule, vitiating his triumphs. In 1200, instead of compensating Hugh of Lusignan for the loss of his intended bride, Isabella of Angoulême, John siezed his duchy of La Marche. This prompted Hugh to appeal to his and John's overlord, Philip of France, thus setting in train the formal confiscation of John's continental lands and the loss of Normandy and Anjou between 1202 and 1204. After the spectacular coup at Mirebeau in 1202, John wilfully alienated William des Roches, seneschal of Anjou. Thereafter, John could no longer rely on the loyalty of the Barons of Anjou. Most damaging was the disappearance and presumed murder inside one of John's prisons of Arthur of Brittany in 1202-3. Rumours swirled around Arthur's death. Hubert de Burgh, custodian of Falaise where Arthur may have been held, denied responsibility for his death. Some accused John's henchman Peter de Mauley of the murder. One account, possibly derived from an eye-witness, accused John in person, saying that he murdered Arthur in a post-prandial alcoholic rage at Rouen at Easter 1203, disposing of the body in the Seine. Whatever the truth, Arthur's fate and John's inability to produce him, lent Philip II a telling propaganda weapon and ensured the hostility of the Bretons.

In dealings with English nobles, John was no less malevolent. Even the loyalist Earls of Chester and Pembroke were harried and threatened for no better reason than that they were powerful. More notoriously, John's former favourite, William de Briouze, was ruined and exiled, his wife and son starved to death in prison. Such violence fostered an atmosphere of fear. It was one thing to execute thirty Welsh hostages in 1212 or allow captives from Mirebeau to starve to death in Corfe Castle after a failed attempt at a mass break-out. But the persecution, without trial, of English barons was different.

Yet this is precisely what John's policy seemed often to be. At every turn he exploited wardship, relief and his sovereignty as king to discipline his nobles. A favoured technique was to force barons to become royal debtors. Again, the Briouze family provides a most dramatic example, Matilda de Briouze being compelled to offer the huge sum of 50,000 marks (equivalent to the Exchequer revenue for one year) for the king's grace (i.e. protection money) when her assets amounted to twenty-four marks and some gold pieces. Geoffrey de Mandeville forced to offer 20,000 marks for John's ex-wife and the earldom of Gloucester. Reliefs varied according to loyalty. 10,000 marks were imposed on William FitzAlan and Nicholas Stuteville, but William de Forz, the son of John's mistress the Dowager Countess of Aumale, inherited for free. The purpose was political control not financial profit. Stuteville had, by 1230, almost £10,000 still outstanding on debts contracted under John. Given the average annual baronial income of £200, very few being worth even as much as £400, the threat of fore-closure was potentially ruinous. If the debtor had recourse to Jewish bankers for a loan, he again con-fronted the king who regularly taxed the Jews and received all their property – including notes of credit – on their deaths. Other avenues of extortion were explored. The venality of Angevin justice and adminis-tration, exactly matching its pretentions, could be turned to the king's advantage. William Mowbray was encour-aged to offer a bribe of 2,000 marks to the king to obtain a favourable outcome in a land suit. John accepted the bribe – and allowed Mowbray to lose the case, insisting he pay up nonetheless. It is unsurprising that the sale of justice, judgement without trial and the cost of reliefs and wardships appeared prominently in Magna Carta.

John's unpopularity went further. His style of rule and his personality repelled affection and loyalty. Even his gambling and drinking crony, his half-brother William of Salisbury, briefly deserted him in 1216. John's sus-picious nature was matched by gracelessness and the insensitivity of a cunning, introverted cleverness. Many of his hobbies were innocuous enough. John was an avid collector of jewels, which he liked to wear round his neck. He drank and gambled and, like his father, was an obsessive huntsman. Well-read and cultivated, he read both French and Latin, possessing his own portable library, including a copy of Pliny. John was also a preda-tory lecher, with a reputation for seducing his nobles' sisters, daughters and wives. He had numerous mis-tresses and at least five bastards. Outrage at John's sexual licentiousness may have added an edge of bitter-ness to political resentment. One of John's alleged intended victims was the wife of the northern baron, Eustace de Vesci, who for no obvious political reason played a central role in stirring rebellion in 1215. John also had a penchant for blackmailing others for their sexual adventures, accepting bribes as 'hush-money'. He may have had a dirty sense of humour, which may explain the famous, if enigmatic entry on the Oblate Roll of 1204: 'The wife of Hugh Neville promises the lord king 200 chickens that she might lie one night with her husband'. Whether or not John was a smutty-minded groper, it does seem that many thought him personally unsavoury. In a world where private relation-ships were the stuff of high politics, that was a distinct problem.

John had a gift for making enemies, but policies as much as personal quirks caused friction. John was deter-mined to recapture his inheritance. Money was raised by any means possible. There were national property taxes in 1203 and 1207. As the latter raised £60,000 it is diffi-cult to argue that the fiscal exactions of the 1190s had bled England dry. However, the political price was high, there being considerable resistance to the 1207 levy. Thereafter, John was forced to more piece-meal exped-ients. As feudal overlord, John levied reliefs, wardships and scutages at unprecedentedly high rates. On top of the scutage, a tax in lieu of military service, calculated on the number of knights owed, each baron had to pay a fine for personal exemption. This was hardly popular. Sheriffs were required to account for every penny owed the Crown instead of, as previously, paying an agreed lump sum (or 'farm'). Inevitably, this encouraged sheriffs to greater rapacity (or efficiency as Exchequer clerks no doubt saw it). Towns were encouraged to purchase mercantile privileges. Infringements of the onerous Forest Laws were assiduously pursued, as were more general profits of justice and the ubiquitous impos-ition of amercements, fines for petty misdemeanours, often merely protection money. To such sources of income were added the profitable campaigns of 1209-11, Jewish legacies and tallages, and the proceeds of the deserted benefices during the Interdict. Small wonder John was accused of being 'a pillager of his subjects'. More dangerous than the pious clichés of monastic chroniclers, such high and persistent demands for money excited concerted resistance and, in 1213-14, refusal to pay the scutage. In the insistence that aids and scutages be levied with the consent of the barons (Clause 12), Magna Carta was passing political judgement on John's preparations for the great reconquest in France. But by then John's hopes had been dashed. The road from Bouvines to Runnymede was direct.

The last years of John's reign were some of the most extraordinary in English history. Confident in his treasure and his own leadership, two obstacles to a return to Normandy remained. To forestall a projected French invasion blessed by the church, in 1213 John submitted his kingdom to the pope to remove both his personal excommunication and the country's Interdict. When Richard I had done homage for England to the Emperor Henry VI in 1194, he gained merely his own freedom. John, by becoming a papal vassal for his kingdom, acquired a staunchly loyal ally which played a crucial role in sustaining the Angevin dynasty. The root of the dispute had been the king's traditional right to appoint the Archbishop of Canterbury, which the pope had contradicted by appointing Stephen Langton archbishop in 1206. Although not overtly a pious man (again like his father), John's response had little to do with religion. At stake was royal control over church appointments which, given the irrevocable increase in the church's estates, was essential for royal authority to be maintained. An independent church or one wholly controlled by an ultramontane papacy would present immense difficulties in ruling England. As it was, the settlement of 1213 acknowledged the pope's legal authority, but with Innocent III (and his successors) committed to support of their newly repentant vassal, there ceased to be any challenge to royal wishes. For most practical purposes, provided the king and pope co-operated, royal manipulation of the church could continue.

Less tractable was the mounting irritation of sections of the baronage. In 1212, there was a plot to assassinate the king. It is significant of what John had to face that one of the ring leaders, Robert FitzWalter, had surrendered the vital town of Vaudreuil to the French in 1204. John's enemies were champions of no liberty except their own. In 1215, FitzWalter trumpeted himself as 'Marshal of the Army of God', yet personal vendetta and grievance not constitutional, still less religious, principle lay at the heart of opposition to John. Neither side could claim the moral advantage. Robert's fellow traitor of Vaudreuil, Saer de Quincy, was another to rebel in 1215. John was confronted by men exasperated but no less duplicitous and self-seeking than he. John's failure was to woo enough interests and individuals to his side. One problem was that his interests and those of his leading barons increasingly diverged. In 1205 and 1213 he was prevented by magnate indifference and hostilty from attacking Normandy. In 1213, his attempt to circumvent the higher nobility and widen the scope of political action by summoning knights from the shires to a national assembly backfired: they were as unenthusiastic as the barons about the French wars. All might have been transformed by victory in 1214. Failure, however, is contagious.

The civil war of 1215-16 showed John at his best and worst. A master of tactics, he wrong-footed his enemies, led by a hard core of northern malcontents, by assuming the protection of the crusader when he took the Cross at Easter. At Runnymede in June, Magna Carta, into which all the baronial fear and distaste for the operation of Angevin government was untidily poured, provided some basis for compromise, except that its final clause (61) provided for a committee of twenty-five barons to supervise government. If implemented (which inevitably it was not), this would have placed the English Crown into commission. Yet at the very time he was ordering his sheriffs to execute the terms of the charter, John was seeking its annulment by the pope. Militarily, John had the beating of the rebels until the invasion on their behalf by Louis of France, son of Philip II, in the summer of 1216. John's characteristic refusal to challenge Louis on the field led to a haemorrhage in his support. Misfortune, such as the loss of some of his treasure near the Wash, and illness took its toll. John himself recognized the desperation of his plight. In his will, dictated on his deathbed, he urged his executors to 'render assistance to my sons for the recovery and defence of their inheritance'.

By October 1216, the central issue in the civil war was no longer Angevin government but John himself. Immediately after his death, the regency, on behalf of the nine-year-old Henry III, issued a modified Magna Carta signalling a new, more consensual style of rule. Already, the image of Bad King John was abroad. Ironically, John is most remembered for Magna Carta, in the drafting of which he was little involved and whose content he quickly repudiated. The true measure of John's reign is not in the temporary truce between two mercenary and self-interested factions, which the charter represented. It lies in the contrast between the magnificent inheritance of 1199 and the legacy of 1216, with the enemy already within the gates and almost ready to take possession. John may not have been the worst English monarch, nor yet the most tyrannical; but it is hard not to judge him, on any terms other than his own, as one of the most unsuccessful. However, John's family did not entirely reject his memory. Fifty years after his death on a windy October night at Newark, John's grandson, the future Edward I, named his first-born son John.

Further Reading
R. V. Turner, *King John*, 1994.
W. L. Warren, *King John*, 2nd edn, 1978.
J. C. Holt, *King John* (Historical Association Pamphlet), 1963.

JOHN, DUKE OF BEDFORD (1389-1435), third son of Henry IV, ruled Lancastrian France for his nephew Henry VI from 1422 to 1435. A thickset man of great strength and a capable soldier, he was also a statesman and diplomat and ranks second in ability among Henry IV's sons. Well-educated like his brothers, he was a man of some culture. He purchased the great library of Charles VI, which he housed in his mansion of Joyous Repose at Rouen, read Latin and Greek classics in French translation, and commissioned illuminated books of his own. His piety emerges from the two monasteries he founded at Rouen, one belonging to the distinctively French order of the Celestines: a choice that shows how French his tastes became during his prolonged sojourn abroad and his contented marriage to Anne of Burgundy. He possessed all the pride and hauteur of his rank, yet was also affectionate, sensitive, and genuinely compassionate to the unfortunate. So successfully did he curb his naturally hot temper that he was considered remarkable for his caution and prudence.

Bedford's political employment long antedated his creation as duke in 1414. He had administrative, diplomatic, military, and even naval experience as warden of the East March against Scotland in 1403-14 and Guardian of England almost continuously from 1415-21. He thus missed Agincourt. Following the deaths of Henry V and Charles VI in 1422, he became Regent of France for Henry VI, and remained in charge, though not as regent, after Henry's coronation in 1431. Although he was Henry V's eldest surviving brother and heir presumptive to Henry VI, he left England to his brother Humphrey, Duke of Gloucester, asserting his priority of birth only twice – in 1425-6 as Protector and in 1433-4 as Chief Councillor. On both occasions he restored harmony and harnessed English resources for his French wars. He accumulated many honours, acquiring two French duchies and six counties, but he had no heir by either marriage. He served his nephew's interests better than his own.

The Treaty of Troyes of 1420 had recognized Henry V as heir to Charles VI in preference to his own son the Dauphin, the future Charles VII. As Charles VI also died in 1422, Henry VI was legitimate King of France and not a conqueror. It was Bedford's responsibility to retain those areas controlled by Henry V, to extend control over the remainder, and to rule the whole on behalf of Henry VI's French subjects. Victories at Cravant and Verneuil in 1423-4 were high points in a steady extension of the conquered area up to the siege of Orleans in 1429, when he was thwarted by 'a disciple and limb of the Fiend, called the Pucelle, that used enchantments and sorcery' (Joan of Arc). He then suffered his first serious reverses, but nevertheless stabilized the position, retaining in 1435 more territory than Henry V had held. He was then deserted by the Duke of Burgundy, whose alliance he had consistently sought to maintain. Bedford lived like a French nobleman, imposed strict discipline on his troops and combated brigands, used French officials and Norman institutions, and – as the war zone shifted southwards – brought peace and prosperity to Normandy. His rule was not just acceptable but even popular to the Normans, whose taxes financed the war. He was a successful ruler, even if he understandably failed to complete his brother's conquests. Clearsighted, singleminded and consistent, he was loyal to his subordinates and earned their confidence. If he lacked Henry V's remarkable personal magnetism, he nevertheless possessed all the qualities needed in a king and was respected by all those whom he encountered. At his death he could not be replaced.

Further Reading
C. T. Allmand, *Lancastrian Normandy 1415-1450: The History of a Medieval Occupation*, 1983.
R. A. Griffiths, *The Reign of King Henry VI 1422-61*, 1981.
E. C. Williams, *My Lord of Bedford 1389-1435*, 1963.

JOHN OF GAUNT (GHENT), DUKE OF LANCASTER (1340-99), third son of Edward III, was the greatest noble in late medieval England. Already Earl of Richmond in 1342, he entered his wife Blanche's vast Lancaster inheritance and became Duke of Lancaster in 1362. After her much-lamented death, he remarried in

1371 to Constance of Castile, elder daughter of King Pedro the Cruel (*d.*1369), and called himself King of Castile and Leon. Invading Spain in 1386, he gave up his realms in 1388 and two daughters became Queens of Castile and Portugal. From 1394 he was Duke of Aquitaine. By marrying his mistress Katherine Swynford he legitimized his Beaufort offspring and eased their promotion in the peerage and church.

Gaunt was a tall, spare, but well-built man, reserved and dignified in manner. 'Conventional in all things', especially in religion, he was typically aristocratic in his love of ceremony and show, his liberality, his love of dicing, falcony, and the chase. Like Edward III and the Black Prince he served in many expeditions from 1355, displayed knightly prowess at Najera (1367), and made his retinue 'a chivalrous company of highly regarded knights conspicuous for their courtly and chivalrous skills' on the model of King Arthur's Round Table. Hence perhaps his sense of honour. Acutely conscious of the dignity of royal and noble birth and rank and the respect due to them, he deeply resented any criticism or hostility from knights, Londoners or other plebeians. Thus he quarrelled with the city in 1377, the Earl of Northumberland in 1381, and King Richard in 1385. Public apologies and ceremonies of reconciliation were required to appease him: from London and parliament in 1377, Northumberland in 1381, the king in 1385 and 1389, and Arundel in 1394. Duties and obligations, like his good lordship to Wyclif, were scrupulously observed. None took priority over allegiance to the Crown: 'the king had no more faithful servant than himself and he would follow wherever he would lead'. Gaunt's haughtiness was disliked in England and misinterpreted as ambition for the Crown, but abroad his grand manner, exalted birth and rank, international connections and outlook were admired.

After 1370 Gaunt was the senior active royal prince and willingly shouldered military and official burdens that successive kings shirked. Although a poor general, he was a good diplomat and councillor. The ill-health of his father and brother forced him to take the military and political lead, to adopt the French and papal policies condemned by the Good Parliament (1376), and to orchestrate the court's recovery. His unpopularity made a regency impossible, thus permitting Richard II's disastrously premature assertion of power, but his interventions were often decisive. Unable to persuade Richard to campaign in France in person, he walked out of the royal council, thereby giving 'great displeasure both to the king and to the whole council. Yet these temporal lords went in constant fear of the Duke of Lancaster because of his great power, admirable judgement, and his brilliant mind'. His seniority, authority, and 200 retainers enabled him to condemn Richard's counsel and government with impunity. No wonder there were plots to kill him. Again in 1394 Gaunt's 'rough and bitter words' in council reportedly prevented others from expressing their views freely. By then, however, Gaunt was recognized as a force for peace and stability and the complaint was quashed. His retainers dominated local commissions because they too contributed to peace and order, for Gaunt, at least, could control his retainers. His absence in 1386 and death in 1399 were followed by political crises.

Further Reading
A. Goodman, 'John of Gaunt: Paradigm of the late Fourteenth-Century Crisis', *Transactions of the Royal Historical Society*, 5th series, xxxvii, 1987.
G. A. Holmes, *The Good Parliament*, 1975.
S. Armitage-Smith, *John of Gaunt*, 1904.

JOHN OF GLOUCESTER (*fl.c.*1245-*d.*1260) was Henry III's master mason in the later 1250s. Already a successful mason in the 1240s, during the following decade he was particularly associated with Henry III's grandiose schemes at Westminster, both at the Abbey and the Palace. But his work for the king also included activity at Gloucester, Woodstock, Windsor, Guildford, Merton, Oxford and Old Sarum, largely on secular buildings. The value placed upon him is reflected in his rewards: he amassed property in Gloucester, Oxfordshire, Middlesex, Southwark, Northampton and Surrey. In 1255, he received from the king robes 'such as the knights of the Household receive'. His duties and presumably skills were many: the supervision of the large number of labourers at Westminster; designing the queen's lodgings at Windsor; general maintenance of the stone fabric of royal dwellings; renewing the drains and sewers at the Palace of Westminster; even constructing lecterns for the king and the Westminster Chapter House. At Westminster, he worked closely with the king's chief carpenter, Alexander (*fl.*1239-*d.c.*1269). Together, they received patents in January 1257 as masters, respectively, of the king's masonry and carpentry. Their positions had earlier been recognized when, in November 1256, they had been ordered to take charge of all royal works in the kingdom because, significantly, the king 'had suffered much damage through causing his works to be carried on by sheriffs and other officers'. Either this can be seen as another encroachment on local power, part of a policy which so irritated the political nation that it led to overt opposition two years later; or Henry, desperately short of money but insistent on maintaining his regality in stones no less than in rhetoric and policy, was determined to avoid the peculation and financial mismanagement inevitable in a localized system of audit and accountability, a problem not unique to Henry III. Whatever the royal motive, John and Alexander set about their new responsibilities by touring the king's works south of the Trent in 1257, viewing not only buildings but the marble quarries at Purbeck. Like many other servants of Henry III, John found that his office was something of a poisoned chalice. The king was nearly bankrupt: in 1259 wages arrears to the Windsor workmen alone had reached £410. It may be that John was expected to cover any immediate shortfall. If so, it ruined him: at his death in 1260 he owed the king eighty marks and the income from his extensive lands was said to reach only two marks a year. This was the grim reality behind the soaring achievement of Westminster Abbey.

Further Reading
J. Harvey, *English Mediaeval Architects*, 1987.

JOHN OF SALISBURY (*c.*1115/20-1180) had an international career typical of the well-connected and highly-educated twelfth-century ecclesiastic. Although in the second rank of academics, lawyers and administrators, John was a prominent member of the closely interlaced clerisy of clever secular clerks who glided seemingly effortlessly between the courts of kings, popes and prelates. John's contacts are a roll-call of the intellectual and spiritual leaders of western Christendom in the mid-twelfth century: Abelard, Pullen, Becket, St Bernard, Eugenius III, Hadrian IV, Alexander III, Archbishop Theobald. John's contribution to this circle was literary and secretarial. Education at Exeter and Paris was followed by travel and employment across Europe. Although no lawyer, he spent much of his career advising on legal matters, for example on appeals from the English church to Rome. An ability to get on with people secured him an ill-defined administrative post at the papal curia in the late 1140s, followed in the 1150s by employment as secretary to Theobald of Canterbury. In England he became a friend of Thomas Becket, whom he preceded into exile in 1164, only returning in 1170. Apart from the letters he composed for his masters, John's main literary works were the *Metalogion*, a defence of the study of the liberal arts; the *Historia Pontificalis* a gossipy account of the papal curia between 1148 and 1152, written in exile during the 1160s; lives of Anselm and Becket; and the *Policraticus*, written in the 1150s, which combines a critique of contemporary rulers with a treatise on political thought. The *Policraticus* presents a moral view of rule. There is a single principle of government derived from the teaching of the church. However, although God's law is sovereign, in the secular sphere the monarch possesses unassailable authority. John describes a republic (i.e. secular state) as a living organism whose head governs the other members. Only where the monarch is illegitimate, and, in John's terms, therefore tyrannical, was there a right to depose or kill him to restore the moral order. The very unoriginal practicality of the *Policraticus* commended it to later humanist lawyers of the fourteenth century and after who were attempting to construct a theory of authority not dependent upon the self-validating minutiae of lawyers and theologians. John's writing was characterized by a lack of dogmatism and a sense of irony, even objectivity in assessing men and events. John's eye for detail, imagery and allusion made up for his lack of intellectual depth, a fact of which he may have been conscious, as a number of his classical references and quotations are entirely bogus. But they look impressive. There is a refreshing humanity in John. An observer more than an actor, when caught up in the century's most famous act of violence, the murder of Becket, he made his position clear to the archbishop: 'We are sinners and not yet prepared to die: I see no-one here except you who is anxious to die for dying's sake'. At the entry of the knights into the cathedral, John quickly hid. Yet his association with the martyr did him no harm, perhaps even identifying him as a candidate for the high office he attained at the very end of his career as Bishop of Chartres. John confessed to another human weakness: drink. He regarded himself as something of a connoisseur of wine, being particularly harsh on Sicilian, Greek and Cypriot wines which he thought lethal. But he was no wine snob. In 1157, he wrote to a friend: 'I am fond of both wine and beer, and do not abhor any liquor that can make me drunk'. As has recently been written, 'John's fame is as a mirror of his age'.

Further Reading
M. Wilks, ed., *The World of John of Salisbury*, 1984.

JOHN THE OLD SAXON (*fl.*887-904) was a German monk and scholar who entered the service of King Alfred and became Abbot of Athelney. Asser tells us that Alfred summoned from abroad a certain John, 'a priest and monk, a man of most acute intelligence, immensely learned in all fields of literary endeavour and ingenious in many other skills'. Elsewhere he informs us that John was 'of Old Saxon stock', that is a native of Saxony in the East Frankish or German kingdom. John was one of several scholars recruited by Alfred from outside Wessex to assist in his plans for the revival of English culture: others were Plegmund, Grimbald and Asser himself. The help these four men rendered the king was acknowledged by him in his preface to his translation of Pope Gregory's *Pastoral Care*. The only other surviving evidence of John's learning consists of three short Latin poems conjecturally attributed to him. However, he may have played a more important part in the Alfredian intellectual revival than this meagre evidence suggests. For example, he may have brought manuscripts with him from East Francia. There is a sense in which John brought back to Wessex elements of the culture, now lost in the home country, which had been exported to Germany by such as Boniface and Lul a century and a half earlier.

Alfred appointed John Abbot of Athelney, in Somerset, probably round about 890, as part of his plan to revive monastic life in Wessex. The experiment was not a success. Because the English were unenthusiastic about monasticism Alfred had to fill the monastery with foreigners recruited by rather dubious means. Two of the Frankish inmates tried to murder their abbot, but he survived. Whether or not John persisted as Abbot of Athelney after this fracas, we do not know. All we do know about his later life is that he outlived his patron Alfred: his name last features among the witnesses of a royal charter of the year 904.

JOHNSON, DR SAMUEL (1709-84), lexicographer, poet, biographer, essayist, was highly regarded in his time for his literary work. The impact of his personality upon his friends was such that he is known to us through an incomparable record of anecdotes and obiter dicta. He attracted a biographer worthy of his subject, whose method it was essentially to let the Doctor speak for himself. Boswell knew him after the great creative period of his life; our image of Johnson is likely therefore to be of a shambling, gruff, opinionated, elder statesman of literature, a polymath, an independent Tory, a law unto himself, a man with time for his friends. This splendidly ripe autumnal figure has passed into legend. There were also years of struggle and doubt which were the making of the great man.

He was born at Lichfield in September 1709, the year in which his father, a bookseller, was sheriff of the city. As a child he was touched by Queen Anne for the King's Evil, his mother making a special journey with him to London for the purpose. He wore his touch-piece round his neck for the rest of his life and never renounced his sentimental attachment to the House of Stuart. His face was pitted by a severe attack of smallpox, he suffered from a pronounced nervous tic or convulsive start and his eyes were weak. He suffered always from periods of depression of spirits and inability to concentrate, but he had a nearly photographic memory, a feeling for words and ability to extract the meaning from the books which he read hungrily but seldom finished. He was educated at Lichfield School, famous for the teaching of Dr Hunter, and briefly at Stourbridge. Unpractical and moody, he made little effort to fit himself for his father's business, though he learned how to bind a book and acquired an extensive knowledge from his father's collection. With a small legacy and help from a friend, Andrew Corbet, he went to Pembroke College, Oxford, with the reputation of a prodigy in classical studies, but found the tutoring indifferent and may not have added greatly to his academic store during his thirteen months of residence. Already he seems to have acquired a habit of procrastination and already he was enduring bouts of introversion and self-examination; later it was said of him that he could not bear to be alone, and he was always at his happiest in company. Tall, raw-boned, shambling, shabby, twitching, embarrassingly clumsy at table, he was sometimes a butt, more usually an object of some awe. He was dogmatic in his talk, but impressive because he knew so much. His choice of friends was catholic and unpredictable. One was Henry Hervey, a good-natured, reckless young ensign of good family; another, Gilbert Walmisley, Register of the Ecclesiastical Court at Lichfield, urbane Whig and scholar. The fees not forthcoming, Johnson did not complete his course at Oxford and was afterwards hampered in his search for employment by his want of a degree; fortunately, since his brief experience as a schoolmaster, at Husbands Bosworth and later at his own small school at Edial House, showed that he had little aptitude for teaching. In 1731 his father died, encumbered in debts. In the following year, after some unhappy months at Bosworth, he went to Birmingham, where he lived for about three years, writing sporadically some essays which have been lost, for the *Birmingham Journal*, and a translation from the French of a Portuguese Jesuit's travels in Abyssinia. The severe but orotund style, the antitheses and stately generalizations, show that Johnson's style was already setting in the mould of his later work.

At the age of twenty-five, without profession or income, he married Elizabeth Porter, a florid widow twenty years older than himself. His friends disparaged her, but she brought him a modest sum and the comfort of a ripe personality. Johnson's exuberant attentions to his wife aroused the ridicule of the pupils of his school, amongst whom was David Garrick, but he seems to have been devoted to his 'Tetty'; later he neglected her at times and she grew difficult with age. Leaving his school, but taking with him the unfinished manuscript of *Mahomet*, a tragedy, he set off for London, in 1737, with Garrick, aged nineteen. Johnson said of London that 'when a man is tired of London he is tired of life' but his early years were spent in 'drudgery and garrets' and he tried to escape by applying for posts as a schoolmaster. In 1738 he began to contribute to the *Gentleman's Magazine*, for Edward Cave, and he soon asserted some literary control over this miscellany of reports, essays and extracts from other works. He was for some time the reporter of debates in the House of Commons. Since, after April 1738, reports were held to constitute a breach of privilege, these were concocted by Johnson from scraps of notes under the guise of '*debates in the Senate of Magna Liliputia*'. The speeches may have borne little resemblance to the originals; Johnson himself never attended the debates and he was Tory in bias ('the Whig dogs shall not have the best of it'): but they attain a consistent level of excellence which is remarkable considering the speed at which they were written, once ten pages between noon and early evening. He abandoned

this work in 1743 when he decided that it was an unjustifiable fraud; but they were long afterwards thought to be genuine; indeed two of his speeches appeared in the collected works of Chesterfield. In April 1739 Johnson produced a political pamphlet, *Marmor Norfolkiense*, and in May the *Compleat Vindication of the Licensers of the Stage*. They were unworthy of his intellectual powers, as were the short biographies he undertook. But towards the end of 1743 he wrote a lively life of his friend Savage, to whom he was attracted, despite his blatant faults, because of his talents and sufferings. The book, acute in its perception of the conflicts within Savage's personality, reveals as much of Johnson as of his subject. It brought some good reviews but little money. While his contributions to the *Gentleman's Magazine* tailed off, he began, at the end of 1742, a venture in bibliography, working upon the Harleian Library for the bookseller, Thomas Osborne. He wrote the *Proposals* for printing the Catalogue of this vast collection by subscription and again for the *Miscellany*, a collection of the scarcer documents. But he left this work in dudgeon, actually coming to blows with his unappreciative employer, and turned to the production of a new edition of Shakespeare. His conception was grand, but he shelved it, after producing an essay on *Macbeth*, when he learned that Warburton was also working on an edition.

Still searching for an enterprise of a heroic sort, he decided upon a dictionary. The plan for this work, so suited to his magisterial, exact mind and his ability to select from a mass of material, was issued in 1747 and addressed to the Earl of Chesterfield. More practical help came from the printer Dodsley, head of the group who sponsored the dictionary. At the cost of grinding toil, Johnson was given a degree of security. He took a house in Gough Square, hired six amanuenses, settled to an immense programme of reading and committed himself to producing something which, in France, a team of forty academicians had taken nearly a century to compile. He still found time to write outside his self-imposed task. In January 1749 appeared *The Vanity of Human Wishes*, the first poem to bear his name, but his second imitation of the satire of Juvenal. Whereas *London*, written in 1738 and praised amongst others by pope, stayed close to its original, *The Vanity of Human Wishes*, ostensibly derived from Juvenal's Tenth Satire, is distinctively modern in its examples of ambition disappointed, essentially Johnsonian in its stoical mood and morality. Johnson believed that much is to be endured, little to be enjoyed in life. After death he feared 'being sent to Hell, and punished everlastingly'. So he equipped himself to meet life's trials, composing prayers for his own use, a scheme of life which enabled him to live chastely amongst the temptations of the town and to overcome his self-confessed enemy, sloth. The sheer output of these years is astounding. In March 1750, he launched *The Rambler*, which appeared twice a week for the next two years: a periodical essay with a limited circulation of about 500 which set a standard of quality to its more popular contemporaries, and eventually attained popularity itself on being reissued in volume form. *The Rambler* invites comparison with the *Spectator*. The stories and allegories suffer from the same weakness that prevented his succeeding in drama: too much logic and too much of the moralist. His characters show a deep knowledge of human nature, but they are too abstract and generalized to make much impact. Addison's purpose had also been didactic but no-one, reading about Sir Roger de Coverley, would guess that he was being taught philosophy or urged to reform. Johnson aimed at 'the propagation of truth' and his serious purpose was obvious even in his lighter passages.

Concluding *The Rambler*, Johnson stated that he had laboured 'to refine our language to grammatical purity, and to clear it from colloquial barbarisms, licentious idioms and irregular combinations'. If this had been the only achievement of the *Dictionary*, which was completed in 1755, it would have been useful as pioneer work in the etymological jungle which had grown up around the rapidly expanding language. But Johnson's *Dictionary* is also a work of art. Aiming to fix the language and preserve its purity, he succeeded in establishing a standard of reputable use. He accepted no authorities earlier than Sidney or Spenser. But with typical lack of pedantry he included dialect words, Scottish in the main but also some from his native country. He used quotations to illustrate the use of words: often from memory, these do not belong to a scientific approach to lexicography but they are usually accurate, an instance of his prodigious knowledge. His great strength lay in definition, for which he had a genius, as readers of Boswell will recognize. He was the first to attempt a thorough distinction between the different meanings of words: *come*, for instance, is subdivided into fifty sections. Sometimes he was sportive, with words which gave him a chance to air his prejudices: *oats*, for instance, 'which in England is given to horses, in Scotland to men', but his definition of the *patron* (with Lord Chesterfield in mind) strikes a harder note. It recalls the wonderful ending of his letter to the neglectful peer: 'for I have long wakened from that dream of hope in which I once subscribed myself. My Lord, your Lordship's most humble, most obedient servant, Samuel Johnson.' The flavour of his definitions remains where the vast *Dictionary* itself has long passed into limbo. But no-one valued it more than those who followed in his tracks and produced more scientific compilations.

Johnson was acclaimed for his production of the *Dictionary* and began to enjoy a licensed lordship in literary circles. That did not prevent him, in 1756, from being arrested for a small debt and released only after the intervention of Samuel Richardson. He still hankered after grand projects, scheming to edit a journal of European studies, then issuing new *Proposals* for an edition of Shakespeare. But most of his work was such as required less sustained effort. He had exhausted himself in his work on the *Dictionary* and suffered acutely from bouts of depression, conscience-stricken during the intervals of leisure which he needed to recover from his intense bouts of work. It was in these years that he became the Dr Johnson known to us through Boswell's pages; sage, philosopher, obdurate Tory, the presiding genius of the 'Club'. Fanny Burney saw a grotesque figure, 'very ill-favoured, tall and stout but stoops terribly' and noticed his body 'in constant agitation, see-sawing up and down'. Besides his talent for conversation, he had a compelling need of company, to ward off his black moods and prevent his mind from turning in on itself. He contributed to Kit Smart's *Universal Visitor* and undertook the control of the *Literary Magazine* (1756-7). The latter saw his celebrated defence of tea, which he preferred to any form of alcohol and drank copiously. He helped friends with their books, wrote a life of Sir Thomas Browne (1756) and of Roger Ascham (1761). He produced a second series of essays in the *Idler* and a section of another journal, *The Universal Chronicle*. Here may be seen a lighter touch than he displayed before and at least one of his characters, Dick Minim the critic, lives as something more than a type. But his single novel, *Rasselas, Prince of Abyssinia* (April 1759), written in haste to pay for his mother's funeral, is less a story or a study of characters than a series of discussions upon the human condition. It is pure Johnson, in style and philosophy, and levies a severe tax upon the reader's patience. He arrives at the end with a stock of aphorisms and a sense of a deeply serious but not unhappy man. Prefaces, dedications, reviews flowed from his pen, but not until 1762 and a sharp attack from the abrasive Churchill, did he resume work on Shakespeare; with a pension of £300, surely the most deserved of royal bounties, and financial independence, he was able to complete it by October 1765. His common sense, his perception of the genius of Shakespeare and his knowledge of Elizabethan English contributed to the value of this edition. Some of his comments are still to be found in modern editions. Of all that had hitherto appeared, this was the most accurate and the nearest to the originals. Some clues to his quality as a man may be seen in his modesty. The 'great Cham', who was so autocratic, even a bully, in his conversation, did not intrude conjectures or prejudices where the evidence did not support them.

In 1763, Johnson met Boswell; in 1764, with his close friend, Reynolds, he founded the Club; in 1765 he met the Thrales who provided a domestic setting for his middle age. In these years he wrote less but lived more richly than before; he was still generous with his time in causes that appealed to him, writing political tracts, dictating arguments for Boswell's law cases, and generous in his purse towards unfortunates, and with his time in conversation, which fortunately has been preserved for us. In the late summer and autumn of 1773 he travelled with Boswell to the Western Isles of Scotland; it was adventurous in a confirmed Londoner of advanced years. The reader finds interest in his comments about the clans, superstition, emigration and other Highland themes, but the fascination of the book arises from the picture that it conveys – at once intrepid, inquisitive and droll, the philosopher not afraid to get his feet wet, to sit in a small boat, or to vault over a fence to show his agility. At Easter, 1777, a deputation of booksellers waited on him to persuade him to write biographical prefaces to a collected edition of the English poets. Conceived in jealousy of a similar project in Edinburgh, the work proved congenial to Johnson and he gave of his best; the prefaces were published in 1781, without the texts, under the title of *The Lives of the Poets*. Earlier, George III, in a happy moment, had proposed that Johnson should write the literary biography of his country. He was specially interested in the man, and the poetry is seen in its relation to the personality and career of the poet. Thus they remain authoritative as biographies, although long superseded as criticism, partly because he did not know enough, partly because he is subjective, at his worst when he does not sympathize with the character of the poet, as with Milton, the puritan, or Swift, the bitter Tory. In the three years of infirm health that remained to him he endured the blows that usually accompany old age, the loss of friends, Thrale of Stretham, Levett and blind Mrs Williams, his pensioners at Bolt Court, with the courage and enterprise that made him such good company for a younger man like Boswell. In July 1785 he set out on a tour of old haunts, Lichfield, Birmingham and Oxford. He came back to London to die, on 13 December. He was buried in Westminster Abbey among some of the poets whom he had so nobly commemorated.

Dr Johnson was a Tory and a churchman. His Toryism may have been based more upon family tradition and an antipathy towards the Whigs than upon serious Jacobite Principles. It was baseness, arrogance, pretentiousness in politics, that he detested; above all anything that smelt of the hireling. His churchmanship stood upon a rock-like sense of the value of order, but it was nourished by regular and sensitive private devotions. He stood at the still centre of the currents of the age: against 'enthusiasm' on the one hand, also against the divagations, intellectual and moral, of the laxer figures of the established church. Sometimes he was unfair: one recalls a devastating judgement upon Fielding, a steely reluctance to see the merit of Gray. Even his lighter prejudices could lead

him into heavy rudeness, to Scotsmen, to Whigs and to nervous tyros. But we should remember that his reputation carries the heavy load of almost verbatim reporting by an uncritical devotee. Furthermore, beneath the orderliness of his definitions, the emphatic dogmatism, lay an inner turbulence. Even his friends complained of his habits; he admitted to having no love of clean linen. But could they fathom the stress of his life, the disorder of emotions, near at times to madness, that his *Journals* reveal? For years the genial house of the Thrales provided him with a secure refuge. But he could never be long with himself. To the end he had to be writing, talking or travelling. Is it the secret of this man's greatness, the note of authority which we recognize even today, that we know that it came from struggle and heartbreak? Dr Johnson lived at the full stretch of his emotional and mental capacity. Feeling vibrates through his most trenchant statements, and these are acceptable because they expose humbug and cant. In life he stood for reverence, for truth and a high standard of decency. His death, wrote Murphy, 'kept the public mind agitated beyond all former example. No literary character ever excited so much attention.'

Further Reading
G. Clingham, *James Boswell: The Life of Johnson*, 1992.

W. J. Bate, *Samuel Johnson*, 1977.

J. L. Clifford, *Young Sam Johnson*, 1955.

R. W. Chapman, ed., *Letters*, 3 vols, 1952.

S. C. Roberts, *Doctor Johnson*, 1935.

G. B. Hill, ed., James Boswell, *Life of Dr Samuel Johnson*, 6 vols, 1887.

JONES, ERNEST (1819-69) was a Chartist leader. When he died, Engels wrote to Marx that 'he was the only educated Englishman among the politicians who was, at bottom, entirely on our side'. This attractively quixotic convert to Chartism, and thence to Socialism, was the son of a cavalry officer, who had been equerry to Victoria's uncle Ernest when he became King of Hanover. Hence his name, and hence, too, a German upbringing which gave him a wider perspective than those of his fellow Chartists. Returning to England aged nineteen, he was presented to the queen and married in the fashionable London church, St George's Hanover Square. He was called to the Bar, and started to practise on the Northern Circuit.

Warm sympathy with the suffering of those at the bottom of the pile in the 'Hungry Forties' drew him to Feargus O'Connor. He discovered a talent for oratory. Though a small man, he had a beautiful voice and an exciting command of language. He also wrote eloquent verse.

> The land it is the landlords',
> The trader's is the sea,
> The ore the usurer's coffer fills;
> But what remains for me?

He had come to Chartism late. Co-editor of the *Northern Star* in 1847, active in the Chartist Petition and the Kennington Common rally in 1848, he was imprisoned for two years for using provocative language. He was kept in solitary and silent confinement, with a large hole in the roof over his bed, through which rain and occasionally snow fell; without heat, and with no books, pen or paper. He survived, though two others died, and for twelve years heroically tried to revive the disintegrating Chartist movement. He lived near starvation on money earned by poems and novels, refused Chartist cash, and turned down an income of £2,000 a year, which his family offered him if he would abjure Chartism. He came to believe, under the influence of Marx, that nationalization of all the means of production and distribution would be the salvation of working people. But the '50s were prosperous. Rebuffs by the budding Trade Unionists and by the electorate drove him to change tack. He returned to the Bar, where he earned money and a high reputation, sought middle-class support and launched the movement for 'registered residential manhood suffrage'. He saw its first breakthrough with the Second Reform Act of 1867, and though he came bottom of the poll at Manchester in the Election which followed, he had just been readopted as the sole Liberal/Radical candidate there when he died.

JONES, INIGO (1573-1652), designer and architect, was a Londoner, the son of a Smithfield clothworker. We know little about the first thirty years of his life. Before 1603 he had been to Italy and learned the draughtsmanship which marked him above his contemporaries. He went there again, in the company of the Earl of Arundel, in 1613-14, visited Rome, read the writings of Palladio and compared the master's drawings of classical buildings with the originals. Jones's copy of Palladio still exists, with his annotations: it symbolizes the injection of classical antiquity into English architecture in 1615, the year in which he began seriously to practise. Hitherto he had been predominantly concerned with designing stage sets, machines and costumes for the masques which James I's queen, Anne of Denmark, enjoyed so much. From 1605 until they quarrelled in 1631 Ben Jonson and Inigo Jones presented at court a series of elaborate shows, and Jones continued as designer until the masques ceased in 1640. He introduced the proscenium arch and such devices as moving shutters, rotating columns and possibly a revolving platform, and his career is of original importance in the history of the English stage.

In 1615 he became Surveyor of the King's Works, and thenceforward until the outbreak of the Civil War he gave most of his time to the supervision and extension of royal buildings. Much of what he did has been pulled down, and some – for example, the proposed immense reconstruction of Whitehall – never got further than the drawings. Among the buildings which survive, revealing the Palladian imprint which Inigo Jones brought to English architecture – and the English feeling which he imparted to Palladian – are the Queen's House at Greenwich, begun in 1617 and finished in 1635; the Banqueting House at Whitehall (1619-22), with its superb proportion; and Marlborough House chapel (1623-7). Jones was also responsible for the layout of the piazza at Covent Garden, an early, if modest, example of town-planning, and for St Paul's Church there, built like a Roman temple; and he was involved in the plans for the rehabilitation of old St Paul's Cathedral. It is significant that he did little for private patrons (though perhaps no English architect has had so many scores of buildings incorrectly attributed to him). This was partly because as Surveyor he necessarily spent much of his time on routine jobs of maintenance; partly, no doubt, because of the insularity of some of the nobility; yet partly also, it has been suggested, because 'a style backed by the prestige of the Crown and the genius of Jones failed to gain the approval of the country as a whole' in a period when 'the court was increasingly isolated'.* Certainly Inigo Jones's fortunes were tied to those of the court. He left London in 1642, and in 1645 was among the royalists besieged in Basing House, when he was captured and 'carried away in a blanket, having lost his clothes'. He was fined and had to compound for his lands. Yet he found a wealthy Puritan patron, for in the last years of his life he was working for the fourth Earl of Pembroke in the rebuilding and decorating of Wilton House. He died at Somerset House in 1652.

Further Reading
John Summerson, *Inigo Jones*, 1966.

JONES, SIR WILLIAM (1746-94) was internationally famous for his learning in several fields. At different times he was a Fellow of University College, Oxford, a practising barrister, reforming politician and Indian judge; he was a notable classical scholar and his legal treatises were definitive; he was no mean poet and a member of Dr Johnson's circle. He mastered a number of oriental languages, began the codification of Hindu law and helped to popularize the themes and literature of the east by his renderings of them into English verse.

His father was a Welshman, self-taught but a brilliant mathematician, recognized by Newton and befriended by Anson who appreciated his work on navigation. He died when William was only three; at seven William was sent to Harrow, where he came under the influence of a fine teacher, R. C. Sumner. His friends numbered the

---

*E. Mercer, 'The Houses of the Gentry', *Past and Present*, No. 5, May 1954, p.27.

future Lord Teignmouth, Governor-General of India and Jones's biographer; Samuel Parr, who was later to destroy his chance of becoming headmaster of Harrow by voting for Wilkes in the Middlesex election; Bennett, a less colourful scholar, whose hobby was tracing Roman roads in Britain, and Halhed, who was to produce the first Sanskrit grammar. They fostered in each other the precocious scholarship and abstruse interests which may have acquired a special savour as a form of retreat from the hurly-burly of the eighteenth-century public school. They mapped out surrounding fields into the Greek states and transformed their games into Peloponnesian Wars. Greece was a natural magnet; it is interesting, too, to see how they were drawn to the east and especially to India, where the British raj was being so rapidly extended.

At Oxford Jones arrived a finished scholar. At this time University College was second to none in academic standards and a nest of lawyers, including Chambers and the brothers Scott. To help keep himself he tutored Lord Althorp, son and heir of Earl Spencer; after three years, in 1769, he went with the child to Harrow: the connection ended when Jones tried to insist upon complete control of his education. The Spencer connection was nonetheless a useful one. Althorp had an energetic career and was First Lord of the Admiralty in Nelson's time. The portrait of Jones by Reynolds can be seen today at Althorp House. Jones used his leisure to widen his knowledge of eastern languages. He was an exceptionally gifted linguist and is said to have known thirteen languages and to have been acquainted with another twenty-eight. He learned Arabic from one Mirza, a Syrian from Aleppo. At the request of the King of Denmark he translated from the Persian the history of Nadir Shah, a seventeenth-century warrior king. His *Poeseos Asiaticae Commentariorum*, in which he made a metrical comparison between the classical poetry and the east, enhanced his academic fame. In 1771 he produced the Persian grammar which was to prove useful to generations of Indian administrators. Linguistic studies were already fashionable: Horne Tooke, Priestley and, of course, Dr Johnson were all formidable grammarians. Now Jones, who corresponded with European scholars like Count Revikski, caught the mood with verses, flowered and fluent. In 1772 he published his very popular *Asiatic Poems*, purporting to be from the original but only flimsily connected if at all. About this time Jones was sometimes to be seen in Persian dress. He enjoyed his cult, but he had sterner ambitions.

He had originally been put off the law by 'the crude and barbarous style' of the lawbook Latin but in 1774 he returned to the Bar. He was appointed Commissioner of Bankrupts and was busy on circuit; altogether these were years of intense activity for he wrote treatises, including one, *Essay on Bailments*, which is a classic account of a

branch of law almost ignored by Blackstone. To add to a picture of a sprightly, well-balanced character, he was a keen horseman who loved hunting – but despised beagling because, as he said, he liked everything big and disliked everything little – enjoyed swimming, skating and dancing: the whole man indeed. He also acquired the liberal views which were to become popular during the American war. It may be that he was affected by the scenes of poverty that he witnessed on his journeys. He certainly seems, like Wyvill, to have believed that the liberties of his countrymen were impaired by a corrupt and oligarchic executive and legislature. In 1780 he stood as the popular Whig candidate for Oxford University but withdrew when he found that he could make no dent upon the position of the official Whig and Tory candidates. Since he lost no chance of urging freedom for the American colonies and the suppression of the slave trade, played with the idea of universal franchise and confessed to being at least a theoretical republican, preferment was delayed; at last, however, in 1783 he became a judge of the Supreme Court at Calcutta. If without financial independence he could make no mark on English politics, there he was superbly equipped for what proved to be his most important work.

When Jones went to India, Hastings was Governor-General; Cornwallis followed him, a great pro-consul who devoted himself to the reform of Bengal upon English principles of government. In 1793 Lord Teignmouth succeeded, and carried on the enlightened work. In the conditions created by these outstanding men, imbued with the spirit of service to the native races, Jones's talents blossomed. He worked hard in the courts, projected and supervised the codification of Hindu law, translated Sanskrit works and elaborated in lectures to the Royal Asiatic Society, of which he was first president, his thesis that Persia was the matrix from which the dispersal of the world's population had begun. His linguistic studies give him some claim to being the founder of comparative philology. As if his central pursuits were not enough, he was an enthusiastic botanist and classified the Indian flora in the terminology of Linnaeus, played skilful chess and, characteristically, wrote a monograph on the Indian game. From his little wooden house outside Fort William he would walk three miles before dawn to the court, proceed by palanquin to the court house, have a cold bath and breakfast, and work for two hours before his five-hour session on the bench. He made a fortune of £50,000 by saving rather than by corruption, but he did not return to England to enjoy it. Just after his resignation, and after he had sent his wife home to recover her health, he died. Like so many Englishmen he had given himself to the east: we are left to speculate what the rest of his career might have been. He was better equipped than Bentham to be a legal reformer; he might have been drawn into radical politics, for he certainly aligned himself with Price and against Burke; he might have preferred to work at law and poetry in some country retreat. It became fashionable among utilitarians, like Mill, to decry his work as superficial. Now, as the dust settles upon the British raj and on debates about its government, we are better able to appreciate not only Jones's pre-eminence as scholar but his value as one of the men who wanted India to be ruled in the interests of its peoples.

Further Reading
P. Brown, *The Chathamites*, 1967.
Lord Teignmouth, *Memoirs of the Life, Writings and Correspondence of Sir William Jones*, 1804.

JONSON, BEN (1572-1637), playwright and poet, was by his own account of Scottish border ancestry, the posthumous son of a minister. Schooled at Westminster, he worked as a bricklayer for his stepfather, fought as a mercenary in the Netherlands, and made an unhappy marriage before he began in 1597 to work for Henslowe's company as actor and playwright. He killed a fellow actor in a duel and turned Catholic during his imprisonment; he abjured Rome twelve years later. His first play, *Every Man in His Humour*, produced in 1598, established his reputation, and it was followed by a succession of others over the next thirty years, of which *Sejanus* (1603), *Volpone* (1606), *The Silent Woman* (1609), *The Alchemist* (1610), and *Bartholomew Fair* (1614) are the best known. From 1605 to 1630 Jonson, with Inigo Jones designing the settings, delighted the court with a series of masques, and apart from a brief imprisonment for libelling the Scots he was in high favour with James I, who in 1616 gave him a pension as 'king's poet'. In 1618 he travelled to Scotland and stayed for some time with the poet William Drummond of Hawthornden. The death of James and the accession of a new king whose tastes were notably different made Jonson's fortunes less certain. Illness overtook him in the later 1620s; his play, *The New Inn* (1629), failed badly; and after his quarrel with Inigo Jones in 1631 he produced no more masques at court. He died in 1637 and was buried in Westminster Abbey. His fellow poets honoured his memory in a collection of verse entitled *Jonsonus Virbius*. The famous inscription on his tombstone, 'O Rare Ben Jonson', was, according to Aubrey, 'done at the charge of Jack Young, afterwards knighted, who, walking there when the grave was covering, gave the fellow eighteen pence to cut it'.

Drummond of Hawthornden painted an unattractive portrait of Jonson at the age of forty-six, saying, 'He is a great lover and praiser of himself, a contemner and scorner of others; given rather to lose a friend than a jest, jealous of every word and action of those about him (especially after drink, which is one of the elements in which he liveth)'. Big, noisy, quarrelsome, generous,

Jonson was certainly a man of extraordinary range, and he dominated the literary life of London for an unusually long time. This was not simply a measure of the variety of his writings, of the lyrics, the epigrams, the splendid blank verse passages. It was first and foremost a reflection of personality. At the Mermaid Tavern in the first years of the seventeenth century he was the central figure of the famous meetings of writers, the scene of the combats of wit between Jonson and Shakespeare described by Fuller in his *Worthies*, and in their later years he was laying down the law to a circle of younger men, 'the tribe of Ben', at the Sun, the Devil, and elsewhere. But his range of friends was by no means confined to young writers in taverns. It included men of such varied brilliance as Donne and Selden, Bacon and Clarendon, the last of whom spoke of Jonson's 'extraordinary kindness for Mr Hyde, till he found he betook himself to business, which he believed ought never to be preferred before his company'; and he enjoyed the country-house patronage of aristocrats like the Sidneys, the Earl of Pembroke, and the Duke of Newcastle. His own remarkable and uneven genius was no doubt self-made. The classical learning he displayed so lavishly in his plays was the product of omnivorous reading in his younger days rather than of his formal education. Yet in many ways – in his self-assertiveness and yearning for supremacy, his zest for life, his blend of coarseness and delicacy, honesty and scandal, erudition and vulgarity – Jonson was peculiarly representative of Jacobean England, or at least of that part of it which was untouched by Puritanism.

Further Reading
J. Palmer, *Ben Jonson*, 1934.
C. H. Herford and P. Simpson, eds, *Ben Jonson: Works*, 1925-52, vols I and II (*The Man and His Work*).

JORZ, CARDINAL THOMAS (*d.*1310) was one of three English Dominican friars who were created Cardinals of Santa Sabina in 1303-10. All three studied at Paris and Oxford, all probably becoming doctors of theology, all three served in the Oxford convent, and all attended councils abroad. Walter Winterbourne (*d.*1305), probably the eldest, and Thomas Jorz were successively priors of the Oxford convent, priors provincial (heads) of the Dominicans in England and confessors to Edward I (1289-1305), to whom Winterbourne was a most trusted servant. Winterbourne probably originated from Wiltshire, William Macclesfield (*d.*1303), probably the youngest, from Cheshire, and Jorz from Wales, but all were obscure in origin. Their careers demonstrate not just that high office in the mendicant orders was exceptionally open to the talents, not just the international rather than insular horizons of such men, but also the higher valuation placed by the papacy in comparison to the English Crown on those from the religious orders.

Several popes and many cardinals were monks or friars and the other two English cardinals of the fourteenth century, Simon Langham and Adam Easton, were Benedictine monks, yet monks and friars were rarely appointed bishops by late medieval English monarchs.

Thomas Jorz was probably known as Thomas the Englishman at Paris, where he is alleged to have studied under Albertus Magnus and to have known St Thomas Aquinas. He was in the Oxford convent in 1292, when he secured his doctorate of theology and became prior, and in 1297 he became prior provincial of the Dominican order in England. In this capacity he attended Dominican synods at Cologne in 1295, Marseilles in 1300, and Toulouse in 1304. In 1305 Edward I sent him to the General Council of the church at Lyons, where he was created cardinal by Pope Clement V, thereafter making his home at the papal Curia.

In the fourteenth century cardinals resigned their existing offices on appointment and took up residence at the Roman court. Only in the fifteenth century were they allowed to retain their preferments and remain in their country of origin. Jorz thus became a papal official, serving on papal commissions and embassies; he was on embassy at his death at Grenoble in 1310. Jorz's influence emerges in his dealings with Walter Stapledon, Bishop of Exeter, to whom he was my 'principal lord and promoter', for whom he intervened to assist with his consecration and to avert a challenge to his election, and from whom in return he exacted a pension for a protégé. Similarly Edward II asked him to press for the canonizations of Robert Grosseteste (1307) and Thomas Cantelupe (1308). If appropriate records survived, Jorz would probably be seen intervening frequently in English affairs. He certainly exercised his influence to advance his friends and relatives, no doubt assisting the advancement of his brothers Walter in 1306-7 and Robert in 1311-21 to the archbishopric of Armagh.

JOWETT, BENJAMIN (1817-93), Master of Balliol College, Oxford, from 1870 until his death, was the most famous university don of Victoria's reign, a national figure. Few would have expected this of the little white-haired lad with high-pitched voice and cherub face, son of a failed printer and an evangelical mother, who went to Balliol as an undergraduate in 1836. Nor did success come easily to him. As Regius Professor of Greek he was notoriously underpaid for ten years, Christ Church wriggling their way out of increasing his stipend until even the queen commented to Tennyson that Oxford had used him shamefully. The Fellows of Balliol rejected him as their Master at his first attempt in 1854.

He had set out to be a theologian, taking up the position that one's religion was the use one made of one's life; that Christ provided the ideal pattern; and that the church was there to make this pattern available to all who sought it. He also made a plea for the use of reason in interpreting the Scriptures, in an essay in the controversial collection *Essays and Reviews*, published in 1860. This 'Broad Church' approach was denounced by both Newmanites and Evangelicals, and a whiff of heresy hung round him. So he gave up theology, and refocused on classical philosophy, completing his translation of the works of Plato, with commentaries, shortly before his death. To us now his life seems narrow indeed. He never left Balliol. Despite occasional spasms of guilt, he largely ignored his family. A brilliant classical scholar, he never went to Rome, let alone Athens. He neither knew, nor wanted to know, anything about the physical sciences. And what would the modern don make of a Master who believed that research should be undertaken in one's spare time, after the central work of teaching had been done? 'How I hate learning', he once rather curiously admitted.

But Jowett was a dedicated teacher, and it was from this that his influence grew. 'To arrange my life,' he wrote in his notebook as he felt his energy draining, 'in the best possible way, so that I may be able to arrange other people's.' He had the streak of eccentricity common to many great teachers, with his piping speech and long silences. He had high expectations of his students, opening questions but never dictating answers, expecting them to make their own discoveries through hard work. He gathered them round him in vacation reading parties and followed their subsequent careers. Balliol had already started to attract gifted undergraduates, when in 1828 it became the first college to open its scholarships to general competition. Jowett's reputation made it the outstanding intellectual centre at Oxford, and his students included Asquith, Grey, Curzon and Milner as statesmen, Gore and Lang as churchmen, Tout and Caird as scholars, leading lawyers and diplomats, and, most unlikely but devoted, the poet Swinburne. He filled the Master's Lodgings with celebrities to provide his star pupils with contacts for their future careers, and made sure, through constant letter-writing, that he was at the centre of the Balliol network. Nor were undergraduates his only admirers. Florence Nightingale asked him to come and administer the Sacrament to her, and they became close friends, though there is no written evidence of the story that he asked her to marry him.

Jowett's influence at the University of Oxford was important. His programme for opening up the entry to it, and for retaining its collegiate structure while spreading its wealth, was largely accepted; so that, with Cambridge, it remains different from all other universities. He also introduced Hegel to British philosophy, thus starting a new Romantic school of thought there. But the ideals which he set his students left their mark outside Oxford and beyond the academic world, and helped to develop the tradition of public service which became a hallmark of later Victorian Britain. The quatrain first published in *The Masque of Balliol* by a group of undergraduates in 1881, and reproduced in many different versions since, sums up the awe, sometimes grudging, in which he was held.

> First come I. My name is J-w-tt
> There's no knowledge, but I know it.
> I am Master of this College.
> What I don't know, isn't knowledge.

Further Reading
G. Faber, *Jowett*, 1957.

JUXON, WILLIAM (1582-1663), Archbishop of Canterbury, was born at Chichester and educated at Merchant Taylors School and St John's College, Oxford, where he studied civil law. President of St John's from 1621 to 1632, he owed much to the friendship and patronage of his predecessor, Laud, whose ecclesiastical views he shared and upheld when in 1632 he became Bishop of Hereford and in 1633 of London. But where Laud was harsh and rude, Juxon was meek and gentle in manner, and contrived to manage his Puritan diocese without arousing widespread enmity. His appointment as Lord Treasurer in 1636 caused surprise and resentment, because he was an ecclesiastic and clearly Laud's nominee. Inexperienced in politics, he was at least refreshingly honest and industrious. And in Philip Warwick's words, 'so well he demeaned himself through his whole seven years' employment, that neither as bishop or treasurer, came there any one accusation against him in that last parliament 1640, whose ears were opened, nay itching after such complaints'. A humble, unambitious man, he was left in peace at Fulham. In the years after 1646 he was in frequent attendance on the king, and ministered to him on the scaffold. During the Commonwealth he retired to his house at Little Compton in the Cotswolds, conducted Anglican services at Chastleton Manor, and spent much of his time hunting, for which he had a passion. Once when his hounds, said to be the finest pack in England, disrupted a Puritan meeting at Chipping Norton there was a complaint to Cromwell, who brushed it aside, saying that Juxon should enjoy his hunting so long as he did not disturb the government. He was the obvious choice for Canterbury at the Restoration, but he was already an ailing man; he took no real part in the work of the Savoy Conference, and died in 1663. As Bulstrode Whitelocke put it, Juxon 'was a person of great parts and temper, and had as much command of his temper as of his hounds. He was full of ingenuity and meekness, not apt to give offence to any, and willing to do good to all.'

Further Reading
Thomas A. Mason, *Serving God and Mammon, William Juxon 1582-1663*, 1985.

K

KEAN, EDMUND (*c.*1787-1833) was the finest tragic actor of his day, a man who lived wildly and dissipated his great talents. The events of his boyhood are uncertain, since the main source is Kean himself – and he liked to embroider a tale. It seems that he was the son of Nance Carey, a strolling actress, who soon abandoned him. He appeared as a stage cupid, received lessons from a ventriloquist uncle and a Drury Lane actress; he went as a cabin boy to Madeira, but soon returned and fell into the life of a stroller. He played Prince Arthur at Drury Lane when about fourteen but went off to take a circus job in Bartholomew Fair. Having broken both legs tumbling in Saunders's circus he returned to less dangerous employment. Engagements included a recitation before George III at Windsor, small parts at the Haymarket and larger parts in the provinces. He married Mary Chambers, an Irishwoman some years older than himself, in 1808, and they lived precariously for some years. He was always impulsive and often drunk. On one occasion, while he was playing in Norwich, he was due to dine the next day with Bishop Bathurst. He had a battle in the street with nightwatchmen and was so disfigured that he was compelled to send his apologies to the good bishop. A large bump on his nose threatened to be permanent. 'No matter,' he said to his wife, 'I shall now have a Roman nose as well as John Kemble' (his greatest rival and leader of the 'declamatory' school of acting).

Dr Drury, the headmaster of Harrow, came across Kean playing at Exeter – and even acting Shylock and Harlequin in the same evening! He got a Mr Grenfell to write to Whitbread about Kean and the manager of Drury Lane Theatre engaged him for three years. When he had managed to extricate himself from another commitment, he appeared in the role of Shylock and was loudly acclaimed. Lewes wrote (*On Actors*) that there was nothing more impressive on the stage than his lines 'Hath not a Jew eyes?' for 'passionate recrimination and wild justice of argument'. There followed the parts of Richard III, Hamlet, Othello and Iago. Hazlitt and Coleridge were among those who praised him. 'To see Kean act is like reading Shakespeare by flashes of lightning', said Coleridge. For Hazlitt he was 'an excellent substitute for the memory of Garrick', but no more than Kemble could he act the perfect Hamlet: 'Mr Kean's Hamlet is too splenetic and rash, as Mr Kemble's is too pointed and formal. His manner is too strong and pointed. He throws a severity, approaching to virulence, into the common observations and answers.' The criticism tells us a lot about Kean, though it should be remembered that Hazlitt thought that there should be 'as much of the gentleman and scholar as possible infused into the part and as little of the actor'. He also said that his acting was 'not much relished in the upper circles. It is thought too undisguised a display of nature.'

Kean's performances would very likely seem to us unsubtle and blustering. He was obviously powerful in stage presence, although quite small, and bandy-legged after his accident. He had a musical voice and a fine head. He was convicted, in a sordid case (*Cox v. Kean,* 1825) and had to pay damages to the man with whose wife he had been having an affair. His reputation never recovered fully from this episode, though he had good receptions in Paris and New York and was elected a Huron chief in Canada. Performances and public reaction were both unpredictable. Acting, in his tempestuous manner, before excitable, impressionable audiences, taxed him physically and emotionally. He would sometimes go for solitary, hectic, midnight rides along the turnpike, returning to sleep in the stable. He built a little cottage in Bute to retreat to in depressed and remorseful moods. There once he tried to stab his wife. His Coriolanus failed, his Lear was a popular triumph. He revelled in Sir Giles Overreach and it is in this part that he is depicted in George Clint's painting at the Garrick Club, one of several which portray his classical roles. He was capable of thrilling audiences to the end in his best roles. He was playing Richard III in the year of his death, and his last illness overcame him when he was acting Othello.

Recklessly generous with the large sums of money he earned in his heyday, Kean offended his admirers by his debauched taste for low company, and he ill-treated his wife. He was ashamed of his origins and he sent his son Charles to Eton. He too became an actor and producer in due course: devoted to his mother, he effected a last-minute reconciliation between his parents.

Further Reading
Raymund Fitzsimons, *Edmund Kean, Fire from Heaven*, 1973.
G. W. Playfair, *Kean*, 1939.

KEATS, JOHN (1795-1821) died four months after his twenty-fifth birthday. His last year was largely consumed by mental and physical suffering. He had not been a precocious boy; nor, until 1817, could he devote himself wholly to writing. Up till that time he had been a student, and latterly practitioner, of medicine. In a short space Keats became one of the world's great poets.

He still lives vividly today, in his letters and some of his poems. He seems to appeal directly to many who can only approach Wordsworth or Shelley as historians or critics. He is also a poet's poet. Tennyson rated Keats above all others of his century. Pre-Raphaelites and aesthetes, Morris, Swinburne, Wilde, saluted him as their master, pioneer of art for art's sake – a prejudiced view for, as another poet, Hopkins, said, dismissing his defects as due to his youth, he was 'made to be a thinker, a critic as much as a singer or artist of words'. A twentieth-century devotee of Keats was Wilfred Owen.

Some prime romantic conceptions appear in Keats in moderate form. He was inspired by nature; he believed in 'the holiness of the heart's affections and the truth of imagination'. 'A fine writer,' he once wrote, 'is the most genuine Being in the world.' But he was temperamentally averse to extremes: he accepted human limits. The elements of didacticism, or escapism that some find disturbing in other romantic poets are absent from Keats. This poet of tender sensibility was also a man of common sense; 'he had flint and iron in him', said Matthew Arnold, after reading Keats's letters.

Keats's mind was a masculine one and he was an excellent critic. As T. S. Eliot said, 'There is hardly one statement of Keats about poetry which … will not be found to be true …' He wins friends, as he did in his lifetime, by his delight in things for their own sake, by his generous feelings for people and by his lack of conceit. As Arnold saw, 'his love of beauty was an intellectual and spiritual passion'. The poet, said Keats, must be a monk in imagination's monastery: he embraces its discipline so that he can more fully comprehend the joy and pain of actuality. Keats did not aspire to be a prophet or crusader. He was a craftsman – and no poet has ever applied himself more intensely to his craft. For him there was 'no fiercer hell than the failure in a great object'. He received two cruel and uncomprehending reviews of his first ambitious work *Endymion*. Yet he went on to what Gittings has called 'the greatest year of living growth of any English poet'.

Heredity rarely explains genius. Keats's forbears only suggest that John, like his brother George, might have prospered in commerce. Thomas Keats married his employer's daughter, Frances Jennings, and came to manage his livery stables at Moorfields, just outside the city. When he died, after a fall from his horse, John, the eldest of his four sons, was eight. His widow, pretty and impetuous, married again; her mother, Mrs Jennings, took the children to live with her at Edmonton. Chancery suits wasted the money intended by Jennings for his wife and children. Frances soon left her second husband and returned to live with her mother and children. Fifteen months later, in March 1810, she died, probably of tuberculosis. John had nursed her tenderly: suffering and responsibility tried him young. At fourteen he was the male head of his family.

Since 1803 John had been at school under John Clarke at Enfield. (There had been talk of sending him to Harrow – where he would have been Byron's contemporary!) He was a lively, popular boy, open and generous but with a sort of 'terrier courage' when he was roused. He once attacked a teacher who boxed his brother Tom's ears; when he was older he trounced a butcher's boy whom he found maltreating a kitten. Cowden Clarke, the headmaster's son, whose later recollections supply much schoolday detail, befriended and tutored him. He read history and classical mythology, storing his mind with narratives and images which were soon to reappear transformed in verse. He began a prose translation of the *Aeneid* (which he completed after he left school) and discovered astronomy, music – and liberalism in the pages of Leigh Hunt's *Examiner*. He soaked himself in books with such delight that they became parts of his creative imagination. Spencer, Chapman and Drayton, later and most important, Shakespeare, were among the authors who became part of this transforming experience. It was when writing about *King Lear* that he wrote of that attitude to life which embodies 'negative capability' and which 'is capable of being in uncertainties, mysteries, doubts, and does without any irritable reaching out after fact and reason'.

The trust fund set up for the Keats children was badly managed: whether Abbey, the active trustee, was dishonest or ignorant or both has been much debated. Keats could have gone to Oxford; instead he was articled to Thomas Hammond, an apothecary surgeon of Edmonton, and stayed with him for four years, studying the theory and practice of medicine. Fortunately Keats was near enough to Clarke to see him regularly, borrow books and talk about poetry. Of all poets Spencer, with his suggestive epithets and rich imagery, was the most attractive. Keats went through the *Faerie Queene* 'as a young horse would go through a spring meadow – ramping'. His first poem was 'Imitation of Spencer', written when he was eighteen. Sonnets and odes that followed in 1814 and 1815 all show the same natural fault of artificiality, the same predictable enthusiasm. Keats was straining to achieve a poetic manner, using a language that may have seemed fresher, less derivative to him than it does to us.

Before he moved to Southwark in October 1815, to complete his training at Guy's Hospital, he was a committed poet. As he worked at practical anatomy, assisting at operations, witnessing pain and death in that grim age when the skilled surgeon was becoming more ambitious, but was still unassisted by anaesthetics, his mind was often elsewhere. We are told that he always sat beside a window, and talked of nothing but poetry. He still fell naturally into stale idioms; he conceived an unfortunate admiration for the verse of Leigh Hunt. It was Hunt, however, who first published a poem, 'O Solitude', by Keats, in the *Examiner*, and his friendship encouraged Keats in fast and fluent writing. Another friend of this time was the painter Haydon, a total artist, passionate and reckless. Keats, who had qualified and been licensed to practice medicine in July 1816, made himself a home with his brothers in Cheapside and announced that he was going to be a poet. His first collection of poems was published in March 1817. One evening that winter Hunt and he were dining together and gave each other crowns of laurel and ivy to wear; visitors called, Hunt was embarrassed and removed his crown; Keats, unabashed, kept his on. He used to write under an engraving of Shakespeare's head; he read Shakespeare with a new determination to master his craft. The result was *Endymion* (April 1817-February 1818), in his own words 'four thousand lines of one bare circumstance', the love of Cynthia for the mortal Endymion. His concern in the poem is human experience raised to the imaginative 'sublime'. There are two distinct themes: 'the gradations of happiness' and the idea that the poet cannot directly realize an abstract ideal but must come at it through common, concrete experience. In the course of writing the poem he wrote to a friend: 'What the Imagination seizes as Beauty must be Truth – whether it existed before or not – for I have the same idea of all our Passions as of Love, they are all in their sublime, creative of essential Beauty … However it may be, O for a life of sensations rather than of Thoughts!'

Hazlitt influenced Keats in his important conception of a poet as a purely creative being without individual character or identity, who passed, as Hazlitt said, 'through every variety of untried being'. The painter Joseph Severn noted his powers of observation: 'Even the features and gestures of passing tramps, the colour of one woman's hair, the smile on one child's face …' The more mature Keats was, however, to recognize the poet's need for an ethical identity. He revered Wordsworth as the great poet of the age and liked to quote from 'Tintern Abbey' or 'Intimations of Immortality'. But he was opposed to 'poetry that has a palpable design upon us' for 'Poetry should be great and unobtrusive, a thing that enters one's soul'. What he admired in a poet was the capacity for sympathetic identification with some object dearer to him than himself. Nor was this theory unrelated to his life. He was by nature generous of time and sympathy towards friends and family. He was at home in the 'racketing' of literary London: there in 1818 he met Wordsworth, Lamb, Shelley and Joseph Severn. But his brother Tom, sickly with tuberculosis, had first claim on him and he went to look after him in Devonshire. In June his brother George left for America with his young wife – a great blow to Keats.

To escape from his sadness and to gain experience he set off on a tour with Charles Brown, walked 650 miles in the now conventional territory of romance, saw the Lakes, Scotland, climbed Ben Nevis and sailed out to Staffa. He returned awakened in sensibility but physically exhausted: Tom was now very ill and until his death at the end of November Keats scarcely left him. Living in the stuffy Hampstead sickroom, serving his brother with tender care, sleeping little, working on the first draft of 'Hyperion', watching the deadly march of consumption, Keats entered his maturity as man and poet. The experiences of twenty-three years had been vivid, exciting, often beautiful, sometimes cruel. One blow he should not have had to suffer was the scornful attack of Lockhart in the August issue of *Blackwood's* magazine. Keats, as the principal representative of the 'cockney school', was told to go back to the shop: 'It is a better and wiser thing to be a starved apothecary than a starved poet.' Croker's criticism in the *Quarterly Review* was even more damaging because more judicious, the work of a critic of sharp intelligence but no spark of poetic feeling. Keats made a defiant response. 'The genius of Poetry must work out its own salvation in a man: it cannot be matured by law and precept, but by sensation and watchfulness in itself.'

1819 was a miraculous year. For a time Keats was happy. He shared a house with Charles Brown; he met Fanny Brawne and experienced the passionate longings of first love. Two intense personal drives merged in one frenzied activity. He wanted to marry Fanny and to write poetry, not only because he loved it – but to live and provide for her. He had debts; George had lost money in America. In the early part of the year he wrote 'The Eve of St Agnes'. With 'Hyperion' this poem shows that he has come of age: Milton and Spencer no longer dominate, the richness is all his own. 'Hyperion' is one of the few great pieces of epic poetry in the language; it can only be called a failure by the high standards that Keats set himself and sometimes attained. The shorter narrative of 'The Eve of St Agnes' speaks of the emotion of young love – and contains the finest description of cold in our literature. It was written fast, but, as always, Keats revised carefully, looking for ways of replacing the general by the concrete and tactile. He was suffering from painful sore throats, but his mood was often elated. 'The faint conceptions I have of Poems to come brings the blood frequently into my forehead', he wrote to Wood-house. In May 1819 he wrote the 'Ode to a Nightingale', and 'Ode on a Grecian Urn', the 'Ode to Melancholy' and the 'Ode to Indolence'. He was obsessed by the transitoriness of love and beauty. The attraction of the urn and the nightingale is that they are above the process of change and decay. In the summer he stayed with Brown on the Isle of Wight: he rewrote much of 'Hyperion', which became 'The Fall of Hyperion', and 'Lamia'. In the latter poems there is a harder brilliance, nearer to Byron's style. Like most of Keats's poems it centres on a conflict (his love of freedom against his love for Fanny?) between idealistic aspiration and realistic disenchantment. In September he wrote the 'Ode to Autumn', his most perfect expression of the elegiac mood: serene but overshadowed by sadness. We can only record these facts and marvel.

A reaction after his labours is not surprising. He and Fanny were tacitly engaged in the winter. His love-letters record his urgent but undirected desires. Then there was the onset of the tuberculosis that he had probably contracted from Tom, and pressing material worries: he had written what he must instinctively have known was great poetry, but he was living by money forwarded by his publishers. He decided to be a journalist 'on the liberal side of the question'. He wrote a satirical piece, 'Cap and Bells', about the marital troubles of the regent. Was Keats, we may wonder, deliberately staying on the surface for fear of letting the intensity of inward experience overwhelm him? As he wrote to Fanny: 'I am very lax, unemployed, un-meridianed and objectless these last two months' (November). George returned in January to raise money from their trustee, Abbey; some of it was Keats's, but he was too diffident in his dealings with Abbey to press his own claims. Soon afterwards he had a bad haemorrhage. He said to the faithful Brown as he coughed up blood: 'I know the colour of that blood; it is arterial blood; I cannot be deceived in that colour; that drop of blood is my death-warrant; I must die.' He was comforted in his slow decline by belated praise for his poems of the previous year. Leigh Hunt took him in till August; then he went to the Brawnes' house, where he had the harrowing experience of seeing Fanny daily, of seeing her drift away from him, and having to release her from the engagement. He was frantic at times with jealousy and despair, but brave and without self-pity. He dreaded having to leave England, but friends arranged for him to sail to Italy with Joseph Severn, who proved a sympathetic companion.

Dying slowly in the house by the Spanish steps in Rome (the house which is still preserved as a Keats museum), tended by Dr James Clark, vomiting blood and kept alive only by the vitality of youth, fully aware from his medical knowledge of what was happening to him, Keats maintained his outward-looking spirit to the end, constantly concerned about Severn's work and the time he had to spend on his patient. He died on 23 February 1821. An autopsy revealed that the lungs were quite gone. 'Tell him', wrote Leigh Hunt to Severn (thinking that Keats was still alive), 'tell that great poet and noble-hearted man, that we shall all bear his memory in the most precious part of our hearts, and that the world shall bow their heads to it as our loves do … Tell him he was only before us on the road, as he was in everything else.'

Further Reading
Robert Gittings, *John Keats*, 1968.
Douglas Bush, *John Keats*, 1966.
W. J. Bate, *John Keats*, 1963.

KEBELL, THOMAS (*c*.1439-1500), serjeant-at-law, typifies the successful common lawyer. Lawyers were commonly of gentle stock and trained in the London inns of court. They conducted lawsuits in the central courts in Westminster Hall, or practised locally, or, like Kebell, did both. The younger son of a Leicestershire squire, Kebell went to the Inner Temple, later becoming reader and bencher. The most important of his Leicestershire clients was Lord Hastings, the king's chamberlain, whose man of business he became. He represented a wider range of clients in Westminster Hall. He became JP for Leicestershire, counsel (1478) and attorney-general (1483) of the Duchy of Lancaster, and serjeant-at-law in 1486, when the Lord Chief Justice invested him with his insignia: the 'cap of white lawn' (coif), scarlet hood, and livery of blue ray. He would have spent 400 marks (£266.66) on his investiture. 'The greatest honour which the law knew was the call to the coif, and this was demonstrated in the magnificence of the ceremonies which marked the occasion.' Royal judges were chosen from serjeants, all serjeants eventually became judges, and serjeants indeed were reserve judges without specific courts who acted as judges of assize. Of the new serjeants of 1486, Kebell was almost last to assume judicial responsibilities and thus had seven years' practice in the court of Common Pleas, the most lucrative court where only serjeants could plead. A judge of assize and king's serjeant handling royal cases in 1495, Kebell became a justice at Chester in 1499, but died before a vacancy for him occurred at any central court.

In payment he received retaining fees and expenses, about which much is known, and fees for cases, about which we know little. Kebell was feed by aristocrats, monasteries, and towns, and in 1494 became recorder of Leicester. He built up a large fortune, which as usual he invested in land, acquiring twenty properties in Leicestershire and others elsewhere. He planned his purchases with a view to ease of administration and improvement by enclosure. From 1476-7 his principal seat was Humberstone manor near Leicester, which was sparsely furnished, apart from the library and notable stores of linen and plate. Kebell succeeded in establishing his son among the county gentry.

Clearly Kebell was able and ambitious. He was fluent in French and Latin and his books included encyclopaedias, fiction and religious works. The presence among the latter of the Bible and sermons point to a more serious religious understanding than the conventional piety of his chapel and chaplains and projected chantry. He had a strong sense of family and neighbourhood and freely remembered his obligations. His culture, imagination, thoughtfulness and humanity all figure in his legal career.

It is the law reports in the Year Books that tell us most about Kebell's personality. They record more direct speech than any other source and Kebell features 314 times from 1481, more than anyone else. Even his losing opinions were respected. He is recorded citing fifty-six statutes and fifty-four precedents, moving from one to another as it suited him. Supremely self-confident, aggressive and assertive, critical of others, unabashed by strictures and unimpressed by the opinions of others, he insisted on having his say. Quick to think and to cite authorities, he was a formidable debater, who enlivened cases with his personal reminiscences, droll hypotheses, and linguistic dexterity. Whilst not 'a major or original legal thinker', he worked within the imperfect legal system that he found, seldom making broad points of principle, but impressing with sayings that were remembered long after. He was a master of procedure, who could make much from the smallest technicalities and taxed even a hostile court with his submissions. He demonstrates what vigour and potential remained in what has often been regarded as a moribund legal system.

Further Reading
E. W. Ives, *The Common Lawyers of Pre-Reformation England. Thomas Kebell: A Case Study*, 1983.

KEBLE, JOHN (1792-1866), priest and poet, was a modest man, inclined to a quiet life, who found himself playing a leading part in the Oxford Movement. He contributed to its beginnings with a sermon, and sustained its principles by his fidelity when others left or despaired. His virtues and his limitations left a lasting impression on the Church of England.

His father, reverent, reticent, a foe to enthusiasm, had a living at Coln St Aldwyns, but lived at nearby Fairford and gave much time to teaching his children. John, the eldest, was precocious. At the age of fifteen he won a scholarship to Corpus Christi College, Oxford; he was the first since Peel to win a double First Class, in both Classics and Mathematics; aged nineteen he was elected Fellow of Oriel. Pointed out to freshmen as 'the first

man in Oxford', he wished no more than to embrace his father's 'dear, delightful profession'. Early years were spent between Oriel, his college duties, and curacies in Gloucestershire. In 1835 he married Charlotte Clarke, accepted a Hampshire living and remained there for the rest of his life. Thus told, the story is simple. Keble could have been one of thousands who brought the scholarship of a larger world and the spirit of pious duty to a simple rural community. Circumstances ensured however that the curate of Eastleach, and vicar of Hursley, became, and remained, a source of inspiration to Christians everywhere; in his unassuming way, a guide, indeed a leader.

In 1827 a small, plain anonymous volume of verses was published by Parker of Oxford. Keble thought that *The Christian Year* would be 'still-born'. He had started writing verses to fill lonely hours at Eastleach; he went on through the church calendar with verses deceptively plain but carefully wrought. He published to please his father. It was a huge instant success. In his lifetime it ran for ninety-two editions. 'No book was ever more to the liking of its own age, less to the taste of the present one' (Battiscombe). Wordsworth thought Keble's poems so good that he wished he could rewrite them! Keble's readers might, however, have been ill at ease with Wordsworth's preference for the natural. They took readily to Keble's religious sentiments arrayed in sober, familiar dress. It was as if Bishop Butler had taken to versifying or as if George Herbert, Keble's model in pastoral duty as in poesy, had been reborn. When, in 1831 he was elected Professor of Poetry at Oxford, lecturing in Latin, as the basis for ideas elaborated in an article for *The British Critic* (1837), he offered a definition which provides a gloss on Wordsworth's 'emotion recollected in tranquillity': 'The indirect expression in words, most appropriately in metrical words, of some overpowering emotion or ruling taste or feeling, the direct indulgence of which is somehow repressed.'

On 14 July 1833, it was Keble's turn to preach in St Mary's before the university authorities and the visiting judge: the Assize sermon. His ostensible subject was the bill to abolish ten Irish bishoprics, not indefensible in itself but an encroachment of state on church: it raised therefore an important point of principle. Keble did not think that he was starting a religious revival, let alone a war. The heart of his message was an affirmation of principles which he, nurtured in the tradition of the Caroline divines, had long espoused: the Anglican church was representative of the whole church, Catholic and Apostolic. To Newman and Froude, that idea was illuminating, a revelation; to Keble it meant the defence of something familiar and dear. The movement would grow unevenly, Newman would continue to see Keble as its 'true and primary author', but Keble, engrossed in his parish, would be the least political of the protagonists.

His, Newman wrote, was 'too subtle and spiritual a light to be seen, unless placed on a candlestick'. It was crucially important, in the fury of debate and pain of defection, that those leaders who remained within the Church of England – Pusey the scholar, Keble, parish priest – represented the finest, most recognizably spiritual, in the tradition.

Where Newman's theory of the 'Development of Christian Doctrine' was evolutionary, Keble's was that of the cautious historian engaged in rediscovery. 'There is no such thing as improvement, discovery or evolution of new truths'; nevertheless 'the monuments of antiquity may disclose to our devout gaze much that will be to this age new'. The veneration of early Christians for the Blessed Virgin Mary was therefore sufficient reason for reviving such veneration in the Church of England. Keble would not allow devotion or doctrine to exceed the limits sanctioned by primitive practice, whereas Newman, armed with his idea of Development, would treat that practice as the germ of such extensions as the Immaculate Conception.

The Kebles had no children, but the house was often full of friends and relations. They describe an atmosphere of serenity and fun – and a most unassumingly holy man. He could be narrow, even stern: towards Hursley Methodists, towards reformers in Oxford, towards liberals who questioned the verbal inspiration of the Bible. His was not a speculative mind; nor was he an energetic scholar. His parishioners always came first. His translation of Irenaeus was not published till after his death. He would be happy however to be remembered for his edition of the works of Hooker (1836): the author of *The Ecclesiastical Polity* could not have been in safer, more sympathetic hands.

Further Reading
Georgina Battiscombe, *John Keble*, 1963.

KEITH, GEORGE, 11th EARL MARISCHAL

(1693-1778) was a gallant Jacobite, later in life the servant and friend of Frederick the Great; a splendid example of the adaptable Scotsman whose life is mostly spent abroad, but who yet retains the independence and toughness of his native country.

He was the eldest son of the ninth earl. His mother was a Drummond. The feudal office had become a hereditary title but the tradition of the Aberdeenshire family was one of loyalty to the Crown. His father had protested against the Union; George, an officer in Anne's army, joined Mar's rising in Scotland, with his brother James. They fought strenuously at Sheriffmuir, urged the army to make another stand and refused to leave with Mar. Eventually they escaped to France and then went to Spain, where Alberoni was planning to use the Jacobites as an instrument in his ambitious schemes. The Earl Marischal, attainted, led the small Spanish company

which landed in Lewis. He established a base at Eilean Donan on Loch Duich, opposite Skye, but was given little support. With Tullibardine and Lord George Murray, he was defeated in Glen Shiel; he returned, wounded, to Spain, only to be coolly treated by James, who thought him an honourable fool; he, in turn, distrusted the prince's councillors. 'Nothing but ill management on this side of the water has kept or can keep the Elector on the throne of Britain.'

Keith opposed the 1745 rising and after its failure went to Vienna. His brother James, meanwhile, had thrived as a mercenary, first in Russian service, then as Field Marshal of Prussia. Keith went to Frederick the Great who employed him as ambassador in France and Spain during the Seven Years' War. Since Frederick was then an ally of England, he was able to secure the reversal of his attainder and the succession to the earldom of Kintore, his by heredity. It was he, in 1760, who gave Pitt news of the signing of the Family Compact between Charles III and Louis XV. After the Peace of Paris he returned to Scotland but was persuaded by Frederick, who seems to have been truly fond of the robust old man, to return to Prussia. He lived on affectionate terms with this lonely and unloved king for the rest of his life, in his villa at Potsdam enjoying a way of life 'half-Aberdeenshire, half-Spanish'. He was by no means the simple person that his manner suggested. He corresponded with Voltaire, and he invented the game out of which Kriegspiel grew.

KEMP, JOHN (*c*.1375-1454), Cardinal-Archbishop of

Canterbury, is the most remarkable instance of a royal civil servant promoted to high office in the English church. The son of Thomas and Beatrix Kemp of Wye in Kent, he proceeded to Oxford University, where he was already Fellow of Merton College in 1395, and graduated as doctor of canon law in 1414. Before then he entered the service of Archbishop Chichele, participating in the trial of Sir John Oldcastle in 1413, and from 1414 he was Dean of the Court of Arches. Already a rector and canon, in 1417 he became an archdeacon, and in 1418 was licensed to perform his duties by deputy. Now middle-aged, Kemp could look forward to a career of moderate distinction in ecclesiastical administration, comparable perhaps with that of William Lyndwood.

Already, however, he had attracted the attention of Henry V. Negotiations with Aragon in 1415-16 were followed in 1417 by appointment as Chancellor of Normandy and in 1418 as keeper of the privy seal. He joined Henry VI's minority council in 1422 and sat on the council of France from 1423-5. Following the Gloucester-Beaufort quarrel, Bedford appointed Kemp as Chancellor of England in 1426, where he remained until dismissed by Gloucester in 1432. Meanwhile Kemp's diplomatic career continued. His firm stance was counterproductive at the Congress of Arras in 1435, but thereafter he was converted to Cardinal Beaufort's peace policy. Gloucester initially persuaded Henry VI to reject conciliatory terms proposed by Kemp, but next year peace became the official policy and Kemp was linked with Beaufort in Gloucester's fruitless denunciations. As Beaufort aged, so Kemp became the dominant force in government, but he too was ageing and by the late 1440s had been supplanted and indeed alienated by Suffolk. The duke's opposition to the promotion of Kemp's nephew as Bishop of London in 1448-50 fostered and may have caused the rift. The murders of Suffolk, Saye, Moleyns and Aiscough in 1450 were accompanied by the resignation as chancellor of Archbishop Stafford. Kemp, his predecessor in 1426-32, succeeded him. An elder statesman enjoying general confidence, Kemp was a force for stability when Henry VI went mad in 1453, but his death early in 1454 precipitated the Duke of York's first Protectorate.

Kemp's political services brought meteoric promotion. He was appointed Bishop of Rochester in 1419 and of Chichester and London in turn in 1421, making him the classic instance of the mercenary churchman skipping to progressively richer sees. In 1425 he became Archbishop of York, in 1439 cardinal, and in 1452 he succeeded Stafford as Archbishop of Canterbury. Whilst Kemp's political commitments restricted the time he spent in his dioceses, Thomas Gascoigne unduly minimizes his periods of residence. To the Yorkshireman Gascoigne, Kemp was an outsider and his officers were foreigners, but there was nothing unusual in bringing in new men and they were certainly competent at their jobs. For long periods all medieval English bishoprics were run perfectly adequately by their permanent officials. Moreover Kemp's concern to defend and extend archiepiscopal rights would normally have been applauded. He persuaded Henry VI in 1441 to extend his franchises, asserted the rights of his fairs at Otley and Ripon to take tolls, and in 1445 threatened excommunication on all those infringing his privileges and franchises. He thus infuriated the Percies. The ensuing riots were not appeased by Kemp's use of royal authority to imprison Northumberland in the Tower and to convict his sons. Conciliation of his most powerful neighbour was to be preferred. A man of conventional piety, Kemp's sense of roots and family emerges both from his foundation of Wye College and his advancement of his kinsfolk. His cardinal's hat was a particular source of simple pride.

Further Reading
R. A. Griffiths, *The Reign of King Henry VI 1422-61*, 1981.

KEMPE, MARGERY (*c*.1373-*c*.1438) is the subject of 'the first biography in English'. This is because she was a highly exceptional woman, but her early life was commonplace enough. Her father, John Brunham, may

have been the richest man in Kings Lynn, where he was mayor five times, alderman and MP. He married her about 1394 to John Kempe, another member of the oligarchy, who was chamberlain of the town, but never achieved the same eminence. Margery criticized him for this and had to pay his debts, but his difficult wife may be behind his failure. Margery bore her husband several children. Like other wives, she pursued her own trade as well, operating for a while as the principal brewer in the town and also as a miller. She wanted to outshine other women by her gaudy and trendy clothes. Her difficult first labour induced a breakdown, from which she recovered. The failure of her businesses, which she interpreted as God's judgement, contributed to her decision to devote herself to religion.

Margery's autobiography records her retrospective account of her experiences much as set down by a not uncritical priest long after most of the events recounted. That it was written at all shows that he at least believed Margery's religious experiences to be genuine and sufficiently important to be recorded. This was open to question, for Margery's vow of chastity during her husband's lifetime, her visions, her wildly fluctuating moods, and above all her anti-social fits of 'plenteous and continual weeping', which occurred as often as fourteen times a day, could be evidence of mental derangement. Her scribe and the local religious houses were aware of this possibility and, after due consideration, rejected it. In the same way those bishops, who examined her for heresy, satisfied themselves about her orthodoxy and let her go. They put up with her denunciations of the conduct of themselves and their servants very well. She was forever condemning immoral and improper behaviour, disrupting church services, or depressing people at mealtimes. We can sympathize with them.

No English writer, hitherto, had committed to writing so intimate, revealing, and human an account of his life and thoughts. The self-portrait of a minor mystic remains, however, the more credible for its merciless honesty and its fidelity to life.

There were not many Margery Kempes. Her autobiography exists because she was unique and thus worthy of commemoration. Her first breakdown, after the birth of her child, lasted for seven months and involved hallucinations, attempted suicide, and self-mutilation. A period of worldly social climbing was followed by a permanent conversion. Lengthy prayer, fasting, mortification of the flesh, weeping, and – from 1413 – celibacy characterized the rest of her life. She now wished to wear a white dress and the ring of Christ, which Bishop Repingdon – recognizing her instability – initially denied her. In 1413-14 she went on pilgrimage to Jerusalem; subsequently in 1417 to Compostella. She spent all her wealth and survived only by the alms of those she convinced. She suffered terribly, because her companionship – especially her weeping – was intolerable to her fellow pilgrims. Back in England, the townsmen of Bristol, Leicester and elsewhere referred her as a suspected heretic to their bishops. For most of her last years she lived at Lynn, where she was admired and respected by local monks and friars and by the theologians who came to visit her, but where she was hated and reviled by many of the layfolk. Was she inspired by God or was she mad?

Further Reading
A. Goodman, 'The Piety of John Brunham's daughter, of Lynn', *Medieval Women*, ed. D. Baker, *Studies in Church History*, Subsidia 1, 1978.
H. S. Bennett, 'Margery Kempe', *Six Medieval Men and Women*, 1955.
S. B. Meech, ed., *The Book of Margery Kempe*, Early English Text Society ccvii, 1940.

KEMPENFELT, RICHARD (1718-82), admiral, is more famous for the manner of his death than for what he did when he was alive. He was in his cabin aboard the *Royal George* at Spithead when, some guns being moved, timbers of unseasoned wood gave way, and the ship heeled over and sank 'with twice four hundred men'. He deserves, however, to be known for his original work as strategist and reformer, for he was one of the most thoughtful seamen of his time.

His outlook was shaped by the fact that he rose without influence, slowly, by professional merit. Born in London, the son of a Swedish father and an English mother, he served under Vernon at Porto Bello, but did not reach post rank until he was nearly forty. In the Seven Years' War he saw service in the West Indies and Manila. In the American War he was captain of the fleet under three successive commanders of the Channel fleet. It may be that under the first two of these, Admirals Hardy and Geary, old men, indecisive and out of touch with tactical developments, he saved the fleet from worse mischance than the somewhat inglorious but undefeated cruisings which kept the French at bay. In these years he wrote letters, mostly to Middleton at the Admiralty, from which much can be learned about his views and methods. He believed that young landsmen 'may in three months, if half that time at sea, be made to know every rope in the ship, to knot and splice, hand and reef, and be perfect at the management of cannon and small-arms'. He constantly preached the gospel of sailing quality. 'We don't seem,' he wrote from the *Victory*, 'to have considered sufficiently a certain fact, that the comparative force of two fleets depends much upon their sailing. The fleet that sails fastest can engage or not as they please, and so have it always in their power to choose the favourable opportunity to attack. I think I may safely hazard an opinion that twenty-five sail of the line, coppered, would be sufficient to hazard and tease this great unwieldy combined Armada.' We are reminded

here that the English ships were inferior to the French, in sailing performance at least, for the most part of the century.

Promoted Rear Admiral, Kempenfelt continued to serve in the Channel fleet and he was on his flagship when the sudden fatal disaster occurred. It has been suggested that the loss was due to serious neglect on the part of some official on the Navy Board and it may be significant that all attempts to raise the ship were frustrated and that evidence given at the court martial was suppressed. The story makes an ironic epilogue to the life of a man devoted to efficiency and to honest service.

Further Reading
David Mathew, *The Naval Heritage*, Chapter 6, 1944.

KEN, THOMAS (1631-1711), most saintly of the Seven Bishops, was the son of a Berkhampstead attorney. Educated at Winchester and New College, and a Fellow of both, he held various livings before becoming Chaplain to Mary of Orange in 1679. Characteristically he reproached William for his 'unkind' treatment of his wife, and equally characteristically, after his return to England, he declined to allow his prebendal house at Winchester to be bespoken for Nell Gwynne during a royal visit to the city. He went as Chaplain on the Tangier expedition of 1683-4, and preached against the 'excessive liberty of swearing' in which the garrison indulged. In 1685 Charles II gave the see of Bath and Wells to 'the little black fellow that refused the lodging to poor Nelly'. Later the same year his diocese was the heart of Monmouth's rebellion, and Ken, whose loyalty was beyond doubt, interceded with James against the brutalities practised by Kirke's soldiery. Two years later he preached at court against Roman Catholicism, and in 1688 he delivered another sermon before the king in which he called for the unity of all Protestants against the claims of Rome. It is therefore not surprising to find this gentle yet courageous man one of the Seven Bishops of 1688. But after the flight of James, Ken voted for a regency and, although he was long in doubt, declined to take the oaths of allegiance to William and Mary. He was therefore deprived of his see in 1691.

He lived on for twenty years, much of the time at the home of Lord Weymouth at Longleat. The mildest, and perhaps the most statesmanlike, of the Non-jurors, Ken did not approve of perpetuating the schism by consecrating further non-juring bishops. Yet he would not yield to Anne's wish (1702) to reinstate him in his see. He accepted a pension of £200 per annum from her government, paid out of the secret service money. Ken's compassion and generosity were well known in his own day. He was an accomplished man, a musician and a poet, and we know him best through the morning and evening hymns which he wrote, 'Awake my soul and with the Sun' and 'Glory to Thee, my God, this night'.

Further Reading
H. A. L. Rice, *Thomas Ken: Bishop and Non-Juror*, 1958.

KENNETH I (MACALPIN) (*d.*858) may be regarded as Scotland's first king. Already King of the Scots of Dalriada in the west, in about the year 843 he also became King of Picts of the east and, crushing Pictish resistance during the period 843-50, established the viability of the kingdom of Alba. As the Gaelic personal names of its earliest kings suggest, the Dalriadan kingship had been imported from Ireland about the sixth century. Little is known about how Kenneth laid successful claim to the throne of the Picts, who were possibly weakened by a defeat at the hands of the Danes in 839; on the other hand, the Scots of Dalriada may have been given assistance from Ireland in 836. At all events, unity was surely impelled by Scandinavian incursions and their expansion into Shetland, Orkney, Caithness and Sutherland and the Western Isles.

The status of the northern Pictish lands of Ross, Moray and Buchan during Kenneth's kingship is uncertain. Strathclyde (sometimes known as Cumbria, but unlikely ever to have stretched further than the Solway Firth) had its own line of kings, but during the ninth century these seem to have been clients of the Macalpin family. Scone, probably the Pictish site of coronations, was retained. But Pictish matrilinearity was not adopted. Instead, from Kenneth, the kingship of Alba descended through adult brothers or cousins, rather than sons or nephews still in their minority. This seems at first to have involved automatic descent through two alternating collateral lines but later, tanistry customs, in which the heir apparent was designated during the lifetime of the king, as fittest to serve, may also have been important. Kenneth Macalpin was succeeded by Donald I who may have been his brother or nephew.

KENT, WILLIAM (1684?-1748) was a painter and a landscape gardener, but is known chiefly as the leading architect of the Burlington school. The early eighteenth century in England witnessed a reaction against the baroque style of architecture whose principal monuments in England were St Paul's Cathedral and Blenheim Palace. Young gentlemen travelling to France and Italy on the Grand Tour contemplated the relics of classical antiquity, and saw that they were good. The publication in 1715 of Colen Campbell's *Vitruvius Britannicus* and of a translation of Palladio's *I quattro libri dell'architettura* reminded connoisseurs of the fundamental canons of classical architecture, as formulated by Vitruvius in the time of the Emperor Augustus, and as resuscitated by Palladio in the sixteenth century. Judged by these canons, the later work of Wren, much of the work of Vanbrugh, Archer and Hawksmoor, indeed all work denoting the baroque style, was seen to be impure,

even barbaric. Of English architects, only Inigo Jones was admitted within the pale; and, under the talented patronage of Lord Burlington (1695-1753), a school of architecture developed in England to a pitch of dominance, which assumed that the architecture of antiquity was a comprehensive system, and regarded as an impertinent solecism any detail which could not be justified by the severe precepts of Vitruvius, Palladio and Jones. In this movement, Burlington's most conspicuous colleagues were Colen Campbell (who rebuilt Burlington House for him) and William Kent.

Burlington had met the young Kent in 1714 in Rome, where Kent had gone to study, not architecture, but painting. In spite of the disparity of rank – for Kent had been promoted from a humble station by the generosity of Yorkshire squires who sent him to study in Rome *'donec Raphael secundus ens'* – a friendship grew up between them which, while it went deeper than a common interest in the arts, bore its most precious fruit in the artistic collaboration of the two right up to the death of Kent in 1748.

Burlington brought Kent home to England in 1719, set him to work on the decorative painting at Burlington House, and soon contrived to have him substituted for Sir James Thornhill, the Serjeant Painter himself, in the painting of the interior of Kensington Palace. But Kent was never more than an indifferent painter; and Burlington, poring over Palladio's drawings, and recognizing perhaps the true direction of Kent's genius, gave him (in 1724) the job of editing a book to be entitled *The Designs of Inigo Jones*. The book was published three years later, augmented with designs by Burlington and Kent, and the work on it seems to have decided Kent's career. Though he continues as a painter and is even appointed Portrait Painter to the King in 1739, he is now properly an architect, and an architect who, on being appointed to high positions in the Board of Works in the 1730s, exhales in all his official tasks (and despite his fifty years of life) the fresh if austere breath of Palladianism. The outstanding products of his official work were the Horse Guards in Whitehall (completed to his designs after his death), the Royal Mews (demolished 1830), and the Treasury Buildings. He projected, but never realized, a new Royal Palace and a new Houses of Parliament.

Meanwhile he had been busy on private commissions also. As early as 1727, he was helping Burlington with the interior of his Chiswick villa, that epitome of English Palladianism, a worthy imitation of Palladio's own Villa Rotonda near Vicenza. He worked on the interior of Sir Robert Walpole's house of Houghton (newly built for him by Campbell) and was then engaged by the Earl of Leicester to design Holkham Hall. Kent's designs were later executed, and even modified, by his pupil Brettingham; but Holkham is Kent's (and, through Kent,

Burlington's) memorial in domestic architecture. The exterior, which is like that of the Horse Guards without the clock-tower, is severe enough, massive and over-plain; but the interior, where Kent allowed himself some deviation from the strictest rules, is very fine, and shows how adroitly and carefully he could realize his idea (which the brothers Adam adopted) that an architect should be responsible equally for the internal details, down to the *trivialia* of furniture. The majestic hall, designed to display Lord Leicester's antiquities, is the *coup de maître* – though it was shortly to be rivalled by Kent's hall at 44 Berkeley Square.

In short, Kent laid a finger of style on houses all over England, and even on cathedrals. But the country houses of England owe another debt to him. For, not content with his architecture and his painting, with designing furniture, with illustrating books, and with sculpture (he designed for Scheemakers and Rysbrack), he conceived a new plan for landscape gardening. The formal gardens of the seventeenth century irked him: the notion that the garden was something distinct, a portion of nature civilized and enclosed from the uncouth wild. Influenced by the landscapes of Claude, he 'leaped the fence, and saw that all Nature was a garden'. It was a pleasure to him to contrast the formality of the great house itself with studied informality in its surroundings; to dislocate the equipment of the formal garden – the ornamental water, the parterres, the temples – and scatter them about serpentine alleys far from the house; and to use sunken fences to prolong the view over the nearer lawns to the sweep of the park beyond. Rousham is Kent's master-piece here.

The artist, versatile if not illustrious, died a painful death, and, as he had long made Burlington House his home, so he was buried in the vault of his patron, fellow artist and friend, at Chiswick.

Further Reading

M. Wilson, *William Kent: Architect, Designer, Painter, Gardener, 1685-1748*, 1985.

KEPPEL, VISCOUNT AUGUSTUS (1725-86),

admiral, was the son of the second Earl Albemarle. He served as a midshipman on Anson's voyage round the world from 1740 to 1744. After this incomparable schooling he rose steadily. He served under Hawke in 1757 and captured Goree with a small expeditionary force in 1758 in one of the raids, perfectly planned and executed, that led to the capture of all the French factories on the west African coast. He was at Quiberon Bay in 1759 and at the capture of Belle Isle in 1761. To cap all this vigorous service he led the expedition which took Manila in 1762.

If Keppel's subsequent career was a disappointing anti-climax, this is more because of his political entangle-ments than any falling off in his professional skill. He

was closely associated with the Whig group which opposed the American War, and was critical of the conduct of Lord Sandwich at the Admiralty, so it was thought surprising that he was appointed commander of the Channel fleet in 1778. Some Whigs, in a spirit more partisan than patriotic, thought that he was to be made a scapegoat, but in fact he was the ablest available man of his seniority. Under him, third in command, was Admiral Palliser who, nonetheless, kept his seat on the Navy Board. On 27 July 1778, the British fleet encoun-tered the slightly superior French fleet under d'Orvilliers and fought a desultory action in which no ships were won or lost. The French had the weather-guage and could break off the action when they wanted. But the English fleet's fire was the more ineffective because of Palliser's failure to obey Keppel's signal to close. Palliser claimed that the foremast of his division's flag-ship was severely damaged. Enraged by news sheets which alleged that he was responsible for the failure to bring the French to action, he used his position on the Admiralty Board to secure a court-martial on Keppel.

Charged by Palliser himself with not marshalling his fleet, careless approach to the battle, scandalous haste in withdrawing from the action, Keppel became the central figure in a drama of personalities, with strong political overtones. It became the talk of fashionable drawing rooms and naval wardrooms alike – that at the height of a war in which England was fighting not only for her colonies but for her life, a Franco-Spanish fleet cruised about the Channel. Thus the nation paid for the political affiliations and interests of her leading seamen. Did not Rodney say that a man was 'nothing without being in parliament'? Palliser's charges were rejected as malicious and ill-founded. The verdict was regarded as a snub to Sandwich. Palliser was then court-martialled and acquitted – with the rider that he should have informed the commander-in-chief of the damage to his ship. He was given the governorship of Greenwich Hospital, but inn signs everywhere swung in honour of 'Keppel's Head'. He resigned, however, and was supported by his friends, Lord Bristol and Barrington, who refused to accept appointments from Lord Sandwich. Admirers such as Jervis and Duncan took his part and perpetuated the feud in the navy.

The genial and courteous Keppel may have been misled; somehow, too, he aroused violent animosity in Palliser, a blunt Yorkshireman, without influence. But he seems, too, to have been badly treated. Recompense came when he was made First Lord of the Admiralty in Rockingham's government of 1782 and luck with it, since the first news received was that of Rodney's vic-tory of the Saints. His subsequent recall of Rodney was ungenerous; once again we see how politics affected the navy. In the circumstances it is remarkable that England emerged from this war with any credit. In December

1783 Keppel was replaced by Howe in Pitt's government; relatively free of political connections, he commanded general confidence and proved a more successful First Lord than Keppel could have been.

Further Reading

A. T. Mahon, *Major Operations of the Navies in the American War of Independence*, 1913.

KET or KETT, ROBERT (*d*.1549), rebel, was put to death in 1549; the date of his birth is unknown. He came from an old Norman family (the name appears down the years as Le Chat, Cat, Kett, Ket, Knight), one branch of which had settled at Wymondham in Norfolk. Robert and his brother William were well-to-do tradesmen who were also landowners. Robert held the manor of Wymondham from John Dudley, Earl of Warwick, the man who in August 1549 came to suppress the rising which now goes by Ket's name. It was only by an accident that Ket became its leader.

On 20 June 1549, a small riot took place in south Norfolk, when the men of Attleborough, Eccles and Wilby threw down the fences with which the lord of the manor of Beckhall in Wilby had recently enclosed part of the common land over which these men had grazing rights. Trouble was also brewing further south, but it was not until 6-8 July that all these men joined hands in a series of attacks on the hedges in various manors. Robert Ket had a long-standing feud with John Flowerdew, a lawyer who had become a landowner. After the Dissolution of the Monasteries the splendid priory church of Wymondham had been bought from the Crown by the inhabitants. Flowerdew, who lived in the neighbourhood, stripped the lead off the roofs and carried away the bells. The Kets resented this. When in July Flowerdew's closes had been thrown down, he bribed the rioters to go and do the same to Robert Ket. On 9 or 10 July Robert Ket led the rioters back in a reprisal on Flowerdew's fences, and thus by accident he became the leader of the insurgents, and he was joined by his brother William.

Ket marched on Norwich, throwing down hedges as he went. On being refused admission into the city, Ket moved to Mousehold Heath, where he and his men encamped for the next six weeks. He soon had 16,000 men under his command. Good order was maintained, law-courts were established and chaplains said prayers every morning, using the new Book of Common Prayer.

On 21 July Ket rejected the government's offer of a pardon, on the grounds that 'kings were wont to pardon wicked persons, not innocent and just men'. Ket now seized Norwich. William Parr, Marquis of Northampton, was sent with 1,400 men to recover the city, which he did without opposition. But on 1 August Ket attacked and after a grim struggle he secured the place. Becoming now more ambitious, he tried to capture Yarmouth, but he failed.

On 23 August the Earl of Warwick arrived at Norwich, where he was joined by Lord Willoughby of Parham. Their joint forces amounted to about 10,000 men, some of them German troops. The offer of a pardon to all but Robert Ket was rejected. On the 24th Warwick got into Norwich. On the 25th the rebels left their camp, since their lines of communication were cut. On the 27th Warwick saw his chance and launching his troops at the rebels he utterly destroyed them. The Kets fled, but were soon captured. Robert was hanged in chains from Norwich Castle, William from Wymondham steeple.

Religion had played little part in the rebellion: Norfolk was a county largely in favour of reform and hence unlikely to rise against Somerset's religious policy. However, complaints against the clergy form a part of the demands formulated by the rebels on Mousehold Heath, and the religious turmoil of Edward VI's reign perhaps stirred the peasants up to political enthusiasm as well. Agrarian grievances, such as enclosure, engrossing, rackrenting and the eviction of tenants, combined with the great distress of 1549, played a major part in driving the peasantry to rebellion. The Tudor system worked well so long as there was sound government, both centrally and locally. Somerset was not providing sound central government; his policies added to the burden on the poor commons, by increasing taxation and causing inflation through debasement. In Norfolk, local government had broken down with the sudden fall of the Howard family in 1546, and by 1549 no county was worse governed than Norfolk. Ket and his followers expected the central government of the 'Good Duke' to back them up in teaching the local landlords a lesson. The principal effect, however, of Ket's Rebellion and of the other uprisings which occurred in other parts of the country in 1549 was to bring about the fall of Protector Somerset, the man to whom the rebels appealed for help.

Further Reading

J. Cornwall, *Revolt of the Peasantry, 1549*, 1977.
S. K. Land, *Ket's Rebellion*, 1977.
S. T. Bindoff, *Ket's Rebellion*, Historical Association pamphlet, 1949.

KETCH, JACK (*d*.1686), executioner, took office probably in 1663. He seems to have been, or to have become, lamentably inefficient – although he is alleged to have gone on strike for higher fees in 1682. He bungled the beheading of Lord Russell in 1683, defending himself (in a pamphlet which he apparently wrote) on the ground that Russell 'did not dispose himself for receiving the fatal stroke in such a position as was most suitable and that he moved his body'. Two years later there was an appalling scene at Monmouth's execution, when Ketch threw down his axe after three unsuccessful blows, crying 'I can't do it'. The sheriffs compelled him to go on, and it took five blows in all and the use of a knife to sever the head. This professional ineptitude, combined with the part he took in the whipping of Titus Oates, gave him such notoriety that the executioner in 'Punchinello' came to be known as Ketch. He died in November 1686.

KIDD, WILLIAM (c.1645-1701), pirate, was born at Greenock, son of a covenanting minister. He went to sea as a boy, settled in the American colonies, and commanded a privateer in William III's war against the French, receiving £150 reward from New York City in 1691. He was recommended in 1695 to the Governor of Massachusetts, who gave him a special commission, drawn under the Great Seal, to seize and hang pirates in the eastern seas, and in 1696 Kidd set sail in the *Adventure*, first to New York and thence to the coast of Madagascar. By 1698 there were stories that Kidd himself had turned pirate, and when he returned to Boston in the summer of 1699 he was arrested. The main complaint against him involved a French vessel, the *Queda Merchant*, alleged to have been carrying £70,000 treasure. Kidd's version threw blame on his own mutinous crew. In 1700 he and his companions were sent to England for trial. It was Kidd's misfortune that his case became involved in the contemporary political attack on Somers, who as Lord Keeper had issued the original commission, and the trial was notably prejudiced. Eventually Kidd was condemned on a charge of murdering one of his crew by hitting him over the head with a bucket, and hanged at Wapping Old Stairs in 1701. Some of the treasure was recovered, and part of it was spent by the Commissioners of Greenwich Hospital on buying the Queen's House, the lovely building by Inigo Jones which now forms part of the National Maritime Museum at Greenwich.

Further Reading
G. Brooks, ed., *The Trial of Captain Kidd*, 1930.

KIFFIN, WILLIAM (1616-1701), Baptist, was a Londoner of Welsh ancestry who was apprenticed to John Lilburne for a short time from 1629. He became a sectary in the 1630s and by 1645 was well known as a 'ringleader' of those who held unorthodox views on baptism. Kiffin was the minister of a London congregation of Baptists and was periodically in trouble either for his religious beliefs (as in 1655, when he was before the Lord Mayor for preaching against infant baptism) or for the political opinions which were thought to accompany them (as in 1660-1, when he was thrice arrested). But he was also a well-to-do cloth merchant, who made money out of contracts in the Dutch War of 1652, and this made him more acceptable to authority, so that he was, for example, able to use his influence with Clarendon to help his fellow sectaries. Charles II once asked him for a loan of £40,000. Kiffin deemed it safer to make

the king a gift of £10,000, thereby, as he observed, saving himself £30,000. Two of Kiffin's grandsons were executed for complicity in Monmouth's rebellion, and he was briefly compelled by James II to serve as a London alderman. Not surprisingly, he was one of the dissenting leaders who put no trust in James, and he successfully advised the Baptist community not to welcome the king's Declaration of Indulgence. Cautious rather than heroic, Kiffin nonetheless played a quietly significant role in the survival of English Nonconformity.

KILVERT, ROBERT FRANCIS (1840-79), clergyman and diarist, was born in a Somerset rectory and followed in his father's steps, to Oxford and to ordination. After assisting his father as curate at Langley Burrell in Wiltshire, he went as curate to Clyro: there, on the Welsh side of the border with Herefordshire, he worked for seven years. Afterwards he had livings at St Harmon's, in Radnorshire, and at Bredwardine, by the Wye in Herefordshire: there he died, only a few weeks after his wedding. An uneventful life, it might seem, in quiet places, with unimportant people. Throughout however he was keeping a diary. It was published, in three volumes (1938-40), after editing by William Plomer. As a record of a human being, devastatingly honest in self-revelation and appraisal, it is fascinating enough. As a picture of the border country and its people before the great social changes of the twentieth century, it is uniquely valuable. And it is a delight to read. Kilvert was conscientious, a faithful shepherd to his flock. He was also an enthusiast. Fortunately too, he had a painter's eye for a scene, a novelist's feeling for an episode. Walks and visits, sermons, frosty mornings, Easter churchyards, cottage sickbeds and comfortable teas, tinkers and old soldiers, girls idealized, girls loved, 'romps', dances, archery, visits to art galleries, observations of nature; scenes embarrassing, scenes moving, some fine prose, some trite: all in all, it is the record of a warm-hearted, hard-working, devoted, vulnerable man.

Further Reading
Grice, *Francis Kilvert and his World*, 1988.

KING, GREGORY (1648-1712), statistician, was born at Lichfield, the son of a mathematician who sent him to school at the age of two and taught him to read the Psalter at three. From Lichfield Grammar School he went as clerk to the antiquary Sir William Dugdale, then Norroy King-of-Arms, and later he was employed by several of the Staffordshire nobility. Going to London in 1672, he worked for John Ogilby the printer, etching plates, making maps and helping to edit Ogilby's Road-Book. He appears also to have acted as a surveyor in planning streets in the Soho district. From 1677, when he was appointed Rouge Dragon Pursuivant, he made his living as a herald, becoming Registrar of the College of

Arms in 1684. He was dismissed in 1694 as a result of quarrelling with the earl marshal over the arrangements for the funeral of Queen Mary, and thereafter seems to have been employed in the Treasury. King was a man of great ability and wide culture, distinguished in his own day. Yet what has made him of interest to later generations, and of high significance to historians, was the pioneering statistical work he produced in 1696, although it was not published until the beginning of the nineteenth century – his *Natural and Political Observations upon the State and Condition of England*. This was the first careful calculation of the population of England and Wales. Using the Hearth Tax returns, King reckoned 5,500,000 in 1688 – a pretty accurate figure (except for a big over-estimate of those more than sixty years of age). Furthermore, he surveyed the distribution of population according to income among the various classes from peers to paupers, and thus provided a range of valuable material about English society at the time of the Glorious Revolution.

KINGSLEY, CHARLES (1819-75), clergyman, writer, lecturer, amateur scientist and ardent naturalist, was a born story-teller who used the novel to teach and persuade, and the moving spirit behind significant reforms. Usually a force for good, he was invariably a force to be reckoned with: a Christian warrior who enjoyed a good fight, but preferred the heat and dust of a day's action to the patient manoeuvring required of a long campaign.

Son of a clergymen, he was born at Holne vicarage, in Devonshire, attended, briefly, Clifton School, then, from 1832 to 1856, Helston Grammar School. The scenery, people and natural history of the west country seized his young imagination. In 1836 his father was appointed vicar of St Luke's, Chelsea; he then attended King's College, as a day student. So he encountered the extremes, the finery and filth, busy commerce and sweated workers, high culture and low life of the city where the London Working Men's Association was first meeting – and young Dickens was writing Oliver Twist. As an experience it may have accounted for as much as the three years spent at Magdalene College, Cambridge. He gained a First Class degree, and devoted himself to rowing. In a revealing Virgilian, never-bettered, account of bumping races he lauded the 'True English stuff' which had 'conquered at Waterloo – which has created a Birmingham and Manchester, and colonized every quarter of the globe – that grim, earnest, stubborn energy which ... the English possess alone of all the nations of earth'.

On the strength of that passage the phrase 'muscular Christian', though not his, might seem apt enough. Patriotism and athleticism were, however, only two articles in an eclectic creed. In the years that followed Cambridge and ordination he became first curate, then

(1844) rector of Eversley in Hampshire. That humble village on the southern fringe of Windsor forest was to be his base for the rest of his life. However busy and involved he was in national causes, however much time he found for writing (his collected works would fill twenty-eight volumes), for his family, friends and his beloved fishing, the needs of his parish were never neglected. Impatient with dogma and ceremony, he drew the villagers to his church, won them by clear, vigorous teaching and assiduous visiting. In the damp, foetid hovels of the agricultural labourers, in their hunger, ignorance and disease, he found material for *Yeast*. First appearing episodically in *Frazer's Magazine*, published in 1851 as a novel, it was written to alert society to the questions 'fermenting in the minds of the young'. It was a powerful tract for its time.

Some of *Yeast* is Kingsley's own story: the beautiful, high-minded Argemone, who converts the hero to higher views of life and duty, may be read as an idealized Frances Grenfell, his wife since 1844. The central theme is the suffering of the rural poor, the neglect that was partly responsible for it and the urgent need for higher wages, better housing and at least an elementary schooling. His fervent prose touched some readers because he was one of them, manifestly a gentlemen, and a sportsman to boot.

A sense of urgency informs most of Kingsley's writing: reform or perish was the message. Kingsley observed the Chartist demonstration of April 1848, wrote political placards for public display and helped found a new periodical, *The People's Friend*. With Ludlow he brought carts and distributed pure water to the cholera-stricken people of Southwark. The instinct to act was typical; so was his determination to know the facts – and the men involved. He befriended Thomas Cooper, shoemaker, poet and Chartist; Walter Cooper, tailor; and Gerald Massey, editor of a working man's journal, *The Spirit of Freedom*. Under the name Parson Lot, Kingsley wrote the influential pamphlet *Cheap Clothes and Nasty*. Determined, as one reviewer wrote, to write books 'with some purpose in them', focusing on aspects of 'The Condition of England Question', he produced *Alton Locke* (1850). The eponymous cockney tailor, poet and Chartist, was gaoled for his part in a farmworkers' riot. Kingsley was too excited by 'the terrible questionings, the terrible strugglings of this great, awful, blessed time' to maintain control over his story.

Yet he struck hard. Offering a wide panorama, from the sweat shops of Bermondsey to the courts of Cambridge, *Alton Locke* so excited the young and idealistic that Henry James could later speak of a disease, 'Kingsley Fever'. The author's exuberance breaks out in assaults and lectures: Sabbatarianism, Nonconformity, Rome, Geology are among topics which convey one side of the debates of the day. Frederick Harrison wrote later of Kingsley as 'splendidly defiant ... of all the ten commandments of British society in 1849'. There is Dickensian power in his 'scene painting' (Wells too comes to mind), as in the tailors' attic, smelling of new cloth, gin and sweat, its windows shut and streaming with condensed breath. In Sandy Mackay, Kingsley succeeded well enough to persuade his mentor, Thomas Carlyle, to praise 'the rugged old hero ... a wonderfully splendid and coherent piece of Scottish bravura' – without recognizing himself in the character.

For a time he was against the forming of a party to promote Christian Socialism. His favoured solutions, co-operative associations, education, sanitary reform, healthy recreation and true religion, were variations on an essentially conservative, clerical theme. 'True socialism, true liberty, brotherhood and true equality ... is only to be found in loyalty and obedience to Christ.' His sermon of 1851, at St John's, Fitzroy Square, on 'the message of the church to labouring men', stressed that systems of society which favour the accumulation of capital in a few hands, or which oust the masses from the soil, are 'contrary to the kingdom of God'. He did not, however, propose political measures. The people were urged to look to 'something nobler than acts of parliament as a cure for their sufferings'. Part of his purpose in writing *Hypatia* (1853) was to illustrate, from the lives of simple Alexandrians of the fifth century, the idea that Christianity was the creed of democracy, fostering social order through the fellowship between social classes, based on 'the rights of man as man'. The novel was a favourite of Queen Victoria.

Two Years Ago (1857) urged patriotism, public health and opposition to slavery. Meredith called it 'a hearty sermon with illustrations'. Increasingly, meanwhile, Kingsley found fulfilment in writing popular historical novels. *Westward Ho!* (1855) is steeped in traditional anti-Catholicism. We see the Kingsley whose ill-judged challenge to Newman (1864), inferring dishonest statements in his earlier Anglican period, was to provoke Newman's magnificent *Apologia Pro Vita Sua*. *Hereward the Wake* (1866) reinforced myths about the Saxon freedom which was the Englishman's birthright. Even *The Water Babies* (1863), most successful of his books for children, was didactic. It was inspired by his interest in evolution. It also aroused concern about child chimney-sweeps and led to a parliamentary act to protect them.

Kingsley came to bask in the optimistic spirit of the '50s. He was moved to tears on entering the Great Exhibition: 'It was like going into a sacred palace.' He came to see himself as 'more of a government man'. He became first professor of Modern History at Cambridge, then tutor to the Prince of Wales. The 'turbulent priest' might seem to have renounced his radical past.

Canonries, first at Chester, then (1873) Westminster, were congenial. He was proud to serve the queen, yet remained robustly independent. He did not cease striving for favourite causes. One of his last publications was *Health and Education* (1874).

Hopkins wrote of Kingsley's 'air and spirit of a man bouncing up from table with his mouth full of bread and cheese and saying that he meant to stand for no blasted nonsense'. He delivered sermons 'like a man wrestling with demons'. His mind, says Chadwick, 'thought in the imperative mood. He rather ejaculated than spoke. His punctuation was littered with notes of exclamation.' Did the emphatic style cover unsafe thoughts? Was it, as Leslie Stephen suggests, just another response to the Victorian crisis of faith? Did his concern with health and sanitation reflect his desire to be well? He was not a strong man: spells of activity were followed by collapses and prolonged retreats. War brought out the patriot: his pamphlet, *Brave Words to Brave Soldiers*, went to thousands in the Crimea. His understanding of evolution lent itself to a crude racism. 'Niggers' were inferior beings. Governor Eyre was wholly right to suppress them with such violence in Jamaica. 'It must be proved that negro life is *human* life.'

By the end of his life it was generally accepted that society must be collectively responsible for public health, that if property owners obstructed, it was the state's duty to intervene. There was a growing appreciation within the church of the need to come to terms with Darwinian science. There was a greater interest in natural history. Kingsley would have been gratified by these trends. He might also have appreciated the verdict of G. M. Trevelyan: 'Kingsley gave to ordinary folk the idea that they could be religious without being gloomy or censorious.'

Further Reading
Una Pope-Hennessy, *Canon Charles Kingsley, A Biography*, 1948.

KINGSLEY, MARY (1862-1900) has left behind, in her *Travels in West Africa*, one of the best books ever written about exploration; a record of daring which caught the imagination even of the saturated Victorian public. This is the more remarkable because she spent the first thirty years of her short life at home, doing the housework for her invalid mother, and undertaking odd jobs to help her restless, scientific father. She never went to school. When both her parents died in 1892 she set off for west Africa feeling unwanted, to tidy up her father's incomplete researches into fish and fetishes, expecting to die there. But she didn't. Instead she survived two notable journeys, one along the coast from Sierra Leone to Angola and back, the other inland into what is now Gabon.

Into these, even though together they lasted for less

than twelve months, she packed the experiences of an explorer's lifetime. She negotiated rapids in an Ogowe canoe, and black oozy swamps on slippery tree-trunk bridges. She waded neck-deep through a ford, to emerge 'horribly infested with leeches, having a frill of them round our necks like astrakhan collars'. She walked into the villages of the Fans, a cannibal tribe, with her four native companions, Grey Shirt, Singlet, Silence and Pagan; and discovered that an unpleasant smell in the hut where she was sleeping came from a bag in which were 'a human hand, three big toes, four eyes, two ears ... The hand was fresh, the others only so-so, and shrivelled'. She faced a gorilla, who got within a yard of her before a Fan shot it, and a crocodile, which had its feet over the side of her canoe before she dislodged it with a paddle. On the way back from her second journey she climbed Mount Cameroon, rising from the sea to 13,760 feet, by a route which Burton had deemed too difficult.

She spoke and wrote about it all in a racy style which packed the lecture halls. In the mangrove swamp, with its noisy nights – 'splashes from jumping fish, the peculiar whirr of rushing crabs, and creaking and groaning sounds from the trees' – there was 'now and again the strong musky smell that meant a crocodile close by, and one had to rouse up and see if all the crews' legs were on board, for Africans are reckless and regardless of their legs during sleep'. Her approach was idiosyncratic by the standards of her day, especially in a woman. She had a high opinion of traders, and was admired by them, and by the natives, for her tough bargaining. She distrusted missionaries, whose religion was foreign to native culture, and who, seldom practical themselves, tried to turn Africans into clerks instead of teaching them agriculture and mechanics. She was an imperialist, but held that it was the first duty of empire builders in Africa to understand the Africans. *Travels in West Africa* is shot through with her own interest and respect for them, tempered with a healthy realism. She planned to go back, but the Boer War intervened. She volunteered as a nurse, and died of a fever caught off one of her Boer prisoner patients. Though she was no feminist, and did not like the suffragettes, her life provided them with powerful ammunition. Her books tell a remarkable story in a remarkable way.

Further Reading
M. Kingsley, *Travels in West Africa*, 1897.

KIRKE, COLONEL PERCY (1646?-91), son of a courtier who was Gentleman of the Robes to Charles I and Groom of the Bedchamber to Charles II, was a professional soldier. Promoted Lieutenant-Colonel in 1680, he was sent the following year to Tangier, whose Governor he became in 1682; there the Governor's Regiment, raised for service at Tangier, had as its badge the Paschal Lamb. No doubt neither Kirke nor his men were

softened by their service against the Moors. They returned home when Tangier was evacuated in 1684, and in 1685 Kirke fought against Monmouth's men at Sedgemoor with parts of his own and of another Tangerine regiment. What made this harsh, hard-bitten man and his 'Lambs' notorious was their summary execution of prisoners, notably in Taunton market-place. Yet Kirke was one of the officers of James II who refused to abandon his Protestantism, and it is possible that he was involved in the plot to kidnap James II when the army moved to Salisbury in the crisis of 1688. Certainly William III gave him promotion, and he was employed in the relief of Londonderry in 1689, where he distinguished himself by his dilatoriness in taking action from Lough Foyle until it was almost too late. In 1691 he went to Flanders with William's forces, and died at Brussels in that year.

KNELLER, SIR GODFREY (1646?-1723), portrait-painter, was born at Lubeck, son of the city surveyor, and studied in Holland and Italy. Coming to England in 1675, he quickly became fashionable, and few artists have had so successful a career in this country. He painted Charles II and James II and was appointed court painter to William III. Naturalized in 1683, he was knighted in 1691 and made a baronet in 1715. Kneller was an arrogant man with a high opinion of his own powers. Like Lely, he made art into an organized industry: his studio was a painting factory, with specialist assistants who each added a particular item, like a wig or draperies, to the basic portrait done by the master himself, and who turned out the numerous copies of Kneller's royal portraits. Inevitably much of his considerable output was mechanical and uninspired. Nevertheless, Kneller had the sharp eye of the great portrait-painter, as he showed, for example, in the famous series of forty-two paintings of the Whigs in the Kit-Cat Club, of which those of Vanbrugh and Wharton are representative. Whatever the artist's judgement upon Kneller's attitude to his sitters, for the historian at least he provides unusually valuable documentary evidence.

Further Reading
M. Whinney and O. Millar, *English Art, 1625-1714*, 1957.

KNOX, JOHN (1512?-72), Scottish Protestant reformer and historian, was born not earlier than 1512 and not later than 1515. He was ordained priest in April 1536; he was an Apostolic Notary from 1540 to 1543; he may have been a clerk in Cardinal Beaton's employ in 1545, but probably was not. He came under the influence of George Wishart, the Scottish Protestant martyr, and his 'acceptable doctrine' and was then accounted an 'apostate priest'. He was saved from Wishart's fate of burning by Wishart's good advice, 'Nay, return to your bairns and God bless you. One is sufficient for a sacrifice.' He was in daily danger of arrest and eventually took refuge in the castle of St Andrews, which was held by the murderers of Cardinal Beaton. When that fell, Knox was sent by its French captors to the French galleys (1547-9). On his release he went to England, where the Protestant reformation under Edward VI was in full swing. He became a licensed preacher at Berwick and then at Newcastle. Here he became acquainted with Mrs Elizabeth Bowes, wife of the captain of Norham Castle, and here he courted her daughter, Marjory, whom he married probably in 1553. But in 1550 he was up in front of Tunstal, Bishop of Durham, to explain his doctrine. Tunstal was a conservative in religion: Knox represented the most advanced side of the Reformation. To him and to Northumberland the Book of Common Prayer of 1549 did not go far enough. In 1552 Knox was appointed one of the six chaplains to Edward VI. He was all but offered the see of Rochester, but he quarrelled with Northumberland and was twice arraigned before the Privy Council. He could have had the living of All Hallows in London, but he refused it. That he had influence in ecclesiastical matters is proved by his success in getting the Black Rubric added to the Second Prayer Book of Edward VI, which laid down that to receive the Communion kneeling did not imply adoration.

Knox disliked Northumberland and he also saw that the duke's days were numbered. On the accession of Mary, Knox (1554) went overseas.

He was one of the leading 'Marian exiles', engaging in an unseemly quarrel with Richard Cox and his followers over the form of service to use. Knox wanted a more extreme Prayer Book even than that of 1552; Cox was content to obey the Edwardian Act of Uniformity. Knox and his supporters withdrew to Geneva, where they drew increasing inspiration from the doctrines and practices of John Calvin.

In Scotland, during the 1550s, Protestants won a degree of toleration from the queen regent, Mary of Guise. It was far safer for them in Scotland than England, and Knox had visited from Switzerland in 1555. There was support among the magnates for religious reform. A number of their leaders banded together in a covenant for religious action, the 'Congregation of Christ'. They wrote to Knox (who on counsel of caution had halted temporarily at Dieppe), to resume his journey back to Scotland, but did not delay to present a programme of projected reforms to the queen regent. (The posting on 1 January 1559 of the 'Beggars' Summons' on friary gates showed the readiness of reformers to mobilize the anti-clericalism of the lower classes against the clergy, should reform be resisted.) In early 1558, Knox had published his famous *First Blast of the Trumpet against the Monstrous Regiment of Women*, whose rule was 'repugnant to nature, and contumely to God'. The work chiefly reflected his hatred

of the Catholicism of Mary I of England and his disappointed hopes of the queen regent, Mary of Guise. Knox's strictures against the frailties of womankind were taken in poor spirit by one of its least frail representatives, Elizabeth Tudor: hardly had his work come off the presses when she succeeded to the English throne. Knox's book thus became an embarrassment to moderate reformers (and even to himself, as his apologies to Cecil testify).

But in Scotland in the spring of 1559, the initiative was not with queens or kings – or even nobles. Much more important then were Knox's *Appellation of the Nobility and Estates of Scotland* and his *Letter Addressed to the Commonality of Scotland*. For these began to theorize the right of a widely defined community to resist the imposition of 'tyranny', i.e. authority not sanctioned by the word of God, and underpinned, in this case, by the power of France and the papal antichrist. In May 1559, Knox arrived with Scotland already in the throes of what at first was a revolutionary reformation; statues were smashed, monastic properties were looted or taken over, factional battles wracked the towns, French troops were imported by the queen regent to fight on the side of the old order.

On 1 August 1560, the Reformation Parliament convened. To Knox's heartfelt disappointment, it refused to adopt the *Book of Discipline* which he and his fellow ministers had drawn up. This envisaged superintendents rather than bishops, placing the chief power in the hands of a biannual General Assembly, with lay and clerical members. The *Book* aimed to enlist the active partnership of the state in a plan for appropriating the properties of the unreformed church in the cause of reform. Reformers were chiefly concerned with the exposition and discussion of the word, a more austere liturgy and more vigilance in imposing godly standards in the lives of the people. For reasons which included alarm at the recent lawless activity against authority, and the need for English help against the French, the estates of parliament reached a compromise which gave Knox and his fellow reformers only part of the true religion they wanted; unreformed clergymen and practices deemed to be ungodly survived in numbers, but those who were hot for reform were given much impetus.

The legislation of the Reformation Parliament was never ratified by Mary, Queen of Scots (who had returned to Scotland in August 1561), and was therefore of dubious legality, but the queen found it best to observe the mass privately, to listen to Protestant advisers, and not to try to alter the Protestant religion now commonly practised. In 1562 better financial provision was made for reformed preachers. None of this much impressed John Knox, who was enraged that a third of the church revenues should be allocated to the maintenance of the Romish queen and much of the rest to her unreformed co-religionists. Knox was for forcing Mary to marry a Protestant and to rule as a Protestant, since he thought it impossible otherwise to guarantee the defence of Scotland's religion. He incubated a devout hatred for Riccio, and had several personal brushes with Mary herself. The queen did not prove receptive to his belief that subjects and sovereigns owed God equal obedience, or to his opinion, made known to parliament, that 'if she will not agree with you in God, ye are not bound to her in the Devil'.

After the deposition of Mary, John Knox preached the sermon at the coronation of her successor, James VI. Though still a radical in spirit, he agreed to further religious compromises, which confirmed the patronage rights of their existing individual owners (rights opposed to the principle of election by congregations) in the hope of investing reformers by indirect means. In the same vein, he approved the Concordat of Leith which conceded Crown appointment of new bishops in exchange for the right of the General Assembly to vet and supervise them. Knox died soon after, on 24 November 1572. Marjory having died in 1560, Knox remarried in 1564, aged fifty, the seventeen-year-old Margaret Stewart by whom he had three daughters. He had two sons by his first marriage.

Further Reading
H. McDiarmid, C. Maclean and A. Ross, *John Knox*, 1976.
J. Ridley, *John Knox*, 1968.

L

LABOUCHÈRE, HENRY (1831-1911), radical MP, journalist, wit, was a cheerful gadfly of the late Victorian political scene, widely known as 'Labby'. He found himself £6,000 in debt after his education at Eton and Trinity College, Cambridge, and went off to Mexico, where he fell in love with a circus lady, and spent six months living in an Indian village. He then joined the diplomatic service, managed for a time to avoid a posting to St Petersburg on the grounds that he had not got enough money for the railway fare; and, when he did have to go there, organized some elementary spying by a laundress. His prospects changed when he inherited a small fortune, but, rather than resign from the foreign service, he got himself dismissed, for accepting a post in Buenos Aires only on the condition that he could perform his duties in Baden Baden.

He found his true métier as a journalist. He became the *Daily News*'s correspondent in Paris during the siege of 1870, recommending 'those who have cats with philo-progenitive proclivities, instead of drowning the kittens, to eat them. Either smothered in onions or in a ragout they are excellent'. Taking care to avoid heroics himself, he pricked the romantic bubbles of glory in others. To him, war was senseless and filled with tedium. He set about exposing fraud and hypocrisy in many walks of life. To do this, he started a weekly journal, *Truth* (1876) which soon became widely read. He loved to stick his neck out, was horsewhipped more than once, and became a familiar figure in the courts defending libel actions.

From 1880 until 1906 he was MP for Northampton, and was able to push his particular brand of radicalism at Westminster as well as in the columns of *Truth*. His credo was that government should interfere as little as possible with human liberty: he was against empires, and against privilege and perquisites. He was also a vigilant guardian of the public purse. He attacked the cost to it of the royal family, describing the Duke of Cambridge, Commander-in-Chief, 'standing at the head of his troops, drawn salary in his hand', and he moved more than 100 amendments to the army and navy estimates. He relentlessly opposed Jingoists. 'Africa for the Africans' was his policy: and 'Ireland for the Irish', too.

There he tried to hold the Liberal/Irish alliance together to achieve Home Rule. He numbered the actor Henry Irving and the artist James Whistler among his friends, and was personally well-liked for his honesty and sense of fun – though not by the queen, who called him 'that horrible lying Labouchère', and refused to allow Gladstone to offer him a Cabinet post in 1892. He remained unembittered and eccentric, wearing a jacket whose lining hung loose in tatters and taking out his teeth when they felt uncomfortable; a free spirit in a conventional age.

LACY, HENRY, EARL OF LINCOLN and SALIS-BURY (*c*.1249-1311) is a prime example of the nobility of service. The eldest son of Edmund, Earl of Lincoln (*d*.1257), he acquired the earldom of Salisbury by marriage to Margaret Longsword. He further enhanced his fortune through royal grants, notably the Marcher lordship of Denbigh. He was the founder of Whalley Abbey and contemplated establishing an Oxford college in 1307. Unfortunately both his sons died prematurely, one falling in a well at Denbigh and another tumbling from the battlements at Pontefract, leaving his daughter Alice as his sole heiress. On her marriage to Thomas of Lancaster, nephew of Edward I and the greatest nobleman of his generation, Henry resettled his lands, granting the reversion in default of children to the house of Lancaster and thus risked disinheriting collateral relatives should Alice die childless, as indeed she did. This risk, Henry evidently considered, was a price worth paying for such a prestigious match.

While Henry's estates, although extensive, did not place him among the greatest of the earls, his continuous record of royal service over many years was quite exceptional. As a soldier he served in Wales in 1276-7, 1282 and 1293-4; in Gascony in 1294-7, latterly as commander-in-chief, where he was defeated at Bellegarde; and in Scotland in the campaigns of Falkirk (1298), Caerlaverock (1300), 1301, 1305 and 1307. He accompanied Edward I to Gascony in 1286-9 and was one of those commissioned to try the judges on their return. Negotiations with Scotland, France and the Papacy occupied him repeatedly from 1290. In 1279 he acted jointly as regent in the king's absence. Perhaps the closest councillor of Edward I in his last years, he was with him on his deathbed, and was among those t he dying king charged with the welfare of his son Edward II.

While Henry honoured his promise to Edward I, he was not uncritical of Edward II's government and particularly of his infatuation with Piers Gaveston. It was Lincoln who assured Edward II of his power to create Gaveston an earl and befriended the young Gascon, but this did not last long as he became 'of all the earls, his greatest enemy and persecutor'. Lincoln recognized the need for administrative reforms, notably of purveyance. He seems to have pressed first for reform by the king and only later, when disappointed, did he become one of the Ordainers imposing Ordinances on the king. Gaveston represented an obstacle to good government and did not endear himself by nicknaming Lincoln 'burst-belly'. Lincoln's opposition was not disloyal. The Ordainers made a distinction between their duties to the Crown and king, which it has been persuasively argued represented Lincoln's position. He campaigned for reform whilst remaining loyal to Edward II, may have restrained hotter heads among his younger fellow earls, and even seems to have been ready to tolerate Gaveston, if his influence could be curbed. Remarkably he enjoyed the confidence of both parties, acting both as an Ordainer and as keeper of the realm for the king in 1310-11. His death thus removed a moderating influence that was to be sorely missed.

Further Reading
J. R. Maddicott, *Thomas of Lancaster 1307-1322: A Study in the Reign of Edward II*, 1970.
J. F. Baldwin, 'The Household Administration of Henry Lacy and Thomas of Lancaster', *English Historical Review* xlii, 1927.

LAMB, CHARLES (1775-1834), essayist, may have, on the score of his published work, a modest place among English authors, but his life and writing evoke a special affection. No-one ever spoke of him without his Christian name. He was a small, clumsy man, who stammered; his eyes were of different colours. De Quincey wrote of his appearance in sleep when his face 'assumed an expression almost seraphic, from its intellectual beauty of outline, its childlike simplicity, and its benignity'. The eyes, however, 'disturbed the unity of effect in Lamb's waking face' and imparted a feeling of restlessness, 'shifting, like northern lights, through every mode of combination with fantastic playfulness', Lamb's personality intrudes excitably into everything that he writes.

The essays, by which Lamb is best known, elaborate upon his letters and conversation. Part of their appeal is that their author appears to talk to us as intimates, standing upon the common ground of shared experiences. Together his essays amount to an autobiography. Lamb was a Londoner and seldom happy for long away from the crowded and smoky streets of Fleet and Strand, Covent Garden, the narrow lanes of the city and the quiet law courts. With Doctor Johnson and Charles Dickens he is one of the three great Londoners of our literature. As he wrote, in a letter to Wordsworth, comparing his love of London with the poet's 'rural emotions': 'The crowds, the very dirt and mud, the sun shining upon houses and pavements, the print shops, the old bookstalls, parsons cheap'ning books, coffee houses, steams of soups from kitchens, the pantomimes, London itself a pantomime and a masquerade – all these things work themselves into my mind and feed me without a power of satisfying me.'

He was born 'under the shadow of St Dunstan's steeple' and lived for seventeen years at the Temple, where his father was clerk and servant to Mr Salt, Bencher of the Temple. John Lamb had literary tastes and wrote light verse. His wife, Elizabeth Field, was the daughter of the housekeeper of a fine house in Hertfordshire; we may read of it, as a child recalled it in 'Blakesmoor in H-shire'. Charles had the run of Mr Salt's library, as valuable, perhaps, as the education he got at Christ's Hospital, where he went at the age of seven. In two of his pleasantest essays he describes the rigours of his boyhood at this school. He became a good Latinist and he acquired an exceptional friend in Samuel Taylor Coleridge. Yet he was unable to reach a university, perhaps because of his stammer. What this deprivation meant to him may be gauged from his essay 'Oxford in the Vacation'. There is pathos in his make-believe: 'When the peacock vein rises, I strut a Gentleman Commoner. In graver moments, I proceed a Master of Arts.'

He went into the East India Company's offices. His brother, twelve years older than he, was already a clerk in the South Sea Company's office where Charles had started. Lamb's essay upon that establishment recalls the best of Dickens and that writer's keen eye for the odd and the archaic. The work in Charles's office was hard. He was there for thirty-three years, six days a week, often working long hours. But in the evenings he lived more agreeably the convivial life of literary conversation. At places like the Salutation tavern in Newgate Street he talked with Coleridge. 'You first kindled in me, if not the power, yet the love of poetry and beauty and kindliness', Lamb wrote when he dedicated his collected works to the poet. There might also be found there William and Dorothy Wordsworth, Keats, de Quincey, Leigh Hunt, Southey, Hood and Godwin. There Hazlitt found Lamb and recalled him for us: 'No-one ever stammered out such fine, piquant, deep, eloquent things in half a dozen half-sentences as he does ... What a keen, laughing, hare-brained vein of home-felt truth! There was no fuss or cant about him; nor were his sweets or his sours ever diluted with one particle of affectation.'

The background of his life was tragic, the protracted sequel to one awful act. In his later years John Lamb's mind became soft: he was no longer the man whom his son sketches, as Lovel, in 'The Old Benchers of the Inner Temple'. On Mary, ten years older than Charles, fell the brunt of looking after her ageing parents. Charles himself spent a few weeks in an asylum when he was twenty and there was a streak of mental instability in the family. One day in 1796 Mary went out of her mind and killed her mother with a knife. Charles was allowed to take responsibility for her and he looked after her for the rest of his life. Whenever she felt that her reason was giving way she went willingly to hospital. When she was sane she was an intelligent and devoted companion who could, as in their joint *Tales from Shakespeare*, share in his work. It may have been for her sake that he never married. At nineteen he fell in love with a Hertfordshire girl who married someone else. Later he wooed, unsuccessfully, the actress, Fanny Kelly. Some of the restlessness of his nature was surely the result of his anxiety about Mary; he played the buffoon, and drank a lot at parties. Fortunately he had a 'genius for friendship' and found solace in his writing for the labours of desk and ledger. Working as hard as he did, reading deeply and caring for his sister, it is extraordinary that he found so much time for his letters. 'Everybody allows that the art of writing agreeable letters is peculiarly female', says Jane Austen's Henry Tilney to Catherine Morland. 'Letter-writing is a private art: and private life is woman's native and triumphant achievement' writes Lord David Cecil. Lamb's letters are then a *tour de force*: feminine in delicacy and perceptiveness but robust, amusing and above all generous. They must have been delightful to receive.

His first published work consisted of four sonnets in Coleridge's volume of poems (1796). In 1798, with his friend Charles Lloyd, he put out a slender volume of verse which contained 'Old Familiar Faces'. But when he turned to prose he found a richer ore. In 1797 he published his prose romance, *The Tale of Rosamund Gray and Old Blind Margaret*. In 1801 came *John Woodvil*, the product of his intensive study of Elizabethan dramatic poetry, which he helped to restore to fashion. In 1807 he caught public attention with the *Tales from Shakespeare* for Godwin's Junior Library. In the next year *Specimens of the English Dramatic Poets* showed his ripening ability. His taste was for the elaborate and fanciful, the older and quainter the better. He did not enjoy the poetry of Shelley, Scott or Byron; he did not even like the Waverley novels which captured the literary and fashionable world. Amongst writers he put Shakespeare first; he also had a vast knowledge of the Elizabethan and Jacobean dramatists. He had

favourites among prose writers. 'Elia' (Lamb) describes himself as 'hanging over (for the thousandth time) some passage in old Burton, or one of his strange contemporaries'.

His library of books, many tattered bookstall bargains, was an extension of his personality. Another form of escape was the theatre, which he dearly loved: 'A mob of happy faces crowding up at the pit door of Drury Lane Theatre gives me ten thousand sincerer pleasures than I could ever receive from all the flocks of silly sheep that ever whitened the plains of Arcadia or Epsom Downs'. All the sadder was the fate of the one of his four plays to reach the stage, *Mr H-* (1806). The first-night audience killed it – and Lamb joined in the hissing.

When his essays first appeared in 1820, under the name of Elia, they were a great success. Since the first essay was 'The South-Sea House' it is not surprising that its authorship did not long remain a secret! The lack of constructive power which was fatal to his efforts as playwright, the somewhat artificial style which would have detracted from a novel, do not matter in an essay when the author is talking freely of himself. Lamb is especially an essayist of the feelings. Lynd says of him that 'He seems to steep his very words in some dye of memory and affection that no other writer has discovered' and, again: 'He is at once Hamlet and Yorick in his melancholy and his mirth.' Through his essays he has become with Dr Johnson and James Boswell the most intimately known character in our literature: how much gentler than Johnson, how much more admirable than Boswell!

Lamb made enough money to avoid debt and provide for his sister (his brother did nothing for her). In their later years, Mary and he adopted a girl, Emma Isola. In 1825, in failing health, he retired from his company and was given a generous pension. He settled in Edmonton, in his beloved Hertfordshire, but separation from his friends made him lonely for the first time in his life. In deepening darkness of mind, Mary was to survive him by nearly thirteen years. In January 1834 Taylor the publisher wrote: 'Poor Charles Lamb is dead – perhaps you had not heard of it before. He fell down and cut his face against the Gravel on the Turnpike Road, which brought on the Erisypelas, and in a few days carried him off.'

Further Reading
E. V. Lucas, *Lamb's Letters*, 3 vols, 1935.
Edmund Blunden, *Charles Lamb and his Contemporaries*, 1933.
E. V. Lucas, *Life of Charles Lamb*, 2 vols, revised edition, 1921.

LAMB, WILLIAM, 2nd VISCOUNT MELBOURNE (1779-1848) was Victoria's first prime minister. He therefore finds his place in the Victorian age: but his style and his attitudes were those of the Regency.

He was born into Whig society, although not as a blue-blooded member of it. His grandfather, a lawyer, had married a Coke, thus acquiring Melbourne Hall in Derbyshire; later he bought Brocket Hall in Hertford-shire. His mother was an attractive, ambitious and gifted hostess. She pushed her sottish husband into first an Irish, and then an English peerage. There were doubts over the paternity of many of their children, and it was commonly held that William's father was Lord Egre-mont. William quickly established himself socially. At Eton, Trinity College Cambridge and Glasgow Univers-ity he showed intellectual curiosity but no application; theological interest but a distaste for religious enthus-iasm; and a zest for the luxuries of life. His intelligence, confidence, wit and mildly eccentric manners were admired by his young contemporaries. When his elder brother died in 1805, and a political career became pos-sible, he gave up the drudgery of the Bar with relief for a seat at Leominster. The Whigs welcomed a promising recruit.

But the next years were dominated by his wife, Lady Caroline. William fell in love with this vivacious sprite, daughter of the Earl of Bessborough and niece of the Duchess of Devonshire, and married her within five months of his brother's death. She rapidly became the most talked-about personality in London society. Her aristocratic upbringing had given free rein to her ego-centric extremes of mood. Early happiness in her marriage was affected by still-born children, and their surviving son was mentally handicapped. William's apparently cool detachment from her dramatic scenes drove her to 'sadder music and stronger wine', as she set out to catch the shooting star of the Regency scene, Lord Byron, who had just published *Childe Harold*. Their romance ended at Lady Heathcote's ball, when she slashed her wrists with a broken glass and a pair of scis-sors. Her autobiographical novel, *Glenarvon*, included offensive satires on leading hostesses, her mother-in-law amongst them. William was loyal to her even when she was at her wildest – she was observed through a window, on their visit to Paris in 1814, throwing ornaments at him. His family persuaded him into a formal separation from her in 1825, but when she was dying of dropsy three years later he came back from Ireland to be with her. His dislike of confrontation and his carapace of irony grew from the prolonged pain of this disastrous marriage.

Melbourne's political career was divided between a period of over twenty years out of office, followed by fourteen years almost continuously in it. As a Whig, he shared their long exile from power. Impatient with Grenville and Grey, the aloof successors of the charis-matic Charles Fox, he left parliament in 1812. Returning in 1816, he came to respect the policies of the moderate Tories, especially those of Canning and Huskisson. In 1827 he agreed to join Canning's ministry as Chief

Secretary for Ireland, but after Canning's death he became one of the group of Canningites who left Wellington's Tory government when the duke refused to give the seats of the disfranchised borough of East Retford to industrial Birmingham. Though he was no enthusiast for parliamentary reform himself, his friends were, and so he went with them. Thus he became avail-able to the Whigs again when they won the election in 1830.

Grey made him Home Secretary. It was a well-judged appointment, for it spared Melbourne the onus of advo-cating reform, but gave him the task of keeping order while the Bill was going through. His view of reform was pragmatic. He disliked the changes, but with melan-choly eloquence urged the House of Lords to 'yield to the popular vote or be annihilated'. Lord John Russell thought him 'very slack' about the measure. But he was not in the least slack about keeping order. This was just as well. Hunger riots swept the country in 1830, and these were renewed with added violence when the Lords threw out the first Reform Bill. Faced by over 1,000 out-breaks, culminating in the centre of Bristol being gutted by the rioters, and by a threatened run on the banks, the magistrates panicked. Melbourne kept calm. He urged them not to hesitate to read the Riot Act; but he refused to hand weapons out to irregular bodies of vigilantes, or to revert to the use of spies. He also kept in touch with potential rebel leaders, such as Francis Place. His energy was unexpected from one whose image was lethargic. He got a reputation for the harsh enforcement of the law, when his Special Commissioners followed up the riots with 500 sentences of transportation.

When Grey resigned in 1834, William IV thought Melbourne the best of a bad lot, and made him prime minister, as the only man capable of holding together a party which included such difficult men as Old Wicked-shifts, the flamboyantly eccentric Lord Chancellor Brougham, with his faint whiff of sulphur; Russell, earnest, tactless and limited; and Radical Jack Durham, immensely rich and explosive. The king was right. Mel-bourne revealed his tactical skills by holding onto power, with one brief hiccough, until 1841.

He was not the natural leader of a reforming govern-ment, however. 'You'd better try to do no good, then you'll get into no scrapes', was his advice to the young Queen Victoria, and he practised what he preached. Among the main measures of his ministries, the Poor Law Amendment Act was virtually complete before he took over, and the Factory Acts did not interest him. He opposed Robert Owen's efforts to develop Trade Unions, and turned some harmless Dorset labourers into the Tolpuddle Martyrs by enforcing their sentence of trans-portation. He did involve himself in the Municipal Reform Bill, but this was because the old Corporations, which it was designed to end, were often Tory strongholds. By sending 'Radical Jack' to deal with the mounting tensions in Upper and Lower Canada, he initiated the 'Durham Report', which paved the way towards a long-lasting constitutional settlement there; but he had no vision of Empire, let alone Commonwealth, and indeed looked back on his choice of Durham as a blunder.

His Irish policy was the exception to his usual deliberate inactivity. As Canning's Chief Secretary there, he had had close acquaintance with Ireland's problems. The Catholic majority did not have the vote, and had to pay tithes and rates to the Anglican Church of Ireland, whose doors they never entered. The land was divided into small, uneconomic plots, with rent paid to absentee landlords: the population was growing dangerously. Melbourne, sceptically tolerant and fair-minded, had opened his doors to Catholics, and voted for Catholic Emancipation in 1829. Daniel O'Connell and his Irish followers now supported him at Westminster, and he was anxious to do more for them. He did not tackle problems of land tenure, but he tried to appropriate some of the money paid as tithes to the Church of Ireland, to be used for the improvement of the condition, educational and social, of Catholics. His measures, however, were all blocked by the House of Lords, and the Irish continued to sustain his government only because they could expect even less from the Tories. The people who gained from his efforts were the Dissenters. He made it legal for them to be married outside an Anglican church, and many more of them got the right to vote locally through the Municipal Reform Act. A non-sectarian college recently founded was incorporated as University College, London, in 1836.

Melbourne's relations with William IV were never comfortable, and the king disliked many of his ministers so much that, when the safest of them, Lord Althorp, succeeded his father as Earl Spencer in 1835, and went to the House of Lords, he dismissed Melbourne and turned to the Tories, only to have to accept him back again when Peel failed to gain enough seats at the subsequent election. But with Victoria, Melbourne straightway established a relationship which was unique. For him it was a natural one. Charles Greville, contemporary diarist, described him as 'a man with the capacity for loving without having anything in the world to love'. He was an instinctive teacher. He enjoyed the company of intelligent and forceful women, and the young Victoria soon showed herself as one of them. It was perhaps more surprising that she became so attached to him, a man who had been sued in the courts for his relationship with their wives by two husbands – admittedly on totally inadequate evidence. But Melbourne was no roué; rather, a man capable of deep affection. He won her trust early, with his famous charm, which he adapted appropriately, sitting upright in her presence instead of in his usual sprawl, and reducing the oaths with which his

conversation was habitually peppered. 'Very honest, good and kind-hearted as well as very clever', she described him in her diary. She came to rely on him completely, expecting him to be at her side for six hours each day at Windsor, and leaving his chair empty when he was absent. Their talk ranged widely. He was often sceptical – on education: 'None of the Pagets can read or write and they get on well enough'; on religion: 'I'm afraid to go to church for fear of hearing something extraordinary'; on honours: 'What I like about the Order of the Garter is that there is no damned merit about it'. Victoria was fascinated, even when she did not agree. His political influence was sometimes for the good. He kept her opinionated and ill-advised mother away from public affairs. He inculcated a sense of duty: 'A queen's life is very laborious … hardly any leisure.' But he did not train her to be above party, and he risked her reputation by encouraging her to cling to him and his failing government.

She showed her party bias over the Ladies of her Bedchamber. First there was the affair of Lady Flora Hastings, from a Tory family, who was wrongly accused of being pregnant and then died of the disease which had caused her swelling. Then, in 1839, the radicals combined with the Tories to force Melbourne's resignation. Victoria sent unwillingly for Peel, but refused to dismiss any of her Whig ladies. Peel felt that he could not accept office under those circumstances, and Melbourne, whose advice to the queen had been at best ambiguous, came back.

It was an unhappy return. The Whigs kept office for two more years, but the country was swinging against them, with a recession and bad harvests. Unemployment was made harder to endure by the new Poor Law, with workhouses replacing outdoor relief. The discontented rallied round the People's Charter. Its demands, ranging from pay for MPs to manhood suffrage, were far from Melbourne's political world. Meanwhile his lack of interest in foreign affairs and in finance got him into serious difficulties. Palmerston, his brother-in-law and Foreign Secretary, alarmed the strong pro-French lobby in the Cabinet by risking war against France in 1840 over her support for Mehemet Ali against the Turks. But it was finance that brought him down in the end. The budget would not balance – the Penny Post, a costly reform at first, was partly responsible – and the Chancellor of the Exchequer proposed to increase revenue from trade by reducing the import duties on foreign sugar, timber and corn. Melbourne met the dangers of the opposition of vested interest at home with a shrug, telling ministers that he did not care whether they raised or lowered the duty on corn as long as they all agreed to say the same thing. Beaten in the Commons, and then, decisively, in the Election of 1841, he handed over to Peel.

Thereafter he aged rapidly. He kept in touch with the queen, writing her three letters a week at first, and not always steering clear of politically controversial issues. But Albert, time, and his own failing powers, weaned her from him. When he died in 1848, he had already become a figure from the distant past, a man who had gained and held power in a narrowly oligarchic arena through his confident calm in crises and his relaxed and attractive personality. He was not, nor ever intended to be, a creative statesman.

Further Reading
Lord David Cecil, *Lord M*, 1954.
Lord David Cecil, *The Young Melbourne*, 1939.

LAMBERT, JOHN (1619-84), ablest of Oliver Cromwell's military subordinates, was a Yorkshireman from Calton in Craven. His wife was a Lister, connected with the Fairfaxes, and Lambert joined the parliamentarian army and became a captain in Fairfax's cavalry. His remarkably swift rise to distinction reflected his military brilliance. He fought at Marston Moor, had a regiment in the New Model Army, and was a Major-General at twenty-eight; he displayed high strategic insight in the early stages of the Preston campaign of 1648; he commanded the left with great courage and resilience at Dunbar (1650); in the summer of 1651 he won a crushing victory over the Scots at Inverkeithing, and pursued Hamilton's army southwards and played a vital part in the victory at Worcester. Among the parliamentarian commanders only Fairfax and Cromwell were more gifted soldiers. Popular with his own rank and file, Lambert seems to have been less disliked by the royalists than most of the parliamentarian leaders. Perhaps this was because he was not very obviously a Puritan. His religious views remain unknown, he was a realist in outlook and often a cynic in speech, he spent a good deal of money on tulips, and he lived in style with his beautiful wife in Wimbledon House. He was ambitious as well as able, and he had a gift for intrigue; his portrait suggests impatience and a hint of arrogance. Many of his contemporaries did not trust him, and Oliver is alleged to have called him 'Bottomless Lambert'.

His first considerable intervention in politics came in 1647, when he helped Ireton draw up the Heads of the Proposals. By accident or design he was out of London at the time of Charles's trial – though it seems likely that he would have followed Fairfax rather than Cromwell on this question. He took the lead among the officers when in 1652 they urged reform upon the Rump, yet he had no sympathy with the radicals like Harrison. It was Lambert, essentially a conservative in outlook, who in 1653 engineered the dissolution of Barebone's parliament and produced the first draft of the Instrument of Government, and he has thus strong claim to be the creator of the Protectorate. He served on its Council of State, he

was its military commander in the north, he seems to have been behind the scheme of 'Major Generals' created in 1655, he was until 1657 clearly its second most eminent citizen. But he opposed the proposals to make Cromwell king and the Protectorate hereditary, and this action – which it is difficult not to attribute to ambition – led to a breach and to his dismissal (on a pension of £2,000 per annum). It was, in a way, the turning-point in his career.

He accepted his enforced retirement for a time, but in Richard Cromwell's parliament he sided openly with the Republican opponents of the Protectorate, and on Richard's overthrow regained his old commands. The Rump, recalled in May 1659, sent him to crush Sir George Booth's royalist rising in Cheshire (August). After a quarrel between parliament and officers over the rights and command of the army, Lambert followed Cromwell's example and expelled the Rump (October). This action brought protests from Monck in Scotland, who crossed the border (New Year's Day 1660) to restore the authority of the civil power. Lambert's army, which had moved north to meet him, melted away as his soldiers deserted, and even his old patron Fairfax brought out the gentry of Yorkshire against him. He was captured and imprisoned in the Tower. He escaped and tried to rally the army in a last stand against the Restoration, but was recaptured, and he was one of those exempted from the Act of Indemnity of 1660. Tried in 1662, he was condemned to death but reprieved and sentenced to life imprisonment, which he spent in Guernsey up to 1670 and on St Nicholas Island (Drake's Island) in Plymouth Sound until his death in 1684. He lived long enough to find a place in the fictitious plots of Titus Oates.

Further Reading
M. Ashley, *Cromwell's Generals*, 1954, esp. Chapter 6.
W. H. Dawson, *Cromwell's Understudy*, 1938.
C. E. Lucas Phillips, *Cromwell's Captains*, 1938.

LAMBERT, JOHN (his real name was Nicholson, but he took the name of Lambert, on his own showing for fear the bishops might murder him) (*d*.1538), martyr, was born at some unknown date in Norwich and was burned at the stake at Smithfield in November 1538. Educated at Cambridge, he became a Fellow of Queens' College in 1521. It is said that Thomas Bilney converted him to Protestantism, but Bilney was never really a Protestant. Lambert, who frequented the White Horse in Cambridge, was ordained priest and had for a time a living in Norfolk, but he was in some trouble through reading forbidden books. The Merchant Adventurers then sent him to be their chaplain in the English House at Antwerp. In 1529 Sir Thomas More and Bishop Tunstal passed through Antwerp and no doubt heard about the Protestant propaganda which Lambert was carrying on. This may well be the reason why More, when he became Lord Chancellor, had Lambert sent back to England (1532).

Lambert was summoned to Lambeth and was confronted with forty-five articles which he answered with great skill and learning. Archbishop Warham saved him and kept him at his own house at Otford. Warham died in August 1532, and Lambert was free. He took up teaching Latin and Greek to children, resigned his priesthood and thought of marrying; he also entered the Grocers' Company. But Lambert was a man who simply could not avoid controversy. He was soon in trouble. In 1535 he was arraigned before Cranmer and Latimer on a charge of denouncing the worship of saints. Latimer was said to be 'most extreme against him', but Lambert won his point that it was not necessary to eternal salvation to pray for the intercession of the saints and therefore it could not be heresy to abstain. But he would not learn: freed from prison on Friday, he was there on Saturday trying to reopen the whole discussion: as a result he was put into prison for a very short time.

Freed again, again Lambert asked for trouble. When Bishop Taylor of Lincoln, almost a Lutheran, preached a sermon on the Real Presence with some of which Lambert did not agree, Lambert was there at the foot of the pulpit and tried to start a dispute there and then. Taylor refused to listen and told Lambert to put his criticisms into writing. Lambert did this and produced a point of view very near to that of the Swiss reformer, Zwingli. At this moment Robert Barnes was sitting on a commission charged with the duty of extirpating these 'Sacramentaries'. Taylor sent Lambert's paper to Barnes, who passed it on to Cranmer. Lambert was summoned to appear before Cranmer: very rashly he appealed from Cranmer to the Supreme Head of the Church, Henry VIII himself.

Henry was at this moment anxious to prove to the world that, although he had repudiated the Papacy, he had not repudiated the Catholic faith. What more convincing way than by personally presiding over the trial of an alleged heretic? The trial took place and Henry presided. The trial was not an edifying spectacle. Only the bishops behaved decorously. The king magnificently dominated the scene, but the occasion and perhaps the too similar characters of king and defendant combined to bring out the worst side of Henry's bullying character. Lambert kept his end up for some time, but after standing for five hours he was too weary to make any answers at all. The conclusion was inevitable. To Henry's question, 'Do you believe that in the Sacrament of the Altar is the Body of Christ?', Lambert infuriated the king by replying, 'St Augustine ... ': 'I do not want to know what St Augustine says. What do you believe?' Lambert answered, 'I deny that it is the Body of Christ.' There was no answer to that except the flames of Smithfield.

Further Reading

A. G. Dickens, *The Reformation in England*, 2nd, revised edn, 1989.

H. Maynard Smith, *Henry VIII and the Reformation*, 1948.

LAMBTON, JOHN GEORGE, 1st EARL OF DURHAM (1792-1840), 'Radical Jack', was one of the architects of parliamentary reform and contributed significantly to the idea of responsible government in the empire. He was the son of William Lambton, a Durham landowner whose coal royalties were to make his son the richest commoner in the country. John Lambton was reared a Whig, though influenced less by his father, who died when he was five, than by his tutor Beddoes. To Beddoes, whose revolutionary sympathies had cost him an Oxford professorship, Lambton may have owed his committed and wholehearted liberalism as well as a breadth of thought and reading which marks him off from some of the narrower Whigs – Grey, Althorp or Melbourne, for example. He married as his second wife Lord Grey's daughter and served Grey's interest keenly, although not always tactfully. He shared with Russell, Althorp and Graham the work of shaping and steering the reform bill of 1832. He was chairman of the committee which drafted the bill. Russell introduced it to parliament. The two men were quite different in outlook and character. Russell's main concerns were the elimination of rotten boroughs and further representation for the propertied classes. Lambton, in his patrician way, accepted some of the arguments for democracy.

Concerned about the well-being of miners on his estates, he offered his pits to Humphry Davy for his safety-lamp trials, founded a collieries association to provide old age, sickness and accident benefits, and provided schools and libraries; he even allowed the miners some share in the running of their association. Fifty thousand workmen turned out to follow the coffin at his funeral. We learn, however, from Greville what mistrust Durham aroused in fashionable drawing rooms. He denounces the vulgarity of the democrats 'who are not only wild to have a lord for their leader, but must also have that lord who is the especial incarnation of all those odious qualities which they ascribe, most unjustly, to the order of which he is a member, to wit ... an overweening sense of his greatness and rank'. Creevey, too, found an objectionable pride in the man whom he called 'King Jog' because in 1821 he had been heard to remark that he considered £40,000 a year a moderate income, such as a sensible man should have no difficulty in 'jogging on with'.

Beyond doubt there was a meretricious strain in Lambton. Delicate, emotional, prone to moods of intense irritability and flashes of wild temper, he echoes Byron in the wilful behaviour of his youth. After Eton, his guardians wished him to go to the university; instead he joined the 10th Dragoons. On New Year's Day he eloped to Gretna Green with Lord Cholmondeley's illegitimate daughter. Recklessly hospitable, flamboyant, a lover of the turf, he was a true son of the Whig plutocracy. Beddoes had remarked of his handsome charge, aged nine: 'He has the greatest sensibility I have ever observed in a child' and declared that he was 'as capable of going as far in good or bad as any human being I have ever beheld'.

Lambton only held one ministerial office: he was made Lord Privy Seal under Grey in 1830. He held tenaciously to the reform proposals against all temptations to compromise. The support of the radicals and the political unions strengthened his position. A speaker at the mass meeting of the political unions of the Midlands in Birmingham, in May 1832, said that 'if from treachery or from any other cause, the Bill was lost, he hoped the country would call on Lord Durham to take the seat of power'. Would he then have assumed the leadership of such a revolutionary movement as might have come about in the summer of 1832, if Wellington had returned to office? He never lacked boldness. Since 1819, when, with little support from the official leaders, he first sketched out his plans for reform, which materialized in an abortive bill in 1821, he had been laying the foundations of his alliance with the radicals, and he had kept in touch with men like Place. He was probably right in his contention that the unions were of value in canalizing and giving respectable form to forces which might otherwise turn to violence.

During the last years of his life Durham was generally out of the country. In 1834 he was excluded from Cabinet office by Melbourne, who decided that a diplomatic post would best suit a man disturbingly keen upon change. His conduct in the later stages of Grey's ministry had been hectic and often intolerable, even to his father-in-law. His avowed grievance seems to have been that he was not given a post with great responsibilities; he also demanded an earldom. He was undoubtedly convinced that his had been the main part in ensuring the passage of the Reform Bill. He suffered from painful neuralgia and he had suffered agonizing blows in the deaths, in 1832, of his elder son (the 'Master Lambton' of Lawrence's tender picture) and his daughter Harriet, from consumption. It explains much to add that his father, his first wife, four altogether of his children and ultimately, he too, died of this disease. How should a man, with so many possessions, and such doubtful expectation of life, be patient?

Lambton had encountered the tsar, Nicholas II, when sent to secure his neutrality in the matter of Belgian independence. In 1835 he went to St Petersburg as ambassador. He returned in 1837. The election that followed the accession of Queen Victoria left an attenuated Whig majority: the balance was held by the radicals.

Lambton was sent out to Canada to practise his constitutional ideas on the Canadians. Risings there in November 1837 failed, but grievances festered. The French of Lower Canada and the British of Upper Canada were restless under administrators appointed by Whitehall. At home some English radicals demanded the severance of ties between Canada and the mother country. Durham was reluctant to go abroad again; his health was declining and he dreaded the cold. Perhaps he resented having to leave England when the political situation was so delicate – and promising – at home; nonetheless he responded to the queen's appeal. Durham reached Quebec in May 1838; at once he dealt tactfully with the threat of American intervention by sending Colonel Charles Grey, his brother-in-law, on a personal mission to President van Buren. Rather than risk acquittals by sympathetic juries or resort to the provocation of courts martial, Durham selected eight of the 161 prisoners awaiting trial for rebellion, secured confessions in return for a promise to spare their lives, and banished them to Bermuda. He had no proper jurisdiction and it was on this ground that he was attacked at home, and his ordinance disallowed. Durham resigned when he learned of the circumstances. Brougham had exposed the weak point in his decree in the House of Lords. Melbourne had given way before the radical storm and abandoned the man whom he had sent to Canada with a promise of 'the most firm and unflinching support'.

Durham had made himself liked in Canada. His journeys about the country showed his wish to find out conditions at first hand. He had founded police forces in Montreal and Quebec, set up an efficient land registration system and appointed commissions to look into immigration. He now intended to further their interests at home. He explained exactly why he had to go home and he left Quebec amid expressions of sympathy and respect; a procession of 3,000 followed him to the quayside at Quebec.

Durham arrived to find that public feeling had turned against Melbourne. Once again he could have been the leader round whom radicals and liberals could gather for the assault upon the old Whigs. He did not accept the challenge. He probably saw his first duty as lying with the Canadians – and he was a sick man. It has been wrongly alleged that he did not write the report that appeared under his name and was laid before parliament in February 1839. Undoubtedly he was materially helped by his friend Buller. His ideas reflected closely the views of the philosophical radicals, Grote and Molesworth. But the report was essentially his; so was the boldness which characterized the document. He was not entirely original in his recommendations. The union of Upper and Lower Canada had been suggested to the Cabinet in 1821. The theory that the mother country should be forbearing in the use of imperial authority was at least as old as

Canning, if not Chatham. The prime value of the document was the firm commitment to an extension of responsible government to Canada by a man who had grappled with the problems on the spot and was at the same time versed in the constitutional practice of the mother country. Its main weakness lay in its assessment of the French Canadian situation. He let himself be persuaded that the French community would lose its distinctive character and culture and be absorbed naturally as the legislative union of the two Canadas bore fruit. So the chance was lost of creating a federal union of all the provinces such as was eventually brought about in 1867. Little harm was done by deferring the grant of responsible government. Under the sensible administration of Elgin (Durham's son-in-law by his marriage to Lady Mary Lambton) from 1847 to 1854, it became a fact, though typically by practice and precedent, not by statute.

In May 1840 Lambton set off for Carlsbad to cure his worsening consumption, but he never crossed the channel. He died in July. Inevitably there is an unfinished look about his career. But it was no small thing to have established the future of colonial self-government when so few men beyond his own circle were interested in the idea.

Further Reading

Cambridge History of the British Empire, vol. vi, *Canada and Newfoundland*, 1930.

C. W. New, *Life of Lord Durham*, 1929.

LANCASTER, SIR JAMES (1554/5-1618), mercantile captain, was the son of James Lancaster of Basingstoke, husbandman. In 1571 he became an apprentice in the Skinners' Company, being 'prentice to Blasse from the feast of John the Baptist for ten years'. He was sworn a Freeman of the Company on 10 March 1579, on payment of 3s.4d. His early life was spent in Portugal.

When the Armada set sail, Lancaster commanded the *Edward Bonaventure*, 250 tons, in the English fleet under Drake, but no details of his service seem to be known.

In 1591 he again commanded the *Edward Bonaventure* in the first English voyage to the East Indies. The general of the expedition was George Raymond in the *Penelope*. The fleet set sail on 10 April, much too late in the year, so that it did not arrive at Table Bay until the end of July, the first visit of any English ships to that port. There was so much sickness on board that a month was spent here, but so many died that the *Merchant Royal* was sent home with fifty men and the rest of the crews were split between the other two ships. The story of the voyage is one of disaster on disaster. The *Penelope* was lost off Cape Corrientes (12 September 1591). On the 16th the *Edward Bonaventure*'s mainmast was struck by lightning and four men were killed. She sailed on to Mozambique and the Comoro Islands, where she lost a third of her crew in a surprise attack by natives. At the end of November Lancaster reached Zanzibar and stayed there till mid-February 1592. His plan was to make for Cape Comorin and lie in wait for the shipping plying between Goa and the Portuguese eastern settlements. The ship lost her course, victuals ran short and Lancaster's attempts to make Sokotra, the Laccadives and the Nicobar Islands all failed. In June he reached Sumatra and then made for Penang in order to prey on Portuguese shipping. He lay there till the beginning of September, but his crew suffered much sickness and was reduced to thirty-four, of which only twenty-two were fit for work. He succeeded in taking a Portuguese ship filled with pepper and another filled with rice, and then one from Goa with a varied cargo. He moved away to the Nicobar Islands to take in supplies and then to Ceylon, but his men now insisted on going home. Lancaster was 'very sick, more like to die than to live', and in no condition to enforce his own wishes. In April 1593 they reached St Helena, where provisions and nineteen days' rest restored the crew, but as their morale rose their discipline fell, they got out of hand and made for England. Foul winds delayed their passage, provisions again ran short and in desperation Lancaster made for Trinidad. No supplies were available here, but in June he reached Mona and was provisioned by some French ships. He then set sail for Newfoundland to make contact with the fishing fleets, but the wind drove him back to the West Indies and he was again at Mona in November. Lancaster and his second in command, Barker, landed in order to get supplies, leaving six sailors on board. These men cut the cable and sailed off to San Domingo, where they surrendered the ship to the Spaniards.

For a month Lancaster and his party of eighteen were marooned with only vegetables to eat. Then twelve were taken off by two French ships, and Lancaster was one of them. They remained off San Domingo until April 1594; then Lancaster and Barker got a passage home in another French ship commanded by Jean Lenoir which reached Dieppe on 19 May. On the 24th Lancaster reached Rye in Sussex after having been away for three years. It is usually said that the voyage was financially a great success. There is not the slightest evidence that this was so. What Lancaster had succeeded in doing was to penetrate into the Indian Ocean as far as the Malay peninsula without any opposition from the Portuguese. Out of the 198 men who set sail only twenty-five returned to England.

Within five months Lancaster was at sea again with three ships financed by London merchants. Lancaster commanded the *Consent*, 240 tons, Barker commanded the *Solomon*, 170 tons, and a third ship went with them, the *Virgin*, sixty tons. The objectives of the expedition were to raid the Portuguese possessions in Brazil (Pernambuco) and to capture Spanish and Portuguese

LANCASTER, JOSEPH / 773

shipping throughout the voyage. This expedition was a great success and paid a high dividend. Pernambuco was reached on 18 April 1595, and the town was taken and held until all the merchandise in the warehouses had been transferred to Lancaster's ships. The booty was far too great for his ships to accommodate all of it. At that moment by good chance Jean Lenoir turned up and joined his ships to Lancaster's. An arrangement was made with some Dutch ships to carry the rest of the spoils home, and Lancaster was just about to sail when he heard that the Portuguese were building a redoubt at the mouth of the harbour. Lancaster was for ignoring it, but his companions thought it necessary to capture it. Lancaster was too ill to lead the attack himself, which he entrusted to Cotton, Barker and Lenoir with some 300 men. He gave them strict orders never to go beyond the range of the English guns. The redoubt was easily taken; then the force began to chase the enemy and soon found itself faced with a superior force far out of range of the English ships. Cotton, Barker and Lenoir were killed and some thirty-five men. Lancaster set sail at once and reached England in July 1595 after a most profitable expedition.

For four years nothing is heard of Lancaster except that in 1598 he was one of the managers of Cumberland's twelfth expedition. Then in 1601 Lancaster was selected to lead the first expedition sent out by the new East India Company.

It is not possible here to give a detailed account of this long and dangerous voyage. It was an aggressive expedition planned with the object of spoiling the Portuguese, and it was much helped by the friendly co-operation of the Dutch, who hated the Portuguese quite as much as did the English (*Mariner's Mirror*, xviii, 4, October 1932). Five ships were employed: Lancaster was 'General of the Voyage' and commanded the *Red Dragon* (this was Cumberland's old *Malice Scourge*, 600 tons). His crew numbered 202 men and the guns forty. In all 480 men set sail, of whom more than 180 died before the ships started back for England and at least half of the 480 never returned home.

The fleet sailed from Tor Bay on 20 April 1601. By September it had reached Saldanha Bay, but all the crews were suffering from scurvy, 'the plague of the sea and the spoil of mariners' (Sir Richard Hawkins). Lancaster's crew was in much better shape than the others because he had taken bottled lime juice with him as an experiment – the first sailor to do this. By 29 October 107 men had died. By Christmas Day eighteen more were lost. Discontent grew among the men, and five men stole a boat and tried to desert, but they were caught. The fleet reached Sumatra in June 1602, and here Lancaster had a most satisfactory interview with the nonagenarian King of Achin, Alauddin, who was delighted with the presents given to him and with the letters which Queen

Elizabeth had sent him. Commercial privileges were easily granted to the East India Company, but very little pepper was to be had. However, on 3 October a rich carrack was captured and the cargo was transferred to Lancaster's ships; the carrack was then returned to the Portuguese, who much appreciated this 'courtesy'.

Lancaster then sailed for Priaman, where he found the *Susan* ready to return to England with a large cargo of pepper and cloves. Sending her home independently, Lancaster moved on to Bantam, 1,000 miles from Achin. The king here was a boy of nine years old, trading privileges were granted; in five weeks the ships were laden with a huge cargo; and the first 'factory' of the East India Company was settled at Bantam.

The return journey was made with the utmost difficulty: bad storms, contrary winds, leaky ships, rudders lost and the ever-present fear of mutiny justified Lancaster's description of the voyage on his return to England in September 1603, when he gave thanks that he had been 'delivered from infinite perils and dangers in this long and tedious navigation'.

Lancaster was knighted in 1603 and gave his time and attention to organizing the affairs of the East India Company. He was also interested in the search for the North-West Passage, and Baffin gave the name of Lancaster to one of the sounds in the north-west (1616). Lancaster died on 6 June 1618, a wealthy man. He left most of his money to charities (he was never married and therefore had no claimants), some of which are administered today by the Skinners' Company.

Further Reading
Sir William Foster, *The Voyages of Sir James Lancaster*, Hakluyt Society, 1940.

LANCASTER, JOSEPH (1778-1838) was a pioneer in the field of elementary education at a time when the growth of population was not accompanied by any serious attempt by church or state to provide teaching facilities. Private enterprise had to supply the need. Whatever his faults, Lancaster was both enterprising and charitable. His father was a private soldier who served in the American War. Joseph was intended for the nonconformist ministry, but at fourteen he left home with the intention, it seems, of going 'to teach poor blacks the word of God'. Penniless at Bristol, he joined the navy; after one voyage he was released from his engagement by friends. He became a Quaker and began a little teaching at home.

In 1801 he opened a school in London, offering free education to those who could not afford his modest fee. To deal with the large numbers who came, since he could not afford to hire an assistant, he set senior boys to teach the junior ones under his supervision. He managed to instil a strong spirit of community and self-help. The instruction was necessarily simple: reading, writing and arithmetic were learned by drill. The children were given flat desks with layers of sand to write on; large letter sheets and printed passages of the Bible were their only aids. There were elaborate punishments on the principle that it was better to shame than to pain. Boys were suspended in cages and tied to pillars; they were also encouraged by orders of merit and systematic promotion, while promising scholars were prepared for teaching.

In 1797 Andrew Bell had written his account of his work in the Madras orphanage where he had used a similar method of pupil-teaching. At first, when he came home, he approved of Lancaster's work. The Quaker found himself famous. Visitors were impressed by the discipline of an establishment of almost 1,000, where a child could be taught for an estimated cost of seven shillings a year. At an audience at Weymouth in 1805 George III told Lancaster that it was his wish 'that every poor child in my dominions should be taught to read the Bible'. The religious argument could also be used against Lancaster. To opponents like the formidable Mrs Trimmer it was the main fault of his system that it was not subject to church control.

Andrew Bell, founder of the 'Madras system' of teaching, became his relentless opponent and with the formation of rival societies a feud developed which enlisted support from nonconformists, Radicals and Whigs on Lancaster's side, Tories and church establishment on Bell's. Brougham saw in Lancaster a leader in the 'march of mind'; Southey admitted that great good had been done, but only in the way that 'the devil has been the cause of Redemption'. Lancaster was copied. In 1810 he claimed to have promoted fifty schools for 14,200 children. The more extravagant his claims, the more unpractical he became about ways and means. In 1808 Fox and Allen, Quaker philanthropists, came to the rescue of his school and the Royal Lancastrian Society was set up with a board of trustees. Lancaster claimed that he was being overruled by the trustees and seceded from his own movement: he set up a school at Tooting, which soon failed.

Thereafter his life was spent in travelling, pontificating about his methods and quarrelling with those who disagreed with him. He was imprisoned for debt and his wife went out of her mind. He found listeners and imitators in the United States, Canada and Venezuela. He established a school, which failed, in Montreal, received promises from Bolivar which led to further disappointment. He wrote pamphlets obsessively and self-pityingly, in the way of a frenzied pedagogue, with plentiful use of italics, capitals and irrelevant biblical quotations. One cannot help but admire his persistence. 'Be assured that the fire which kindled Elijah's sacrifice has kindled mine', he wrote. Wherever he was, even when he was alone, he would keep his Quaker Sunday morning of silence and 'waiting on the spirit'. In October 1838 he died of injuries received in a street accident in New York. We should look away from the forlorn end to the earlier achievement. His intentions had been unselfish, his method both original and, within its limits, effective. His schools at their best were comradely places of mutual instruction. He had done much to reveal the need and had pointed to ways in which it could be met.

Further Reading
M. G. Jones, *The Charity School Movement*, 1938.
D. Salmon, *Joseph Lancaster*, 1904.

LANDOR, WALTER SAVAGE (1775-1864) was a gifted author; also a fine-looking, thin-skinned, irascible man, whose life was much taken up with quarrels: with his father, Rugby schoolmasters, Oxford dons, wife, Welsh tenants – indeed any person or authority in a position to offend him; also, however, a man whose long life was adorned by some notable friendships in his literary world.

Standing eccentrically alone, having the means to buy the estate of Lanthony with its ruined abbey, and to write without needing to, he was a compound of classic and romantic: an accomplished Latinist, his choice of classical subjects was conditioned by romantic influences. Neither his epic *Gebir*, for example, nor his drama *Count Julian*, is classical in shape or spirit. Some of his early lyrics, plays and heroic poems were translations from his own Latin. His aim in poems was to achieve perfection of form and it was only in disenchanted middle age, as he despaired of winning readers, that he affected to regard poetry simply as an amusement. To the last, to quote George Sainsbury, who finds felicities in the shorter poems, even in single lines in the longer, uneven works, 'he retained that strange occasional command of perfect phrase which was his special merit and privilege'.

It is, however, for his prose that Landor is now best remembered, and the best of it is to be found in *Imaginary Conversations*. Two volumes appeared in 1824, a third in 1828, and he went on adding to them almost to the end. Again the reader has to be selective, allowing for the crotchets and prejudices, the kind of impetuous harangue that Dickens portrayed – and it was instantly recognized – in *Bleak House*'s Mr Boythorne. He may find himself in the impressive train of admirers, from Southey and nearly all of the romantic generation, to Browning, Tennyson and Dickens and, most enthusiastic of all, Swinburne. Or he may be one of the many whom this most fastidious of writers expected to remain uncharmed. They may indeed miss in Landor, among so much that is pretty and charming, that which is to be found in the best critics: the comment that is truly enlightening, and the passion that can communicate at the deepest level of feeling. It is significant that Hazlitt, who was such a critic, found him wanting in those respects. But Landor, who looked always to have the last word, should be allowed it here: 'I shall dine late but the room will be well lighted and the guests few but select'. This was the man who had written to the Bishop of St David's, ungraciously tardy in reply to Landor's offer to restore Llanthony church: 'God alone is great enough for me to ask anything of twice.'

Further Reading
Malcolm Elvin, *Landor*, 1958.

LANDSEER, SIR EDWIN HENRY (1802-73), animal-painter, was born into a family of artists. His father was a well-known engraver, his eldest brother became another: and two other brothers were artists. His mother had sat to Sir Joshua Reynolds.

As soon as he could walk, he was taken by his father to Hampstead Heath to sketch animals. Drawings now in the Natural History Museum show that he was an excellent draughtsman before he was ten. He exhibited at the Royal Academy first at the age of thirteen; at fourteen he became a student there. He was a favourite pupil of the great Fuseli, who would look about the crowded drawing-school, and ask: 'Where is my curly-headed dog-boy?'

Meanwhile, he was drawing the wild animals kept (in those days) in the Tower of London and in the other menagerie at Exeter Change. He went further, and dissected every animal whose carcass he could obtain. He and the artist J. F. Lewis bought a newly-deceased lion from the menagerie, and worked on it until the neighbours revolted at the smell. And Charles Dickens, much later, used to relate how Landseer's manservant had come in on Landseer and a company of guests, to say: 'Did you order a lion, sir?' The result of all this preparation was an uncanny dexterity in depicting animals. He came to know his subjects – his 'sitters' – so well that he could work very fast from memory, and yet with meticulous accuracy, in the drawing of fur, feather or pelt, musculature and anatomy. He was spoken of as a second Stubbs. His fame spread rapidly, as his father and brother distributed engravings of his work.

In 1824 he sold *The Cat's Paw* for £100: a sum sufficiently large (though later he could charge ten times that) to enable him to buy No. 1 St John's Wood Road, where he lived for the rest of his life, surrounded (he never married) by various members of his family. But it is the subject of *The Cat's Paw* – the story of the monkey who forces a cat to rake for him roasted chestnuts out of a hot fire – that proclaimed not only an artist with an unusual knowledge of animal anatomy, but a shift of direction in his style. From now on, Landseer moves away from painting animals as animals per se: they come to be used as vehicles for the expression of sentiment –

and his sentiment descends sometimes to sentimentality. In particular, he begins to give animals *human* feelings and qualities: pity, nobility, irony, vulgarity. A painting of 1839 shows two dogs sharing a kennel, and is called *Dignity and Impudence*. Thus strict observation and 'naturalness' yielded to a style which was criticized as tendentious, but won immense popularity for the artist – from a public who either loved animals or hunted them for sport. Eventually, the Victorian traveller was accustomed to find in every parlour a print of *Jack in Office* (1833), for example, or *The Old Shepherd's Chief Mourner* (1837), *The Stag at Bay* (1846) or *The Monarch of the Glen* (1851). The last two are triumphant tributes to the animal aristocrats of the Highlands.

Stories are told of his incredible speed of execution, and of his dexterity: how he once drew simultaneously, for a lady who said it was impossible, an antlered stag with one hand, and the head of a horse with the other. The Royal Collection has a very remarkable painting of his. The famous lion-tamer Isaac van Amburgh lies in a cage surrounded by lions, a tiger and two leopards. At his side he consoles a lamb, who is surprised to find himself in this savage company. The colouring is dull – sober browns and reds: Landseer was no colourist. But the painting of the 'great cats' is a perfect illustration of Ruskin's view that 'There is in every animal's eye a dim image and gleam of humanity, a flash of strange light through which their life looks out and up to our great mystery of command over them, and claims the fellowship of the creature if not of the soul'.

Landseer was a portrait-painter too, and a landscapist. He first went to the Highlands of Scotland in 1824, was captivated, and returned as often as he could. There are in the Tate Gallery some affectionate sketches from these holidays; and of course landscape plays an important role in some of his best known pictures. He was also a sculptor. The Duchess of Abercorn, going to visit him at St John's Wood, found him in the garden, working from a ladder on a huge mass of clay. Also in the garden was a full-grown lion – at liberty – brought up from the Zoo for the day: fortunately 'an elderly and peculiarly docile lion', who was modelling for his bronze brethren, known the world over, who guard the base of Nelson's Column in Trafalgar Square.

Landseer was a favourite of Queen Victoria and Prince Albert, and was knighted in 1850. In spite, however, of his success, and of an amusing, buoyant temperament which won him countless friends, he suffered from periodic depressions and even breakdowns. This probably accounts for his refusing the Presidency of the Royal Academy when he was offered it in 1865. He was badly knocked around in a railway-accident in 1868. In his last years, he became dangerously deranged, and would have been confined if he had not been accompanied night and day by medical attendants – and by a

Mrs Pritchard, an elderly neighbour, almost the only person who could control him by her tongue alone.

Further Reading
Richard Ormond, *Sir Edwin Landseer*, 1981.

LANFRANC OF PAVIA (*c*.1010-89; Archbishop of Canterbury 1070-89) by circumstance and skill was one of the most influential Archbishops of Canterbury. After the Norman Conquest, his political alliance and personal friendship with William I reset the pattern of church/state relations which, despite a few well-publicized exceptions, were characterized by co-operation. Lanfranc maintained the intimacy between king and archbishop which had been established by Dunstan and Edgar a century earlier. Jealous of his authority within the church, where his concentration on rights and canon law bred episcopal arrogance and rancour, when the ecclesiastical and secular worlds met, Lanfranc saw his role as the king's adviser, not challenger or competitor. He expressed this policy succinctly, the Latin giving a flavour of the clarity and vigour of his mind: '*contra preceptum regis nil rogare et nil iubere praesumo*' ('I cannot take the responsibility for giving any directive or order that is contrary to the king's instructions').

In 1070, William I engineered the deposition of Archbishop Stigand, ostensibly on the canonical grounds of irregular appointment and pluralism, but in reality because of Stigand's suspect loyalty. The king's choice of successor was risky yet understandable. Lanfranc was an ageing monk and scholar whose administrative and political experience had been confined to the world of Norman monasteries. Yet, as abbot of the ducal foundation of St Etienne at Caen, he was an intimate of William's household and family. From William's perspective, Lanfranc offered the moral integrity of a monk; the personal devotion of a friend; and the clarity of intellect and purpose of a lawyer. Although Lanfranc was never really at home in England, he effectively managed to mould the English church as he and his master desired.

Lanfranc's early career was not one which suggested his later hierarchical eminence. In the early eleventh century important western European bishops were usually from the ranks of the high nobility and, except in tenth-century England, tended to be secular clerks, not monks. Even in England, the habit of appointing monks as bishops was waning in the decades before the Conquest. Lanfranc, from an urban professional background, had begun his career as a student of law in northern Italy. About 1030, he crossed the Alps into Burgundy and France where he seems to have studied and perhaps taught the traditional trivium – grammar, rhetoric and logic – before settling to teach at Avranches *c*.1039. Around 1042, Lanfranc underwent a conversion and

joined the religious community at Bec where, despite his complaints about its lack of eremitic rigour, he stayed for twenty years, from *c*.1045 as prior. During the 1050s he resumed teaching, his interests still centred on law, grammar and rhetoric, traditional subjects to which he contributed little that was not soon superseded. Although he engaged in controversy, attacking Berengar of Tours' views on the Eucharist in the 1060s, Lanfranc as an academic, and later as a churchman, was a conservative. Unlike his successor as Prior of Bec and archbishop, Anselm of Aosta, Lanfranc did not engage in the higher flights of speculative philosophy or theology. However, as an expert in canon law, Lanfranc was concerned with ecclesiastical discipline and the moral standard of the clergy. In this he was in tune with contemporary church reformers who enjoyed the support of Duke William and made him a suitable candidate in 1063 for the abbacy of the duke's Abbey of St Etienne, the so-called Abbaye-aux-Hommes, at Caen.

As in Normandy, Lanfranc's policies in England were those of an old-fashioned reformer, looking to a partnership with the secular ruler to achieve an improvement in the organization, manners, morals and buildings of the clergy. In his insistence on legal precedent and rights, Lanfranc had much in common with the reformers who, in the late 1040s had captured the papacy, their vociferous campaign against the abuses of simony, lay investiture and clerical marriage reaching a crescendo during the pontificate of Gregory VII (1073-85), after whom the movement is commonly known. But on the issue of authority and the subjugation of temporal to spiritual power, Lanfranc parted company with the Gregorians who wished to enforce fealty from secular rulers and subservience from the ecclesiastical hierarchy. Thus in 1080, Lanfranc was not prepared to agree that the King of England was, by virtue of the payment of Peter's Pence, an annual gift to the pope, a papal vassal. Equally, within the church Lanfranc respected the pope's position, but not without qualification. As he wrote to Pope Gregory: 'I am ready to yield obedience to your commands in everything *according to the canons*' (italics added). Throughout his reign, Lanfranc maintained mutual support with the king and the independent rights of Canterbury.

Lanfranc's rule of the English church mirrored and sustained the secular conquest of the country. Like the king, he pursued his rights through law and, failing that, violence. In 1088, when meeting resistance from the monks of St Augustine's, Canterbury to his nominee as abbot, he dispersed some of them, imprisoned others and had one publicly flogged: 'thus did Lanfranc enforce obedience, and so long as he lived he broke down the opposition of the rest by dread of his name'. He presided over an almost wholesale exclusion of Englishmen from the highest posts in the church: not one native was appointed to a see during his nineteen years at Canterbury. He sponsored the introduction of continental monastic practices, and even some foreign monks. Where William built castles, Lanfranc encouraged the construction of new cathedrals which in their size and austere regularity of design were visible symbols of the new order in church as in state. Using the model of his abbey at Caen (and importing stone from there too), Lanfranc rebuilt his own cathedral in the 1070s on a grand scale, dedicated to Christ Himself. At Canterbury, he disparaged English saints, removing their relics from the cathedral and their names from the calendar of feast days. Even St Dunstan was demoted in this fashion and he thought so little of local sentiment that Archbishop Aelfheah, murdered by the Danes in 1012, only narrowly avoided a similar fate. Some of his early predecessors and other saints from the heroic age of the Conversion Lanfranc moved to his new foundation of St Gregory's which thereby was lent an instant, potentially lucrative, if spurious aura of venerable sanctity. At the very least there was an intrusively abrasive quality about Lanfranc's behaviour. As the Canterbury monk Eadmer (who revered Aelfheah as a 'holy martyr') commented, Lanfranc was 'a somewhat unfinished Englishman' (*quasi rudis Anglus*). In this he was just like most of the others who ruled the kingdom after 1066.

Yet if he had little time for English customs, he was unflagging in establishing what he saw as the traditional rights of his office. Claiming primacy over all Britain, in addition to English prelates he consecrated, either personally or by delegation, Irish and Orcadian bishops. In 1072, he secured a papal judgement acknowledging the supremacy of Canterbury over York, although this failed to resolve what became one of the longest running ecclesiastical feuds in Europe. The method of establishing Canterbury's primacy shows Lanfranc at his most characteristic. The case was heard at a council presided over by the king, held at Winchester, at which Lanfranc, the lawyer to his core, produced an impressive array of evidence, including chronicles, Bede's *Ecclesiastical History*, and papal privileges (possibly forged for the purpose).

Canterbury's temporal rights were not neglected either. At the famous trial at Penenden Heath (1072 or, possibly, 1075/6), Lanfranc not only made good his claim to certain estates in Kent against Odo of Bayeux and others, but also, in the words of one account, 'vindicated afresh the liberties of his church and the customary jurisdiction which he was entitled to exercise' over his lands. The judgement effectively recognized the immunity of Lanfranc's lands from the scrutiny of royal officials.

In ruling the church, Lanfranc was equally keen to establish a legal basis, often agreed at church councils, of which he held seven. At Winchester in 1072, apart from the dispute with York, issues of the church

calendar, simony, wandering clergy and monks, treason and an instruction to secular priests to say masses for the king (an extension of tenth-century English practice) were discussed. The Council of London in 1075 was the largest of the reign chaired, in the absence of the king, by Lanfranc himself. The main business was the transfer of sees, usually to towns, a sign of both political necessity and the growing urbanization of England: Sherborne to Old Sarum; Selsey to Chichester; Lichfield to Chester; Dorchester-on-Thames to Lincoln and North Elmham to Norwich. Characteristically, justification for these removals was found in precedent and canon law. The latter also provided the basis for decisions on pastoral care; discipline of the clergy; good order within monasteries; lay marriage customs; and, even, prohibitions on white magic : 'the bones of dead animals must not be hung up anywhere as a charm against cattle-disease'.

However, despite such admirably reformist procedures, it is salutary – and very far from the Gregorian ideal – to note that the removal of spiritual pleas from secular to episcopal courts 'according to the precepts of the holy canons' was ordered by royal writ. All that Lanfranc achieved was in the context of royal power. Whatever independence he had in church matters was delegated from the king, a situation typical of both England and the continent over the previous century and more. What was different was Lanfranc's insistence upon legal, canonical precedent and his grip of the church structure expressed through patronage, regular meetings with his fellow bishops and occasional church councils.

Much of this successful exercise of archiepiscopal *auctoritas* depended on Lanfranc's own personality and his willingness to identify his interests with those of the king. At least twice, in facing down the serious rebellion of 1075 in the king's absence and in the securing of the succession of William II in England in 1087-8, his active political support for the monarch was crucial. His loyalty, on a public level, is understandable. One great advantage Lanfranc had as archbishop was that he had no independent network of influence, patronage or power. He had no family or landed connections in the Anglo-Norman nobility. He was unaffected by faction as all he had came from the king's favour. Thus isolated, Lanfranc, as has recently been written, 'could only be the king's man'.

That he embraced this position with enthusiasm cannot be doubted. He was one of the few men that William I trusted and cherished: on one occasion Lanfranc was forced to rest and submit to a medical régime 'on the king's orders'. No less important was his concept of obedience and hierarchy. At the trial of the rebel Bishop of Durham in 1088 against William II, Lanfranc adopted a position entirely at odds with Gregorianism: 'We judge the bishop not as a bishop but as a vassal, as we judged

Odo of Bayeux [in 1082] … by his original breach of faith and by accusing the king's magnates of deceit the bishop has lost the safe-conduct which he has invoked'. This outburst provoked spontaneous applause from the king's barons who shouted 'Seize the bishop! The old bloodhound's right!' For Lanfranc, the right order of the world was one which recognized the importance of the secular ruler in maintaining peace: that was not a function of a monk. Early in the 1070s he summed up his view: 'While the king lives we have peace of a kind, but after his death we expect to have neither peace nor any other benefit'. Lanfranc saw temporal things as ephemeral, papal pretensions to dominate the world no less transitory than those of princes.

From the sources, Lanfranc does not emerge as a particularly warm or attractive personality. He was apparently uninterested in the spiritual life of the laity, more concerned with legally proper forms of administration and organization. His contempt for local English cults is revealing. Even his apparently generous gesture in allowing women who had fled to nunneries 'for fear of the Normans' to re-enter the world and marry was dictated by pragmatism and an acknowledgement of the legal as well as emotional fragility of vows made under exceptional compulsion. To Lanfranc's obsession with legality and rights and his creation of an ambitious, able but self-conscious episcopal elite has been attributed one of the least creditable yet most tenacious aspects of the post-Conquest church; the endless round of infra-ecclesiastical litigation and bickering over shares in the church's chest of temporal wealth, jurisdiction, status and power. Lanfranc could be cruel and, if not necessarily vindictive, then sternly unyielding. Small wonder he and William I got on so well. Yet although he contributed much to royal government, for all his forensic intellectual skills and his legal clarity of language, he kept his independence. Unlike Geoffrey of Coutances or Odo of Bayeux, he was never a glorified member of the king's administration. He rarely even witnessed royal charters.

The apparent contradictions of medieval monks who adopted public roles are probably impenetrable to modern observers. Yet for all his worldly prestige, wealth and power, Lanfranc's monastic vocation was central to his personality and, hence, his effectiveness. Unlike some famous medieval holy men, he did not flaunt his spirituality. Neither did contemporaries accuse him of hypocrisy. He belonged to a generation of monks less self-consciously obsessed with their own virtue than their successors. He reconciled his public labours and private faith through a sense of rectitude which could be unforgiving but was untainted by self-righteousness. In England he was able to avoid the posturing of the continental Investiture Contest partly because he achieved what the militants of Gregorianism missed entirely. He was able to see that necessary political action for the benefit, as he saw it, of God's church was not dependent on the constant scrutiny of first principles which owed nothing to accepted precedence, custom or efficiency. If anything, his legacy to the church in England consists of a pragmatic and independent appreciation and application of universal canon law which encompassed both royal control and ecclesiastical autonomy.

Further Reading
H. Clover and M. Gibson, *The Letters of Lanfranc*, 1979.
M. Gibson, *Lanfranc of Bec*, 1978.

LANGLEY, THOMAS (*c*.1360-1437), Bishop of Durham from 1406, was propelled to high ministerial office by the Lancastrian usurpation of the Crown. Apparently a younger son of a cadet branch of a gentry family from Langley near Manchester, he proceeded via the service of the Radcliffes of Radcliffe into that of John of Gaunt and the Lancastrian kings. 'To No-one of these Duchy servants was the triumph of Henry of Derby to bring greater success than to Thomas Langley'. Appointed his secretary, he became keeper of the privy seal – third of the great ministers of state – in 1401, and Chancellor of England and principal royal diplomat in 1405-7. He had accompanied Henry to Scotland in 1400 and to the battle of Shrewsbury in 1403. He was again the leading diplomat in 1412-17, served again as chancellor in 1417-24 – an exceptionally long term distinguished by the marked expansion of the court of chancery – and was a royal councillor until finally allowed to retire in 1433. Diplomatic duties on the northern border continued until death. Essentially an administrator devoted to the house of Lancaster, he avoided taking sides in the crises of 1410-12 and 1426 and was rightly trusted by each master in turn. He was executor of John of Gaunt, Henry IV and Henry V, and continued settling their affairs until at least 1436, 1429, and 1435 respectively.

Langley was bearded and had an aristocratic love of the chase and splendour rather than the noble connections and university education increasingly expected of a bishop. Obviously he was not illiterate. He acquired a collection of books useful to his position and patronized schooling for others. His first rectory at Radcliffe in 1385 was followed by two prebends, thanks to John of Gaunt, but it was only after 1399 that his ecclesiastical career really took off. Chief among his new positions were the archdeaconry of Norfolk and deanery of York, which he seems, unusually, to have treated as more than sinecures, but he had to wait for his bishopric. Pope Innocent VII thwarted him at London and York before he secured the important and valuable bishopric of Durham in 1406. This was obviously a reward for administrative services, but he took his responsibilities more seriously than most, for he went to Durham twice a year even when chancellor, spent long periods there at other times, and showed close and continual interest in its management. He overhauled the administration of his see, enjoyed good relations with his cathedral priory and contributed generously to its building operations. In his last years he rebuffed Sir William Eure's attack on his regalian rights as Count Palatine of Durham. 'The most outstanding feature of Langley's episcopate was his work to reform the secular foundations.' This was designed to adapt outdated institutions for modern needs. Earlier he had helped Lord Delaware to found Manchester College and Henry V to found Syon Abbey and he himself established chantries and schools both at Durham and Middleton (Lancs.). He even shone on the international ecclesiastical scene, for he attended the council of Pisa in 1409 as representative of the northern province and attorney for fourteen bishops and 103 abbots and priors, and he was offered the cardinalate in 1411, which Henry IV declined on his behalf. He was a civil servant who proved a thoroughly worthy bishop.

Langley was conscientious and meticulous over every detail. He possessed great physical and mental energy and enjoyed good health until the very end. He was trustworthy and thus a frequent choice as executor. Rigid on principles and harsh with the unrepentant, he possessed the flexibility necessary for a diplomat and the patience required of a pastor. He remained loyal to Lancashire, liked to have Lancashiremen about him, and genuinely cared what happened to old friends and to members of his household on his death. In a lifetime in politics he made no personal enemies.

Further Reading

R. L. Storey, *Thomas Langley and the Bishopric of Durham 1406-1437*, 1961.

LANGTON, STEPHEN (*c.*1165-1228; Archbishop of Canterbury 1207-28), one of the foremost biblical scholars of his time, found himself, through little fault of his own, one of the most controversial Archbishops of Canterbury at the centre of the most serious and acrimonious dispute between the King of England and the pope in the Middle Ages. Born in Lincolnshire, Langton studied in Paris in the 1180s, remaining there to teach and write. The schools of Paris then attracted the intellectual and ambitious elite of western Europe. One of Langton's fellow students was a well-connected Italian nobleman, Lothar dei Conti of Segni who, as Pope Innocent III (1198-1216), was to determine the course of his later career. Together, the two of them may well have visited the Canterbury shrine of Thomas Becket, a saint for whom Langton held a persistent, patriotic admiration.

Langton's academic studies were mainly scriptural. Although his *Quaestiones*, which revealed a practical mind when applied to textual or theological problems, were popular, his fame rested upon his preaching and his work as a biblical commentator, his reorganization of the

chapters of the Bible in the late 1190s gradually winning general acceptance across the whole of western Christendom. His other works included religious verses such as the hymn *Veni, Sancta Spiritus*. A later English chronicler ascribed to Langton, somewhat improbably, a life of Richard I. Orthodox and unoriginal, it is unlikely that it was his pedagogic influence that led to his only pupil known by name, one Master Guerin of Corbeil, to be condemned for heresy in 1210. Langton, whose academic reputation was recognized by preferment to canonries at Paris and York, was typical of a group of his Paris contemporaries, including fellow Englishman Robert of Courçon (i.e. Curzon). Not satisfied with purely speculative theology, Langton and his colleagues were concerned with the systematizing of doctrine and its application to the actual world: one of his own famous sermons was on usury. Of particular relevance to the future was Langton's teaching at Paris that it was lawful to resist a tyrannical king who acted by his own will, not the law, a precept he had to defend in practice as King John's archbishop.

This pragmatic quality, allied to occasionally inflexible intellectual rigour, was characteristic of a generation of ecclesiastics which came to the fore under Innocent III. Among these Langton was prominent. In 1206, he was appointed Cardinal Priest of St Chrysogonus (an obscure, possibly fictional martyr of the early fourth century), testimony to his Parisian eminence. The timing was fortuitous. By the end of the year Langton had been elected Archbishop of Canterbury after an almost unprecedented display of papal authority. After the death of the previous archbishop, Hubert Walter, in 1205, one faction among the monks of Christ Church, Canterbury had elected their fellow monk Reginald, another the king's candidate, John de Gray. The parties appealed to Rome, where Innocent set aside both candidates and presided over the election, by the Canterbury monks present at the Papal Curia, of Cardinal Langton, who was in Rome at the time. The new archbishop was consecrated by the pope at Viterbo in June 1207. According to the agreements reached between English kings and the papacy over the previous century, although the election by the monks was canonical, the consecration, without royal assent, broke accepted precedent. King John felt his rights of patronage and hence control over the English church were threatened; he refused to recognize Langton as archbishop.

This led to a bitter six-year conflict, with Langton, except for a brief foray to Dover in 1209, exiled from England. Significantly and deliberately, he spent much of this period at the Cistercian monastery at Pontigny where Becket had stayed in the 1160s. King John was excommunicated and England placed under a papal Interdict. Deadlock was only ended in 1213 by the pope's threat to depose John at the very time the king's plans to recover his lost patrimony in France were nearing fruition. Faced by a possible papally sponsored French invasion, King John yielded in May 1213, receiving absolution from Langton himself in July.

Having been a symbol of a papal vision of ecclesiastical authority, Langton in office proved to be his own man. From 1213-15, he clashed with successive papal legates, a result of the novel and anomalous circumstance of the king having submitted his kingdom to papal overlordship as a price of reconciliation in 1213. From being the traditional head of the church, the archbishop now had to contend with a papal representative whose main brief was to support a now-faithful papal vassal, the king. In 1213/14, Langton clashed with Legate Nicholas over the extent of royal patronage. During the early months of 1215, Langton attempted to mediate between John and the rebellious magnates. According to the unreliable St Albans chronicler, Roger of Wendover, Langton suggested the Coronation Charter of Henry I as a legitimate basis for the baronial demands against the king. This is credible, if only because two years earlier Langton had presided over the council of St Albans where John had sworn to abide by the laws of Henry I, by which may have meant the Coronation Charter. Whatever his role in drafting Magna Carta, Langton's failure to support the king wholeheartedly excited the anger of the pope and led to the archbishop's suspension by Legate Pandulf and summons to Rome. After attending the Fourth Lateran Council, Langton remained abroad from 1215 until 1218. He had demonstrated that, like other occupants of the chair of St Augustine, he possessed inconvenient singlemindedness.

The political landscape to which he returned was very different from that which he had left. The minority government of William Marshal operated on the basis of consent rather than coercion. After the Marshal's death in 1219, Langton continued as an ally of the justiciar, Hubert de Burgh, in protecting the authority of the Crown, in particular against former partisans of King John such as Falkes de Bréauté. He remained wedded to finding just agreement between magnates and king: between 1221 and 1223, he played a leading role in mediating between the young Henry III's counsellors; in 1223, he called for the reissuing of Magna Carta, as he did again in 1225 in return for support for a fifteenth for a campaign in Poitou. In 1223, in order to bolster the independent effectiveness of the king's government, he helped secure the papal bull which granted Henry III control of his own seal.

As archbishop, Langton proved loyal to the traditions of his office and the national church. He recrowned Henry in 1220 (the Legate Guala and the Bishop of Winchester had performed an unavoidably perfunctory ceremony in the dark days of 1216). In 1221, he persuaded Pope Honorius III (1216-27) to remove the resident papal legate; to limit papal provisions in England, a system whereby the pope imposed candidates to benefices, often absentees or papal cronies; and to restate the superiority of Canterbury over York. In 1226, Langton further emphasized his independence by resisting an attempt to reserve a prebend in each collegiate church for papal funds. In tune with the reforms encouraged by Innocent III at the Fourth Lateran Council, probably at an assembly held at Osney Abbey near Oxford in 1222, Langton issues a set of Constitutions concerning ecclesiastical discipline and organization which were widely imitated across the English dioceses over the next generation.

By the time of his death in 1228, Langton had shown himself as a constructive church leader and a politician of pragmatism. He was no Becket. Unlike the martyr, whose relics he moved to a new shrine amidst great ceremony in 1220, he sought to translate general principles into effective practice. If he lacked the silken skills of the adept political infighter, he also lacked the brittle priggishness of many intellectuals in public life. It is rare for such a distinguished academic to cope even as well as Langton with the pressures of political leadership, but in this, as in much else, Langton conformed to the reforming approach and programme of his circle of Parisian scholars and of Innocent III in particular. It is often said that Innocent's pontificate marked the apogee of papal monarchy in the Middle Ages. If so, his success and lasting influence depended on men of the calibre of Stephen Langton.

But Langton was not simply a general in the papal army, however much he came to symbolize the pope's claims to authority in Christendom during the dispute with King John. As a figurehead for Innocent III's vision of the world order, he could encounter trouble, as on the occasion one of his sermons was heckled shortly after his return to England in 1213. But in contrast to any identification with the ultramontane implications of Innocent's policies, Langton was proud of his Englishness. Like many exiles through choice or compulsion (and Langton was both), he lauded his love of his country. In 1207 he declared that 'from our tender years we have loved our kingdom with a natural love'. This may have been no more than politic for the newly appointed ex-patriot archbishop establishing his local credentials. But it was a theme to which he returned. At the translation of Becket's relics in 1220 he talked of 'the triumph of an Englishman' and in a sermon of 1224 he referred to men like Falkes de Bréauté as 'the affliction of the natives to whom the people of England were so often given over as booty … take heed so that aliens are no longer permitted to act against you'. The thirteenth century saw a growing awareness amongst the political elite of national identity. It is entirely in keeping with this development that Langton, one of the most cosmopolitan of archbishops, should have issued, in January 1215, a charter in Anglo-Norman French, one of the first such documents not written in Latin, the universal language of government, law and religion, since the reign of William I.

Stephen Langton was neither a hero nor a saint. He was at times as much a victim as a champion of the cause he was chosen to represent. From his politics, sermons and writings, he emerges as a highly practical man, of sharp but flexible intellect, who preferred to achieve than to strike propagandist poses or escape into intellectual obscurantism. To have helped compose Magna Carta or to have reorganized the Vulgate text of the Bible would each have been notable: to have done both was remarkable.

Further Reading
F. M. Powicke, *Stephen Langton*, 1928.

LANGTON, WALTER (*d*.1321), Bishop of Lichfield from 1296 until his death, was 'the first treasurer of the Exchequer who was in fact, if not in name, the king's chief minister' (Tout). Probably from Leicestershire, he entered Edward I's service as a youth, establishing mutual trust that lasted all the king's life, and worked his way up the wardrobe from clerk (1281) to keeper (1290-5), serving as treasurer of the Exchequer in 1295-1307, ironically as the Scottish war enhanced the financial importance of the wardrobe. Minor reforms at the wardrobe and minor economies in the royal households are attributable to Langton, but his main achievement was the highly efficient management of the Scottish war in spite of escalating royal debts. He was also a frequent ambassador and government spokesman. His devotion to Edward I's interests meant he would go to any lengths, even crime, to achieve his wishes. In return, he enjoyed the complete confidence of the king, who found him 'conspicuous in the maturity of his counsel and full of discretion, useful, nay necessary, to us and our realm', and backed him against all comers.

What this meant in practice emerged at Langton's trial under Edward II. Forty-eight charges alleged all kinds of abuse of power: manipulation of justice, maintenance, extortion, arbitrary seizures and imprisonment. Langton admitted six charges of champerty, the most serious perversion of justice, and was convicted in at least twenty-four other cases, damages being awarded against him. His mastery of financial and legal technicalities recalls Adam Stratton a generation earlier, but Langton's repertoire was wider. Moreover as treasurer he had more scope: he could exploit royal debts, pressurize sheriffs accountable to him for arrears, and even join the bench to judge his own case. His absolute assurance of royal support and of retrospective pardons when he went too far gave him self-confidence in his immunity and added insolence to his power. Not surprisingly, Langton

became very rich, spent lavishly on building (including two churches at his reputed birthplace), acquired extensive estates worth £1,300 a year to pass on to his brother Robert Peverell and nephew Edmund, and later claimed to have lost £20,000 by his trial. Langton's corruption was perhaps not unique, but its scope must have been: surely Langton himself could not have brought all his affairs to a conclusion. The charges of simony, homicide and devil worship of which he was acquitted at his trial pale beside his documented career as 'the most successful profiteer in the royal administration'. Imprisoned in 1307-8 and in 1311, he was briefly treasurer again in 1312, but thereafter lapsed into political obscurity.

Langton's dishonesty and greed hardly fitted him for an ecclesiastical career. Certainly he was a pluralist and nepotist, perhaps kept a mistress, and must have been normally non-resident as bishop. Yet his cathedral chapter described him as 'a God-fearing man of pure life and devoted to his ministry' and he was remembered, with some justice, as a benefactor to the church of Lichfield. Not only did he defend the rights of his see, but he built a new palace at Lichfield, reconstructed Eccleshall Castle, and built extensively at his house in the Strand and his manor houses. At the cathedral he founded a chantry, erected the Lady Chapel, walled the cloister, enhanced the common fund, and left plate, jewels etc. in his will. He erected a bridge in the town. Tout's comment that he saw 'his bishopric rather as a reward for his administrative skill than as an ecclesiastical obligation' was less than just.

Further Reading
M. Prestwich, *War, Politics and Finance under Edward I*, 1972.
A. Beardwood, 'Trial of Walter de Langton, Bishop of Lichfield 1307-12', *Transactions of the American Philosophical Society*, new series 54(3), 1964.

LATIMER, HUGH (1485?-1555), Bishop of Worcester, martyr, was born probably in 1485 at Thurcaston in Leicestershire. The clearest portrait of Latimer is to be obtained by allowing him to speak for himself. 'My father was a yeoman and had no lands of his own, only he had a farm of three or four pound by year at the uttermost and hereupon he tilled so much as kept half a dozen men. He had walk for a hundred sheep and my mother milked thirty kine. He was able and did find the king a harness with himself and his horse. I can remember that I buckled his harness when he went unto Blackheath field (1497). He kept me to school or else I had not been able to preach before the king's majesty now.' 'In my time my poor father was diligent to teach me how to shoot as to learn me any other thing. He taught me how to draw; how to lay my body in my bow, and not to draw with strength of arms as other nations do, but with strength of body.'

In 1506 Hugh was sent to Cambridge, where he was elected to a Fellowship at Clare Hall in 1510. In 1516 he took holy orders and in 1524 he became BD. That Hugh was still a believer in the old religion is proved by the sermon he preached that day against the teaching of Melanchthon. One of his hearers was Thomas Bilney, who was so much struck by the sermon that he called on Latimer. 'Bilney was the instrument by which God called me to knowledge; for I was as obstinate a Papist as any was in England. Bilney heard me at that time and perceived that I was zealous without knowledge, and he came to me afterwards in my study and desired me for God's sake to hear his confession. I did so, and by his confession I learned more than before in many years. So from that time forward I began to smell the word of God and forsook the school-doctors and such fooleries.' The use of such words as 'smell' and 'fooleries' is typical of Latimer's racy and arresting English, touched sometimes with what we today might regard as coarseness.

In 1525, according to one story, Latimer preached in the university church and the Bishop of Ely was present. He suspected that Latimer had Lutheran tendencies and he inhibited him from preaching in the diocese. Latimer was also examined by Wolsey's chaplains, but he disowned all connection with Lutheranism and was given permission to preach throughout the kingdom. He was soon again in trouble on account of two sermons he preached 'on the card', in which he explained allegorically how men could win salvation by playing trumps. He had also given much offence by deprecating what he called 'voluntary works', such as pilgrimages, in comparison with works of faith, e.g. of mercy (1529). Nor was his popularity at all increased when it was known that he strongly favoured the king's side over the divorce of Catherine of Aragon. But he won the favour of Henry VIII when he denied the validity of the marriage before the committee which Gardiner took to Cambridge in 1530 to ascertain the opinion of the university divines. He was at once appointed to preach before the king (1530). As a reward he was given the living in Wiltshire of West Kington, to which he was instituted in 1531. A few months later he preached in a neighbouring parish and gave much offence by denouncing all the bishops and clergy in England as being, not shepherds entering by the door, but thieves whom there was not enough hemp in England to hang. In 1532 he was accused of preaching that the Virgin Mary was a sinner, of denouncing invocation of saints and denying purgatory and hell fire. The Bishop of Salisbury, in whose diocese West Kington lay, was Campeggio, an Italian and an absentee. After a delay of almost a year Latimer was cited to appear before the Bishop of London. At first he refused to sign the articles which were presented to him, but ultimately he made a complete

submission. Foolishly he wrote a letter denying that he had confessed to any error of doctrine, only to indiscretion. For this he was compelled to admit to Convocation that he had erred in doctrine.

In 1533 he was again in trouble over a sermon he preached at Bristol, and he was inhibited by the Bishop of London. But he had good friends at court and he regained the king's favour, so that he was commanded to preach before Henry on Wednesdays in Lent (1534), and in 1535 he was made Bishop of Worcester in direct succession to four consecutive absentee Italians. Perhaps he owed these favours to the support which he gave to the marriage of Anne Boleyn with Henry VIII.

From now onwards his preaching became more outspoken. In 1536 he denounced the luxury of the bishops, abbots and 'other strong thieves'. At a meeting of Convocation he asked the clergy what they had done to benefit the poor during the last seven years. They had burned a dead man (Tracy) and tried to burn a living one – meaning himself. More and more in his sermons he dwelt upon the poverty of the poor and the wealth of the rich. And he moved more and more towards Protestantism. It is to be noted that when the Pilgrimage of Grace broke out, the rebels repeatedly demanded that Latimer and Cranmer should be handed over to them.

In his diocese Latimer worked hard. He issued orders that every priest was to possess a whole Bible in English, or at any rate a New Testament: he commanded his clergy to pay first attention to preaching, to admit No-one to the Communion who could not say the Lord's Prayer in English, and to instruct the children in their parishes to read English. He had a statue of the Virgin in Worcester Cathedral – 'our great Sibyl', as he called it – stripped of its jewels and ornaments, and was anxious for it to be burned: 'she herself with her old sister of Walsingham, her young sister of Ipswich, with their other two sisters of Doncaster and Pentice would make a jolly muster in Smithfield.'

In 1538 he was on a commission to examine John Forest, and at the execution he preached a sermon, or (as he put it either callously or in the Pauline sense of 'I speak as a fool') 'played the fool after my customable manner'. In the same year he sat on a commission to investigate the famous miracle of the 'Blood of Hailes' and found it to consist of a yellowish gum. When in 1539 there was passed the Act of the Six Articles, Latimer and Shaxton, Bishop of Salisbury, resigned their sees. For more than twelve months he was a prisoner in the house of Sampson, Bishop of Chichester. He was then released, but he was forbidden to preach in or to visit London, either university, or his late diocese. For the next six years his life becomes a blank: then in 1546 he was brought before the Council on a charge of having encouraged his friend Crome, who was in trouble over his preaching. Latimer was put in the Tower and remained there until he was released by the general pardon at the accession of Edward VI.

Latimer set to work at once. His servant said of him, 'then most of all he began to set forth his plough and to till the ground of the Lord and to sow the good corn of God's word … preaching for the most part two sermons every Sunday … For he being a sore bruised man and above three score and seven years of age took notwithstanding all these pains in preaching, and besides this every morning ordinarily winter and summer about two of the clock in the morning he was at his book most diligently.' He refused to go back to his bishopric, but he became the most notable of preachers. Of all his sermons the most famous is still that 'of the Plough', in which he attacked unpreaching and non-resident bishops, citing the devil as the best example of a diligent bishop: 'He is the most diligent preacher of all other; he is never out of his diocese; he is never from his cure; he is ever in his parish; the diligentest preacher in all the realm; he is ever at his plough.' In another course of sermons he took as his main subject the oppression of the poor by the rich, and included eulogies of Somerset's government. Latimer worked in concert with Hales and the 'commonwealth men' on behalf of the poor. Nothing could more vividly picture for us the effect Latimer's preaching had on his congregation than the entry in the church warden's accounts at St Margaret's, Westminster, in 1549, one shilling and sixpence paid for 'mending divers pews that were broken when Dr Latimer did preach'.

When Mary came to the throne Latimer was well aware of the danger in which he stood. On 4 September 1553 a summons against him was issued, but he was given six hours' notice beforehand to give him a chance to escape. He refused to take it. In March 1554 he, together with Ridley and Cranmer, was sent to Oxford to take part in a dispute on the doctrine of the Mass. He was condemned for heresy and was handed over to the secular arm to be burned. Ridley was at the same time condemned. On 16 October 1555 – after so long a delay – they were both led to execution in Oxford 'upon the north side of the town in the ditch over against Balliol College'. They were fastened to the stake with a chain round the middle of both. Bags of gunpowder were hung round their necks and the fire lighted. 'Be of good comfort, Master Ridley and play the man,' said Latimer, 'we shall this day light such a candle, by God's grace, in England as I trust shall never be put out.' Latimer died quickly with little suffering.

Latimer was a man sincere, courageous and full of vitality. His manner was aggressive, his style of preaching extremely effective, his English racy, easily understood, arresting and prone to become even harsh. His mind was clear but not subtle: he saw things in black and white. Being supremely self-confident he was often rash in his decisions, bold but ill-advised in utterance. As a reformer he had no patience with conservative bishops who had been trained as lawyers in the canon law. He was perfectly right in thinking that these men, men like Bonner and Gardiner, would always see the lawyers' or legalistic side of the Reformation as at least equal with the doctrinal or spiritual. He could not tolerate their readiness to compromise and comply. On the other hand, he had no understanding at all of what was involved in government or diplomacy, which are based on compromise, and he misunderstood the nature of law, which aims not at prefection but at the enforcement of order.

It was impossible for such a mind to yield to the will of the majority in order to achieve unity, at the expense of his convictions. That is why he opposed the *Bishops' Book*, which he looked on as a temporary expedient to secure unity. In his refusal to believe in purgatory he was wholly logical: 'The founding of the monasteries argued purgatory to be; so the pulling down of them argueth it not to be. What uncharitableness and cruelness seemeth it to be to destroy monasteries, if purgatory be!' His denunciation of images, pilgrimages and other traditions was not merely iconoclastic. The reformer Hilsey said of him, 'I have perceived that his mind is much more against the abusing of things than against the things themselves.'

Latimer's attacks on enclosures and the new landed interest were not directed solely against their cupidity. He felt their actions to be immoral and irreligious. 'If ye bring it to pass that the yeomanry be not able to put their sons to school … and that they be not able to marry their daughters to the avoiding of whoredom; I say ye pluck salvation from the people and utterly destroy the realm. For by yeomen's sons the faith of Christ is and hath been maintained chiefly.' Yet for all his preaching, he probably achieved more for Protestantism by the nobility of his death.

Further Reading
H. R. Trevor-Roper, *Historical Essays*, 1957, pp.85-90.
A. Chester, *Hugh Latimer*, 1954.
H. S. Darby, *Hugh Latimer*, 1953.
R. Demaus, *Hugh Latimer*, 1869, abridged edition 1935.

LATIMER, LORD WILLIAM (1330-81) was the villain of the Good Parliament of 1376. Although he succeeded to his father's Yorkshire barony when only five, his mother's longevity – she died only in 1384 – deprived him of most of its income and made him dependent on the royal favour that he earned by a distinguished career of public service. He was repeatedly in France from Crécy in 1346 until 1381 and was the king's principal representative in Brittany from 1359-67, acting as king's lieutenant from 1361 and sharing in Duke John IV's decisive victory at Auray. He served in Scotland in 1356 and was an active diplomat from 1369. Returning home about 1368, he attended the Lords assiduously, usually as trier of petitions, was a regular royal commissioner, became steward of the household in 1368, chamberlain in 1371-6, executor of Edward III, and councillor both to him and the young Richard II. Always a key officer, the chamberlain controlled 'both written and personal access to the king', which was particularly important in the 1370s as Edward III increasingly lost his grip on affairs. Latimer may therefore have become 'the man most intimately involved in the organization of the renewed war effort from England'. Certainly he was constantly engaged in mustering and paying troops and administrative tasks of all kinds. Inevitably the government's failures and unpopular policies were also attributed to him and were charged to his account at the Good Parliament of 1376. Latimer pleaded that decisions of policy had been made by the whole council and indeed most charges could not be substantiated.

Latimer undoubtedly profited from his service. He received a £333 annuity during his mother's lifetime in 1354, became a Knight of the Garter about 1362, captured the Count of St Pol and others for ransom, acted as captain of St Sauveur-le-Vicomte and lived off the country, was appointed warden of northern forests (1368) and of the Cinque Ports (1372), and purchased several valuable wardships. Hence the wealth that enabled him to lend money to the Crown at interest. This loan, supposed to be to the king's loss as another lesser loan without interest was declined, was made a charge against Latimer at his impeachment. So too was his sale of licences to export wool free of custom, which he claimed to have paid into the chamber at a profit, and his purchase of royal debts at a discount, a common enough practice. What was behind these charges was the belief that Latimer exploited his privileged position to profit from the Crown at a time of great financial stringency. Such claims could not then be substantiated and cannot now, but they secured Latimer's conviction, fine and loss of office. That was the real intention. The financial and other charges were pretexts to destroy Latimer, Perrers and others who ruled in Edward's last years and whose policies were unpopular. Latimer quickly recovered Edward's favour and resumed his interrupted military and political career, though no longer as chamberlain of the royal household.

Latimer's reputation has been sullied both by his impeachment and by his malicious portrayal by the St Albans chronicler. He may, of course, have been as sexually immoral, avaricious and deceitful as accused, but he was certainly no coward – his military career speaks for itself – and his pious intentions belie the charge of irreligion. On balance it is only the events of 1376 that separate his notoriety from the adulation that befell his colleague at arms and fellow Yorkshireman Richard Lord Scrope of Bolton.

Further Reading

C. Given-Wilson, *The Royal Household and the King's Affinity: Service, Politics and Finance in England 1360-1413*, 1986.

G. A. Holmes, *The Good Parliament*, 1975.

LAUD, WILLIAM (1573-1644), Charles I's ecclesiastical champion, was born at Reading, the son of a clothier. From Reading Grammar School he went in 1589 to St John's College, Oxford, of which he was successively scholar, Fellow and (1611) President. Whether or not the long years that he spent as a don unfitted him for a courtier's life, as many writers from Sir Philip Warwick onwards have implied, it was certainly at Oxford that he developed the vehement anti-Puritanism that was his most obvious characteristic when he became a prince of the church. In the first years of the seventeenth century the Arminian tide was beginning to flow at Oxford, not least at St John's, the college of Campion and other recusants a generation before. So it is perhaps not surprising that in 1603 we find Laud, as Proctor, involved in a doctrinal brush with the vice-chancellor, the Puritan George Abbot. Promotion in the wider world came to Laud through a leading Arminian, Richard Neile, Bishop of Rochester, to whom he became chaplain in 1608. Neile got him appointed a royal chaplain in 1611, yet not until ten years later did Laud get a bishopric. In the interval he had become Dean of Gloucester (1615) and signalled his arrival by having the communion table moved from the centre of the cathedral to the chancel and converted into an altar. His slow advance reflected the hostility of Abbot who in 1611 had succeeded Bancroft as Archbishop of Canterbury, and – perhaps even more – the doubts of James I about Laud, expressed in the famous comment 'he hath a restless spirit, and cannot see when matters are well, but loves to toss and change and bring things to a pitch of reformation floating in his own brain'. Neile moved upwards in preferment, to Lincoln and then (1617) to Durham, and the Arminians grew stronger and more claimant. But it was attachment to a patron at once far stronger and less reputable than Neile, the king's favourite, Buckingham, that gained for Laud the bishopric of St David's in 1621. He paid two visits to this remote and poor see during the six years for which he held it.

The death of James I in 1625 and the accession of Charles was as decisive in the career of Laud as in the history of the English constitution. To a king who distrusted him there succeeded one whose ideas on doctrine and church government were in entire harmony with his own – and one, moreover, who was to prove as naive politically as Laud himself. It was Laud who preached the sermon, in terms stressing the divine origins of royal authority, at the opening of Charles's first parliament in 1625; Laud who supplied

Buckingham with lists of Arminian churchmen to promote and Puritans to hold back; Laud who became the director of the king's ecclesiastical policy. In 1627 he became Bishop of Bath and Wells (which he never visited), and in 1629 of London. His rise was assisted by the troubles of Abbot, who had been suspended from office in 1627 for his opposition to Charles's arbitrary policy. Laud was one of the commission of five bishops appointed to carry out the archbishop's duties, and although Abbot recovered favour with the king, Laud was now evidently the dominant figure in the Church of England. When Abbot eventually died in 1633 Charles greeted Laud with the words 'My Lord's Grace of Canterbury, you are very welcome'. He remained archbishop until he was executed in 1645, although he achieved little after the outbreak of the Scottish Wars in 1639, and for the last three and a half years of his life he was a prisoner, almost forgotten, in the Tower.

Laud was an unattractive man. Red-faced, short, harsh of speech, bad-tempered, fussy, humourless, he was little liked by contemporaries, whatever their religious opinions. Courtiers thought him a low-born upstart and found him something of a vulgarian. Clarendon, whose verdict is friendly and who pays generous tribute to Laud's courage, draws attention to his vindictiveness. His relations with women were never easy, and he did not win the queen's trust. Dedicated to his task of restoring the Church of England to greatness, temperamentally welcoming the routine and details of business, Laud had little time and less capacity for affability. His devotion to the policy of 'Thorough' – a policy which was quite unrealistic in the atmosphere of the Stuart court – ensured him enemies among those who administered the law as well as among those who suffered from it. Laud's mind was blinkered and unimaginative. His defects were not those of the authoritarian who loved power for its own sake. He enforced formality and pomp because he believed them appropriate to the church and the episcopal order to which he belonged, not to satisfy his own love of authority; indeed, he was personally austere to the point of meanness. His narrowness was entirely that of a man who cannot understand why others sincerely differ from him. As to his unimaginativeness, Clarendon's comment goes deep. 'He was a man of great parts, and very exemplary virtues, allayed and discredited by some unpopular natural infirmities; the greatest of which was (besides a hasty, sharp way of expressing himself), that he believed innocence of heart, and integrity of manners, was a guard strong enough to secure any man in his voyage through this world.'

For Laud was an idealist with a closed mind. His ideal was reactionary, the restoration of the church in England to its medieval power and status, subject only to the authority of king instead of pope. It was a response to the challenge of Puritanism; 'with Laud the forces of conservatism found their most determined leader'.* So his activities in the years after 1629 ranged over an immense field. As Bishop of London he cleared the gossips and businessmen out of St Paul's and set Inigo Jones to begin the restoration of the fabric; suppressed Puritan preachers' arid lectureships; and in the Instructions to Bishops (which Charles compelled Abbot to send out) required bishops to reside in their sees and not to lease their lands, and to tackle the problem of Puritan lecturers throughout their dioceses. From Canterbury after 1633 he launched his Metropolitical Visitation of his province, in effect an inquisition into every detail of church life – conduct of services, state of buildings, vestments, sermons, behaviour of the clergy – whose purposes included the imposition of Arminian orthodoxy and the restoration of uniformity in externals. Throughout his time at Canterbury he tried strenuously to raise clerical incomes by the recovery of impropriated tithes and other church property. His attacks upon Puritan propagandists – like the punishment of Prynne, Bastwick and Burton – were merely the most spectacular incidents of his policy.

Laud, who joined the Privy Council in 1627, was no politician, yet the attainment of his ideals in the church depended wholly on royal authority; moreover, he became deeply involved in the secular policies of the 1630s. He was prominent – not least by his severity – in Star Chamber as well as upon its ecclesiastical counterpart, High Commission. When Portland died in 1635 Laud was the main figure in the Commission which took over the Treasury, until he got his own nominee, Bishop Juxon, appointed in 1636. For a time he was head of a junto for foreign affairs. His friendship and alliance with Strafford necessarily involved him in politics, for he saw himself as the champion of Strafford's Irish policy – and of 'Thorough' in general – against the 'Lady Mora', the procrastination and corruption of the courtiers. And the problem of Romanism became a political issue also. Laud, who had engaged in a celebrated controversy with the Jesuit Fisher in the last years of James's reign (and apparently thereby rescued Buckingham for Anglicanism), was as hostile to Rome as to Calvinism; but he was in a difficult plight, for Henrietta Maria made the court the effective hub of English Romanism. The offer of a cardinal's hat, made immediately upon Abbot's death in 1633, helped to strengthen the widespread Puritan suspicion that Laud himself was a papist.

When the non-parliamentary régime collapsed in 1639-40 Laud's power and policy vanished. He resisted the inevitable recall of parliament as long as he could, for he was essentially an authoritarian; as Trevor-Roper puts it, 'Laud had a natural antipathy to discussion'. Indeed, his church policy had contributed much to

---

*Christopher Hill, *Economic Problems of the Church*, 1956, p.339.

786 / Laud, William

the unpopularity and to the failure of the régime. Arminianism smelt of popery; the attempt to recover church lands and income threatened property-owners; Laudian episcopacy was inextricably committed to arbitrary government, to Star Chamber and Ship Money and the other features of the régime. So the power of the hierarchy was destroyed, and Laud himself was packed off to the Tower, to remain in cold storage until he went to the block early in 1645. When in 1660 Anglicanism came into its own again, it was an Anglicanism very different, politically and constitutionally if not ceremonially, from that which Laud would have imposed. It was compelled to acknowledge the existence of organized dissent; and it was firmly subordinated not only to the central government but to the gentry in the countryside. Only in Oxford did William Laud's work survive. There the lectureship in Arabic in which he installed Edward Pococke (1636), the new Statutes which he gave to the university, and – most notable of all – the superb Canterbury Quadrangle with which he endowed St John's have provided a lasting memorial.

Further Reading

C. Carlton, *Archbishop William Laud*, 1987.
Kevin Sharpe, 'Archbishop Laud', *History Today*, August 1983.
H. R. Trevor-Roper, *Archbishop Laud (1573-1645)*, 2nd edn, 1962.

LAW, WILLIAM (1686-1761), mystic, non-juror, wrote about Christianity in works both practical and controversial. He was a profound theologian, but his own saintly character was as good an argument for his faith as anything he wrote.

He was the son of a grocer in Kingscliffe in Northamptonshire. At Emmanuel College, Cambridge, Puritan in tradition, evangelical in spirit, he was ordained and elected Fellow. When he refused to take the oath of allegiance to George I he lost his Fellowship and chance of preferment in the church. For a time he served as curate of Fotheringhay. In 1727 he was chosen to be tutor to Edward Gibbon, father of the historian; after his pupil had gone abroad he remained with the family at Putney, their cherished friend and spiritual director. He had already made a name as defender of non-juring principles. In his *Three Letters to the Bishop of Bangor* (1717-19), Law demolished Hoadly's arguments for a church without authority for bishops or creeds. His *Remarks on the Fable of the Bees* (1724) was a caustic answer to Mandeville's poem and its moral – that 'private vices are public benefits'. *The Case of Reason* (1731) is a more profound work, and was an extended argument against deism as it was expressed in Matthew Tindal's *Christianity as Old as the Creation*. To the Deist idea of God, standing apart from a universe which was governed by a fixed order of creation 'both plain and perspicuous', Law opposed a living God who could only be understood by the intuitive, spiritual faculty.

Law was a mystic, but a man of his age too in his common sense. His *Christian Perfection* (1726) and the *Serious Call to a Devout and Holy Life* (1728) were concerned with the question of how to live in accord with the teaching of Christ. With wit and tender but cogent reasoning he expounded a way of Christian living based upon a new principle of life. In an age of tepid views Law's masterpiece, the *Serious Call*, reached the hearts of thousands. John Wesley criticized it on the grounds that, although he put a high ideal before men, he omitted to emphasize that the only means of attaining it was through the atonement of Christians. But he spoke of it as 'a treatise which will hardly be excelled, if it be equalled, in the English tongue, either for beauty of expression or for justice of thought'. The book had most appeal to the evangelical. But men of cooler temper were also captivated, for its appeal was as much intellectual as emotional. Dr Johnson, who claimed that his reading it 'was the first occasion of my thinking in earnest about religion', Gibbon the temperamentally sceptical, Lyttelton, all felt its power. 'Though deep, yet clear his system', wrote the poet Byron. No other book, after the Bible itself, played such a part in moulding the religious thought of the time.

In 1737 Law settled at Thrapston, subsequently at Kingscliffe again, with Mrs Elizabeth Hutcheson and Mrs Hester Gibbon, the historian's aunt. The trio resolved to live a religious life, to devote the ladies' wealth to charity, to put into practice the principles of the *Serious Call*. From a window in the manor house Law distributed charity to all comers. The quiet Northamptonshire countryside soon swarmed with beggars, the villagers protested, the vicar denounced indiscriminate giving from the pulpit. Law was, however, no sentimentalist. When he received £1,000 from an anonymous donor he used it to start a school for the village girls. Mrs Hutcheson added a boys' school and an almshouse; there the old people still talk of Law as if he were alive. He founded a library used and visited by his devotees today, especially Americans. Tradition has it that he was plump and round-faced, but there is no certain record, for he would not allow himself to be painted. As he grew older his mystical preoccupations deepened. Boehme's writings appealed especially to his 'hunger of the soul'. When he first read the works of that shoemaker of Görlitz (c.1733) he was put into 'a perfect sweat'.

Law's own later works, *Appeal to all that doubt* (1740), *The Spirit of Prayer* (1749-50) and *The Way to Divine Knowledge* (1752) were not widely popular or understood. They are based on the idea that nature and law are one; nature is God's book of revelation, His outward manifestation of what He inwardly is – and is able to do. Exceptional in its combination of lucidity and vision, Law's mind is expressed in prose as fine as any of the century: explicit, rhythmic and witty. Excelling in the use of simile and analogy, he could be severe or tender, homely or elevated, ironic or plain. If, as Leslie Stephen said of the *Serious Call*, its power could only be 'adequately felt by readers who can study it on their knees', it is also true that his closely logical habit appealed to those who were unable to share his devout frame of mind. In an age that looked askance at enthusiasm he made religious feeling respectable and desirable. It was in character that he should have died, after a short illness, almost in the act of singing a hymn.

Further Reading
A. K. Walker, *William Law, His Life and Thought*, 1973.
J. H. Overton, *Law, Non-juror and Mystic*, 1881.

LAWES, HENRY (1596-1662), musician, born at Dinton in Wiltshire, was associated with the Chapel Royal in various capacities from 1626 onwards, losing his official posts during the years of the Civil Wars and Interregnum and recovering them at the Restoration. Contemporaries thought very highly of him both as singer and as composer. In 1633 he wrote the music for Thomas Carew's masque *Coelum Britannicum*, and in 1634 for *Comus*, which he seems to have suggested to Milton and in the first performance of which at Ludlow he played the part of Attendant Spirit. Lawes also set the verse of Herrick and other Caroline poets to music. He published several books of songs and wrote a number of anthems, notably 'Zadok the Priest', composed for the coronation of Charles II. Perhaps no single Englishman did as much as Lawes to establish traditional modes and rules for the setting of his native language to music, and in this sense he did much to make the achievements of Purcell possible.

Further Reading
W. M. Evans, *Henry Lawes*, 1941.

LAWRENCE, SIR HENRY (1806-57) and **LAWRENCE, LORD JOHN** (1811-79) were the sixth and eighth sons of an Anglo-Irish soldier, and closely-bonded brothers. They went through the East India Company's training schools, Henry at Addiscombe and John at Haileybury: and both found their way to posts in India, Henry a military and John a civil one, through the influence of a family friend, who was a director of the company. In the course of careers that were to make them famous they showed marked family resemblances. Both were men of action, powerful leaders from the front. Both read their Bibles regularly and held simple Christian beliefs which guided their everyday lives: after a rare loss of control over his strong temper, Henry was seen kneeling by his bedside, his hands covering his face. Each married the daughter of a clergyman. Their

religion was personal and private. They were not dogmatic, and had a respect for the beliefs they encountered in India, as long as these did not conflict with Christian morals. They shared a fundamental goodwill towards the people they ruled, but combined it with controlled harshness in times of crisis. Both had to work through periods of severe illness, Henry suffering from the effects of a vicious malaria contracted in Burma in his first campaign, and John struggling with blinding headaches. They were driven by a strong sense of duty, but also by a love for India and its people. 'If I cannot live in India I must go and die there', said John, when told by his English doctor that he ought not to return after a period of leave.

Yet you have only to look at portraits of them to see the differences, all the more striking in two such strong personalities. Henry has much the finer face. 'Sir Henry looked to Heaven and stroked his beard and then he knew what to do', said an Indian. He was sensitive to others' feelings, not least to those of the native aristocracy. He ruled from the saddle rather than from the desk, knew his people and was loved by them. But he could also be oversensitive to criticism, and while he was a hero to the able young men who worked for him, he was prickly with his equals and superiors. John's rougher, simpler nature is reflected in his more coarse-grained features. He was a first-class administrator, who drove others as hard as he drove himself and had an exceptional grasp of detail. 'Jan Larens knows everything', they said. He kept a tight hold of the purse strings. He liked to be firmly in control of everything for which he was responsible. To the people of Kangra who showed signs of joining the hostile Sikhs he wrote: 'If you have any grievance let me know it, and I will try to remove it … If you will excite rebellion, as I live I will surely punish you.' The echoes of the Old Testament were characteristic. He was respected rather than loved, but when the crisis of the Mutiny came, he kept the Punjab loyal and rescued Delhi. 'But for him,' wrote the Governor-General, 'the hold of England over Upper India would have had to be recovered at a cost of English blood and treasure which defies calculation.'

Despite their different career paths, each of them had both civil and military experience. Henry, involved in campaigns in Burma and Afghanistan and the Sikh wars, also organized a revenue assessment in the north-west provinces, and was resident in Nepal. There he and his devoted wife Honoria, the first white woman to come to Nepal, started the Lawrence hill schools for the children of Europeans, some of which still provide a 'public school' type of boarding education. John, in the course of his work as magistrate and collector in Paniput, caught the eye of the Governor-General Lord Hardinge by the efficiency with which he organized ammunition and transport for Gough's army in the Second Sikh War.

So they were both well equipped when they came together in the Punjab.

The work they did there provided the model for the Indian Civil Service in the century which followed. The British had been drawn into the Punjab through a political power vacuum following the death of the mighty Ranjit Singh. The Sikh army, without a responsible leader, became a maverick menace. Hardinge tried to avoid annexation, and after the First Sikh War (1845-6) sent Henry Lawrence as his Agent, and then as Resident with the power of a regent. Only after a rebellion while Henry was away on leave, and the Second Sikh War (1848-9), did the new Governor-General, Dalhousie, take the country over. He determined to restrain Henry's increasingly independent policy and methods by setting up a Board, with Henry as its President and John as one of the two other members. There followed a period of tension between the two brothers, with the third member (who was Field Marshal Montgomery's grandfather) acting as the channel for their correspondence. In land settlements, John backed the peasants against their former rulers, while Henry was tender towards the old chiefs. But it was creative tension. By themselves it was said that Henry would soon have had to close the Treasury and John would have had a full revenue but a mutinous country. Between them they achieved what Henry described as 'a light and agreeable assessment, a strong police and a quick hearing in all cases'. They produced a large surplus of revenue over expenditure while building thousands of miles of roads and digging canals, for irrigation as well as transport. They also managed to disband a proud army and disarm a warlike population. They did all this through District Officers. These were given responsibility on the spot, and areas small enough to enable them to know the people with whom they were dealing. The house which the Lawrences built in the Punjab was so strong that it stood when the flood of the Mutiny rose around it.

Eventually the tension between the brothers became intolerable, and Henry went off to be agent amongst the princes in Rajputana. Canning, succeeding Dalhousie as Governor-General, summoned him back as he was starting for leave in England in 1857, to be Chief Commissioner for Oudh. It proved to be a death sentence. When the Mutiny exploded he chose a good defensive position in the Residency at Lucknow, and collected enough stores to withstand a siege of months. The government designated him the new Governor-General should anything happen to Canning. But he never heard this. His room was hit by a shell, and he was fatally wounded. The soldiers who were asked to move his body, 'lifting the covering sheet, one by one lovingly and reverently kissed his face'. John's closing years gave him more power but were more prosaic. He stayed in the Punjab until he left India in 1859, returning to a hero's welcome,

a peerage and a place on the new India Board, set up when the East India Company handed India over to the state. In 1863 Palmerston sent him back as Viceroy. He did what was hoped by keeping out of north-west frontier entanglements. 'Let us only be strong on this side of the passes,' he wrote, 'and we may laugh at all that goes on in Kabul.' But financial problems weighed heavily on him, and when he found that he could not exercise the same personal influence that had served so well in the Punjab, he fell back on cautiously rigid bureaucratic control. Florence Nightingale, who had seen in him the man to bring the new sanitation to all India, was angrily disappointed. There was peace, however, and in the last decade of his life after his final return to England in 1869, he had the satisfaction of watching the Indian Civil Service, which he and his brother had done much to shape and to inspire, attracting some of Britain's most talented and idealistic young men.

Further Reading
M. Edwards, *The Necessary Hell: John and Henry Lawrence and the Indian Empire*, 1958.

LAWRENCE, STRINGER (1697-1775) has been aptly called 'the father of the Indian army' for he started a tradition of strenuous soldiering which lasted as long as the British Raj. Under him and his fellow officers, Indians who could be inept and cowardly under their own countrymen fought superbly. He served at Gibraltar, in Flanders and on the field of Culloden before being sent to India as 'major in the East Indies only' to command all the company's troops, in 1747. He was captured by the French at Madras but released at the peace of Aix-la-Chapelle. In 1749 he was made civil governor and military commandant of Fort St David. Although Clive's seizure and defence of Arcot steals the fame, Lawrence taught Clive much about commanding small bodies of troops. He was responsible too for the forward policy of co-operation with such Indian princes as would be friendly. In 1752 with Clive he defeated the French-backed Chanda Sahib and restored Muhammed Ali as Nawáb of the Carnatic. When war was renewed in 1757 he was made brigadier-general and in the following winter he commanded Fort St George in its successful resistance to siege. He left India in 1759. Eyre Coote succeeded him and completed the discomfiture of the French by the victory at Wandewash.

LAWRENCE, SIR THOMAS (1769-1830), portrait-painter, was the grandson of clergymen on both sides, but his father descended to keeping a public house in Bristol, where Lawrence was born. In 1772 the family took The Black Bear at Devizes, an inn frequented by fashionable travellers on the Bath Road – to whom the infant Lawrence exhibited his astonishing precocity at drawing likenesses. He was a public figure before he was ten; his talents were in demand at Oxford and at Bath, to which successively the family migrated; and by the time Lawrence began his brief stint at the Academy Schools in London at the age of eighteen, he had had an education which barely extended beyond the perilous arts of ingratiating himself with his patrons. But there is no minimizing the impression he made on London. This was something new, a virtuoso who was not only young but extremely good-looking. Sir Joshua was sage; the court was charmed. Lawrence painted the queen at Windsor – that familiar portrayal of the plain lady in white silk which, for a lad of twenty, is simply a master-piece – and although the painting failed to please their Majesties, the royal favour was exerted, first in pressing Lawrence on the Academy as early as 1790, and then (1792) in appointing him to succeed Reynolds as Painter-in-Ordinary before he was even elected RA. From here success was assured him, even if death had not deprived him of his rivals, Reynolds in 1792, Rom-ney in 1802, Hoppner in 1810. The prince regent made an exception to his rule of enmity to his father's friends; honoured Lawrence with knighthood in 1815; and com-missioned him to anticipate the camera by painting the portraits of the monarchs, statesmen and generals who had made the allied victory in the late war. Thus the Emperor of Russia and the Holy Roman Emperor, Blücher and Suvarov, Richelieu and Tschernitschev, and the rest of the heroes who at London in 1815, and at Aix in 1818, met to parcel out Europe, gave sittings in turn to Lawrence, and were gathered once and for all to the walls of the Waterloo Chamber at Windsor. From Aix, Lawrence went on to Vienna, to paint the Archduke Charles; and to Rome, to paint Cardinal Consalvi and what is perhaps (for its revelation of character) his chef-d'oeuvre, the crafty-benign portrait of Pope Pius VII. On the night of his return to England in 1820, he was elected PRA to succeed Benjamin West; in 1823 he advised on the purchase, from the estate of his late friend Angerstein, of the collection which made the nucleus of the National Gallery; and so he continued, in a position of unapproached authority, until his sudden death, leaving 1,700 brushes in his studio and a very valuable collection of old-master drawings.

Apart from his art, he was a fencer, a boxer and a billiards-player. He was curiously unable to keep himself financially solvent – which his taste for drawings only partly explains. He was a lonely man and probably unhappy. Despite or because of early affairs with the daughters of Mrs Siddons, he remained a bachelor – but a bachelor who was qualified to gladden the hearts of ladies of rank, and even used the opportunity of doing so: he was, in short, something of a philanderer.

In his painting the reading of character tends to be skin-deep only: expert in depicting courtliness and all the superficial graces of the Regency period, he seldom comes up to the qualities of wisdom, long-suffering or magnanimity (his *Warren Hastings* is an obvious exception). The deficiency can hardly have been one of education (as has been suggested), since it was least obvious in his earliest work: *William Lock of Newbury* (1790), *Captain Moore* (1792), *Viscount Barrington* (1792), are as profound as they are brilliant. But later, whether from overwork or from that degeneration which commonly afflicts the manhood of infant prodigies, the perception is slacker, and there is more truth than falsehood in Haydon's ungentle criticism that Lawrence 'flattered the vanities of the age, pampered its weakness and met its meretricious tastes. His men were all gentle-men with an air of fashion and the dandyism of high life – his women were delicate but not modest – beautiful but not natural, they appear to look that they may be looked at and to languish for the sake of sympathy.' However that may be, the best of his works are so striking as to have become part of the very language of portrait-painting; and *Elizabeth Farren* (which, with *Pinkie*, opened the door to romantic portraiture), *Princess Lieven*, *Lord Mountstuart*, *William Lamb* and the various paintings of the Duke of Wellington and the prince regent, are as distinctive emblems of their age as Hilliard's *Young Man* or Van Dyck's *Charles I* of theirs.

Further Reading
K. Garlick, *Sir Thomas Lawrence*, 1954.
D. Goldring, *Regency Portrait Painter*, 1951.

LAYARD, SIR HENRY (1817-94), archaeologist and diplomat, became world-famous when he published *Nineveh and Its Remains* in 1848. He put the ancient biblical cities of Mesopotamia on the map, and aroused British interests in the Arab world, in a way which influ-enced her policies there through two world wars and beyond. Between the Tigris and the Euphrates, great mounds stood up from the desert, one as much as four miles in circumference. On 9 November 1845, Layard began digging into the side of one of them, and before the day was out had exposed a chamber formed of marble slabs, each covered with cuneiform inscriptions. It was part of a six-and-a-half acre Assyrian palace built in the seventh century BC. Friezes, bas reliefs and sculp-tures were quickly revealed. Then he was met by two Arab horsemen, shouting: 'Hasten, O Bey, for they have found Nimrod himself.' What the diggers had actually unearthed was a huge winged bull, its head five feet high. Later, other magnificent sculptures emerged, including two lions, eleven feet long and eleven feet high. Three hundred men dragged the bull onto an immense cart, and then onto a raft, which took it 600 miles down the Tigris to the Persian Gulf. In this way did the Assyrian trophies, undisturbed for twenty-eight centuries, travel to the British Museum, where they can still be seen. Meanwhile, the cuneiform inscriptions were being deciphered by Henry Rawlinson. Soon, more was known about the Mesopotamian civilization than the Romans and Greeks had known.

Layard was lionized when he got home. His story was worthy of the *Arabian Nights*, his favourite reading as a boy. He was a fine horseman, and had won the confidence of the Arabs by mastering their language, wearing their clothes and studying their history. He was something of a polymath; artistic and a business man, with political ambitions. Russell made him Under Secretary for Foreign Affairs, and later he was briefly Commissioner for Works and Buildings. But he got on much less well with Westminster politicians than with Bakhtiari Arabs. He was opinionated, cocksure, and saw everything in black and white. He turned the general criticisms which he made into personal attacks – on Aberdeen, Palmerston and Gladstone in particular. His enemies dubbed him 'Mr Lie-Hard'. So he never had the influence which his fame might have achieved for him, even when he was ambassador to the Porte in the critical period leading up to the Congress of Berlin in 1878. He ended his life, disappointed and on the shelf, in Venice.

Further Reading
G. Waterfield, *Layard of Nineveh*, 1963.

LEAR, EDWARD (1812-88), artist and writer, was best known in his lifetime for his humorous verse. But he was also a highly entertaining letter-writer and an unwearying traveller, who published the descriptions of his travel with illustrations done by himself. Above all, he was an artist, perhaps the best topographical artist of his time, who painted nearly 10,000 watercolours and more than 300 oil-paintings.

He was the twentieth of twenty-one children, and brought up by a sister. His unsettled childhood perhaps contributed to the depressions which visited him throughout his life. He was also a lifelong epileptic; and, because epilepsy was then thought shameful, the secrecy he had to practise isolated him socially, and made him shy and eccentric. To his friends and his patrons (they were often the same people), he was warm-hearted, very amusing, but also exigent – he tended to ask too much of them. Nevertheless, for someone who was reclusive by nature, and who spent much of his life abroad, he had an astonishing number of friends, with whom he corresponded when he could not see them. But 'social life' he disliked; it was the freedom from the restraints and obligations of society, quite as much as the delight of artistic engagement with remote and beautiful landscapes, that prompted his almost incessant travelling. He wrote in his diary: 'The Elements – trees, clouds, &c – silence … seem to have far more part with me or I with them, than mankind.'

Very early, he made himself into a superb drawer and painter of birds. At the age of nineteen, he published *Illustrations of the family of Psittacidae, or Parrots*, one of which – the Red and Yellow Macaw – was praised as 'equalling any figure ever painted by Audubon'. Many of the paintings in John Gould's great *Birds of Europe* (1832-7) are by Lear (though unacknowledged). His power in this field was recognized by Lord Stanley, who succeeded in 1834 as the thirteenth Earl of Derby, and was the father of the prime minister. He invited Lear to Knowsley, to paint the animals of his menagerie. From then on Lear had the friendship and the patronage of the Stanleys; and it was for the grandchildren of the thirteenth earl that he wrote *The Book of Nonsense* (1846), which has gone through countless editions, and delighted children of all ages. It was this book, with Lear's development of the 'limerick' form, and its successor books of Nonsense, that gave him what fame he enjoyed during his life. And one has only to hear the verbal music of *The Owl and the Pussy-Cat*, or

> Far and few, far and few
> Are the lands where the Jumblies live;

to be back in a world of glorious, melodious unreason. Lear wrote his Nonsense because he understood children, and never ceased to be a 'child' himself. But he wrote it also as a liberalizing protest against the formality, the Evangelical gravity, of Victorian society – which helps to explain why it was so popular.

In the late 1830s, Lear abandoned his career as an animal-painter, and turned to landscape. He spent ten years in Rome, improved his skill, sold his work, prospered for a time. *Illustrated Excursions in Italy* (London, 1846) was his first published travel-journal. It caught the eye of the queen, and led her to invite him to Osborne House to give her drawing lessons. In 1849, feeling in need of instruction himself, he submitted to a year at the Royal Academy Schools; and then took lessons from Holman Hunt, deriving from him a pungent use of colour.

Now Lear's travels began in earnest. Over the years he went from Italy to Greece and the Ionian Islands, to Turkey, Syria, Palestine, the desert of Sinai, Egypt, Albania, Corsica, Malta – and finally (when he was over sixty) to India and Ceylon. Further illustrated travel-journals appeared. These show that, although the Indian journey was undertaken at the invitation of the Viceroy, Lord Northbrook, Lear journeyed mostly as a pioneering adventurer. Although he himself makes light of them, one can picture the difficulties that an invalid, a vulnerable man, met in coping with the primitive conditions, the loneliness, and the dangers from nature and men. Of course he had his servant Giorgio, a Suliot from Corfu, as companion on all his travels. But Lear himself was a man of tough resolution. His close friend Sir Franklin Lushington wrote of him: 'From first to last he was, in whatever circumstances of difficulty or ill-health, an indomitable traveller. Before visiting new lands, he studied their geography and literature, and then went straight for the mark; and wherever he went he drew most indefatigably and most accurately.' It is clear this was the life for him, a life in which he could 'find himself'.

The sketches that he did on these journeys, and the paintings that he made from them, are amongst the most romantic landscape paintings ever made. It is customary now to value the sketches more highly; and certainly Lear was inclined (like Constable) to over-elaborate the 'finished' painting, and thus to lose the power of spontaneity. He was a very fine draughtsman; and that, and his genius for quickly establishing the composition of a picture, make even his 'rough' sketches sufficient as pictures. And he gave to these real landscapes a breath of the same air, of the Golden Age or of Eden, that Claude had given to the landscapes of his imagination. When Lear describes the 'sights' of Corfu, he is expressing the nature of much of his subject-matter: 'You may pass your days by gigantic cliffs with breaking foam-waves below them ... – or on hills which overlook long seas of foliage backed by snow-covered mountain ridges ... or beneath vast olives, overbranching dells full of fern & myrtle & soft green fields of bright grass: or in gardens dark with oranges & lemon groves, those fruits sparkling golden & yellow against the purple sea & amethyst hills: – or by a calm sandy shore below aloe-grown heights – rippling – sparkling curves of sea sounding gently around all day long.' And Tennyson's response to Lear's *Journals of a Landscape Painter in Albania &c* (1851) was the verses entitled 'To E.L. on his travels in Greece', with their mention of 'Illyrian woodlands' and 'the vast Akrokeraunian walls'.

No wonder that he chose to live where he could see the Mediterranean. In 1871 he built a house at San Remo on the Italian Riviera. But his last years there were lonely and rather sad, as he became unable to return to London each summer, and as the failure of his eyesight curtailed his letter-writing as well as his struggles to complete a set of 200 drawings as illustrations to Tennyson's poetry. For various reasons – not least because he had depreciated his own oeuvre by painting 'potboilers' ('Tyrants', he called them) in order to pay his bills – he never found the fame, or the fortune, as a landscape painter that he thought he had deserved. Faithful Giorgio died. Foss, his faithful cat, died. And, when Lear himself died, not one of his friends was able to attend the funeral. Lushington however wrote of him: 'Apart from all his various qualities of genius, I have never known a man who deserved more love for his goodness of heart and his determination to do right.' He and the others would certainly have echoed Lear's own words – 'How pleasant to know Mr Lear!'

Further Reading
Vivien Noakes and others, *Edward Lear 1812-1888*, (Catalogue of the Royal Academy of Arts Exhibition, 1985).
Vivien Noakes, *Edward Lear, The Life of a Wanderer*, 1968.

LEE or LEGH, ROWLAND (*d.*1543?), Bishop of Coventry and Lichfield and Lord President of the Council in the Marches of Wales, was the son of William Lee of Morpeth, Northumberland, and of Isabel Trollope of Thornley in Co. Durham. The date of his birth is unknown: he probably died in 1543. He first entered public life in 1528 under Wolsey. He shared with Stephen Gardiner and Thomas Cromwell in the suppressing of those monasteries whose wealth Wolsey required for his foundation of Cardinal College at Ipswich. After Wolsey died, Lee stuck to Cromwell, who put his son under Lee's charge, and he became one of the principal agents between the king and Cromwell and the clergy, and in the matter of the king's divorce; and for his many services he received frequent preferments. It is possible that it was Lee who secretly married Henry VIII and Anne Boleyn on 25 January 1533. His final reward was the bishopric of Lichfield and Coventry, known in those days as Chester, on 10 January 1534. This appointment caused much offence to at least one person. Stephen Vaughan, a close friend of Cromwell's, wrote to him: 'You have lately holpen an earthly beast, a mole, and an enemy of all godly learning, into the office of his damnation, *a papist*, an Idolater, and a fleshly priest' (Ellis, *Original Letters*, 3rd series, ii, p.285).

In May 1534 he was appointed President of the King's Council in the Marches of Wales with the object of restoring law and order, which had broken down under Voysey, Bishop of Exeter. He owed his appointment to Cromwell, who seems first to have recognized the need for a new and consistent policy in Wales. Lee proved himself a man of loyalty and of resolute energy, 'stowte of nature, readie-witted, roughe of speeche, not affable to any of the Walshrie, an extreme ponisher of offenders, desirous to gain credit with the Kinge and comendacon for his service' (Gerrard to Walsingham). There is some evidence, not above suspicion, that he hanged 5,000 criminals.

When Henry VIII and Cromwell began to carry out a reorganization of government in Wales and introduced the shire system from England and appointed Welshmen as JPs, Lee opposed the policy, since he did not think Welshmen would be impartial in administering justice and he himself was not 'of that perfectness to know what shall chance in time coming'. We know little about the last three years of his Presidency and very little of interest about the last years of his life. He died at Shrewsbury probably on 28 January 1543, and is buried there in the church of St Chad's.

Further Reading
J. F. Rees, *Tudor Policy in Wales*, Hist. Assoc. pamphlet, 1935.

LEGGE, GEORGE, 1st LORD DARTMOUTH (1648-91), son of a devoted royalist of the Civil Wars, was educated at Westminster and King's College, Cambridge, and served briefly on land and sea in the Dutch Wars. James, Duke of York, was his patron, and Legge, though a determined Protestant, stood firmly by him throughout his changing fortunes in his brother's reign. Legge was created Baron Dartmouth in 1682 and commanded the expedition sent to evacuate Tangier in 1683-4. When James came to the throne in 1685 he appointed Dartmouth Master of the Horse and Governor of the Tower. In September 1688, when the threat of William of Orange's invasion was evident, James removed the Catholic Strickland from command of the fleet and appointed Dartmouth in his place. Dartmouth's conduct thereafter, except in one respect, was ambiguous and remains controversial. It is possible, though by no means certain, that decisive action on his part could have destroyed the Revolution, either by intercepting the Dutch flotilla on its voyage, or by attacking it in Torbay and thereby awakening English hostility to the invaders. He failed to take that action, for one or more of several reasons. His own naval experience was very limited; he could not rely upon the loyalty of his captains, and there was traditional and strong anti-Catholic feeling among the seamen; both James's own instructions and those from the Navy Board encouraged him to be cautious in risking battle. The easterly winds which drove the Dutch down Channel, within sight of the English fleet, held Dartmouth at his moorings in the Downs, and even when he got out as far as Beachy Head he was driven back again to the Downs by a south-westerly gale. He eventually arrived at Torbay a fortnight after the Dutch, yet failed to engage them there; it is hard to account for this particular decision except on the hypothesis that Dartmouth believed that his captains would not obey an order to attack. Finally he took the fleet back to Spithead, where it surrendered to William five weeks after the Dutch landing. One action only of Dartmouth's was unambiguous: he firmly declined to obey the king's order to escort the infant Prince of Wales to France from Portsmouth, saying that such a step would be 'treason to the known laws of the kingdoms', and he took strict measures to ensure that the yacht which was to carry the child did not sail. Dartmouth was a man caught in the toils. His long record of personal loyalty to James and the tone of his letters to the king throughout this time forbid us to explain his inaction in terms of treachery. He did not long outlive what for him was a tragic choice of disloyalties. Relieved of his command, he took the oath of allegiance to the new sovereigns, but was soon imprisoned on a baseless charge of plotting to hand over the defences to France. In 1691 he died of apoplexy in the Tower.

Further Reading
M. J. Sydenham, 'The Anxieties of an Admiral', *History Today*, October 1962.

LEIGHTON, LORD FREDERIC (1830-96), painter and sculptor, dominated the artistic world in London in the last quarter of the nineteenth century – not only by his work (though that was majestic enough) but by his patrician, leonine presence, and his leadership of the Royal Academy.

He seemed to burst into notice fully-armed, like Athena from the head of Zeus. His first major work, *Cimabue's Madonna*, a huge and very ambitious painting of a procession in Florence in which the central figures are Cimabue and his pupil Giotto, was exhibited in London in 1855 at the Royal Academy, when Leighton was still living abroad. It created a sensation, and was bought by the queen – on the advice of Prince Albert, who recognized (no doubt) the arrival of a genius, but must also have seen that the antecedents of the painting were German. For, although Leighton had been born in Yorkshire, at Scarborough, he had travelled with his family all round the continent. He had learnt his trade in Berlin, Rome, Florence, Paris – and in Frankfurt, where, during the most important period of his education, he was the pupil of Eduard von Steinle, a leader of the Nazarene School, which both anticipated and greatly influenced the Pre-Raphaelite Brotherhood by seeking to revive German art in the pure, ideal pattern of the early Renaissance.

It was, then, the 'foreign-ness', as well as the brilliance, of *Cimabue's Giotto* that attracted Prince Albert's patronage. But the same 'foreign-ness' caused Leighton to be suspected by xenophobic critics and conservative Academicians. In spite of a series of paintings which showed a mastery of his art, including the magnificent *Syracusan Bride* (1866), a procession like *Cimabue's Madonna*, but this time of beautiful women going to the wedding in the company of some dangerously frisky tigers and leopards – in spite of these, it was not until 1868 that he was elected RA. But the next year he served on the Hanging Committee of the Academy; was soon added to the Council; and in 1878, on the death of Sir Francis Grant, was chosen President (and knighted by the queen).

His distinguished appearance alone seemed to qualify him for the position. He had helped to form the Artists' Rifles in 1860, and in 1869 he became its commander – a tribute to his natural authority. But so many were his abilities that Whistler, once hearing them enumerated, said: 'Hmm. Yes. Paints a bit too, don't he?' Leighton was the best President of the Academy since Sir Joshua Reynolds: a new broom in the administration, an opener of windows on stuffy prejudices, a consistent and generous advocate of younger, unknown, perhaps avant-garde artists (whom he often helped from his own pocket though he might not sympathize with their work). Both by personal example, and by making changes which were at first resisted, he greatly improved the teaching in the Academy Schools. For nearly twenty years, he 'was' the Royal Academy – when the Royal Academy 'was' British painting. He stands as the central figure in Frith's *The Private View of the Royal Academy in 1881*. But he drove himself beyond his power: he had never been robust. Angina struck him in 1894, and helped to bring him to his death in 1896. At that last New Year, he became the first and only artist to be raised to the British peerage.

The wonderful thing is that, all the time that he held these offices, he had continued to produce a stream of paintings. The artist who was so prolific lived a concentrated and disciplined life. Although he had a large number of friends and in the highest places, he seems to have been reluctant to enter an intimate relationship with anyone. He never married; and, when he built his 'Aesthetic Palace' in Holland Park – now known as Leighton House and open to the public – he provided for reception rooms, for a huge studio with picture gallery, for a breathtaking 'Arab Hall', but no guest bedroom. He employed only two living-in servants, so as to avoid the fuss of a larger establishment.

His principal relaxation was to travel – and to paint as he travelled. He followed the principle he jotted down in his sketchbook: 'Art is the utterance of our delight in the phenomena of nature and an endeavour to communicate to others and perpetuate that delight.' He went abroad almost every year in the late summer; and the paintings he made are delightful. Small in size, fresh and unlaboured, with brilliant effects of light, they are close relations of Corot's Italian landscapes (1825-8). They were useful also as 'evidence' for the landscape backgrounds of his 'serious' work.

For pure landscape painting was still unregarded, even disdained, in official circles; and Leighton bowed to a convention which Edward Lear and other landscape painters struggled against. In any case, he was ambitious. The great paintings of his middle years consolidated his reputation for loftiness of sentiment and an almost magical craft. His technique, beginning with very careful drawing, was elaborate and painstaking to a degree unique in British art, and was generally followed through in every area of the painting. Thus one finds in his work, as in the work of the Venetian masters of the sixteenth century (whom he greatly admired), colouring which succeeds in being both brilliant and subtle. One finds a genius for large-scale composition. And one finds the very high degree of finish which characterized his work and was later criticized. In this respect he was the

English Ingres. He was urged to leave parts of a painting *un*finished, so that the viewer could share in the act of creation. But that was not his way. It is in the drapery of his figures – where the accumulation of folds and pleats and creases becomes superfluous – that one sees most clearly his obsession with completeness, as well as a regal zest in the bounteous demonstration of his powers. Yet he was not satisfied: every painting was to some extent a failure: 'With every painting I complete, I follow the funeral of my ideal.'

His subjects were taken mostly from classical mythology and the Old Testament. The procession of his paintings can be studied in galleries on both sides of the Atlantic. Finally his treatment of the subject becomes largely symbolical: e.g. *The Return of Persephone* (1891) and the famous *Flaming June* (1895). But the best of his last paintings is *Captive Andromache* (1888, Manchester City Art Galleries), the climax of his processional paintings, and a wonderful exercise in colour and chiaroscuro with (at the centre) the dark, grief-laden figure of Andromache,

> The wife of that same Hector that fought best
> Of all the Trojans when all fought for Troy.

Among Leighton's portraits is the early, full-length study of *May Sartoris* (Fort Worth, Texas), showing a fifteen-year-old girl dressed in a heavy riding-habit of darkest blue and black slashed by a scarlet scarf: it is a living, breathing refutation of the notion that Leighton's characterization was passionless. The National Portrait Gallery holds the incandescent features of Sir Richard Burton, the traveller (1876). And there is a self-portrait (painted, signficantly, against a background of part of the north frieze of the Parthenon) in the Uffizi Gallery, Florence.

It is curious that Leighton gave the title of 'England's Michelangelo' to his friend and neighbour, G. F. Watts. Some of those last paintings of Leighton's – *Flaming June* included – derive from a study of Michelangelo more obviously than anything of Watts's. But both artists had studied Greek sculpture, and had casts of the Elgin Marbles in their studio; which accounts for the static, sculpturesque quality of some of Leighton's drapery, and for the frieze-like character of his processional paintings. And Leighton, like Watts, executed a handful of distinguished sculptures: his powerful *Athlete Wrestling with a Python* (1877) can be seen in the Tate.

In fact Leighton both led and inspired contemporary British sculpture – the so-called New Sculpture; but, in the field of painting, his very 'perfection' turned away followers, and he left no heirs of importance. Even his own work was after a time forgotten. The tantalizing story of *Flaming June* is now well known. It vanished from sight in 1930. It reappeared in 1963 – when it could have been had for £50 or less (with frame). Finally it was bought by a connoisseur, the then Governor of Puerto Rico, for his Museum at Ponce. There it resides today, and one would find it hard to overestimate its value. The reputation of its creator has apparently followed much the same course.

Further Reading
Stephen Jones and others, *Frederic Leighton 1830-1896* (Catalogue of the Royal Academy of Arts Exhibition, 1996).

LELY, SIR PETER (1618-80), painter, belonged to a Flanders family, although he was born at Soest in Westphalia, son of a captain in the Brandenburg army. He studied at Haarlem and first came to England in the 1640s. Turning from landscape to the more profitable task of portraits, he painted the children of Charles I in 1647. The coming of the Republic did him no harm, nor did the Restoration. He painted Oliver Cromwell early in the Protectorate, by which time he was firmly established in upper-class favour; yet in 1661 Charles conferred a pension of £200 per annum on him, recognizing him as the successor to Van Dyck, and in 1662 he was naturalized. Until his death in 1680, just after his knighthood, Lely continued to be the leading artist in his adopted country, turning out a long succession of society portraits. Like Kneller after him, he developed a kind of studio factory, employing assistants to add details and background, and as with Kneller the result was a great quantity of mediocre work. Yet there were striking exceptions, notably perhaps when he escaped from the languid female fashions of the Restoration: the portraits of admirals which he did during the Second Dutch War (now at Greenwich) reveal Lely at his shrewd and vigorous best. In the history of English portraiture the pattern developed by Lely lasted for over a century.

Further Reading
R. B. Beckett, *Peter Lely*, 1951.

LENTHALL, WILLIAM (1591-1662), Speaker of the Long Parliament, was a barrister, born at Henley-on-Thames of gentry stock and educated at St Alban Hall, Oxford, and Lincoln's Inn, who had already done well in his profession and bought country estates (including Burford Abbey from the Falkland family), before entering the Commons in 1640 as member for Woodstock. He is celebrated for his adroit reply to Charles I when the king entered the House with an armed retinue in January 1642 and demanded to know where the Five Members were: 'May it please your Majesty, I have neither eyes to see nor tongue to speak in this place but as this House is pleased to direct me, whose servant I am here; and humbly beg your Majesty's pardon that I cannot give any other answer than this to what your Majesty is pleased to demand of me'. The remainder of his long record as Speaker is not glorious. He sided with parliament against the king in 1642 and with the army against

the Presbyterians in 1647. He accepted Pride's Purge in 1648 and, although he was not a member of the court which condemned the king, he showed no reluctance to be the nominal chief magistrate of the Republic. He was turned out with the Rump in 1653, when he put up a token resistance and compelled Harrison to help him down from his chair, but he was back again as Speaker of the first Protectorate Parliament next year. In the parliament of 1656 Lenthall had a seat but not the Speakership, and was one of those who urged Oliver to take the Crown; yet in 1659 he came back leading the Rump. At the Restoration he backed Monck. But fortune deserted him: he got no seat in the Convention and although his life was secure he was excepted from the Indemnity. A testimonial from Monck saved him from imprisonment, and he returned to his estates at Burford to die in 1662. It was no doubt a measure of his fears for his own safety that he stooped to give evidence against one of the regicides, of words spoken in the Commons.

LEOBA, ST (*d.c.*780) was a native of Wessex who went out to Germany to assist Boniface and ended her life as Abbess of Tauberbischofsheim in Franconia. As a young girl she was placed in the monastery of Wimborne in Dorset which had recently been founded by the sisters of King Ine of Wessex. When she grew up she spent some time pursuing her studies at the Kentish monastery of Minster-in-Thanet. It was from there that Leoba first wrote to Boniface, to whom she was related through her mother, in about 732, introducing herself, asking for his prayers and proudly sending him some of her Latin verse. She seems to have returned to Wimborne shortly afterwards, for it was to her abbess there that Boniface addressed himself a few years later, probably about 738, to ask her to allow Leoba to come to join him in Germany. Boniface founded a nunnery at Tauberbischofsheim and placed Leoba in charge of it. She remained there as abbess for the rest of her life.

Leoba's career furnishes another example of the important role played by women in the early Anglo-Saxon and Anglo-German church. In addition to being a highly competent abbess, Leoba was remarkable for her learning. Her ninth-century biographer, who had access to the recollections of four of Leoba's pupils, tells us that to a good knowledge of the scriptures 'she added by way of completion the writings of the church fathers, the decrees of councils and the whole of ecclesiastical law'. Her personality was as formidable as her learning. Her pupils remembered reading to her at night when she was old. Even when she seemed to nod off to sleep she never relaxed her vigilance and would be quick to pounce on any mistakes made by the reader. Sometimes they made mistakes on purpose, to test her, but never did they go undetected. Leoba was one of the first in that long (and continuing) tradition of distinguished but sometimes alarming academic ladies who have contributed so largely to English intellectual life.

Further Reading
The ninth-century life of Leoba is translated by C. H. Talbot, *The Anglo-Saxon Missionaries in Germany*, 1954.

LEOFRIC (*d*.1072), Bishop of Exeter from 1046 until his death, is chiefly remembered today for the book-collection he amassed and left to his cathedral library. Leofric was apparently a native of Cornwall, but he was brought up and educated in Lotharingia, that is, roughly speaking, the western parts of the Rhineland. At that period Lotharingian cathedral communities and religious houses were renowned as centres of learning, spirituality and ecclesiastical revitalization. Bruno, Bishop of Toul from 1027 to 1048, was not untypical of the sort of churchmen under whose influence Leofric may have come; as Pope Leo IX (1048-54) Bruno was to become a famous reformer. In addition to receiving a good education and becoming acquainted with the latest tendencies in continental church life, Leofric seems also to have met and entered the service of the exiled Prince Edward (later to be known as Edward the Confessor). Leofric seems to have been in Edward's entourage when he returned to England in 1041. After his accession to the throne in 1042 Leofric was one of the 'king's priests', i.e. an important minister and civil servant. He was rewarded with a bishopric in 1046.

The bishopric established at Crediton early in the tenth century by Archbishop Plegmund had responsibility for the whole vast area of Devon and Cornwall. At some point in the tenth century a separate diocese for Cornwall had been established, rather precariously, at St Germans, just across the river Tamar from Plymouth. Leofric decided to concentrate the two, to fix the seat of the diocese at an important urban centre, Exeter, and to reform the way of life of the cathedral community by introducing canons living according to the rule of Bishop Chrodegang of Metz (*d*.766). (In the middle years of the eleventh century this was a cathedral constitution much favoured by reforming churchmen in Lotharingia and Germany.) The approval of Pope Leo IX was secured in 1049 and of King Edward in 1050. Within four years of his appointment Leofric had carried out a major reform in his diocese.

He also made it his task to put the finances of his bishopric on a secure footing. This he did partly by consolidating and extending its landed endowments, partly by instituting regular arrangements for sharing the income therefrom between on the one hand the bishop and his household and on the other the community of canons who formed the cathedral chapter. This, again, was a common concern of ecclesiastical reformers of the period. It also displays the disciplined planning of the

former civil servant. Like his contemporary Ealdred of York – though not on Ealdred's princely scale – Leofric undertook also to embellish his church by stocking it with treasures. These included vestments, bells, processional crosses, silver plate, carpets and other hangings; also such curiosities as three bear-skins, a 'fyrdwain' (or 'army-cart' – whatever that might have been) and a silver pipe through which consecrated wine could be sucked from a chalice as through a straw (an instrument technically known as a fistula).

He also left to his church a very considerable library of over sixty volumes. About half of these were service books of one sort or another. Also represented were canon law, and some of the works of Pope Gregory I and Bede. Some of the books were in Old English. These included the translation of Boethius by King Alfred and 'a big English book on various subjects written in verse'. This volume, happily still where Leofric left it, is the manuscript known as the Exeter Book, one of the principal collections of Old English poetry. It contains, among much else, two of the poems of Cynewulf and such other deservedly famous pieces as *The Wanderer*, *The Seafarer*, *Widsith*, *Deor*, *The Wife's Lament* and *The Ruin*.

After his death in 1072 Leofric was remembered as a good man and an active pastor. Bishops such as he give the lie to the Norman propaganda myth that the late Anglo-Saxon church was somehow 'decadent'. Nothing could be further from the truth.

Further Reading
F. Barlow and others, *Leofric of Exeter*, 1972, is a pleasing collection of essays. Nearly all the poems in the Exeter Book have been translated (into prose) by S. A. J. Bradley, *Anglo-Saxon Poetry*, 1982.

L'ESTRANGE, SIR ROGER (1616-1704), journalist, was born at Hunstanton, member of a well-to-do Norfolk royalist family. He served under Rupert, and was in a parliamentary prison for three years under sentence of death for his part in a plot to recover Lynn for the king. On his release in 1648 he at once promoted a futile royalist rising in Kent, and then fled abroad, returning in 1653. In 1659 he was busy pamphleteering against Lambert and in favour of the monarchy, and at the Restoration he came into his own, combining the occupations of government spy and editor of a semi-official newspaper. L'Estrange, an accomplished musician and a scholar who wrote translations from the Spanish and published a very large collection of *Aesop's Fables*, a man in Pepys's words 'of fine conversation … most courtly', was also the holder of firmly reactionary opinions, and in 1663 he wrote a pamphlet denouncing the liberty of the press. As a result he was in the same year appointed 'Surveyor of the imprimery and printing presses', and he held the office – in which he was responsible for hunting down illicit presses and pamphlets – almost continuously until the Revolution of 1688. He used his powers vigorously, employing informers and corruption and aiming particularly at Republicans and Dissenters. One printer of a seditious pamphlet, John Twyn, was hanged, drawn and quartered on l'Estrange's evidence; and in 1670 he claimed to have suppressed over 600 pamphlets. Yet it is clear that he was in fact very unsuccessful, partly perhaps because, so it was said, he was too susceptible to female blandishments. In 1680 he ran into trouble over the Popish Plot, when a false witness was employed against him, and he fled abroad, while the London mob burned his effigy. He returned in 1681, soon recovered his authority, and did much to get Oates convicted of perjury. James II knighted him, but this did not prevent l'Estrange, characteristically, from attacking the king's proposals for religious toleration. Inevitably the Revolution brought his dismissal, and within a few years the lapse of the system of licensing of the press. His last years were unhappy ones, marked by short spells of imprisonment (he was suspected in 1696 of a share in the Assassination Plot) and by financial trouble caused by a wife addicted to gambling.

Further Reading
G. Kitchin, *Sir Roger l'Estrange*, 1913.

LIGONIER, JEAN-LOUIS (1680-1770), general, was born at Castres, the son of Huguenot parents of good stock. In 1698 he followed into exile others of his family who had left after the Revocation of the Edict of Nantes. From Holland he went to Ireland, whence, after four years of obscurity, he turned up in England, became a naturalized Englishman and joined, as a volunteer, the army of the Duke of Marlborough. He showed courage and discretion in the campaigns of Flanders and Germany. He was the first man through the breach into Liège in 1702 and was allowed to buy himself a company in the Tenth Foot. In 1706, for dashing leadership of assault troops in the attack on Menin, he was promoted major. At Malplaquet he showed once more the courage for which he became renowned; after the battle he counted twenty bullet holes in his clothing. After the Peace of Utrecht, in 1713, he was given the governorship of Fort St Philip in Minorca. He was adjutant-general to the force which captured Vigo in 1719 and in 1720 acquired his own regiment, the Eighth Horse. Thus, without favour or private income, he made his mark. Stationed in Ireland from 1720 to 1724, the Black Guards, as they were called, became known as an elite force, so that men paid for the privilege of being a trooper and later distinguished themselves in the Flanders campaigns of 1742-5. Ligonier did not marry, but kept a mistress in Southwark, by whom he had several children. He had, nevertheless, some standing in Irish society; he seems to have been a man of much charm, generous, vivacious and hospitable.

Circumstances favoured him in the War of the Austrian Succession. In the small army allowed by peacetime economies there was a shortage of good regimental officers who had taken pains to study their craft, or had much fighting experience. That the supreme command in Flanders went, after the resignation of Stair in 1743, first to the septuagenarian Wade, then, in 1745, to the Duke of Cumberland, twenty-five years old, speaks for itself. Again Ligonier, as a relative outsider, was by necessity a professional whose prospects were unprejudiced by political affiliations. He knew, too, how to make himself agreeable to George II and accompanied him as a personal staff officer, liaising between the king, the Cabinet and Lord Stair. At Dettingen, in 1743, George II was so taken with his conduct that he wished to make him a Knight Banneret on the field; he was subsequently made a Knight of the Bath. In 1744, because of Wade's indisposition, he was for long periods virtually commander-in-chief. By contrast with his fellow general Hawley, he was humane: 'it is with the greatest reluctance I set my name to a death warrant'. At Fontenoy in 1745, under Cumberland, he was in command of the British infantry who were praised throughout Europe for their gallant advance and disciplined retreat. Their training, and their handling on the field, saved the army from the effects of Cumberland's careless reconnaissance and rash orders.

Ligonier preceded Cumberland home after the Jacobite landing later in the year but, after organizing the army which was to have confronted Charles Edward if he had marched upon London, he played no part in the subsequent Scottish campaign. It is typical of Ligonier that he should have provided for an issue of blankets for his troops against the hazards of winter in the Highlands – the first time that this was done. Earlier he had paid out of his own pocket for an extra doctor for his regiment, got Treasury approval for the issue of wheat instead of rye for soldiers' bread, and instituted regimental hospitals in Flanders. At Roucoux in 1746 it was his handling of a much smaller force that saved the allies from a severe defeat. He was captured at Laffeldt in the following year, ironically, after his greatest feat of arms. By his advice to Cumberland to hold the village of Laffeldt – which inflicted heavy casualties on Saxe – and by his superb use of the cavalry, he enabled the infantry to extricate themselves from a tricky situation. The devotion of young Lord Henry Campbell, who met his death scouring the battlefield for his chief, is a tribute to Ligonier's power to inspire young officers. Saxe, who had lost about 10,000 men, far more than the allies, is said to have presented him to Louis XV as 'a man who has defeated all my plans by a single glorious action', to which Louis replied, 'The English have not only paid all but fought all'. Ligonier was subsequently released on exchange.

Peace, in 1748, brought recognition of his services. He entered parliament for Bath. He seems to have taken some interest in the affairs of the growing town and was a close friend of Ralph Wood, after Nash the principal organizer of Bath society, but never spoke in parliament. Another unsolicited honour was election to the Royal Society, a remarkable honour for a Frenchman and a soldier, although he had cultivated tastes and an extensive library. In the same year he became lieutenant-general of the Ordnance, the highest professional military position in the peacetime army. It was of this period of his life that Horace Walpole wrote: 'He had all the gallant gaiety of his nation. Polished from foppery by age and by living in a more thinking country, he was universally beloved and respected'. He was also very busy. As President of the Board of Officers, he was concerned during these years with the standardization of dress, drill and tactics. During this period, the Ordnance Survey was begun and the Corps of Engineers developed as a military body. When war broke out again in 1756, and after the severe economies of the Pelham administration and the mistakes of men on the spot, Byng and Braddock among them, the ministry found itself faced with a crisis of nerve and resources, it was lucky that Pitt had as adviser a man of Ligonier's calibre.

It is difficult to apportion credit for the remarkable victories of 1758-62 between the politician Pitt, and the soldier Ligonier, who was the equivalent of a modern chief of general staff. Ligonier left very few papers; advice taken over the dinner table leaves no mark in history. But both Corbett, naval historian of the period, and his own biographer Whitworth, make large claims for him. In two ways particularly he was of service. The precise and ambitious plans for the reconquest of North America were his work, and the appointment to independent commands of relatively junior officers such as Forbes, Wolfe and Amherst reflects his own knowledge of the service. Amherst had been on his staff; he was a brilliant success in Canada. He was also largely behind the policy of diversionary attacks on the French coast. Tactically, they can be criticized for waste of precious resources, but they helped to relieve the pressure on Frederick the Great. More effective in this way were the continental campaigns of Ferdinand of Brunswick. Again Ligonier pressed for full support in these operations, against a sometimes reluctant Pitt. Brunswick had under him, at one point, more redcoats than ever Marlborough did. The glory of the battle of Minden has to some extent obscured the success of later actions, but the brilliant performances of the Marquis of Granby, and Brunswick's victories, proved the wisdom of Ligonier and the quality of English troops. Again and again the French were defeated; after 1758, Frederick had no

French troops to face. 1762, the year after Pitt's retirement, brought victories as fine, in their way, as 1759. The achievement of a man of his age, at a time when staffs and secretariats were minimal, in planning a global war effort, places him among the few great chiefs of staff. The success of the British in this war was owed largely to the fact that there was an overall strategic direction from a soldier, familiar both with the problems of the soldier in the line and the commissariat at home.

When Ligonier became a baron, he was dismissed as Master of the Ordnance by Bute's government in 1763 (one of the charges of the *North Briton*): he had been an Irish peer since 1757. In 1766, when he was superseded by Granby as Commander-in-Chief, he was raised to an earldom. He lived four more years, single to the end although he nearly made a match with a widow before she discovered that he was over eighty at the time. His reputation for gallantry received unpleasant twists from a scurrilous satire which suggested that he employed a valet to procure girls for him. He may have been licentious. He could also be hard: in 1759 he ordered the court martial sentence upon Sackville, dismissed the service for disobedience to orders at Minden, to be read out to all regiments as an example, 'so that officers may be convinced that neither high birth nor great employment can shelter offences of such a nature'. But his name was secure with the British soldier whose interests he had always made his first concern. An obituary notice said of him: 'In him the soldier has lost a real friend: one who in public and private life did honour to humanity'.

Further Reading
R. Whitworth, *Field Marshal Lord Ligonier*, 1958.

LILBURNE, JOHN (1615-57), the most spectacular champion of individual freedom in the English Revolution, was probably born in Sunderland, of a well-to-do family of the lesser gentry of north-eastern England. Educated at Bishop Auckland Grammar School and the Royal Grammar School, Newcastle-upon-Tyne, he was sent to London about 1630 as apprentice to a clothier, and quickly fell under its Puritan influences. In 1636 he was taken to see John Bastwick, in prison for his tracts against the bishops. Lilburne plunged with enthusiasm into the enterprise of getting copies of Bastwick's scurrilous *Letany* printed in Holland and smuggled into England. He was betrayed, and in 1638 haled before the Star Chamber, to face the first of a series of trials and imprisonments. From the start he displayed that blend of acumen and impudence which drove his judges to despair, and that flair for publicity and sense of an audience which made him the hero of the age with thousands of Londoners. On this occasion 'Free-born John', as he was quickly nicknamed, declined to swear the ex officio oath, under which he might be compelled to condemn himself or others. He was sentenced to a fine of £500, to be whipped from the Fleet prison to Westminster and there pilloried, and to be kept in prison until he conformed to the law.

He remained in prison until the meeting of the Long Parliament, when he was released on a petition presented by Oliver Cromwell. Despite the appalling conditions of the Fleet, where he was shackled and in ill-health, he employed his martyrdom in two related activities which were to form parts of the pattern of his entire career. He wrote several pamphlets, on his trial and in support of the Puritan cause, and he organized petitions for his release. In 1641-2 he took part in the demonstrations and riots with which Londoners welcomed the condemnation of Strafford and the widening breach between king and parliament. For a short time he ran a brewery, and he got married; but when the fighting began in the summer of 1642 he went off to the wars, with a captain's commission in Lord Brooke's regiment of infantry. Nearly all the Lilburnes were for parliament; his brother Colonel Robert Lilburne had a distinguished military career, defeating the royalists of Northumberland in the Second Civil War and Derby's Cavalier force at Wigan in 1651, and signed the king's death-warrant in 1649. John fought at Edgehill and at Brentford, where he was taken prisoner and sent to royalist headquarters at Oxford; here he narrowly escaped trial for treason, but was eventually exchanged. Joining the army of the Eastern Association, he fought as a Lieutenant-Colonel of dragoons under Manchester at Marston Moor, and received the surrender of Tickhill Castle. But in 1645 he declined to take the Covenant, and left the army.

This action marked the beginning of Lilburne's courageous yet hectic and futile political career as the leading figure among those who from 1647 came to be called the Levellers. Hostile to the Presbyterians, a champion of freedom of conscience and of the press, Lilburne was in no sense a man with a political programme, still less a political organizer. He was by temperament an individualist and a propagandist, believing passionately in freedom, to which he and the Levellers gave a wider political content than the parliamentarian leaders. In 1645 he came into collision with the Presbyterian majority in the Commons, and was imprisoned in Newgate for two months. His fame spread – partly at least because of the way in which he dealt with committees who examined him, reading Magna Carta to them and to the Sergeant-at-Arms – and crowds followed him everywhere. His activities brought him into contact with the abler minds of other leading radicals, William Walwyn and Richard Overton, and he widened the scope of his pamphleteering, publishing in October *England's Birthright Justified*, which denounced such popular grievances as monopolies, tithes and the excise, and demanded toleration, freedom of speech, annual parliaments and the rule of law.

Here was an outline of the Leveller programme. But in 1646 Lilburne was in trouble with the House of Lords, initially over a libel on the Earl of Manchester. Before them he refused to kneel, he put his fingers in his ears, and he appealed to the Commons. The Lords despatched him to the Tower, whence he continued to produce pamphlets, this time demanding a reform of the government of the city. In February 1647 he managed to get a Commons committee to examine him – with the doors open to the public. By this date Leveller ideas were gaining ground, not only in London but also among the common soldiers of the army, alarmed about the arrears of their pay and about the hostility of the Presbyterians in parliament to independency in religion. Lilburne turned to the army for support. He had hopes of the officers, and in March he wrote a remarkable letter to Cromwell, warning him against his parliamentary advisers in a splendid phrase ('O Cromwell, thou art led by the nose by two unworthy covetous earthworms, Vane and St John') and appealing to him to resist the 'tyranny' of parliament. More important, he was in touch with the Agitators appointed by the regiments. In August 1647 the army entered London. But Lilburne was not released from the Tower, and he took no part in the Putney Debates of October and November on *The Case of the Army*. He remained in prison until August 1648, and after his release he clashed over liberty of conscience with the leaders of the army, now triumphant in the Second Civil War.

Lilburne opposed the trial and execution of the king. He had been in contact with royalist fellow prisoners in the Tower; and he realized that the destruction of the king did not solve his own problems or those of the common soldiers. The way was now open to the new and more powerful tyranny of the army commanders. Characteristically, he soon appeared before the Rump with an outspoken petition entitled *England's New Chains*. Scarcely surprisingly, the government struck back. The three chief Levellers, Lilburne, Overton and Walwyn, were arrested in March, and when the Leveller-mutineers were crushed at Burford in May a special force of troops was sent to make sure Lilburne did not escape from the Tower. There was widespread unrest this year, with rumours of an alliance between the Levellers and the royalists, and not until August, after he had bitterly denounced Cromwell and the army leaders in *An Impeachment of High Treason*, was Lilburne put on trial for high treason. It was an extraordinary trial, with the judges and prisoner shouting at one another, Lilburne using every technicality and delay (at one point he sent for a chamber pot and used it), the Guildhall packed with his supporters. The jury of Londoners acquitted him, with immense popular rejoicing.

But it was a hollow triumph – a personal victory for Lilburne, not for the cause for which he stood. The

Leveller movement was dead, and the remainder of Lilburne's career has the air of anticlimax and disillusion. He started business as a soap-boiler; he got (through Cromwell) a grant of lands in Durham; and he acted as a pleader in the law-courts for other men's cases. One of these brought disaster, for he published a pamphlet in a case against Sir Arthur Hasilrige, a leading parliamentarian and an old enemy of the Lilburne family; the Rump took exception and banished him, in December 1651. He went in 1652 to Amsterdam and then to Bruges; hobnobbed with royalists, notably the Duke of Buckingham; and inevitably wrote a pamphlet, *Lieutenant-Colonel John Lilburne Revived*, against the army and Cromwell. When the Rump was turned out in 1653, he returned without official authority and was arrested. Put on trial again for breaking his banishment, he once more attracted immense popular support, and was again acquitted by the jury. But this time the government, alarmed by the popular enthusiasm, did not release him. Instead they sent him in 1654 to the remote fortress of Mount Orgueil in Jersey, where his old adversary Prynne had once been incarcerated, and there, deprived of crowds of fellow prisoners and visitors, far away from any means of popular appeal, his spirit began to change. In October 1655 he was brought back to Dover Castle, and was converted to Quakerism, becoming dead, as he put it in a last pamphlet, *The Resurrection of John Lilburne* (1656), to 'carnal sword fightings and fleshy buslings and contests'. He was allowed free on parole a good deal; but he was now worn out by the strains and sufferings of his career, and in 1657 he died at Eltham.

Lilburne, who was the father of ten children and who lost an eye in an accident in 1645, was a remarkable man – tough, sincere, a gifted pamphleteer, a natural lawyer, a man with a vision of the needs of others. Yet he achieved nothing and he founded no lasting movement. This was partly no doubt because the Leveller movement rested on too narrow a social basis: it offered nothing to the great mass of the poor, it frightened the property-owning class, it depended too much on London craftsmen and small freeholders in economic difficulty. And the Levellers were outmanoeuvred as well as overpowered by Cromwell, Ireton and the other army leaders. Yet the causes of Lilburne's failure lay in great part in himself. He was an individualist, with the power to defy but not to construct; far more a showman than a statesman, he performed heroically and brilliantly, yet always on issues of other men's choosing. Turbulent and impetuous, a classical case of the man who is always against the government, he roused opinion without organizing it, and his legacy is only the memory of a hero.

Further Reading
Pauline Gregg, *Free-Born John*, 1961.

LINACRE, THOMAS (1460?-1524), physician and classical scholar, was born probably in 1460 and died in 1524. Nothing is known for certain about his family origins or his early life. About 1480 he went to Oxford, but to which college is not known. He became a Fellow of All Souls in 1484. It is possible that he learned the elements of Greek from the Italian scholar Vitelli, who was then at Oxford, and that he attended lectures given by Grocyn, with whom he became an intimate friend.

Perhaps Linacre obtained his earliest education from William de Selling, Prior of Canterbury, who may have been his uncle. We know for certain that Linacre accompanied Selling when the latter travelled to Rome in 1485 as Henry VII's ambassador. Probably they parted company at Bologna and Linacre attached himself to the great Italian classical scholar, Poliziano, and went with him to Florence. Linacre at once attracted attention by his quick and intelligent mind. He shared his studies with Lorenzo de Medici's two sons, one of whom later became Pope Leo X and did not forget this early friendship.

At some unknown date Linacre visited Rome, where he met the classical scholar, Hermolaus Barbarus, and it is more than probable that it was Barbarus who first turned Linacre's attention to the study of medicine. It may have been Barbarus also who gave Linacre his accurate and critical knowledge of Aristotle.

In 1495 Linacre was in Venice where he lived with Aldus Manutius, the founder of the Aldine Press and the greatest of the Italian printers. Aldus was devoted to Greek scholarship, especially to Aristotle rather than to Plato. He published the first volume of the Aldine edition of the works of Aristotle in 1495: the third volume appeared in 1497 with a tribute in the preface to the scholarship of Linacre. Aldus paid a further tribute to him when he published in 1497 Linacre's translation of Proclus's work *de Sphera*.

Linacre was at Padua, the most famous university in Europe for medicine, late in 1495. On 30 August 1496, he took his MD at Padua and Richard Pace has recorded the vivid impression which Linacre made on his examiners by his learning and his quickness. The next year he set out for England and on his way he visited at Vicenza the greatest of the Italian medical scholars, Leonicenus, who was the author of the first treatise on syphilis, the new disease which was beginning to attack Europe.

The precise date of Linacre's return to Oxford is not known, but after he was back, on the strength of his degree in medicine at Padua, he was given an MD at Oxford. He soon established a high reputation as a lecturer on medical subjects, and he probably also lectured on Greek subjects, especially on Aristotle. From Linacre Thomas More learned Greek; Erasmus owed much to his friendship and inspiration; and Colet was one of his closest friends until an unfortunate quarrel over a Latin grammar which Linacre wrote for Colet's new school of St Paul's. It is not improbable that Linacre spent a time at Cambridge, according to Dr Caius (the refounder of Gonville Hall under the name of Gonville and Caius College), and the fact that Linacre founded a lectureship at Cambridge suggests that he had some reason for remembering that university.

In 1500 or 1501 Linacre became tutor to Prince Arthur, but the prince died in 1502, so that Linacre's post was a short-lived one. In 1509 he was appointed physician to Henry VIII at a salary of £50 a year. This entailed his leaving Oxford and living almost exclusively in London, where he soon acquired a large and distinguished practice as a doctor: his patients included Wolsey, Warham, Fox, Colet, More, Erasmus and many others.

It is probable that Linacre was ordained deacon in 1511, but he was not admitted priest until 1520. Even before 1511 he was receiving many ecclesiastical benefices, and after 1520 he was given many more. He never resided in them: it was a common thing to present these livings to distinguished men who then sold them to clergy who were willing to pay for a living. Thus Linacre built up a considerable fortune which later he decided to use for the public advantage. About 1520 Linacre gave up his medical practice so as to have more time for literary work. Sir John Cheke tells a story that late in life Linacre took up the New Testament for the first time in his life and on reading the Sermon on the Mount exclaimed, as he threw the book away, 'either this is not the Gospel or we are not Christians'.

In 1523 he was appointed tutor to the Princess Mary, when she was five years old. But he died on 20 October 1524, and was buried in the old Cathedral of St Paul's. He died of the stone, the medical name for which was calculus. Linacre was a noted grammarian, and it is likely that it was Linacre whom Browning had in mind when he wrote his *Grammarian's Funeral*:

> Back to his book then; deeper dropped his head;
> Calculus racked him.

Although Linacre was a priest, although he was a very considerable classical scholar with great interest in Latin grammar, he cannot be called typical of the Oxford humanists who were his contemporaries, for his chief interest was not in theology but in medicine. His principal claim to fame lies in the immense amount he did to further medical knowledge in the sixteenth century by translating several of the medical works of Galen out of Greek into Latin, thereby making them more widely understandable, and to make possible further advances in medical knowledge by his founding the College of Physicians in 1518, and by the foundation of two lectureships in medicine at Oxford and one at Cambridge. In his own day it was as a classical scholar that he was revered by such men as Erasmus. His most important contribution to scholarship was his treatise *De Emendata Structura Latini Sermonis*, published in the year of his death, 1524, printed by Richard Pynson.

The queen owns a portrait which is said to be of Linacre and to have been painted by Quentin Matsys.

Further Reading
R. Weiss, *Humanism in England during the Fifteenth Century*, 3rd edn, 1967.
R. J. Mitchell, *English Historical Review*, 1935.
J. F. Fulton, *New England Journal of Medicine*, 1934.
W. Osler, *Linacre Memorial Lecture*, 1908.
J. N. Johnson, *Life of Linacre*, 1835.

LIND, JAMES (1716-94), physician, has an honoured place in the history of the navy as the man who did most to combat the scurvy and other deficiency diseases which lowered the efficiency of ships on long voyages. He served with Vernon in the West Indies in 1739-41 and later off the coast of Guinea. For the sufferings of men with scurvy, the reader should turn to Smollett, also for a time a naval surgeon, and the adventures of Roderick Random. Lind was subsequently physician to the Naval Hospital at Haslar and able to deepen his study of illness on board ship. We may wonder how men survived at all in the cramped, reeking quarters of these ships, on a diet that was too often reduced to weevily bread and biscuit, maggoty salt pork and brackish water. Lind was not alone in realizing the importance of balancing the diet. But he brought scientific observation to bear, wrote treatises on the subject, and influenced thoughtful seamen like Anson and Cook. In 1754 he published his *Treatise of Scurvy*, suggesting green vegetables, fresh fruit and lime juice as preventives. In 1768 he presented a fuller survey in his *Essay ... for preserving the life of Seamen*. If it were no longer true at the end of the century that, as Lind said, 'the number of seamen in time of war who died by shipwreck, capture, famine, fire or sword, are but inconsiderable in respect of such as are destroyed by the ship diseases and by the usual maladies of an intemperate climate', this was a fine memorial to him. His work was carried further by Gilbert Blane (1749-1834) who obtained free issues of soap and medicines for seamen.

Further Reading
N. A. M. Rodger, *The Wooden World: An Anatomy of the Georgian Navy*, 1986.

LINGARD, JOHN (1771-1851), the son of a Lincolnshire carpenter, and a Roman Catholic, was the first English historian to make a principle of writing from authentic sources. His twelve volume *History of England from the first Invasion by the Romans to the Revolution of 1688*, begun in 1811, in progress for most of the rest of his life, and last printed in 1914, was the most popular history of England until the appearance of

Green's (in 1874). Although somewhat unbalanced in areas of treatment (the last 200 years occupy more than two-thirds of his volumes), it still merits respect for its scrupulous accuracy and pleasing style.

Lingard was sent to Douai, the English College in Flanders where Daniel O'Connell was among his fellow students. When the college was suppressed by the revolutionary government in 1793 he came to Crook Hall in Durham, with a number of fellow students and masters. Ordained in 1795, he taught there and at Ushaw, whither the college moved in 1808. In 1811 he was appointed to serve the mission of Hornby, near Lancaster in the valley of the Lune. This quiet place was his home until his death and here he wrote pamphlets expounding the Catholic position in politics, letters of counsel to other Catholic leaders ('almost the oracle which our bishops consulted' said one of them), a prayer book, a translation of the gospels from the Greek, hymns – and his great history.

Lingard would not accept a bishopric though he was created, by Pope Leo XII, a cardinal in petto. He was far however from being a recluse. His relations with the Protestants among whom he lived were most cordial: indeed they placed a tablet to his memory in their parish church. As his personality was modest and direct, so was his writing. He wrote of the Reformation with what one reviewer called 'placid neutrality' and he strove to be impartial in all controversial matters. Lingard's work is therefore scientific in a way that makes both Macaulay and Froude seem tendentious and unsound. His style won general approval from fastidious readers who looked for classical periods and clear expression. Indeed Hallam said of Lingard's account of the plague in 1665 that it 'may even fairly challenge comparison with the well-known account of the plague at Athens by Thucydides'. In an age which saw a revival of prejudice against Roman Catholics and in which politics were seriously embittered by this feeling, the scholarly, judicious work of a great Catholic historian was of incalculable value.

LISLE, ALICE (1614?-85), was the widow of John Lisle, the regicide and Cromwellian who was shot dead by an Irish royalist in Switzerland in 1664. Living at Moyles Court, near Ringwood in Hampshire, she was well known for her dissenting views and her readiness to help the persecuted. In 1685 after Sedgemoor, she gave refuge to John Hickes, a minister who had fought for Monmouth. Arrested by royal troops under Colonel Penruddock, whose father John Lisle had sentenced to death for leading a rising in 1655, she was tried before Jeffreys on a charge of harbouring a traitor. Despite her plea that she had merely thought Hickes was in trouble for illegal preaching, she was found guilty and sentenced to be burned alive, Jeffreys crying 'Had she been my own mother, I would have found her guilty'. The sentence was commuted to beheading, and Alice Lisle, aged over seventy, was executed at Winchester, the first victim of the Bloody Assizes.

LISTER, LORD JOSEPH (1827-1912), the man who transformed surgery by developing antiseptics, had the right background for success as a professional man and a scientist in Victorian England, for his father was a scientifically minded Quaker, who gave him a broad education and financial support. He emerged from University College, London, as a qualified surgeon, and surgery remained his first love, with his experiments and ideas growing out of it. He was exact and careful, more at ease with the details of his craft than with general principles. In the words of his biographer, he 'preferred the slog up the mountain to the view from the summit'. From James Syme, the professor for whom he worked in Edinburgh, he learnt his skill as a teacher, his courage as a surgeon and, less happily, his lack of tact in controversy. He also married Syme's daughter Agnes, a severe lady but a close companion in his work, in whose handwriting are most of the entries in the Commonplace Book in which his ideas and experiments are recorded.

Between 1860 and 1869 he was Regius Professor of Surgery at Glasgow. There, disturbed by the high death rate from the putrefaction of wounds after surgery, and appalled by the conditions in the Glasgow Royal Infirmary, where mounds of cholera corpses were discovered only a few inches beneath the ground outside the accident wards, he decided that infection in wounds was caused by the atmosphere: and then, after reading Pasteur's work on fermentation, that vital germs in the air did the damage. To destroy these he used carbolic acid on dressings. The first 'Listerian' operation was on a compound fracture. Soon he was opening up abscesses, performing a mastectomy on his sister, and doing plastic surgery. Experiments on absorbable ligatures followed, to prevent the damage caused by the traditional silk threads. His later operations included resections – joining nerves and tendons – and brain surgery. Few would have been worth risking without antiseptics.

Lister was an austere man, who expressed himself clumsily on paper and often felt embattled. His fellow surgeons in Britain took to his ideas more slowly than did those in France or Germany. In St Bartholomew's Hospital, one of them mockingly used to tell those entering the operating theatre: 'Shut the door quickly or one of Mr Lister's microbes will come in.' He made mistakes: the use of a carbolic spray to kill germs in the air was a waste of time. His strongest support came from his students, in Edinburgh and King's College London. But he had many other powerful allies, including the queen, who allowed him to remove an abscess from her armpit.

Gradually it was realized that the range and safety of surgery had been transformed by his methods. Between 1859 and 1870 hospital mortality after major operations was 45.13 per cent: between 1886 and 1890 it was 7.1 per cent. Though a sad near-recluse after the death of his wife, Lister was enshrined in his lifetime in the Pantheon of his profession; the first medical Peer, and one of the original twenty-four people to receive Edward VII's Order of Merit.

Further Reading
H. C. Cameron, *Joseph Lister, The Friend of Man*, 1948.
Sir Rickman Godlee, *Lord Lister*, 1917.

LIVINGSTONE, DAVID (1813-73) is the only missionary to have been honoured with a national funeral in Westminster Abbey. The prime minister attended and the queen sent a wreath. The service took place eleven months after his death: his body had been brought back from Chitambo, a village in the heart of what is now Zambia, by his devoted African followers. A spirit of emotional uplift warmed the whole country, and Florence Nightingale called him 'the greatest man of his generation'.

Livingstone was in many ways a proper hero. He was cast in the right mould, this Scottish lad from Blantyre, who had learnt his Latin from a grammar book propped up on a frame in the cotton factory where he worked his fourteen-hour day. He saved enough money to train as a medical missionary in Glasgow, joined the London Missionary Society with the intention of going to work in China, but was guided towards Africa by a fellow Scot, Robert Moffat. North of Moffat's mission station at Kuruman, Africa was still 'the Dark Continent'. Already a loner by instinct, Livingstone soon became restless, made long forays into the Kalahari desert, and in 1847 established his own station at Kolobeng, in the south of what is now Botswana. 'All my desires tend forwards towards the north,' he wrote. 'Why, we have a world before us here.' In 1848 he joined two big game hunters on an expedition. Thereafter he was an explorer until he died.

He went first to Lake Ngami, near the Okavango Delta, to the Makololo tribe. There he learnt of a great river to the north. In 1851 he found it, the Zambezi, at the point in the modern Caprivi Strip where it is 500 yards wide. In 1853 he set out to find a route from there to the west coast, to open up the heart of Africa to British traders and missionaries. With only a few Makololo porters, and often gripped by malaria, he struggled through tribes who grimaced at him with filed cat-like teeth, and demanded tolls which he could not pay; through thick forests, rivers, and waist-deep marshes; through scorching sun and blinding rain; until he reached the coast at Luanda. There, unwilling to abandon his porters, and hoping to find a better entry into Africa from the east, he

refused the offer of a ship to England and set off back across the continent. On the way, he discovered the Victoria Falls. He was also able to chart the Zambezi along almost its whole length. It was a journey of 4,000 miles, through country largely unexplored by any Europeans. The story which he had to tell when he got back to England in 1856 stirred the country.

His next expedition was government-sponsored. It was much less happy and successful. The Zambezi proved impassable for boats – Livingstone had unluckily taken a short cut and missed the section which included the Kebrabasa Rapids – so in 1850 he turned north up the Shire River, and reached Lake Nyasa. He never got as far as its northern end, and, even before he was recalled by the government in 1863, he had abandoned his attempt to get his boat up onto the lake. Bishop Mackenzie, heading the mission which was part of the enterprise, had shocked public opinion back home by using firearms in his 'holy war' against the slavers, and had then died of malaria. Finally Livingstone's wife Mary, who had come out to join him, also died. He returned to England, sad but unquenchably restless. He set off again in 1866, intending to examine the hydrography of the watershed of the African uplands in order to find the sources of the Nile and the Congo. But his journeying became wandering. Recurring fever, dysentery, tropical ulcers and bleeding sapped his energy. He trudged round Central Africa for seven years, believing that God would direct his steps, to fulfil His purpose. In all that time, he saw only one other white man: Stanley, sent out as a journalist to find him, caught up with him at Ujiji on the western shore of Lake Tanganyika. The meeting is now a legendary picture in history: Stanley in his smart white flannels and shining boots dismounting from his horse, Livingstone under a mango tree, gaunt, grimy, and near death through haemorrhage. 'Dr Livingstone, I presume.' 'Yes, that is my name.'

Livingstone was not always a hero. Indeed, his achievements had not measured up to that description, against his declared aims. Going out to Africa as a worker for the London Missionary Society, he only converted one man. He had failed to end the Arab slave trade, and near the end of his life had to watch helplessly as Arab slavers massacred Africans at Nyangwe. His claim to have found in the Zambezi a navigable route into the heart of Africa, along which commerce could flow, settlement develop and Christian civilization spread, was proved false. His picture of African natural resources was sensationally overpainted – patches of cotton became huge fields, and scrawny cattle prize beasts – while he underestimated the problems of disease and the hostility of the Portuguese. As for the Nile, Speke had in fact already discovered its true source further north, and Livingstone got it wrong. Many who travelled with him became disillusioned: his swings of mood may have been cyclothymic. Though his grief at the death of his wife was deep and long-lasting, he often treated her and their children as an encumbrance. She was 'my dear Rib', and he complained about her pregnancies.

Yet he had qualities which put him apart from the other explorers of his era. He looked the part. 'There was something powerful about him,' recalled a sailor, 'that drew men to him, black and white alike … and withal he was gentle as a child.' His deeply furrowed and tanned face and the gleam in his eye held his British listeners, even though he was a hesitant and awkward public speaker, who had been rejected by the Missionary Society for this clumsiness when he first applied. His speaking tour round Britain in 1857 was a *tour de force*, and the enthusiasm at Oxford and Cambridge led to the Universities Mission to Central Africa. His *Missionary Travels* was a best seller, written at speed from his journals, and telling the dramatic story of his cross-African journey with plain spontaneity and a lyrical enthusiasm for the Africa he had discovered. Like Burton (whom he disliked and deplored), he was a man of many parts: ornithologist, astronomer, doctor whose use of quinine opened up malarial areas to travellers. But unlike him, he was God's man, chosen to raise the Africans (whom he regarded, not as genetically inferior, but as a fallen people) to the level of Christian civilization. This was what won the heart and the imagination of the Christian optimists of mid-Victorian Britain.

Further Reading

Oliver Ransford, *David Livingstone, the Dark Interior*, 1978.

David Livingstone, *Narrative of an Expedition to the Zambezi and its Tributaries*, 1865.

David Livingstone, *Missionary Travels and Researches in South Africa*, 1857.

LLOYD, EDWARD (d.1713) was keeping a coffee-house in Tower Street, London, in 1688, and he moved to larger premises in Lombard Street in 1692. Four years later he began to publish every three weeks a paper called *Lloyd's News*, which contained a good deal of special information about shipping as well as more general news from home and abroad. This lasted only a few months, being apparently brought to an end because of a protest from the House of Lords over an erroneous item, and it was not revived for nearly forty years, when it took the form of *Lloyd's List*, devoted to material about shipping. Little is known of Edward Lloyd; but by the time of his death in 1713 his coffee house was already prospering, as the *Tatler* and *Spectator* showed, and was firmly established as a centre of marine insurance.

LLYWELYN AP GRUFFYDD (Llywelyn II) (d.1282) began his political career inauspiciously, as ruler of only a part of Gwynedd. By 1267 his dominion extended to by far the greater part of Wales but his death in 1282 anticipated by only a few weeks the extirpation for more than a century of the dream of establishing a state independent of the English. Some brief account of Llywelyn's immediate family may help explain his later dilemmas and this historic failure.

Llywelyn was the second of four sons of Gruffydd (d.1246), himself the son, by Tangwystyl of Rhos, of Llywelyn ap Iorwerth (Llywelyn I). In 1240, upon the prince's death, Gruffydd was proclaimed King of Gwynedd, but the throne was also claimed by his half brother Dafydd, son of Joan, daughter of King John. Gruffydd, though supported by most of the Welsh lords, was unable to prevail. One reason was the opposition of Henry III, who was able to extract from Dafydd, as the price of supporting his candidature in Gwynedd, his acceptance of English overlordship of Welsh territories outside it. Gruffydd was arrested, and died in 1244 trying to escape from the Tower of London. Dafydd's cession of overlordship no longer seemed a good bargain, and hostilities with the English were renewed. But Dafydd himself died childless in 1246, and the succession passed to the sons of Gruffydd. It was initially shared between Owain, the eldest, and Llywelyn; later the two younger sons, Dafydd and Rhodri, sought to advance their claims.

Llywelyn had already shown political aptitude, attracting followers in Clwyd. Now, given the weakness of Gwynedd and Henry's determination to maintain heavy military and political pressure, he and his brother Owain had no alternative but to acknowledge English suzerainty. They appeared before Henry at Woodstock in April 1247 and agreed to provide military service. In 1250-1, however, they quietly began to build links with other powerful men in north and central Wales which could form the basis of a future coalition against the English. Henry III, meanwhile, was busy laying the basis for Edward I's later conquest of the country. Ruthless in exploiting Crown rights in English feudal law, and adept in the use of local concessions designed to foment dissension among his enemies, Henry was able to extend his landholdings, to assert his judicial supremacy, and to strengthen his political and military position in Wales. Henry's forward policy alienated many of the Norman lords and the Welsh land-owning families with which they were often intermarried, in Wales and the Marches, making them receptive to anyone who might appear as a counterweight to the heavy hand of the English Crown. English law and taxes were often imposed aggressively by royal justiciars; resentment extended downwards into Welsh society.

Llywelyn showed himself brilliantly able to capitalize on these difficulties and to take the opportunities which now presented themselves. In 1255, when his brother Dafydd sought a repartition of Gwynedd, Llewelyn felt strong enough to ignore Henry's claim, as overlord, to settle the dispute in his court. Defeating and imprisoning Owain and Dafydd, he now established himself as sole ruler of Gwynedd. Earlier diplomatic efforts began to bear fruit. Between 1256 and 1258, Llywelyn reasserted control in eastern Gwynedd and moved into Gwrtheyrnion. Under his leadership, native dynasties recovered Powys Wenwynwyn (southern Powys), Ceredigion and Ystrad Tewi; disaffected lords, notably in Deheubarth and northern Powys were transferring their allegiance to the new prince. This coalition was able to inflict upon Henry a series of military reverses. His commanders suffered a devastating defeat near Llandeilo, his invasion of the north was ineffective, and political opposition grew in England. In June 1258 a truce was agreed.

Llywelyn had already displayed remarkable political skill, and now commanded enormous personal loyalty and respect in Wales. Combining deft diplomatic manoeuvres with ruthless action, he had assembled a fragile coalition of lords and princelings and welded it into an effective operational force. The patriotic sentiments of his troops, stirred by the trampling of Welsh laws and customs, blossomed with success, and their commander deployed his military forces flexibly, with an eye to the importance of popular sympathy. All this contrasted sharply with the disunity and lethargy of his enemies. Now de facto overlord of much of Wales, Llywelyn felt able, in an appeal to the Scots, to refer to himself as its prince. From 1258 to 1262 his main aim was to win Henry III's formal recognition of his position. This was refused, but Llywelyn tightened his grip over errant allies and took Builth from the Mortimers. This region of central Wales was vital to Llywelyn's security. In 1262-3 he pressed eastward into the lordships of Maelienllyd and Brecon almost as far as Abergavenny, capturing the remaining isolated English outposts in the north. Henry was unwilling to agree comprehensive peace, but his difficulties were much increased by the struggle with the barons, some of whom had been provoked by royal policy in the Marches, and whose party, led by Simon de Montfort, was especially strong there. In 1263 Llywelyn sent troops to help de Montfort; an alliance followed and, in June 1265, at Pipton, Simon recognized Llywelyn as the Prince of Wales and overlord of its magnates. De Montfort was dead within three months, but Llywelyn had been astute enough to insure himself against this, promising to hold his position and his dignities in Wales as a vassal of the king, to pay him £20,000 over ten years, and to withhold payment if the English should repudiate the treaty.

The English did not. On 27 September 1267, beset with internal difficulties and under pressure from the papal legate, Henry III signed the Treaty of Montgomery. This confirmed the right of Llywelyn and his heirs to the title Prince of Wales. It conceded to him the overlordship of Powys, Ceredigion and parts of Deheubarth and extensive lands in the Marches, including property owned by Crown supporters Mortimer and Bohun. Llywelyn promised to allot lands to his dissatisfied brother Dafydd, who had defected in 1263, but their affairs were to be subject to the final arbitration of Welsh courts. He agreed not to help the king's enemies and to pay him 25,000 marks over eight years.

The gains of the Treaty of Montgomery were great, but so were the burdens. Slender resources had hampered the ambitions of the most capable Welsh leaders. A second problem, of the succession, also returned to plague Llywelyn, and it may be that there was a connection between the reappearance of these two besetting difficulties. Llywelyn's lack of a son made it hard to deny the claims of his brothers. His failure to marry was perhaps connected to his desire for an alliance which might reflect and so help secure his hard-won status; but princesses of royal blood did not come cheap. In these years, Llywelyn was at the apex of his power, commanding 200,000 or more subjects. But his income is unlikely to have exceeded £6,000, and large sums were owed to the English. Heavy payments – £11,500 was handed over from 1267 to 1272 – forced him to press down hard on his lordly allies and to alienate some, in Powys and Deheubarth, who owed him homage. Over time, though sensible of the need to maintain the willing consent of what was still, in part, a coalition, it seems that Llywelyn began to adopt a greater degree of coercion in dealing with his subordinate lords and to centralize juridical authority in his courts. Gradually, Llywelyn's coalition began to loosen, friendships cooled, enemies began to detach themselves from the ranks of the neutral, and relations with the English Crown deteriorated.

In the east and south, where the allegiances of Welsh landowners were very unsettled, the provisions of the Treaty of Montgomery, and its ambiguities, were tested by renewed pressure from the Marcher lords such as Bohun and Mortimer. In 1267-71 Llywelyn sought to enforce his overlordship in parts of northern Glamorgan, to which his rights were not explicitly set out in the Treaty. When this drive was extended to Senghennydd, which stretched all the way down to the Severn Estuary, and threatened to cut off access by land to the southern lordships not held by him, it was met with determined resistance by the Clare family from its stronghold of Caerphilly castle. Llywelyn's relations with the church also ran into difficulties. He had been in correspondence with Pope Gregory X who was sympathetic to him, and enjoyed good relations with the Franciscan, Dominican and Cistercian friaries. But there was friction between the claims of Welsh secular law and canon law, the problem of relations with Canterbury, and with bishops as feudal lords. All of these helped fuel a damaging quarrel with Anian, the Bishop of St Asaph who in 1275-6 won the English king's confirmation of the liberties of his diocese, and stirred the pot of renewed contention with the Prince of Wales. Even more seriously, there was discovered in 1274 a plot to murder Llywelyn hatched by his ubiquitous brother Dafydd and Gruffudd ap Gwenwynwyn, the disaffected ruler of southern Powys, whose domains were now ruthlessly absorbed by Llywelyn. He and Dafydd had found it expedient to take shelter from the Welsh courts, and they found it in England. In all these matters, Llywelyn complained, the English monarch winked at his opponents and laughed at the Treaty.

By now Edward I, king since 1272, having returned from the crusade, was stung by Llywelyn's repeated refusal to attend him. Llywelyn's marriage plans helped widen the rift further. Perhaps as a response to his brother's treachery, Llywelyn now activated a plan to marry Eleanor de Montfort. Eleanor's attractions included one imperial and two royal uncles, but the plan had perhaps been originally conceived at the time of English disintegration as a means to further it. Anyway, the only effect of the de Montfort name in 1275 was to enrage Edward and when Eleanor sailed from France in 1275 he seized the ship and imprisoned her at Windsor. This in turn enraged Llywelyn, and brought the two leaders to the brink of war. Edward now denied the validity of the Treaty of Montgomery; his grounds, that Llywelyn was not entitled under the Welsh laws of partible inheritance to sole control of Gwynedd, simultaneously supported the claims of his guest Dafydd.

By now, in all the dealings between them, Edward openly sought to treat Llywelyn as vassal, and Llywelyn as clearly insisted on his own princely status. The dispute was ostensibly about dignity, but it also concerned the power of ultimate decision in Wales. Negotiations on such fundamentals proved fruitless, and in November 1276 Llywelyn was declared a rebel. Acquiescing in the reconquest by Marcher lords of lands from Powys to Glamorgan, Edward, in the spring of 1277, deployed an army of 800 knights and 15,000 foot. The territories of Llywelyn's allies fell or capitulated during the summer. Edward's troops entered Gwynedd in August and also invaded Anglesey by sea. Llywelyn was forced to sign a treaty at Aberconwy on 9 November 1277 which confined his authority to Gwynedd west of the Conway and to share some of it with his brothers. The treaty effectively stripped Llywelyn of the substance, though not the shadow, of his claim to the principality, and imposed upon him vassal status; he paid homage in December 1277, and married Eleanor in the English king's presence at Worcester in 1278.

In the next years, Edward implemented legal, political and military measures which enormously strengthened the Crown's position in Wales and extended the reach of his courts even into Gwynedd; his intrusions into affairs local to north Wales and into Llywelyn's arrangements with his wife and his brothers seemed calculated to stress the Welshman's subordinate status. Llywelyn kept his temper and patiently sought to pick up the strands of his old diplomacy, and in 1281 even made a pact with his old enemy Roger Mortimer. But it was too late. A dispute between Llywelyn and the returned Gruffydd Gwenwynwyn concerning control of Arwystli on the Gwynedd-Powys border raised the question of whether it should be resolved under Welsh or English law. Edward became involved in the case, seeking to assert his own right, as a king, to try the case and to command the presence of the litigants. Humiliating to Llywelyn, Edward's attitude also seemed increasingly to call into question the validity of Welsh law. The effect was to politicize the issues and to provide a focus for the re-emergence of local resentment at the aggressive imposition of royal authority in Wales by arrogant English officials.

Ironically, the rebellion was initiated by Dafydd, in March 1282, and Llewelyn claimed to have had no prior knowledge of it. However that may be, the revolt spread through north and central Wales and generated enormous popular support, though some few princelings stayed in the royal camp. Edward launched a force of overwhelming strength, which once more swept back the opposition into Gwynedd. Archbishop Pecham's peace plan of October little delayed the English king. He had determined to treat Llywelyn as a traitor and now sent armies to complete the destruction of his power base. Llywelyn's desperate attempt to break out of Snowdonia by opening hostilities in the south-east led to the end of military resistance, for its single defeat, at Builth in December 1282 also resulted in the prince's death. The laments of the poets accurately reflected the military and political finality, despite Dafydd's brief resistance, of this event.

LLYWELYN AP IORWERTH (Llywelyn I) (1173-1240), also known as Llywelyn the Great, was the grandson of Owain Gwynedd and Marared, daughter of Madog ap Maredudd (the last King of all Powys 1132-60). Twice in his long life, he was to achieve control of almost all Wales outside Dyfed and Glamorgan. Llywelyn's rise began in 1195 when he won from his uncle Dafydd control of east Gwynedd. He took west Gwynedd in 1200, south Gwynedd in 1202, south Powys in 1208 and became overlord of Deheubarth in 1216. Under his control, and partly through his agency, especially in Gwynedd, feudal relations came to permeate the old society. But Llywelyn's tactical acceptance of the feudal overlordship of King John won him neither the trust of the English king nor, at first, the allegiance of his own barons, who feared the royal enemy at home more than they did his rival across the Marches. John's invasion and occupation of much of Powys and Gwynedd in 1211-12 helped change their minds. With the support of Philip Augustus of France and Pope Innocent III, Llywelyn was able to mobilize powerful supporters in Wales. His capture of Shrewsbury indirectly helped the English barons in their efforts, which culminated in Magna Carta, to bridle the English king. But it strengthened Welsh monarchical power. Freed from English royal pressure, Llywelyn was able to engineer the partition of Deheubarth and to secure the homage of its lords and of the Kings of Powys. In 1218, the government of the young Henry III signed the Treaty of Worcester, which went far in accepting Llywelyn's predominance in much of Wales outside Dyfed, Gwent and Glamorgan. William, Earl of Pembroke successfully reoccupied Camarthen and Cardigan castles in 1223, but when the justiciar Hubert de Burgh sought to reassert control in Powys, Llywelyn was able to defeat him at Ceri in 1228, proceeding three years later to raid Brecon and south Glamorgan. Llywelyn's position as direct ruler or overlord in much of central Wales was ratified by the English in the Treaty of Middle in 1234.

Such concessions reflected the strength of Llywelyn's position during the early part of the reign of Henry III. The few extant documents indicate that from the reign of Llywelyn I there were already evolving some of the features of a state, with such key offices as chancellor at its core, and orderly methods of administration, including the issuing of royal orders and letters under the prince's great and privy seal. Llywelyn evolved an acute sense of his own dignity and the status of his principality, and there were efforts to underpin this by the invention of historical myths as well as through the imposition of homage upon other dynasts, and through the authority of his courts. The prince's policy would not have succeeded without a readiness to mobilize military force. But it also involved a skilful blend of marriage alliances with powerful families of the Marches, the ruthless imposition of feudal obligations upon lesser Welsh lords and kings, and a willingness to acknowledge a loosely defined fealty to the English king, which he hoped would not be used to undermine his own position among his feudal dependents.

The early success of these tactics was much facilitated by Henry's difficulties with his barons, which precluded any major military effort in Wales. Henry III also acquiesced in the succession to Gwynedd of Llywelyn's son Dafydd, by Joan, illegitimate daughter of King John. This issue was very important to Llywelyn, and in 1222 he was successful in persuading Pope Honorius III to remove possible legal uncertainties by legitimating Joan. Dafydd's claim to Gwynedd, however, was disputed by his half brother Gruffydd. When Llywelyn died in April 1240, Henry III quickly made it clear that the price of his support for Dafydd was his confinement to Gwynedd. Llywelyn had aroused violent antagonisms among those proud Welsh lords who yet called themselves kings, in southern Powys and Deheubarth, and had bridled the ambitions of the Marcher families. Henry's action was well calculated to mobilize such bitter frustrations in a bid to establish his own predominance in Wales, his success undermining the achievements of Llywelyn the Great.

LOCKE, JOHN (1632-1704), philosopher, was a Somerset man, born at Wrington, the son of an attorney and small landowner. There was Puritanism on both sides of the family. His father fought, extremely briefly, as a Captain in the parliamentary army in the Civil War, and his father's Colonel nominated John to a place at Westminster School, whither he went in 1647. Thus he was one of the numerous distinguished pupils of Dr Busby, that formidable royalist who kept his place despite the wars and taught his pupils to question the foundations of authority. A King's Scholar in 1650, John Locke went up to Christ Church, then the most notable of Oxford colleges under the headship of John Owen, in 1652. In 1658 he became a Senior Student (i.e. a Fellow) of Christ Church. In 1660, like nearly everyone else in Oxford, he welcomed the Restoration; and the evidence is, according to Maurice Cranston, that at this time John Locke was 'a man of the Right, an extreme authoritarian'.

Yet already there were portents of change. Most notably, Locke was dissatisfied with the Aristotelian logic and medieval disputations of Oxford, and had turned to an interest in science and in medicine. Here was study based upon experience, and here he would discover his approach to the principles upon which knowledge was founded. During the 1660s Locke liberalized and deepened his mind, partly by study of science and medicine under Robert Boyle, partly by his first trip abroad (a short one in 1665 to Protestant and tolerant Brandenburg), most of all by his relationship with Lord Ashley, formerly Sir Anthony Ashley Cooper, whom he first met in 1666. The following year he gave up his work as college tutor at Christ Church, although he remained a Senior Student, and went to live at Ashley's house in London as the latter's personal physician, performing a successful operation on him soon afterwards. In this same year 1667 Locke wrote a manuscript essay on toleration which reveals a substantial widening of his views since 1660. It reflects also the fact that he had been brought by his residence with Ashley into direct contact with the political realities of Charles II's England – for this was the year of the fall of Clarendon and the rise of Ashley to power.

London also provided other opportunities for Locke to display his intellectual strength. He became a Fellow of the Royal Society; he wrote a considerable part of a book on the rate of interest, his only economic work of consequence (it was not published until 1692); he was appointed secretary to the Lords Proprietors of Carolina, colonial territory in which Ashley was interested, and helped to frame for it a constitution, which never came into effect. He gave some time at least to the medical care of his patron's own household: thus in 1671 we find him looking after Ashley's newborn grandson, the future third Earl of Shaftesbury. Most important of all, he wrote in 1671 the first drafts of the *Essay Concerning Human Understanding*. This, Locke's philosophical masterpiece, was not published until many years later, years in which Locke's own fortunes had been closely linked with those of his patron.

During the 1670s Locke, rather intermittently, was in some sense a political adviser to Ashley, who in 1672 was created Earl of Shaftesbury. These were the years when Shaftesbury, at first (1672-3) Lord Chancellor and ready to collaborate with Charles II, moved into opposition and became the first organizer of party in English political history. Locke's role in these developments is hard to discern and easy to exaggerate. From 1673-5 he was Secretary of the Council of Trade and Plantations; from 1675-9 he was in France, probably for his health, although it is at least interesting that these were precisely the years of secret negotiations between Louis XIV and the English opposition. He returned to England at the time of the Popish Plot and was at Shaftesbury's side during the Exclusion crisis. The year 1681, the year of the Oxford Parliament and of the collapse of the constitutional policy of exclusion, was of immense significance in the lives both of Shaftesbury and of Locke, and in the relations between them. For Shaftesbury, arrested by the government but freed by a London jury, decided to organize revolution, and Locke, himself in danger – watched by the Librarian of Christ Church, who was acting as an unpaid government spy – wrote his most celebrated work, the *Two Treatises of Government*. In form they were a refutation of the divine right philosopher Filmer's *Patriarcha*. Their central theme was a defence of the right of subjects to rebel against an arbitrary prince, and thus they were, to say the least, highly relevant to the schemes of Locke's patron. They were not in fact published until 1689, when they served to justify the 'Glorious Revolution', to provide the theoretical framework within which the political life of eighteenth-century England was conducted, and to stimulate the American colonists to revolt. Yet in their original intention the *Two Treatises* were 'not the rationalization of a revolution in need of defence but a demand for a revolution yet to be brought about'.*

---

*Peter Laslett, 'The English Revolution and Locke's *Two Treatises of Government*', *Cambridge Historical Journal*, vol. XII, No. 1, 1956.

Shaftesbury's revolution never came off. In 1682 he fled to Amsterdam where he died in January 1683. His body was brought home to Dorset for burial and Locke attended the funeral. He was still suspect and spied upon, and after the Rye House affair he deemed it wise to slip across to Holland that autumn. There he remained until 1689. His exile, spent mostly in Amsterdam and Rotterdam, was not disagreeable: he had numerous friends, he had taken steps to secure sufficient cash (Locke was in no way vague about money), and Holland was Protestant, tolerant, and clean. There was some peril, for James II's government, which had deprived him of his Studentship at Christ Church, attempted to have him extradited, and for a time he hid under the pseudonym of Dr van der Linden, but the Dutch authorities declined to hand him over. Certainly his exile was fruitful in writing. These were the years of his letters to English friends which later (1693) were published as *Thoughts concerning Education*, in some ways perhaps the most notable work any Englishman has ever written on the subject, and certainly one which is perennially refreshing in its individual humanity and freedom from humbug. In 1686 he wrote his *Letter on Toleration*, first published in Latin at Gouda in 1689, a sane and moderate attempt to define the proper limits of both governmental and ecclesiastical interference with freedom of conscience: it won him widespread fame in a Europe overshadowed by Louis XIV's Revocation of the Edict of Nantes. Above all, in the same year he completed the book on which his eminence as a philosopher rests, the *Essay concerning Human Understanding*, whose object was 'to take a survey of our own understandings, examine our own powers, and see to what things they were adapted'. His approach to these problems in the *Essay*, above all his theory of knowledge with its foundation of empiricism, established him as one of the great creative philosophers of modern history.

Naturally Locke rejoiced in the Revolution of 1688, which both represented the triumph of his ideas and opened for him the way of return to his native country. 1689 was indeed *annus mirabilis* for John Locke. Not only did he come home in the convoy that brought Queen Mary to England, where he took up residence in London and accepted a minor government post, he also had in the press in that one year all three of his greatest works, the *Two Treatises*, the *Essay concerning Human Understanding*, and the *Letter on Toleration*. These publications firmly established his reputation in educated circles in the English-speaking world and in Europe. From 1691 Locke lived for most of the time at the country house of Otes in Essex, the home of Sir Francis and Lady Masham, a bachelor savant with his 4,000 books, his telescope, meteorological instruments and botanical specimens, rather fussy, yet as always courteous, humane and modest. He indulged in literary controversy, notably in connection with his *The Reasonableness of Christianity*, which he published – anonymously – in 1695 and which, for all his formal Anglicanism, was remarkably Unitarian in flavour. In 1696 he was appointed a Commissioner for Trade: the pay was good, but the work in London was arduous, especially for an ageing asthmatic, and he resigned in 1700. He died at Otes in 1704, and lies buried in the churchyard of High Laver nearby. Locke is one of the giants of the seventeenth century, for, like Bacon and Newton, he asked new questions and created a new arena of thought.

Further Reading
Maurice Cranston, *John Locke*, 1957.

LOCKHART, JOHN GIBSON (1794-1854) was for twenty-seven years the successful editor of the *Quarterly Review*, the journal which competed for literary excellence, critical impact and political influence with the Whig *Edinburgh Review*. He is best known, however, as the biographer of Sir Walter Scott, his father-in-law. Besides numerous occasional pieces, some ballad poems and four novels he wrote lives of Burns and Napoleon. Clever, fluent, aggressive or sympathetic as occasion demanded, in none of that varied work did he excel. In the seven volumes of *The Memoirs of Sir Walter Scott* (1836-8) subject and biographer interacted to produce a masterpiece. The second half of the twentieth century has seen a flowering in the genre of literary biography: with new techniques, insights and resources come different critical standards. In the ample, traditional style, within its conventions, Lockhart can be placed on a level with Boswell: two Scotsmen – and two writers who so knew and revered their subjects that they lived, felt, thought and spoke for all time. No less than Boswell, he had the talent, and tact, to depict genius.

Lockhart was the second son of a Lanarkshire minister. His precocious scholarship set him, aged fifteen, on the high road that other clever Scotsmen have trodden: from Glasgow High School and University to Balliol College, Oxford. He won a First, went to Germany, and paid the obligatory visit to Goethe at Weimar. At the Scottish bar he was unsuccessful, so his thoughts turned to literature. With John Wilson he became the mainstay of *Blackwood's* magazine. His caustic wit was well suited to the thrust and parry of Edinburgh's intellectual journalism. In 1818 he first met Scott who recommended him to Ballantyne, the publisher, and suggested that he take over editing the *Edinburgh Annual Register* which Scott was keen to relinquish. In 1820 he married Scott's eldest daughter, Sophia.

In 1825 he went to London, to the *Quarterly Review*, and a wider fame. His *Life of Scott*, known to many in the abridged version of 1848, brought acclaim, though some thought that his account lacked reverence. He was faithful to his declared intent of 'making use, wherever possible, of his own letters and diaries'. It was his wish 'to let the character develop itself'. So the reader comes, not only to know the man, but to see the growth of the writer. Let one passage speak for the whole. There is a dinner party on a warm Edinburgh night in June 1814. The young men go to the library; it has a north window which looks obliquely upon Castle Street, and so on another lighted window where a hand can be seen writing, writing, pausing only to place another sheet upon the pile. Is it an attorney's clerk finishing some work? 'No, boys,' the host exclaims: 'I well know what hand it is – 'tis Walter Scott's.' 'This,' comments Lockhart, 'was the hand that, in the evenings of three summer weeks, wrote the two last volumes of *Waverley*.'

Sir Walter expected to found a dynasty of Scotts at Abbotsford. Yet of his four children, the elder son died soon after their father: both Lockhart's sons died also. By 1854 only Lockhart's daughter, and her daughter, remained of the family. His own health was broken, his spirit crushed. He travelled to Rome but returned to Abbotsford to die.

LOMBE, JOHN (1693-1722) and his half-brother **THOMAS LOMBE** (1685-1739) are among the less well-known figures of the industrial revolution, but they deserve notice for they erected, on an island in the river Derwent, the first factory in England and gave an enormous impetus to the development of industrial capitalism.

English manufacturers of silk were confronted by great difficulties: they had to buy their raw silk abroad and when they tried to make their own thrown silk (the thread made by twisting together the filaments from the cocoons), smugglers put such cheap thread on to the market that they were badly undercut. It was rumoured that there were, in Italy, machines for throwing silk but they went unseen until, in 1716, John Lombe penetrated into a building in Leghorn where they were used. With the help of an Italian priest he secretly made some drawings and sent them to England hidden in pieces of silk. When he was re-embarking, a brig was sent after him and he only narrowly escaped. Soon after his return home, however, he died, a victim to Italian poison, so rumour had it. Meanwhile he had set up, in 1717, silk-throwing machines upon the Italian model. His brother supplied the necessary capital and in 1718 obtained a patent for fourteen years. Soon afterwards the famous factory was built, a huge barracks, 500 feet long, five or six storeys high, with 460 windows. The machines were very tall, cylindrical in shape and they rotated on vertical axes; several rows of bobbins received the threads and gave them the required twist by a swift rotary movement. At the top the thrown silk was automatically wound on a winder, ready to be made up into hanks for sale. The machine was a complex one. Defoe, who visited the factory on one of his tours, said that there were '22,586 wheels and 97,746 movements, which work 73,726 yards of silk thread every time the wheel goes round, which is three times in one minute, and 318,504,960 yards in twenty-four hours'. The whole mechanism was worked by one water wheel. The workman's main task was to retie the threads whenever they broke; each man had charge of sixty threads.

This factory employed 300 workmen. In a short time Thomas Lombe made a fortune, became an alderman and a sheriff and was knighted. When parliament refused to renew his patent in 1732, he was given £14,000 indemnity. He did not live long to enjoy his success but he had the satisfaction of knowing that he, with his brother, had pioneered an entirely new form of industrial organization.

Further Reading
A. E. Musson and E. Robinson, *Science and Technology in the Industrial Revolution*, 1969.

LONGCHAMP, WILLIAM (*d.*1197; Bishop of Ely 1189-97), who briefly ruled England during Richard I's absence on crusade 1190-1, was one of the most vilified public figures of the Middle Ages. Not content to demolish his policies and motives, his enemies portrayed him as a physically grotesque, ugly, misshapen, dwarfish, leering, pot-bellied pederast. Whether or not Longchamp resembled a gargoyle or could not, as some alleged, be trusted with the sons of the nobility, his chief failings were political tactlessness and personal arrogance which, in the eyes of his employer, King Richard, were, initially at least, outweighed by his effectiveness in conducting royal business. A Norman clerk and expert in civil law, he graduated from Henry II's chancery to the service of the future Richard I, rising to be his chancellor before 1189. After Richard's accession, Longchamp, now the royal chancellor in England, was selected as the king's chief representative in England, being appointed joint justiciar and Bishop of Ely, the traditional civil servant's see. The following year Longchamp ousted his colleague, Hugh of Le Puiset, Bishop of Durham, leaving himself supreme. Richard clearly calculated that he needed a viceroy of complete personal loyalty, without existing potentially conflicting ties of interest. To provide the necessary institutional status, Richard not only agreed to the demotion of Le Puiset but secured (for a cool 1,500 marks) Longchamp's appointment as papal legate. This concentration of authority was no irresponsible whim: Longchamp's power over church and state was replicated after 1194 in Richard's appointment of Hubert Walter as Archbishop of Canterbury and justiciar.

In his eighteen months in power (March 1190-October 1191), Longchamp proved himself vigorous and effective. The central administration continued to function smoothly, Longchamp's management even provoking what passed for humour from one of his bureaucrats compiling the Pipe Roll: 'The Bishop of Ely owes £20 of that (i.e. Welsh) scutage on account of his knights. But he had them and a great many more in that same army in the king's service. And therefore with angels and archangels he is quit'.

Longchamp pursued royal rights energetically, especially in controlling strategic castles. In 1190, he toured the north, disciplining royal officials who had allowed the massacre of the Jews in York and dissidents at Lincoln. He twice campaigned in the Welsh Marches. He held a church council at Westminster in 1190. As measure of his success, the majority of the bishops supported his petition to the new pope, Celestine III, in 1191 for his legation to be renewed and he retained the support of senior barons, such as the Earls of Warenne and Aumale.

Longchamp's tactics were no more Draconian than those of Henry II's servants, but in the absence of the king he was vulnerable. Office had not yet been divorced from person, and baronial resentment at government action could express itself more easily against a parvenu minister rather than the king. Longchamp fell foul of the xenophobic snobbery of the English elite, which, rather than nascent constitutionalism, was an increasingly marked feature of this period. Longchamp also had to contend with the restless ambition of Richard's surviving brother and adult heir presumptive, John, to whom the king had alloted considerable estates in England. Together, John and discontented barons set out to destroy the chancellor, whose high-handed methods proved poor politics. In the summer of 1191, civil war was only averted by a treaty between Longchamp and John mediated at Winchester by the king's special envoy, Walter of Coutances. The compromise included criticism of arbitrary disseisin by royal officers, an anxiety which reached mature expression in Clause 39 of Magna Carta. Certainly, Longchamp had, with Hugh of Le Puiset, Gerard de Camville or Roger Mortimer, acted ruthlessly on his own authority, but it could be argued that was what he had been appointed to do. His opponents talked of his disregard of what they described as the legitimate customs of the realm, but their motives were hardly altruistic. John wanted to run England by and for himself. His chief propagandist, Hugh of Nonant, Bishop of Coventry, was a self-important, opportunist turn-coat whose main talent, it seems, lay in the invention of colourfully venomous anecdotes about the chancellor.

Longchamp's fall was dramatic. In trying to prevent the king's half-brother, Geoffrey, Archbishop of York, from entering the country, some of Longchamp's men had violently dragged him from sanctuary into custody. Geoffrey and his allies ensured that no-one would miss the parallels with Becket's murder. Although politically trivial in itself, the incident provided an excuse for all

Longchamp's enemies to combine to force him from office. This they achieved by mid-October 1191, when Longchamp surrendered the seal. According to Hugh of Nonant, Longchamp's initial attempt to flee the country disguised as a woman – 'a sex which he always hated' – ended in humiliating farce: waiting on Dover beach, he was picked up by a fisherman whose attempted rape was only thwarted after he lifted Longchamp's skirts.

Although excluded from England, Longchamp retained Richard's favour and continued to show his worth. In 1193, he arranged terms for the king's release from captivity in Germany and visited England to arrange payment of the ransom of 100,000 marks. He was in England again during the king's visit in 1194. As a servant of the king, Longchamp showed skill and tenacity, two traits which especially irritated the factious barons and prelates he so conspicuously failed to control during his period of office in England.

Further Reading

J. Gillingham, *Richard the Lionheart*, 1978.
W. Appleby, *England without Richard*, 1965.

LONGESPEE, WILLIAM (*c*.1212-50) rather unexpectedly became one of the most famous Englishmen of the thirteenth century. An unlikely candidate for immortality, William was the son of Ella, Countess of Salisbury in her own right (*c*.1191-1261), founder and later Abbess of Lacock abbey (Wiltshire) and William Longespee (*d*.1226), a bastard son of Henry II. Despite his lineage and the favour of his cousin Henry III, his achievements were less than modest. He campaigned regularly with the king, sharing in the failures in Brittany (1230), Wales (1233) and Gascony (1242-3). He was unable to obtain recognition as Earl of Salisbury after his mother took the veil (1237). A companion of his other cousin, Richard of Cornwall, on crusade in 1240, he briefly rose to prominence as leader of a substantial English contingent that joined Louis IX of France's crusade in 1249. Heavily subsidized from central funds for hiring knights and serjeants, William left England, we are told, his saddlebags stuffed with cash. His availability to lead the English crusaders suggests that he was a very minor political player. The crusade was a disaster. He quarrelled with his French colleagues and was killed at the battle of Mansourah in the Nile Delta (February 1250). Yet whatever his insignificance in life, in death William found apotheosis as an English martyr. At the hands of mythmakers, including Matthew Paris, within two generations William had become a national hero, specifically manufactured to stand in contrast and indictment to the French who were portrayed as panic-stricken cowards. By the early fourteenth century a poem in French detailing William's self-sacrificing heroism was circulating and he featured in the Middle English epic *Richard Coeur de Lyon*. William became a symbol and a barometer of a growing literary fashion for nationalist anti-French feeling. William was a specifically English hero, signifying the beginnings of the development of a national consciousness which was to be such a feature of English history in the later Middle Ages.

Further Reading

S. Lloyd, 'William Longespee II: The Making of an English Crusading Hero', *Nottingham Medieval Studies* xxxv, 1991.

LOPEZ, RODRIGO (*d*.1594), Physician-in-Chief to Queen Elizabeth I, came of a Portuguese Jewish family. Little is known of his early life. He married the eldest daughter of Gonsalvo Añes, more usually known as Dunstan Añes, by whom he had two sons and three daughters. His brother-in-law was Alvaro Mendez, councillor to Sultan Murad, who created him Duke of Metilli. Thus Lopez had distinguished relations in many parts of Europe. He was driven from Portugal by the Inquisition and settled in England in 1559. Lytton Strachey in *Elizabeth and Essex* calls him a practising Christian, but Lucien Wolf in his *Jews in Elizabethan England* quotes evidence to show that Lopez was a practising crypto-Jew and that Burghley was well aware of it.

Lopez set up in London as a doctor and was so successful that he became the first house physician at St Bartholomew's Hospital. Leicester and Walsingham became his patients, and in 1586 he was appointed Physician-in-Chief to the queen, who treated him with great generosity. He was now a well-known and prosperous man, with a son at Winchester College, a house in Holborn, and an assured position at court. His very success, however, and his being a foreigner and a Jew, brought him many malicious enemies.

After Spain had incorporated Portugal in the Spanish Empire, the pretender to the Portuguese throne was Antonio Perez, known as Don Antonio. Lopez, of course, sided with Antonio against Spain. It was partly on the advice of Lopez that Elizabeth sanctioned the Drake-Norris expedition of 1589 to restore Don Antonio to the throne. That expedition was a failure, and the Earl of Essex, who was the leader of the anti-Spanish party in England, brought Antonio back to England in 1590 to act as a cat's-paw in his political ambitions. Lopez got to know Essex at court and agreed to act as interpreter between the earl and Antonio. Relations between Lopez and Essex soon deteriorated, and in 1593 Lopez rashly criticized the earl to Antonio, who passed on the criticism to Essex.

Spanish spies were all the while plotting to get Antonio's servants to murder Antonio and the queen. Lopez became involved in the first part of the plan, but he showed no sympathy with the idea of murdering Elizabeth. The plot reached the ears of the Council, Lopez was at once under suspicion, and Essex saw his chance to have his revenge on the Jew. When he examined Lopez's papers nothing incriminating was found, but that did not deter Essex. Some of Antonio's servants were arrested, and under torture they brought charges against Lopez which led to his arrest. He was put in the Tower (1594) and was tried by a special tribunal over which Essex himself presided. Inevitably Lopez was found guilty and condemned to death. For three months the queen delayed signing the death warrant, but she gave way at last, and on 7 June Lopez was drawn on a hurdle to Tyburn, where he was hanged and quartered. Camden records that on the scaffold Lopez declared that 'he loved the queen as well as he loved Jesus Christ, which from a man of the Jewish profession moved no small laughter in the standers-by'. There can be little doubt that Lopez was sacrificed largely to satisfy the vanity of Essex, but a point of view more hostile to Lopez will be found argued by A. Dymock.

Apart from the dramatic interest of Lopez's rise and fall, he has a claim to be remembered on another score, for there are considerable grounds for thinking that Lopez is alluded to in Shakespeare's Shylock.

Further Reading
Lytton Strachey, *Elizabeth and Essex*, 1928.
Lucien Wolf, 'Jews in Elizabethan England', *Transactions of the Jewish Historical Society*, 1924-27.
Martin Hume, *Transactions of the Jewish Historical Society*, 1919.
A. Dymock, *English Historical Review*, 1894.
S. L. Lee, 'The Original of Shylock', *Gentleman's Magazine*, 1880.

LOSINGA, ROBERT, i.e. the Lorrainer (*d*.1095; Bishop of Hereford 1079-95) was a distinguished mathematician, computist, chronologist and astronomer (i.e. astrologer). An unusual choice as a post-Conquest bishop, he was neither a royal clerk nor a Norman monk, his experience being of scholarship not administration. To England and his diocese, Robert brought a range of influences. Notably, he rebuilt Hereford Cathedral on the model of Aachen and attempted to popularize the eccentric chronological system of the Irish recluse Marianus Scotus (*d*.1082). (This added twenty-two years to the AD calculation.) Robert sent a copy of Marianus's *Universal Chronicle* to his friend Wulfstan of Worcester in 1082, where it was incorporated into the cathedral chronicle, and himself wrote a commentary on it, wrongly described as *Excerpts* from Marianus, in 1086. This included a uniquely contemporary description of the Domesday Survey then in the process of being conducted. Perhaps Robert's greatest fame came from his study of the stars, by which he claimed to have successfully predicted the future, famously when he declined to set out for the consecration of Lincoln Cathedral in 1095 because he rightly foresaw it would not take place. It is possible that Robert also introduced the western, two-dimensional abacus into England, thus facilitating the computing revolution which transformed royal and baronial auditing in the following century, the abacus being a chequered cloth which gave its name to the Exchequer. It is likely that Robert's brand of cosmopolitan learning would have reached England regardless of the Conquest, but the employment of Robert reveals how closely England was drawn into movements of European culture. Rather than his acknowledged skill at computing time and numbers, where his high reputation despite gross error made him a model of academic achievement, perhaps Robert's main attraction to William was his expertise as an astrologer. If so, Robert was not alone. The Conqueror's doctor, Gilbert Maminot, Bishop of Lisieux (1077-1101), a scholarly sybarite who spent much of his time gambling and hunting, was also a *sagax horoscopus*, a learned astrologer. Medieval monarchs were nothing if not superstitious; they greatly favoured those who convinced them that divination was a science.

LOVELESS, GEORGE (1797-1874) was the leader of the group of Tolpuddle labourers who were sentenced to transportation for administering illegal oaths. Because of the publicity aroused by the case, the subsequent reprieve of the men, and the stimulus that their 'martyrdom' gave to radical movements, the Tolpuddle men have an honoured place in English social history.

Undoubtedly they were doing more than they realized when they met on 9 December 1833 for a ceremony of initiation into the 'Tolpuddle Friendly Society'. It was hoped that it would become part of a Dorset network of such societies which would eventually be incorporated into the Grand National Consolidated Trades Union – that ambitious organization whose collapse in 1834 was to be such a serious setback to the growth of trades unionism. An informer, present at the meeting, supplied details to the local magistrate. The six principals (one of whom, James Hammett, was not present at the meeting) were sent for trial at Dorchester Assizes. They were found guilty and, on 19 March 1834, sentenced by Mr Baron Williams to be transported 'to such places beyond the seas as His Majesty's Council, in their discretion shall see fit, for the term of seven years'. The indictment was based upon a strained interpretation of the Mutiny Act of 1797 which had been passed to cope with mutinous seamen in wartime. The government, prompted by an energetic magistrate, James Frampton, decided to use the trial as a means of checking what they regarded as a contagious spirit of village democracy. With this policy Williams, a newly appointed judge and a keen Whig, was fully in sympathy. The trial was therefore a political demonstration as much as an exercise in law.

Loveless, married, with three children, was the best educated of the group, having taught himself to read and write. Like his brother he was a Methodist. A local preacher of some renown, he had even managed to acquire a small theological library. To zealots like Frampton, to parsons like Dr Warren (the vicar of Tolpuddle whom the men accused of letting them down after undertaking to see them righted), to be a Methodist was to defy the proper ordering of village life under squire and parson. Loveless's record speaks for his determination and intelligence; he was a sober, earnest and purposeful man. Orator though he was, only exceptional circumstances made such a man into a militant radical. The 'Captain Swing' riots of 1830 had been a desperate movement of protest against intolerable conditions. Rising population, the effect of enclosures in grain producing districts and the introduction of new labour-saving machinery combined to bring a docile peasantry to mobbing and organized destruction. Nowhere in England were agricultural wages lower than in Dorset – or in Dorset than in the Tolpuddle district. When local farmers reduced them from nine to eight shillings, at the end of 1832, a deputation of villagers, with Loveless as spokesman, met the magistrates and farmers. They went back to work, apparently expecting some improvement. But wages were further reduced. Loveless may be believed when he said that it was 'impossible to live honestly on such scanty means'. By October 1833 he had made contact with Owen's Union. A meeting to hear officials from London was held in Tolpuddle. Since the repeal of the Combination Acts there was nothing illegal about such a proceeding, but the men needlessly exposed themselves by holding an initiation ceremony. Below an imposing painting of Father Time, as a skeleton with a scythe in his hand, the initiates took an oath not to reveal the members or the activities of the society. It was the oath that betrayed them.

Loveless's colleagues went to Australia, he, in 1834, to the penal sub-colony of Van Diemen's land. Discipline was ferocious: in 1834 there were 15,000 convictions and 50,000 lashes were inflicted upon a convict population of 15,000. At home the London Dorchester committee was founded to obtain redress. Thomas Wakley MP marshalled a campaign of petitions and pressed the new Home Secretary for a reprieve. Russell, unlike his predecessor Melbourne, was sympathetic. Eventually a free pardon was conceded (March 1836). Despite frustrating delays the men were traced. Loveless with his brother and their families, and James Brine, went to Greensted in Essex where an eighty-acre farm had been bought for them by public subscription. Loveless was welcomed in Chartist circles: his experiences were incendiary material for the advancing democratic movement. His pamphlet, the *Victims of Whiggery*, attacked the political establishment and exposed the cruelties of transportation and the conditions of the penal settlements. It was perhaps, however, to escape from politics and publicity that the Loveless family, with the other Tolpuddle men (except for Hammett) decided to emigrate to Canada (1844).

There Loveless farmed and prospered, and built a Methodist church. Before his death an Act of Parliament had set the British trades unions upon a sound legal footing (1871). In 1872, Joseph Arch, another Methodist, founded the National Agricultural Workers' Union. Loveless had the satisfaction of knowing that – to quote the words of his memorial in Siloam cemetery: 'The case of the Tolpuddle martyrs became a turning point in labour laws and practices in the United Kingdom.'

Further Reading
Joyce Marlow, *The Tolpuddle Martyrs*, 1971.
J. L. and Barbara Hammond, *The Village Labourer, 1760-1832*, 2 vols, 1911.

LOVETT, WILLIAM (1800-77) drafted the first People's Charter, and has thus earned his place amongst the heroes of the Chartist Movement. He was a hero more in the mould of the little men of H. G. Wells than of the giants of his contemporary, Carlyle. Brought up in Cornwall by his mother, a strict Methodist, he was never particularly successful at the various trades which he tackled. He abandoned fishing because he was sea-sick. Ropemaking was a declining industry, so he became a cabinet maker, and moved to London. He married, after a hiccough over theological incompatibility, but lost his savings in a pastry-cook business, which his wife had persuaded him to start. This led him to accept the post of storekeeper to the first London Co-operative Association, and from that base he developed an interest in Robert Owen's Co-operative Movement. He also became involved in the struggle for the liberty of the Press, as Secretary to the Victim Fund for those who were imprisoned for defying the stamp duties, which were crippling the publication of newspapers. In 1831 he was imprisoned himself for refusing to serve in the militia.

In 1836, following the collapse of Owen's trade union, he founded the London Working Men's Association. This took its shape from his interests. It was an educational society for skilled artisans like himself, aiming at self-improvement in political understanding and status. It was small, never having more than about 200 members. It was against all forms of violence. Although he was prepared to ally, for tactical reasons, with the enfranchised middle classes on the one hand, and the rougher elements of the industrial workers on the other, Lovett essentially stood apart from them both. His movement spread, and within a year there were over 150 similar associations. In 1837, a public meeting was called by the LWMA at the Crown and Anchor tavern in the Strand, which led to a petition to the House of Commons, and in the following year this became the basis for the People's Charter, drafted by Lovett and published on 8 May 1838.

The Charter proposed a vote for every adult man, a secret ballot, annual parliaments, equal electoral districts, the payment of MPs, and the ending of any property qualifications for them. It became the rallying point for movements for political reform, and within the next century all its ideas except annual parliaments were to be adopted. It was the product of a short-lived combination of political groups whose aims were diverse. Improvements in factory working conditions, the abolition of the new Poor Law, currency reform, trade union rights, the freedom of the Press, workers' education; all might be achieved if the People had the Vote. The next step was a National Convention, with Lovett as its secretary, and the preparation of a National Petition.

But the 'Physical Force' groups in the Chartist movement gained ascendancy, with talk of a run on the banks, and a 'sacred month' general strike if the Petition were rejected. Lovett spent a month in Warwick Gaol, for describing the 'Peelers', Peel's police, as 'a bloodthirsty and unconstitutional force'. When he came out, he moved away from the Chartists, though not from the Charter. During the next upsurge of Chartism in 1842, he attempted, unsuccessfully, to ally with a middle-class parliamentary group. Feargus O'Connor, by now the dominant figure in the Movement, denounced him for being out of touch with the poor, a lackey of the well-to-do, and an abstract theorist to boot. Increasingly Lovett focused on educational work. He was a pioneer in this field, but he never achieved the mass penny contributions which he hoped would turn his scheme for the education of workers into a national movement. This mild, kind, earnest and rather melancholy man was a thorough organizer, but no leader. But he lived to see his class enfranchised by the Second Reform Act in 1867.

Further Reading
G. D. H. Cole, *Chartist Portraits*, 1965.

LOWE, ROBERT, VISCOUNT SHERBROOKE
(1811-92) was a stormy petrel in the middle of the political scene. He was a remarkable man to look at, an albino with a large white head who peered out at the world beneath eyelids nearly closed. 'I am told we've got an Albanian now amongst us,' muttered an old Tory when he joined the House of Commons. He was no respecter of convention, and could be seen pedalling a huge tricycle, and later a tandem. He was formidably intelligent, and contemptuously cutting about the less quick-witted, even when they were political allies, like W. E. Forster, 'a bumbler and a boor'. Instinctively he was an extremist, who enjoyed pushing policies through against opposition, and often made this more difficult by the intemperance of his language. Add to this his energy, impatience, and a humour which was often cruel and

sometimes bawdy – he was pleased to be nicknamed *Rabellaise au lait* – and it is easy to understand why Palmerston and Gladstone were not sure whether it was riskier to have him in or out of their ministries.

The son of a parson and handicapped by his inadequate eyes, he had to fight his way to the top, achieving political fame and wealth during eight years in Australia (1844 to 1852), when he was frustrated as a don and a lawyer in Britain. Back in England he quickly made his mark as a leader writer for *The Times* (he had been Delane's Oxford tutor), and held office in the Indian Board of Control, the Board of Trade and the Board of Education, before becoming Gladstone's Chancellor of the Exchequer in 1868. He features in the history books chiefly as the leader of a Whig group, dubbed by Bright 'the Adullamites' for the successful opposition they organized from their 'Cave' to the Reform Bill which Russell and Gladstone tried to get through in 1866. His speeches against democracy during the debates on the Bill were famous in Victorian parliamentary history. Lowe was a Benthamite liberal, who believed that good government should aim for the greatest happiness of the greatest number, but that democracy would subject the country to the tyranny of an ignorant and venal majority, which would always fall for the quick fix at the expense of long-term prosperity. He was an élitist, one of the first to campaign for a meritocracy. He worked with Macaulay to open the Indian Civil Service to competitive entry through examination, and then achieved the same for almost all the English Home Civil Service. Thus he helped to lay the foundations for the modern executive. He proclaimed the importance of education for the democracies which he saw must eventually emerge: 'I believe it will be absolutely necessary that you should prevail upon our future masters to learn their letters.' But he earned the reputation of an educational Gradgrind for his stress on useful subjects, and on payment for teachers by the results they could achieve for their pupils in central examinations.

For his tough-minded approach, Palmerston had chosen him to push through reforms which would reduce the cost of education to the state, and Gladstone had the same reason for making him Chancellor of the Exchequer. There he carried the Liberal policies of Free Trade and low taxation to their furthest extreme, before the need to raise more money for defence after the Franco-Prussian war forced him into the unwise imposition of a match tax, which led to a popular demonstration. The Latin pun which he planned to put onto the revenue stamps on the match boxes, '*Ex luce lucellum*' – 'From light a little gain' – earned him no plaudits, and his arrogance drew the fire of his enemies when his department made other mistakes. Gladstone had to move him to the Home Office in 1873, and he was never a minister again. He was at once too blunt and too sharp to be a successful politician. But although he was the Cassandra of democracy, he also helped to create the conditions to make it work.

Further Reading
Asa Briggs, *Victorian People*, 1954.

LUDLOW, EDMUND (1617?-92), regicide and Republican, was a Wiltshire man from Maiden Bradley, educated at Trinity College, Oxford, and the Inner Temple. He became a member of Essex's life-guard, and fought with some distinction in the Civil War, reaching the rank of colonel. His father had been MP for Wiltshire and an extreme parliamentarian; Ludlow succeeded to his seat in 1646 and outdid him in extremism. He supported the Independents, he warmly approved of Pride's Purge, and he seems to have had doubts about Cromwell at an early stage. In 1649 he signed the king's death-warrant and he became a member of the Commonwealth Council of State. For four years from 1641 he was in Ireland, serving as Lieutenant-General, and it was Ludlow who in effect completed the Cromwellian conquest. In his absence Oliver dismissed the Rump and set up the Protectorate. Ludlow's hostility was so plainly stated that he was arrested when he landed in England. He was wholly unwilling to accept the new régime. When Cromwell demanded of him 'What is it that you would have?' he answered 'That which we fought for, that the nation might be governed by its own consent'. In 1659 he helped to remove Richard Cromwell and was made a member of the Council of State. Almost alone he recognized the need for army and parliament to co-operate if the Republic was to survive. In 1660 he was elected to the Convention, and actually took his seat; but when it was evident that his fate would be execution, he managed to get away and take ship to France. By 1662 he had taken refuge in Vevay in Switzerland, and there he remained for a generation, writing his memoirs. The royalists plotted against his life and managed to murder one of his fellow refugees, John Lisle. The Revolution of 1688 stirred the old man, and he returned to England in 1689. At the instigation of Sir Edward Seymour a proclamation was issued for his arrest, and he once again escaped, making his way back to Vevay, where he died in 1692. He was a thorough-going and stubborn Republican, and his *Memoirs* are most valuable for the light they throw on the collapse of the English Republic after the death of Cromwell.

Further Reading
A. Worden, ed., *A Voice from the Watch Tower*, 1978.
C. H. Firth, ed., *Memoirs of Edmund Ludlow*, 1894.

LUDLOW, JOHN MALCOLM FORBES (1821-1911), born in India but brought up in Paris, derived from his French upbringing an original angle from which to approach the religious and social questions that occupied him during a long life. Not till 1843, and marriage, did he feel that England, not France, was his 'heart's home'. He remained detached in spirit from English empiricism, a believer in planning. In the Huguenot church in London he looked for 'the real Christianity' of the gospels. He read principally French and German authors, but it was also under the influences of Thomas Arnold, as interpreted by his biographer Dean Stanley, and Frederick Maurice, that he came to his distinctive programme for social action. Its triple foundations were democracy resting on universal suffrage, the all-embracing socialism advocated by Proudhon and Fourier, and Christianity, as supremely relevant to the nation's health.

A shy, studious man, Ludlow did not shrink from learning, through visiting, about the plight of the poor. He also gave himself unstintingly to the labours of writing and administration that would earn from Edward Norman the measured tribute: 'arguably the most important of Christian Socialist leaders of the whole century.' Disillusioned, after 1848, about political prospects, Ludlow declared that 'social reform alone was worth living for'. Society he saw in organic terms. Moral worth could not be 'fixed at any particular degree in the mere scale of wealth'. What criterion then should be adopted? An idea can be gleaned from his seminal article (1850), *Labour and the Poor*: The remedy to social ills 'lies not in any system or theory, not in any party cry or economical machinery, but in a thorough change of spirit'. To the whole nation, the call must be: 'Make me a clean heart O God, and renew a right spirit within me.' He challenged the competitive system as 'the devil's own work'. The answer lay in the principle of association, 'the only effective remedy against the fearful beating down of wages'. Rejecting emphasis on rights, he urged that men consider their social duties: a principle to be applied 'not in one shape but in a thousand'. One of these was the Trades Union. He assisted in the early development of the Amalgamated Society of Engineers. Another was the Friendly Society. After drafting the defining act of 1875, he acted for seventeen years as chief registrar of Friendly Societies. He took part in the meeting of the Christian Social Union of 1889 and was heartened by the new vitality in a movement he had done so much to promote. In his signally useful life Ludlow showed the way to realize, in community, St Paul's noble injunction: to be members one of another.

Further Reading
N. C. Masterman, *John Malcolm Ludlow, The Builder of Christian Socialism*, 1963.

LULLUS, ST or LUL (*d*.786) was the successor of Boniface in the see of Mainz. Lul was a native of Wessex and had been brought up in the monastery of Malmesbury. It is possible that he was a distant kinsman of Boniface, and fairly certain that several of his relations worked alongside Boniface in the German mission-field where so many men and women of Anglo-Saxon stock achieved prominence. Lul probably joined Boniface in about 738-9. He rapidly distinguished himself as a man of outstanding talents and emerged as the favourite disciple of his master's old age. By 747 he had become Boniface's archdeacon (a bishop's most important subordinate). In 751 he represented Boniface on a mission to the pope. In 752 he was consecrated a bishop in order to act as an assistant-bishop to Boniface. In 753 when Boniface set out for Frisia on his last missionary journey he designated Lul his successor in the see of Mainz, although to do this was in breach of the law of the church governing episcopal elections. On Boniface's death in the following year Lul became Bishop of Mainz, apparently with the support of the Frankish king, Pippin III. He retained the see of Mainz for the remainder of his life.

Lul's personality and achievements have almost inevitably been overshadowed by those of his great predecessor. He has suffered neglect also because the sources bearing upon his career as a bishop are hard to interpret. For example, it was for long believed that Lul engaged in unseemly quarrels with Sturmi, the abbot of Boniface's monastery at Fulda; but it seems that this episode has been much exaggerated. It has been argued that the popes were distrustful of Lul because of the manner in which he had come to episcopal office, and it is indeed true that they did not grant him a pallium (the symbol of an archbishop's authority) until about 781; but we cannot be sure that this delay arose from suspicion. It has been suggested that Lul was inactive in the mission-field; on the contrary, however, it seems that he was urging upon Pippin's son Charles (that is, Charlemagne) more vigorous steps for the evangelization of Saxony and that Charles was responding eagerly to his teaching.

These matters remain uncertain. What we can be sure about is that Lul maintained contact with friends in England. The evidence comes from surviving letters to and from him, numbering about forty. To an even greater extent than the letters of Boniface, Lul's correspondence bears witness to the transmission of books from England to Germany. He asked for the works of Aldhelm. Abbot Cuthbert of Jarrow and Archbishop Albert of York were asked to send certain of the works of Bede. Lul did not confine himself to requests for recent works of Christian scholarship. To Bishop Cyneheard of Winchester he wrote asking for works of secular learning, instancing books on medicine. It is likely that it was through Lul's agency that certain works by classical authors reached medieval Germany. For example, the minor works of Tacitus (including his life of Agricola) have been transmitted to us by way of a ninth-century manuscript from the monastery of Hersfeld; and Hersfeld had been founded by Lul. The letters of Lul show him as an active patron of learning and serve as further reminder of the degree to which the scholarship of the Carolingian Renaissance rested on the intellectual resources of Anglo-Saxon England.

Further Reading

W. Levison, *England and the Continent in the Eighth Century*, 1946.

LUMLEY, RICHARD, 1st EARL OF SCARBOROUGH (*d.*1721), one of the seven signatories of the invitation to William of Orange, came from a family which had fought for the king in the Civil War. Brought up a Roman Catholic, he served Charles II as a soldier and in 1685 led the Sussex militia against Monmouth, who was captured by some of his men. But he disapproved of James II's policy; deprived of his regiment in 1687, he became a Protestant. He was one of the three Tories who signed the invitation to William in 1688, and he played an active part in the revolutionary movement in the north, occupying Newcastle-on-Tyne for the new régime. A Privy Councillor in the reigns of William, Anne, and George I, he was created Earl of Scarborough in 1690 and he fought at the Boyne and against the French in Flanders in the War of the League of Augsburg.

LYDGATE, JOHN (*c.*1370-1449), monk of Bury St Edmunds, was one of the most prolific of poets. He came from Lidgate near Bury in Suffolk, became a monk of the great Benedictine abbey there by 1382, and attended Gloucester College, Oxford about 1406-8. He read widely but less than has often been supposed: he was no humanist and knew the classics mainly through French translations. Contemporary appreciation of his poetry gave him a highly unusual career for a monk, for without apparently holding high office at Bury he spent much of his lifetime outside the cloister. He lived some years in London and in Lancastrian France. He was absentee prior of the alien priory of Hatfield Broadoak in Essex from 1423 until 1434, when he returned to Bury for his old age. His principal works were his *Troy Book*, commissioned by Prince Henry in 1412 and completed in 1420, his *Siege of Thebes* (1421-2), and the *Fall of Princes* (1431-8) commissioned by Humphrey, Duke of Gloucester. There is also a mass of poetry relating to particular occasions – for Lydgate acted like a poet laureate – and much love and religious poetry, most of it commissioned by his patrons. These included King Henry VI, Queen Katherine, the Earls of Salisbury and Warwick, the Countesses of March, Shrewsbury, Stafford, Suffolk and Warwick, St Paul's Cathedral chapter and several London companies. He was unrivalled in his own day and was considered the equal of Chaucer, a judgement no longer accepted.

Lydgate may have known Chaucer, certainly admired him, and constantly borrowed from him. 'From him he took his style, his verse-forms, his metre, and many of the genres in which he wrote'. He imitated and tried to improve on the master, tackling the same topics and seeking to surpass him. By our standards he failed, but our standards are not Lydgate's. Lydgate and his age did not admire Chaucer's originality, freshness and realism as much as we do, but commended instead his moralization and rhetoric. Lydgate constantly moralized and amplified, writing at inordinate length in ornate language. He was the equivalent in verse of the prose-writer Abbot Whetehamstede. He was the master of saying nothing at excessive length and showed no fear of repetition when drawing a moral. A 'profusion of surface decoration' takes priority over any meaning. Plot, realism, narrative flow, and drama are lost in a mass of words. Thus his *Troy Book* is 'homily first, an encyclopaedia second, and an epic nowhere'. It makes Lydgate's poetry too long-winded, dull and tedious for us, but it was what contemporaries admired.

No doubt the appalling amount he was required to write largely explains occasional technical deficiencies, such as loose syntax and lame metre. Yet most of his work is competent – he had remarkable facility in versifying – and little falls disastrously short. Moreover his best work contains good lines, near-flawless craftsmanship, high rhetorical flights, genuine eloquence and feeling. He was never an innovator. 'He can never, even at his best, rivet us with the uniqueness of his language or enrich our awareness of words.' His verbosity, his inability to select, and his tendency to make everything seem the same are the marks of a profoundly unoriginal mind. They indicate in him:

total acquiescence in the conventions and demands of his age. Like any competent professional, he did what was asked of him, and working within an established literary tradition he had neither the desire, nor the incentive, nor the creative power to make things new.

This makes him typical of his age, not untypical. It is no disgrace to fall short of the standards of Chaucer, particularly when the character of Chaucer's genius was still imperfectly understood.

Further Reading
D. Pearsall, *John Lydgate*, 1970.

LYELL, SIR CHARLES (1797-1875), geologist, was the author of the *Principles of Geology* which may be compared with Darwin's *Origin of Species* as a contribution to the great earthquake in nineteenth-century thinking about the universe, the creation and the nature of God. It dealt a mortal blow to the old 'catastrophic' interpretation and to the idea of universal and immutable

laws of the universe, though these laws continued to be stoutly, sometimes (as by Gosse) eccentrically, defended.

Lyell was the eldest son of Charles Lyell, botanist and student of Dante, of Kinnordy in Forfarshire. The family lived in the south of England during his boyhood and the son's taste for natural history was encouraged by his father's interest and by the freedom of his life in the New Forest and Sussex. At Exeter College, Oxford, he was an indifferent classic but a keen student of entomology until Dr Buckland's lectures attracted him to geology. The discovery of the difference between successive faunas was then so enlarging the subject that a correct understanding of its principles had become essential to the zoologist who wished to understand the relations between existing genera and species. Lyell's whole scientific work stemmed from the notion that the processes of the past must be judged by those currently in progress. 'We must preach up travelling as the first, second and third requisites for a modern geologist.' This dictum of Lyell's later life was based on his own experience of extensive travel: in 1817 he was in the Grampians, Mull and Staffa; in 1818 he inspected the Juras and the Alps.

He intended to study for the bar but weak eyesight thwarted him. He worked for the Geological Society, carried out intensive field studies and corresponded with foreign experts. In 1827 he was briefly on circuit, having taken up legal practice, but geology had already become his life. His enthusiasm was matched by a scholarly caution in the face of conflicting evidence; when he came to conclusions they were magisterial in argument and style. In the autumn of 1828 he was to be found walking and riding mule-back around Sicily, studying the evidence of recent mountain building. He realized that the relative ages of the later deposits could be established by the proportion of living to extinct molluscan species which they contained; hence came his division of tertiary strata into eocene, miocene and pliocene. This long-accepted classification, and his account of the way in which fossiliferous deposits could have been slowly raised above the sea appear in his *Principles*, published by Murray in successive volumes between 1830 and 1834.

From the start the book, constantly revised by Lyell, enjoyed wide circulation: the twelfth edition was issued in 1875. Some criticized Lyell for taking insufficient notice of Hutton's work: since Hutton, however, the science of paleontology had introduced a new field of evidence. Lyell's appeal to existing causes may suggest that his 'uniformitarian' doctrine is opposed to that of evolution – and he certainly opposed Lamarck's theory of transmutation of species until Darwin produced what seemed to him to be convincing evidence. Darwin himself paid tribute to his work, though Lyell's book *The*

Antiquity of Man (1863) treated the theory of the origin of species with reserve.

Lyell was unusually open-minded, always ready to alter his position in the light of new evidence. Though contemporaries used to talk of his 'Lord Chancellor manner', his was a liberal and tolerant mind. Dean Stanley wrote of him: 'From early youth to extreme old age it was to him a solemn religious duty to be incessantly learning, constantly growing, fearlessly correcting his own mistakes … Science and religion for him not only were not divorced but were one and indivisible.' All his life he continued to travel and study. He was a sociable man of wide sympathies; in friendships, as in intellectual pursuits, he ranged beyond his own circle and subject. Charles Darwin was to speak affectionately of his 'morning house of call' when he lived at 16 Hart Street, London. Lyell was not a tall man but an unusually high, wide forehead would have given him a fine presence if his very short sight had not made him stoop and peer.

Further Reading
T. G. Bonney, *Charles Lyell and Modern Geology*, 1895.

LYNDWOOD, WILLIAM (*c*.1375-1446), Bishop of St David's from 1442, was a great canon lawyer and 'stood head and shoulders above the rest of fifteenth-century English and Welsh bishops'. The son of a woolman from Linwood near Market Rasen in Lincolnshire, he attended Gonville Hall and perhaps Pembroke Hall, Cambridge University, and graduated as doctor of canon law in 1407. A career in ecclesiastical justice and administration duly followed. He must have had some such experience before 1414, when he became chancellor to Henry Chichele, Archbishop of Canterbury and auditor of causes. From 1417 to 1431 he was official principal (chief judge) of the court of Canterbury, and in 1419-26 he was prolocutor (speaker) of the Canterbury convocation. He thus presided over all litigation at the provincial court for fourteen years, including several important heresy trials. He was 'a notable heretic-hunter'. In 1433 he represented the English at the General Council of the church at Basle. By the end of his term nobody can have known more about the canon law of the province of Canterbury and certainly nobody was better able to codify it than Lyndwood, whose great *Provinciale* digests and explains in five books the decrees of the province of Canterbury from the time of King John to Archbishop Chichele. It was and is the main source for English medieval canon law.

As early as 1402 William Lyndwood had been described as a king's clerk and he was regularly employed on diplomatic missions from 1417 to 1441. Only in 1431, however, did he transfer formally from the archbishop's service to that of the king. Due to the chancellor's indisposition, Lyndwood preached his sermon at the opening of parliament. He then joined the young King Henry VI in France, where he was a councillor and acted as clerk of the privy seal. On their return to England in 1432 he was appointed by Gloucester as keeper of the privy seal – the third minister of state. He remained in office until 1443, probably only resigning in order to devote himself to his distant diocese. His exceptionally long appointment demonstrates both that he was acceptable to all and also how well he filled his office. So belated a promotion to such a poor, remote and generally unattractive see indicates, however, how limited was his political stature. Lyndwood, in short, was a highly efficient bureaucrat, but not a political figure of the front rank.

Lyndwood's long and valued service for a variety of masters brought him many different livings from 1397 on culminating in the archdeaconry of Stow in 1434. He may have taken a drop in income on his promotion as bishop. Generally, no doubt, he was non-resident, but that he had some pastoral experience and concerns is suggested by a licence to preach in 1417. His educational interests were expressed also through the king's foundations at Eton and King's College, Cambridge, whose statutes he helped to draft, and through the benefactions to Gonville and Pembroke halls in his will. Such legal erudition and such experience and capacity for ecclesiastical administration surely fitted him ideally for a bishopric, but this came only late in life for political services. Bishoprics were no longer allocated primarily for spirituality or services to the church. What ranked highest in Lyndwood's own estimation and what he wished to be remembered for was his *Provinciale*, a chained copy of which he directed to be available at the chantry founded for him by his executors in the crypt of St Stephen's Chapel, Westminster. His wish was granted. This is his claim to fame.

Further Reading
R. A. Griffiths, *The Reign of King Henry VI 1422-61*, 1981.

LYONS, RICHARD (*d*.1381), vintner and alderman of London, was impeached in the Good Parliament of 1376 and murdered in the Peasants Revolt four years later. Lyons's origins are obscure: perhaps from Winchelsea and certainly illegitimate, he was buying property in London from 1359, when he had presumably completed his apprenticeship and established himself as a vintner. By 1365 he was prominent enough to take a lease of the three London taverns selling sweet wines. He was still principally a vintner in 1376, when he was owed £518 for wine supplied. Like most successful merchants, he extended his interests into other areas: in 1376 he owned a ship, iron valued at £198, cloth worth £649, lead worth £103, stocks of timber, and was lending to both the Crown and private individuals (like the Duke of Brittany) on security. To redeem his loans to the Crown he was appointed farmer of the petty customs and subsidy throughout England, which inevitably involved him in other areas of royal finance. He was sheriff of London in 1374 and alderman from then until dismissed in 1376, following his impeachment and forfeiture. He was back in business as a royal lender in 1379 and may have been richer at death than in 1376. He was knight of the shire for Essex in 1380.

Lyons's rapid increase in wealth is illustrated by his purchase of property in London from 1359, of the manor of Overhall-in-Leiston in Essex in 1365, and many other properties from 1375. At his death in 1381 he held thirty houses, sixty shops, twelve cellars, and six gardens in London and its suburbs north of the Thames, two shops and seven gardens in Southwark, three manors and other land in Essex and Kent. Most apparently escaped forfeiture in 1376 because held in trust. Moveables worth £2,443 had then been discovered in London alone, much of it in stock, but much comprising the contents of his house in the parish of St James Garlickhithe. Although he had been divorced in 1363, he was childless and presumably lived only with servants, his house contained a hall, parlour, five chambers, chapel, wardrobe and little wardrobe, pantry, buttery, kitchen and stable. These rooms were richly furnished with tapestries, chandeliers, and elaborate beds. The wardrobe and little wardrobe contained £87 worth of armour, linen and clothes, including a long list of colourful and furred gowns. Much of this was secured by the Duke of Gloucester on Lyons's fall. Lyons was probably not one of the richest aldermen and fell far short of the capital resources of the high nobility, yet his lifestyle was remarkably opulent.

It was Lyons's financial dealings with the Crown that justified his impeachment in 1376 and his consequent unpopularity that led to his murder. Yet the charges are not particularly convincing. Lyons lent money to the Crown at interest and may well have bought up old royal debts for less than their face value, but neither of these activities was illegal. No doubt, of course, he secured preferential terms for repayment, but all royal creditors sought to insist on that. 'Ambitious Lyons certainly was, and unscrupulous he may have been, but the evidence does not seem to justify the description of him as an "arch-thief".' Some charges were apparently made maliciously by smugglers to divert attention from themselves, but the main reason for Lyons's impeachment seems to be political – because he was too intimately connected with the unpopular and unsuccessful policies of Lord Latimer and Alice Perrers in the mid 1370s. Like Gilbert Maghfield somewhat later he found trade and politics did not mix.

Further Reading
A. R. Myers, 'The Wealth of Richard Lyons', *Essays in Medieval History presented to Bertie Wilkinson*, ed. T. A. Sandquist and M. R. Powicke, 1969.
S. Thrupp, *The Merchant Class of Medieval London*, 1962.

LYTTELTON, GEORGE, 1st BARON (1709-73) was the son of Sir Thomas Lyttelton of Hagley in Worcestershire, a gentleman of some standing and electoral influence in the county, and of Christian, daughter of the Earl of Cobham. He was, besides this connection with the Temple family, also related to the proud Grenvilles, since Christian's sister was the wife of Richard Grenville. An ancestor had been the legal expert and author of Lyttelton's *Tenures*.

After Eton, Christ Church and the Grand Tour he entered parliament in 1735, sitting for Okehampton, in the same year as William Pitt, who was also linked to the 'Cobham cousinhood' by his brother Thomas's marriage to Lyttelton's sister. With this militant group he attached himself to the interest of the Prince of Wales, becoming his secretary, less because he admired Frederick than because he could attack Walpole. The destruction of this minister was the prime object of the 'Cobham Cubs' for seven years, but after his fall Pitt continued to inveigh against the war policy of Carteret. Lyttelton was overshadowed by the ability of Pitt, but he found office before him, in December 1744, as a Lord of the Treasury. When Pitt continued to attack this ministry, he suffered from some embarrassment. One of Henry Fox's letters describes him sitting 'silent and uneasy' on an occasion when he had voted against the government. But Pitt, too, joined the ministry in 1746 and Lyttelton himself retained his office until 1755, when he was made Chancellor of the Exchequer by Newcastle. This involved him in a more lasting breach with Pitt which was not healed until 1763. Since he had a notorious incapacity for arithmetic, he was unhappy in his post and resigned it the following year, with a peerage. Lord Hervey said of him that he had a flow of words, uttered in a lulling monotony, commonplace in the moralisms and maxims which were his stock-in-trade. Horace Walpole, who did not love him, declared that 'absurdity was predominant' in his constitution. 'With the figure of a spectre and the gesticulations of a puppet, he talked heroics through his nose, made declamations at a visit, and played at cards with scraps of history.' Yet he allowed that 'he was far from wanting parts; spoke well when he had studied his speeches; and loved to reward and promote merit in others'.

Lyttelton approached literature with the same solemnity that amused Walpole. His verse contains many of the mannerisms of the Augustans and little that is specially pleasing or interesting. But some of the stanzas in the *Monody*, written in 1747 in memory of his wife, Lucy Fortescue (a selection of which may be found in the *Oxford Book of Eighteenth Century Verse*), invite comparison for feeling and elegance with the best of his time. In his prose works he shows the influence of the French master: Montesquieu, for instance, in his *Persian Letters*, sprightly and deist in turn; Fénelon, in

Dialogues from the Dead, in which the tone is more serious, as benefited an ardent convert to Christianity. He was a zealous amateur historian and wrote a *Life of Henry II* which is, by all accounts, a heavy and uninspiring compilation. His letters, to his father and others, show, however, historical imagination and an excellent topographical sense. The man who helped James Thompson with *The Seasons*, to whom Fielding, his fellow Etonian, dedicated *Tom Jones*, was worth something more, perhaps, than Lord Chesterfield's observation that he looked as if his head had already had one chop on the block, for it hung always on one shoulder or the other, or the devastating remark of Dr Johnson about the *Dialogues*: 'He sat down to write a book to tell the world what the world all his life had been telling him.'

Further Reading
S. C. Roberts, *An Eighteenth-Century Gentleman*, 1936.

LYTTON, ROBERT, 1st EARL OF LYTTON (1831-91) was a dangerously exciting Viceroy of India between 1875 and 1880. His was a strange appointment, for he was a diplomat who would rather have been a poet. Son of the romantic novelist, Edward Bulwer, Lord Lytton (qv), he had vivid blue eyes, curly hair and beard, and a lofty brow. Disraeli and Salisbury asked him to move to Delhi from Lisbon, where he was ambassador, because Bulwer had given the young Disraeli introductions to the beau monde, and because the Lyttons, at Knebworth, were neighbours to the Cecils at Hatfield. He was their fifth choice. The splendour of the orient and the powers of the Viceroy attracted him. His instinct for theatre helped to make the most of Victoria's decision to be proclaimed Empress of India. Disraeli wrote to Salisbury: 'Lytton's proclamation schemes, tho' they read like The One Thousand and One Nights, I believe are judicious.' He and his family processed on elephants to the Imperial Assemblage, where sixty-three Ruling Chiefs received banners, and the celebrations lasted for a fortnight. He was never afraid of acting decisively, and embarked on the government's forward policy on the north-west frontier with enthusiasm. Russian expansion in Asia had brought them near to Afghanistan and the passes through to India. After earlier disasters there, the Liberals had preferred to let the Russians struggle to control the mountain Afghan tribes, without interfering. Lytton sent a resident British Agent to Kabul, who was soon murdered. A full-scale invasion had to follow. The expense was great, the future uncertain, and when the Liberals won the election of 1880, Lytton resigned before he was recalled. He was not the last to underestimate the ferocity with which Afghans are ready to fight foreign invaders. Lytton eventually became ambassador to Paris, after a romantic affair with the novelist Ouida, who urged him to elope to a Sicilian palace. His wife helped him through bouts of the 'Black Care', which dogged him all his life. One of their sons-in-law left a more lasting mark on India; Edwin Lutyens, architect of New Delhi.

M

McADAM, JOHN LOUDON (1756-1836) was a road-builder whose name became a part of the English language. He was born at Ayr, went to New York at the age of fourteen, became a successful merchant, and returned to his native country in 1783 and bought an estate at Sauchrie in Ayrshire. As deputy-lieutenant of Ayrshire and trustee of a turnpike trust he encountered problems of road-making. He spent thousands of pounds on his own experiments and travelled widely, inspecting roads.

In 1798 he moved to Falmouth as agent for re-victualling the navy. In 1815 he became surveyor to the British Turnpike Trust and, using his own system, set about rebuilding 180 miles of local roads. His method was relatively cheap since he believed that the hard-laid stone base, as used by Telford, was unnecessary. 'As no artificial road can be made so good as the natural soil in a *dry state*, it is necessary to preserve this state.' The earth had to be properly drained and kept dry by spreading on it a layer, about ten inches deep of small graded stone chips. After this had been flattened by traffic, two additional layers were put down. The result was 'a solid road, of clean, dry stone, or flint, so selected, prepared and laid, as to be impervious to water; and this cannot be effected unless the greatest care be taken that no earth, clay, chalks or other matter, that will hold water, be used with the broken stone; which must be so laid, as to unite by its own angles into a firm, compact and impenetrable body'.

He was impoverished by his single-minded efforts and in 1820 he petitioned parliament for compensation. A special investigation was made and a report recommended his methods. Parliament voted a grant of £2,000, hardly over-generous in relation to the social value of his work. In 1827 he was made Surveyor-General of Metropolitan Roads. His methods were soon widely adopted and the basic principle was retained even when tar was added to make tarmac. It was his new roads that made possible the express coach services, the best in Europe, with an average speed of nine to ten miles an hour.

Further Reading
R. Devereux, *J. L. McAdam*, 1936.

MACAULAY, LORD THOMAS BABINGTON (1800-59), historian and politician, was one of the most widely read writers of the Victorian age, outselling even his hero Sir Walter Scott. His popularity owed much to his opinions. He was a man of his time, confidently proud of his country. He was the son of Zachary, a leading Evangelical. He became acceptable in Whig circles, although no heir to land or mansion, through the influence of the friends he made during a brilliant career at Cambridge. There he was as famous for his waistcoats as for his wit. He was also spectacularly clumsy, but a razor gash, a knotted mess of cravat, habitual spillings and breakages, were readily attributed to his concentration on higher things. In 1830 Lord Lansdowne provided him with the pocket borough of Calne to get him into the House of Commons. In a formidable oration, he proclaimed the aim of the Great Reform Bill of 1832 – 'Reform that you may preserve'. Though his style was awkward and his voice harsh, the seemingly effortless trawl of relevant facts, the vivid illustration, the relentless logic, compelled the admiration even of opponents: Peel said that 'portions of that speech were as beautiful as anything I ever heard or read'.

In 1834 he accepted a place on the Supreme Council of India, to secure himself financially. There he established English as the official language, and British Common Law as the basis of the legal system. He also drafted a penal code which was to become the basis of Indian criminal law: 'the pacific triumphs of reason over barbarism', he believed. He shared Palmerston's forthright patriotism. 'Wherever the Englishman may wander, he is followed by the eye and guarded by the power of England.' This was virtuous power, for England was showing the world how to change without bloody revolution. He returned from India in 1838 with the outline of a History of England already in his mind, and also its theme. 'For the authority of law, for the security of property, for the peace in our streets, for the happiness of our homes, our gratitude is due, under Him who raises and pulls down nations at His pleasure, to the Long Parliament, to the Convention and to William of Orange.' The writing of English history had been dominated by the

Tories, from Clarendon to Hume. This was to set the record straight.

Although he resumed his parliamentary career as Member for Edinburgh, and was Secretary at War (1839-41) and Paymaster General in 1846, Macaulay rarely spoke in the Commons, and never, after being made a peer in 1857, in the Lords. He put his History first. After suffering a coronary thrombosis, he abandoned his original plan to span the period from the 1688 Revolution to the death of George IV, and the four volumes he had time to write before his early death only took him to the Peace of Ryswick (1697). But they were best sellers. This was as much to do with their style as with their content. Macaulay had already made his reputation as a writer, with literary and historical essays for the *Edinburgh Review*, of which the first, on Milton, made him famous overnight, and with his *Lays of Ancient Rome*. He had the gifts of a great narrative historian: a photographic memory (which enabled him to learn a Shakespeare play in an evening), an orderly mind, and the ability to pace his story. His research was energetic, if random, and his trudges round Sedgemoor and Derry, Killiekrankie and Glencoe, brought colour to his setpiece descriptions, which move forward compellingly to their climaxes. His judgements were simple and forceful. Strafford had been 'the lost Archangel, the Satan of apostasy', Cromwell 'had a high stout English heart'. He also included, the first English historian to do so, a long chapter of social history.

He has been much criticized subsequently; for taking sides, for distorting the past by interpreting it in the light of the present, for his sentimental picture of English society. His own character prevented him from appreciating the sensitivities of many about whom he wrote, for after a precocious youth he never fully grew up. Unmarried, he focused his affections on his sisters. His opinions, too, did not change: he was a man with few doubts and little subtlety. But he well earned two posthumous tributes: burial in Westminster Abbey and, which he would have appreciated even more, his nephew George Otto Trevelyan's *Life and Letters*. It is there that he can still be found: there and in his writing, for he is the most readable of all the Victorian historians.

Further Reading
O. Dudley Edwards, *Macaulay*, 1988.
J. L. Clive, *Macaulay: The Shaping of the Historian*, 1973.
J. H. Plumb, *Men and Places*, 1963.
Sir G. O. Trevelyan, *The Life and Letters of Lord Macaulay*, 2 vols, 1876.

MACBETH (*d*.1057) was King of Scotland from 1040 until his defeat by Earl Siward of Northumbria in 1054 effectively removed him from power. Before his accession Macbeth had been *mormaer* of Moray. This is a Gaelic term meaning 'great steward', in theory indicating some degree of subordination to the king. However, the *mormaers* of Moray were pretty independent men with regard to the rulers who called themselves Kings of the Scots whose seat of power lay much further to the south. In attempting to bring Macbeth to heel, King Duncan I (*r*.1034-40) was defeated and killed. Macbeth took the kingship and Duncan's sons fled into exile.

Scottish history before *c*.1100 is pathetically ill-documented. Macbeth's reign is no exception. We know that, like his slightly elder contemporary Canute in 1027, Macbeth went on a pilgrimage to Rome in 1050, where 'he scattered money like seed to the poor'; readiness to leave the country might indicate a degree of confidence about the stability of his rule. We are told that he was a generous benefactor to the religious community on St Serf's Island in Loch Leven. He is described by a contemporary as a generous king, the 'ruddy-complexioned, yellow haired tall one in whom I shall rejoice'. We hear that he fought against the English on at least one occasion before 1054, though we know nothing of the circumstances. Siward's invasion of 1054 led to a hard-fought battle in which Macbeth was defeated but managed to escape to the north. Siward installed Malcolm, son of Duncan I, as king; his authority presumably ran only over southern Scotland. Three years later, in 1057, Macbeth was cornered at Lumphanan, about twenty miles west of Aberdeen, where he was defeated and killed.

Macbeth's wife was a lady with the unlovely name of Gruoch. Nothing to the discredit of the real Lady Macbeth is told in the reliable sources; but then, practically nothing of any kind at all is told of her. Macbeth's evil reputation is owed entirely to the imagination of fourteenth- and fifteenth-century chroniclers.

Further Reading
A. A. M. Duncan, *Scotland: the Making of the Kingdom*, 1975.

MACDONALD, FLORA (1722-90) was the daughter of Ronald Macdonald of South Uist; he died when she was a child and her mother married again – Sir Alexander Macdonald. She was brought up in turn by Clanranald, Chief of the Clan, and Macdonald, and sent to finish her education in Edinburgh. In June 1746 she happened to be staying on Benbecula. Her stepfather was at the time in command of the militia out looking for Prince Charles Edward, fugitive since Culloden. On 21 June Captain O'Neil, an old acquaintance, asked her to help to convey the prince to Skye. She arranged for a pass from her stepfather for herself, manservant, 'Betty Burke' (an Irish spinning-maid, needed, she said, to help her mother) and six boatmen. They crossed the Minch and, after being first driven off by some militia-men, safely reached the house of Lady Macdonald. Sir Alexander was serving with Cumberland's army, but she agreed to shelter the prince. He stayed at the house of her factor, Macdonald of Kingsburgh. On 30 June Flora accompanied the prince to Portree and saw him off to Raasay. He had weeks of anxiety and concealment to endure before he returned to France. But she had done more than anyone to save his life.

Flora Macdonald was arrested on her return to Benbecula and sent to the Tower. On her release she was adulated in society but was in no way affected by this. She had acted, she said, not from any high-flown loyalty but as she would 'for any person in distress'. In 1750 she married Allan Macdonald of Kingsburgh; it was then that she received the celebrated visit of Dr Johnson and Boswell, who recorded that she was 'a little woman of a genteel appearance and uncommonly mild and well-bred'. In the following year, impoverished like so many Highlanders at this time, she and her husband emigrated to North Carolina. He was a loyalist in the Rebellion and was captured; she returned to Scotland and was wounded on the way in a fight with a French frigate. Reunited with her husband after the war she lived for the rest of her life in Skye. In either army or navy, all her five sons served King George III.

Further Reading
F. McLynn, *Charles Edward Stuart*, 1988.
Eric Linklater, *The Prince in the Heather*, 1965.

MACPHERSON, JAMES (1736-96) was a literary impostor, but not a literary charlatan. He presented his own poems as the work of Ossian; this was a sort of fraud, but his works had an influence and a merit which justifies his fame as an original artist. Dr Johnson declared that *Fingal* was 'as gross an imposition as ever the world was troubled with'. Had it been an ancient work, 'a true specimen how men thought at that time, it would have been a curiosity of the first rate. As a modern production it is nothing'. Dr Johnson spoke with the indignation of a literary man and a purist in the heat of an argument which now makes pleasant reading in Boswell's account of the *Tour of the Hebrides*. Thousands of less critical readers were attracted by the epic quality of *Fingal*, its notes of romance and sensibility.

Macpherson was born in 1736 at Ruthven near Kingussie, the son of a small farmer. At the University of Aberdeen he acquired literary tastes and ambitions that could not be satisfied by his work as schoolmaster in his native parish. In 1758 he published a poem, *The Highlander*. He became tutor to the son of Graham of Balgowan; when he accompanied him to Moffat he met there John Moore, author of *Douglas* and an ardent fancier of Highland life. Macpherson was already acquainted with the Gaelic fragments of the period of Ossian but believed that he could do better. For his friend he wrote *The Death of Oscar*, then other romantic stories. In 1760 appeared *Fragments of Ancient Poetry collected in the Highlands of Scotland, and translated from the Gaelic or Erse language*. Persuaded by 'several people of rank, as well as taste', he travelled around the Highlands and Western Isles: the fruit of his travels, and the patronage of some Highland lairds, was *Fingal: an ancient epic poem in six books*. In the following year, *Temora*, another poem, was published, in eight books. Macpherson was borne on by a mixture of conceit, real feeling for the new idiom, and a gale of popular acclaim, and he was undismayed by the heated argument about the authenticity of his poems. He promised to publish the originals but of course never did. He had taken only such expressions and themes from the Gaelic as suited his own epic purpose. Rejecting the Irish Finn in favour of Fingal, conqueror of the Romans and native hero, he slighted Irish scholars as much as he offended the sceptical critics of England. When in 1805 Laing published an edition of Ossian (and of Macpherson's own poems) the extent of his borrowings and of his originality was revealed. By then his Ossian had swept Europe. Goethe and Napoleon read it, and many others who were entranced by the new cult of medievalism and liked his wild, misty melancholy, regretful and sombre, couched in a rhythmic language that was as near to the familiar cadences of the Bible as it was to any Celtic bard.

Macpherson wrote a *History of Great Britain* (1660-1714) and an unremarkable translation of the *Iliad*. He was active as a politician, was made Surveyor-General of the Floridas in 1764 and sat in parliament for Camelford from 1780. He lived out his last years at Belleville, the house he built for himself at Badenoch. He did not underestimate his own abilities. It was at his own request and cost that he was buried in Westminster Abbey.

Further Reading
J. S. Smart, *Life of Macpherson*, 1905 and some lively passages in Boswell's *Tour to the Hebrides*.

MACQUEEN, ROBERT, LORD BRAXFIELD (1722-99), the most arresting figure amongst the legal portraits in Cockburn's *Memorials of his Time*, achieved a notoriety outside his native Scotland by his conduct of the treason trials of 1793-4. 'But the giant of the Bench was Braxfield. His very name makes people start yet.' Political temper was charged with furious anti-Jacobinism in these years. Reformers and radicals whose activities were in some way suspect to the government might expect to encounter biased juries. In Scotland, however, the judges themselves failed to maintain impartiality. Foremost among these was Braxfield, who presided at the infamous trials of Muir, lawyer and founder of the Scottish Friends of the People, and Palmer, a leading Scottish Unitarian, sentenced to fourteen and seven years' transportation respectively. In Braxfield's view the Constitution was perfect, and it was seditious, therefore, even to propose change. He was exceptionally well-versed in the details of the law; at the same time he was a boor and a bully. 'Strong built and dark, with rough eye-brows, powerful eyes, threatening lips, and a low growling voice, he was like a formidable blacksmith. His accent and his dialect were exaggerated Scotch; his language, like his thoughts, short, strong and conclusive.' His gross repartee provides the Scottish bar with some of its best stories. Even if he was not, as has been said, the judge who told a former chess crony whom he had sentenced to be hanged, 'That's checkmate to you, Matthew,' he did make a habit of adorning his judgements with a mordant humour all his own. To a clever culprit he once said: 'Ye're a vera clever chiel, man, but ye wad be nane the waur o' a hanging.' With reference to his aged and trusty clerk, he used to boast: 'Hoot! just gie me Josie Norrie and a gude jury and I'll do for the fellow.' Others too in that robust age doled out brutal punishments without regard for their victims' feelings. The particular blot upon the record of this masterly lawyer is that he gloried in the prejudices that could make a travesty of justice. His eminent career reveals the rough underside of the civilization of the eighteenth century – and in Edinburgh at that.

Further Reading
W. F. Gray, ed. and abridged, *Henry, Lord Cockburn: Memorials of his Time*, 1946.

MAELGWYN GWYNEDD or MAELGWYN FAWR or MAGLOCUNUS (*d.c.*549), appears in the sixth-century chronicle of Gildas as a powerful ruler of the north-western kingdom of Gwynedd, which included the fertile land of Anglesey and extended beyond the boundaries of present day Gwynedd. Maelgwyn ruled from Degannwy (near Conway) but the court later took up residence in Anglesey at Aberffraw, which may already have been a centre in Maelgwyn's time. His power extended to Ceredigion (roughly Cardiganshire) and perhaps even further south. His death corresponded roughly with the start of a new struggle, in the north of England, where his descendants fought a long and unavailing rearguard action against the insurgent Anglo-Saxons; a seventh-century descendant was Cadfan, a tyrant chronicled by Bede, and his grandson Cadwaladr, the legendary last British king.

Maelgwyn is listed as a descendent of Cunedda. The pottery and glassware discovered at Degannwy prove conclusively that during Maelgywn's reign in the early to middle sixth century, his kingdom maintained contact with the Mediterranean world. At the court at Degannwy he was attended by musicians and poets, who sang of military heroes and their exploits. None of their verses seems to have been yet written down and the poet was expected to memorize the epics crafted by his predecessors. Maelgwyn had once taken monastic vows, and may

have been a patron of Celtic style Christianity. But Gildas lamented that the ruler came to listen too much to the vain poets of his court, so that 'the vessel, once prepared for the service of God, is changed into an instrument of Satan'. Maelgwyn now appears as a prodigious sinner: the 'island dragon ... first in evil, mightier than many both in power and malice, more profuse in giving, more extravagant in sin'. He is reported to have died *c.*549 of the plague.

MAGHFIELD, GILBERT (*c.*1340-97), ironmonger and alderman of London, is representative of the lesser trades of the city. He had presumably completed his apprenticeship by 1367, when he was acting for another merchant at Danzig in modern Poland, and he established himself as a leading merchant during the next decade. He concentrated on the iron trade to the Basque port of Bilbao in northern Spain and to Bayonne in south-west France. Relatively little of his imports were sold directly to blacksmiths, as he dealt mainly with other wholesalers. He normally bought and sold on credit and by about 1390 had an annual turnover of about £1,150, compatible with total capital of £1,000-£1,500 and comparable to members of the city's ruling oligarchy. His standing was recognized by his election as alderman in 1381 and as sheriff and alderman in 1392. He also entered royal service, acting as custodian of the seas along the east coast in 1383 and from 1385 as collector of customs at Southampton and Boston. Royal favour and involvement in politics distracted his attention from business and/or damaged his trade and his credit collapsed. Without credit, he was forced to curtail his foreign trade, he was driven into moneylending, got behind with his customs payments, and ran into debt. His fortune was eroded, his goods and a surviving account book were seized by the Crown as security, and at death he can have been worth no more than £500. Medieval trade was a speculative and uncertain activity. It was as easy to lose everything as to make a fortune and there must have been many failures like Maghfield, few of whom can be studied as he can be. Despite his misfortunes, 'this early ironmonger must at one time have been typical of the outstanding group of London merchants who together created the immense prosperity of the city at the end of the fourteenth century'. He has also been considered, somewhat implausibly, as the model for Chaucer's Merchant in *The Canterbury Tales*.

The ships that imported Maghfield's iron also carried his cargoes of grain and woollen cloth, the latter being overwhelmingly the most important English export. Iron was Maghfield's main import, but woad and alum – ingredients in clothmaking – were of secondary importance. He sold them mainly to country clothiers and to a lesser extent to London grocers. Other minor imports were beaver, saffron, licorice, wax, copper, millstones, greenginger and canvas. He also dealt in fish, as befitted a resident of Billingsgate, the city of London's fish-market. His varied business shows him to be representative of 'a large group of merchants who, while specializing to some extent in one trade, also dealt in a wide range of miscellaneous merchandise'.

By 1390-5 Maghfield no longer ventured overseas, but directed operations from his London home, where he maintained a substantial household including butler, cook, and two maids. The house was leased in 1372, lay between Thames Street and the river, and possessed a private quay. By 1386 he had also acquired a neighbouring wharf and six shops at Billingsgate. Other property in London and lands in Woolwich, Middlesex, Kent and Buckinghamshire completed his estate: a clerk and three valets were needed to administer it for him. Like so many successful city businessmen he had obviously invested the profits of trade in real estate, which was more secure and which offered an income, albeit a relatively low one. Rents bulked larger in his finances in his last years, although unable to avert his decline. Even if his misfortunes disqualified him from the London aldermanry, his eventual estate compared very favourably with those of leaders of the less prosperous provincial towns.

Further Reading
M. K. James, *Studies in the Medieval Wine Trade*, ed. E. M. Veale, 1972.
E. Rickert, 'Extracts from a fourteenth-century account book', *Modern Philology* xxiv, 1926-7.

MAITLAND, JOHN, 2nd EARL and 1st DUKE OF LAUDERDALE (1616-82), member of the Cabal and ruler of Scotland for most of Charles II's reign, was a great nephew of Maitland of Lethington, the Scottish politician of Elizabethan days. A big, heavy, red-haired man, with a tongue too big for his mouth, which, as Burnet put it, 'made him bedew all he talked to'; broad Scots in pronunciation, rough and often passionate in manner; he had nevertheless an able mind, extraordinary memory and shrewd judgement, and was profoundly learned, in Hebrew as well as in the classical languages. His record in Charles II's reign indicates that he had few scruples and a cold heart. Pepys, supping at Lauderdale's house one night, was taken aback to hear him say 'that he had rather hear a cat mew than the best music in the world'. Brought up a Presbyterian, and equipped with a legal training, Lauderdale was a prominent Covenanter in the 1640s, a Commissioner in England for the Solemn League and Covenant (1643-6) and one of the Scottish members of the Commission of Both Kingdoms, the 'War Cabinet' set up in 1644. As one of the Scottish representatives in England, he shared the responsibility for handing Charles over to parliament in 1647.

Yet like all Scots at this time, Lauderdale had to face the dilemma created by the political intervention of the English army and the collapse of Scottish hopes of imposing Presbyterianism upon their southern neighbours. Like many Scots, he solved it by returning to the support of the Stuarts. As events were to show, Lauderdale's return was complete and without reservations. He was one of the Commissioners who concluded with Charles I the Engagement (December 1647) which precipitated the Second Civil War. He backed the agreement with Charles II, helped to crown him at Scone in 1650, and was captured at Worcester in 1651. For the next nine years he was a prisoner in England, and when he was set free at the Restoration he made haste to demonstrate an extreme royalism. As Clarendon, the recipient of some of this obsequiousness, observed, 'He was very polite in all his discourses, called himself and his nation a thousand traitors, and Rebells' and 'seemed not equally delighted with any argument, as when he scornfully spake of the Covenant, upon which he brake a hundred jests'. Charles II made him Secretary of State for Scotland in 1660, and from about 1663 he was the dominant figure in the government of Scotland, becoming Lord High Commissioner in 1669. He has been called 'the crudest but most dependable tool in the Cabal',* and Charles three times ignored an address from the Commons asking for his removal. His direct influence upon English affairs was slight, although he seems to have taken care to keep in close touch with the king, who for his part found him an amusing oddity and something of a butt in council. Lauderdale's doctrinal beliefs remained in some ways Presbyterian: his conduct, notably his deep thinking, won him a reputation as a debauchee.

The years between the Restoration and the Revolution were some of the darkest in Scottish history, the time of savage persecution of Presbyterians, and of the merciless prosecutions by the formidable Lord Advocate, 'the Bluidy' Sir George Mackenzie. Much of the responsibility for these things rested upon Lauderdale, the loyal executive of Stuart policy, whose dexterity as a manager stifled opposition in the Scottish parliament. He had, indeed, no great enthusiasm for episcopacy himself, and for a few years after the Pentland Rising (1666) he pursued not so much a policy of moderation as a tactic of realism, attempting to win Covenanting support by a Letter of Indulgence in 1669. This was unsuccessful, and in the early 1670s he went back to persecution, with such steps as the Letters of Intercommuning (1675) which boycotted individuals by government order, and the planting of the Highland Host (1678) upon the peasantry of the south-west. The results were seen in the events of 1679 – the murder of Archbishop Sharp, and the Covenanting rebellion which Monmouth defeated at Bothwell Brig; and when Lauderdale resigned office

*D. Ogg, *England in the Reign of Charles II*, 1956 edn, vol. I, p.329.

through ill-health in 1680 his policy could hardly be said to have succeeded in its aims. Nor were its wider implications and results beneficial to the Stuarts. It aroused hostility in England because the opposition in the Commons suspected that it provided a foretaste of Stuart policy in this country, and it did much to ensure the success of the appeal of William of Orange to lowland Scotland in 1689.

Further Reading

July Buckroyd, *Church and State in Scotland, 1660-1681*, 1980.
D. Ogg, *England in the Reign of Charles II*, 1956 edn, vol. II, pp.400-20.

MALCOLM II (Malcolm Mackenneth) (*c.*954-1034) played an important role in the formation of Scotland, even though he may perhaps have been compelled to recognize the ultimate overlordship of Canute, the monarch of Denmark and England. The heartlands of his kingdom lay between the Forth-Clyde line and the Mounth, known as Fortriu, with its capital in Fife, perhaps at Dunfermline. But victory over a Northumbrian army at the battle of Carham on Tweed (1018), confirmed Malcolm's control of Lothian. Furthermore, since he was known as 'King of the Mounth', it is clear that Malcolm's dominion also extended north of the Grampians. It has been argued that he acted as an over-king in Moray, a role perhaps cemented through the marriage of his sister to the *mormaer*, or great steward, of Moray, and that he may also have been responsible for initiating the use of thanes as royal agents in his domains. He was certainly a Christian, who contributed to the monastic settlement at Old Deer in Buchan. Malcolm settled the Crown upon Duncan, the son of his daughter Bethoc and of Cronan or Crinan, the Abbot of Dunkeld, a move which, whatever its legal novelty, helped achieve the political unification of his realm with that of Strathclyde (also known as Cumbria).

MALCOLM III (Canmore) (*c.*1031-93) was the eldest son of Duncan I. The name Canmore (Ceann Mor) was not a surname but a soubriquet, meaning Big Head, though we do not know if it referred to brain or skull. He succeeded to the throne of Alba after killing Macbeth and Macbeth's stepson Lulach at Lumphanan (August 1057) and Essie in Strathbogie (March 1058) respectively. Malcolm was assisted in his seizure of the Crown by Siward, created Earl of Northumbria by Canute; and their campaign had been launched on the orders of Edward the Confessor. Macbeth included Norman mercenaries among his troops; Malcolm and his ally had mobilized a force of Norse, English and Scottish soldiers.

About 1065 Malcolm married, first, Ingibjorg, widow of the Norse Thorfinn, Earl of Orkney and Caithness, probably an enemy of Macbeth; politically the move may have been inspired by the need to secure Malcolm against trouble from Moray, or from Northumbria. There, after the death of Siward in 1055, Edward the Confessor had installed Tostig, brother of his heir apparent Harold Godwinson, as the new earl. Malcolm, possibly because he saw this as a threat, invaded Northumbria in 1061. Tostig, however, was overthrown, and in 1066 quarrelled with Harold, now the English king. That year, with Malcolm and Harald Hardrada of Norway, he conceived a plan to invade and partition England, probably allotting Northumbria to Malcolm. But of all these protagonists, only Malcolm survived the year. His two allies were dispatched at Stamford Bridge by Harold, but three weeks later the Englishman lost his own life, and his kingdom, at Hastings.

Malcolm's second marriage, *c.*1070, registered the dynastic effects of this cataclysm. His bride was Margaret, sister of Edgar Atheling (prince), who now found themselves both forced to flee from the Normans. Malcolm was deeply suspicious of Norman intentions, and the match ensured that his feelings were reciprocated. The tension improved the prospects of the Wessex royal house, for William's position was at first insecure, facing stubborn opposition in the north in 1068-9, and the Scottish hostility to the Normans translated into a willingness to shelter their enemies. More than realpolitik was involved however, for Malcolm was much taken with Margaret. Her piety and influence upon him helped to open Scottish society and religion to English and continental ideas and practices. Most of their eight children were given names of English origin, but soon discovered the need to adapt to the political realities of Norman hegemony.

At first, however, relations with the Normans were frosty. Their reduction of Northumbria may well have encouraged Malcolm to fear for the safety of his own domains. In 1070, he launched raids south of the border. In 1072 William gathered together a large land army, supported by ships, and pursued Malcolm as far as Abernethy on the Tay. Here, claims the Anglo-Saxon chronicle, Malcolm became William's 'man', or vassal, though it is unclear whether his words amounted to the cession of feudal fealty or military capitulation in the face of overwhelming force. Malcolm certainly did not feel constrained by the promises undertaken at Abernethy, even given the danger posed to the life of his son Duncan, surrendered there as a hostage. For in 1079, whilst William was away in Normandy, he launched a new raid into Northumbria as far as the Tyne; the following year at Gateshead, the Northumbrians massacred the Bishop of Durham and several Norman knights. A new army was sent, but its commander, William's son Robert Curthose, apparently aimed to contain Malcolm, rather than to destroy his kingdom. Accordingly, a conference was held at Falkirk but no agreement seems to have been reached here, and on his return journey, Curthose built a New Castle, on the north bank of the Tyne, to strengthen English defences.

The cycle was repeated in 1091, when the new king, William Rufus, also found it necessary to visit Normandy; and Malcolm, incited by the Atheling, returned to Northumbria. Soon pursued into Lothian by a new army, Malcolm once more found it expedient to agree to mend his ways, swearing fealty to the English king in exchange for manors in England. This agreement seems to have broken down, and William occupied (English) Cumbria (below the Solway Firth), driving out its local lord and building a castle at Carlisle. Malcolm travelled to Gloucester to seek conference, but was rebuffed. He returned to Scotland and launched the final invasion which led to his death at the River Alne at the hand of Morel, nephew of Robert de Mowbray, Earl of Northumbria.

Grief at this news is said to have killed the queen. It led to a sharp reaction against foreign influences through which (despite hostilities) feudal customs were beginning to challenge traditional values based on kinship. Among these unpopular imports was the principle of primogeniture. Passing over Malcolm's sons, and expelling both Normans and the friends of the Saxon royal house, the Scottish lords chose his brother Donald Ban as the new king, though this was disputed (successfully for some months in 1094) by Duncan II, Malcolm's son of his first marriage, who had been released from captivity in England about 1087. Donald Ban was restored but deposed again in 1097 by Malcolm's son Edgar with the support of William Rufus. In other ways the trend towards Normanization gathered pace. Malcolm's daughter Matilda or Maud (née Edith) married Henry I and Mary married the Count of Boulogne. Donald Ban was the last of Scottish kings to buried at the ancient site in Iona; Malcolm and his heirs found their resting place in Dunfermline.

MALCOLM, SIR JOHN (1769-1833) was a leading figure in India in the period of the Maratha wars: a time of expansion, conquest and pacification. He was a straightforward, brave, honourable man, one of the select company who made British rule synonymous with justice and humanity. 'The universal greeting to an Englishman was: "Atul Raj! May your rule last for ever".' If this was anything but a figment of the reporter's imagination, it was to men like Malcolm and his contemporaries, Munro and Elphinstone, all Scotsmen, that it was due.

Malcolm's grandfather was a minister, his father a small farmer of Eskdale who had seventeen children and fell on bad times. When he was thirteen, John was sent for interview to the Directors of the East India Company.

'Why, my little man,' one of them asked, 'what would you do if you met Hyder Ali?' 'I would draw ma sworrd and cut off his heid', the lad replied. He was given his commission at once. With an open delight in life that invited the nickname of 'Boy Malcolm' he missed no chance of distinction. For a time at fifteen he had command of two companies of infantry. He lived well, became a fine horseman, did not despise the dancing girls. Boisterous practical jokes or 'Malcolm riots' were a hazard that his friends learned to accept. Startled envoys were roused from their grave discussions by a cry of 'Tiger! Tiger!' and swept off to shoot the animal. No doubt it was a useful diversion at a tricky stage in negotiation. For Malcolm was shrewd. He moved from the military to the civil branch, where service was more regular and interesting. He learned Persian and was secretary to successive commanders-in-chief.

The arrival of Lord Wellesley as Governor-General was a great event for him. A hard driver of loyal lieutenants, Wellesley was 'the glorious little man' to Malcolm and his set. Malcolm served on special missions requiring enterprise and understanding of the Indian. He was successfully Resident to the Nizam of Hyderabad and envoy to Persia. When he went to Persia he was thirty-one; he went with a train of 500 assistants and servants. The company was disturbed – but Malcolm got a treaty of friendship with the Imam of Oman and leave to establish an English resident at Muscat. As Wellesley's private secretary, 1801-2, he was privy to the government's plans to deal with the Marathas. After a short time as Resident in Mysore, he went on campaign with Arthur Wellesley, as his political adviser. When he crossed the Governor-General (on the matter of the cession of Gwalior to Scindia) he received an imperial, Curzon-like rebuke. But their relationship was repaired by mutual courtesies. When Wellesley went home, the best part of Malcolm's career seemed finished. The Directors identified him with Wellesley's grandeur.

When after five years' leave he returned to India in 1817 he took an active part in the third Maratha war as brigadier in the army of the Deccan. He won a battle, leading his troops, sword in hand; then took part in the negotiations. He took over Malwa in Central India, territory of Rajput chiefs, whose boundaries had dissolved in the Maratha invasions: hunting-ground of bandits and hell for peasants. To these little states 'shaken as if from a pepper-pot', he brought order and peace. The peasants reappeared to till the soil. 'The fellows that I was hunting like wild beasts are now all tame and coming in declaring I am their only friend.' He was always ready to hear and talk to natives then – and later when he returned to India, after some years of leave and writing in England, to be Governor of Bombay, 1826-30. His predecessor there had been Elphinstone. The district was well governed. He built roads and telegraphs, but much time was taken up with a quarrel with the Supreme Court.

He was a tired man when he came home for the last time. He was MP for Launceston for a year in the last unreformed parliament. He had the satisfaction of seeing his book *The Administration of India* published before he died. It is a quarry for students of the old India. His life of Clive was completed by another hand and posthumously published; it provided the occasion for Macaulay's celebrated essay. Malcolm and Macaulay lived in different worlds. Malcolm might be selected as the type of thousands in India. He revelled in hoghunting and shooting. He enjoyed his 'mulligatawny at tiffin'. He was a long way removed from the earnest administrators of the generation that was established when he left. His own nature, we are told, was 'joyously generous'; he used to deplore the remoteness and coldness of some of the new men. His own strength was in natural, unself-conscious relations with the natives. He could find a homely phrase that cut through mistrust and carried conviction. And he earned respect as a man of action. A robber chief told him that he knew it would be useless to resist for 'such is your reputation that the sword that is drawn against you will be weighed to the earth by curses'.

Further Reading
P. Woodruff, *The Men who Ruled India*, vol. 1, 1953.
J. W. Kaye, *Life of Sir J. Malcolm*, 2 vols, 1856.

MALORY, SIR THOMAS (*d*.1471) was the author of the *Morte d'Arthur*, a literary masterpiece and a work of remarkable scale for any medieval layman to produce. Clearly the author was literate in French and English, the language of his sources, but also unpractised in writing. His power of composition grew as the work progressed but his prose style remained simple, colloquial and direct, probably much like his speech. To Malory the romances contained 'unalterable historical fact' about a real Arthur and his court. It was thus history that Malory recast into chronicle, excluding verbiage and description in favour of sober narrative and moral significance. The *Morte* is a repository of chivalric and religious ideas that the author himself must have shared. It is concentrated, unified and powerful.

The identity of the author has been much disputed. He himself tells the reader that he was a knight prisoner, who completed it in custody in 1469-70. Almost certainly, therefore, he was the Sir Thomas Malory excluded from the 1468 general pardon with Lancastrian conspirators implicated in Cook's plot and probably also he was Sir Thomas Malory of Newbold Revel (Warw.). This has posed considerable problems to modern scholars, for this Malory's notoriety for violent crime conflicts wholly with the values of the *Morte* and he appears unexpectedly old to be the author. If he was

indeed already campaigning in 1414, he could hardly have been less than his mid-seventies and may have been much older, but this might have been some other Malory.

This Malory's continuous career begins only in 1439, perhaps when he returned from France following the death of Richard Beauchamp, Earl of Warwick and lieutenant of France, whose retainer he may have been. The *Morte* reveals him critical, appropriately for a veteran, of the loss of English possessions in France. The death of his father in 1433-4 had brought him a substantial estate in Warwickshire, which may have been unusually unstable during the 1440s due to the youth of Earl Richard's son Duke Henry (*d*.1446) and the latter's daughter Anne (*d*.1449). Malory was politically active, becoming MP for Warwickshire in 1445-6. He was feed from the Beauchamp estates, but we cannot be sure of all his affiliations or their priority. Local politics rather than criminal proclivities probably explain the crimes he committed from 1444, from his raid on the Peto lands to his attacks on the Duke of Buckingham and Combe Abbey, and his thefts in Essex in 1454. He was 'a rapist, church-robber, extortioner, and would-be murderer'. Although his indictments were made by his enemies and must be treated with caution, he does seem to have behaved quite without discretion and forfeited the confidence of all parties. Suggestions that he became unhinged or senile are surely disproved by the *Morte d'Arthur*. However that may be, this unlucky and incompetent politician was almost continually in prison throughout the 1450s, escaping briefly in 1459-60. Under such circumstances, it is hard indeed to identify his national political affiliations, but his pardon in October and military service in Northumbria in November 1462 has parallels among erstwhile Lancastrians who were allowed to buy their way back into favour. At peace with the government thereafter, he was perhaps embroiled in Cook's conspiracy in 1468, for which the circumstantial evidence is strong but the facts weak. Imprisoned again, like Sir Thomas Gray he turned to writing and earned undying renown.

Further Reading
P. J. C. Field, 'The Last Years of Sir Thomas Malory', *Bulletin of the John Rylands Library* 64, 1982.
M. C. Carpenter, 'Sir Thomas Malory and Fifteenth-Century Local Politics', *Bulletin of the Institute of Historical Research* liii, 1980.
P. J. C. Field, 'Thomas Malory: The Hutton Documents', *Medium Aevum* 48, 1979.
P. J. C. Field, 'Sir Thomas Malory MP', *Bulletin of the Institute of Historical Research* xlvii, 1974.
P. J. C. Field, *Romance and Chronicle: A Study of Malory's Prose Style*, 1971.

MALTHUS, THOMAS ROBERT (1766-1834), political economist, was the second son of Daniel Malthus of Albury in Surrey, a gentleman of scholarly tastes and a firm believer in 'the perfectibility of man'. As befitted a friend of Rousseau he undertook Thomas's education himself; thereafter it was entrusted to tutors. Richard Graves was followed by Gilbert Wakefield, whom Malthus accompanied to Warrington Dissenting Academy when Wakefield was appointed its classical master. The views of the adult Malthus, logical and systematic but stronger, perhaps, in statistical calculation than in human understanding, must surely be related to this careful education. He was not unduly precious, however; it is recorded that he was fond of rowing. Intensive tutoring taught him, too, to think for himself. When he went to St John's, Cambridge, he read widely, won classical prizes and was ninth Wrangler in the mathematical tripos. He became a Fellow of the college and was ordained. A curacy at Albury was followed by a living in Lincolnshire but the villagers of Walesby were left to a curate's care. His religious views were utilitarian, unenthusiastic. 'Parson Malthus' was to become a natural bogey-figure to warm-blooded traditionalists. His theories seemed to be at variance with his Christian vocation. Yet, in the face of declining real wages and a system of poor relief that threatened to pauperize the agricultural labourer, his concern about the rise in population was not extraordinary. The population of Europe had risen in the twelve centuries before 1800 to a total of 180 millions. Between 1800 and 1914 its population increased from 180 to 460 millions.

In 1796 Malthus wrote a pamphlet entitled *The Crisis*. In deference to his father he did not print it, but he continued to study questions of population and poor relief. A discussion of Godwin's *Political Justice* and that author's optimistic dream of social equality led him to clarify his own views. So he wrote the *Essay on the Principle of Population* in 1798. Godwin dreamed of social equality in a society from which vice and misery had been banished. Malthus declared that, even if the ideal society could be established, it would soon be ruined by excess of people. Population, he said, tended to double itself every twenty-five years, increasing by geometrical progression, while resources, at best, increased only by arithmetical progression. He later modified his argument in a second edition of the book (1803) in which he explained that the 'checks' of famine, epidemics, natural disasters and 'vice', to which he ascribed such an important role, were not insuperable obstacles to social improvement; rather they were dangers to be overcome, if society were to be bettered. His own panacea was 'prudential restraint', which should delay marriages to a later age than had been customary among the poorer classes. He later added the idea that it would be to the ultimate benefit of labourers to remove gradually the protection afforded by the Poor Laws, which seemed to encourage procreation and therefore an over-stocked labour-market.

Malthus was certainly influential. He claimed Pitt among his converts. In 1805, after marrying the year before and resigning his college fellowship, he acquired a regular audience for his views as professor of history and political economy at the new East India Company's college at Haileybury. Those who were going to govern India's teeming millions might be expected to listen attentively to 'Pop' Malthus. His lectures led him to consider the theory of rent: he published his conclusions in two pamphlets and the tract *The Nature and Progress of Rent* (1815). Ricardo largely accepted his doctrine and it proved less controversial than his theories about population. These were attacked on grounds of common sense and humanity by men of such different views as Cobbett, Coleridge and Southey. Godwin damaged the statistical case (with the assistance of Booth, a respected mathematician) by demonstrating (in *Population*, 1820) that the growth of population in America, the main source of Malthus's evidence, was largely due to immigration, while in a settled country, such as Sweden, the population had but doubled in a century – and there the standard of living had risen as well.

Malthus, though 'one of the serenest and most cheerful' of men, as his friend Harriet Martineau wrote, and acutely sensitive to the abuse which his doctrines provoked, was beyond doubt more dogmatic and 'feeolosophical' (to borrow Cobbett's word) than the facts warranted. He did not allow for the effects of industrialization, the exploitation of the waste and underdeveloped areas, or the effect of education and the acquisition of property in cultivating a sense of personal responsibility. There was also something grimly patronizing about his advice to the poor. But it was scarcely inhumane. Cottage budgets of the time showed that every succeeding child after the third plunged the family into deeper distress. Malthus could argue that his was a more constructive contribution to the problem of the poor than soup or blankets from the manor house. Maynard Keynes once pointed out that the world would have been wiser and richer if it had taken its economics from Malthus rather than from Ricardo. Francis Place stressed the urgency of the matter: 'All were opposed to the Malthusian doctrine … All disregarded the fact that the people had increased and were increasing and overrunning the means of subsistence.' Country tombstones tell the tale of nature's means of birth-control in Malthus's time. Today once more the debate which Malthus initiated is relevant and alive.

Further Reading

Patricia James, *Population Malthus: His Life and Times*, 1979.
A. Flew, ed., *T. R. Malthus, An Essay on the Principle of Population* and *A Summary View of the Principle of Population*, 1970.
Talbot Griffiths, *Population Problems in the Age of Malthus*, 1967.

MANBY, GEORGE WILLIAM (1764-1854) was one of the first pioneers of rescue work at sea. He was born at Downham Market in Norfolk. Having joined the militia, he was appointed in 1803 to be barrack master at Yarmouth. He often heard of shipwrecks and, like other people, he at first regarded them as unavoidable. Dickens in *David Copperfield* paints an unforgettable picture of a storm shipwreck on this stretch of coast and in 1807 many witnessed just such a scene. The gun-brig *Snipe* was wrecked and sixty-seven persons perished within sixty yards of the beach. After the gale had subsided 147 bodies were washed up on thirty miles of coast. It occurred to Manby that a line might be thrown to a threatened vessel from a gun. In 1783 he had fired a line over Downham Church from a mortar and he began a series of trials based on this experiment. It was difficult to attach a rope to the shot without its snapping, but at length strips of raw-hide closely plaited were used. In 1808 an opportunity came for him to test his invention. The brig *Elizabeth* was discerned about 150 yards from the beach, helpless in a gale. The crew were lashed to the rigging with no means of rescue and great waves were breaking over them. The mortar was brought, a line thrown over the ship, a boat hauled off by it and seven men brought to land.

In 1810 a grant of £2,000 was made for Manby to research into sea-rescue. He was commissioned to report on the dangerous stretches of coast from Yarmouth to the Forth and as a result fifty-nine mortar stations were erected. Manby also attempted to devise shells filled with burning composition so that a crew could see the trajectory of a line being fired towards them. When quite old he made a journey into the northern seas in order to test a new kind of harpoon. He also attended to improvements in lifeboat methods. He became a Fellow of the Royal Society and received several foreign awards and decorations for his life-saving inventions.

MANGNALL, RICHMAL (1769-1820) was the author of *Questions*. Hers was a name of power in the nineteenth-century schoolroom. Her little book, privately printed in 1800, then taken up by the shrewd firm of Longman, had appeared by 1857 in eighty-four editions. It was the stand-by of generations of governesses and other teachers, especially in girls' schools like that at Crofton Hall, where Miss Mangnall was for many years headmistress. The confident style of the answers, expressing truths assumed to be beyond questioning, evokes the spirit of the Enlightenment. Judgements are level, plain, humane. Opinions presented as facts are an easy target for a scientific age. Miss Mangnall would not have liked later tendencies to doubt, to qualify, 'to be fair'. Fairness for this high-minded lady was to give to child and teacher the gist of current knowledge and the best of her understanding, patriotic, protestant and humane. She believed in 'the superior excellence' of the British constitution. She was also proud of her country's claim to have 'struck off the chains that galled the African slave'. She paid stately homage to the hero. In praise or censure she sought to improve the occasion. So the Duke of Wellington 'rebuked by his conduct restless vanity, and reprimanded the morbid sensibility of irregular egotism'. The works of Rabelais, 'a Frenchman', were 'greatly deficient in that delicacy without which genius may sparkle for a moment, but can never shine with pure, undiminished lustre'.

Pupils may have wished to know more about 'the abominable Sylla'. They may not have cared 'Whence are cocoa-nuts procured?', nor shared Miss Mangnall's liking for classification games: 'Name the four most ambitious men in Rome'. Her name, and her questions, may have been hateful to them. The answers still had to be learned. Looking at the Victorian age we seek cultural influences among the great, a Coleridge, a Carlyle. We should not forget Miss Mangnall.

MANNERS, JOHN, 7th DUKE OF RUTLAND, (1818-1906) is best known as Lord John Manners, the beau ideal of the Young England group in the 1840s. He was the prototype gentleman: handsome, courteous, high principled, loyal, modest and not too clever. At Cambridge his ideas were formed in the company of his brilliant but reckless friend, George Smythe. They reacted against the middle-class Gradgrinds from the industrial heartland, and the Utilitarian Chadwick with his cruel Poor Law; and against the Whigs, who treated the church as if it were merely a subordinate branch of the state. They were fascinated by the political writing of Bolingbroke, the novels of Scott (Manners went to the queen's Fancy Dress Ball as a character from *The Talisman*), and the Gothic Revival in architecture. They were inspired by the High Church preaching of Frederick Faber in the romantic Lakeland setting of Ambleside. There they saw their world as did Peacock's Mr Chainmail in *Crotchet Castle*. 'Now we all wear one conventional face; we have no bond of union, but pecuniary interests, ... no nature, no simplicity, no picturesqueness; everything about us is as artificial and as complicated as our steam-machinery.' So they looked back to a golden age of feudalism, when the poor were peasants, who served happily and healthily in their communities, protected by their overlords and worshipping in parishes which formed part of a universal church. Entering the House of Commons when they were little more than undergraduates, they found a hero in Disraeli, whose style and ideas matched theirs, and whose ambitions had recently been thwarted by Peel. With him, and another Cambridge friend, Baillie-Cochrane, they formed a quartet in 1843, to put their ideas into practice and rescue the Tories from the humdrum and heartless materialism of Manchester.

The main impact of the group was literary rather than practical. From the ideas they tossed around together came Disraeli's trilogy of novels, and from one of these, *Sybil*, emerged the One Nation vision which became one of Disraeli's main themes, his belief in the natural alliance between the Tories and the British workman, and which has survived in Conservative Party manifestos to this day. They did warmly support the Ten Hour Bill for factory workers, and they secured some modifications in the new Poor Law. Most of Lord John Manners's hobby-horses were eventual winners: allotments, holy-days as holidays, museums, sports. But these were slow starters, and some, such as his campaign for maypoles on village greens, were mocked. As a political group, Young England was short-lived. Disagreements soon divided the four, and when Smythe backed and Manners opposed the Repeal of the Corn Laws in 1846, they broke up.

Manners remained loyal to Disraeli, and lived to serve as a useful and reliable minister for seventeen years. A good speaker, and commanding wide respect for his integrity, he could have held high office, the more so because of the shortage of talent amongst the rump of the Tories after the split with the Peelites. Smythe saw him as 'the Philip Sydney of our generation', and Disraeli, who was keen to promote him, told him that he might become prime minister one day. But he was diffident. As the second son of a duke in a culture of primogeniture, he was also impecunious, and had to turn down for financial reasons the chances of becoming Governor General of Canada and Viceroy of India. Finally, the romantic flatulence of some of his youthful writing clung to his reputation. One couplet proved unforgettable:

> Let wealth and commerce, laws and learning die,
> But leave us still our old Nobility.

His chosen haven in Cabinets was First Commissioner for Works, whence his taste for Gothic architecture has left its mark on public buildings. He moved out of it to become Postmaster General only when he had to – although he showed unlikely enthusiasm for the telephone while he held that office, and, much more characteristically, earned the affectionate respect of Post Office employees. Normally he preferred lost causes. Of the many which he had backed in his youth, from Don Carlos in Spain to the ancient custom of Montem at Eton, he remained loyal to one larger one through his long political life, the protection of British farming. He developed the theme of Imperial Preference in the 1880s. From Belvoir Castle, where he succeeded his brother as Duke of Rutland (1888), he had the satisfaction, before he died, of seeing Chamberlain start the overthrow of the Free Trade dogmas which had dominated his times.

Further Reading
Richard Faber, *Young England*, 1987.
Charles Whibley, *Lord John Manners and his Friends*, 1925.

MANNERS, JOHN, MARQUIS OF GRANBY (1721-70) was commander of the British contingent under Ferdinand of Brunswick from 1759 to the end of the Seven Years' War. His force, larger than the British contingent which had served in Marlborough's army, won a series of remarkable victories, small in scale but important in the overall strategy of the war. Today only the expert has heard of Warburg and Kloster Kampfen, Vellinghausen, Emsdorff and Wilhelmstal, but swinging inn-signs recall the name of a brave and spectacular general.

Granby was the elder son of the Duke of Rutland and went to Eton and Trinity College, Cambridge. He had a seat in parliament from 1741 to his death. Wealth and influence smoothed his way but a blockage occurred when Ligonier was preferred for the colonelcy of the Blues: George II disliked his father. He raised a regiment in 1745 to fight against the Jacobites; later he served in Flanders. A lieutenant-general in Germany under Ferdinand, he had the mortification of sharing in the failure of the cavalry to complete the splendid victory of Minden. Sackville, commanding the cavalry, would not move; Granby, in command of the second line, was about to charge on his own initiative when Sackville rode up and ordered him not to. What the troops thought may be considered unprintable; what Ferdinand said was that, had Granby been in command, the French would have been annihilated. Sackville was dismissed and Granby succeeded him. In the next four years, with the intelligent backing of Ligonier at the War Office, he won a series of battles, usually against odds.

If it is true that 'Canada was won on the banks of the Elbe', then not only Frederick the Great but Ferdinand and Granby should share the credit. The cavalry were brought to a high pitch of efficiency, and Granby led them with tactical skill and reckless daring. 'One could see nothing finer and more fit,' said Ferdinand in 1760 of the cavalry. Waldegrave's infantry battalions were also impressive. The battle of Warburg in 1760 affords a good example of this army in action. When it was obvious that the infantry could not catch the French, Ferdinand ordered Granby to move against their flank. Two hours' riding with cavalry and horse artillery brought them to the French corps of 20,000. Then a massive attack shocked the French into rout. Granby led his men in bare-headed. They drove the French back to the river Diemel, where they were decimated by Phillips's artillery; in all they lost about 8,000 men. Of his performance at a later battle, Wilhelmstal, in 1762, Ligonier wrote: 'No man ever acted with more courage or more like a commanding officer. The Blues did almost beyond what was ever done by a cavalry regiment.' His only criticism of Granby was that he was too bold, 'exposing himself like a hussar'.

In 1763 he was recalled to be Master of the Ordnance; in 1767 he was made commander-in-chief. He was a poor administrator, however, and his later years were inglorious. He had spent a fortune on his own regiment, largely recruited from Belvoir tenantry of Leicester and Rutland, he drank too much, and he died heavily in debt. He was also a victim of Junius's acid pen. It was an unequal encounter: he was happier with the sword.

Further Reading
R. Whitworth, *Field Marshal Lord Ligonier and the British Army, 1702-70*, 1958.

MANNING, CARDINAL HENRY (1808-92), Cardinal Archbishop of Westminster, was head of the Roman Catholic church in England, into which he was received as a convert from the Church of England, from 1865 until his death. Godson of a prime minister, nephew of a Lord Mayor of London, and son of an MP who was also Governor of the Bank of England, he was educated at Harrow and Balliol. Gladstone thought him one of the three handsomest men at Oxford. Though he initially preferred sport to scholarship, he became President of the Oxford Union, was awarded a First Class Degree, and would have embarked on a political career had his father not lost all his money. Instead, under the influence of the evangelical Favell Bevan, he was ordained in 1833, joining the parish of John Sargent, and marrying his daughter Caroline. Sargent died within months, and Manning succeeded him as Rector of Lavington. There he showed courage for a young man, in criticizing the Duke of Richmond, big landowner in the parish, for 'the sin of exacting the largest rents and doing the least repairs'. The sympathy he felt for the lot of the agricultural labourer stayed with him: in 1872 he was to share a platform with their leader, Joseph Arch. Four years after her father, Caroline died too. He wrote sermons by her grave, and kept the book into which she wrote her meditations next to his bed for the rest of his life.

But his own religious beliefs moved on. He was already sharing many of the views of Newman, and saw the Church of England as the true vessel of the Apostolic tradition, the *via media* between Roman corruption and Protestant heresy. His move to Rome was slower than Newman's. He was emotionally bound to Lavington, and his prospects in the church were bright. But state interference in the church was anathema to him. The appointment of the heretical Hampden as Bishop of Hereford was bad enough, but it was the Privy Council's action in overruling the ecclesiastical Court of Arches in

the Gorham case which finally drove him to seek a church which stood 'high above the craft and meddling of ministers and kings'. He was received into the Roman Communion on Passion Sunday, 1851.

It was natural, therefore, that once a Roman, he should become a whole-hearted supporter of the pope's authority. He had already met Pius IX and fallen for his charm, and he was instinctively at ease among Italians and in Rome. Pius made him Provost of the Westminster Chapter in 1857, and in 1865 chose him personally as archbishop on Cardinal Wiseman's death. It was an astonishingly swift rise for a convert. In 1875 he became a cardinal, and was even considered a possible successor to the pope himself. He looked the prelate that he had become. The handsome young man had developed a high forehead, finely carved profile, imperious mouth, deep-set eyes. The pink silk riding breeches of the undergraduate had given place to a crimson skull cap and biretta. His authority was formidable: 'when he turns his eye on you, oh my! don't you shiver!', recalled a boy who attended him at Mass.

This was no Madame Tussaud cardinal, however, but a man of action. 'To be in the world and yet dead to it is the highest reach of faith', was Manning's ideal. His image obscures the work and achievements of a remarkable social pioneer. The condition of the poor was his deep concern, in terms of both personal salvation and social stability, for he saw the body and soul as interdependent, and the slums as potential breeding grounds for secular revolutionaries. There were plenty of impoverished Roman Catholics in England: in the 1851 census, 500,000 of the 700,000 registered were Irish immigrants. Manning raised the money to get 70,000 Catholic children into Catholic schools; he shared platforms with Salvation Army temperance campaigners (he called drink a 'gangrene' on society); he was friendly with radical reformers such as Dilke, Stead and Josephine Butler; he supported early Trades Unions. When he was over eighty he brought the bitter and crippling 1889 London Dock strike to an end through tireless conciliation. 'Remember, Ben', he said to the dockers' leader, Ben Tillett, 'If you want to wear the crown, you must learn to bear the cross.' To his critics he replied: 'People call it socialism. I call it Christianity.' When he died, the four mile route from Brompton Oratory to Kensal Green was lined by mourners without a gap.

But there were many even then who did not mourn. When Pius IX restored the Roman Catholic hierarchy in England in 1850, he created fresh stresses for Catholics there. The Old Catholics, some from great families and comfortable in their ways, disliked Manning for supporting Papal authority against national traditions. They had their own hero in Newman. Newman and Manning were very different, the thinker versus the politician, the man of influence versus the man of power, the liberal versus the authoritarian. Newman wanted Catholics to be able to go to Oxford, but was blocked by Manning, who wanted them educated separately. Manning started a Catholic university college at Kensington, intended as the first of a federation, only to have it wrecked by the opposition of the Jesuits and of Newman. Manning campaigned for the declaration of Papal Infallibility in 1870; Newman believed in the infallibility of the church, but feared the hard dogmatic assertion of Papal authority. The disagreements between them were deep, temperamentally and politically, and though Manning often tried to heal them, Newman's comment summed up his own attitude: 'I cannot trust the archbishop. He never wishes to see a man except for his own ends.'

As is often the case, the master of words has won the verdict of posterity, the more so because Manning was damned by his biographer, Purcell, who hijacked his papers without approval as soon as he was dead. But if Manning's assertion that seekers after truth were sickened by the 'chaos of innumerable sects and the lack of any tribunal able to teach with authority' will appeal to some but not to others, his dedication to better education and conditions for the poor gave a lead which the whole Roman Catholic church in England has followed ever since.

Further Reading
D. H. Newsome, *The Convert Cardinals: John Henry Newman and Henry Edward Manning*, 1993.
Sir Shane Leslie, *Henry Edward Manning, his life and labours*, 1921.

MANSEL, JOHN (*d.*1265) was one of Henry III's most accomplished and versatile servants, particularly expert in the conduct of foreign policy. From humble origins, educated at court, by 1234 he was employed in the Exchequer. For the next thirty years Mansel acted variously as royal secretary, councillor, keeper of the Great Seal, legal agent, diplomat and ambassador. His rewards were lavish. The clerical son of a cleric, he was a prodigious pluralist, his income from benefices allegedly running into thousands of marks a year. He wore his clerical garb lightly. Until a stone crushed his leg during the Gascon expedition in 1243, Mansel had made a name as a soldier, in Italy in 1238 and again on the 1242-3 French campaign. Unlike other contemporary bellicose clerics (e.g. Boniface of Savoy, Archbishop of Canterbury), Mansel actually fought, on one occasion unhorsing his opponent, the seneschal of the Count of Boulogne. After 1243, he had to content himself with administration and luxurious living. A member of the king's council from 1244, he held the Great Seal 1246-7 and 1248-9, but his main expertise was in foreign affairs. Here his achievement was remarkable, including the treaty and marriage alliance with Castile (1254); the Sicilian agreement with Innocent IV (1254); the election

of Richard of Cornwall as King of the Romans (1257); the Treaty of Paris (1259); the papal absolution of the king's oath to support the Provisions of Oxford (1261); and the Mise of Amiens (1264). Mansel became an almost indispensible adviser to the king, reflected in his taking the Cross with his master in 1250 despite recurrent poor health. There were few issues concerning royal interests on which Mansel was not employed. One modern writer has called him 'almost the Wolsey of his age'. Unsurprisingly, he became a focus for the hostility of government critics, such as Matthew Paris and the baronial reformers of 1258-9. In 1263 he was forced into exile by Montfortian rebels, dying abroad two years later. How far he influenced or merely executed royal policy is obscure. Although his skill as a negotiator was, judged by results, exceptional, his own attitudes are hidden. It is intriguing that one of his friends and an executor to his will was Robert Tweng, a veteran nationalist, anti-papal terrorist directly opposed to most of the foreign policy initiatives so smoothly operated by Mansel himself. This alone suggests that there was more to the politics of Henry III's reign than met the eyes of royalist or baronial apologists.

MAP, WALTER (*c.*1130/35-1209/10) was a successful royal clerk and church administrator who gained a great reputation as a raconteur. Many of his stories are preserved in his *De Nugis Curialium (Courtiers' Trifles)* compiled between 1181 and the early 1190s. Born in the Welsh Marches (Map = ap = son of in Welsh), his family had served Henry II before 1154. Educated at Gloucester and in Paris, he became a canon of Hereford under the patronage of Gilbert Foliot. In the king's service by 1173, when he was an itinerant justice in Gloucestershire, he remained a prominent royal clerk for the rest of Henry II's reign. Walter attended the Third Lateran Council in 1179 as one of Henry's representatives and was attached to the household of the Young Henry until the prince's death in 1183. As his official career developed, he amassed a comfortable living as a pluralist. Already a canon, in 1186 he became Chancellor of Lincoln and precentor in 1189. In 1196 he was appointed Archdeacon of Oxford. By this time, he had finished *De Nugis*, a rambling compendium of court gossip and satirical anecdotes, with as much organization, Walter himself admitted, as a timber yard. At its serious moments it compares with a parody of the *Mirror of Princes* genre supported by edifying moral or cautionary tales. Walter attempted some historical portraits, all worthless except his vivid, surprisingly unbiased and convincing description of his patron Henry II – an objectivity which may account for Walter not publishing it. *De Nugis* sheds light on the rather chaotic mind of a leading member of the chattering classes of the late twelfth century. His interests are human; his education classical; his style urbane, witty, informed and spacious, devoid of the portentous anxiety or academic pretentiousness displayed by so many of his contemporaries. One curiosity is that *De Nugis* is the earliest known work to nickname Ethelred II 'the Unready' or, more properly '*un-raed*', bad counsel, a pun which would have been right up Walter's street.

Further Reading
Walter Map, *De Nugis Curialium*, ed. M. R. James, C. N. L. Brooke and R. A. Mynors, 1983.

MARGARET, LADY HUNGERFORD (*d.*1478) illustrates the capacity for business and politics of medieval women that is normally hidden from the historical record. She was daughter and heiress of William Lord Botreaux (*d.*1462) and wife of Robert, Lord Hungerford (*d.*1459). Forty years of marriage and motherhood have left almost no record, but her husband's death exposed her as a historical individual. Like many widows, she wanted to prepare for salvation and depicted herself as kneeling in prayer with a book on her lap. What she 'desired above all things earthly' was to complete an almshouse at Heytesbury (Wilts.) and to found a chantry at Salisbury Cathedral. Literate in English and French, she was up-to-date with the latest innovations in services, had clearly defined preferences – notably the chastity of the Virgin and Five Wounds of Christ – and devised services, furnishings and decoration to fit her taste. From these conventional materials, she produced something discriminating, coherent, sophisticated and highly individual. Determined not to spoil her chances by obstinacy and wilfulness, she cultivated humility and resignation at the same time as compiling statutes for her foundations that left nothing to chance. Her example shows the scope for religious individuality among even ordinary Christians unable to cultivate the mysticism of Cecily, Duchess of York.

Margaret's achievement is the more remarkable in view of the enormous problems left her by her menfolk. Her husband left her responsible for the enormous ransom of their son Moleyns, whose Lancastrian politics led to increased debt and the confiscation of the family estates. Moleyns was executed in 1464, his son in 1469, and Margaret herself was imprisoned three times. These were not uncommon misfortunes for Lancastrian women under the Yorkists, some of whom were rendered almost destitute. Margaret, however, fought back with amazing resource and tenacity. She appealed to king and parliament, lobbied and bribed her way through the corridors of power, persuaded the great that her interests were theirs, played off opponents, argued her legal rights, and glossed over or faked weaknesses in title. She kept debt under control by selling land and plate, curtailing expenditure, and by closing an almshouse of her father's that represented a permanent drain on her income. Twice

she rebuffed her opponents, once she drove a hard bargain with Richard, Duke of Gloucester, and at the end almost the whole inheritance was saved for her heirs from the forfeiture that should properly have befallen it. She had also managed to liquidate the enormous burden of debt. But her hands could not be clean.

Margaret was actuated by two motives, her sense of inheritance and her piety, and it was the latter that took priority. She had chosen to pay off debts that could have been evaded rather than leave a stain of guilt on her husband's soul. That and her religious foundations had cost more money than her income could stand and so she had sold land that her heirs should have inherited, which they strongly resented and threatened to recover in the courts. Fearful for the repercussions for her soul, Margaret appealed to the next generation, her infant granddaughter, putting her own one-sided version of events. It is one of the first English autobiographies. Faced by a choice between responsibility to God and to her heirs, she had chosen God. Her rather colourless spouse cannot have dominated her as the law permitted during those forty unrecorded years.

Further Reading
M. A. Hicks, 'The Piety of Margaret, Lady Hungerford (*d.*1478)', *Journal of Ecclesiastical History* xxxviii, 1987.
M. A. Hicks, 'Counting the Cost of War: The Moleyns Ransom and the Hungerford Land Sales', *Southern History* viii, 1986.
M. A. Hicks, 'Piety and Lineage in the Wars of the Roses: The Hungerford Experience' in *Kings and Nobles in the Later Middle Ages*, R. A. Griffiths and J. W. Sherborne, eds, 1986.

MARGARET, MAID OF NORWAY (1283-90) was the only child of the marriage in 1281 of King Eric II of Norway to Margaret, daughter of Alexander III, King of Scotland, by his first wife, also Margaret. Her mother's death (apparently in childbirth) was the first of a catastrophic series. Alexander's younger son David followed, aged eight, in 1281. When the king's elder son also died childless at the age of twenty in February 1284, the magnates of Scotland met at Scone and, apparently at the behest of Alexander III, acknowledged the Maid, now the only remaining direct descendant of the king, as his heir. But others, notably Robert Bruce and John Balliol, had their own claims. Bruce averred that the problems posed by a female successor had some years earlier prompted the magnates to nominate him against another female claimant (Dervorguilla). Even for those who accepted the Maid, there were hard questions to resolve. Who would govern during her minority? Who would choose her husband, and on what terms? In 1284 Alexander himself had written to Edward I in terms which suggested that though the Maid was his heir, her marriage to an English prince would bring 'much good', a tacit admission of the dangers otherwise posed.

At the end of March 1286, Alexander fell from his horse and was killed, and the magnates of parliament hastened to nominate the Maid as queen in her absence. The following month, however, Yolande, the second wife of Alexander III, was found to be pregnant. What if the baby should be male? The bishops and barons who now foregathered swore a new oath to an unspecified heir, and appointed two barons, two bishops and two earls to rule in the interim. The child was stillborn, and Bruce of Annandale launched a rising in the south-west. Though his attempt failed, Bruce's supporters remained as strong as those of another claimant, John Balliol, son of Dervorguilla; in 1287, given the threat of civil war between these equally matched forces, the government decided to reaffirm the decision of 1284 in support of the Maid. In November 1289, in the Treaty of Salisbury, the Scottish, English and Norwegian governments set out the arrangements for the Maid's marital future. Norway promised to convey her to England by 1 November 1290 'free and quit of all contract of marriage'; England undertook that if Scotland was at peace, they would return her there still unmarried; the Scots vouched for the tranquillity of their kingdom when its new queen should arrive, and promised not to marry her off without the agreement of the others.

The need for such elaborate provisions arose partly because the marriage proposal long since initiated by Alexander III, and supported by Scots who were not partisans of Bruce or Balliol, was that the Maid should marry Edward's son (later Edward II). But the Maid's grandmother, Margaret, had been the sister of Edward I. This made the boy second cousin to his 'intended', a breach of canon law. Fortunately for all parties, Pope Nicholas IV was amenable to a dispensation. The news was well received among the Scottish magnates, and a letter was sent asking Eric to dispatch the Maid to England. Terms were agreed with the English in the Treaty of Birgham of July 1290. Scotland was to retain its own laws and remain separate from England. If Edward and Margaret had no heirs, the kingdom was to revert to claimants unspecified but 'wholly, freely, absolutely, and without any subjection'. Edward's appointment of Anthony Bek, Bishop of Durham, as guardian of the pair may suggest a sceptical view of such phrases. In any case, the agreement was soon worthless. Margaret sailed from Norway in September 1290, but died at Kirkwall in Orkney. She was buried in Bergen. Throughout her short life, the Maid was the object of manoeuvres relating to the future of the Scottish monarchy. It was plunged into crisis by her death.

MARGARET, ST (*c*.1046-93), the sister of Edgar Atheling, was brought up in Hungary, where Canute had condemned their father Edward the Exile, nephew of Edward the Confessor. It was during this exile that Margaret absorbed the piety of a nation only recently converted under the leadership of St Stephen. Margaret

and Edgar were able to return to England in 1057, but in 1066, found themselves pursued by new enemies. In 1068, as William's troops moved into Northumbria, they fled further northwards to Scotland. King Malcolm III was much enamoured with Margaret, and they soon married. The new queen exerted much influence, bringing to Scotland something of the customs of Wessex and the evangelical zeal of Hungary. Margaret founded a priory at Dunfermline and engaged in correspondence with Lanfranc, and her confessor was Turgot, later Bishop of St Andrews. The Pictish church in Scotland had adopted the Roman system and the skeleton of its episcopal system remained. Margaret's concerns were chiefly in the area of establishing the observance of certain rites along Roman lines, and this helped begin the long process of building an 'orthodox' diocesan system. For her piety and active concern for the church Margaret was canonized in 1250.

Margaret's monastic foundations largely followed a traditional pattern, quickly overtaken in the twelfth century by new houses organized on the reformed Benedictine lines exemplified by the Citeaux foundation (Cistercians), and by the semi-secular Augustinians.

Margaret, and the new influences she brought, surely helped to dispose both her husband and their six sons and two daughters towards the establishment of links with important Norman families; the Norman connections and upbringing of David I may be seen as especially significant. It is said that Margaret 'was distressed even to death' at the news of Malcolm's death. If this may suggest that their relationship was a close one, the impression is reinforced by the English names given to the six sons of the marriage; this alien influence appears to have been resented by many.

MARGARET OF ANJOU (1430-82) exercised unusual political influence for an English queen. Part of the package that brought Henry VI a French truce, she also brought the exalted connections of one of the European nobility. She was the younger daughter of King René, Duke of Anjou, Bar and Lorraine, Marquis of Provence, and titular king or claimant to Sicily, Jerusalem, Hungary, Aragon and Majorca. Still in her teens, she was a good looking girl, vivacious and spirited, who loved romances and the chase. Her household account of 1452-3 reveals her fondness for splendid clothes and jewels and her extravagance. She also shared her new husband's interest in education, accepting the patronage of what became Queens' College, Cambridge. She quickly won a place in his affections and ensured he kept his foolish promise to Charles VII to surrender Maine, whose count was her uncle Charles. Her extravagant husband endowed Margaret more generously than he could afford and she enlarged her resources as opportunity permitted. The succession question, already acute at her marriage, was solved by Prince Edward's birth only in 1453, when her husband's breakdown put his succession in doubt.

This breakdown plunged Margaret into English politics. Her application for the regency was set aside in favour of the Duke of York as Protector in 1453-4 and 1455-6. Now a formidable politician, she saw York as a threat and determined to manage affairs herself. Since Henry was too easily influenced, he must be removed from Westminster and from the duke into her control. She settled at Kenilworth and Leicester castles, which she fortified and backed by a Cheshire-based retinue. Henry performed some ceremonial functions and indulged his religious obsession, much of it in monasteries, while Margaret presided over the court. She insisted that Coventry render her the honours properly due to the king. Virtually bankrupt, her government could do little. It cannot strictly be claimed that 'the queen and her affinity ruled the realm as she liked'. As parliament was avoided and access to the king restricted, national politics almost ceased until York's next coup in 1459. Margaret followed York's defeat by his condemnation, but next year the Nevilles won possession of King Henry. The compromise reached in parliament, which made York into Henry's heir and effective ruler, disinherited Prince Edward and was thus unacceptable to Margaret. She rallied opposition in the north, wreaked revenge on York at Wakefield, defeated Warwick in 1461, but suffered decisive defeat at Towton shortly afterwards.

Margaret escaped with her son, her hope for the future, and continued resistance for ten years. Initially she sought support abroad, willingly hazarding Calais and Berwick as diplomatic counters, but realized how hopeless it was by 1463. At that point she retired to St Michel in Bar with her son and other Lancastrians, where a shadowy and impoverished government in exile was maintained. They plotted continuously, spinning elaborate and impractical combinations of rebellion and invasion, even speculating on an alliance with Warwick the Kingmaker. Impossible when first devised in 1468, this became reality on the earl's exile in 1470, when Margaret married her son to his daughter Anne Neville. She herself did not reach England in time to celebrate Henry VI's second accession but only for the desperate pursuit that ended at Tewkesbury with defeat, her son's death, and her capture. Days later Henry VI was murdered and the Lancastrian cause died with him.

Premature mortality and Louis XI's designs on their inheritances meant that the house of Anjou had almost expired by 1475, when Margaret was returned to France under the treaty of Picquigny. Edward's condition was that she renounced her English rights, Louis XI's terms that she gave up her Angevin ones. Her father, King René, supported her in Reculée Castle until his death in 1480, when she was thrown on the charity of a gentleman at Dampierre. Fortunately she soon died.

Further Reading

A. R. Myers, *Crown, Household and Parliament in the Fifteenth Century*, 1985.
R. A. Griffiths, *The Reign of King Henry VI 1422-61*, 1981.

MARGARET TUDOR (1489-1541), Queen of Scotland, was the eldest daughter of Henry VII and Elizabeth of York. She was born on 29 November 1489, and she died on 18 October 1541. She was two years older than her brother, Henry VIII. She was not so well educated as the rest of the Tudors, but she could write, though only what she called 'an evil hand', and she could play on the lute and the clavichord. In 1495 Henry VII tried to arrange a marriage for Margaret with James IV of Scotland, in the hopes of thus cutting off Scottish support for Perkin Warbeck. This attempt failed, but after long negotiations the marriage was finally arranged in 1502. Margaret arrived in Scotland on 27 June 1503, and the marriage was celebrated at Holyrood Abbey on 8 August 1503. The event was recorded in 'The Thrissil and the Rois' by William Dunbar.

James IV died at the battle of Flodden in September 1513. James's and Margaret Tudor's son James was only one year old. James IV's will nominated Margaret as the guardian of the little James V, a position which in practice conferred an important part of the state power. There was much discontent among the Scottish nobility that, after the calamitous defeat at Flodden, respect for Scottish independence was not to be expected of the sister of the victorious English king. There were also friends of an English alliance, but these must have been sadly disappointed at Margaret's maladroitness in politics and her lack of consistency of purpose, even in the cause of friendship with Henry. In August 1514, the queen married Archibald Douglas, sixth Earl of Angus. If this was an expression of love or lust, it did not last long; if it was designed to strengthen the hand of the anglophile faction with which Douglas was identified, it backfired, because her first husband's will had stipulated that remarriage would disqualify her from continued guardianship of the new king. Margaret was forced to surrender her three-year-old son to Albany and an attempt at abduction failed, enforcing the couple's departure to England. Here, she gave birth to Margaret, her only child by Douglas, later mother of Lord Darnley.

Margaret Tudor's political actions hereafter almost defy logic. By 1519, she was already at loggerheads with Douglas, pressing Henry VIII to secure her a divorce; his refusal drove her to ask the same favour of the man who had disposssessed her of her children, Albany (who was related to Pope Clement VII). When the logic of his French alignment was translated in summer 1522 into an Anglo-Scottish war, Margaret betrayed Albany's plans.

When his second effort to mobilize the Scottish nobility for war failed in 1524, Albany left for France. Margaret returned to Scotland, resumed possession of her young son James, and had him crowned king in an elaborate ceremony which signified nothing more than that Margaret herself was in charge. This, however, had been made possible only by revulsion at Albany's anti-English policy, which also led to the return of Margaret's despised husband, the leading anglophile Douglas. The following year, Albany prevailed on Clement VII to grant Margaret her divorce from Douglas, calculating that it would weaken the anglophile faction; it certainly weakened Margaret, and probably played a part in the kidnap in 1526 of the young king by her ex-husband.

That year, Margaret was married for the third time, to Henry Stewart, younger son of Lord Avondale, later created Lord Methven, but she had by now lost all political influence. In 1538, in a bizarre attempt to regain it, she sought to have her marriage to Methven anulled – with a view to remarrying Douglas, presumably in the hope of strengthening the anglophile interest. King James was at the time engaged in a vendetta against the relations of Earl Douglas; whatever he thought about the proprieties of Margaret's attempt, he opposed its politics. Margaret was forced resentfully back to Methven, and died in 1541.

Further Reading
P. H. Buchanan, *Margaret Tudor: Queen of Scots*, 1985.

MARLOWE, CHRISTOPHER (1564-93), playwright, was the son of a prosperous Canterbury shoemaker. He was educated at the King's School, Canterbury and at Corpus Christi College, Cambridge, where he stayed for seven years (1580-7) and graduated both BA and MA. It is possible that at first he intended to follow a career in the church, but he probably took up writing before he left Cambridge.

At Cambridge he was not an unruly student and certainly profited from the classical elements in his education. But even before he went down from university, he seems to have been involved in one dangerous escapade, for it is likely (although not certain) that he was employed by the Privy Council to spy on the Catholic seminary at Rheims. His whole short life was to be peppered with dangerous and disreputable activities of this sort.

From Cambridge he went, as an aspiring writer, to London. It seems likely that his classical translations date from this early period, when his university education was still fresh in his mind. He translated Ovid's *Amores* as *All Ovid's Elegies*, a work which was burnt on the orders of the Archbishop of Canterbury because of its salacious content. Less controversial was his translation of Lucan's first book of *Pharsalia*, published in 1600 after Marlowe's death.

Marlowe made his name, however, not as a poet but as a playwright, and he did so very quickly on coming to London. His first play was *Dido, Queen of Carthage*, based on the *Aeneid*, perhaps commenced while he was still at Cambridge, and in part also the work of Thomas Nashe. His next work, almost certainly dating from 1587, was a great London stage hit, *Tamburlaine the Great*. At an early performance of this work, an actor accidentally killed a pregnant woman and her child in the audience when he fired a loaded 'calyver' at the Governor of Babylon tied to a stake and missed. This incident gives a good taste of what Marlowe's plays were like: full of energy and what we might call 'special effects'. So popular was *Tamburlaine* that Marlowe rushed out *Part Two*, where he stretched the factual, biographical basis of the play beyond breaking point. The problem was that he had told Tamburlaine's life-story fully in Part One and now had to rely on imagination.

In 1589 Marlowe wrote *The Famous Tragedy of the Rich Jew of Malta*, another very popular play which gave Shakespeare the idea for the *Merchant of Venice*. There then followed two history plays. First, in 1592, *Edward II* and, secondly, in 1593 *The Massacre at Paris*, which dealt with the St Bartholomew's Day Massacre in Paris. Perhaps his greatest was *The Tragical History of Dr Faustus*, which is dated 1588-9 by some authorities or 1592 by others. The play was based on a recent German work and its tale of demoniacal magic has since exerted a powerful influence on a variety of European artists.

In addition to this prodigious output of plays and translations, Marlowe found time to compose a number of poems, most notably 'Come live with me and be my love', which has remained popular ever since, and an epic, *Hero and Leander*.

Marlowe led a troubled, violent life as a London playwright. In 1589 he was imprisoned briefly in Newgate Goal for his part in the death of an inn-keeper's son in a street brawl. In 1592 he was bound over to keep the peace in the sum of twenty pounds. In the same year he was deported from the Netherlands for attempting to pass forged gold coins. In 1593 he was in trouble with the Privy Council for being an atheist. It is likely that he and a number of other intellectuals in the circle of Sir Walter Ralegh were free-thinkers, and after Marlowe's death accusations of this sort were made by his former friends. Whether the author of *Dr Faustus* also dabbled himself in the black arts is unclear. It seems highly probable that he was a homosexual.

Marlowe's death might have fitted well into one of his own plays. We only have his killer's side of the story, of course. According to this, Marlowe and two dubious associates, a slimy Catholic-baiter and spy called Robert Poley and one Ingram Frizer, spent 30 May 1593 at Eleanor Bull's tavern in Deptford Strand. After a convivial lunch, followed by a convivial supper, a quarrel developed over the bill. Marlowe was lying on a bed, with his two friends sitting on the bed's edge, their backs towards him. Marlowe drew a dagger from the back of Frizer's belt and cut his face slightly. In the struggle which followed, Frizer killed Marlowe. The coroner's jury returned a verdict of self-defence, and Frizer escaped unpunished.

Marlowe was under thirty when he died and some of his admirers have claimed that, had he lived, he would have written plays which might have matched those of Shakespeare. He was a pioneer: the first great English playwright for the Elizabethan stage, and Shakespeare benefited from his path-finding work. But,

> Marlowe was happy in his buskined Muse,
> Alas, unhappy in his life and end.

Further Reading
F. Boas, *Christopher Marlowe*, 1964.
M. Poirier, *Christopher Marlowe*, 1951.
A. L. Rowse, *Christopher Marlowe*, 1940.

MARSH, ADAM (*d.*after 1259) was an early Franciscan scholar whose friendships with Robert Grosseteste and Simon de Montfort linked the new Order with innovative academic investigation, ecclesiastical reform and radical politics. His reputation relies chiefly on his surviving correspondence: very little of his academic work remains or has been identified. Marsh appears as a confidant and adviser, not a leader or shaper of the destinies of others. Preferment within the church may have been denied him by his own volition, by his friar's vocation or by political suspicion of his purist views.

He had the credentials for a successful ecclesiastical career. A nephew of Richard Marsh, Bishop of Durham (1217-27), after education at Oxford, where he became a leading Master of Arts, he sustained his position as a wealthy secular clerk and scholar by holding the living of Wearmouth. From this period dates his connection with Grosseteste who became a close friend. The original contact may have been when Grosseteste gathered around him a group of scholars, including Marsh, to translate the newly available Greek philosophical and scientific texts. Marsh possibly encountered the Franciscans in Oxford through Grosseteste who was their patron and regent of the Oxford Franciscans 1229-35. Seeking fresh ways of understanding the temporal world, Grosseteste's group was infected by the new way of religious life offered by the Mendicant Orders. Marsh's secretary abandoned the academic life for that of a missionary friar and this influence may have persuaded Marsh, already a famous teacher, to take the Franciscan habit *c.*1232.

Such a translation scarcely interrupted Marsh's career. At Oxford he continued to lecture and write on a range of subjects from biblical commentaries and works on

penance to mathematics, languages and natural philosophy (i.e. what passed in the thirteenth century for science). Between 1247 and 1249, he was regent of the friar's school at Oxford, the first of the Order to be so. Roger Bacon, an Oxford near-contemporary and fellow Franciscan, loyally coupled Marsh with Grosseteste as the two leading philosophers of his time. Within the Order, Marsh took a stand against excessive erosion of the original Franciscan ideal of poverty, although accepting the need for secular proctors to handle money for the necessities of life. There was inevitable compromise between St Francis's precepts and the realities of running an international organization whose functions expanded beyond those of local charity or missionizing. Whatever his theoretical position, Marsh's own career pointed up potential contradictions and tensions which were to split the Order in the early fourteenth century and lead to some so-called Spiritual Franciscans, who followed their founder's Rule with pristine severity, being condemned as heretics.

Away from Oxford, he moved freely in the greatest secular and ecclesiastical circles. An observer at the trial of Simon de Montfort for maladministration of Gascony in 1252, Marsh developed an intense admiration for him, acting almost as his secretary as well as spiritual and political adviser. Marsh was one of the earl's executors in 1259. He also facilitated contacts between Simon and Grosseteste, whom he assisted in the administration of the diocese of Lincoln up to 1253. Marsh's influence and abilities were recognized by the king who appointed him to an embassy to France in 1257 to discuss a possible settlement of outstanding territorial disputes. Although exerting much influence as a devout and rigorous friar, Marsh hardly conformed to the pattern of life followed by St Francis. Yet his career was a model of how the new Mendicant Orders could adapt and play a significant role in the wider life of the church and Christendom.

Further Reading
A. G. Little, *Franciscan Papers*, 1943.

MARSHAL, WILLIAM (1147-1219) had a most remarkable career. Born the son of a prosperous minor baron, he made his name first as a roistering but shrewd manager of a team of tournament fighters. With good looks and a loyal disposition, he established an enviable reputation for the newly fashionable qualities of courtliness and chivalry. The protégé successively of Eleanor of Aquitaine, her son the Young King Henry and Henry II, the originally landless William netted one of the greatest heiresses in the Angevin Empire. Prominent in the service of Richard I and John, despite the latter's ingratitude, William stood firm in support of the king in the years of disaster for the Angevins 1213-16, so much so that when John died, leaving as heir a child of nine, the septugenarian William became the young Henry III's protector and Regent of England for the last three years of his life.

William's distinctive life was nonetheless a palimpsest upon which were successively written the obsessions of his age and class: war; tournaments; courtly intrigue; the caprice and generosity of the great; pilgrimage to the Holy Land; the hunt for heiresses; the hard choices of men with more than one lord; loyalty; dynastic greed; and the balance of rule between monarchs and their nobles. That William, despite nasty setbacks, emerged triumphant in most of these itself deserved notice: he was clearly more than a pretty face, a silver tongue and a strong right arm. There is a tenacity of ambition and ruthless determination which framed and lent purpose to the outward glitter of his life.

No less remarkable is that William was the subject of the first medieval biography of a layman who was not a king. The *Histoire de Guillaume le Maréchal*, a vernacular poem of over 19,000 lines finished between 1226 and 1229, was written by a member of the marshal's circle, called John. The author is hardly objective; but he is informative. Behind the glamorous veneer, a man considerably less of a bland archetype can be detected, one whose deeds nevertheless inspired enough interest and devotion to warrant such a unique surviving tribute.

Although not from one of the great landed dynasties of Anglo-Norman England, William spent his whole life in or near royal courts. In 1152, still a very young boy, his pro-Angevin father, John Marshal, gave him as a hostage to King Stephen to buy more time at the siege of Newbury. William later recalled that in his tent Stephen played him at 'knights', a tournament game with straw men, a scene which says much about the amiability of the king and the charm of the child.

In the decade before his death in 1165, John Marshal's fortunes declined so much so that William was left nothing. Entering the household of William de Tancarville, in 1167 he was knighted, and for the first time saw action (at the battle of Neufchâtel-en-Bray) and fought in a tournament. Despite earning praise for his courtliness, William lacked cultural refinement. Nicknamed 'gaste-viande' (i.e. 'guzzle-guts'), he was unusual for one of his background in never learning to read or write. His education was more or less exclusively fitted for a career as a professional soldier. Yet he was quick-witted enough to spend his life extracting profit from tournaments and royal service.

After spending a couple of years attached to the court of Eleanor of Aquitaine, in 1170 William joined the extravagant and glamorous entourage of the Young King Henry, where, while keeping up his semi-professional tournament business, he fulfilled the role as the prince's tutor-in-arms. Henry was a tournament fanatic, so William's place in his favour was sure. In 1173, William's prestige was singularly recognized when he knighted the Young King, a ceremony which he repeated in vastly different circumstances for young Henry's nephew and namesake forty-three years later. Except for a brief period in the early 1180s, William remained close to the Young King, but Henry's death in 1183 transformed prospects. Entrusted with carrying the dead prince's cloak bearing his crusader's Cross to the Holy Land, William received a promise of employment on his return from Henry II. William brought back with him in 1186 the rich cloth which was to serve as his own pall thirty-three years later.

Having lost the reversionary interest of the Young Henry, William rapidly compensated by service to the Old Henry. The secure foundations of his later grandeur were laid in 1186-9. He made close contacts with influential members of the king's household, such as the future Justiciar Geoffrey FitzPeter and began to receive patronage, in the form of lands, lucrative wardships and the promise of the hand of Isabel, heiress to the extensive lands in the Marches, Wales and Ireland of Earl Richard of Striguil. On Henry II's death in 1189, despite having been unhorsed by William in a recent encounter at Le Mans, the new king, Richard I, confirmed and extended his father's grants on both sides of the Channel. On his marriage to Isabel of Striguil, William at last entered the baronage and independence.

However, he owed his fortune to his loyalty. Richard I had elevated him for a purpose, to help guard his dominions during his absence on the Third Crusade. This proved a test of William's political skill and prescience, as the conflict between the chancellor, Longchamp, and Prince John careered towards civil war. William backed John and led the movement which ousted Longchamp in October 1191. Although faithful to King Richard, remaining at his side through his French campaigns of 1194-9, William kept in with John. In 1194, he refused homage to Richard for his Irish lands, instead reserving it for John, as Lord of Ireland. Such ambivalence had a precise purpose. As his enemy Longchamp acutely remarked 'Planting vines, Marshal?'

After Richard's unexpected death in 1199, William harvested the fruits of his husbandry. Instrumental in securing John's succession, he was rewarded with the earldom of Pembroke and a significant extension of his estates, especially in Wales and Ireland. Enjoying the favour of a new and grateful king and the friendship of both justiciar (Geoffrey FitzPeter) and chancellor (Hubert Walter), William appeared at the summit of his career. But his self-interest could not long remain compatible with that of a monarch whose power was crumbling and whose suspicion was pervasive and venomous. William played a vigorous if unavailing part in the defence of Normandy. But when Philip II gained control of the duchy in 1204, William looked to his own, managing to negotiate a deal with Philip in 1205 whereby he did the king liege homage for his French lands. This implied that William would be unable, on risk of forfeiture, to fight Philip in France. As the recapture of his French lands was King John's central policy, William's homage to Philip at one stroke questioned his loyalty and negated his usefulness. Between 1205 and 1212, William suffered the humiliations and political insecurity of loss of royal favour. Initially, he was not even allowed to retire peacefully to his possessions in Ireland, as John was fearful for his own lordship there. When summoned to court in 1207-8, it was to be publicly humiliated, personally teased, politically undermined and legally threatened. From 1208, William lived in retirement in Kilkenny, for the first time acting as a settled ruler of his estates, as well as indulging in a favoured pastime of beating up the native Irish: as the imaginative Matthew Paris put it a generation later, he was 'a Saturn to Ireland'.

The extraordinary transformation of William's fortunes between 1212 and 1216 from distrusted exile to Regent of England reveals the extent of the collapse of John's authority as well as Marshal's almost robotic loyalty. Yet even in his late sixties, William never altered his conviction that the greatest rewards were to be found at the hands of the richest provider, the king. He, as very few then did, remembered the failure of the 1173-4 rebellion and the ultimate futility of hoping for preferment in opposition to the monarch. If he had been tempted to forget, his experiences of 1205-12 served as a raw reminder. When, in 1212, magnate discontent with John's methods of rule expressed themselves through an ill-concealed assassination plot, William ensured that Ireland stayed loyal. In a sense he had no option: a successful coup would not have advantaged him much more than a vengeful king. As for John, the plot of 1212 and the opposition to the French campaign of 1213-14 demonstrated that there were fewer and fewer men of substance and experience on whom he could rely. Patronage in the Middle Ages was never entirely efficient in binding the loyalty of subjects, but it was with William Marshal, perhaps because he had started with nothing.

Returning to England in 1213, William immediately began to reap the landed rewards of service. He also emerged, with the Earl of Chester, as the leading loyalists among the magnates as the English baronage slid from the defeat in France in 1214, to the failed compromise of Magna Carta and open civil war in 1215. Nevertheless, whether by accident or design, family interests were protected by William's eldest son's support for the baronial side. As the crisis deepened for the Angevins, William's importance grew. He organized the royalists in the southern Marches and Wales. In 1216 he unsuccessfully tried to dissuade Philip II from sending his son Louis to England: such an invasion obviously placed

William in a uniquely difficult position. But he did not flinch in his adherence to John. After the king's death in October, when to many it must have seemed that a Capetian triumph was inevitable, William assumed guardianship of the young Henry III and, with the approval of the Earl of Chester, the regency: 'rector noster et regni nostri' as he was styled in royal documents. The sight of the venerable warrior, who had buried three kings (four if you include the young Henry), whose memories stretched back to King Stephen, with the boy-king was the stuff of romance – and maybe of actual emotion. There is a Churchillian sentimentality in William's recorded remarks to three friends the evening of his acceptance of the regency: 'If everyone abandons the boy but me, do you know what I shall do? I will carry him on my back, and if I can hold him up, I will hop from island to island, from country to country, even if I have to beg for my bread'.

The first task facing the new regent was survival. This William achieved in 1217 primarily through military victories over the French and the rebels at Lincoln and in the Channel. At Lincoln, William himself fought energetically, forgetting his helmet in his eagerness for the fray in which he killed Robert of Roppesley. The naval battle off Sandwich he merely observed with the king from the cliff-tops. But the royalist success was consolidated by a lack of vindictiveness. Already in November 1216 he had Magna Carta reissued, a symbol of a fresh start and a more consensual method of governing. Now, after the French defeat, William negotiated the withdrawal of Prince Louis for the sum of 10,000 marks. As Louis was the son of William's French overlord, perhaps this generosity was not wholly altruistic.

In the last two years of his life, William laid the foundations for the rebuilding of royal authority. Given the poverty of the Crown and the divisions of the civil war, it was inevitable that he had to conciliate rather than coerce. Magna Carta was again reissued in 1217; the Exchequer was restored; the judicial bench returned to Westminster in 1217, with salaried justices to minimize corruption; a general eyre was instituted in 1218-19; and regular councils gave the magnates the impression that they were involved in rule through common consent. Helping the regent were the papal legates, Guala and Pandulf; the Justiciar Hubert de Burgh; and the Bishop of Winchester, Peter des Roches. But none of them could (or were to) inspire wide enough confidence, especially vital as there was no prospect of effective independent royal government dealing with intransigent rebels or grasping partisans of the late king, not least because of the failure to restore royal finances. Of course, William never ignored the interests of his family: in 1217 he recovered Marlborough which his father had lost almost sixty years before. But whatever the limitations of his rule, William had kept the centre intact. By the time he died in 1219, there was a system of royal government for others to expand and develop.

The verse biography of William Marshal makes it both easier and more difficult to approach the man as an individual. Opinions and remarks attributed to him have to be treated with care. But something of the private man can be detected. He seems to have been a faithful and certainly uxorious husband: he and Isabel had ten children. Although over forty when he married, he left no recorded bastards. He was a brave, vigorous and deadly fighter into his seventies. He turned his prodigious skill at tournaments (he claimed to have taken prisoner over 500 knights) into a thriving business in the 1170s, with his Flemish partner Richard de Gaugy: they had a disciplined team with a deliberate strategy calculated to maximize captives and minimize risk of injury, all conducted on a professionally commercial footing. Of his dynastic ambition there can be no doubt: it provided the most prominent leitmotif of his life. His success can be judged that when he died, possibly of cancer, on his own manor, surrounded by his own extended household, he had made his family one of the greatest in the British Isles. His loyalty was not disinterested. Neither, presumably, were his extensive religious donations. He died, in the habit of a Templar, the model of a good Christian lord and knight, firm in his faith and his social position. Rather typically, the biographer's account ignored the inconvenient detail that William died still under excommunication by the Irish Bishop of Ferns, a penalty dating back to some Irish-bashing of 1212.

William's political apotheosis was the result of longevity – he knew personally all the kings who ruled England from 1135 to 1272 – and clear political vision. It may also have been because he was liked. William had the qualities contemporaries admired and a personality to match. He was no routine toady: on his deathbed, holding Henry III by the hand, he prayed that the king's life might be short if he followed the example of '*alcun felon ancestre*' ('a certain criminal ancestor'). Famously impassive in public, here the dying courtier perhaps let slip his true feelings for at least one of his Angevin masters. William's life shows that there was more to being a courtier than literature might imply. In warfare, chivalry, politics, faction, intrigue and self-advancement, William Marshal fought his way to the top and managed to stay there. As Richard I once said of him, he was indeed '*molt corteis*', most courtly.

Further Reading
D. Crouch, *William Marshal*, 1990.

MARSHALL, MARGARET, DUCHESS OF NORFOLK (*c*.1320-99) was a dowager 'of remarkable business acumen and spirit' who 'has left distinctive and lasting traces of her colourful career'. Her father was Thomas of Brotherton, Earl of Norfolk and Earl Marshal

(*d*.1338), son to Edward I by his second marriage to Margaret of France and half-brother of Edward II, so Margaret was first cousin of Edward III. The successive deaths of her brother Edward by 1337, her sister Alice and her stepmother by 1362, and her niece in 1375 left Margaret ultimately as sole heiress of her father. This was recognized by the Crown, which henceforth entitled her Margaret Marshall – holder of the dignity, but not the office, of Earl Marshal – and Countess of Norfolk. Since her father had been amongst the most generously endowed of the earls and since she also enjoyed dowers from her two husbands John Lord Segrave (*d*.1354) and Walter Lord Mauny (*d*.1372), Margaret was the greatest dowager of her time. She outlived all her children and many other descendants, who never realized their hereditary expectations, and thus epitomizes 'the problem of late medieval dowagers' to noble families. Her eventual heir at death was a great-grandson. In 1397, when her grandson Thomas Mowbray was created Duke of Norfolk, Margaret was created Duchess of Norfolk in her own right – a remarkable mark of distinction and very welcome to her.

Medieval wives were subject to their husbands and little can be learnt about them. In Margaret's case we know only that she bore each husband a son and a daughter, that she married Lord Mauny from personal choice without royal licence, and that she went overseas in 1350 in defiance of a royal prohibition, perhaps to seek a divorce from Lord Segrave. Edward III's anger was not allayed by her prevarications and she spent several months in detention. Past the age of childbearing by 1372, she deliberately chose to remain single and independent for her last twenty-seven years.

Like other great dowagers, Margaret possessed the resources of great magnates, but not their inclination for high politics. Her acute sense of her exalted ancestry, high rank, and royal connections caused her to seek implementation by the Crown of endowments promised to her father and to secure privileges and possessions as Earl Marshal. Both claims apparently failed. To her tenants she probably appeared no different from male lords: like them she was well-served by professional administrators and was concerned to run her property efficiently. One estate exemplifies 'her grasp of administrative affairs; her pursuance of her rights and dues; and a certain harshness stemming from keen self-interest'. She was mean about inessential expenses, such as payment of annuities, and vigorous in enlarging her resources, if necessary by fraud or violence. She could thus afford to live in state at Framlingham Castle very much like the Lady of Clare a generation earlier, entertaining lavishly and pursuing her religious interests. She made no new foundations, but gave generously to several existing ones, including the houses of Minoresses at Bruisyard and Aldgate so fashionable with noble ladies at this time. These gifts were apparently connected to patronage to William Woodford, a Franciscan theologian, and to her provision of stalls for Greyfriars, London, where she chose to be buried. Without obvious functions in their last years, dowagers commonly dwelt on the good of their souls and could afford to satisfy their spiritual as well as their earthly aspirations. If it is therefore strictly true that Margaret 'used her wealth' purely for 'personal advantage', it is also true that some of her activities – such as defence and pursuit of her rights – were of equal or greater value to her successors and their benefit may indeed have been intended.

Further Reading
R. E. Archer, 'Margaret of Brotherton c.1320-1399', *Historical Research* lx, 1987.

MARTEN, HENRY (1602-80), wit, Republican and regicide, the son of a distinguished civil lawyer, inherited wide estates in Berkshire. Educated at University College, Oxford, and by travel abroad, he was in Aubrey's phrase 'as far from a Puritan as light from darkness'. Aubrey has a story that 'Henry was in Hyde Park one time when his Majestie was there going to see a Race. The king [Charles I] espied him, and sayd aloud, Let that ugly Rascall be gone out of the Parke, that whore-master, or else I will not see the sport.' Cromwell, too, when he ejected the Rump in 1653, called Marten a 'whore-master'. Elected MP for Berkshire in 1640, he was violently anti-royalist, and one of the earliest Republicans. Clarendon records Marten saying to him at this time (1640-2): 'I do not think one man wise enough to govern us all'; and in 1643 the House sent him to the Tower for saying that it were better one family were destroyed than many. A brilliant talker with a gift for repartee, the records suggest that he was the wittiest member of a parliament that badly needed wit but did not always appreciate it. When a godly MP moved that all 'profane and unsanctified persons', a category for which the deist wencher Marten was admirably qualified, be expelled, Marten's counter-motion that all fools might be put out likewise, 'and then there would be a thin House', can scarcely have endeared him to his colleagues.

He raised troops for parliament in both Civil Wars but his part in the fighting was undistinguished. His role in the conflict with the king was that of pamphleteer and speaker. He may have been the author of *A Correction of the Answerer*, a tract of 1646 demanding the condign punishment of Charles, and in 1647 he moved in the Commons for 'no further addresses' to the king, a motion lost by thirty-four (among them Blake) to eighty-four (including Cromwell). This year also saw Marten collaborating closely with the Levellers and supporting the army in its quarrel with parliament. With the

Levellers he shared not only their wish to deal sternly with Charles but also a good deal of their political and social programme. He was probably one of the three authors of the Leveller *Remonstrance of Many Thousand Citizens* (1646) and he certainly had a hand in drafting the democratic constitution, *The Agreement of the People* (1647). Marten was liberal-minded enough to demand (with John Selden) toleration for Roman Catholics, and – though not himself a Leveller – sufficiently radical in social outlook to write in 1648 the tract *England's Troublers Troubled, or the just resolutions of the plain men of England against the rich and mighty*, a satirical onslaught upon the London capitalists. It was about this time too that he told a jury at a trial to put their hats on to show that they, not the men on the bench, were 'the chief Judges in the court'.

Marten sat on the court which tried Charles I, and signed the death-warrant; and a royalist witness attributed to him the formula on which the court based its authority, 'in the name of the Commons in parliament assembled and all the good people of England'. After 1649 he was a member of the Council of State and in that year proposed the abolition of imprisonment for debt; one of those who thought that the Rump should perpetuate itself, he broke with Cromwell and was turned out in 1653. During the Protectorate he was out of politics, and seems to have spent some time in prison as a result of the debts he had incurred on the parliament's behalf in the wars. In 1659 he returned with the Rump. When the Restoration came he was put on trial and defended himself with courage and ability; yet according to Aubrey, his life was spared through a wit similar to his own, Lord Falkland saying, 'Gentlemen, yee talke here of makeing a Sacrifice; it was the old Lawe, all Sacrifices were to be without spott or blemish; and now you are going to make an old Rotten Rascall a Sacrifice'. Marten was imprisoned for life, in the Tower, at Windsor, and finally at Chepstow, where he died. Many royalists saw him as 'that pernicious Catiline', in the phrase of one of their pamphleteers. Aubrey, more kindly, calls him 'a great and faithful lover of his Country … a great cultor of Justice, and did always in the House take the part of the oppressed'.

Further Reading
C. M. Williams, 'Henry Marten', in *Puritans and Revolutionaries*, ed. Donald Pennington and Keith Thomas, 1978 (pp.118-138).

MARTIN, RICHARD (1754-1834) was much loved for his compassionate and generous nature and earned the name 'Humanity Martin' for his work for animal welfare. As benevolent Irish landowner and diligent parliamentarian he might be honoured above those less scrupulous about how they used their rental incomes. More especially he should be remembered as the founder, in 1824, of The Royal Society for the Protection of Animals.

From County Galway he went, like other scions of Ascendancy families, to Harrow and Trinity College, Cambridge. He returned to the Irish Bar and parliament, and management of the 200,000 acres around his family seat, Ballinahinch Castle. He was a keen supporter of the Act of Union and, from 1801 to 1826, represented Galway at Westminster. Like some other Protestant landowners who knew their Catholic tenants and sympathized with their aspirations, he supported emancipation. George IV was otherwise inclined, but appreciated Martin's wit and remained his friend. 'I hear you are to have an election in County Galway. Who will win?' he asked. 'The survivor, sire,' replied Martin. He was known as a man of quick temper and fought more than one duel.

Unusually at a time of lavish promotion among Irish families, Martin refused the offer of a peerage. But it was his constancy in cherished causes that made the greatest impression. In 1822 he saw through parliament a law that made Britain the European leader in the field of animal welfare, 'to prevent the cruel and improper treatment of cattle'. He was no less zealous in following up and prosecuting breaches of the Act.

MARTINEAU, HARRIET (1802-76) was, for a time, the leading woman writer of the day. She owed it to her exceptional intelligence and, as her *Autobiography* reveals, a sense of mission fortified by her experience of illness, belated recovery and subsequent resolve, having abandoned religious faith, 'to hold tight where she had got footing' – to a creed of scientific materialism.

She was born to a family of Huguenot origins in Norwich and lived there till she was thirty. Her father, a manufacturer of army cloth, was left without business by the end of the Napoleonic Wars. Bank failures completed the family's ruin and it became clear that she must earn her living. She had been deaf since the age of nineteen. Encouraged by her brother James to 'leave it to other women to make shirts and darn stockings', she had already written articles on diverse topics when, in 1832, her *Illustrations of Political Economy* made her famous. Twenty-four didactic stories exemplified the teaching of Adam Smith, Malthus and Ricardo. After two years (1834-6) in America, she returned, a convinced abolitionist, and found publishers competing for her *Society in America*. She was also commissioned to write a novel. Attributes of *Deerbrook*, 'this outstanding novel', include, in Horsman's view 'a persistent power of giving crisp actuality to everyday things'; he points to 'scenes which rival George Eliot herself'. After its publication her health broke down and she spent invalid years, 1839-44, at Tynemouth. She recovered, she thought, through Mesmerism: her belief in its therapeutic powers puzzled

some of her friends, but she was sure. 'A new light spread through my mind, and I began to experience a steady growth of self-command, courage, and consequent integrity and disinterestedness.' There was indeed little left of her early Unitarianism but the persuasive working of 'the religion of duty'.

From 1845 she lived at Ambleside, with nieces, whom she treated as if her daughters, and maids – who were schooled with the nieces. She knew most of the most important people of the day: they came to the Knoll to listen to a crisp monologue about factory laws, school provision, the latest scientific theory – or novel – and, if bold, venture their opinion into her ear-trumpet. She wrote on subjects ranging from the history of the *Thirty Years' Peace, 1816-46*, to domestic management. Education was a special interest. She was awed by no-one. She was capable of implacable hatreds, as for George Lewes, whose companion, George Eliot, spoke of being repelled 'by the vulgarity (I use the word in a moral sense) of her looks and gestures'. She later wrote of Harriet's 'wonderful fluency and eloquence, her animal spirits as unflagging as her intellectual powers'. But, like many, women especially, she was appalled by her views. Martineau collaborated with H. G. Atkinson in writing *The Laws of Man's Nature and Development* (1851). It was avowedly agnostic. She wrote of her relief at renouncing the painful anxiety of feeling that her salvation depended on her own will or on God. The materialism of *The Laws* was advanced as a new gospel, with – her critics said – a sense of superiority over still benighted believers. In 1853 she consolidated her position with an abridged translation of Comte's *Philosophie Positive*.

Martineau's feminism was inconsistent, both radical and conservative: she held it important for women to have political knowledge and views – but thought that few successful women were happy in their personal lives. For all her courage and probity, her cleverness and her genuine interest in 'the questions of the day', such as slavery in America, she never seemed to escape entirely from the 'philosophic radicalism' of her youth – at least from its spirit. Coleridge had said to her: 'You seem to look on society as an aggregate of individuals.' 'Of course I do', she replied. By 1850, between Benthamites and Coleridgeans, the latter were winning the struggle for the Victorian mind. One of them, Matthew Arnold, referring to the herd instinct 'so eminently a vice of the English', wrote what might serve as her epitaph. 'I cannot but praise a person whose one effort seems to have been to deal honestly and sincerely with herself.'

Further Reading
R. K. Webb, *Harriet Martineau: a Radical Victorian*, 1960.

MARVELL, ANDREW (1621-78), poet and politician, was born near Hull, son of the moderate Puritan master of the Hull Charterhouse, and was probably sent to Hull Grammar School. After going to Trinity College, Cambridge, he travelled abroad during the Civil War years. His most celebrated single poem, the *Horatian Ode upon Cromwell's Return from Ireland*, with its lines on the execution of Charles I, was written in 1650. From 1651 to 1653 he was tutor to Fairfax's daughter at Nunappleton in Yorkshire, and probably wrote there many of his agreeable lyrics in praise of gardens and rural life. He is always likely to be remembered for his poem *To His Coy Mistress*, with its lines,

> But at my back I always hear
> Time's winged chariot hurrying near.

After a period as tutor to Cromwell's ward, William Dutton, he became in 1657 Milton's assistant as Latin Secretary to the Council of State. From 1658 to his death in 1678 Marvell was MP for Hull, and looked after the needs of his constituents vigorously. A member of Harrington's Rota Club in 1659-60, Marvell defended Milton after the Restoration, standing by him at the time of his prosecution and writing the preface in his praise for the second edition of *Paradise Lost* in 1674. He grew increasingly hostile to the government in the 1670s, attacking the persecution of dissenters, inventing the nickname 'Cabal' for the group of ministers from 1673 to 1678, and denouncing the pro-French and pro-Catholic policies. His anonymous pamphlet *Account of the Growth of Popery and Arbitrary Government in England* created a sensation when it appeared in 1677, and the government offered £100 for the name of its author. As the *Horatian Ode* indicates, Marvell was more ready than many of his contemporaries to sense the values of both sides in the great conflict of the seventeenth century.

Further Reading

Robert Wilcher, *Andrew Marvell: an Introductory Study*, 1986.
R. L. Shaw, ed., *Andrew Marvell: Essays on the Tercentenary of his Death*, 1979.
Christopher Hill, 'Society and Andrew Marvell', *Puritanism and Revolution*, 1958.
M. C. Bradbrook and M. G. Lloyd Thomas, *Andrew Marvell*, 1940.

MARY I (1516-58), who became Queen of England in 1553, was the third child of Henry VIII and Catherine of Aragon and the only one to survive infancy. For the first years of her life she was given into the charge of the Countess of Salisbury.

For the first twelve years of her life she was Henry's 'pearl of his kingdom'. To begin with, Catherine supervised her education, entrusting it to Linacre and commissioning the great Spanish scholar, Vives, to recommend a curriculum. Mary was well educated, but showed little aptitude for learning, except perhaps in music. She mastered Latin and French, but never learned to write or to speak Spanish. Catherine was educating her, after all, to be an English princess.

Very early in life she became a pawn on the chessboard of international politics. In 1518 she was promised in marriage at the age of two to the newly-born Dauphin of France: that was broken off and she was promised to the twenty-two-year-old emperor, Charles V. Mary was then six. Charles chose instead to marry Isabella of Portugal, whereupon Mary was offered to James IV of Scotland and then to Francis I of France, who was thirty-two in 1527.

In 1526 Mary was sent as Princess of Wales to Ludlow, where a court was established for her, her education provided for, and instructions were given to the Countess of Salisbury, mother of Reginald Pole, and to Mary's chamberlain, John Dudley (who later as Northumberland was to try to prevent her from succeeding to the throne) that the princess was to have plenty of good food, clean linen, dancing and open air exercise. It is likely enough that these next two years were to be the happiest in Mary's life.

In 1528 the first suggestions of the divorce were mooted. From 1528 to 1530 Mary hardly ever saw her parents. In 1531 she was separated from her mother, she was forbidden to write to her, and she never saw Catherine of Aragon again. The next year began the unhappiest part of Mary's life. In 1532 Henry VIII spent on his daughter one-fifth in the whole year of what he spent in one day on Anne Boleyn. In 1533 Mary was deprived of her title of Princess of Wales: when in the same year Elizabeth was born to Anne Boleyn, Mary was declared a bastard and cut out of the succession to the throne by Act of Parliament. Her household was broken up, the Countess of Salisbury was sent away, and Mary was relegated into the new household set up for the new Princess Elizabeth.

The years 1534-6 were probably the most cruel time that Mary had to endure. Henry was determined to break what he called her 'Spanish pride' and force her to agree to the royal supremacy and her own bastardization. This became a major political problem for the king and his minister, Thomas Cromwell. In the end, after intense pressure had been applied, Mary gave in to her father, largely because of the death of Anne Boleyn in 1536, which Mary hoped might pave the way to better relations with Henry if first she submitted to him. So Mary capitulated to the demands Henry made upon her. She even acknowledged her own bastardy, that 'the marriage heretofore between his majesty and my mother ... was by God's law and man's law incestuous and unlawful'. Mary is not to be blamed for this. One may guess how great a support Catherine had been, but she was dead now. Even Mary's cousin, Charles V, advised her to yield.

Mary's cup of sorrow was not yet quite full. Henry

seemed very ready to restore Mary to his favour. The arrival on the scene of Jane Seymour brought her a good friend. And even Cromwell, always a swimmer with the tide, made her a present at the New Year. But there were still crosses to be borne. In 1540, her old tutor, Dr Featherstone, and her mother's chaplain, Abell, were burnt at the stake. But worst of all was the wholesale attack made on the Pole family, so that among other sufferers Mary's best friend, the Countess of Salisbury, was executed.

That Henry's treatment of his daughter may have been only politic and even repugnant to him may be perhaps supported by his treatment of her after the execution of Anne Boleyn – which removed Mary's most bitter and dangerous enemy. It is said that Anne contemplated the murder of Mary by poison. At any rate from 1536 to 1547 Mary lived a life of ease and contentment, with apparently enough money to allow her to enjoy herself at the gaming tables and to indulge her love of giving presents to her relatives, friends, and especially her godchildren (Madden, *Privy Purse Expenses of the Princess Mary*, 1831).

In 1544, Mary was restored to the succession, after Edward, but before Elizabeth, by the Act of Succession and by Henry's will. Between 1547, when her father died and 1553, when she ascended the throne, her difficulties continued. She had much affection for Edward VI, little liking for his religion. Her quarrels were mostly with the Council, not with Edward. The Council demanded conformity to the new Protestant religion. Mary stood up superbly, imperturbably and invincibly to all the attempts made to bring her to accept the new Protestant religion. By the time Edward died, Mary had conceded nothing and maintained her own position intact, without falling out herself with Edward VI, although after 1551 she did forgo the public celebration of the Mass, restricting herself to Catholic services in private.

In July 1553 Edward VI died and Northumberland made his desperate bid to substitute his daughter-in-law, Lady Jane Grey, in place of Mary as the new queen. Mary was at Hunsdon when a message came from the Council telling her to visit her brother, who was very ill. On her way she was warned that the king was already dead. She rushed to her own house at Kenninghall in Norfolk, whence she wrote to the Council, promising a general pardon if she was proclaimed at once. Then she went with all the local supporters she could raise to Framlingham and there she proclaimed herself queen. Her standard was hoisted over the Gatehouse and she announced that 'The queen is not fled the realm, nor intendeth to do, as is most untruly surmised'. On 19 July, so swiftly did the nation react to her courage, she was proclaimed in London. On 3 August she entered London triumphantly as queen, Northumberland having already

been arrested at Cambridge. Her reign had begun and she had the whole nation at her feet.

Mary's marriage was in personal terms a disappointment, even a failure. The decision to marry her cousin, Philip, heir to Spain and Burgundy, can be defended on several counts. An alliance with the enemies of France suited English national feeling and it was by any standards a good match. Grave difficulties surrounded a marriage with an English noble, and though English xenophobia was aroused by the marriage to Philip II, this was less dangerous than the civil discord which could ensue from a domestic match. For Mary the wedding with Philip may have represented a return to her Catholic, Spanish roots, but most important she hoped to establish the succession as soon as possible by giving birth to a child, preferably of course a son. The marriage treaty with Philip (1554) was highly favourable to the English, since it would give to the future King of England born to Mary and Philip, possession of the Netherlands, even perhaps (if Philip had no further children) the whole Spanish empire. In the end, however, the marriage was fruitless and unpopular. Philip spent only two brief periods in England and there was to be no child, only a number of phantom pregnancies, which made Mary ridiculous, symbolizing her desperate desire for an heir, but underlining clearly her failure to bear one.

Mary's religious policy was at first something of a success. The restoration of religion as Henry VIII had left it at the end of his reign was in tune with the religious feelings of the majority of the nation, especially after the extremism of Edward VI's reign. In November 1554, Cardinal Pole arrived in England to reconcile the country to the pope, but he accepted parliament's insistence that there should be no attempt to restore the property of the monasteries: in itself, a realistic acceptance of the facts of political life and one which does the régime credit. However, although well-intentioned, Pole had neither the time nor perhaps the energy to undertake a revival of English Catholicism in the spirit of Catholic Reform. The counter-reformation was visible in Mary's religious policy most clearly only in the persecution of heretics. All told, at least 274 were burnt at the stake in the years 1555-8. This was the fiercest bout of religious cruelty England ever witnessed and it had a profound and harmful effect on the Catholic cause which Mary so strongly supported. It failed to remove the canker of religious non-conformity, instead it strengthened Protestantism and gave to Roman Catholicism the stigma of tyranny and extremism, especially through the writings of John Foxe and of later historians, by which medium it became a long-lived, and not yet quite extinct, myth. The centre of the persecution was the capital itself, especially the Smithfield fires, and the diocese of London accounted for nearly half the total of those executed

(112); this strengthened the Protestant cause in the most dangerous place. Catholicism was further weakened and heresy strengthened by the exile of about 800 Protestants in Mary's reign, who were allowed to escape to the continent. Many of them found their way to Germany and Switzerland, where they strengthened their faith and made it purer by association with John Calvin and other continental reformers. This gave to the English Protestant tradition a new and potentially dangerous twist.

Mary's third great failure was in foreign affairs. In 1557 she allowed herself to be drawn through the Spanish alliance into war with France. Of course, there was nothing very new or alarming in this; indeed, this was probably at first popular with the upper classes since it allowed them to rally round a patriotic cause and to sink their religious differences in the queen's service. English forces acquitted themselves well at the Battle of St Quentin, where the Spanish defeated the French. But the war was costly and led to heavy taxation, debts and popular discontent as the burdens on the poor commons increased. The great disaster came early in 1558, when a series of English blunders and a brilliant surprise attack by the Duke of Guise led to the loss of Calais, the last remnant of the great English empire in France.

In some less spectacular areas, Mary's reign scored some successes. Government ran smoothly enough under an effective Privy Council, and parliament in the main co-operated with Mary. The reform of the financial system projected under Northumberland was brought to completion and there was a general drive against corruption, for example in the administration of Crown Lands and in the Court of Wards under Sir Francis Englefield. The Customs were reformed when a new Book of Rates was issued in 1558. An important Militia Act was passed in 1558, the foundation for the Elizabethan and early Stuart armies, and national defences were built up. Exploration and trade were fostered and a charter granted which incorporated the Muscovy Company in 1555. A number of parliamentary acts tightened up in the field of public order and strengthened the hand of the Justices of the Peace.

Mary was the first female ruler England had had since Matilda in the twelfth century, and it is perhaps surprising that in such an age of male chauvinism she was not less successful than she was. She prepared the way for the more spacious days of her sister and both Mary's successes and failures helped give Elizabeth some advantages in 1558. It is difficult to pass final judgement on Mary; she had only five years of government and given more time she might have been able to build on some of her sound beginnings. As it was, her brief reign must on the evidence before us be accounted a failure, but by no means an unmitigated disaster.

Further Reading
D. M. Loades, *The Reign of Mary Tudor*, 2nd revised edn, 1991.
R. Tittler, *The Reign of Mary I*, 1983.

MARY II (1662-94) was the elder daughter of James, Duke of York, and Anne Hyde. Brought up a Protestant at Charles II's insistence, despite the conversion of both her parents to Romanism, she was married to William of Orange in 1677. In 1678 she had two miscarriages, and thereafter remained childless. Sincerely as well as dutifully accepting her husband's attitude to her father's policy on the English throne after 1685, she joined him in condemning the Declaration of Indulgence and supporting the Seven Bishops. Mary accepted the Revolution and the deposition of her father as necessary to the security of Protestantism. Nor had she any doubts that William must rule as king, and she turned down Danby's plan that she should be sole sovereign with the words 'I shall take it extreme unkindly, if any, under pretence of their care for me, should set up a divided interest between me and the prince'. As queen she played no significant part in the making of political decisions. Yet as regent during William's frequent absences she was a calm and dignified head of state, not least in the crises of 1690 and 1692. She died of smallpox in 1694.

Few women in English history have been so important as Mary II, who made possible the curious form taken by the English Revolution of 1688-9, and also made her highly unpopular husband acceptable to the English people, in particular to the moderate Tory leaders. Yet her importance lay in her mere existence rather than in her qualities, with one significant exception – her devotion to Protestantism. Owing much to those two very different yet practical divines Compton, her childhood tutor, and Burnet, her adviser at The Hague, she firmly resisted her father's efforts to win her to Rome. In her way Mary was as much a symbol of Protestantism as the last English woman who had been Queen of England before her, Elizabeth I. With something of the primness of her grandfather Clarendon, almost morbidly conscientious about her own conduct, Mary found in a practical religion, appropriate to the temper of the late seventeenth century, the way of expressing a deep natural kindliness. She was a patron of the movement which led to the Society for Promoting Christian Knowledge (SPCK), and she originated the project of Greenwich Hospital which William carried out as a memorial to her. Her graciousness and sincerity made her popular both in the Holland she grew to love and in the England which she came to dislike.

A precocious and lively child who grew into a sensitive and intelligent woman, she suffered bitterly in her personal life as a result of her public role. She had been her father's favourite child, and the prolonged crisis of

1688-90, ending only with the Boyne, was a torment to Mary, prevented by her duty to William from showing any sign of her sorrow for her father. James, characteristically, solemnly cursed and disowned her. Her sister Anne, self-centred and unimaginative and in this period dominated by Sarah Churchill, disliked William intensely, and the disgrace of Marlborough in the 1690s led to a complete break between her and Mary which was never healed. Nor were Mary's relations with William easy. The evidence suggests that she had had no wish to marry and that the barren match which was of such decisive importance in British and European history and by which she sacrificed so much came near to shipwreck. There was his attachment to Elizabeth Villiers; probably more important, there was the difficulty, felt by all who knew him, of understanding William's whole complex and awkward personality. Yet Mary came to love him with 'a passion that cannot but end with my life', triumphing by her almost puritanical sense of duty and her capacity for affection. Moreover, it seems certain that the outward signs of disharmony, of which Jacobite gossip made the most, reflected William's temperamental reserve and boorishness rather than any deeper failure. His grief at her death was frightening to observers. Its intensity, in this strange man in whom public and private feelings were so inextricably blended, may not improperly be regarded as a measure of his adopted country's debt to the most honest and attractive of Stuart monarchs.

Further Reading
Hester W. Chapman, *Mary II, Queen of England*, 1953.

MARY, QUEEN OF SCOTS (1542-87) was the third child and only daughter of James V of Scotland and of his wife, Mary of Guise. The rout of the Scottish army at Solway Moss had taken place on 24 November and Mary was born on 8 December. It is said that in his despair over the military defeat James V, on hearing the news of the birth of his daughter, cried out, 'it came with a lass and it will gang with a lass', and turned his face to the wall and died on 14 December. Mary was, therefore, one week old when she became Queen of Scots. Negotiations at once began for her marriage with Edward VI of England, but these were frustrated on religious grounds by Cardinal Beaton. On 10 September 1547 Protector Somerset, determined to bring about the marriage, defeated the Scots at Pinkie Cleugh. The Scots now made a marriage alliance with the French, and on 7 August 1548, at the age of six, Mary sailed for France to marry the Dauphin, Francis, son of Henry II and Catherine de Medici.

Mary was brought up at the French court with the children of the royal family. Her education was carefully supervised and gave her all the Renaissance accomplishments. Throughout her life she wrote French most easily, although she was, of course, fluent in Scots and even learnt some English while in captivity here. The French court was soon impressed by her intelligence, her charm, her beauty and personality. She was brought up a strict Roman Catholic in the midst of a cultured and far from strict court, but the freedom of the court would seem to have affected her more than the strict discipline of the church, if one is to judge by her later history. Yet, in truth, her position was an impossible one. She had never known Scotland, yet she was queen of that country: she married on 24 April 1558 a weak and sickly husband, Francis, heir to the French throne. She might thus combine the two kingdoms of France and Scotland, and she was heir to the throne of England. Yet before her marriage she had signed away Scotland to France, on the terms that if she died without an heir Scotland was to go as a free gift to the King of France, with all her rights to the English throne, and any assent she might be compelled to make to any different arrangement by the Scots was to be null and void from the start. That that was a betrayal of her native country cannot be denied, but what did her native country mean to a girl of sixteen who had left it at the age of six?

In the year when Mary married Francis (1558) Mary I of England died and the Protestant Elizabeth came to the English throne. Mary at once claimed the English throne on the grounds of Elizabeth's illegitimacy. She quartered the arms of England with those of France and assumed the style and titles of the ruler of England – and she used them even after her accession to the French throne, on the death of Henry II, in 1559. The English queen was not unreasonably incensed.

On 10 June 1560 Mary of Guise died, which removed the regent and created a feeling in some Scottish minds that the real queen ought to return. On 5 December Francis II died and Mary was left a widow at the age of eighteen, with no throne in France, excluded from court by the jealousy of the regent, Catherine de Medici, and with the prospect of returning to Scotland, where the Roman religion was proscribed and the Reformation was in full swing under John Knox. The Protestant lords were trying to arrange a marriage between James, the second Earl of Arran, who was heir to the Scottish throne after Mary, and Elizabeth of England. Scotland was a wild, uncivilized and heretical country, turbulent and split into factions. To return from France to Scotland was an act of great courage, especially as few of the lords seemed to want Mary. Elizabeth refused the Arran marriage: at once a reaction in favour of Mary set in.

The period of the negotiations for her return shows Mary at her best. She offered to forget all troubles of the past, she wanted to be recalled by the Scots, and she agreed not to interfere with the new Protestant religion of Scotland. But even at that moment she was playing a double game. She had not made up her mind to go back.

She was desperately anxious to marry. The Guises backed her, hoping to recover their influence in French politics. But all proposals for Mary's marriage were thwarted by Catherine de Medici. At last Mary determined to go back to Scotland. It was an inauspicious moment from the point of view of Elizabeth. Mary was heir to the English throne: she was a Catholic, and the treaty of Edinburgh between Elizabeth and the Scottish Protestant lords was as yet unsigned. Trouble was bound to ensue.

Mary sailed from Calais on 15 August 1561. She had a cheerless journey, she was delayed outside Leith by a dense fog (Knox saw in this 'the sorrow, dolour, darkness and all impiety' which her arrival betokened), and no preparations had been made for her at Holyrood. Mass was said in her private chapel on the first Sunday, which resulted in a stormy interview between Mary and Knox, who came away impressed only by 'her proud mind, crafty wit and indurate heart'. (Knox is no reliable witness.) And indeed her passions – always so much stronger than her political judgements – led her into a great error. She had told Moray that she did not want to interfere with the religion of Scotland: but in fact she had already told the pope that she meant to restore Catholicism to Scotland. And now she burst out at Knox: 'Ye are not the kirk I will nourish. I will defend the Kirk of Rome, for I believe it is the true Kirk of God.'

Efforts have been made to see Mary as a successful ruler of Scotland in the years 1561-7. She did not convince Knox, who noted that 'in the council she kept herself very grave: but as soon as ever her French fillocks and fiddlers and others of that brand gat the house alone, then might be seen skipping not very comely for honest women'. Knox thought that rather than work at the business of being a queen, she preferred to 'shoot at the butts' and to hawk. It is true that Mary's *politique* policy restored a degree of religious peace to Scotland, and that for a while she was able to keep order among the troublesome Scottish nobles. She established quite friendly relations with Elizabeth of England, but her negotiations failed to obtain any recognition of her claims to the English succession, and Elizabeth remained suspicious of her. Within a short time, Mary's government in Scotland was to be challenged, especially after her disastrous marriage to Darnley.

Mary's prime objective when she returned to Scotland was marriage. She wanted at first to marry Don Carlos, son of Philip II, and thus to combine in her own person the thrones of England, Scotland and Spain. To accomplish this she was ready to restore Catholicism in Scotland. But the Guises were opposed to and prevented the marriage. Elizabeth suggested Robert Dudley, Earl of Leicester, but in 1565 there arrived in Scotland Henry Stuart, Lord Darnley, the elder son of the Earl of Lennox and Margaret, daughter of Margaret Tudor, sister of Henry VIII, and the Earl of Lennox. Thus Darnley was heir to the English throne after Mary herself. He was aged nineteen, extraordinarily handsome, very athletic, of the meanest intelligence, arrogant, wilful and vicious. Whether Mary did in fact fall in love with Darnley has been disputed. That she did would seem to be her only justification. If the marriage was simply a political move to strengthen her claim to the English throne, her intelligence failed to reveal to her that Darnley, a Catholic, could only further bind together the English and the Scottish Protestants, could only alarm the Scottish Protestant lords for the safety of their lands, and threaten the hopes of the Hamiltons of reaching the throne of Scotland. At any rate, she married him, perhaps secretly in March, certainly publicly in July 1565. From this ill-judged marriage sprang most of Mary's future troubles.

Darnley was hateful to the Scottish lords, largely on account of his arrogance, his imprudence and his viciousness. Hateful also was David Riccio, one of Mary's musical quartet whom she now raised to be her Foreign Secretary. Moray headed a rebellion, which Mary succeeded in putting down, but she had already found out her mistake in marrying Darnley. His discontent that she refused to give him the Crown Matrimonial (that is, official recognition by parliament of his position as her equal as king and the reversion of the throne to him, were Mary to die first), his weakness of character, and his accusations that she was Riccio's mistress, soon turned her love to hatred. The murder of Riccio in 1566 was followed by the imprisonment of the queen by the lords, but Mary escaped with Darnley, with whom she put up as well as possible until her son was born in June 1566. It is at least probable that she was already in love with Bothwell and anxious to be rid of Darnley. He had just married Jane Gordon, sister of the Earl of Huntly, but within a matter of weeks he had made up his mind to secure the Scottish throne by marrying Mary. When Darnley fell ill at Glasgow – it was said of smallpox, almost certainly of syphilis – Mary attended him frequently, then fetched him away to an isolated house outside Edinburgh, Kirk o' Field, where he might have better air than in the city, the arrangements being left in the hands of Bothwell. She left Darnley there late in the evening of 9 February 1567 and went in the company of Bothwell to Holyrood. Early in the morning of the 10th the house at Kirk o' Field was blown up and the body of Darnley was found under a tree, uninjured by the explosion: he had been strangled before the explosion took place. There is no proof that Mary had any hand in the murder of her husband, or that she even knew it was to take place, since the only purported evidence contained in the Casket Letters must on the whole be rejected. Yet, if she was wholly innocent, her subsequent behaviour with the universally accepted murderer, Bothwell, requires much more explanation than has so far been forthcoming. She made no attempt to exonerate herself when the populace was vociferously accusing her, as she went through the streets. She showered favours on Bothwell, probably agreed to a collusive abduction, and within three months of Darnley's death she had married the by then divorced Bothwell (16 May 1567). Never had Mary behaved with less wisdom or discretion.

Once again Mary's passions had outrun her judgement – or so one is justified in saying, until further evidence in her favour is available. Fairly or unfairly, all Europe turned against her – France, Spain, the pope and her own subjects. The Scottish lords raised an army against her, Mary and Bothwell gathered a small force (mostly adherents of Bothwell's) to meet them. At Carberry Hill, seven miles outside Edinburgh (June 1567), the two sides met, but Mary's army dwindled away without any battle being fought. She was forced to abdicate and was imprisoned in a castle on Loch Leven. Bothwell escaped to Norway. In 1568 Mary escaped from Loch Leven, raised a force to meet her half-brother, the regent, Earl of Moray, but she was defeated at Langside, and then crossed the border into England. Mary is sometimes described as 'fleeing' into England, but she could safely have stayed in Scotland, where her supporters were rallying, or have returned to France, to seek the help of her family. To put herself into Elizabeth's hands was to commit an act of gross political miscalculation. Elizabeth never released Mary, keeping her in one place of imprisonment or another for the next nineteen years. For the first few years, Elizabeth entered into discussions with the Scots and French to achieve Mary's restoration to the throne of Scotland, but all negotiations of this sort failed.

Mary now became the centre, witting or unwitting, of Catholic plots against the life of Elizabeth. Without doubt the extreme Catholics used her for their own ends: without doubt Mary was a party to their plots. She came to approve political assassination too many times for Elizabeth to feel safe or for anybody to believe her protestations. When her brother Moray was murdered (1570), she wrote to Cardinal Beaton that 'she was the more indebted to the assassin that he had acted without her instigation': but she told Moray's widow that the murder was done 'against our will'. She agreed to the plot by which she was to marry the Duke of Norfolk: she was a party to the Ridolfi plot (1571) which was linked with Norfolk's plot: she was pleading with Elizabeth for kindness and at the same moment she was hand in glove with Throckmorton in his plot for the invasion of England and the taking off of Elizabeth (1583): by her own actions she hopelessly entangled herself in the Babington plot (1586), for she dictated a letter to Babington which gave her consent to a rising on her behalf which was to include the murder of Elizabeth. Her arrest, trial

and condemnation followed inevitably. For a long time Elizabeth refused to sign the death warrant, but at last she gave way, and Mary was beheaded at Fotheringay Castle on 8 February 1587.

It is doubtful, however, whether the plots in which Mary engaged were very dangerous to Elizabeth, and Mary's imprisonment in England made the task of conspirators more, not less difficult. Elizabeth gained a great deal from having Mary in prison in England; above all, it tied the Scottish opponents of Mary closely to the English side, and it established a close, lasting alliance between Scotland and England for the first time in the history of what had previously been extremely hostile nations.

Mary has been fortunate in her biographers beyond her deserts. Largely through her dignity and courage at her execution, the spell which she failed to exert on most of her contemporaries she has succeeded in casting on her modern biographers. Mary, Queen of Scots, has become a legendary figure, a shamefully wronged woman, beautiful (Clouet has done his very good best for her), pathetic, romantic and pitiable. Swinburne wrote of her that 'the world never saw more splendid courage at the service of more brilliant intelligence'. That is a travesty of the truth.

It is doubtful how much intelligence she had: it failed her over Darnley and over Bothwell. She had some courage, as in deciding to return to Scotland from France – but what other choice was open to her? That courage failed her after Carberry when, in the Provost's house in Edinburgh, she was seen at the window half-naked and screaming for help. It failed her again after Langside, when she fled to England as fast as a horse could carry her, before her cause was irretrievably lost. And it is difficult not to feel that much of her behaviour in prison in England was unheroic.

It is easy to say that no woman, placed in Mary's circumstances, could have succeeded where she failed. It is as easy to say that in any other circumstances Mary would as surely have ruined her own life. She was a woman destitute of all moral sense, incapable of self-sacrifice, concerned only with her own selfish ends. It is not even true that she remained faithful to the Catholic religion: she abandoned it in order to get the Scottish throne; she would have abandoned it, if there had been the slightest chance of her winning the English throne through the English Protestants. And she, the queen, had not enough authority or will to marry Bothwell according to the Roman ceremony. Mary, Queen of Scots, is pitiable in that she had not enough character to control her passions: it is only by falsifying values, Protestant or Catholic, that she can be called admirable.

From her folly and suffering, however, the union of England and Scotland, in the person of her son, James VI and I, was to be born.

Further Reading

J. Wormald, *Mary, Queen of Scots: a Study in Failure*, 1991.

M. Lynch, ed., *Mary Stewart*, 1987.

G. Donaldson, *Mary, Queen of Scots*, 1974.

A. Fraser, *Mary, Queen of Scots*, 1971.

G. Buchanan, *The Tyrannous Reign of Mary Stewart*, ed. Gatherer, 1958.

MARY BEATRICE OF MODENA (1658-1718), second wife of James II, was the daughter of Duke Alfonso IV of Modena. She had been brought up in a convent and wanted to become a nun; at the time (1673) of the marriage, which was the work of French diplomacy, she was 'but fifteen years old, and so innocently bred that till then she had never heard of such a place as England, nor of such a person as the Duke of York'. The marriage of the heir to the throne to a Catholic in the year of the Test Act could not be popular, and it contributed fuel to the explosion of the Popish Plot five years later. Mary Beatrice acquired a reputation for haughtiness, scarcely surprising in a girl of her background suddenly translated to a strange land full of heretics. Gracious in manners apart from the occasional outbursts of a furious temper, she was quick-witted rather than intelligent. Her piety was deep and genuine, and it is clear that the influence she gradually acquired over James strengthened rather than restrained his Catholicizing zeal. She was apt to make scenes about his continuing attachment to Catherine Sedley and other mistresses, yet she stood firmly and loyally by him, both in the days of his unpopularity during the Exclusion Crisis and in the shadows from 1688 onwards. The birth of her son James Edward in 1688, after the deaths of her five previous children, was received with widespread scepticism which found expression in the 'warming pan' legend; there can be no doubt whatever that the child was genuine. At the Revolution Mary Beatrice seems to have been the principal influence in persuading James to flee his country, and she and the baby prince preceded him to France. In her long exile in France she remained proud, dignified and increasingly devout, a far more spirited figure than the apathetic James, whom she outlived by seventeen years.

Further Reading

Carola Oman, *Mary of Modena*, 1963.

MARY OF ST POL, COUNTESS OF PEMBROKE (1304-77), foundress of Pembroke College, Cambridge and Denney Abbey (Cambs.), was fourth daughter of Guy de Châtillon (*d*.1316), Count of St Pol and a granddaughter of Henry III. The Châtillons and Valences, her husband's family, were both of European importance. On the childless death of her husband Aymer, Earl of Pembroke in 1324, she received for life lands in England, Wales and Ireland worth £750 and more in France. Young and rich widows normally remarried and indeed her marriage was granted to a son of the Earl of March in 1327, but she remained single throughout her fifty-three-year widowhood. Although defrauded by the Despensers of property later valued at £20,000, this does not adequately explain why Aymer's will remained unsettled in 1377. The estates she bought, her religious foundations, and her evident wealth indicate the low priority given to the husband she scarcely knew.

Mary had four French ladies in her entourage in 1325 and always employed French clerks. She made four lengthy visits to France and bequeathed to the king a sword without a point, a clear indication of her preference for peace rather than war. She provided Pembroke College with external rectors as at the University of Paris and urged it to recruit French scholars. Ultimately forced by the Hundred Years' War to choose between England and France, she opted for England, where she had more property, and where her high standing is shown both by the favours received from Edward III and her selection as custodian of the young Princess Joan of Woodstock. She pestered successive popes for a stream of privileges for her clerks, her foundations and herself. Her land transactions and her ruthlessness towards the recalcitrant nuns of Waterbeach show her capacity to manage her affairs and have her own way. She remained single because she preferred the independence that her wealthy widowhood gave her.

Mary's foundations comprised a chantry at Westminster Abbey, a house of Franciscan nuns (Minoresses) at Denney, and Pembroke College, Cambridge, besides lesser donations and two abortive Carthusian monasteries. The Minoresses were a highly aristocratic, exclusive and strictly enclosed order originating in a nunnery at Longchamp founded with a special papal rule in 1263 by Louis IX's (St Louis) sister the Blessed Isabella. Two English houses were founded in 1293 at Aldgate in London (the Minories) and, by Denise Munchensy, at Waterbeach (Cambs.). Initially Mary patronized Waterbeach, then founded Denney (1339) and forcibly transferred the nuns there from Waterbeach. Denney received more land and privileges, becoming a major house with forty-one nuns in 1379. Mary's Hall of Valence Marie of 1347 at Cambridge, later Pembroke College, received generous endowments of £106, a chapel, and other privileges. When aged only twenty, Mary took sixteen Franciscans to France and always kept several absentee parsons with her. The pope allowed her first to enter nunneries with female attendants (1333), then with ladies and knights (1334), then with her household, and then to eat and sleep in houses of both men and women (1364). She even built private quarters in Denney Abbey. The final stage in her religious progress was her choice in 1377 to be buried in the habit of a Minoress. Her piety was not the product of old age and proximity of death, but was already present in her twenties.

Further Reading
M. A. Hicks, 'The English Minoresses and their Benefactors 1281-1367', *Monastic Studies – The Continuity of the Tradition*, ed. J. Loades, 1990.
J. R. S. Phillips, *Aymer de Valence, Earl of Pembroke 1307-24: Baronial Politics in the Reign of Edward II*, 1972.
H. Jenkinson, 'Mary de Sancto Paulo, Foundress of Pembroke College, Cambridge', *Archaeologia* lxvi, 1914-15.

MARY TUDOR (1496-1533), Queen of France, Duchess of Suffolk, grandmother of Lady Jane Grey, was born probably early in March 1496, and she died in 1533. She was the second daughter of Henry VII and Elizabeth of York, and therefore sister of Henry VIII. In 1508 she was betrothed to Charles of Castile, afterwards the Emperor Charles V. In 1509 her father died and her brother succeeded as Henry VIII. In 1514 arrangements were all but completed for her marriage to Charles, but the Emperor Maximilian I, Charles's grandfather, played false and the marriage never took place.

Henry VIII was not the man to lie down under such an insult. Swiftly and secretly he made peace with France and compelled his sister, who was eighteen years old, to marry Louis XII of France, an enfeebled and sickly old man of fifty-two. Mary was much in love with Charles Brandon, Duke of Suffolk, and she only agreed to marry Louis XII on condition that, were he to die, she should be free to marry whom she would. Her marriage with the French king lasted only eight months, for Louis died on 1 January 1515. Left alone in France, Mary was in a perilous position. To save herself from being compelled to make another political marriage either by Francis I or by Henry VIII, she persuaded Suffolk (who had pledged his word to Henry not to marry Mary without his consent) to marry her secretly in Paris, probably in the last week of February 1515. Henry was furious, not because he disliked the marriage, but because Suffolk had broken his word and the marriage was made without Henry's consent, and he was only placated by a present of £24,000 and 200,000 French crowns and all the plate, jewels and rich clothing which had formed part of Mary's dowry.

The marriage was generally unpopular in England, and therefore the duke and duchess retired into private life in Norfolk. During a short visit to London in 1516 Mary gave birth to a son. A year later she entertained Catherine of Aragon on her way to Walsingham (March 1517). In July she was at court, whence she moved to Hatfield, where she stayed in order to have her second baby, Frances, who became the mother of Lady Jane Grey. The king's anger over the marriage was short-lived: he had a deep affection for his sister Mary, much more than he had for his other sister, Margaret, the Queen of Scotland, and Mary was frequently at court. Her health was never strong, and she was from time to time seriously ill, but was able to meet her one-time affianced husband,

Charles V, when he visited England in 1520; she was able also to accompany Henry VIII to the Field of Cloth of Gold, during which a treaty was made with Francis I which restored a great part of her dowry.

When Henry entered on his divorce from Catherine of Aragon, Mary was strongly on the side of the queen, largely because she could not tolerate seeing Anne Boleyn, once one of her ladies-in-waiting, raised to the position of queen above herself, who had once been a queen.

The rest of her life is historically unimportant. She died on 24 June 1533 at Westhorpe in Suffolk and was buried in the abbey of Bury St Edmunds. That monastery was dissolved in 1538, and the coffin was moved into St Mary's church. It was opened in 1784 and Horace Walpole and the Duchess of Portland took away some locks of Mary's hair.

Mary Tudor was an exceptionally beautiful woman, not only physically but also in character. Her beauty of face was known throughout Europe: she never lost the deep feelings which Henry had for her: she won the hearts of all France by her devoted treatment of Louis XII. Her family life with Suffolk was one of untarnished happiness. Like all the Tudors she loved music and was an accomplished musician. She had a gay nature and a light step for dancing, she adored beautiful clothes and enjoyed to the full the fun and pageantry of the life into which she was born. She had also strength and courage to tell her formidable brother just how far he could go, and to fight for what she thought to be due to the meanest of her servants. No wonder that Mary Tudor has gone down in history and in modern literature as the most romantic of a hard-bitten family.

Further Reading
J. Gainey, *The Princess of the 'Mary Rose'*, 1986.
M. C. Brown, *Mary Tudor, Queen of France*, 1911.
M. A. E. Green, *Lives of the Princesses of England*, vol. 5, 1850-55: an admirable essay.

MASCA, PANDULF (*d.*1226) was an Italian papal official who, between 1219 and 1221, in the words of T. F. Tout, 'almost acted as King of England' and, unlike some who actually wore the crown in this period, did so with considerable skill and success. A sub-deacon of the Roman church, Pandulf first came to England in 1211 on an unsuccessful mission to negotiate an end to the Interdict, earning notoriety and praise for apparently resisting John's attempts at physical intimidation. Two years later, in very different circumstances, Pandulf was back to receive John's submission and cession of the kingdom to the pope. From 1213 to 1215, Pandulf continued to act as a papal agent in England, for some of the time under the Legate Nicholas (1213-14). His reward, illustrating the new Angevin-papal alliance, was his election to the see of Norwich in 1215. In the same year he returned to

Rome to attend the Lateran Council and resume work in the papal chamber. Although in the confidence of the new pope, Honorius III, with whom he may have worked at the Curia, Pandulf never became a cardinal. When, in 1218, he was appointed to succeed the distinguished Cardinal Guala as Legate to England, he had to rely on his personality, ability and the full papal authority ('*plenarium potestatem*') Honorius granted him in matters spiritual and temporal.

In the first few months as legate, Pandulf made such a good impression that in April 1219 the dying regent, William Marshal, commended the young Henry III to his guardianship, despite the furious protestations of the king's tutor, Peter des Roches. After the regent's death, a governing triumvirate emerged of the legate, Peter des Roches and the justiciar, Hubert de Burgh. Unlike Guala, Pandulf was an experienced administrator who concerned himself closely in government. While consulting meticulously with his colleagues, as legate and guardian of the king he took the lead. It was his implementation of the papally inspired policy of resumption of royal castles, lands and rights and renewed control over local agents of the Crown that gave the Minority government its direction and objective. Under the slogan Pandulf used to the justices of the bench in 1220 'royal rights are to be preserved' and publically stated in repeated papal bulls of 1219, 1220 and 1221, this policy provided the foundation upon which Angevin government could be rebuilt.

Pandulf was not shy in getting involved in specific cases, but his activity was inevitably wide. He initiated talks leading to peace with the Welsh and the 1220 truce with Scotland. To underpin the campaign for restitution of the king's rights, he organized Henry III's second coronation in 1220 in a more orthodox ceremony than the hugger-mugger affair of 1216. Typical of his diplomatic treatment of colleagues, Pandulf allowed the sensitive Archbishop Langton to exercise his traditional right to crown the king. As legate, as well as controlling ecclesiastical patronage, Pandulf lent material support to the régime. Where lay taxation, such as the scutage of 1217 or the 1220 carucage, produced meagre sums, his profitable tax for the crusade allowed him to give loans to the government, thus, in D. Carpenter's words, becoming its paymaster as well as director.

By 1221, central authority was becoming more accepted; the policy of resumption was beginning to bear fruit and, especially important, royal income was at last rising substantially (the £8,000 raised in 1220 was £3,000 more than the previous year): and it never looked back. Politically, however, Pandulf's position in both church and state was becoming increasingly anomalous in the face of the growing authority of Langton and Hubert de Burgh, or so, at least, Langton on a visit to Rome, seems to have persuaded the pope. On the

archbishop's return to England in July 1221, Pandulf resigned, not to be replaced. Back in Rome in 1222, he was finally consecrated Bishop of Norwich. His interest in English affairs remained to the end. In 1225, he was encouraging Hubert de Burgh in his handling of the rebels of 1223-4, urging him to ensure that 'the pride of the traitors does not ascend further than is expedient'. However, Pandulf did not meddle after his retirement. He was in no position to, as his authority had always been that of a representative, never wielded in his own right. He remained simply a bishop *in absentia*. In 1226 his body was brought to Norwich for burial in the cathedral he had never entered as bishop in life. Like so many of his contemporaries, Pandulf's career knew no nationalities. With his predecessor Guala, Pandulf, despite his relatively modest status, put into practice the rhetoric of papal monarchy as effectively as anyone in the Middle Ages. This may explain his relative neglect by champions of an insular reading of English history. It is ironic that so many of those who in these years stood between England and factional anarchy were not natives. But unlike many of the others, Pandulf earned the accolade of local praise: even Matthew Paris had a good word to say for him.

Further Reading
D. Carpenter, *The Minority of Henry III*, 1990.

MASHAM, ABIGAIL (née HILL) (*d.*1734) was a distant relative of Sarah Churchill, Duchess of Marlborough, who crowned many kindnesses to her and to her brother Jack by obtaining for her the post of Woman of the Bedchamber to Queen Anne. She may also have been related to Robert Harley, who used her to break the long-standing and intimate friendship between the queen and the Marlboroughs. A plain red-nosed woman, Abigail Masham was determined, even-tempered, patient and of Tory opinions. Trevelyan calls her 'mean-souled', 'an adventuress, a listener at keyholes'. Even without these qualities she would no doubt have provided something of a relief to the queen from the outbursts and hectorings of Sarah; with them, she was an excellent tool for a politician anxious to end the domination of Marlborough. In 1707 she married Samuel Masham, Groom of the Bedchamber to Prince George. By the November of that year Sarah, only too well aware of what was happening, was writing of 'the black ingratitude of Mrs Masham, a woman that I took out of a garret and saved from starving'. Within two years more, Abigail, in command of 'the back way into the queen's closet', had almost achieved her design, assisted by the stormy anger of the woman she was supplanting. In January 1710 there was a political crisis brought about by Anne's offer, without consulting Marlborough, of a regiment to Jack Hill. The duke threatened to resign unless Abigail was dismissed. The dispute was patched up: Abigail kept her post, Jack did not get his. Yet the end of the Marlboroughs' power was within sight. In April came the last meeting of Sarah and the queen, and four months later Anne dismissed Godolphin, the other pillar of the duke's power at court.

It is arguable that the effect of Abigail Masham's intrigues may easily be overrated, and that the unpopularity of the war at this stage would have brought Godolphin and the Marlboroughs down before long. To Harley, the prime mover in the affair, Abigail Masham was as much a political fact at this stage of British political development as the unsatisfactory nature of Marlborough's victory at Malplaquet. But Harley, like Sarah, was himself to suffer from Abigail's lack of gratitude. When in 1711 the gulf between Harley and St John began to grow, she began to turn to St John, who was adroit enough to win her support by backing, against Harley's wishes, the unsuccessful Quebec expedition of that year, whose military commander was Jack Hill. In 1712 her husband, thanks to Harley, became Lord Masham, one of the dozen peers created to get 'peace without Spain' through the lords. Yet in the rivalry of the last years of Anne's reign Abigail, characteristically, employed her malice, her talents for intrigue, and her influence over her mistress against Harley. There were rumours that she was profitably involved in dubious transactions in the South Sea Company, rumours only scotched by Anne's prorogation of her last parliament. For her, as for St John, success came too slowly this time. The death of Anne in 1714 threw Abigail Masham into the obscurity of private life.

MASON, SIR JOSIAH (1795-1881), designed and manufactured steel pen-nibs. A Kidderminster boy, he had an inventive turn of mind, and created a split key-ring which could be produced by machinery. In 1829 he sent three sample pens to a Mr Perry in London. Two days later, Mr Perry was in Birmingham, and Josiah Mason was a pen-maker. He used cedar-wood holders, with metal receptacles for the 'slit' nibs. The scale of his production grew rapidly, and by 1874 his annual output was said to be 234 million nibs with more than three tons of steel being rolled each week for his 1,000 workers: this despite the appearance of John Joseph Parker's 'fountain', or 'reservoir', pens in 1835. He branched out into electro-plating and the manufacture of india-rubber bands, and used some of his wealth to found a College of Science in Birmingham in 1879, which helped to prompt the founding of Birmingham University. Despite the spluttering and scraping of crossed or bent nibs, the speed with which the quill was replaced by the steel-nibbed pen showed the importance of the achievement of Mason, and his rival Joseph Gillott, in producing 'the knitting-needle of civilization'. The queen, who used her own pens more than most, properly recognized this by

knighting him. He remained a Midlander all his life, and died in Erdington.

Further Reading
Asa Briggs, *Victorian Things*, 1988.

MATILDA (1102-67), for a few months in 1141, seemed about to become the first queen regnant in English history. Her failure to do so rested as much on her own mistakes as on the deep-seated misogyny of twelfth-century public life. Two of her contemporaries, Urraca of Castile (in 1109) and Melisende of Jerusalem (in 1131) inherited their fathers' crowns, although not without controversy. Matilda's inability to make good her claim may have been predictable, but not inevitable. Her career falls into three periods: marriage to the Holy Roman Emperor (1109-25); heiress and claimant to the Anglo-Norman realm (1127-42); patroness of the inheritance of her son, Henry, in England (1142-8) and Normandy (1148-53). Like all noble heiresses outside the cloister, Matilda's life and actions were defined by men: her father, husbands, rivals, allies and son. Unlike many, however, Matilda played an active role in her own destiny, provoking one contemporary to call her 'a woman of the stock of tyrants'.

The eldest child of Henry I, Matilda received a bluestocking education, first in England at the cultivated court of her mother, Queen Matilda, then, after 1110 and her betrothal, in Germany by Archbishop Bruno of Trier. This training for a politically influential life was hard, Matilda later recalling being beaten regularly by a terrifying aunt. The marriage alliance with Germany, concluded in 1109, was of considerable diplomatic importance for Henry I, witnessed by the dowry of 10,000 silver marks he offered. Henry stood to gain an ally against the King of France and, equally important to a monarch whose authority rested on coup d'état and military conquest, enhanced status as the emperor's father-in-law. For Matilda, her marriage to Henry V, solemnized in 1114, was a defining moment. Although she survived Henry by over forty years, took another husband, and identified herself with Normandy and England, she retained the title of empress: her son by her second marriage was known as Henry FitzEmpress. Matilda was no passive consort; she witnessed royal *acta*; channelled petitions to the king; performed as titular regent in Italy (1118-19); corresponded with her father; and, on her husband's death from cancer in 1125, was entrusted with the imperial insignia. On the election of Lothar of Supplinberg as the new King of Germany, Matilda returned to her father, laden with jewels and relics, ready to be groomed for a new, no less exalted position than the one she left behind.

In 1120, Matilda's brother, William, drowned in the White Ship, leaving her Henry I's sole surviving legitimate child. Although he remarried in 1121 (Matilda's mother having died in 1118), Henry had no more legitimate children, nor, by 1126, as he neared sixty, was he likely to after five years of childless marriage. Henry's choices were limited. His elder brother, Robert, was still in one of his prisons and, unsurprisingly, the king rejected Robert's son, William Clito. Of his own bastards, the eldest, Robert of Gloucester, was suitable in all things except his unacceptability to the church and, increasingly, to a lay baronage whose titles to land rested on legitimacy. Henry had showered lands and honours on his nephew, Stephen of Blois, son of his sister Adela, but more as a means of building up a loyal family block of support for his designated heir rather than as a signal of preference for the inheritance itself. His choice was eased by what he may have seen as his daughter's aptitude for public business. Her training had ensured she had a mind of her own and sufficient, perhaps excessive, self-confidence to act independently. Whatever his emotional attachment (hardly strong in practice as he had scarcely seen her between her ninth and twenty-fourth year), Henry decided that his dynasty was to hold the throne, not those of his siblings.

His decision is explicable in the context of his rise, against expectations, to power through his own initiative and skill. It was also not unique. At precisely the same time, another self-made monarch, Baldwin II of Jerusalem, was facing death with no sons. Like Henry, he settled the succession on a daughter, Melisende. The parallel was hardly coincidental, as the Jerusalem and the Anglo-Norman arrangements were closely linked. To secure Matilda's succession, two things were necessary: her formal acceptance by the magnates and a husband, to provide heirs and military leadership. Henry extracted oaths of allegiance to Matilda in 1127, 1131 and 1133 (and possibly 1128); and in 1128, she was married to Geoffrey of Anjou whose father, Count Fulk, departed immediately after the ceremony to become the consort of Melisende of Jerusalem, leaving Geoffrey as Count of Anjou and, thus, a suitable match for Henry I's heir. There was, however, a difference in Baldwin's and Henry's succession settlements: under the former, Fulk became King of Jerusalem on Baldwin's death alongside his wife; Geoffrey was designated no such status, the allegiance sworn to Matilda in 1131 being to her alone. She was to be more than the vessel of the dynasty's continuity.

In fact that continuity was by no means easily secured. Matilda had been reluctant to marry Geoffrey, a decade her junior. The match made good diplomatic sense, protecting Normandy's southern flank and balancing the perennial hostility of Capetian France and the prospective antagonism of Blois. But the Angevins were traditionally suspect to the Norman baronage, with whom, especially with loyalists such as her half-brother Robert and Brian FitzCount, Matilda had forged close political links. Matilda possibly contrasted the status and surroundings of her two husbands. Equally, she had a notoriously sour nature and he a famously shallow one. Despite the urgency to provide Henry I with a grandson, they lived apart between 1129 and 1131 and perhaps only the prospect of the succession to Anjou going to his Jerusalem half-brothers in Palestine (the first of whom was born in 1131) persuaded Geoffrey to a reconciliation. More certain was Henry I's hostility towards Geoffrey which could only be assuaged (and then only partially) by producing the desired heir. Thus a combination of duty and greed led to the births of Henry (1133), Geoffrey (1134) and William (1136).

While Henry I denied his son-in-law any influence in Normandy, still less England, Matilda spent much time at Rouen where her father and his ministers could introduce her to government administration. But Henry's preparations came to nothing after his death in December 1135, his failure to admit Geoffrey into favour being perhaps crucial, as it left the field free for Stephen of Blois's coup d'état. By Easter 1136, only one English tenant-in-chief had not acknowledged Stephen as king, including those most closely associated with Matilda. Her attempts to reverse the decision of 1135-6 were hampered by the fact of Stephen's coronation and anointing; the near-unanimity of secular and ecclesiastical acceptance of his title once he had been crowned; and Geoffrey's lack of interest in England: throughout his marriage his main concern was to further Angevin interests by annexing Normandy.

If Stephen had proved a successful ruler, Matilda's claim would have languished and lapsed. But a series of mistakes, blunders and defeats, most notably the failure to gain firm control of Normandy in 1137, opened a path for Matilda to contest the throne. Although the Welsh and Scots, whose king, David, was Matilda's maternal uncle, failed to dent Stephen's régime in 1138, disaffection grew in 1139, encouraging Matilda to assert her rights. Landing in Bristol in September 1139, she attracted the support of former allies, officials and favourites of Henry I, including her half-brothers, Robert of Gloucester and Reginald of Cornwall; Baldwin de Redvers; Miles of Gloucester; Bishop Nigel of Ely and Brian FitzCount. Her followers shared no obvious guiding principle (although political disappointment and the desire for recognized tenurial legitimacy have been suggested) other than loyalty to Henry I's wishes – and self-interest. Matilda's power was confined largely to the west country and her supporters' estates. For most of the next decade, victory or defeat were impractical, as neither Matilda nor Stephen attracted overwhelming baronial backing. The king usually enjoyed majority allegiance, but Matilda's adherents were a powerful, loyal and tight-knit group that could not be destroyed by the royalists. In addition, after 1137 Stephen could not rely on Normandy, which was finally lost to Geoffrey in 1144. Military equilibrium was matched by political impasse. There were no grounds for compromise. Either Stephen was king or not: only death or decision of war could alter that.

The stalemate was briefly broken in 1141 after the defeat and capture of Stephen at the battle of Lincoln (February). From his prison at Bristol Stephen released his vassals from their allegiance; his brother, the papal legate Bishop Henry of Winchester, accepted Matilda as 'Lady of the English' in March; Stephen's party began to collapse; Normandy rapidly gave way to Count Geoffrey, who overran the duchy except for some pockets of resistance only finally overcome in 1144. But Matilda's support was fragile. There was a disappointing attendance at an assembly at Winchester intended to confirm her authority (April) which was disrupted by royal partisans who were being rallied by Stephen's wife. More serious was Matilda's failure to secure the surrender of significant garrisons between her and London, notably Wallingford and Windsor. With Kent and London itself in the hands of royalist sympathizers, Matilda's hopes of coronation at Westminster depended on further appeasement. In June, she bought the adherence of Geoffrey de Mandeville, castellan of the Tower. This allowed her in June to establish herself temporarily at Westminster. Here her high-handedness, arrogance and lack of tact alienated baronial support and infuriated the Londoners. She even managed to fall out with Henry of Blois, on whose continued support she depended for her chance of success. When she haughtily threatened the Londoners with a heavy tax, they attacked Westminster, forcing her to flee unceremoniously to Oxford. A few weeks later, the Rout of Winchester (August), from which Matilda herself barely escaped, reversed the verdict of Lincoln with the capture of Robert of Gloucester. By the end of 1141, after the exchange of prisoners, Stephen was restored and, if anything, Matilda's position was worse than it had been twelve months earlier. Her behaviour, domineering towards allies and vindictive towards opponents, exacerbated doubts as to the suitability of a woman as monarch.

Although remaining the focal point of resistance to Stephen until 1148, Matilda's chance of the throne had gone. A new pattern emerged. After her dramatic escape through enemy lines from Oxford on a snowy winter night in December 1142, Matilda maintained her base at Devizes. The beneficiary of Stephen's political mistakes, such as his ill-judged mistreatment of Ranulf of Chester (1146), she was unable to make headway against secure royalist domination to the east and north. Her pleas for assistance to her husband, who completed the conquest of Normandy in 1144, were ignored. From the moment of his perilous landing in England in November 1142, Matilda's hopes were concentrated on her son, Henry.

Increasingly irrelevant to the future of English politics, in 1148, a year after the death of Robert of Gloucester, Matilda settled in Normandy leaving her son to make good his own claim in England. It might have been more prudent for Henry I to have designated his grandson heir in the first place: perhaps his daughter refused to countenance being by-passed; it would have been in character.

The rest of Matilda's life was spent nurturing her son's interests, as vice-regent in Normandy and in diplomatic dealings with Germany and France. To the end of her life, when she attempted to mediate between Henry II and Louis VII of France, she refused to embrace dignified inaction. Perhaps that was one of her problems: against the logic of the times she had insisted on an effective political role as the head of her own party. By doing so, in some eyes she compromised her cause. Her qualities of energy, arrogance, bravery, commendable in a man, were condemned in a woman. In all senses she could not win. Described by contemporary writers as a striking, forceful and unbending woman, her attempts to rule were seen as unfeminine. On the other hand, she successfully retained the loyalty of important English magnates and displayed considerable tenacity in adversity. It was her failure to match this with charm and magnanimity that sealed her fate. Constitutionally, it is hard to see that Matilda represented anything except herself and her family interest. Her eagerness to disinherit Stephen and his heirs of the Honour of Boulogne in 1141 demonstrated she stood for no principle of inheritance or legitimacy. Her career emphasized that, in spite of largely clerically-inspired theories of election and consecration, and the secular lip-service paid to inheritance and designation, royal power depended chiefly on occupancy. This Stephen achieved in 1135-6 and Matilda failed to grasp in 1141. Yet her career was not entirely unsuccessful: all subsequent monarchs of England have been her descendants, not Stephen's.

Further Reading
M. Chibnall, *The Empress Matilda*, 1991.

MATILDA OF BOULOGNE (?1103-52; Queen of England 1135-52; wife of King Stephen) was the daughter of Eustace III, Count of Boulogne. Matilda proved herself a vigorous and effective politician in her own right, one of a number of such tough twelfth-century bluestockings such as her namesake and rival the Empress Matilda; Eleanor of Aquitaine; or the two Languedoc Ermengards, of Narbonne and Béziers. As well as being heiress to one of the more strategic counties of north-west Europe and a large fief centred on Essex, Matilda was closely related to the Kings of Jerusalem, the Counts of Flanders, and the Kings of Scotland (Malcolm III was her maternal grandfather). Through her mother she was a direct descendant of

Ethelred the Unready: through her father, of Charle- magne. Married to Stephen of Blois in 1125, Matilda brought to her husband spectacular lineage, significant wealth and a determination and energy which he often lacked. It was from her county that Stephen launched his successful coup in 1135. In 1138, Matilda supervised the capture of Dover castle from the empress's partisans. The following year, she negotiated a treaty with her uncle, David I of Scotland. In 1140, she arranged a mar- riage alliance with France and discussed the prospects of peace with Robert of Gloucester at a conference at Bath. In 1141 Matilda's role was crucial for the survival of Stephen's cause. She rallied his supporters after the king's defeat and capture at Lincoln; harried diplo- matically the turncoat Bishop of Winchester, finally win- ning him back to Stephen's side; manipulated the favours of the Londoners against the empress; and played an important role in the rout of the king's enemies at Winchester. The royalist *Gesta Stephani* admiringly described Matilda as 'a woman of subtlety and a man's resolution' who 'bore herself with the valour of a man'. In later years she seems to have concentrated on the prospects of her children, in particular her son and heir, Eustace. In her vigorous pursuit of her family's interests and her ability to replace her husband when required, Matilda conformed to a type of medieval heiress far removed from the blushing, playful, politically neutered objects of contemporary romancers' imagined devotions.

Further Reading
R. H. C. Davis, *King Stephen*, 1967.

MAUDSLAY, HENRY (1771-1831), inventor, was the son of William Maudslay, a joiner by trade who made textile machinery before joining the artillery as a wheel- wright; he was wounded and discharged but found work at the Woolwich Arsenal. Henry was born there and his first job was making and filling cartridges. He moved to the blacksmith's shop and acquired local fame as a metal worker; when he was eighteen Joseph Bramah, the Barnsley inventor, sent for him. He was received sus- piciously by the foreman because he had not served an apprenticeship. He proved his skill on the spot by renovating an old vice. At twenty-eight Maudslay was Bramah's head foreman. He had helped to make the first Bramah safety lock and he had married Bramah's housemaid, Sarah Tindel. But he was refused a rise in wages – he was paid 30*s.* a week – and so he left and set up his own workshop and smithy just off Oxford Street. He later moved to a larger workshop in Cavendish Square, where he eventually employed eighty men.

His first important improvement was the slide rest ('Maudslay's go-cart' and a boon to operatives who hitherto, when using a lathe, had to hold the cutting tool against the revolving metal, which made it hard to maintain level pressure and was also very tiring). His

screw-cutting lathe was produced in about 1800. Leonardo da Vinci had first designed some such machine. The Frenchman Senot had produced a model in 1795. Maudslay's was enormously superior, combining slide-rest lead screws and change-gears in a screw- cutting lathe that could achieve remarkable accuracy. Hitherto, every screw thread had to be made by hand and each nut was different from another. It was left to his pupil Whitworth to standardize screw threads. One feature of Maudslay's lathe is that it is made entirely from metal; it marks the abandonment of wood in the construction of metal-working machines. Accuracy was the hall-mark of all his work. His bench micrometer, which served as the ultimate standard in his work- shops, was a court of appeal, and he called it the Lord Chancellor.

Maudslay's biggest commission came from the admir- alty during the war. They wanted pulley blocks in large numbers: one battleship alone used 1,400 blocks. Marc Brunel designed a labour-saving machine for making them and Maudslay was commissioned to put his designs into effect. He completed the task in six years. There were forty-three machines to carry out each oper- ation from cutting the elm logs to completing the pulley blocks – machines for sawing, boring, mortising, shaping, rounding and milling, all worked by a thirty- two h.p. steam engine. The machines were successful and costs and time were cut; some of the machines were still in use until recently at Portsmouth dockyard.

Among the patents Maudslay took out were a calico printing machine, a differential gear hoist, and a machine for softening water by aeration. He had eventually to move his expanding business to a disused riding school in Lambeth. There the sign of 'Maudslay, Sons & Field' was erected. In 1826 Thomas Allen described his 'exten- sive factory … steam engines, tanks for shipping, and all works connected with various factories, are here executed in the best manner. They occasionally employ upwards of 200 men'. The eldest son managed the busi- ness after his father's death. Clement, inventor of the metal-planing machine, Whitworth, who standardized screw threads and exhibited at the Great Exhibition a measuring machine capable of measuring to one- millionth of an inch, and Nasmyth, inventor of the steam hammer, were the most famous of Maudslay's pupils. Nasmyth recalled his insistence upon the strictest accu- racy: 'No-one that I ever met could go beyond Henry Maudslay himself in his dexterous use of the file. By a few masterly strokes he could produce plane surfaces so true that when their accuracy was tested by a standard plane surface of absolute truth, they were never found defective'.

Henry Maudslay, who liked to remind his employees of the virtues of economy and simplicity – 'Put to your- self the question, "What business has it to be there?", avoid complexities, and make everything as simple as possible' – was the perfect model for Samuel Smiles and his theme 'self help'.

Further Reading
K. R. Gilbert, *Henry Maudslay*, Science Museum booklet, 1971.
J. B. Jeffreys, *The Story of the Engineers*, 1945.

MAUNY, LORD WALTER (*d.*1372), founder of the London Charterhouse, was the most distinguished of the Hainaulters who accompanied Queen Philippa of Hainault to England in 1327 on her marriage to Edward III. Although then only an esquire, he was of noble birth, the son of John le Borgne de Mauny, Lord of Mauny near Valenciennes, and a relative of the Counts of Hainault themselves. He inherited lands from both parents in Hainault and continued to visit them even after he became an important landowner in England. His English possessions were the rewards of royal service and of his marriage in 1352 to the great royal heiress Margaret Marshall, Dowager-Lady Segrave and eventually Duchess of Norfolk (1397). This was no més-alliance, for Mauny was knighted in 1331, summoned to parliament as a baron in 1347, and became a knight of the Garter in 1359. He was the oldest and perhaps the ablest of Edward III's outstanding military commanders.

Mauny's first campaigns from 1332 were with Edward Balliol in Scotland and from 1337 at sea as admiral. He attacked the Isle of Cadzand at the mouth of the Scheldt, securing prisoners worth £8,000 and grants of land in reward from Edward III. Henceforth until 1360 he campaigned almost continuously in Brittany (1342), Gascony (1345), Calais (1347), the Low Countries, Scotland and at sea, always with distinction, but without participating in any of the great battles. He was also frequently engaged in diplomacy with the French. His disgrace in the crisis of 1340 was brief indeed and he held office in Wales and even, in 1368, in Ireland. Resumption of hostilities saw him as second-in-command, in spite of his advanced age, in the expedition of John of Gaunt in 1369, his last campaign.

Mauny was a hardened professional soldier, who made his fortune from war, but he also built up an international reputation for chivalry. He was, we are told, 'one who loved honour more than silver', and his career was punctuated by the quixotic acts of individual courage and prowess that contemporaries so admired. In 1342, for example, when he sallied with a few companions from a Breton castle to destroy a French siege-engine, he was attacked by the French, whom he could easily have evaded. Vowing instead to unhorse one of them, he engaged in unnecessary close combat, and thus had considerable difficulty in returning to the security of the castle. Again in 1346 he released a Norman knight without ransom in return for a safe-conduct from Gascony to Valenciennes. Captured by Philip VI, who wished to execute him, it was only the intervention of the future John II that prevented an abrupt end to his career. In spite of such counter-productive episodes, his career, like those of the Black Prince and Sir John Chandos, shows how the English, unlike the French, somehow reconciled chivalric ideals and individual feats of arms with the organization and discipline necessary for victory in battle.

Mauny, characteristically, was also a man of deep piety. In 1349 he acquired lands near Smithfield, London for a burial ground, where 50,000 plague victims were reputedly buried. There he built a chapel of the Annunciation of the Blessed Virgin Mary, which Pope Clement VI agreed could become a secular college of thirteen chaplains. Mauny, however, changed his mind by 1361, when he transferred the property to Michael Northburgh, apparently as trustee. Instead in 1371 Mauny secured a licence to found on the site a house of Carthusian monks, the strictest contemporary religious order, still to be dedicated to the Annunciation (*La Salutation Mère Dieu*), and left £2,000 in his will for its implementation, which Northburgh duly completed. Mauny was buried in his new monastery.

Further Reading
J. H. Harvey, *The Black Prince and his Age*, 1976.

MAURICE (*fl.*1174-87) was probably responsible for building two of the most impressive English stone keeps of the twelfth century, at Newcastle-upon-Tyne and Dover. Described in 1174-5 as a *cementarius* (mason) at Newcastle, he may have been involved throughout its building 1171-7. Between 1181 and 1187 he was in charge of construction at Dover as an *ingeniator* (engineer), being paid at the unusually high rate of one shilling a day. In 1181, he received over £3 as a gift from the king. This value placed on his work and the similarities of design between Newcastle and Dover points to Maurice as their architect. In style, both are dominated by traditional donjons: regular, rectangular stone towers, like the Tower of London of the previous century. These were being superseded by polygonal keeps (such as at Orford 1165-73) which gave defenders greater coverage of besiegers. Nevertheless, Maurice's keeps were impressive defences. They were also very expensive: Newcastle cost up to £1,000, while the price for Dover was nearly £4,000, perhaps a quarter of the English king's annual income. Maurice has been described as 'the greatest, as he was the last, of the exponents of the square donjon'.

That financially hard-pressed monarchs were prepared to spend such vast sums on castles demonstrates their importance as centres of administration, political control, military garrisons and defence. From William the Conqueror's makeshift pallisades at Pevensey and

Hastings in 1066, to the motte and baileys which helped secure the French conquest of England, to the great stone fortifications at London, Colchester, Rochester, Windsor, Winchester, Nottingham or Norwich, castles played a crucial role in English political life. Henry II spent over £20,000 on some ninety castles over thirty-three years. Much more than success in set-piece battles, control of castles formed the pivotal objectives of kings and their opponents in every major crisis of the period, for example the establishment of William I's power 1066-9 and Henry II's in the 1150s or the civil wars of 1088, 1139-53, 1173-4, 1215-17 and 1263-5. The royal garrison at Orford effectively hampered Hugh Bigod's manoeuvres in East Anglia in 1173-4, while, on the other hand, Brian FitzCount's castle at Wallingford in Stephen's reign, Falkes de Bréauté's fortress at Bedford in 1224 and the Montfort stronghold at Kenilworth in 1265-6 proved intractible obstacles to royal supremacy. Thus the work of servants such as Maurice was central to royal government, a role brought to its apogee by the building of the Edwardian castles in north Wales, symbols of almost imperial might, by the Savoyard James of St George in the 1270s and 1280s.

Further Reading
J. Harvey, *English Mediaeval Architects*, 1987.

MAURICE, FREDERICK DENISON (1805-72) was a theologian of remarkable originality and breadth of mind, whose concern about social justice led him to espouse co-operative socialism and schemes for adult education.

He was born near Lowestoft, in Suffolk where his father was a Unitarian minister. There was discomfort in belonging to a small sect: defensive attitudes within the circle; outside it, prejudice and rejection. His mother and sisters, also bruised, moved towards Anglicanism. His was a more complicated journey. Intelligence and ambition took him to Trinity College, Cambridge, and the study of law, but scruples prevented his graduating: he refused to subscribe to the Thirty-Nine Articles. He went to London to pursue a literary career, wrote an autobiographical novel, *Eustace Conway* (1834), and for a time edited the *Athenaeum*. His sense of vocation persisted, nurtured by the Platonic philosophy taught by his Cambridge tutor Julius Hare, with its sense of unifying principle. So he was drawn to Oxford and to ordination as priest. He became chaplain to Guy's Hospital (1837) and to Lincoln's Inn (1841-60). In 1840 he was appointed Professor of Literature at King's College, London. There, from 1846 to 1853 he was Professor of Theology.

Such appointments provided the framework for his main work. 'I was called from my cradle to the pursuit of unity': the more comprehensive the church, he argued, the more powerful for good in the world. *The*

Kingdom of Christ (1838), written in the form of letters to a Quaker, defended the Church of England's theological stance: the Catholic church for the English nation. Transcending the diversity of sects and creeds, the church is the chief sign of the divine order, above family and nation. 'The World is the Church without God; the Church is the World restored to its relation to God ...' Christ came to found not a religious sect but a kingdom.

For Maurice, God is in everything. He challenged the Evangelical premises which made them stress sin and the Fall. His God made the world, and made it basically good. Through Christ God had restored the world to a right relationship to Himself. The grace of God is greater than the sin of man. Rather than try to rescue individuals from an assumed fate, Christians should seek to realize the *one-ness* of humanity in Christ. Maurice saw in Chartism a social crisis reflecting the moral bankruptcy of capitalism. He joined with men like Kingsley and Ludlow to teach – and act. In May 1848 he began to edit *Politics for the People*. For this he would be honoured by later generations of churchmen, Westcott, Gore and Temple, as founder of Christian Socialism.

Socialism was but a phase in a search for social justice. Maurice was a socialist because he was a Christian. To be regenerated, society must find in God 'the law and ground of its order and harmony, the only secret of its existence'. Inevitably however, his political involvement, together with his rational approach to theology, exposed his flank to critics. In 1853, following the publication of *Theological Essays*, in which he expressed disbelief in the eternity of hell, he was dismissed from King's. This released him for a larger role, when he became first Principal of the Working Men's College. He taught there; also at his other foundation, the Queen's College for Women. In 1860 he left Lincoln's Inn, and with it, the remaining constraints on his venturesome theology. At St Peter's, Vere Street, he found a congenial base for his teaching. In 1886 he became Professor of Moral Philosophy at Cambridge. It is ironic that Maurice, so staunch for the established church, should find himself working on its margins. 'He did not wish the church to shut itself inside its private life' (Chadwick). Some honoured him for his prophetic courage and tried to follow the subtleties of his arguments. For a modern historian his importance is beyond doubt: 'Most modern theology is in some way indebted to Maurice's clear and courageous thinking' (Moorman).

Further Reading
A. R. F. D. Vidler, *Maurice and Company*, 1966.

MAURICE OF LONDON (*d.*1107; Bishop of London 1086-1107) was one of those public servants whose private life, although notorious and scandalous, scarcely interrupted his successful career. A Norman by birth, he was appointed Archdeacon of Maine as part of William the Conqueror's annexation of the county after 1063. He became William I's chancellor *c*.1078, an office he held until his appointment to the see of London in 1086. Evidently an efficient organizer, he reconstructed his Cathedral of St Paul's on a lavishly grand scale. His legal experience failed to prevail, however, in 1094 when he unsuccessfully contested Anselm's right to consecrate the parish church of St Mary's in the archbishop's manor of Harrow. In 1100, he played a central role in the succession of Henry I to the throne after the sudden death of William Rufus, crowning the new king only three days after his brother died. His influence in royal administration is reflected here and in the earlier rise to dominance of his protégé, Ranulf Flambard. Like Flambard, Maurice, even though not in full priestly orders until shortly before his consecration as bishop, was a libertine, his pursuit of women attracting considerable monkish condemnation. Apparently, Maurice justified his sexual exploits by claiming that, on medical grounds, they were essential to his health.

MAXIMUS, MAGNUS CLEMENS (*d*.388) ruled as usurping Roman emperor from 383 to 388. Of Spanish birth, Magnus Maximus served in the Roman army in Britain from 367 and rose to high military command. In 383 he proclaimed himself emperor, crossed the Channel with an army and established his rule over Gaul and Spain. In 387 he moved into Italy but in 388 was defeated by the rightful emperor, Theodosius I, and executed at Aquileia. His significance in British history is twofold. First, his withdrawals of troops from Britain made the province even more vulnerable than it already was to Pictish, Irish and Saxon marauders. Secondly, he was remembered (under the name Macsen) in medieval Welsh tradition as the ancestor of several British princely dynasties. Precisely what significance this may have is not clear, but it is possible that Maximus established reliable native subordinates for defensive purposes in positions of authority that later became hereditary. On both counts his unwitting contribution to the confused process called for convenience 'the end of Roman Britain' was considerable.

Further Reading
J. Matthews, *Western Aristocracies and Imperial Court* AD *364-425*, 1975.

MAXWELL, JAMES CLERK (1831-79) is, for many physicists, a name ranking in eminence with Newton and Einstein. His theory of electromagnetism was a landmark in the history of science. In its day it had a greater impact on scientific thinking than any work since Newton's. Yet Maxwell never acquired the wider fame of Faraday and, astonishingly, did not appear in the queen's list of famous members of the Royal Society at its 1960 tricentenary celebration.

He was the son of a Dumfriesshire laird, spoke with a Galloway accent and kept the family house all his life. Socially conservative, he held to the orthodox Scottish Calvinism of his upbringing, and his horizons were not broadened by his wife, who suffered from a psychosomatic illness. But from childhood he was intellectually curious. 'What's the go o' that?' he would ask with wearing persistence. His contemporaries at The Edinburgh Academy nicknamed him 'Dafty': but Cambridge undergraduates, while baffled by his odd ideas, and enraged by his habit of taking exercise by running up and down staircases at 2.00 a.m., enjoyed his quirky sense of fun and recognized his genius. He became a Fellow of Trinity, and then a Professor at Aberdeen University in 1856. He was just twenty-five.

Thereafter his career was not smooth. Aberdeen made him redundant when it combined two colleges. Edinburgh rejected him. King's College, London, selected him as its Professor of Physics and Astronomy in 1860, but he resigned in 1865, and worked from home until 1871, when he became the first Professor of Experimental Physics at Cambridge. There he played a central part in the design of the Cavendish Laboratory, which had just been given to the university by the Duke of Devonshire. Maxwell's trouble was that he was a very bad lecturer. He was diffuse, inaudible, and far too quick. Being casual over details, he also had his full share of misfortunes on the blackboard.

But it was a different story when he put pen to paper. There his lucid style, sometimes enlivened by wit and even romantic imagination, revealed to the full his philosophical cast of mind and his conceptual insights. He often started with analogies, and used them as a scaffolding for his concepts, to be discarded later. At the Cavendish he wrote, for his inaugural address, of 'the difficulty of recognizing, among the concrete objects before us, the abstract relation we have learnt from books, and the distracting pain of wrenching the mind away from the symbols to the objects, and from the objects back to the symbols'. He used his own intuitive ability to move easily between the two in the study of many fields, including molecular physics, where he established in part the Maxwell Boltzmann distribution of molecular velocities in a gas. He is regarded as the co-founder, with Clausius, of the kinetic theory of matter. His most profound work, however, was to lead to an understanding of electromagnetic waves.

In the early nineteenth century it had been thought that there were two different types of electricity: one responsible for electrostatic phenomena, like hair standing on end when combed in a dry atmosphere, and the other associated with magnetism – electromagnets, for example. Scientists from many different countries contributed to the advance of knowledge from this point. The American, Franklin, showed lightning to be concerned with electricity. Thereafter the impetus came from Europe. The Italian, Volta, invented the cell which produced the first continuous source of electricity; the Dane, Ørsted, found that electric currents generated magnetic fields; the Frenchman, Ampère, measured and calculated these. The Englishman, Faraday, showed that changing magnetic fields can generate electric currents and, crucially, postulated 'lines of force', in place of the traditional 'action at a distance', to explain electromagnetism. All this experimental evidence provided data for Maxwell's theoretical analysis.

Maxwell's equations put into precise mathematical form the relationships between changing electric and magnetic fields as described by Faraday. But Maxwell found an inconsistency in his equations which could be eradicated by including an additional term. He identified the property of this as a displacement current whenever an electric field is changing. Then he went further to derive the equations of electromagnetic waves, and in 1864 he obtained the theoretical value of their speed in space, which closely matched the value for the speed of light already obtained experimentally by Fizeau.

The understanding that light might be described as electromagnetic waves has led over the years to the discovery of the remainder of the electromagnetic spectrum and its applications, including radio, radar and television. Indeed, Einstein's Special Theory of Relativity can be thought of as a generalization of Maxwell's equations extended to all matter. It was said some years ago that in different parts of the natural sciences courses at Cambridge University Maxwell's equations were taught eighteen times, a tribute to their clarity, conciseness and range of application.

Maxwell's predictions of 1864 were remarkable, since the existence of electromagnetic waves was not confirmed experimentally until the demonstrations of Hertz in 1886. It was sad that he did not live to see this fulfilment of his work. With good reason he has been described as the greatest theoretical physicist of the nineteenth century.

Further Reading
J. Crowther, *British Scientists of the Nineteenth Century*, 1936.

MAYNARD, SIR JOHN (1602-90), Serjeant-at-Law, was a Devonian, born the son of a barrister at Tavistock and educated at Exeter College, Oxford, and the Middle Temple. He was called to the bar two years before the Petition of Right, and lived to become a Commissioner of the Great Seal after the Glorious Revolution. Thus his career spans the century of revolution as that of no other Englishman in public life. He sat for Devon constituencies in the Short and Long Parliaments, in Oliver's last parliament, in the Convention of 1660, in Charles II's Cavalier parliament, in James II's only parliament, and in the Convention of 1688-9. Maynard prosecuted Strafford in 1641 and Stafford in 1680; he was a manager in the impeachment of Laud, Counsel for the Crown against Sir Henry Vane, leader in the case against Edward Coleman. Such a career required dexterity as well as longevity, professional skill as well as political sagacity. Maynard was a moderate parliamentarian in the 1640s, critical of the Cromwellians and an opponent of the execution of Charles I. He took the Engagement to the Commonwealth, yet he defended Lilburne successfully in 1653 and was sent to the Tower because he pleaded Habeas Corpus in the Cony case of 1655. Like many shrewd men, he adjusted wisely in 1659-60; Protector's Serjeant in 1658, he became King's Serjeant, and got a knighthood into the bargain, at the Restoration. In Charles II's reign he took a moderately Whig line and made profitable use of his learning and of his oratory during the Popish Plot. At the Revolution he was on the side of the angels, seeing the victory of William as the triumph of the rule of law and achieving high office for the first time at the age of eighty-six.

MAYNE, CUTHBERT (1544-77), the first seminary priest to be executed in England, was born in the parish of Sherwell, near Barnstaple, in 1544. He was sent to Oxford by his uncle, who had conformed to the Anglican church; he was at St John's College, which was at that time much affected by the Catholic revival – Edmund Campion was at that college – and Mayne became a Catholic. He took his BA in 1566 and his MA in 1570, but when the Bishop of London, on evidence contained in some letters from Mayne's friends overseas, sent to arrest him, Mayne left Oxford and went abroad to the English seminary college at Douai. He spent three years there (1573 to 1576), was ordained priest in 1575, took his BD in 1576 and in April of that year he returned to England secretly on missionary work.

Arriving safely in England, Mayne went to his own west country and became chaplain to the Catholic Francis Tregian in his house, Golden, in Cornwall. For a year he lived there in safety, in the guise of Tregian's steward, and during this time he travelled about from house to house, administering the sacraments, comforting Catholic families and reclaiming the relapsed. Inevitably news of his presence in Cornwall leaked out. The Sheriff was Sir Richard Grenville. After consultation with the Bishop of Truro Grenville set off with an armed force for Golden: he knew the house well and had not any difficulty in arresting Mayne. He found him wearing an *Agnus Dei* (a wax imprint of a lamb). Mayne's papers were confiscated and among them was found a Papal Bull of Indulgence dated 1575, the Jubilee Year, 'divers other relics used in popery ... with a special treatise against the Book of Common Prayer'.

Mayne's trial followed the usual course and he was condemned for treason for possessing the Bull. There was a difference of opinion among his judges, because it was claimed that the Bull expired in 1575, but the verdict went against Mayne. He was executed on 30 November 1577, with all the horrible customs of those days.

Mayne was the first of the Catholic martyrs, neither the most distinguished nor the most important, but he was among the simplest and the most forthright. What Burghley and Walsingham needed to know was how Catholics would behave, if England were to be invaded by a Catholic power. Mayne did not hesitate: at his final examination he said, 'If any Catholic prince took in hand to invade any Realm to reform the same to the authority of the see of Rome, that then the Catholics in that Realm invaded by foreigners should be ready to assist and help them.' Mayne was a brave man who died for his religion: he also provided the justification for the acts of a government responsible for the safety of the realm and of its religion as established by law.

Further Reading
A. L. Rowse, *Tudor Cornwall*, pp.347, 1941.
A. L. Rowse, *Sir Richard Grenville*, pp.134, 1937.

MEIKLE, ANDREW (1719-1811), millwright, invented the first effective threshing machine. Improving upon earlier designs, it could be driven by steam, by water, by horses or by hand. The long process of threshing with flails and winnowing by draught created by a hand-turned wheel was shortened by this machine. Its widespread adoption in the corn lands of southern England led to much hardship among the labourers who had grown to depend on threshing employment in winter and it was one of the causes of the revolt of 1830. Meikle, a Scotsman, had already invented a machine for dressing grain and made unsuccessful efforts to produce threshing machines before arriving at the drum type, which made its first appearance in 1786. It contributed greatly to the improvement of agriculture, if not to the well-being of the labourer.

MELTON, WILLIAM (*d*.1340), Archbishop of York from 1317 until his death, was both a model civil servant and a model archbishop. Of modest origin, he was one of the many Yorkshiremen recruited into government by Edward I and Edward II. A financial expert, whose first post was usher of the wardrobe to Edward I, he acted as cofferer to Queen Margaret (1298-1300), chamberlain of Chester (1301), controller of the wardrobe to Edward II as prince (1304-7) and king (1307-14), and keeper of the wardrobe (1314-16), which he resigned on his election as archbishop. Subsequently he returned for two spells as Treasurer of the Exchequer in 1325-6 and 1330-1 and one as chancellor (1333-4), when the royal chancery was at York. His administration was distinguished both by efficiency and honesty, so that he was acceptable both to

the king and the Ordainers, and in 1325-6 he was responsible for reforming the Exchequer.

A cleric like most civil servants of his time, Melton became a prodigious pluralist, being promoted to a range of ecclesiastical benefices in which he was non-resident, several of which, such as the deanery of St Martins-le-Grand in London and provostship of Beverley, were normally reserved for royal clerks. Nominated by the king to the archbishopric of York, he immediately resigned his royal offices and departed to his province, where he resided almost continuously till his death. There he proved himself 'one of the best of the medieval Archbishops of York' (Grassi), devoting himself to tiresome episcopal duties such as the confirmation of boys and visitation of his parishes, asserting his authority over rival jurisdictions such as the Archdeacon of Richmond and York Cathedral chapter, and assisting the poor, particularly relieving those poor tenants who could not pay him their debts. He was severe, it was reported, only to the contumacious and to rebels and he tried unsuccessfully to protect the north against the Scots.

Both as minister of the Crown and archbishop, Melton patronized his family and fellow Yorkshiremen. In government he was at the 'very centre of the York group', the 'archetype of all the York clerks' (Grassi), and recruited many other Yorkshiremen to royal service, among them a successor as chancellor and archbishop in John Thoresby, who had been receiver of his chamber. Melton was thus largely responsible for the prominence of Yorkshiremen in royal administration for the rest of the fourteenth century. As archbishop, he made at least 388 loans totalling £23,551, some perhaps usurious and others to the Crown, but most apparently designed to assist northern monasteries and noblemen through their financial difficulties. He financed the education of his nephews and nieces at Newark, leaving substantial bequests to each of them, and built up a private landed estate for his nephew William, thus raising the Meltons from obscurity into a leading county family. Clerics who were kinsmen or neighbours were promoted to benefices in his gift. As the careers of Anthony Bek and Walter Stapledon show, such nepotism was normal for his time and Melton was even praised for it by the chronicler of the Church of York. By promoting to royal office Yorkshiremen who were both able and thoroughly worthy, Melton was arguably acting in the public interest.

Further Reading
J. L. Grassi, 'Royal Clerks from the Archdiocese of York in the 14th Century', *Northern History* iv, 1968.
R. M. T. Hill, *The Labourer in the Vineyard: The Visitations of Archbishop Melton in the Archdeaconry of Richmond*, Borthwick Paper 35, 1968.
L. H. Butler, 'Archbishop Melton, his neighbours and his kinsmen, 1317-1340', *Journal of Ecclesiastical History* ii, 1951.

MEREDITH, GEORGE (1828-1909), poet and novelist, gained a following among discriminating readers which grew until in honoured old age he was lauded as the 'grand old man of letters'. It was to be his fate to be more read about than read. He was, and has remained, par excellence, 'the writer's writer'. If, however, a writer's importance be gauged by his influence on other writers, Hardy, Gissing, Stevenson, Woolf, Joyce and Lawrence among them, he deserves our attention as well.

His own life contained material for several novels. He was born at Portsmouth, the son and grandson of tailors. The unappreciated worth and social disadvantages of the business were a source of his cultivation of the style of a gentleman. Its aspirations and pains are reflected in his account of a tailoring family, in *Evan Harrington* (1860). His mother died when he was five: a small legacy assured him a superior education at a local school. He then spent two adolescent years at a Moravian school in Germany. From an unorthodox education, laying stress upon creative pursuits, he emerged, aged sixteen, with a romantic view of life and an earnest commitment to literary self-expression. Yet, like other great Victorian novelists, he was essentially self-educated.

To be a poet offered escape from the projected career in law. Marriage to a widow, eight years older than he, beautiful but demanding, care for a stepdaughter and their own son, framed a life of lodgings, the casual journalism he detested, penury, creditors and quarrels. When, in 1858, his wife left him for the artist, Henry Wallis, he found solace in his work. His poetry contained some striking phrases. The imagery could be memorable. There are strength of observation and touches of pathos in *Modern Love* (1862) for example. In his poems can be seen some of the ruling ideas of the novels to which he turned (the reverse of Hardy's literary odyssey) for ampler expression of his themes. For this 'prose Browning' all perception was worthwhile for its own sake. 'The harvest was enough in itself, before it was turned into bread' (Beach Thomas).

George Eliot saw in *The Shaving of Shagput*, a fantasy out of the *Arabian Nights*, that 'significant humour' which would often leave the reader puzzling, perhaps discouraged. First reviewers linked *The Ordeal of Richard Feverel* (1859) to *Tristram Shandy*. It was one of several variations on the comic theme. The 'test of true comedy', as he would later write in his lecture 'On the Idea of Comedy and of the Uses of the Comic Spirit' (1877), was that it should 'awaken thoughtful laughter'. Its 'flourishing' formed 'one excellent test of the civilization of a country', for it was only in 'a society of cultivated men and women' and one 'where women are on the road to an equal footing with men' that the thought with which 'true Comedy' informs laughter could be awakened. So 'Philosopher and Comic Poet' were 'of a cousinship in the eye which they cast on life'.

Among later novels three seem best to have fulfilled his ideals: *Beauchamp's Career* (1875), the most elegantly constructed, *The Egoist* (1879), remorseless in its study of a refined selfishness, and *Diana of the Crossways* (1885), where he is most tenderly elegiac. His later works suffered from too overt a preoccupation with the questions of the day. Some would say that he donned too eagerly the prophetic mantle. But devotees who strode with him about Surrey heaths and hills found inspiration. 'He talked with a kind of swagger,' wrote one. 'I am every morning on the top of Box Hill', wrote the sage, 'as its flower, its bird, its prophet … I shout ha ha to the gates of the world.' It was what Carlyle called his 'wind in the orchard style'. He came to be isolated by deafness but there was still a rich human experience to flavour the monologues. There was tragedy behind the striking looks – 'the noble, ravaged handsomeness' – and dancing wit. In 1864 he married Marie Vulliamy – but would outlive her by twenty-four years. He quarrelled with his eldest son; when he died Meredith did not go to the funeral; nor did he heed his first wife's appeal to visit her as she lay dying. There was a brittle pride in his conduct which in his novels he holds up to ridicule. Sidney Colvin wrote of his 'elaborate high courtesy and unsparing raillery'. As in his novels, the straining for effect, love of elliptical statement and elaboration of language, could be more tiring than uplifting.

'Meredith was his own great subject' (Robert Lynd). It is insufficient as verdict on a rare talent. He is wonderfully quotable. Of a lady, he wrote: 'a woman who has never had the first tadpole wriggle of an idea.' Diana Warwick stepped out into the dawn: 'she is bird-song and the light of morning and coming of flowers.' No wonder the generation of G. M. Trevelyan and the Edwardian literati adored him, that novelists as different as Henry James and E. M. Forster acknowledged him as master. Pleasing by his wit and teasing by his convoluted prose he chartered a course for the psychological novel of the next century.

Further Reading
Siegfried Sassoon, *Meredith*, 1948.

MERTON, WALTER (*c.*1205-77), Bishop of Rochester (1274-7), was the founder of Merton College, Oxford. His career illustrates how men frequently gravitated from private to royal service, how administrative service to the Crown normally led to promotion in the church, and how churchmen habitually invested their income and employed their patronage to the advantage of their relatives. Born at Basingstoke to prosperous freeholding parents, the only son among seven sisters, Walter was probably not a scholar himself, but was the friend of scholars. Initially known as Walter of Basingstoke, he changed his name about 1236, when in the service of Merton Priory, Surrey, transferring thence to the chancery of the priory's patron, King Henry III, perhaps through the patronage of Ralph Neville, Bishop of Chichester. From 1242 he was chancellor of Nicholas Farnham, Bishop of Durham (1241-9). He reappeared in the royal chancery in 1255 and in 1258-9 was the normal deputy of the chancellor. Thwarted of the chancellorship of England by a baronial candidate in 1260, he was chancellor as the king's nominee in 1261-3, but thereafter he gave way to Thomas Cantelupe. Continued employment in the public service led to an unexpected second term as chancellor in 1272-4 during the absence of Edward I, when he was virtually Regent of England.

From 1233 Walter was rector of the church of Cuddington (Surrey), where he endowed a light before the high altar in 1274 and whose church he probably rebuilt. Successive patrons rewarded him for his administrative services with further livings, which he held in plurality. Thus in 1246 the pope dispensed him to hold three rectories and in 1268 he held four, certainly without papal approval. From 1259 he was also a canon of St Paul's, opting to live in a prebendal house nearby, convenient for his work in chancery. In 1274, like most chancellors, he was given a bishopric and was appointed Bishop of Rochester. A superb conveyancer, he was dealing in land in Basingstoke before inheriting his parents' estates and ultimately purchased a large estate for his foundations, besides leaving the large sum of £5,000 in his will.

In accordance with his parents' wishes, Walter established his hospital of St Mary and St John, Basingstoke in 1240-5 for the poor and clergy 'whose strength is failing'. When it ran into difficulties in 1262, he transferred the patronage to the king. Merton College originated in 1262-3 as the 'House of the Scholars of Merton' at Malden in Surrey. Consisting of a warden and priests, its role was to support twenty scholars at Oxford. Walter drew up statutes to this effect in 1264, but subsequently changed his mind, transferring the college to its present site in Merton Street, Oxford, and compiling new statutes in 1274. Most students at medieval universities lived in rented lodgings or hall and had to support themselves through their studies, often through non-residence in their benefices. Colleges were endowed halls. Founders established colleges like Merton with sufficient endowments to provide free food and accommodation for their scholars, who were normally graduates with arts degrees reading for higher degrees in theology, law, medicine or music. Walter's scholars, his statutes clearly reveal, were to be drawn mainly from his kin, the numerous offspring of his aunt and seven sisters, whose marriages and dowries he had earlier arranged. Founder's kin came first, other scholars from the diocese of Winchester afterwards, a pattern also found in most other early colleges. Walter did not anticipate that Merton College would become an educational institution open to all.

Further Reading

C. A. F. Meekings, *Studies in Thirteenth-Century Justice and Administration*, 1981.
J. R. L. Highfield, ed., *The Early Rolls of Merton College, Oxford*, Oxford Historical Society, new series, xviii, 1964.

METCALF, JOHN (1717-1810), 'Blind Jack of Knaresborough' as he is better known, provides a rare example of spirit and achievement in the face of physical handicaps. As a constructor of roads along the boggy moors and uplands of the Pennine country which lay athwart the busy industrial areas of Lancashire, Yorkshire and Derbyshire, he was a pioneer of real importance.

Metcalf was completely blinded at the age of six after an attack of smallpox, but people tended to forget his disability when they encountered him. He was at various times a horse-dealer and carrier, and thus well acquainted with the mud, ruts, stones and dust of eighteenth-century roads. He was prodigiously active and once for a bet raced a friend from London to Harrogate: on foot, he took six days; his friend, in a carriage, took eight. He was a notable horseman and an accomplished fiddler, much in demand at fashionable spas such as Harrogate. He married a beautiful girl, Dolly Benson, after a characteristic elopement. In 1745 he joined his county volunteers and served in the subsequent Scottish campaign under the Duke of Cumberland. At one time he seems to have thought of setting up as a spinner, but his great work was to be as road-maker.

A contemporary, Hew, described how he had seen Metcalf, 'with the assistance only of a long staff', working on his roads, 'ascending precipices, exploring valleys, and investigating their several extents, forms and situations so as to answer his designs in the best manner'. When Hew inquired about the new road 'it was really astonishing to hear with what accuracy he described the courses and the nature of the different soils through which it was conducted'. Between 1760 and 1790 he constructed roads from Wakefield to Doncaster, Bury to Blackburn, Ashton to Stockport, Skipton to Burnley, Macclesfield to Chapel-en-le-Frith and Whaley Bridge to Buxton, 180 miles of turnpike in all. His method was to dig out the soft soil, to spread out bunches of heather and broom on the earth-bed, and to cover them with stone and gravel on the surface, with a gentle convex slope so that rainwater ran off into the ditches on either side. He was taciturn about his ways and means, however, and preferred to make his surveys alone, so there is some doubt about his methods. There is none about his success or its importance in the evolution of the industrial north of England.

Further Reading
E. Pawson, *Transport and Economy: The Turnpike Roads of Eighteenth-Century Britain*, 1977.

METCALFE, CHARLES THEOPHILUS, 1st BARON METCALFE

METCALFE, CHARLES THEOPHILUS, 1st BARON METCALFE (1785-1846) was the younger son of a major in the Bengal army who later rose to be a director of the East India Company. His mother, in the forthright words of his biographer, was 'grim' but 'a woman of strong understanding'. Charles was neglected and snubbed. At Eton, he was once seen riding a camel, from which his tutor deduced that he was 'orientally inclined'. And he found satisfaction in a life of service in India – 'happiness' would be too strong a word for this withdrawn, somewhat enigmatic figure, who has been called the greatest Indian official of his generation.

Though he bemoaned 'an ugly phiz', he made his mark early. 'The ugliest and most agreeable clever person – except Lady Glenbervie – in Europe or Asia', Lord Minto once wrote of him. He was called 'the little stormer' after he had volunteered to lead an assault against an Indian fortress. He gained the alliance of Ranjit Singh, the Muslim Prince of the Sikhs, which Lord Minto believed was vital to British security. He returned from dealing with the most formidable prince in India, with an alliance which endured – and a Sikh mistress who gave him three Eurasian sons. At the age of twenty-seven he was given charge of Delhi. In theory he was but Resident at the court of the Mogul emperor. In reality the emperor ruled over nothing but his court. Metcalfe was responsible for a great area, besides relations with other nominally independent princes whom he had to cajole and persuade as best he could. Thompson no doubt exaggerates when he calls Metcalfe's administration of Delhi 'the greatest single administrative work put through by a single British ruler'. Comparable results were achieved elsewhere. But his work was distinctive. He ended hanging and flogging and the selling of slaves. He forbade suttee – widow-burning – and set an example which the Governor-General would one day have to follow. He carried out a great work of pacification. Indian boys caught pilfering were sent to a special camp where they could be taught a trade. He was also severely practical: his revenue rose nearly fourfold in six years. He rejected the Cornwallis scheme and treated the tax-collecting zamindar strictly as an agent of government. Furthermore his collectors were also magistrates; he would have none of Cornwallis's division of executive and judiciary. His recommendation that there should be small districts, in each of which a European should have general authority with Indian aides, was broadly embodied in the Act of 1833.

Metcalfe subsequently worked with the Governor-General as Secretary in the secret, foreign and political departments. Then he went as Resident to Hyderabad (1820-7). He found there an eighteenth-century situation where the Resident and an enterprising gentleman 'not of pure European blood' were managing the Nizam's affairs to their own monetary advantage. Hastings, the Governor-General, was content (for peace and quiet) to overlook the peccadilloes. Metcalfe took a lofty line and acted with his usual vigour. Though rebuked by Hastings he had the support of the supreme council. He himself became a member of the council in 1827. He was Bentinck's right-hand man during most of his forward-looking government. For a year, 1835-6, he acted as provisional Governor-General, between the administration of Bentinck and Auckland. He was unlucky not to be confirmed in office. In the case of Lord Auckland the tradition of sending out an English grandee, so often beneficial, was to have an unhappy result. Because of Metcalfe's liberal views about censorship, the Directors held him to be unsound. They passed him over for the governorship of Madras – and he sailed home. He had been in India for thirty-seven years without break.

His career had postscripts. In 1839 he was made Governor of Jamaica. In 1843 he became Governor-General of Canada. He resigned after two years. Essentially he is to be judged, as he would wish, as a servant of the British Raj, one of those men who gave meaning and substance to the ideal that is expressed in Ellenborough's famous statement: 'We have a great moral duty to perform in India.'

Further Reading
E. Thompson, *Charles, Lord Metcalfe*, 1937.
J. W. Kaye, *Life of Metcalfe*, 2 vols, 2nd edn, 1858.

MIDDLETON, SIR CHARLES, 1st LORD BARHAM

MIDDLETON, SIR CHARLES, 1st LORD BARHAM (1726-1813), naval administrator, prepared the navy for its crucial role in the Revolutionary and Napoleonic wars. On the main staircase at Exton Hall in Rutland there hangs a picture of the fleets at the close of the battle of Trafalgar, painted for presentation to Lord Barham who was First Lord of the Admiralty in the year of the battle of Trafalgar.

Born in 1726, Middleton entered the navy as a 'Captain's servant' at the age of fourteen. He had no special chance of distinguishing himself in the Seven Years' War and for twelve years afterwards he lived on half pay. He was recalled for active service again in 1775 and commanded in turn the *Ardent* and *Prince George* battleships. In 1778 he was appointed Comptroller for the navy. His mother was a cousin of Lord Advocate Dundas and his immediate sponsor was Lord Sandwich, the First Lord. Middleton rose by the conventional path of patronage, but his appointment came at a critical moment in England's affairs. Jealousies amongst senior officers, exacerbated by the Keppel and Palliser courts martial, and incompetence and graft at the lower level of administration and supply, threatened the efficiency of the navy just when it was called on to fight France, Spain and the Americans with a fleet which had undergone two decades of peacetime economies. The timber shortage was all the more acute because of the cessation of supplies from America. An alternative source was found in Nova Scotia, better terms were offered to ease the transport of domestic timber. By all means possible, reserves of hemp, pitch and masts were built up, while an urgent programme of building was mounted in the dockyards. Copper-sheathing became general practice when, at Middleton's suggestion, a preservative was applied which made it possible to use the sheathing with iron bolts without corroding them. The use of the carronade, a short-range gun made at the Carron ironworks, gave British ships superiority in close actions. The hasty expedients of war were not all satisfactory – the use of unseasoned timber, for instance, was bad – it might have caused the loss of the *Royal George*. But the lessons learned were valuable.

After the war the fleet was systematically re-equipped and rebuilt; timber was given time to season and reserves of material were built up. At the same time Middleton tackled the complex weaknesses in naval administration. The political climate was favourable to reform. In 1785 a commission was set up to inquire into the fees and gratuities received in public offices. Besides prohibiting fees, the Commission accepted his plan that the Board, essentially unchanged since the Restoration, should be divided into three committees: Correspondence, Stores and Accounts. A Deputy Comptroller should be appointed to assist him, a Secretary and Surveyor of Civil Architecture added to the Board. Unfortunately these proposals were not implemented by the government until 1796. Middleton, an avowed reformer amongst colleagues, some of whom stood to lose by his reforms, was in an exposed position. In March 1790 he resigned. He was recalled briefly to serve as senior naval member of the Board of Admiralty, in May 1794.

It was to Middleton's credit that he was able to leave a well-equipped navy. Compared with 1775 or 1755, the transition from peace to war was easy. But things went awry again under the lax comptrollership of Sir Andrew Hamond and Lord St Vincent stirred up a hornets' nest when he became First Lord in 1801. He himself was much to blame for his misjudgement when he cut down stocks after the Peace of Amiens, and Middleton inherited an awkward situation bedevilled by complaints and inquiries, when he was recalled in January 1805 to be chairman of yet another reforming Commission. Three months later he became First Lord himself, when Melville was forced to resign after criticism of his handling of naval accounts while he was Treasurer of the navy. In this way, with the debris of administrative scandals all round him, Lord Barham, as Middleton now became, rose to be head of the navy. After anxious

months came the glorious day, when England 'saved herself by her exertions' and Nelson destroyed the French fleet, and the vestiges of Napoleon's invasion with it, at the battle of Trafalgar. It is uncertain how much Barham was responsible for Nelson's strategy. But it was lucky that the country had this man, with his large experience, at the head of operations. He retained all his vigour of mind and capacity for decision. Indeed, after his resignation, almost unnoticed, in February 1806, he continued to act as chairman of the Commission which, when it completed its work, had drawn up comprehensive rules for the whole of naval administration. He retired in 1807 to enjoy six years upon his country estate at Teston in Kent.

His voluminous papers are a fascinating source for this rich period of naval history. He was the confidant of such men as Hood and Kempenfelt. His real influence was far greater than his official work would suggest, for he was consulted by seamen and politicians on the many points on which he had expert knowledge. Austere, religious – he was a friend of Wilberforce and an early opponent of the slave trade – outspoken, he was sometimes an awkward colleague, but he was always a great public servant.

Further Reading
J. K. Laughton, *Letters and Papers of Charles, Lord Barham*, 3 vols, 1907-11.

MILES OF GLOUCESTER (*c*.1100-43) was a leading protagonist in Matilda's attempt to win the English throne. Sometimes regarded as one of Henry I's 'new men', Miles was the hereditary sheriff of Gloucestershire and castellan of Gloucester, position first acquired by his grandfather, Roger of Pitres, in the reign of William the Conqueror. Miles succeeded his father, Walter, sometime before 1126. By marriage, he secured the Welsh lordship of Brecknock and from Matilda in 1141-2 the sub-tenancy of Abergavenny. His power in the west was consolidated by his acting as local justiciar. Loyal to Henry I, he nevertheless soon recognized Stephen and by Easter 1136 was acting as his constable. Miles remained close to Stephen in the early years of the reign, playing an important role in the supression of the Welsh rising of 1136.

In 1139, however, he joined Matilda almost as soon as she landed. Given the adherence to Matilda of Miles's more powerful neighbour, Robert of Gloucester, this change of allegiance may have been prompted by self-preservation as much as legitimist devotion. Whatever his motives, Miles proved one of Matilda's most effective commanders: in 1139 alone he secured Gloucester and Hereford; relieved Wallingford and sacked Worcester. In 1141, however, he only managed to flee the Rout of Winchester by abandoning his weapons and stripping off all his armour so that he arrived at Gloucester 'weary, half-naked and alone'. Earlier that year, at the height of her power, Matilda had created Miles Earl of Hereford, confirming his position as a sort of military viceroy in the southern Marches. One of his duties was to raise finance for Matilda's campaigns, but he encountered stern opposition when he attempted to tax the church. Even though supported by Gilbert Foliot, then Abbot of Gloucester and his protégé, Miles was placed under an interdict by Robert of Béthune, Bishop of Hereford. Such fiscal expedients, common to both sides in a civil war, no doubt played a part in colouring the gloomy and hostile tone of ecclesiastical commentators on the conflict. Few issues aroused the moral indignation of medieval established clergy more certainly than heavy financial exactions levied on their institutions. Miles himself came to an unfortunate end, accidentally shot dead by one of his companions when out hunting in the Forest of Dean, an accident eerily reminiscent of the death of William II.

Despite his apparent fickleness, Miles was far from being a representative of any so-called 'feudal anarchy'. His local authority depended on his maintenance of a combination of public justice, royal favour and private acquisition of land; thus did he calculate his political advantage. Once decided, he seems to have acted with conspicuous loyalty. Nearly the last thing he, or his fellow magnates, wanted was a baronial free-for-all with its promise of the last thing they wanted, loss of estates and titles.

Further Reading
D. Walker, 'Miles of Gloucester', *Bristol and Gloucester Archeological Society*, 1958-9.

MILL, JAMES (1773-1836), Indian administrator and economist, was the son of a shoemaker, near Montrose. He studied for the Presbyterian ministry at Edinburgh and was licensed to preach in 1798, but in 1802 he came to London to earn his living by his pen. He soon lost his interest in theology and took up a sceptical position. His acute and practical mind found in Bentham a stimulating tutor and in India a great subject.

After editing and writing for various periodicals, in 1806 Mill began work on his great *History of British India* (published in 1817). His aim was to give India 'a good system of judicial procedure' on Benthamite lines. As Bentham said, 'Mill will be the living executive – I shall be the dead legislative of British India'. His huge volumes are a remarkable essay in scientific history but they suffer from serious defects. Typically Mill argued that his never having been to India was an advantage: while the historian must understand 'the laws of human nature' in abstract and must study the principles of human society and 'the machinery of government', he must also eschew the detailed and picturesque. His approach was explicitly western, insensitive to the

differences between one Indian and another, the subtleties of caste and the tensions that arose from the conflict of races. The book has become a memorial to the strengths and weaknesses of the 'Utilitarians'. Macaulay called it the greatest historical work since Gibbon but Maine said that its inaccuracy was equalled only by its bad faith. Mill's 'emphatically polemical' intellect (his son's words) may have been less suited to history than to the political and social analysis in which he excelled. He was writing, primarily for a British readership, a critique of current attitudes towards colonies – a source of patronage and power for ruling élites, producing, or prolonging, bad government.

In 1819 Mill, radical though he was known to be, was made assistant examiner by the Directors of the East India Company. In 1832 he became chief of the examiner's office. Effectively he controlled all departments of Indian administration. He continued to study and write. In 1821 he published *Elements of Political Economy*. The greatest of Bentham's disciples, Mill showed in this work, and in his *Essay on Government* (ed. Barker, 1937), that he had his own great contribution to make. 'Philosophic Radicalism' was only for the few. Indeed, as Coleridge said, 'to the immense majority of men, even in civilized countries, speculative philosophy has ever been, and must remain, a *terra incognita*: the minds that govern and influence society are always few.' Some of the few were captured. 'There is now nothing definite in politics except Radicalism', wrote Mill's son John Stuart to Thomas Carlyle, in May 1832. Radicals were to find the aftermath of the Reform Bill disappointing; it was rather as a third force than a third party that they were to be effective. Turning to what John Stuart Mill called 'the root of the evil' they tackled education, colonies, the problems of poverty and of public health.

There was a fearless quality about James Mill. In his notorious 1824 essay on Colonies for the *Encyclopaedia Britannica* (where many of his most important articles appeared), he hinted broadly at the desirability of birth-control – at a time when the subject was taboo. He advocated independence for Canada and the West Indies at a time when liberals could look no further than free trade. He was nothing if not public-spirited, and took a leading part in founding University College, London. He idealized his son and trained him to be a paragon. Under the sole tutelage of his father, the boy began Greek at three! At fourteen he was deep in logic and political economy. He 'never was a boy'. At seventeen he joined a 'Utilitarian' society which met at Bentham's house. He was recognized as the coming leader; but at twenty he had a nervous breakdown. Of this we read in his autobiography: it presents a revealing portrait of his father. We learn of the hours spent on the teaching of his children, his fanatical insistence upon a life of ordered usefulness, his truly Scottish delight in struggle, and praise of men who overcame adversity. Every walk was an opportunity for catechism on the day's learning, every book contained a moral or political economic message – and through all ran the insistence upon logical analysis. He carefully shielded his son from contact with other boys – 'the contagion of vulgar modes of thought and feeling'. Decisive, overbearing, confident, he sought to reproduce his character and philosophy in that of his son.

John Stuart Mill recovered. He achieved greatness. His *Essay on Liberty* is better perhaps than anything his father wrote. It represents a triumph of the human spirit and intelligence over an oppressive training. His proud tribute to his father deserves also to be remembered. 'During his later years he was quite as much the head and leader of the intellectual radicals in England as Voltaire was of the *philosophes* of France.'

Further Reading
E. Halévy (translated by M. Morris), *The Growth of Philosophic Radicalism*, 1928.
Alexander Bain, *James Mill*, 1882.

MILL, JOHN STUART (1806-73) has a unique place among the intellectuals and writers of Victorian England. In an age when human knowledge seemed to lie within the grasp of a single mind, he was foremost in the developing studies of logic, psychology, political science and political economy. 'Utilitarian' was his name for the society which he formed to promote discussion of philosophical ideas in relation to the issues of the day. But no single word – 'utilitarian', 'liberal', 'rationalist' – can convey the range of his ideas.

He was the eldest son of the historian, economist and philosopher James Mill, Scottish-born but a Londoner perforce, by reason of high office in the East India Company. John Stuart could also be called a Londoner, though he was to spend his later years in the south of France. In truth he inhabited an intellectual castle of his own: from its ramparts he looked out at his countrymen in a spirit of mild detachment, their religion, political system and society seen as belonging to another, unsatisfactory world. Only for his father's friends, or a few younger and like-minded, Grote, the Austin brothers, Macaulay, could the drawbridge be raised. That young Mill could be regarded as an insufferable prig who could write that 'everybody [English] acts as if everybody else … was either an enemy or a bore'; that he suffered a kind of breakdown, emerged as a more rounded person; that he came to have great authority in public life, were all attributable to the schooling devised and managed by his father.

It was perhaps 'the most severe and painful discipline which any great mind has survived' (Arthur Salter). Greek began at three. By twelve his classical reading would have been impressive in an undergraduate. It was reinforced by history, philosophy, higher mathematics and foreign languages. 'No holidays were allowed lest the habit of work should be broken.' One excursion, to Devonshire, in 1813, memorable for its rarity, was shared with his father and Jeremy Bentham, doyen of rationalists. Otherwise, there were improving walks, with lessons recited as father and son strode out towards London's fields. Mill owed much to the Benthams: Jeremy's brother, General Bentham, was his host for some time in southern France. He was fourteen when he came to breathe its 'free and genial atmosphere' and to acquire a continental perspective. Law, his intended career, now took second place to the philosophers, notably Hartley, Helvetius, Dumont and, all-pervasively, Jeremy Bentham, who would lead his mind towards the comprehensive rationalism of his life's work.

Mill's *Autobiography* records his mental odyssey and the concerns of 'philosophical radicalism'. 'The autobiography of a steam engine', wrote Carlyle: it is dispassionate, analytical, only incidentally revealing about his personality. Neither mother nor younger children figure at all. After a friendship of twenty-one years, two years after her husband's death, he would eventually marry Harriet Taylor. He describes a paragon of virtue, a beacon of intelligence, a profound, awakening influence: she scarcely emerges as a human being, nor he as having known more than a meeting of minds. He was aware of the strengths, as well as the oppression of his schooling. His father 'had scarcely any belief in pleasure' but encouraged botany: it became a life-long interest. Understanding was the aim: it was 'not an education of cram'. John had to read to his father the manuscript of his great *History of British India* while he corrected the proofs; so he acquired a knowledge of that land, 'eminently useful to my later progress'. He was so trained that all subjects would be grist to his analytical mill. He did not rebel against his father's teaching or fail to capitalize on it by 'voluntary exercises'. Inevitably however there was a price to pay.

In the autumn of 1826 he gave way to blank depression: 'The whole foundation on which my life was constructed fell down.' His education had failed to foster feelings strong enough 'to resist the dissolving influence of analysis'. He had 'a well-equipped ship and a rudder, but no sail'. He had established his Utilitarian Society (1822-3), and begun writing for *The Westminster Review*. New contacts made him realize how odd he was; admired for his precocious knowledge but ill-formed for social life. Carlyle had been an unlikely friend, finding common ground in love of truth and dislike of cant, though (said Carlyle) 'he cannot laugh with any compass'. Now however: 'he seemed to be withering … into the miserablest metaphysical *scrae* ['old shoe'] body and mind. His eyes go twinkling and jerking with wild lights and twitches; his head is bald, his face brown and dry – poor fellow after all.' He was rescued by poetry, 'Medicine for my state of mind'. Wordsworth's poems spoke 'of thought coloured by feeling, under the excitement of beauty'. With them came that arousal of imagination, and the sensitivity which won Gladstone's warm tribute: 'a saint of rationalism'.

In 1835 Mill became editor of Molesworth's *London Review* and began 'to fight the deep slumber of public opinion'. He was becoming convinced that political philosophy was 'something much more complex and many-sided than he had previously had any idea of, and that its office was to supply not a set of model institutions, but principles from which the institutions … might be deduced'. Considering the dogmatic tendency in radicalism, Mill's contributions to the current debate were significant. Among the most important are 'Thoughts on Poetry' (1833), 'Bentham' (1838), 'Coleridge' (1840) and 'Michelet's History of France' (1844): the titles convey the breadth of his interests and anticipate the books in which he was to bring order to moral and social questions. Inspiration came from two main sources: the line of thinking that ran back to Hume, Locke and Newton, the work of the *philosophes*, and now that of the positivist, Auguste Comte. He set out to supply a valid method of proof for conclusions in moral and political science. In 1843 were published the two volumes of his *System of Logic*. In the last section, book VI, he formulated a logic of the human sciences, history, psychology and sociology among them: that it is now widely criticized does not detract from its contemporary importance.

Mill had been tutored in the economic theories of Ricardo. His subsequent interest in economic questions had been reinforced by social concerns: in particular the famine in Ireland and problems there of land-holding. He felt compelled to separate questions of production and distribution when the evidence showed that present systems left hosts of his fellow countrymen defenceless before market forces. He did not become a socialist, but he did review the foundations of society. He tested the principles of 'the dismal science' against the realities of life: no-one was better qualified to do so. In the Victorian intellectual world he was an insider: all the greater his influence.

Since 1823, Mill had been at India House. Since 1836 he had charge of the East India Company's relations with the Indian states. After the Mutiny he was the man chosen to defend the company's administration against the proposed transfer of its powers. When, in 1858, it was dissolved, he was offered a seat on the new council, but chose to retire with a pension sufficient for independence. Soon his wife died and he lived mainly in France, returning only occasionally to his house at Blackheath. His noble *Essay On Liberty* (1859) was dedicated to Harriet. Reviewing 'the nature and limits of power which can be legitimately exercised by society over the individual', it set out, reasonably and eloquently, the libertarian case. His essay on 'The Enfranchisement of Women' seems to reflect Harriet's thinking on social issues. Questions remain. What did she feel about her self-sufficient husband? What room was left for the expansion of her mind, the pursuit of her interests, let alone the intimacies of married life, when he was so much taken up with his work for India and for humanity?

Mill seemed latterly to be returning to the thinking of Bentham and of his father. He was elected to parliament, for Westminster, and sat for three years. He refused to attend to constituents' business. In parliament however he secured concessions during the passage of the Second Reform Bill (1867). The reduction of the National Debt, and representation of women were among projects in which he remained interested after electoral defeat in 1868. He was an uncomfortable political ally to orthodox liberals. In his writing too the utilitarian and the liberal, the agnostic and social idealist, the free trader and advocate of co-operative agriculture sit uncomfortably together. The whole may be less impressive than the parts. He showed, however, that it was possible to be both earnest and tolerant, rational, yet humane. As Morley wrote, he offered 'the strength of an ordered set of convictions, with that pliability and that perceptiveness in face of new truth, which are indispensable to those very convictions being held intelligently …' Wherever there is injustice or oppression it is still to Mill that people turn for the most rational, often the most eloquent of arguments for freedom, toleration and the decencies of public life.

Further Reading
Maurice Cranston, *John Stuart Mill*, 1958.
J. S. Mill, *Autobiography*, ed. H. J. Laski, 1924 (orig. pub. 1873).

MILLAIS, SIR JOHN EVERETT (1829-96), the most popular painter of the Victorian age, was born to a family who had long been natives of Jersey. By the time he was nine, his artistic talent was so pronounced that his parents were persuaded to take him to London. They entered him at the 'best' drawing-school; from which he proceeded to the Royal Academy Schools in 1840 – at eleven, the youngest pupil they had ever taken. Here he won all the prizes. His admiring fellows recognized his precocity by calling him 'the Child'; and it is indeed hard to believe that *Pizarro seizing the Inca of Peru*, exhibited at the Academy in 1846, was the work of a sixteen-year-old: or that he could be so self-confident as to supply, in the following year, a canvas fourteen feet by ten (*The Widow's Mite*) for the Westminster Hall competition.

But then he changed direction. In 1848, he joined with William Holman Hunt, Dante Gabriel Rossetti, and several others, in forming the Pre-Raphaelite Brotherhood: an association of young artists who aimed to effect a small revolution in British painting by reverting to the naturalism, the simplicity, brilliant colouring, and moral symbolism of early Italian-Renaissance painting (sc. before the time of Raphael).

Millais's first-exhibited painting in the 'new' style was *Isabella*, the banquet-scene from Keats's poem: a painting of great virtuosity, with an unorthodox composition, perfection of detail, 'real' faces, glowing colours – and the Brotherhood's initials 'PRB' carved on Isabella's stool. The 'real' faces were taken from his friends and family, though Isabella's sinister brother bears the features of a bully from whom Millais had suffered at the Academy Schools. But critics and public were puzzled; and they were repelled – 'disgusted' – by Millais's next 'Pre-Raphaelite' offering, *Christ in the House of His Parents*, in which the realistic depiction of the Holy Family was felt to be blasphemous. Dickens condemned the picture in words of which he should have been ashamed. But Ruskin, whose *Modern Painters* had supplied or confirmed many of the Brotherhood's ideas, predicted that they would lay 'the foundations of a school of Art nobler than the world has seen for 300 years'.

Nevertheless Millais himself was dismayed by the public reaction. He began to go in for 'safer' subjects, and to paint in a more sentimental vein. Sentiment was a string on which he played all his life. As he put it, 'Pathos is my poetry': excessively so, by present standards, but not by the standards of his age. So *Ophelia*, and *The Return of the Dove to the Ark*, were followed by *The Huguenot*, *The Order of Release*, *The Blind Girl*, *The Black Brunswicker* – each overtly appealing to the emotions of the viewer, each telling a story which would be instantly understood. *Autumn Leaves* (1856) is less narrative: an elegy for the departure of summer, and a captivating evocation of twilight. But in any case it is the *painting* of these pictures, rather than their 'message', which is more admired today. It is hard to imagine that the flowery banks, the dell through which the crystal stream bears Ophelia's body, could be bettered for accuracy of observation; the humble straw on the deck of the Ark (in *The Return of the Dove*), or indeed the rocks which bear up Ruskin in Millais's famous portrait of him (1854).

It was Millais who said that the dominant aim of the Pre-Raphaelites was 'to present on canvas what they saw in Nature'. But by 1860, Millais (along with most of the others) was moving away from the ideals of the Brotherhood. His colouring becomes softer. His brushwork, now looser and broader, suggests rather than elaborates detail. 'Truth to nature' had meant that the model for Ophelia (Elizabeth Siddal, later the wife of Rossetti) must be immersed for hours in a bath warmed by lamps below; and the landscape background of that painting

had occupied Millais for weeks spent beside a Surrey stream. Now his marriage, and the birth of children, gave him economic as well as artistic reasons for painting faster. What is lost is not just the refinement of detail, but the extreme (and, it must be said, unnatural) clarity of perception which gives these earlier paintings a dreamlike quality.

But Millais's popularity increased from year to year. Because he was to a great extent the representative Englishman of the Victorian age, he had a genius for catching the public mood. Thus *The North-West Passage* (1874) is a tribute to the Arctic explorers of the mid-century: it even has the subtitle: 'It must be done, and England should do it.' Then, he made himself a superb painter of children: *The Princes in the Tower*, *An Idyll of 1745*, and – more obviously sentimental – *My First Sermon*, *Cherry Ripe*, and *Bubbles* (1886) – the last a portrait of his grandson, and a comment on the transience of youth, which became even more widely known when (to Millais's displeasure) it was bought by Pears Soap, and used as an advertisement. Meanwhile, his portraits of the good and great – Gladstone, Carlyle, Tennyson – became familiar to the man in the street by reproduction. And he did a great deal of book-illustration in the 1860s: eighty-seven drawings for Trollope's novels alone.

Millais's portrait of Ruskin was begun in 1853, in the Trossachs of Scotland, where Millais was on holiday with the champion of the Pre-Raphaelites and his wife Effie, who had modelled for *The Order of Release*. The Ruskin marriage had already come to grief. Millais and Effie were attracted to each other, but kept a decent distance apart until the Decree of Nullity had been granted and the portrait finished. Their marriage was happy and fruitful. Two of their eight children appear as the boys in the famous *Boyhood of Raleigh* (1870), and others elsewhere. The family spent part of every year in Perthshire, Effie's home country; and it was there that Millais painted his 'pure' landscapes, such as *Chill October* and *Lingering Autumn*.

In London, Millais built himself a mansion at 2 Palace Gate, Kensington: it was a time when successful artists were very well-rewarded – not least through the reproduction of their works in engravings and colour prints. In 1885, he was created a baronet. And since – from the days of 'the Child' onwards – he had served the Royal Academy and been served by it, so it was the very proper climax that in February 1896 he was elected President in succession to his old friend Lord Leighton. But, like Leighton, he too was dying of cancer; and, when the end came, in August, he was buried beside Leighton in St Paul's Cathedral.

The man who had painted these instantly-memorable pictures (for, once seen, they do not go away) was widely mourned. One of the many tributes to him, written soon after his death, is worth quoting because it is characteristically Victorian: '[His] sterling qualities had attracted a host of friends. His frankness and honesty, his geniality and kindliness, and, above all, his manly wholesomeness, without taint of modern decadence or morbidity, endeared him to everyone with whom he came into contact. He was typically English, in the best sense, with all the physical and mental attributes that have enabled our race to dominate the world, a lover of the country, a good shot, a keen fisherman, and a fearless horseman. The very look of him, with his stalwart, well set-up figure and handsome, self-reliant face, conveyed the impression of perfect health of mind and body, and declared the inexhaustible vigour of his nature.'

Further Reading
Benedict Read, *Millais*, 1993.
Keith Roberts, *Millais*, 1967.

MILTON, JOHN (1608-74), Puritan poet and pamphleteer, a Londoner born in Bread Street, Cheapside, was the son of a well-to-do scrivener who was a considerable amateur musician. Sent to St Paul's, he showed literary promise and linguistic gifts as well as a passion for study. Thence he went in 1625 to Christ's College, Cambridge, where he wrote a number of poems in English and in Latin. *On the Morning of Christ's Nativity* was written in 1629, the year of his graduation. Nicknamed 'the lady' at Cambridge because of his fair complexion and slight build, Milton was an austere young man, strict in his Puritanism and dedicated early to using his gifts for the forwarding of the divine plan. He had intended to take orders but felt unable to do so in face of the growing Laudianism of the church. 'Church-outed by the prelates', he turned instead to poetry as his chosen task, and in 1632 withdrew to Horton in Buckinghamshire, where his father had retired from business, and devoted himself to a strenuous course of study of the classics and ancient history in preparation for his writing. In 1632 he composed *L'Allegro* and *Il Penseroso*, neither of them published until later; in 1634 his masque *Comus* was presented at Ludlow Castle; and in 1637 he wrote *Lycidas* in memory of a Cambridge friend drowned in the Irish Sea. During 1638-9 he travelled in Italy, and when he returned to England in July 1639 it was clear that a political crisis could not be long delayed. That same month Charles sent for Wentworth from Ireland.

The crisis transformed Milton's career, turning him into a pamphleteer and, later, a civil servant; for twenty years he wrote no poetry except sonnets and Latin verses. He settled in London, taking his two nephews as resident pupils in 1640, and next year he opened his campaign for the Puritan cause with a series of pamphlets attacking episcopacy. In 1642 he married the daughter of a royalist magistrate of Forest Hill in Oxfordshire.

After about a month she went home on a visit and declined to return to Milton; not until 1645 did she eventually do so, and then Milton supported her family, whose fortunes had been broken by the war. Shortly after her departure Milton chose to publish a tract in defence of divorce (1643) which caused an outcry among his fellow Puritans. Two of his finest pieces of prose-writing appeared in 1644 – the severe essay *Of Education* and the great defence of freedom of the press, *Areopagitica*, with its celebrated imperative 'Give me the liberty to know, to utter, and to argue freely, according to conscience, above all liberties'. The opinions expressed in *Areopagitica* were not acceptable to the Presbyterian supporters of revolution, while for his part Milton, as he said in 1646, believed that 'New Presbyter is but old Priest writ large'. His Independent sympathies led him to support the army leaders against parliament in the quarrel which developed after the defeat of the royalists in the First Civil War, and he went on to accept the extreme Republican doctrine and the execution of the king. This action he defended in 1649, both in *The Tenure of Kings and Magistrates*, justifying the deposition and punishment of tyrants, and in the *Eikonoklastes*, his notably unsuccessful reply to the *Eikon Basilike*. Milton's services and importance to the Puritan cause were recognized by his appointment (1649) as Latin Secretary to the Commonwealth Council of State, the post which he held until the Restoration. By now his eyesight was failing, and he became totally blind in 1652, the year also of his first wife's death. The Council retained him in his post, although they provided him with assistants (among whom was Andrew Marvell) and reduced his salary. He married again in 1656, but his second wife died in 1658. Towards the end of the Commonwealth he returned to pamphleteering, with attacks on compulsion in religion and upon tithes, and two months before Charles II was restored he wrote his last plea for Republicanism, *The Readie and Easie way to establish a Free Commonwealth*.

As a defender of regicide Milton was in grave peril in 1660. He was arrested and imprisoned, but thanks probably to the intervention of Marvell and other friends, suffered no more than a heavy fine. With his hopes for the Puritan state destroyed, Milton turned back to the great task he had set himself as a young man, to use poetry to

> ... assert Eternal Providence
> and justify the ways of God to men.

Paradise Lost includes a little material written at the beginning of the Civil Wars; according to Aubrey, Milton began the body of the poem in 1658 and completed it in 1663. Not until 1667 did he find a publisher, who paid him £10 for the manuscript. *Paradise Regained* and *Samson Agonistes* followed in 1671, three years before his death. In his last years Milton, who had married a third wife, thirty years his junior, in 1663, lived in quiet retirement, taking no part in public affairs.

Aubrey, in a sympathetic description, tells us that Milton's 'harmonical and ingenious soul did lodge in a beautiful and well-proportioned body'. Not all his contemporaries were so charitable, and, indeed, Aubrey goes on to admit that 'he was much more admired abroad than at home'. There were aspects of Milton which they, as well as later generations, found somewhat repellent – the savagery of some of his invective, the harshness of the discipline visited upon his daughters and pupils, the pride which was always present in his austerity and which often ran into vanity, the narrowness of his personal relationships. And there was much that Milton was not. He was no democrat: his ideal of government seems to have been rule by an oligarchy of rich Puritans. He was not entirely consistent even in his superb championship of toleration, for he was at times willing to concede that it might be necessary in the national interest to forbid Roman Catholic worship. Yet when all qualifications are made Milton stands out as one of the dominant figures of his century. Had he died when he was thirty, *Comus*, *Lycidas* and his other early poems would have assured him immortality. He is one of the supreme political pamphleteers, not so much for his prose – which is unequal – as for the timelessness and the challenging force of the argument for social and civil freedom which is at the heart of his writing. *Paradise Lost*, an epic unparalleled in English, the finest achievement of his genius, uniting his vast classical and Renaissance learning with his extraordinarily sensitive ear and his tremendous imaginative force, was also the noblest expression of the concern of seventeenth-century Puritanism with the eternal issue of Good and Evil.

Further Reading

Christopher Hill, *Milton and the English Revolution*, 1977.
J. H. Hanford, *John Milton, Englishman*, 1950.
F. E. Hutchinson, *Milton and the English Mind*, 1947.

MINTO, GILBERT ELLIOT, 1st EARL OF MINTO

(1751-1814), Governor-General of India, had a liberal and cosmopolitan upbringing. He was the son of Sir Gilbert Minto, third Baronet of Minto, politician, scholar and wit, a leader of Edinburgh society. He chose his friend David Hume to tutor his son; he also attended the Pension Militaire at Mirabeau. Minto brought an open and inquiring mind and liberal principles to his political career. After being at Christ Church, Oxford and Lincoln's Inn he became member for Morpeth in 1776. He was a hot Whig and a friend, among others, of Burke; he shared Burke's views upon India, carried a motion condemning the conduct of Elijah Impey at Fort William and shared in the impeachment of Warren Hastings. Like Burke he parted company with Fox over the Revolution. He was employed by the government as negotiator at

Toulon after Hood had occupied the town in 1793. Experience in administration came in 1794 when he was made governor of Corsica. In that unlikely spot he experimented with constitutional government, set up a parliament and expelled General Paoli, 'the liberator'.

In 1798 he received a peerage and in the following year was appointed ambassador at the court of Vienna, where it was his delicate responsibility to preserve good relations with our strongest ally. He was for a short time President of the Board of Control; then the 'Talents' ministry made him Governor-General of India. He was there from 1807 to 1813. He followed the autocratic Wellesley, who had dealt with the problems of India in the strategic context of the war against France – and taken advantage of the brief interlude of peace to make war upon the Marathas. Wellesley had behaved as the servant of the government rather than of the East India Company. The Directors were alarmed by the extent of their new responsibilities after two decades of conquest. Minto's mission was to consolidate and pacify, a role well suited to his easy and rational temper. He was not content, however, with a passive role. The Russian bogey raised its head when Napoleon made his treaty with the tsar at Tilsit (1807). Minto countered threats of Russian activity in Central Asia by a triple diplomatic move. Malcolm was sent to Persia, Elphinstone to Afghanistan, Metcalfe to the Punjab, to construct alliances. The work was skilfully done. Ranjit Singh of Lahore proved a loyal ally. Shujah Shah of Afghanistan was soon, however, to lose his throne. The emphasis of policy was on security against external threats. In central India the peace that Cornwallis had patched up with the Marathas had left the inhabitants defenceless against marauding Rajpur or Maratha chieftains. The Pindaris, Pathan mercenaries formerly employed by the Maratha chiefs, formed robber bands. It was left to Minto's successor to deal with them.

Minto appreciated clever and imaginative men. He was quick to appreciate the quality of Elpinstone and Metcalfe. He gave warm and practical support to Raffles, whose plans fitted in with his own desire to seal off the Indian ocean from the French and their Dutch puppet-allies. He actually accompanied Raffles on his expedition to Java (1811) and, after its successful conclusion, was able to write: 'An empire has been added to the dominion of the British Crown and converted from a seat of hostile machinations and commercial competition into an augmentation of British power and prosperity.' Remembering perhaps his Corsican days, he stayed for some weeks with Raffles, helping him to establish its government on liberal principles. The exertions of this year may have been responsible for his decline in health. He died the year after his return from India.

Humane and broad in his interests, Minto strengthened a good tradition. He was genuinely interested in the

Indians and ready to learn from India. He went deeply into the beliefs and customs of Hindus and Moslems. In the view of English evangelicals he was sadly tepid in support of Christian missions. But he projected the establishment of colleges for Moslems. He was no Wellesley to take bold military initiatives, no Bentinck to defy unpopularity and tackle abuses in a radical way, but he was ready to back good and active men.

Further Reading
John Buchan, *Lord Minto*, 1924.

MITFORD, MARY RUSSELL (1787-1855) was born at Alresford in Hampshire, the only child of Dr George Mitford. He was a cultivated man but childishly un-stable, petulant and irresponsible. He was ambitious in his choice of acquaintances (Fox, Sheridan, Cobbett were among them). Unfortunately he loved coursing, whist, and conversation better than his medical practice. To sustain himself he relied on a diminishing stock of capital. He received one fortune from his wife. There was another windfall when Mary, aged ten, chose him a lottery ticket which won £20,000 and enabled him to build a house at Reading fitting what he imagined to be his station. Mary was indulged and happy in childhood, allowed to read as much as she wanted and she went to a school in Chelsea, run by a French émigré, where the arts and graces were encouraged. But she grew up to a life of vicissitudes of wealth and poverty.

Gambling and extravagance so reduced the family that they had to move to a cottage at Three Mile Cross, a village between Reading and Basingstoke, where they lived for the next thirty years. To support her father Mary turned to writing. Her *Poems* appeared in 1810. Her tragedy *Julian* was performed at Covent Garden in 1823 with Macready in the title role: later *Foscari* (1826) and *Rienzi* (1828) were still more successful. *Charles I* was actually banned by the licensee, George Colman, which shows how fear of republicanism lasted in England after the Napoleonic Wars. She could never earn enough to support her feckless father, who had to be thwarted in his attempt to borrow from a trust fund set up to protect the family and to be traced to, and rescued from, a gaming saloon in London. Mary's mother died in 1830, her father lived on till 1842; he was nearly arrested for debt in the last year of his life.

Sadly the writing that she wished to indulge in for art and pleasure became a compulsory labour. She wrote poems and plays, potboilers for the public taste, reflect-ing the zeal for improvement and concern for outward propriety that was becoming fashionable. She had been reared in a more easy-going tradition and she always resisted the extremes of evangelical fervour and doc-trine. 'God forbid that I should be a canter', as she said when deploring Byron's 'want of purity'. Lamb, Eliza-beth Barrett and Landor were among her correspondents

and she was never wholly isolated. Her relatively retired life in a Hampshire village and her need perhaps to find some stable and secure ground in a life of shifts and emergencies led her to write letters describing her life in which the reader may find the genesis of her master-piece. The series of sketches that first appeared in the *Lady's Magazine* (between 1824 and 1832) and which make up *Our Village* are justly famous. Her skill is unassertive, the style is quietly unself-conscious, that of a good letter-writer. Her theme is 'country scenery and country manners as they exist in a small village in the south of England'. Elizabeth Barrett wrote with justice that Miss Mitford, 'a sort of prose Crabbe in the sun, but with more grace and less strength', wrote prose better than poetry, 'and transcends rather in Dutch minuteness and high finishing, than in Italian ideality and passion'. George Baxter's drawings well catch that 'minuteness'. She excels in the minute delineation of landscape. Effects are sometimes avowedly 'pretty' and she likes to describe what she finds agreeable, but her keen painter's eye saves her scenes from being merely sentimental. Like her landscapes, her characters are based on what she observed. She can be mildly caustic or urbanely detached in the manner of an Addison while her delight in life's small corners and curiosities recalls Lamb. *Our Village*, together with *Sketches of a Country Town* (based on Reading), affords a fair reflection of the character of a brave and amiable woman.

Mary Mitford was so exhausted at the time of her father's death that she wrote little thereafter. Remaining debts were paid off by public subscription. In 1851 she moved to the village of Swallowfield. In the following year her pony-carriage overturned and she only made a partial recovery from the accident. Her fragile health was a poor reward for her unselfish life but her spirit was indomitable. Charles Kingsley visited her soon after the accident: 'I can never forget the little figure rolled up in two chairs in the little Swallowfield room, packed round with books up to the ceiling, on to the floor … some-where out of the upper end of the heap, gleaming under a great globular brow, two such eyes as I never, perhaps, saw in any other Englishwoman …'

Further Reading
Vera Watson, *Mary Russell Mitford*, 1949.
Constance Hill, *Mary Russell Mitford and her Surroundings*, 1920.

MOLEYNS, ADAM (*c*.1400-50), Bishop of Chichester from 1445, distinguished himself both as a politician and as a Renaissance humanist. The younger son of a Lancashire knight, he prepared for a career in the church by studying at Oxford University, where he graduated as doctor of civil law in 1435. Long before then, in 1429, he was at the papal Curia in Italy, where he not only ingratiated himself with the pope, but mixed with

Poggio and other Renaissance humanists. He was appointed papal chamberlain and clerk of the apostolic chamber in 1435, when he acted as royal proctor at the Curia. He visited the Council of Basle on his way home to pursue an administrative career in England. He was clerk to the royal council from 1436-42 and was employed on frequent diplomatic missions from 1438. His appointment as king's secretary in 1441 involved close contact with Henry VI. Moleyns won his trust – witness his involvement in the foundation of Eton College – and established considerable influence over the impressionable monarch. In 1444 he achieved ministerial rank as keeper of the privy seal. Capable and diligent, he made himself indispensable to the Duke of Suffolk by the late 1440s, becoming intimately and emotionally involved with his policies. Hence his rash accusations of financial maladministration and favouritism against the Duke of York as lieutenant of France in 1446. The fall of Rouen in 1449 and the Crown's virtual bankruptcy represented complete failure and discredited him politically, as Moleyns recognized. To escape the inevitable storm, he resigned his ministry in December 1449 and planned to go on pilgrimage abroad. Before going, however, he went to Portsmouth to pay the troops, was accused of treachery for losing Normandy, and was murdered on 9 January 1450. Suffolk's impeachment followed.

Moleyns's aristocratic connection contributed to his lightning promotion, but his ability and literary accomplishments mattered more. He

successfully cultivated an elegant Latin style free from the conventions of Latin prose as taught during the Middle Ages. Moleyns appears to have been on the same level as most Italian humanists of the time and by far superior to any of his English contemporaries, Beckyngton included.

Since such skills had become essential for diplomacy, they brought Moleyns rapid ecclesiastical promotion. His first rectories in the 1420s presumably came through family connections, but those that followed were the rewards of papal and royal service. Altogether he enjoyed fourteen rectories and twelve canonries, archdeaconries and deaneries, not all at once. He duly became Bishop of Chichester in 1445.

As Chichester was a poor bishopric, Moleyns, who was certainly ambitious and reputedly covetous, could expect promotion to a better see in due course. Suffolk indeed proposed him unsuccessfully for the bishopric of London. In the meantime Moleyns applied himself to improving Chichester's rights and amenities. He secured royal exemption from the court of admiralty on his lands and in 1447 was licensed to include 12,000 acres of land in his parks and to crenellate twelve manor houses. Even after returning to England, he maintained his classical interests, corresponding with the noted humanist Aeneas Sylvius Piccolomini (later Pope Pius II 1458-64), but he

was far too eminent and busy to teach or write. Like other early English humanists he found that his intellectual accomplishments were worth more in politics than education and brought rapid promotion to positions of responsibility that prevented further study.

Further Reading
R. A. Griffiths, *The Reign of King Henry VI 1422-61*, 1981.
R. Weiss, *Humanism in England during the Fifteenth Century*, 3rd edn, 1967.

MOLEYNS, SIR JOHN (*d*.1361) made his fortune from royal service and crime in the early fourteenth century. The son of a Hampshire MP and thus of gentle birth, Moleyns shared such aristocratic tastes as fighting, jousting, hawking and the chase. He was also literate. As a younger son, Moleyns made his way in life by undertaking difficult and potentially violent tasks, such as arresting people or ships and debt-collection. He entered royal service about 1325 during the Despenser régime and participated in both the revolutions of 1326 and – as Montagu's protégé – of 1330. Just as Montagu rose to be Earl of Salisbury, so Moleyns was in high favour of earl and king in the 1330s, becoming esquire of the household, knight (1334), master of the royal goshawks, and recipient of frequent licences to crenellate, impark and alienate. He went with Salisbury and Edward III to the Low Countries in 1338, travelling frequently to and fro as intermediary with the government in England, but suffered from Edward's wrath against Archbishop Stratford in 1340. His trial, like that of John Oxenford, brought many misdeeds to light. Taking flight, he was pardoned only in 1345 but rapidly recovered his former favour thereafter. He was summoned to a great council as a baron in 1347 and became steward of the queen's household in 1352, but he failed to answer further charges in 1355, pleaded benefit of clergy in 1357, and died in prison in 1361.

John married Gill Mauduit, granddaughter – but not heiress – of Robert Poges of Stoke Poges. During the disturbances of 1326 he murdered Gill's uncle, *induced* her grandfather to surrender Stoke Poges to him, and suborned the judge sent to investigate. This was merely the first of a whole series of crimes including kidnapping, chicanery, seizure of lands, abuse of office and forest offences. Since he was a royal servant, none of his victims dared complain until 1340. He thus resembles the unjust sheriff John Oxenford and the notorious Folville and Coterell gangs of gentlemen-bandits that terrorized the Midlands at this time. By 1340 his lands were worth about £800 a year, he had stocks of armour, plate, jewels and wine, and several hundred pounds in coin, which took several days for royal agents to list. In 1357 he was charged both with abuse of office – notably paying himself excessive wages – and straightforward crime, notably horse-theft. The speed of his second fall suggests improved standards of public order: certainly the criminal gangs declined, partly due to alternative profitable employment as soldiers in France. Moleyns's recall and promotion, like those of Hengham and Stratton somewhat earlier, indicates that Edward III was no more scrupulous about employing discredited servants than his grandfather Edward I. Despite his second fall, Moleyns's heirs succeeded to Stoke Poges and his other estates.

Although ruthless and self-interested, Moleyns performed valued services for others and had genuine religious feeling. He was the benefactor of houses of Augustinian canons at Southwark and Oxford and founded chantries at Burnham Abbey, of which he was patron, Stoke Poges and Ditton. Evidently he was more than merely a man of violence.

Further Reading

N. M. Fryde, 'A Medieval Robber Baron: Sir John Moleyns of Stoke Poges, Buckinghamshire', *Medieval Legal Records*, ed. R. F. Hunnisett and J. Post, 1975.

G. R. Elvey, 'The First Fall of Sir John Moleyns', *Records of Buckinghamshire* xx.ii, 1972.

J. G. Bellamy, 'The Coterel Gang: An Anatomy of a Band of 14th-Century Criminals', *English Historical Review* lxxix, 1964.

E. L. G. Stones, 'The Folvilles of Ashby-Folville, Leicestershire and their associates in crime', *Transactions of the Royal Historical Society*, 5th ser. vii, 1957.

MONCK, GEORGE, 1st DUKE OF ALBEMARLE

(1608-70), was born at Potheridge near Torrington, of a landed family long established in Devon, connected by marriage with the Grenvilles. There is a tale that at the age of sixteen he thrashed the under-sheriff of Devon, who had arrested his father for debt (after being bribed not to do so), and he was certainly packed off on Buckingham's expedition to Cadiz under Sir Richard Grenville in 1625. This episode began a career of fighting which took him to La Rochelle in 1627-8 and to the Low Countries in the 1630s. In 1638 he returned to England a skilled soldier, distinguished by the courage which he had shown in the capture of Breda (1637) and by the seriousness with which he took his profession. He took part in the Bishops' Wars (1638-9); like Fairfax, he saw his troops routed at Newburn. In 1642 he commanded a regiment of Foot against the rebels in Ireland, and in 1643 he was one of the royalist commanders defeated and captured by Fairfax at Nantwich. Sent to the Tower, he remained there until the end of the First Civil War, consoling himself by writing a book, *Observations upon Military and Political Affairs*, and by making love to his laundress, Mrs Nan Ratsford, a blacksmith's daughter. From 1647 to 1649 he served parliament as Major-General in Ulster, returning to England after making an armistice with the rebel leader Owen Roe O'Neill; this incident temporarily clouded his reputation, but not with Cromwell, under whom he fought at Dunbar (1650); and it was Monck who reduced Scotland to order by the end of 1651.

In the following year Monck, at the age of forty-four, became an admiral, in the First Dutch War. His ignorance of nautical language was a joke; his Chaplain and first biographer, Thomas Gumble, says that when the seamen, according to their terms of art, cried 'starboard and larboard', he always cried, 'Ay, boys, let us board them.' Yet he proved a successful naval commander in action, displaying his natural vigour and courage and also considerable strategical and tactical insight. His victory in the battle of the Gabbard (1653), after his fellow admiral Richard Deane had been killed by his side, was a convincing one; and later in the same year off Scheveningen he deliberately employed the manoeuvre of 'breaking the enemy's line from to leeward' to cut the Dutch fleet in half and win the battle in which the great Dutch admiral, Van Tromp, was killed. This practically ended the war, and in 1654 Monck returned to Scotland as Governor – a mark of the trust which Cromwell, now Lord Protector, placed in him. He ruled with moderation and was not unpopular. Yet the real significance of this part of his career lay in its ending; for his authority in Scotland, his army and the full treasury which he built up, gave him a central position in the crisis which gradually developed after Cromwell's death in September 1658. For six months George Monck was to be the dominant figure in England, and the use he made of his power was decisive in our history.

He accepted and supported Richard Cromwell, and when Richard departed he submitted to the recalled Rump, writing to the Speaker in June 1659 'obedience is my great principle, and I have always, and ever shall, reverence the parliament's resolutions in civil things as infallible and sacred'. Later that summer he showed no sympathy with the royalist intrigues which caused Sir George Booth's futile rising. What moved Monck to intervention in England was the breach between parliament and the army commanders headed by Lambert and Fleetwood, who in October expelled the Rump. Monck purged his army of disaffected elements and prepared to march south; the unpopularity of military rule led the commanders to change their mind and recall the Rump in December; whereupon Monck, crossing the Tweed at Coldstream on New Year's Day, 1660, moved on London. The army which Lambert led north to halt him melted away in Yorkshire, with Fairfax taking the field against it. On his way Monck declared firmly against monarchy, but committed himself to nothing else; his remarkable natural taciturnity was no doubt invaluable, yet it seems likely that he had at this stage no definite policy. After his arrival in London (3 February) he submitted at first to the Rump's orders to punish the city for its defiance; but seeing how bitterly resented this action was, he turned on his masters with an ultimatum and on 21 February readmitted the members excluded by Pride's Purge twelve years earlier, a tremendously popular step which enabled parliament to dissolve itself and opened the way to a free election. At the same time, convinced that only the return of the king would prevent anarchy, he consented at last to receive a letter from Charles II, now in Holland. 'Cautious to the end, he refused to commit anything to paper, but sent some valuable advice orally.'* The advice was the basis of the Declaration of Breda (April), itself the foundation of the Restoration settlement. The elections held later that month returned a strong royalist majority, and Monck at last made clear to parliament his approval of the return of the monarchy. Appropriately, it was George Monck who welcomed Charles II on the beach at Dover in May and, in effect, handed his kingdom back to him.

The great moment of his career was over. Loaded with honours and created Duke of Albemarle, he served Charles II well for ten years. Modest in his tastes, careful with his accumulated wealth, old-fashioned in his standards, he was out of place at the Restoration court; and so was the Duchess of Albemarle, the former laundress of the Tower, who had been his mistress and whom he married in 1654 after the death of her farrier husband. Little attention was paid to his political views; but in military matters he was regarded with respect. It was Monck who presided over the disbandment of the greater part of the Cromwellian army in the months after the Restoration. He went to sea once more, against De Ruyter in the Second Dutch War (1664-7), but with little success; nor could he prevent the disaster of the Dutch attack on the fleet in the Medway, though his appointment to command did much to quell panic in London. He died in 1670 and was buried in high state in Westminster Abbey.

Charles II's government was too poor to build a monument for Monck; and later historians have tended to neglect him. In many ways he was easy to poke fun at, and to underrate. His lady, something of a scold, besides her lowly origins; his homely establishment; his slowness of speech; his total lack of brilliance; his equally total lack of political ambition – these things, in different ways, made contemporaries underestimate him. Pepys (24 October 1667) could write: 'I know not how, the blockhead Albermarle hath strange luck to be loved, though he be (and every man must know it) the heaviest man in the world, but stout and honest to his country'. Thomas Gumble assessed him differently, saying 'his Judgement was slow but sure, he was very cogitative, and of a great natural prudence and cunning in his own affairs'. There is a measure of irony about Monck's career. Essentially a professional soldier, dedicated to his

calling, he achieved little in land warfare; his campaigns in Ireland were abortive, he was defeated in his only battle in England and spent the remainder of the Civil War in the Tower, his main achievement in Scotland was as a proconsul rather than as a general. On the sea, by contrast, where he was an amateur, he may be regarded as an innovator – the founder of the mêlée school of naval warfare, anticipating Rodney by over a century. Above all, at the climax of his life, it was Monck's interpretation of the proper role of the army in the state which put an end to the Commonwealth and to military rule in England. For he believed simply and profoundly that soldiers should be the servants of civil authority, not the instruments of generals ambitious for dictatorship. 'I am engaged,' he said, 'in conscience and honour to see my country freed from that intolerable slavery of a sword government, and I know that England cannot, nay, will not endure it.' Monck presided over the Restoration, ensuring that it was peaceful. By the manner in which he achieved this he achieved something which, on a long view, was much more important than the return of the Stuarts; on the morrow of the triumphs of the Cromwellian army, the most remarkable army in English history, one of whose leading commanders he had been, he established the tradition that the British army is non-political. No doubt George Monck owed a good deal to luck, to the realism of Charles II, to the blunders of Lambert and the other generals. But it is not easy to dispute the force of Gumble's rambling observation: 'His prudence was a Virtue Paramount in him and Mistress of all the rest, and this appeared that after the exclusion of Majesty, and put out of the Throne for many years, he restored it without one drop of blood, and made them his instruments, who had been the excluders, and having to doe with so many various interests and factions, (all striving for the Power) he managed them so well that they were all serviceable to his ends, and those children of the Serpent, with all their little Policies and cunning, could never give him the Go-by, but he out-witted them all.'

Further Reading
Maurice Ashley, *General Monck*, 1977.

MONTAGU, CHARLES, 1st EARL OF HALIFAX (1661-1715), the statesman responsible for the foundation of the National Debt and the Bank of England, was born at Horton, in Northamptonshire, of a cadet branch of a family already prominent in seventeenth-century England, and was educated at Westminster and Trinity College, Cambridge, of which he became a Fellow. A clever and witty young man, he wrote with Matthew Prior in 1687 *The Town and Country Mouse*, a successful burlesque of John Dryden's recently-published *The Hind and the Panther*. Elected MP for Malden in 1689, he was an able debater and rose very swiftly to

*G. Davies, *The Early Stuarts*, 1959 edn, p.257.

eminence, becoming a Commissioner of the Treasury in 1691 and Chancellor of the Exchequer in 1694. He held these offices until 1699, and he was in that time the main figure responsible for a series of financial reforms as important as any in our history. These measures, adopted initially to finance William's War of the League of Augsburg (1689-97), made it possible in the next reign for Godolphin to pay for Marlborough's war; and they provided the structure within which British public finance has been conducted ever since. They included the creation of the National Debt arising from the long-term loan of 1693; the establishment in 1694 of the Bank of England, itself the product of another loan; the beginning of the system of a general fund, consolidating the national finances; the great recoinage of 1696, carried through in co-operation with the new Master of the Mint, Montagu's old Trinity friend Sir Isaac Newton, and paid for by the imposition of the window tax; and the first issue of Exchequer bills. Not the least important feature of these measures was that for the first time they gave the man who lent to the state a real sense of confidence, secured on assets more stable than the whim of a monarch. Thereby perhaps Montagu did more than any other man to establish the Revolution Settlement.

Montagu, who sat in the Commons until he got his peerage in 1700, was an adroit parliamentarian, and has been described by David Ogg as 'our first real Cabinet minister, because he headed a great department, and had to defend his conduct of that department in the Commons'. In 1698 he was responsible for the setting-up of the 'new' East India Company. He was a Whig leader, a member of the Junto of five, and was one of those let into the secret of the Partition Treaty of 1699. In the anti-Whig reaction of the last years of William's reign this, together with the grants of Irish land which he received, provided an excuse for his impeachment in 1701; the Lords dismissed the charges.

The writer of the *Dictionary of National Biography* article on Halifax observes in a crushing sentence that 'his ambition was great, his vanity excessive, and his arrogance unbounded'. There is some evidence that success went to his head. It seems likely that personal qualities account for the fact that he held no great office in Anne's reign, even in the years of Whig supremacy, although he was one of their leaders in the Lords' debates. He was one of the English Commissioners appointed to negotiate the Union with Scotland, and in 1706 he went on a Whig diplomatic mission to see the Electress Sophia in Hanover. In 1714 he was one of the regents named by George I to administer the kingdom, and he was at the Treasury again for a few months before his death in 1715. A man of taste, Halifax was not unimportant as a patron of literature; for all Swift's hard comment that what Halifax gave to literary men was 'good words and good dinners', it is clear that he did much more than this for Addison.

Further Reading
D. Ogg, *England in the Reigns of James II and William III*, 1955, Chap. 14.

MONTAGU, EDWARD, 1st EARL OF SANDWICH

(1625-72), admiral and patron of Pepys, was the son of the member for Huntingdonshire in the Long Parliament. His father was a royalist, but the family was divided, and Edward Montagu followed the lead of his cousin the Earl of Manchester. He was at Marston Moor and at Naseby, and he succeeded his father as the county member. In Barebone's parliament he was prominent among the moderates, and under the Protectorate he was strongly attached to the cause of his neighbour Oliver Cromwell, whom he wanted to take the Crown. In 1656 he was appointed joint General-at-sea, although he had no naval experience. He went over to royalism in 1659 after the fall of Richard, and brought his fleet back from the Sound in the hope of supporting Sir George Booth's rising. He arrived too late, but luckily the government was too busy coping with Lambert's activities, and Montagu was merely allowed to resign. Next year he was given joint command of the fleet with Monck, whom he detested, and purged it of Republicans and sectaries, before sailing to Holland to bring Charles II home on his flagship the *Naseby*, renamed *Royal Charles*. His reward for his services was the earldom of Sandwich.

Sandwich had a somewhat chequered career in Charles II's reign. The picture of him which emerges even from his kinsman and protégé Pepys's *Diary* is not over-attractive. He was extravagant and much in debt, and in 1663 Pepys took it upon himself to write a 'great letter of reproof' to Sandwich about his conduct with his mistress, Mrs Becke of Chelsea. As an admiral he fought well at Lowestoft in 1664 under the Duke of York, breaking the Dutch line. But in 1665 he was in trouble over his handling of prize-goods, alleged to have been plundered by himself and his officers, and he was deprived of command and sent off on an embassy to Madrid. He returned to the sea in the Third Dutch War, and in 1672, having fought with great courage in the battle of Solebay, he was drowned after his ship was blown up. His body was later picked up and he was buried in Westminster Abbey.

Further Reading
R. Ollard, *Cromwell's Earl: a Life of Edward Montagu, 1st Earl of Sandwich*, 1994.
F. R. Harns, *Edward Montagu, 1st Earl of Sandwich*, 1912.

MONTAGU, EDWARD, VISCOUNT MANDE-VILLE and 2nd EARL OF MANCHESTER (1602-71), parliamentarian commander, came of a great

Huntingdonshire family, and like the lesser Huntingdonshire squire who was three years his senior, Oliver Cromwell, went to Sidney Sussex College, Cambridge. He was given a barony in his own right, and took the courtesy title of Viscount Mandeville, when his father was created Earl of Manchester in 1626. According to Clarendon, he won court favour early through Buckingham, from whose family his first wife came. But he married five times; his second wife was a Rich, the daughter of the Puritan Earl of Warwick, and thenceforward he moved in Puritan circles unfriendly to the Crown. Austere, formal, kindly, gentle, Mandeville seems also to have had a flair for political organization, and his house in Chelsea became a centre for Pym and his supporters. The fact that he was the only peer whom Charles attempted to arrest together with the Five Members in January 1642 is a measure of his importance in the opposition. Although he had no military experience, he was given high rank in the parliamentary army. His father died in 1642 and it was as Earl of Manchester that he became, in 1643, Major-General of the army of the Eastern Association, with Cromwell as his subordinate. His record until after Marston Moor was no bad one, though until the summer of 1644 he remained anchored to the eastern counties. But the scale of parliament's triumph at Marston Moor transformed the future, opening up a prospect of total victory. Men like Oliver welcomed this, sensing it as realism in dealing with Charles I; but it horrified a cautious aristocrat like Manchester, who wanted a negotiated peace. As he said in a council of war that winter, 'I beseech you let's consider what we do. The king cares not how oft he fights, but it concerns us to be wary, for in fighting we venture all to nothing. If we fight him a hundred times and beat him ninety-nine, we shall be hanged – we shall lose our estates, and our posterities be undone'.

So the military opportunity created by Marston Moor was lost. Lethargy and procrastination governed Manchester's conduct, reaching a climax in the delay which allowed the royalists to escape at the second battle of Newbury. Cromwell could not tolerate this, and in parliament denounced Manchester's 'backwardness to all action'. Behind the clash of personalities and the opposing strategies lay the widening conflict between the Independents and the Presbyterians, with all its implications in politics, religion and social class, and here Manchester's attitude was plain. When the Self-Denying Ordinance of 1645 brought his military career to an end he returned to parliament as a leading Presbyterian peer. He was bitterly opposed to the king's trial, he took no part in public affairs under the Republic, and he welcomed the Restoration. Charles II made him Lord Chamberlain and gave him the Garter. He died in 1671, and Burnet and Clarendon alike eulogized him, the former as 'both a virtuous and a generous man', the latter as

'of all men who had ever borne arms against the king … the most worthy to be received into the trust and confidence in which he was placed'.

MONTAGU, JOHN, EARL OF SALISBURY (1351-1400)

was 'one of the few genuine friends that (King) Richard had' in 1399 and is supposedly the only one motivated by 'love rather than self-interest'. Six generations of Montagus gave loyal service to the Crown. The third generation had been represented by the first Earl of Salisbury, John's grandfather; the fourth generation by the second earl – a soldier of distinction – and by John's father John Lord Montagu, soldier and steward of Richard II's household; John himself was the fifth; and his son Thomas, the great earl, the sixth. The younger John distinguished himself militarily in France in 1369 when only eighteen, securing several ransomable captives, went on crusade to Prussia against the Slavs in 1391-2, and succeeded his uncle as knight of the Garter in 1397-8. He was a member of the royal household – a king's knight – by 1383, during his father's stewardship, but he was not yet important enough to be appealed at the Merciless Parliament of 1388. More influential later, he was then one of the so-called Lollard knights who protected heretics from persecution, associated with other Lollard knights like Clanvowe and Sturry, and wrote highly-regarded poetry – 'ballads, songs, rondels, and lays' – all of which are now apparently lost. Although only once a diplomat, sent in 1398-9 to thwart Bolingbroke's second marriage, he 'seems to have had unusually close relations with the French court'. Soldier, courtier, crusader, and poet, he 'belonged to the international chivalrous class and spoke its lingua franca'.

Yet Salisbury was an earl only for the last three years of his life. His father was a younger son, whose barony and offices were earned by arduous service to the Black Prince, Edward III and Richard II. Unable to endow his son generously, he doubtless gave him access to military and courtly circles, whilst overshadowing him for many years. How much the younger John needed independent means is suggested by his marriage to the twice-widowed daughter of a London mayor: Maud, daughter (but not heiress) of Adam Francis (d.1375), widow of the grocer John Aubrey and Sir Alan Buxhull KG. His chosen residence was her manor of Shenley in Hertfordshire. He was the first earl to marry into mercantile stock, though he was not then an earl. His cousin's death in 1382 made him heir presumptive, but not until 1397 did he succeed his uncle as third earl. No longer the vast inheritance of 1337, shorn of Denbigh and the Isle of Man, the earldom of Salisbury nevertheless remained an outstanding west country estate sufficient to transform Montagu's status, prosperity and political career.

Montagu first came to the forefront of the political stage in 1397, when he was one of eight noblemen who appealed Gloucester, Arundel and Warwick of treason. He was not one of the *duketti* – little dukes – selected for further promotion, but the king did back his claims to the great lordship of Denbigh, though significantly not to the point of success: Earl Roger Mortimer's death in 1398 reduced the value to the king of Montagu's rival claim. Montagu accompanied King Richard II on his second expedition to Ireland in 1399 and was sent back on Bolingbroke's invasion to recruit in north Wales. He failed. The Welsh would not join him, even the forces he brought deserted, believing the king to be dead, and he withdrew with only a small force to the security of Conway Castle, where King Richard joined him and where he surrendered to his enemies. Montagu was briefly imprisoned but released in time to join Exeter in the abortive rebellion of 1400 against Henry IV, which resulted in his lynching at Cirencester and the forfeiture in parliament of his estates. Montagu's heir, however, was allowed to succeed in 1409 and lived up to the family tradition of good service, this time to the Lancastrian dynasty.

Further Reading
J. A. Tuck, *Richard II and the English Nobility*, 1973.
K. B. McFarlane, *Lancastrian Kings and Lollard Knights*, 1971.
A. B. Steel, *Richard II*, 1941.

MONTAGU, JOHN, 4th EARL OF SANDWICH

(1718-92), First Lord of the Admiralty, 'Jemmy Twitcher', because of the fads and failures which characterized the last years of his long control of the admiralty, has not received the credit that he deserves for devoted administration at a time when the government was more interested in reducing taxation than in maintaining the armed forces. Indeed, he is dismissed thus by a biographical dictionary: 'The scandalous fourth earl, invented sandwiches to eat at the gaming table.' Some rehabilitation may be required.

After early service in the army, Sandwich received political preferment in 1748 when he became First Lord. His prime political interest was henceforward naval administration and he was First Lord, in all, for fifteen years. Newcastle actually wanted to make him Secretary of State in this year, having a high opinion of the young landowner who had three boroughs at his disposal and was a close adherent of the Duke of Bedford. But he dismissed him in 1751 in order to force Bedford to resign from the secretaryship. On the accession of George III Sandwich moved towards the court, to enjoy a share of the patronage which the king was bent on controlling and to mend his fortune, ravaged by gambling losses. His affairs being, he said, 'in the most confused condition', he accepted the post of ambassador to Spain. In 1763 he became First Lord again and then, in Grenville's ministry, Secretary of State. As such he belonged to the comparatively small group which decided major issues under Grenville's severe direction. The House of Lords witnessed an incongruous scene when Sandwich, acting for the government, read out passages from an obscene poem, the *Essay on Woman*, which Wilkes had printed. The government's intention was to discredit Wilkes's radicalism by tainting him with pornography, but some recalled that Sandwich – 'Jemmy Twitcher' as he was called – had been an intimate of Wilkes and the Hell Fire Club. Sandwich was mainly concerned, however, with foreign policy: alarmed by the isolation of England after the Peace of Paris he wished to make some alliance with Austria. Austria, however, saw little advantage in this and Grenville refused to provide subsidies. Friction between Sandwich and Grenville increased and was one of the causes of the ministry's downfall in 1765.

In 1770, when North was seeking to broaden the basis of his government, he brought Sandwich back to the office of Secretary of State. In the following year he became again First Lord of the Admiralty; once more he was handicapped by the economizing spirit of his superiors. North tried to cut expenditure on the navy, but Sandwich made the most of limited resources. Copper bottoms were given to existing ships. But the penalty for North's retrenchments was paid in the American war, when the navy proved too small for the demands of a war against the American colonists, France and Spain together. A fleet cannot be expanded in a few months. Problems of manning and of raw materials took years to solve. Meanwhile Sandwich believed that the threat of France was of the first importance. Graves had to meet the activities of scattered American privateers with a small fleet while a larger force patrolled the Channel. In the event the French controlled American waters for long enough to have a decisive influence on the colonial war and the home fleet failed to inflict a proper defeat upon the French. Admiral Rodney's victory of the Saints (April 1782), which restored naval control of the Atlantic and ended the French threat to the West Indies, came too late to help Sandwich's reputation, for North's government had resigned a month before.

Sandwich had already been the target of a pamphlet war and the central figure in a crisis of confidence. As never before rivalries among senior naval commanders reflected political differences. The quarrel of Keppel and Palliser and the courts-martial which followed their indecisive battle of Ushant in July 1778 were embittered by the fact that Keppel was closely bound to the Whig opposition; his sister was married to the Duke of Bedford's heir. He became a public hero, many of the captains took his part and some refused to serve; aged admirals were sent out to sea, men such as Hardy and Geary, unfitted for active service. Fortunately, however, these political strains hastened the emergence of a new type of naval officer of the middle class, professional in outlook, often sons of the vicarage, like the Hood brothers or Nelson. Meanwhile distrust was engendered by the suspected corruption and known inefficiency of the Navy Board. Horace Walpole wrote of Sandwich's 'passion for maritime affairs, his activity, industry and flowing complaisance' but he went too far when he said that this 'endeared him to the profession'. Sandwich's sophistication, the courtly air of effortless authority which is expressed by Gainsborough's celebrated portrait in Greenwich Hospital was a further irritant to those who loathed the politics of North and the patronage of the court. Furthermore Sandwich was himself too much a product of the system to be able to carry out the radical reforms which were needed to transform the navy of 1780 into the navy of Nelson and Collingwood. He seemed to be more preoccupied with patronage than with policy. In his correspondence with Rodney occur constant requests to forward the career of some protégé or other. 'There is,' wrote the First Lord, after a reference to Lord Charles Fitzgerald, 'another young officer of fashion now in your squadron. You will infinitely oblige me. I mean Lord Robert Manners.' Lord Sandwich was an amiable man, obliging, zealous for the navy. But he never quite emancipated himself from the image of the dilettante. Indeed, with his adored mistress, Martha Ray, whom he surrounded with pet dogs and parrots, with his taste for fine clothes, he lived in a very different world from the seamen whose operations he controlled.

Further Reading
N. A. Roger, *The Insatiable Earl, a life of John Montagu, fourth Earl of Sandwich*, 1993.
G. R. Barnes and J. H. Owen, eds, *The Private Papers of the Earl of Sandwich*, 4 vols, 1932-8.

MONTAGU, THOMAS, EARL OF SALISBURY

(1388-1428) and Count of Perche was *the* great Earl of Salisbury. He was the outstanding English commander in France in the 1420s. He alone was undefeated and he alone could rival the prestige of King Henry V. As a contemporary wrote, 'he was accounted in his time throughout France and England the most expert, subtle and successful in arms of all the commanders, who have been talked about in the past hundred years'. Relatively few noblemen were professional soldiers like Salisbury, who served almost continuously in France from 1415 to his death. In 1415 he fought both at Agincourt and in the Duke of Bedford's naval victory over the Genoese. He returned with Henry V to Normandy in 1418, serving both with the king and on detached missions, and in 1419 was singled out to be lieutenant-governor of Normandy. He emerged with credit from the Duke of Clarence's unnecessary defeat at Baugé in 1421. From being one of the Regent Bedford's commanders, he became his principal field commander. When the English took the initiative and advanced southwards in 1423,

Salisbury took the lead. In that year he defeated a Franco-Scottish force at Cravant, next year he participated in Bedford's even greater victory at Verneuil, he helped conquer Maine in 1425, when he captured both Le Mans and Mayenne, and was commander of Upper Normandy in 1427. He was 'a sound strategist, an excellent tactician, and an expert in the use of artillery. Like all great commanders, he had the gift of inspiring confidence in his men and filling them with the confidence of victory'. But his career was tragically cut short and what he could have achieved is forever hidden from us. It was almost certainly his strategy that led to the siege of Orleans, which it is clear he knew how to undertake and that his successors did not. His death right at the start of the siege deprived the English of their direction, even before the intervention of Joan of Arc exposed them to defeat, and marked the military turning point. He proved to be an 'irreplaceable loss'.

Yet Salisbury was a most unlikely Lancastrian devotee. His father, Earl John, had been Richard II's friend and died in rebellion against Henry IV. John had suffered forfeiture, but in 1409 his son Thomas was allowed to recover his earldom and those lands that were entailed. Only in 1421 did he secure the full restoration, which he had earned by outstanding service. Long before then, however, he had become a model of Henry V's well-attested willingness to win over potential troublemakers by friendship and trust. Thus Salisbury was elected a knight of the Garter as early as 1414, became a royal councillor in 1417, was employed as diplomat, and received military responsibilities. During the 1420s he was one of Bedford's councillors in France and one of Henry VI's minority council in England. He was rewarded with a French county, lordships and garrison-captaincies in France, and was appointed warden of the New Forest and to other offices in England. Even when restored, however, his inheritance was modest for an earl and was supplemented by his marriage to two heiresses. The first, Eleanor Holland, co-heiress of the Earl of Kent, bore him only a daughter, so he remarried to Alice Chaucer. She was a connection of the Beauforts and the royal family and so too was his son-in-law Richard Neville, so Thomas was integrated with the house of Lancaster and identified with its interests by kinship as well as service. Since neither marriage brought Salisbury a legitimate son – he already had a bastard son John – his augmented inheritance passed to the Nevilles and his widow to his less fortunate colleague-in-arms the Earl of Suffolk. Despite his sense of dynasty, Thomas was thus to be the last Montagu Earl of Salisbury.

Further Reading
E. C. Williams, *My Lord of Bedford 1389-1435*, 1963.

MONTAGU, WILLIAM, EARL OF SALISBURY

(1301-44) is 'the most conspicuous example in the

fourteenth century of a sudden rise to greatness by royal favour and patronage'. Although established in Somerset by 1086, the Montagus owed their rise to prominence entirely to royal service and patronage. Simon Montagu (*d*.1316), the first earl's grandfather, had a long military career in Wales, Ireland, Scotland and Gascony, was custodian of Corfe (1299) and Beaumaris (1309) castles, sheriff of Somerset and Dorset, and an MP. Apart from military service, his son William (*d*.1319) was in Edward II's household by 1306, became captain of his knights in 1315 and steward of the household in 1316. As such, he was one of the new court party, labelled with Audley and Damory as 'worse than Gaveston', and in 1318 was transferred to Gascony as Seneschal. He tripled the family's manors to eighteen and sat in parliament as a baron. The family remained, however, of purely local importance.

Such royal connections explain the future earl's admittance whilst still a minor to the royal household. At first a yeoman, by 1326 he was a knight, and in 1328 a banneret. He established a close personal relationship with the somewhat younger Edward III that lasted all his life. It was Montagu who, on a mission to Avignon in 1329, established a secret mode of communication for Edward with the pope. It was he who devised and led the coup d'état that overthrew Isabella and Mortimer in 1330. Interrogated beforehand by Mortimer, Montagu boldly declared that he had done nothing against his allegiance, then told the king privately 'that it was better that they should eat the dog than the dog eat them', and personally led the dangerous adventure. His reward was an immediate grant of land worth £1,000 a year. He never looked back.

Montagu's career after the coup was marked by continuous service and striking royal favour. He fought in Scotland from 1333-7, sometimes in command and not always successfully, went on diplomatic missions to both Scotland and France, accompanied Edward to the Low Countries in 1338-40, when he was one of his inner council of four and was left as a hostage, and served in Brittany in 1343. He was one of Edward's constant companions, 'always encouraged him to excellence, honour, and love of arms', and escorted him on his secret mission to the French court in 1331. So close was their tie that Montagu was allowed to adopt the king's crest of an eagle, became godfather to his son Lionel of Antwerp, and persuaded Edward to lay the foundation stone of his new priory. Created Earl of Salisbury in 1337 and Earl Marshal in 1338, he was endowed 'with the largesse expected of a chivalrous master' twice as generously as the other five new creations. Besides enhanced west country holdings, he received the great Marcher lordship of Denbigh, the lordship of Wark-on-Tweed, the Isles of Lundy and Man, and (for life) the Channel Isles. For his son he secured the hand of the Monthermer heiress and

a daughter married the future Earl of March. As final evidence of his new status, he founded, built and endowed a new priory of Augustinian canons at Bisham as the family mausoleum, where he was buried following a jousting accident when still only forty-three. Such a flow of favours enabled him to meet without apparent accident the ransom he incurred about 1340. His career demonstrates how one individual 'might make the fortune of his family in one career of brilliance at court and on the battlefield'. His son, less favoured, lost much of his gains.

Further Reading
G. A. Holmes, *The Estates of the Higher Nobility in Four-teenth-Century England*, 1957.
R. Douch, 'The Career, Lands and Family of William Montagu, Earl of Salisbury, 1301-44', London MA thesis, 1950.

MONTAGUE, RICHARD (1577-1641), controversialist and bishop, was the son of a vicar of Dorney in Buckinghamshire; educated at Eton and King's College, Cambridge, he became a Fellow of both and in 1617 was appointed a canon of Windsor. A considerable scholar, he was ready to defend – with a sarcastic pen – the Church of England against both Catholics and Puritans. His views were Arminian, and before the end of James I's reign his sermons had been attacked by the Puritans. In 1625 he wrote, *Appello Caesarem*, condemning Puritanism and Popery alike. The Commons committed him to custody; released on bail, he was made a royal chaplain by Charles I. Next year the Commons put in a petition that the book should be publicly burned and its author punished. Characteristically, Charles made him Bishop of Chichester in 1628, and here he remained until his translation to Norwich ten years later, a firm disciplinarian on the Laudian pattern. In the 1630s Montague was concerned in the tentative negotiations with the pope for reunion. He died in 1641 shortly after the Long Parliament had set up a commission to consider his offences.

MOORE, SIR JOHN (1761-1809), general, was the son of a Scottish doctor and writer, whose novel *Zeluco* suggested to Byron the idea of *Childe Harold*. He took his son, who had been at Glasgow High School, on a long tour to learn foreign languages and ways. At Berlin the boy saw the ageing Frederick the Great and the celebrated Prussian manoeuvres: 40,000 men engaged in the field exercises of the kind that the methods of the French army were soon to make obsolete. At Vienna he was offered a commission in the Imperial army of Joseph II himself. He joined the British army at the age of fifteen, and thereafter the army was his life.

Moore was a complete professional soldier, an intelligent student of war and of the men who were lucky enough to come under his command. He saw his first service in the American war. On his return home he entered parliament for a Scottish constituency; he was a Pittite during his short career in the Commons (1784-90). When the French war started he was a lieutenant-colonel and was soon employed in the attack upon Corsica; there his skill in the training of troops was noticed, and he became adjutant-general to General Stuart. In 1796 he went under Abercromby to the West Indies; when his general was ordered to go to Ireland to suppress the rising there he took Moore with him. In the following year, 1799, he was Abercromby's right-hand man in the invasion of Holland and was badly wounded in that abortive operation. In Egypt, in 1801, it was his brigade that led Abercromby's army to victory at Aboukir. He was again wounded, and his commander, the valiant old Scot, who taught Moore much about caring for troops, was killed. On his return home, he was given the chance to put his ideas into practice.

In 1799 an experimental rifle corps had been formed and trained in mobile tactics. It was reconstituted in October 1802 and sent to Shorncliffe for special training under Sir John Moore, as he now was, along with the 14th Light Dragoons and two regiments of the line. The brigade thus formed was to be the spearhead of the force that was being mobilized to resist invasion. Moore made it into an élite body, so distinctive in discipline, morale and tactics that today his name is honoured as the founder of the light infantry. The essence of his system was that every soldier should know his own part, and to this end he insisted that his officers treat their men as human beings. The drill was practical rather than merely ceremonial: by insistence upon physical fitness, by rewards for good conduct, by example and encouragement, he sought to make his men proud, though they were recruited at the alehouse door, from Irish cabins and the London slums. That this worked is a tribute to the high standard of Moore's officers, inspired by the example of a selfless commander who had a craftsman's eye for the handling of his material. The men were made to march fast, 'to bring down the feet without shaking the body' – the words will appeal to all who have stamped on a parade ground. Above all they were trained to be crack shots, to kill at 300 yards, to use cover and not to waste a round. They were told 'to inflict death upon the enemy rather than to confound, astonish and intimidate'. They were expected to be self-reliant as well as tough, to cook and to mend; the officers were made to race their commander up hills.

Such tactics might cause offence, especially since Moore was brusque with what he regarded as false parade. When asked once if the hussars were to wear their pelisses, he replied, 'Oh, yes, and their muffs too.' But most were enthusiastic, like the future historian Napier, who was a subaltern under Moore and who said that at Shorncliffe 'officers were formed to command

and soldiers acquired such discipline as to become an example to the army and proud of their profession'. Another soldier wrote, 'The 52nd is at this moment one of the first corps in the Service' although 'the cat-o'-nine-tails is never used'. The same regiment especially distinguished itself in the rearguard of the great retreat to Corunna.

It was tragic that Moore and many of the troops that he had trained so skilfully were spent in a campaign that was nearly a disaster. Moore had a soldier's suspicion of politicians, and was at odds with Castlereagh during the Spanish operations, but it was not the government's fault that these operations began with misfortune. Neither the collapse of a promising Spanish resistance, nor the fact that Napoleon would be free to move with a quarter of a million troops were anticipated, when Moore was told to take command of the army in Portugal and to support the Spanish as best he could. He had been on frustrating service in Sicily, and Sweden, whence he had to escape in disguise. Meanwhile Wellesley's troops had shown at Vimiero that the French could be beaten. In October 1808 Moore found enthusiasm for his command among the troops, who had been sickened by the convention of Cintra; but he realized that he must take a great risk, to unite with Baird's force in northern Spain before Napoleon could crush the Spanish revolt. He marched; at the same time the Spanish armies caved in before the French. He waited for news of them in mid-November, when he reached Salamanca. Not realizing how serious their situation was, he decided to risk a coup against Napoleon's line of communication between Madrid and France.

That, he probably realized, would draw upon him the whole French army. Did he sufficiently weigh the risk to his own army, the only British army at that time in fighting trim? Did he under-estimate the effect of the mountains and climate upon his troops in retreat? It turned out to be a very near thing, almost a debacle. After Moore had joined Baird and struck east towards Burgos, Napoleon turned. Moore retreated precipitately by the direct route, across the mountains to the sea: 250 miles of terrible country in bitter cold. His troops drank, looted, and alienated the inhabitants; but they remembered how to fight. A fine sustained rearguard held Soult at bay, and significantly the rearguard lost less men than any other division. When the battered force reached Corunna they defended the town and on 16 January 1809 repulsed the French with loss. Twenty-four thousand out of 30,000 were then evacuated but not their commander. He was mortally wounded in the fight which saved the army from shame. 'Not a drum was heard, not a funeral note' as his shrouded body was consigned to its grave.

There is room for dispute about his handling of troops. Should he have turned to fight more often? Need he have pushed on so fast? He himself deplored the collapse of discipline, but could anything else be expected of troops who felt cheated of battle? His bold march seriously disrupted Napoleon's plans. The campaign provided valuable battle experience and Wellington, essentially cautious in his strategy, gained much from it. Politicians criticized Moore's strategy but his men had nothing but praise for him. He was a great trainer of troops, from whom in recent times Montgomery and Paget borrowed ideas and methods. The laments of his troops, their sense of loss, are witness enough to the character of the man.

Further Reading
Carola Oman, *Sir John Moore*, 1953.
Beatrice Brownrigg, *The Life and Letters of Sir John Moore*, 1923.

MOORE, THOMAS (1778-1852), poet and friend of poets, was born in Dublin. His father was a grocer, afterwards an army quartermaster. As a boy he tried his hand at sonnets. Trinity College was opened to Catholics in 1793, so Moore was able to go there. In 1799 he came to London to study law, but hoped to keep himself by the pen, and the patronage of Lord Moira: that produced a valuable post in Bermuda with duties which he could exercise through a deputy. Early poems, with his musical talents, opened doors at fashionable houses. In 1806 his two volumes of *Odes and Epistles* were sharply criticized in the *Edinburgh Review*. Moore called Jeffrey out to a duel at Chalk Farm. Neither was hurt and they afterwards became friends. He wrote an opera entitled *MP or the Blue Stocking*, married an actress, Bessy Dyke, in 1811, and came to the notice of Holland House.

He still wrote mainly to entertain. Typical of his easy, light, rather soulless style was his *Twopenny Postbag* (1812). Meanwhile he was working on something more ambitious. *Lalla Rookh* (1817) came at the right time. India was topical, and this romance, with its rich descriptions of eastern life, had an instant appeal. It ran to twenty editions in his lifetime; translated into Persian it found an oriental market. Stendhal claimed to have read it five times. Moore stood next to Byron in popular fame. Briefly he was wealthy; then he faced ruin when his deputy in Bermuda incurred debts for which he was responsible. He now wrote for solvency, his family, and the Wiltshire cottage he had bought in 1811. Neither a novel, *Epicurean*, nor his *Life of Sheridan* made much stir. But his *Life of Lord Byron* (1830) was another matter. Everybody wanted to read about the hero of Missolonghi. A pension from the Whigs, in 1835, rewarded his satirical poems on their behalf. By then the flow was drying up.

Moore was essentially a fashionable poet. He had a good ear for melody and the rhythms of a song. He was a natural writer – yet took little trouble to improve his technique or enlarge his experience. Those privileged to hear him sing his lyrics after dinner may have had the best of him. Few of his works are read today.

MORDAUNT, CHARLES, 3rd EARL OF PETERBOROUGH (1658-1735), the hero of Barcelona, was the son of a Cavalier conspirator, Viscount Mordaunt, and served in the navy as a boy. As a young man in the 1680s he was an outspoken member of the Whig opposition; he left for Holland in 1686 and accompanied William of Orange throughout the enterprise of 1688. Created Earl of Monmouth in 1689, he was for a short time First Commissioner of the Treasury. Vain, boastful, dishonest, reckless, above all fickle and unstable in opinions and purposes, he was 'a skeleton in outward figure' (Swift), a man of wit and charm, courage and high talents, who infuriated everyone with whom he had dealings. His thoroughly disreputable attempt to incriminate Shrewsbury and Marlborough in the Fenwick conspiracy (1696) landed him in the Tower. Inheritance of the earldom of Peterborough (1697) did something to restore his credit, but not until the War of the Spanish Succession did he achieve the celebrity to which he believed himself entitled. In 1705 he was appointed, with Admiral Sir Clowdisley Shovell, joint Commander of the expedition sent to win Spain for the Archduke Charles, and in an assault in which he showed reckless personal gallantry his forces captured Barcelona, the strongest fortress in the country. He followed this up by overrunning the province of Valencia, and thereby committing his country to the Carlist cause and the ruinous doctrine of 'No peace without Spain'. These activities, related to the public in the exaggerated *An Account of the Earl of Peterborough's conduct in Spain*, by Dr John Freind (1707), made him a national hero. This was the limit of his achievements. His quarrelsomeness, levity and capacity for mischief made him impossible to work with; in September 1706 Marlborough was writing 'I do not think much ceremony ought to be used in removing him from a place where he has hazarded the loss of the whole country', and in 1707 he was recalled. A long series of official inquiries into his conduct did little except enable the Tories to use him as a propagandist counterweight to Marlborough: Swift in particular lauded his generalship in his political pamphlets. But when the Tories came to power from 1710 they employed him as a diplomatist rather than as a soldier, and then for motives clearly stated by Queen Anne when she wrote to Harley, 'I think he should be sent somewhere, for I fear if he comes home while the parliament is sitting he will be very troublesome'. Peterborough's official career ended with the coming of the Hanoverians in 1714. His capacity for mischief did not. His activities included dabbling in European politics, in which he claimed to have caused the fall of Alberoni, who called him 'a most pretentious fool and consummate blackguard'; thrashing an Italian tenor for insolent behaviour to the singer Anastasia Robinson, whom he eventually married; and writing his memoirs, which so shocked his widow after his death that she burned the manuscript at once. He lived on, a patron of letters and a friend of Swift, Pope and Gay, travelling abroad a good deal, until he died at Lisbon in 1735.

Further Reading

For the Spanish campaign, see G. M. Trevelyan, *England under Queen Anne: Ramillies and the Union with Scotland*, 1932, Chaps. 4 and 7.

MORE, HANNAH (1745-1833) was a pioneer in writing about religious matters in a popular way; she was also influential in the movement for religious education of the poor. Her activities may suggest a woman of narrow absorption and a presumptuous piety. Brave, devoted, idealistic though she was, the evangelical, elitist tone of her writing, with its pervasive sense of class, is not appealing. Set in her own time against the degradation of many of the poor, and the indifference of many of the rich, her work and personality acquire new significance. The youthful friend of Dr Johnson and David Garrick, the flirtatious bluestocking and author of the *Bas Bleu* (a description of the life of the literary ladies of London), she retained much of her liveliness as the serious part of her personality emerged and she sought to 'escape from the world'. A sense of humour becomes, however, more difficult to trace in 'Saint Hannah' (who said that she would derive more gratification from being able to lower the price of bread than from having written the Iliad), the sabbatarian who wrote of Pitt's duel on Putney Heath: 'to complete the horror, they chose a Sunday'.

Her father, a Norfolk gentleman who had been reduced by the failure of a law-suit to take the mastership of a school near Bristol, sensibly brought up his daughters so that they could earn their own living. Hannah was precocious, a voracious reader and anxious to write. She improved her French by talking to French prisoners on parole. In 1757 she joined her elder sister, who had set up a school in Bristol, continued her education and later taught there. In about 1767 she received her first proposal of marriage from a Mr Turner, a Bristol merchant about twenty years her senior; he prevaricated strangely and after six years the engagement was broken off, though he provided her with a small annuity. She would never afterwards listen to talk of marriage. She was excited by her meeting with Dr Johnson who, with amiable hyperbole, declared that she was 'the most powerful versiatrix in the English language'. Garrick persuaded her to write a play: *Percy*, for which he wrote both prologue and epilogue, ran for twenty-one nights at Covent Garden. She afterwards said that she had liked Garrick despite his profession, that she never saw cards

– and but one other actor in his house! She enjoyed her *succès d'estime*, and only gave up writing plays when Garrick died (1779). Her *Sacred Dramas* (1782) were not intended for the stage.

In 1784 Hannah More left London, renounced its dinners and routs and settled in a cottage she had built at Cowslip Green, ten miles from Bristol. There she gardened, wrote, observed the world and considered her spiritual position. In 1788 there appeared anonymously the result of her reflections: *Thoughts on the Importance of the Manners of the Great to General Society*. Meanwhile the state of the Somerset poor had attracted her attention. In Cheddar and Blagdon, Shipham and Rowberrow, the people were almost pagan, wild and depraved in morals.

Following the example of Robert Raikes, Hannah and her sisters founded schools for village children and gave them respectability in the eyes of the prejudiced or cynical by assuring them (as in a letter to a bishop who was perturbed by the possibility of 'enthusiasm') that she taught on weekdays only 'such coarse work as may fit them for servants ... only habits of industry and piety'. Of course she was accused of 'methodism', a useful bogey word for idle clerics – but also a growing movement, a living reproach, if not a threat, to the establishment of what Brougham called a 'quiet and somewhat lazy church'. In the Mendips, thirteen adjacent villages were without resident clergy. She was also attacked by local farmers, who thought that religion would 'ruin agriculture' and by mothers, who wanted to be paid for sending their children to school. She was actually summoned before the Dean's Court to answer the charge that a school she had started at Blagdon was a conventicle and was illegal because unlicensed! By the time of this 'Blagdon controversy' (1800-02) she had moved on to the national stage – at least to that wing of it occupied by the evangelicals.

After the success of *Village Politics* (1792) she wrote a series of tracts, secured the backing of committees all over the country and the formation (1799) of the Religious Tract Society. To a man like Bishop Porteous of London, who caused a theatre manager to drop the curtain in the middle of a ballet at midnight on Saturday rather than face prosecution for playing on the sabbath, Hannah was a valued spiritual adviser. An aunt was distressed by her niece's 'seriousness' until she was relieved – and converted – by reading Hannah More's *Coelebs in Search of a Wife* (her most popular book, published in 1809): one of thousands affected similarly by the new puritanism. In an age of extremes she found a popular medium for an acceptable message. The novelist Jane Porter wrote, in 1815, 'of the state of morals and religious opinions amongst all ranks of person in the country' twenty years before, when 'the poor were in profligate innocence – the rich in profligate apostasy'.

The melodramatic contrast is typical, also the sense of critical tension of opposites. Hannah More wrote in 1817 of the death of Princess Charlotte, for whom she had written *Hints towards Forming the Character of a Young Princess*, that it was a punishment for the national lack of piety. The next year she wrote: 'It appears to me that the two classes of character are more decided than they were; the wicked seem more wicked, and the good better.' If the 'good' were indeed 'better', or if there seemed to be, as a clergyman correspondent of hers wrote, 'a more lively impression of the importance of Christianity among the great', this determined lady had had some part in it.

Further Reading
M. G. Jones, *Hannah More*, 1952.
M. G. Jones, *The Charity School Movement*, 1938.
Brimley Johnson, ed., *Letters of Hannah More*, 1925.

MORE, HENRY (1614-87), theologian, came from a gentry family at Grantham and was educated at Eton and Christ's College, Cambridge. Elected a Fellow of Christ's in 1639, he remained a don: a shy and saintly man who disliked controversy, he rejected several offers of deaneries and bishoprics. Brought up a Calvinist, he came to be a firm champion of the moderate Anglicanism expounded by Hooker. More is perhaps the most representative figure of the group known as the Cambridge Platonists. Tolerant and mystical rather than dogmatic, emphasizing the spiritual values of religion and the duty of man to employ reason, 'the candle of the Lord', to discern his faith, they continued in the second half of the seventeenth century the teachings of such men as Chillingworth before the wars. Their doctrines did a good deal, in their influence upon individual clergy, to make Anglicanism at once more liberal and more confident, and to prepare it for 'the Age of Reason'. More's own writings were to win the approval of such diverse men as Wesley and Coleridge.

MORE, SIR THOMAS (1478-1535), Lord Chancellor, was the son of the judge, Sir John More by his first wife, Agnes Graunger. After beginning his education at St Anthony's school in Threadneedle Street, he was then put to live in the household of Archbishop Morton, who was also the Lord Chancellor. More would have been about twelve years old then and he spent two years in the Morton family, where he soon made a reputation for his intelligence, wit and liveliness. Years afterwards he paid a tribute to the archbishop, for whom he always had much affection and respect, in his *Utopia*. About 1492 More went to Oxford, almost certainly to Canterbury College, later to be incorporated into Christ Church. Here he came under the influence of the New Learning, studying Greek and Latin and French, theology and music. After two years or less he returned to London to

study law (1494); he became an intimate friend of Colet and in 1499 was first introduced to Erasmus, who became his lifelong bosom friend. He began his legal life at New Inn, but in 1496 he was transferred to Lincoln's Inn, where he had a rapidly successful career.

In 1499, however, More began to have doubts whether he ought to follow a legal career and ought not to become a priest. For some four years he seriously examined this possibility and for a time lived in close touch with the brothers of the Charterhouse. In the end (1503) he abandoned the idea of an ecclesiastical life and turned with renewed energy to the study of law, in which he was quickly and brilliantly successful.

In 1504 he was elected to parliament, but his constituency is not known. It is said that in this year 'as a beardless boy' he opposed and 'clean overthrew' the king's demands for a huge sum of money to cover the marriage of the Princess Margaret to the King of Scotland. Henry in fury revenged himself by keeping John More in the Tower until he paid a fine of £100. (Pollard in his *Wolsey* denies this story.) The next year (1505) More married Jane Colte and settled in London in Bucklersbury. During the next six years he lived a quiet and enjoyable life, rejoicing in his four children, dividing his leisure time between developing his home and literary pursuits. Twice Erasmus came to visit him: in 1508 More went to Paris and Louvain, but he returned convinced that Oxford and Cambridge were superior universities. In 1511 his wife died, and within a month he had married again, this time a widow, Alice Middleton, who had one daughter. Alice was seven years older than More and proved to be a capable housekeeper rather than a sympathetic wife. More now moved from Bucklersbury to Crosby Place in Bishopsgate Street, where he remained until he bought land in Chelsea and built for himself what was to become one of the famous houses of England.

All this time he had been proving himself a notable lawyer: he was made under-sheriff of London (1510) and he soon came into close relations with the new and young King Henry VIII, who professed for More much affection. More never allowed himself to be blinded by this and he never put much trust in the king's protestations. 'If my head should win him a castle in France, it should not fail to go.'

The year 1516 saw the publication of *Utopia*, a literary masterpiece which, under the guise of representing an ideal society, was in fact a bitter attack on the political and social evils of the day.

In 1517, More became a royal councillor. He was an astute politician, who rose rapidly in royal favour, largely because of the king's personal friendship for him, but also because Wolsey trusted him. He acted as unofficial secretary to the king, and was rewarded with a knighthood in 1521 and the office of Chancellor of the

Duchy of Lancaster in 1525. In 1521 he was called in by the king to help him in writing his book on the seven sacraments against Martin Luther. Later Henry was to accuse More of having 'villainously and traitorously' provoked him to write this book in defence of the Papacy and thereby to put a sword in the pope's hands to fight against himself. More replied that he had been 'a sorter out and placer of the principal matters' after the book was finished, 'wherein when I found the Pope's authority highly advanced, and with strong arguments mightily defended, I said unto his Grace "I must put your Highness in remembrance of one thing, and that is this. The pope, as your Grace knoweth, is a prince as you are, and in league with all other Christian princes. It may hereafter so fall out that your Grace and he may vary upon some points of the league, whereupon may grow breach of amity and war between you both. I think it best therefore that that place be amended, and his authority more slenderly touched".' In 1523 More became Speaker of the House of Commons. Up to this point More had himself been in favour of reform, but he always envisaged the reform of the church as coming from within and he was utterly opposed to reform by revolution. For this reason he himself wrote a letter against Luther, and in 1528 he wrote his *Dialogue* against the English reformers, especially against Tyndale.

On the fall of Wolsey in 1529 More was appointed Lord Chancellor. He must be regarded as one of the greatest of chancellors, both for the unassailable integrity with which he conducted his court, for the unequalled rapidity with which he discharged the cases, and for the great labour with which he applied himself to the job of providing justice. In the words of a recent student of More's career (Dr J. A. Guy), 'It was as a judge, not a politician, that his reputation stands highest.' Part of More's drive against lawlessness and a part which suited his religious outlook was his encouragement of censorship of the press, and of the persecution of heretics. It has been charged against him that he was implacable against heretics and sent some of them to the stake. It is true that he was stern against seditious heretics, those who stirred up strife. To others, he was lenient and helpful, as he was to his future son-in-law, Roper.

More resigned the chancellorship in 1532 because he found himself increasingly out of sympathy with the king's policy over the divorce and towards the church: the last straw was when the clergy were forced to subscribe the Submission in answer to Cromwell's Supplication of the Ordinaries. For the next two years he continued to write his pamphlets against heretics, in some of which he sank to the lowest depths of vulgar abuse and vindictive wit, especially against Tyndale. In 1533 he became for a short while embroiled in the episode of the Nun of Kent, Elizabeth Barton, and his name was included in the Bill of Attainder, but it was removed at the third reading. More himself said that his danger was only postponed, not removed, and when on 30 March 1534 a new Act of parliament required an oath to the succession of Anne Boleyn's children, More knew that his end was very near. He was willing to accept the altered succession, as a matter within the powers of parliament to deal with, but he refused to take the oath which also in effect repudiated the Papal supremacy. He sought to avoid execution by not making an open declaration of why he refused the oath, but was tricked by Sir Richard Rich into explaining his position. He was committed to the Tower in April 1534, charged with high treason and tried at Westminster on 1 July 1535. He was, of course, found guilty and was executed on Tower Hill on 6 July. Thomas More died protesting that he was 'the king's good servant but God's first'. As he had said to Thomas Cromwell before his trial, 'though I was a prisoner and condemned to perpetual prison yet I was not thereby discharged of mine obedience and allegiance upon the King's Highness'. He was canonized by Pope Pius IX in 1935.

Of More's execution it must be said that the law was strained to breaking point in order to secure a 'legal' conviction. Even so, it is possible on purely political grounds to make out a case on Henry's side. Henry was always a political realist and never a man of moral principle. The need for an indisputably legitimate heir to the throne, and a male heir at that, was paramount in his and in most people's view. More was a 'wise, righteous and brave man who went to his death for his conscience' (J. D. Mackie, *History*, June 1936). He was a first-class scholar, a man of the highest principles, a practising Christian, a faithful husband, a devoted father; his capacity for friendship, his wit, his hospitality, his kindness to servants, his love of music, his affection for animals (as his menagerie at Chelsea proves), his powers of conversation, made and still make him a great and good and lovable man. But More was also a saint, and like many other saints there was in him a hard core of granite, a fibre strong as steel, which made him a formidable opponent in controversy, a severe critic where he felt his principles to be outraged, and which gave his saintliness that almost fanatical desire for martyrdom which one sees in men like Southwell. It was not that he was impervious to the reasonable arguments of his friends and of his beloved daughter Meg: rather, he simply declined to listen to argument; one almost has the feeling that he feared he might lose the martyr's crown. It is claimed for him that he died in order to save the Papacy and the unity of Christendom. Yet there is a curious letter which he wrote to Cromwell when he was in prison in which he urges the king to pursue his idea of a General Council on the grounds that the present pope might be deposed and a new pope appointed with whom

His Highness might be well content; 'never thought I the pope above the General Council' (Eng. edn of More's works, 1557, p.1,427). Perfection is not given to man, and More was not perfect. The shock which his execution caused throughout Europe is the measure of his status and reputation in his own day.

Further Reading
R. Marius, *Thomas More*, 1984.
A. Fox, *Thomas More*, 1982.
J. A. Guy, *The Public Career of Sir Thomas More*, 1980.
E. Surtz and J. H. Hexter, eds, *Utopia*, 1965.
W. Roper and N. Harpsfield, *Lives of More*, Everyman edn, 1936.
R. W. Chambers, *Thomas More*, 1935.

MORGAN AP OWAIN or MORGAN HEN or MORGAN THE OLD (*c*.930-74) was one of the dynasty of Meurig ap Tewdrig which had emerged in Glywysing (roughly south Glamorgan and Gwent) from the seventh century, but whose territories became fragmented under the control of many brothers and cousins. Morgan ap Owain became predominant among them about the mid-tenth century. The Morgan name passed through dynastic successors to the lands which they ruled – Morgannwg, or Glwad Morgan, later Glamorgan, though it has been suggested that the name may have already been derived from Morgan ap Athwrys (*d.c.*655), an earlier ruler of the Tewdrig dynasty.

MORGAN, SIR HENRY (1635-88), buccaneer, came from Llanrhymney, in Glamorgan. There are several tales to account for his presence in the West Indies: it seems most likely that he went on the expedition of Penn and Venables which captured Jamaica in 1655. He fought in the Second Dutch War (1644-7), commanding a ship in an attack on Curaçao. In 1668 he was chosen 'admiral' of the buccaneers, and his period of authority marks the climax of the power of this group of lawless seamen of all nations who ranged the waters of the Caribbean, terrorizing the inhabitants of its coasts. Under Morgan's leadership they carried out exploits of equal bravery and brutality. In 1668 his force of 400 men took and sacked Portobelo, the fortress-base of the Spanish silver fleets, and carried off a quarter of a million pieces of eight. Next year they broke into Lake Maracaibo and plundered its shores. Finally, in 1671, they captured Panama, a city of 30,000 people, killing several hundreds of its defenders for the loss of only six of their own number, and looting the country for sixty miles round. Evelyn complacently observed that 'such an action had not been done since the famous Drake'. Certainly Morgan's actions gave the *coup de grâce* to all real Spanish power in the Caribbean. Some of our information about Morgan comes from a dubious source, *The Buccaneers of America*, an account, first published in 1678, by a Dutchman named Esquemeling, who certainly exaggerated both the heroism and the plundering. Morgan was an intrepid and ingenious leader, but he was also a mean and treacherous scoundrel who even cheated his own men out of their share of the Panama loot. In 1672 his buccaneering career ended when the British authorities in Jamaica sent him home under arrest. But he managed to win Charles II's favour, and returned to Jamaica in 1674 as Deputy Governor. Suspended from office in 1683, he seems to have spent most of his last years drinking and gambling. He was reinstated a month before his death in 1688.

Further Reading
P. K. Kemp and Christopher Lloyd, *The Brethren of the Coast*, 1960.
C. H. Haring, *The Buccaneers in the West Indies in the Seventeenth Century*, 1910.

MORGAN, WILLIAM (*c*.1541-1604), Bishop of St Asaph, was educated at St John's College, Cambridge, and between 1575 and 1588 he held four livings in Wales. He made a translation of the Bible into Welsh, but he met with much local opposition and he was delated to the bishop, who refused to take any action. Morgan was then reported to Archbishop Whitgift and was summoned to Lambeth. He succeeded not only in convincing Whitgift that he was perfectly capable of making a sound translation, for he knew both Greek and Hebrew, but he also won the support of the archbishop, who promised to defray all the expenses of producing the book. The Bible was published in 1588, an independent translation made directly from the original. Many of the changes made in the English Revised Version were taken from Morgan's translation.

In 1595 Morgan was made Bishop of Llandaff and he was translated to St Asaph in 1601. He proved himself an admirable bishop, a sound administrator and a firm and incorruptible man, but he seems to have had a good many quarrels with people who were less scrupulous than himself. He died on 10 September 1604. There is a biography of him by C. Ashton published in 1888 to commemorate the tercentenary of the Welsh Bible.

Further Reading
F. O. White, *Lives of Elizabethan Bishops of the Anglican Church*, 1898.

MORLAND, GEORGE (1763-1804), painter of rustic subjects, exhibited his first drawings at the Royal Academy at the age of ten. His father was old when he was young; and, being himself an artist and the son of an artist, educated the young Morland, under the strictest regimen, exclusively in art. Young Morland was compelled to copy incessantly, to the perfection of his technique, but to the wearying of his spirit. At nineteen he escaped from domestic tyranny, and reacted against it as strongly as the son of any moralist is supposed to do.

Thereafter his story is one of increasing degradation: of thraldom to picture dealers who plied him with drink in exchange for his art, while they multiplied his paintings by copying them behind his back; of financial extravagance indulged even in the debtors' prison, even while he painted against time and invention to relieve the debt; of low company and rewards, of strength and opportunities lost – a story relieved only by some steadiness at the time of his marriage (to the sister of the artists William and James Ward) and by the pleasures which, however transitory, he found in the most adventurous of his dissipations. (And could a man have been wholly unhappy who painted pictures of such engaging innocence?) He was released from debtors' prison under the Insolvent Debtors Act of 1801; died under confinement in a sponging-house in 1804; and his wife, falling into convulsions at the news of his death, died four days later.

The unscrupulous copying of Morland's paintings, and completion of his sketches, make it hard to number his huge output of paintings and engravings. In the last eight years of his life he is said to have painted 100 pictures a year, quite apart from his drawings, and at one time he kept his 'models' (pigs, foxes, goats and a horse) in his very house. He had not only to satisfy creditors and feed the dealers who fed him, but cater for the public demand for his pictures. It was as if the people had premonition of the plunder of the English countryside, and desired a memento of the England that was passing: they certainly liked to be assured that the English peasantry were not made on the French model, carrying revolution in their hearts. For Morland's work is rustic painting of the most comfortable kind. His animals have none of the sleek, nervous breeding of those Stubbs painted; his country people are stock characters, who gather at the stable or the village inn. This was art for the ordinary man, and must have made the fortune of the dealers. One is tempted to say that Morland put out potboilers: the wonder is – which is also a tribute to his art – that he hardly did so. The quality which he maintained under severest stress speaks of a mastery of paint which, had he ever paused to strike out afresh, had he ever given himself time to invent, or to refurnish his pictorial imagination, might have raised him to a high, if not the highest, rank.

Further Reading
Ellis Waterhouse, *Painting in Britain 1530-1790*, 1969.

MORLEY, VISCOUNT JOHN (1838-1923) was a Radical who reached politics by way of high-class journalism; a thinker first and a statesman later. He commanded amongst Gladstonian Liberals something of the respect held for Keith Joseph by the Thatcherites. The son of a north country surgeon, he made his name as editor of *The Fortnightly Review* from 1867 until 1882. At a time when periodical journals had nationwide influence, Morley assembled a glittering collection of contributors, men of letters and of ideas: Mill, Huxley, Bagehot, Pater, Swinburne, Trollope, D. G. Rossetti and Mazzini, to name only a few. He also wrote extensively himself. He was an agnostic; a believer in constitutional reform; eventually a pacifist. The queen therefore regarded him as a Jacobin, but he was no democrat, and had little interest in social reform, let alone Socialism.

Gladstone was his hero. Entering parliament in 1883, he started as a close ally of Chamberlain, but broke from him over Home Rule, which Morley believed to be the only solution to Ireland's problems. He became Gladstone's Chief Secretary for Ireland in 1886, and again in 1892, so he was in the forefront of the parliamentary battles over the Home Rule Bills. After Gladstone's death he wrote his biography, which sold 130,000 copies. Like Gladstone, he became more radical as the years went by. In the Liberal governments after 1905, he was responsible, as Secretary for India, for the legislation which introduced an elective element into both the Viceroy's Council and the Council for India in London, the start of the long progress to Indian self-government and independence. In 1910 he urged that the king should create as many new peers as would be needed to carry the parliament bill, which limited the powers of the House of Lords: a body about which he had, back in 1884, coined the slogan 'Mend them or end them'. In 1914, he led the opposition within the Cabinet to entering the war, and he resigned when he lost. Morley was at his most influential among men of letters. Although he loved to be in the middle of the political world, he was not so effective there: altogether too prickly and even old-maidish. His ideas and opinions made him the touchstone of the Liberal Party after Gladstone. They became increasingly alien to the voters of industrial Britain.

MORRIS, WILLIAM (1834-96), best known a hundred years after his death for his designs for wallpaper and materials, was a craftsman with many gifts and enormous energy, a voluminous writer, and a pioneer British socialist. He was also a bundle of contradictions: a capitalist who proclaimed Marxism, a medievalist who looked forward to the millennium, a man who preached that the worker should master all the skills of his trade but who practised the division of labour in his firm. Yet no-one thought him bogus. He was consistent all through his life in his enthusiasms, his friendships and his frailties. His personality, as well as his ideas and activities, made him a powerful influence in his own day, and he became an even more important one thereafter.

The child was father to the man. 'It is the child-like part of us that produces works of imagination', he wrote later. Brought up in a Georgian mansion on the edge of Epping Forest, young Morris roamed the woods and saw the flowers, bushes, trees and birds with sharp eyes and accurate memory. He also read – all of Scott's novels by the age of seven, he claimed. Such romances filled his mind. He idealized women, Guineveres to his King Arthur; but he was close to only one, his sister, Emma. When she married an evangelical clergyman, he felt deserted, and his loss is reflected in many of the stories in his poetry, where men adore women whose love is given elsewhere.

When he went up to Oxford his band of friends nicknamed him 'Topsy' because of his thatch of thick curly hair. He was a figure of affectionate fun as they fought soda-water battles and played practical jokes on him, taking a tuck in his waistcoat when he was beginning to worry about his spreading girth. He was clumsy and strong, and had an explosive temper. Kicking in door panels was almost a habit, and he once hurled a fifteenth-century folio at the head of a workman. When, enlisted by their hero Rossetti, he and his friends decorated the new Oxford Union building, Morris wore a suit of armour of his own design; but he could not lift the visor, and was seen dancing with rage, and roaring inside it. The outbursts were quickly over, however, and Burne-Jones and the others of the 'Oxford Brotherhood' were inspired by his energy and enterprise. And so it went on. After his death Yeats wrote: 'You saw him producing everywhere organization and beauty, seeming almost in the one instant helpless and triumphant; and people loved him as children are loved.'

Emotional immaturity led to an unhappy marriage. Jane Burden, the daughter of a stableman and a model for Rossetti, fitted Morris's vision of the perfect woman, a working-class girl who looked like a medieval queen. He got his architect friend Philip Webb to design for them the Red House on Bexleyheath in Kent – Gothic with its high-pitched roof and over-arched windows, but practical, spacious and solid. This he filled with his own designs and furnishings. Later the family homes were in London, near his works, and at Kelmscott, his country paradise on the upper reaches of the Thames near Lechlade. But he and Janey were never close, and life became complicated by Rossetti's attentions to her, to which she responded. She became an invalid, only healthy when he was away. He remained a loyal husband and a devoted father. Their elder daughter was an epileptic, which made her almost a social outcast in Victorian times, but his letters to her are full of sympathy and love.

Morris soon became a craftsman with many skills. After briefly training as an architect under Street, he turned to painting, under the influence of Rossetti, and then to decorative arts. In 1861 he founded the firm, famous as Morris & Co., of 'Fine Art Workmen in Painting, Carving, Furniture and the Metals', with the names of Madox Brown, Burne-Jones, Rossetti and Webb amongst those on its prospectus as partners. Moving from Red Lion Square to Queen Square and eventually to Merton Abbey, it expanded to include stained glass,

tiles, embroidery, tapestry and carpet weaving, and the printing of material and wallpaper designs. Morris had the sense to employ businessmen to keep its affairs in order, but he himself provided most of the finance, since he was for many years a wealthy man, with an annual income of £900 from shares in a Devonshire copper mine, inherited from his father. He did much of the design work himself, ran looms, learnt about dyes, painted tiles, worked out colour schemes for the windows and put in their lead lines. Later he turned to illuminating manuscripts, became a skilled printer, and near the end of his life set up the Kelmscott Press, where, with his own design of heavy Gothic type, he produced famous work, including his edition of Chaucer, with Burne-Jones's woodcuts. He also campaigned against the wholesale restoration of churches, by which Gilbert Scott and others were reducing the work of individual craftsmen over the centuries to a flat mediocrity.

Meanwhile, he found time to write copiously – poetry, prose romances, epics and Utopian dreams. *The Earthly Paradise* (1868-70), for which he was best known in his lifetime (and better known than for any of his craft work and design), is a huge poem of 42,000 lines. There are twenty-four stories in it, wonderfully atmospheric. To borrow Flecker's words, these are:

> Tales, marvellous tales
> Of ships and stars and isles where good men rest,
> Where nevermore the rose of sunset pales,
> And winds and shadows fall towards the West.

Much of his writing is of a remarkably high quality, considering the speed at which it poured out. When his Oxford friends proclaimed him a poet on the strength of some early verses he said: 'Well, if this is poetry, it's very easy to write.' This facility made his imagery less concentrated, and less memorable, than, say, Tennyson's. There are few 'great' lines to arrest one's progress along the agreeable road of the unfolding stories. Moreover, though he liked to think that he was a story-teller in the manner of Chaucer, he showed nothing of Chaucer's depth of characterization, and nothing of his sense of humour. But he could scale the heights of *Sigurd the Volsung* (1877), a saga composed within the torrent of excitement generated by his visits to Iceland, before returning to the plains of prose, to express the Utopian ideals which began to take over his life.

Morris's life's work was governed by his hatred of industrial ugliness and impoverishment. Inspired by Ruskin, he spoke at Oxford in 1883, in a lecture on Art and Democracy, of 'whole counties of England' disappearing 'beneath a crust of grime': of 'a love of dirt and ugliness for its own sake' so that 'the well of art is poisoned at its spring'. He looked back to the time when commerce was made for man, not man for commerce, and when workmen were artists and craftsmen, not 'hands' in one section of an industrial machine. In the same year he joined Henry Hyndman's Democratic Federation and became a Socialist. Then he read *Das Kapital* (in French) and was converted to Marxism. For the next ten years he was a prominent speaker on socialist platforms, in Hyde Park and elsewhere. He financed two socialist papers, *Justice* and *The Commonweal*, and was urged to become leader of the Independent Labour Party. But he had little long-term influence on the development of the Labour Party or on socialist thought. He hated the 'shilly-shallying of politics'. He quarrelled with Hyndman, too dictatorial and jingoist, and his later efforts to hold different factions together brought him no satisfaction or success. His rural Utopia meant nothing to the workers for whom he imagined it, though they held him in honour. His intellectual appeal, then as now, was to the middle classes. As prosperity has broadened these, so his vision has grown more influential. Today he would surely be the leader of the Green Party. Words he spoke over the grave of a young man killed in the Trafalgar Square riot of 1887 – Bloody Sunday – came from his heart. 'Our friend who lies here has had a hard life; and if society had been differently constituted, his life might have been a delightful, a beautiful and a happy one. It is our business to begin to organize for the purpose of seeing that such things shall not happen; to try to make this earth a beautiful and happy place.'

Further Reading

Exhibition Catalogue, *William Morris*, 1996.
F. MacCarthy, *William Morris: a life for our time*, 1994.
E. P. Thompson, *William Morris: romantic to revolutionary*, 1955.

MORSE, HENRY (1595-1645), born at Broome near the Suffolk-Norfolk border, entered Corpus Christi College, Cambridge, in 1612, and two years later fled to the English seminary at Douai, where he was received into the Church of Rome. Henceforward, as novice, priest and Jesuit, he dedicated his life to his faith, partly on the continent (he spent five and a half years at the English College in Rome), partly on a series of missions to his native country. His experiences were typical enough – the escapes from pursuivants and informers, the hourly peril sharpened by the growing Puritanism of the age, the administration of the sacraments to loyal Catholic households, the imprisonments, the strengthening of faith by constant spiritual exercises. What makes Morse's story peculiarly attractive is his devotion to the poor and sick and his universal charity, qualities which found their noblest expression in the years 1633-7 when he served as Catholic priest in the poor parish of St Giles-in-the-Fields. In 1635-6 London suffered from a severe visitation of the plague. Morse, nursing the sick, administering the sacraments to the dying, visiting Protestant and Catholic poor alike, organizing financial help from country Catholics and from Queen Henrietta Maria and her co-religionists at court, was heroic and untiring in his work. He also made numerous converts, and this led to his arrest and trial at the Old Bailey. A pardon from the king, at the queen's instigation, saved him on this occasion. But so zealous a missionary was unlikely to survive, particularly in the Civil War years. After further adventures and exile, he fell into parliamentarian hands near Newcastle-upon-Tyne late in 1644, and he was hanged at Tyburn in 1645.

Further Reading

Philip Caraman, *Henry Morse, Priest of the Plague*, 1957.

MORTIMER, ROGER, EARL OF MARCH (*c.*1286-1330) moved unexpectedly from the Celtic periphery to the centre of the national stage in 1326, when he became the 'power behind the throne' during Edward III's minority. The Mortimers had been Lords of Wigmore since Domesday Book and Roger Mortimer could claim descent from both the Welsh princes and William Marshal, Earl of Pembroke. His wife brought him Ludlow, making him a more potent Marcher lord, and he was an obvious candidate to be joint justice of north Wales with his uncle Roger Mortimer of Chirk. Conventionally enough he founded a college of nine priests at Lentwarden and another of two chaplains in Ludlow castle. From his wife he had also inherited extensive lands in Ireland, where he was king's lieutenant in 1315-18, defeating Edward Bruce, and justiciar from 1319. If account is taken also of his service in Scotland (1308-10), Gascony (1313), against Llywellyn Bren (1315) and Bristol (1316), he emerges as the outstanding soldier of Edward II's reign.

His Marcher origins explain his participation in the Despenser War in 1321 and in the defeat next year, when he was spared his life and imprisoned perpetually. Edward's decision to execute him prompted his escape abroad to Hainault, and his alliance with Queen Isabella and Hainault made Edward II's overthrow possible. Thereafter he was an increasingly dominant political figure, initially as Queen Isabella's lover, and latterly as the brute force needed to defeat opponents. Mortimer took his opportunity to enrich himself and revenge himself on his enemies, showing flagrant disregard for the law. He arranged the execution of the Despensers. He is usually held responsible for the very necessary murder of Edward II and the death of his brother, the Earl of Kent, but not for the details of policy that remained in Isabella's hands. His abrupt fall in 1330 was followed by his brutal execution as scapegoat of the régime. Edward III ignored Isabella's pleas for clemency.

1326-30 were crucial years in 'the most striking rise in the fourteenth century of political acquisition of property'. Starting the century merely as Marcher lords, the Mortimers ended it with 'an inheritance second only to Lancaster'. Mortimer's rewards from his successful invasion were concentrated in Wales, where he was granted many royal and forfeited lordships, some of which his heirs retained, and the justiciarship of all Wales with power to appoint all officers except the chamberlains. 'They took unto them castles, towns, lands and rents in great harm and loss unto the Crown, and of the king's estate also, beyond measure.' In 1328 he was given the new title of Earl of March. So immensely proud was he of his title that, like Gaveston, he insisted on its use rather than his own name. He traced his shadowy connections with the Lusignan Counts of La Marche, claimed descent from the legendary King Arthur and King Brutus, and entertained Edward III and Isabella at Wigmore, where he held a Round Table. A son was married into the blood royal and other children into other great families, alliances that endured and stood his heirs in good stead after his fall. Contemporaries remarked on his pride and arrogance, the splendid and exotic clothes that he wore, and found him as insufferable as the Despensers whom he had destroyed. He shared their fate and thus brought the see-saw of political violence to an end.

Further Reading

N. M. Fryde, *The Tyranny and Fall of Edward II 1321-26*, 1979.

P. C. Doherty, 'Isabella, Queen of England 1296-1330', Oxford DPhil thesis, 1977.

G. A. Holmes, *Estates of the Higher Nobility in Fourteenth-Century England*, 1957.

MORTON, JOHN (1420?-1500), Archbishop of Canterbury and cardinal, was born probably in 1420 at Milborne St Andrew, near Bere Regis in Dorset. He was the son of Richard Morton, of a Nottingham family, and Elizabeth, daughter of Richard Turburville and Cecilia Beauchamp, being the eldest of five sons. He was educated at the Benedictine Abbey at Cerne, from which he went to Balliol, Oxford. He took up law, but he also took orders, and in 1446 he appears among the vice-chancellors of Oxford, known also as commissaries. He moved to London and practised as a lawyer principally in the Court of Arches, and became a Privy Councillor and Chancellor of the Duchy of Cornwall. From this moment he became a great pluralist and might almost be said to have collected offices and livings. All these appointments were ecclesiastical, but Morton's work was almost wholly legal or political, and there is little evidence that he resided in any of his livings.

During the Wars of the Roses Morton was mainly on the Lancastrian side, but he managed to keep in with the Yorkists when they were in the ascendant. He was present at the battle of Towton and at one point had to fight for his life: he was wrongly reported to have been taken prisoner (1461). He escaped to the north and sailed for Flanders, not to return to England for ten years. He was in 1461 attainted, convicted of treason and sentenced to lose all his possessions. While he was abroad he attended the Queen Margaret, first at Bruges and later at Louvain. He played a large part in reconciling Warwick and Clarence to the Lancastrians, and when they sailed for England (1470), Morton went with them, landing at Dartmouth on 13 September. He was present at the battle of Barnet (April 1471), after which he hurried to Weymouth to meet the queen and her son, who were expected there. He took them to Cerne Abbey and thence to Beaulieu.

The battle of Tewkesbury put paid to Lancastrian hopes, and Morton now (1471) reconciled himself with the Yorkists. Edward IV evidently looked on Morton as a trustworthy and valuable servant; he reversed the attainder and in 1472 appointed him to be Master of the Rolls. In a short time Morton held many prebends and five archdeaconries. One sign of the king's confidence in Morton may be seen in the embassy which Edward entrusted to him to bring the emperor and the King of Hungary into an alliance against the King of France, Louis XI (1474). The next year he was one of the negotiators of the Treaty of Picquigny where peace was made with Louis XI, and he received as his share of the spoils a pension of £2,000 a year.

In 1478 he was appointed Bishop of Ely. On the day of his enthronement, after a night of prayer, Morton walked from Downham to Ely with his head uncovered, bare-footed and barelegged, with his beads in his hand, saying his Paternosters. He now gave up the Mastership of the Rolls and to a great extent devoted himself to religious duties. He also became tutor to the Prince of Wales. At his palace in London he held reading parties both for young and promising scholars and also for men of learning, English and foreign: he set about reforming his diocese and he revived his connection with Oxford. When Edward IV died in 1483, Morton was one of his executors, but he refused to act on the grounds that he was not given large enough powers to act effectively.

When Richard of Gloucester began to scheme to seize the throne from his young nephew, Edward V, Morton was in a difficult and dangerous position. He was present at the council meeting at which Richard's plans began to make themselves known, a meeting made famous by Shakespeare's dramatization of it, in the course of which Richard refers to one of Morton's favourite hobbies, the growing of fruit:

> My Lord of Ely, when I was last at Holborn,
> I saw good strawberries in your garden there:
> I do beseech you send for some of them.
> *(Richard III, 3.4.)*

That Morton at once went to order some did not save him from arrest: he was put into prison, but he was released on a petition from Oxford University on behalf of 'our dearest son' and allowed to reside with

Buckingham at Brecknock Castle. Buckingham had already been forming his own plans against Richard, which he now divulged to Morton. Morton himself had almost certainly come to the conclusion that the hopes for the country rested now, not on Richard, but on Henry of Richmond. He approved of Buckingham's plans and he became the intermediary between Buckingham and Reginald Bray, and this brought him into touch with Margaret Beaufort, Countess of Richmond, mother of Henry Richmond, later Henry VII. It is possible that it was Morton who first implanted in Margaret Beaufort's mind the idea that her son should marry Elizabeth of York, daughter of Edward IV, and thus end the feud of the Roses. If this is true, it goes a long way to establishing Morton, rather against the factual evidence, as being a clear-sighted and honest man, who did his best in the most difficult times for his country. A rising was planned to take place in the west. Morton decided that he ought to be at Ely: it is possible that he distrusted the success of a purely local rising and wanted to be in the east of England to raise forces there. Buckingham was suspicious of allowing so important a personage to leave his side. Morton escaped secretly by night and went to Ely. Shakespeare records for us Richard III's feelings:

Ely with Richmond troubles me more near
Than Buckingham with his rash-levied strength.
(Richard III, 4.3.)

Buckingham's rising failed, Henry of Richmond's expedition from Brittany had to turn back, Buckingham was arrested and executed. Morton had gone to Flanders and was there till after Bosworth, except for a visit to Paris where he met Richard Fox, later Bishop of Winchester, and won him over to Henry's side. Morton was able to warn Henry that the Duke of Brittany meant to betray him to Richard III and thus to advise him to fly into the realm of the King of France.

In 1485 Henry Richmond invaded England and won the throne. Morton came back; his attainder was again reversed; he was made a Privy Councillor; in 1486 he was Chancellor and Archbishop of Canterbury. From that point on until his death in 1500 Morton was, under Henry VII, the most important and powerful man in the kingdom. He was supreme, except for the king, in church and state. He now set himself to remedy the abuses in both: immorality in the monasteries, over-mighty subjects in the state. He reformed clerical abuses, even down to the form of dress: he ordered residence for those with care of souls: bishops were to take trouble in selecting clergymen. He set out on visitations (1490) to Lichfield, Coventry, Bath and Wells, Winchester, Lincoln, Exeter. He petitioned the Papacy to canonize Henry VI, in which he failed, and Anselm was canonized instead. In 1493 Morton was made a cardinal. His position now was something like a foreshadow of Wolsey's

position later on: Morton was head of the church as primate, cardinal and legate; he was chief administrator in the state as Chancellor of England, especially in the law; he was Chancellor of Oxford University; he opened parliament for the king and defended policy, especially taxation, in speeches more like modern speeches than those in the past; he received foreign embassies; he persuaded the pope to allow some modification in the laws governing sanctuary.

In the realm of finance there seems little doubt now that Morton's position was extremely difficult. The king had to have money, and left to himself Henry might have pursued a much more heavy-handed and even tyrannical policy than he did: he was restrained by Bray and by Morton. 'Morton's Fork' or 'Crutch' has passed into history, but it looks as if he accepted all the unpopularity for financial measures which would have been worse but for him, in order to save the reputation of the king. And he had to bear the burden of unpopularity for the many 'benevolences' which were raised out of the nobility.

In one respect Morton was a herald of the future: he was an indefatigable builder. He repaired the palace at Canterbury; the Manor House at Lambeth, where the Gateway is his work; the episcopal residences at Maidstone, Aldington Park, Ford, Charing: his arms are on the tower at Wisbech: he built what is now the old part of Hatfield House: restored Rochester Bridge; put the splendid roof on to the nave of Bere Regis church. In addition he cut a great canal from Peterborough to Guyhirne near Wisbech, known as Morton's Leame, which brought the High Fen into cultivation amounting to 4,387 acres: this canal was forty feet wide, four feet deep, with new outlets to the sea, and forty miles in length. It lasted until 1725.

In legislation his most famous Act is that of 1495 to protect from the penalties of treason those who act under a de facto king, in order to protect all who had supported or were serving Henry VII.

Bacon records of him that 'he was a wise man and an eloquent, but in his nature harsh and haughty, much accepted by the king, but envied by the nobility and hated of the people'. In that tribute there is nothing to persuade us that Morton was not a highly valuable statesman in harsh and difficult days. But Sir Thomas More, who as a boy was brought up in Morton's household, puts into the mouth of Hythlodaye in *Utopia* a more generous tribute: 'a man not more honourable for his authority than for his prudence and virtue ... In his speech he was fine, eloquent and pithy. In the law he had profound knowledge; in wit he was incomparable; and in memory wonderful excellent. These qualities, which in him were by nature singular, he by learning and use had made perfect. The king put much trust in his counsel: the weal public also in a manner leaned unto him.'

The general opinion nowadays is that Morton was not,

and Sir Thomas More was, the author of *The History of Richard III*, both in the Latin and English versions (Chambers, *Thomas More*, p.55).

Morton died on 15 September 1500, at Knowle in Kent.

Further Reading
C. Harper-Bill, *Journal of Ecclesiastical History*, 1978.
R. I. Woodhouse, *Memoir of Morton*, 1895.
T. Mozley, *Henry VII, Prince Arthur and Cardinal Morton*, intro., 1878.

MOWBRAY, THOMAS, EARL OF NOTTINGHAM and DUKE OF NORFOLK (*c*.1366-99) was 'an intensely ambitious young man with a taste for intrigue'. A younger son, he succeeded in 1383 to his father's modest barony and became heir apparent to the Segrave and Norfolk estates of his grandmother Margaret Marshall. Her longevity kept him relatively poor and dependent on royal favour. He was brought up with the king, who immediately made him an earl, a knight of the Garter, and married him to a short-lived heiress. Mowbray had a private apartment at King's Langley palace and shared in Richard's plot to murder John of Gaunt in 1385. He served with the king as Earl Marshal in Scotland and shared a naval command with Arundel in 1387. The advance of Robert Vere as dominant favourite apparently involved the eclipse of Mowbray, whose victory off Margate and unlicensed marriage were both ill-regarded by the king. Rivalry with Vere may explain why late in 1387 he joined the three original Lords Appellant: Gloucester, Warwick, and his father-in-law Arundel. Factional strife rather than constitutional principle probably impelled him into opposition and rapid reconciliation with the king followed the ruin of his rival Vere.

Whereas Gloucester, Arundel and Warwick were dismissed on Richard's majority in 1389, Mowbray returned to favour. He was appointed warden of the East March and captain of Berwick and Roxburgh in 1389. He exchanged these posts for the captaincy of Calais in 1390, supplanted Gloucester as justice of Chester and north Wales in 1394, and in 1397, with royal help, wrested Gower from Warwick, another fellow Appellant. As a diplomat he negotiated Richard's second marriage. As a former Appellant of 1388, he had a key role as one of the king's own Lords Appellant in 1397. It was Mowbray who arrested Gloucester, imprisoned and murdered him at Calais; who as Earl Marshal supervised the execution of his father-in-law Arundel; and who was rewarded by a dukedom (Margaret Marshall became duchess), recognition as Earl Marshal, and by the grant of large parts of the estates of Arundel and Warwick. He was now a magnate of the front rank.

Yet his fall was abrupt. Exiled for life in 1398, he died at Venice next year, still only thirty-three years old.

Behind his fall lay the conversation with Hereford that prompted each to accuse the other of treason. Mowbray had been the proudest and most presumptuous of courtiers of the 1390s, the most deserving and best rewarded of Richard's Appellants, yet he never enjoyed Vere's proximity to the king and never knew Richard's innermost thoughts and ultimate intentions. Apparently he still feared vengeance for his actions in 1388 and invoked it to excuse Gloucester's murder. 'And he swore great oaths swearing that he would answer before God that it was never his will that he should be killed but only for dread of the king and eschewing of his own death.' Whether indeed Mowbray plotted further treason, his exile shows that he was not indispensable and perhaps even an embarrassment to Richard, who seized the chance to be rid of him. He thus lost a formidable adherent and further fuelled the dangerous uncertainty of his last years.

Yet Mowbray was more than a 'self-seeking renegade'. He was literate, probably appreciated music, and was pious. His patronage of monasticism included the foundation of a Carthusian house at Axholme. Reputedly a chivalrous knight, he patronized a new crusading order in 1395, planned a pilgrimage to Jerusalem in 1399, and heard three masses at the Coventry Charterhouse before his abortive duel with Hereford. To gauge his complex personality accurately requires a precise assessment of the boundary between his sincerity and commitment and his ambition, self-interest and devious subtlety.

Further Reading
J. A. Tuck, *Richard II and the English Nobility*, 1973.
A. Goodman, *The Loyal Conspiracy: The Lords Appellant under Richard II*, 1971.

MUGGLETON, LODOWICK (1609-98), sectary, was the son of a farrier, born in the Bishopsgate district of London, who became a journeyman tailor. Like many others of his class, he was much moved by extreme Puritan ideas in the disturbed 1640s. Neither Presbyterianism nor the ordinary forms of independency satisfied him. Like George Fox he sought to live 'an honest and just natural life', yet the fear of hell-fire was strong with him, and he was much impressed by the Ranter John Robins, especially perhaps by the latter's claim to be able to damn his opponents to all eternity. In 1651-2 he had a series of revelations. So did his cousin, John Reeve, personal ones 'by voice of words' from Jesus Christ; the two claimed to be the 'two witnesses' of Revelation xi. 3, and quickly acquired a following. Reeve died in 1658, and the sect came to be known as the 'Muggletonians'. Their beliefs were eccentric even among the sectaries of the time. God was one and eternal, with a material body larger than that of a man: he had come to earth as Jesus, and left Elijah in charge of the universe. The devil was a human being. Men were divided into the blessed and the cursed, and Muggleton had a divine commission – which he used with a will – to bless or curse to eternity. The Muggletonians neither prayed nor preached. Not surprisingly, he was several times in trouble with the authorities, both of Commonwealth and monarchy, for blasphemy, and in 1677 he was put in the pillory and had his writings publicly burned. He had a furious controversy with the Quakers, whom he denounced as 'serpents' and damned with enthusiasm in apocalyptic phraseology. Muggleton was a tough, shrewd character, who dealt firmly with schisms among his followers, condemned the sins of the flesh, enjoyed a pipe, and lived to eighty-nine.

Further Reading
C. Hill, W. Lamont and B. Reay, *The World of the Muggletonians*, 1983.
C. E. Whiting, *Studies in English Puritanism*, 1931, chap. vi.

MUN, THOMAS (1571-1641), economist, was the son of a London mercer. Mun went into trade early, particularly with the Levant and the Italian cities, and became a prosperous merchant. He was chosen a member of the committee of the East India Company in 1615, and his first book, published in 1621, was a defence of the company against the charge that they exported too much specie in order to pay for their imports of luxuries. His second and most famous book, *England's Treasure by Foreign Trade*, was probably written before 1630 but was not published until 1664. In this he generalized the theme behind his earlier work, and laid down the doctrine of the 'balance of trade', a doctrine whose fulfilment required us 'to sell more to strangers yearly than we consume of theirs in value', i.e., to ensure that the balance was tilted in our favour. Mun, whose own business success lent much weight to his theorizing, wrote in an age when foreign trade was growing rapidly in importance, and was felt to add mightily to the strength and reputation of the country, and he was the first considerable exponent in England of what came to be known as the 'mercantile' system of political economy.

MURDAC, HENRY (*d.*1153; Abbot of Fountains 1144; Archbishop of York 1147-53) took full advantage of the brief period when the Cistercian order combined political power and moral authority to achieve high ecclesiastical office in the face of royal hostility and local opposition. A Yorkshireman who held lucrative preferments under Archbishop Thurstan, he abandoned teaching as a secular clerk to enter Clairvaux under its charismatic and forceful abbot, St Bernard. Murdac, a man of intellect, asceticism and conviction, became one of Bernard's favoured disciples, being appointed successively Abbot of Vauclair and then Fountains, in his native Yorkshire. At Fountains, Murdac proved himself combative, rigid in imposition of strict Clairvaux rules

and entrepreneurial. Daughter houses were sponsored, even as far away as Norway. Locally, he began to assert Cistercian influence beyond the cloister in opposing the election as Archbishop of York of William FitzHerbert, a secular clerk and close relative of King Stephen. In his campaign Murdac was able to recruit his patron Bernard, seen by many – himself included – as the conscience of Christendom, and, crucially, Bernard's pupil, Pope Eugenius III (1145-53). At one point in the conflict, William's men sacked Fountains itself: they knew who their enemy was. Murdac's motives may or may not have been selfless. What is certain is that after William's desposition by Eugenius in 1147, Murdac attracted enough support in a divided election for the same pope and fellow Cistercian to appoint him archbishop in William's stead.

As archbishop, as when abbot, Murdac scarcely conformed to the often proclaimed Cistercian model of the retiring eremite, shunning the world, finding spiritual fulfilment only in the cloister. Despite the refusal of the king and the York clergy to accept him, Murdac pursued a vigorous policy of asserting archiepiscopal rights often in the direct interests of the Cistercian order. He also maintained close control over the affairs of Fountains, using his archiepiscopal authority as a cover for hiring and firing a series of abbatial stooges. Recognized by the king in 1151 in return for his help in persuading Pope Eugenius to consecrate Stephen's son king, Murdac remained energetic in imposing what he saw as the highest ecclesiastical standards throughout the church, but his effectiveness was limited and transitory. After his death, a non-Cistercian pope, Anastasius IV, restored Archbishop William. Murdac, for all his personal qualities, exposed flaws in Cistercian policy eagerly siezed upon by opponents. His rectitude appeared self-righteous; his probity smug; his conviction arrogance; his actions no better than those of any other self-interested ecclesiastical faction. Such were the contradictions of success. To them Murdac added his own abundant taste for acrid controversy. York never again had a Cistercian archbishop.

Further Reading
F. Barlow, *The English Church 1066-1154*, 1979.
D. Knowles, *The Monastic Order in England*, 1949.

MURDOCK, WILLIAM (1754-1839), mechanic and inventor, introduced lighting by gas. During his work in Cornwall, as works manager for Boulton and Watt he conducted experiments with a view to using inflammable gas obtained from coal for lighting. He successfully lit his own house and later installed gas lighting in Boulton's Soho works. The peace of Amiens (1802) was celebrated with a brilliant display of new lighting, to 'the astonishment and admiration' of the people of Birmingham who went to see it.

Murdock's father was a Scottish millwright. William followed the same trade, but in 1777 he came south, looking for experience, and in particular for work on one of the new steam engines. When Boulton interviewed him he noticed him twiddling his hat: it was made of wood to his own design. Boulton took him on and sent him to oversee the firm's machines in the Cornish mines. Not the least of his duties was to watch for patent infringements. Murdock had to be tough as well as devoted. He seemed to live for his machines. He was once found asleep, heaving at his bed post, calling out, 'Now she goes, lads, now she goes!'

Murdock did not, as is often supposed, invent the steam locomotive, although he was one of several who were experimenting with such machines at the time of Trevithick's successful invention. To steam engine construction he did however contribute the 'sun and planet' motion and the 'bell-crank' engine. In 1810 he took out a patent for making stone pipes and the invention of 'iron cement' is also attributed to him. A story is told of him that well illustrates his resourceful character. On a visit to Manchester, one of the first cities to be lit by gas, he was invited to the house of a friend who lived outside the illuminated part of the city. Murdock walked with his friend past the gas works. He went in, took a pig's bladder from his pocket, filled it with gas, placed the stem of an old tobacco pipe into the neck of the bladder, and thus produced a flow of gas and a flare of light to guide them along the dark roads. As he grew older Murdock became modestly prosperous, but he went on working. On the lawn of his house at Handsworth stood a quaint garden ornament. It was 'the first piece of iron-toothed gearing ever cast'.

MURRAY, LORD GEORGE (1694-1760), Jacobite general, was a son of the Duke of Atholl. He spent an unruly youth, failed to settle at Glasgow University and went into the army. He gladly exchanged a cornetcy in George I's army for a colonelcy in 'James III's', but his participation in the revolt of 1715 led to exile, and he did not improve his position by acting with his brother William, Marquis of Tullibardine, as leader of the abortive rising of 1719. A dominant motive in his life was service to the exiled king, whom he came to see as personification of Christian hero and knight. In 1725, however, he secured a pardon and came to live at Tullibardine Castle. In 1739, in the interests of his family, he at last took the oath of submission to the Hanoverian king. He believed that the Jacobite cause was moribund and wanted to serve his country. He even suggested the employment of Highland troops in the government service.

The events of 1745 seem to have taken Murray by surprise, and the landing of the prince may well have appeared a forlorn adventure. He was drawn to engage himself in the Cause by his brother William, who had remained chivalrously loyal to the prince, by his own military ambitions and by a strong sense of honour. At Perth, in September, he was appointed joint Lieutenant-General of the army, with Lord Perth, under the prince. From the start his position was difficult. The only experienced soldier, he had to bear the garrulous advice of Mr O'Sullivan, self-appointed military adviser, Quartermaster-General and Adjutant-General, but ignorant of war and the country, as well as the uncertain whims of the prince. The Highland army of about 3,000 was as undisciplined as it was brave; that it did not behave worse was owing largely to his sensible discipline. Because Murray was forthright with the prince, who liked the flattery of the Irish group, he was subsequently held to have been disloyal. But this came with the bitterness of defeat and exile, and during the early campaign disagreements were stilled by victory at Prestonpans and the exhilaration of the march to Derby. In December the lack of recruits compelled him to counsel retreat, with the approval of the rest of the Council; thereafter the prince blamed him for all that went amiss.

The splendid victory at Falkirk showed that, in Lord Mahon's words, the prince had a general with whom none could vie 'in planning a campaign, providing against disasters, or improving a victory'. Perhaps ultimate disaster was inevitable in the face of the larger, well-found force of Cumberland; but there is little doubt that the overwhelming defeat of Culloden was caused by the constant interference of the prince, too sanguine to the last, and especially by his insistence upon battle at Culloden on 16 April 1746, when his troops were exhausted and starving. The conduct of the battle is still surrounded by controversy. Lord George Murray emerges, however, as a commander of foresight and bravery, 'first and last upon the field'. After the battle he remained in hiding for eight months in the hills near Tullibardine. Then he took ship and landed in Holland on Christmas Day. Charles Edward refused even to receive him, but he settled down to live contentedly enough in exile near Cleves.

Further Reading
J. Black, *Culloden and the 45*, 1990.
Katherine Tomasson, *The Jacobite General*, 1958.

MURRAY, WILLIAM, 1st EARL OF MANSFIELD (1705-93) was a great Lord Chief Justice; for thirty-two years he sat on the King's Bench. In all that time the court was only twice divided in opinion, and only two of its judgements were reversed in the House of Lords. His wisdom, fairness and perseverance in difficult cases epitomized the finest qualities of English law.

Murray was a Scotsman by birth, younger son of Lord Stormont and of Margery Scott. He was born at Scone, but went to Westminster School and to Christ Church, where he became known as a consummate and elegant scholar. When he entered the House of Commons in 1742 his legal reputation was already made. He became Solicitor-General and lent weight unquestioningly to successive governments. It was perhaps unseemly that he should have led for the Crown in the Jacobite trials of 1746-7, but his view of his rebel countrymen was not a sentimental one; the ministry had been severely shaken by the '45 – and the charge was treason. In the Commons he steadily enhanced his position. 'Silver-tongued' Mansfield could speak with sense and style about any matter of law, economics or politics. After he became Attorney-General in 1754 he was Newcastle's prop and partisan in the Lower House. Two years later he accepted the Chief Justiceship, which was his highest ambition. Offered the Great Seal, he twice refused; he filled briefly the office of Chancellor of the Exchequer, but he took a diminishing part in politics.

Upon Mansfield fell the onus of passing judgements in the several stages of the Wilkes case. These seem to show a bias in favour of prerogative, but when, for instance, he reversed Wilkes's outlawry for the technical reason that the writ was wrongly made out, he was more the cautious lawyer than the supple politician. Indeed, his procedure throughout was influenced by precedents rather than by his instinctive conservatism. Yet Wilkes accused him of subverting the law and 'Junius' complained, in his most venomous manner, that he was importing the civilian (Roman) doctrines into English law. He certainly reduced the scope of the jury in libel cases, holding that their only job was to decide the fact of publication; after the special verdict returned in the case of *Rex v. Woodfall*, newspaper editor, he ordered a new trial. Deliberate and wary though he was, Mansfield did not hesitate, when he felt that a principle should come before precedent no decision was more crucial than that of 1771 in the case of the negro James Somersett, that slavery could not exist in Great Britain. In another important case, *Campbell v. Hall*, he deprived the Crown of its powers of legislation by Order in Council over a colony to which a legislative assembly had been granted. By the sort of ingenious fiction in which Common Lawyers delight, he ruled in *Fabrigas v. Mostyn* that the island of Minorca was for legal purposes deemed to be 'within the ward of Chepe'.

Lord Mansfield won respect by his manner, for he was *gravitas* personified, and by his magnanimity. During the Gordon Riots a wild Protestant mob wrecked his house and destroyed his precious library, but he subsequently presided with conspicuous fairness over the trial of Lord George Gordon. Judicial manners in those days were not perfect and we are told that, like other judges, he would read a newspaper during counsel's speeches, if he believed that the evidence was closed and that counsel was wasting public time. He made however some useful reforms in procedure. He put an end to the practice of allowing any number of counsel on the same side to address the house and thus delay business excessively; he also used to deliver judgement whenever he believed there was no need for reconsideration, where formerly it had been customary to reserve it. His greatest achievement was, however, in the field of commercial law. Before his time commercial cases hardly ever came into the courts; he gradually attracted to the King's Bench a mass of business from the city. He empanelled a special jury of business-men who attended regularly so that the judge came to know them well; he would talk freely with them in court and some would become habitués.

Mansfield became an earl in 1776, but he did not resign his office until 1788; he spent his later years serenely at his house at Caen Wood, near Hampstead. Boswell spoke of his 'air and manner which none who ever saw or heard him can forget'. His courtesy, ease of manner and graceful speech were as impressive as they were unusual in an eighteenth-century lawyer.

Further Reading
C. H. S. Fifoot, *Lord Mansfield*, 1936.

MYNN, ALFRED (1807-61), cricketer, was a yeoman of Kent and among the greatest of early cricketers. Others could be chosen to represent the early days of the game, for instance, Beldham, one of the heroes of Hambledon so graphically described by John Nyren: 'Michael Angelo should have painted him … great in every department, but his peculiar glory was the cut. His wrist seemed turned on spring of the finest steel. He took the ball, as Burke did the House of Commons, between wind and water; not a moment too soon or too late'. From the start cricket tempted men to such rapturous prose and flights of imagination. Alfred Mynn had no Nyren to celebrate his skills but he was the first to be generally acknowledged among cricket's champions. He was rather over six foot tall, and twenty stone in weight, but 'there was nothing clumsy about him. He was stately and dignified at all times'. Tall-hatted, he managed to deliver, round arm, at a disconcerting pace (the bowler's arm was not allowed to rise above his shoulder till 1835). There is some evidence that he could also bowl a leg-break. How he dominated the rough pitches of those days and impressed his personality on fellow players can be judged from these memorial lines, by W. J. Prowse: no other game could inspire such a requiem.

> With his tall and stately presence, with his nobly moulded form,
> His broad hand was ever open, his brave heart was ever warm.
> All were proud of him, all loved him. As the changing seasons pass,
> As our champion lies a-sleeping underneath the Kentish grass.

N

NAPIER, SIR CHARLES (1782-1853) was the Irish general who conquered Sind. He was descended from Charles II through his mother, who, as Lady Sarah Lennox, was the girl George III wanted to marry. He wore his hair long in honour of his cavalier ancestry, and was appropriately uninhibited and eccentric in other ways. 'What a life he has led', said Dalhousie, 'what climates he has braved, how riddled and chopped to pieces with balls and bayonet and sabre wounds he is!' A small man with a beaked nose, with steel-rimmed spectacles perched on it, he grew huge extravagant whiskers to match his straggly hair. Women made him 'all about fire' – the devil himself, he said was 'not more flaming' – and he had a long, passionate liaison with a Greek girl, Anastasia. He and Byron took to each other, sharing a sardonic humour and a romantic love of Greece, and he was invited to lead the Greek army in their war of freedom against the Turks. A warm heart and a strong temper led him to strike a camel driver, who was maltreating his animal, so hard that he had to fight a battle next day holding the reins of his horse with a broken hand. He was equally angry with the mill owners of the north of England for the suffering of the handloom weavers. 'Hell may be paved with good intentions, but it is assuredly hung with Manchester cottons.'

He owed his opportunities partly to his hero Wellington, and partly to his widely recognized intelligence. His interests were broad. After burning towns in the American War of 1812 he studied agriculture, building and political economy. He read much and wrote powerfully. In 1822 he was sent out to the Ionian Islands, where the governor made him Resident in Cephalonia. There he proved an enlightened despot. He drained marshes: he built a new harbour, schools, hospitals, markets, prisons and barracks, and a network of roads spanning the mountains. It was the happiest part of his life, but it came to an end typically. He quarrelled with the governor, who found him high-handed and odd, and ordered him to shave. Napier obeyed, sent the hair in a parcel to the governor, and departed on leave. He was not allowed to return. After a long spell on half pay from 1830, he was given the Northern Command in 1839, as a general who would handle the Chartist riots with discretion. He went to Chartist meetings in mufti, got introductions to their leaders and assured them of his sympathy for their cause if peacefully pressed, but of his determination to put down riot ruthlessly. His part in preventing violence was recognized then and since.

He went to India in 1841 in order to provide for his daughters, in whose interests he had already remarried twice, widows of over sixty. The new Governor General, Ellenborough, clever, direct, outspoken and mistrustful of commercial interests, recognized a kindred spirit and sent him to take political as well as military charge in Sind, the land round the Indus between Afghanistan and the sea. The massacre of their forces in Afghanistan had just shaken the confidence of the British throughout northern India, and Napier was determined not to be 'Cabooled'. It was also his responsibility to keep a route open into Afghanistan from the south. Ellenborough was out to impose control over the Amirs who ruled in Sind. When they hesitated to sign a tough treaty, Napier advanced on them, and won two decisive battles at Miani and Dubba in the spring of 1843. The annexation of Sind followed, which Napier had expected. 'We have no right to seize Sind, but we shall do so, and a very advantageous, useful, humane piece of rascality it will be', he wrote in his journal; and as its new governor he set about improving the lot of the peasants, repeating his building and irrigation achievements and setting up a civilian police force, as well as abolishing suttee, the Hindu practice of burning widows when their husbands died.

He got a bad press back in England through James Outram, later hero of the Mutiny. Outram had been the political officer in Sind before Napier arrived, and favoured a 'softly, softly' policy. He spread exaggerated stories of the savagery of Napier's troops in battle and of their looting and rape in the harems afterwards. Napier's cause was not helped by the hype of his historian brother William, a fiery controversialist. His victories received no salutes, and he never got a peerage. But Wellington hailed him as a great commander, and got him sent back, against the protests of the East India Company, to be

Commander-in-Chief under Dalhousie in 1849. Inevitably sparks flew between two powerful characters. 'This little goose is quite unfit for his place', wrote Napier. But Dalhousie was the boss and Napier resigned. Death caught up with him at last three years later. There was no mourning amongst the evangelicals and the men of commerce; but many then and since have seen him as the most intelligent and unusual of Victoria's generals.

Further Reading
P. Napier, *Raven Castle, Charles Napier in India 1844-51*, 1991.
P. Napier, *I Have Sind, Charles Napier in India 1841-44*, 1990.

NAPIER, JOHN (1550-1617), inventor of logarithms, was a Scottish laird, born at Merchiston Castle near Edinburgh and educated at St Andrews. He seems to have travelled abroad for some years before settling on the family estates. Napier was a man of tough practical mind, and of a varied genius, unusual among the Scots gentry of James VI's time. A firm Calvinist, in 1594 he published *A Plain Discovery of the Whole Revelation of St John*, a very successful piece of anti-papal propaganda. An inventive landowner, he obtained a patent in 1597 for a device, based upon a hydraulic screw, to check flooding in coalpits; and about the same time he sent Francis Bacon's elder brother a detailed project for making new weapons of war, including great mirrors as burning-glasses and a musket-proof metal chariot. An amateur mathematician, even more of an amateur than Englishmen like Wallis and Barrow fifty years later, Napier made use of a set of rods, known as 'Napier's Bones', to work out sums, and commended an arrangement of metal plates in a box which served as a kind of calculating machine. But what brought him immediate and lasting fame was a highly utilitarian mathematical discovery, the development of the theory of logarithms, which he expounded after twenty years' work in his *Mirifici Logarithmorum* of 1614. Their rapid adoption – in an age which for purposes of astronomy and navigation, taxation and banking, was growing increasingly in need of easier methods of calculation – was largely the work of a Cambridge mathematician, Henry Briggs, who proposed ten as the base and worked out elaborately detailed tables.

Further Reading
W. Brownlie Hendry, 'John Napier of Merchiston, *History Today*', April 1967.
E. W. Hobson, *John Napier*, 1914.

NASH, JOHN (1752-1835), architect, was with Sir John Soane the principal exponent of that phase of neo-classicism which is called the Regency style. Architects working in the Regency style combined a scrupulous eclecticism with a splendid bravado: like the pure 'Grecians' of the time, Wilkins and Smirke for example,

they went back further than the Romanism of Sir William Chambers and the Adam brothers, to the fountainhead of the classical style, the Greek columns and entablatures – but then they proceeded to take liberties with them; and, not content with that, they went on to borrow, and often to mix with their neo-Grecian endeavours, the outstanding features of the Gothic style and of those styles which Sir William Chambers and others had made familiar, the Chinese, the Indian and the Egyptian. For this work Nash, with his abounding self-confidence, was peculiarly well-fitted; and fortune gave him the largest opportunities.

But he was in his mid-forties before he came to the public notice. He had studied architecture in his youth; then with the help of a small legacy, he had set up as a builder in London, but had gone bankrupt, and taken refuge in Wales and the west country. Here he began to prosper, and in 1796 he returned to London to work in an informal architectural partnership with Humphrey Repton, the landscape-gardener. Two years later he married a Mary Anne Bradley, who seems to have been on intimate terms with the Prince of Wales, for from now on he was assured of royal favour, and was soon able to part company with Repton and to set up on his own account.

It was now that he began to design the small country houses – 'villas' – which improved roads were bringing within the range of city-workers; to embellish older houses with Gothic additions in the manner of Wyatt; and to exercise great ingenuity in planning country cottages which should be ornaments to the estates on which they were scattered (and of which the most coherent group is that of Blaise Hamlet, near Bristol).

Wyatt's sudden death in 1813 benefited Nash in two ways. He became (with Soane and Smirke) one of the three new Deputy Surveyors to the Board of Works. And, having already worked for the prince at Carlton House, he was naturally chosen in Wyatt's stead to carry out the desired 'improvements' to the Brighton Pavilion. By 1818, the Pavilion had emerged in its present form; and the bizarre exterior, which has echoes of the Taj Mahal but partakes of a score of other influences too, is largely Nash's own.

By 1818, Nash was already far advanced with a more grandiose scheme. In 1811 the lease of 'Marylebone Park' reverted from the Duke of Portland to the Crown; and it was proposed that this land should be developed and linked to Whitehall by a great north-south route. In July 1811 the whole scheme was entrusted, by the influence of the prince (now regent), to Nash. It was a wise choice; for perhaps only Nash had the scale of vision (he was never one to become enmeshed in detail), the toughness and tenacity (for his plan involved widespread demolition of property), and the entrepreneurial capacity (he risked his own fortune on what was technically an official scheme) to complete the undertaking. The speed with which the work progressed is the best evidence of his capacity. Of course he was assisted by modern materials: stucco is used throughout, and many of the columns are of cast iron. And the design of the individual houses was left to fellow architects. But Nash was the overall director and, if the finished work seems ill-considered and sometimes negligent, that was the price paid for his energy.

Of course, Nash's plan was never completed. He and the prince intended that it should eclipse Napoleonic Paris. It never did that: the geometric regularity of large-scale town-planning has never appealed to the British genius. But even today, after redevelopment and blitzes, enough survives of what was completed to enable us to see the degree of originality and adventure. Nash intended that the route should run from Carlton House, on the north side of St James's Park, to the new Regent's Park. But in 1825, the prince (now king), tiring of Carlton House and its associations, ordered its destruction. In its place were built the great Carlton House Terraces. They formed the southern terminus of the route, which then proceeded northwards through Waterloo Place, Lower Regent Street and Piccadilly Circus (truly a circle in those days). Then came the first bend to the left, up the famous colonnaded quadrant of Regent Street (but Regent Street has been entirely remodelled in this century). Crossing Oxford Street at Oxford Circus, the route took a second leftward bend in Langham Place (where Nash's new church of All Souls closed the view up Regent Street), and proceeded along Portland Place (already built by the Adam brothers). Here Park Crescent and the terraces facing Park Square made – and make – a splendid entrance to the park, which is itself bordered by Nash terraces. It is amusing to follow this route and see how much of Nash's work survives. Cumberland Terrace, flanking the park on the east side, is perhaps the finest, for it was intended to face a 'villa' to be built in the park for the prince himself. But the spirit of Nash's London can still be caught by one who stands in Waterloo Place.

The third large item of royal patronage was the rebuilding of Buckingham House, which George IV wished to occupy as a palace in place of Carlton House. But, because of the high cost, Nash's commission was suspended on the king's death (1830) and his operations obscured by his successor. The Marble Arch, which he intended as an entrance, has found another resting-place. In 1835 Nash died in his Gothic castle on the Isle of Wight, and with him finally died the Regency.

Further Reading
J. Summerson, *John Nash*, 1935.

NASH, RICHARD (1674-1762) was King of Bath at a time when this city was the 'queen of spas'. The eighteenth century in England was an age of watering places where the affluent went to purge themselves, to ease their gout and to enjoy the diversions of social life with their fellow sufferers. The oldest of the spas was Bath, and at Bath for many years the presiding genius was 'Beau' Nash. Carmarthen Grammar School and Jesus College, Oxford, nurtured this supple Welshman. He studied law at the Middle Temple after a brief period in the army, made a name as a dandy and paid his bills by lucky gambling. Early in the century he fixed on Bath which had been visited by Queen Anne and was frequented by invalids and quack doctors but was still a shabby place; the waters were dirty and the amenities few. An easy and negligent manner concealed in Nash a talent for planning and persuasion and within a few years a new city rose round the 'reaking steam' of the baths. There was a new pump room and a theatre; round about villas sprang up. The key to the success of the spa was easy transport, so Nash raised money to improve the Bath Road and others leading to the town.

For forty years Nash reigned unchallenged. Street lighting and a night watch were among the improvements ordered by the town council under his instructions. He assisted in the foundation of a hospital, opened in 1742. His insistence upon order, space and elegance, together with the genius of the Woods, father and son, architects of the North and South Parades, Queen's Square and the Circus, made a complete and beautiful town. He had the gift of being able to make himself agreeable to the visiting gentry and indispensable to the town council. As Master of Ceremonies he assumed the role of enlightened despot. The insulting behaviour of the chairmen was corrected. His code of dress and deportment dealt with such matters as requests to dance and the summoning of footmen. One may be quoted to show their flavour: 'That no gentleman gives his tickets for the Balls to any but Gentlemen. N.B. Unless he has none of his acquaintance'. He did not hesitate to enforce his rules. When the Duchess of Queensberry appeared in a white lace apron of which he was known to disapprove, he tore it from her and threw it into the back benches where the ladies' maids were sitting. He waged a campaign against the wearing of boots in the Assembly Rooms; if any person erred in this way, Beau Nash would ask him, in the most public way, where he had hidden his horse. He grew more tyrannical with age, and would embarrass young ladies by inquiring why they were not dancing, or press dowagers to subscribe to some new charity.

As a shareholder in the gaming tables, and in other ways which he did not reveal, Beau Nash made a splendid living out of his private empire. But he did not want Bath to become a mere gambling den and he intervened personally on occasion to save young gamblers from ruin. The same mixture of good nature and business sense led him to ban duelling in Bath. About this time it became unfashionable for men to carry swords and the practice of duelling declined; a step towards civilization for which Nash must have some credit. A unique feature was that it was customary for visitors to attend daily morning service at the Abbey, where now the marble tablets, row upon row, commemorate the fashionable worshippers who died in Bath. In his heyday Nash was a magnificent figure in his white hat and his extravagant clothes, preceded when he travelled in his post chariot by outriders, footmen, French horns and similar pomps. The Gaming Act of 1739, which made illegal private lotteries and the games of Basset, Hazard, Faro and the Ace of Hearts, was, however, a setback. Ultimately he lost his money and died poor.

Further Reading
Edith Sitwell, *Bath*, 1932.

NAYLER, JAMES (*c.*1618-60) was a leading apostle of the early Quaker movement. He was of yeoman stock from Woodchurch, near Wakefield in Yorkshire, served for some eight years in the parliamentary forces, and was a member of an Independent church. When he left the army he went back to the land. Thence, like so many in that age of religious ferment, he felt himself called to the work of God. 'I was at the plough', he told a magistrate some years later, 'meditating upon the things of God, and suddenly I heard a Voice, saying unto me "Get thee out from thy kindred and from thy father's house"'. Soon afterwards he met George Fox, and joined him in spreading the message of the Inner Light, the 'Christ within'. He was a man of attractive manner and appearance, the most persuasive of early Quaker preachers, and did much to evangelize the north of England in the early 1650s. Like his fellows, he suffered for his preaching; a mob beat him at Walney Island in 1652, and in 1653 he was imprisoned at Appleby on a charge of blasphemy (even though he converted one of the judges on the bench). But in Derbyshire in 1655 he confounded 'seven or eight priests' in a dispute, the people crying out 'A Nayler, a Nayler, hath confuted them all'. Later he moved southwards to London where at first he won many adherents to the Quaker faith.

It was at this point that what is known in Quaker history as 'the fall of Nayler' took place. He evidently became mentally unbalanced, carried away by the success of his preaching and by the flattery of some of his women followers. As George Fox put it, 'James ran out into imaginations, and a company with him'. Fox and others rebuked him, but this led only to division in the movement. Eventually on 24 October 1656, Nayler was led riding into Bristol, his followers strewing garments in the way and singing 'Holy, holy, holy, Lord God of Sabaoth'. He was arrested by the authorities and brought before the House of Commons, who debated the case for nine days. Nayler himself, sincerely enough, claimed

that he had not been allowing himself to be worshipped but 'the appearance of God in him'. Lambert, who had been his commanding officer, urged leniency, and so did others, but the House resolved that Nayler was guilty of 'horrid blasphemy'; and, quite unconstitutionally, for it had no judicial powers under the Instrument of Government, and against the wishes of the Lord Protector, proceeded to pass a savage sentence. He was to be set in the pillory for two hours and then to be whipped through the streets; two days later he was again to be pilloried, his tongue was to be bored with a hot iron, and his forehead branded with the letter B; then he was to be sent to Bristol, carried through the city on horseback, facing backwards, and whipped; finally he was to be kept in solitary confinement, without pen, ink, and paper, until the Commons chose to release him. The sentence was carried out in full, despite petitions from various sources, some pointing out the dangers of making parliament 'a court of will'; 'we are', claimed one member, 'God's executioners'. Nayler was kept in gaol until 1659, when the Rump set him free; he showed remarkable courage throughout his ordeal and an equally remarkable spirit of forgiveness after it. He was reconciled to Fox and to the Quaker movement, to which the whole episode had done a great deal of damage by causing internal divisions and much public scandal and distrust, and he ought more properly to be remembered for his evangelism and for his devotional writings – which were numerous and contain passages of great charm – than for his fall. Nayler resumed his preaching and service to Friends; but in 1660, on his way northwards, he seems to have been set upon by robbers, and he died near Huntingdon.

Further Reading
W. C. Braithwaite, *The Beginnings of Quakerism*, 1959 edn, esp. Chap. 11.
M. R. Brailsford, *A Quaker from Cromwell's Army*, 1927.

NEEDHAM, MARCHAMONT (1620-78) was an unscrupulous journalist whose career illustrates the opportunities given to what was virtually a new occupation by the English Revolution. He came from a gentry family of Burford in Oxfordshire, was a chorister at All Souls, tried his hand at teaching at Merchant Taylors School, studied law and medicine, and then turned to journalism, editing from 1643 *Mercurius Britannicus*, whose aim was to counteract the royalist *Mercurius Aulicus*. It was a satirical and scurrilous sheet, and its editor was a brazen liar. 'As the war progressed the duel of wits between *Aulicus* and *Britannicus*, challenging, deriding and scoring off each other week by week became an accepted and enlivening accompaniment to the conflict.'* But in 1646 Needham offended the House

*C. V. Wedgwood, *The King's War*, 1958, p.166.

of Lords, who sent him to prison, and in 1647 he changed sides and produced a new sheet, the *Mercurius Pragmaticus*, even more abusive. It was in this that he called Cromwell 'the town-bull of Ely'. Not surprisingly, he was again imprisoned, and in 1649 he changed his colours again, took the Engagement, and wrote a pamphlet commending the Commonwealth as an earnest of new-found loyalty. Its line, appropriately, was that the man of sense ought to accept the new régime and avoid trouble. In 1650 he produced a third newspaper, *Mercurius Politicus*, and devoted his talents to backing the shifts and turns of Oliver's policies. He was also (1653-60) editor of the official *Public Intelligencer*. At the Restoration he lost his job and, backing a loser at last by writing against the return of the king, fled abroad. He was pardoned and came back to England, but henceforward earned his living by practising medicine. Yet he could not resist one or two forays into his natural profession, writing pamphlets advocating reforms in education and in medicine, and he was even employed by Danby's ministry to write against Shaftesbury.

NELSON, VISCOUNT HORATIO, DUKE OF BRONTË (1758-1805) was born at Burnham Thorpe Rectory in North Norfolk, the third son to survive but the fifth to be born to the Reverend Edmund Nelson, a quiet man, distantly related to the Walpoles. He died in the cockpit of the *Victory*, at the moment of a memorable triumph in the greatest battle in British naval history. His personality is hard to convey through the facts of his life, romantic and heroic as these are. Nelson's greatness was recognized by many who had to deal with him, as well as by people to whom he was but a name. He had always a strong sense of his destiny. Like other great men, he had an actor's flair for improving upon the occasion. He was intensely imaginative, in his writing and conversation, in his professional duty and in the manner in which he enacted the important scenes of his life. It is not surprising that, as he himself complained, every portrait of him showed a different man.

His career began as it was to continue, with a restless eagerness to be doing great things. On a winter's morning, with his brother William, he found the way to their school at North Walsham blocked by snow. Their father urged them to make one more attempt. When William thought the time was come to give up, Horatio insisted upon pressing through: 'Remember, brother, it was left to our honour.' He wanted to follow his uncle Maurice Suckling to sea. This uncle, captain of the *Raisonnable*, upon which Horatio sailed as midshipman in 1771, and subsequently Comptroller of the navy, was able to launch him on his career. On Suckling's suggestion he went on a merchant vessel to South America to acquire practical seamanship. Then, in 1773, he accompanied a North Pole expedition for scientific research, under the

Hon. Daines Barrington. In 1775 he joined the *Seahorse*, frigate, on a voyage to the East Indies, but this unfortunately brought fever which recurred at intervals through his life. His slight, fragile-seeming build might have been the legacy of this illness, which nearly killed him. So, he confided later in life, was his resolution to be a hero: 'confiding in Providence, I will brave every danger'.

In 1777 he went to Jamaica on the *Lowestoft* frigate as lieutenant; with war came quick promotion and in 1778 he became Commander, in the following year Post-Captain. In 1780, commanding the frigate *Hinchingbrooke*, he led the naval force in the expedition against Port Juan. Strenuous exertions in nightmarish conditions were followed by a further visitation from 'Yellow Jack' and he was invalided home. In 1781 he was appointed to commission the *Albemarle*, a converted French merchantman and poor sailer. In this vessel he served on the American station and there made the acquaintance of Hood, whom he greatly admired, but he did not take part in the major fleet actions. In 1784, though it was peacetime, he contrived further employment, enforcing the Navigation Act against the Americans in the *Boreas*. In March 1787 he married a young widow, daughter of a planter in the Leeward Islands, Fanny Nesbit. With her he settled down to five years on half pay, the regular lot of a naval officer in peacetime, at Burnham Thorpe. The company of a lady, invalidish and tending to low spirits, who bore him no children, the mild amusements of Norfolk society, coursing and birds'-nesting, were not enough for him. After much frustration he got command, in 1793, of the *Agamemnon*, sixty-four guns, at the outset of a war which was to provide unparalleled challenges and opportunities to the navy and its young captains.

Nelson went with Hood to the Mediterranean. With him sailed a neighbouring rector's son, William Hoste. In the letters of this young midshipman, who followed him from the *Agamemnon* to the *Captain*, we learn of the respect, amounting to adoration, that Nelson inspired amongst those he commanded. 'Was there ever such a man in our navy before, or can you imagine that there ever will be one to equal him?', he was later to write. Nelson now showed his heaven-sent gifts of command, quick imaginative strokes, a longing for glory, the ability to transmit his ardour to his men, an unusual generosity in his interest for others and readiness to praise them. In 1800 he was to write to Lord Spencer from the *Foudroyant*, 'Not for all the world would I rob any man of a sprig of laurel – much less my children of the *Foudroyant*. I love her as a fond father, a darling child, and glory in her deeds.' This was unusual language for a sailor to employ in writing to the First Lord. In a reticent service, Nelson's uninhibited, warm personality made its mark because it went with superb technical virtuosity. He expected to succeed; with his men stirred by his confidence, happy in his trust, it is not surprising that he did.

Nelson was employed in the blockade of Corsica and then commanded the naval brigade at the reduction of Bastia and Calvi; here a blow from a stone, thrown up by shot, destroyed his right eye. In 1795 he was present at Hotham's two small victories outside Toulon, but thought them insignificant, though he captured the *Ça Ira* in a memorable duel; already he conceived of battle in terms of destroying the enemy. His chance came in February 1797 at the battle of Cape St Vincent, where he was commodore under Jervis; it was his boldness in breaking the line that transformed a line battle into sharper action of a more destructive sort. When the *Captain* was laid alongside *San Josef* to board, he followed the soldiers in to receive the swords of the Spanish officers. Though Jervis's dispatch was reserved, he appreciated that the victory owed much to Nelson. In the fleet, enthusiasm was boundless; at home his reputation was made. He was promoted rear admiral and received the Order of the Bath. His fame was not lessened by the gallant failure of his attack upon a richly laden Spanish ship at Santa Cruz in July. But he lost his right arm, shattered at the elbow as he was about to draw his sword, in a boat just off the mole of Santa Cruz.

His fortieth year brought greater glory. In March he hoisted his flag on the *Vanguard* and took a small squadron into the Mediterranean to watch the French. Damaged by a storm, the *Vanguard* was forced to put into San Pietro while the French squadron was bound for Egypt. During the weeks of searching, his fleet actually sailed so close to the French, at night in a fog, that the French admiral heard their signal guns and hastily altered course. How history would have been changed, if Nelson had met Napoleon that night, we are left to guess. Eventually he learned that they had gone to Egypt and tracked them down in Aboukir Bay where, against Admiral de Brueys with seventeen ships against his twelve he won a classic victory, as daring as Quiberon Bay – and even more complete. De Brueys made the mistake of relying on the reefs which protected his position. Nelson risked going into a strange bay at dusk, without charts or pilots. The wind blew along the French line, so he concentrated his attack on the weather end, then creeping down the line, captured or destroyed the whole fleet, except for two frigates. The scene, with the darkness lit up by the fire of the drifting ships, was unforgettable. The high moment came at ten p.m. when the flagship, *l'Orient*, 120 guns, blew up in an explosion which was heard ten miles away. Nelson was wounded in the head but remained active. Morning dawned, heavy with smoke upon a scene of carnage; the French had lost over 5,000 – taken, drowned, burned or missing. At home Lord Spencer, who had been distracted by rumours

of mishaps and by Nelson's apparent failure to meet the French fleet, was told that the victory had been gained without the loss of a ship and he fainted with relief. Nelson, meanwhile, sailed to Naples and into the arms of Lady Hamilton.

The wife of the English ambassador, she was a low-born beauty, much painted by Romney, appealing in a reckless, vulgar way, and brave. Nelson was enslaved by her and the liaison that followed lasted until his death. His letters reveal a complete infatuation. His cold and scornful attitude to his wife, on top of desertion, is the most unattractive feature of the affair. Lady Hamilton became somewhat blatant and her flattery disgusted Nelson's friends, but the affair is redeemed from squalor by Nelson's naive, unquestioning devotion to the woman who destroyed his reputation, and very nearly his career. When Nelson, who had been made Duke of Brontë by the King of Naples, evacuated the king from Naples to Palermo and subdued the insurgents, he was ordered by Lord Keith, commander-in-chief in the Mediterranean, to sail to Minorca. Nelson refused; when the order was repeated he sent his second-in-command, Duckworth, himself remaining to control the blockade of Malta from Palermo. He was censured by the admiralty for his conduct, resigned his command and came home, with the ambassador and Lady Hamilton. Arriving in England in November 1800, he saw his wife for the last time; the interview was unhappy.

The Duke of Wellington recorded later his impressions of a meeting with Nelson. At first – when Nelson did not know who he was – he talked like a charlatan, in 'a style so vain and so silly as to surprise and almost disgust me'. Then – when he realized that he was talking to Wellesley – 'he talked like an officer and a gentleman' so that the general saw, after all, that he was 'a very superior man; but certainly a more sudden and complete metamorphosis I never saw'. The strain of long years at sea upon an imaginative nature, the innate tendency to dramatize situations, the ambition suddenly and brilliantly realized at the Nile – all help to account for the almost bizarre personality of these years. With his insensitivity to society's views, his habit of plain speaking and his reputation in the service for arrogant disobedience, it is not strange that he was looked on coldly by some of his superiors. Nelson acted on the principle that he once outlined to his father: 'I always act as I think right.' When he had bought a property in Surrey at Merton where he could live with Lady Hamilton, he wrote to her: 'Have we a nice church at Merton? We will set an example of goodness to the under-parishioners.' In the same way he was probably unaware of the feelings he aroused in Sir Hyde Parker, to whom he was vice-admiral in his next employment, a punitive expedition to the Baltic.

On 2 April 1801, Nelson took twelve ships of the line

and the smaller vessels into Copenhagen harbour. Hyde Parker, who was always cautious, following up Nelson's attack according to plan, was disturbed by the hot reception Nelson was receiving and signalled for withdrawal. Nelson had just remarked that this was 'warm work' – then 'but mark you, I would not be elsewhere for thousands'. The signal was reported to him. He walked about, working the stump of his right arm in agitation. Then, after saying that he would be damned if he would leave off the action, he said, 'You know, Foley, I have only one eye. I have a right to be blind sometimes.' He raised his spy-glass to his right eye and announced, 'I really do not see the signal'. Heedless of the fact that three ships had run aground, he persevered in the face of heavy fire from the shore batteries till he had sunk, burned or taken all the seventeen Danish ships. He was shocked by the carnage of the action – but it was entirely successful. The Northern League was dissolved; a code was agreed to govern the searching of ships and the definition of contraband – the causes of the dispute. Nelson, who had been made baron after the Nile, now became a viscount and succeeded Parker as commander-in-chief, but a bout of influenza caused him to return to England. Ordered to look after the defence of the coast, on the prospect of a French invasion, he planned an attack upon the flotilla at Boulogne, which failed with some loss.

When war was declared again in April 1803, Nelson went back to the Mediterranean in the *Victory*, which had served as flagship for Keppel and Kempenfelt, Howe, Hood and St Vincent. For the next eighteen months he cruised about Toulon; he was briefly absent for the first time when in March 1805, Villeneuve slipped out of port and sailed for the West Indies. Meanwhile Napoleon had 90,000 men and 2,000 transports ready at Boulogne. He ordered the admirals to assemble and return to Europe to clear the Channel of such English ships as remained. But when Austria declared war on France, his invasion plan was put off. Trafalgar was thus a postscript. But the sequence of events that led up to it was dramatic. Nelson searched for Villeneuve blindly, following intuition: at first, wrongly, to Sardinia; thence to Egypt; then, on the second break-out, correctly, to the West Indies. The courage that dictated his decision to follow Villeneuve there, leaving the Channel unguarded, is typical: 'If they are not gone to the West Indies I shall be blamed: to be burned in effigy, or Westminster Abbey is my alternative.' He passed Gibraltar on 7 May, a month behind Villeneuve. He returned, having taken only twenty-four days to cross the Atlantic, hard on his tracks. For two years he had not set foot outside the *Victory*. He was still concerned about the Mediterranean. Fortunately Barham had ordered Calder to block the French en route for Brest. On 22 July, the day after Nelson reached Gibraltar, Calder fought the French off Finisterre. He did not destroy them, but they retreated

back to Ferrol under cover of fog. In August they went on to Cadiz. Nelson arrived there on 28 September with carte blanche from the admiralty to fight as he wanted.

On 20 October the French came out, with thirty-four ships of the line. The next day the British, with twenty-seven ships, came up with them off Cape Trafalgar. The enemy were extended in a half-moon. Nelson's original plan was carried out to the extent that his ships split one-third of the French line from the rest. But it developed into the pell-mell battle that he liked to see, relying upon the gunnery of British ships and the competitive fighting spirit of the crews. They did not need his celebrated signal, 'England expects that every man will do his duty', to spur them into action. Eighteen of the French ships were sunk or taken; none of the remainder ever fought again. The enemy lost in killed and wounded nearly 6,000 men. But Nelson did not live to enjoy this consummation of his tactics and spirit. At about 1.30 p.m. he was hit in the spine by a sharp-shooter from the *Redoutable* while he stood on his quarter deck, unmistakable in his decorations. At about three, Hardy came below to tell him that they had 'twelve or fourteen of the enemy's ships in our possession'. At about 4.30 he died.

The glory and pathos of the scene – the dying admiral in Hardy's arms, his delirium, his words, 'Kiss me, Hardy' – can move us still, so we are not surprised to read, in a sailor's letter, his feeling of agonized loss: 'I should like to have seen him, but then, all the men in our ship who have seen him are such soft toads, they have done nothing but Blast their Eyes and cry ever since he was killed. God bless you! chaps that fought like the Devil, sit down and cry like a wench.' When, after terrible storms had delayed the sending of dispatches, the nation heard about the victory, on 6 November, the news was received with a sense of national loss. Men could only say 'Alas poor Nelson'. Later, they were able to express their respect in a state funeral of unprecedented pomp. The only sound from the crowd beside the procession was like a 'low murmur', which arose from their removing their hats. Sailors of the *Victory*, his 'band of brothers', tore apart one of the ship's flags to secure mementoes of their captain. Later, Nelson's elder brother was made an earl, money was voted to him and to his sisters. But Lady Hamilton and his daughter Horatia, so confidently entrusted to the nation in his last note, written on the morning of battle, were left without provision.

Further Reading
T. Pocock, *Horatio Nelson*, 1987.
Oliver Warner, *A Portrait of Lord Nelson*, 1958.
Carola Oman, *Nelson*, 1948.
R. Southey, *Life of Nelson*, 1911.

NENNIUS (early ninth century?) was the name of a Welsh ecclesiastic to whom is ascribed authorship of the work known as the *Historia Brittonum* ('History of the

Britons'). The *Historia* was put together in the form in which we have it in the first quarter of the ninth century. The attribution to Nennius is not attested in all surviving manuscripts, so it is not clear whether Nennius, whoever he may have been, was the original compiler or a later editor. The *Historia* is an assortment of texts – genealogical, annalistic, hagiographical, geographical – assembled on no very clear principle. It preserves early chronicle material, some apparently from the seventh century and some conceivably from the fifth, which has historical value. It also contains a good deal of legendary matter about Julius Caesar, Magnus Maximus, St Germanus, Ambrosius Aurelianus, Arthur, St Patrick and others. The *Historia Brittonum* is of interest as presenting a distinctively British perspective on the events of the fourth to the seventh centuries and as indicating what materials were available early in the ninth to a Welsh antiquarian looking at the British past.

Further Reading
John Morris, *Nennius. British History and the Welsh Annals*, 1980.

NETTER, THOMAS (*c*.1370-1430) of Walden was 'perhaps the most distinguished friar of any order between the age of Ockham and the Dissolution'. He was born to humble parents at Saffron Walden in Essex, probably about 1370, and became a Carmelite friar. Of the four principal orders of friars in England – Franciscans (Friars Minor), Dominicans (Friars Preachers), Augustinians and Carmelites – the Carmelites were the smallest. He was in the London convent in 1396 when ordained priest. It was probably before this that he met the Franciscan William Woodford, who contributed to his theological orthodoxy, and subsequently he attended Oxford University, becoming a bachelor of theology (1409) and a doctor somewhat later. He was a theologian of great learning and skill. He attended the General Councils of the church at Pisa (1409) and Constance (1414-17). From 1414 until death he was provincial of the English Carmelites, exercising office efficiently and justly and devoting himself to the improvement of discipline and observance. He preached at the funerals of both Henry IV and Henry V and was confessor of Henry V from 1414 and Henry VI, accompanying him to France in 1430 and dying there.

The friars, especially the Carmelites and above all the East Anglian Carmelites, were the principal bulwarks of orthodoxy against heresy in late medieval England. Among them Netter stands out 'as the theologian who gave a full and final answer to the Lollards'. This was in his *Doctrine of the Catholic Faith against the Lollards and the Hussites (Doctrinale)*, the Hussites being heretics from Bohemia (now Czechoslovakia) who were strongly influenced by Wyclif's teachings. Netter was too young to have been taught by Wyclif himself, but he attended Oxford when the heretic's works were still in current use and some of his followers were still teaching. When he first encountered Wyclif's logic and speculative philosophy, he was most impressed:

Whilst at first I thought of this in silence, afterwards in my early years I lent credulous ears to his logical teaching. I was quite astounded by his sweeping assertions, by the authorities cited and by the vehemence of his reasoning.

Moving on to the study of theology, Netter found Wyclif to be 'an open counterfeiter of Scripture' and devoted himself to the destruction of Lollardy. Whilst still at Oxford he discomfited the future Hussite Peter Payne, and he participated in a succession of trials of leading Lollards. As preacher at St Paul's Cross and as royal confessor he urged stronger measures against Lollardy and in 1419 went on a mission to eastern Europe to drum up Polish and Lithuanian support for Emperor Sigismund's crusade against the Hussites. It was King Henry V who encouraged him to write his *Doctrinale*, which he presented in 1426-7 to Pope Martin V, who received it with enthusiasm.

Netter brought an excellent knowledge of Lollardy to his task. He read most if not all of Wyclif's philosophical and theological works, he was familiar with much of the literature compiled by his followers including items since lost, and he had participated in many heresy trials and had access to records of them. In Book I of his *Doctrinale* he laid bare the roots of Wyclif's philosophy as preliminary to its comprehensive refutation and in Books II and III firmly rebutted Wyclif's deductions from his philosophy, reasserting a whole range of traditional Catholic doctrines in the process. He wrote clearly and directly, eschewing scholastic jargon, and his book may well have discouraged new recruits to Lollardy among academics. No Lollard replied: perhaps no reply was possible.

Further Reading
J. Robson, *John Wyclif and the Oxford Schools*, 1966.

NEVILLE, CECILY, DUCHESS OF YORK (1415-95), the mother of Edward IV and Richard III, lived a life of such piety that it became a model for other noble ladies. This was during her last years. It had not always been so. What we know of her earlier career, like most noble ladies, is little more than a catalogue of birth, connections, and childbearing. Last of the twenty-three children of Ralph Neville, Earl of Westmorland (*d*.1425), she was married as a child to Richard, Duke of York. She accompanied him as king's lieutenant to France and Ireland, bearing children both in Rouen and Dublin, and living in regal state. Perhaps to receive the new queen, Cecily commissioned a marvellous dress, mantle and hood of crimson velvet and ermine, for which 325 pearls and 8oz. of gold were required. Hence expenditure on clothing in 1443-4 of £608, almost the income of an earl, and her husband's appointment of someone to watch over her spending. Whilst York engaged in English politics in the 1450s, his duchess lived mainly at Fotheringhay (Northants.) with her younger children. In 1459, when he fled abroad, she was placed in the custody of an elder sister, and in 1460 a brief triumph was followed by Richard's death. During her sons' reigns she lived mainly at Berkhamsted (Herts.) and Baynards Castle in London off her extensive dowerlands, apparently involving herself seldom in politics, but frequently in royal christenings and other family events. It seems clear that she objected to Edward IV's marriage to Elizabeth Wydeville, allegedly stating 'in a frenzy' that he was no son of hers and perhaps thus giving rise to the (presumably apocryphal) rumour repeated in 1469, 1477-8 and 1483-4 that 'the late King Edward was not begotten by Richard, Duke of York but by some other, who privily and by stealth had knowledge of his mother'. Reputedly she indignantly denied the story after Richard III used it to justify his usurpation.

Cecily outlived all but two of her children. Her husband, three sons, four grandsons, and other kinsfolk died violently, but there remained many grandchildren in whom she interested herself. It was therefore not to escape from personal tragedies that she took to religion. Her piety was too active and positive for that. Her daughter Margaret of York could have learnt her own remarkable piety from her mother, but it is for Cecily's last decade that we are informed. 'I trust to our Lord's mercy that this noble princess thus divides the hours to his high pleasure,' wrote someone describing the régime of these years. Between 7 a.m. and 8 p.m. she heard three services of matins, three low masses, and three evensongs, some in private and others in chapel. Arduous and extensive though such activities were, they are purely conventional. What distinguishes Cecily is the time given to private meditation and the spirit in which she undertook it. The books of mysticism in her chamber – unusual in themselves – included advanced works of great depth and complexity, such as those by St Catherine of Siena and St Bridget of Sweden. For a laywoman like Cecily voluntarily to read them every day and extract enough to explain afterwards at table demonstrates both an advanced spirituality and a 'deep and personal love of mysticism'. Cecily's spiritual exercises, like those of Margaret Beaufort and Margaret Hungerford, did not conflict either with conventional observance, great wealth, or the demands of household, estate and family that she continued to fulfil. Only leisure made them possible, however, so such practices were probably confined to nuns and clergy, to dowagers without children to bring up like Cecily and the two Margarets, or to men who shirked their responsibilities, like Henry VI. The new piety could not be open to all.

Further Reading
T. B. Pugh, 'Richard Plantagenet (1411-60), Duke of York, as the King's Lieutenant in France and Ireland' in *Aspects of Late Medieval Government and Society*, J. G. Rowe, ed., London 1986.
C. A. J. Armstrong, *England, France and Burgundy in the Fifteenth Century*, 1983.

NEVILLE, GEORGE (*c.*1432-76), Bishop of Exeter (1455-65) and Archbishop of York (1465-76), is the outstanding example of a political bishop of noble birth. As the son of Richard, Earl of Salisbury and of royal blood, he was guaranteed high office in the church. A degree had become an essential qualification for a bishop, so he attended Oxford University, which pandered to his rank by shortening the courses leading to his BA and MA and his regent mastership and elected him as its chancellor in 1453, when he was only twenty-one. From 1442 he rapidly accumulated benefices, including the 'golden prebend' of Masham in 1447, and a bishopric duly followed. It was his father, then Chancellor of England, who persuaded the royal council in 1454 that George's 'blood, virtue and cunning' deserved the next see, and though under canonical age he became Bishop of Exeter in 1455, his consecration being delayed until he was twenty-seven! Following their victory at Northampton in 1460, the Neville earls appointed George as Chancellor of England, a post he held throughout Edward IV's critical early years. He was rewarded in 1465 with the archbishopric of York, which lay in his home area and complemented the local resources of his brothers. He aspired to become cardinal, but when the pope made his decision in 1467 it was the Archbishop of Canterbury who was promoted. That same year he was dismissed as chancellor and his royal grants were taken back, as King Edward transferred his favour from the Nevilles. After initial mediation, George supported Warwick's resort to force in 1469. He had secretly obtained the licence for the marriage of Clarence to Warwick's daughter, he conducted the ceremony, his name appears on their manifesto, and it was he who actually arrested the king. After this scheme broke down and Warwick went into exile, George supported the return of Henry VI and was his chancellor during his Readeption. His failure to hold London in 1471 contributed substantially to the defeat and death of his brothers and the last Lancastrian claimants. Yet George continued plotting in 1472, apparently pointlessly, was indicted, and was imprisoned in Hammes Castle, Calais. Edward IV would have liked to deprive him of his see, but could not. Instead Richard, Duke of Gloucester secured his release, so George, now sick and discredited, could die at liberty.

Clearly George Neville was an ambitious prelate with aristocratic tastes: his favourite residence at Ricksmansworth was his own and he had his own private estate; his enthronement was of legendary scale and splendour; and he reputedly possessed moveables worth £20,000 in 1472. He was a competent administrator and diplomat, and an astute politician and schemer. His political stance was unprincipled and was determined by his brother Warwick the Kingmaker: hence, perhaps, his confusion after Warwick's death. But he was not merely a noble politician in ecclesiastical garb. He could preach and had sufficient theological interest to be outraged by Pecock's contempt of the early Christian Fathers. He joined Warwick in founding St William's College for the chantry priests of York Minster in 1461. His intervention saved Lincoln College, Oxford from dissolution and he served four terms of seventeen years as Chancellor of Oxford University. His own course of study, though confined to a curtailed arts course, brought him into contact with John Free at Balliol and introduced him to Renaissance scholarship. Though never as learned as his kinsman William Grey, George Neville was a patron of humanism and humanists, protecting a Greek, Emanuel of Constantinople, and selecting as secretaries men who could write letters in classical Latin. He himself read classical literature and acquired a basic knowledge of Greek. It was a mark of his depression in prison that he abandoned his literary studies.

Further Reading

M. A. Hicks, *False, Fleeting, Perjur'd Clarence: George, Duke of Clarence, 1449-78*, 1980.
C. D. Ross, *Edward IV*, 1974.
R. Weiss, *Humanism in England during the Fifteenth Century*, 1967.

NEVILLE, RICHARD, EARL OF SALISBURY

(*c*.1400-60) turned Richard, Duke of York from an ineffectual protester into a realistic pretender for the Crown. Salisbury was the eldest son of Ralph Neville, Earl of Westmorland (*d*.1425) by Joan Beaufort (*d*.1440), legitimated daughter of John of Gaunt. From his father he inherited the great northern lordships of Middleham, Sheriff Hutton (Yorks.) and Penrith (Cumbs.). Like him, he was warden of the West March towards Scotland in 1420-34 and from 1443. His mother's royal and Beaufort connections secured him his earldom in right of his wife in 1429 and his victory over his nephew, the second Earl of Westmorland. The claims of birth were supplemented by good service on the borders, in France (1431, 1436), and from 1437 as a councillor. To both parents he owed exceptionally wide connections: his brothers were the Bishop of Durham and three barons and his many brothers-in-law included the Duke of York. Outstandingly able, he capitalized fully on his financial and military resources, court connections, and the marriages of his siblings and children.

Salisbury was first and foremost a great northern nobleman. His wife's southern inheritance was a source of cash spent in the north. So too was his border wardenship, which he converted into 'a principal buttress of dynastic policy'. His own lands were concentrated in the West Riding, but he built on the wardenship, the promise of favour at court, his brother's bishopric, the custody/lease of Barnard Castle (Durh.), and his capacity to pay retainers to extend his power into Cumbria and County Durham, and throughout Yorkshire. Hence Westmorland's unwilling surrender in 1443 and the feud with the Percies provoked by trespassing on their preserves both in Cumbria and Yorkshire. Their quarrel was pursued not by Salisbury or Northumberland but by their sons. Beginning after 1450, the violent clashes culminated in a private battle at Stamford Bridge in 1454.

The Neville-Percy feud was the chief single factor which turned political rivalry into civil war. Richard of York could not have renewed his challenge to Somerset without the Neville alliance. The first battle of the St Albans was the immediate outcome of the harnessing of this private quarrel to the central issue between the two royal dukes.

That had not been Salisbury's intention. He backed the king in 1452, whilst striving to temper York's punishment. He had too much to gain from his court connections. But these were strained by his son's dispute with Somerset over his Warwick inheritance and Henry VI failed to intervene on his behalf in the Percy feud. York did, however, during his first Protectorate. Salisbury was then a generally acceptable nominee as chancellor, but was replaced on Henry VI's recovery by a council that included, significantly, his rival Northumberland. Salisbury was therefore at York's side at the first battle of St Albans, where significantly Northumberland as well as Somerset was eliminated. A twenty-year extension of his Marcher wardenship and his son George's promotion to a bishopric during York's second protectorate showed York rather than the court to be best able to serve his interests. Salisbury and his son Warwick shared York's defeat, exile and forfeiture in 1459. They defeated their enemies at Northampton in 1460 and placed the king in protective custody. As in Buckingham's case a tension between allegiance and faction remained. It was the Nevilles who blocked York's usurpation late in 1460, substituting recognition as King Henry's heir, and Salisbury died with York when this unworkable compromise was decisively rejected by Margaret of Anjou at Wakefield. Without the Nevilles, York could achieve nothing, but at the crucial moment their support faltered. Consequently Salisbury's son saw York's son to the throne.

Further Reading

A. J. Pollard, *North-Eastern England during the Wars of the Roses*, 1990.
R. L. Storey, *The End of the House of Lancaster*, 2nd edn, 1986.
R. A. Griffiths, *The Reign of King Henry VI 1422-61*, 1981.

NEVILLE, RICHARD, EARL OF WARWICK and SALISBURY

NEVILLE, RICHARD, EARL OF WARWICK and SALISBURY (1428-71), alias Warwick the Kingmaker, was the supreme example of an overmighty subject. Ineligible to reign himself, he made and unmade kings because none served his purpose. Of royal and aristocratic descent, he was eldest son of Richard Neville, Earl of Salisbury (*d.*1460) and thus heir to the northern Neville estates and the custody of the West March. He benefited most from the Neville marriages, acquiring in 1449 the earldom of Warwick and lands yielding £4,000 mainly in the west Midlands and south Wales. He had to defend his title against Henry VI's favourite Somerset and thus aligned himself with his father with the Duke of York. During the 1450s father and son proved determined, decisive and ruthless. Somehow they found preemptive strikes and assassination compatible with their allegiance and self-interest with constitutional principle. Initially deferring to his father, Warwick familiarized himself with warfare on land and sea and was the more forceful by 1460. After thwarting York's usurpation in 1460, he engineered Edward IV's accession next year.

King Edward depended on the military and political support of the Neville brothers: George was chancellor, John military commander in the north, and Warwick was everywhere. Now Earl of Salisbury too, he was by far the richest nobleman of the decade. He kept a splendid household, retinue, fleet of ships, and train of artillery. Edward gave him many confiscated estates and exalted offices: Great Chamberlain and Admiral of England, Warden of the Cinque Ports and Captain of Calais, Chief Steward of the Duchy of Lancaster, Warden of the Marches and King's Lieutenant in the north. He used royal favour to marry off his sisters to coming men. His brothers were promoted. He appeared the arbiter of English policy.

Of course he was not. As the Lancastrians were defeated, so Edward preferred his own men and ideas. He listened to Warwick's advice, treated him indeed as his most trusted councillor, but did not always do as he wished. Warwick thought this ingratitude. So extensive were his interests, that to advance anyone anywhere anyhow appeared an attack upon him. He could not satisfy himself with what he had and was offended by Edward's veto of his marriage of his daughters to royal dukes and his pro-French foreign policy. He dropped neither. Self-confident and self-righteous, pained and angry, he denounced Rivers and Pembroke as evil councillors and resolved as in the 1450s to eliminate them and place the king under restraint. Always a risk policy even with Henry VI, it failed with Edward IV. Firmly excluded from power, Warwick then backed Edward IV's brother George, Duke of Clarence for the Crown – an unforgivable and unsuccessful step. Exiled again, he increased the stakes by placing Henry VI on the throne, an expedient already faltering before his defeat and death at Barnet in 1471.

Yet in many ways Warwick was a conventional enough aristocrat: in his piety and recreations, building and display, pride of lineage and arrogance to parvenus. His plans for Warwick involved improvements to Guy's Cave and the Beauchamp Chapel and a new almshouse for old retainers. Such aspirations help explain the undoubted popularity that he so assiduously cultivated. He was the most ambitious and daring of politicians, strategists and pirates, but his disastrous over-caution as a tactician lost him all his battles. Ultimately therefore his great estates, retinue and popularity were all for nought. But his real error was he forgot that prime duty of allegiance that he forced on the Duke of York in 1460.

Further Reading

R. L. Storey, *The End of the House of Lancaster*, 2nd edn, 1986.

M. A. Hicks, *False, Fleeting, Perjur'd Clarence: George, Duke of Clarence, 1449-78*, 1980.

C. D. Ross, *Edward IV*, 1974.

P. M. Kendall, *Warwick the Kingmaker*, 1957.

C. L. Scofield, *Edward IV* i, 1923.

C. Oman, *Warwick the Kingmaker*, 1891.

NEVILLE OF RABY, RALPH, EARL OF WESTMORLAND

NEVILLE OF RABY, RALPH, EARL OF WESTMORLAND (1354-1425) defeated the Percy rebels under Henry IV and made himself 'supreme everywhere north of the Humber'. A series of successful marriages had built up estates extensive enough for an earl before Ralph's succession as sixth Lord Neville of Raby in 1388. These included the four castles of Raby and Brancepeth in County Durham and Middleham and Sheriff Hutton in Yorkshire. By then he had already served in France in 1380, on diplomatic missions to and campaigns against the Scots, and had been warden of the West March in 1385. He deputized as constable of England both in 1391 and 1497. All this time he was a trusted retainer of John of Gaunt, Duke of Lancaster, and in 1397 he married as second wife Gaunt's bastard daughter Joan Beaufort, who was legitimated with her brothers that same year. This marriage transformed Neville's career. He was created Earl of Westmorland and in 1399 he supported the usurpation of Gaunt's eldest son as Henry IV. Joan was in turn half-sister, aunt and great-aunt of the three Lancastrian kings and Ralph, who was generally called the king's brother under Henry IV, was councillor to all three. The connection bore immediate fruit in his grant for life of the marshalcy of England and honour of Richmond. His brother Thomas Lord Furnivall became treasurer of England in 1404-7. A string of other grants followed. More important, Westmorland established the Nevilles as natural wardens of the West March and secured a string of wardships that largely explains the remarkable series of marriages that he arranged for his twenty-two offspring – many of them while they were still children. The matches contracted for Ralph and Joan's sons made them Earl of Salisbury, Lords Fauconberg and Abergavenny respectively, while daughters became Duchess of Buckingham, Norfolk and York. By the 1450s the Nevilles were related to almost the whole peerage and one line was powerful enough to act as kingmakers. That not all Nevilles co-operated was also largely Westmorland's fault, for he transferred his principal lands from his eldest son's Westmorland line to Joan's eldest son Richard Neville, Earl of Salisbury. His heir was left with less land as earl than his father had inherited as a baron and a violent feud ensued. Ralph's new-found eminence was marked by the new college he established at Staindrop, where he was buried.

John of Gaunt's vast estates had supported the most powerful retinue in medieval England. Henry IV and Henry V succeeded both to the Duchy of Lancaster and the Lancastrian retinue, which they assiduously cultivated as essential buttresses to their throne in spite of repeated criticisms of its cost by the House of Commons. The careers of John Norbury and Thomas Chaucer illustrate their reliance as kings on family retainers. Only during Henry VI's minority was the Lancastrian connection allowed to decay. Nowhere were the Duchy estates more concentrated and the retinue stronger than in northern England, where John of Gaunt had overshadowed both the Percies and Nevilles. It was this connection – which included Westmorland – that enabled Henry IV to take the crown and subsequently defeated the Percy rebellions in 1405 and 1408. Numerous and important though the Yorkshire followers of the Percies were, they were not so many or so powerful as the Lancastrian retainers in the same county. Westmorland was the Percies' principal rival in the north and his appointment as constable of Roxburgh in 1401 may have been a factor in the Percy rebellions. It was Cheshiremen whom Hotspur led to defeat at Shrewsbury in 1403, but subsequent risings were centred in Yorkshire. It was essential for Northumberland to eliminate Westmorland in 1405, but the latter evaded capture, organized resistance, quickly contrived the capture of Archbishop Scrope and the dispersal of his forces, and drove Northumberland northwards into exile. Similarly Westmorland held the north for Henry IV in 1408. His loyalty was crucial in the survival of the Lancastrian dynasty.

Further Reading
J. A. Tuck, *Richard II and the English Nobility*, 1973.
J. L. Kirby, *Reign of Henry IV*, 1970.

NEWBERY, JOHN (d.1584), traveller. Virtually nothing is known of the early life of this very interesting, intrepid and important man. There is a slight possibility that he was related to Ralph Newbery, who published Hakluyt's *Principal Navigations*: he may also have been in his early years in Holland and have learned Dutch

(Foster, *England's Quest of Eastern Trade*, pp.79 and 94). He first appears in history in 1579 as a 'citizen and merchant of London', 'desirous to see the world'. He made three remarkable journeys which give him the right to a place in any dictionary of biographies: his only failure is not to have found a place in the *Dictionary of National Biography*.

The first voyage, 1579. Newbery left London in March and travelled overland to Marseilles. Thence he sailed to Tripoli in Syria; from there he took ship to Jaffa and then went on to Jerusalem, where he visited 'the monuments of those countries'. The return journey to England was made via Jaffa, Tripoli, Marseilles, Paris to London. Newbery had been away for eight months.

The second voyage, 1580. Newbery left England on 19 September in an English ship bound for Tripoli. He arrived there in January 1581, and went northwards to Aleppo. Here he dressed himself as a Mohammedan trader, provided himself with a Greek servant and on 19 March set out for the Portuguese port of Hormuz at the southern end of the Persian Gulf. The next day he was at Bir, where he took a boat down the Euphrates to Fallujah and thence by land to Baghdad (15 April 1581). After staying there for nine days he went by boat down the Tigris to Basra (May). Here he changed boats and went down the Persian Gulf to the island of Kishm. On the way the party was all but taken and made into slaves. From Kishm Newbery crossed over to Hormuz (22 June). At Hormuz he took a house and stayed there for six weeks. The Portuguese at that time had no objections to the English visitor, but the Venetian merchants were very jealous of him. One of them, Michael Stropene, seduced Newbery's Greek servant 'to understand my secret purposes'.

On 1 August 1581 Newbery left Hormuz and made up his mind to go home by land through Persia. He knew a little Arabic, but he had no European companion, only a servant, this time a Persian Jew. On this journey he carried with him a small stock of cloves as merchandise. On 6 September he reached Shiraz, where he spent sixteen days, and Isfahan on 4 October, where he stayed three days. He then travelled north to Kashen (12 October) and he spent more than three weeks in this important trading centre. His next move was north-west to Tabriz, where he arrived on 23 November. He left Tabriz on 1 December 1581 for Julfa, arriving eventually at Erzerum on 21 December. Here he spent Christmas and arrived at Erzingan on 3 January 1582 and Constantinople on 9 March.

Most people would have taken ship for Venice and then have travelled to England overland, but that was too easy for Newbery. He decided to go straight across Europe northwards to Dantzig on the Baltic Sea and then home by ship along the northern European coast. On 4 April 1582 he sailed into the Black Sea, where he encountered a violent storm. On 25 April he reached Reni at the mouth of the river Pruth, where he was fascinated by the methods of making caviare. On 1 May he left for Jassy, then on to Kaminietz on the Russo-Polish frontier. We know next to nothing about his journey from there to Dantzig, but we do know that he picked up a boat at Dantzig and reached London on 31 August 1582. His journey had taken all but two years. By the end of it he was the first Englishman to have travelled down the valley of the Euphrates; probably the first, certainly the second, if not the first, to set eyes on the famous depot of Hormuz; the first to cross southern Persia and to visit Shiraz and Isfahan; the first to reach Constantinople from Persia via Asia Minor: the first to sail on the Black Sea and to travel through the Danubian countries to Poland and the Baltic.

The third voyage, 1583. In the autumn of 1582 a plan was formed by the New Turkey Company (later the Levant Company) for reaching Cathay by way of Hormuz and India. Newbery was selected to lead the party and to carry letters from the queen to the Great Mogul and to the Emperor of China. No-one was better fitted for the post, for Newbery could speak Arabic, he was already on good terms with the governor of Hormuz, and his courage and business ability had been fully proved. The Hakluyts were involved in the plan and Newbery had been in correspondence with the younger Hakluyt, for he had written to him from Aleppo as 'Right wellbeloved and my assured good friend'. Hakluyt had given him a note from the writings of a Portuguese pilot, Fernando Fernandez, and a letter from Thomas Stevens to his father, containing valuable information about sailing by the Portuguese route round the Cape. Stevens was a Jesuit, which proved valuable later, for otherwise 'we might have rotten in prison' (Taylor, *Tudor Geography, 1485-1583*, p.136). Newbery was also to find a second copy of *The Geography of Abulfeda*. He failed to find one in Syria, but he wrote hoping for success in Baghdad or Persia. Hakluyt did get a copy, probably not from Newbery.

Newbery was to lead a party of six to Baghdad: there, two were to stay with part of the stock-in-trade: the four were to go on to Basra, and there two were to stay to trade: Newbery and Ralph Fitch were then to take £300 or £400 worth of stock and 'so to go for the Indies'. There also accompanied the party a gem-polisher named William Leeds, and a painter of the name of James Story, who went at his own expense for the fun of it.

The party sailed from London in the *Tiger* on 13 February 1583 ('Her husband's to Aleppo gone, master of the *Tiger*', Macbeth, 1.3), but a storm drove the ship into Falmouth, and it was 11 March before they got away again. They arrived at Tripoli in Syria at the end of April, stayed there for a fortnight and then went on to Aleppo. At the end of May they set out for Baghdad, travelling to

Bir on camels, by boat down the Euphrates to Felujah, then on camels by night because of the heat to Baghdad, where two of the party remained. On 6 August the rest reached Basra, where two more remained with some of the stock: Newbery and Fitch set off with £400 in goods and money, accompanied by Leeds and Story.

In mid-August they embarked at Basra for Hormuz, where they arrived on 5 September. Unluckily, there was a new governor who knew not Newbery, and he had the party arrested and thrown into prison. This was the work of Michael Stropene, who denounced them as spies, and the governor sent the four travellers off to Goa to be dealt with by the Viceroy (29 November 1583). Here they were interrogated to see whether they were heretics, but nothing was proved against them, and they were released on bail. It was here that Thomas Stevens came to the rescue by helping to find the surety. Story had been taken up by the Jesuits, who persuaded him to paint their church and to join their order as a probationer, and he was free as air: Newbery, Fitch and Leeds were freed on condition they did not leave Portuguese territory. They now hired a house and began to trade and felt pretty confident that all was now well. After a few months they asked that their bail should be cancelled and the money returned to them. To their surprise the Viceroy threatened them that they 'should be better sifted before it were long and that they had further matter against them'. The three of them, therefore, turned their money into jewels, left their shop open with all the goods displayed for sale and slipped away (April 1584).

Newbery led his companions into south India to Bijapur, the capital of the kingdom of that name. They moved on to Golconda, famous for its diamond mines, in order to investigate the possibilities of trading in precious metals and stones, since Leeds was an expert in these things. We know nothing of what transpired there: the next matter of interest is that they came to Agra to the court of the great Emperor Akbar, but finding he was away at Fatehpur Sikri, they travelled twenty miles and obtained an interview with Akbar and presented Queen Elizabeth's letter. We have to deduce a personal meeting from Fitch's account of the emperor's dress and court, but he does not specifically state that they met the Mogul in person.

In September 1584 the trio separated: Leeds remained as an expert on jewels to the emperor: Fitch went on down the Ganges and Newbery set off home to England to plan fresh travels. On 28 September the three parted company. Newbery on his way home met a lonely death, nobody knows where or how. He deserves a memorial.

Further Reading
The above account owes everything to W. Foster's *England's Quest of Eastern Trade*, 1933, supplemented by E. G. R. Taylor's *Tudor Geography 1485-1583*, 1930.

NEWBERY, JOHN (1713-67), publisher, was a quaint character, friend of many notable writers such as Goldsmith and Dr Johnson. He was for a time the assistant editor of the *Reading Mercury*. When he came to London he published some standard works such as the *Guide*, a gazetteer of buildings and monuments, and the *Medicinal Dictionary* in three volumes (1743-5). He made patent medicines and sold Doctor James's Powders, an infamous compound of antimony and phosphate of lime, in St Paul's Churchyard. He found fame in writing, or at least presenting, books for children, using them sometimes to advertise his medicines. With Mrs Margery (or Goody) Two-Shoes, Giles Gingerbread and Tommy Trip and his Dog Jowler reaching an avid public, Newbery may claim to be the discoverer of the profitable market in books that were written specially for the young.

Further Reading

Austin Dobson, *Eighteenth-Century Vignettes*, vol. 1, p.118, 1892.

NEWCOMEN, THOMAS (1663-1729) was a blacksmith or ironmonger of Dartmouth. He was a skilled craftsman and no scientist, yet it is of considerable interest that in the 1680s he was corresponding with Robert Hooke about atmospheric engines and about the steam-pump invented by the Huguenot refugee, Dr Papin, a friend of Hooke. His invention of the atmospheric engine was in essence simply an improvement upon the 'fire engine' patented (1698) by another Devonian, Thomas Savery, the military engineer. The Newcomen engine, made in 1705, was a reciprocating engine intended to drive pumps for draining mines. It used steam-power to create a vacuum upon which the pressure of the atmosphere would act and so move the heavy beam connected with the pumping rods. It was widely used during the eighteenth century, in the coalpits of the north and midlands as well as in the tin-mines of Cornwall, and also as an indirect source of power by driving water-wheels for ironworks. Its weakness, seriously felt in Cornwall if not on the coalfields, was its inordinate consumption of fuel, and this led in the later years of the eighteenth century to its transformation by Cornish engineers such as the Trevithicks and its replacement by James Watt's steam-engine.

Further Reading

L. T. C. Rolt and J. S. Allen, *The Steam Engine of Thomas Newcomen*, 1977.

L. T. C. Rolt, *Thomas Newcomen: the pre-history of the steam-engine*, 1963.

NEWMAN, JOHN HENRY (1801-90), priest, theologian, philosopher, poet and prophet, was a leading figure in the 'Oxford Movement' within the Church of England; became the most celebrated of converts; and devoted his latter years to the service of the Roman Catholic church. When he died, *The Times* declared that 'a great man has passed away, a great link with the past has been broken'. Since then his personality, thought and spirituality have been studied exhaustively. In the mind of Catholics, Anglican and Roman alike, he stands as high as ever. Few others would question the contemporary judgement.

A highly imaginative child, John, the eldest of six, grew up in a substantial London household. His father, also John, was a banker. His mother came of Huguenot stock. Religion, Anglican, tinged by his mother's evangelical spirit, was important, not overwhelming. Until his father's financial downfall in 1816 brought anxieties, John's life had provided the happy memories on which he would later draw for reassurance. The benign establishment of Dr Nicholas in Ealing, where good teaching was accompanied by a mild discipline, was ideal for a boy who could appeciate Cicero but find time for his violin, for long walks and boating. He was ill at the end of his last term. Lonely days in the sickroom brought the spiritual experience, when 'God mercifully touched his heart': not the sudden revelation that the evangelical might hold valid, but 'a change of thought'. It was one of those crises of development to which he was later to attach great significance.

His father, setting out with John, but still undecided between Oxford and Cambridge, encountered a friend, took his advice, drove west and placed him at Trinity College. Sixteen years old, shy and studious, he surprised his tutor, Mr Short, by the extent of his reading, and undergraduates by his self-possession. In Newman's 'deep imagination' God willed him to lead a single life. Reading *The Force of Truth* by Thomas Scott implanted the idea of religious truth as a quest, and understanding of it as a personal development. 'Unhumbled reason' was the root of all heresy. For Newman, whose theology would develop from such insights, growth was 'the only evidence of life'. Most influential was his discovery, through Milner's *History of the Church*, of the Early Fathers. It was 'a paradise of delight' in which he saw an analogy with his experience of the form and emotion of music: Greek clarity of reasoning fortified by the material imagery of the Hebrew.

The iron will that underlay Newman's gentle manner was tested when he broke down through overwork in his final examinations: a place 'under the line' in the lower part of the second class might have suggested an end to Oxford. Instead he toiled towards that coveted prize, a fellowship at Oriel College. Aged twenty-one, Newman entered the most distinguished Common Room in Oxford. Few of its clever, earnest members, tending to liberalism, were his natural allies. Keble was mainly absent, ministering in his father's parish. But Richard Whateley, first logician of his day, under whom he was

Vice-Principal of the tiny St Albans Hall, taught him to think accurately: 'he was the first who taught me to weigh my words.' Provost Hawkins's sharp mind helped him shed the last of his evangelical notions. Encountering worldly undergraduates or, as curate of St Clement's, people beyond the city walls, he acquired the self-confidence that would help him endure rebuffs. In 1826, he was appointed a college tutor: he saw it as an office of pastoral care.

Encouraged by Keble, two followed him in this line, Robert Wilberforce and Hurrell Froude. Provost Hawkins feared that it would lead to the cultivation of a few, the neglect of others. In 1830 he banned the group from acting as tutors. Newman was freed for what he would see as a greater work. He was by then vicar of the university church of St Mary's.

In its pulpit his ever-deepening scholarship, creative theology, pastoral intuition and artistic sensibility came together with memorable force. He was of fair height, slender, with a wiry strength: grey-blue eyes, a prominent nose, strong chin and full mouth. 'I seem to hear him still', Matthew Arnold would write of those days. His voice was low and musical, 'silvery' it was often called; his style, deliberately cultivated, echoed the cadences of Gibbon and Hume: the poetry rarely obscured the force and rationality of his thought. 'The English sermon had never before and has never since attained such psychological intensity and subtlety' (Ian Ker). Some much-loved prayers originated in his closing perorations. Central themes were the nature of the visible church, with its sacraments and rites the channels of invisible grace, and the authority, Catholic and Apostolic, by which it lived, and taught.

Already a group was forming round Hugh Rose, who founded *The British Magazine* to stir opinion to the dangers of liberal theology and political control. The growth of Nonconformity; a church in a state of what Newman called 'do-nothing perplexity'; the prevailing idea of the cure of souls as a form of private property; the Tory 'betrayal', Catholic Emancipation, which had led Newman to oppose Peel's candidature for Oxford University in 1829; patronizing or cynical attitudes in high Whig circles: such factors ensured that the relationship of church and state would be an issue. A proposal to abolish ten bishoprics of the Church of Ireland and Keble's Assize sermon in 1833 on 'National Apostasy' brought it to the fore. The 'Hadleigh conference' which followed, a gathering of friends at Rose's Essex vicarage, helped make a party out of a cause.

So Newman came back from his Italian journey with the Froude family to find that Oxford men looked to him to lead. In Sicily he had nearly succumbed to fever. The experience strengthened his sense of vocation. Returning home he composed 'Pillar of the Cloud' and 'Lead Kindly Light'. There was however more of polemics than of poetry in the spirit in which he and Froude entered the lists. For Froude, dying of tuberculosis, there was too little time. For Newman 'there was a work to do', for the church – and for Froude. As a friend wrote: 'everything, humanly speaking, is darkening round the church.' 'Choose your side,' declared Newman, and wrote *A Tract for the Times*. 'Are we content to be the mere creation of the state?' The rhetorical question launched the Tractarian or 'Oxford Movement'. Two ideas merged, a theological and an aesthetic. The first was a catholicism not Roman, not primarily medieval, but patristic, grounded in the Early Church and the writing of the Fathers. The second, in tune with the romantic spirit of the age, conducive to the movement's spread beyond academic circles, was a yearning for the Gothic and its religious ethos.

While Oxford steamed, England watched – and read. Tract followed tract, as Pusey and others plied their pens. Of Pusey, with his professorial position and influential connections, Newman wrote that 'his simple devotion to the cause of religion overcame me'. Newman himself wrote twenty-two tracts, besides his *Lectures on the Prophetical office of the Church*. That classic statement of the High Church doctrine of authority was the foundation of what he called 'a large, bold system of religion, very unlike the protestantism of the day but … concentration and adjustment of the statements of great Anglican authorities'. So the party grew; more became convinced of the apostolical authority of the church; more aspired to the beauty of holiness in church services; more offered and received regular communion. More, however, clamoured against what they saw as Romish inclinations, as revealed by the publication, by Newman and Keble, in 1838, of Froude's *Remains*, in which the Reformation was passionately denounced. Protestant suspicions were confirmed, in 1841, by the publication of *Tract 90*, in which Newman sought to reconcile the Thirty-Nine Articles with the teaching of the ancient church. Some read into his argument the view that they were also compatible with the post-Reformation doctrines of the Catholic church: one was W. G. Ward, extreme in discipleship as later in opposition to Newman. The Bishop of Oxford requested that the *Tracts* be suspended. Newman yielded, but his critics were not assuaged. He was appalled by the government's support for the establishment of an Anglo-Prussian bishopric in Jerusalem – as if Lutheran heresies did not matter! That was, he said, 'the beginning of the end'. He retired to his chapelry at Littlemore, outside the city but in St Mary's parish. There he gathered a handful of his followers in a quasi-monastic régime and pondered the question of allegiance.

In September 1843 Newman resigned his living of St Mary's, then preached his last Anglican sermon in Littlemore Church, 'The Parting of Friends'. There was drama in the event as in the title; no less characteristic was the heart-searching, as Newman strove to reconcile the principles of the Early Church with those of Rome. His idea of development, in line with current debate about evolution, showed him a way along which the Roman Catholic church could be said to have travelled. By contrast the Reformation represented a clean break, in doctrines, liturgies and practices. On 9 October 1845, at Littlemore, Newman was received into the Roman Catholic church; a few weeks later he published his *Essay on the Development of Christian Doctrine*. It did not assuage the sense of loss, even betrayal, felt by Keble, Pusey and others who remained within the Anglican fold. Nor could Roman Catholics believe that Newman had shed his Anglican attitudes. Only five years before, he had written: 'We English like manliness, openness, consistency, truth. Rome will never gain on us till she learns these virtues.' Soon he would write a novel, *Loss and Gain* (1848), the story of a young man's search for faith amid the competing calls of Oxford spiritual factions. If there was pain, there was also humour, a free-ranging mind.

The Roman Catholic years saw the alternations of achievement and failure, acclaim and hostility, hope and despair, that he had already known. Since the French Revolution conservative attitudes had predominated within the church. After 1848 Pope Pius IX had good reason to fear nationalism, and therefore national attitudes within the church. A party in England, reinforced by converts like Manning, Faber and Ward, followed him uncritically. Old Catholics, however, confident in their own tradition, preferred to keep their distance from Roman bureaucrats and Irish 'bog priests' alike. Lord Acton, trained in the German school of historical criticism, gave them intellectual leadership. The arrival within this disparate fold of a man of genius, who would not treat theology as if it were a closed system, nor was blind to the implications of scientific discovery, caused discomfort. Rome could not find a suitable role for Newman. When he found his own he met with difficulties at every turn.

After ordination at Rome he founded the Oratory at Birmingham, believing that its free form of association was suited to industrial cities and for men of different capacities. A centre of learning and teaching, it also catered for the city's poor Catholics. It would be his retreat, virtual home, for the rest of his life. He was content there, not quiet. He was long at odds with Faber, founder of the London Oratory, as to the rule of the daughter house. A libel case brought by a former priest, Achilli, whom Newman had exposed as a charlatan, brought an adverse judgement, and glee to Newman's baser critics. He was called to Ireland to be first Rector of the new Catholic university. He might have little to show in Dublin for many journeys across the Irish sea

and wrangles over its constitution: for a wider public there were the influential lectures and essays on the values of a liberal education, brought together in *The Idea of a University*. Ker calls it 'a triumph of literary art, perhaps the finest extended example of non-fictional prose in the English language'. For G. M. Young it was 'the final utterance of Christian humanism, as if the spirit evoked by Erasmus had found its voice at last'.

Newman's role as editor of the Roman Catholic monthly, *The Rambler*, also proved vexatious, not least because of the hostility of Manning, soon to be Archbishop of Westminster. He respected Newman but feared what he stood for: 'an English Catholicism, of which Newman is the highest type. It is the old Anglican, patristic, literary Oxford tone transplanted into the church.' *The Rambler* was suspect to theological conservatives as representative of Lord Acton's belief in the importance of critical scholarship. Newman's article, 'On Consulting the Faithful in Matters of Doctrine', was reported to Rome on suspicion of heresy. His attempt to found a Catholic hostel in Oxford was thwarted by the hierarchy: would Oxford contaminate the faithful? Humble, prayerful, but sensitive to slights real or supposed, Newman plainly wished to obey, yet found it hard when cherished plans were blocked. There was a fierce side. He had already shown himself to be vehement in debate, master of logic and irony, not always charitable. Now he was challenged by Kingsley to justify the honesty of his life as an Anglican. In response he wrote *Apologia pro Vita Sua* (1864). It won friends beyond the bounds of the Roman communion by the candour and grace of his writing.

Following the definition of Papal Infallibility in 1870, Gladstone questioned its effect on Catholic subjects faced by a conflict of loyalties. Newman believed in the doctrine, opposed its definition, and seized his chance to explore the theological issue. He had always thought that teaching was his real vocation and the philosophical defence of Christian belief his principal mission. *The Grammar of Assent*, considering the nature of faith, shows that faith can possess certainty when it rises out of evidence that is no more than probable.

In 1879 Pope Leo XIII made him cardinal. In the course of his long pilgrimage he had transformed the Church of England and helped Catholic theology to come to terms with critical scholarship and scientific advance. A hundred years later he may be best known for the poem that inspired Elgar's great work *The Dream of Gerontius*. As that work of genius transcends questions of doctrine to present spiritual aspiration in its noblest form, so his theological writing escapes the tyranny of logic and rises above traditional concerns. It was, as he said, for factory girls as well as philosophers. It is for Protestants as well as Catholics. It is indeed for all who value the spiritual element in their cultural inheritance.

Further Reading
David Brown, ed., *Newman, A Man for Our Time: Centenary Essays*, 1990.
Ian Ker, *John Henry Newman: A Biography*, 1980.
Meriel Trevor, *Newman: The Pillar of the Cloud; Newman: Light in Winter*, 1962 (abridged as *Newman's Journey*, 1974).

NEWNES, SIR GEORGE (1851-1910), known as 'Not Out Newnes' on the cricket field of the City of London School, grew to become a pioneer of modern journalism. In 1881 he launched the newspaper *Tit-Bits*, which was to earn him a fortune and develop the techniques of the popular press. He aimed it at the new market of 'junior clerks and the like'. Despite some starchy reactions to its name (Newnes was shocked when the double entendre was explained to him), it achieved a national circulation of 850,000 within seven years. He attracted gifted contributors: W. T. Stead, Arthur Pearson, Alfred Harmsworth. He used innovative publicity techniques: insurance for any reader killed in a railway crash, prize competitions with Tit-Bits Villa as one of the prizes, buried treasure (500 sovereigns), with clues in the paper. But it was the human interest stories and the short news items which sold it. Harmsworth went off and created a whole new paper out of 'Answers to Correspondents' which he had worked on for *Tit-Bits*, and then started *The Daily Mail*, while Pearson founded *The Daily Express*. Later Newnes launched the *Review of Reviews* with Stead, *The Strand Magazine*, where the Sherlock Holmes stories were first published, and *The Westminster Gazette*, a Liberal organ which lost money. He became a Liberal MP. His was one of the early houses in Putney to have electricity; he worked for half the week from home by telephone; and he bought a motor car from Paris when there were few on the road. But he was happiest to have brought 'entertainment to crowds of hard-working people craving for a little fun'.

NEWTON, SIR ISAAC (1642-1727), greatest of English scientists, was born on a farm at Woolsthorpe Manor, seven miles from Grantham in Lincolnshire. His father was already dead, and the outward record of Newton's career is a classical example of the widow's son from a humble home who makes good by sheer intellectual ability. He went from King's School, Grantham, to Trinity College, Cambridge, as a sizar in 1661, and his outstanding qualities of mind were quickly discerned by an eminent scholar, Isaac Barrow. In 1667 he became a Minor, in 1668 a Major, Fellow of Trinity, and in 1669, at twenty-seven, he succeeded Barrow, at the latter's wish, as Lucasian Professor of Mathematics. The Royal Society elected him a Fellow in 1672. His magnum opus, the *Principia*, perhaps the greatest scientific work ever written, which he completed in eighteen months, was published in 1687, and won him immense prestige at once. He represented the University of Cambridge in parliament in 1689 and in 1701-2. In 1696 he became Warden of the Mint (and Master from 1699 for the rest of his life) and carried through the most important recoinage in modern English history. From 1703 onwards he was President of the Royal Society. In 1704 his notable work on light, the *Opticks*, was published. Next year Queen Anne visited Cambridge, and conferred a knighthood on him at Trinity. In his old age Newton was recognized as one of the giants, and at his death in 1727 his body lay in state before burial in Westminster Abbey. His statue by Roubiliac, done some twenty years after Newton's death, stands in the place of honour in the ante-chapel of Trinity, the college also of Francis Bacon, J. J. Thomson, and Rutherford.

Yet behind this outward success lay a complex character. Newton was a withdrawn man whom his contemporaries found hard to understand. Few felt affection for him, though nearly all felt respect. He was in part the absent-minded don whom his Cambridge assistant, Humphrey Newton (another Lincolnshire man but no relation), describes, 'thinking all hours lost that was not spent in his studies', neglecting his meals and his dress, and the like. Beyond this superficial characteristic – which itself contrasts very sharply with the businesslike efficiency which Newton displayed in the affairs of the Mint – there were deeper difficulties. Temperamentally lonely, perhaps frustrated, he remained a bachelor all his days – though the sole suggestion that he ever thought of becoming anything else rests upon an old lady's gossipy recollection. Certainly he seems to have been puritanically fearful about sex: Brewster, his nineteenth-century panegyrist, relates that when his chemist friend Vigani told a coarse tale about a nun, Newton 'broke off all acquaintance with him'. He was morbidly sensitive to criticism, and his irritability led often to spitefulness. His scholarly career was punctuated by a series of unedifying controversies, each extending over several years, with Hooke, Flamsteed, the first Astronomer Royal, and Leibniz, the German philosopher. None of these men was faultless in the disputes, but neither was Newton. He was always ready to believe himself deceived or persecuted, and in 1693-4 he had a nervous breakdown in which, as his curious letters to Locke at the time show, he was clearly suffering from some form of paranoia. Yet he was a man of contrasts. He was always generous with money to others, living plainly himself. He retained throughout his life a simple and pleasing affection for Lincolnshire and Lincolnshire people. He was no time-server, and was active in opposition to James II's Catholicizing measures in Cambridge. Everything we know of him indicates that he was a man whose religious views were held with complete sincerity; these views were Arian ones which prevented him from subscribing to the Thirty-Nine Articles and thus from taking orders, a fact which was something of a barrier to earlier preferment.

The careers of seventeenth-century scientists were widely varied, as the lives of Wren and Petty show. There were no established narrow channels, for science itself was still in its infancy. Yet Newton's scientific career had a strangeness all its own. He produced a considerable proportion of the original ideas which are the essence of his legacy to mankind in the course of eighteen months which he spent alone at Woolsthorpe in 1665-7, when Cambridge was virtually closed by plague. He was then twenty-four: in his own words long afterwards, 'in those days I was in the prime of my age for invention, and minded mathematics and philosophy more than at any time since'. At the heart of these ideas was his hypothesis about the role of gravitational attraction in the universe. But he took it no further for thirteen years because of the mathematical difficulties which it raised. Instead he turned to other branches of science, in particular to optics, and this provided the subject of his first paper to the Royal Society, in 1672 when he was thirty. Newton seems to have had little sense of any need to publish the results of his investigations at any time, and the criticism and controversy which publication aroused disturbed him quite disproportionately. In 1676 he wrote of bidding adieu to science eternally 'excepting what I do for my private satisfaction', and during the next few years he had hardly any connection with the Royal Society. It was a dispute with Hooke which drove him back to the question of gravity in 1679, and to providing mathematical proof of the part played by the inverse square law in the mechanics of the heavens. He found his solution, and then seemingly forgot about it for five years, until Halley's visit to Cambridge in 1684 to ask for his opinions on the movements of the planets; and even then he could not lay his hands on it. It was Halley who persuaded him to write the *Principia*, and undertook the financial risk, as well as the labour, of seeing the book through the press. Once it was published, 'Newton's life became more full of incident, and more empty of science'.* He deliberately refrained from publishing the *Opticks*, most of which had been written before 1690, until after the death of his critic Hooke in 1703. He continued to devote long hours to study, and he left huge quantities of manuscript material at his death. But hardly any of it concerned the physical and mathematical science in which the *Principia* had revealed his pre-eminence. This was not because of any serious failure of power to handle this subject; the Queries which he added to the first Latin edition of the *Opticks* when he was sixty-four contain some remarkable insights. His interests now lay elsewhere. Some of the material –

about half a million words – dealt with chemistry and alchemy, to what precise end nobody has ever been able to explain. Some of his labours were given to problems of ancient chronology. Most of the material concerned religious questions, in particular the intellectual implications of Christianity as these were revealed by exhaustive study of the Bible.

Newton the scientist was fortunate in his age. Born in the year of Galileo's death, he built upon the work of such predecessors as Kepler and Descartes (even where he proved them wrong), and he benefited from that of older contemporaries like Barrow, Wallis and Boyle. The contemporary development of mathematical techniques, the rise of scientific societies, the widespread interest in experiment, the relevance of astronomy and mathematics to the practical needs of navigation, war and craftsmanship, the whole freer intellectual climate brought about by the Puritan revolution – all these things worked directly or indirectly to his advantage, making his work both possible and more fruitful. Yet Newton dominated by his own extraordinary combination of qualities – his formidable power of concentration, his brilliant mathematical skill, his exceptional precision in experimental work and (some would add) his remarkable scientific foresight. So it came about that as a young man in his twenties he grasped the principle of universal gravitation and moved behind Kepler's Laws to the inverse square law; worked out the prismatic theory of colours and was led to construct the reflecting telescope, using mirrors instead of lenses; and discovered the binomial theorem and formulated the principles of the differential and the integral calculus. By the time of the publication of the *Principia* he had worked out a rigorous proof of the inverse square law. Thus in that book he stated his three Laws of Motion and went on to explain the orbits of the planets in terms of universal gravitation. He explained under one threory the motions of the planets, the precession of the equinoxes, the ebb and flow of the tides, and the orbits of comets. The *Principia* was predominantly theoretical and mathematical, but in parts of it Newton described his use of experimental methods. In his second book, the *Opticks*, he provided detailed experimental proof of the prismatic theory of light. To Newton light consisted of corpuscles travelling at high velocity, whereas Huygens had proposed a wave theory.

The French mathematician Laplace, living a century after Newton, wrote that 'the *Principia* is pre-eminent above any other production of human genius'. Its implications for the range of the human mind were vast. Starting from the basic hypothesis, confirmed by mathematical proof, that every particle of matter attracts every other particle with a force directly proportional to their masses and inversely as the square of the distance between them, Newton had provided man with a new

---

*A. R. Hall, *The Scientific Revolution, 1500-1800*, 1954, p.249.

framework of thought. He had brought all the physical phenomena of the universe, from the falling of the apple to the movement of the planets in their orbits, into one system, a system governed by mathematical law. This was the achievement which provided the universality of Newton's work, gave him primacy among the scientists of his day and justified the phrase 'the Age of Newton'. Newton's inclusion of both terrestrial and celestial phenomena within one theory was aptly named by A. N. Whitehead 'the first physical synthesis'. In Pope's famous couplet

> Nature and Nature's Laws lay hid in Night,
> God said, Let Newton be! and all was Light.

'Light' also implied, in Newton's own words, that 'an entire liberty must be allowed in our inquiries': so prodigious a demonstration of scientific and rational truth made nonsense of intolerance. Moreover, the consequences for the development of science itself were immense. Besides providing a remarkable example of scientific method at the highest level, Newton had defined terms like mass, force, and momentum, and provided the essential foundations of theoretical physics as a mathematical science. Astronomers for the next century and a half would follow the highway which Newton had illuminated for them, and not until the end of the nineteenth century would the Newtonian system of the universe be challenged.

Newton himself appeared to take a modest view of his achievement, saying not long before he died 'I do not know what I may appear to the world; but to myself I seem to have been only like a boy, playing on the seashore, and diverting myself in now and then finding a smoother pebble or a prettier shell than ordinary, while the great ocean of truth lay all undiscovered before me'. And on one issue of fundamental importance which arose from his revolutionary discoveries he was himself entirely clear. He saw no antagonism at all between religion and science, no incompatibility between Christianity and the implications of the law of gravitation. Although he told his friend Richard Bentley in 1692 that in writing the *Principia* he 'had an eye upon such principles as might work with considering men, for the belief of a Deity', he believed firmly that it was not the scientist's task to discover final causes. Physics and theology were separate studies. Yet to Newton, God was the Final Cause, and the study of what he called 'the most beautiful system of sun, planets and comets' was the study of the divine craftsmanship. Just as in his labours in physics and mathematics he had sought, and found, the key which would unlock the mysteries of the physical universe, so in the work upon the prophesies of the Book of Daniel and of the Revelation which occupied so much of the second half of his life he was seeking the key to the mystery of God.

Further Reading

G. E. Christianson, *In the Presence of the Creator: Isaac Newton and His Times*, 1985.

R. S. Westfall, *Never at Rest: A Biography of Isaac Newton*, 1980.

NIGEL OF ELY (*d.*1169; Bishop of Ely 1133-69) was a member of the remarkable family of royal administrators established by his uncle, Roger, Bishop of Salisbury, Henry I's justiciar. This included his brother, Alexander, Bishop of Lincoln; his cousins, Roger and Adelelm, respectively chancellor and treasurer in the early years of Stephen's reign; and his own illegitimate son, Richard FitzNeal, treasurer to Henry II and Richard I. Educated at Laon under the renowned *magister* Anselm and his brother, the mathematician Ralph, Nigel became treasurer to Henry I in the mid-1120s, the post probably being created for him by his uncle Roger when (1123-6) viceroy of England. As treasurer, Nigel, who may have picked up the latest computing techniques at Laon, coordinated the financial operations of the king's chamber and the treasury. He remained at the heart of government after his appointment as Bishop of Ely in 1133 until he shared in his uncle's ruin in 1139. Nigel's response to Bishop Roger's arrest was characteristic. Used to a substantial military entourage, Nigel withdrew to Devizes castle prepared to fight, only surrendering when the king threatened to hang his cousin Roger. Excluded from court and stripped of office, Nigel retained his see and from there continued to resist Stephen, hiring troops and fortifying the Isle of Ely. Driven out by royalist forces, Nigel joined Matilda in the west country, being at her side throughout the triumphant months of 1141. When the pendulum swung against the empress, Nigel became an especial target of the king, fearful lest the bishop combine with other East Anglian rebels. In 1143, Nigel was forced to appeal to Rome against charges brought by the papal legate, Stephen's brother, Henry of Winchester. On his return in 1145, he made peace with the king, giving his teenage son Richard as hostage.

In 1154, at the repeated and urgent requests of the new king, Henry II, he came out of retirement to help reconstruct administration at the Exchequer which had been severely run down during the civil war. Nigel's reluctance was understandable. Most of his new colleagues, including the two justiciars, had served Stephen, one of them, Robert of Leicester, being implicated in the coup of 1139. The urgent problems at the Exchequer were re-establishing control over sheriffs; restoring procedures of effective audit; and the revival of clear, comprehensive and coherent records on the Pipe Rolls. All these, by the time Nigel retired through ill-health in 1164-5, had, to a great extent, been achieved.

For Henry II, Nigel represented expertise and experience. In the flattering account by his son in the *Dialogue of the Exchequer*, he appears as a master of procedure and Exchequer business. Although his position was informal, Nigel was influential enough to be able to give the justiciar, his old enemy Robert of Leicester, a severe dressing down when he breached precedent over Exchequer privileges: the exchange must have given the aged bishop some pleasure. The impression given in the *Dialogue* that Nigel recreated the Exchequer is probably untrue, but he did restore it on the same lines as it had operated under his uncle, providing Henry II with effective means to implement his wishes. To his son, Nigel was a heroic bureaucrat. He certainly was industrious. At Ely, he instituted inquests into the see's lands; established a diocesan Exchequer; and vigorously pursued resumption of estates lost in the severe depredations of the civil war. Combined with his actions under Stephen and his charters, the evidence shows Nigel to have been, as his enemies portrayed him, a man more adept at secular lordship than spiritual leadership.

NIGHTINGALE, FLORENCE (1820-1910) had to fight her way out of the chrysalis of her family. She was the elder daughter of well-connected parents with large houses, Hurst Lea in Derbyshire and Embley in the New Forest, who expected her to behave like a good Victorian daughter until they married her off. 'What is my business in this world, and what have I done this fortnight?' she wrote in 1846. 'I have read *The Daughter at Home* to Father, and two chapters of McIntosh; a volume of *Sybil* to Mamma. Learnt seven tunes off by heart. Written various letters. Ridden with Papa. Paid eight visits. And that is all.' Her sister Parthenope ('Parthe') was intensely possessive, and used ill-health as a weapon to keep her close. Even when she was over thirty her letters were read, her movements controlled, her invitations monitored by others. Yet she was such a striking personality that she already counted as friends George Eliot, Shaftesbury, Palmerston and a future cardinal, Manning. As early as 1837 she had felt a calling for some great work. In 1844 she knew that it was nursing. Yet only in 1853 did she finally make the break, after a number of nervous prostrations. There is much to be learnt about Victorian attitudes from this long and painful saga.

Nursing was then a degraded occupation, filled with Mrs Gamps, prostitutes and drunkards. Florence Nightingale had to go to a religious community at Kaiserswerth for some training. When her father finally gave her an allowance, and she went to take charge of 'The Institution for the Care of Sick Gentlewomen in Distressed Circumstances', her declared aim was to establish the reputation of nursing as a profession. She quickly showed herself to be a first-class administrator and a determined politician. When Sidney Herbert, Secretary at War, looked for someone to take charge of the nurses who were desperately needed for the troops in the Crimea, he turned to her. She grasped her opportunity

and made it the basis of her life's work. The hospital at Scutari, to which the British casualties had to be ferried across the Black Sea, was a Turkish artillery barracks, with no beds, no kitchens and privies without water. When the forty nurses arrived, they found a dead Russian general in one of their rooms, and the decaying body of a horse polluting the main water-channel. The transformation which Florence Nightingale and her 'Angel Band' achieved was the result of sustained hard work on a heroic scale, and it all depended on her own strength, leadership, command of detail, and diplomacy. She would not allow her nurses to start work until a doctor invited them to do so, and insisted that all requisitions for equipment were made through the proper channels, complex and slow though they were. She got things done because she had come out with the funds to pay for the equipping of the wards: describing herself as 'a general dealer in socks, shirts, wooden spoons, tin baths, cabbages, operating tables, bed-pans and stump-pillows'.

Her stamina was extraordinary. When a fresh intake of wounded arrived she was on her feet for twenty-four hours at a stretch. Working in the midst of diarrhoea and vermin, she survived attacks of dysentery and Crimea Fever. She never let any of her patients die on their own, and the strength 'The Lady with the Lamp' gave to soldiers as they endured amputations without anaesthetic soon became famous. But while she was doing this, she was also coping with a crushing burden of administration, without a secretary: acknowledging gifts, making requisitions, writing reports to Sidney Herbert, sending back to their homes the messages of dying soldiers. On top of all that, she was fighting the army's Chief of Medical Staff, Dr Hall, who had reported before she arrived that nothing was lacking in the hospital at Scutari. 'Knight of the Crimean Burialgrounds I suppose', she wrote when he was made a KCB. During those eighteen months there she stamped the profession of nursing with her own image, and taught officers and officials to treat soldiers as Christian men, and not as 'the scum of the earth enlisted for drink'.

She did all this at the expense of her own health. For much of the rest of her long life she was confined to her room. From it, however, she conducted a series of ambitious and influential campaigns. She was never a feminist, preferring the company of men to women, and using her personal magnetism to the full. Her pen flowed across the paper, with evidence to Royal Commissions; books; and, above all, letters, often written from five in the morning and as many as 100 in a day, browbeating slothful or cautious ministers like Lord Panmure – nicknamed 'The Bison' – and urging allies to ever greater efforts. Of these the closest was Sidney Herbert, heir to Wilton, *chevalier sans peur et sans reproche*. Together they set up a Royal Commission on Army Medical

Organization, packed it with reformers, and got most of its recommendations accepted. Barracks were made sanitary, an Army Medical School was founded, and a Statistical Branch, to provide the information on which future reforms would depend. The soldier's health, physical, moral and mental, was their concern, as well as his sickness. Concerts, lectures and workshop training were started, as alternatives to the demoralizing 'dram shop'; and recreation rooms were built. Traditionalists and economizers, Gladstone among the latter, used the techniques of bureaucracy to resist and delay, but Miss Nightingale's relentless drive pushed things through. She drove Sidney Herbert to an early death. Blinkered in her single-minded determination, she made him work on as Minister at War and Chairman of the Royal Commission, when he knew he had an incurable kidney disease. 'It is not true that you cannot (sometimes) absolutely mend a damaged organ', she wrote to him. When he finally resigned, eight weeks before his death, she told him: 'No man in my day has thrown away so noble a game with all the winning cards in his hand.' When he died, she turned on God. Herbert's death involved 'the misfortune, moral and physical, of five hundred thousand men', and it would have been 'but to set aside a few trifling physical laws to save him'.

She found new helpers, and carried on with fresh tasks. Her *Notes on Hospitals* revolutionized hospital building: the new St Thomas's Hospital at Lambeth was the jewel in her crown. After her *Notes on Nursing* a Training School for Nurses was founded with money raised by her Nightingale Fund. Mrs Wardroper, the Matron at St Thomas's, was its first Superintendent, and from St Thomas's above all developed the modern nursing profession. Then Florence Nightingale took on the enormous task of sanitizing, not only the Indian army, but India itself. The statistics she prepared for the Royal Sanitary Commission on the Health of the army in India filled two large vans when she moved house, and the digest of them which she published, complete with woodcut illustrations, shocked public opinion. Only the loss of the Viceroy's report (pinned to the wrong set of documents by the India Office!) delayed the setting up of a public health service for India: but this proved a fatal delay when her ally Lord de Grey lost office with the fall of the Liberal government in 1866.

Some may have groaned: 'Another shriek from Miss Nightingale', but, as her close friend Jowett, Master of Balliol, wrote to her: 'A poor sick lady, sitting in a room by herself, and ministers have only not to go near her and not to read her letters … and yet you seem to draw them.' It was indeed *de rigueur* for newly appointed Viceroys to visit her before they set out for India. Henry Dunant, the Swiss founder of the Red Cross and author of the Geneva Convention, spoke of her as his inspiration. She drafted sermons and prayers for Jowett at

Balliol. Eventually, after the death of her parents and her sister, serenity stole into her. During this Indian summer she grew close to Sir Harry Verney, widower of her sister, and spent much time with him in his beautiful Buckinghamshire family house, Claydon. She became a legend before her death. At the Victorian Era Exhibition for the queen's Diamond Jubilee, her bust was bedecked each day by an unknown hand with fresh flowers. In 1907, Edward VII conferred on her, as the first woman to receive it, the Order of Merit. 'Too kind, too kind', she murmured. The fire had at last gone out.

Further Reading
C. Woodham-Smith, *Florence Nightingale*, 1950.

NINIAN, ST or NYNIA (fifth century?) was a British bishop of the sub-Roman period. Our information about Ninian is extremely fragmentary, the only faintly reliable early sources being two sentences in the *Ecclesiastical History* of Bede and a tortuous Latin poem of the eighth century known as 'The miracles of Bishop Nynia'. Modern scholars are prepared to accept that Ninian was a Briton who became bishop of a Christian community established in what is now Galloway; in Bede's day his cult was celebrated at Whithorn. It is impossible to date his episcopate precisely. The literary evidence, such as it is, suggests that Ninian flourished about the middle of the fifth century. The surviving archaeological evidence is congruent with such a dating: that is, the remains of an early Christian cemetery beneath the medieval Whithorn Priory church, the inscribed stone commemorating a Christian named Latinus at Whithorn, and the comparable stone erected in memory of two bishops (successors of Ninian, perhaps) at Kirkmadrine in the Rhinns of Galloway. Bede reported – somewhat cautiously ('as they say') – that Ninian had converted the southern Picts to Christianity. Whom he meant by the southern Picts is by no means clear; possibly he intended the peoples living about the Firth of Forth. It is not impossible that Ninian preached Christianity to them. We simply do not know.

Further Reading
C. Thomas, *Christianity in Roman Britain to AD500*, 1981.

NOLLEKENS, JOSEPH (1737-1823) was the foremost portrait sculptor of his day; his working life neatly bridged the interval between Roubiliac and Chantrey. His father and grandfather were painters from Antwerp; and he himself was apprenticed at thirteen to the immigrant Antwerp sculptor, Peter Scheemakers, whose statue of Shakespeare for Westminster Abbey (1740) had been uniquely popular. For ten years from 1760 Nollekens laboured in Rome, making sketches, 'restorations' and copies of ancient statuary, and imbibing that science of the antique which, while it coloured his work, has too readily been assumed to be the leading characteristic of it. It was in Rome that Garrick, out of kindness, became his first sitter; but it was the bust of Laurence Sterne, done also in Rome and now to be seen in the National Portrait Gallery, which declared his talent. His reputation was published, and he returned to England in 1770 to engross the stage of sculpture. Only two years later he was elected RA, and married into the Johnson circle. He made it his interest to become a rich man, which he notably achieved. When his tremendously active life closed in a cloud of senile dementia and paralysis in 1823, his estate was found to have reached the mountainous size of some £200,000. In *Nollekens and His Times* is stigmatized the avarice of the sculptor; but the author of that 'biography' was disappointed at receiving a mere £100 as Nollekens's executor, and his strictures must be taken with a handful of salt. Undoubtedly Nollekens practised economy as a virtue; but the scale of his fortune is the scale of his professional success; and it is simply a token of the increasing popularity of portrait sculpture that he was able to charge as much as 150 guineas for a single bust, four or five times what Rysbrack had charged in the 1730s.

More than eighty funeral monuments he has to his credit, a large enough achievement for any sculptor. But these often disappoint: they reiterate motifs which were in any case borrowed from his predecessors – the orthodox pyramid for a background, and in front the lachrymose woman, and the boys who hold up medallion portraits of the deceased. And it is not surprising, in such a number, to find that the modelling has been skimped, or that (especially in the drapery) it is over-complex in a stylized way.

But that is only a portion of his work: it is as the sculptor of busts that we honour Nollekens. He has been hailed as a neo-classicist; Flaxman said he was the only English sculptor before Banks who had 'formed his taste on the Antique and introduced a purer style of art'; but though Nollekens dwelt in the tents of the neo-classicists and carved works (such as the goddesses for Wentworth Woodhouse) which, but for a certain wryness, would decidedly be taken for revivals of the antique, his talent was too various to be neatly labelled, and many of his busts are as unpretentiously realistic as those of Rysbrack or Roubiliac. The bust of Sterne has been mentioned: the bare shoulders and the prominent bonework, the style of the features, are Roman of the Republic; but the face that confronts you is an unidealized, scrupulous study of a humorous and masterful man; and although the eyeballs are incised according to Nollekens's usual practice, there was no need of that to animate the cast of features on which the currents of character had been so unmistakably traced.

Nollekens was known for his skill at taking likenesses, at sifting the essential features from the secondary. Although he made a point of modelling from the life, the effect of a Nollekens bust is as if the sculptor had gathered from the painted portraits and concentrated into one head the traits which each painter had separately noticed as the most distinctive in the subject – and this at the time of the zenith of English painted portraiture. Thus – in the case of the king or Rockingham, of Pitt or of Fox – not all the painted portraits look like the bust, but the bust looks like all the painted portraits. Friends must have come upon the busts with the shock of recognition; for us they are the nearest thing to flesh-and-blood acquaintance with the sitters.

NORBURY, JOHN (*c*.1350-1414), esquire, was one of those Lancastrian retainers, whose career was transformed by Henry, Duke of Lancaster's accession as King Henry IV in 1399. Though of gentle birth from Nantwich in Cheshire, he was merely the younger son of a younger son. Lacking his own inheritance, he had to make his own way, initially as a soldier of fortune and latterly, perhaps, as an administrator. He was already experienced militarily by 1385, when he was a mercenary captain in the decisive Portuguese victory over Castile at Aljubarrotta. He crusaded with Henry, Earl of Derby (later Henry IV) in Lithuania in 1390. Norbury also became one of the many members of the great retinue of Henry's father John of Gaunt, Duke of Lancaster and married his daughter to the treasurer of the ducal household. This points to no more than respectable affluence, for Norbury was still merely a minor middle-aged Hertfordshire squire in 1399. He joined Henry IV before his formal accession and immediately afterwards the new king appointed him Lord Treasurer, keeper of the privy wardrobe, captain of Guines, and a permanent councillor. A wide variety of administrative tasks were crowded on him, so that he went on diplomatic missions, received custody of royal lands, was Henry's creditor and commissioner. He married again, this time to the sister and widow of the peerage, sired sons, and built up estates in the shires. This 'stern round of new duties' and opportunities lasted only a decade, for by 1409 Norbury had effectively retired from public life.

It must have been prior personal service that had earned Norbury the complete confidence of Henry IV by 1399. From then on he was constantly with the king, receiving his commands by word of mouth and undertaking the most secret business. King Henry even stood godfather to Norbury's son and gave him his name. Yet the man so honoured remained no more than an esquire. His case illustrates in an extreme form the medieval king's right to seek advice where he chose and to favour his own servants over his greatest subjects. An insecure king rated personal loyalty to himself higher than the mere allegiance due to him as king and Henry relied heavily for support and service on the great Lancastrian affinity built up by his father. 'Henry IV's position as king was strengthened by the local service of many who had served him and his family before 1399'. Norbury's transition from ducal to royal servant made his fortune and defeat for the House of Lancaster would have entailed his fall. Such considerations made him 'at every turn the king's man. Thus the king's cause was his own and the king's profit his own profit'. He was far from alone. No wonder Henry IV resisted so firmly all the Commons' efforts to cut the cost of his Lancastrian connection.

In 1399 Norbury was a widower with one married daughter and no obvious incentive to marry again. It was the rewards of royal service that gave him the means and desire to father a second family. Similarly it was royal service that made him a man of account at court. Hence, perhaps, the rapidly accumulated wealth that he was able to lend to the king and to invest conventionally in substantial country estates that made his heirs into a county family of standing. Hence also his rapid acceptance into the highly interdependent society of local landowners in Hertfordshire. Norbury was a commissioner both there and in Kent and served his gentry neighbours as a valued trustee. Whilst royal patronage came too late to lift him into the peerage, it carried him far indeed from his unpromising origins and even from the position he had attained in 1399.

Further Reading
M. Barber, 'John Norbury (*c.*1350-1414): An Esquire of Henry
    IV', *English Historical Review* lxviii, 1953.

NORTH, FREDERICK, 8th LORD NORTH and, two years before his death, second Earl of Guilford (1732-92), was prime minister, in a limited sense, for twelve years. He owed his power to the support of the king, to his administrative talents, and especially to his hold over members of the House of Commons. He appears, however, to have been inadequate in the face of the grave problems of the later years of office, Ireland, the reform movement and the American War. He himself felt that he was unsuited to the demands made by war, and posterity has confirmed his estimate.

He was educated at Eton and Trinity College, Oxford. At twenty-two he entered parliament for Banbury, whose corporation was always amenable to the head of the family at neighbouring Wroxton Abbey. In 1759 he became a Lord of the Treasury under Newcastle and remained there through the ministries of Bute and Grenville. Removed by Rockingham, he was further advanced by Chatham, who made him Chancellor of the Exchequer after the death of Townshend in 1767. In 1770 he took on the leadership of the ministry relinquished by Grafton. He spoke well and wittily; he was efficient and sensible about financial matters. In his reluctance to be committed ahead and in his political shrewdness he recalls

Walpole, but time was to show that he lacked that minister's energy and ruthlessness. It is fair, too, to suggest that North's rapid rise owed much to luck. Chatham's physical collapse, Grafton's embroilment in the Wilkes case, and Rockingham's party ties, left the field open to a minister who would put the conduct of government before consistency of principle. North had no large personal following, but this enabled him to secure the sympathy of independent backbenchers and to enlist in his ministry men from all connections. The Grenvillites felt free to return to office; one of them, Suffolk, became Secretary of State in 1771. Grafton himself was Privy Seal, Dartmouth, who had been a Rockinghamite, became Secretary of the Colonies, and Sandwich, who had been associated with Bute, went to the admiralty. North took a modest view of his own role. His executive authority was only that of his department, the Treasury, and in the Cabinet he did not press his views. At first the administration basked in the favour of the king, business and city interests, and a majority in parliament. The prime concern of merchant and landowner was a return to what they saw as normal budgeting, with the reduction of the debt and of rates of taxation swollen by war. That this involved reductions in the army and navy did not concern them, except when some flurry, such as the Spanish attack on Port Egmont in the Falkland Islands in 1770, revealed shortcomings. North sought to avoid entanglements abroad and thus to find a million pounds a year for the reduction of the debt. Eventually this might have led to the reduction of the Land Tax; meantime North pegged it at 3*s*.

North's talent for the conciliation of interests can be studied in his handling of the complex Indian problem. Here action was called for, because of the boom and subsequent slump of East India stock, caused by widespread buying for influence and patronage in the lucrative affairs of the company. The problem was made more acute by the fact that against the private fortunes of speculators and exploiters there was a serious imbalance of trade which threatened the company's future. Furthermore, the company, which was wading deep in Indian native politics, had to be subjected to some measure of control. Out of this situation, following inquiries which emphasized the corruption of company officials and a vote upon the specific case of Clive (in which North voted against him, but seems to have been relieved that the censure motion was lost), emerged the Regulating Act of 1773. This secured the immediate financial future of the company, by a compulsory loan and by freeing the tea trade from duties payable on re-export. There was to be a supreme court of justice and supreme Presidency, Bengal being elevated above Madras and Bombay and placed under a Governor-General and council of four, appointed by parliament. The scheme represents a typical compromise between the extremes of commercial independence and state control. Because of the value of the patronage and the persistence of problems inherent in the company's expansion, India was to be the subject of further legislation in 1783 and 1784. But North, who showed moderation in the face of the temptation to increase the patronage of the Crown, had achieved his object: the stability of the company and thus of England's position in India.

America offered still more intractable problems. Here North reaped the harvest of earlier and hasty sowings, notably Townshend's duties of 1767. It may be argued that there could be no solution, in the long term, other than independence, but it does seem that North's administration, unimaginative before, feeble during the war, had the worst of both worlds. The unloading of tea in America to help the East India Company's trade balance, and the subsequent dispute with Boston in December 1773, may be laid, moreover, at North's door. The closure of the port of Boston merely served to unite that town with other colonies which had hitherto disapproved of extreme measures. It is ironic too that the colonists' suspicions were increased by a measure which was statesmanlike in itself. The Quebec Act gave Canada a legislative council and allowed the French to keep their own laws and priests, but it guaranteed also the extension of Canada down to the Ohio and thus barred the expansion westward of the coastal colonies. So New England puritans and property agents convinced themselves that North intended to enslave them. He, myopic and badly advised, believed that he had only to coerce Massachusetts for the disturbances to subside. From the meeting of the pan-colonial congress in 1774 to the skirmish of Lexington in April 1775, the battle of Bunker Hill in June 1775 and the Declaration of Independence in July 1776, North was but a spectator of events. His amiable weaknesses were exposed as the administration drifted from expedient to expedient, discovering too late the cost of military unpreparedness. Gage advised the government to send large forces at once; but the army was too small for effective land war and the navy was hampered by a shortage of commissioned ships. Since North would not dictate a policy his ministers pursued several policies at once. Lord George Germain wanted swift military blows; Sandwich, afraid of invasion from France, wished to keep the fleet at home. North himself hoped for effective action by the loyalists. He was always obsessed with the problem of national debt, knowing that his majority depended upon his reputation for economy.

Howe demanded 20,000 troops for 1777, received only 2,500 and felt himself unable to act at a time when the Americans were relatively weak. In October 1777 Burgoyne had to surrender at Saratoga, victim of casual and over-optimistic planning. A big naval and military effort was planned for 1778; at the same time commissioners were sent to treat with Congress. But in that year French forces came to tilt the scales. In the following year Spain entered the war and Gibraltar was besieged. The navy was precariously stretched and not yet effective. The recriminations which followed the indecisive battle of Ushant in 1778 between Keppel and Palliser and the former's trial weakened the ministry. By 1779 Howe was defeatist and urged the ministry to come to peace. But George III was convinced that there was principle at stake in what had become a global war. North's political survival became the king's obsession. He begged to resign. 'I am not equal in abilities to the station which I ought to hold, as the place next the director of publick affairs at this time,' he wrote to the king in November 1779. He was accurate as well as modest in his analysis of the weakness of a government of separate and squabbling departments: 'In critical times, it is necessary that there should be one directing minister'. He was, however, culpably weak, even negligent. Robinson said in 1779 that he was 'the original cause of the bad situation of everything'. He could not or would not make a decision, preferring to trust to time to provide a solution. 'Nothing can goad him forward,' said the Attorney-General Thurlow in January 1780; 'He is the very clog that loads everything.'

Ireland meanwhile displayed trends uncomfortably close to the American pattern. The American war, moreover, produced a depression in those trades which exported to America or France. The Protestant gentry formed volunteer associations to take over home defence and release regular troops for service abroad. But when Lord North failed to remove some of the restrictions upon Irish trade, as Buckingham, the Lord Lieutenant, wished, this force became a weapon in the hands of Irish patriots. Flood, Grattan and their followers called for freedom of Irish trade and greater constitutional independence. Moreover they were encouraged by Fox and his Whig friends to see their challenge in fundamental terms of liberty and oppression. In 1780, too late to assuage Irish discontents, North made concessions: the right to trade freely with the colonies, freedom of wool and glass exports and the restoration of the bounty of her coarse linen sent into England. Irishmen were left to yearn for legislative security, Englishmen to grumble at North's apparent weakness.

Opposition was given further punch by a revival of radicalism. In the south, Wilkesites led by Jebb were advocating a more popular constitution, with more seats of the Westminster type. In Yorkshire, Christopher Wyvill's Association became the prototype of similar movements for franchise reform all over the country, and propertied men lent their support. To a general disquiet at the handling of the war was added a feeling that the influence of the Crown, through a subservient minister and his handling of the patronage, in the words of

Dunning's famous motion, 'has increased, is increasing, and ought to be diminished'. Old Whig prejudices were reinforced by the discontents of the gentry who wanted America beaten but taxes reduced, and by radicals who urged the need for more independent country members. North, ever at home in the House of Commons, did not lose his grip. The fury of the Gordon Riots in June 1780, irrelevant as they were to the main issues, strengthened arguments for stability. The violence of Fox went further than the squires would accept. North met petitions with bland talk and his majority in the Commons survived all attacks. In April 1780 Dunning was defeated by 254 to 203. In the election of that year, the government actually improved its position. North continued in power throughout 1781, the year of the surrender of Yorktown. 'Oh God, it is all over,' said North when he heard the news, but he did not resign until March 1782. Then, as Rigby put it, he had 'to give the thing up' because peace in America was necessary if England were to defeat her foes in Europe, reinforced now by Holland; and North was disqualified for this task by his commitment to war.

Jenkinson, who knew him well, suggested that North was insincere in his constant pleas to resign. The argument that he craved for power, despite the humiliations that this entailed and the additional handicap of failing sight, is strengthened by his conduct in 1783. After the death of Rockingham, and Shelburne's failure to muster enough support, Fox and North came together in a surprising tandem. The king regarded North's defection as an unforgivable piece of treachery and waited for his chance to destroy the coalition. This came, over the vexed position of India. The Regulating Act, which North had always regarded as a provisional measure, had not been working well. Warren Hastings had acquired the odium of many Whigs during his bitter contests with his council. The defence of India against the revenge of France could not be left with safety to a private company. The India Bill of Fox provided for the transfer of the whole territorial responsibilities of the company to a board of seven commissioners. Fox and Burke claimed that public control had been secured, free of executive corruption, but their enemies pointed to an extension of Whig patronage. 'Carlo Khan', monstrous and greasy, replaced North as the satirists' butt. With the king's encouragement, the Lords voted against the Bill and, in December 1783, Fox and North resigned and Pitt became First Lord of the Treasury.

North had lost reputation by this brief episode; it helps him little to add that he may have conceived that it was his duty to assist in the forming of some government, when all the groups were so much at variance. The cartoonist's portrait – pop eyes, pouting lips and round belly, the sprawling, somnolent figure on the Treasury Bench, the king's puppet of Whig legend and the insensate tyrant of American tradition – these figures have obscured the North of history. His reputation might have been secure if he had resigned at the start of the American War. At the height of this war he was able to present budget speeches of a lucid and masterly sort. As a war financier he would have stood higher if he had seen to it that his schemes were not marred by dishonest clerks and contractors, but even here he was unfortunate. In 1779 he had set up the Committee for Examining the Public Accounts: its reports were later to be the basis of Pitt's reforms and North got no credit for them. In his last years he was of no political consequence. He went completely blind and lived only four years to enjoy t he earldom that he inherited in 1788 from his aged father.

Further Reading
P. D. G. Thomas, *Lord North*, 1976.
I. R. Christie, *The End of Lord North's Ministry*, 1958.
H. Butterfield, *George III, Lord North and the People*, 1949.

NORTHAMPTON, JOHN alias COMBERTON (*d.*1397-8), draper of London, led the attack on the victualling monopolies and on the political dominance of the great merchants within the city during the 1380s. His origins are uncertain, for we know only the Christian names of his parents James and Mariota, although they were probably residents of London where he had many relatives. John himself was a tradesman prominent enough to be one of four upholders of his guild (livery company), but he owned no ship, did not trade abroad, and lacked foreign contacts. His brothers William and Robert, respectively skinner and esquire, were of little account. John's career was transformed in 1371-5 by his second marriage to Petronilla, a wealthy heiress and widow, who brought him extensive urban property yielding rents of £120 a year and the substance to qualify as an alderman. It was probably this marriage, in short, that gave him the means to champion the smaller masters and retailers with whom he properly belonged. He had become 'a man of position and of considerable, though not of great wealth. His supporters were insignificant in both respects'.

Like all corporate towns, London was ruled by a self-perpetuating oligarchy of the richest merchants. Their power was attacked by two changes to the city consti-1tution in 1376 that introduced annual election of aldermen and transferred election of common councillors from the wards to the guilds. These reforms widened the group of officeholders without breaking the dominance of the plutocrats. Northampton, who first became alderman in 1375, may have initiated these changes and certainly exploited them. When elected mayor in 1381 in the aftermath of the Peasants' Revolt, he employed his authority first to break the power of the fishmongers, whose monopoly over fish-sales and virtual independence of the corporation were universally unpopular. His attacks on immorality and on the level of ecclesiastical fees also enjoyed widespread support. Hence his re-election in 1382. When he abandoned caution to attack the other victualling trades, however, he overstretched himself, alienating the most powerful guilds and the greatest merchants. The 1383 election was disfigured by violence and Northampton lost to Nicholas Brembre. Northampton admitted defeat only reluctantly, spurned reconciliation, and sought to recover power by seeking to have the election annulled, by plots, and by a mass demonstration of lesser guildsmen. He became associated with threats to the peace and social revolution. The Crown intervened, he was tried and imprisoned at Tintagel, his patron John of Gaunt securing his restoration only in 1390. By then, however, Northampton's cause was lost. The old constitution had been restored and the oligarchs had recovered their monopoly of power. Northampton's only lasting achievement was to curb the independence of the fishmongers, although he himself, unlike his rival Brembre, died peacefully in his bed.

Evidently Northampton was something of a demagogue, who drew the lesser masters and trades into London's politics to secure lower food prices and a greater say in city affairs. Shrewd and clear about his objectives, he was resolute and inflexible in their pursuit and did not flinch from the use of force. Contemporaries were uncertain whether he sought personal power or whether he was motivated by abstract principle. While he inspired considerable loyalty among his partisans, he never enjoyed the united support of the non-victuallers, of the lesser crafts, or among their aldermen. In other ways, he appears a conventional merchant-capitalist, founding a chantry in Elsingspital and patronizing both the Benedictine nuns of Cheshunt and the newer and more otherworldly Carthusians.

Further Reading
S. Thrupp, *The Merchant Class of Medieval London*, 1962.
R. Bird, *The Turbulent London of Richard II*, 1949.

NORTHCOTE, SIR STAFFORD, 1st EARL OF IDDESLEIGH (1818-87) was a natural political second-in-command who allowed his head to emerge above the parapet and suffered a harsh end. Son of a Devon squire, he rose through his conscientious efficiency, friendly good nature and Etonian connections. He became private secretary to Gladstone and secretary to the Committee which ran the Great Exhibition. Then he and Sir Charles Trevelyan produced a seminal Report on the Civil Service (1854), which recommended entry by competitive examination into a policy-making stream; the outstanding quality of the British Civil Service springs from this Report. Northcote also, as a member of the Public Accounts Committee, exposed some of the shambles of the old administrative machinery. He

was one of the Peelites who moved back into the Conservative Party. Disraeli organized him into the pocket borough of Stamford in 1858, and Northcote became his loyal adviser, valuable as a tactful moderate and a capable financier. Briefly President of the Board of Trade and Secretary for India, he became Chancellor of the Exchequer, where Disraeli had wanted him, in 1874. There he cut income tax and created a new Sinking Fund to reduce the National Debt.

So far a happy and worthy story. But when he took over as leader in the Commons after Disraeli became Lord Beaconsfield, his lacklustre oratory, which had benefited little from lessons in elocution, depressed a Party which had been used to their Chief's stylish defusing of the Gladstone thunderbolts. When Beaconsfield died, Northcote and Salisbury shared the Party leadership. Northcote had a lingering reverence for Gladstone, and believed in selective and constructive opposition. But the 'Fourth Party' on the Conservative back benches, led by Lord Randolph Churchill, who nicknamed him 'the Goat' because of his long beard, soon made his life humiliatingly uncomfortable. The next Conservative government was therefore led by Salisbury. Northcote retreated to the Lords as Foreign Secretary. In 1887 he learnt through reading a newspaper that he had finally lost his place in the Cabinet. Very soon afterwards, he had a heart attack in the ante-room of 10 Downing Street, and died in the presence of the prime minister.

NOTHELM (*d.*739) was Archbishop of Canterbury from 735 until 739. While he was a priest in London Nothelm was employed by Albinus of Canterbury to convey to Bede information about the early history of the church in Kent. Afterwards Nothelm visited Rome, probably between 715 and 725, and transcribed letters from the papal archives, which also he took to Bede for use in the preparation of the *Ecclesiastical History*. Bede recorded his gratitude to Nothelm in the preface. In 735 Nothelm was consecrated Archbishop of Canterbury. Little is known of his brief archiepiscopate. He visited Rome again in 736. He held a church council, probably in 737. Boniface, leader of the English mission to Germany, corresponded with him. He is remembered chiefly for the assistance he rendered to Bede.

NOWELL or NOEL, ALEXANDER (1507?-1602), Dean of St Paul's, author of much of the Prayer Book Catechism, was born perhaps in 1507 or 1508 (1506, 1510, 1511 have also been given) at Whalley, in Lancashire. He was educated at Brasenose College, Oxford, became a Fellow of the college, Public Reader of Logic in the university, and after he was ordained he became Master of Westminster School and Prebendary of the Abbey (1551). Being given a licence to preach, Nowell soon acquired a great reputation as a preacher, and during the reign of Edward VI he 'preached in some of the notablest places and auditories in the realm'. When Mary came to the throne, Nowell was returned to parliament as member for Looe in Cornwall, but he was not allowed to take his seat on the grounds that 'having a voice in Convocation' he was not eligible to sit in the House of Commons. He then went abroad and joined the Marian exiles. On Mary's death Nowell returned to England and was made Archdeacon of Middlesex, a canon of Canterbury and a canon of Westminster.

In November 1560 he was recommended by Elizabeth 'for his goodly zeal and special good learning, and other singular gifts and virtues' for election as Dean of St Paul's. Nowell soon afterwards married, and Archbishop Parker wrote that, if the queen would have a 'married minister' for Provost of Eton, there was none comparable with Nowell. The queen would not have a married minister. Some of Nowell's sermons were bold rather than tactful and he was in trouble more than once. On 1 January 1562 he placed a richly bound prayer book with pictures of the saints and martyrs on the queen's cushion in St Paul's as a New Year's gift: Elizabeth sent the verger to fetch her old book, and after the service was over she went to the vestry and soundly rated the dean for infringing her proclamation against 'images, pictures and Romish relics'. In 1564 he was preaching a Lenten sermon before the queen and spoke slightingly of the crucifix. The queen called out, 'To your text, Mr Dean – leave that, we have heard enough of that', and so confounded was Nowell that he could not finish his sermon.

His boldest sermon was that in which he took the queen to task for not marrying and providing an heir to the throne, with the queen sitting listening. 'All the queen's most noble ancestors have commonly had some issue to succeed them, but Her Majesty yet none.' ... 'If your parents had been of your mind, where had you been then?'

In 1562 he became Rector of Much Hadham, Canon of Windsor in 1594 and Principal of Brasenose in 1595. He died in 1602. He was twice married, but he had no children. He was a fine scholar, a skilful debater, a learned theologian: he was held to be an authority on educational matters and he endowed a free school at Middleton. He was also a devoted and accomplished fisherman and is said accidentally to have invented bottled ale, for when one day he was fishing in the Ash at Much Hadham he left a bottle of ale in the grass beside the river and a few days later found the contents effervescent.

Nowell is to be remembered as the author of three catechisms: (1) the 'Large Catechism' approved by Convocation in 1563 and printed in 1572; (2) the 'Middle Catechism', an abridged version of the Large; (3) the 'Small Catechism' of 1572, which was almost identical with that in the 1549 Prayer Book and of which Nowell was probably the author: he was also the author of the first part of our present catechism, the second part being added in 1604 as a shortened and altered version of Nowell's.

Further Reading
R. Churton, *Life of Nowell.*

O

OASTLER, RICHARD (1789-1861), the Factory King, was a romantic Tory Yorkshireman. Like his father before him, he was steward of the estates of the absentee Thornhill family, and lived in their mansion, Fixby Hall. There he put into practice his belief in the obligations of landowners, and kept open house for the tenants. He also proclaimed his views on such issues as Queen Caroline (pro) and the Reform Bill (anti) in stentorian tones. Wesley had taken him in his arms as a baby and blessed him, and though he became a strong churchman, he retained the Methodist's fervour. The campaign for the abolition of slavery had aroused his early enthusiasm. In 1830, a worsted manufacturer showed him that crueller things were going on in the factories of his own county. From then on, Oastler made factory reform his cause.

He was the Danton of the movement. His commitment was complete, his attacks fearless, his voice loud for the 'thousands of little children … daily compelled to labour from six in the morning to seven in the evening, with only – Britons, blush while you read it – with only thirty minutes allowed for eating and recreation'. When Whig legislation to improve conditions was restricted to cotton mills, which were less at risk from foreign competition than the woollen textiles, Oastler made the 'Fixby Hall Compact' with the Huddersfield woollen clothworkers, and started Short Time Committees to keep up the pressure from the factory floor. Later, when manufacturers were not putting into practice the small improvements which the government did extend to all factories, he incited the children to use their grandmothers' knitting needles to wreck the spindles. In Yorkshire he became The King – later The Old King.

For reformers of a different ilk he had no time. He stood apart from Robert Owen's Trade Union campaign, opposed any moves to enlarge the franchise, regarded both the spirit and the practice of the new Poor Law with disgust, and believed that Peel had sold the soul of the Tory Party to the money-loving materialists of Manchester. So he had no time for either the Chartists or the Anti Corn Law League. Thornhill dismissed him in 1838, and he spent three years in the Fleet as a debtor. Thenceforward, ill-health dogged him. But his campaigns bore fruit in the Factory Acts of 1844 and 1847: and his hierarchic philosophy, 'a place for everything and everything in its place', was taken up by Young England, and enshrined in Disraeli's novels.

Further Reading
C. H. Driver, *Tory Radical: the life of Richard Oastler*, 1946.

OATES, TITUS (1648-1705), perjurer, was born at Oakham, son of a parson who had become an Anabaptist. Expelled in his first year at Merchant Taylors School, he attended two Cambridge colleges (Caius and St John's) without attaining a degree, but he managed to get himself ordained, and in 1674 he became curate to his father, who had reverted to Anglicanism and held a living at Hastings. Before long both of them were in gaol for perjury in bringing false charges against a local schoolmaster. Titus escaped from Dover prison, spent some months as a naval Chaplain, and then became Chaplain to the Protestants in the Duke of Norfolk's household at Arundel. About this time he met Israel Tonge, a London vicar, and the two of them decided that fortune and fame were to be had by discovering and if necessary inventing Catholic, and preferably Jesuit, plots. To pick up titbits of information which would add verisimilitude to his tales, Oates haunted the coffee houses where Catholics met, and the queen's chapel in Somerset House. Then he persuaded the Catholics that he wished to be reconciled with Rome, and in 1677 was admitted to the Jesuit college, at Valladolid in Spain. After five months he was expelled, and he left Spain claiming a bogus degree as Doctor of Divinity of Salamanca. Next he managed to gain acceptance at the English Catholic seminary at St Omer, in the Netherlands, where he survived six months before expulsion.

In 1678 he was back in England, and he and Tonge set to work. The outcome was the celebrated 'Popish Plot' which, retailed to the magistrate Edmund Berry Godfrey and then to the council, and heightened in its effect by the mysterious murder of Godfrey, filled London with terror in 1678-9. The details, outlined originally in forty-three articles which Oates later expanded, included the murder of the king and the entire council, a French invasion of Ireland, a general massacre of Protestants, and the installation of the Duke of York on the throne; Oates swore that the whole project had been planned by the Jesuits at a general 'consult' at the White Horse Tavern in the Strand on 24 April 1678, at which he himself had been present. The thing was a tissue of absurdities and lies: the Jesuits had never met at the White Horse, Oates himself had been in St Omer on that date. But it was believed by nearly everybody in a London ridden with anti-Catholic prejudice, and it brought affluence and power to its inventor. This extraordinary scoundrel, short in the neck and outrageously long of chin, with his strange nasal drawl, foul language and obscene wit, unlimited in his effrontery, quickly became the man of the hour, 'the saviour of the nation'. Lodged in Whitehall, and provided with a generous salary, cheered by the mob as he went about the town dressed in full canonicals, accompanied by special guards, and ordering arrests, he dined with the king, and was fêted by Shaftesbury and the Whig aristocrats.

A series of state trials of Catholic suspects followed, with Oates as the principal witness for the prosecution, aided by a crop of lesser informers like William Bedloe. It has been estimated that in these trials some thirty-five men were judicially murdered, beginning with the execution of Coleman, the Duke of York's secretary, in December 1678. In April 1679 Oates published his *True Narrative* of the plot. In July his career of triumph was interrupted at the trial of the queen's doctor, Wakeman, when some of his lies were exposed and Chief Justice Scroggs directed the jury to acquit. Although Oates turned public fury against Scroggs, the pace of terror slowed. But it did not stop, and through 1680 Oates continued to flourish, his perjury culminating in the evidence upon which the House of Lords condemned the innocent Catholic Viscount Stafford in December. A quarrel with Tonge at a public dinner, at which each of them claimed to have invented the plot, did not discredit Oates, though it embarrassed his supporters, and the death of Tonge prevented further trouble from that quarter.

But in 1681 the tide turned against him. Oates's political importance lay in the fact that his activities provided an ideal background for the Whig campaign to exclude the Duke of York from the succession, and when that campaign collapsed at the Oxford Parliament (March 1681) his day was done. Charles's government was slow to act against one who had been so popular; and Shaftesbury and the Whig leaders were more important targets. But in 1682 Oates's pension was reduced and then stopped, and he was forbidden the court. In 1684 he was arrested under the medieval law of *Scandalum Magnatum* – whereby peers could bring a criminal action against commoners for words spoken against them – and cast in damages of £100,000 for calling the Duke of York

a traitor. And after York had come to the throne in 1685 Oates was tried and convicted for perjury. Jeffreys imposed a sentence of calculated barbarity, including deprivation of his clerical habit, a heavy fine, five appearances in the pillory annually, a whipping from Aldgate to Newgate on 20 May 1685 and a whipping from Newgate to Tyburn on 22 May, and – if he survived the whippings – imprisonment for life. The whippings were carried out mercilessly, yet Oates survived. He spent James II's reign in Newgate, where he contrived to write an anti-Catholic pamphlet and, if Anthony à Wood is to be believed, to get one of the prison bedmakers with child.

He was released shortly after the Revolution, and given a modest pension. There was little general sympathy for him: his character was too disgraceful, and his existence reminded too many men of their own weakness ten years earlier. In 1693 he married a well-to-do widow, and in 1698 the government gave him £500 to pay his debts. He became a Baptist preacher and employed his talents upon the congregation of Wapping Chapel. But he ran true to form to the end, for in 1701 the Baptists expelled him as 'a disorderly person and a hypocrite'. He died in 1705.

Further Reading
John Kenyon, *The Popish Plot*, 1972.

O'CONNELL, DANIEL (1775-1847), 'the Liberator', Irish lawyer and popular leader, was responsible, more than any other man, for the act of Catholic emancipation. To reverse the Act of Union was beyond his powers, but his campaigns for the betterment of his countrymen made him for many years 'the uncrowned king', if not of all Ireland, certainly of the Catholic peasantry of that impoverished land. He was the eldest son of Morgan O'Connell of Cahirciveen, in Kerry, and the nephew and adopted son of Maurice O'Connell of Darrynane. He was educated at Cove near Cork and then abroad, at St Omer and Douai. As a devout Catholic he was appalled by the irreligious spirit of the French revolutionaries. Back in Ireland he was called to the Bar (1798) and soon made his name in the courts as a pleader and cross-examiner. In Lecky's view he had repeal of the union in mind from the start: he brought new dimensions to the argument. Grattan had never appealed directly to priests and people. O'Connell deliberately did so. He was a tall man, of splendid appearance and voice, and he spoke to the people in their native Gaelic. He saw that the priests, mostly of peasant stock themselves, often ignorant men but the natural leaders of their villages, must be mobilized in the cause. And the masses had to be taught the value of emancipation: for the educated it meant an entrée to commissions and civil posts, for the peasant an end to oppression. Under O'Connell the peasant learned to reject the leadership of landowner and bishop. Stirring the people to action, O'Connell helped to destroy their feudal loyalties.

In 1802 he married his cousin, who gave him five sons and three daughters. He acquired a vast practice on the Munster circuit: swaggering confidence, a caustic wit and a quick eye for his opponent's weakness made him a formidable advocate. Sometimes his bold tongue got him into trouble. His attacks on 'the beggarly corporation' of Dublin (an Orange stronghold then) brought a challenge from a Mr d'Esterre; in the subsequent duel he shot his antagonist. Peel, then Secretary for Ireland, called him out later in the year, but O'Connell's wife informed on him and had him bound over to keep the peace. O'Connell comes badly out of this story. He provoked the duel, seeking political capital out of a personal challenge. His behaviour was crudely aggressive. He was known to be a good shot, who was reputed to keep his eye in by shooting stray curs when he was out riding on circuit. In Peel, the good Protestant, his behaviour aroused the greatest distaste. The incompatibility of the two men was significant. They clashed again when Peel was Home Secretary, most seriously when he became prime minister. It is to O'Connell that we owe that devastating remark about Peel – that his smile was like the gleam of silver plate on a coffin lid. He was later to attack the young Disraeli (who had already attacked him) as 'heir-in-law of the blasphemous thief who died upon the Cross'. Such was his style of controversy.

In 1823 O'Connell set up the Catholic Association to press for emancipation and repeal of the Act of Union. In 1824 he began to levy his 'Catholic rent' of one shilling a year on the members of his association. In that year he was prosecuted, and acquitted by Attorney-General Plunket, for having expressed the hope that 'another Bolivar might arise to vindicate the rights of the Irish people' (about the same time that Canning was recognizing the revolted Spanish American colonies!). The association was suppressed in 1825, whereupon it was reconstituted in new form as 'the Order of Liberators' with the object of promoting 'concord among all classes of Irishmen'. The government could no longer shelve the emancipation question: the population was rising fast and pressed grimly on land resources. There were reports of arson and brigandage from many areas; secret societies flourished and civil war seemed likely. An election in 1826 showed that tenants were beginning to assert themselves against landlords: at Waterford Lord George Beresford, whose family owned a large part of the county, was defeated by the liberal Protestant Villiers Stuart. O'Connell watched the English situation closely. It was always his policy to exploit English political differences for Irish advantages. In May 1828 Wellington had to reconstruct his Cabinet after the withdrawal of the Canningites and he put Vesey Fitzgerald, member for Clare, at the Board of Trade, which meant that he had to

seek re-election. As he was an emancipationist no difficulty was anticipated. But O'Connell chose to make this the time and place to issue a historic challenge. He stood as a Catholic candidate, received a majority (2,057 votes to 982) and thereby served notice upon the British government that, unless they were prepared to see the same thing happen in other Irish seats, they must concede Catholic emancipation.

Wellington and Peel acted to prevent the breakdown of government. Many of their followers felt betrayed. The king threatened to retire to Hanover; 142 members voted against the bill, but it was passed, in March 1829, and the king tearfully accepted what 'was considered by the Cabinet to be for the immediate interest of the country'. The government was hardly generous: the forty shilling freeholder lost the vote and the franchise was raised to £10. But except for the offices of king, regent, Lord Lieutenant of Ireland and Chancellor of England, the constitution of Great Britain was opened to Catholics. The Ascendancy did not, of course, lose its hold overnight. Nor did the reformers of the thirties appease Irish discontents. In 1831 Chief Secretary Stanley introduced a system of national education to meet the need for religious instruction. English alone was used in the new elementary schools. O'Connell approved, since he, like many of the priests, regarded Irish as an obstacle to progress. Nationalism became a more coherent political force, ironically enough, just as the distinctive Irish culture was being destroyed.

In English politics the result of the Reform Act was to create an 'Irish Party', led by O'Connell and able to hold the balance between the two parties. He personally nominated about half the candidates returned; three of his sons and two sons-in-law composed his 'household brigade'. Forty-five of 105 Irish members were 'repealers'. He fought fiercely against the Coercion Act of 1833, but tried to restrain his more impulsive followers from acting prematurely to get repeal. Melbourne won O'Connell's support by the 'Litchfield House Compact'; in return for parliament votes, he pursued a policy of conciliation. Mulgrave, the viceroy, and Drummond, his under-secretary, with O'Connell's support, attacked terrorism by means of the newly enrolled Royal Irish Constabulary. The Tithe Act of 1838, which merged tithe in rent, removed one bitter grievance. The Poor Law Act of the same year, extending to Ireland the English system, aroused O'Connell's condemnation. After Peel succeeded Melbourne in 1841 O'Connell waited until he had finished his year of office as Lord Mayor of Dublin, then redoubled his efforts to restore 'the Old House on College Green'. Vast meetings met and marched and listened spellbound to violent oratory. O'Connell believed in the weight of numbers as a political argument, but he eschewed violence. The Lord Chancellor of Ireland wrote: 'The peaceable demeanour of the assembled multitudes is one of the most alarming symptoms'. The garrison troops were reinforced; at one time there were more than in India!

On the hill of Tara a quarter of a million are said to have heard O'Connell. On 8 October 1843, the greatest meeting of all was to be held at Clontarf, where Brian Boru had routed the Norsemen 800 years earlier; belatedly the government prohibited it and barred the approaches with troops. O'Connell ordered the people to disperse and they did so peaceably. In his words, 'human blood is no cement for the temple of liberty'. He was tried for conspiracy with five others, by a Protestant jury in Dublin, and condemned. The verdict was reversed in the House of Lords in September 1844. But O'Connell lost his hold. He left prison after fourteen weeks' incarceration to find that he was being outflanked by the militants, the 'Young Ireland Party' of Davis, Duffy, Mitchell and Fintan Lalor. Some were Protestants who resented the Catholic bias of his campaign, others looked back regretfully to the principles of Grattan and Tone and sought inspiration in the Gaelic past. Many were prepared to countenance physical force in the manner of 1798. The government had been unwise to arrest O'Connell: his words had aroused the masses, but he had the courage to try to direct their protests into constitutional channels.

In January 1847 he withdrew suddenly from political life. By then he had witnessed the distressing ravages of the potato blight and the 'Great Hunger': a million of his compatriots were dead. He had seen and deplored the growth of a secular spirit: one of his last campaigns was directed against Peel's provincial non-sectarian colleges – 'Godless colleges' he called them. Everything combined to vex and harry him. His superb physique collapsed at last. He sailed to Italy to recover his health. Five months later, on 15 May 1847, he died at Genoa, on the way to Rome. His heart was taken to Rome and buried in St Agathe's. O'Connell had cut away decisively from the Irish establishment and taught the people to feel their power. It is hard to distinguish between his patriotic sentiment and love of his own voice and power. But some of the worse faults of the democratic politician cannot be attributed to him. He believed imaginatively in Ireland and in his church; he was lion-hearted and generous, a man of heroic stature.

Further Reading
R. B. McDowell, *Public Opinion and Government Policy in Ireland, 1801-46*, 1952.
D. Gwynn, *Daniel O'Connell*, 1930.

O'CONNOR, FEARGUS (1794-1855), Chartist leader, was every Englishman's idea of an Irishman. He liked to claim descent from the Kings of Connaught, and he looked the part, with his brawny figure and his red locks hanging over the collar of his coat. He had the gift of the gab, and more than a touch of the blarney. Son of a Protestant landowner who had joined the rebel United Irishmen, he was radical by nurture as well as by nature. In the midst of the rollicking life of a young squireen, he got to know leading English reformers: Burdett was his patron. In 1832 he won a sensational election victory, by unseating the traditional aristocratic family in County Cork, without financial backing, through the power of his oratory. At Westminster, he backed all the radical causes: disestablishment of the Church of Ireland, repeal of the Act of Union, and the abolition of the Poor Law, of stamp duty on newspapers, of the Combination Acts and of the press gang. When his leader, O'Connell, made his pact with the Whigs, O'Connor would have none of it – 'the moment they get to Whig Cross, they bid us goodnight' – and the Liberator eventually had to denounce his turbulent follower.

By then, O'Connor had won a reputation in the heart of industrial Britain. On speaking tours in Yorkshire and Lancashire, he stirred the men of fustian jackets and unshorn chins with his full-blooded attacks on the hated Poor Law, and all the other wrongs of the evil Malthusian society under which they suffered. 'You were charmed with the melodious voice ... the astonishing volubility ... and the gallant air of bold defiance with which he assailed all oppression and tyranny,' wrote a contemporary. He was coarse-grained enough for the roughest of listeners. So, when barracked: 'You gentlemen belong to the big-bellied, little-brained, numskull aristocracy. How dare you hiss me, you contemptible set of platter-faced, amphibious politicians?' Spicy anecdotes and inflammatory rhetoric, delivered with an enormous voice, conveyed the warmth of his sympathy towards the down-trodden of the new industrial society, the handloom weavers and the Glasgow spinners. He used the press as well as the platform. His *Northern Star*, first published in 1837, was an immediate success. By 1839 50,000 copies were being bought each week, taken into the workshops and spread around the clubs, reading rooms and taverns where working men met.

In 1838, O'Connor threw his considerable weight behind the People's Charter. He addressed nearly all the mass meetings held to elect delegates to the Chartist Convention and to get signatures for the Petition, constantly emphasizing the national nature of the movement, however varyingly local its well-springs might be. His message was that universal suffrage would open the door to all the other reforms. But it soon became apparent that there was no hope of getting this by peaceful means: and when parliament rejected the Petition, O'Connor's lead became erratic. His language was violent, but he opposed the National Holiday (general strike) as being inadequately prepared, and so without prospect of success. He was against any sort of armed rising unless it were to be fully national – which he knew to be impractical. He held torchlight meetings, with the sound of pistol shots in the background, but they were all bluff, and he steered clear of the one serious rising, at Newport. He launched a National Charter Association, but could not fund it. He gathered three million signatures for the Petition of 1842, but he had already scared off the middle-class support which was essential if it were to muster votes in parliament.

When it was rejected, he began to look elsewhere for a panacea for industrial suffering, and started the Chartist Co-operative Land Society in 1845. Members were to be given between one and four acres of land when their names came up in the ballot, in return for subscriptions varying from threepence to a shilling a week. O'Connor hoped that England would be covered with peasant smallholdings; that industrial wages would rise as the number of workers available to the factories dropped; and that the quality of life for all the working classes would be transformed. By 1847, over £80,000 had been subscribed, and six estates were bought, the first at Heronsgate, near Rickmansworth.

In 1847, O'Connor won another parliamentary seat at Nottingham, and next year, the year of revolutions in Europe, he masterminded the last great Chartist Petition. But again he baulked at violent confrontation, and when Wellington called out the troops he cancelled the mass march across the Thames from Kennington and brought the Petition to Westminster in a few cabs. From then on, it was downhill all the way. The finances of the Land Society became chaotic. The *Northern Star* had to close, and O'Connor himself lost the threads of policy, and eventually of reason, and was detained as insane. He has had a bad press from historians, and he made many enemies within the Chartist movement itself. But, warm-hearted as well as muddle-headed, he gave the Chartist movement a national focus which none of its other leaders could have achieved.

Further Reading
G. D. H. Cole, *Chartist Portraits*, new edn, 1965.

ODA (*d*.958) was Archbishop of Canterbury from 941 until his death. He was of Anglo-Scandinavian origin. The biography of his nephew Oswald by Byrhtferth of Ramsey tells us that Oda's father had come to England with the Danish army led by Halfdan in the third quarter of the ninth century. It is of great interest that a second-generation immigrant, son of a father who had presumably been born a pagan, could rise to the highest ecclesiastical office in the land; and it may have something to suggest to us about the nature of English society in the tenth century. As a young man Oda attached himself to the household of a certain Athelhelm, presumably the man of that name who was successively Bishop of Wells (909-23) and Archbishop of Canterbury (923-6). Oda's rapid rise in the English church must have owed much to the interest of so distinguished a patron. Oda accompanied Athelhelm to Rome in 923 and shortly after his return was promoted by King Athelstan to the bishopric of Ramsbury. As tenth-century bishops were expected to be, Oda was a diligent servant of his king. The witness-lists of charters show that he was a regular attender at the royal court. In 936 he was entrusted with a delicate diplomatic mission to France. He may have accompanied the English army to the battle of *Brunanburh* in 937. Athelstan's successor King Edmund continued to favour Oda. In 940 he negotiated a treaty with the Danish kingdom of York. In the following year Edmund promoted him to Canterbury.

Not a great deal is known of Oda's archiepiscopate, but enough evidence survives to indicate its importance. He resumed the practice of holding church councils and issuing ecclesiastical legislation, thus providing leadership and direction for the English church. He re-established a bishopric in East Anglia. Since the destruction of Christian institutions there by the Danes in the 860s – some of them, perhaps, Oda's kinsmen – the church life of the region had been supervised by the Bishop of London. However, such a situation was obviously unsatisfactory and Oda set about remedying it by re-establishing the bishopric of Elmham (which later moved to Thetford and finally to Norwich). At Canterbury Oda carried out major alterations to his cathedral church, heightening its walls by twenty feet, presumably for the insertion of a clerestory. He made important additions to Canterbury's relic collection. The body of St Wilfrid was brought from Ripon probably in 948, and at some date unknown the relics of St Ouen (or Audoin) were brought from Rouen in Normandy. Oda was a patron of learning. The deacon Frithegodus, who wrote poems in honour of these two saints in astonishingly complicated Latin, was remembered at Canterbury as a famous teacher. His name was not Old English but German, so it looks as though Oda – like King Alfred before him – looked to the continent for scholars to revive English learning.

Oda also concerned himself with monasticism. He had himself taken the monastic habit – in an act of personal piety, not as a formally professed monk – at the famous monastery of Fleury (now St Benoit-sur-Loire), possibly at the time of his embassy to France in 936. It was to Fleury that he sent his nephew Oswald for training in the monastic life. It was not by chance that it was during Oda's archiepiscopate that his friend King Edmund initiated the monastic revival by appointing Dunstan Abbot of Glastonbury; and that Edmund's successor Eadred followed this up by appointing Ethelwold Abbot of Abingdon. It is possible that Oda intended to refound the monastery of Ely. He received a generous grant of land there, enough to endow a monastic house, from King Eadwig in 957. But whatever plans he may have had for

Ely were cut short by his death in 958.

The great trio of reforming churchmen in the second half of the tenth century, Dunstan, Ethelwold and Oswald, did not start from scratch. They built upon foundations laid by the prelates of the generation preceding their own, among whom Oda was the most distinguished.

Further Reading
Oda deserves more attention than he has yet received from historians. For the present, see the few pages devoted to him in N. Brooks, *The Early History of the Church of Canterbury*, 1984.

ODO (*d.*1200; Abbot of Battle 1175-1200) provides an example of the two faces medieval abbots can show posterity. For the writer of the *Chronicle of Battle Abbey*, Odo was a figure of spiritual power, simplicity, eloquence, humility and learning, the leader who worked and ate with his community and only refrained from sleeping in the common dormitory because of an unpleasant bowel condition. It is of this man that Dom David Knowles waxed lyrical: 'one of the most attractive of all those that appear in the literature of the time … had others cultivated the simplicity and sobriety of Odo the subsequent history of the monastic order in England would have been happier and more peaceful'. Yet Odo, as sub-prior and prior of the monks of Christ Church, Canterbury, played an active and distinctly equivocal, if minor role in the Becket affair. It was his business acumen as much as his sanctity that appealed to the monks of Battle when they elected him abbot in 1175. No man who twice was considered for the archbishopric of Canterbury or who provoked papal accusations of conspiracy to murder was entirely unworldly.

Already prominent in Canterbury circles by 1159, Odo became the leading figure in the Canterbury Priory at a time when all the attention was sought and taken by the secular clerks of the households of Archbishops Theobald and Becket. Yet Odo was not overawed in such company. John of Salisbury respected his quality and, in 1163, as sub-prior, Odo acted as Becket's proctor in Rome in the dispute with York. Becket's absence (1164-70) presented the monks with a severe conflict of loyalty, to their archbishop or convent. Odo seems to have been faithful to his institution. In 1166-7, he co-operated with the king's agent Richard of Ilchester and in 1167 was chosen as prior without Becket's approval. Although Odo temporarily withdrew from Christ Church in 1169, this did not spare him from coming under suspicion of collusion with the archbishop's enemies in 1170. Yet Becket's disciples were predominantly members of his household without permanent status or affiliation at Canterbury, so during the vacancy 1170-3, the convent, led by Odo, once again assumed prominence. Although passed over for Richard of Dover in 1173, Odo contin-

ued to act as Christ Church's business manager and legal spokesman. As such he attracted the notice of the monks of Battle.The abbey of Battle acted as both a war memorial and, as the justiciar Richard de Lucy observed, a symbol of Norman victory and legitimacy. As abbot, Odo continued his predecessors' defence against the Bishop of Chichester's claims to jurisdiction. Although again losing out at Canterbury to Baldwin of Ford in 1184, Odo established a reputation for holiness partly through his public sermons, in which he expounded the scriptures with clarity and style. To his monks he spoke in Latin or French; to the people he spoke in English. That we think of Odo as a saint rather than a man of affairs reflects not a dichotomy in twelfth-century monasticism so much as the slant of our records. Odo may have been an admirable man – although not all contemporaries thought so – but he was also an effective manager of a monastic community and its secular interests.

Further Reading
D. Knowles, *The Monastic Orders in England*, 1949.

ODO OF BAYEUX (early or late 1030s-97; Bishop of Bayeux 1049/50-97) was one of the most powerful men in England in the twenty years after the Norman Conquest. Although famously ambitious, ruthless and energetic, Odo's position depended on his half-brother, William the Conqueror. To him Odo owed the immensely lucrative see of Bayeux when he was still a teenager. After playing an active part in the Conquest, Odo was granted the strategically important earldom of Kent as well as vast estates throughout England which, by the 1080s, were worth over £3,000 per annum, making him the richest tenant-in-chief in the kingdom. In the king's absence, Odo regularly acted as one of his deputies in England. Unlike other magnates, Odo travelled the kingdom settling, ostensibly in the king's name, small land disputes, of which there was no shortage in the messy aftermath of conquest. His motives were hardly altruistic, his intervention in land tenure becoming notorious. As a man and a politician Odo acquired a bad reputation for luxury, vice and cruelty. Viewed objectively, he was both wealthy and efficient: he reorganized the diocese and extended the chapter at Bayeux; he proved a vigorous military commander in the north of 1080; and he increased the yield from his own demesne in England by forty per cent in twenty years. However, his power relied entirely on royal favour. Unlike the prince-bishops of the Rhineland, he had no real independence. In 1072, he lost claims to lands in Kent against Lanfranc by the judgement of a royal agent. In 1082, for reasons still obscure, but possibly connected with Odo's continental ambitions or his support for William's impatient eldest son, Robert, the king decided to destroy his brother. He was arrested and spent the rest of William's reign a prisoner at Rouen. Although restored by Rufus, Odo rebelled in 1088 with other members of the 'old guard'. His defeat led to the final confiscation of his English lands. His last years were spent on the continent, presiding over a thriving cathedral community at Bayeux. In 1095, he cut an incongruous figure at the Council of Clermont, at which Urban II proclaimed the First Crusade. Odo embodies much of what the reforming popes detested: lay appointment; secular office; a love of material wealth and power; a layman in all but dress and, perhaps, education. Nonetheless, Odo, seeing his favoured nephew lose his grasp on Normandy to Rufus, joined Robert on crusade. Odo got no further than Palermo, where he died early in 1097 while visiting a Norman soul-mate, the tough, successful adventurer Roger, the Great Count of Sicily. Odo's career touched greatness but ended in failure. His lasting achievements came from his local power: his endowment and building at Bayeux; his probable sponsorship of the Bayeux Tapestry, almost certainly embroidered in Kent; and, above all, his patronage of gifted secular clerks from Bayeux who went on to scale the heights of church and state, including three Archbishops of York (Thomas I, 1070-1100; Thomas II, 1109-14; Thurstan 1114-40); William of St Calais, Bishop of Durham (1080-97), the compiler of the Domesday Book; and Ranulf Flambard, Rufus's feared chief minister. They formed a fitting epitaph for a man described a generation later as 'more given to wordly affairs than spiritual contemplation'.

Further Reading
D. Bates, 'Odo of Bayeux', *Speculum*, 1975.

OFFA (*d*.796) was King of Mercia from 757 until 796, the builder of the biggest earthwork in early medieval Europe – Offa's Dyke – and by common consent the most imposing Anglo-Saxon ruler before Alfred. Like Ethelbald, his predecessor as King of Mercia, Offa claimed descent from a brother of King Penda. He fought his way to the kingship of Mercia against a rival named Beornred in 757. Mercian hegemony over southern England had crumbled after Ethelbald's murder. Offa gradually put it together again. He seems to have established lordship over Kent by 764 and over Sussex by 771. Beorhtric of Wessex (786-802) was a client-king who married one of Offa's daughters – often a token of political subjection – in 789. Offa had power over East Anglia, and even Northumbria may have submitted to him, for its king, Ethelred, married another of Offa's daughters in 792. From 774 onwards he was frequently styled *Rex Anglorum*, 'King of the English', in his charters. Like any other ruler of his age, Offa had to fight hard to achieve and maintain his supremacy. Kent caused him a great deal of trouble: Offa's army was defeated at Otford in 776 and from then for perhaps as much as nine years Mercian ascendancy over Kent was

suspended. Offa exiled Egbert, an anti-Mercian claimant to the kingdom of Wessex. He executed a King of East Anglia, Ethelbert, later to be venerated as a saint, in 794. He extinguished local dynasties in small kingdoms such as Sussex and Lindsey.

Thus far, Offa looks like any successful warlord. But there was more to him than this. Consider first the Dyke. Offa's Dyke is an earthwork defining the frontier between Mercians and Welsh, consisting of a ditch to the west and a bank which originally rose up to twenty-five feet high to the east, the whole being about sixty feet wide. The bank may have been surmounted by a wooden palisade, possibly even in some places by a stone wall. The frontier it defined or defended was about 150 miles long: twice as long as the frontier guarded by the Wall of Hadrian. It was an astonishing achievement, not simply in physical but also in organizational terms. Its administrative implications are thought-provoking: speculation continues. It was no ordinary king who could plan and execute a work of engineering on this scale. (For comparison: Charlemagne planned and began the digging of a canal to link the rivers Danube and Main in 793; the project was abandoned before 1,000 metres had been dug.)

The same impression of order and efficiency, of a government which could make plans and then carry them through, is suggested by Offa's coinage. In the third quarter of the eighth century the Kings of Kent began to issue a new coinage of silver pennies (or *denarii*), partly modelled on new Frankish coins and differing in weight, fineness and design from previous Anglo-Saxon issues. When Offa re-established his control of Kent in about 785 he took over the mint at Canterbury and had its moneyers start striking coin in his name. There were several other mints which struck for him, in Mercia, East Anglia and Wessex. When early in the 790s Charlemagne slightly increased the weight of the Frankish penny, Offa followed suit in England. These developments are evidenced by the surviving coins themselves. They constitute unimpeachable testimony to firm royal control over the coinage.

The existence of the mint at Canterbury was one reason why Offa was so eager to maintain control of Kent. Another was the presence of the archbishopric. Archbishop Jaenberht (765-92) was probably among the leaders of Kentish opposition to Offa in the 770s and 780s. Offa's riposte was drastic. A papal legation visited England in 786 and was brought to sanction a revolution in English ecclesiastical organization. In the following year, at a church council described as 'contentious', Offa forced through a decision to raise the bishopric of Lichfield to archiepiscopal rank. This created a new metropolitan province in the Mercian territory of midland England – at the expense of Canterbury. The archbishopric of Lichfield did not last long – it was wound up shortly after Offa's death, in the years 801-3 – but while it did it materially increased Offa's power over the church. One of its first-fruits was the anointing of his son Ecgfrith as king in 787. This was the first time, as far as we know, that a king's son had been anointed in England. Offa was probably copying the example of Charlemagne who had had his sons anointed in 781. The purpose was clear: Offa was trying to establish his dynasty as a hereditary monarchy hedged about with the sanction of the most solemn Christian ritual. (It is of some interest that the genealogy of the Mercian royal family seems to have been recorded in writing for the first time, at Lichfield, at about this date.)

Offa's desire to secure a Mercian archbishopric was not simply political. The multiplication of metropolitan or archiepiscopal provinces in the interests of pastoral efficiency was a concern of contemporary reformers in Charlemagne's realm, among whom, we should remember, there were Englishmen known to Offa, such as Alcuin – who had accompanied the papal legates to Offa's court in 786. Offa was a responsible Christian ruler. The council which he held with the legates enacted reforming legislation. He founded monasteries, for example at St Albans. He embellished the tomb of St Oswald – and his interest in the cult of a saint who was a soldier-king is noteworthy. Offa is known to have possessed a copy of the *Ecclesiastical History* of Bede, and that work may have influenced his thinking about kingship. Stray references and survivals indicate a flourishing Christian culture in eighth- and ninth-century Mercia. It is sobering to consider how different Offa's Mercia might look to us had one of the great midland monasteries Repton, say, or Breedon – produced a continuator of Bede to tell us about it. If any such work were produced it must have perished in the wreckage of Mercian culture inflicted by the Vikings.

We can sense, then, a certain statesmanlike quality about Offa, co-existing – not necessarily uneasily – with the warlord roistering with his thegns about him in his mead-hall. This impression of shrewdness and sophistication is borne out by what we know of his dealings with Charlemagne. Anglo-Frankish contacts were undoubtedly more intense than the surviving sources show. Cross-Channel trade was even more important in Offa's day than it had been in the time of Ine or Ethelbald. If, as seems likely, there were something in the order of five million silver pennies of Offa in circulation in England about the year 790, we must ask ourselves where the bullion came from, for English native deposits of silver are negligible. Commodities must have been exported to cause an influx of silver in return. Fortunately we know from a letter of Charlemagne to Offa in 796 that English textiles were exported to Francia. It is our first certain evidence of what was to become one of the great staples of English commercial life – the export of wool or woollen cloth yielded by English sheep. That Charlemagne and Offa could correspond about trade is another indication of its importance. They were in contact with each other about other matters: the possibility of a marriage alliance, the harbouring of English political exiles in Francia, the exchange of diplomatic gifts, the passage of pilgrims to Rome through Frankish territory, and so forth. Frankish churchmen attended the English church council of 786; English churchmen attended Charlemagne's council of Frankfurt in 794. Of course, the Francia of Charlemagne was a vastly bigger affair than the Mercia of Offa; but not necessarily a more complex one. As kings, Offa and Charlemagne were cast in similar moulds.

Further Reading
Although there is a large periodical literature devoted to Offa there is as yet no modern book on him: in its absence, the reader may turn to the fine chapter in J. M. Wallace-Hadrill, *Early Germanic Kingship*, 1971.

OKEY, JOHN (1606-62) was a ship's chandler who was Colonel of a regiment of dragoons at Naseby (the only dragoons in the New Model) and who signed the death-warrant of Charles I. In 1649 the University of Oxford made him a Master of Arts after he had crushed the Leveller mutineers at Burford. He took part in Cromwell's Scottish campaign of 1650-1, and was prominent in the storming of Dundee. In 1654 he was a member of the first Protectorate parliament, and he was one of the Three Colonels (the others were Alured and Saunders) who put forward a petition against the Instrument of Government, asking for the summons of a full and free parliament. As a result he was court-martialled, and although he was acquitted of treason he lost his commission. He was a member of Richard Cromwell's parliament of 1659. In 1660 he fled abroad. Two years later he was captured at Delft through the agency of Sir George Downing (Pepys thought Downing behaved 'like a perfidious rogue'), brought home and tried as a regicide, and hanged, drawn and quartered. Okey, an Anabaptist and a diehard Republican, was a man of courage and cheerfulness, as his account of the battle of Naseby suggests.

Further Reading
H. G. Tibbutt, *Colonel John Okey, 1606-1662*, 1955 (Bedfordshire Historical Record Society, vol. XXXV).

OLDCASTLE, SIR JOHN, LORD COBHAM (*c*.1378-1417) led the first Lollard revolt in 1414 and was burnt as a heretic in 1417. Yet his origins were quite conventional. The Oldcastles were substantial gentry in Herefordshire and John was not the first to be a knight, sheriff or MP. That Marcher gentry were remote from central government is shown by his presence in the Scottish campaign in 1400 in the retinue of a minor nobleman Lord Grey of Codnor. The Welsh revolt of Owen Glendower made such men strategically important. Oldcastle knew Wales: his seat at Almeley was on the western edge of Herefordshire, his wife had a Welsh name, and so he could probably speak Welsh too. A succession of campaigns, custodies of castles, and commissions brought Oldcastle the favour and friendship of the future Henry V and a European chivalric reputation. Hence his part in jousts at Lille in 1410 and in the Burgundian victory at St Cloud next year. Hence also his choice as fourth husband of the great heiress Joan de la Pole and his acquisition in her right of the title Lord Cobham and extensive Kentish properties including the new castle of Cooling. No longer an obscure Herefordshire squire, Oldcastle was an important magnate. A dazzling military career with Henry V beckoned.

Presumably already a Lollard in Herefordshire, Oldcastle was certainly one in Kent. He was literate and acquainted with Lollard doctrine, which he could expound at length; he owned and read Lollard tracts; he harboured Lollards in his household; and he condoned attempts to convert his tenants and neighbours. He was thus a late example of the Lollard knights so important under Richard II and it was apparently 'His social position rather than any peculiar fitness (that) made him the leader of the Lollard party'. He had apparently attained this position by 1409, when he was corresponding with the Hussites in Bohemia. When his Lollard connections came out in 1413 and the clergy wished to try him, Henry V offered him time to reconsider. Oldcastle, however, was adamant and scorned to recant. Although given every chance to withdraw, Archbishop Arundel found in Oldcastle a Lollard of principle and foolhardy courage, whose temper several times betrayed him into heretical outbursts. Repeatedly pressed, he denounced the pope as the head of Antichrist, the archbishops and bishops as his limbs, and the friars as his tail. Even after his condemnation, Henry V postponed his execution, hoping for recantation. Instead Oldcastle was rescued from the Tower, hid in London, and organized his rebellion. This was designed to capture the king. What else was intended is unknown: the authorities thought that it aimed to kill the royal family, the nobility and clergy, and divide England into smaller principalities. The plot was exposed, the few hundred insurgents were easily defeated, but Oldcastle himself escaped. His last years were spent in hiding: in the West Midlands in 1415 and in 1417 near Welshpool. There he was overpowered and thence he was taken to London for execution.

That Lollardy was a sect with an organization and structure is suggested by what we know of Lollard texts. These were systematically researched and written, apparently at Oxford, mass-produced and distributed to Lollard congregations, all of which thus shared the same beliefs. By purging Oxford, Archbishop Arundel destroyed academic Lollardy and ended Lollard book production. Oldcastle apparently used the Lollard communication network to enlist support in many cells and exposed them to persecution. He revealed them to be few and humble, nothing for the king to fear, and by identifying them with treason he discredited them with the propertied élite. After Oldcastle and his friends, no noblemen nor gentry are known to have been Lollards. The movement degenerated into isolated cells, secret and humble, often out of touch with one another. Its organization was destroyed.

Further Reading

K. B. McFarlane, *John Wycliffe and the Beginnings of English Nonconformity*, 1952.

W. T. Waugh, 'Sir John Oldcastle', *English Historical Review* lv, 1940.

ORDERIC VITALIS (1075-1142/3), author of the *Ecclesiastical History of England and Normandy*, was one of the most important chroniclers of the Anglo-Norman empire, a union he embodied in his own life. He was born at Atcham, near Shrewsbury, but spent the whole of his career as a monk at the Norman abbey of St Evroul. Orderic's father, Odelerius, was a Frenchman who had come to England to increase his fortune with Roger de Montgomery between 1066 and 1068. His mother was English and, as must have been common for children of such mixed marriages, until he was ten Orderic probably knew no French. His separation from his family in 1085 left its emotional scars. Over fifty years later Orderic recalled the moment when his father 'weeping … gave me, a weeping child, into the care of the monk Reginald, and sent me away into exile for love of God, and never saw me again. And so, a boy of ten, I crossed the English channel and came into Normandy as an exile, unknown to all, knowing no-one.' The habit of sending children away, tenacious in the English upper classes, had, for Odelerius, a positive justification: 'he promised me that if I became a monk I should taste of the joys of Heaven with the Innocents after my death.' St Evroul provided Orderic with the surroundings, the books, the time and the incentive to write history, often in his own hand. The description of him as 'one of the finest calligraphers of his day', is borne out by his own holograph manuscript of the *Ecclesiastical History* which survives in the Bibliothèque Nationale in Paris. Orderic began writing history before 1109. The *Ecclesiastical History*, commissioned by the Abbot of St Evroul, was begun in 1114/15 and completed in 1141. The original scheme was to include a history of Normandy and the Normans in England to the reign of Henry I. In 1136, he added two books of universal history and, at about the same time, inserted a digest of earlier Anglo-French history. He also included, at the request of the monks of Crowland whom he visited in

1115, 'Lives' of their patron, St Guthlac (*d.c.*714), and their benefactor, Waltheof (*d.*1076). Certain passages were revised in 1141. Initially conceived for the community of St Evroul, as it grew the *Ecclesiastical History* became a history of the Normans for the Normans. Orderic's main inspiration was Bede's *Ecclesiastical History*, of which he made his own copy. His researches were extensive: documents; over fifty literary sources; and oral evidence. St Evroul attracted important visitors and Orderic himself travelled in Normandy, England and France gathering material. Safe in his cloister, Orderic attacked the lax morals of courtiers and nobles, writing with some objectivity about the Anglo-Norman kings. Like Bede, he was careful to establish the provenance of his oral information: for example his information on the White Ship disaster (1120) came from the sole survivor, Berold, a butcher from Rouen, who apparently did the rounds of the duchy relating his ordeal to packed houses. Orderic's attitude to the English was understandably equivocal: he attacked the violence and greed of the Norman conquerors; but condemned the English as degenerate and justified the Conquest as providing necessary church reform. Orderic's vision of the secular world is in the mainstream of Christian historiography: the wages of sin are death; there is no help in this world even for the most powerful. Thus, in a typically vivid passage, William the Conqueror's naked, abandoned and rotting corpse testifies to the transience of earthly glory. History was didactic, a series of examples to inspire men to reform their lives. Anglo-Norman society gave Orderic plenty of scope.

Further Reading
M. Chibnall, ed. and trans., *The Ecclesiastical History of Orderic Vitalis*, 1969-80.

ORLETON, ADAM (*c.*1275-1345), Bishop of Hereford (1317-27), Worcester (1327-33) and Winchester (1333-45), was one of the first bishops to be translated (moved) from one see (bishopric) to another. Later a commonplace way of promotion to richer sees, at first it led to charges of greedy careerism, particularly as Orleton's appointments were made against royal wishes by Pope John XXII while he was on missions to the papal Curia. Greed, however, is not the only or perhaps even one explanation. It was papal policy to foster translations and thus strengthen papal control over appointments and increase papal revenue. John XXII was a lawyer who favoured lawyers, particularly Orleton, who had elevated views of the dignity of popes and bishops. A strong pope, he frequently overrode the weak kings with whom he coincided. Later the balance of power shifted decisively, so that popes were reduced to confirming nominees that they did not approve.

Orleton's origins are exceptionally obscure. Born somewhere in Herefordshire and educated at an unknown university, he was an MA by 1301 and a doctor of canon law by 1307. Law, so useful for the government of church and state, became increasingly the route to advancement in the church and theologians were restricted at best to peripheral and poorer sees. Orleton's legal expertise was appreciated simultaneously by the Bishop of Hereford (1311-13), the future Archbishop Reynolds as Bishop of Worcester (1311), as official to the Bishop of Winchester (1312-15) and as a royal diplomat from 1307. Such service took him to the papal Curia and General Council of the church at Vienne, where in 1311 he was made a papal chaplain. Later he became an auditor of the sacred palace, and ultimately a bishop.

Lawyer-bishops are often charged with legalism rather than a genuine concern for souls, but this is not true of Orleton. Inevitably often on diplomatic business before 1336 and increasingly ill thereafter, 'at many points Orleton is to be found engaged in parochial, judicial and administrative activity'. Visitations, monastic reform, the suppression of illicit pluralism, the encouragement of study, defence of episcopal rights, confirmations and preaching are all recorded. The high point of his episcopal career was the canonization of Thomas Cantelupe in 1320.

Orleton's reputation has suffered from the enmity of one particular chronicler. Most charges against him are demonstrably unfounded and indeed exaggerate his importance. It is clear that he was never a politician of the front rank. If he did meet Mortimer in 1322, it was not necessarily treasonable, and he was only tried on Mortimer's escape. His conviction proves nothing, for he did not plead, claiming immunity as bishop, and the king shamelessly manipulated the process. His lands and chattels were seized. He hoped for reconciliation and did not plot, but he joined Isabella and Mortimer before victory was assured. Briefly their treasurer, he was sent to the Curia, where he was again promoted. Mortimer's anger at this resembled Edward II's in 1317 and 1333, when Archbishop Stratford was also hostile. Hence, perhaps, Orleton's last brief public appearance to attack Stratford in 1340-1. Blind by then, he resided continually at Farnham Castle and had a coadjutor to assist him with his duties.

Further Reading
R. M. Haines, *Church and Politics in the Fourteenth Century: The Career of Adam Orleton c.1275-1345*, 1978.

OSBORNE, SIR THOMAS, 1st EARL OF DANBY (1632-1712), statesman, was a Yorkshireman from Kiveton, whose father had been Vice-President of the Council of the North under Wentworth and a royalist in the Civil War. He succeeded to the baronetcy and estates in 1647. His neighbour Buckingham was his patron in his early career. In 1665 he became MP for York, in 1668 joint Treasurer and in 1671 sole Treasurer of the Navy, and in 1673 Lord Treasurer. Created Earl of Danby in 1674, he was evidently chief minister by 1675. This rapid rise resulted in part from a plausible manner, not unwelcome to the king in the days of Buckingham and Shaftesbury. Behind this, and far more important at a time of chronic monetary difficulty for the Crown, lay astute financial skill and business competence. After paying off the navy's debts and reorganizing its accounting, Danby as Lord Treasurer set about a policy of retrenchment. He reduced the rate of interest on government loans, secured stricter control over the customs farmers and more favourable terms from the excise farmers, and increased the yield of the hereditary revenues. This policy was highly acceptable to Charles II, for, besides its material returns, which were boosted by an improvement in trade in the mid-1670s, it pointed towards the financial independence of the Crown.

Danby used the whole patronage of the Crown – honours, offices, promotions, contracts – to build up a Court party with a numerical majority, especially in the Commons. Yet his policy was not merely financial, nor were its foundations solely material. He wanted a strong monarchy based upon traditional Cavalier loyalty and uncompromising Anglicanism, and this meant firm enforcement of the penal laws against Dissenters and Catholics. Abroad he was anti-French, reversing the policy hatched at Dover in 1670. Thus the Third Dutch War came to an end in 1674, and in 1677 Danby arranged the master-stroke of his term of office, the marriage of William and Mary. Yet the very success of this policy created enemies on every hand, ranging from Louis XIV to the Country party in parliament, men who saw a rising threat of royal absolutism. Proud, avaricious and smooth, Danby never enjoyed popularity or widespread trust. Moreover, like every minister for almost a century to come, he was at the mercy of his Sovereign. Despite his own anti-French views, he had taken part in the king's secret negotiations to secure a subsidy from Louis XIV, and in their course written to Ralph Montagu, the English ambassador in Paris, letters which in certain circumstances might be highly incriminating.

In 1678 these circumstances came about, when the Popish Plot created an atmosphere of wild anti-Catholicism and political irrationality. From the start Danby blundered in his handling of the Plot; he showed scepticism about Oates and Tonge, and allowed his opponents led by Shaftesbury to seize the tremendous weapon it offered. The unholy alliance of Louis XIV and the Country party against Danby found its opportunity in the dismissal of Ralph Montagu from his embassy in 1678. In return for a French pension, Montagu produced Danby's letters before the Commons, and the minister was impeached on a variety of charges, including one to the effect that he was a papist sympathizer and had con-

cealed evidence about the Plot. Charles, behind whom Danby made no effort to shelter, tried to save him by dissolving parliament and by removing him from office (1679), but the newly-elected Commons proceeded to attainder. In the upshot Danby was sent to the Tower and stayed there until 1684, hated as much by James, Duke of York and by 'high' Tories like Rochester as by the Whigs.

His career seemed over. After his release he lived largely in retirement, either in Yorkshire or in his mansion at Wimbledon. Nevertheless, as the architect of the Orange marriage of 1677, with all its implications for the safeguarding of English Protestantism, Danby could not be other than an opponent of James II's Catholicizing despotism. In 1687 he was in touch with William through the latter's agent Dykveld, and in 1688 he was one of the seven signatories of the famous invitation. Nor did he fail in action in the crisis of that autumn. It was Danby, full of schemes and energy, who brought the north of England out on William's side, outwitting James's supporters and seizing the city of York. No Whig in outlook, Danby wanted Mary to be regent, but found himself compelled to accept the joint sovereignty. His reward was great: in 1689 he was created Marquis of Carmarthen and appointed Lord President of the Council, and he received an imposing array of powers and dignities in the three Ridings of his native county. Moreover, from 1690 to 1694 he was once more the chief minister of the Crown, responsible for the government of England during William's frequent absences on campaign in Ireland and in Flanders. Once again his old unpopularity appeared. He quarrelled with Halifax, the Whigs denounced him, he was lampooned as 'Tom the Tyrant', and he eventually ceased to be of much use to William. Once again, in 1694, he was impeached, this time on a charge of receiving a bribe of 5,000 guineas to obtain a new charter for the East India Company, and although the impeachment came to nothing it marked the end of Danby's political greatness. He hung on to the Lord Presidency until he was dismissed in 1699, and he continued to appear in the Lords from time to time. As late as 1710 he spoke in debate, on the Sacheverell affair. He was over eighty when he died in 1712.

Danby died a duke: in 1694 'the white Marquis' of Carmarthen, as he was called from the dead-white pallor of his face, was translated into the Duke of Leeds. This enthusiasm for outward honours suggests why men disliked him. Danby was vain, pompous, too obviously fond of money; and, like Walpole, he distrusted colleagues with ability. In a sense both parts of his career ended in failure, the first in a spell in the Tower, the second in lasting neglect. Yet his importance in English history is great, and his services to his country are often overlooked. First, in the reign of Charles II he was a minister of a new kind, illustrating, in the words of

David Ogg, 'the change whereby the purse-bearer displaced confessor, favourite and lawyer'.* He was a business minister, the forerunner of Walpole, whom he anticipated in reliance on a blend of corruption and common sense. Secondly, his support of the House of Orange, in 1677 and 1688, was of decisive consequence for the liberties of Englishmen. Even James II recognized this, when in 1692 he included Danby among the few men whom he was not prepared to pardon. It would be unjust to deny him the title of patriot. Thirdly, he has a significant, though somewhat ambiguous, role in the history of political party in England. He led the 'court' party of the 1670s as an alliance between Crown and church, thus establishing an age-long 'Tory' tradition. He was a successful pioneer in the craft of political management. And it might even be held that Danby did more than anyone else to stimulate the Whig party into existence, by presenting the Commons with a profound constitutional challenge in the 1670s.

Further Reading
A. Browning, *Life and Letters of Sir Thomas Osborne, Earl of Danby*, 3 vols, 1944-51 (vol. I contains the *Life*).

OSMUND OF SALISBURY (*d.*1099; Bishop of Salisbury 1078-99) was probably a distant relative of William the Conqueror whom he accompanied to England as a chaplain. From c.1070-8 he was the king's chancellor, head of the small writing office which drew up royal documents, mainly charters and writs. Described in the Northamptonshire Geld Roll (*c.*1070/78) as the king's *writere*, it is even possible that during his chancellorship he was effectively the sole court scribe, the rest of the writing for the government being farmed out to cathedral and monastic scriptoria. Certainly, William of Malmesbury later described Osmund as bookish who, even as bishop, 'did not disdain writing or binding books'. In his time as chancellor, Latin fully replaced English as the sole official language of government. Following almost invariable custom, Osmund's reward for his services came in the form of a bishopric. At Salisbury (what is now Old Sarum), he built a new cathedral and reformed the cathedral chapter, installing a hierarchy of officials and thirty-two secular canons. Osmund does not appear to have played a very prominent part in national or ecclesiastical politics. However, he was closely involved in planning Domesday Book, probably being a commissioner for the survey of south-western counties, now contained in the so-called Exon Domesday which may have been written at the Salisbury scriptorium. Of even more lasting significance was his institution of new orders for liturgical services, the so-called 'Use of Sarum', a compilation designed to establish uniformity of worship. Whether or not it was introduced in response

to the reluctance of English clergy to adopt Norman styles of chanting, the Sarum Use, with emendations especially in the thirteenth century, came to dominate the liturgy of the English church for the rest of the Middle Ages. When Osmund was finally canonized in 1457, the work he had started almost four centuries before had left an indelible mark on the religious life of his adopted country.

OSWALD, ST (*d.*642) was the son of King Ethelfrith and King of Northumbria from 634 to 642. During the reign of Edwin he lived in exile among the Irish and the Picts. In the course of this exile he was converted to Christianity through the agency of the Irish-Scottish churchmen of Columba's monastery of Iona. In 634 he returned to Northumbria and defeated and killed Edwin's slayer, Cadwalla of Gwynedd, near Hexham.

According to Bede, Oswald exercised an overlordship even more extensive than Edwin's. To the peoples under Edwin's sway he added lordship over the Irish settled in western Scotland and over the Picts. His authority in Wessex is indicated by his co-operation in the establishment there of Bishop Birinus in about 635. But Bede presented Oswald as much more than just a powerful king. He was 'beloved by God', a saint as well as a king, the model of what a Christian ruler should be. Not only was he active in the spreading of the faith – for example, by bringing Aidan to Northumbria – but he was notable also for his exercise of Christian virtues, humility, charity, piety. He won victories under the sign of the Cross. It was because he was so good a Christian, Bede seems to urge (no doubt with an eye to the somewhat less than godly kings of his own day), that he was so great a king. Bede could present his death in battle at the hands of Penda, probably near Oswestry in Shropshire, as a kind of martyrdom.

After his death his cult was promoted partly under the influence of Wilfrid, partly through the actions of King Oswy of Northumbria and his daughter Osthryth. The cult mattered to the family: a royal saint could shed lustre on a dynasty. Oswald's miracle-working relics became a focus of eager interest. His head was buried at Lindisfarne; the skull found inside the coffin of St Cuthbert when it was opened in 1827 was probably his. His hands and arms were buried at the royal residence of Bamburgh. The rest of his body was laid in a shrine at the monastery of Bardney in Lincolnshire. Early in the tenth century the Bardney relics were removed to Gloucester by Ethelflaed, the daughter of King Alfred, where the church of St Oswald which she built in the saint's honour has recently been excavated. Meanwhile the cult of Oswald had been exported to the continent by English missionary churchmen such as Willibrord. Throughout the Middle Ages and beyond Oswald remained a popular saint in Germany and Italy.

*D. Ogg, *England in the Reign of Charles II*, 1956 edn, vol. II, p.527.

OSWALD, ST (*d*.992), Bishop of Worcester and Archbishop of York, was together with Dunstan and Ethelwold a member of the trio of ecclesiastical reformers who dominated English church life in the second half of the tenth century. Like the other two men Oswald was well-connected: Archbishop Oda of Canterbury was his uncle. Oswald was probably a native of the eastern Danelaw. He received a good education, though we do not know where. His uncle Oda's patronage enabled him to buy – yes: a strong whiff of an unreformed church – a minster church in Winchester and he settled among the community of clergy attached to it. He could hardly have failed to make the acquaintance of Dunstan and Ethelwold who were both much at court in this the first city in the kingdom and recipients of the patronage of Bishop Elfheah of Winchester. After some time Oswald desired to go abroad to learn the true principles of the monastic life. Oda advised him to go to the celebrated monastery of Fleury, on the Loire, where he himself had adopted the monastic habit, probably in 936. Fleury, recently reformed under the influence of Cluny, was at the height of its renown as a model monastic house following the Rule of St Benedict, whose mortal remains, removed from Monte Cassino to Fleury in the seventh century, were a focus of pilgrimage. Dates in Oswald's early life are non-existent. He probably went to Fleury in the first half of the 950s, when he was perhaps aged about thirty.

After some years at Fleury Oswald decided to return to England to teach true monastic observance there. On his arrival back in his native land Oswald found that his uncle Oda had just died (2 June 958), so he addressed himself instead to Oscytel, Archbishop of York (956-71), who was another kinsman. Oscytel brought him and Dunstan together. It was Dunstan who was responsible for Oswald's promotion to the bishopric he had recently vacated, Worcester, in 961.

Oswald remained Bishop of Worcester for the rest of his life. To it he added the archbishopric of York in 972, holding the two sees in plurality for twenty years. Much of his energies went into monastic foundations. The first monastery he established was at Westbury-on-Trim, in the extreme south of his diocese, in 963. It was followed by several more in the diocese of Worcester over the next few years – Evesham, Pershore, Winchcombe and perhaps Deerhurst. At Worcester itself Oswald gradually transformed his cathedral chapter into a monastic priory, as Ethelwold had done at Winchester in 964. Outside the diocese his most famous foundation was at Ramsey in the Fens in 968: the initial endowments were provided by Ethelwine, Ealdorman of East Anglia from 962 to 992, one of the sons of Athelstan Half-King. Oswald was probably involved in the refoundation of Crowland – formerly the hermitage of St Guthlac – whose first abbot was another kinsman. He may have tried, though unsuccessfully, to re-establish Northumbrian monastic life at

Ripon. At several of these houses the influence of Fleury can be detected. Germanus, an Englishman who had been at Fleury with Oswald, was the first Prior of Ramsey and went on to become the first Abbot of Winchcombe. Abbo, a prominent monastic reformer and intellectual, later to be Abbot of Fleury from 988 to 1004, spent two years teaching at Ramsey (985-7) where he composed his life of St Edmund, the East Anglian king killed by the Danes in 870. (Abbo was murdered by the monks of La Réole in Gascony who were reluctant to accept his reforms: a reminder that the career of a tenth-century monastic reformer could be dangerous.) Monks from Fleury advised in the drawing-up of the document known as the *Regularis Concordia*, commissioned by Ethelwold of Winchester, which laid down the rule of life to be observed in the reformed English monasteries.

A large number of documents, for the most part leases of land, issued by Oswald while Bishop of Worcester, has survived. They are of great interest for their information about the tenure of land in later Anglo-Saxon England. They also testify to Oswald's efficiency as a man of business in the administration of Worcester's endowments. Comparable documents from York have not survived, though a few estate-surveys and memoranda about endowments suggest that Oswald was equally careful in the management of his northern diocese. Byrhtferth of Ramsey, his earliest biographer, laid stress on Oswald's energetic diocesan administration.

Oswald was a man of aristocratic temper. He was a lavish spender on his journey to Rome in 971, like Dunstan ten years beforehand. He showered gifts of books, vestments, plate upon his monasteries. At Ramsey he would feast 'royally' with plenty of wine drunk from horns chased with gold and silver to wash down the banquet. Of the gorgeous trappings of this great prelate's life little now remains. The magnificent Ramsey Psalter, now in the British Library, was probably made for him (and one of its artists, interestingly, also worked at Fleury). But we must try to be aware of these trappings. The reformers of the tenth century may at heart have been holy and humble men of God. But they moved through their world like princes. To lose sight of this is to miss more than just the style of the late Anglo-Saxon church.

Oswald's career, not surprisingly, had many features in common with those of Dunstan and Ethelwold. We can sense the presence of a group of kinsmen about him: Archbishop Oda, Archbishop Oscytel, Abbot Thurcytel of Crowland, and numerous relatives who feature as beneficiaries of or witnesses to the series of Worcester leases. Oswald was sustained by a group of kinsmen and in his turn sustained them. The same sense of a small, close-knit clique emerges from study of his network of connection among the highest circles of church and state: Dunstan, Ethelwold, Ealdorman Ethelwine, and of course King Edgar who promoted Oswald to Worcester and York and actively encouraged the establishment of the new monasteries.

Wealth, might and magnificence: powerful family clans; the forceful support of the king. This is what we can read in and sometimes between the lines of our sources. These sources were uniformly favourable to the reformers. It is always useful to ask the question, what do they *not* tell us? They drop barely any hints that the reform was not plain sailing through unruffled waters. But was there any opposition? It is easy enough to see who gained by it. Who lost?

The essential point to grasp is that the tenth-century reform was not just about monastic observance but about property-rights and patronage as well. The unreformed religious communities were for the most part closely integrated into local aristocratic society; their inmates the members of prominent local families, these families in varying degrees the beneficiaries of a legal interest in the communities' endowments. For its victims reform was often an attack on entrenched property-rights, family expectations and local sentiment. Ethelwold's expulsion of the secular chapter from Winchester in 964 was an act of expropriation without legal justification. Dunstan's mastery of the art of patronage must have disappointed expectations not just of ecclesiastical office but of material gain. Oswald's kin from eastern England who received lands on the Worcester estates in the west displaced existing tenants drawn from local gentry families. Many people suffered from the reform movement. It is not surprising that there was an anti-monastic reaction after Edgar's death.

However, the three leaders were survivors. Not for them the grim fate of Abbo of Fleury. Oswald survived the longest of them. He died on 29 February 992.

Further Reading
E. John, *Orbis Britanniae*, 1966, contains a collection of stimulating essays mainly focused on the tenth-century reform, and some specifically on Oswald's part in it.

OSWY (*d*.670) was the son of King Ethelfrith and King of Northumbria from 642 to 670. According to Bede, Oswy was the seventh Anglo-Saxon ruler to exercise overlordship: like his brother Oswald he held sway over English, Britons, Picts and Irish-Scottish. It was a supremacy for which, like other seventh-century kings, Oswy had to fight hard, not only against neighbours like Penda of Mercia whom he defeated and killed in 655, but also against princes of his own Northumbrian dynasty. In 651 he was guilty of what Bede called the shameful murder of Oswin of Deira at Gilling, where he subsequently founded a monastery in expiation for his crime in which Ceolfrith first experienced the monastic life. Oswy founded several other monasteries, notably

Whitby in 657. Whitby was closely associated with the Northumbrian royal family: its first abbess was a Northumbrian princess, Hilda; it served as a royal mausoleum – the body of King Edwin was removed there; and in 664 it was the meeting-place of the council under Oswy's presidency at which the issues between Roman and Irish churchmen which had troubled Northumbria since the time of Aidan were debated and resolved in favour of Rome. Oswy's Roman allegiance was pleasing to Bede, who tells us that the king had intended to lay aside his kingdom and travel to Rome, accompanied by Wilfrid, there to end his days; though his death in 670 prevented this. Bede also approved of Oswy's active propagation of Christianity. The king was instrumental in the conversion of Sigebert, ruler of the East Saxons, and of Peada, the son of Penda of Mercia; he took counsel with the King of Kent about the appointment of an Archbishop of Canterbury. But in the last resort Bede had his reservations. Careful as always in his choice of words, for him Oswy was a 'most noble' king but not a 'most Christian' one: Oswy was not an Oswald.

OVERBURY, SIR THOMAS (1581-1613), victim of the greatest scandal of James I's court, was the son of a landowner of Bourton-on-the-Hill in Gloucestershire. Educated at Queen's College, Oxford, and the Middle Temple, he was a good-looking, tall young man with some literary talent and an abundant natural vanity. He served in the office of the Secretary of State under Robert Cecil, who sent him to travel in France and the Low Countries; but his rise to high influence, and his doom, came through his connection with Robert Carr, later Earl of Somerset. He had first got to know Carr, a younger man than himself, and a less intelligent one, on a visit to Edinburgh in 1601, and when Carr suddenly became the favourite of James in 1607 it was to Overbury he turned as friend and confidant. As the king's devotion to Carr increased, so Overbury grew in power and in wealth as 'the man behind the favourite'. A natural careerist, he was appointed Server to the King and he became the channel through which those who wanted to use Carr's influence had to apply. He seems to have become insufferable in behaviour and generally unpopular – in the words of Bishop Goodman, 'a very witty gentleman, but truly very insolent'. In 1611 he was involved in a quarrel with the queen (who the year before had cried out on seeing Carr and Overbury strolling outside her window, 'There goes Carr and his governor') and had to flee to Paris to avoid the Tower, but was allowed to return because Carr was unable to handle the business of state without him.

The comedy of Overbury turned to melodrama when Carr fell in love with Frances, Countess of Essex. Overbury encouraged the affair, but opposed it when in 1612 the lovers decided to open the way to marriage by divorcing Frances from her husband, for he feared the replacement of his own influence over Carr by that of the Howard family to which Lady Essex belonged. As a result he incurred the hostility of the Howards, headed by the Earl of Northampton, who got Overbury put into the Tower after he had declined to go as an ambassador to Russia, and kept there while the divorce proceedings began. Lady Essex then decided to poison him, and this she finally achieved, after some ineffectual attempts, by getting sublimate of mercury put into an enema administered to him. This sordid crime was kept dark for two years, during which time Carr, created Earl of Somerset, married Lady Essex, released from her husband after divorce proceedings which James did his best to facilitate. The revelation of the truth ruined the Somersets and lowered even further the shoddy reputation of the court of James I. The murder and the discovery gave to the literary works of the victim – notably his poem 'The Wife' and his essays *The Characters* – a publicity and a fame which, on their merits, they scarcely deserved; indeed, writers of the eminence of Donne and Sir Henry Wotton found it worthwhile having their poems published with those of Overbury in order to get into print.

Further Reading
William McElwee, *The Murder of Sir Thomas Overbury*, 1952.

OVERTON, RICHARD (*fl*.1645-63), Leveller, emerged in the 1640s from a very obscure background. He had lived in Holland, he was a Baptist of unorthodox views, and he was an unlicensed printer. By 1645 he was a notorious pamphleteer, Martin Mar-Priest, who enjoyed slinging mud at Prynne and the Presbyterians as well as at Anglicans, and the first of whose tracts, *The Arraignment of Mr Persecution*, was a wide-ranging defence of toleration which demonstrated the cruelties of Protestants as well as of Papists. He had also written a piece called *Man's Mortalitie* which revealed a scepticism and materialism rare, or rarely expressed, in the seventeenth century; he held the Mortalist theology, that man's soul died with his body. With the arrest of Lilburne in 1646 Overton turned to politics, and for the three short years of the Leveller movement's existence he was one of its leading figures, probably its most vigorous exponent of Republicanism. His most characteristic pieces were *A Remonstrance of Many Thousand Citizens* (1646), perhaps the best expression of the Leveller creed, and *The Hunting of the Foxes ... By Five Small Beagles* (1649), an ironical attack on the army leaders. Arrested with Lilburne and Walwyn in 1649, Overton took the engagement to the Commonwealth. He defended Lilburne in 1653, but thenceforward turned to shadier courses, offering in 1654 to become a Commonwealth spy and joining Sexby in royalist conspiracy in 1655. Twice more he turns up, in 1659 and 1663, each time in gaol. After that no more is heard of him.

Further Reading
H. N. Brailsford, *The Levellers and the English Revolution*, 1961.
Joseph Frank, *The Levellers*, 1955.

OVERTON, ROBERT (*c*.1609-68), Cromwellian general, was a Yorkshireman from Easington who had been a student at Gray's Inn. He fought at Marston Moor for parliament and was in 1647 Governor of Hull. In 1650 he was with Cromwell at Dunbar, and for the next three years he was one of the main figures of the army of the Commonwealth in Scotland – acting as Governor of Edinburgh, conquering Orkney and Shetland, and commanding in western Scotland. From 1653 to 1654 he was back in his old post at Hull, then returned to Scotland to serve under Monck. At this point he was arrested and sent to England in connection with a mutinous movement among a group of officers in Scotland, and he remained in prison without trial, first in the Tower and later in Jersey, until 1659. It is not certain exactly what Overton had been doing. But he had made it clear to Cromwell that he disapproved of the Protectorate; he had got mixed up in the obscure plottings of the Leveller John Wildman; and he was probably a Fifth Monarchist and thus suspect to the authorities. Parliament released Overton and reappointed him to Hull in 1659. He refused obedience to Monck and after the Restoration he was again imprisoned on suspicion of being involved in Fifth Monarchy conspiracy. He spent much of the remainder of his life in prison, in the Tower, in Chepstow and finally in Jersey once more. Overton was a scholar as well as a soldier, a friend of Milton, sincere and utterly disinterested, yet evidently hesitant and uncertain in political action. A correspondent of Cromwell's wrote in Overton's defence, 'I am confident that he had never continued so obstinate if it had not been for the imperious spirit of his wife'.

Further Reading
M. Ashley, *Cromwell's Generals*, 1954.

OWAIN GLENDOWER (*c*.1354-*c*.1415) had the best claim of any Welshman to the title 'Prince of Wales'. From his mother, through the House of Deheubarth, and from his father, through the kings of Powys, Owain's descent could be traced back to Hywel Dda and beyond. His family had once fought for Llywelyn ap Gruffydd and still retained lordship over northern Powys. In 1390, Iolo Goch celebrated Owain's ancestry in verse, and helped establish his reputation as an historic representative of Welsh nationhood. But patriotic poets were less proud of more recent events.

For many years, the rulers of Powys had bought survival through clientage with the kings of England and marriage alliances with the Norman aristocracy of the March lands. One of Glendower's grandmothers was a

Lestrange. In 1328, the family had secured its estates through entail; thus, its property rights came under the protection, in theory at least, of the English state. Owain himself lived the life of a squire. He enjoyed an income of £200 a year, attended one of the Inns of Court, married the daughter of Sir David Hanmer of Flintshire, and arranged the marriage of his own daughter into the powerful Scudamore family of Herefordshire. Anxious to serve the kings of England, Owain fought in the Scottish campaign of 1385 on the side of Henry Bolingbroke, son of John of Gaunt, Duke of Lancaster. When Gaunt died in 1399, King Richard II tried to seize his estates. The resultant conflict with Bolingbroke led to Richard's deposition and murder, and to the coronation of his opponent as Henry IV, in September 1399. The following month, Bolingbroke's son, later Henry V, was invested as Prince of Wales.

His elevation was not greeted with unalloyed joy in Wales. Colonial rule in the days since the English conquest of 1282 had been especially severe under the strong monarchies of Edward I and III. Neither Edward II nor Richard II was as well able to control his squabbling magnates, and the effect was to relax somewhat the pressure of English authority in Wales. During Richard's reign, laws which discriminated on the basis of race and language were enforced rather less brutally, and more Welsh administrators were employed. These men, such as the sons of Tudur ap Goronw, supported Richard politically against parliament, and feared the consequences of his deposition. It was in these circumstances that Owain's life became part of the history of his country. As the new régime settled itself, he accused his neighbour, Reginald de Grey, Lord of Ruthin, of stealing common land. Unfortunately, Grey was a close ally of the new king. Owain could get no satisfaction from the courts, from King Henry, or from parliament. Outraged and offended, whether as a chivalrous Marcher lord or as a traditionalist Welshman, jealous at the *sarhad*, or slight, upon the honour of his family, Owain and his relations unfurled the standard of their revolt on 16 September 1400. They were quickly able to mount effective attacks on the urban centres in which English power and privilege were concentrated – on Ruthin, and then Denbigh, Flint, Oswestry and Welshpool.

The conflict was immediately sparked by jealousy between two litigious lords, but its roots lay much deeper. Many Welsh gentlemen were excluded from jobs and influence, but Owain also drew support from aggrieved lords (such as the Hanmers) of Norman descent. But his cause was no mere baronial putsch. It aroused passion and great hopes, sustaining its partisans through a decade of hardship against a much more powerful opponent. The rebels were able to tap deep wells of popular resentment. In many parts, during the years of occupation, discriminatory laws had served to nurture with grievance an older sense of Welshness. Owain seems to have sought to lend historic and cultural depth to this identity by invoking the ancient British traditions of King Arthur. There is evidence that he had sounded out potential allies outside his own area before September 1400; certainly, his followers proclaimed him Prince of Wales from the start. It seemed at first that the revolt would quickly be snuffed out. By October 1400 Henry IV had mobilized and deployed a large army, which swept all before it in north Wales. Influential rebels hastened to capitulate. Most of these were pardoned by Henry Percy, 'Hotspur', the man charged with mopping up; but the recalcitrant were ruthlessly dealt with. The official Prince Henry sat comfortably in his headquarters in Chester, whilst the unofficial Prince Owain, with by now only seven men, spent the winter in the mountains.

In the spring, however, he marched southwards into the central Pumlumon range, inspiring wide popular support, recruiting thousands of soldiers, and winning a victory over English troops at Mynydd Hyddgen. Meanwhile, in the north, his supporters Rhys and Gwilam Tudor were able to mount a successful surprise attack on Conwy castle. A new revolt around Carmarthen triggered the despatch of a new royal army, which occupied the monastery of Strata Florida in autumn 1401. But the main rebel force had already passed northwards, arriving at Carnarvon by November. From now on royal expeditions would struggle to deal with opponents practised in guerilla tactics. Owain's forces learned to refuse open combat, to use their knowledge of the terrain and the sympathy of the population to mount surprise attacks, before vanishing into the mist. But the insurgents also used coercion against their own countrymen; the struggle was a civil war. Amongst the Welsh, Owain's cause divided families, though English town-dwellers, whom colonial policy had granted trading privileges, were overwhelmingly hostile. In 1401, for the first time, many Welsh gentlemen, realizing that Owain had a real chance, threw their weight on the insurgents' side. He won support, too, from the lesser secular clergy and from the strong Cistercian houses, which operated outside the control of Canterbury. The Welsh army was chiefly composed of peasants and labourers. Owain sought to consolidate popular sympathies by ending the exactions of the Crown and its allies. The English parliament was in no doubt about the national character of the revolt. In September 1402, it introduced new and draconian penal laws, which further restricted the access of the Welsh to towns and jobs and forbade them rights of assembly.

Owain's position continued to improve. In 1402-3, as English armies were repulsed, the rebel leader was enthusiastically greeted in Glamorgan and Gwent, and dissension grew amongst the English lords. The powerful Percy family of Northumberland moved into opposition to Henry IV. In the Marches, Owain captured and ransomed Reginald de Grey and Edmund Mortimer, uncle of the dispossessed heir of Richard II. Grey's freedom was bought, but Henry refused to pay for Mortimer. Owain took rapid political advantage, securing Edmund's agreement to defend his claim in Wales and sealing the bargain with the marriage of his daughter, Catherine, to his powerful new ally. Hotspur too rebelled against Henry, though he was quickly defeated and killed at Shrewsbury in July 1403. By now, however, English forces in Wales commanded little but their garrisons and a few coastal areas. Amongst the lords and gentlemen of the Marches and in the English shires of Shropshire, Herefordshire and Gloucestershire there was sympathy for a peace with the powerful Welsh prince. In 1404, even the great stone castles of Cardiff, Aberystwyth and Harlech, which had been supplied from the sea, fell to Owain.

Now in possession of secure territory in the west, Owain was able to assemble a staff and tackle the question of finance. He summoned a parliament to Machynlleth, and was perhaps formally crowned Prince of Wales there. Efforts were made to attract international backing. Dr Gruffyd Young and John Hanmer travelled to Paris and persuaded Charles VI to send a naval expedition, though it was militarily ineffective. In February 1405 Owain and his domestic allies signed an extraordinary agreement to partition England and Wales between them. The younger Edmund Mortimer was to take the south of England and its Crown, the Percies were to rule the north and Owain Glendower was to reign in Wales and the Marches. A second parliament in Harlech, with four representatives from each commote, was called to vote money for the northern part of the enterprise. But only the Welsh third of the bloc proved effective; Mortimer was held in England and the northern rising proved abortive. An effort to enlist Scottish support also foundered. However, in 1404 a formal treaty with Charles VI of France was signed. At a synod near Machynlleth, the Welsh clergy agreed to his proposal to adhere to the Avignon papacy. Thus, in spring 1406, Young was able to contact Benedict XIII with the request that the Welsh church be governed separately, by its own Metropolitan at St David's, that revenues should be spent in the country and that its clergy should speak Welsh; two new universities would produce Welshmen of learning.

Earlier, in August 1405, a French force had landed at Milford Haven and marched as far as Worcester. But the French expedition could not easily be maintained and its internal conflicts multiplied. In 1406, continuing English military pressure resulted in the loss of coastal areas from Gower to Anglesey. Henry expelled John Trevor from St Asaph and installed his nominee in St David's.

Eventually the resources of the English state, especially its sea power, told against Owain; heavy losses, of life and property, sapped the morale of his followers; the country yearned for peace. The castles of Aberystwyth and Harlech fell in 1408-9, and men of substance increasingly came to repudiate their leader as a dangerous popular hero. Owain was once more forced into the hills; here, he was able to evade capture. His final military thrust, into Shropshire, ended with the execution of his chief lieutenants, Rhys the Black, Philip Scudamore and Rhys Tudor, though Gruffydd Young still sought support in France. In Wales, Owain was no longer a serious threat after 1410, but his rebellion survived the death in 1413 of the English king who had helped provoke it. Henry V took Owain's son Maredudd into his service, perhaps intending to force a humiliating capitulation from the father. But Owain had vanished. Historians now think he died in July 1415, perhaps in Herefordshire. But the poets of the time did not believe it; they long continued to prophesy that one day he would return to claim his country.

Further Reading
Glanmore Williams, *Owen Glendower*, 1966.

OWEN, JOHN (1616-83), Independent theologian, of Welsh stock, son of an Oxfordshire vicar, graduated at Queen's College, Oxford, and read widely in mathematics and philosophy as well as in theological studies. Hostile to the Laudian statutes, he left Oxford in 1637 and wrote tracts against Arminianism. In the 1640s he moved from Presbyterian to Independent views and in 1646 became minister of a congregation at Coggeshall in Essex. He was Chaplain to Cromwell during the campaigns in Ireland and in Scotland, and Preacher to the Council of State (1649-50), and in 1651 was intruded as Dean of Christ Church. From 1652 to 1658 he was Vice-Chancellor of Oxford and was the chief agent of the attempt to make the university Puritan. It was in part at least his doing that, in Clarendon's words, Oxford during the Commonwealth 'yielded a harvest of extraordinary good and sound knowledge in all parts of learning'. He was a firm disciplinarian, brisk in manner, though Anthony à Wood, a hostile witness, noted that he 'weared for the most part sweet powder in his haire, sets of points at his knees, boots, and lawn boothose tops, as the fashion then was for young men'. At national level Owen may be regarded as the outstanding ecclesiastical statesman of the Commonwealth era. He was chiefly responsible for the scheme of church settlement which was debated in the Rump and the Nominated Parliament and which eventually took shape, with modifications, in Cromwell's ordinances setting up the 'Triers' and 'Ejectors'. Owen was also prominent in opposing Cromwell's acceptance of the Crown. Ejected at the Restoration, he refused to conform; yet he had influential friends at court and he escaped severe persecution. In 1673 he became the minister of an independent congregation in Leadenhall Street. He wrote a good deal at this time in favour of toleration and against Catholicism. His extensive doctrinal treatises were among the most distinguished produced by seventeenth-century Puritanism, and the personal influence of his teaching, for example, on men so different as Cromwell and the young William Penn, was considerable.

OWEN, ROBERT (1771-1857), self-made manufacturer, factory reformer, educationalist and utopian socialist, spent much of his life in the search for a 'new society'. His writings and experiments were of little consequence when measured against his exalted hopes. He was so original in his plans that he may be termed a revolutionary, yet he was more assiduous than dynamic; he was neither upset nor stimulated by practical setbacks – as if nothing could gainsay the validity of his ideas. He was among the first English thinkers to recognize the moral and social benefits that industrialism could bring, and he was modern in his concern with what might be called the psychology of environment.

New Lanark was an experiment of seminal importance. Yet Owen was stubborn and blind in whole areas of life. His understanding of human nature was limited, his political sense deficient. His experience of succeeding in life by his own enterprise, and of managing large numbers of workmen in the new disciplines of the mechanized mill, with his interpretation of the eighteenth-century philosophers and their view of human nature, combined to produce an idea of a society which could be improved and transformed by the application of rational rules. This view never evolved significantly. Once he had discovered the principles of social regeneration the facts of social life became less important to him.

Owen was born at Welshpool, Montgomeryshire, the fourth surviving son of Robert Owen, a saddler. He was a clever schoolboy and at the age of seven was already assisting the local schoolmaster. At nine he left school to work in a draper's shop. He went to London, the next year, to join his saddler brother. Thence he soon took himself to Stamford and the draper's shop of Mr McGuffog who was so impressed by his assistant that he later offered him his daughter – and a partnership. Owen rejected both. He learned the cotton business: in 1791 he set up as a master-spinner. Then he became manager for a Mr Drinkwater, who had a large and well-run mill in Manchester; Owen won the workers' confidence and instilled sound discipline. He was no radical but an observant and humane businessman. He was apparently unmoved by the French revolution but showed an enlightened interest in science, as a member of the Manchester Board of Health and the Literary and Philosophical Society. What he was in Manchester he would

always, in essentials, remain: a self-made paternalist who believed that workers' efforts and morale depended on their environment. When he bought the New Lanark mills from David Dale (he soon afterwards married Dale's daughter) he could create a new kind of environment that was both disciplined and wholesome for his 1,500 workers.

He stopped the employment of pauper apprentices and refused to take any child under the age of ten (six or seven was usual before). New Lanark was a virtually closed society and the workers lived on the site in specially constructed houses. Owen wanted his men to develop 'habits of attention, celerity and order'. He improved houses, streets and sanitation, built company shops and schools, and organized every detail of the employees' lives. Fines imposed for immorality and swearing went to a fund for medical care. 'Silent monitors', coloured boards beside each bench, recorded the worker's behaviour and progress. (His wife was meanwhile being encouraged to look after her home by the award of prizes.) Owen cared that workers should be contented and should have a pride in their work, their labour bearable within the requirements of factory discipline. There was no question, however, of consultation – indeed no formal representation of the men's interests. They were virtually his serfs and he was master of their lives. In 1823 his men complained to the partners about his attitude: they were 'compelled by Mr Owen to adopt what measures so ever he be pleased to suggest on matters that entirely belong to us' which was 'degrading to our characters as free-born sons of highly favoured Great Britain'. Owen once observed, during a visit to the West Indies, that the slaves' 'worst enemies would be those who tried to free them'.

New Lanark convinced Owen that education was the key to social progress. Education for him was training for life. He wished 'to remoralize the lower orders'. In his *New View of Society* (1813) he expanded upon the idea that children had a plastic quality and could be moulded: 'any general character from the best to the worst, from the most ignorant to the most enlightened, may be given to any community … by the application of the proper means'. The curriculum of his schools was severely practical and contained 'elementary social and economic facts'; emphasis was also placed on such activities as knitting, sewing and botanical walks; both sexes were to be formed into companies for marching practice which, Owen believed, fostered discipline and harmony of body and mind. He was also original in advocating nursery schools where the first rule was to make the children happy. Inspectors of Owen's schools reported a 'general spirit of kindness and affection' and the appearance of 'one well-regulated family'.

At the end of the French war Owen thought that the government should spend money on 'a national system of training and education for the poor and uninstructed'. Nothing of the sort was done, so he turned to his own plans for 'villages of co-operation'. These were self-supporting rural colonies: their purpose, to provide employment and the setting for a good life. They were constructed on a square, with lines of public buildings, school, library, a 'place of public worship' and a communal restaurant. Cobbett spurned these 'parallelograms of paupers' but the Duke of Kent declared his interest, Napoleon is supposed to have read the *New View* in exile, and Owen toured Europe and had an audience with the future king, Louis Philippe. The messianic strain became more pronounced. He promised 'to let prosperity loose upon the country'. On the analogy of the advances accomplished by inventions in industry he forecast that knowledge and moral improvement would leap forward as well. He argued vaguely for a new religion of truth (which meant living in conformity with the demands of the laws of nature). He took his idea of the formative influence of environment to the point of denying, not only responsibility before God, but even the sovereignty of the individual will. Anticipating that science would so increase the amount of wealth produced that the acquisitive instinct would disappear, he outlined equitable ways of distributing produce. In his rational society class distinction would be unknown. Where love failed, marriages should be understood to have ended.

Owen was soon abandoned by his grander patrons when his naive views became known. He would have alarmed politicians, if they had taken him seriously. He was disillusioned by politics. His proposals for a factory bill were unrecognizably reduced by the time they reached the statute book in 1819 (the elder Peel's Act). Leading radicals had rejected his advances when he addressed them in 1817. His newspaper, *The Crisis*, with its revealing subtitle *The Change from Error and Misery, to Truth and Happiness*, its motto 'If we cannot yet reconcile all opinions, let us endeavour to unite all hearts', and its cover design of a rectangle of buildings, 'a community of 2,000 persons, founded upon a principle commended by Plato, Lord Bacon, T. More and R. Owen', blandly ignored the political excitements of the time. Owen was concerned with psychological change: a new spirit of rationality would make political moves irrelevant. The criterion would then be what was good for the human race.

He was naturally attracted to America. In 1824 he visited the United States and met many famous Americans. In 1825 he opened his Community of Equality at New Harmony, Indiana. He hoped for 'the industrious and well-disposed of all nations'; inevitably drop-outs, criminals and drunkards arrived as well. Neither a democratic assembly nor Owen's fussy attempts at autocratic rule met the community needs; nor did it pay its way. In 1827 Owen conceded failure, blaming the strength of 'the individual system, founded as it is upon superstition'. He was still ready with advice and schemes and planned a chain of Owenite communities in Texas. He was discredited – and impoverished – by the New Harmony debacle. He had to sell his remaining shares in New Lanark. But his own confidence was unimpaired. Owenite societies borrowed his name and ideas: he had already used the term 'co-operative' and, when he returned from America, societies had been formed, in support of co-operation, with co-operative shops and 'labour exchanges' for the marketing of goods; the word 'socialism' was being widely used. Owen was not greatly interested in the co-operative movement: buying and selling were not in his scheme of things. He was enthusiastic, however, about the National Equitable Labour Exchange, opened in London in 1832, since it was based on the ideas already propounded in his *Report to the County of Lanark* (1820) that all wealth proceeded from labour and knowledge, that labour and knowledge were remunerated according to the time spent in manufacture – in an age of technological advance a vulnerable notion – and that time should be the measure of wealth. The Exchange failed. Characteristically, Owen dismissed the experiment as if it were irrelevant – 'It was a mere pawnbroker's shop in comparison with the superior establishments which we shall speedily have it in our power to institute' – and it confirmed his belief that improvement must await a revolution in men's hearts.

Owen played, however, a large part in the formation of the Grand National Consolidated Trades Union (1833). His hope was to abolish the distinction between masters and men: the idea of co-operation along these lines had already interested him in the proposals of the Operative Builders' Union. His idea of the Grand National was one of co-operation on the national scale, with every craft and trade incorporated in one body. He convinced himself that the lower orders were not the passive objects of improvement that he had hitherto known but active, energetic and ready to assume responsibility. That they should therefore want to promote their own craft at the expense of others, that they should want to use the strike weapon at once to initiate the golden age, he did not allow for. Premature strikes weakened many unions; in several cases office-holders absconded with the funds. Owen quarrelled with Morrison and Smith, advocates of the national strike; the movement disintegrated amidst confusion and recrimination, while Owen turned to constructing an organization which should reflect his purer ideals: the British and Foreign Consolidated Association of Industry, Humanity and Knowledge. He did ride at the head of a great procession of London workers (April 1834) protesting against the barbarity of the Tolpuddle sentences. But he soon returned from action to the idea, more important to him than any organization. He would not compromise and he could not share or sympathize with the material hopes of the workers whom he addressed so loftily – as they saw it, condescendingly.

The last part of his long life was spent in travelling about the world, reaffirming obsessively, in word and print, the principles of his rational society. He became a spiritualist. He had always presented a broad front to admirers and critics. The very imprecision of his theories of change in society meant that they were adaptable to different groups of people. Men could choose their own inspired interpretation of his new Jerusalem in England's blighted land; or they could see him as an amiable crank – or even a self-important prig. For all his moral earnestness he was not big or clever enough to see or admit his own shortcomings. His wife Caroline gave him eight children and had the spirit to hold to her Presbyterian convictions. He let her drift out of his life. It seems that he could feel more for people as abstractions than as human beings. But he took trouble to answer the letters of simple men when they wrote for guidance. He was an incomparably zealous propagandist. His confidence could be infectious: 'I therefore now proclaim to the world the commencement, on this day, of the promised millennium, founded on rational principles and consistent practice' was his message, on May Day 1833, to the National Equitable Labour Exchange. Engels, who rejected his thesis, paid him the tribute of describing him as 'a man of almost sublimely child-like simplicity of character and at the same time a born leader of men'.

Further Reading
John Butt, ed., *Robert Owen, Prince of Cotton Spinners*, 1971.
Sidney Pollard and John Salt, eds, *Robert Owen*, 1971.
Margaret Cole, *Robert Owen of New Lanark*, 1953.

OXENFORD, JOHN (*fl.*1327-48): his 'eccentric and yet typical career' so vividly illustrates the scope for corruption in local government that he has been proposed as the model for the sheriff of Nottingham in the ballads of Robin Hood. Apart from their routine administrative, judicial and financial duties, sheriffs were the obvious people to undertake any exceptional tasks for the Crown. All such activities offered opportunities for oppression and profit so tempting that from at least 1170 to 1451 there were constant complaints against sheriffs and repeated attempts to control them through legislation. John Oxenford was repeatedly sheriff of Nottinghamshire and Derbyshire in 1334-9. Commonplace offences that he committed included accepting a bribe to release a thief from prison to the peril of the jurors who indicted him, refusing bail except for payment, charging for the delivery of writs, collecting royal debts more than once, seizure of property, and four times returning himself as MP for the county. Further opportunities were offered by the renewal of war with Scotland and from 1337 with France, which resulted in constant instructions to sheriffs to collect and despatch supplies to the forces, payment to be made later. Oxenford, it appears, took foodstuffs from at least forty-three villages without payment in 1338, much of it, it was alleged, for his own rather than the king's use. Wheat, malt and oats levied for the garrison of Perth were instead sold overseas for Oxenford's profit, so that Perth fell. His claim that the supplies were lost in the River Humber was questioned by the Exchequer, but fortunately his stepfather John Shoreditch was the Exchequer baron assigned to hear the case, not only letting his stepson off, but securing £100 for his losses and trouble. An informer was bribed. Oxenford also seized 200 oxen and 12,000 sheep, afterwards selling them back to their owners, but not before several had been put out of business. 'Even in an age when venality and profiteering were endemic among local officers, Oxenford seems to have been particularly corrupt,' yet he was repeatedly reappointed and even escaped unpunished with a pardon from the special inquiry of a fearsome commission of trailbaston in 1341. It may be that Shoreditch secured his appointment, protected him in office, and secured his pardon, or perhaps he had more powerful protectors. Robin Hood, if he existed, lived before 1262, but his ballads were amplified later and may well draw on Oxenford's discreditable and highly unpopular career.

Oxenford was a surprising choice as sheriff. He was the son of Nicholas Aurifaber or Sudbury, who was bailiff and in 1289 mayor of Oxford, and his wife Helen, who remarried to Shoreditch, then an Oxford doctor of civil law, but later a knight, royal councillor and Baron of the Exchequer. John Oxenford married a widow by 1327 and thus acquired her dowerlands in Owthorpe (Notts.). Although these qualified him for office-holding in Nottinghamshire, their value – a mere £8 a year – was far below the normal income for a sheriff or knight. Oxenford was besides a townsman and an interloper. No wonder he needed to maximize the illicit profits of office to support himself. Dismissed in 1339, outlawed for non-appearance in court in 1341, and bereft of Owthorpe by 1341, probably by his wife's death, he returned to Oxford to take up his inheritance by 1342, when it was seized as security for his royal debts. He had sold it by 1345, contracted a further debt of £150 in 1348, and thereafter disappears into impoverished obscurity. His origins and fate are thus unusual, but his misconduct in office was exceptional only in scale and fully explains why 'men still had a justifiable distrust' of sheriffs.

Further Reading
J. R. Maddicott, 'The Birth and Setting of the Ballads of Robin Hood', *English Historical Review* xciii, 1978.

P

PAINE, THOMAS (1737-1809) wrote *The Rights of Man*, a textbook for the extreme radicals in the England of his day; he was also an international figure held in high repute by American rebels and French revolutionaries alike. Both in France and in America, however, there was a reaction: he was imprisoned by Robespierre and looked at askance by Americans, who found that the extreme views which had been serviceable during the War of Independence were inappropriate to more sober times. In writing and character he was bold and uncompromising to the point of pig-headedness. It was precisely that inability to see more than one side of the question that made him such an effective propagandist. He was not, except in his manner, original, but he was very influential.

Paine was born in the small Norfolk town of Thetford, where his father farmed in a small way and made stays. Thomas was much influenced by the Quakerism of his father, though he was confirmed in the Church of England. Because the Quakers did not approve of the Latin books used at school, he would not learn Latin. Apprenticed stay-maker, he went off to sea at the age of sixteen and served, by his own account, on the privateer *Terrible*, commanded by Captain Death! He soon returned to stay-making, set up his own business, and married; but his business failed, his wife died, and in 1761 he obtained a job on the excise. He was early in trouble for neglect of duty, but he survived in this service until 1774, when he was dismissed for voicing the grievances of the excise men in a tract. In the same year he separated from his second wife and sailed to America. Here he edited a magazine, *Pennsylvania Magazine or American Museum*, wrote articles for it condemning slavery and advocating republicanism and expressed the sentiment, which few as yet dared openly voice, in favour of complete independence for the colonies. In *Common Sense*, which appeared in January 1776, he argued, with a crudely forceful eloquence and logic, his case against the English constitution.

His writings were received with acclaim by the colonists. He was engaged in intelligence and staff work in 1777-8; on one occasion he distinguished himself by carrying a message in an open boat under a cannonade from the British fleet. In January 1779 his indiscretion landed him in trouble, and he had to give up his post as Secretary to the Committee for Foreign Affairs, when he made embarrassing revelations about the French alliance and American profiteering at a time when the French government was anxious to preserve a guise of neutrality. He was more a journalist than a public official and at heart an anarchist with a strong distrust of authority: 'Government, like dress, is the badge of lost innocence; the palaces of kings are built on the ruins of the bowers of Paradise.' Another sample of his writing gives an idea of his terse style: 'Society is produced by our wants, and government by our wickedness; the former promotes our happiness positively by uniting our affections: the latter negatively, by restraining our vices. The one encourages intercourse, the other creates distinctions. The first is a patron, the last a punisher.' In the English government Paine had, of course, admirable material for his superficial and scornful analysis and the occasional trumpet-call to sedition: 'Of more worth is one honest man to society, and in the sight of God, than all the crowned ruffians that ever lived.' Paine wrote for ordinary men who could not fail to understand his meaning.

Once the war was over, Paine travelled in France and England, chiefly with a view to publicizing and selling plans for an iron bridge. The outbreak of the French Revolution ensured a second career for him. The events were stirring, their implications far-reaching; in Edmund Burke, author of the conservative, romantic *Reflections on the French Revolution*, he had a target who was brilliant, eloquent and famous. Burke's appeal to the past, his idea of society as an organism and a mystical communion of living, dead and still unborn, were nonsense and anathema to Paine. Paine was prone to oversimplify, but Burke was simply ignorant of the conditions which had produced the Revolution. Burke's sympathies were therefore, in Paine's view, romantically misplaced: 'He is not affected by the reality of distress touching his heart, but by the showy resemblance of it striking his imagination. He pities the plumage, but forgets the dying bird.' *The Rights of Man* came out in

March 1791. In it Paine argued that the civil rights of man were a natural growth from the rights that men enjoyed as human beings: Burke venerated the English constitution, but what sort of constitution was it that denied the mass of the people the exercise of these rights? Paine's history with stock references to the Norman Conquest and the Glorious Revolution might be vague, but his arguments were sharp-edged. He was able to expose the persistent injustice and inequalities in England and to question hallowed conventions: hereditary monarchy and 'mixed' government among them. In some points he was, however, cautious. Republican though he avowed himself, he was no extreme democrat, for he wanted to link the possession of the vote with the payment of taxes.

The first part of *The Rights of Man* was a success, though its vehement attack upon cherished English illusions roused fury. The publication of the second part, in February 1792, forecast, in a somewhat superficial way, that there must be revolutions to sweep away the old order. At the same time there would evolve a new idea: 'Government founded on a moral theory, on a system of universal peace, on the indefeasible hereditary Right of Man.' Paine was naive in his conception of man standing on the brink of a terrestrial paradise: would his nature change so much that 'to be free it is sufficient that he wills it'? But in his enthusiasm for international co-operation, the rule of reason, even Free Trade, he embodies much of what is best in the thought of his time and anticipates the idealism of the Victorians, Mill, Cobden and Gladstone. He was practical too in his analysis of domestic problems: he wanted graduated taxation, compulsory popular education, provision for the aged, a child allowance and reform of the Poor Law. 'The poor, as well as the rich, will then be interested in the support of the government, and the cause and apprehension of riots and tumults will cease.'

Paine had written a book which was both radical and positive. To his admirers he was an apostle of hope; to his detractors he was a dangerous, subversive traitor. His simple pronouncements appealed dangerously to simple men: no democratic thinker has been more challenging. Even Fox's liberalism was inhibited by the fears of men of property; he thought *The Rights of Man* a seditious libel. Indeed Paine's conduct invited criticism. When the French monarchy fell he was elected a delegate to the first Assembly of the Republic. While his book was being proceeded against in London, he enjoyed the welcome of his constituents in Calais and entered into the debates of the Convention. Events were disillusioning. Bravely Paine opposed the spirit of revenge that seemed to prompt the enemies of Louis XVI and voted against the sentence of death. He was temperamentally and ideologically out of tune with Robespierre's Jacobins, and grew isolated; he was imprisoned, threatened with

the guillotine. Illness and good luck, not the American ambassador, saved him. Paine emerged from this experience harrowed, with incipient persecution mania, and he worked off his feelings by devising invasion plans against England. Then he published *The Age of Reason*. Its tone was polemical, popular, mocking. He affirmed a benevolent deism and denounced all churches as enemies of the individual conscience. 'My own mind is my own church,' he said, a Quaker idea. Revelation he discounted, the Virgin Birth and Resurrection he dismissed in a facile way. For the Bible and revelation he substituted nature. Much of this book is shallow. Paine was a great propagandist, because he was so unsubtle; for the same reason he was incapable of appreciating the complexities and depths of religious feeling. *The Age of Reason* is weak tea, well sugared; but it sustained radicals in their suspicions of the church establishment. He offered what seemed to be wanted and needed: an undemanding, diluted humanist faith for the common man.

Paine was both enterprising and brave; he met his end with fortitude: 'I have lived an honest and useful life to mankind; my time has been spent in doing good, and I die in perfect composure and resignation to the will of my creator.' He never indeed underestimated his own worth, nor his services to mankind. In several ways his life was significant. He disseminated hostility towards authorities in church and state, scepticism about institutions and dogmas; he expressed a potent faith in the natural goodness of men; especially he invited the common man to interest himself in politics. In him the inarticulate found a voice and a sense of direction, stirred by his conviction that the happiness of individuals is the only test of the validity of governments.

Further Reading
J. Fruchtman, *Thomas Paine: Apostle of Freedom*, 1994.
C. Bonwick, *English Radicals and the American Revolution*, 1977.
H. H. Clark, ed., *Paine's Writings*, 1961.
A. O. Aldridge, *Man of Reason*, 1960.

PAKEMAN III, SIMON (*c*.1306-76) represents the many minor gentry who ran noble estates and local government in the fourteenth and fifteenth centuries. The Pakemans were a long established family of substantial freeholders from Kirby Muxloe near Leicester. Overshadowed locally by the knightly Herle family, their social contacts comprised families of similar status from their immediate area. Simon Pakeman II held seventy-five acres in demesne at his death in 1313, when his son Simon Pakeman III was a minor. His wardship was acquired by the Herles, who probably provided him with a legal training. By 1337 he was an attorney in the court of Common Pleas, where Sir William Herle was Chief Justice. There is no evidence that Simon received any training at arms or that he ever served abroad. Throughout his career he acted for Leicestershire clients in the central courts. Although he was knight of the shire for Leicestershire in 1334, an unusual choice, his career really took off only after 1340.

In 1340 Henry, Earl of Lancaster appointed him steward of the honour of Leicester, which comprised estates in Leicestershire and adjoining shires, and from 1341 he served the Earl of Warwick, becoming steward of his manor of Kibworth Beauchamp and of Merton College's adjoining manor of Kibworth Harcourt. It was presumably such contacts that explain both the widened geographical scope of his activities, as he served on commissions in Warwickshire and Lancashire, and his greater weight in Leicestershire itself, where he became a regular commissioner and served twice more as knight of the shire in 1346 and 1348. Such royal commissions continued in spite of his replacement as steward of Leicester honour in 1346 by Henry of Grosmont, next Earl of Lancaster, who may however have employed him in some other capacity, and the termination of his Warwick stewardship in the late 1350s. He became steward of Leicester honour again in 1362 following the succession of John of Gaunt as Duke of Lancaster and served on his council and in many other capacities up to his retirement in 1375. During these years, Pakeman was continuously employed in local government, sat twice more as knight of the shire, and widened his circle of clients to include Lancaster's retainer, Lord Ferrers of Groby, appearing frequently as executor, feoffee and attorney.

Pakeman was thus one of the indispensable experts on whom royal and noble administrations relied. Service to his lords involved him in affairs outside Leicestershire and gave him a prominence in administration of his home county that owed nothing to his personal rank and wealth. Aptitude and expertise were evidently accompanied by a willingness for hard work, which his social superiors eschewed in favour of more aristocratic employment and pursuits. Pakeman's motive was presumably financial. His salaries as estate officer must have brought in much more income over many years than his paltry inheritance. Yet his social position changed little. He extended his lands somewhat, but not substantially. The social status, contacts and outlook of his heir remained those of the minor Leicestershire gentleman. Presumably Pakeman preferred a higher standard of living to investment of his salaries in land. Historians have understandably concentrated on the tiny minority of outstanding successes, who transformed their social position and became national figures like Robert Holland and Thomas Hungerford. Those who did not are less well-documented, more obscure and therefore difficult to study, but there were certainly many more like Pakeman, who enjoyed successful careers without radically altering their social status, landed estates, or provincial horizons. Such people were the mainstay of provincial society and government.

Further Reading
G. G. Astill, 'Social Advancement through Seigniorial Service? The Case of Simon Pakeman', *Transactions of the Leicestershire Archaeological and Historical Society* liv, 1978-9.

PALAVICINO, SIR HORATIO (*c*.1540-1600), financier and diplomatist, was born at Genoa about 1540, the son of Tobias Palavicino, a member of the wealthy, aristocratic banking family in northern Italy, which was closely connected with most of the powerful Italian banking firms. The family business was based on handling the Papal monopoly in alum, a commodity greatly in demand in the Netherlands and England for the cloth trade. In 1578 Horatio sold the family stocks of alum at Antwerp to the Dutch rebels in return for an import monopoly which excluded all future farmers of the Papal alum monopoly. The Dutch did not pay cash: Queen Elizabeth of England underwrote the loan in order to keep the Dutch revolt against Spain alive. In other words, she borrowed from Palavicino £29,000. In 1579 Sir Thomas Gresham, the English government's chief financial agent, died. It was necessary to find a successor, a man who had intimate knowledge of international high finance, who was an expert in currency exchange, who could handle the transfer of large sums of money from one financial centre to another, to ambassadors and secret agents, who could find the ready cash for subsidies to allies, who was ready and able to turn ambassador (or spy) himself, and whose reputation created confidence and credit. Only Horatio Palavicino fulfilled all these requirements, and on top of this he could at need act as a secret agent.

In 1586 he was given a full diplomatic mission as ambassador to the Protestant princes in north-western Europe to raise an army for the invasion of eastern France. He became a naturalized Englishman and was knighted by Elizabeth. He lost the queen's favour when she discovered the profits Horatio had made out of the 1578 loan. He had lent her £29,000: in 1592 she repaid him £4,425 of the capital, the only repayment she ever made. But by that time Horatio had cleared £41,053 in interest alone. Between 1594 and 1600 he was engaged in increasing his own wealth and investing it in land. His methods were ruthless, unsavoury and highly successful. He speculated in corn and earned great hatred for the distress he caused in time of famine by raising the price. He bought *objets d'art* for his clients; he arranged the ransom of prisoners, notably Spanish prisoners from the Armada; he lent money on the most exorbitant conditions; he tried to make a corner, but failed, in the world supply of pepper. By the time he died in 1600 he was the richest commoner in the land, worth at least £100,000, and he had accumulated 8,000 acres in three counties. He was interested in sheep-farming and devoted some 2,600 acres to pasture. At his home at Babraham in Cambridgeshire he was something of a pioneer in agriculture, in experimenting in irrigating his meadows.

Palavicino was an unpleasant man, ruthless in pursuit of wealth, harsh as a landlord. He was impetuous and emotional, but also cold and calculating. He remained on friendly and even affectionate terms with the Cecils and the Earl of Shrewsbury, yet he was notorious for the duplicity with which he treated his debtors. His intellectual powers were considerable, his abilities enormous. He spoke six languages; his interests were wide and varied – for example, he studied naval and military affairs and served at sea against the Armada. He began life as a Catholic and changed over gradually to the new faith, influenced by the cruel treatment meted out to his brother by the pope at the time of the alum crisis in 1578 (his brother was tortured), but doubtless as much influenced by the £29,000 owed to him by a Protestant queen. After his death his second wife married Sir Oliver Cromwell of Hinchinbrook, his son Henry (aged fourteen) married Catherine, Sir Oliver's daughter by a first marriage, his son Toby married her sister Jane, and his daughter Baptina married her brother Henry. Sir Oliver was the great-uncle of Oliver Cromwell, the Protector.

Further Reading
Lawrence Stone, *Sir Horatio Palavicino*, 1956.

PALEY, WILLIAM (1743-1805), Archdeacon of Carlisle, was the author of textbooks upon moral and religious subjects which so successfully defined the thinking of the time that he influenced a generation – the last generation of the age which has been described (by Whitehead) as 'an age of reason based on faith', and the last which was prepared to take seriously books which 'proved Christianity to be true'. His *Principles of Morals and Political Philosophy* (1785) was adopted as a textbook at Cambridge and went through fifteen editions in the author's lifetime; it provoked Bentham to write his celebrated *Principles of Morals and Legislation*. Frankly utilitarian but ready to compromise between orthodoxy and rationalism, lucid in exposition and edifying in tone, Paley served a readership which wanted to be reassured. *Evidences of Christianity* (1794), his best known book, countered the shocks of revolution with the quiet arguments of the eighteenth-century divine for whom God was not mysterious, for whom the consequences of men's actions provided the safest test of virtue. He defined virtue as 'doing good to mankind in obedience to the will of God and for the sake of everlasting happiness'. Some of his adherents, like Jebb, became unitarian. Paley remained orthodox, saying, when urged to support a move for the relaxation of the terms of a clergyman's subscription to the Thirty-Nine Articles, that 'he could not afford to keep a conscience' and on another occasion that the Articles were merely 'articles of peace'; they contained 'about 240 distinct propositions, many of them inconsistent with each other' so that no-one could expect any man to believe all.

Paley was the son of the headmaster of Giggleswick: the family had been settled in the neighbourhood for many generations. His father had the highest opinion of his talents: 'He has by far the clearest head I ever met with in my life', and William never lacked confidence, though he was a clumsy fellow and cut an odd figure at Cambridge – absent-minded, liable to fall off his horse or lose his notes. He was laughed at when he recited a prize essay in the Senate House. He never lost his strong Yorkshire accent, but he became a popular lecturer when he became a Fellow of his college, Christ's, in 1768. With his friend John Law he did much to raise the standard of tuition: indeed, he presents a pleasant picture of the friendly young don, an intellectual all-rounder, interested in his pupils and more conscientious than his somewhat cynical utterances might suggest. He was less at home, perhaps, in the country living that he accepted after his marriage to Jane Hewitt (1775). He divided his time between his parishes (he usually had two), his public interests (he was an early opponent of the slave trade) and his writing. *Reasons for Contentment* was the title of one of his more complacent books (1792). He had good reasons. Preferment came steadily to him as his services as defender of the establishment became recognized. In 1795 he became rector of Bishop Wearmouth, worth £1,200 a year – an immense sum for those days. He had eight children by his first wife. He married again, four years after her death, in 1795. Latterly he grew very stout.

Paley was exceedingly fond of fishing, but most of his time was given to writing and he was always jotting down stray thoughts, until his notebooks became a 'confused, incoherent and blotted mass'. His thinking was plain enough, however, and his style was warmly praised by Pitt, whose judgement we may respect. As to his religious teaching there must be reservations. It was a short step from this Christian utilitarian to James Mill, who excluded orthodox religion from thought as unworthy of serious thought, and to evangelicals who excluded thought from religion. Perhaps, as Coleridge said: 'belief in God could not be intellectually more evident, without becoming morally less effective'.

PALMER, JOHN (1742-1818) by his vision and good planning achieved almost single-handed a revolution in transport. The son of a well-to-do brewer of Bath, he came to realize the inefficiencies of the post when he helped his father with the management of his theatre at

Bath. The Post Office messengers seldom kept time and, being unarmed, were an easy prey to highwaymen. Robberies were frequent and the service was slow. Palmer, who was both self-confident and persistent, worked out a scheme for a fast mail-coach service on the same lines as the stagecoach, with an armed guard and four passengers to defray the expense. Pitt, Chancellor of the Exchequer under Shelburne in 1783, saw the possibilities of the plan. When he became prime minister in 1784, he ordered a trial, against argument and obstruction from the Post Office. Long sunk in bureaucratic sloth, postal officials were driven to advise clients to cut their banknotes in half before sending them by post, and they continued to intrigue against Palmer, despite the success of the new mail-coaches. From about three days the journey from London to Bristol was cut to sixteen hours, an hour shorter than the stagecoach. The journey was not comfortable, but it was reliable, except in winter, and safe. Pitt, who was aware of the value to the country of this service, made Palmer Surveyor and Comptroller-General of the Post Office. Though he was compelled to dismiss him in 1793 because of indiscreet attacks upon his superior, Lord Walsingham, he compensated him with a pension of no less than £3,000 a year.

PALMER, SAMUEL (1805-81), landscape-painter and etcher, was a visionary, like his friend and mentor William Blake; and the best of his visionary paintings were done before the accession of Victoria. Thereafter his life (for forty years) seems something of an anticlimax, in terms of experience as well as of expression – though he created some most lovely pictures, and though there was a 'sunset-touch', a few years at the end during which he recaptured much of his earlier vision.

He grew up on the southern edge of London, where the countryside invaded the town: the son of a bookseller. Both father and mother were Baptists; and although Palmer later joined the Church of England – as the church which most appealed to his romantic temperament by colour, liturgy, music, architecture – yet the strict religion of his early home profoundly influenced his life. His mother died when he was thirteen; but her place was taken by the remarkable Mary Ward, his nurse, devoted friend, and (to a degree) inspirer.

His father was that unusual thing: a father who *wanted* his son to be a painter, and was prepared to support him until he was successful. He also instilled in him a strong love of Nature. In his fourteenth year, the boy had three pictures accepted for exhibition at the Royal Academy, and two at the British Institution. His friendship with the landscape-painter John Linnell helped to form his taste by pointing him towards the Renaissance masters. To that he added a devotion to poetry, especially that of Milton, and especially Milton's own landscape, of dewy mornings, of shepherds sheltering from the heat of noon, and (above all) the magic of night, of woods and pastures sunk in darkness

> ... till the moon
> Rising in clouded majesty, at length,
> Apparent queen, unveil'd her peerless light,
> And o'er the dark her silver mantle threw.
> (*Paradise Lost*, IV.606-9)

It helped of course that Milton was a Christian, and his great poem a Christian document; for thus his high authority could be cited for Palmer's lifelong certainty that the purpose of art is religious. 'Genius', Palmer wrote, 'is the unreserved devotion of the whole soul to the divine, poetic arts, and through them to God; deeming all else, even to our daily bread, only valuable as it helps us to unveil the heavenly face of Beauty'.

Linnell introduced Palmer to older artists: to William Mulready, to John Varley, and (during 1824, at Fountain Court, in a meeting which was the most important of Palmer's life) to William Blake himself. To say that Palmer was captivated is hardly enough. Was not Blake the complete visionary, who as a boy had seen God looking in at the window, and the trees in Peckham thronged by starlike angels? Was he not a metaphysical poet? Was he not the illustrator of Milton, of Virgil, Dante, and of the Bible itself? Was he not also a transparently good man, indifferent to money or fame, whose life was simple and spent in the world of spirit?

Under Blake's influence, Palmer's leading motives were drawn together, as yarns are twisted to make a strong rope. Blake taught him to perceive 'the soul of beauty through the forms of matter'. From there it was a short step to holding that beauty was an aspect of God, art a sacrament, and the artist a kind of priest. Blake wrote: 'Prayer is the study of art; praise is the practice of art'. This idealism appealed to friends of Palmer also (he had a gift for making and keeping friends). A group of artists came together – including George Richmond and Edward Calvert, distinguished both then and later – who had fallen under Blake's spell, and by whom the primacy of the imagination, and its religious task, were unquestioned. Paradoxically in view of their youth and optimism, they called themselves the Ancients.

In 1826, for the sake of Palmer's health, his family moved out of London, to Shoreham in Kent. This opened the brightest period of Palmer's life, and the years in which he did much of the work which was unique to him (though it must be said that the *most* idiosyncratic – the haunting drawings done only in sepia mixed with gum – were created before the move to Shoreham). The place itself was still a rural paradise. The Ancients came down in force, for longer or shorter visits. They prayed together, worked at their painting, walked the hills at night like the exiles in the Forest of Arden, 'fleeting the time carelessly as they did in the golden world'. Palmer was happy – never so happy as during those few years at

Shoreham; and he did a series of paintings which are among the best things of the nineteenth century: ideal landscapes of a world of innocence, rich fields and ancient woods lit by sun, moon, stars, bright clouds – all 'charged' (in the words of his contemporary, Hopkins) 'with the grandeur of God'.

It goes without saying that these pictures – and most of his later works – are quietist if not escapist. He loathed the creeping industrialization of England – the 'uglification' of a supremely beautiful countryside. The coming of the railways appalled him: what would he have made of the motorcar with its crude intrusions into the privacy of the human soul?

Then, in the early 1830s – the idyll ended. Palmer was very hard up. His father and his brother had returned to town. The circle of the Ancients dispersed. Palmer's own vein of high inspiration seemed to be exhausted. Finally, in 1834, he too went back to London. He was only twenty-nine.

And three years later, the beloved Mary Ward died. With no-one to look after him, Palmer at last married Hannah, the daughter of John Linnell. They scraped together enough to allow them to spend two years in Italy. But they returned to poverty, and the confinement of London. Linnell proved to be a difficult father-in-law; and Hannah and Palmer were never really *ad unum* – except in the black days after the death of their elder son, a boy of great promise, in 1861, at the age of nineteen. (They had already lost their daughter at the age of three.)

Italy had turned Palmer's work in a new direction. He was excited by the landscape of the Campagna, its Virgilian echoes, and the treatment of it by Poussin and Claude. He made some marvellous paintings in Italy (there are two panoramas of Rome to be seen in Birmingham, and a third in Cambridge); but the note which was Palmer's alone has gone from his work. From now on, he is a watercolourist – and a colourist – of the very first rank, but not alone in that; and his pictures, though wonderfully poetic, are less obviously pictures of his dreams.

At last, an enlightened lawyer (who was Ruskin's solicitor) commissioned Palmer to do a series of etchings illustrating Milton's *L'Allegro* and *Il Penseroso*. It was four years since the boy's death; Palmer's religious faith was stronger again; he had moved back to the country, to Redhill; and he entered with delight into this work. Then he began also to etch illustrations to a translation he had made of Virgil's *Eclogues*. He lavished care on these series, so that they occupied him until his death. He was treading in the steps of Blake once more; and his landscapes now show touches of Claude. But also – in *The Lonely Tower*, *The Bellman*, in *Opening the Fold* – we are back in the unmistakably Palmerian world, of shepherds folding their sheep under starlit skies, of a village sunk in sleep or waking to the dappled clouds of morning. The magic has returned. The ordinary is transfigured, idealized.

Dressed often in an ankle-length coat and a beaver almost as high as himself, Palmer made an eccentric figure, and there is no doubt that he was an oddity. But his jolly companionship, his sense of the ridiculous, his sheer goodness, as well as admiration for his artistic powers, won and kept him many firm friends – of whom the most faithful of all, George Richmond, was beside him at his death.

One child survived, Arthur, and wrote his father's *Life*. Some of Palmer's best work is in the Ashmolean Museum, Oxford.

Further Reading
Raymond Lister, *The Paintings of Samuel Palmer*, 1985.
Lord David Cecil, *Visionary and Dreamer*, 1969.

PARIS, MATTHEW (*c*.1200-59) is one of the most distinguished English historians. Prolific, opinionated, erudite, his chronicles have for centuries shaped views on his period, not least because his prejudices – snobbish, conservative, xenophobic – mirrored those of so many of his successors as historians of thirteenth-century England. In 1217, Matthew became a monk at St Albans, where, with the exception of visits to some important ecclesiastical functions in England and a trip to Norway in 1248, he spent the rest of his life. Although cloistered, Matthew was in no way isolated. St Albans was a wealthy monastery, conveniently situated on Watling Street within easy reach of London, its guest-house well-used by the great, the good and the exotic: the abbey hosted Armenians in 1228 and 1252. Among Matthew's informants, many of whom must have stayed at the abbey, were Richard of Cornwall, the king's brother; Hubert de Burgh, the justiciar; Peter des Roches; Robert Grosseteste; and royal officials such as John Mansel. Between 1216 and 1252, Henry III visited St Albans nine times. In 1247, Matthew attending the ceremonial reception of the Holy Blood at Westminster Abbey, talked to the king who asked him to record all that he had seen and invited him to dinner. On the king's visit to St Albans in 1257, Matthew hung around the royal guest and dined at his table. The chronicler was obviously something of a celebrity, historiographer to the nobility as well as his monastery.

Matthew's output was prodigious. On the abbey's history he wrote the *Gesta Abbatum (Deeds of the Abbots)* covering the period from the alleged foundation in 793 to 1255 and the *Vitae Offarum (Lives of the Offas)* about Offa of Mercia, the supposed founder of the abbey, and his ancestor Offa of Angeln. For these Matthew, an enthusiastic, if uncritical, believer in thorough documentation, plundered the abbey's archives. His hagiography, which he composed both in Latin prose and, for a lay audience, in French verse, reflected his historical interests, his subjects including St Alban, Edward the Confessor and, for Matthew, the politically correct Archbishops Becket, Langton and Rich, all opponents of royal authority. His masterpiece was the *Chronica majora (Greater Chronicle)*. Begun in 1240, it covered the period from the Creation to 1259. To 1236, Matthew was chiefly dependent on the *Flores Historiarum* of a fellow St Albans monk Roger of Wendover which Matthew edited and expanded. For the last twenty-three years, however, Matthew was his own source, maintaining an original and almost contemporary account and commentary of events of a range and depth unparalleled in medieval England. His approach was encyclopaedic, cosmopolitan and judgemental. An artist of distinction, Matthew embellished his text with painted heraldic devices, maps (e.g. of Palestine, England, Scotland and the world) and numerous vivid marginal line drawings illustrating the narrative. The *Chronica* became bloated by his voracious appetite for information, so around 1250 he began writing shortened versions (the *Flores Historiarum* and *Abbreviatio Chronicarum*); a volume of extracts concerning English history (the *Historia Anglorum*); and a separate book of documents, the *Liber Additamentorum*, which he cross-referenced with the *Chronica majora*. Not only was this a massive historical enterprise, Matthew's original 1236-59 section alone comprising 300,000 words, but much of the actual writing and drawing was done by Matthew himself. On top of this, he found the time to illustrate the works of others.

What prevents this vast enterprise from sinking beneath its own weight is Matthew's readability. This not only turns on the marginal notes and the attractive, almost comic-strip drawings, but also on his style and what he has to say. Matthew's Latin is clear, his narrative easily followed. There are chapter headings, annual summaries of events and neat character sketches of leading figures. He was an early master of the succinct obituary and the telling epigram. Above all, he was an historian, not just a chronicler: he had a definite view on the events he described. His lack of objectivity forms his strength and weakness: it lends intellectual coherence to his work while seducing the reader into accepting his opinions as fact. Like many of his generation, surrounded by the seemingly endless conflicts of church, nobles and king, Matthew had a deep suspicion of any central authority, royal or papal, which appeared to infringe the traditional rights and habits of locally established hierarchies, noble, clerical or monastic. Although he came to moderate his vilification of Henry III, perhaps as he got to know the king personally, his antagonism to the court runs behind all his political analysis. From Matthew, rather than the documents of government, derives the familiar picture of Henry III as extravagant, petulant and easily-led, especially by parasitic Savoyard and Poitevin

relatives. As 1258-9 showed, this view was partly shared by some baronial opponents of royal policy, but it cannot be accepted as objective. Matthew's fulminations against the papal curia were, unlike those of Robert Grosseteste, based on institutional self-interest. Matthew feared papal power because of the possible encroachments, through patronage of foreigners and taxation, on the freedom (i.e. usually, income) of the English church. It is no coincidence that the *Chronica majora* appealed to Elizabeth I's Protestant Archbishop Parker of Canterbury who collected two of Matthew's autograph copies, now at Corpus Christi College, Cambridge. But Matthew's vision of the English church in danger and his insinuation that there was widespread anti-papalism should be treated with caution. Matthew's cynicism at royal and papal motives may appear justified, but not because of Matthew's witness.

Matthew was a traditional Benedictine, proud of an Order somewhat left behind by the new Orders of monks and mendicant friars. The latter were a pet hate: new, ultramontane, and successful. Matthew's political and ecclesiastical model seems to have been that of a Benedictine abbey, autonomous, run by an abbot according to custom and the Rule, with established, immutably defined and mutually recognized obligations to superiors in church and state. This was a central theme of almost all his historical and hagiographical work. What catches the eye may be the descriptions of buffalo; the drawing of the elephant given to Henry III by Louis IX in 1255; the marginal cartoons; the interest in heraldry, art, architecture, and natural science; above all the sheer scale and bulk of the narrative. What cannot be denied is the nature of the literary achievement: the most original and, in the concept of the illustrated chronicle, innovative historical enterprise of its time. Matthew Paris was a historian on the grand scale, amongst Englishmen on a par with Bede, William of Malmesbury, Clarendon and Gibbon. When Matthew's continuator in 1259 claimed he was unworthy to undo the tie of Matthew's shoe, he said no more than the truth. After Matthew, monastic historiography in England, as elsewhere, began to decline. At St Albans in the fourteenth century there was a revival with Thomas Walsingham, but he was a pale shadow of Matthew Paris.

Further Reading
R. Vaughan, *Matthew Paris*, 1958.

PARK, MUNGO (1771-1806), pioneer of African exploration, was born at Foulshiels in the Yarrow valley. He was the seventh son of a family of thirteen, but his father managed to send him to the grammar school at Selkirk. Only intelligence and enterprise could make a career for a farmer's son; there was no room on the land except for the eldest. He studied medicine at Edinburgh, but without distinction, and was lucky, on coming to

London in 1791, to secure an introduction through his brother-in-law, the botanist James Dickson, to Joseph Banks, who was a member of the 'African Association', which sought geographical knowledge and commercial opportunities from African exploration. Park went to the Far East as surgeon on an East Indiaman; then, in 1795, he accepted the Association's commission to explore the interior of Senegal.

Earlier attempts sponsored by the Association had failed. It is likely that Houghton, Park's immediate precursor, had been murdered, because he carried too much merchandise. Park therefore travelled light, accompanied by a man and a boy, both negroes, with a handful of trade goods, some survey instruments and a smattering of the Madingo dialect. He lived frugally on the milk, corn and ground nuts of the natives. He was captured and kept prisoner for three months by Arab slave-traders. Houghton had established the fact that the Niger flowed eastwards. But its course and destination remained uncertain; did it join the Nile or the Congo, or did it evaporate in the Sahara? Few accepted what proved to be correct – that it flowed into the Gulf of Benin. Park struck the Niger at Segu, followed it far enough to confirm its eastward flow, then managed to walk back most of the way, until he fell in with a trading caravan. He returned to England and published an account of his journey which ran into several editions (1799). Objective and bald, this is a classic traveller's tale. In its restraint of manner and absence of moralizing it is very much of the eighteenth century. We learn more of the country than of the author, but a picture emerges – stoical, deeply religious in a simple, Calvinist way, full of curiosity and capable of patient endurance.

Park married Alison Anderson, the daughter of his former master at Selkirk, and they had three children. He became a doctor at Peebles. Amongst his friends there was Sir Walter Scott, who was much taken with his knowledge of border ballads. Africa had entered his blood, however, and he seized the opportunity offered, this time by the government, to lead an expedition to follow the whole course of the Niger. He set out at the beginning of May 1805, with his brother-in-law Dr Anderson, Lieutenant Martyn – a hearty fellow, given to shooting natives – some naval artificers and thirty-five volunteers from the garrison of Goree. His instructions, as laid down by the Secretary of State for the Colonies, were 'to pursue the course of the river to the utmost possible distance' and 'to establish communication and intercourse with the different nations on the banks'. Unfortunately he started only just before the rainy season (in April 1805). 'Now the rain had set in I trembled to think that we were only halfway through our journey.' Most of the soldiers died on the march to Segu. Anderson had died of dysentery. Park had managed to cure himself by a dose of calomel so strong that his

mouth was ulcerated and he could not sleep for a week. At Segu he parleyed with Chief Mobidine and constructed a forty-foot flat-bottomed boat. He sent his servant Isaaco back to the coast with his letters and journal, then continued down the Niger with his few remaining companions. He seems to have thought that his best hope was to press along the river.

Park simply vanished into a mist of folk tales and speculation. It seems, by the account of the devoted Isaaco about six years later, that he and the remaining three white men were killed by natives as they tried to negotiate their canoe past a rock obstacle by the village of Boussa. (A chief of that region is said to wear Park's ring at the present day.) They were then only some 250 miles from the mouth of the river, having travelled over 1,000 miles. Park's last journals were never recovered and there survives from this second journey only a diary up to November. His was the sort of bravery that puts him in the class of Anson, Cook, or Scott of the Antarctic. His own laconic account is his best memorial: he knew what the hazards were, but his notes were calm and orderly to the end.

Further Reading
E. W. Bovill, *The Niger Explored*, 1965.
W. H. Hewitt, *Mungo Park*, 1923.

PARKER, MATTHEW (1504-75), Archbishop of Canterbury, was born on 6 August 1504, at Norwich. He came of a well-to-do family, but little is known of his origins and early life. He went to Corpus Christi College, Cambridge, in 1521, where he took his BA degree in 1525, perhaps in 1524. He was ordained in 1527 and in that year was elected a Fellow of the college, having refused an offer to migrate to Wolsey's new foundation of Cardinal College, Oxford. For the next seven years he studied the early centuries of church history. During this period Parker consorted with the reformers who met at the White Horse Inn, and became firm friends with people such as Bilney and Latimer, but Parker differed from some Cambridge reformers in that he was never a controversialist. The debates and disputes in which he took part served only the more to turn him back to finding out historic facts, not other people's opinions. Too many of the reformers came to look on religion as a thing to be debated and not a life to be lived: Parker never fell into that error, 'he was never drawn aside into undisciplined enthusiasm' (Kennedy, p.34). He became a popular and influential preacher in and around Cambridge, but he was once (in about 1539) attacked before Lord Chancellor Audley for alleged heresy. Audley dismissed the charge and urged Parker to 'go on and fear no such enemies'. One other fact in Parker's early days at Cambridge was to have immense influence on his later life – he became the firm friend of William Cecil (Lord Burghley) and Nicholas Bacon.

In 1535 Parker was reluctantly persuaded to accept the office of chaplain to Anne Boleyn, who gave him the deanery of St John the Baptist College, Stoke-by-Clare in Suffolk, where he spent what were probably the happiest years of his life pursuing his interests as a scholar, improving the college and saving it from dissolution when Henry VIII attacked the monasteries. Anne also before her execution commended her daughter Elizabeth to his care. This peaceful and busy life went on until 1544, when Parker was appointed Master of his old college at Cambridge, Corpus Christi. He became vice-chancellor of the university and also Dean of Lincoln. His period as vice-chancellor involved him in some stormy episodes: he quarrelled with Gardiner, the Chancellor of Cambridge, over the performance of a scandalous play at Christ's College, and Gardiner never had a good opinion of Parker from that time onwards. He had to withstand an attack on the revenues of the Cambridge colleges by the Crown which he warded off with great tact and skill. But perhaps in the long run the most important single event in Parker's life took place on 24 June 1547, when he married Margaret Harlestone of Mattishall in Norfolk. They had been betrothed for seven years, but as long as the law forbade the marriage of clergy Parker was doomed to celibacy: in anticipation that the law would be amended by the Lower House of Convocation, Parker married this remarkable and admirable woman. The marriage led them both into great difficulties when Mary Tudor came to the throne, and the outspoken objections of Elizabeth, when she became queen, to married clergy caused both Parker and Margaret great pain and trouble. But Margaret proved herself equal to all occasions and roused the admiration of Nicholas Ridley to such a pitch that he inquired of Matthew Parker whether Margaret had a sister, for if he himself were ever to marry he could not hope for a better wife than a lady like Mistress Parker. Even Elizabeth I was compelled in later years to acknowledge the worth of Mistress Parker. Parker was a modest and far from self-confident man and much of his success was due to his wife: it is noticeable that when she died his powers began to fail quickly.

When Ket's rebellion broke out (1549) in Norfolk, Parker happened to be in Norwich. As the rebels used the English Prayer Book and allowed licensed preachers to address them, Parker went to the camp and preached a sermon from the 'Oak of Reformation'. He gave them excellent advice, not to destroy the crops, not to shed human blood, and not to distrust the king. It was a rash sermon to preach in the circumstances and Parker escaped the fury of the rebels only 'by the judicious raising of the *Te Deum*' (Kennedy, p.62). His purpose probably was then, as always later when he was archbishop, to support law and order.

It is not possible to deal fully here with Parker's relations with Bucer, but it is necessary to record that he became a great friend of the German theologian – Parker preached the sermon at Bucer's funeral – and there is little doubt that Bucer had considerable influence on Parker's views on the Sacraments. Both were by nature moderate men of the *via media*, gentle and sincere (see Kennedy, pp.65-9).

When Mary Tudor came to the throne in 1553, Parker as a married priest was deprived of his preferments and he had to disappear into obscurity. He lived with a friend and thoroughly enjoyed his retirement from public life and administrative duties, but he suffered an accident when one day he fell from his horse, and for the rest of his life suffered from a strangulated hernia which brought him incessant ill-health and eventually killed him.

In 1558 the accession of Elizabeth opened a new chapter in Parker's life. He himself would have liked to return to Cambridge and restore the university, which had fallen into decay. But the problem of the Anglican church prevented this. Elizabeth and Cecil were faced with the difficulty of holding the balance between the old Roman Catholics who still accepted the pope as head of the church, the Henrician Catholics who accepted the Catholic religion but repudiated the Papal supremacy, and the extreme Protestants who were now returning from exile on the continent. It was essential to find the right man as Archbishop of Canterbury. Only a man of balanced judgement, of deep learning, gentle yet firm, conciliatory yet courageous, could successfully fill the office: only Matthew Parker had all the qualifications. He tried desperately to avoid the responsibility, but the queen and Cecil knew that he was the right man and they compelled him to accept. Years later Parker declared that 'if he had not been so much bound to the mother (Anne Boleyn), he would not so soon have granted to serve the daughter'. He was consecrated in Lambeth Palace Chapel on 17 December 1559. This consecration by four bishops surviving in England, though without sees, is the connecting link between the old and the new succession of Orders in the Church of England.

Parker's first important piece of work was the Metropolitan Visitation of the southern province in 1560-1 to investigate how far the Act of Uniformity and the Injunctions of 1559 (a code of orders to protect the new church from Catholic 'superstition' – e.g. the cult of saints, reverence for relics: to ensure that only sound Protestant doctrine should be taught: 'to plant true religion') were being carried out and to correct moral offences among clergy and laity. At that moment things seemed to be quiet and the nation to be accepting the new order.

By 1563 signs of the coming storm were evident. Both parliament and Convocation were worried by fears of Papal intrigues, of the hostility of France in the south and of dangers from Mary, Queen of Scots, in the north. Measures against the Romanists were stepped up and Parker was much troubled by the prospect of religious persecution. He took pains to ensure that the measures were leniently enforced, so that for the first ten years of Elizabeth's reign life was not made too difficult for the Romanists.

With the revival of the Council of Trent, with the increase in Papal propaganda by introducing into England controversial books, and with the Puritan propaganda which was being broadcast by the Protestant refugees and with which even some of the Anglican bishops were sympathetic, Parker set out to provide uniformity in doctrine for the Elizabethan church. He accordingly reduced Cranmer's Articles of Religion (1563) from forty-two to thirty-eight in number (in 1571 they became the Thirty-Nine Articles) and various Homilies and Catechisms were also issued. All were intended to lay down the fundamental points of belief.

Another problem with which Parker had soon to deal was the dispute over ceremonial and ritual. There was a large party in Convocation which would have liked to destroy the whole settlement about ritual made in the Prayer Book and the Injunctions. Many clergy were taking the law into their own hands and were pulling down rood-lofts, destroying chancels and some were even turning the organs out of their churches. Similarly there was no uniformity in the vestments which the clergy wore or refused to wear. In other words, Parker was now faced with the problem of Puritanism. For the rest of his life he was continuously harassed by the disobedience of many of the clergy, by the irresolution of the queen, and by the hostility of such courtiers as the Earl of Leicester. Parker dealt with these conflicting opponents mercifully and reluctantly. His 'Advertisements' (1566) were a compromise on the question of vestments, laying down that the surplice should be worn in the parish church and the cope in the cathedrals. He then set about seeing that these instructions were carried out. 'Execution, execution, execution of laws and orders must be the first and the last part of good governance, although I yet admit moderations, for times, places, multitudes.'

Each year the situation became more difficult, the Puritans increased in numbers and in fanaticism, and the Papacy grew more aggressive. The Rebellion of the Northern Earls in 1569, the Bull of Excommunication (1570), the massacre of St Bartholomew (1572), persuaded the gentle Parker that strong measures were necessary and that Mary, Queen of Scots, (by now a prisoner in England) would have to be eliminated: 'If that only desperate person were away as by justice soon it might be, the Queen's Majesty's good subjects would be in better hope and the papists' daily expectation vanquished.' By dint of patience, tact, firmness and adaptability Parker had saved the Prayer Book from the attacks of the Genevans; he had built a new church delicately poised on the foundations of the old; a sterner policy was now needed to defend that church, a Whitgift rather than a Parker to direct the battle.

One other achievement belongs to Parker, perhaps his greatest. He had always made it his business to see that this 'new' church was not in fact a new church, that it should be the old, original church revived. His study at Cambridge of the early centuries of the church's history, his refusal to be moved by anything other than historical facts, his study of the Anglo-Saxon language, his collecting of ancient documents, were all directed towards one end, to prove that the 'new' Church of England was in truth the old Catholic church purged from the abuses and innovations of the Middle Ages. In 1566 he paid out of his own pocket John Day to cut in brass the first Saxon type for the publications of *A Testimonie of Antiquitie*, showing 'the ancient faith of the Church of England touching the Sacrament of the Body and Blood of the Lord ... above 600 years ago'. The book proved that it was a medieval innovation which forbade the clergy to marry and which restricted the receiving at the Communion to one kind.

Between 1563 and 1568 Parker was a moving spirit in preparing the Bishops' Bible, although he had not much time to give to the actual translation. He was, as Strype said, 'a mighty collector of books', not as a mere bibliophile but for a practical purpose, to help the Church of England in its struggle against Rome and the Puritans. The historian Freeman once said of Matthew Parker that it was owing to him, more than any other man, 'that there is anything to edit and anything to read about the early history of England'.

Although Parker was a modest and retiring man, hating publicity and ostentation, he had a proper regard for the office of archbishop and for his duty as a hospitable host. He himself was very sparing in his diet, but he entertained liberally and his home life was organized on a spacious scale: he was given special leave by the queen to maintain a body of forty retainers in addition to his regular servants. Among the many visitors who came to Bekesbourne Parker was once compelled to entertain the French ambassador. Parker was highly suspicious of his guests, whom he looked on as religious and political spies. Parker was in many ways naive, but he was also shrewd and he kept a close watch on the Frenchmen. After the party had left, Parker sat down and counted his spoons and was surprised to find that none had disappeared.

Parker died on 17 May 1575, worn out by pain and toil. He had endured much, for the queen left him to take all the blame when he carried out her orders and they proved unpopular. He was buried in Lambeth Church and his tomb was desecrated by the Puritans in 1648.

When Sancroft became archbishop, Parker's bones were recovered and reburied, with the epitaph, *Corpus Matthaei Archiepiscopi hic tandem quiescit.* He is not the best known of the archbishops, yet among the long line of St Augustine's successors none has served the Church of England more faithfully and more profitably than this gentle, modest, wise and saintly man.

Further Reading

V. J. K. Brook, *Archbishop Parker*, 1962.
Canon C. Smyth, *The Listener*, 30 October 1947.
E. W. Perry, *Under Four Tudors*, 1940.
W. M. Kennedy, *Archbishop Parker*, 1908.
W. E. Collins, *Typical English Churchmen*, 1902.
F. O. White, *Lives of the Elizabethan Bishops of the Anglican Church*, 1898.

PARKER, RICHARD (1769-97) was a ringleader in the most serious naval mutiny in the history of the navy. On 16 April 1797, a mutiny had broken out in some of the ships stationed at Spithead: the men registered their complaint against harsh conditions but behaved with restraint and weakened their own position by stating that they would go back to fight the French if the occasion should arise. When the red flag fluttered out on the *Sandwich*, flagship of Vice-Admiral Buckner, on the Nore station on 2 May, ten days after the settlement of the Spithead mutiny, the government had greater cause to be alarmed. For these men were more militant and better organized. Whether or not they were Jacobins, whether there were French or Irish agents at work, cannot be established. Individual Corresponding Society members contacted ship's delegates and addressed mutineers. A 'gentleman in black' was reported to be in touch with Parker. The mutineers were affected by talk of liberty and some of their leaders were desperate enough to talk of sailing out to hand over their ships to the French. With Duncan blockading Camperdown and Jervis on his uncomfortable station off Cadiz, the collapse of naval discipline threatened the war effort – and the whole social order. 'Without trusting entirely to a navy whom we may not be able to pay, and on whose reliance no firm loyalty can be placed, how are we to get out of this cursed war without a revolution?' wrote Cornwallis, not normally an alarmist.

A committee of delegates had elected Richard Parker to be their 'President' on 10 May. The son of an Exeter corn dealer, he had served in the navy as a midshipman and been dismissed for insubordination. In about 1791 he had married Anne MacHardy and settled in Scotland as a schoolmaster. After being imprisoned for debt, he had taken the government's quota money to secure release. Just before this his daughter had died. He arrived aboard the *Sandwich* in February; it was a foul and over-crowded ship, there was discontent on board and disturbing news from Spithead. It is not difficult to see why these men mutinied, nor why Parker became their leader. He was vain, excitable, but not necessarily insincere in his idealism. He played the mutineer with style, maintained an admiral's state and never stirred abroad without music and banners. He concealed from his men the vital information that the government had decided to increase naval pay. Keeping his hat on in the best Jacobin manner, he eventually presented to Admiral Buckner articles ranging from reasonable requests to an affirmation of the right of seamen to dismiss their officers! Since the admiralty declined his invitation to parley, the mutineers took the offensive: on 24 May they despatched delegates to Yarmouth to urge men of the North Sea fleet to join them. Admiral Duncan was unable to prevent the infection spreading through his fleet: one after the other his ships sailed away as he stood out for the Dutch coast, leaving him only his flagship, the *Venerable* and the *Adamant*. 'I am sorry,' he wrote, 'that I have lived to see the pride of Britain disgrace the very name of it.'

On 28 May the First Lord of the Admiralty went to Sheerness, but he learned that Parker's support was patchy and he resolved to hold out: parliament passed stern measures, including a bill extending the death penalty to persons who had any intercourse with mutineers. The troops were stiffened by promises of extra pay and middle-class citizens manned gunboats for the defence of London. The mutineers set up a blockade of the Thames and the East India Company placed its fleet at the admiralty's disposal. Soon there were no more brass bands playing 'Rule, Britannia' or gangs of sailors roaming the waterfront enjoying an unexpected holiday. Hungry, cooped up in their ships, uncertain of the future, they rounded on their leaders. 'Dam my eyes,' wrote one man to the admiralty, 'if I understand your lingo or long Proclimations but in short give us our Due at Once and no more at it, till we go in search of the Rascals the Eneymes of our Country.' On 5 June they celebrated the king's birthday; on 6 June they were formally declared rebels; on 9 June Parker ordered the fleet to the Texel: no ship obeyed. On 15 June the crew of the *Sandwich* turned against Parker and sailed under the guns of Sheerness. Some of the leaders escaped to France. Parker, less fortunate, handed over to the military by his men, was tried by court martial, found guilty and, with fifty-eight others, condemned to death.

He spent his last hours penning a justification of his own actions and a denunciation of his followers: 'him whom they have exalted one moment as their Demagogue, the next they will not scruple to exalt upon the gallows'.

Further Reading

G. E. Mainwaring and B. Dobrée, *The Floating Republic*, 1935.
C. Gill, *The Naval Mutinies of 1797*, 1913.

PARNELL, CHARLES STEWART (1846-91), Irish leader, was described by Asquith as 'one of the three or four men of the Nineteenth Century'. During the long, dark, stormy history of Anglo-Irish relations a shaft of light has occasionally broken through, to bring short-lived hope. One significant gleam in Victoria's reign came with the leadership of Parnell. He was an unlikely champion for the downtrodden Irish: a Protestant land-lord who spoke with an English accent, son of an Angli-can clergyman and owner of 4,000 acres in Co. Wicklow, where he was also High Sheriff and captain of a cricket side. But he was descended through his mother from 'Old Ironsides', an American admiral who had fought the British in 1812. His sojourn at Magdalene College, Cambridge, where the English gentry predominated, was cut short by a fight. When in 1875 he was elected MP for Meath, it was with the backing of the Home Rule League. His impact at Westminster was immediate. Within a year a minister was saying 'something must be done about Mr Parnell'. Such was the persistence of his questions and speeches that he often kept the House up deep into the night. During the debates on flogging he intervened 250 times, and waved a cat-o'-nine tails over his head. His cautious leader, Isaac Butt, was embar-rassed, but Dublin loved it. In 1878 he forged links between the Irish at Westminster, the extremist Irish Republican Brotherhood, and the ex-Fenians in Amer-ica. It was the alliance on which his career was thence-forward based, and which he held together with tactical genius. After the Election of 1880 he became Chairman of the Home Rule Party. He was only thirty-four.

'Master Charley is born to rule,' said his nurse. Tall, slim and handsome, he had the self-confidence of an aristocrat. His gentleness, courtesy and winning smile impressed even his opponents. He was by instinct reserved; feared because people did not know what he was up to. As a speaker he used clear logic rather than rhetoric. His self-control hardly ever broke, yet all were aware of the fierceness of his devotion to Ireland, 'a vol-cano capped in snow'. An Englishman visiting Dublin thought his popularity there greater than anything Glad-stone had experienced in Midlothian: 'Parnell's journey can be compared only with the progress of Caesar', he wrote.

The journey was purposeful, to win Home Rule for Ireland. When he started, this seemed a pipe-dream, Home Rule motions in the House of Commons being thrown out by huge majorities. Yet eleven years later, in 1886, a Home Rule Bill was introduced by the British government itself, and this was largely Parnell's achievement. He created the disciplined prototype of the modern political party. He then forced Irish grievances onto the attention of the House of Commons, by filibus-tering so successfully that the Speaker had to change its rules, a forty-one-hour session on a Coercion Bill being

the climax. He consolidated his support from the extrem-ists by getting himself arrested for the violence of his attacks on coercion. They 'clapped the pride of Erin's isle into cold Kilmainham gaol'. But while he was there he came to an agreement with Gladstone. Parnell agreed to back Gladstone's second Land Act, which gave Irish tenant farmers secure tenure and fair rents; and to try to end the boycotting of landlords and their collaborators, which had escalated into violence. For his part Glad-stone agreed to repeal the Coercion Act and work with Parnell for justice for Ireland. This informal alliance proved the breakthrough. It survived even the horror of one of the worst acts of terrorism in the whole of Ireland's history, when the new Chief Secretary, Lord Frederick Cavendish, brother of the Whig leader Lord Hartington and married to Gladstone's niece, was hacked to death with his Under-Secretary in Phoenix Park, by 'Invincibles' armed with long surgical knives bought in Bond Street. Parnell's political position was strengthened by the forming of the Irish National League, which gave his party a constituency organization throughout Ireland; and also by the Third Parliamentary Reform Act, which enfranchised the agricultural labourer. Crucially, the General Election of 1885 left the Irish holding the balance of power between Liberals and Conservatives. As crucially, Gladstone was committed to pacifying Ireland, and had come to feel that Home Rule was the only way to do so. So Home Rule came onto Westminster's political agenda. Although Gladstone could not keep enough Liberals with him to carry the Bill through the Commons, it seemed only a matter of time before it got onto the Statute Book.

Had this happened, the clouds might have cleared away and the subsequent history of Ireland been differ-ent. But it needed Parnell's continuing leadership, and that was not to be. A catastrophe in his private life destroyed him as a public figure. He had triumphantly survived one personal attack, when letters condoning the Phoenix Park murders, said to have been written by him, and sent to *The Times* by Richard Pigott, a nationalist newspaper owner, were shown on their publication to be forgeries. But in 1889 Willie O'Shea, Irish MP and former army captain, sued his wife Katie for divorce and cited Parnell as co-respondent. Katie and Parnell had indeed been devoted to each other since 1880, and had had three children. Theirs was a domestic relationship, and Katie was the one real love of Parnell's life. He wrote to her as his 'Wifie' and shared her house as often as he could when Willie was away, which he normally was. How much Willie knew is still debated. Probably he was turning a blind eye from 1886, and with good reason, for Katie was due to inherit a substantial fortune from her Aunt Ben, which would not have come her way if scandal had tainted her. Soon after Aunt Ben's death

Willie sued. Parnell, confident as only a national hero could be, wanted the divorce to go through so that he could marry Katie: and the case was therefore uncontested. But he had underestimated the Victorian attitude to adultery, and overestimated his own prestige in Ireland, where he had not spoken for five years. The Catholic church abandoned him. Gladstone believed that the Nonconformists in the Liberal Party would not accept a continued alliance with the Irish if they were led by an adulterer. The Irish knew they could only get Home Rule through Gladstone. So they deposed Parnell.

The epilogue to the tragedy was bitter, for the Home Rule Party which Parnell had created was destroyed. He himself had been torn for years between his love for Katie and his ambitions for Ireland. Now he had chosen Katie, and for him it may have been best that heart disease killed him quickly, for despite his fierce campaigning, his candidates were losing by-elections to Irish opponents. He died in her arms. There was no other Irish leader remotely as strong to take his place.

Further Reading
F. S. L. Lyons, *Charles Stewart Parnell*, 1977.

PARR, CATHERINE (1512-48), Henry VIII's sixth and last wife, was born in 1512 and died on 7 September 1548. She was the daughter of Sir Thomas Parr, Controller of the Household to Henry VIII. Her father died in 1517, and Catherine was brought up by her mother, who was twenty-two years old at the time of her husband's death. Her education was careful and thorough and she became an accomplished scholar in Greek and Latin and modern languages.

When she was twelve years old an offer of marriage was made for her for Lord Scrope's son, but the offer was declined as not fulfilling the conditions laid down in her father's will. At some unknown date later she married Edward Borough, of whom nothing is known. Her second husband was John Neville, Lord Latimer, who had already been twice married and had two children by his second wife. He took some part in the Pilgrimage of Grace, but he escaped punishment and was held in favour by the king. He died in 1542 or 1543, and Catherine was at once sought in marriage by Sir Thomas Seymour, brother of Jane Seymour. She intended to marry him, but she was 'overruled by a higher power', which was in fact Henry VIII, whom she married on 12 July 1543. Catherine was physically a small woman, but she had character, spirit and much shrewdness, besides great kindness of heart. She managed Henry more successfully than any other of his wives: it was probably she who persuaded him to restore to Mary and Elizabeth the rank of princess, which had been taken away from them as being bastards: she interceded for the victims of the persecution under the Six Articles: and she took much interest in the education of

Elizabeth and of Edward, her stepchildren. For three months in 1544, while Henry was abroad invading France, she was Regent of England.

Henry's temper in his last years was very unreliable, for he was irritated by religious dissensions and in constant pain from an ulcer on his leg. Catherine nursed him and sometimes discussed religious questions with him. Once she differed from him. 'A good hearing it is,' Henry said, 'when women become such clerks; and a thing much to my comfort to come in mine old days to be taught by my wife.' It is said that a charge of heresy was brought against her and was signed by the king without her knowledge. But she got to know of it and fell ill with anxiety. Henry sent his doctors to her and also visited her himself. When she recovered she went to see the king and explained that she had only meant 'to minister talk' and not to assert opinions of her own. 'Is it even so, sweetheart? Then perfect friends we are now again', said Henry. But the next day she was walking with him in the garden at Hampton Court when the Lord Chancellor arrived with forty of the King's Guards to arrest her. Henry took the chancellor aside, and all that Catherine could hear was 'Knave! beast! and fool!' Catherine interceded for the chancellor, if he had done anything wrong. 'Ah poor soul!' said Henry, 'thou little knowest, Kate, how ill he deserveth this at thy hands. On my word, sweetheart, he hath been to thee a very knave.'

Henry VIII died on 28 January 1547. At once Sir Thomas Seymour, who had lately been created Baron Seymour of Sudeley, asked Catherine to marry him. Their engagement is certain, and Seymour passed several nights with her at Chelsea. Royal assent had not been yet asked for: when it was, the Protector was hostile to the marriage, but Edward VI in the end took Seymour's part and the Protector became reconciled to the event. On 30 August 1548 Catherine gave birth to a girl, but she died on 7 September from puerperal fever. Catherine lies buried in the chapel at Sudeley Castle.

Further Reading
A. Martienssen, *Queen Katherine Parr*, 1973.
Jean Plaidy, *The Sixth Wife*, 1953.

PARRY, SIR HUBERT (1848-1918), musician, led the revival of British music at the close of the nineteenth century. He commanded respect, within and beyond the musical world, through his position in society, his intelligence and his weighty and serious approach, as well as by his technical competence. From Eton and Oxford, he studied music in Germany under Edward Dannreuther. He made his name with works for the voice; cantatas and songs. An early success was his *Blest Pair of Sirens*, a setting of Milton's poem, *At a Solemn Music*, to which his style was well suited, and which is still in the choral repertoire. Most of his early writing, indeed, was for use in churches, and his *Scenes from Prometheus Unbound*, composed in 1880 for the Gloucester Festival, was acclaimed a masterpiece. Later he was to catch the mood of the nation at the coronation of Edward VII with his anthem, *I Was Glad* (sung at subsequent coronation services), and again in 1916, the year of the Somme, with his *Songs of Farewell*. His setting of Blake's *Jerusalem* could well be the national anthem if England were to become a republic.

Parry thought hard and wrote clearly, notably in his *Life of J. S. Bach*, and in *The Art of Music*, into which he introduced the Darwinian concept of evolution. He was Director of the Royal College of Music from 1894 until his death, and Professor of Music at Oxford. His knighthood was a proper recognition for raising the nation's musical standards – from a low level – in composition, performance, criticism and education.

Further Reading
C. L. Graves, *Hubert Parry: his life and works*, 2 vols, 1926.

PARRY, WILLIAM (*d.*1585), conspirator, was the son of Harry ap David of Flintshire, a man of good family, and his second wife, Margaret, daughter of the Archdeacon of St Asaphs. His original name was William ap Harry. According to his testimony, his father died about 1566, aged 108, leaving fourteen children by his first marriage and sixteen by his second. No date is known for William's birth. He was executed on 2 March 1585.

William was educated at a grammar school in Chester, from which, after several attempts, he escaped and went to London. Here he married a widow, Mrs Powell, who brought him some wealth. He entered the household of William Herbert, the first Earl of Pembroke, with whom he remained until the earl died in 1570, when Parry entered the queen's service. A second marriage with a widow, Catherine Heywood, brought him several manors in Lincolnshire and Kent, which involved him in some litigation in 1571. He was a profligate and extravagant young man and he very soon squandered all his resources and was being pursued by creditors. He therefore applied to Burghley to be employed as a spy abroad, doubtless in order to elude the creditors. He tried to ingratiate himself with the English Catholics abroad, to worm out of them their secrets which he could send on to Burghley. He returned home in 1577 and was constantly applying to Burghley for financial help. In 1579 he suddenly disappeared overseas without a licence to leave the country: he was home again in 1580. Pestered again by creditors, Parry violently assaulted one of them, Hugh Hare, for which he was convicted and sentenced to death, although he complained that the Recorder 'spake with the jury and the foreman did drink'.

Pardoned by the queen, Parry in 1582 asked leave to travel abroad. He continued to pretend that he was searching out the secrets of exiled Catholics, but in fact he was beginning to take the Catholic side. He urged a more lenient policy towards them in England and he pleaded for a pardon for some of the best of the exiles. Then he fell in with Charles Paget and Thomas Morgan, agents in Paris of the Queen of Scots. After reading some of the writings of Cardinal Allen, Parry allegedly began to ponder on the lawfulness of murdering princes for the sake of religion, with special reference to Queen Elizabeth. But he still played a double game: on 10 May 1583 he wrote to Burghley: 'If I am not deceived, I have shaken the foundation of the English Seminary at Rheims and utterly overthrone the credit of the English pensioners at Rome.'

In January 1584 Parry was again in England. He went straight to court and had an interview with Elizabeth. To her he confessed that he had had dealings with the pope, Paget and Morgan to attempt 'somewhat' against her life, but he protested that he had done this only in order to 'discover the dangerous practices devised and attempted against her Majesty by her disloyal subjects and other malicious persons in foreign parts'. In March he received a letter from Cardinal Como which gave some colour to this story. This letter Parry showed to the queen, who pardoned his offences and provided him with a seat in parliament (1584). He at once got into trouble for violently opposing an anti-Catholic bill and he was imprisoned for a few hours until released at the command of the queen.

Short once more of money, Parry took up spying again. He selected a man named Edmund Neville, who may have been a cousin of Parry's, and to him he proposed a plot to assassinate the queen. It is possible that Parry was only trying to extract from Neville some admission which could be used against him. Neville, however, revealed Parry's suggestion to one of the courtiers, who at once went with the information to Elizabeth. Parry was arrested, accused of compassing the queen's death, partly on Neville's evidence, chiefly on the evidence provided by Parry himself in his confession to the queen in January 1584.

It is difficult to be sure that Parry was really guilty. That he was technically guilty in discussing the murder of the queen without any authority from a minister to do so as a trap is certain. Whether he ever intended to murder the queen is another matter. Parry was a vain, weak and vacillating man, with an inflated idea of his own importance. It is unlikely that he would ever have had the resolution to carry out such a deed. When he was examined by Walsingham, he passionately protested that he had never mentioned such a matter to anybody since his return from France. He spent the night at Walsingham's house: next morning he asked for an interview and told Walsingham that he now remembered that he had mentioned to a kinsman of his a statement he had read in a book about the lawfulness of killing princes for the sake of religion. Confronted with Neville, he denied again that he had talked of murdering Elizabeth. Examined a third time, Parry made a full confession, wrote it out and confirmed it in a letter to the queen. The most charitable thing is to suspect that he was not entirely sane. He was hanged at Westminster on 2 March 1585.

Further Reading
Conyers Read, *Sir Francis Walsingham*, 1925.

PARSONS or PERSONS, ROBERT (1546-1610), Jesuit, was born at Nether Stowey in Somerset in 1546, and died in Rome in 1610. He was the son of a blacksmith who had eleven children, of whom Robert was the sixth. He was educated at Stogursey, then at Taunton, went up to Oxford, first to St Mary's Hall, then to Balliol, of which college he became a Fellow. At heart he was a Catholic, but he twice took the Oath of Supremacy. In 1575 he left Oxford after a quarrel with his colleagues who are said to have resented his popularity with his pupils. For five months he lived in London, then he went to Padua to study medicine: after two or three months there he went on to Rome, and on 4 July 1575 he was received into the Society of Jesus.

Parsons was ordained in 1578 and was put in charge of the second year novices. It was probably Parsons who originated the idea of sending Jesuits into England. Much to his surprise he was among the first to go and was appointed the Superior of the party. Parsons, Campion and seven others set out from Rome on 18 April 1580, mostly on foot, having only a few horses. They took six weeks to arrive at Rheims, and here the party split up. Parsons travelled to St Omer with Campion. 'He was dressed up like a soldier, such a peacock, such a swaggerer,' wrote Campion, and in the disguise of a captain returning from Flanders, Parsons arrived at Dover on 16 June alone (Campion was to follow). He moved to Gravesend and thence by boat to London, where he failed to find any lodgings; therefore he went to the Marshalsea, where he knew there were many Catholics. One of them found him a home, and he summoned a synod of Catholic priests in London to meet him at Southwark, where they discussed many points of importance to the Jesuit mission.

On 18 July Parsons and Campion (who had arrived safely) met by night to say goodbye to each other. They were joined by Thomas Pound, at whose suggestion Campion wrote his *Decem Rationes* and Parsons wrote his *Confessio Fidei*. He then began his tour of Northampton, Derby, Worcester, Gloucester, preaching and administering the sacraments from house to house. In October he was back in London, but he found that the hue and cry after the Catholics was at its height, so that he never dared stop more than two days in any one place. At last he set up a home in Bridewell, which acted as a secret centre for Catholic priests. The persecution increased, for the government was faced with a Catholic

rebellion in Ireland, backed by Spanish troops, Spain was now in possession of Portugal, there was a threat from Scotland and Catholicism was on the increase in England.

At this point (1580) Stephen Brinkley set up a secret printing press near Barking, and in spite of great difficulties and dangers he succeeded in printing Parsons's *A Brief Discourse containing certain Reasons Why Catholics refuse to go to Church*. The press was removed to Stonor, near Henley (1581), where Brinkley printed Campion's *Decem Rationes*, but this led to a search at Stonor and to the capture of Campion. Parsons was at the time in Windsor Forest and he thought it safer to retire to Sussex for a short while, after which he left England and arrived on 30 August at Rouen. Here he spent the winter, his chief activity being the founding of a school at Eu, near Dieppe, for English boys. This was the first of such schools: later it moved to St Omer, and later still it became the College of Stonyhurst in England. But Parsons was immensely busy in other directions. He was writing incessantly; he was the first man to see the necessity for saving Catholicism in Scotland, if it was to survive in England, and therefore he was negotiating with Lennox to send a Jesuit to Scotland. Meantime the Papacy and Spain were negotiating for the Enterprise – the invasion of England – without much success. Parsons determined to take a hand in the work.

From June 1582 Parsons was in Spain until April 1583, but his efforts to persuade Philip II to take active measures failed. He fell dangerously ill in Madrid and all but died. In May he was in Paris and then he met Allen at Rheims. He then travelled to Rome for three or four weeks, during which visit he extracted from Pope Gregory XIII two briefs, one to re-excommunicate Elizabeth, and one to make Allen Bishop of Durham, but these were neither published nor put into operation. In October he was in Paris, then he went into Flanders to advise the Duke of Parma about the number of English Catholics in that country and there he spent the winter. Most of 1584 was taken up in Paris with organizing the coming and going of English Catholics, sending off books, vestments, chalices, in close co-operation with Allen. It is said that at one point he was in great danger of being murdered at the instigation of the Earl of Leicester. This was because Parsons had taken the major part in publishing a libellous pamphlet called *Leicester's Commonwealth*, which was full of scurrilous abuse directed against the royal favourite and his influence over the queen. For some months of 1585 Parsons was at St Omer, but in September he and Allen went to Rome. The pope was now Sixtus V, and Parsons wanted to do his third year of probation before taking his final vows as a Jesuit. Allen went to discuss the financial difficulties of the seminary at Rheims; but there is no doubt that both went in order to persuade the new pope of the importance of the Enterprise.

For the next three years Parsons was living in Rome, first at the English College and then as Latin Secretary to the General of the Society. He took his last vows in May 1587 and he became Rector of the English College in 1588. During these years he directed the Jesuit mission to England and it was he who sent Father Garnet to England. He poured out a good deal of advice to Philip II on the invasion of England, but in fact he had little influence in getting the Armada despatched. It was certainly through his activity that Allen was made a cardinal. Less than a month after the news reached him of the destruction of the Spanish Armada Parsons left Rome and went to Spain, where he passed the next eight or nine years in founding and managing English seminaries there. He also spent much time in inciting Philip II to renew his attacks upon England, but he also warned him that no attack would be successful unless it was supported by a strong party of Catholics inside the island. He was perfectly well aware that some of the Spanish policy had only alienated English Catholics, but there are grounds for thinking that it was Parsons's intrigues abroad which greatly contributed to English Catholics' lukewarmness towards Papal and Spanish policy. In 1594 he published his *Conference about the next Succession*, a masterly work of political philosophy in which Parsons set out the case against the theory of the divine right of kings and also argued that on Elizabeth's death, the rightful heir to the throne was Philip II's daughter, the Infanta Clara Eugenia.

After Parsons returned to Rome as Rector of the English College there in 1596 he faced a number of 'domestical difficulties', divisions within the English Catholic movement. His appointment of Blackwell as archpriest or superior of the mission in 1598 led to a long and bitter dispute with those among the secular clergy who resented Parsons's influence. They sent two delegates to Rome to dispute the appointment: Parsons dealt with them high-handedly and shut them up in the English College. A further delegation was sent and the matter was not finally resolved until the reign of James I. Parsons died in Rome on 15 April 1610 and lies buried beside Cardinal Allen in the church of the English College.

Parsons played perhaps the most active part of anyone in the tragic history of Catholicism in England in the reign of Elizabeth. He was committed to the restoration of what he regarded as the true faith to his motherland. He sought to achieve this by devoting his energies and talents wholeheartedly to this end. He was one of the greatest political and religious writers of his age, he was a gifted diplomat and an educator and administrator of genius. In the end, his efforts were unsuccessful, and so for four centuries most English historians have dismissed him as a traitor.

Further Reading
P. J. Holmes, *Recusant History*, 1979, 1981, 1985.
P. J. Holmes, *Elizabethan Casuistry*, Catholic Record Society, 1981.
P. J. Holmes, *Historical Journal*, 1980.
Leo Hicks, *Letters and Memorials of Father Robert Parsons, SJ*, Catholic Record Society, 1942.
J. H. Pollen, *The Memoirs of Father Robert Parsons*, Catholic Record Society, 1907.

PASTON, JOHN (1421-66), esquire, is perhaps the best known late medieval gentleman and has often indeed been taken as representative of his whole class. This is due to the survival of the incomparable Paston letters. Approximately 1,100 items in all, these constitute by far the most extensive collection of contemporary letters, larger by far than those of the Celys, Stonors and Plumptons. They are also the most interesting and significant. They date mainly from the years 1450-80 and it was evidently John I who first systematically hoarded them.

It was John's father William (*d.*1444), a royal justice, who first raised the family into the ranks of the gentry by the profits of law and by the marriage of his son to Margaret Maltby, an important local heiress. John too received a legal training at the Inner Temple and was a practising lawyer as well as a landowner. His most important client proved to be Sir John Fastolf (*d.*1459) of Caister (Norf.), an old, childless and extremely rich ex-soldier, whose last, oral, will gave all his East Anglian lands to Paston on condition of the foundation of Caister College and a payment of 4,000 marks (£2,667.33). This lifted the Pastons into the front rank of the Norfolk gentry, justifying John's appointment as sheriff and his repeated election as knight of the shire. It also precipitated a series of disputes, conducted at law and by force of arms, that lasted for the rest of John's life, perhaps precipitating his death, and even beyond. Fastolf's oral will was not universally accepted as valid: it may have been fabricated by John Paston or else resulted from undue pressure on the old knight. It certainly brought John endless trouble and expense, three terms in the Fleet prison, and ultimately secured for the family only part of the lands at issue. Rigid, resolute and calculating, Paston does not appear even through his own correspondence as the most attractive and sympathetic of the participants.

The Paston letters are full of information on many topics. They have been ransacked by historians for information on love and marriage, religion, relations of landlord and tenant, and many other topics. Their principal value, however, is as a source for the politics, local government, law and order in East Anglia. As a new family, the Pastons had to defend their status and possessions against rivals: thus John himself was accused, wrongly, of being a serf; his title to his father's lands was contested; and he was engaged in litigation in several courts over the Fastolf lands. A good title was not sufficient, for the legal system could be perverted by bribery, influence and threats; it could be circumvented by violence in the locality or by influence at court. John Paston had a good title to Gresham (Norf.) in 1448, when it was stormed by Lord Moleyns, who could not be prosecuted because he was backed by the Duke of Suffolk, who was supreme both locally and nationally. Later Suffolk's son demolished John's lodge and the Duke of Norfolk besieged Caister Castle. Political fluctuations, calculations and tactics are faithfully mirrored by the letters. The impression is of a society where might rather than right prospered, where local government and justice were corrupt, and where gentlemen had to engage in politics, had to find a lord to depend on, and had to fulfil his wishes however outrageous they might be. This, it is often supposed, was the pattern everywhere. It may well be, however, that East Anglia was exceptional or that Paston's abrasiveness made him the centre and the cause of the trouble the letters depict. Perhaps some contemporaries even in East Anglia, such as John Hopton, managed to live more peaceful and trouble-free lives. But in their vivid details and lively language the Paston letters evoke the fifteenth century as no other surviving records do.

Further Reading

C. Richmond, *The Paston Family in the Fifteenth Century: The First Phase*, 1990.

J. Gairdner, ed., *The Paston Letters 1422-1509*, 1904; repr. 1986.

N. Davis, ed., *Paston Letters and Papers of the Fifteenth Century*, 2 vols, 1971-6.

H. S. Bennett, *The Pastons and their England*, 1932; repr. 1968.

PASTON, MARGARET (*c.*1420-82), wife of John Paston I (*d.*1466), illuminates the world of the married woman. The legal subjection of women first to fathers and then to husbands meant that most cannot be studied by historians and that those women who are best known are predominantly rich widows, whose property and behaviour was no longer controlled by men. Margaret Paston is immortalized by the Paston letters. She was born Margaret Mautby of Mautby in Norfolk and was a considerable heiress. Hers was an arranged marriage, but one in which Margaret willingly accepted her husband's superiority and in which convenience blossomed into affectionate companionship between the two partners. She bore her husband John Paston seven children and instilled in them respect and obedience to their father even after they had grown up. She deferred to John's wishes, accepted his priorities, and sought to fulfil them even after his death, when she upbraided their eldest son for falling short. Yet even Margaret did not *wholly* identify herself with John. It is striking that in 1482, forty-two years after her marriage, she chose to be buried not at Paston but in the parish church of Maltby, her original home, which she improved and beautified.

Margaret's 104 surviving letters and those to her and about her cast a flood of light on the life of the fifteenth-century gentlewoman. They illuminate the upbringing and education of her children, relations with them before and after marriage, the material considerations behind the arranged marriage, and the traumas attendant on romantic love. The fifteenth-century gentlewoman was above all a housewife, responsible for running a household of considerable and fluctuating size. She was responsible for catering and clothing. Much had to be bought outside, some at local markets, luxuries from further afield, and much – like fish in Lent and livery cloth – requiring bulk orders in advance. She was responsible for the operation of the brewhouse and bakery, the home farm and dairy, for preserving what was perishable and for making cloth into garments for the whole household. It was no sinecure. Housewifery had to be learnt and called for considerable administrative ability and foresight on the part of gentlewomen everywhere.

But Margaret also had other responsibilities. The Paston letters exist because the family did not continually live together and therefore needed to correspond. Margaret's husband practised law in London and was frequently absent on his own business or in prison. In his absence, Margaret took responsibility, for example in estate management, and he sent her instructions on a wide variety of topics for her to act upon. She, in return, kept him informed about local developments. That was in normal times, but times were not normal. Margaret was also involved in Paston's political activities, his litigation, and his struggles with the local nobility. She was actually within Gresham manor house when it was stormed by Lord Moleyns and it was she in person who appealed to the local justices when nobody else dared. She showed herself to be a formidable operator, no less shrewd and resolute than her husband, and perfectly capable of filling his place. Margaret's experiences were exceptional, but she was probably far from unusual in her capacity to cope, which widows had to do as a matter of course.

Further Reading

J. Gairdner, ed., *The Paston Letters 1422-1509*, 1904; repr. 1986.

N. Davis, ed., *Paston Letters and Papers of the Fifteenth Century*, 2 vols, 1971-6.

H. S. Bennett, *The Pastons and their England*, 1932; repr. 1968.

H. S. Bennett, *Six Medieval Men and Women*, 1955.

PATER, WALTER (1839-84) was a notable critic and essayist whose uncompromising aesthetic stance left its mark, not only in the work of Pre-Raphaelite painters, but also poets like Swinburne, and those younger men of the *fin de siècle* who responded rapturously to his call to value 'art for art's sake'.

School and undergraduate days at King's School, Canterbury and Queen's College, Oxford, grounded him in the classical studies that were to inform his writing, but left him hypersensitive about his supposed plainness and deformity, so hurtfully different from the beauty he studied in sculpture and painting. With a fellowship at Brasenose he began the writing for reviews that was collected and published in 1873 as *Studies in the History of the Renaissance*. Paradoxically, the apostle of beautiful form displayed more of style, in the choice of words and phrases, than of shape or coherence in argument. Pater was sustained in his sense of mission by an admiring coterie, and the sheer volume of his work conveys stamina. He was no dilettante. Yet an impression of shallowness persists. He found cats easier to love than human beings. Sharp little jokes helped him to find an audience and keep morbid fears at bay. His treatment of great themes – birth, death and faith – reflects his limited experience.

In all the minutely observed and delicately phrased studies of particular artists, in his novel *Marius the Epicurean* (1885), his *Imaginary Portraits* (1887) and his ventures into philosophy, notably *Plato and Platonism* (1893), the central theme was that art existed for the sake of its beauty: neither moral standards nor utilitarian functions were relevant. It was not due to Pater's writing about art so much as to his conviction that a man should treat his own life as a work of art, to be shaped according to art's, not society's rules, that his teaching was misappropriated, as by Max Beerbohm's 'comely ragamuffins in velveteen, murmuring sonnets, posturing, waving their hands'. Pater's injunction to Oxford men 'to burn with a hard gem-like flame' invited misrepresentation. Perhaps it was inevitable that aestheticism's appeal to the *haut monde* should become 'the patter of the boudoir' (Holbrook Jackson). Latently, even blatantly homosexual attitudes, frivolity and flamboyance among the more outré of his admirers, might caricature, but should not obscure a significant achievement. Pater supplied a valuable contrast and corrective to the tendency of his time to evaluate art on the basis of its moral and educational value.

PATERSON, WILLIAM (1658-1719), company-promoter, was a Scot from Dumfriesshire who came to England as a boy, prospered in trade, especially with the West Indies, and by the 1690s was well known in the City of London. An odd mixture of shrewdness and folly, Paterson belonged to the race of 'projectors' who flourished in the later seventeenth century and for whom the trade boom of the early 1690s provided scope and temptation. He is associated in British history with two ventures of this period, and it was characteristic of this imaginative and unlucky man that he withdrew early from the highly successful Bank of England and persevered to the end in the disastrous Darien scheme. Paterson is generally called 'the founder of the Bank of England', and he was indeed the leading figure of the mercantile group who put forward and negotiated with Charles Montagu, Chancellor of the Exchequer, the scheme on the lines of which the Bank was created. But he failed to pay up all his subscription, quarrelled with his fellow directors over policy, and resigned in 1695. By this time he was becoming heavily involved in the development of the Company of Scotland Trading to Africa and the Indies, the so-called Darien Company, whose creation was authorized by an Act of the Scottish Estates that May. Paterson had a well-warranted confidence in the economic prospects of Scotland. Unhappily, misled by his own successes in the Caribbean and by the superficial merits of the site of Darien, set between two oceans, he gave his energies – and much of his own cash – to sending his fellow countrymen down a road which was a ghastly dead end. The withdrawal of the English half of the capital and his own impeachment by the Westminster Parliament in 1695 increased his resentment against a country which he believed had undervalued his own financial acumen, and whetted his enthusiasm to found a Scottish colony in Panama. He himself went to Darien; fever made him desperately ill and killed his wife, but neither this experience nor the expulsion of the colonists by Spain convinced him of the folly of the enterprise. Like most Scots, he blamed William III and the English. He was wise enough in Anne's reign to support the Act of Union (1707), realizing its advantages for Scottish economic development. Yet even here Paterson was unlucky, for it was some years before he got his share of the 'Equivalent' which England paid to solace the investors in the Darien Company.

Further Reading
John Prebble, *The Darien Disaster*, 1970.
G. P. Insh, *The Company of Scotland Trading to Africa and the Indies*, 1932.

PATRICK, ST (*c*.415?-93?) was a British missionary bishop in Ireland, commonly though not very accurately termed the 'apostle of Ireland'. Patrick is the earliest native of Britain who can still speak to us directly, so to say, about himself. We possess two documents, undoubtedly genuine, of his own composition: the *Epistola* or 'Letter' addressed to a British king named Coroticus, and the *Confessio* or 'Declaration', a justification of his career and conduct. The *Confessio* is a kind of spiritual autobiography and is the prime source of evidence about his life. It is short, simple, awkward and oddly moving. Anyone who seeks to understand Patrick should start (and finish) by reading the *Confessio*.

Patrick was born into a well-to-do landed Romano-British and Christian family, probably somewhere in the north-west of the province of Britannia and perhaps not far from Carlisle, at some point in the first quarter of the fifth century. (The chronology of his life has generated long and sometimes fierce controversy. This essay follows the reconstruction suggested by Professor Thomas (see below) whose arguments are persuasive.) He evidently received some schooling, though of a fairly rudimentary kind: throughout his life he remained pathetically ashamed of his lack of learning, which is evidenced in the very simple Latin which was all that he could command. At the age of sixteen he was captured by raiders from Ireland and spent six years in captivity there working as a herdsman for his master 'near the forest of Foclut which is near the western sea', an area tentatively identified as the region of Killala in County Mayo. At the end of this period he escaped and managed to take ship to Gaul. It is possible that he spent some time at an ecclesiastical centre in Gaul such as Tours or the Auxerre of St Germanus, though all he himself tells us is that after a few years he returned to his family in Britain. This may have been somewhere about the year 440.

It was then that Patrick saw a vision in which he was summoned to return to Ireland: a man from Ireland appeared to him proffering a letter headed 'the voice of the Irish', and as he read it he heard voices crying, 'We beg you, holy boy, to come and walk again among us.' That Patrick experienced some sort of call is in no doubt. But there may have been rather more prosaic reality behind his mission as well. Patrick was consecrated a bishop before his return to Ireland, so we must allow further time in Britain for ecclesiastical training; he can hardly have gone back to Ireland before c.450 at the earliest. Furthermore, it is likely that he was despatched by the British church authorities, answerable to them, not with a roving commission to convert the heathen but as the bishop of an existing Christian congregation. Where this group was we do not know, though it is more likely to have been in the northern than in the southern half of Ireland. (The connection with Armagh is not claimed before c.700 and must be regarded as unproven.)

Patrick spent the rest of his life as a bishop in Ireland, ministering to his congregation and also enlarging it by evangelization. Of his activities in detail we know very little. We hear of large numbers of converts drawn from all ranks of the Irish social hierarchy; of the ordination of clergy; of travels to remote parts hitherto untouched by Christianity; of the foundation of religious communities. We also hear of dangers and tribulations; among these, criticisms levelled at Patrick and his conduct of the mission by the clergy in Britain, whose accusations the *Confessio* was seemingly designed to

rebut. Undeterred by difficulties, Patrick worked on in Ireland to the end of his life, in his own words 'a slave in Christ to a foreign people'. We do not know where he was buried, though his cult was later based at Armagh. The fine hymn known as 'St Patrick's Breastplate' is a later composition incorrectly attributed to him. To strip his career of its accretion of legend and to deprive him of the 'Breastplate', as modern scholarship has done, is in no way to diminish his achievement. Patrick and his anonymous fellow workers and successors laid the foundations on which the justly acclaimed achievements of early medieval Irish culture were raised.

Further Reading
The most recent translation of the relevant texts may be found in A. B. E. Hood, *Saint Patrick: His Writings and Muirchu's Life*, 1978. There is an excellent commentary upon them in the final chapters of C. Thomas, *Christianity in Roman Britain to* AD500,1981.

PAULINUS (*d*.644) was a missionary to Northumbria and the first Bishop of York. A native of Rome, he was sent by Pope Gregory in 601 along with other Italian ecclesiastics to reinforce the Kentish mission of Augustine. After the partial conversion of King Redwald of East Anglia at the court of Ethelbert of Kent it seems likely that Paulinus accompanied the king back to his kingdom; he probably encountered the exiled Edwin there. When Redwald relapsed into paganism we may assume that Paulinus returned to Kent. In about 619 he accompanied the Kentish princess, Ethelburga, to Northumbria when she was betrothed to King Edwin, and remained at his court slowly working towards his conversion which finally came about in 627. Paulinus had been consecrated a bishop in 625 and Edwin established an episcopal see for him at York. During the remainder of Edwin's reign we catch glimpses of Paulinus preaching and baptizing at Yeavering, Catterick, Lincoln and elsewhere. When Edwin was defeated and killed in 633 the church nurtured by Paulinus in Northumbria was almost blotted out. Leaving ecclesiastical direction there in the hands of his assistant James the Deacon, Paulinus withdrew to Kent with the queen and what remained of the royal family. There he was given charge of the vacant see of Rochester which he administered until his death in 644.

PAXTON, SIR JOSEPH (1803-65), the Duke of Devonshire's gardener, and designer of the Crystal Palace, had a career that was only possible in an aristocratic society. The 'Bachelor Duke', sixth Duke of Devonshire, was a princely figure in Regency and early Victorian times, a lavish host and extravagant patron, who inherited large estates and many houses, including Chatsworth in Derbyshire and Chiswick House to the west of London. Paxton, a garden boy without any known education, had, through his green fingers and lively intelligence, become a foreman in the Horticultural Society's gardens at Chiswick. There the duke talked with him, and, on a sudden whim, asked him to become Head Gardener at Chatsworth. He was twenty-three. His start was dramatic. Arriving at 4.30 a.m. he climbed over the gate, put the men to work when they appeared, and went off to breakfast with the housekeeper and her niece. 'The latter fell in love with me and I with her, and thus completed my first morning's work at Chatsworth.' They married, and she proved a devoted wife and an exceptional business woman.

Speaking of the duke at a dinner after the Crystal Palace had made him famous, Paxton put his own life into perspective. 'It is to his fostering hand that I owe all I possess.' The duke thought big, and spent extravagantly. Paxton organized expeditions to get plants from Burma and Canada, which were the envy of his rivals: though the *Amherstia Nobilis* from Burma would never flower at Chatsworth, and the two young gardeners leading a trans-Canadian venture were drowned in the Colombia River. He moved to Chatsworth, from an estate in Surrey, a giant palm weighing twelve tons. His conservatory to house the plants was the largest glass building in the world. Over his huge rockery fell a cascade of water piped in from the moors. His fountain threw water 267 feet into the air, nearly eighty feet higher than any other. The displays he laid on for the duke's visitors were famous. 'I should have liked that man of yours for one of my generals,' said Wellington to his host after accompanying the queen to one of them.

For an especially precious plant, the giant lily *Victoria Regia*, he created in 1849 a new glass house. This gave him the idea for the Crystal Palace. The Great Exhibition planned by the prince consort was in danger of foundering, partly because of the cumbersome design for the building favoured by its Committee. On a train journey Paxton roughed out his own design, in glass and iron, on a piece of blotting paper, and showed it to a committee member, the engineer Robert Stephenson. It won his enthusiastic support, was eventually adopted, and was one of the reasons for the Exhibition's acclaimed triumph. Especially remarkable were Paxton's preparation of detailed drawings within a week, to be in time for their submission to tender; the design of the whole building in multiples of eight, to make possible the mass production of its parts; and the height of the central transept, to enclose elm trees which the organizers were forbidden to cut down. But it was the use of glass which caught the public's imagination. On May Day 1851 the Exhibition was opened by the queen, with the short tubby figure of Paxton leading the procession. The garden boy became Sir Joseph.

Something of a polymath, he was already wealthy, through shrewd speculation on the railways: he bought the shares and his wife sold them. Their timing was impeccable, and theirs was a partnership of trust. His friends numbered both George and Robert Stephenson and the railway magnate George Hudson. He put his business acumen to the service of the debt-burdened duke, some of whose Yorkshire estates he persuaded Hudson to buy. He had literary interests and was friendly with Dickens, who became the (unsuccessful) first editor of *The Daily News*, which Paxton founded. Accompanying the duke almost everywhere he went, he became an enthusiast for the antiquities which they encountered on a Grand Tour. He also proved a keen fisherman and a first-class shot. He moved the Crystal Palace to its new site in Sydenham, intending it as a leisure centre for working-class families. He became MP for Coventry, and organized a corps of navvies to build roads in the Crimea during the war. He floated some imaginative ideas. His Great Victorian Way to relieve traffic congestion would have been a glass enclosed boulevard, 100 feet high and seventy feet broad, encircling London from the Royal Exchange via Rotherhithe, Lambeth, Westminster, Victoria, Kensington, Paddington and Islington. This was too much for his contemporaries to digest, and eventually the Metropolitan Line was built instead. That was probably fortunate. But, *mutatis mutandis*, Britain could do with another Paxton in the twenty-first century.

Further Reading
V. Markham, *Paxton and the Bachelor Duke*, 1935.

PAYNE, MASTER PETER (*c*.1380-1455) was the last of the academic Lollards at Oxford and was a vital link between the English Lollards and the Hussite heretics of Bohemia (modern Czechoslovakia). He was born at Hough-on-the-Hill near Grantham in Lincolnshire to a French father and English mother and was educated at Oxford University, where he became a master of arts but never apparently qualified in theology. In 1408 he was renting White Hall and from 1411 he was principal of St Edmund's Hall, one of the fifty private hostels for students at the university. Payne fled abroad in 1413 and spent the rest of his life in Bohemia.

Wyclif was an Oxford academic before he became a heretic and his early followers were concentrated in Oxford. Archbishop Courtenay tried to purge the university of heretics in the 1380s and many of Wyclif's theological tenets had been condemned. Such efforts, however, failed to eradicate heresy from Oxford. Wyclif's philosophical works, which contained the seeds of his theology, remained uncondemned; copies of his theological works survived; and there were still academic Lollards to prepare further Lollard tracts and to convert new generations of heretics. Peter Payne presumably encountered Wyclif's philosophy on the arts course before he was converted by the Lollard Peter Patrich. According to Thomas Netter, he then became the worst of the Oxford Wycliffites. Translation of the Bible from Latin into English, which Payne defended in 1405, was a respectable view not yet confined to heretics, but in 1406 it was apparently he who used the university seal to commend the life and teachings of Wyclif. This letter was carried by two Czech scholars, who had visited Oxford to secure Wycliffite literature, and marks Payne's first contacts with the Hussites. He failed to appear for a public disputation on Lollard theology with Thomas Netter of Walden and in 1410 was acquitted of heretical opinions about the sacrament of communion. By then, however, control of Oxford's heresy was moving from the university to Archbishop Arundel, who secured the condemnation of 267 errors of Wyclif and thoroughly purged the university. Wisely Payne declined to stand trial and fled abroad, reaching Bohemia by 1415.

Payne brought to Bohemia a thorough knowledge of Wyclif's writings, both philosophical and theological, and of later Lollard literature. He is supposed to have taken further books there, but there is no direct evidence of this. His distinctive handwriting shows that he annotated many surviving Wycliffite books in Bohemia and he has been credited with indexing some for easier use. Almost at once Jan Hus was burned by the Council of Constance, the Hussite revolution followed, and Payne was thrust into the theological and diplomatic limelight. In 1421 he was engaged in mediating between the moderate Ultraquists, who wanted communion in both kinds (bread *and* wine), and the more radical Taborites and was engaged in offering the Crown of Bohemia to the King of Poland. He was one of the Hussite delegation to the Council of Basle in 1432, he became vicar-general of Archbishop John of Rokycana, and in 1451 he was sent on a mission to Constantinople. Even by Bohemian standards, however, he was a theological radical, who associated himself with the Taborites, and his safety was far from assured. He was a fugitive in 1437-9, when he was captured and could have been deported to certain death in England, but was instead ransomed by the Taborites. He shared in the decisive defeat of the Taborites in 1452, but was allowed to live at peace in Prague until his death three years later.

Further Reading
R. R. Betts, *Essays in Czech History*, 1969.
S. H. Thomson, 'A Note on Peter Payne and Wyclif', *Medievalia and Humanistica* xvi, 1964.

PEACOCK, THOMAS LOVE (1785-1866), novelist, was born at Weymouth, the only child of a London glass merchant who died when he was three. His mother was a woman of intelligence whose favourite reading was Gibbon; his grandfather, Thomas Love, a retired, one-legged navy man, was also influential in his upbringing. He left school at thirteen and was thereafter self-educated. He became nonetheless an accomplished Grecian. Hellenism seasoned his writing but did not provide the main inspiration. His novels are largely conversation pieces in which story and scene play a subordinate part. Indeed, they can be called criticism in novel form. In the process of exposing the foibles and fallacies of others, Peacock reveals a great deal about himself: a Regency Aristophanes, a witty egotist, with a good deal of Rabelais thrown in – and a strong line in eighteenth-century Gibbonian rationalism.

Peacock did not depend solely on writing for a living. For a time (1808-9) he was a merchant, then undersecretary on a warship. From 1819 to its demise in 1856 he was an examiner in the East India Company. This occupation left him a good deal of time for writing. His friendship with Shelley, too, undoubtedly stimulated him: later he described, in *Fraser's Magazine*, his friendship with the poet between 1812 and 1822. Shelley, who provided him with the original of Skythrop in *Nightmare Abbey*, needed practical and patient friends in his intense and restless existence. Peacock was a good companion to him because they were so different in character and ideas. He appreciated Shelley the more because he did not agree with him. It was his cool and original appraisal of poetry as a primitive thing, and of the present age of poetry as an age of brass, in *The Four Ages of Poetry* (1820), that provoked Shelley to write his *Defence of Poetry*. Peacock was not entirely serious in his part of philistine, though he had a great aversion to the poetry of Wordsworth. We need not regret that he wrote *The Four Ages* since it elicited such a lyrical response, a piece of prose in its way as fine as anything that Shelley ever wrote. Idealist and cynic – it was an improbable relationship, but not an unfruitful one.

Peacock produced his first poems in 1804 and wrote at intervals afterwards. His best lyrical poems are scattered through his novels, however. All but one of the novels were written between 1816 (*Headlong Hall*) and 1831 (*Crotchet Castle*). *Gryll Grange*, which some find the most enjoyable, is a *tour de force*, an old man's book, written in 1860. What will the reader find in these books, which are different from anything else in our literature? The contemporary debate is presented in terms of comic exaggeration which anticipates Dickens but draws upon the novels and plays of the past, the tradition of Fielding and Ben Jonson. The characters are often easily recognizable because of the simplification and prejudice which is perhaps Peacock's limitation as a critic, though part of his merit as a satirist. Mainchance Villa (in *Melincourt*) is the new residence of Peter Paypaul Paperstamp, with whom Mr Feathernest, Mr Vamp, Mr Killthedead and Mr Anyside Antijack discuss a letter from Mr Mystic, of Cimmerian Lodge. They are considering the best means to be adopted for finally and totally extinguishing the light of human understanding. Mr Forester (Shelley) and Mr Fax (Malthus) arrive: the latter is the champion of pure reason. Soon Paperstamp, whom the reader may already have identified as Wordsworth, and Feathernest (Southey) raise the cry, 'The church is in danger'. Vamp (a Tory reviewer) applauds: 'It is an infallible tocsin, for rallying all the old women in the country', and Paperstamp observes that 'a little pious cant goes a great way towards turning the thoughts of men from the dangerous and jacobinical propensity of looking into moral and political causes for moral and political effects'. Thus Peacock canes the romantic poets, as elsewhere the political economists, high and dry Tories (as in the amusing arguments against parliamentary reform in the *Misfortunes of Elphin*), or, in relatively gentle mood, in *Gryll Grange*, the high fanciful idealist, Mr Falconer, far-gone in hagiolatry, living in a tower, chaste but attended by seven beautiful sisters.

Two of Peacock's novels are different from the others: *Maid Marian* (1822) and *The Misfortunes of Elphin* (1829) are romantic stories, the first derived from Robin Hood, the second from Celtic legends. Peacock married a Welsh girl, Jane Gryffydh, and knew a little Welsh. There are pastoral scenes and verse in these books, besides satire. As a form of bardic light opera, the 'War Song of Dinas Vawr' in *Elphin* is very fine. Irony prevails, however, and the romance is never offered straight. Moreover the characters are mostly shadows. Professor Saintsbury, who was an ardent Peacockian, held that his 'extraordinary' style, 'full-blown and splendid', was to be found in *Elphin*: 'The epigram is not fired off point-blank at the reader' but 'slips easily off the pen, and is accompanied by the best Swift or Lucianic absence of insistence and waiting for applause'. For most people, however, the novels of talk will give most pleasure. The reader may look in vain for depths in Peacock. He perceives very clearly the antagonistic forces in the world about him: 'The sentimental against the rational, the intuitive against the inductive, the ornamental against the useful, the intense against the tranquil, the romantic against the classical' (*Crotchet Castle*). When we think of Hazlitt or Coleridge, however and the way in which their thought reached beyond this opposition, we see that the entertaining Peacock but skimmed the surface of his times. As his granddaughter recorded, 'He would not be worried'.

Further Reading
O. W. Campbell, *Thomas Love Peacock*, 1953.
J. B. Priestley, *Life of Thomas Love Peacock*, 1927.

PECHAM, JOHN (*c*.1230-92) is the only Franciscan friar to become Archbishop of Canterbury. The case for the thirteenth century as 'golden age of the medieval church' owes much to the triumphal progress of the friars, which was sealed in England by the succession as primates of the Dominican Kilwardby and the Franciscan Pecham in turn. Born at Patcham in Sussex about 1230, Pecham was already an Oxford graduate, when he joined the Franciscans in the 1250s. The preaching of the friars relied on academic training in theology and so Pecham was sent to study and teach first at Paris (*c*.1259-72), then at Oxford (*c*.1272-5), and finally at the papal curia (1277-9). Later entitled the 'ingenious doctor', he wrote extensively on theology, criticizing the theories of both the Latin Averroists and St Thomas Aquinas, and contributing to the controversy between the mendicants (friars) and the secular clergy. His sermons are simple and powerful, his poems and hymns deeply religious and technically perfect. He knew the Bible intimately and meditated on the crucifixion, redemption, and on the power and mercy of God. Contemporaries admired as saintly his rigorous fasting and chastity, which caused him to eschew the company of women. To his intellectual and imaginative gifts, he added administrative experience as provincial of the English Franciscans and a range of contacts in academic and papal circles. To the English church establishment he was an outsider and an unlikely papal choice as archbishop in 1279. His role was to initiate reform and to restore ecclesiastical liberties.

As archbishop, his concern for souls extended even to pluralists, he strove to secure the poor their due, and his charity was exceptional in spite of constant financial difficulties. Vigorous, meticulous and efficient, he visited every diocese in his province, a unique achievement, established new training for the parish clergy, sought to exclude the unworthy from bishoprics, and strove to stamp out pluralism and non-residence. His antecedents explain his defence of friars against seculars, his refusal to shorten monastic church services, his correction of theological errors at university, and his anxiety to prevent monks going there from acquiring dangerous learning they did not require. His defence of the Church of Canterbury brought conflict with his subordinate bishops and the Archbishop of York. Almost all such actions brought controversy, litigation, and unwanted expense. Often overbearing and caustic, he did not foresee the offence he caused. Naturally irritable, sensitive and impatient of criticism, he responded to challenges with invective, often spoiling a good case through intemperance, and sought to crush his opponents. He lacked tact, forbearance and the spirit of compromise. His concessions were spoiled by the bitterness with which they were made.

Pecham's defence of ecclesiastical liberties began at the Council of Reading (1279), but Edward I compelled Pecham to retract some canons as infringements of his prerogative, ignored Pecham's subsequent assertion of his prime duty to God, and stepped up royal encroachments on the church courts into outright attack. But Pecham's patient negotiation produced a satisfactory settlement in the writ *Circumspecte Agatis* (1285), which defined spiritual jurisdiction generously and precisely. This was perhaps the high point of Pecham's archiepiscopate, as thereafter his physical strength and mental equilibrium declined, leaving him lonely, embittered, and wrongly feeling a failure and betrayed.

Further Reading
P. Heath, *Church and Realm 1272-1461*, 1988.
D. L. Douie, *Archbishop Pecham*, 1952.

PECOCK, REGINALD (*c.*1390-1460), Bishop of St Asaph (1444-50) and Chichester (1450-8), was the only bishop convicted of heresy in late medieval England. A Welshman and Oxford graduate, Pecock held rectories in Gloucester (1424) and London, where he was also master of Whittington College (1431), before becoming in turn Bishop of St Asaph in 1444 and Chichester in 1450. Convicted of heresy in 1457, he was forced to recant to escape the flames, his books were burnt, he had to resign his see (1458), and he was confined to Thorney Abbey, where he was allowed

a secret close chamber (having a chimney) and convenience within the abbey, where he may have some sight to some altar to hear mass and that he pass not the said chamber. That he have no books to look on, but only a breviary, a mass book, a psalter, and a Bible. That he have nothing to write with; no stuff to write upon.

Pecock's loyalty to the church explains both his submission and his life's work. Firstly, he defended the church against criticism, as in his *Repressor of Overmuch Blaming of the Clergy* and his defence of non-preaching bishops, whose many essential duties, he argued, did not include preaching. Secondly, he wrote to improve lay understanding of Christianity and to convert heretics to orthodoxy. To reach such audiences, he wrote in English – the first theologian to do so – and relied overwhelmingly on logical reasoning. Lollards, he appreciated, rejected the authority of Catholic theology and tradition, interpreted the Bible for themselves, and therefore needed to be persuaded of the reasonableness of the official position. He was too serious about his subject and too respectful to his readers to simplify and wrote at whatever length was needed to make his meaning clear. The result was 'monumental, heavy, massive, dull and sometimes, but not always, wearisome and lacking in originality'. It was too excessively academic and technical for any but intellectuals. They, however, objected to his refusal to insist on unreasonable beliefs, such as Christ's descent into hell, and his determination to prove by logic what was already supported by Scripture, the early Christian Fathers, or tradition. In his recantation they forced Pecock to admit to 'presuming of mine own natural wit, and preferring the judgement of natural reason before the New and Old Testaments, and the authority and determination of our mother, Holy

Church'. Apart from attributing to him certain doctrines that he never taught, his critics failed to realize that 'the authority of the Bible was for Pecock unquestionable' on matters of faith. As his arguments probably passed unnoticed by those for whom they were intended, Pecock's sufferings were in vain.

It was not what Pecock said, but how he said it that led to his downfall. He was handsome, dignified, and immensely vain. Although not particularly learned or original, he exaggerated the value of his work – never had Christianity been expounded 'so clearly, so feelingly and comprehensively' – and wrongly thought his arguments irrefutable. He was extremely critical and historically acute, rejecting the Donation of Constantine, parts of the Creed, and even the Ten Commandments for his own Four Tables! He was amazingly tactless and did not understand the strength of hostility to him or its source. Such grave personal defects obscured his utter sincerity, intellectual honesty, and ardent sense of mission. His English prose and sense of the past are more memorable than his theology.

Further Reading
C. W. Brockwell, *Bishop Reginald Pecock and the Lancastrian Church*, 1985.
E. F. Jacob, 'Reginald Pecock, Bishop of Chichester', *Essays in Later Medieval History*, 1963.
V. H. H. Green, *Bishop Reginald Pecock*, 1945.

PEEL, SIR ROBERT (1788-1850) became a Victorian hero. He was a scion of the Industrial Revolution, his family from Lancashire and his wealth from calico. The Peel family success story warranted four pages in Samuel Smiles's *Self Help*. He was serious and public spirited. His family life was close, with regular family prayers. He was a pillar of the Church of England, but disliked dogmatic extremes. His splendidly comfortable manor at Drayton gave him roots in the English countryside. He had the technological interests of the age, and was President of the Royal Society, as well as an eclectic collector of paintings. Though he made bitter enemies, his effective administrative reforms, his belief in sound money, and above all his drive for Free Trade, were felt to have laid the foundations of British prosperity. Albert thought the world of him, and won the queen over to him. Crowds cheered him along the streets as he rode to Westminster to make his resignation speech, and when he died, statues of him sprang up in towns and cities all over the country. Historians have confirmed the verdict of his contemporaries, and the Tory party has performed with its customary skill the conjuring trick of putting the two severed halves together again in the box, and claiming both the pragmatic Peel and his leading critic, the romantic Disraeli, as part of its ancestry.

He had the nature and the nurture of a budding leader. His father was one of the richest of the cotton magnates, had bought the parliamentary borough of Tamworth, and told young Robert: 'Bob, you dog, if you are not prime minister some day, I'll disinherit you.' Educated amongst the gentry at Harrow and at Christ Church, he was the first to be awarded a Double First at Oxford in Classics and Mathematics. He was well built and handsome, with striking auburn hair. When his father organized him into the Irish Borough of Cashel, aged twenty-one, he caught the eye of Perceval, one of the four other Harrovian prime ministers who overlapped him in the House of Commons, and by 1812 had risen to the key Irish post of Chief Secretary. Only the younger Pitt had climbed faster.

Ireland featured large and fatefully in Peel's political life. In his six years as Irish Secretary, he made his name amongst the Tories by creating the Irish Constabulary ('Peelers'), by successfully renewing the Insurrection Act when his colleagues were wobbling, and by leading the Protestant opposition whenever Catholic Emancipation was proposed in the House of Commons. The Catholic leader, Daniel O'Connell, described him as 'a raw youth, squeezed out of the workings of I know not what factory'; a duel was only prevented when O'Connell was arrested. He became 'Orange' Peel. He believed that Catholic Emancipation would inevitably lead to the dissolution of Ireland's Union with England, and the issue drew him apart from Canning, otherwise his friend and ally. Oxford University honoured his Protestantism by choosing him as their Member of Parliament. So when, in 1829, he and Wellington carried Catholic Emancipation through a shocked and taunting parliament, he was marked as a turncoat. He justified the Act on pragmatic grounds. The popular landlord, Vesey Fitzgerald, had been routed at a by-election at Clare by O'Connell, who, as a Catholic, was not allowed to take his seat in the House of Commons. A repetition of this result on a national scale would have made Ireland ungovernable: yet only he and Wellington could get Emancipation through parliament by bringing enough Tories with them. To some, nevertheless, this was 'miserable, contemptible hypocrisy'. Oxford rejected him.

Before then, he had won a high reputation as Home Secretary, an office which he held under four prime ministers, between 1822 and 1830. Following years of repression, Peel set about clearing the undergrowth of an archaic collection of criminal laws. His method was to prune and to graft, not to plough up and replant. He reduced a mass of obsolete legislation to a handful of intelligible statutes. He also tackled, cautiously, the problems of enforcing the law. English mistrust of arbitrary government made the introduction of a centrally controlled police force deeply suspect. It was to Peel's credit, as politician as well as administrator, that he got as far as creating the London Metropolitan Police. In their blue uniforms and iron framed top hats, they were so well run that they were soon imitated all over the country. The age of the beadle and the spy was over, and the Bobby on the beat (nicknamed after his creator) had arrived.

In 1830 the long era of Tory power came to an end. The liberal Canningites had already resigned from Wellington's government, leaving Peel as almost its only minister of top calibre in the House of Commons. The Whigs, in a Britain which seemed to be lurching from riot to revolution, pushed through the First Parliamentary Reform Act. Peel was at first appalled by the scale of the changes, speaking sometimes with the 'incoherent red-faced rage' of an often hot-tempered man. But once the Bill was carried, he set about making the new House of Commons work. Its mood, and that of the electorate, was in fact more attuned to the Lancashire cotton merchant than to the Whig aristocrat. In the Tamworth Manifesto, written to his constituents before the next General Election in 1835, Peel showed how well he had grasped this, by appealing to 'that great and intelligent class of society … which is far less interested in the contentions of party than in the maintenance of order and the cause of good government'. By then he had actually become prime minister. In 1834 he was given the chance to form a government and show that a Tory administration could work, when William IV dismissed his Whig ministers, and summoned Peel back from an Italian holiday. Although he did not gain enough seats to win a majority at the subsequent election, his hundred days in office established the new Conservatism in the eyes of the electorate, and his party's strength in the House of Commons was increased from 150 to 290 members.

In opposition again, he showed such tactical skill, not least in restraining the Tory majority in the House of Lords from irresponsible treatment of government measures, that he won back many of the former Canningites, led by Stanley. The Conservative party, as it was becoming known, was developing an effective organization, centred on the Carlton Club and the work of Bonham, its electoral expert. In 1839, when Melbourne resigned, everyone expected the Whigs to go out. Their departure was delayed by the young queen, who refused to change any of the Whig Ladies of her Bedchamber. Peel properly refused to take office without some gesture of royal confidence. He had contributed to the crisis through his stiff and shy manner towards Victoria, but Melbourne should have persuaded her into more constitutional behaviour, and he paid the penalty in 1841, when the Conservatives were returned to power with a solid majority. By then, Peel was seen as the natural prime minister, and the Conservatives as the party of the future, transformed in a decade from the helpless opponents of the national will by his leadership.

He took office in difficult circumstances, at the start of the 'Hungry Forties', with bad harvests, trade depressed, industry stagnant, and the Chartists turning violent. The Whigs had left a government deficit of £7.5 million. Against that background, Peel's fiscal achievements were remarkable. In his great budget of 1842 he repealed the duties on all British manufactures, reduced those on imported raw materials to five per cent or less and on foreign manufactured goods to twenty per cent or less. He paid for this by reintroducing income tax. This was a bold move, for it had previously been levied only in wartime: yet one Whig MP commented: 'One felt all the time he was speaking, "Thank God Peel is Minister".' His policy led to the expansion of trade, and the gradual growth of a budget surplus. In 1845, thus encouraged, he abolished the import duties on more than half the items still on the tariff book, and drastically reduced the contentious sugar duties. Britain was poised to take full advantage of its head start over the rest of the world in the techniques of industrial production. And with his Bank Charter Act (1844), he provided sound money to back the manufacturers. The Currency Act of 1819, known as Peel's Act because he chaired the Committee which shaped it, had put Britain back onto the gold standard, but there was no restriction on the issue of notes, and 400 banks could print them. Result – four major financial crises. The Bank Charter Act limited the issue of notes by the Bank of England, and terminally curtailed the issue by private banks. Only three times in the next eighty years did a government have to take emergency powers to extend the issue.

Free Traders have usually advocated a peace-making approach to foreign policy, and Peel's Foreign Secretary, Aberdeen, was notably trusting in his diplomacy. Peel often took a stronger line, and in 1845 launched a £1 million naval rearmament programme which nearly led to Aberdeen's resignation. He also halted the Repeal Association in Ireland, in the middle of what it had proclaimed as 'The Year of Repeal', by having O'Connell arrested, a bold, and well timed, decision which ended the Liberator's career as an effective leader. He achieved much of what he set out to do in Ireland, conciliating the Catholics by opening up opportunities for higher education for them, with new colleges to be grouped into a new university, and increased endowments for the Catholic seminary at Maynooth. His confidence grew with his successes.

But there loomed all through the years of his government the problem of the Corn Laws, and the Anti Corn Law League made sure that they were never far from the foreground of politics. How could a free trader like Peel accept duties on foreign corn, which pushed up the price of bread, and discouraged improved techniques in agriculture, and which did not even benefit the farm workers, who suffered like everyone else from the high cost of food? Peel himself felt the dangers of the growing isolation of a landed aristocracy defending its privileges.

At the end of one of Cobden's speeches he turned to his neighbour on the Front Bench, saying: 'You answer this, for I cannot.' But the Tory party was the landed party, wedded to agricultural protection. From his dilemma as its leader, Peel hoped to escape by reducing duties on foreign corn gradually.

But, with corn as with Catholics, his hand was forced, and again it was the Irish who forced it. The total failure of the potato crop had created famine there. The government had to let foreign corn into Ireland free. Could the duties in England be maintained? Peel felt not. He attempted to get the Whigs to take office, but Russell returned what Disraeli dubbed 'the poisoned chalice', and Peel embarked on his second major reversal of policy. This time he split his party. Always hypersensitive to criticism, he had already shown arrogance towards his back-benchers when testing their church loyalty over the Maynooth grant, and had only forced them to accept the reduction in sugar duties by threatening resignation. He now expounded a constitutional doctrine which did not sit easily with the party feelings which were emerging after the Reform Act. 'I claim for myself the right to give my sovereign … that advice which I believe the interests of the country require.' Party policies should take second place to good government if circumstances changed. The restless landed MPs found an unlikely leader in Disraeli, who savaged the prime minister, who had earlier ignored his requests for office, in a series of brilliant speeches. His theme was clear. 'Let men stand by the principle by which they rise.' 'A Conservative government is an organized hypocrisy.' The Repeal of the Corn Laws (1846) was carried with Whig support, but two-thirds of the Conservatives present voted against it, and soon afterwards the government was beaten and Peel resigned.

He broke his party. Nearly all his ablest ministers stayed loyal to him, leaving the Protectionist majority of the Tory gentry almost leaderless. He refused to form a new party himself, preferring the role of a national statesman. But he did not live long into the period of political instability which followed. Physical exhaustion had already taken its toll; he had suffered from noises and pains in his head ever since a shooting accident. His early death in 1850 was caused by a fall from his horse, which stumbled over him after it had thrown him. His political career, however, had already come to an end with his resignation. There was, and is, dispute about whether the emergency of the Irish famine required the Repeal of the Corn Laws: but not over his motives. 'Good God!' he exclaimed in the Commons, 'Are you to sit … and calculate how much diarrhoea, and bloody flux, and dysentery, a people can bear before it becomes necessary for you to provide them with food?' The country at large recognized the Repeal as the climax of his efforts to bring prosperity to Britain, and its leading newspaper called him 'the greatest statesman of his time'.

Further Reading
N. Gash, *Sir Robert Peel* [1830-], 2nd edn, 1986.
N. Gash, *Mr Secretary Peel* [-1830], 2nd edn, 1985.
N. Gash, *Peel* (a condensed version of *Mr Secretary Peel* and *Sir Robert Peel*), 1976.

PELAGIUS (*fl.c.*380-420) was a Christian teacher, theologian and heretic. A native of Britain, where he received what was clearly a very good education – a point of some importance for our understanding of the intellectual culture of Roman Britain – Pelagius settled in Rome about 380, lived there until about 409, and then moved by way of north Africa to Palestine where he is last heard of in 418. It was in the course of his long residence in Rome, where he was taken up by the high-minded, pious, Christian aristocracy, that he developed the views which the ecclesiastical authorities, notably Augustine of Hippo, were to condemn. Pelagius's teaching, often misrepresented, was that man's God-given nature permitted and indeed obliged him to achieve perfection; and that this should be sought by the layman through living a life of stern, austere, ascetic Christian rectitude. In developing his ideas he was led to question the doctrine of Original Sin and it was this that attracted the condemnation of the church. In the land of his birth Pelagian ideas became sufficiently widespread to bring St Germanus twice to Britain in the second quarter of the fifth century to combat them. In some form or another Pelagius's teaching has remained influential from his day to our own. He is the first native of Britain to have made an enduring contribution to the intellectual and religious culture of Europe. He is also, coincidentally, the first native of Britain of whose physical presence we can form some idea. Pelagius was a great big man, fat and bull-necked; oddly enough, in defiance of all subsequent changes of race and custom, the first 'John Bull' figure in British history.

Further Reading
P. Brown, *Religion and Society in the Age of Saint Augustine*, 1972.
P. Brown, *Augustine of Hippo*, 1967.

PELHAM, THE HON. HENRY (1695-1754) had an unspectacular career and personality. In the words of his biographer, Coxe, 'his understanding was more solid than brilliant'. He himself disclaimed 'court ambition' and had 'very little interested views' but made reduction of the nation's debt the main aim of his administration. Yet 'Harry the Ninth' was a leading minister from 1743, when he was promoted from Paymaster to First Lord of the Treasury and Chancellor of the Exchequer, until his death in 1754; from 1746 at least he was in effect prime minister, as his brother acknowledged. During this period he established such an ascendancy in the House that opposition virtually ceased. In November 1753 there were no amendments to the royal address. In his time, more than even in Walpole's, stability was achieved by a minister who enjoyed the confidence both of king and parliament. This was the Whiggery, 'the politics of stock-jobbers, and the religion of infidels' which the Tory Dr Johnson denounced. The collapse of opposition had an unhealthy aspect. It was the triumph of a system which depended upon securing personal allegiance by individual bargains: 'men before measures'. At the same time the system provided a period of tranquillity during which useful reforms could be promoted. Such measures as there were bore the stamp of Pelham's sane and reasonable mind, even where he did not initiate them. He was not a great man, but a deservedly well-liked one. He had the tenacity of Walpole, his mentor, who had made him Paymaster in 1730, but without his coarseness and greed; the patience of Newcastle, his brother, to whose grasp of the system he owed his position, but without his pettiness. There was also tragedy in his life: after the death of his two sons in 1734 work may have been anodyne.

On 10 February 1746, after George II had proved more than usually difficult, Newcastle and Harrington, Secretaries of State, were followed into resignation by Pelham, Bedford, Gower, Monson and Pembroke; the larger part of the ministry. Two days sufficed to show that George could not have an alternative ministry. The Pelhams therefore returned on their own terms: the supporters of Bath and Granville were dismissed. Pitt was brought in as paymaster and appropriate honours were distributed among 'the old gang'. It was a decisive political victory for the old Whigs against the new, as well as a constitutional event of some note. By 1746, every important politician had been drawn into the Pelham circle. The Pelhams were effective because they operated as leaders of the group in which every man had his place. Henry Pelham confirmed the mastery of the group by his skilful conduct of business in the Commons; it was also a tribute to him that George II came not only to accept but apparently to trust his administration. There were tensions such as arose over the disagreements about foreign policy between Newcastle and Harrington and the fall of the latter after Newcastle's persistent interference in his business. In this Newcastle was acting, in his own intrusive and fussy manner, in the interests of George II. On the whole, however, the triumph of the Pelhams was owing to the fact that Henry Pelham had the trust both of the king and of parliament. He had temporarily solved the dilemma of the century, the legacy of the Glorious Revolution.

Pelham regarded peace as worth almost any price and celebrated the treaty of Aix in 1748 with drastic reductions in the size of the armed forces: the navy from

51,000 to 10,000 in two years, the army from 50,000 to 18,850. He balanced the budget within four years and was able to reduce the Land Tax. Unpreparedness for the next war was the price of these economies, but they found general favour. He simplified the management of the National Debt, swollen alarmingly to £77 million, and secured the reduction of the interest to a uniform three per cent: the 'consols' as the new consolidated stock came to be called. This involved him in a running battle with the vested interests in the city, the financial rings which had floated loans on the basis of a closed subscription. His success in the battle, gained by conciliation and firmness, provided an example of the good effects of continuity of administration of the sort that the Pelham system provided.

Pelham promoted measures to stimulate trade: he supported Oglethorpe's bill of 1750 creating the Free British Fishery Company to develop the herring industry, and allowed the export of wool from Ireland, hitherto forbidden. Despite his brother's nervous warnings about the indignation of the populace, he supported Chesterfield's measure for reform of the Calendar and he spoke warmly in favour of the Jew Naturalization Bill in 1753, aware perhaps of his obligation to Gideon, the city banker, for support of his policy; but he allowed his brother, and mob clamour, to cause its repeal in the same year. Whig oligarchs could not afford to be insensitive to public opinion in the year before an election. The growth of gin-drinking had not been checked by Walpole's Act of 1736 and its degrading effects were brought home to public opinion, already conscious of the brutality and violence among the lower classes in the larger towns, by the satirical prints of Hogarth. 'Gin Lane' and its illicit vendors were brought under control by Nugent's bill, the Tippling Act of 1751. In 1753 Hardwicke, Lord Chancellor and the faithful ally of the Pelhams, steered through his Marriage Act to control clandestine and irregular marriages. Henry Fox, though a member of the administration, defended the 'Fleet marriages' and labelled Hardwicke 'a giant spider'. There was room for public as well as personal disagreements within the loosely bound administrations of the time. Much of the legislation of the years of the Pelham supremacy was humdrum, much directed towards private interests, enclosure, turnpike road building. Some was directed towards the perennial problem of the smuggler; there was a medley of measures to deal with specific problems: the width of wagon wheels, for instance. The record reveals a steady advance in the economic strength of the country and a slow-growing interest in the morality of society. Respectable, amiable but shrewd, Pelham was a loss to his friends and to his country. He was the only eighteenth-century 'prime minister' to die in office. Now there ensued a prolonged period of political instability. His king recognized his worth and his

comment is no bad memorial: 'Now I shall have no more peace.'

Further Reading

J. Wilkes, *A Whig in Power, The Political Career of Henry Pelham*, 1964.

J. B. Owen, *Rise of the Pelhams*, 1957.

Coxe, *Memoirs ... of Henry Pelham*, 2 vols, 1829.

PELHAM-HOLLES, THOMAS, 1st DUKE OF NEWCASTLE (1693-1768) was fortunate to live in the eighteenth century when the political system was such as to afford his talents the widest scope. George II thought him unfit to be a chamberlain at a minor German court, but was forced to accept him in high office throughout his reign. The man who was derided by the wits and snubbed by his fellow ministers has left an imposing answer to his critics. He was Secretary of State from 1724 to 1754, with a break of only two days, in February 1746, and one shift, from south to north, in 1748. Then he was First Lord of the Treasury from March 1754 to November 1756 and again from June 1757 to May 1762. It is a unique record. Newcastle had the means to make himself indispensable even if he did not have the personality to make himself respected. Wealth, borough influence, understanding of the workings of patronage, a readiness to serve abler men, and to betray them when necessary: all these contributed to his position. But more important than anything was his passionate interest in the political game. To stay at the centre of affairs he seems to have been ready to make any sacrifice of pride.

Newcastle canalized the various sources of influence that were available to governments of the time: boroughs, places in dockyards, excise and institutions under the Crown, grants from the civil list or secret service money, clerical and academic preferment. He directed them to the one end of securing a parliamentary majority. But he was no mere political jobber. Despite the flurry and effusion of his huge correspondence, the apparent lack of sense of proportion, the moments of timidity and the obsessive jealousies that made him such a tiresome colleague, Newcastle had a talent for management, patience, subtlety, a good memory and insight into political behaviour. He also delighted in electioneering. In every election from 1715 to 1761 he took a prominent part, in his own counties, Sussex, Nottinghamshire, Lincolnshire and Yorkshire, but also as general agent for the government throughout the country. His guidance of the riotous elections of 1734 was perhaps his masterpiece; the opposition had a good cry in 'No excise' while bad harvests and trade were damaging government prospects; the ministers yet secured a comfortable majority.

Newcastle had been Lord Chamberlain in 1717. In 1724 he became Secretary of State in place of Carteret and despite Pulteney, who must have hoped for the position. Townshend snubbed him as Carteret did later, but he played a leading part in the downfall of that minister in 1730. Besides his encyclopaedic handling of the patronage he made himself useful to Walpole by his sensible debating. He was at his best when he could accept the dominance of a greater man. But when first Carteret, and then his brother Henry Pelham, led the administration, Newcastle's phobia about being left out of things became a menace. With Carteret (1742-4) he was especially uneasy, for he rode roughshod over even the formalities of Cabinet consultation and committed the economical Pelhams to lavish expenditures. In August 1743 he complained 'No man can bear long what I go through every day, in our joint audience in the Closet'. The king might humiliate Newcastle in the closet, but he could not impair his hold upon the House; he was forced to accept Carteret's resignation in November 1744. Unless power in the House and favour in the closet could be combined, eighteenth-century government was impossible: this is the reason for the power of the Pelhams. They were at least prepared to compromise, to reconcile the opposites of Hanoverian king and anti-Hanoverian parliament, to prosecute a war while looking for peace, to bring even Tories like Phillips and Cotton into minor ministerial posts. Because they were interested as much in power as in measures, they made government possible. In 1748, Newcastle overcame his phobia about sea travel to conduct negotiations at Aix-la-Chapelle. Louisburg, England's only conquest of the war, was handed back to the French; Don Philip got the Duchies of Parma and Piacenza. In India the status quo was restored. England kept Gibraltar and Minorca; Prussia kept Silesia. '*Bête comme la paix*' was the saying in Paris. But Newcastle was pleased with his efforts to end the war which, in Carlyle's phrase, was 'an unintelligible, huge, English-and-Foreign Delirium'. Frederick the Great knew what he wanted, a greater Prussia, for the present Silesia – and he got it. Charles Emmanuel of Savoy was bent, in Gibbon's phrase, upon 'plucking more leaves of the Italian artichoke'. France was 'consulting her traditions rather than her interests'. Unfortunately the loose ends left untied by the peace of Aix-la-Chapelle were to cause another war. Newcastle could not prevent it, since it was desired by both France and Austria. Culpably he did nothing to prepare England for the resumption of the war. He neglected the vital task of building up the navy. He was affected by George's anti-Prussian prejudices. While Kaunitz, disenchanted with the English alliance, set the diplomatic revolution in train, Newcastle busied himself with his 'Great System, the great object of my life, in foreign affairs': this was to secure, by lavish bribery, the election of Maria Theresa's son as King of the Romans. Henry Pelham grumbled about this expensive 'moonshine', Frederick was self-righteous about interference in German affairs,

the Austrians themselves contemptuously rejected the scheme as an impertinence and came to terms with France.

Hard hit by his brother's death in 1754, Newcastle pressed on with his System. Russia was brought in by a defensive treaty in September 1755, then Prussia, alarmed by the prospect of attack from Russia, by the Convention of Westminster. France and Austria then made their alliance, to be joined by Russia. Newcastle was gullible in supposing that his treaties with Prussia and Russia were not incompatible; a more serious objection voiced by Pitt was that the centre of England's diplomatic interest appeared to be Hanover. When England floundered into war in 1756 it was to the accompaniment of disasters for which Newcastle was responsible; the defeat of Braddock, the wrong type of general, sent too late; the abortive naval action of Byng and the subsequent loss of Minorca. 'Indeed he shall be hanged' said the agitated Newcastle, after the debacle – he was shot. But the poor state of the navy and the confused orders given to England's naval commanders can be laid at the minister's door. Pitt had been dismissed from the Paymastership in November 1755 and had since been jeering at Newcastle's alliances and followers, 'Xerxes's troops'. Now Newcastle was forced to come to terms with him. At first Pitt attempted to rule without him, from November 1756 to April 1757. Against the king, against the closet, against Newcastle, and denied the boon of early victory, he was ineffective. From 6 April, when he was dismissed, until 29 June, when he joined with Newcastle, the country was without a government. The country wanted Pitt, but he could not have a free hand in parliament or enjoy the confidence of the king without Newcastle. From 1757 to 1761, the partnership subsisted on this uneven basis. The accession of George III, Pitt's determination to carry the war into a further phase by attacking Spain and his haughty and uncooperative ways were among the causes of his fall in October 1761; Newcastle did not wish it, for all their differences of policy. George's determination to recover control of the patronage meant that Newcastle's own days were numbered. In the negotiations which led to the Peace of Paris he fought for recognition of the claims of Frederick without success; opposed in everything and edged out of power, he eventually resigned in May 1762.

Some of the best stories of the eighteenth century are told about Newcastle. Horace Walpole's account of his conduct at Westminster Abbey during the funeral of George II is typical: 'He fell into a fit of crying at the moment he came into the chapel, and flung himself back into a stall, the archbishop hovering over him with a smelling-bottle; but in two minutes his curiosity got the better of his hypocrisy, and he ran about the chapel, with his glass to spy who was or who was not there, spying with one hand and mopping his eyes with the other. Then returned the fear of catching cold; and the Duke of Cumberland, who was sinking with heat, felt himself weighed down, and turning round, found it was the Duke of Newcastle standing upon his train, to avoid the chill of the marble.' The accounts of Hervey, Waldegrave and Smollett show that it was fashionable to laugh at him. The solemn Lord Wilmington said possibly the truest thing about him: 'The Duke of Newcastle always loses half an hour in the morning, which he is running after the rest of the day without being able to overtake it'. His worse fault was meddling. During the peace negotiations of 1746-8, properly the province of his fellow Secretary of State, Harrington, he corresponded secretly with the envoy in Holland and sent instructions contrary to those of Harrington. He could not leave well alone and it was his mother, to whom he was devoted, who spoke of him 'perpetually fretting your friends with unjust suspicions of them'. He was easily agitated. Of a dinner party with Granville he wrote: 'My Lord President had dined and talked very unguardedly ... I was frightened the whole time'.

Newcastle always showed, however, a high conception of public duty. If it was his fault that he thought himself indispensable, he had the talents to make himself so. He devoted himself to the handling of pension and place, but he made nothing from it for himself; considering the fortunes made by lesser men, like Henry Fox, we may respect his self-denial. His kindness and his patriotism deserve better from the historian than they received from contemporaries.

Further Reading
R. Browning, *The Duke of Newcastle*, 1975.
J. B. Owen, *The Rise of the Pelhams*, 1957.

PENDA (*d*.655) was King of Mercia from 633 to 655, a lifelong heathen at a time when the conversion of the English to Christianity was proceeding apace, and a formidable ruler who rivalled the power of the Northumbrian kings. In 633 he defeated and killed Edwin and in 642 Oswald. It was only with great difficulty that Oswy managed to serve Penda the same way at the battle of the river *Winwaed* (unidentified, probably one of the tributaries of the Humber) in 655. Bede never refers to Penda as enjoying an overlordship of the type he attributes to these three Northumbrian kings: but he reveals that Penda had power, at least from time to time, over Wessex and East Anglia, and Welsh tradition recorded by Nennius recalled that British kings could be counted among Penda's subjects.

Penda's power might have been based in part upon peaceable relations with his British neighbours in Wales. It is significant that he threw off the overlordship of Edwin and established himself as King of Mercia in alliance with Cadwalla, King of Gwynedd. Mercia's westward expansion under Penda may have been a matter of diplomacy as much as of war. Early Mercia could have been as 'Anglo-Celtic' as the Northumbria of Ethelfrith or the Wessex of Ine.

Penda is notorious, thanks to Bede, for his heathenism. He did not forbid Christian missionaries such as Cedd to preach in his dominions and he even tolerated the conversion of his son Peada in 653. But for himself, he preferred to stick by his ancestral gods and did so until his death. The conversion of Anglo-Saxon kings to Christianity was not a walkover.

PENN, SIR WILLIAM (1621-70), admiral, was a Bristolian, the son of a merchant, and was brought up to the sea. He served in the parliamentarian navy, and by 1651 was commanding a squadron in pursuit of Rupert in the Mediterranean. He fought with distinction in the First Dutch War, notably in the actions of 1653 which ended with the death of Tromp, and was appointed a General of the Fleet and a Commissioner of the admiralty. In 1654-5 he commanded the Fleet in the unhappy expedition which failed to take Hispaniola but secured Jamaica instead; like its military commander Venables, with whom he quarrelled, Penn was briefly imprisoned on his return. In disgrace, he withdrew to the estates he owned in County Cork, and it was here that his son William first came into contact with Quakerism. Restored to favour and knighted at the Restoration, he became a Commissioner of the navy, the role in which he appears so frequently in the pages of Pepys, who first enjoyed him as 'a merry fellow and pretty good natured, and sings very loose songs' but later came to think him a dissembler and 'a very villain'. Penn served under the Duke of York in the Second Dutch War and took part in the action off Lowestoft in 1665. He died in 1670 and was buried in St Mary Redcliffe at Bristol.

PENN, WILLIAM (1644-1718), founder of the Quaker colony of Pennsylvania, was the son of Captain (later admiral) Penn. Born in a house on Tower Hill, he went to school at Chigwell. When the admiral fell into disgrace in 1655 because of the failure to capture Hispaniola, the family moved for some years to their estates in Ireland. The Restoration brought the admiral back to favour, and William went to Christ Church. Later he was to talk of the 'hellish darkness and debauchery' of Restoration College; while there he seems to have been a royalist and something of a dandy, yet also to have fallen under the Nonconformist spell of Dr John Owen, who had been the Cromwellian vice-chancellor of the university. Penn was fined for non-attendance at chapel and sent down; he had a row with his father, who sent him to Paris. After a taste of court life and a duel he settled to study for two years (1662-4) at the Huguenot College of Saumur, where he was deeply affected by the tolerant and liberal theologian Moyse Amyraut. On his return to England he studied at Lincoln's Inn; in 1666 he went again to Ireland on business connected with the family estates, and in Ireland he was converted to Quakerism. As a boy of eleven he had been to a meeting in Cork where the preacher, Thomas Loe, had deeply moved him; now, in 1667, he heard Loe once more, and henceforward he was a Quaker.

To join a sect which was eccentric in dress and language, whose meetings were illegal and whose members were persecuted both by the law and by public opinion, was strange conduct for a gentleman born into the ruling class. The admiral certainly thought so, but eventually recognized his son's decision before he himself died in 1670. Penn was imprisoned three times in three years: in 1670 the jury's verdict when Penn was on a charge of riot (they found him guilty of speaking in Gracechurch Street and in effect acquitted him; he had in fact been taking part in a Friends' meeting outside their meeting-house, closed under the Conventicle Act of 1670) was the occasion of Brushell's Case (1671), which established the freedom of juries. In 1672 Penn married Guli Springett in Bristol. He wrote extensively in these years, most notably, *No Cross, No Crown* (written in the Tower in 1669), a prophetic defence of Christian self-denial, and *The Great Case of Liberty of Conscience* (1671); used such influence as he had at court on behalf of his fellow Quakers; and took part on the Whig side in politics during the Exclusion Crisis (1678-81), acting as agent for Algernon Sidney in two elections. But increasingly his mind was turning towards the opportunities which the American colonies seemed to offer, both of providing a refuge where his Quaker brethren could find and practise toleration, and of establishing a 'Holy Experiment', a state living by Christian principles. In 1676 he was one of the Trustees of the colony of West New Jersey; and in 1680 he petitioned Charles II for a grant of land in America in payment of a debt of some £16,000 owing to the admiral. The result was the colony of Pennsylvania, named after the admiral, and founded in 1681. Penn drew up its constitution, the Frame of Government, providing for an assembly elected by all taxpayers, complete religious toleration, no oaths, and the death penalty only for wilful murder or treason. He was himself its Governor, and he was reponsible for the famous peace treaty of 1683 with the Delaware Indians. But he spent in all only four years (1682-4, 1699-1701) there. This was one of the reasons why his later relations with the colony were not easy, involving litigation and political disputes. Nevertheless, Pennsylvania prospered more rapidly than any other of the early colonies, attracting a variety of settlers – Quakers from every part of England, Welsh and Irish, Dutch and Germans. Its capital, Philadelphia, the City of Brotherly Love, grew swiftly, in schools and hospitals and culture as well as in material wealth, and before Penn died it was challenging Boston as the greatest of colonial towns. Voltaire and the other philosophers of eighteenth-century Europe were full of admiration for Pennsylvania, as a testimony to the virtues of toleration and good sense.

Some of Penn's activities in the second half of his life brought difficulties upon his colony and his fellow Quakers as well as upon himself. He had been something of a Whig under Charles II; under James II he became very much a Jacobite, a familiar figure at court, accepting James's offers of religious freedom to Dissenters at their face value, acting as go-between to James and the Fellows of Magdalen, and going on a mission on the king's behalf to William of Orange. He backed James's Declaration of Indulgence in 1688, no doubt in the interests of the religious and political toleration in which he believed and which he had advocated in a pamphlet (*Good Advice to the Church of England, Roman Catholick and Protestant Dissenter*) in the previous year. Macaulay, in a famous passage of his *History of England* (Vol. I, Chap. 4) savaged Penn; the attack is open to much criticism in detail, yet one phrase – 'He had no skill in reading the characters of others' – strikes home. Penn's misjudgement of James II led him into trouble after the Revolution. He was before the Council in December 1688; he was in danger of arrest in 1690-2, because he had been in communication with the exiled king, and for a time went into hiding; for two years, 1692-4, he was deprived of the governorship of Pennsylvania. He recovered public esteem in the later part of William III's reign. But there were private troubles, too; Penn had lived on a generous scale at Holland House, and ran into debt, and at one time he was a prisoner in the Fleet. Nevertheless, he continued to write; his *Essay towards the Present and Future Peace of Europe* (1693) is a fine plea for international understanding. And he remained deeply respected among Quakers, untypical though he was of them in some ways. Swift in the *Journal to Stella* tells us (1712) of what may have been his last public appearance: 'My friend Penn came there, Will Penn the Quaker, at the head of his brethren, to thank the duke for his kindness to their people in Ireland. To see a dozen scoundrels with their hats on, and the duke complimenting with his off, was a good sight enough.' Later in this same year Penn had a stroke. He lingered on in a second happy childhood until 1718. He lies now by the Jordans Meeting House at Chalfont St Giles.

Further Reading
Mary Maples Dunn, *William Penn: Politics and Conscience*, 1956.
Catherine Owens Pease, *William Penn*, 1956.
J. W. Graham, *William Penn*, 1916.

PENRUDDOCK, JOHN (*d*.1655), of Compton Chamberlayne in Wiltshire, has given his name to the only royalist rising against the government of Oliver

Cromwell. Penruddock's Rising, or the Wiltshire Rebellion, of March 1655, was a small affair involving less than 400 men and it was easily crushed. The rebels seized Salisbury; proclaimed Charles II at Blandford; completely failed to rally the support they anticipated in Dorset; and were broken by a troop of regular cavalry in three hours' fighting in South Molton. Penruddock was beheaded at Exeter after a fair trial, about fifteen others were put to death, and many more were sent to Barbados as indentured servants. Behind this hopeless episode lay a widespread royalist conspiracy. Late in 1653 a secret group, the Sealed Knot, was formed to organize an armed restoration of the monarchy, and its plans for 1655 envisaged a major rising in Yorkshire, with simultaneous movements against the Commonwealth in Lincolnshire, Cheshire, and Shropshire, and the south-west from Hampshire to Cornwall. But the Sealed Knot was excessively cautious. The government got on the track, strengthened its own forces, and arrested many royalists; the projects in the north and along the Welsh border fizzled out; and Penruddock's futile rising was virtually all that happened. The whole episode lowered the morale, never very high, of the more active royalists. More important, it gave Cromwell's government the opportunity to introduce, in the autumn of 1655, the most unpopular of all its devices – the system whereby England was divided into eleven areas with a Major-General set over each, a system in effect of government by the sword.

Further Reading
A. H. Woolrych, *Penruddock's Rising*, 1655, Historical Association Pamphlet, G.29, 1955.

PENRY, JOHN (1563-93), martyr and founder of Welsh Nonconformity, came of a well-to-do family and in 1580 he went up to Peterhouse, Cambridge. In 1586 he transferred to Oxford, probably to join in a Puritan movement which was beginning there. He took to preaching, and finding that his native Wales was exceptionally backward and ignorant, he decided to approach the government. From this moment he developed into a pamphleteer with a most forthright and rash style. He attacked those whom he believed to be the cause of the evils with violence and a total disregard for the possible consequences, including even the queen herself in his diatribes. Between 1587 and 1590 he printed in the secret press of Robert Waldegrave a series of pamphlets which, among other things, attacked especially severely the bishops. In 1588 there came from his press, and the proofs of it were certainly corrected by Penry, the first of the Marprelate tracts, known as *The Epistle*. In the next twelve months several more appeared. Penry was helped by John Udall and Job Throckmorton. Nobody to this day has discovered for certain who Martin Marprelate really was. Penry suffered persecution more than once, and he was ultimately arrested and condemned to death

for treason, not for the Marprelate tracts. He himself denied that he was Marprelate, and the evidence against him was to a large extent extracted from witnesses who had been put on the rack. The article in the *Dictionary of National Biography*, written between 1895 and 1896, accepts Penry as the author: this account should be compared with *The Notebook of John Penry 1593*, published by the Camden Society in 1944, where credence is given to Professor Dover Wilson's theory that the real author was Sir Roger Williams, although this view is not now popular. Penry was an unwise, but a highly courageous, controversialist, who was ready to die for his opinions. He was tried for treason on 21 May 1593, and was condemned to death. On 29 May, while he was having his dinner, he was suddenly told that he was to die that day. At five o'clock in the afternoon he was hanged.

Further Reading
The Notebook of John Penry 1593, edited by A. Peel for the Camden Society, 1944.
Dover Wilson in *The Library*, October 1907.

PEPYS, SAMUEL (1633-1703), diarist and naval administrator, was a Londoner, born in the parish of St Bride's, the fifth child of a tailor. His paternal ancestors were from Cottenham in Cambridgeshire, and he spent a year or two of the early 1640s in Huntingdon and attended the school where Oliver Cromwell had been a generation before. But he was brought back to London and went to St Paul's School; and in 1649, a boy of strong Puritan feelings, he saw Charles I executed. Next year he went up to Magdalene College, Cambridge, graduating in 1653. In the later 1650s he took service under his cousin, Edward Montagu, that loyal Cromwellian who in 1656 was appointed joint Commander of the English fleet. In 1658 Pepys was successfully cut for the stone, and in that year too he began, in effect, his career as a civil servant by becoming a clerk to one of the Tellers of the Exchequer, George Downing. Yet the great turning-point in his life came in 1660 when, after sailing to Holland as Montagu's secretary in the fleet that brought the king home, he was appointed Clerk of the Acts to the Navy Board, and thus was launched on the course that made him the most distinguished civilian naval administrator in English history. And it was on 1 January 1660, too, that he began to keep a diary.

The *Diary* was written in the shorthand devised by Skelton some twenty years before. Since it was first deciphered and published (in part) in the early nineteenth century it has become much the most popular of all the source-works of English history. Its value to historians lies partly in its information about the leading personalities and events of Restoration England, partly in the light it sheds on social life in Charles II's London. These things have attracted the general reader also, yet what has fascinated him at least as often has been the

Diary's revelation of its author in all his rich humanity. Gossip, amours, friendships, quarrels with his wife; music and sermons and plays; snobbery, delight in being in the know, patriotism, devotion to work; an endless pleasure in small things, a sense of the great occasion – all are there. As a diarist Pepys was lucky, with the Restoration, the Plague, the Fire, and the Dutch raid on the Medway to record from intimate knowledge as his framework of public events. Yet he used his luck with a superb blend of art and artlessness. Perhaps what has made the *Diary* so permanently attractive is that it was the work of a young man. He stopped writing it in his thirty-seventh year, on 31 May 1669, because he believed himself to be threatened with blindness. Later that same year the death of his wife was a shattering blow.

Yet an exciting and hazardous public career, of high significance to posterity, lay ahead of him. As Clerk of the Acts, Pepys had already made his mark. He had begun to tackle corruption in the dockyards; had become treasurer of the committee responsible for Tangier; had, like his fellow diarist Evelyn, with whom he had so little in common, stayed at his post throughout the Plague; and had in 1667-8 done his best to defend the Navy Office from Commons' criticism for the disasters of the Dutch War. Thus by 1669 he was an established public servant distinguished for zeal and shrewdness. His great achievements as a naval administrator came after 1673, when the Test Act compelled the departure of James, Duke of York, from the post of Lord High Admiral. Charles II put the admiralty into commission and appointed Pepys as Secretary. He retained the office until 1688, apart from an interval from 1679 to 1684, and during these years he carried out or inaugurated a series of reforms. Some, like his detailed dealings with naval contracts or his development of the convoy system in the Third Dutch War, were of immediate significance; others, like his reorganization of officers' ranks and his preference for 'tarpaulins' as Commanders were the beginnings of long-term developments. All contributed to making the admiralty an effective department of state and thus to laying the administrative foundations for the naval glories of the following centuries.

His work was not done without fierce opposition, and this did not come only from those whose jobbery Pepys ended and who disliked spending £600,000 on the thirty new ships of the line he demanded in 1677. For Pepys had long abandoned his Republican enthusiasm of 1649, and had become very much a supporter of the court; no doubt his royalism was sharpened by James's own interest in the navy. So it is scarcely surprising that Shaftesbury and his followers went for Pepys as soon as he was elected MP for Castle Rising in 1673, accusing him of popery, or that at the height of the Popish Plot scare in 1679 they got him dismissed from his post and sent to the Tower on a similar bogus charge. Although he was freed within a year he had been in dire peril. In James II's reign Pepys was in effect the civilian head of the admiralty, and in the crisis of the Revolution he remained loyal to the king – although, characteristically, he did not reproach Dartmouth for his failure to challenge William's landing. Inevitably he was dismissed, and in 1689 he was again arrested and accused of passing naval information to the French. But the charge was soon dropped, and Pepys spent the remainder of his days in retirement at Clapham, publishing *Memoirs of the Navy* in 1690 and devoting some of his energies to Christ's Hospital, of which he was treasurer.

Further Reading
Richard Ollard, *Pepys*, 1974.
R. C. Latham and W. Matthews, eds, *The Diary of Samuel Pepys*, 11 vols, 1970-83.
Arthur Bryant, *Samuel Pepys: The Man in the Making*, 1933; *Samuel Pepys, The Years of Peril*, 1935; *Samuel Pepys, The Saviour of the Navy*, 1938.

PERCEVAL, SPENCER (1762-1812), who had been prime minister for three years, was shot dead in the lobby of the House of Commons on 12 May by a bankrupt merchant, John James Bellingham. His shocking end is perhaps better known than his steady life. Yet it is likely that, but for a madman's bullet, he would have earned a large place in political history, as the prime minister who rode out the storm – and brought the ship safely into harbour. He was only fifty when he was killed, physically robust and active, politically secure and respected. Napoleon was preparing to march on Moscow, Wellington to take the initiative in the Peninsula. Indeed, in Fortescue's words, he had 'endured the dust and heat of the race without earning the immortal garland'.

He was the younger son of the second Lord Egmont, who was celebrated for his glum appearance; he died when Spencer Perceval was eight. The boy was sent to Harrow which was just then attracting the notice of parents away from Eton and Westminster and entering its golden age as a nursery of politicians. Under Heath and Drury he became a competent classical scholar, made some life-long friends, among them Dudley Ryder, the future Lord Harrowby and a staunch political ally, and acquired a lasting affection for the school. At Trinity College, Cambridge, he became a confirmed evangelical, living in a world apart from the majority of undergraduates, a world of earnest manners and set opinions. He could be thoroughly eccentric in his religious concerns – as when he indulged in his taste for prophetic calculations about the end of the world and the identity of the creatures in the book of Revelation. He did not hesitate to use his parliamentary influence to promote legislation on moral questions such as adultery and divorce. Yet he was almost unmarked by the less attractive features of contemporary evangelicalism. There was little of that priggishness that men noted about the 'Saints'.

For lack of means, Perceval had to go straight to a career. Decisive, tough-minded and methodical, he rose rapidly in his Bar practice. In 1796 he became member of Northampton after a fiercely contested election in that notoriously radical borough. He enjoyed the support of the Castle Ashby interest, but his constituency, with its 1,000 electors, was no pocket borough. He was a conscientious member and had no trouble in keeping this seat for the rest of his life.

It was about this time, when he was making his way, that Romilly wrote of 'his excellent temper, his engaging manners and his sprightly conversation'. Like many small men (he was little more than five feet tall) he was also thrusting and tireless. He wooed Jane Wilson and married her against the wishes of her father, who did not see a future Attorney-General in this impecunious barrister. He received a pleasant sinecure, the Surveyorship of the Maltship and Clerkship of the Irons, and he was orthodox on such sensitive questions as the revolution and the constitution. But all was founded on hard work and good advocacy. From the start he was a fervent Pittite and spoke effectively for the ministry in critical debates. At the same time he was entrusted with the prosecution in important state trials, such as that of Binns of the London Corresponding Society (who was acquitted after a brilliant defence by Romilly). His legal and political careers thus advanced together, and in 1801 he became Solicitor-General in Addington's administration. He had no qualms about taking office under Pitt's supplanter, since he did not hold with Pitt's policy of Catholic emancipation. In his immovable opposition to any concession to the Irish Catholics he drew largely on the views of his intolerant brother-in-law, Lord Redesdale, and he overrated the threat of the pope as the instrument of a hostile power. But his views were grounded on his faith in the Church of England. Unlike many evangelicals he was utterly opposed to the liberal idea that any body of Christians is a church in itself and entitled to full social and political rights in the state. It was in the name of the Church of England – envisaged as a positive moral force in the nation – that he opposed the Roman Catholic claims, framed his education policy and also projected reforms which would purify his church and make it more effective. Though he was widely regarded as a fanatic, his was a positive and idealistic view.

When Pitt was on his way in 1798 to fight the duel with Tierney that might have ended his life, and was asked about a possible successor, he told Ryder, his second, that 'Mr Perceval was the most competent person, and that he appeared the most equal to Mr Fox'.

It is a remarkable judgement upon a man who has been so often dismissed as a political hack, a stop-gap or, with memorable unfairness by Sydney Smith, who could not bear the 'sepulchral Spencer Perceval', as having 'the head of a country parson and the tongue of an Old Bailey lawyer'. In fact Perceval's qualities did not amount to genius, but they were largely what was needed in the situation created by the exigencies of war, the weakness of the Whigs and the intransigence of the king on the question of Catholic emancipation. He was therefore promoted from Solicitor-General to Attorney-General in 1802, in which office he remained under Pitt after 1803. After Pitt's death he was considered to be the leader of 'Pitt's friends'. A brief period in opposition was followed by two years at the Exchequer, from March 1807 until he succeeded Portland in October 1809. Because of Portland's inability to transact any business in the latter months of his administration, Perceval acquired independence and authority. When he became prime minister, few were surprised and George III was delighted. But the position was deplorable in all respects. The reckless behaviour of Canning had removed not only himself, but also for the time being Castlereagh, from the political scene. Rivalries went so deep that the main question in choosing new ministers was less that of fitness for the job than willingness to work with colleagues. Perceval had also to consider the blocks of votes that belonged to leading contenders for office. His first duty was to see that his government was viable in parliamentary divisions.

In the end his Cabinet was less than impressive. Lord Chancellor Eldon laid twenty to one that the government would not even face parliament. A typical Whig reaction was Grey's: he was torn between admiration for Perceval's courage and indignation that he should dare to form a ministry at such a time. Wynn found a disturbing feature: 'In the whole of the list there is not one man of old property, weight and influence in the country but that idiot Lord Westmorland.' Auckland argued that none of the ministers, except for Perceval, was able enough to devise a strategy to contain Napoleon, to find means to implement it, and to combat the French economic campaign without crippling the country's own economy. Fortunately Wellington was capable of holding his own in Spain, Liverpool proved a capable war minister, Napoleon contributed to his own defeat and Britain's economic strength enabled it to survive the continental decrees.

At the start, however, the government's prospects were bleak. That it survived, and with some credit, was due mainly to Perceval. His resilience was exactly what was required. The ministry survived the inquiry into and debates on the Walcheren expedition. Somehow money was found to pay for the Peninsular War. Wellington saw mainly the shortcomings of the Treasury but ministers deserved praise for their efforts to find the money which maintained the war from day to day. These were, in Gladstone's phrase, 'the heroic days of war finance'. In the detailed business of the Exchequer Perceval owed much to talented subordinates, notably Huskisson and Herries. He tended to act as he thought his mentor Pitt would have done. All the responsibility and much of the work was, however, his. He remained Chancellor of the Exchequer after becoming prime minister, despite prolonged efforts to find someone to relieve him of a burdensome post, and his five budgets are models of sound finance. Between 1808 and 1812 the supplies needed exceeded those of any comparable period and a greater proportion than ever before was raised by taxation. The total of new debt contracted between 1803 and 1807 was £156,000,000; from 1808 to 1812 it was but £123,000,000. After Perceval's assassination it rose again steeply. The chancellor had stood firm against the defeatism of those who believed that it was impossible to finance continuous operations on the continent, and against the caustic attacks of the bullionists.

Perceval's ministers made some capital out of George III's fiftieth jubilee in 1810. They were justified in hoping that some of the old king's popularity would rub off on them. The king's sons were nothing but an embarrassment. In May 1810, when the Duke of Cumberland's valet was found dead, the verdict was that he had made an attempt on his master's life. The popular verdict was the opposite. The Duke of York had been forced out of the Horse Guards after revelations about the sale of commissions by his mistress, Mrs Clarke. Perceval, who defended him stoutly at that time (1808) insisted upon his reinstatement in 1811. When in the summer of 1811 George III relapsed into insanity, the question of regency was raised again. Perceval followed the precedents of Pitt, went on with his work, and had the satisfaction of being confirmed in office. As Perceval survived crisis after crisis his reputation advanced to a point at which 'plucky Perceval' could be described (by J. W. Ward) as 'the most popular man in England'. He worked incessantly and felt the strain, though, said Long, he was 'as hard as iron'. Only Sunday morning service at St Margaret's, Westminster, with his large brood of children in attendance, and occasional informal parties, provided relaxation; but a tranquil home provided the ideal background for his labours. He would often slip quietly into the nursery to see his children, for 'he was never so happy as when playing in the midst of them'.

In 1812 Wellesley resigned after prolonged intrigues. Talk of coalition was largely a screen for his own ambition to be prime minister. The regent very properly stood by Perceval who was able to strengthen his administration by bringing back Castlereagh to the Foreign Office and Sidmouth as Lord President; Castlereagh brought talent, Sidmouth votes. In the country at large,

however, these manoeuvres looked insignificant beside dangerous outbreaks of popular violence. A trade depression in 1811 had brought unemployment; the Orders in Council were widely blamed, machines and stocking frames were smashed. One of Perceval's last acts was to set up a special commission in Lancashire to deal with the Luddites.

Bellingham, who had suffered imprisonment in Russia, where he had represented a firm of Liverpool merchants, may have thought that Perceval was the member for Staffordshire, and former ambassador to Russia; he was certainly deranged and it is only the loosest link that connects his murderous act with the distresses of merchants and weavers. But mobs assembled that night in London to exult, bonfires were lit and flags waved in Nottingham and Leicester. Some were convinced that an English revolution was beginning. In fact the country was quiet. The administration survived under Lord Liverpool, whose capacities were at least equal to those of Perceval. But the old Toryism had received a mortal blow. 'The most reactionary prime minister of the century' (Aspinall) was certainly a defender of the status quo in church and constitution. Liverpool, also opposed to Catholic emancipation, may have been a better man to lead the Tories into the politics of transition after the end of the war.

In another view (Roberts) Perceval was 'hardly equal to the responsibilities of his post'. This is surely to overlook the particular needs of these years. That slight figure, that good-tempered spirit, that clear-sighted pursuit of England's essential goals, above all the unselfconscious probity, appealed to independent country members and to declared opponents. He was that rarest of political leaders, one who is entirely trusted. He died practically penniless, though his family were generously compensated by parliament. George III said of Perceval that he was 'perhaps the most straightforward man he had ever known'. Wilberforce's tribute sounds uncomfortably in modern ears: never had he known any individual die 'of whose salvation he entertained less doubt'. Wilberforce touched, nonetheless, upon the heart of the matter. The faith was the man.

Further Reading
Denis Gray, *Spencer Perceval*, 1963.

PERCY, HENRY, 1st EARL OF NORTHUMBER-LAND (1341-1408) raised the Percies into 'the most powerful magnates on the Scottish border', made Henry IV king, and died in rebellion against him. The Percies of Alnwick already had large estates in Yorkshire and Northumberland before his second marriage brought much more in Cumberland and Northumberland. Initially he rose as a Lancastrian retainer, serving in France under successive dukes in 1359-60, 1369 and 1373, but his interests focused on the borders, where he was repeatedly diplomat and warden of the Marches. The warden system enhanced the Percies' local authority and financed an inflated private army of retainers. 'During the reign of Richard II it is clear that they aimed to control Border politics and administration through securing the Wardenships of both the East and West Marches towards Scotland'. His son Hotspur was defeated at Otterburn in 1388, they were victorious at Homildon Hill in 1402, and their exploits against the Scots were celebrated by the border ballads. They jealously protected their monopoly of power against John of Gaunt and Richard II's termination of their tenure of both wardenships in 1396 may explain their rebellion in 1399. Henry IV restored both offices and authorized them to conquer much of southern Scotland, but he would not finance their conquests. As these could only be realized with royal finance, they tried to replace King Henry by the young Earl of March in 1403.

Percy's career was not confined to the north. He campaigned and negotiated abroad, was Marshal of England in 1376-7 and constable in 1399. He was created Knight of the Garter in 1366 – Hotspur became one in 1388 – and earl in 1377. Hotspur (1364-1403) fought in Scotland, Prussia and Flanders, was Marcher warden and lieutenant of Aquitaine, justice of Chester and north Wales, and from 1402 commander against the Welsh revolt of Owain Glendower. Northumberland was an astute politician and a moderating influence under Richard II. He served on commissions of reform, declined to attack Arundel and told Richard that the Appellants were loyal subjects with whom he should negotiate in 1387, found Brembre not deserving of death in 1388, and yet interceded for Gloucester and Arundel with the royal council in 1389. He was 'one of the honest brokers of politics in 1388 and 1389'.

Richard II purged many noblemen, took others to Ireland, and several were killed in 1400. Together these circumstances enabled the Percies to play a bigger political role than their actual power justified. Their support in 1399 ensured the success of Bolingbroke's invasion, they captured Richard II, and they immediately received lavish rewards, which makes it hard to believe their claim that they did not intend to make Henry king. He made them completely dominant on the borders and north Wales, gave priority to their salaries as far as his straitened finances permitted, and allayed other sources of friction. Yet in 1403 Hotspur launched a rebellion from Cheshire. He was defeated at Shrewsbury before Glendower or Northumberland could assist, he and his uncle Worcester were killed, but Northumberland himself was acquitted. Rebelling again in 1405, Northumberland was frustrated by Westmorland and fled into exile. Now a convicted traitor and fugitive, Northumberland rebelled again in 1408, but was easily defeated by the sheriff of Yorkshire at Bramham Moor. The family

was restored in 1416, but never again were the Percies the national arbiters of power that they *appeared* in 1399-1408.

Further Reading

P. M. McNiven, 'The Scottish Policy of the Percies and the Strategy of the Shrewsbury Campaign', *Bulletin of the John Rylands Library* lxii, 1980.
J. A. Tuck, *Richard II and the English Nobility*, 1973.
P. McNiven, 'The Betrayal of Archbishop Scrope', *Bulletin of the John Rylands Library* liv, 1971.
J. M. W. Bean, 'Henry IV and the Percies', *History* xliv, 1959.

PERCY, HENRY, 4th EARL OF NORTHUMBERLAND (*c*.1449-89) contributed to Richard III's usurpation and deposition, but his priority was to restore the Percies to a dominant position in northern England. From the 1450s the Percies were contesting Neville dominance in the region. Their private feud spilled over into civil war and led to total disaster. Henry's grandfather, the second earl, was killed in 1455, his father, the third earl, in 1461, the earldom and estates were confiscated and given to Clarence and the Nevilles, and finally in 1464 Warwick's brother John was created Earl of Northumberland. Henry's prospects were limited to his mother's lands. Respect for inheritance was such, however, that almost all heirs of Lancastrian traitors were ultimately restored and hopeful fathers made a speculative investment of marrying their daughters to them. Thus Lord Herbert secured Henry Percy for his daughter Maud. Weakness in the north revealed by Warwick's rebellions in 1469-70 prompted Edward IV to restore Percy to the earldom of Northumberland. He came through the revolutions of 1470-1 unexecuted and systematically reconstructed his retinue and authority throughout the 1470s and 1480s.

The Nevilles were dead, but their lands, retainers, and ambitions were inherited by Warwick's daughter Anne Neville, whose husband Richard, Duke of Gloucester was more than a rival to Northumberland. As both reconstructed their shattered inheritances they clashed, Gloucester having a big advantage as the king's brother. To protect himself Northumberland became the duke's retainer. Gloucester thereafter left him in control in Northumberland and the East Riding, whilst he himself was supreme elsewhere. All the other northern nobles also took service under Gloucester, whose domination of the whole region was recognized in 1482 as king's lieutenant in the north. The relationship operated on a basis of mutual respect and warmth and worked well in practice. Percy served under Gloucester in the Scottish war of 1480-3 and in 1483 assisted Richard's usurpation as Richard III by executing Earl Rivers and by bringing a northern army south to overawe London.

Northumberland did well out of Richard III's accession, but not as well as he probably hoped. It did not mean the end of the Neville hegemony. Richard's power rested so heavily on his own dominance of the north that he was not prepared to delegate it to Northumberland. The earl sat on the new Council of the North as a simple member, not president, and his authority was restricted to what it was before. Such considerations disillusioned him and doubtless explain why he defaulted at Bosworth and assisted in Richard's defeat.

The new king, Henry Tudor, had known Percy as a boy and did not trust him. He needed him, however, to rule the north, but kept him under a tighter rein than earlier kings. The earl was able to expand into Cumbria, where he had large estates, to dominate Yorkshire, and to attract into his retinue many former supporters of Richard III. They, however, were jaundiced by his 'disappointing of King Richard at Bosworth field' and were unenthusiastic about suppressing rebellions raised by those former associates, who remained loyal to Richard's memory and sought to place his heir on the throne. Apart from crushing rebellions, the earl favoured a conciliatory policy to disarm the opposition and to encourage the north to accept Tudor rule. Henry VII, however, asserted his authority and insisted on tough action. In 1489, much against his better judgement, Northumberland was obliged to suppress a popular uprising against heavy and unprecedented taxation. The retainers he took with him agreed with the peasants, had no love for the earl, and left him to be lynched. This enabled Henry VII to impose an outsider on the north and led eventually to the Percies becoming the natural opponents to northern government rather than that government itself.

Further Reading
M. A. Hicks, 'Dynastic Change and Northern Society: The Career of the Fourth Earl of Northumberland, 1470-89', *Northern History* xiv, 1978.

PERCY, THOMAS (1729-1811) published the *Reliques of Ancient Poetry*, which were a mine of riches for the romantic imagination to work upon, a work of scholarship and the start of a literary movement. Percy was a grocer's son of Bridgnorth in Shropshire, who went from the local grammar school to Christ Church, where he showed an interest in early literature. He had already made a collection of Chinese poems and proverbs when he made the discovery which led to his great work. Staying with his friend Humphrey Pitt at Shifnal, he found on the floor a dusty manuscript volume which a maid had been tearing up to light fires. There remained, in a Jacobean hand, nearly 200 sonnets, ballads, historical songs and metrical romances from the time of Chaucer to the seventeenth century. With this for a beginning, Percy collected and edited assiduously. The *Reliques* (1765) were followed by *Northern Antiquities* in 1770. As more and more readers turned from the artificiality of contemporary verse to the Gothic and romantic of a less settled age, and antiquarian pursuits became

fashionable, taste was prepared for Sir Walter Scott, and Percy was rewarded with preferment in the church. He became Dean of Carlisle and, in 1782, Bishop of Dromore, where he added a new transept to the cathedral. His last years were bleak, since he lost his sight in 1805 and his wife in 1806. But a Percy Society was founded to keep his name alive and his portrait was painted by Reynolds. Few men who have not themselves been original artists have had such an effect upon the culture of the time. Though he expended some time upon a fruitless attempt to show that he was descended from the Northumberland Percys, he was a modest man and a true scholar.

PERRERS, ALICE (*c*.1345-1400), notorious mistress of Edward III, first appears in history about 1365 as damsel of Queen Philippa. She must have been of gentle birth and may have come from Hertfordshire. Although not beautiful, she was apparently Edward's mistress well before the queen's death in 1369 and enjoyed his unwavering fidelity thereafter. She bore him at least two children: a son John Southerey born about 1364-5 and knighted in 1377, who died obscurely, and a daughter Joan. Another daughter, Joan the younger, was apparently sired by the Westmorland knight William Windsor (*d*.1384), later a baron, whom she married about 1377, but may have been betrothed to much earlier. Neither daughter was acknowledged by Windsor, who left all his property to three sisters, and both married relatively humbly.

The height of her influence in the 1370s coincided with the king's galloping senility. He treated her with chivalric honour, holding tournaments for her benefit, heaped her with gifts including royal jewels formerly belonging to Queen Philippa, and allowed her to exercise authority within his household like a queen. Her sway over him gave her an influence over his decisions deplored by Bishop Brinton: 'It is not fitting or safe that all the keys should hang from the belt of one woman.' She was apparently uninterested in foreign affairs, but involved herself in court intrigue and distribution of patronage. She was later convicted of preventing investigation of Windsor's misdeeds as ruler of Ireland and of securing a pardon for the merchant Richard Lyons in defiance of parliamentary decree. Descriptions of such events reveal the essentially informal nature of her influence, exercised in Edward's chamber or sitting on his bed, and shows how difficult it was to detect or counter.

Her obscure birth and limited means gave Alice more excuse than most favourites for her rapacity. Certainly she pursued her own advantage single-mindedly and with a shrewd business sense. Edward gave lands and moveables to her, others she borrowed and let him buy, yet others she bought with Exchequer loans that he later pardoned. Much else was secured by purchase, in return for influence or by moneylending. She accumulated twenty-two manors, lands in seventeen counties, and a London house. The poet Langland may have made her model for his Lady Meed and the Speaker in the Good Parliament in 1376 declared that 'it would be a great profit to the kingdom to remove that lady from the king's company so that the king's treasure could be applied to the war and wardships in the king's gift be not so lightly granted away'. She also corrupted justice: 'This Alice de Perers had such power and eminence in those days that no-one dared prosecute a claim against her.' When not at court, she lived in considerable luxury in her manor of Pallenswick in Hammersmith.

Alice's political influence and greedy self-interest help explain her impeachment in the Good Parliament of 1376 and resultant forfeiture, sentences rapidly revoked by Edward III, but repeated next year after his death. Evidently even her associates disliked her. Although the latter sentence too was set aside, partly because she was tried as single when actually married, Alice did not recover all her wealth despite extensive litigation and died in 1400 a woman of only moderate wealth at her home at Gaynes Park, Essex. She had not forgotten or forgiven her losses, transmitting her by then futile claims to her daughters.

Further Reading

C. Given-Wilson, *The Royal Household and the King's Affinity: Service, Politics, and Finance in England 1360-1413*, 1986.

G. A. Holmes, *The Good Parliament of 1376*, 1975.

G. Kay, *Lady of the Sun: The Life and Times of Alice Perrers*, 1966.

PETER, HUGH (1598-1660), the Puritan preacher, was born of a well-to-do mercantile family at Fowey; his paternal ancestors were Flemish Protestant refugees of the previous century, his mother a daughter of long-established Cornish gentry. In 1613 he went to Trinity College, Cambridge, as a sizar, and between then and his ordination as priest ten years later he acquired non-conformist views of a congregationalist kind, and the patronage of the Puritan Earl of Warwick. By 1628 he had a considerable notoriety in London as a converting preacher; his attacks on the popish practices of Queen Henrietta Maria got him into trouble with his bishop, leading to suspension from preaching and to flight to the Netherlands. There he spent six years, mainly as minister to the congregation of English merchants in Rotterdam. He saw service with Dutch troops against the Spaniards and also, for a month, with the army of Gustavus Adolphus in Germany, he helped to organize supplies of Puritan literature for England, and he conducted his ministry on Puritan lines, until the inquisitive arm of Archbishop Laud reached the Rotterdam church

and compelled Peter in 1635 to migrate once more. This time he went to New England, succeeding Roger Williams in 1636 as minister at Salem. He played an important and constructive role in the early establishment of the Massachusetts Bay Colony; he was, for example, prominent in the foundation of Harvard College. Yet he is principally celebrated at this time for his zealous enforcement of a narrow congregationalist orthodoxy, and for his part in the condemnation and banishment of Anne Hutchinson, who had dared to accuse him and other ministers of preaching the doctrine of salvation by works.

In 1641 he returned to England as an agent of the Colony, deputed to obtain financial and other assistance. It was an hour of hope and challenge for the Puritan cause, and Peter welcomed the opportunity to 'further the reformation of the churches' in England. He was never to go back to New England; as with Oliver Cromwell, an era of revolution was to sweep him into directions of which he had not dreamed. After the outbreak of the Civil War in 1642 he became a vigorous propagandist, 'roaring it up and down' England for parliament's sake, an extraordinary mixture of preacher, recruiting officer, pamphleteer, election agent, official reporter and counterspy. Violent in speech, often heartless in manner, given to buffoonery in his sermons, something of a rabble-rouser, he was nonetheless effective and sincere in his devotion to the cause of 'the Saints'. As a Chaplain in the New Model Army he took part in the victorious campaigns of Naseby and Langport and from 1646 onwards he was a powerful champion of Independency, denouncing Presbyterians and royalists alike. After the outbreak of the Second Civil War he spoke strongly in favour of bringing the king to trial; he defended Pride's Purge; and on the eve of Charles's execution he preached in St James's Chapel on 'the terrible denunciation to the King of Babylon' (Isaiah xiv, 18-20).

As for so many Puritans, the years 1649-60 were for Peter a time of anticlimax and of some disillusionment. Before the establishment of the Protectorate (1653) he was a busy servant of the new Republic, sitting on committees, going to Ireland with the army of conquest, acting as Chaplain to the Council of State, disputing with John Lilburne, spreading the gospel in south Wales; and in 1654 he was appointed one of the triers who were to license clergymen. But he was not on good terms with the Protector and his government, and periodic illness and the trend of public events made him despondent in the later 1650s. When the crisis of 1660 came he tried in vain to win favour from Monck. Although Hugh Peter was not technically a 'regicide' he had clearly done more than most men to 'encompass' the death of Charles I; he symbolized 'the rule of the Saints', and he was a natural and easy target for Presbyterian hostility. He was exempted from the Act of Oblivion and Indemnity, and executed for high treason at Charing Cross on 16 October 1660.

Hugh Peter is in many ways an unattractive character, even if we do not accept the massive contemporary vilification and even if many worse men made their peace on handsome terms with the Restoration government. Yet he is one of special interest for two reasons. First, he was one of the numerous figures of the revolutionary era to put forward projects of extensive social reform. In his *Good Work for a Good Magistrate, Or a short cut to great quiet* (1651), he advocated the establishment of new universities, a reform of the poor law, a national bankruptcy law, changes in the law of entail, municipal banks, a standard system of weights and measures, a national land registry, a radical revision of the tax structure, and the replanning of London. Secondly, his career as a whole – the mercantile port-town origins, the Cambridge influence, the early Congregationalism, the patronage of a Puritan aristocrat, the experience of the Netherlands and of Massachusetts, the gradual fusing together of Independency and the war-effort, the eventual concentration of hostility upon the person of the king, the disunity and despondency that came with the political problems brought by victory – summarizes a great deal of that seventeenth-century politico-religious movement which we call Puritanism.

Further Reading
R. P. Stearns, *The Strenuous Puritan*, 1954.

PETER OF BLOIS (*c.*1130-1212) was one of the most popular western writers of the Middle Ages: over 500 manuscripts of his works survive. After a conventional upper-class education in law, at Bologna, and theology, at Paris, Peter became a freelance tutor, lawyer, and attendant cleric to any household willing to employ him. His story was that he spent his time warding off would-be patrons. He held an influential post at the Sicilian court (1166-8), acting as keeper of the royal seal and tutor to the young William II. In the 1170s he was attached to the households of the Archbishop of Rouen; Reginald FitzJocelin, Archdeacon of Salisbury; and, from 1174, the Archbishop of Canterbury, Richard of Dover, whose chancellor Peter became. He also made contact with the royal court. In 1182, FitzJocelin, now Bishop of Bath, appointed Peter his archdeacon. Between 1184 and 1190, Peter worked for the new Archbishop of Canterbury, Baldwin of Ford. He was closely involved in presenting Baldwin's legal case against the monks of Canterbury, in which cause he was prepared to lie in court and tamper with evidence. He accompanied Baldwin on crusade in 1190. Thereafter, he drifted between service to Eleanor of Aquitaine, Hubert Walter and Archbishop Geoffrey of York. Further preferment came with the deanery of Wolverhampton and the archdeaconry of London, but despite these and other benefices, Peter complained of poverty and neglect. What he really wanted was a bishopric. His inability to speak English – and his refusal to learn – may have played a part in this.

Peter was in the second or third rank of secular clerks, competing for but never achieving high office. Perhaps because of this, he became a more or less professional writer of letters, pamphlets and short treatises. Some, such as the panegyric on Henry II *c.*1174, were designed to impress potential patrons. Others, such as his three tracts on the Third Crusade, had a wider purpose, to influence opinion. In 1184 he compiled a collection of his letters to which he added over the next decade. They formed the basis of his posthumous reputation, and were read into the fifteenth century as models of style as much as anything more profound. Peter was not an original thinker: for his treatise on friendship he plagiarized Ailred of Rievaulx. His strength was rhetoric. In many of his letters he advocated moral reform, a return to individual apostolic poverty as a protection against the evils consequent on material extravagance. Whether this implied indigence or humility is not entirely clear, nor is it plain to what extent Peter's arguments were personally felt or literary exercises. Well-travelled, vain, self-righteous, a regular in the ante-chambers of the great, Peter was a twelfth-century pundit, a sort of proto-journalist. Like a modern leader-writer, he took an event, for instance the rebellion of 1173-4 or the death of Raynald of Châtillon at the hands of Saladin (*Passio Reginaldi* 1187/90), and proceeded to tell his audience what its significance was and what they should think and do about it. He articulated ideas for others to use.

Further Reading
R. W. Southern, *Medieval Humanism and other Studies*, 1970.

PETER OF SAVOY (*d.*1268; Count of Savoy 1263-8) was one of the brothers of Henry III's mother-in-law. On his marriage in 1236 to Peter's niece, Eleanor of Provence, Henry eagerly employed her uncles to further his expansive international schemes and provide political ballast at home. Peter's elder brother, William, Bishop-elect of Valence (*d.*1239), was briefly a dominant figure in royal councils 1236-7. His clerk, Peter d'Aigueblanche stayed in England to become one of Henry's most valued officials and diplomats, as well as Bishop of Hereford (1240-68). Another brother, Boniface, became Archbishop of Canterbury (1241-70). On Peter were lavished the largest secular rewards, including the honour of Richmond and the wardenship of the Cinque Ports. Knighted by Henry in 1241, Peter, while never abandoning his continental interests, became an influential English courtier and magnate. As such, he attracted the opprobrium of nationalist observers, such as Matthew Paris who invented scurrilous stories of Peter importing bevies of foreign ladies to corrupt English aristocrats. Henry found in Peter a diplomat, whose existing European experience was usefully employed on his behalf. It is a sign of how Henry mismanaged his affairs that Peter was one of the original seven nobles, led by another foreigner Simon de Montfort, who in April 1258 formed a sworn commune to reform English government. Although Peter soon abandoned the opposition, with the rest he had acted out of resentment at the favours given to the king's Lusignan relatives. Reconciled with Henry, Peter was active on his behalf before leaving England in 1262. The following year he succeeded his nephew as Count of Savoy. Although resented by insular chroniclers and jealous rivals within the English nobility, Peter's energy, administrative proficiency, wide geographical range of action and military skill earned him the nickname of 'little Charlemagne'. The role that Peter and his Savoyard brothers played in English political life exposed a gulf which divided the cosmopolitan Angevin monarch from the majority of his English nobles. Of these relatives, Peter was possibly the ablest. Whether Henry was wise to promote him, especially in view of his actions in 1258, is less obvious.

PETRE, FATHER EDWARD (1631-99), James II's Jesuit adviser, belonged to the Essex branch of a prominent Roman Catholic family. Born in London and educated at St Omer, he entered the Society of Jesus in 1652 and was sent on mission to England about 1679. He spent a year in Newgate at the time of the Popish Plot, and was again in prison from 1681, when he was appointed Vice-Principal of the English Jesuits, until 1683. Petre was zealous for his faith and plausible in speech, a member of the aggressive party in the church, and James II welcomed him at court from the start of the reign, putting him in charge of his chapel and installing him in his own former lodgings in the Palace of Whitehall. He became an ally of Sunderland and a member of the informal inner council; in 1687 he was formally sworn of the Privy Council and he was active in the purging of the corporations and the expulsion of the Fellows of Magdalen. Petre appears to have been a vain and headstrong man who gave imprudent counsel. Yet it is easy to exaggerate his influence, and he was rather the tool of Sunderland than an *éminence grise*. His public admission to the Council probably did far more harm to the king's cause than any advice he gave. In his own person he illustrated the conflict between James II's policy and that of the Papacy, for he was not popular at Rome and Innocent XI firmly declined the royal suggestion that Petre be given a cardinal's hat. In the crisis of 1688 Petre was one of those who advised James to stay in England. He himself made a secret escape, going back to St Omer, whose rector he became in 1693, and remained abroad for the rest of his life.

PETTY, SIR WILLIAM (1623-87), founder-member of the Royal Society and pioneer of the use of statistics, was the son of a small clothier in Romsey, Hampshire. He learned Latin at school in Romsey; went to sea as a cabin boy at thirteen, broke his leg, and was put ashore in Normandy; became a pupil at the Jesuit College at Caen, paying his way by trade; served three years in the navy, studied medicine in Holland, and worked as a journeyman-jeweller; acted as amanuensis for Thomas Hobbes in Paris; studied at Brasenose, and earned a living in oddments of laboratory work in Oxford and London; made a number of unprofitable inventions, including a double-writing instrument; and in 1650 became a Doctor of Physic of the University of Oxford, where he spent the better part of the next two years. Petty was one of the Fellows 'intruded' by parliament into the governing body of Brasenose, and was shortly appointed Professor of Anatomy; he was also made Reader in Music at Gresham College in London. Public fame quickly came to him by chance through the strange affair called 'The Raising of Ann Green', in which he 'restored' a servant girl who had been hanged for abortion and coffined before life was entirely extinct. It was more important that at Oxford he was a member of the small group of scientists, including men like John Wilkins, John Wallis and Jonathan Goddard, out of which the Royal Society was later to grow, and which sometimes met at Petty's lodgings near All Souls.

Yet his stay in Oxford was short. In 1652 Petty was appointed physician to the Commonwealth army in Ireland, and he spent many of the remaining thirty-five years of his life there. Land, not medicine, was his main concern, in this period of plantation after the Cromwellian conquest. His survey of twenty-two counties, the Down Survey, was the best for almost two centuries; in the 1660s he completed an impressive map of Ireland; a friend of Henry Cromwell, he did well for himself in the land market, owning perhaps 30,000 acres, many of them in Kerry, at his death. Acquisitive, pushing, and indiscreet, he frittered away much time and talent in financial and political feuds in Ireland. Yet it was probably his Irish experiences that directed this 'person of a stupendous invention and of as great prudence and humanity', as Aubrey calls him, into the particular form of social thinking which has made later generations interested in him.

Like many who had prospered under the Commonwealth, Petty adjusted himself comfortably to the Restoration, and was knighted in 1661. He was one of the twelve founder-members of the Royal Society, and a man of many projects. He had a passion for navigation and shipbuilding, and devised a double-bottomed boat, a controversial and not very happy experiment. But he was above all a pioneer in what we should today call the social sciences, interested in the application of quantitative analysis to social and economic problems. Much influenced by contemporary Dutch practice and ideas, by some of the trends of thought of the Commonwealth period, and by his friend John Graunt, he ranged not very systematically over a variety of social questions – unemployment and productivity, taxation, the penal code, land registration and planned care for the sick among them; his conclusions were usually of little value, although he sometimes produced anticipations of later approaches, as, for example, of the labour theory of value. From a later standpoint, by far his most interesting work concerned population statistics, to which he gave the name *Political Arithmetic*, writing an essay with this title in 1682 and a rather fuller work published three years after his death. Petty was one of the first men to recognize the importance of statistics in connection with such problems as taxation, employment, life insurance and the size of armed forces. His contemporaries found this short-sighted, heavy man, with his streak of vulgarity and his greed for worldly success, rather tiresome and slightly comic. The actual consequence of his work for the future can easily be overrated. Nevertheless, the pattern and direction of Petty's interests and thought provides an illuminating example of the new social and intellectual climate of late seventeenth-century England, a climate very different from that of the days of the early Stuarts.

Further Reading

K. Theodore Hoppen, 'Sir William Petty', *History Today*, February 1965, pp.126-134.
E. Strauss, *Sir William Petty*, 1954.
Sir George Clark, *Science and Social Welfare in the Age of Newton*, 2nd edn, 1949.

PETTY, WILLIAM, 2nd EARL OF SHELBURNE (1737-1805) was one of the most intelligent politicians of the eighteenth century. Intellectual in his tastes, original in his views as in his choice of friends, ambitious to succeed and brave in his policies, it was his fate to arouse widespread suspicion among his associates, to be limited to but two short periods of high office and to see promising plans miscarry or come to fruition under another man's direction.

He was born in Ireland and lived there until he was sixteen, receiving an irregular education in a semi-feudal household – a setting in which an original talent may grow more strongly than under conventional schooling. He went to Christ Church in 1755 and joined the army in 1757. He served with enough distinction to be promoted ADC to the king after the battle of Kloster-Kampfen. He sat for a short time as member for High Wycombe and meanwhile took advantage of his position at court to further his career; unfortunately at this time he fell foul of Henry Fox, acquiring a name for deviousness in the process which became a byword in the circle of Fox and

his son. As an ally of Bute, however, he was rewarded by the Presidency of the Board of Trade which he accepted on the condition that he should have 'equal access to the king with other ministers'. He resigned in September 1762, but meanwhile played a vital part in the publication of the Board's important report which led to the ban upon settlement beyond the headwaters of the Appalachian Mountains.

For the next three years he cultivated the acquaintance of Pitt, whom he admired intensely. This seems to have been a political liaison which never ripened into a friendship, but Pitt respected the younger man's intelligence and rewarded his zeal with the post of Secretary of State for the Southern Department in his administration of 1766. He conceived the colonial section of his department to be the most important; again American affairs preoccupied him. Because of Pitt's collapse and virtual withdrawal from responsibility, Shelburne was left to shape his own policies, but he was hampered by the fact that he shared responsibility for the colonies with the Board of Trade. Furthermore he was unable to prevent Charles Townshend from imposing duties upon the colonies which ran counter to his policy. He worked hard for conciliation. He now wished to encourage the westward expansion which had been stopped in 1763. He was unusual too amongst English politicians in being ready to listen to American views. Franklin, colonial agent for Pennsylvania, was a frequent visitor, so was 'omniscient Jackson', former agent for Massachusetts. He also hoped that the financial problem could be solved by taking the quit-rents for new colonies. But his perhaps too optimistic proposals were rejected by the Board of Trade. So Shelburne failed to prevent the growth of tension on this crucial issue.

Though he acquired the name of being the colonists' friend, this was of no assistance to him in domestic politics; he was gradually isolated. As early as June 1767, Grafton was expecting him to go, 'considering the little cordiality shown by his lordship towards myself and others of the Cabinet of late'. At the end of the year Grafton moved towards an understanding with the Bedford Whigs who were resolved to make no concessions to the colonists. He sensibly proposed dividing the American business from the other functions of the Southern Department. But Shelburne kept the Southern Department, without the 'American business', the confidence of his fellow ministers or indeed of the king. In October 1768 he resigned, to be followed by Chatham.

He held no office again for fifteen years. He gave up his correspondence with Chatham and watched the American colonists move into positions of defiance without being able to do more than register occasional protests. Burke and Fox would not collaborate with him, while some moderate men came to oppose American claims as a mark of patriotism. Later he went so far as to say that 'the right of taxation had, from the first, been chimerical'. But he held, like Chatham, to the idea of reconciliation and hoped for 'a fair, honest, wise and honourable connection, in which the constitutional prerogatives of the Crown, the claims of parliament and the liberties, properties and lives of all the subjects of the British empire would be equally secured'. While military disasters were spoiling the prospect of such generous ideals ever becoming accomplished fact, Shelburne was active in other ways which antagonized politicians otherwise amenable to his ideas. Always somewhat outré in his methods and his friends, he used agents in the city, like Alderman Sawbridge, to intrigue for him in London, and he secured influence in the East India Company through purchase of stock by agents. It is not surprising, in view of Shelburne's secretive ways, as well as his grudge against Grafton, that he has been credited with the authorship of the letters of 'Junius' (though the evidence is stronger for Philip Francis). More surprisingly he resorted to the duelling sword to settle his differences with a Scottish MP. In 1780, distrusting the party claque of Rockingham and the wild oratory of Burke and Fox, he employed Price, Priestley and Jebb to prepare a programme of economic and administrative reform. In employing skilled advisers outside the charmed circle of parliament, he anticipated the methods of some twentieth-century politicians. His ideas were more thorough-going, more in line with the thinking of the 'physiocrats', in his anticipation, for instance, of free trade, than those of Burke and his friends who looked back to a parochial tradition. But this free and unprejudiced habit of thought was of no advantage to him in a close political world where personal relationships counted for so much.

Shelburne did, however, have one great asset when, after Yorktown, it became evident that the American War must be decently ended. He was an acknowledged expert in American affairs, he had the trust of a number of Americans who associated his name with the tradition of Chatham, and he was not inhibited, as was North, by his previous actions, from approaching the Americans with a free hand. In March 1782, he became Secretary of State for Home, American and Irish affairs in Rockingham's ministry. His role was to make a separate peace with the Americans while Fox, the other Secretary of State, had charge of the other negotiations with the foreign powers, France, Spain and Holland. These, naturally, opposed the idea of a separate American peace. Fox and Shelburne worked through separate agents. The situation would have been difficult even without the intense mutual dislike of the two principals. When Rockingham died in July, and Shelburne, upon whom the king now leaned since he was known to oppose full independence, became First Lord of the Treasury, Fox resigned.

Shelburne was thus left to carry the load of an unpopular treaty himself. In the circumstances he achieved a tolerable settlement, and in a manner which went some way to assuaging old wounds. He had to abandon his cherished dream of a Federal Union. Instead, faithful to his Free Trade principles, he tried to associate the idea of mutual trade benefit with a peace which otherwise could be none other than a recognition of defeat. In the event Britain recognized American independence and ceded much of the disputed territory in the north-west. The confiscation of loyalists' property was to end, but the request to the individual state legislatures that they should make adequate restitution of properties already confiscated was not given proper sanctions. In the end, perhaps inevitably, the loyalists were sacrificed. France, in the treaty of Versailles, took Goree and Senegal, Tobago and St Lucia; Spain, Florida and Minorca. But Shelburne was shabbily rewarded for his services. He seems to have believed that George III's influence, together with the basic division of North and Fox, would be enough to ensure his majority. When, improbably, Fox and North combined and the peace terms were debated in the Commons, the ministry was defeated (April 1783). Perhaps Shelburne could have carried on; but he believed, wrongly, that George III had let him down. George in fact accepted the new coalition with revulsion. Fox and North promptly sanctioned the peace which they had formerly rejected; only their dislike of Shelburne had prompted their censure. The defeat of the American Intercourse Bill, in 1784, completed his apparent failure. But the wisdom of the policies that he had tried to implement was seen by the younger Pitt who, like Shelburne, professed himself a disciple of Adam Smith. He had also been Shelburne's Chancellor of the Exchequer and his Free Trade Treaty of 1786 with France might have been Shelburne's work.

In 1784 Shelburne was made Marquis of Lansdowne, but he played no further part in politics. His relative failure remains one of the puzzles of the time. Assessing his influence on the younger Pitt, Disraeli called him one of the 'suppressed characters' of history. He could be patient, generous, sympathetic. Yet his was a temperament basically unsuited to the eighteenth-century political game; he was an example, not the last, of the disabilities of an intellectual in politics. He never lived down the taunt of 'the Jesuit of Berkeley Square'. His manner was unfortunate, sometimes obsequious, sometimes arrogant. Neither the boldness of his ideas, nor his willingness to change his mind, nor his habit of making fine qualifications and distinctions upon matters which seemed plain to less subtle minds, inspired the confidence without which no statesman can do much for long. He found compensation for his departure from political life in his library and pictures at Bowood and Lansdowne House. Besides these two great houses and their treasures, he bequeathed a political tradition: the third and fifth marquises both became Cabinet Ministers.

Further Reading
R. A. Humphreys, 'Lord Shelburne and British Colonial Policy, 1766-8' from *Ec. H.R.*, reprinted in *Essays in Eighteenth-Century History*, 1966.
J. Norris, *Shelburne and Reform*, 1963.

PHILIPPA OF HAINAULT (*c*.1314-69), queen of Edward III, is representative of the majority of late medieval English consorts, who played no significant part in English politics. Typically she was of foreign birth. She was the daughter of William the Good (*d*.1337) and Jeanne of France (*d*.1342), Count and Countess of Holland and Hainault. A match between Prince Edward and a daughter of Count William, probably her elder sister Sibylla, had been mooted before the visit of Queen Isabella and Prince Edward in 1326, when Edward and Philippa's betrothal and Hainaulter support for Isabella's invasion of England were agreed. Philippa, it is recorded, wept on Edward's departure, so fond of him had she become in their week's acquaintance, and on his accession their marriage was contracted by proxy at Valenciennes and then concluded in person in 1328 in York Minster. Her coronation and endowment were delayed by Queen Isabella, who understandably did not want to be eclipsed as queen mother, and did not take place until 1330, only shortly before the birth of the Black Prince. Altogether Philippa bore her husband twelve offspring, seven sons and five daughters, thus fulfilling to excess the prime function of any medieval English queen and supplying Edward with endless material for diplomatic marriages.

Philippa was not beautiful, but tall and handsome in her youth, a plump and somewhat heavily-built woman in later life. She was unusually well-educated, writing French and speaking Dutch fluently. Her piety is revealed by her patronage of the hospital of St Katherine by the Tower, St Stephen's College Westminster, and Queen's College Oxford. The latter was founded by the Cumbrian clerk Robert Eglesfield, who persuaded Philippa to give it her name and patronage. She it was who secured Edward's licence for the foundation, the appropriation of various churches, and the diversion to it of other endowments. Such patronage was valuable and perhaps essential, but it involved little loss to the queen except an annuity of £13 from Richmond honour.

Philippa shared in her husband's visit to the Low Countries in 1338-41, supervised the defeat of the Scots in 1346, and witnessed the defeat of the Spanish off Winchelsea in 1350. She apparently shared Edward III's chivalric interests, presiding over many tournaments, and appears to have managed her affairs competently and with due regard for the law. Her best documented quality was compassion, which caused her to intercede for carpenters responsible for staging that collapsed under her at the Cheapside tournament of 1331 and again for the unfortunate burghers of Calais in 1347. Another Hainaulter Jean Froissart, who claimed her patronage but scarcely knew her, praised her as:

Tall and upright, wise, gay, humble, pious, liberal and courteous, decked and adorned in her time with all noble virtues, beloved of God and of mankind … And as long as she lived, the kingdom of England had favour, prosperity, honour and every sort of good fortune; neither did famine or dearth remain in the land during her reign, and so you will find it recorded in history.

Barring the Black Death, this is a description difficult to fault, but so conventional as to add little to our knowledge. Philippa gave Edward little trouble, contributed scarcely at all to national politics, and her kinship network was a diplomatic asset. Their marriage was apparently affectionate. Later when her health gradually faltered, the result of a riding accident and 'dropsy' (1367), she did nothing to impede the transfer of the king's affections to her attendant Alice Perrers, his mistress and dominant influence over him during his last decade.

Further Reading
B. C. Hardy, *Philippa of Hainault and her Times*, 1910.

PICTON, SIR THOMAS (1758-1815), general, was the son of a country gentleman of Pembrokeshire. He entered the army at the age of thirteen, he died on the field of Waterloo. He was unusually tall and strong, and stories collected round his name in profusion. In 1783 he checked a mutiny by striding into the ranks, grabbing the ringleader by the scruff and marching him away. Unconventional about clothes, he fought at Busaco in a red nightcap, at Waterloo in a top hat. He was alleged to be rough, even cruel, but he was trained in a hard school. In 1797 he was made military governor of Trinidad, in 1801 civil governor of that wealthy island. He built roads and developed trade. His brisk methods made enemies, however, and in 1802 commissioners were sent out by Addison's government to inquire into alleged injustice. When he returned in 1803 he was arrested and held to a large bail. Three years later the action of *Rex v. Picton* was begun. The charge was that he had allowed the torture of a mulatto woman accused of robbery, under the existing Spanish law; the juristic question was whether, when a country came under the sovereignty of Britain, the Common Law immediately replaced any previous system. Found guilty on a technical point, Picton was tried again in 1808 and acquitted. Nevertheless the charge stuck to his name and Picton had no active service until 1809 when he went with Chatham as Major-General in command of a field brigade in the Walcheren expedition.

In 1810, on Wellington's request, he was appointed to

command the Third Division in the Peninsula. In the daring escalade at Badajoz, in cool retreat at El Bodon, in gallant attack at Vittoria, Toulouse and Ciudad Rodrigo, in a dozen scrapes and sallies, always in the thick of the action, Picton inspired his troops. Foulmouthed but genial, at his best in danger, he was too independent to please his superiors. Wellington was often cold towards him, the government niggardly. Twice he received the thanks of the House, but he was refused a peerage. His statue at Carmarthen commemorates Britain's Marshal Ney, 'the bravest of the brave'. In 1815 he was appointed to the command of the Fifth Division; he joined the duke the day before Quatre Bras. There he had some ribs broken, but only his servant was told. He was so wounded at the outset of Waterloo that he would probably have died, even if he had not received a musket ball while leading a victorious charge against the French.

Further Reading
Michael Glover, *Wellington's Peninsular Victories*, 1963.

PIERCE or PEARCE, EDWARD (*d.*1695), sculptor, was the son of an artist who had worked for Van Dyck. We know nothing of his training as a sculptor, and, indeed, he seems to have spent most of his working life as a mason. From 1663 to 1665 he was employed as mason and carver for Sir Roger Pratt, at Horseheath. After 1671 he was working in various capacities in the rebuilding of London. He was paid £50 apiece for the bronze dragons at the base of the Monument; he worked as a mason on the south side of St Paul's; and he is said to have rebuilt St Clement Danes from Wren's plans. He designed the Bishop's Palace at Lichfield, and his work in wood or stone, such as pulpits and staircases, may be found in a number of buildings in the Midlands and southern England. In practice he can have found little time for sculpture, of which art he was the most distinguished exponent in his century. No doubt he found little demand: he was a victim of that return to foreign fashions and practitioners in the arts which was one aspect of the Restoration. He produced several statues for the Royal Exchange, some work for the City Companies, and busts of Cromwell and Milton. Perhaps his greatest as well as most appropriate achievement was the superbly sensitive bust of his master, Wren, in 1673, a piece which is outstanding among the portraits of the century.

Further Reading
June Seymour, 'Edward Pierce: Baroque Sculptor of London', *Guildhall Miscellany*, i (1952), p.10.

PITMAN, SIR ISAAC (1813-97), who invented phonographic shorthand, started his working life as a teacher. He was a man who was always ready to experiment, became a vegetarian, and was dismissed from his first school for joining Swedenborg's New Church. Later he unsuccessfully promoted the duodecimal system and a longer alphabet. But by then he had developed the idea which made his name: a shorthand based on sound. It first appeared in 1837, in *Stenographic Soundhand*, which he was so busy writing that he did not have time to celebrate Queen Victoria's coronation. With paired consonants and different shadings of the same pen stroke for different letters, it proved decisively speedier than any of the previously established methods of abbreviation. Pitman was a good business man. He used the Penny Post to distribute his second edition in 1840, and got his five brothers to work for him. By 1867 his work had run to twelve editions. It spread to the USA and Australia, and eventually into other languages, world-wide. There was an international congress, a jubilee and a knighthood. It took the dictaphone to challenge his pre-eminence.

PITT, WILLIAM, 1st EARL OF CHATHAM (1708-78), the elder, statesman, was born into a family already established by the efforts of his remarkable grandfather, Governor Pitt. Thomas Pitt had made his fortune in India, first in profitable operations outside the East India Company, later more respectably, poacher turned gamekeeper, as Governor of Fort St George. Fierce and eccentric in temper, he returned to see to the advance of his family. He had prepared the way by the acquisition of estates and a rotten borough, Old Sarum. Wealth drew his children into aristocratic marriages: a daughter to Earl Stanhope, his short-lived eldest son Robert to Elizabeth Villiers. His family were, however, difficult; they were extravagant, while he was overbearing to the point, it seemed, of insanity. Only in Robert's younger son William did he find a kindred spirit. At ten, William was sent to Eton. Afterwards he was to say that a sensitive boy was cowed there for life; but he made friendships, notably with the Grenville brothers and George Lyttelton, which served him well. 'He is a hopeful lad', wrote his grandfather, 'and doubt not but that he will answer yours and all his friends' expectations'. In the year of his grandfather's death 1726, William went to Oxford. Already he suffered from the gout which had tortured his grandfather, though he did not yet show signs of the family temper. Governor Pitt never knew the meaning of repose; he described his own wife as mad, though she was no more than flighty. Elizabeth Villiers came from a family of genius and alarming instability. Most of Robert's fortune went to the elder son, Thomas, and William was forced to make shift with an income of about £200. Fortunately Thomas helped him to complete his education.

From Oxford William went to Utrecht but made no serious preparation for any profession. In 1731, by the patronage of Lord Cobham, a connection by the marriage of his elder brother to Christina Lyttelton, he was made cornet in Cobham's Regiment of Horse; his military duties did not prevent him from making a foreign tour in 1733. On his return he found politicians embroiled in the Excise Question. The great house which Lord Cobham had just restored was the centre of a circle of his relations and dependants. Here Pitt met the leaders of the opposition whose views coincided with his own and whose plans fired his ambitions. In 1735 he became member for the family borough. He quickly revealed a talent for debate which raised him to the leadership of the 'Cobham's cubs'.

Historians have found it difficult to account for the power of Pitt. Using the language of psychology, one has called him 'manic depressive', accounting for the intense force and passion of his rhetoric by saying that this derived from an uneven tempo of life: one phase of exaltation, insight and energy being followed by another of dark, withdrawn depression. Others have stressed the gout which caused periods of agony and collapse. It seems that, for all his friendships, he was a lonely figure. He gained his effects in the House by studied and histrionic language, but its note of prophetic authority came from a sense of destiny which set him apart. The formal manner which kept ordinary men at their distance may have been his defence against his periodic awareness that he was not well.

The enmity between George II and his son Frederick gave Pitt his first chance to attract the attention of parliament and the divided court. In 1736 Frederick married Augusta of Saxe-Gotha. The ministry avoided giving the matter space for debate, but Pitt used a congratulatory address to make the opposition's point in a speech of masterly sarcasm. For all his show of loyalty he cannot have been surprised when Walpole deprived him of his cornetcy. 'Who will rid me of this terrible cornet of Horse?' George II is supposed to have said; but Pitt was to pay a higher price in exclusion from high office, for George had a keen memory for insults. Soon there was a greater occasion for oratory, and a real division of principle. The affair of Jenkins's Ear gave the opposition an excuse to hound the reluctant ministry into war with Spain (1739). Pitt believed that England's future lay in her pursuit of overseas trade: decadent Spain was in no position to resist the advance of England's merchants, if they were backed by the English navy. When he spoke of Walpole's Convention of Pardo as 'a stipulation of national ignominy' and declared that 'the complaints of your despairing merchants – the voice of England – has condemned it', he was rousing a spirit as old as Elizabeth, lifting the greed of merchants and the opportunism of politicians to a level of patriotic principle.

Walpole clung to power until January 1742. Carteret, his successor, secured the temporary neutrality of Frederick, built up the 'Pragmatic Army' and looked forward to the defeat of France in the manner of Marlborough. In Pitt's view, however, England's war was concerned primarily with Spain and with winning her trade: if France had to be fought, it should be by sea. Since Carteret was reckless in his use of subsidies and high-handed in his approach to colleagues and to parliament, Pitt found ready ears for his attacks. 'Neither justice nor policy required us to be engaged in the quarrels of the continent … the confidence of the people is abused by making unnecessary alliances; they are then pillaged to provide the subsidies. It is now too apparent that this great, this formidable kingdom is concerned only as a province of a despicable electorate'. Philippics of this sort helped to destroy Carteret and made the fortune of Pitt's group. Chesterfield, Cobham and Lyttelton came to the Pelham administration after the fall of Carteret in November 1744; Pitt was kept out by the king. After the disasters and shocks of the Jacobite rebellion in 1745, the Pelhams made a strong case for his inclusion. George II was adamant against his having the office of Secretary at War. But after the manoeuvres of February 1746, when the Pelhams resigned to prove that they were indispensable, George was compelled to accept him: first as Vice-Treasurer for Ireland, then, in May, as Paymaster-General.

Eighteenth-century paymasters were able to speculate privately with the money which passed through their hands between the receipt of army pay and the arrival of the bills; they received a lucrative cut from such transactions as the granting of foreign subsidies or the raising of mercenary troops. Pitt, however, lodged his balances with the Bank of England. Though the step was taken with a typical flourish and an eye on the public outside the House of Commons, it was also a sincere sacrifice. Despite an eccentric legacy from the Duchess of Marlborough, Pitt was a relatively poor man, but he was interested more in power than in profit.

Paymaster for nine years, he made constructive use of the office, in the two years of war that ended with the peace of Aix-la-Chapelle in 1748, and in the years of diplomatic activity that led towards the next war which most people considered inevitable. He kept in touch with his agents abroad and studied the commercial statistics of England and France. Through such contacts as William Beckford, a London sugar magnate, Cumming, a Quaker with African interests and William Vaughan, a fish merchant of New Hampshire, he gleaned information about the French colonies and planned a comprehensive strategy of empire. While he might not agree on all points with such advisers – Beckford, for instance, opposed the capture of French sugar islands on the grounds that a glut of sugar would lead to a fall in price – and while the interests of colonists could not always be reconciled with those of merchants, there was a general agreement in Pitt's circle upon the main theme: trade must be made to flourish by war.

Attacks of gout and recurring depression could not always be countered by the distraction of work. After the removal of Henry Pelham's restraining hand, in 1754, he was disturbed by the trends of Newcastle's foreign policy. Newcastle's great system took no account of the determination of Austria to be revenged upon Prussia; when Newcastle eventually turned to Prussia as an ally, *faute de mieux*, he was only doing what Pitt had long urged. England drifted towards a war, crippled by the economies which had reduced her fleets and armies, without certain aim or emphatic leadership. Pitt was meanwhile made happier in his private life by his marriage in November 1754 to Lady Hester Grenville. With relish he turned to attack the government. He demanded a secretaryship of state and a change of policy: tortuous negotiations occupied the summer of 1755. In November he denounced the government's German subsidy treaties, urging an alliance with Frederick even if this meant a break with Hanover, and a policy which gave priority to the defeat of France overseas in the interests of the colonists, 'those long-injured, long-neglected, long-forgotten people'. He was dismissed. The alignment was clear. He had the support of most in the city and of merchants everywhere. He had made himself once more obnoxious to the king and embarrassing to Newcastle. He could only be accepted if some national disaster forced the king to listen to the indignation of the public to whom Pitt, 'the great commoner', spoke.

The Convention of Westminster (January 1756) secured the alliance of Prussia on terms which included a guarantee for Hanover's neutrality. But the Seven Years' War started with set-backs. In Canada, General Braddock was defeated and killed. In the Mediterranean, Admiral Byng failed to defeat the French squadron which was covering the expedition to Minorca, leaving the island's garrison to its fate. In December the king gave way to Pitt's conditions: he was to be Secretary of State with direct access to the king and responsibility for the formulation of policy – yet Cumberland, commander-in-chief of the allied land forces, refused to receive his orders. In April Pitt was dismissed, but the weeks that followed only proved that Newcastle could not form a ministry without him. While the country demonstrated its support with petitions and the freedom of cities, a coalition was devised. Newcastle, as First Lord, was to manage parliament and find the money. Pitt, as Secretary of State, was free to run the war. Pitt had at last achieved real power, but on Newcastle's terms: only success could justify him and give him security of tenure. Fortunately he did not lack confidence: 'I know that I can save this country and that I alone can'.

In his first months of power, Pitt had remodelled the instructions to his commanders, but new plans and new men could not mature at once; the pace of war was slow in the eighteenth century. In India, luckily, the East India Company had a man who needed no order from England. Clive, victor of Arcot, as Pitt recognized, was 'a heaven-born general'. After Calcutta had been captured by the French, acting in concert with Admiral Watson, he counter-attacked, recaptured Calcutta and Chandernagore and in June 1757 defeated the huge army of Surajah Dowlah at Plassey. The victory enabled Pitt to concentrate his attention on what he considered the vital spheres: Canada and the West Indies.

Pitt's measures were inspired by two basic needs: to keep Frederick in the war and to secure the supremacy of the sea. To protect the country against French invasion and at the same time make available an army to protect Frederick's flank, he raised a militia from the counties and two regiments from the Highlands. Frederick was to receive subsidies and the French were to be distracted by a series of amphibious attacks upon her coastline. At sea, he set up a close blockade of the French bases, Brest, Rochefort and Toulon. At first it was not apparent that much was being achieved by his 'blue water' policy: the ships were in poor shape and French reinforcements slipped out of port to Canada and the West Indies. The operation against Rochefort was a fiasco and so was the first attack against Louisburg, in both cases because of incompetent commanders. Pitt ignored the rules of seniority and looked for commanders of initiative; his clear orders and confidence in victory encouraged them to be bold. He backed Grenville's Navy Bill (1758), which enhanced the attractions of naval service by speeding up the payment of seamen's wages. At home his determination to be honest, even about defeats, made for confidence: 'I despise your little policy of concealments.' Cumberland was defeated by the French at Hastenbeck and made his peace, but Pitt disowned his action as being authorized by the Elector of Hanover, and put his army under Ferdinand of Brunswick.

Success came first, in 1758, in Canada, where Pitt's scheme was grandiose, planned for total victory, risking disaster. Abercrombie was to move up the Hudson valley to Montreal. A combined force under Amherst and Boscawen was to reduce Louisburg, sail up the St Lawrence and attack Quebec. Forbes, a tough veteran, was to attack Fort Duquesne. Abercrombie was checked at Ticonderoga. Amherst captured Louisburg, after a careful siege. Forbes took Fort Duquesne, renamed it Pittsburgh, and died there. For the following year, Pitt shifted Amherst to the command vacated by Abercrombie. The army of the St Lawrence he gave to the impetuous Wolfe. This officer, mortally sick with tuberculosis, shared Pitt's craving for victory and had also a keen concern for discipline, training and commissariat. The naval force, under Admiral Saunders, co-operated closely and intelligently. After long delays, Wolfe decided to gamble on a night attack by way of the supposedly inaccessible face of the Heights of Abraham, and was justified by complete victory. In the following year Amherst and his fellow commanders converged upon Montreal. The surrender of the city in September marked the end of French rule in north America.

Meanwhile Pitt's forces had been successful in west Africa. In 1758, Fort Louis, on the Senegal river, and Goree (Dakar) were captured, and with them the gum and slave trades. The price of slaves rose in the West Indies, where Pitt also had designs. General Hopson failed at Martinique, which was then left until 1782, but captured Guadeloupe, reckoned to be worth nearly ten million pounds. These victories overseas reflected the failure of the French navy to evade the stringent Mediterranean fleets – thus to protect invasion, which Choiseul planned in 1759, and leave a free hand to commanders across the Atlantic. Here Pitt was superbly served by his seamen. Maintaining the blockade of Brest and Toulon in all weathers, Hawke and Boscawen had already played their parts; then Hawke won a famous victory at Quiberon Bay, in the face of a gale (November) amongst the shoals of a treacherous part of the Brittany coast. He destroyed the Brest fleet which had finally run the blockade. Boscawen sank a large part of the Toulon fleet which he had chased to Lagos. News of Minden, where (August) Ferdinand of Brunswick won a great victory over the French, completed the 'wonderful year'. Pitt was idolized by the populace and respected even by the old king, not insensible to the glory of his nation.

Attention to detail, a strong nerve, an infectious craving for victory and a sound grasp of the principles of strategy – all played their part in Pitt's success as a war minister. So, it should be added, did the work of Anson, First Lord, and Cleveland, Secretary, at the admiralty. In his political management he was less happy. He treated Newcastle, Hardwicke and, more justifiably, Bute, the chief adviser to the Prince of Wales, with sarcasm and condescension. Yet Newcastle served him well, finding the money for schemes in which he did not believe, under the most provocative circumstances, for Pitt did not hesitate to criticize his financial management. The accession, in 1760, of George III, prone to see political questions in personal terms and taught to believe that Pitt had 'the blackest of hearts', created a raw situation. In March 1761, Bute became Secretary of State. Pitt could not work with a man whom he knew to be inexperienced and believed to be in office primarily to find means of ending what George III, in his first speech, had called a 'bloody and expensive' war (Pitt substituted for 'bloody' the words 'just and necessary'). Pitt appreciated that Frederick the Great, even after his victory at Torgau in November 1760, was near the end of his tether, but when talks began in 1761 he was primarily concerned with

winning more counters for peace. In June naval and military forces captured Belle Isle at the mouth of the Loire. In July came news of the occupation of the island of Dominica and Pondicherry on the coast of India. Pitt was thus strengthened in his haughty tone and unbending attitude. Over the question of the Newfoundland fisheries, which Choiseul was driven by French commercial opinion to demand, he would not budge. Cod was Britain's gold. Sure that Spain was planning to come into the war (and rightly) he wished to strike first. His fellow ministers demurred at his proposals. 'Being responsible, I will direct, and will be responsible for nothing that I do not direct', said Pitt, and resigned his seals and his war. The almost hysterical notes of humility with which he accepted from his ungrateful king £3,000 a year from the sugar duties and a barony for his wife suggest a man near to the end of his tether. His judgement may have been astray too in his attitude towards peace. Newcastle and Hardwicke knew the discontents of the squires who paid the Land Tax, and they appreciated the dangers of abusing a strong position: the classic mistake of victorious statesmen. Ultimately, however, Bute made a peace which only seemed to the Pittites a feeble one: the sugar islands were returned, with the trading stations in west Africa and fishing rights in Newfoundland. Pitt attacked these concessions in a speech of three hours: France, he urged, had been given the means to become once more formidable on sea, while England's ally Frederick had been betrayed.

He only commanded sixty-five votes in the House; but in the streets the crowd shouted for him. Political power, however, called for some readiness to meet colleagues halfway, to work inside the system and not merely to ignore it. Pitt's physical and mental condition combined to deprive him of that patience and tact which were required. At times now he was a caricature of himself, in his appearances in the House, gaunt, pale, legs wrapped in rolls of flannel, or in Dorset at the house at Burton Pynsent, left to him by a wealthy admirer, where he directed ambitious projects of landscape gardening without thought of the cost. A devoted wife, four children and a beautiful house provided a background in which he sometimes relaxed. But his usual manner, strained, unnaturally histrionic, lay on the surface of a manic frenzy. The ostentation of his household, his postilions in blue and white, armies of servants around his children, were the outward signs of a restless ambition. Neither content to retire nor competent to play the exacting political game, he wished to be a force in politics, operating from the outside: 'unattached to any party I am, and wish to be, entirely single'. He was splendidly inconsistent: at first standing out for Newcastle, later refusing to work with him. He was determined, if he were to return to office, to do so on his own terms. That he could still rise to a great occasion he showed when he made a fine speech upon the Stamp Act, in January 1766, urging that there should be no taxation of free subjects without representation. The Stamp Act was repealed, but he was unable to dissuade parliament from provoking the colonists by unnecessary assertion of the principle that it had the right to tax them; so the Declamatory Act was passed.

In July 1766 he got at last the sole and unconditional direction of affairs. The problems which faced the government were those which he was specially fitted to tackle: the observance of the Treaty of Paris by France and Spain, the tension between the American colonists and the mother-country, and the status of the East India Company. He made several striking appointments: Charles Townshend went to the Exchequer and Shelburne to order American affairs. He set about his duties with tempestuous energy. Yet in October 1768 he resigned after a catastrophic ministry. What had gone wrong? He had embarked upon an experiment in rule, not only without party but almost without Cabinet: 'sole minister' indeed. Then he became really ill and so remained, on the threshold of madness, for the rest of his ministry.

He selected his ministers upon their merits, so far as he knew them, without regard for their connections. That Charles Townshend was unreliable was unfortunate; with careful handling he might have made great use of his talents. But it was Townshend who complained that Pitt treated his ministers 'like inferior animals'. His brother-in-law Temple, proud himself, refused to serve, anticipating that he would, like the rest, be regarded as a subordinate official. If he had stayed in the Commons he might still have held together 'an administration chequered and speckled', as Burke called it, 'patriots and courtiers, king's friends and republicans; Whigs and Tories; treacherous friends and open enemies ... indeed a very curious show'; but in the most surprising act of his life he took an earldom, removed himself from the sphere where he ruled with acknowledged mastery, and forfeited the sympathy of the people, for the doubtful advantages of the authority of a title and the pleasure of a king whom, with his veneration to royalty, he proposed to serve by 'destroying all party distinctions'. After a month Chatham collapsed. He made a show at first of ruling the country from Bath, where he wintered in 1766-7, and then from his house in Hampstead. But he was unable to impose his authority upon his ministers. When Townshend produced his unfortunate duties, in May 1767, light but offensive to the colonists whom Chatham understood so well, the prime minister was out of touch, so distracted that he would not even see his wife, sunk in agonized brooding, a prey to sudden whims such as pulling down some house which obscured his view. Grafton described his condition in shocked words: 'his nerves and spirits were affected to a dreadful degree

... his great mind bowed down'. But the king clung to the hope that he would recover, while the ministry drifted rudderless; eventually Chatham himself, emerging from his shadows, forced his resignation upon the king.

It was a sad episode. The damage done was immense, ironically greatest in his special sphere of interest. As he realized the gravity of the American situation, partly restored to his former spirit Chatham once more played an active part in the opposition. He was delighted by the letters of 'Junius', akin to his style in their fierce, polemical tone. He declared that 'he would be in earnest for the public' and 'a scarecrow of violence to the gentle warblers of the grove, the moderate Whigs and temperate statesmen'. But the latter had found a prophet in Edmund Burke who wrote of Chatham at this time, that he wanted 'to keep hovering in air, over all parties, and to swoop down where the prey may prove best'. Over the renewed case of Wilkes and the question of general warrants, he did indeed come near to destroying the ministry of Grafton. It was a cause after his own heart, with a smell of injustice, a threat to the liberties of the subject and a wider audience outside parliament listening angrily to his words. He was eloquent and Grafton resigned, but in Lord North George III found a successor more pliable and more amenable to his wishes.

With North secure, and little scope for effective opposition, after this brief resurgence of effort, Chatham retired to a watchful isolation. He pushed no further his suggestions for a modest reform of parliament. He pressed warmly the case for reform in India, where the less scrupulous servants of the East India Company were making fortunes for themselves at the expense of good government and the good name of the mother-country. For a time he turned to active farming, and housed his cows in typically palatial stalls. Debts and mortgages piled up while the creditors were warded off by his indulgent and determined wife. His warnings about the condition of America went unregarded until the eve of war. Then brave efforts to present his case, passionate and deeply pondered, for the concession to America of the fundamental liberties – no taxation without consent, independent judges and trial by jury, along with the recognition of Congress – foundered upon the ignorance and prejudice of parliament. His intuition that France was waiting to exploit the crisis, his intimate knowledge of the American colonies, lent passion to his words. In his last years he found again a certain nobility and showed that he had not lost the stagecraft of his great days. But in January 1775 the House rejected his Bill for securing a reconciliation. Then after war had broken out he warned the Lords that America could not be conquered. He still, however, clung to the view that reconciliation was possible. In April 1778, he went once more to the Lords where the Duke of Richmond was pressing a motion to grant American independence. His mind wandered, he was incoherent, sometimes inaudible; only phrases here and there recalled the passion and intellect of the statesman. It was a speech of hopeless resolution. His last words before he collapsed were: 'My Lords, any state is better than despair; if we must fall, let us fall like men.'

Carried from the House, he was driven to Hayes, his favourite home. His eldest son he sent back to his regiment at Gibraltar. William read Homer to him, the passage about the death of Hector; so heroically he died and was buried in Westminster Abbey with fitting pomp. In the Guildhall Burke's inscription summed up what he had meant to the city; he was the minister by whom 'commerce was united with and made to flourish by war'.

Further Reading
Jeremy Black, *Pitt the Elder*, 1992.
R. Middleton, *The Bells of Victory: the Pitt-Newcastle Ministry and the Conduct of the Seven Years' War*, 1985.
S. Ayling, *The Elder Pitt, Earl of Chatham*, 1976.
J. Brooke, *The Chatham Administration, 1766-8*, 1956.
Basil Williams, *William Pitt, Earl of Chatham*, 2 vols, 1913.
Lord Rosebery, *Chatham, Early Life and Connections*, 1910.

PITT, WILLIAM (1759-1806), statesman, was born on 28 May at Hayes in Kent, the second son of William Pitt and Hester Grenville. By the end of that year his father had been immortalized by a succession of splendid victories; despite the vicissitudes of his later career, nothing could detract from the prestige of his name. Resolute, efficient, devoted to her husband, Hester Grenville embodied the better qualities of her proud family and provided her son with a more stable inheritance than that of the Pitts – erratic, violent, sometimes brilliant but sometimes mad. William was notably sane. He announced, when his father was made Earl of Chatham and he was but seven, that he was glad that he was the second son, for he wanted to follow his father's course in the House of Commons. Shy and uneasy in his relations with people, he seemed always to possess the conviction that he must do great things.

Chatham recognized the quality in his son and sought to train his mind. He taught him to think on his feet, by making him read aloud in English from foreign texts; when he came to a difficult passage he would pause until the right words came. He was taught by a tutor, Edmund Wilson, at a pace which invited reaction. At the age of fourteen he went to Pembroke College, Cambridge, in Wilson's words 'to be admired as a prodigy; not to hear lectures, but to spread light'. There his tutor, Tomline, could hardly contain himself: 'his parts are astonishing and universal' – but Pitt fell ill and had to convalesce for six months. The doctor prescribed early rising, daily riding, and port. Thereafter his health remained sound though he came to rely increasingly on his port. In 1776

he took his degree by privilege, but stayed at Cambridge. By now he was an accomplished mathematician and linguist, steeped in Newton, Locke and Hume. Later he was to be an admirer of Paley whose reasoned statement of the *Principles of Moral and Political Philosophy* accorded with Pitt's temperament and views.

He chose law for his profession, went to Lincoln's Inn and was called in 1780. To this period belongs the encounter with Gibbon whom he so worsted in argument that the historian left in a pique and would not return. Since his father's death Pitt was poor and had to be assisted by Earl Temple, his uncle. His early debts were to grow steadily all his life. He practised on the Western Circuit but he was set on politics. In 1780 he came bottom of the poll at Cambridge, but was promptly provided with a seat for the amenable borough of Appleby by Sir James Lowther. His training for politics had been almost entirely academic. With his strict up-bringing and his own deliberate preparation, he was markedly different from the man who was to be his greatest rival: Charles James Fox had already acquired a host of friends and debts and was in the course of softening mind and will by reckless dissipation.

Pitt attached himself to that section of the Whigs who adhered, under Shelburne, to Chatham's conception of colonial policy and had therefore opposed the government of Lord North. In February 1782 North fell at last and was succeeded by Rockingham, who did not offer Pitt a post, despite the latter's interest in parliamentary reform. He had already announced that he would not accept 'a subordinate situation', but after Rockingham's death in July, Shelburne made him Chancellor of the Exchequer. 'He is not a chip off the old block; it is the old block itself,' said Burke after listening to him speaking. Pitt's mature reasoning impressed the House; as compared to the dazzling style of Fox it was especially the architecture of Pitt's speeches that compelled attention. Shelburne valued his talents, his independent views and the patriotic appeal of his name. Fox, who seems to have hoped that Pitt would incline towards his group, was affronted by his decision to serve under Shelburne: his subsequent alliance with North destroyed Shelburne's government. From March 1783 until the end of the year, Pitt was therefore free to take his own line again, knowing that he stood well with the king who had pressed him to succeed Shelburne. Unpopular in the country, detested by the king, the Fox-North coalition was too strong in parliament to be defied at once. Pitt stood back and waited for power on his own terms. He took up one of his father's interests when, in May 1783, he introduced proposals for parliamentary reform in alliance with Wyvill and the Yorkshire Associations. They were rejected, though Fox spoke for them; so was his bill for reform of the abuses of administration. In the autumn Pitt travelled to France and met Talleyrand and

Necker, whose wife tried to arrange a marriage with her daughter. Pitt seems to have been unaware of what was intended and the future Mme de Stael was left to find her match elsewhere. He never went abroad again.

On 17 December Fox's India Bill was defeated in the Lords and on the following day George III commanded his ministers to give up their seals. Temple became Secretary of State and Pitt moved into the centre of the storm with the office of First Lord of the Treasury. The risk was great, for the cry of royal tyranny still carried weight in the House. The kingdom 'was trusted to a schoolboy's care'; he was the head of a 'mincepie administration' and the wits had a field day. But he was heartened by Robinson's estimate of voting prospects and gambled on the effect of royal patronage and a turn of opinion in the constituencies. His ministers were weak in talents even before the resignation of Temple, who should have led the Lords. But Pitt stood firm against the opposition's gibes. They weakened their case by their vehemence; division after division their majorities fell. Pitt refused the sinecure of the Clerkship of the Pells. It was vital for him to appear to be independent of the court since in reality he relied so heavily upon it. He presented his own India Bill which provided for the public control which Fox's bill had proposed, through a Board of Control, without giving that body the patronage which made Fox's bill so vulnerable.

The bill was only defeated by eight votes; by March the difference had narrowed to one vote. Fox was discredited by the hooligans who attacked Pitt's coach outside Brooks's Club; Robinson, meanwhile, prepared the ground by discreet use of the king's known favour. On 24 March, parliament was dissolved and, in the election that followed, Pitt won a triumph which reflected both careful political management and a surge of popular feeling; 160 supporters of Fox and North lost their seats. Returned head of the poll at his beloved Cambridge, Pitt remained its member for the rest of his life.

The next five years, the most satisfying of Pitt's life, saw a series of measures designed to restore England's reputation and finances. The last four years of war alone had cost £80,000,000; the debt stood at £231,000,000. Discontent in Ireland, administrative disorder in India, threatened further expense, if not actual war. Abroad England had no friends. To set against the problems, one hidden advantage must be recorded. The industrial revolution was entering upon its most dynamic phase. The wealth was being created which, tapped by loans and taxes, was to enable England to survive the unparalleled burdens of the Napoleonic Wars. Nonetheless, Pitt's talent for financial administration was a factor in the recovery of the economy in the five years before the French Revolution. 'So perfect a knowledge of the Commerce, Funds and Government of the country,' wrote Lady Gower, 'that one must imagine that he had the experience of fifty years.' Largely unoriginal in his measures, he went a long way to implement the free trade advocated by Adam Smith. Like his mentor Shelburne, he paid heed to the views of the intellectuals. At a dinner party in 1787 he complimented Adam Smith thus: 'Nay, we will stand until you are seated, for we are all your scholars.' He showed also a Walpolean grasp of political realities and eschewed the grand projects of the more doctrinaire sort of reformer. He hit smuggling by reducing the duty on tea and other essential imports and simplified the method of collection. The yield on such dutiable goods as wine, spirits and tobacco rose sharply. By an extension of the Hovering Act (1780) he empowered officials to search ships up to four leagues out to sea. Further duties were added, to make up for the deficit arising from the reductions, upon a wide assortment of goods – hats, ribbons and hair powder, linens, calicoes and candles, paper, bricks and tiles, horses and even servants. In general this represents a trend which students of modern governmental finance will recognize: the government seeking to profit from the growth of consumption in an expanding economy.

The fashionable process of 'economical reform' was carried further by an inquiry into 'fees, gratuities, perquisites and emoluments'. The system of government borrowing was altered when loans were raised by tender, and he initiated a modest reform of archaic revenue procedures by creating the statutory Commission for Auditing the Public Accounts. By such measures an annual deficit was turned to a surplus and the means made available for the reduction of the National Debt. For this, Pitt instituted a sinking fund, similar to that outlined by Price. He did not, however, as Price proposed, borrow money at simple interest in order to invest at compound interest. He set aside a surplus £1,000,000 a year from the annual revenue. It did pay off several millions of debt, but its greatest service was to restore confidence in the government's solvency. (Pitt was later criticized for clinging to the system in wartime when he had to borrow at high rates in order to maintain the fund.) His triumph of financial understanding and parliamentary stamina was the Consolidation Bill of 1787, containing 2,537 separate resolutions. By the consolidation of customs duties, national book-keeping was vastly simplified. The Treasury account books were reduced from sixty folios to about a dozen. On the eve of war with France, Pitt was able to forecast a continuance of surpluses. It had been an astonishing achievement.

Pitt acquired at once an authority in the House which enabled him to persist in measures which he believed to be justified. Fox and his friends drew upon a fund of anti-French prejudice when they attacked the Free Trade treaty of September 1786. But Pitt had the manufacturing interest behind him and he carried it through with lofty contempt for the arguments of the opposition: 'to suppose that any nation could be unalterably the enemy of another is weak and childish'. Of course the English gained by a treaty which reduced duties on French wines, vinegar and oil and linens, and, correspondingly, duties upon English cottons, woollens, muslins, saddlery, porcelain and pottery. The French came to see the treaty as being the cause of their complex economic misfortunes and Robespierre even claimed that Pitt had deliberately precipitated the Revolution.

Pitt was less resolute in pressing schemes which promised no material advantage. He was not at heart a radical. Reforms, however desirable, had to be placed in the balance with all the needs of government. Few prime ministers have been ready, like Gladstone over Home Rule, to jeopardize a government for a single principle. Advocates of abolition of the slave trade and of the reform of parliament had to make their way as best they could. Although he consciously tried to lead and direct his ministers, Pitt was forced, perhaps even content, to accept the system of his time, and there was no unanimity in his Cabinet about reforms. Furthermore there was no party discipline which could enable Pitt to impose his point of view. He had only some fifty personal adherents as against more than twice that number who could be called Foxites. In 1785 he presented a scheme for the reform of parliament by the disenfranchisement of thirty-six boroughs, the distribution of seventy-two seats between the larger counties and the cities of Westminster and London and the admission of copyholders in the counties to the franchise. Boroughmongers were to be compensated handsomely; Fox opposed it, but most men accepted the idea of a borough as a piece of property. Pitt was defeated by seventy-four votes and introduced no further scheme for reform. Since Wilberforce, author of the movement to end the slave trade, was ill, Pitt himself introduced the motion for an inquiry in May 1788. Later the movement ran into entrenched opposition from commercial interests. In 1792 Pitt spoke eloquently for total abolition but the House preferred the compromise of Dundas – regulation of the trade. There the matter was left until 1806.

When Pitt took office, the state of Ireland was alarming. The antagonism of Grattan and Flood and the quarrel about the emancipation of Catholics divided the legislature, while the people suffered from poor trade and welcomed the actions of extremist groups. Pitt saw free trade as one solution, the precursor of that union which he thought must come. His proposals were opposed by the Whigs on the grounds that they would ruin British industry. Fox was fêted in Manchester and Pitt modified his proposals: the Navigation Laws were to be binding in both kingdoms and duties were not to be reduced below ten per cent. It was then the turn of the Irish to protest against what seemed to be a betrayal, and

of Fox to declare that he would not 'barter English commerce for Irish slavery'. The problem was therefore allowed to lapse and the distresses of Ireland continued to fester for want of intelligent and enforceable legislation. In Canada, however, in 1791, far-sighted action was taken to avoid racial dispute by the division into Upper or British and Lower or French provinces, each with its elected assembly. The French community remained, however, obstinately separate; and the problems outlined in the Durham Report of 1839 remained to be solved by the Act of 1840.

In 1784 Pitt secured the passage of his India Act. Whigs felt cheated – and made Warren Hastings the target of their revenge, hoping that Pitt would be drawn into the struggle. He, however, voted for indictment on the Benares charge. Justice could therefore take its course without reflection upon the government. As Pitt hoped, Hastings was eventually acquitted upon all charges. Pitt had acted as a politician and sympathy was subdued by calculation. We may recall his action in the first months of his administration when he upheld the election scrutiny against Fox: technically he was right, but it was a time for generosity. Pitt's stature could not be denied; but even his friends wished sometimes that he would glance towards the ground.

Pitt's style of leadership was unusually detached. In Cabinet he was uncommunicative. He entertained little. In the Commons he seemed scarcely to acknowledge the existence of his back-benchers. He detested the business of patronage which had been meat and drink to Walpole and North. But success justified his cautious handling of affairs. His integrity and commanding air earned loyalty, if not love. He could be counted upon not to be extreme. His lavish promotion of peers (119 in his time as prime minister) did indeed cause alarm. Pitt was uneasy about it himself, but he was also largely indifferent to the idea of nobility as a caste. He had to balance the Whigs and to compensate for the abolition, in the course of reform, of other forms of patronage. As in other matters he judged every case on its merits.

Under his armour there was a good-natured man, gentler and more uncertain when confronted by a contrary opinion than many supposed. Dundas once warned him of 'the unyielding nature of your temper when you are anxious upon a subject'. His instinct for perfection was constantly challenged by his insight into problems and understanding of what was possible. He did not spare himself the trouble of mastering subjects which he held to be important. Dealing with the Hastings case, he shut himself up with Dundas for ten days to study the intricacies of the Bengal revenues.

In foreign affairs Pitt devoted himself to altering Britain's condition of isolation. In 1783 the emperor had voiced a common opinion when he said that the country had descended forever to 'the rank of a second-rate power like Sweden or Denmark'. A crisis arose in 1787-8 from the quarrel in Holland between the Republican party and the Stadholder. When collision point had been reached the Cabinet backed the Stadholder with a subsidy and held the fleet in readiness, while Prussian troops marched to defend him. The French accepted the defeat of the republicans whom they had formerly upheld.

Spain, too, yielded to British power. After arresting British ships in Nootka Sound (1790), they subsequently admitted the British right to navigate the Pacific. The Eastern Question cast a larger shadow. After Suvaroff's victories over the Turks in 1791 Pitt became alert to the danger of Poland and the Turkish Empire being dismembered between Russia, Austria and Prussia. He demanded that Russia should restore her conquests, notably Okzakoff, but the Whigs protested and the Cabinet was divided. Pitt had to retreat: the price paid was the secret partition of Poland in 1793. Nonetheless Pitt was reducing armaments up to the outbreak of war with France in that year.

One of Pitt's recurring problems was caused by the precarious mental balance of the king. Between October 1788 and February 1789, when George III regained his sanity, his future seemed to hang upon the Regency Bill. Essentially Pitt was conducting a delaying action in his search for precedents and his desire for a formula which should give the regent powers adequate for an emergency. Fox stood for the regent's inherent right but spoiled his case by careless preparation. When the king recovered, the Regency Bill had not become law, the Whigs were 'un-Whigged' and Pitt could justly claim that he had stood both for the rights of the king and for the privileges of parliament against a prince whose personal conduct did not commend him to sober citizens. As a gesture of independence he had returned the offer of £100,000 from the merchants of London – though he was short of money as always. His personal reputation was by now secure. Indeed, a note of awe creeps into contemporary accounts of 'the good minister'. His slender figure, the long, haughty nose above a disdainful mouth, his proud and absorbed public manner; his seeming indifference to women and simplicity of life were all so different from the lavish style of Fox. Pitt's friends knew a more spontaneous person – witty, a man who loved children and read the poems of Burns, went dutifully to church but liked to argue points of doctrine; a delightful companion at the dinner table. Richard Wellesley, about this time, described his manners as 'perfectly plain' and thought him endowed 'beyond any man of his time … with a gay heart and a social spirit'.

In his appraisal of the French Revolution Pitt stood halfway between Fox, who welcomed it effusively, and Burke, who warned of the tyranny that would ensue. He was pragmatic as ever, sympathizing first with the creation of a limited monarchy, then shrinking from the extremes of violence. He judged what was happening in France by its effect upon England. He welcomed Burke's defection from the Whigs but remained unimpressed by his flights of rhetoric and prophecy. The effect of the Revolution was to create a new Toryism, thus seemingly to make Pitt's position impregnable. As the war developed after 1793, Fox's attitude became increasingly unpopular: for some years the opposition virtually withdrew from parliament. As a war leader Pitt enjoyed the support that men give when faced by a common danger and he could count on patriotic sentiment and generous loans. The price was heavier, however, than even the mounting figures of the National Debt could show. Schemes of reform wilted in the prevailing mood of anti-Jacobinism. Pitt gave expression to this spirit and seldom gave way to its excesses. He was little suited, though, to the needs of 'this war of armed opinions'. It was Pitt's tragedy no less than Fox's; it consumed his spirit.

Pitt upheld the Scottish judiciary in 1793 after treason trials of notorious severity with biased judges. He seems for once to have capitulated before popular opinion. But he panicked less than his associates in the face of the symptoms of social revolution and his 'reign of terror' was relatively mild. There was widespread acquiescence in the anti-Jacobin agitation of 1792-9 – the Aliens Act, the Seditious Meetings Act, the Treasonable Correspondence Act, the suspension of Habeas Corpus and the anti-combination laws. His position was not easy for he was associated with the establishment of wealth and privilege by those who protested against the high price of food. 'No war! No famine! No Pitt!' was the cry of the London mob in 1795.

He always kept negotiated peace in mind but unfortunately the British did not achieve enough success to give them a strong position. Pitt was not a gifted strategist; he seemed to be unable to devise an over-all strategy. He can be criticized for failing to appreciate the impoverished mentality of revolutionary governments who were unconcerned by the loss of sugar islands and trading posts. Their acquisition was moreover of doubtful benefit to England. In the West Indies 40,000 British troops died of disease. Nor did economic warfare bring the success expected; only slowly did Pitt accept that France would not be destroyed by inflation.

Pitt was ill-served by his continental allies, who accepted his subsidies but could not match the spirit of the French armies, the administration of Carnot or the genius of Napoleon. Successive coalitions were bedevilled by the failure of the powers to act together. English military intervention was also inglorious: the Duke of York's expedition of 1793 to France had to be withdrawn, the Quiberon Bay expedition of 1795 was a fiasco. In 1795 Prussia and Spain left the coalition; in 1796 Spain joined France. The campaigns of Bonaparte smashed the Austrians in Italy and in the autumn of 1797 Britain stood alone and consols fell to forty-eight. Could 'the efforts of a free, brave, loyal and happy people', in Pitt's words, check France? France came to mean Bonaparte, First Consul in 1799, emperor in 1801. To his credit Pitt had exempted the navy from his peacetime economies. In Sir Charles Middleton, at the admiralty, he had a great administrator. England's strength was at sea but, as the naval mutinies of 1797 showed, even there lay danger. The victories of St Vincent and Duncan restored confidence, however; the brilliant success of Nelson at the Nile in 1800 gave Napoleon a salutary lesson in the importance of sea power, and his victory at Copenhagen in 1801 showed neutral powers what to expect if they took sides in the Great War. These were dour years for Pitt. Long, wearing hours were spent poring over maps, consulting with ministers and commanders, writing and reading correspondence, wrestling with the problems of war finance. He had the moral stature to promote such unpopular taxes as, in 1798, an income tax rising to 2s. in the pound for all above £200 a year. He was hissed by the mob, but the burden was placed fairly on the shoulders of the rich when he raised the land tax; his appeal for an extra voluntary subscription was received with enthusiasm and large loans were floated.

Pitt bore the burden alone. It was expected that he would marry Eleanor Eden, but for some reason, although he seems to have been in love with her, he decided against marriage. His own affairs were utterly confused, debtors pressed. It is odd that he who devoted so much care to the nation's finance could not order his own. Did he foresee that his life would be one of unrelieved cares leading to an early death? Was he unusually considerate – or unfeelingly cold, as his enemies said? He remained a bachelor, living at Downing Street and Walmer Castle (as Warden of the Cinque Ports), with his niece Lady Hester Stanhope as housekeeper. His health deteriorated, he drank deeply but without the gaiety of earlier years. Dundas claimed that he divided his time 'between cellar and garret'. Never methodical, and a neglectful correspondent, he now became increasingly casual about political and personal business. In 1806 there were still odd documents of the 1780s lying about his room. He was usually calm but one incident showed that he could crack: in May 1798 he fought a duel with Tierney on Putney Common after a violent exchange in the Commons.

Negotiations for peace brought their own strains. Fox urged the ministers on with brilliant speeches but others condemned the very idea of parleying with unstable revolutionaries: predictions were hazardous, treaties unreliable. Between the iron obstinacy of Grenville and

the wishful thinking of Fox, Pitt had to steer a middle course. As it turned out, Pitt was not the man who made peace.

The problems of Ireland did not wait upon the events of war. By the impetuosity of Earl Fitzwilliam in 1795, who introduced a bill in the Irish parliament for full civil equality for Catholics and Protestants, he was embroiled in a struggle whose outcome, he believed, must be political union. In an hysterical atmosphere calm measures were spurned. Pitt offered a charter for Maynooth College – but Catholic feeling could not be assuaged. The United Irishmen planned a republic, but fortunately for England their title was a misnomer. The Catholic rising in Leinster and Wexford was less a republican movement than an agrarian *jacquerie* fortified by religious fanaticism and, belatedly, by French troops. Hideous atrocities embittered both peasants and troops before the rising was put down by Lake and Cornwallis. Pitt was impressed by the military danger and the cost of 40,000 troops, as well as by the distresses of Ireland. In January 1800 he presented the case for Union in a speech which was masterly, humane, comprehensive. To persuade the Irish borough-mongers to give up their interest, £10,000 was given for each borough; sinecures, titles, further sweetened the pill. The total bill for disenfranchisement was £1,260,000, forty-six promotions to the peerage and twenty ecclesiastical appointments. The resolution passed the Dublin parliament in the spring of 1800. Then Pitt ran upon the rocks.

Loughborough, his Lord Chancellor, aroused the king's anxieties about Catholic Emancipation. When Pitt put this before the king the latter talked of conspiracy and insisted upon his oath: he saw the issue, as always, in personal terms and spoke of loyalty. Pitt felt that he was committed to the Catholic cause by the previous transactions, though no formal promise had been given. In February 1801 he resigned. George III lapsed into insanity. Pitt promised that he would not raise the question of Catholic Emancipation again in George III's lifetime. Addington was left to negotiate the peace of Lunéville. Pitt continued to give support as a private member. Just as he had never seen himself as being, in a modern sense, head of a party, so now he would neither lead any systematic opposition nor listen to suggestions of a compromise ministry. He was reticent in these months to a point that exasperated his friends. They longed, in Canning's words, for the return of 'the pilot who weathered the storm'. He seems to have waited for a spontaneous rush of public opinion and he suffered in health from sudden release from the tensions of high office. Visits to Bath were needed to relieve his gout and biliousness. Only a private subscription among friends saved him from his creditors, but he had still to sell Holwood, his country house.

In May 1803 war was resumed after deadlock had been

reached upon the question of Malta. As Colonel of the Kentish Association and Warden of the Cinque Ports, Pitt drilled volunteers. 'He absolutely goes through the fatigue of a drill sergeant' reported Hester. At first he seems to have supported the government. He seems to have hoped for a coalition, but the government's naval policy alarmed him. Then Fox joined him in voting against the Militia Bill and Addington's majority sank. At the end of April 1804 he resigned. George III resisted Pitt's request to have Fox in – and Grenville stayed out in sympathy with Fox. Pitt shouldered his burden with only Dundas close enough to him to be of much use. The impeachment and disgrace of Dundas was a shattering blow. But Pitt planned for a decision: the navy's part, planned by Barham at the admiralty, was to annihilate the French and Spanish fleets, while on the continent Austria and Russia were to bring the French to action in Italy. The Mediterranean was the strategic centre. In the event, Napoleon's invasion plans were thwarted, but Trafalgar brought grief as well as the exhilaration of complete victory. Pitt, who admired Nelson intensely, could not sleep the night he heard the news. Napoleon's sea power was destroyed but on land the triumphs of Ulm and Austerlitz were to spell the destruction of Pitt's laborious and expensive design.

In November 1805 he went to the banquet at the Mansion House; the mob untied the horses and dragged his carriage themselves. To the Lord Mayor's toast to the 'saviour of Europe' he simply replied: 'I return you many thanks for the honour you have done me; but Europe is not to be saved by any single man. England has saved herself by her exertions and will, as I trust, save Europe by her example.' The frail figure seemed to embody the collective will of the nation. In December, however, came the news of Austerlitz. He may not have said 'Roll up the map of Europe, it will not be needed these ten years', but he seems to have believed it. Wilberforce spoke of his 'Austerlitz look'. His last weeks were passed in physical agony and the heartbreak of a disappointed patriot. In his last delirium listeners caught the cry 'Hear! Hear!' and later, 'Oh! my country! How I leave my country!' He died in the early morning of 23 January 1806. His last thoughts seem to have been of the Commons, and of the country which he had so nobly served.

Many wept. Lord Malmesbury vowed that in his whole future life he would always act as he believed William Pitt would have wished. For a political following, more generally for a political class, Pitt became, more than a memory, an idea. Because his mind had been so open, his policies so pragmatic, his appeal was broad. It was that which had frustrated Charles James Fox; and it was he who said, after his rival's death, that 'it seemed as if there were something missing in the world'.

Further Reading
J. Ehrman, *The Younger Pitt*, vol. I, 1969; vol. II, 1983; vol. III, 1996.
J. Holland Rose, *William Pitt and the National Revival* and *William Pitt and the Great War*, both 1911.

PITT RIVERS, AUGUSTUS (1827-1900), archaeologist, general and flamboyant polymath, was born Lane Fox, but changed his name in 1880, on inheriting the 27,000 acre Rivers estate on Cranborne Chase from a cousin. He was the worst sort of Victorian father, a large, imposing man, who banished one son from his house and struck his daughter with her own riding crop when she went out to meet her brother in the grounds. 'Damn it woman, you shall burn,' he told his wife, when she asked for burial rather than cremation. Mrs Pitt Rivers was a mean woman, who once recycled the bacon and eggs which a guest left unfinished, and their home was not a happy one. But outside it, Pitt Rivers used his energies creatively in many fields. As a soldier, he helped to pick the rifle-bored musket which the army adopted in the Crimean War, and trained the troops to use it. As an anthropologist, he formed a collection which he passed to Oxford University, where the Pitt Rivers Museum was created to house it. As an educator, he converted Farnham House on his own estate into a new type of popular museum, with plentiful descriptions and models. He set up a pleasure ground near it to draw the crowds, with a hotel, picnic bowers, an open air theatre, a bandstand, Indian houses, a race track, and eventually a golf course. He kept a menagerie of 'yaks and zebras and so on', as a local put it, for cross-breeding experiments.

But archaeology became his compelling interest. Cranborne Chase was an archaeologist's paradise; a royal hunting ground, which until 1830 had been preserved from change since the Middle Ages. In a field where the gentleman amateur predominated, Pitt Rivers, though one himself, set new standards in section drawing, the labelling and arranging of finds, and the establishing of their chronology. He broadened the objects of excavation from burial mounds, to forts, dykes and settlements. He appreciated more than his contemporaries the interrelationship of archaeology and anthropology. Profoundly influenced by Darwin, he saw his discoveries as revealing the truths of gradual evolution. The political and social moral of them was clear to him. 'The law that Nature makes no jumps' should make men 'cautious how they listen to scatter-brained revolutionary suggestions'. There spoke the general and the landlord.

Further Reading
M. Bowden, *Pitt Rivers: his Life and Archaeological Work*, 1991.

PLACE, FRANCIS (1771-1854), radical politician, was the son of Simon Place, a baker who became bailiff to the Marshalsea and keeper of a 'sponging house' in Vinegar Yard, Drury Lane. At fourteen the boy was apprenticed to a leather-breeches maker. At nineteen he married Elizabeth Chadd, two years younger than himself. They set up house in one room in a 'rookery' off the Strand and Place set himself, energetically and frugally, to make a living out of a declining trade.

When, in 1793, the leather-breeches workers struck work, Place was chosen to be their organizer. The strike was sponsored by the Breeches Makers' Benefit Society, which had managed to collect £250 to back their action. Place, who had started to work on cloth breeches to make more money, found that the breeches makers were making common cause: indeed, he learned about the strike, when his master refused to give him any more work, alleging that the cloth-breeches makers were supporting the others from their earnings. He resolved, therefore, to counter the masters' strategy by broadening the struggle. Some of the London men were induced by seven shillings a week strike-pay to tramp into the provinces, armed with their Society's certificate, to secure hospitality from local societies. Place also opened a shop to sell 'Rag Fair Breeches' at a special price. Thus he circumvented the employers, prolonged the strike and exposed himself to reprisals, when at last the men accepted defeat. He was given no work for eight months and had to pawn his belongings. In 1795, with trade temporarily brisk and a reformed society, of which he was secretary, the workers managed to get the conditions – for which they had struck before – this time without a struggle. Persistence, co-operation and boldness had shown the way.

Place had meanwhile become a member of the London Corresponding Society and was active as unofficial adviser of clubs. He was much influenced at this time by Tom Paine's *Age of Reason* and its anti-authoritarian message. In 1796 we find him arranging for the production of a cheap edition of the book. He won the friendly respect of James Mill, Robert Owen, whom he helped with his *Essays on the Formation of Character*, and Jeremy Bentham. He stayed for some months in 1817 (leaving his business in the care of his eldest son) with Bentham and Mill at Ford Abbey, and busied himself there with learning Latin grammar. Romilly met him there and declared him 'a very extraordinary person' as well as a disciple and admirer of Bentham's. 'He is self-educated, has learned a great deal, has a very strong natural understanding, and possesses great influence in Westminster – such influence as almost to determine the elections for Members of Parliament.' He used this influence to help independent reformers like Hobhouse, winner of the Westminster election in 1820, and Joseph Hume, who drew heavily upon Place's parliamentary records for his political campaigns. He was also a voluminous writer; there are seventy-one

volumes of manuscripts and materials in the British Museum: he tended to be prolix in argument and laboured in style.

In later life Place supported many causes, birth control among them. In 1823 he was responsible for the distribution of handbills on this subject. He had two great triumphs. In 1824 he succeeded in getting the law against combinations of workmen repealed. In the following year he prevented their re-enactment: the Amending Act of that year left combination lawful. With Hume he had managed to pack the parliamentary committee, presented it with carefully collated evidence from employers and workmen, and rushed the act through before the government realized its significance. Place's methods were masterly: for example, he prevented extreme opponents of the laws from appearing, lest they should spoil the case by overstatement.

His motives should be understood. As a Benthamite, who believed in 'cheap and simple government', he hoped that trades union action would be discouraged because workers would learn, in their new freedom, the futility of combining in the face of the inexorable 'laws' of political economy, and the better course of collaborating with employers in increasing the 'wages fund' that depended on employers' profits. At the same time he approved of the activity of the small unions whose concern was with conditions of labour. On the whole, however, he was careful not to become involved in any directly subversive activities. He saw the role of working-class reformers as accessories to those who could obtain a hearing in parliament. He had been a member of the Corresponding Society since 1794 and an official since 1795. He seems to have wanted a sober, orderly *conversazione* with other 'inquisitive, clever, upright men'. He later idealized this side of the society. It taught men 'to think, to respect themselves, and to desire to educate their children'. There was also a rowdier, impatient element; in 1796 he resigned his post and in 1797 he left the society altogether.

When some of his colleagues were languishing in gaol, Place was laying the foundations of a business. In April 1799, with a fellow workman as partner, he set up a tailor's shop in Charing Cross Road. Within two years he was on his own and employing more than thirty workmen. He did not lose sight of political issues or political friends. He managed the collecting of subscriptions for the prisoners' families. But he believed that agitation was hopeless at that time; when he intervened it would be from the base of a flourishing business. The cause of reform was best served by mobilizing public opinion so as to bring pressure on parliament – and he could do nothing effective in this way until he had secured his own position as a prosperous tradesman. He had a large family – ten out of fifteen survived infancy – and he provided for them well. He also read widely, collected the library which was to become the regular resort, club and committee room of reformers, and awaited his chance to intervene.

In 1807 Sir Francis Burdett stood for Westminster and Place helped to direct a campaign which, because it was devoted to the bread-and-butter business of canvassing and registering, was cheaper than previous campaigns in this turbulent constituency. Burdett came top of the poll, radicalism obtained a loud voice in the Commons – and Place was established, in the niche which he occupied until the passing of the Reform Bill, as organizer and oracle of Westminster radicalism. He quarrelled with Burdett in 1810 when the latter refused to lead the procession which Place had arranged to celebrate Burdett's release from the Tower. Like other radical leaders of these pioneer days, Place was sensitive about his status in the movement. He was by temperament a committee man, a student of the art of getting things done.

After the introduction of the Reform Bill in 1831 Place's library became again the meeting place of the extreme reformers. Years of research and study of the mechanics of popular politics now bore fruit. The various leaders of radical and liberal opinion made common cause. He wrote of events across the Channel that they had 'produced a very extraordinary effect on the middle classes, and sent a vast number of persons to me, with all sorts of projects and propositions'. By May 1832 Place was making active preparations for the expected civil war. Placards, devised by him, bore the slogan 'To stop the duke, go for gold', which produced a run on the banks. Had this not achieved its effect he planned a collective refusal to pay taxes. There was talk of barricades and pikes, but moderate counsels prevailed. Cocksure and self-important as he was, Place was no revolutionary.

Place's triumph, ironically enough, reduced his political influence, since Westminster was partially disenfranchised by the ten shilling clause and no longer held its peculiar position as a popular constituency. Place lost most of his money by the mistakes of a solicitor and was forced to exchange Charing Cross for a house in Brompton Square. He was still active in the back rooms of politics. He helped Joseph Parkes prepare the municipal corporations report in 1835 and drafted the 'People's Charter' for his friend William Lovett in 1838. But the Chartism of O'Connor and O'Brien owed little to Place: he was altogether too bourgeois for them. In 1840 he became chairman of the Metropolitan Anti Corn Law Committee. But in 1844 a tumour on the brain incapacitated him, though he lived for ten more years. In 1851 he was separated from his second wife. He died on New Year's Day of 1854 in his daughters' house in Hammersmith. In his lengthy autobiography (unpublished) Place overestimates his importance in the reform movement as a whole. But in Westminster, for two decades, he was keeper of the radical conscience and the most effective promoter of the cause.

Further Reading
Dudley Mill, *Francis Place*, 1988.
Graham Wallas, *Francis Place*, 1898.

PLEGMUND (*d.*923) was Archbishop of Canterbury from 890 until his death. He was a native of Mercia. Later tradition asserted that he had lived as a hermit at Plemstall, near Chester. There is no means of testing this tradition, but it should be noted that the earliest recorded form of the place-name is *Plegmundes stow*, 'the holy place of Plegmund'. At some time unknown, but before 887, he was attracted to the court of King Alfred, by whose agency he was promoted to the archbishopric of Canterbury in 890.

Plegmund's archiepiscopate was long and important. It is unfortunate that we know so little about it. What we do know suggests that Plegmund was an active and creative figure in the life of the English church. His most enduring contribution to that life was an administrative one. Between 910 and 918 he subdivided the two enormous dioceses of Wessex, Winchester and Sherborne, and created three additional ones. Seats for bishops were established at Crediton (with a diocese embracing Devon and Cornwall), Wells (Somerset) and Ramsbury (Wiltshire and Berkshire); Sherborne was thenceforward left with Dorset alone, and Winchester with Hampshire and Surrey. In its main lines the administrative reorganization lasted for nearly 1,000 years. Whether or not it owed something to Plegmund's reading of what Bede had had to say about Archbishop Theodore – and it may well have done – Bede would have approved of it. He would also have approved of the fact that Plegmund undertook it after consultation with the pope, whom he had visited in 908.

There are some other indications that Plegmund was a churchman of reforming temper. Archbishop Fulk of Rheims (883-922) wrote to Plegmund at some point, apparently – for we know of the letter only through a tenth-century chronicler's précis – congratulating him on his attempts to extirpate clerical marriage among the English. It is likely that this refers to legislation issued by Plegmund, presumably in an ecclesiastical council. We also possess the text of a letter from Pope Formosus (891-6), whom Plegmund may have visited in 896, which seems to suggest that the English bishops were taking steps under their archbishop's guidance to convert the Scandinavian settlers in the Danelaw to Christianity – a tantalizing allusion to an important but obscure activity.

Plegmund's reforming initiatives, administrative and otherwise, could only have been undertaken with the active support of the two kings he served, Alfred and Edward the Elder. Of his relations with Edward we know practically nothing: the civil government of that king is very ill-documented. But we are better informed about his association with Alfred. In the preface to the translation of Pope Gregory's *Pastoral Care* into Old English, attributed to Alfred, the king thanked four men for their assistance: Plegmund, Asser, Grimbald and John. We may take it that Plegmund was closely involved with Alfred's educational plans. This is confirmed by the evidence of surviving documents written at Canterbury. The charters of the period between about 850 and 890 were drafted by men who were barely literate: knowledge of Latin was shaky, calligraphic standards abysmal. And this at the oldest seat of English Christianity – one is put in mind of Alfred's observation that at the time of his accession in 871 there were very few people left in England who could understand the services of the church or translate a document from Latin into English. But under Plegmund there came a change for the better, which it is surely correct to attribute to his initiative. Basic literacy returned; Latinity and script improved; the modest yet firm foundation for the tenth-century intellectual revival was laid down.

Plegmund was associated with Alfred's other projects. In 898 he attended a meeting called by the king, along with Ealdorman Ethelred, his wife Ethelflaed and Bishop Werferth of Worcester, to discuss what was described as the *instauratio* of the city of London; by which was probably meant such matters as planning and fortification in the wake of Alfred's takeover of London from the Danes in 886. Plegmund acquired property in the city, including a river-frontage, for his church of Canterbury. He had therefore close connections with the Alfredian programme of urban renewal and defence.

Legislation was another area of activity where Plegmund might have been of service to Alfred. The king's code of law, issued probably in the 890s, was more intellectually elaborate than any of the codes promulgated by previous Anglo-Saxon rulers and more deeply impregnated with Christian values. It is difficult to believe that churchmen of high rank did not have some say in drafting it. (Wihtred and Ine had legislated with the advice of their bishops, and Archbishop Wulfstan was to draft a whole series of codes for Ethelred II and Canute. Again, Alfred's Catolingian contemporaries across the Channel were accustomed to receiving episcopal guidance and admonition.) The case is strengthened by the circumstance that some of the linguistic usages of Alfred's lawcode display Mercian rather than West Saxon forms of Old English. The mind turns irresistibly to Alfred's Mercian Archbishop of Canterbury.

This is as much as we can know, and reasonably infer, about Archbishop Plegmund. The sketch is necessarily indistinct. But we can sense the outlines of a statesman who was a sturdy prop of the Alfredian and Edwardian régime.

PLUNKET, LORD WILLIAM (1764-1854) was one of the most aggressive politicians of his time. Irish questions gave him much scope for advocacy and rhetoric. His father was a Unitarian minister in Dublin, least advantageous of positions. He died in poverty and William's education was paid for by fellow Unitarians. From Trinity College, Dublin he went on to the Irish Bar and to a borough in the pocket of Lord Charlemont. When Pitt proposed the Act of Union and Castlereagh set about the abolition of the Irish parliament, Plunket was in his element. In 1798 the Union was enacted – but Plunket's speeches, cold, bitingly witty, made him a hero in Ireland.

In 1803 Robert Emmett appeared in court charged with being leader of a band of men who had murdered the Irish Chief Justice. Plunket knew his father and was popularly associated with the rebel cause. However he led the prosecution; Emmett was hung. Cobbett would revive the charge of early sympathy with revolution and Plunket would have to bring an action to clear his name. Meanwhile, however, he was the government's man. He became Solicitor-General for Ireland. After 1812 he was member for the University of Dublin. From the Grenville Whigs he moved to Lord Liverpool's Tories.

A small man, he was impressive by sheer power of argument, and a controlled vehemence of speech. Canning said that his speeches brought back the best days of Burke, Pitt and Fox. In 1822 he became Attorney-General for Ireland. He became a convinced advocate of Catholic emancipation. Canning held that Plunket did more for the Catholics than any other politician: more than Grattan, even O'Connell. Prime Minister in 1827, Canning made him Chief Justice of Common Pleas in Ireland and raised him to the Lords. There he helped Wellington to secure the passage of the Catholic Emancipaton Bill. The duke asked him to sit beside him on the Treasury bench and advise him step by step as the Bill edged its way through an unhappy house. His performance there, and his forensic skills, led the Whigs to give him office. From 1830 to 1841 he was Lord Chancellor of Ireland. Fierce and sharp in debate he was warm-hearted and generous in private life. It is typical of him that, with his brother, a doctor, he paid back every penny subscribed to the education of which he had made such remarkable use.

POCOCK, SIR GEORGE (1706-92), admiral, was a capable seaman who did valuable service without achieving any notable or decisive victory. He joined the navy in 1718 and received swift promotion. He was in chief command in the Leeward Islands, 1747-8, where he captured a French convoy of forty ships. Upon the outbreak of war again, he got his flag and was sent to command the fleet on the East India station in 1758. Off the Coromandel coast, in three successive actions, he battled with d'Aché, the competent French commander, for the mastery of the sea which was so vital to land operations. The third time, in September 1759, after two indecisive encounters, Pocock fought a formal line engagement which shattered many of the French ships, though none was sunk. The battle displayed the limitations of the old rule about not breaking the line. Pocock could, one feels, have been more enterprising. But it was his duty to keep his fleet intact. Moreover d'Aché subsequently withdrew his fleet and the English were able to capture Pondicherry. Pocock became admiral and KB in 1761. In the following year he commanded the fleet in the exemplary amphibious operation that led to the capture of Havana and was rewarded by prize money of £122,697. He retired in 1766 after a career which had amply demonstrated the value of sea power when put to intelligent use.

POCOCKE, EDWARD (1604-91), Oxford orientalist, born in the city and educated at Thame Grammar School and Magdalen Hall, became a Fellow of Corpus Christi College. He began oriental studies as a young man, and at the age of twenty-four published an edition of four previously unprinted epistles from the Syriac New Testament. From 1630 to 1635 he was Chaplain to the English Turkey merchants at Aleppo, learning Arabic and collecting manuscripts and coins, and on his return Laud had him appointed to the Lectureship in Arabic which he had just founded at Oxford (1636). In 1637 Pococke went again to the east, living mainly at Constantinople, and when he came back in 1641 Laud was in the Tower: he rejected the scholarly advice, based upon successful experience, which Pococke brought him from Grotius, to have himself smuggled out in a box of books. Pococke himself, installed in a country living in 1642, ran into trouble with his parishioners because of his Laudian background, and only the intervention of Selden and others saved his lectureship. Pococke declined the oath to the Commonwealth, but managed to continue his studies in peace, publishing his masterpiece *Specimen Historiae Arabum* in 1649. After the Restoration he lived at Christ Church as a canon and as Professor of Hebrew, and on his death at the age of eighty-six his fine collection of oriental manuscripts was bought for the Bodleian.

POLE, REGINALD (1500-58), Cardinal and Archbishop of Canterbury, was born in March 1500 and died on the night of 17 November 1558, aged fifty-eight years. He was the son of Sir Richard Pole, who had married Margaret, Countess of Salisbury, the daughter of Edward VI's brother, George, Duke of Clarence. He was, therefore, one of the Yorkist claimants to the throne. It was this relationship to the reigning king in England which made him so important in the eyes of foreign rulers. Henry VIII showed him considerable kindness and made generous grants of money towards the cost of his education at the Carthusian school at Sheen, at Magdalen College, Oxford, and at Padua University. In addition he made over to him ecclesiastical revenues to ensure him an income equal to his rank. At Oxford his teachers were Linacre and Latimer, in Italy the great scholars Longolius, Leonicus and Bembo. He also corresponded with Erasmus, met John à Lasco, the Polish reformer, and paid a visit to Rome. He proved himself a man of great intellectual qualities, brilliant in debate, and ultimately an admirable teacher, but he was never a learned theologian.

Pole was in Italy from 1521 to 1527. He was back in England by 1527 and was cordially welcomed by the king. But Pole disliked life at court and retired to Sheen to pursue his studies. Pole was much opposed to the divorce from Catherine of Aragon which Henry was planning, and when the king sought his advice, he got leave to go abroad to Paris. But when he was there, Henry demanded that he should obtain the views of Paris University. Thanks to the influence of Francis I the opinion was favourable. Recalled to England, Pole was, on the death of Wolsey, strongly urged to accept either the bishopric of Winchester or the archbishopric of York. Henry was anxious to have him on his side in his quarrel with Rome, but Pole would not accept on those terms. In an interview with the king, Pole behaved tactlessly and violently, the king lost his temper and almost hit Pole, finally leaving him dissolved in tears. The quarrel was soon mended, and in 1532 Henry allowed him to go abroad to Avignon and then to Padua.

Up to 1536, the year in which Pole visited Rome and became a cardinal, Henry made many attempts to win him over, for he recognized the danger to England which might come from a hostile Yorkist. But Henry's impatience and Pole's inflexibility always prevented a reconciliation, which was at last made impossible by the publication of Pole's *De Unitate Ecclesiae*, in which discretion was thrown to the winds and abuse was poured out on Henry. From that moment Pole revealed his inherent lack of political insight. He thought the Pilgrimage of Grace was symptomatic of all England; he was prepared to become a traitor to his own country and to urge France and Spain to invade England, and he advocated a commercial blockade of England.

Henry retaliated by executing Pole's brother and his mother, although he may have been justified in suspecting them of being directly involved with Pole in treasonable conspiracy. The king may even have tried to have Pole murdered, but it may be that Pole only imagined this. Henry took all possible steps to obstruct Pole's legatine missions; that is, his missions from the pope to England and to foreign powers to depose Henry.

Foreigners also recognized the importance of Pole in the diplomatic world. His dynastic position became a reason for trying to arrange a marriage between him and Mary Tudor, and the pope gave him a legateship to sustain English rebels with money. Nor did the pope underrate the value of Pole's scholarship. From 1536, when he became a cardinal, to 1549, when it looked as if Pole was likely to succeed Paul III as pope, Pole's career was distinguished and he was probably happier than he was either before or after. Twice he presided over the Council of Trent and he was made Governor of the Patrimony of St Peter, while he enjoyed the friendship of the most famous woman of Italy, Vittoria Colonna. But in truth he was losing ground. He belonged to the liberal Catholics, who hoped for reconciliation between Lutheranism and the Catholic church, and when this party failed to secure control of the church, and the more extreme party was successful at the Council of Trent, Pole's own influence began to wane. He bowed to the inevitable and accepted the papal authority. He was not a strong enough man to oppose the policy of the papacy on principle and risk exile a second time. He had been exiled from England for denying the Royal Supremacy, he now accepted the Papal Supremacy. He was within an ace of being elected pope on the death of Paul III; but although he was supported by the imperial cardinals, that inevitably put the French cardinals against him, while the Italian cardinals wanted an Italian pope.

On the accession of Mary Tudor it was only a question of time before Pole would return to England. He was appointed the new Archbishop of Canterbury. But his return for various reasons was delayed, and it was not until 20 November 1554 that he landed in England. He at once set about restoring England to the Catholic fold, reorganizing the church and preventing the later succession of Elizabeth. Up to this moment he was still only in deacon's orders; on 20 March 1556 he was ordained priest and the next day, when Cranmer was burned, Pole as archbishop celebrated Mass for the first time in his life. For two years the government of England was very largely in the hands of Pole, who busied himself both in religious and secular affairs. But although the ecclesiastical settlement of Henry was reversed by Act of Parliament and Pole enforced many reforms which he wanted, he failed in the end both in making England Roman Catholic and in keeping Elizabeth off the throne. He must accept his share of responsibility for the burnings. All his life he hated extreme measures, but he dared not oppose the persecutions. He died the same night as Queen Mary, with his work unfinished.

Reginald Pole was a sincere and single-minded man, a passionate believer in the Christian religion, a man of perfect integrity and unblemished morals. He had a genius for friendship and he was intimate with the best spirits in Italy, men like Contarini, Priuli and Sadoleto, women like Vittoria Colonna. But he was intransigent and inherently weak; he dreaded holding public office,

and although he was able to speak his mind fearlessly and even violently, as he did to Pope Paul IV, he often shirked his clear duty, as he did when he failed to withstand the Marian persecutions. Yet he saw clearly the dangers inherent in the growing modern state and he took his stand courageously and consistently in defence of religion and the church. It is his chief claim to be remembered that he also saw the need for reform in the Catholic church, tried patiently to achieve reform and by his example and work made the ultimate reforms of the Jesuits the easier to achieve.

Further Reading
R. H. Pogson, *Historical Journal*, 1975.
D. Fenlon, *Heresy and Obedience in Tridentine Italy*, 1972.
W. Schenk, *Reginald Pole, Cardinal of England*, 1950.
W. G. Zeeveld, *Foundations of Tudor Policy*, 1948.
P. Hughes, *Rome and the Counter-Reformation in England*, 1940.
K. B. McFarlane, *Cardinal Pole*, 1924.

PONET, JOHN (variations in spelling are **POYNET**, **POINET** and **PONNET** but he always used the form **PONET**) (1516-56), Bishop of Winchester, was born in Kent in 1516 (not 1514). Little is known of his early life. He arrived in Cambridge at the Queens' College about 1528, took his BA, became a Fellow in 1532, MA 1535, bursar 1537-9, dean 1541-2. He was ordained in 1536 and took his DD in 1547. At the time of his arrival at Queens' that college was the most advanced in the university in its theological opinions, but Ponet was a member of a group of young men who were more distinguished for their humanistic interests than for theological opinions. His friends included John Cheke, Roger Ascham and William Cecil.

Ponet made good use of his time at Cambridge. He was a man with considerable intellectual abilities, he had a mind which ranged over many interests and he had great facility in learning languages. 'It was no sluggish attention which he gave to learning languages – Latin, of course, Greek, Italian, and at last German' (Bale). He was said to be an excellent mathematician and he was greatly interested in astronomy. As bursar of Queens' he designed the complicated sundial which is still in the front court there, and he gave a copy of it to Henry VIII for Hampton Court. 'It shows not only the hour of the day, but also the day of the month, the sign of the moon, the ebbing and flowing of the sea, with divers other things as strange.' In addition to all this he made a greater study of the Scriptures and of the Church Fathers than any of his contemporaries with the exception of Cheke.

In about 1547 he became chaplain to Cranmer and he quickly acquired much influence with the archbishop. He was said to have advised him 'in the hidden secrets of divine mysteries' and there is no doubt that Cranmer came to rely on Ponet more and more.

In 1549 Ponet wrote a tract defending the marriage of the clergy (Cranmer was a married man). On 23 February 1550 he was nominated to succeed Bonner as Bishop of London, but in March he was nominated to Rochester and he was consecrated in June. Within a year he was translated to Winchester in place of the deprived Gardiner. He was compelled to surrender the enormously wealthy revenues of that see and he received in exchange a fixed income of 2,000 marks a year.

At some point he seems to have been married to a butcher's wife at Nottingham while her husband was still alive. Machyn in his *Diary* records: 'The 27th day of July (1551) was the new Bishop of Winchester divorced from the butcher's wife with shame enough,' and he was ordered to pay the butcher an annual pension as compensation. Ponet then married again, and when Mary Tudor came to the throne in 1553 he was deprived of his bishopric as a married priest. He took part in Wyatt's rebellion, and when he saw that it was a failure he fled overseas to Strasbourg.

Little is known of his life abroad. He became involved in a dispute with Dr Martyn over the marriage of clergy (1556) and he also wrote in the same year his *Short Treatise of Politike Power*. He died in Strasbourg in 1556.

Ponet has acquired a bad reputation among historians. The *Dictionary of National Biography* calls him 'clever, but somewhat unscrupulous': Miss Garrett in her *Marian Exiles* writes that 'of John Ponet the man there is little good to be said: he was quarrelsome, avaricious, unscrupulous and a coward'. Later writers tend to take a more generous view of his character and a higher view of his importance. Probably he was rather above than below the average standards of his time in character and integrity. His literary style was pungent, his mind vigorous and even aggressive, but he had a generous spirit and much magnanimity of heart. He has been called 'the highest ranking English churchman in Germany' during his exile, in daily touch with the humanists like Cheke and Morison (Zeeveld). His *Short Treatise of Politike Power* was the 'most important contribution of the exiles to the history of English thought' (Zeeveld). 'He was laying down a principle which anticipated by almost a hundred years Milton's declaration of the individual's independence from the state' (ib.); and the American John Adams calls him 'the theorist whose *Politike Power* contains all the essential principles of liberty which were afterwards dilated upon by Sidney and Locke'. Ponet's main thesis is that rulers, just as much as subjects, have the duties of Christians and of citizens to obey the laws of God, of Nature and of men. Their position is one of trust and it may be forfeited, for 'all laws do agree that men revoke their proxies and letters of attorney when it pleaseth them, much more when they see their proctors and attorneys abuse it' (C. Morris,

Political Thought in England: Tyndale to Hooker, p.152).

Further Reading

J. W. Allen, ed., *History of Political Thought in XVI Century*, 1954.

C. Morris, *Political Thought in England: Tyndale to Hooker*, 1953.

W. G. Zeeveld, *Foundations of Tudor Policy*, 1948.

W. S. Hudson, *John Ponet, Advocate of Limited Monarchy*, 1942.

POPE, ALEXANDER (1688-1744), greatest of the Augustan poets, was the son of a linen draper who retired to the country at the age of forty-two with a modest fortune and a newly-married wife, a witty, gracious woman in her mid-forties and, like her husband, a pious Roman Catholic. Alexander was the only son of this contented late marriage and she was passionately fond of him. Alas, he grew up a stunted, meagre cripple, about four foot six high, suffering from a tubercular infection which led to curvature of the spine. Ultra-sensitive, driven in on himself by self-consciousness, he found relief in intense absorbed reading and in the conversation of a few sympathetic adults. After unsatisfactory experiences at several private schools he was largely self-educated, but his creative urge was all the stronger for this, and he was writing poems by the age of twelve and planning for himself the life of a poet.

He came to London in 1704, the year of Blenheim, and was soon taken up by William Wycherley, who gave him his tired lyrics 'to mend', and by other literary men who were pleased by his fragile precocity. So he was drawn into a world of coffee houses and cultivated talk, where literature was respected and genius could flourish. 'Knowing' Walsh, a busy poetaster, declared portentously that 'there was but one way left of excelling: for though we had several good poets, we never had one great one that was correct' and he desired Pope to make that his study and aim. This correctness has the wrong meaning for us, as it may have had for Walsh. Pope was indeed to be the most 'correct' of poets, but his ideal was not the cold, inhuman compression of feeling and image into a conventional frame that much of eighteenth-century poetry may seem to be. Pope was 'correct only in that he was a laborious perfectionist, acutely, even agonizingly, sensitive in ear and eye to the form, texture and rhythm of verse. His search for the right and the best informed his life and affected his relationships and his attitudes to people and things. The suffering dwarf with his lustrous eyes and fine-drawn features, constantly in pain from the headaches and rheumatism that affected his "little crazy carcase", so thin-skinned that everything that was not a compliment seemed to be a slight, should be judged in the light of this search. His art was his life.'

When he was twenty-one his *Pastorals* appeared in Tonson's *Miscellanies*: they foreshadowed the delicacy and musicality of his mature work. Here indeed was the born poet who, however he might borrow from other writers, such as Dryden, could not but 'lisp in numbers'. In 1711 came the *Essay on Criticism*, an ambitious attempt to distil in 750 lines the essence of critical thought since Aristotle. There was little that was original, but this was no mere academic dissertation: with a felicity of phrase that has given many lines to dictionaries of quotations, Pope put warmth and even, sometimes, lyrical feeling into commonplace ideas. His own couplet expresses exactly the brilliance and the limitations of the Essay:

> True wit is Nature to advantage dress'd,
> What oft' was thought, but ne'er so well expressed.

That he was perfectly master of his craft he demonstrated with *The Rape of the Lock*, which was published in its first state in 1712. His theme was magnificently trivial: an event in Roman Catholic society, the cutting of a lock of Miss Fermor's hair by Lord Petre. The poem was added to and polished by Pope as if he knew that it was a masterpiece, but in everything but Clarissa's speech it was complete by 1714. This poem can be enjoyed at several levels: as an occasional piece, a witty diversion, a satire of society's values, a criticism of the heroic manner, even a heartfelt lament for the ephemeral. 'I am charmed', wrote Berkeley, 'with all those images, allusions, and matters inexplicable, which you raise so surprisingly, and at the same time so naturally out of a trifle'.

Pope was an amateur painter and for a time he studied under Jervas and made his home with that painter. *Windsor Forest*, which he published in 1713, is full of epithets of colour which show the painter's eye. It is a complex and closely-wrought 'place' poem which drew upon Denham's *Cooper's Hill*, the Elizabethans Drayton and Spenser, besides being soaked in the feeling and imagery of Ovid and Virgil. This is not, as might be guessed from Pope's view (recorded by Warton) that a poem wholly of description would be as 'absurd as a feast made up of sauces', a poem about nature alone: its allusions remind the reader of the work of man who was himself part of nature, and its climax, when Thames speaks of his glories and the historic pageant passes before him, expresses a glorious vision of the role of Great Britain, the bringer of peace and the gifts of civilization to all the world.

Pope's energies were long occupied with his translation of Homer's *Iliad* which appeared between 1715 and 1720. 'It's a very pretty poem, Mr Pope, but you mustn't call it Homer', said the great Grecian Bentley. Modern readers would agree but it was Pope's purpose to create a poem of his time. He discerned in Homer a 'plentiful river' in which we 'are borne away by a Tide of Verse, the most rapid, yet the most smooth

imaginable'. It is best now to treat Pope's *Iliad* as a poem in its own right, redolent of the ethos of the eighteenth century, neo-classical rather than classical in spirit. Pope was sufficiently encouraged by the reception of the poem to embark upon the *Odyssey*, with the aid of assistants. He grew rich enough to buy himself a villa at Twickenham, where he was to spend the rest of his life. But fame brought envy and his own sharp pen drew cruel reprisals from rivals and victims. At times he seems to have lived in a perfect frenzy of controversy. It would be tedious to record the details of the feud; they are best left in the gutters of Grub Street. King in his world of letters he might be, but beyond the toil and stress of composition, the exacting search for the *mot juste*, we can see the taut nerves of a creative spirit, always ready to be hurt and always ready to hit back, even to anticipate the assailant's thrust. In his appalling attack upon Sporus (Lord Hervey) he expressed characteristic venom.

> Sporus, that mere white curd of Ass's milk!
> Satire or sense, alas! can Sporus feel?
> Who breaks a butterfly upon a wheel?
> Yet let me flap this bug with gilded wings,
> This painted child of dirt, that stinks and stings.

Pope could be servile too. He secured presentation at court, he ate at the table of Robert Walpole; but he parodied the royal family and joined in the throng of Walpole's enemies. He relished obscenity and he grew deceitful to the point of addiction. He was, however, no stranger to love; his passion for Martha Blount was at least returned in steady friendship: she became his constant companion. An early essay *Against Barbarity to Animals* expressed humane feelings unusual in his time: his Great Dane, Bounce, was one of the joys of his life. Then he was often kind to people in difficulties, Savage for instance. Among his close friends was Bolingbroke, whom he appreciated for his vitality and wit. 'I never in my life', said Bolingbroke, 'knew a man that had so tender a heart for his particular friends, or a more general friendship for mankind'. Pope was brave above all, and to help a friend would do anything. His *Epistle to Lord Oxford* (1721) paid tribute to a man in disgrace and invited suspicion of Jacobite sentiments. He gave evidence for Bishop Atterbury at his trial for treasonable correspondence with the Pretender. He once wrote to Gay that it was his desire 'to fix and preserve a few lasting dependable friendships', and to Swift: 'I never aimed at any other fortune than friends.'

For all the exuberance of fancy in the *Dunciad* (1728 but subsequently recast) we may regret that so much of Pope's energy was spent in personal satire. Some of its allusions foxed contemporaries; they are lost on us. But all but the obvious victims enjoyed it and so can the modern reader, for Pope is at his sprightliest even when he is being subtle in parody and riddle. The *Dunciad* enabled him to work off some of his rage. For a time he went around with a pistol in his pocket but soon, on the prompting of Bolingbroke, he was working in calmer mood on the *Essay on Man*. It was an ambitious philosophical project, never completed. The first parts appeared in 1733-4: it summed up the popular philosophy of the day, in elegant pentameters which are often as forceful and lovely in form as they are trite in idea and sentiment. Let him who doubts it study the passage that begins: 'Know then thyself, presume not God to scan'. Throughout the poem there runs a cool vein of irony which, though Pope could sometimes still work up a white-hot blaze of contempt – as in his assault on Sporus – is typical of most of his later work, and notably the *Imitations of Horace* with which he was agreeably occupied in these years.

To the end Pope's life was strangely compounded of serenity, pleasant days with his friends and his garden at Twickenham, and frenzy. Paranoiac in suspicions, he embroiled himself in rows about the publication of his correspondence and a clash with Colley Cibber, which closed resoundingly with Pope's new version of the *Dunciad* (1743), in which Cibber was raised to the dubious status of principal dunce. His gnawing consciousness of inferiority gave him little rest: did he not falsify addresses, destroy some and rewrite others of his letters, to leave a better image of himself to posterity? He was often hurt, but he invited it in such a masochistic way that we may sympathize with Cibber's remark: 'You seem in your *Dunciad* to have been angry with the rain for wetting you, why then would you go into it?'

In attack or defence, Pope used all the literary weapons: irony, caricature, even forgery. Much may be forgiven the man who was so pre-eminently the voice of his generation's culture, this fiery, quivering, indomitable spirit, whose poems have preserved for us 'the feast of reason and the flow of soul' which above all things he epitomized and valued.

Further Reading
F. Rosslyn, *Alexander Pope: a Literary Life*, 1990.
G. Sherburn, ed., *Correspondence of Pope*, 5 vols, 1956.
B. Dobrée, *Alexander Pope*, 1951.
E. Sitwell, *Alexander Pope*, 1930.

POPHAM, SIR HOME RIGGS (1762-1820), admiral, was a fine navigator, an enterprising commander and a man of ingenious bent whose most lasting contribution to the navy was a new code of signals.

His father was British consul in Morocco; he was educated at Westminster and he went to sea at sixteen. While serving the East India Company between 1790 and 1793 he used his position as naval officer to facilitate private trade: law-suits and some discredit ensued. In 1794 he was in charge of gunboats under the Duke of York; the expedition failed, but Popham was promoted to post-captain. In 1799 he put his mastery of coastal survey and

navigation to good effect with the expedition to north Holland; in 1800 he was operating in the Red Sea. After he was charged with excessive expenditure a committee of the House of Commons was set up. His name was cleared, but he always had a reputation for being too fond of prize money. A certain recklessness also invited criticism. He was sent in charge of a small squadron to secure the Dutch colony at the Cape. The mission accomplished, he sailed across the Atlantic and in June 1806 seized Buenos Aires. His troops were soon overcome there by a Spanish force and Popham was court-martialled. His unauthorized act was rash. But he achieved by his surprise attack with 1,500 men what cost over 2,000 casualties in the following year, when the government sent an expedition to recapture the city. He was reprimanded, but he was too valuable to the government to remain unemployed. In 1809 he skilfully piloted Strachan's fleet carrying the Walcheren force up the Scheldt. In 1812 he assisted Wellington by blockading the small ports held by the French in northern Spain.

Nothing hampered the naval commander of the eighteenth century so much as the lack of an efficient signalling code. Howe first found an answer to the problem in the 1780s. But Popham did more; he devoted much time to the study of flag signals and in 1800 he produced his first *Vocabulary Signal Book*. In successive dictionaries he listed nearly 2,000 words and 1,000 sentences of common use which could be indicated by three flag hoists. The most famous signal ever sent, on 21 October 1805, used the code of Popham. Before he died he had worked out a means of obtaining 11,000 combinations of three flags. Battles would no longer be lost through inadequate signals. The commanding officer could resume tactical control of the fleet.

Further Reading
M. Lewis, *The Navy of Britain*, 1948.

PORSON, RICHARD (1759-1808), classical scholar, was born on Christmas Day at the Norfolk village of Ruston and was educated at the village schools of Bacton and Happisburgh. His father, an intelligent man, was parish clerk, but it was a curate, Mr Hewitt, who gave the boy a grounding, and a neighbouring squire, Mr Norris, who got him a place in College at Eton. Some friends of Norris (who died in 1777) provided for him to go to Trinity, Cambridge, where he won the Craven and First Chancellor's medal and became a Fellow of the college. At Cambridge Porson showed that his friends' enlightened trust was justified, for he displayed a powerful mind, prodigious memory and an acuteness of judgement that made him a formidable critic. He contributed to reviews and magazines and acquired a name for caustic truthfulness, wit and penetration. He had scruples about orthodox belief which are sometimes found amongst men who are passionately concerned with the validity of texts, and he would not follow the usual academic path of ordination. He therefore lost his Fellowship in 1792, but was provided by friends with a small annuity and was also made Professor of Greek, at £40 a year. In 1796 he married a widow, but she died within a few months. He then lived in chambers in Essex Court in the Temple. In 1806 he was made librarian of the newly founded London Institution. Two years later he died, leaving a library of valuable books and a reputation for robust eccentricity.

Porson's accomplished work was less than his reputation for learning would suggest, but everything he did was of the highest quality. Restricted somewhat in imagination, he was unequalled in judgement and his critical emendations were based on solid reading and thought. His favourite tragedian was Euripides. He hoped to be remembered as 'one who had done a good deal for the text of Euripides' and his editions of *Hecuba*, *Orestes*, *Phoenissae* and *Medea* justify his ambition. He also collated the Harleian manuscript of the *Odyssey* for the Oxford Homer. Like A. E. Housman, whose character and work recalls traits of Porson, he did not confine himself to academic studies. His *Letters to Travis* in which he belaboured an unfortunate clergyman who had criticized Gibbon, and a letter in the *Morning Chronicle*, in which he made fun of Ireland's forgeries on Shakespeare, show the delight he took in exposing what he took to be fraud. His mordant wit, and his puns, often in Greek, have a place in scholarly legend. He was often unwashed and unkempt, frequently rude and neglectful of ordinary civilities, and seldom wrote letters, even to foreign scholars who corresponded hopefully with him. He developed a famous thirst, but it may be that he drank to overcome the distress of chronic asthma and insomnia. Though he was a strong man who could walk in a day from London to Cambridge, he wasted much of his time in periods of inertia. His uncompromising honesty was perhaps his most attractive feature. 'He had no equal', wrote a fellow scholar, 'in the most pure and inflexible love of truth'. It would have pleased him to know that he would be buried near to Bentley, in the antechapel of Trinity.

Further Reading
J. E. Sandys, *History of Classical Scholarship*, 1903-8.

PORTER, ENDYMION (1587-1649), courtier, born of Gloucestershire gentry but with a Spanish grandmother, was brought up in Spain and became a page in the household of the statesman Olivares. In England as a young man he took service with Buckingham, was employed in the Spanish marriage bargaining, and accompanied Prince Charles and the favourite to Madrid in 1623. After the war with Spain he took part in the peace negotiations which led to the treaty of 1630. During the next ten years 'Dim' Porter was perhaps the most intimate confidant of the king, whose cultivated enthusiasm for art and literature he shared, and whose great collection of paintings he helped to build up. Yet, as C. H. Firth put it, 'Porter's rewards more than kept pace with his services'. Besides generous payment for his diplomatic activities and his pension as Groom of the Bedchamber he drew fees as collector of fines in the Star Chamber and surveyor of petty customs in the Port of London; got long leases of land at low rentals and shares in such monopolies as soap and white writing paper; and was a member of Sir William Courteen's Association to break into the East India trade. His wife was a Catholic, notorious for her proselytizing activities. When the Long Parliament met Porter was elected for Droitwich. He was one of the courageous minority who voted against Strafford's attainder, and the Commons later named him as one of the eleven delinquents they were not prepared to pardon. He was certainly involved in the Army Plots against parliament, and was suspected of having instigated the Irish Rebellion. During the First Civil War he was with Charles at Oxford, and in 1645 he escaped abroad, first to France and then to the Spanish Netherlands. He returned to England in 1649 and compounded for his estate, but died later that year. The client of Buckingham and the loyal and trustworthy friend and servant of Charles I, Endymion Porter, wirepuller, monopolist and patron of the arts, with his Catholic wife and Spanish sympathies, personified many of the grievances and suspicions which Puritan Englishmen harboured against their second Stuart king.

Further Reading
Gervas Huxley, *Endymion Porter*, 1959.
The article in the *Dictionary of National Biography* is by C. H. Firth.

PORTER, GEORGE RICHARDSON (1792-1852), statistician, was author of a seminal book, *The Progress of a Nation in its Social and Economic Relations to the Present Time*, of which contemporaries would speak in the same breath as Adam Smith's *Wealth of Nations*. Claiming that 'all the elements of improvement are working with incessant and increasing energy' it provided the keynote for 'The Age of Improvement'.

Porter was first a sugar broker, an unsuccessful one. In 1834 he helped found the Statistical Society of London. It was as an already well-known expert in statistical collation and analysis, in 1843, that Gladstone brought him into government. Gladstone had been disappointed with his own appointment to the Board of Trade, 'governing packages'. He soon realized, however, that it was of fundamental importance, underlying the fiscal revolution of Peel's ministry. In 1844 he gave Porter the superintendance of a new statistical department. It was a significant move towards 'scientific government'. Its central assumption was that policy should be based on the most complete possible statistical evidence. What today seems obvious was then novel. In that lies the importance of this devoted servant of facts and numbers. What then was coming to seem obvious, because of 'the visibility of progress' (Porter's phrase) – that the process was unstoppable, the possibilities boundless – would later be questioned. Meanwhile Porter was both representative of his time, and a prime contributor.

POWELL, VAVASOR (1617-70), Welsh preacher and Fifth Monarchist, was born at Knucklas in Radnorshire. His uncle, the Vicar of Clun, sent him to Jesus College, Oxford, and he later became a schoolmaster at Clun, in trouble for Puritan opinions. After Naseby, parliament attempted to evangelize Wales, a royalist stronghold, and Powell was sent as a missionary to north Wales, where he was not very successful. In 1650, under the influence of Thomas Harrison, the Rump passed an act for the propagation of the gospel in Wales. Under this nearly 300 Welsh clergy were ejected; Powell was prominent in this enterprise as one of the 'approvers' appointed to provide their successors. These were not easy to find, and the 'approvers' used itinerant evangelists instead, of whom Powell was the chief, travelling and preaching between 1650 and 1653 on a scale comparable with that of Howell Harris in the next century. But Powell, like Thomas Harrison, became a Fifth Monarchist and came out in opposition to the Protectorate. Preaching in London in December 1653 he called Oliver 'the dissemblingest perjured villain' and told his congregation to go and pray 'Lord, wilt Thou have Oliver Cromwell or Jesus Christ to reign over us?' He fled to Wales, was captured and released, and continued his preaching, issuing in 1655 an attack on Cromwell called *A Word for God against wickedness in High Places*. At the Restoration he was soon arrested, and he spent most of the last ten years of his life in prison, refusing to swear allegiance to the monarchy. He wrote in prison a moving account of the persecution of Puritans called *The Bird in the Cage, Chirping*.

Further Reading
Thomas Richards, *Religious Developments in Wales, 1654-1662*, 1923.
Thomas Richards, *History of the Puritan Movement in Wales*, 1920.

PRESTON, JOHN (1587-1628), Puritan divine, the son of a 'decayed' Northamptonshire gentleman farmer, was educated at Northampton Grammar School and King's and Queens' Colleges, Cambridge, becoming a Fellow of the latter. He contemplated a diplomatic career, but after hearing an evangelical sermon by John Cotton in 1611 devoted himself to Calvinist divinity. Able, witty, highly effective as a tutor and lecturer, he quickly became a leading Puritan. In 1615 he distinguished

himself when James I visited Cambridge by an ingenious argument for the view that dogs can reason. Some years later he gained the favour of Buckingham whose influence got him appointed in 1621 as a chaplain to Prince Charles and in 1622, aided by Preston's own flair for academic intrigue, election as Master of Emmanuel, a notably Puritan college. For some years Preston, who in 1621 had written a paper against the Spanish marriage project, was a leading figure in a scheme to win the favourite's support for an anti-Spanish foreign policy and a plan of church reform at home, involving the confiscation of the lands of deans and chapters, which would be financially profitable to the Crown. Buckingham took the idea seriously; war with Spain broke out – because of the fiasco of Charles and Buckingham's visit to Madrid – in 1624; and Preston for a time seemed on the verge of great political influence. But the death of James I and the accession of the Arminian Charles transformed the situation. Laud was predominant in ecclesiastical affairs, and Puritan reforms were condemned. Preston lost Buckingham's favour and for the short remainder of his life (he died from tuberculosis in 1628) supported the parliamentary opposition to the favourite. He was prominent in setting up the Feoffees for Impropriations (1625-6) who purchased advowsons and impropriate tithes in order to instal Puritans in livings and lectureships. Yet his true historical importance lies neither in this nor in his abortive political project, but in the long-term consequences of his preaching. As preacher at Lincoln's Inn from 1622 until his death, he had in his congregation many who were to be prominent on the parliamentary side in future. His sermons, posthumously published, were of continuing and inspiring influence in spreading the covenant theology, that central and explosive doctrine of seventeenth-century Puritanism. Few men did more than John Preston to toughen the king's opponents for the struggle.

Further Reading
Christopher Hill, *Puritanism and Revolution*, 1958, pp.239-74.
Irvonwy Morgan, *Prince Charles's Puritan Chaplain*, 1957.

PRICE, RICHARD (1723-91) was a Nonconformist minister and radical whose versatile writings earned him a controversial fame in his lifetime. At the end of his career he had the misfortune to provide a chopping block for Edmund Burke; since his views were either unfashionable or reviled he passed quickly from memory. Today we can see his importance more plainly in the light shed by new studies of the radical and Nonconformist minorities of the reign of George III.

Price was born in Wales, though, like many able Welshmen, he soon left it. The son and grandson of Calvinist ministers, he was perhaps lucky to escape from the cold comforts of his home; his father was a rigid moralist but somewhat concerned, too, about his social position. When he died in 1739, leaving his property to his elder son, Richard came penniless to London, where he met a mellower tradition of dissent in the shape of Samuel Price, his uncle, assistant to Isaac Watts at his chapel in Monk Lane. He was well taught at Hoxton Academy, one of those small dissenting schools like Daventry and Warrington which made such a large contribution to English middle-class culture; there, too, he met John Howard, whose letters about prisons he was later to revise and prepare for the press. Subsequently Price became chaplain to Mr Streatfield, a wealthy dissenter, who left him some money on his death in 1756; the next year he married and set up a happy but childless home at Newington Green. At a succession of places, notably after 1769 the Grand Pit Meeting House at Hackney, he impressed small but thoughtful congregations with his sincerity and originality. His preaching was the central activity of his life: other interests were diversions to be guarded against. In theology he occupied the middle ground of the moderate rationalists between the scepticism of the deists and the fervour of the new Methodists. In manner, men of his persuasion, mostly substantial and intelligent townspeople like Thomas Rogers, John Aiken and the American Benjamin Franklin, were distinguished by a certain savoir-faire: restraint rather than rigour, reason rather than fanaticism, above all open-mindedness, set them outside the puritan tradition. They were sober, but they were not saints – nor did they aspire to be.

Price's major contribution to philosophy was his *Review of Principal Questions in Morals* of 1758, which challenged the Lockean theory of ideas, that all thinking was the effect of notice taken by the impact of objects on the senses. Against the idea that the materials of reason and knowledge were limited to experience, which permeated so much of the thought of the time, Price set his belief in the existence of an independent faculty capable of grasping the 'universal' ideas which experience could not impart. The ability to judge between right and wrong came from this faculty. Further, Price argued that moral consciousness was a common endowment irrespective of belief or unbelief. In his theology can be seen the same desire to maintain the freedom of manoeuvre. Politically underprivileged, dissenters like Price were naturally sceptical of any establishment or any system of dogma imposed by an establishment; they valued the more the intellectual freedom which was the envy of *philosophes* across the Channel. Price was influenced, too, by an emotional reaction against the Calvinist doctrines of original sin and election. Accepting everything short of the divinity of Christ, he admitted the supernatural element and the possibility of divine intervention. His emphasis, however, was on a Christ who as reformer and teacher did not impinge upon the moral autonomy of the individual.

Price's concern with politics was not inconsistent with his moral and philosophical position. He had a natural sympathy with the claims of the American colonists and with the movement for the reform of parliament which coincided with the American war. He was patronized first by Shelburne, then by the younger Pitt, though in some measure disappointed by both: the former was devious, the latter cautious, both were imprisoned as much by the political ethos as by the system. Price first made common ground with Shelburne over the Stamp and Declaratory Acts. He was active in the petitioning and lobbying which preceded the Dissenters' Relief Act of 1779. His *Observations on the Nature of Civil Liberty* was more influential than perhaps it deserved to be: its loose definitions and simple arguments appealed to radicals of all sorts and especially to Americans, whose idealism and virtue he certainly exaggerated. A parliament directly dependent upon popular suffrage was the crux of his political programme; here he is nearer to Rousseau than to the property-conscious Locke. There is, however, a saving individualism, a common sense about Price. He touched the political yearnings of an awakening middle class but he never came near to such an abstraction as the general will. His ideas influenced reformers such as the Unitarian Jebb and the Yorkshire squire Wyvill. For political action, however, it was on Shelburne's ministry of 1782-3 that his hopes were focused: its relative failure and the apostasy of Fox disappointed him. He preserved the illusion that Pitt was a reformer for some years. His main link with the young prime ministers was, however, provided by his essays as an economist.

Price was not alone in being alarmed by the size of the national debt (£72.5 million in 1759, £231.8 million in 1783), but his concern was characteristically a moral one: his view was that of a puritan who deplores the effect upon the family of an indebted and spend-thrift father. He was also fascinated by the actuarial problems. His interest in life insurance went back to 1761 when he first worked out a formula for determining the probability of the recurrence of particular events. He had subsequently supplied the Equitable Assurance Society with calculations, based upon his study of the inhabitants of Northampton (a town that seemed suitably central in position and middling in size), in the form of the *Northampton Tables*, which, using bills of mortality, compared actual with expected deaths, and which remained in general use for half a century. Price's *Observations on Reversionary Payments* was the first published treatise on life insurance: he may well claim to be one of the founders of this service. In his idea for a sinking fund he may have been less original. Walpole had created one for redemption; the idea at least was a familiar one. His observations about the economy owed more to guesswork than to science: he thought he saw evidence for a declining population in window tax returns and seems to have been blind to accumulating evidence of a spectacular growth of wealth and investment. He was not an economist like Adam Smith, or even his Anglican counterpart Dean Tucker, but a moralist. He could claim, however, as author of *An Appeal to the Public on the Subject of the National Debt* in 1772 and subsequently as adviser to Pitt, for whom in 1785 he drew up four alternative schemes, to have influenced that statesman's much-vaunted, and later much-derided, sinking fund.

In 1787 Price became one of the directors of the new Academy at Hackney: founded to provide a liberal education for Nonconformists, it failed because of unrealistic management and poor discipline. In 1789, however, Price's attention was drawn to France and the revolution which to men like him announced the dawn of a better age. He was on the committee of the Revolution Society of London which commemorated 1688 but celebrated its centenary by enunciating principles which were more democratic than Whiggish. Price's celebrated *Sermon* in praise of the Revolution, preached on 4 November, was a rallying call to dissenters, the dispossessed and radicals of all sorts in a society which wanted 'the grand security of public liberty'. In this political testament all the strands of Price's thought were drawn together. He denounced the luxury and greed and the venal and militarist politics of a selfish and wealthy oligarchy. He stated three principles which he believed the British constitution failed to uphold: the right to liberty of conscience in religion, the right to resist power when abused and 'the right to choose our own governors, to cashier them for a misconduct, and to frame a government for ourselves'. In a fine passage he urged the case for liberal government: 'enlighten them and you will elevate them. Show them that they are men, and they will act like men.' The words are worthy of the robust old moralist who used to spend some weeks every year by the sea, a pioneer in his enjoyment of sea-bathing. In 1790 he took his holiday as usual, at Bridgend. But in the following February he caught a cold while taking a funeral; in April he died.

Further Reading
A. Lincoln, *Some Political and Social Ideas of English Dissent, 1763-1800*, 1938.
C. B. Crune, 'Richard Price and Mr Pitt; Sinking Fund of 1786', *Ec. H. R.*, 2nd series, IV, No. 2.

PRIDE, COLONEL THOMAS (*d.*1658), was a man of obscure origins, perhaps the son of a drayman or brewer, who fought well for parliament at Naseby, Bristol, Preston, Dunbar and Worcester. He was one of the officers most hostile to the Commons in 1647, and on his record he was a very appropriate choice to carry out the 'Purge' of 1648 which has immortalized his name. He signed the king's death warrant in 1649. Although he took little part in the politics of the Republic, he seems to have been the instigator of the officers' petition which finally determined Cromwell not to take the Crown in 1657. Pride was a firm exponent of Puritan social policy. He suppressed bear-baiting and wringing the necks of the cocks. It is of greater interest to the economic historian that in 1650 he was the head of the syndicate which took over the contract for victualling the navy. The syndicate had its ups and downs, but Pride did well enough to buy the Palace of Nonesuch, and in 1656 he was given a knighthood to dignify his rise.

PRIESTLEY, JOSEPH (1733-1804), nonconformist theologian, radical in politics and tireless experimenter in natural science, was the son of a Yorkshire cloth-dresser, but brought up by an aunt of Calvinist persuasion, whose home was a centre for local dissenting ministers. He suffered from poor health as a boy and though he was sent to Batley Grammar School and to the Dissenting Academy at Droitwich, he owed his precocious knowledge of languages, including Hebrew and Arabic, and his interest in science, to his own intensive studies. He early rebelled against some of the strict tenets of Calvinism, but he remained a Puritan in his outlook. Plays and novels he deplored; a useful and busy life was his ideal. He is sometimes described as a *philosophe* and his range of intellectual interests may tempt us to align him with Diderot and d'Alembert. His was indeed an original mind and he was impelled in everything by a fervent love of truth; in his political and theological writings alike he would follow where logic led him. He sought for others the liberty of thought which he needed for himself. Though his investigations in chemistry were hampered by his obstinate adherence to the old theory of phlogiston, or 'the matter of fire', he did not usually succumb to the temptation to follow in well-worn paths. Rather, he would observe and note from many sources in books and nature, until he had conceived a new synthesis.

In 1755 he became Presbyterian minister at Needham Market, but he soon found himself drawn to rational and liberal views that were inconsistent with conventional theology. He wished to study the scriptures free from the constraining influences of the creeds. Though he stood firm on evidences for God's existence and power, he denied that Christ's death was a sacrifice, and rejected in turn the Trinity and Atonement. In the end he adopted the Unitarian position after having been at different times a determinist, an Arian, a Socinian and a materialist. He should be regarded as the author of the modern Unitarianism, which he regarded as the teaching of Christ and the Apostles before the perversions of Hellenistic and oriental influences. This Unitarianism was a middle-class version of that deism which was already strong in universities; in Priestley it took a very tolerant shape. He could have been embittered by misunderstanding and abuse, for he was branded as an atheist despite the firm arguments of his *Disquisition relating to Matter and Spirit* (1777). He was a pleasant-natured man, however, and never let his own convictions make him contemptuous of others. He even advocated the toleration of Roman Catholics.

Priestley had many friends. Two notable ones were Benjamin Franklin, whom he met when he came to London on yearly visits from Cheshire, where from 1763 to 1767 he made a living by tutoring at Warrington Academy, and Shelburne, the philosophically inclined politician, whom he accompanied on a continental tour in the capacity of literary companion and served for a time as librarian. Others were Burke, Banks, Price and Wedgwood: it is a fair roll call of the genius of the time. Honours accrued at home and abroad: in 1766, Fellow of the Royal Society, later member of both the French Academy of Sciences and the St Petersburg Academy. In 1780 he became minister of a chapel at Birmingham and he was living there when the French Revolution broke out. He had revived his notoriety amongst the orthodox with the publication of his *History of Early Opinions concerning Jesus Christ* in 1786, but the 'church and king' rioters who sacked his house, with his library and laboratory, and forced him to seek asylum in the United States, were animated more by political prejudice than theological fervour: he had replied in reasoned terms to Burke's magnificent conservative effusion, *Reflections on the French Revolution*. After the riots he tried to live down his false fame, and he refused the embarrassing honour of election to the National Convention of France. He could not, however, rent a house, cartoonists pilloried him – one saw him as 'Dr Phlogiston', brandishing a political sermon and standing on a tract entitled 'Bible explained away' – and his effigy was burned alongside Paine's.

In 1794 Priestley sailed to America, whither his three sons had already migrated while his fellow Unitarian, Coleridge, denounced 'the statesmen bloodstained and priests idolatrous' who had driven him away. Priestley had sympathized with the colonists at the time of their rebellion; now he looked forward to peaceful exile in the rough hinterland of Northumberland, Pennsylvania. He grew lonely, however. His conversation did not entrance his hosts, even his preaching palled. He was involved in controversy, not only with Americans but also with his fellow émigré, Cobbett, a very different sort of radical who, amongst many wild charges, actually declared that he was in league with the Jews. President John Adams, once his friend, came to regard him with contempt: 'his influence is not an atom in the world', he wrote, when declining to execute the alien law against him. Adams's successor, Jefferson, however, championed him and he

lived out his last years in peace, writing, reading and experimenting. He had been disillusioned in his belief that America might become a pastoral utopia, a land of self-sufficient farmers unconcerned with world power or trade.

The list of Priestley's published works on theology, philology, history, political and moral science fills nearly six columns in the *Dictionary of National Biography*. Two other columns record his scientific writings. The latter suffer from the diversity of his interests: he was also preacher, teacher, philosopher, grammarian, a great talker and an accomplished player on the flute. But several of his observations in the 1770s and 1780s, those great decades in the history of science, were fruitful. He improved the technique for studying gases. He showed that green plants gave off a respirable gas. He isolated oxygen by heating certain oxides and investigated nitrogen and silicon tetrafluoride. He does not, however, stand quite in the forefront with Cavendish or Black, Scheele or Lavoisier. He would not pursue any single line for long enough for his temperament was restless; moreover he would never believe that natural science was as important as the study of God.

Further Reading
Basil Willey, *The Eighteenth-Century Background*, 1953.
A. Lincoln, *Some Political and Social Ideas of English Dissent 1763-1800*, 1938.
Anne Holt, *A Life of Joseph Priestley*, 1931.

PRIMROSE, ARCHIBALD, 5th EARL OF ROSEBERY (1847-1929), Victoria's youngest prime minister, enjoyed a gilded youth. At Eton, where he was happy, he was considered gifted but idle – 'original all day long: too original to be very popular', wrote his tutor. Oxford he left without a degree, when the Christ Church authorities told him that either he or his horse must go. 'Dear Mother,' he wrote, 'I have left Oxford. I have secured a house in Berkeley Square; and I have bought a horse to win the Derby. Your affectionate Archie.' He inherited the title from his grandfather when he was twenty, and his considerable wealth became exceptional when he married Hannah Rothschild ten years later. She brought Mentmore and its treasures with her, to add to the Rosebery estates. These included Dalmeny near Edinburgh, and the two houses of which he was most fond, the Durdans at Epsom and Barnbougle, a gaunt castle on a promontory of the Firth of Forth, which he rescued from decay and from whose windows he could gaze out alone across the sea. To land, title and wealth he added a lively intelligence and wide interests. He had youthful good looks and an effective speaking voice, deep and melodious. He developed, apparently effortlessly, a political power base in Scotland. When Gladstone accepted the invitation to stand for Midlothian, and made Dalmeny his home for the campaign there in 1879 which opened a new era in political demagogy, Rosebery was at his side, used the experience from his American travels to help with the organization, and was hailed by the Scots in his own right with deep-throated cries of 'Rozbury, Rozbury', which were to greet him at political meetings in Scotland for the next twenty-five years.

From then on many saw him as Gladstone's heir. He became Under-Secretary at the Home Office with special responsibility for Scotland in 1881, and entered the Cabinet as Lord Privy Seal in 1885. In Gladstone's brief third administration in 1886 he was Foreign Secretary; he returned to the Foreign Office in 1892, and finally succeeded the Grand Old Man as prime minister in 1894. En route, he served as the first Chairman of the London County Council in 1889, and settled a major coal strike by negotiation. Power enhanced his reputation, especially his handling of foreign affairs. Gladstone's earlier efforts to reassert Liberal pacifist ideals, after Disraeli's flamboyant imperial advances, had brought death to General Gordon and shame on his party. Rosebery, by contrast, had a more assertive policy. When the Khedive of Egypt removed the pro-British chief minister, he promptly reinforced British troops there. When the East Africa Company got into financial difficulties, he took over its responsibilities by annexing Uganda. In both cases the majority of the Cabinet was against him: but he insisted on complete independence as Foreign Secretary, and got it. His realism was closer to the policy of Lord Salisbury than to Gladstonian ideals. 'We cannot afford to be the Knight Errant of the World,' he wrote to the queen, 'careering about to redress grievances and help the weak.' He exercised tight personal control over ambassadors, enjoyed the work and was in tune with the national mood, imperialist in Africa but avoiding commitments in Europe.

Yet there were warning signs a-plenty that his would not be a smooth ride as prime minister. Gladstone's Home Rule commitment had smashed the alliance between Whigs and Liberals, and most of the Whig aristocrats were following Hartington as Liberal Unionists into partnership with the Conservatives. Nonconformist liberals and egalitarian radicals, who now formed the bulk of the Liberal Party, were not always comfortable together, and both suffered from the defection of Chamberlain and the disgrace of Dilke. Rosebery's chief rival, Sir William Harcourt, was a quarrelsome rhinoceros under whom few Cabinet ministers would agree to serve, but he was more popular in the rank and file of the party than Rosebery, who had never sat in the House of Commons. Only a man with Machiavellian political skills could have reunited the old Liberal Party: only an inspiring radical leader could have mapped out a place for the new one on the political landscape. Rosebery was neither. Indeed he was disastrously unsuited to the task. He hated politicking. 'He would not stoop: he did not

conquer', was Winston Churchill's verdict. All through his life he was moody, switching from lively charm to silent arrogance, rude even to his devoted Hannah, whose early death in 1890 left him devastated and drove him into solitude. He was often hard to find, as he flitted at whim from one of his houses to another. Sensitive to criticism, he was profoundly out of sympathy with the boorish Harcourt. An aristocrat who owned a string of race horses and could not resist flippant comments on serious issues ('laid-back' long before the epithet was coined), he was mistrusted by the dominant Nonconformists.

So his ministry only lasted for sixteen unhappy months. He started by making a damaging mistake when he told the Lords that England 'as the predominant member of the Three Kingdoms' would have to be convinced of the merits of Home Rule before it could be passed, thus enraging the Irish allies on whom his parliamentary majority rested. His attempt to initiate a reform of the House of Lords fell flat. His secret agreement with the Belgians about spheres of influence in Central Africa had to be abandoned under pressure from Harcourt, and so did negotiations with France about Egypt. The one significant and seminal achievement of his government, the budget introducing graduated death duties on all forms of property, was Harcourt's; and Rosebery did not like it. Suffering from debilitating insomnia he seized the opportunity of a snap defeat in the Commons to persuade the Cabinet to resign.

The last thirty-five years of his life were a long-drawn-out anticlimax. The Liberals were routed in the 1895 Election, and Rosebery resigned the leadership next year. When the Boer War broke out, Liberal imperialists such as Asquith and Grey looked to him to re-emerge as their leader, but though he accepted the Presidency of the new Liberal League, a catch-all to hold together the opponents of the old-fashioned pacific policies of his successor, Campbell-Bannerman, he remained as remote as ever. By the time the Liberals regained power in 1905 he had distanced himself too far to be considered for office. He had become contemptuous of Party, and his political interventions were limited to the occasional big speech preaching Efficiency. He was a recluse long before his death.

Intelligent contemporaries and the bright young men of the next generation found him fascinating, with his well-stored mind, his gift for words and his wide range of interests. The most famous of these was the Turf. Though a poor judge of a horse, he won the Derby three times, twice when he was prime minister. He relished the excitements of the races, the early morning matches on Epsom Downs, and the company of the whole racing world, jockeys, trainers and owners. But he was also no mean historian, a magpie collector and a vivid writer. 'The Past stood ever at his elbow', wrote Churchill of him. His library included first editions of the Authorized Version and the 1549 Book of Common Prayer, a copy of Shakespeare's First Folio, and the manuscripts of Dr Johnson's last prayer and Disraeli's *Vivian Grey*. He wrote a best-selling life of Pitt, and books on Lord Randolph Churchill, the early Chatham and Napoleon in exile, which are well-informed and refreshingly readable. A diary entry after he had met Newman in old age catches his style. 'The cardinal like a saint's remains over a high altar, waxy, distant, emaciated, in a mitre, rich gloves whereon the ring (which I kissed), rich slippers ... And this was the end of the young Calvinist, the Oxford don, the austere vicar of St Mary's. It seemed as if a whole cycle of human thought and life were concentrated in that august repose.' It was sad that so gifted a man as Rosebery himself should have lived the long evening of his own life cast down by his sense of failure.

Further Reading
R. Rhodes James, *Rosebery: a biography of Archibald Philip, Fifth Earl of Rosebery*, 1963.

PRIOR, MATTHEW (1664-1721), diplomatist and poet, the talented son of a joiner at Wimborne, in Dorset, went to London as a boy and was educated at Westminster and St John's College, Cambridge, by the patronage of the Earl of Dorset. In 1687 he joined Charles Montagu in writing *The Town and Country Mouse*, a successful parody of Dryden's *The Hind and the Panther*. He became a diplomatist in the reign of William III, going to Holland and France, where he was Portland's secretary, and taking part in the negotiations at Ryswick in 1697. In 1701 he was elected MP for East Grinstead. A witty companionable man, Mat Prior enjoyed the friendship of Marlborough as well as that of Montagu (now Earl of Halifax), and got a minor post as Commissioner of Trade. But a reshuffle of the government in 1706 deprived him of it, caused him financial hardship, and drove him into the ranks of the Tories, even though he was essentially a man of moderate opinions. In 1711 St John, anxious to bring the War of the Spanish Succession to an end, sent Prior to France to open peace talks. He showed himself an adroit and tough negotiator – though the Mayor of Dover upset the plans for secrecy by detaining him as a suspected French spy. Prior accompanied St John to Paris when the formal negotiations started in 1712 and played a vital role in the Utrecht settlement, although the queen did not think his birth good enough for a post of the first rank. Prior was not a Jacobite and did not involve himself in the project, which the French were pushing, to put the Old Pretender on the throne after Anne's death. Nevertheless, the Whigs imprisoned him for some time in 1715-17. After his release a subscription edition of his poems brought him a large sum, and with this and a gift of £4,000 from Lord Harley he bought an estate in Essex, where he lived until his death in 1721. As a writer Prior is most distinguished for his witty epigrams and short familiar poems, like the charming *To a Child of Quality*.

Further Reading
L. G. Wickham Legg, *Matthew Prior*, 1921.

PRYNNE, WILLIAM (1600-69), Puritan pamphleteer, born at Swainswick near Bath, the son of a gentleman-farmer, was educated at Bath Grammar School and Oriel College, Oxford, and became a member of Lincoln's Inn. Much influenced by the sermons of John Preston, he began his career as a pamphleteer in the Puritan cause in 1626. Altogether he wrote some 200 pamphlets and books, and according to Anthony à Wood, writing just after Prynne's death, there were thirty-six volumes of his works at Lincoln's Inn. Prynne was always prolix and often scurrilous; many of his earlier writings were directed against 'externals' which offended Puritans, like long hair, bowing in church, and the drinking of toasts, and the most celebrated of his writings, *Histriomastix* (1633), was an assault as abusive as it was learned, over 1,000 pages long, on the stage and everything associated with it, and on many things rather tenuously associated with it, such as organs, paintings in church and May Day festivities. Published at a time when Henrietta Maria was about to take part in a play and containing in the index the item 'women actors notorious whores', it brought Prynne into the Tower and before the Star Chamber, where he was condemned to the pillory, the cropping of both ears, life imprisonment and a fine of £5,000. Prynne retaliated with a series of pamphlets against the bishops in general and Laud in particular for which in 1637, in company with Henry Burton and John Bastwick, he was once more brought before the Star Chamber, and once more condemned to the loss of both ears (or what was left of them) in the pillory, life imprisonment and a fine of £5,000, in addition to being branded 'S.L.' (for Seditious Libeller; Prynne's version was Stigmata Laudis) on his cheeks. The savage sentences made Prynne a popular martyr; handkerchiefs were dipped in blood from his ears, and his journey to imprisonment in Caernarvon Castle (whence he was later moved to Mount Orgueil in Jersey) was a triumph.

Released in 1640, he became a prosecutor for the parliament and conducted proceedings against Laud with malicious relish. But he soon found himself in opposition again, pouring out his writings against the army, the Independents, the execution of the king, the extreme claims of the Presbyterian ministers, and Oliver Cromwell (whom he compared with Richard III). Not surprisingly, he was a victim of Pride's Purge in 1648, and in prison once more from 1650-3. In 1659-60 he was strongly in favour of the return of the monarchy, and in February 1660 he was prominent among the secluded members who re-entered the Commons. Charles II made him Keeper of the Records in the Tower. The Clarendon Code brought him out against the bishops once more, and Pepys records him as 'every day so bitter against them in his discourse in the House'.

Aubrey speaks of Prynne's 'strange Saturnine complexion' and quotes Wren's remark that he had 'the countenance of a witch', and calls him 'a learned man, of immense reading, but is much blamed for his unfaithfull quotations'. Pepys's friend Finch described him as a man of mighty labour and reading and memory, but the worst judge of matters, or laying together of what he hath read, in the world', a verdict which Pepys did not believe. Anthony à Wood, more authoritatively, noted that most scholars thought Prynne's works rather 'rhapsodical and confused than in any way polite or concise'. Maitland paid tribute to his work in calendaring the records in the last years of his life. Sheer persistence, in antiquarianism as in controversy, was Prynne's greatest quality, as the epitaph Aubrey quotes suggests:

> Here Lyes Will. Prinne
> Bencher of Lyncoln's Inne
> Who went through thick and thin
> Alwaies out and alwaies in.

Further Reading
William Lamont, *Marginal Prynne*, 1963.

PUGIN, AUGUSTUS WELBY NORTHMORE

(1812-52) designer and architect, was the son of an aristocratic émigré from the French Revolution, who had worked as a draughtsman in John Nash's office, and later became an authority on Gothic design (a renewed interest in which was beginning to come into fashion). This enthusiasm he passed on to his son, who otherwise had no formal training as an architect. The younger Pugin had total visual recall. He was able to remember everything about a building and could draw it in precise detail. A precocious youth, he had carried out many commissions before he was twenty-one, including the design of some furniture for Windsor Castle and stage sets for Covent Garden. He was a restless young man with a passion for the sea, causing his parents great concern when he was shipwrecked in the Firth of Forth. He enjoyed wearing unusual clothes, as can be seen from his statue on the Albert Memorial.

The turning point in his life came in 1834 when he was converted to Roman Catholicism. From then on he was as fervent in his religion as in his devotion to Gothic architecture. Following the recent Act of Catholic Emancipation there was a big demand for new Catholic churches, and Pugin designed many of them. He received commissions for Anglican churches too, and also for schools and houses. He built in the second pointed style, that is to say late thirteenth-century to early fourteenth-century, which he regarded as the only true religious architecture. He received considerable

fame from his book *Contrasts* (1836) which drew comparisons between contemporary buildings and the glories of a Catholic past, and from *True Principles of Pointed or Christian Architecture* (1841), where he pleaded for 'honest expression' of construction. In his opinion a building was irregular because functions demanded it: variety of functions could not be contained in a symmetrical frame. He practised what he preached, becoming increasingly innovative in his designs; for example, placing church towers in asymmetrical positions.

He was interested in interior decoration too. To avoid having to rely on suppliers who did not share his own high standards, he started, with John Hardman, a metalwork manufacturing firm, adding stained glass for windows to the business. He also designed furniture, fabrics, wallpapers, tiles, sculpture and embroidery. Often he was working with limited funds, but sometimes he had a rich patron – for example the Earl of Shrewsbury when he built St Giles, Cheadle – and then he filled his building with colour and splendour.

When he was a young man, he helped Barry with some of the designs for the rebuilding of the Houses of Parliament. Later he did more work on gothic details for the facade and designed many of the furnishings inside, including candelabra, doorplates, hatstands and inkwells, which can still be seen there.

From the list of his achievements it could be assumed that he had a long life. In fact he died at the age of forty. He had often suffered from ill-health and he finally drove himself too hard. He went mad and was put in Bedlam, though he was brought home to die in the house he had built for himself at Ramsgate, by the sea he loved so much. It was a sad end for a man who has subsequently come to be regarded as a pivotal figure in the development of the Gothic Revival.

Further Reading
Kenneth Clark, *The Gothic Revival*, 1950.

PULLEN, ROBERT

(*d.* 1146) was one of the very few English cardinals in the twelfth century, but his domestic fame rests more with the assertion that he was one of the earliest Masters at the embryonic University of Oxford. The truth is more prosaic. Born in Dorset, he studied theology in northern France before returning to England as an itinerant scholar. By 1133, he was teaching in Exeter, presumably at the cathedral school at which Baldwin of Ford (Archbishop of Canterbury 1184-90) was educated, almost certainly after Pullen's time. Between 1133 and 1138/9, Pullen taught Scriptural theology at Oxford and acquired the archdeaconry of Rochester before moving to Paris, where he taught 1139-44. Among his pupils there was John of Salisbury. In 1144, he was summoned to Rome to become papal chancellor. In this position he probably attracted a number of Englishmen to the papal curia, including, perhaps, the future pope, Nicholas Brakespeare. Although highly spoken of by Bernard of Clairvaux, Pullen remains a shadowy figure. He is said to have refused a bishopric offered by Henry I: but such claimed refusals, in all ages, tend to indicate ambition or reputation rather than actual fact. As a scholar, his theological works follow the critical methods of Abelard, although his own *Sentences of Theology* were soon overtaken by those of Peter Lombard. He evidently gained renown as a teacher, as the Parisian schools of the early 1140s were not for the second-rate, although they were, in the aftermath of the recent condemnation of Abelard, a place for the orthodox. Pullen must have had a reputation for administrative as well as intellectual skills to become papal chancellor: we know from Bernard of Clairvaux's correspondence that he had influential friends. The significance of his time in Oxford is clearer. The only previous known Master to teach in Oxford had been Theobald of Etampes, who seems to have lectured on the liberal arts from before 1100 to the early 1120s. There was no continuous school at Oxford. Pullen had no successor until late in the century, the university being a creation of the early thirteenth not early twelfth century. Many English towns boasted academic Masters: Northampton, for example, gaining an earlier reputation for its schools than Oxford. But Pullen's presence in Oxford coincided with the residence there of men such as Geoffrey of Monmouth and suggests that the town, with its many religious foundations, castle and royal palace, was beginning to be attractive to scholars and their clients.

Further Reading
J. Catto, ed., *History of the University of Oxford*, vol. i, 1984.

PULTENEY, SIR JOHN (*c.*1290-1349) may have been the richest London merchant of the fourteenth century. The son of Adam Neale of Clipston (Sussex) and grandson of Hugh Pulteney of Pulteney (Leicestershire), he was of gentry stock on both sides, yet was nevertheless apprenticed to a London draper. By 1330 he was already a substantial merchant. Characteristically he broadened his activities to include a fulling mill at Stepney, dealt in meat and grain, of which he had £258-worth in store at his death, and high finance. Like William de la Pole, he lent money to the king and several times negotiated with the Flemings on behalf of the king or city. His eminence in London was recognized by the aldermanry he held almost continuously from 1327-38 and his three mayoralties in 1331-2, when he was also escheator, 1334 and 1337. Several times he was a commissioner of oyer and terminer in the London area, he was justice of peace for Middlesex, and in 1337 he was knighted with the Black Prince by Edward III – a rare distinction for a townsman – and was granted £66

a year to support his new dignity. No doubt his aristocratic birth, upbringing and tastes were accompanied by aristocratic manners.

Traditionally trade was considered socially demeaning and those engaged in it were social inferiors of their equals in wealth in the countryside. Investment in trade was speculative and risky and required constant vigilance if losses were to be avoided. Although less profitable, land was a more secure investment and carried with it higher status than trade. Successful tradesmen in medieval England habitually bought land, often becoming substantial landowners, and their sons frequently abandoned trade for the higher social status of rural gentry. As London was the greatest English medieval city and the centre of English overseas trade, it was Londoners who generally made the largest fortunes and therefore Londoners who built up the largest rural estates of all townsmen. Sir John Pulteney was much richer than leading provincial townsmen like Adam Horder and Thomas Rent and was perhaps also the greatest citizen landlord of the fourteenth century. He had a head start on others, for he inherited substantial lands from his mother Maud Napton in Leicestershire and Northamptonshire, but in addition he was buying land as early as 1329. By his death, after he had alienated much in mortmain, he still possessed twenty-three manors in five counties and had lands in Middlesex, Kent, Cambridgeshire, Leicestershire, Warwick, Suffolk and, of course, London.

Of gentle birth and evidently aspiring to be a gentleman, he also spent his money in an aristocratic way. Much was dispensed in the religious foundations which he endowed so lavishly: the chantry of Corpus Christi in St Lawrence's church, Candlewick Street, established for a master, thirteen chaplains and four choristers; the smaller – but still substantial – chantry of three priests in St Paul's Cathedral; and the Carmelite friary at Coventry. His plutocratic lifestyle also emerges in his buildings: the church of All Hallows, Lower Thames Street, and his three houses. 'There is no finer or more complete fourteenth-century manor house than Penshurst Place' (Pevsner), Pulteney's favourite rural seat built about 1341 and later inhabited by John, Duke of Bedford (*d.*1435). Coldharbour, near Dowgate, became the city residence of the Earls of Salisbury and George, Duke of Clarence, and Pulteney Inn was to be the London house of the Black Prince and his stepson the Duke of Exeter. Pulteney's buildings, estates, and the inventory of his possessions illustrate the remarkable wealth to be accrued by the most successful Londoners, which made them the equals in income and acceptable socially to the greatest noblemen as colleagues and associates, if not yet as marriage partners.

Further Reading
S. Thrupp, *Merchant Class of Medieval London*, 1962.

PULTENEY, WILLIAM, 1st EARL OF BATH (1684-1764) possessed talents enough to make him a great parliamentarian. It has sometimes been assumed that he would also have been a statesman if it had not been for the implacable opposition of Robert Walpole; for this, however, there is little evidence.

His education at Westminster and Christ Church left him with an abiding love for the classics and a facility in the sort of oratory that was specially admired by his contemporaries. In Lecky's view he was 'probably the most graceful and brilliant speaker in the Commons in the interval between the withdrawal of St John and the appearance of Pitt'. He entered parliament an ardent Whig, upheld Walpole in debate and visited him in prison after his disgrace in 1712. After the Hanover Succession he was rewarded by Walpole's former office of Secretary at War; with Walpole and Townshend he resigned his office in the Schism of April 1717. He did not, however, return to greatness with his allies in 1721; in 1723 he was fobbed off with the small but lucrative office of Cofferer of the Household. Walpole may have hoped that his well-known 'instinct for accumulation' might prove stronger than his political ambition. But he was not so easily assuaged and he lost the office in 1725 after vehement attacks on Walpole's financial arrangements.

Pulteney had been left the borough of Hedon and a fortune by an early patron, Henry Guy, Secretary of the Treasury under William III – and he married another. He was therefore as independent as he was ambitious; not the man whom Walpole would choose for running partner in the administration – he preferred Newcastle. But it is not certain that Pulteney would have made the better minister. He had a large share of the 'spirit of faction' that characterizes the years of the Whig supremacy. Hervey had good reason to emphasize his nuisance value for he had been gratuitously offensive to this 'delicate Hermaphrodite' as he called him and they subsequently fought a bloodless duel. He was not, however, rancorous in his references to Pulteney and his opinion is revealing: 'a man of parts but not to be depended upon; one capable of serving a minister, but more capable of hurting him from desiring to serve himself'. Pulteney's talents were not limited to oratory. He had an excellent head for figures and a clear understanding of the problems of foreign and domestic policy. He proved himself, too, an adept political journalist. With Bolingbroke he inspired *The Craftsman* and from 1726 to 1736 he was one of its most effective contributors. In its pages may be seen the attitudes of the Old Whiggery which Pulteney came to represent: it was the tradition of the country party, not so very different from the new Toryism which Bolingbroke fostered after his return from exile, opposition to the court, the financiers and to the corruption which was thought to fester in the seats of power. To this

was added the notion of the Patriot: in Walpole's view, a man who has been refused a favour, but in Pulteney's, one who stands apart from the court, who opposes 'arbitrary power' (as in the case of the Excise) and stands for a robust foreign policy. It was the latter, expressed in the clamour over Jenkins's Ear and the demand for war with Spain in 1739, that provided the occasion for one of the parliamentary scenes in which Pulteney excelled and was the long-term cause of Walpole's fall. But when that happened in January 1742, Pulteney declined to form the 'broad bottom' ministry which Argyll and the Prince of Wales wanted: 'The heads of parties, like the heads of snakes, are urged on by their tails.' Morley speaks of 'the sense of shame that made him hesitate at turning courtier after having acted the patriot for so long'. If true, then enough is said of the failings of the attitude and of the man. It may, however, be merely a sign of the weariness that he referred to in a letter to George Berkeley after 'the struggle against universal corruption'. He had no wish 'to be the Whig who undermined Hanoverian Whiggism' (Langford).

He accepted a peerage in this year, along with Walpole, to be greeted by his rivals with the words: 'You and I, My Lord, are now two as insignificant men as any in England'. In 1746 he did make an abortive attempt to form a ministry with Granville; perhaps at that juncture it was well that he failed. Without the largeness of spirit of a Pitt, or the application of a Henry Pelham, it may be that he had fulfilled the role for which he was best qualified, that of leader of opposition. It was an important one in an age when oligarchic government could easily have declined into a conspiracy to defraud the nation. He challenged the unhealthier aspects of Walpole's monopoly, even if he seemed at times, in his animosity against Walpole, to be narrowing political life to the petty conditions of the duel. By the manner in which he fought the duel he quickened the sluggish pulse of parliament and earned the tribute of Shelburne: 'the greatest House of Commons orator that had ever appeared'.

Further Reading
L. Colley, *In Defiance of Oligarchy*, 1982.

PURCELL, HENRY (1659?-95), musician, was probably born at Westminster of a Shropshire family. His father became a gentleman of the Chapel Royal in 1660, and Purcell himself was a chorister there. He was appointed composer-in-ordinary to the king in 1677 and organist of Westminster Abbey in 1679. By this time he had already written a number of anthems, including possibly 'They that go down to the sea in ships'. Certainly in his early twenties Purcell was already active in the full range of his very varied compositions, writing fantasias for stringed instruments, odes and 'welcome songs', and musical dramas. In 1682 he was appointed organist of the Chapel Royal, and in 1683 his first printed composition, a group of sonatas, appeared, as well as the first of his 'Odes for St Cecilia's Day'. For the coronation of James II in 1685 he wrote the anthem 'My heart is inditing'. The years 1688-90 saw the writing and production of the opera *Dido and Aeneas*, and in 1691 came *King Arthur*. For the funeral of Queen Mary, early in 1695, he wrote 'Thou knowest, Lord'. Purcell himself died later that same year. He was still only in his middle thirties, and his output had been immense, including seventy-nine anthems and other sacred works, over fifty dramatic pieces and thirty-two odes, as well as numerous fantasias, sonatas, harpsichord pieces, and songs of various kinds. Purcell was both a gifted singer and an erudite musician much influenced by French and Italian work. In vocal and choral music he has remained unrivalled by any Englishman: the death-song of Dido – 'Dido's Lament', a splendid example of a ground bass – revealed his extraordinary mastery of song, while his use of choruses had substantial influence upon Handel. His work as a whole illustrates the curious balance which late seventeeth-century England struck between the sacred and the secular. In some ways he began a new age, for while his anthems maintained the tradition of Byrd and Gibbons, his dramatic and operatic work pointed to the future. Purcell's achievement was a peak from which there was a sudden descent, for no English composer of comparable genius was to appear for 200 years.

Further Reading
Curtis Price, *Henry Purcell and the London Stage*, 1984.
A. K. Holland, *Henry Purcell*, 1948.

PUSEY, EDWARD BOUVERIE (1800-82), priest and theologian, was one of the principal figures in the Oxford Movement. When his initials appeared under his tract on Baptism (previous tracts having been anonymous) those who sympathized with the movement's aims became known as 'Pusey-ites'. Some became converts to Roman Catholicism. He remained faithful to the Church of England and by his leadership helped ensure that Tractarian principles would have a lasting influence.

His father had assumed the name Pusey when he inherited the family estates in Berkshire. At Eton and Christ Church, Oxford, Edward's ability promised distinction but it was disappointment in love that made him give up a season's hunting to devote himself, sixteen hours a day, to the work that brought a First Class degree and, in 1823, a Fellowship at Oriel College, where Keble and Newman were already established. Both his father and hers had opposed his engagement to Maria Barter, daughter of a neighbouring squire. Two years in Germany (1825-7), where he became an accomplished Semitic scholar, followed by appointment to the university chair of Hebrew, brought a change of parental heart. His had been constant. A decade of happiness was

followed by tragedy. His wife died in 1839; an infant too had died; crippling illness incapacitated a son; only his daughter Mary would survive him. Thenceforward a kind of pious passion informed his lonely life: an extreme austerity would be his defence against the grief that threatened to unhinge a powerful mind; defence of his church and the promotion, within it, of Catholic principles, would be his chief concerns.

When Keble raised the question of church authority in his Assize sermon (1834), and Newman had entered the lists with his tracts, they found in Pusey a formidable, though independent-minded ally. He had an imposing vantage point in his professorship and canonry at Christ Church: aristocratic connections, scholarship and piety added weight. Typical contributions were his tract, *Fasting* (1834) and exhaustive study, *Baptism* (1835). His stamina was remarkable; it was required of his readers too. In 1836 he instituted the Oxford Library of the Fathers, to which his own chief contributions were editions of Augustine's *Confessions* and several works of Tertullian. In that year he was the archbishop's choice for the vacant Regius Professorship of Divinity. Instead Lord Melbourne, with provocative disregard for ecclesiastical judgement, appointed the Low Churchman, Hampden. It was the defining moment when, in R. W. Church's view, the issue of authority became inescapable and the Oxford Movement began.

After Maria's death, men would see a bowed figure, avoiding the sights that might offer solace. Had he lost his sense of proportion? There had never been much sense of humour. But there was a noble side: some looked for a leader and found a saint. Pusey's character came to matter almost as much as his message. He never lost heart. In 1843 his sermon on the Real Presence was delated to the vice-chancellor for heresy. He was denied a hearing before his 'assessors' and suspended from preaching for three years. Before his sentence was over Newman had left the church. The power of the civil courts shown by the Gorham case, and the continuing antagonism of the authorities towards the 'Puseyites' brought further conversions, led by Archdeacons Wilberforce and Manning. Undeterred, Pusey continued to work for the Catholic principles and practices which he held compatible with Anglicanism, and to condemn what he saw wrong in the Roman church, like its teaching about purgatory and indulgences. Neither his writings, for example, *The Doctrine of the Real Presence* (1855), and *Eirenicon* (1865-70), affirming the distinctive position of the Church of England in the context of the question of reunion with Rome, nor his valued practice of hearing confessions, were calculated to save him from suspicion. He fitted too well the popular notion of a Romish priest.

Pusey had been the celebrant at Newman's last service at Littlemore. For Pusey it was a parting of minds, only a temporary parting of friends, and they remained in touch. This truly humble and generous man was as loyal to his friends as to his church and university. During early years as professor he had toiled thanklessly on the cataloguing of the Arabic manuscripts in the Bodleian Library. He opposed, but could not prevent, the reforms which destroyed the intimate bond between the university and the Anglican church. More constructive was his work on the Hebdomadal Council and his remarkable pamphlet on *Collegiate and Professorial Teaching*. His generosity was limited only by his means: to communities of sisters, notably that of the remarkable Priscilla Sellon at Devonport, and to new churches like that at Leeds. Fighting for the soul of the church he had sometimes seemed weighed down. But he lived to see sympathetic appointments to the bench of bishops, notably by Gladstone; and the church strong again in principled leadership, devout lives, and pastoral zeal reaching out to the poorest in the land. He might be concerned about the kind of 'modernism' that he saw in Jowett whom, untypically, he attacked for his commentary on St Paul's epistles. But he was too scrupulous a scholar to be dismayed by the advance of science and he could look for comfort to the new generation of high churchmen: that of Canon Liddon, his disciple and biographer, who would have been a bishop if the queen had not thought that 'he would ruin and taint the young men, like Pusey'; of Edward King, much loved model of episcopal care; and of Charles Gore, first principal of Pusey House, founded after Pusey's death, as resource and inspiration to future generations.

PYM, JOHN (1583-1643), the most effective parliamentary opponent of the Stuarts, was born at Brymore near Cannington in Somerset, an estate owned by the Pyms since the thirteenth century. He was an infant when his father died and his mother married Anthony Rous of Halton St Dominic in east Cornwall; thus John Pym was brought up in a Puritan household close to Plymouth in the days of the Armada, close also to the Tavistock estates of the Russells, the richest Puritan magnates of the south-west. In 1599 he went with his stepbrother Francis Rous to Broadgates Hall (later Pembroke College), Oxford, although he took no degree there, and in 1602 he was admitted to the Middle Temple. Presumably he spent a good deal of his early manhood administering the wide estates he owned in northern Somerset; at some date between 1605 and 1613 he gained profitable – and, in view of his later political activities, useful – government employment as Receiver of Hampshire, Wiltshire and Gloucestershire.

His House of Commons career began in 1621 when he sat for Calne in James I's third parliament, making his mark as a moderate member of the opposition, yet one who was strongly anti-Spanish and anti-Catholic. He

was important enough to be placed under house arrest after the Commons Protestation of 1621. In 1624 he sat for the Russell seat of Tavistock, which he continued to represent in the five more parliaments of his life. By 1629 he had emerged as one of the leaders of the Commons, a principal figure in the impeachment of Buckingham and in the Petition of Right and a vigorous foe of the Arminian clergymen, Montague and Manwaring; an energetic committee-man and a weighty speaker, yet far more moderate and less prominent than the emotional Eliot, whose martyrdom in 1629 he did not share. In the eleven years of non-parliamentary rule (1629-40) many of the opposition, for motives part commercial and part religious, turned their attention to colonization in the New World: Pym was treasurer of the Providence Island Adventurers and also a grantee of lands in Connecticut. The significance of the Providence Company's activities was greater in domestic history than in the Caribbean. The colony, never very flourishing, was lost to Spain in 1641, but the board meetings of the company, attended by such eminent Puritans as the Earl of Warwick and Viscount Saye and Sele, seem to have been used, particularly at the time of the Ship Money crisis in 1637, to concert opposition to the king's activities.

The year 1640 brought Pym national opportunity and responsibility when Charles I was compelled by the Scottish crisis to summon parliament; for of the main figures of the Commons of the 1620s Coke and Eliot were dead, Wentworth was now the king's servant, and Pym alone remained. He took his chance and showed his power by a masterly statement of the nation's grievances in the opening debate of the Short Parliament, and thereafter his leadership was assured. The era of 'King Pym' had begun. After the dissolution of the Short Parliament (May) Pym established contact with the Scots, and when the royal failure in the Second Bishops' War was evident he was prominent in drawing up the Petition of the Peers (August) which led to the summoning of another parliament (November). In the election campaign which preceded this Long Parliament, the most celebrated in English history, Pym, in the phrase of Anthony à Wood, 'rode about the country to promote the elections of the puritanical brethren to serve in parliament', and he was prompt and decisive in action when the Commons met, turning its members' burning sense of misrule into the attack on the apostate Strafford, in Pym's words 'the greatest enemy to the liberties of his country, and the greatest promoter of tyranny, that any age had produced'. Much of his energy in the first session went into the impeachment of Strafford; and when that was clearly breaking down, he rapidly accepted the plan of attainder proposed by others and carried it mercilessly through, taking full advantage of the rumours of army plots and of the tension of the London mob to compel Charles to sign the death warrant. Meanwhile he was prominent in what came to be the lasting constitutional work of the Long Parliament, the series of laws prohibiting arbitrary taxation and destroying the prerogative courts. In these matters Pym acted in harmony with the great majority of the Commons. But the second session brought division, and Pym's course, hitherto set within a traditional interpretation of the constitution, moved into revolutionary directions. The central issues upon which the Commons divided were three. One was religious: Pym moved from acceptance of a limited episcopacy to support for the 'Root and Branch' policy, which would have destroyed the ancient system of church government. The second and third were political. Pym insisted that command of the army – not merely of the force to subdue the Irish rebels – could be entrusted only to men acceptable to parliament, and this struck at the very heart of royal sovereignty. Further, he demanded that the king should 'employ only such counsellors and ministers as should be approved by his parliament'. This challenge to royal authority and the established constitution gave Charles a party in the Commons; Pym's appeal to the people, the Grand Remonstrance, with its catalogue of royal misgovernment and its famous demand for the employment of ministers 'as the parliament may have cause to confide in, without which we cannot give His Majesty … supplies for the support of his own estate', was carried by a majority of eleven votes only. In January 1642 came Charles's essay at a coup d'état, the attempted arrest of the Five Members. Pym and the others (Hampden, Hesilrige, Holles and Strode, together with Lord Mandeville from the Upper House) took refuge in the city, returning to Westminster in triumph a week later. Charles had left his capital the day before. The lines of civil war were being drawn.

The final phase of Pym's career began in January 1642; it was the period in which the Commons' majority turned itself into an executive government, preparing for and conducting a war. Pym was the central figure in this government, responsible for the Militia Ordinance (March 1642), for the Nineteen Propositions (June) which Charles rejected, and for the establishment of the Committee of Safety (July) of fifteen members on which he served. After the fighting began in the summer, his principal contributions to the parliamentary cause were in finance and in diplomacy. The creation of the excise tax in 1643, so vital to victory, sprang originally out of a proposal by Pym. Even more important were his negotiations with the Scots, for these led in September 1643 to the signature of the Solemn League and Covenant, the treaty which opened the way to Marston Moor and the parliamentarian capture of the north. It was Pym's final achievement. He died of cancer in December 1643 and was buried in Westminster Abbey.

No Englishman of the seventeenth century left so deep a mark on the development of his country's political life and institutions as John Pym. Pym, not Cromwell, was the architect of revolution and of parliamentary supremacy. Yet he remains something of a mystery. There are patches of his career of which we know little; of his inner and personal life, unlike that of Cromwell or even of Strafford, we are almost entirely ignorant; and he has not been the subject of a major biography by a modern historian. In his last three years of intense political activity (1640-3) it is difficult to assess Pym's work separately from that of other parliamentarian leaders. What we do know of him is often unattractive. He appears as a tough, subtle, unscrupulous politician, evidently moved by rancour as well as by fear in his dealings with Strafford, ready enough to whip up the London mob as a weapon against Charles and all who supported him or seemed likely to do so. And there is no doubt truth as well as bitterness in Clarendon's comment that he 'had observed the errors and mistakes in government, and knew well how to make them appear greater than they were'. Yet the starting-point of any verdict on Pym's political career must be that he was – like Clarendon himself – essentially a moderate, in the early 1640s as in the 1620s; a moderate whose aim was to restore what he believed to be the Elizabethan constitution in church and state. More logical and a good deal more ruthless than men like Clarendon, the men whom he carried with him in his attacks on Strafford, on unparliamentary taxation and on the prerogative courts, but who recoiled from an assault on the central citadel of royal supremacy, Pym clearly came to believe in the autumn of 1641 that the king could no longer be trusted. It is unlikely that he realized the constitutional implications that followed from this: for he was firmly in the parliamentary tradition which in some measure he created, empirical and opportunist. Carried forward on the swell of a revolutionary tide, Pym was yet no Robespierre driven by dogma and vanity. He was throughout his life deeply hostile to Arminianism which, like most contemporary English gentry, he tended to equate with popery, and to its exponents like Montague and Laud, and this was certainly a powerful – perhaps the decisive – motive in his opposition to a king whose court seemed thick with Arminians and Catholics. It is usual to regard him as a Puritan, yet he did not regard himself as one; he was no sectary, and, indeed, he saw himself as a conservative in religion, restoring the sound Protestantism of Elizabethan days. As a practical politician he was outstanding, genuinely 'a great House of Commons man'; a cogent speaker, sensitive to the moods of the House and masterly in the marshalling of argument; a superb tactician in his management of business and an expert in finance; highly successful in the manipulation of public opinion, creative in the development of the committee system. Above all, there is the claim Pym put forward in his speech to the City of London shortly after the battle of Edgehill: 'We shall pursue the maintenance of our Liberties, Liberties that may not only be the Laws and Statutes, but Liberties that may be in practice, and in execution.' These 'Liberties' were the liberties and privileges of a small class of subjects, in the context of the seventeenth century; Pym and his supporters were neither democrats not egalitarians in any sense. Yet their defence – and expansion of these liberties in parliament and through the Civil War became the basis of parliamentary democracy. The challenge which 'King Pym' threw down to King Charles is the central fact of English constitutional history.

Further Reading

Anthony Fletcher, *The Outbreak of the English Civil War*, 1981.
Conrad Russell, 'The Parliamentary Career of John Pym, 1621-29' in P. Clark, A. G. R. Smith and N. Tyacke, eds, *The English Commonwealth, 1547-1640*, 1979.

J. H. Hexter, *The Reign of King Pym*, 1941.

PYTHEAS OF MARSEILLES (*fl.c.*310BC) was a Greek navigator, astronomer and explorer to whom we owe the earliest written account of the British Isles by a traveller from the civilized Mediterranean world. His work has not survived, so we are dependent for our knowledge of it upon a summary preserved by the historian Polybius, who was writing about a century and a half after Pytheas's day. Some authorities, both ancient and modern, have been sceptical about the voyage of Pytheas but others have been more charitable. It seems reasonable to suppose that it did indeed take place, that Pytheas sailed up the Atlantic coasts of Spain and France, visited Cornwall (whose tin-mines he mentioned), explored some at least of the south and east coasts of Britain and heard stories of an island somewhere to the north named Thule (possibly Shetland).

R

RADCLIFFE, JOHN (1652?-1714), physician and benefactor of Oxford, was a Yorkshireman, the son of a Wakefield attorney whose Puritan sympathies seem to have secured him the post of Governor of the local House of Correction. Educated at Wakefield Grammar School and University College, Oxford, he was elected a Fellow of Lincoln in 1669. Turning to the study of medicine, he began to practise in Oxford in 1675, and moved to London in 1684, settling first in a house next door to Kneller in Covent Garden and later in Bloomsbury Square. Radcliffe seems to have been a highly successful doctor from the start, and at the height of his career in London was said to be making £7,000 per annum. His success certainly did not rest upon profound knowledge. It came rather from a flair for diagnosis and a contempt for many of the orthodox remedies of his day. Like Sydenham he advocated fresh air, he disliked the custom of bleeding patients, and he recommended his 'bitter', a tincture which, it was claimed, 'corrects all irregularities of the Head and Stomach by hard drinking or otherwise'. Moreover, he won royal patronage quickly, becoming Physician to the Princess Anne in 1686 and to William III after the Revolution. Consciously a 'character', Radcliffe was arrogant, rude and outspoken, particularly in his cups. He lost his appointment with Anne in 1694 when he told a messenger who interrupted a drinking-party to summon him to the princess that 'her Highness's distemper was nothing but the vapours'. He sat in the Commons as a High Tory and his political sympathies were Jacobite: he had been a pupil of Obadiah Walker, the Master of University College and James II's chief agent in the attempted Romanization of Oxford, and befriended him after his downfall. On his death in 1714 he left £140,000, and Oxford was his principal legatee, gaining in particular the Radcliffe Camera as an addition to the Bodleian Library, and the Radcliffe Infirmary.

Further Reading
C. R. Hone, *The Life of Dr John Radcliffe*, 1950.

RAEBURN, SIR HENRY (1756-1823), portrait painter, called 'the Scottish Reynolds' (though Romney was a closer parallel), was born in Edinburgh, to which his father had come, as the last of a line of Border farmers, to set up in a mill in Stockbridge on the Water of Leith. Raeburn was left an orphan at the age of eight and grew up under the gentle care of his adult brother. He was apprenticed (like several of the Renaissance painters) to a goldsmith, who encouraged him in miniature painting. In 1778 he married Ann Leslie, a prosperous widow; she brought him an estate adjoining his brother's in Stockbridge, and great domestic happiness. To visit London in 1785 was, for an artist, to visit Reynolds; and Reynolds sent Raeburn on to Rome for two years. In 1787 he returned to Edinburgh, which had entered on its golden age. Of this happy period Raeburn was for thirty years the biographer in paint: in nearly 700 portraits he commemorated those who in talents or birth were then 'the most virile and unspoilt aristocracy in Europe'. 'I could see none of my old friends,' said an elderly lady returning to Edinburgh in the 1870s 'until I went into the Raeburn Gallery, and found them all there.' Of course, he sometimes desired to loose the bonds of his provincial limnership. He must have yearned to work in London, to refresh his own brushwork by painting with his peers, to have Fox, Nelson or Canning as his sitter. But he was dissuaded; and the result is a corpus of the features of a single society, completer even than the Holbein drawings of the court of Henry VIII. Raeburn was elected RA in 1815, and knighted by George IV, when the king made his famous visit to Edinburgh in 1822. He died in the following year, from a cold caught while visiting St Andrew's in the company of Walter Scott.

There was nothing bohemian about this artist. He golfed, fished and played the archer with his friends. He took his young son Henry on Highland expeditions to gather material for his landscape backgrounds. Not content with painting, he acted as architect; and the names Raeburn Place and Ann Street recall where he laid out a part of Edinburgh's new town on the family's Stockbridge properties.

Had he been a scientist too, he might have become a parent of the photographic camera; for as artist he was preoccupied (like Wright of Derby) with the effect of light falling on the human figure. Form in a Raeburn portrait is expressed in terms of chiaroscuro, by broad areas of light and shade spread out with crisp, decisive brushstrokes. As he worked without assistants, he painted the whole picture himself, and he painted with assurance and speed (his method of work is splendidly described by Stevenson in *Virginibus Puerisque*). But facility is frequently dangerous. In Raeburn's case it too often barred him from exploring the depths and complications of character. And in any case the sun of his own disposition cancelled all that was dark or weak or vicious in others. It seems he 'never saw an ugly face'; and he crowns his sitters with virtues to which many of them can have aspired only in their happiest moments. Qualities of nobility, benevolence and grace are dealt out pretty justly here and there, but sit uneasily – almost vulgarly – on the more homespun of his clients. Raeburn was too kind to be candid. But there they stand or sit, in novel attitudes, in romantic surroundings, looking down their noses, a race of demi-semi-gods. What masterpiece has *Lt. Col. Lyon* been caught sketching? Is there any secret of the world or the law that *Adam Rolland* is not privy to? Can benign *Dr Adam*, Rector of the High School, really have died of apoplexy? (We know he did.) Here *Dr Spens* draws an arrow which cannot miss its mark; here *The Revd Robert Walker* is one with the north wind, as he skates on Duddingston Loch. On this side *The MacNab*, in full panoply, has hurried to the studio straight from a gathering of his clan; on that, the lovely *Mrs Scott Moncrieff* confounds the assertion that Raeburn could not paint a young woman. There breathe the Judges, rosy and affable – but in truth, as soon as you start to look, you forget how to cavil.

Further Reading
Theodore Brotchie, *Henry Raeburn*, 1924.

RAFFLES, SIR THOMAS STAMFORD (1781-1826), administrator, orientalist, naturalist and patron of science, is best known as the founder of Singapore. He was also an enlightened governor of Java during the British occupation of that island, 1811-16. A versatile, far-sighted man, Raffles was perhaps, as G. M. Trevelyan has suggested, 'the first European who successfully brought modern humanitarian and scientific methods to bear on the improvement of the natives and their lot'.

The son of a sea captain, born off Port Morant in Jamaica, he became a secretary at the age of fourteen in the East India House. In 1805 he went to be assistant secretary to the new establishment at Penang. At this time Napoleon hoped to take over the Dutch colonies in Asia; the British were resolved to prevent his doing so. In 1806 the Dutch fleet was destroyed by a British squadron in Batavia harbour; in 1808 the Moluccas were occupied. Raffles meanwhile had mastered the Malay language and delved into their history. When in 1810 he went to Calcutta to offer his services to Lord Minto, the Governor-General, he had already made his mark as an expert in that little-known region. In a letter to his wife Minto described him as 'this very clever, able, active and judicious man, perfectly versed in the Malay language and manners'. Minto commissioned him to prepare the way for a military expedition to Java, where the Dutch governor had declared for France. Besides the most thorough preparations for invasion, including extensive propaganda for the benefit of the Rajahs of Java, Raffles was busy collecting specimens, insects, moths, fungi, shells, and manuscripts and poems about the Malays. 'Mr Raffles,' said his clerk, 'took great interest in looking into the origin of nations, and their manners and customs of olden times.' In June 1811 he left his headquarters at Malacca, with Lord Minto; in August the troops landed, under the command of Sir Samuel Auchmuty: in a month 3,500 troops had destroyed a Franco-Dutch army of 10,000. Java had capitulated. Lord Minto decided to hold the island, though his instructions were only to render it militarily useless, and he appointed Raffles governor.

He dealt with native resistance by a successful attack on the Sultan of Djogjakarta. His power once secured, he made good use of it. A convinced free-trader, he ended the Dutch system of monopoly and introduced free trade – with small duties to raise sufficient revenue. He looked forward to the growth of trade between Java and Britain. He worked out a new system of land rents: essentially this meant the end of the Dutch system of forced labour and compulsory cultivation of certain crops such as coffee. Rents were to be fair and some initiative was left to the peasant. Raffles showed in all his projects a respect for freedom and for the individuality of the six-and-a-half million people under his government. His approach was sensitive and scholarly, his interests varied, but he was no dilettante; on the contrary, he was as practical as he was energetic. He revived the old Batavian Society of Arts and Sciences and made it a centre of research. From India came the director of the archaeological survey to study the remains of Hindu temples. The temple of Borobodur emerged from its cocoon of black lava. Dr Horsfield, the future keeper of the company's museum, one of the foremost botanists in the world, worked with him. As a young clerk in London Raffles had been inspired by the anti-slavery movement; he kept an interest in this cause until his death. In Java the main social problem was not slavery but the apathy of people long used to feudal conditions. Raffles sought to give more power to the people. The village elders were allowed scope to make judicial decisions while circuit judges, as in India, dealt with major cases.

Raffles's governorship was to prove but an interregnum since the island was handed back to the Dutch, with most of their other possessions, in 1815. Some indication of his feelings can be gathered from what he later told a deputation from the Asiatic Society. 'There was Java, an island of rice; and Borneo, an island of gold; and Banca, an island of tin; and the Celebes, islands of spice' – enough, as he said, 'to supply the rest of the world for all ages, all recklessly abandoned to the Dutch by a government that knew neither *why* nor *what* they were giving'. Raffles at least had the satisfaction of knowing that the Dutch accepted his institutions and methods. In 1810 he had written of the Dutch policy in Java that it was 'a more cold-blooded, illiberal and ungenerous policy than has ever been exhibited towards any country, unless we except the conduct of the European nations towards the slave-coasts of Africa'. 'A modern colonial administration,' wrote a Dutch historian, 'was forced on us from outside.' On his way back in 1816 he interviewed Napoleon on St Helena. When he arrived in England he married his second wife and devoted himself to the monumental *History of Java*. In two volumes he described the history, society and literature of Java, with engravings and line drawings. The book was deservedly well reviewed; Raffles was honoured bv a levée at Carlton House and a twenty-minute speech by the prince regent. He was knighted and made a Fellow of the Royal Society.

His scientific pursuits did not satisfy Raffles's ambition. He had experienced the pleasures of administration and he had a vision of liberal imperialism which the indifference of governments could not impair. He was appointed governor of Bencoolen in Sumatra which had remained British. Before he left he wrote a state paper to Canning arguing that a new base should be found as 'an entrepôt for our merchandise', Bencoolen and Penang being too far away from the Malayan archipelago. But Canning was not then foreign minister and Castlereagh was preoccupied with Europe: he did not wish to offend the Dutch. The directors of the East India Company regarded Bencoolen with disfavour since it was of little value as a trading station. Raffles and his wife found themselves in a 'den of ravenous dogs and polecats'. Raffles set about making this unpromising place a centre of British trade and influence. He freed the slaves and set up a school for the children of slave parents. There were protests from traders and other injured interests. This energetic, idealistic governor was becoming a nuisance.

It was Raffles's habit to go to the man in power. In 1818 he secured from Lord Hastings, Minto's successor in India, instructions to secure 'the establishment of a station beyond Malacca such as may command the southern aspect of these straits'. Hastings soon revised his orders: Raffles was to desist from the attempt to found a settlement – but when this postscript arrived, Raffles had already planted the British flag upon the ancient Malayan city of Singapura and was planning its development. 'With this single station alone I would undertake to counteract all the plans of Mynheer.' So Lord Hastings and the governors of the company were presented with a *fait accompli*. The company's council denounced him – but some individual directors acclaimed his vision and Hastings stood by him. Raffles spent three more years at Bencoolen cultivating pepper and collecting specimens. In October 1822 he returned to Singapore and spent six months working intensively on the planning of the city: harbour, roads, administrative quarter, Chinese quarter. The port was to be free of duty, open to all. There was to be a Malay college where Malays could advance in their own language and others could study it.

It is almost incredible that so much was done in six months; it was the hectic work of a sick and distressed man. Three of his five children had died of fever in Sumatra. He endured violent headaches. Fortune was persistently cruel: on his way to England he lost all his possessions by fire on board ship – his notes for a history of Sumatra, thousands of drawings and a menagerie of wild animals. He was treated ungratefully by the company. After he settled near London, the India House demanded £22,000 from him on account of excess salary paid many years before. He was appreciated, however, by the leaders of the anti-slavery movement. He had shown that it was feasible to abolish slavery. In the Abbey his monument by Chantrey stands alongside those of Wilberforce and Buxton. There is also a bust of Raffles in the Lion House at the London zoo. This commemorates the founder and first president of the Zoological Society 'for the introduction of living animals, having the same relation to zoology as a science that the Horticultural Society does to botany'.

Raffles died at Hendon less than two years after his return to England. In post-colonial Singapore his name and memory live. In Java, too, he is 'the great Raffles'. He taught Malays, Chinese and Javanese to think of the Englishman as just, liberal and sympathetic. He ranged in mind and action beyond the conventions of his time and the limits of the system he served.

Further Reading
Emily Hahn, *Raffles of Singapore*, 1948.
R. Coupland, *Raffles: 1781-1826*, 1926.

RAGNAR LOTHBROK (*d*.852-6?) was a Viking freebooter who was active in the second quarter of the ninth century. Most historians of the Viking age would agree that Ragnar existed and that he lived about this period; but his origins and doings remain almost impenetrably obscure. It is not that we lack information about him. On the contrary, there survives a superabundance of materials relating to his career. The trouble is that nearly all the sources are late and legendary. The few that are early are laconic and resist easy interpretation. Plausibility is all that may be claimed for what follows.

Ragnar was a leading member of the Danish-Norse warrior aristocracy. His zone of influence may have centred upon Zeeland and other islands of the Kattegat, the water which separates Denmark from southern Sweden. His power depended therefore on the possession of ships and command of the sea. The young warriors who manned his ships and fought for him expected adventure and profit: these rewards were the condition of their loyalty. (One is reminded of Anglo-Saxon warbands of an earlier age, such as that led by Guthlac before his conversion.) That meant piracy. The Vikings were parasitical upon the rich lands beyond the North Sea, to which their ships gave them access. Ragnar can be traced in the Orkneys and Hebrides. It is possible that he is to be identified with the Viking leader named *Reginherus* in contemporary Frankish sources who led a fleet up the Seine to plunder Paris in 845. It is reasonably certain that he was active in Ireland in 851-2 where he seems to have been fighting against the Norwegians who had founded Dublin in 841. Ragnar met his end shortly afterwards, possibly while campaigning in Anglesey or north Wales.

Ragnar's by-name Lothbrok means 'shaggy breeches' and refers to his clothing of leather boiled in pitch which had the magic property of making him invulnerable. According to legend he met his death at the hands of King Aelle of Northumbria, who discovered the secret of his magic clothes, stripped him of them and flung him into a snake-pit where he was killed. The story is a fiction, probably invented at a later date to provide a retrospective justification – revenge for their father's murder for the invasion of Northumbria by Ragnar's sons in 866. However, it is not impossible that Ragnar campaigned in Northumbria at some stage of his career.

The first accurately datable Scandinavian attack on England occurred in 793 when the monastery of Lindisfarne was sacked, though it is likely that sporadic raids of which we know nothing had been taking place for half a century or so before that. There exists no simple explanation of the Viking movement overseas. The diffusion of the use of iron in Scandinavia gradually made possible more intense agricultural exploitation. This in turn permitted demographic growth which would in time press upon the limited resources of the Scandinavian environment. Technical advances in shipbuilding, which would produce such masterpieces of strength and elegance as the Gokstad ship (*c.*880), opened the seaways of the North Sea and the Atlantic to Viking enterprise. The influx of silver bullion from the Islamic Middle East, well-attested archaeologically and attracted by trade in slaves, furs and timber with the distant lands of the caliphate in Iran, may have had far-reaching consequences for Scandinavian society. It provided capital

for shipbuilding, weaponry and trading ventures. It drove a wedge between those who were its beneficiaries and the rest. An élite of wealth and status emerged, competitive and acquisitive, whose members attracted retinues of unruly young warriors on the make; and these men in their turn, as we have seen, had to be rewarded. The emergence of stronger kings in Denmark and Norway, for reasons not unconnected with this new wealth, could make life at home difficult for these turbulent nobilities. It is to some such cluster of factors as these that we should attribute the beginnings of Viking activity in western Europe.

There is, finally, the consideration that the English, Frankish and Irish kingdoms were rich and vulnerable, attractive to predators. Who would settle in Orkney or Iceland when Lincolnshire, Leinster or Normandy lay open? Who plunder the humble churches of the Hebrides when Jarrow or Kells or Noirmoutier were there for the picking? The appearance in western waters from the 830s onwards of large Viking fleets, carrying well-equipped armies several thousand strong under the leadership of high-ranking aristocrats, bent on systematic plunder, was the response to these opportunities. Ragnar was one of these men. In the next generation they would go a step further and carve out territorial principalities for themselves.

Further Reading
A. P. Smyth, *Scandinavian Kings in the British Isles 850-880*, 1977.

RAINSBOROUGH or RAINBOROW, THOMAS

(*d.*1648), parliamentarian soldier, the son of a naval Commander, was brought up as a sailor. The family had connections with Puritan New England and his two sisters married Winthrops from Massachusetts. After a short spell at sea in 1643 as vice-admiral, Rainsborough was commissioned as a Colonel and spent the remainder of the Civil Wars serving parliament on land. He raised a regiment under the Earl of Manchester, officered it mainly with returned emigrants from New England, and won a reputation by capturing Crowland Abbey. Appointed to command a regiment in the New Model, he fought at Naseby, Bridgwater and Bristol in 1645 and captured Woodstock in 1646. A tall man of powerful build and impulsive daring, skilled in siege operations, he was noted for the stern discipline he imposed on his own men and the ferocity he displayed towards the enemy; after taking Prior's Hill Fort at Bristol, he 'immediately put to the sword almost all in it', as Cromwell said in his report to the Commons.

But Rainsborough's interest for the historian lies not so much in his exploits in battle as in his part in the Putney Debates of 1647. The leading Republican among the officers and the one field officer with views sympathetic to those of the Levellers, he opposed reconciliation with

RALEGH, SIR WALTER / 1021

the king and demanded a new constitution based apparently upon a suffrage without property qualification. He had a flair for the cogent statement of his beliefs. The claim for political equality has rarely been put more straightly than in his statements, 'For really I think that the poorest he that is in England hath a life to live, as the greatest he; and therefore, truly, Sir, I think it's clear that every man that is to live under a government ought first by his own consent to put himself under that government'; and 'I do not find anything in the law of God that a lord shall choose twenty burgesses and a gentleman but two, or a poor man shall choose none'. Rainsborough was a hot-tempered man, and at one point in the debates stormed at Cromwell, shouting 'one of us must not live' and threatening to impeach him. After a reconciliation with Cromwell, Rainsborough was ordered to take up command at sea, but the fleet mutinied, refused to have him on board, and declared for the king (1648). So he fought on land again in the Second Civil War, taking part in the capture of Colchester, where he was responsible for the execution of Sir Charles Lucas and Sir George Lisle. He was killed in the same year at the siege of Pontefract, murdered by two royalists who found him unarmed in his room. His funeral at the Independent Chapel in Wapping provided a great demonstration for the Leveller movement. 'Rainsborough, the just, the valiant, and the true', as his epitaph called him, long remained a hero to the younger radicals.

Further Reading
Hugh Ross Williamson, *Four Stuart Portraits*, 1949.

RALEGH, SIR WALTER (this spelling pronounced *Rawley*, was the one he mostly used after his father's death in 1581; although the whole family used more than seventy variations, he himself is not known ever to have used the usual modern form of **RALEIGH**) (1554?-1616), poet, historian, explorer, sailor, soldier, courtier, was the second child of Walter Ralegh by his third wife, and he was thus half-brother to Sir Humphrey Gilbert, his mother's son by her first husband. He fought as a volunteer in the Huguenot armies at the battles of Jarnac and Monconteur in 1569, and went to Oriel College, Oxford in 1572. In 1578 he joined with Humphrey Gilbert on an unsuccessful expedition bound for the Azores and West Indies against Spain. In 1580-1 he saw military service in Ireland, after which he returned to England to the court at Greenwich. The story that he spread his cloak 'in a plashy place', 'whereon the queen trod gently over, rewarding him after with many suits for his so free and seasonable tender of so fair a foot cloth' does not occur before the mid-seventeenth century. He remained at court for many years as a favourite frequently and richly rewarded. In 1584 he was knighted.

In 1583-9 he sent out at his own expense of £40,000 six expeditions to plant a colony overseas in America, and later he sent out others, the last in 1603, but all were failures, the only tangible result being that the potato and tobacco were introduced into England and Ireland.

In 1588 he took no active part in the fighting against the Armada. In 1591 he published anonymously an account of Grenville's last fight in the *Revenge*, which later became the basis for Tennyson's poem. In 1592 he was imprisoned for misbehaviour with one of the queen's maids of honour, Elizabeth Throgmorton, but he was soon released. They were married and lived at Sherborne. In 1594 he sent an expedition to reconnoitre the river Orinoco, and in 1595 himself went in search of the fabulously wealthy city of Manoa in South America, known as El Dorado. The expedition was a failure. On his return he played a leading part in Essex's expedition against Cadiz. 1597 saw him back at court and reconciled with the queen. He then took part in Essex's abortive expedition against Spain, but his conduct led to a violent quarrel which was never healed.

When James I came to the English throne his mind had already been poisoned against Ralegh, who soon found himself in the Tower on a charge of being implicated in Watson's plot 'to surprise the king's person'. Ralegh was tried for high treason, convicted, condemned to be executed, reprieved and shut up in the Tower from 1603 to 1616. During his imprisonment he wrote his *History of the World*, beginning at the Creation, but he only got as far as 130BC. In 1616 he was released in order to go on an expedition to find El Dorado, on the condition that, if he failed, he would return. He set sail from Plymouth on 12 June 1617. The expedition was a disastrous failure, and a fight took place with the Spanish just at the time when James I was trying to negotiate a Spanish marriage for his son, Charles, Prince of Wales. True to his promise, Ralegh returned to England, and James had him executed, largely at the demand of the Spanish ambassador (29 October 1618).

Ralegh was an intellectual genius, witty, brilliant, graceful, a poet and a great writer. He had a fearlessly independent mind, a bitter tongue and a scornful use of repartee. He was rapacious, restlessly energetic, ambitious for power and fame, an unscrupulous schemer in pursuit of success. Yet he was also extravagantly generous, adored by his wife, beloved by his servants. He never attained to political power, because the queen never trusted his judgement, however much she enjoyed his company. He was accused of being an atheist, whereas in fact he only refused to accept without criticism orthodox opinions, and his *History of the World* proves him to have been deeply religious. His ideas were ahead of his times – he held that colonies (he would have called them plantations) would absorb surplus population, reduce unemployment at home and stimulate trade. When he laid his head on the block on the scaffold, somebody asked him if he would not rather lie with his head to the east of Our Lord's arising. Ralegh's answer was, 'So the heart be right, it is no matter which way the head lieth.'

Further Reading

S. Coote, *A Play of Passion: the Life of Sir Walter Ralegh*, 1993.
N. L. Williams, *Sir Walter Raleigh*, 1988.
A. M. C. Latham, *Sir Walter Raleigh*, 1964.
A. L. Rowse, *Ralegh and the Throckmortons*, 1962.
D. B. Quinn, *Raleigh and the British Empire*, 1947.
E. Thompson, *Sir Walter Raleigh*, 1935.
V. Harlow, *Introduction to The Discovery of Guiana*, 1928.

RALPH OF BETHLEHEM (*d.*1174; Bishop of Bethlehem 1156-74), an Englishman, was chancellor of the Latin kingdom of Jerusalem for the last thirty years of his life. The Queen Regnant Melisende, his patroness, had tried unsuccessfully to appoint him Archbishop of Tyre, the second see in the kingdom, in 1146. It was said by his successor as chancellor that Ralph owed his promotion to Bethlehem in 1156 to being a fellow countryman to the then pope, Hadrian IV. A learned but worldly man, Ralph played a significant role in the affairs of the kingdom as administrator, diplomat, even military commander: he was wounded on campaign in Egypt in 1165. Under Bishop Ralph the remarkable Byzantine mosaics were installed in the Church of the Nativity in Bethlehem, which survive to this day: Greek designs, commissioned by an English bishop for a Latin church in Palestine, symbols of the cosmopolitan world which allowed Ralph to find employment 2,000 miles from his homeland. Ralph was a Levantine counterpart to Thomas Brown, the English minister of Roger II of Sicily. It is likely that Ralph came from a noble family who, frustrated by career prospects in Europe, sought his fortune in the less congested ecclesiastical world of Outremer where western also-rans could come in winners. Ralph was not the only successful Englishman in the east. Another was William, Prior of the chapter of the Holy Sepulchre who became the first Latin Archbishop of Tyre in 1128. The horizons of twelfth-century Europe were widening, offering, as Ralph's career showed, new and attractive opportunities for the educated, well-connected and pushy.

Further Reading

B. Hamilton, *The Latin Church in the Crusader States: The Secular Church*, 1980.

RALPH OF COGGESHALL (*d.*after 1224) was abbot of the Cistercian abbey of Coggeshall in Essex from 1207 until ill-health forced him to resign in 1218. He gave his name to a *Chronicon Anglicanum*, covering the years 1066-1223, the last section of which, 1187-1223, he wrote himself. Although head of an obscure provincial house, through extensive personal contacts with the nobility and the international Cistercian network, Ralph

was well informed. His information about the Third and Fourth Crusades, for instance, came from returning crusaders and monks. Much of his chronicle is based on oral evidence, which lends it a diffuse character. Not a witness of political standing or academic distinction, Ralph displays the orthodox prejudices of a conventional monk content to follow the harsh judgemental view of a sinful world familiar to his predecessors. The great, Richard I or Hubert Walter, are punished for their vanities or sins; the Jews deserved death in the massacres of 1190. His portraits of Richard I and John may represent a barometer of contemporary opinion, moulded by the hindsight of events. Richard is a flawed hero, his chivalric reputation sullied by greed and anger. Ralph's dislike of John grew as his reign progressed, until by 1216, he is shown as a bad-tempered liar, cheat, glutton and coward. Henry III's minority, however, is regarded more positively, perhaps because of the reconciliation between royalists and most of the baronial opposition between 1217 and 1219. Ralph's description of the ravages of the civil war of 1215-17 explains his enthusiasm at the return of peace. He, like many others, transferred their loyalties from the baronial faction to the royalists, a conversion tinged with overt nationalism. Just as Ralph was suspicious of John's foreign officials, such as Peter des Roches, so he scorns the French Prince Louis as one 'who had come to destroy the English people'. Such xenophobia, initially useful in rallying support behind Henry III, was to grow to deafening, irrational proportions in the hands of later writers, such as Matthew Paris, and some discontented politicians in the late 1250s. Ralph's nationalism suggests that the future of an Anglo-French Angevin empire would have been precarious regardless of the outcome of John's battles with Philip II of France, a fact largely lost on the cosmopolitan courtiers of Henry III.

Further Reading

A. Gransden, *Historical Writing in England c.550-c.1307*, 1974.

RAMSAY, ALLAN (1713-84), portrait-painter, was born in Edinburgh, where his father's poetry was almost the first fruit of that grand literary harvest of the eighteenth century. Young Allan studied art in London (attending Hogarth's St Martin's Lane Academy for some of his time) and in Italy; and from 1738, though he had and used a studio in Edinburgh, he worked chiefly in London. The foreign timbre of his work, the lack of which kept Hogarth unfashionable, and the patronage of Dr Mead (who had cared for the consumptive Watteau in 1719) helped him to early popularity. By 1751 the critic Vertue thought his pictures 'much superior in merit than any other portrait painter's'. In the same year Ramsay, who had lost by death his first wife and their three children, eloped with Margaret Lindsay, later to be the subject of *The Painter's Wife*, the flower of his work. He took her to Rome from 1754 to 1757, and it must have been her example which formed in his head that marvellous vision of womankind which he realized during the following years, and which prompted Horace Walpole to say that Ramsay was 'formed' to paint women. He had painted George III as Prince of Wales and had reached an intimacy with him which was continued on the prince's accession: Ramsay was created Painter-in-Ordinary, and had to employ a throng of assistants to meet the overwhelming orders for royal portrait-copies to be sent, as imperial symbols and as marks of favour, to the furthest parts of the world. At about the same time his star became eclipsed by those of Reynolds and Gainsborough; and when an accident to his arm (*c*.1733) made painting difficult, he moved gracefully from the world of artists to the world of philosophers and littérateurs. Now he travelled for health and diversion, and his struggle to return from Italy (to die at Dover) in 1784 is reminiscent of Scott's last return to Abbotsford.

Ramsay was a man of great charm, an accomplished scholar, who spoke several languages, exerted himself as an essayist, and was welcome to men of learning everywhere. He knew Rousseau and Voltaire; corresponded with Diderot; was specially appreciated – 'loved' – by Dr Johnson; entered the group which surrounded Mrs Montagu; and in Edinburgh formed the Select Society, members of which were Hume, Adam Smith, James Adam the architect, William Robertson the historian, Lords Kames and Monboddo, and Boswell.

His portraiture is uneven in quality. It is also undramatic. He was a 'still-life' artist: his subject-figures, though full of potential vitality, do not 'move'; they are caught in moments of repose, not in action, but they are caught with loving care. Ramsay later made a habit – which was uncommon at the time – of doing chalk-studies before setting to work in paint. Thus his painting is peculiarly disciplined and delicate. He made some memorable male portraits: *Dr Mead* (for the Foundling Hospital), *David Hume, Rousseau*. But in his portraits of women – where from billowed costumes of lace and coruscating satin there looks out all that is most lovely, most frail, and most tender – he touches the heights.

RAMSAY, JAMES, 1st MARQUIS OF DALHOUSIE

(1812-60) was a strong Governor-General of India, but a might-have-been statesman at home. His ability was recognized early. Son of a soldier who became Governor-General of Canada, he went from Harrow to Christ Church, where he was a contemporary of Canning and Elgin, who were in turn to follow him in India. He married Lady Susan Hay, became MP for Haddington in 1837, succeeded to his father's title next year, was chosen to assist Gladstone as Vice-President of the Board of Trade in 1843, and took over from him as President in 1845. There he showed formidable mastery of the details of the railway schemes which were proliferating all over the country, and which it was his task to license, often working until two or three in the morning. He would have liked government control over these, 'directly but not vexatiously exercised', but the tide of laissez faire was against him. As a Tory, he turned down Russell's offer of a place in the Whig Cabinet which replaced Peel's, but agreed to succeed Hardinge as Governor-General of India in 1848. At thirty-six, he was the youngest ever to be appointed.

Though his doctor remarked with awe that no loose papers could ever be seen on his desk, Dalhousie was no mere administrator. Small and slight in build, he nevertheless had an air of natural command, and could be irascible when crossed. 'The Lord Sahib is a pepper pot', said Sir John Grant. He wanted 'a proper maintenance of the authority of a mighty office'. He often despised the Directors of the East India Company: 'they write in a tone which no Secretary of State would address to the Lieutenant Governor of the bulls and bisons of the Falkland Islands.' The military had to be subordinate. 'There can't be two masters here and there shan't be,' he wrote to Gough, and Napier resigned as Commander-in-Chief when Dalhousie banned him from altering the pay structure of the native troops without his approval. With the elder Pitt he might have said: 'Being responsible, I will direct.' And direct he did. Frontier wars against the Sikhs and in Burma were followed by annexation, against the advice of many on the spot but in the interests of good government. To the same end he also absorbed seven native states which had been set up within the borders of British India. He used the doctrine of 'lapse', by which sovereignty lapsed to the paramount power in default of a male heir to the ruler; and he refused to recognize the last-minute adoptions by which infertile Hindu rulers circumvented this. Oudh he annexed without any such excuse, after many warnings had failed to persuade its king to govern by standards acceptable to Victorian Britain.

Throughout the lands for which he was responsible, Dalhousie set out to raise these standards. His aims were lofty, his energy and drive at a level which eventually destroyed his health. Much was started: village schools and a college of engineering, prison reforms, irrigation and the Ganges Canal, the freeing of trade, a modern post. Nearest to his heart were properly thought-out plans for a railway system, based on the political and commercial needs of the country, to be built by private firms backed by government financial guarantees. These plans were adopted after the Mutiny. More was intended. One of his lucid despatches outlined an educational scheme for the whole of British India, and he urged, unsuccessfully, an increase in the proportion of European troops in the army.

He was asked to stay on, and did so for two years beyond his allotted span, although India had killed his wife and crippled him, as it did Lord and Lady Canning and Lord Elgin after them. He returned to England, in 1856, to die, aged only forty-eight, four years later. Acclaimed when he got back, he had before his death to face the blame for the Indian Mutiny. He was certainly responsible for disaffection amongst native princes, especially in Oudh, where the Mutiny was centred; but he should also be credited with the loyalty of other parts of India, particularly of the Punjab, where the Board he set up after its annexation had been governing as he hoped. Lord Curzon regarded him as the ablest of his predecessors: it was the admiration of one great pro-consul for another.

RAMSDEN, JESSE (1732-1800), optician and inventor, was renowned throughout Europe for the quality of his instruments. He was remarkably versatile. He set up as an engraver in 1762; later he took out patents for important improvements in astronomical and surveying equipment. In 1774 he brought out his Equatorial, by means of which a telescope can be made to follow, by clockwork, the apparent motion of any point in the heavens towards which it is directed. The most modern telescopes still embody this mechanism in some form. He also produced an engine for the mathematical gradation of a circle. The traditional surveyor's instrument for measuring angles, the theodolite, that had been used since the sixteenth century, was transformed by him. His 'great instrument', which proved itself capable, in the primary triangulation of England, of measuring angles at a distance of seventy miles to two seconds of arc, is the prototype of the modern theodolite. He was devoted to his craft and would never raise his prices, so that from all his inventions he made but a modest fortune.

RANULF FLAMBARD (c.1060-1128; Bishop of Durham 1099-1128) was one of the most powerful and controversial figures of the reign of William II. His actions and personality excited resentment, admiration and anecdote. His character and reputation are suggested by his nickname, 'Flambard': flamboyant, fiery, glittering, scorching, prompting William of Malmesbury's pun, 'a torch of iniquity'; definitely dangerous to know if he were against you, but a generous benefactor to family and friends. His work for William Rufus earned him the obloquy of ecclesiastical commentators but his monks at Durham remembered him with affection. The remarkable attention lavished on him by contemporary writers suggests that Ranulf was not easy to ignore. Ranulf is one of the few people of his generation (barring saints) for whose personality there is plentiful and plausible evidence. From the excavation of his tomb, it is possible to know what he chose for his episcopal staff and ring and even what he looked like. Five foot nine tall, he had a short, broad head, a strong jaw and sloping forehead: witnesses thought him good-looking.

The son of Thurstin, an obscure parish priest in the diocese of Bayeux, Ranulf was probably introduced to the royal court by Odo of Bayeux. By 1086, as well as a royal chaplain, he had become Keeper of the King's Seal, working under Maurice the Chancellor. Already Ranulf had amassed lands, houses and churches across southern England worth about £30. For Ranulf, royal employment was always a means to profit. It is characteristic that when Maurice, now Bishop of London, reputedly denied him a deanery, Ranulf looked elsewhere for patronage. Precisely what tasks he performed for William I is unclear, but it is likely he was involved in producing and executing royal writs, and hence in legal business and finance. By 1087 he may have had experience in what became one of his specialities, the administration of vacant churches on behalf of the Crown.

After 1087 Ranulf rose rapidly in the household of the new king. The two men were of a similar age; neither, in the words of R. W. Southern, 'can be called respectable'; they shared a certain exuberant enjoyment of life. Although Ranulf was always a servant, and their relationship never reached the intimacy of that between Henry II and Becket, they got on well. In his unceasing search for money and the exploitation of royal rights, Rufus had, in Ranulf, an agent as predatory as himself.

Within the royal household, although never holding any office other than royal chaplain, Ranulf soon emerged as a key administrator. Regularly witnessing royal writs, in 1093 his name appeared immediately after the bishops and chancellor; in 1096, his name headed the witnesses to a writ ordering tenants of Worcester to pay a relief to the king. It may be no coincidence that these years saw an increased use of the writ for communicating royal orders to the localities, there being a substantial fine of £10 imposed for non-compliance. Throughout William II's reign, Ranulf witnessed more writs than anybody else (thirty-five), but he acted as part of a team of officials, including the grand curial bishops William of St Calais of Durham and Walkelin of Winchester, and the household servants: the chancellors William Giffard and Robert Bloet; the stewards Eudo and Haimo; and Urse d'Abitot. Ranulf's dominance was, perhaps, exaggerated by later chroniclers searching for a scapegoat for Rufus's harsh ecclesiastical exactions, but Ranulf did emerge in the 1090s as the king's leading man of business. In part, this was because he was unafraid to appear in public on his master's behalf, as in 1093 when he appeared at Canterbury to serve a writ on Anselm on the very day of the archbishop's enthronement. Ranulf was also able to roam across a wide area of royal administration, unhampered by any formal designated duties, when, in 1097-9, he acted as one of the regents left in England during the king's absences.

Contemporaries were in no doubt about his power, calling him 'justiciar' and *totius regni procurator*, titles later applied to Henry I's chief minister, Roger of Salisbury. The two areas beyond the royal household in which Ranulf was most active were finance and the law, both liable to provoke hostility and publicity in equal measure. Although Orderic Vitalis portrayed Ranulf as measuring England with a rope in his eagerness to reassess royal dues, most evidence comes from the exploitation of existing feudal incidents, such as reliefs, and the exploitation of the church. As bishops and abbots technically were tenants-in-chief of the king, during vacancies the Crown had the right to administer the church's lands. That this was profitable, and that William to some extent manipulated his rights by delaying appointments, was widely recognized, even if exaggerated, especially when compared to the similarly lucrative secular custodies which, affecting lay lordships, failed to incite the chroniclers' corporate wrath. Ranulf was appointed administrator of Ely Abbey possibly by William I. During Rufus's reign he was involved in the custody of Ramsey; New Minster, Winchester; Christ Church, Canterbury; and the bishopric of Worcester in 1095. Between 1096 and 1099, Ranulf made £300 p.a. as custodian of the see of Durham. Other abbeys which fell under Ranulf's frankly commercial control included Thorney, where he ordered a reassessment of services (presumably upwards), and Hyde Abbey which he sold to a close associate, Herbert Losinga, in 1090. It is small wonder that Ranulf was seen by monkish chroniclers as a rapacious asset-stripper.

Called by some the king's *placitator* or advocate, Ranulf was equally heavily engaged in the endless litigation involving land rights and jurisdiction. Whatever else, the Norman Conquest and subsequent land settlement had left uncertainty and, as Domesday revealed, a host of disputes, many involving the Crown. Part of Ranulf's job was to travel the realm in pursuit of royal claims. This line of business took Ranulf to Canterbury in 1093 and Bury St Edmunds in 1095; in 1096, he toured Devon and Cornwall asserting royal rights to lands in a manner which looked back to the circuits of Odo of Bayeux under the Conqueror and forward to the itinerant justices of Henry I and Henry II. Ranulf's handling of suits demonstrated that medieval royal justice usually meant deciding cases in favour of the Crown, its friends and its allies. Justice was neither neutral nor blind. As with ecclesiastical and secular custodies, the currency of civil law was property; so were the profits, to king, to Ranulf and to his associates. Ranulf, as the king's representative, could intimidate or favour litigants.

It is hardly surprising that such a vigorous royal servant should be feared. However, he was resented because he was a parvenu who lined his own pockets. Whether or not in 1094 he took a cut of the money he received from the fyrd of Hastings in lieu of military service, he certainly exploited his custodies and amassed a fortune in lands, revenues and ecclesiastical preferment. Archbishop Anselm called Ranulf a prince of publicans, implying that he exploited royal taxes for his own advantage. By the late 1090s, Ranulf enjoyed a string of lucrative benefices across southern England, as well as canonries at Salisbury, London and Lincoln. These last perhaps indicate a network of old government hands with whom Ranulf had worked, including the three former royal chancellors, Bishops Osmund of Salisbury, Maurice of London and Bloet of Lincoln. Ranulf also took care of his family, including his own sons, his brothers and nephews for whom he worked hard, and with some success, to place throughout the Anglo-Norman church. However, the gravy train of government service had a precise destination. Hitherto wholly dependent on royal favour, in 1099 Ranulf bought himself independent power and position with £1,000 for the bishopric of Durham. The arriviste had arrived.

Just as suddenly, Ranulf's career as royal minister was ended with the death of his master on 2 August 1100. Within a fortnight, Ranulf was arrested, deprived of his bishopric and sent to the Tower of London, earning himself the distinction of being the first political prisoner to be incarcerated there. His fall was primarily symbolic. In tune with his coronation Charter of Liberties, Henry I was trying to distinguish his régime from that of his predecessor in order to garner the widest support for his coup. Ranulf, more than any of Henry's subsequent favourites, a man 'raised from the dust', was expendable, whereas, for example, his former boss, Maurice of London, or Rufus's last chancellor, William Giffard, were not, and were received into Henry's favour. Ranulf's reaction to adversity showed his mettle. In February 1101 he escaped from the Tower (later romancers said by rope) and placed his services at the disposal of Robert Curthose in Normandy in attempting to unseat Henry from the English throne. Ranulf may have acted as one of Curthose's leading advisers for the invasion of England in 1101 which led to the inconclusive Treaty of Alton, but was probably unimpressed by the quality of his new master. Once peace had been agreed, there was a reconciliation with Henry which restored Ranulf's bishopric and his English lands. An unspoken condition seems to have been that Ranulf stayed in Normandy as a double-agent for Henry in the methodical campaign to annexe the duchy. He visited his see only occasionally, as in 1104 for the translation of relics of SS Cuthbert and Bede, despite his apparent doubts as to their authenticity. Meanwhile, he exercised his energies in administering the diocese of Lisieux, which he attempted to convert into a family sinecure, first for his brother, then his son.

After 1106, and the successful conquest of Normandy by Henry I, Ranulf returned to Durham for good. No longer the king's protégé, materially in reduced circumstances, Ranulf set about organizing the monastic priory at Durham which his predecessor, William of St Calais, had founded. Inevitably, as in most medieval cathedrals, there were disputes between bishop and chapter over money, in this instance over the income from priory lands to be used to pay for the building of the great new cathedral church. The row emphasized the straitened circumstances of the northern diocese. The idea of the wordly former civil servant cloistered with his monks inevitably gave rise to ribald stories. On one occasion it was alleged the bishop provided a lavish meal of food normally forbidden the monks served by waitresses in tight fitting clothes; Ranulf sat back watching the brothers' surreptitious glances at the women and chiding them for their hypocrisy. In fact Ranulf was generous to his monks and relations were normally good. Ranulf's business acumen brought stability to Durham's finances; he attracted scholars to his household, including the future Archbishop of Canterbury, William of Corbeil. He was a friend and benefactor of the influential and respected local hermit, Godric of Finchale. In Durham and the surrounding area, Ranulf was remembered with affection. There is a flattering portrait of him in a later twelfth-century *Life* of St Godric by one Durham monk; another recalled: 'that was our golden age, under Ranulf our bishop'.

That Ranulf was heartily disliked by many cannot be denied. Yet hatred and condemnation were often tinged with respect, as in the story of his escape from kidnap and attempted murder by Thames pirates when Keeper of the King's Seal or in the account of his daring escape from the Tower. He lived life to the full. Handsome, intelligent, witty, he was an attractive figure, fond of clothes, food, drink and sex. His attempted seduction and failed rape of his wife's niece Theodora in 1114 has become notorious because his intended victim later became the well-known hermit, Christina of Markyate. Yet after he had become a bishop he provided for his wife Aelfgifu by respectably marrying her off to a prosperous man in Huntingdon. He neglected neither her nor his children. In the eleventh century, for able children of humble parents like Ranulf, the only hope of advancement lay either in the church or in especial skill at martial butchery. Inevitably religious vocations could be affected or strained. Yet in all the calumny heaped on Ranulf, nobody accused him of hypocrisy, for which he was perhaps too honest, too aware of human weaknesses, both excellent credentials for his role as royal extortioner. Ranulf's sins were venal and venial. To compensate for social insecurity he sought to establish a dynasty. He understood that to be great a man had to be generous, as his household and monks as well as his family discovered. He fascinated even those whom he terrorized. The monk Simeon of Durham, who knew him, summed up his quality: 'impatient of leisure, he went on from labour to labour, thinking nothing done unless new enterprises pressed on the heels of those already accomplished'. To this restless energy was allied acute intelligence and organizing genius. His career had a wider significance than that of Rufus's henchman. Again in the words of Southern, 'the great line of administrators who fashioned and finally destroyed the medieval system of government in England begins with Flambard'.

Further Reading
F. Barlow, *William Rufus*, 1983.
R. W. Southern, *Medieval Humanism and other Studies*, 1970.

RANULF II, EARL OF CHESTER (before 1100-53), nicknamed *aux Gernons* (i.e. moustaches), played a prominent and vacillating part in the civil war of Stephen's reign, his actions, in common with most of his peers, springing from personal grievance rather than dynastic loyalty or principle. Ranulf's father, Ranulf I, had been granted the earldom of Chester in 1121 after his maternal uncle had drowned in the White Ship disaster (1120) but, in return, had been compelled to surrender Cumberland and his patrimony of Carlisle. The restoration of these lost estates was the mainspring of much of Ranulf II's political life. Inheriting the Chester earldom in 1129, he initially supported Stephen as king after 1135. However, successive treaties between Stephen and King David of Scotland in 1136 and 1139 gave the Scots large tracts of lands in Cumberland coveted by Ranulf who reacted by seizing the town and royal castle at Lincoln in 1140. Stephen retaliated early the following year by driving Ranulf from the town and besieging the castle. Ranulf now allied with the Empress Matilda in defeating the king at Lincoln in February 1141. Ranulf's association with the Angevin party was cemented by his marriage in 1141 to the daughter of Robert of Gloucester. However, his territorial ambitions were no closer realization, as the King of Scots was also a close ally of Matilda. In 1145, Ranulf was reconciled to Stephen. However, there was no love lost between Ranulf and the king's entourage, many of whom had suffered at his hands. In August 1146, at Northampton, Ranulf was suddenly arrested and put in chains when he refused the king's demand to restore all lands he had taken. He was only released when he surrendered all former royal property, including Lincoln. Stephen's arrest of Ranulf was a public relations disaster. He had broken his oath of reconciliation of 1145 and his own promise of protection, thus detering any more defections from the Angevin faction. Stephen had breached a central tenet of effective medieval rule, that of being a good – i.e. fair – lord. In 1149, Ranulf joined Henry FitzEmpress and was reconciled with David of Scotland who, in return for the lavish grant to Ranulf of most of Lancashire, retained Carlisle. But Ranulf was never a party man. His priorities remained centred on his own territorial and dynastic advantage, as shown by his *conventio* with a leading royalist, Baron Robert of Leicester (1149/53). Under this treaty, the two magnates, independently of their rival liege-lords Stephen and Henry FitzEmpress, agreed to limit any hostilities forced between them by their masters and to protect their respective tenurial positions. Ranulf's career, notorious for his arrest in 1146, is more significant as evidence that the drama of high politics was played against a dense background of baronial competition for rights, lands and inheritances which took precedence over any claims of royalty.

Further Reading
R. H. C. Davis, *King Stephen*, 1967.

RANULF III, EARL OF CHESTER (*c*.1170-1232) was one of the old school of Anglo-Norman barons whose loyalty to the Angevin dynasty was consistent but contingent on the receipt of lucrative favours. Bishop Stubbs described him as 'almost the last relic of the great feudal aristocracy of the Conquest' and, however his career is viewed, he was – and thought himself – very grand. Small in physical stature, he was a giant in terms of family relationships and estates, the twin pillars of his ambition and political career. Succeeding to the earldom as a minor in 1181 and attaining majority and control of his estates in England and Normandy in 1187, in 1189 he married Constance of Brittany, widow of Henry II's son Geoffrey (*d*.1186) and mother of Arthur of Brittany, with whom King John contested the Angevin succession 1199-1202. Although bringing Ranulf control of the honour of Richmond in England as well as the duchy of Brittany, the marriage was not a success, being finally dissolved in 1199. The following year Ranulf cemented his power in Normandy by marrying Clemencia of Fougères. Relations with John were initially tentative. Ranulf had opposed John's attempted coup of 1193-4; he retained many contacts with partisans of his former stepson, Arthur; and his second wife's family joined Philip II. Spending most of 1199-1204 in France, Ranulf's continued loyalty was bought by John with further patronage. But the king was suspicious of Ranulf (as, indeed, he was of most people), perhaps with reason. In the winter of 1204-5, Ranulf, suspected of dealings with the rebellious Welsh and of contemplating revolt himself, had extensive estates temporarily confiscated by the king. The episode demonstrated the limits of independent action even by the most powerful English magnate, which may have persuaded Ranulf that loyalty was good business. Thereafter, Ranulf basked in an uninterrupted

flow of royal favours. In return, he fought John's Welsh wars 1209-12; helped secure the peace with the pope in 1213-14; and was with the king in Poitou in 1214. Loyal to John in 1215-16, one of the few barons to witness Magna Carta of 1215 *ex parte regis*, Ranulf played a leading military role in the civil war by virtue of his extensive estates and numerous castles. On John's death, Ranulf's influence increased further. Although he stood aside to allow William Marshal to assume the regency for the young Henry III, he put his political weight behind the reissuing of Magna Carta (1216 and 1217); his military experience in defeating the rebels at Lincoln (1217); and his diplomatic skill in negotiating the treaty with Louis of France (1217) and peace with the Welsh (1217/18). His rewards from the government he partly ran were immense, including the earldom of Lincoln, a clutch of sheriffdoms and estates in the north, East Midlands and East Anglia. In 1218, his decision to honour the crusade vow he had taken in 1215 may point to a genuine piety beyond that of the customary ecclesiastical patronage expected of the great. It may also reflect a degree of thwarted ambition: relations with the regent were not always easy. In the east, Ranulf played a leading role in the Fifth Crusade's siege and occupation of Damietta (1218-19). On the Crusade's failure, he returned to England in 1220, to find William Marshal dead and the government in the hands of Hubert de Burgh. Ranulf was not alone in finding the shoals of faction difficult to navigate in 1220-4 as tensions grew between government officials and old John loyalists. These flared into open conflict in the winter of 1223-4 when Ranulf, among others, briefly tried to resist de Burgh's policy of resumption of sheriffdoms and royal castles. Ranulf's final years saw him acting as an elder statesman, witnessing the 1225 reissue of Magna Carta; playing a prominent role in the dispute in 1227 over Forest Laws; and, as a veteran, leading Henry III's army on the ill-fated Poitou expedition of 1230-1. He never lost sight of his private advantage. In 1220, some of his estates avoided the carucage; the 1225 Aid was not levied in Cheshire; and in 1229, he successfully resisted the ecclesiastical tax collector. It may have been a sign of age and declining influence that he failed to stop the levy of the 1232 fortieth on his lands. The whole of Ranulf's career had been determined by the maintenance and acquisition of rights and property. It must therefore have been galling that he had no heir, on his death his estates being divided between his four sisters. Ranulf's political career reinforces the folly of historical periodization. Knighted by Henry II, with estates on both sides of the Channel, Ranulf cut a European figure after 1204, on crusade 1218-20 and on two campaigns in Poitou, 1214 and 1230-1. A witness to all first four issues of Magna Carta, he had little thought of running his estates according to new constraints of political or legal behaviour. Historians seek the origins of change: in Ranulf III of Chester they have a good example of the tenacity of tradition.

Further Reading
J. W. Alexander, *Ranulf of Chester*, 1983.

RAWDON-HASTINGS, FRANCIS, 1st MARQUIS HASTINGS (1754-1826), Governor-General of India,

was the eldest son of John Rawdon, first Earl of Moira. He was educated at Harrow. It is said that when he went back there, a renowned statesman, he 'tipped' every boy in the school. After a time at University College, Oxford, he went into the army and served with credit in the American War. In 1778 he was made adjutant-general to the forces in America. In April 1781, in a small fight at Hobkirk's Hill, he defeated the American General Greene. He gained in America a reputation for strategy remarkable in one so young, and his experience in irregular warfare was to be useful to him later in India. He was a martinet and his severity aroused comment: he even set a price on the heads of rebels. What a soldier he might have become can be gauged from his victory at Hobkirk's Hill, described by Cornwallis as 'by far the most splendid of this war'. He received a peerage in 1783. At first he was a supporter of Pitt, but friendship with the Prince of Wales drew him into the Whig camp. He championed the prince over the regency question but he was only intermittently involved in politics. In 1790, in conformity with his uncle's will, he took the name of Hastings. In 1793 he succeeded to his father's Irish earldom. In 1794 he successfully led a supporting force through Belgium to join the Duke of York. The ultimate failure of the duke's campaign obscured the tactical skill of that operation, carried out in the teeth of a large French army.

He was a strong supporter of the Catholic cause in Ireland and one of the main opponents of the Act of Union. His military career advanced by way of home appointments which gave him practice in administration. In 1803 he became commander-in-chief in Scotland. In 1806 he was made Master of the Ordnance and sat in the Cabinet of 'the talents'. He was active on behalf of the Prince of Wales in investigating the conduct of the princess. He took a leading part in the negotiations of 1810-12: first over the revived question of the Prince of Wales's regency; later, in the abortive attempts to found a coalition in which at one stage he tried, with Wellesley, to form a ministry. In outlook he resembled Wellesley. Of all the Governors-General who succeeded the 'little lord' he came nearest to him in style and achievement.

He went to India in 1813. His predecessor, Lord Minto, had pursued a policy of appeasement in accordance with the wishes of the Directors. But territorial advance could not be halted so easily: intervention which, in theory, as a good Whig, Hastings deplored, became inevitable

when neighbouring states were misruled. In this land, where 'gold is won by steel' (Walter Scott), annexation was sometimes a safer way than alliance with corrupt or unstable states. The frontiers of British rule were strategically unsound. For 700 miles along the valley of the Ganges the frontier was open to northern hill tribes who would not learn peace except by conquest. India's political decay had left many petty sovereignties: régimes of conquest, sustained by plunder, innocent of administration. The amirs of Sind who controlled the lower waters of the Indus tolled river traffic and plagued their subjects. Maratha chiefs in the country north-east of Bombay backed or acquiesced in the Pindaris, robber bands who terrorized central India. Treaties with such men were of little use: rulers succeeded rulers with bewildering frequency. Only the great Ranjit Singh of the Punjab maintained a steady power. He was a staunch ally of the British – but it was to satisfy him that Lord Auckland later devised his unhappy scheme of invading Afghanistan. There were obvious benefits in direct rule.

Hastings's time was spent in the consolidation of British rule. In November 1814 he set about the Ghurkas of Nepal, difficult neighbours and great warriors. The British commanders fumbled at first; there were reverses. The patient tactics of General Ochterlony brought success in the end. Simla was left in British possession, the hill town that generations of British officers were to know so well; henceforward it was part of army training to go up to the hills in the Indian summer. The Ghurkas, moreover, were to prove valuable allies and soldiers. In 1817 Hastings decided to attack the homelands of the Pindaris. He had to keep the Marathas quiet while the Pindaris were dealt with. Gwalior was bound by a treaty, Baroda dared not move, three other Maratha chiefs rose and were defeated; meanwhile the robbers were encircled, killed or dispersed. His two armies performed nobly despite floods in the Deccan and an outbreak of cholera. The peace established in 1820 made the British government the sovereign power south of Sind and the Sutlej, and brought nineteen small Rajput states under British protection.

In matters of government Hastings's approach was sometimes that of a soldier rather than an official charged with the well-being of the inhabitants. When Metcalfe was trying to reform the government of Hyderabad where he was Resident, Hastings censured him for actions which would 'estrange and irritate the better classes'. In this case, where an experienced administrator was battling against a corruption which 'tainted the whole atmosphere', Hastings seemed content to advise: leave well alone. Nor can he be allowed much credit for the foundation of Singapore by Raffles in 1819 for, though Raffles obtained his consent to establish a base, only his speed in doing so prevented Hastings, who had had second thoughts about it, from cancelling his instructions. In 1821 he resigned on a trivial issue. He had made the mistake of allowing a native bank in which he had an interest to lend money to the state of Hyderabad. The Directors accused him of corruption; he was cleared, but his action in making the loan was censured. Like so many of the upper classes of his generation he was casual about money matters; he was also generous. He spent large sums on establishing schools and missions; he also lived in splendid style. He once lent his country home to some French émigrés: in his guests' rooms he left signed, blank cheques which they could fill up at pleasure. It is not surprising that when he left India he was a poor man and that he was content to accept for his old age the governorship of Malta, where he spent the years 1824-6. He died at sea in the latter year. He left directions in his papers that his right hand should be cut off and preserved until the death of the marchioness, then to be placed in her coffin.

Consistency was not his prime virtue. He had once denounced the British government of India in unbridled terms: 'It was founded on injustice and had originally been established by force.' He had now proved himself a strong and imaginative administrator. A tall, athletic man with a stately and impressive manner, Hastings could have been a great soldier, possibly a prime minister. In India he was able to use his talents to the full.

Further Reading
Major Ross, *The Marquis of Hastings*, 1893.
Marchioness of Bute, ed., *Private Journal of the Marquis of Hastings*, 2 vols, 1858.

RAY, JOHN (1627-1705), naturalist, the son of a blacksmith at Black Notley in Essex, went to school in Braintree and thence to Cambridge. A Fellow of Trinity, lecturing in Greek and Mathematics like his contemporary and friend Isaac Barrow, he turned to the scientific study of plants during an illness. In 1658-62 he travelled over much of Britain from southern Scotland to Land's End collecting specimens and recording information, and his earliest published work (1660) was a record of the plants in Cambridgeshire, in effect the first 'county flora'. Under the Act of Uniformity of 1662, Ray, a dissenter, resigned his fellowship, yet he was fortunate in having friends willing to help him financially, and in 1663-6 a long continental tour, ending at the University of Montpellier, enabled him to accumulate what was for that time a unique knowledge of the flora and fauna of western Europe as well as a great store of material. Elected a Fellow of the Royal Society in 1667, Ray – assisted by his well-to-do friend Francis Willughby until the latter's death in 1672 – gave the remainder of his days to a systematic survey of plant and animal life and to the publication of a remarkable series of classificatory and historical volumes. A modest, unambitious, profoundly religious man who had been much influenced

by the Cambridge Platonists, Ray lived at Black Notley from 1680, working with unremitting diligence and corresponding with savants and scientists throughout Europe. Perhaps the most notable of his many books were his three great folios on the *History of Plants* (the first of them appearing in 1686) and his *Synopsis of British Plants* (1690), the first scientific English flora; yet his publications also included works on animals, reptiles, and insects, as well as the books on birds and fishes which appeared under Willughby's name although they were, in fact, written by Ray. His classificatory work, based on accurate observation and identification and a complete rejection of the mythological material which had hitherto befogged botany and zoology, laid the foundations upon which Linnaeus built in the next century; although his classification was essentially artificial, based sometimes on single characters, it does in many instances result in fairly natural groupings. His experimental work was limited, yet Ray was far more than a superb cataloguer who turned natural history from a hobby into a science. He welcomed new ideas like those of Grew on sexuality in plants or of Redi on 'spontaneous generation', and in his philosophical writing, *The Wisdom of God* (1691), he discussed the adaptation of organisms to their environment and thus pointed to one of the central issues of later biological work. The greatest of the earlier English naturalists, Ray was a worthy contemporary of Isaac Newton.

Further Reading
C. E. Raven, *John Ray, Naturalist*, 1950.

REDWALD (*d*.627?) was King of East Anglia and according to Bede the fourth English ruler to exercise overlordship over all the Anglo-Saxon kingdoms south of the Humber. In 616 he defeated and killed Ethelfrith of Northumbria and thereby assisted Edwin, whom he had harboured as an exile, to gain power there. Redwald was converted to Christianity, apparently at the court of Ethelbert of Kent, but on his return to East Anglia had been led away from the faith 'by his wife and by certain evil teachers'. Bede tells us that in his temple he set up a Christian altar alongside a pagan one. For him, Christianity meant the acceptance of an additional god, not the abandonment of his ancestral heathen ones, a not uncommon phenomenon in barbarian 'conversions' of the early Middle Ages.

It is likely, though not certain, that it was Redwald who was interred in the magnificent ship-burial at Sutton Hoo discovered in 1939. There he was deposited in the ship which was to convey him to the next world (with money to pay the steersman and the rowers), with all the equipment he would need: helmet, armour and shield; weapons and jewellery; silver spoons and plate; bronze cauldrons, drinking horns, wooden buckets and cups; a harp and a lamp; and more mysterious objects whose significance is not clear, such as a large whetstone in mint condition, decorated at each end with carved and painted human faces, one end surmounted by a bronze statuette of a stag. These treasures are of a splendour unparalleled in the early medieval archaeology of Europe. Like the remains of Edwin's great hall at Yeavering they convey something of the magnificence of seventh-century kingship. Most interesting is their revelation of the cosmopolitan world in which Redwald lived. His helmet and shield were Swedish; possibly his ancestors too. The great silver dish came from Constantinople; a bronze bowl from Alexandria; the coins from Gaul; the hanging bowl perhaps from Ireland. How these objects were acquired can only be a matter for conjecture. Most of them were too luxurious to have been the fruit of mundane commerce. Heirlooms? Plunder? Tribute? Presents acquired in the course of diplomacy? We cannot say. But it is not irrelevant to bear in mind that Redwald's East Anglia, like the Kent of Ethelbert, was rich in part at least because of trade. Recent excavations at Ipswich, only seven miles from Sutton Hoo, have revealed a thriving emporium with trading connections across the North Sea with the Rhineland and a native pottery industry whose products – the consumer goods of the seventh century – were widely distributed in eastern England.

Further Reading
The Sutton Hoo finds are superbly displayed in the British Museum, whose booklet, *The Sutton Hoo Ship-Burial*, is the best introduction to them.

REGENBALD (*fl.*1050-67; *d.* after 1086) was the head of Edward the Confessor's writing office, in effect, and possibly in name, his chancellor. He seems to have continued in this office under William I until replaced in 1067, in which year the new king confirmed all his previous holdings and added some estates formerly held by Harold II. Regenbald still held extensive benefices and property in 1086 when he was described in Domesday Book as *canceler*. A clerk, who under Edward the Confessor enjoyed the status although not the office of a bishop, his retention of land suggests he may have done the new régime some service as an agent of administrative continuity. His wealth and power in 1066 reflects the growth of a central royal writing office whose professionalism was reflected in the well-fashioned writs of the last Anglo-Saxon kings, an administrative tradition exploited and extended by the Norman rulers. His estates in 1086 indicate that the Norman tenurial revolution had limits. Regenbald, perhaps originally German, had another qualification to be an adhesive tenant. He was Vicar of Bray. His acceptance of the changing governments of the 1060s merely foreshadowed his two more notorious successors, Simon Aleyn, who survived the religious upheavals of the 1530s to 1560s, and Francis

Carswell, who trod delicately through the ecclesiastical minefields of late Stuart and early Georgian England. Aleyn was supposed to have denied being a turncoat: 'I alwaies kept my Principle, which is this, to live and die the Vicar of Bray,' the exact sentiments attributed to Carswell in the famous eighteenth-century song. Regenbald would have recognized their achievement.

Further Reading
S. Keynes, 'Regenbald The Chancellor (sic)', *Anglo-Norman Studies* x, 1988.

RENNIE, JOHN (1761-1821), engineer, was born at Phantassie in Haddingtonshire. He was a typical product of the thorough education available to Scottish boys at this time. From his father's farmhouse he went to a parish school at Prestonkirk and thence to the burgh school at Dunbar. He also learned practical skills from a millwright on the Phantassie estate, Andrew Meikle, inventor of the threshing machine. From Edinburgh University he went to England to study the work of Brindley, Boulton, Watt and other pioneers. In 1783 he encountered Watt, another Scotsman and it was for him that he executed his first important commission, the Albion flour mill at Blackfriars. Remarkable for the use made of iron, as well as of steam power, this mill laid the base of Rennie's career. From the experience gained in its construction he was able to design other mills; amongst other projects were new machinery for the Mint, and sawmills for Archangel. In an age of expanding demand and a lack of trained engineers a man like Rennie could not be a specialist. Transport in general and canals in particular, however, provided the richest opportunities. In 1804 his Rochdale canal was opened; its digging along a hilly Pennine route had necessitated the construction of elaborate works to maintain the water level. He also made the Lancaster canal, with an aqueduct over the Lune 600 feet long and simple in design.

Miles of rich, brown farmland, now many feet below the level of the fenlands roads, attest to the success of Rennie's drainage work in south Lincolnshire. More imposing memorials are however to be found in the London bridges which he designed and built. Early essays in the analysis of the problems of span and tension and some designs for other bridges which were not carried out preceded the maturity of his best work. His first important bridge, at Kelso, had the elegant semi-elliptical arches and Doric ornamentation which later characterized Waterloo Bridge. The roadway was level, instead of the steep crown typical of most earlier bridges; this is to be found, too, in his first English bridge, over the Wytham at Boston. The Waterloo bridge was designed to harmonize with the river front of Somerset House, for Rennie was a man of his time in appreciating that utilitarian structures should be in harmonious relationship with near-by buildings. He was remarkably resourceful in the face of technical problems. His bridge, founded on coffer dams, 120 feet in span, had nine arches; the piers were ornamented with Doric pilasters. When he came to design a second Thames bridge, at Southwark, authorized by parliament in 1814, he found the river very deep and the tides rapid at the point chosen for construction. To obtain the widest possible waterway he therefore built a bridge of only three cast iron segmental arches; the central one, of 240 feet span, sprang from robust stone piers and was the largest yet attempted in cast iron. When the old London Bridge was found to be unsafe, Rennie, asked to report on the situation, declared that an entirely new bridge was wanted. He completed a design just before his last illness. Appropriately his son, John Rennie, thirty years old when the first pile was driven in March 1824, carried out the work. Five semi-elliptical arches in Yorkshire grit-stone and hard granite composed a design of strength and some grace. At its opening in 1831 he received the knighthood which his father had earlier declined for himself, the first civil engineer to be honoured in this way.

Rennie encompassed an enormous amount of work. At the New London docks he made extensive use of steam engines for pumping and pile-driving. At the East India Docks, he had cast iron in the roofing of warehouses, railways and machinery for handling the heavy goods. He improved the navigation of the River Clyde, re-modelled the harbours of Holyhead and the docks of Grimsby and Hull. For one gigantic work there is no certain evidence that he was mainly responsible. It seems likely, however, that the Bell Rock Lighthouse was his, and he certainly was the main authority behind the building of the Plymouth breakwater which, when it was completed in 1848, had used 3,760,444 tons of stone. He would have shrunk from no undertaking, if he thought that the plan was workable and the results useful. He was made a Fellow of the Royal Society in 1798 and on his death was buried near London Bridge at St Paul's. Simple, unassuming, downright in character, he really lived for his work and refused to believe until the week of his death that his illness could be fatal. Upon his single visit to France, he went at once with the younger James Watt to look at engine works at Dunkirk. It remains to record the one noble project that wilted for want of support: a waterway for ships from Portsmouth to London. There survives but a forlorn piece of this conception in the weed-strewn Wey and Arun Canal.

Further Reading
L. T. C. Rolt, *Great Engineers*, 1962.
C. T. G. Butcher, *John Rennie*, 1960.

RENT, THOMAS (*c.*1260-1323) of Ipswich was 'in many ways typical of the class which directed borough administration in the early fourteenth century'. Like Adam Horder in Southampton, John Rent and his son Thomas apparently moved to Ipswich about 1280 and in 1283 both were taxpayers there, John paying more than average and Thomas somewhat less. Presumably Thomas succeeded to his father's fortune, which he then transformed. The list of his possessions drawn up at his death indicates wide-ranging interests. He then held six messuages (houses and adjacent land), six shops, a workshop, quay, garden, and two vacant plots of land in Ipswich itself; another messuage, some woodland, 120 acres of arable land, five acres of meadow, and seventeen acres of pasture at neighbouring Stoke. Together these lands and other rents, mainly acquired in the early fourteenth century, had a rentable value of £10.7s.4d. a year, a substantial amount, but not all were rented out. Certainly not his own house in the town; not the quay where he kept his boat, probably used for fishing, and stored his timber, perhaps from his own woodlands; not the fifty-four acres of land sown with wheat and barley; and not the meadow and pasture where he kept his eighty sheep. The list reminds us that even the larger towns of late medieval England like Ipswich were small in population and physical size by modern standards and lay among their own fields, enabling townsmen to be part-time farmers or to keep a few animals on the commons. Thomas Rent was also a customs collector from 1304-20, a post with a salary and scope for illicit profit that he apparently exploited. His brewhouse and bakery probably served more than his family and trading activities are hinted at by his constant suits for debt. Whatever he was trading in, he was a slow payer, exploiting free credit for as long as possible, and building up by his death goods and chattels worth the large sum of £118, including £4 in cash and £27 in growing crops. Typically much of his wealth was in moveable goods rather than tied up in land, typically he bought land as a safer form of investment than trade, and typically he lived in considerably more comfort than rural neighbours of similar wealth. His total capital was less than his half-share of the £666 fine levied by the Exchequer and £200 demanded by the Younger Despenser for his misconduct as royal customer. His partner was pardoned but Rent was not, dying in 1323. His son John was a prominent citizen, but not in the same class.

As a wealthy citizen, Rent naturally became one of Ipswich's ruling clique. His first known appointment was to a committee to revise the town customs in 1291. He was one of the two bailiffs on twelve occasions in 1297-1321, coroner from 1312, and in 1313 and 1315 represented Ipswich in parliament. His record was exceeded only by Thomas Stace, bailiff eighteen times in 1295-1321, coroner twice, and MP ten times. Their monopoly of power, perhaps secured by fixing their annual elections, offered chances for corruption and culminated with reforming ordinances in 1321. They were charged with extorting inordinate fees for use of the common seal of the borough, for using it without common consent, and for levying taxes, some of which they diverted to their own use. Such charges were made in many towns and cannot be proved. The remedies were also commonplace: the appointment of clavigers to keep the keys to the common chest and thus control the use of the common seal and the nomination of chamberlains to control the borough's money. It can be shown however that they admitted new burgesses without common consent and pocketed the entrance fines. Rent, Stace and their clique did not concede victory to the burgesses, but objected vigorously. Rent's house was looted and the Crown, accustomed to such urban disturbances, appointed a commission of inquiry. Rent's disaster followed.

Further Reading

S. Alsford, 'Thomas le Rente: A Medieval Town Ruler', *Proceedings of the Suffolk Institute of Archaeology* xxxv.ii, 1982.

REPINGDON, PHILIP (*c*.1340-1424), Bishop of Lincoln from 1404 until 1420, was the only Lollard to become a bishop in late medieval England. He entered the Augustinian abbey of St Mary-in-the Meadows at Leicester by 1369, when he was ordained a priest. The Austin canons were not an enclosed order and could act as parish priests: Repingdon had considerable pastoral gifts and became an able preacher. Before then, however, he was despatched to Oxford University, where he distinguished himself, becoming in 1382 a doctor of theology and being selected by Robert Rigg, chancellor of the university, to preach on the feast of Corpus Christi in the Austin priory of St Frideswide's (now Christchurch Cathedral). It was apparently at this point that Repingdon joined other young scholars convinced by the theology of John Wyclif, notably Nicholas Hereford, John Aston, and Laurence Steven alias Bedman. Whereas Wyclif wrote abstrusely and was content to be read only by academics, his disciples propagated his message openly, both at Oxford and on preaching tours in the provinces. They have been credited with making Lollardy into a movement. Repingdon may have made Leicester into a Lollard centre; certainly he preached heretically on the Holy Communion both at Brackley (Northants.) and at Oxford, where his sermon was applauded by the chancellor and university authorities. In 1382, however, Archbishop Courtenay's Earthquake Council struck at the Oxford Lollards: Rigg was humiliated into submission, the errors of Repingdon and his associates were condemned, and they were required to submit. At first all refused, Repingdon and Hereford appealing both to John of Gaunt and to Rome, and were excommunicated. Repingdon then submitted, abjured his errors, and was absolved, thus reopening the promising career that he had apparently thrown away. He

became Abbot of Leicester in 1393, Chancellor of Oxford University in 1400, Bishop of Lincoln in 1404 – exceptional for an Austin canon – and in 1408 was created cardinal – but not generally recognized as such – by the anti-pope, Gregory XII. His conversion was complete. No bishop, according to Archbishop Arundel, was more vigorous in his attacks on heresy.

Repingdon was indeed an excellent bishop, who 'strove for order, reform and unity within the church' and whose 'work as diocesan surely entitles him to rank high among the churchmen of the later Middle Ages'. He administered his see efficiently, can be shown to have visited much of his vast diocese three times, and sought to settle differences between the cathedral dean and chapter. He promoted orthodoxy and sought to root out the heresy that he may have founded at Leicester in his visitation there in 1413. His concern for ecclesiastical standards and discipline, for example by encouraging university education and fulfilment of parish duties, was motivated by pastoral concern for the spiritual well-being of ordinary Christians. Hence, too, his encouragement of preaching. Such conduct suggests that his recantation in 1382 involved only Wyclif's theology and that his dissatisfaction with clerical abuses and commitment to improved pastoral provision for the laity remained. His career thus confirms that Lollard strictures against the church were widely shared and that it was their speculative theology that overstepped the bounds of orthodoxy. Unlike those other bishops, like Orleton and Wykeham, whose last years of physical incapacity were spent still clinging to office and income, Repingdon resigned in 1420 in a final expression of missionary idealism.

Further Reading

M. Archer, 'Philip Repingdon, Bishop of Lincoln and his Cathedral Chapter', *University of Birmingham Historical Journal* iv, 1953-4.

K. B. McFarlane, *John Wycliffe and the Beginnings of English Nonconformity*, 1952.

REYNOLDS, SIR JOSHUA (1723-92), portrait painter, though not the greatest English painter, did more than any other to make English painting great. He gave it stature. Before him, we speak of English painters; but after him, of English painting, an indigenous gamut of art fit to be compared with the great European schools. For nearly forty years he worked in London at the hub of society, a bachelor, stable and industrious, highly influential, widely respected. In his old age he was described by Boswell as 'he who used to be looked upon as perhaps the most happy man in the world'.

He was born in Devonshire, the son of a clergyman who was also headmaster of the local school. His father rewarded the boy's talent by sending him to London as apprentice to Thomas Hudson, then a luminary in the world of painting. After four years, Reynolds returned to the west, and it was not until he was twenty-five that he had the good fortune to be taken to Italy by Captain Keppel (whom he later painted with distinction). He spent three years in the study of the Italian Masters and must have used his time well, for on his return to London he made an immediate success. In 1755 he had 120 sitters for portraits; by 1764 he was earning £6,000 a year by his brush. From 1760 he kept a large house, including studios and a gallery, in Leicester Square, where he entertained liberally and played host to a galaxy of acquaintances. His friendships with the great Whigs deprived him of the favour of the court; but when the Royal Academy was instituted in 1768 and Reynolds's stature was such that he was seen as the only possible President, the king was obliged to acquiesce in the election, and indeed knighted Reynolds in the following year. Thereafter he was zealous in the work of regulating the Academy and organizing its schools, and was a constant contributor to its exhibitions. To the Academy he delivered his *Discourses*, which were probably polished by Burke and Johnson so that they can still be read with pleasure as well as profit, and which yet bear wonderfully little relation to Reynolds's own practice.

The number of his portraits declined a little with his absorption in the Academy, and with the reasonable preference of would-be sitters to entrust their immortality to artists technically more 'safe'. But he remained the doyen of English painters until in 1790 his eyesight failed and he was compelled to cease working. After a melancholy period he died in 1792; and was borne to St Paul's by a party which included three dukes and two marquises.

His spectacles and ear-trumpet (deafness began with a cold caught while he was copying the Raphaels in the Vatican) make him conspicuous in the group portraits of the day. Some critics have found it difficult to believe that his character was as delightful as it seems to have been. Thus, because he was a rich man, he is said to have been avaricious; because he preferred good society, he is said to have been a snob. The truth is that he liked to live in style; that he was generous, though not to a fault; and that he frequented high places because he was welcome there. The man who was at the same time intimate with the Whig lords and with Wilkes, with Mrs Siddons and Horace Walpole, had reason to be proud of his social versatility. He was no mere lion-hunter: he cared for Goldsmith when Goldsmith was a nobody; and Johnson, who knew nothing of pictorial art, must have loved the man and not the artist ('There goes a man not to be spoiled by prosperity,' he said of Reynolds). It is clear, however, that he was somewhat jealous of his position; and the coolness towards Gainsborough (dramatically dissolved on Gainsborough's deathbed) was largely the result of the latter's antagonism to Reynolds's beloved Academy.

In the reports of the immortal conversations of the Literary Club (later simply The Club), which he joined in founding in order, he said, to give Johnson unlimited opportunities for talking, and of which Burke, Goldsmith, Garrick and Boswell were also members, Reynolds appears now as pacemaker, now as peacemaker, and always his presence was grateful. In Boswell's *Life* his name appears less frequently than Johnson's alone.

As artist, he was portrait painter first and foremost. His excursions into religious painting, into allegory, landscape and history painting, are not to be considered beside his portraiture, but he painted portraits, not as portraits alone, but in terms of those other branches of painting. Thus his great portraits are highly allusive, and if we miss the spiritual in them – well, it was an unspiritual age. He excelled in painting men of authority and action (*Lord Rodney*, *Lord Heathfield*) and young children (*The Strawberry Girl*, *Miss Bowles*, *Lady Betty Hamilton*). In composition, as in all his art, he was often faultless, but often a borrower. So individually, however, did he treat his borrowings from earlier masters as to suggest that he seriously undervalued his own power of originality. 'Damn him, how various he is!' said Gainsborough. The modest ambition of his youth was to be the successor of Kneller; but his true exemplar was Titian. Unfortunately he carried his devotion to the Venetians into the realm of chemistry, and in searching for the 'Venetian secret', which to him was a kind of philosopher's stone, he made such rash experiments with his materials, using vehicles and pigments not only improper and unstable in themselves but mutually antagonistic, that much of his best work was the early victim of time. He himself jokingly admitted that he came off with 'flying colours'. But what colours! Ruskin called him one of the seven supreme colourists. And yet there was no-one living to teach him such colours. Had he not experimented, he might have remained too truly the successor of Kneller and robbed our eyes for ever of the brilliant flesh colours, and the triumphant golds and reds, which illuminate the work of his maturity.

Further Reading

R. Wendorf, *Sir Joshua Reynolds: The Painter in Society*, 1996.
N. Penny, ed., *Reynolds*, 1986.
F. W. Hilles, *The Literary Career of Sir Joshua Reynolds*, 1936.

RHODES, CECIL (1853-1902) must feature as a Victorian Englishman, even though he won his fortune and fame in southern Africa, for he was arguably the chief British Empire builder and its most ambitious visionary. He caught the imagination of the public. Son of the Vicar of Bishop's Stortford, he was sent out to join his brother in South Africa for his health. His arrival coincided with the discovery of diamonds and the prospecting which led to the Big Hole at Kimberley. There Rhodes went digging. He linked up with a digger on a neighbouring plot, Charles Rudd, and together they prospered in the amalgamations which followed, until, helped by winning a monopoly of the water-pumping systems, their De Beers Mining Company became the leader in the field. Perseverance in buying out competitors was Rhodes's secret, but when the stakes became larger his alliance with the gifted financier Alfred Beit of the rival French company became crucial. 'What is your game?', Rhodes asked Beit. 'I am going to control the whole diamond output', came the reply. 'That's funny,' said Rhodes. 'I've made up my mind to do the same: we had better join hands.' Together they ruled the diamond world. The famous cheque for £3,338,650 with which in 1889 Rhodes bought the Central Mining Company from his flamboyant rival, Barney Barnato, to complete the consolidation, has been preserved. It was eighteen years since he had dug for his first diamond.

With the huge fortune thus acquired (he never had the same success with gold) the vicar's son set out to create a mighty empire for Britain in Africa. As early as 1877 he had entrusted the executors of his will with the establishing of a secret society, whose object would be 'the extension of British rule throughout the world'. Money to him meant power, and the Big Hole was a means to an end. His first aim was to bring about a federation of the four states of southern Africa: the British Cape Colony and Natal, and the Boer Orange Free State and Transvaal. He entered the Cape Colony Assembly in 1881, and by 1890 had become prime minister, forming an alliance there with Jan Hofmeyr's Afrikaaner Bond. Meanwhile he was also looking beyond the Transvaal up to central Africa, where the European powers were staking out their claims on the heels of the missionaries and the explorers. The search for gold and the dreams of empire led him to form the British South Africa Company to push northwards into the lands of the Ndebele and the Shona tribes. In 1889 he obtained a Royal Charter for the company. 'All this is to be painted red', he declared, sweeping his hand across a map from the Cape to Cairo, and as a start he sent a column of settlers through to Mashonaland, to lay claim to the mining rights granted to them by Chief Lobengula. There they built Fort Salisbury.

But in Mashonaland and the Transvaal alike it proved difficult for the gold diggers to live at peace with the older occupants of the country, and it was no part of Rhodes's plans that they should do so. First, the Ndebele Chief Lobengula, a twenty-stone warrior, was driven into exile and died. His Matabeleland was joined to Mashonaland and the settlers named them Rhodesia. Then the mining community in Johannesburg, the uitlanders, sought political rights from the Boer President of the Transvaal, Kruger. Rhodes, who by this time saw himself swimming with the tide of history and who was suffering ever more seriously from the heart disease which was to kill him, tried to force the pace. He organized military support for a planned uitlander rising, and his close friend Dr Jameson sat poised on the Transvaal border. But the uitlanders lost their nerve. Rhodes tried to abort the plan, but Jameson had set off. His 'Raid' ended in defeat and capture. Rhodes resigned, and his hopes of getting a peaceful federation of Boer and British South African states ended. Hofmeyr became a bitter opponent.

From then on Rhodes's aim was to keep the Royal Charter for his company. In this he was successful. Chamberlain backed him in exchange for his silence over how much Chamberlain had known of Jameson's Raid. Moreover, Rhodes's own popularity was unimpaired. What was meant to be a full parliamentary investigation into his part in the Raid became what contemporaries punningly called 'a Lying-in-State at Westminster'; while in Cape Town there was a public holiday to greet his return. But without Hofmeyr he was politically emasculated and had little to do with the events leading up to the Boer War. When it broke out he went straight to Kimberley, where he threw his weight around and made life difficult for General Kekewich, who was commanding its defence during the siege. His heart gradually failed, not helped by the machinations of Princess Radziwill, an outrageous society lady who set her cap at him and tried to blackmail him when he repulsed her. He died at his cottage by the sea at Muizenberg, and Dr Jameson told the crowds outside that his last words had been: 'So little done, so much to do.'

Rhodes never cut a heroic figure. He had a high-pitched voice, his clothes were scruffy, his manners casual: he was gauche with women, only relaxing in the company of the young men whom he picked to work for him, and with one or two of whom he had romantic, though sexually repressed, relationships. All the more remarkable, then, was the power he exerted over his contemporaries. His business efficiency and energy were ruthless, but they were combined with a physical zest for life, expressed without inhibition, and with an overarching vision. His imperial dreams had Roman inspiration: he had all the classical authors mentioned in Gibbon's *Decline and Fall of the Roman Empire* translated for his library. He loved Africa, creating a beautiful house in the Cape Dutch style at Groote Schuur, and choosing to be buried where the view from a hill in Matabeleland had enthralled him. He used his wealth unsparingly to achieve his aims. Although Rhodesia has left the map, the Rhodes Scholarships survive, founded and funded by him to promote a union of English-speaking people, by giving potential leaders amongst their students all over the world (including a President of the USA) an education at Oxford, where he had worked for his degree in the intervals between making his fortune at Kimberley. But his influence on the course of the history of South Africa proved to be baleful.

Further Reading
B. Roberts, *Cecil Rhodes, Flawed Colossus*, 1987.

RHODRI MAWR (*d.c.*877), or Rhodri the Great, was the first High King of Wales. He appears to have been descended from Maelgwyn Gwynedd, and was himself the grandfather of Hywel Dda (Hywel the Good). He succeeded to Gwynedd in 844 by descent from his grandmother. His defeat in 856 of the Danish leader Horn, or Gorm, was widely known and acclaimed. Increasingly, however, the British inhabitants of Wales had also to deal with the Saxons of the earldom of Mercia, under Wessex suzerainty from 829. It may be that these external threats hastened attempts at political unification. However, Rhodri sought to found his claims to the territories later acquired upon legitimate succession; he seems to have been adept at converting opportunity into military and political success. Thus, in 855, he was able to make good his claim to Powys through his mother Nest, and in 872 he established his rule over Seisyllwg, which extended from Ceredigion to Gower. By this time the authority of Rhodri extended over all of Wales except Dyfed, Glamorgan, Gwent and Brycheiniog (roughly the former Brecknock, from whence it draws its name). Forced out of Gwynedd by the Vikings, he and his son died in the defence of Powys from the Mercians in 877 or 878; a second son, Cadell, became King of Seisyllwg. Generations of the rulers of all the kingdoms of Wales traced their descent from Rhodri Mawr.

RHYS AP GRUFFYDD (The Lord Rhys) (*d.*1197) was the child of a marriage alliance between Gruffydd son of Rhys ap Tewdwr, exiled in Ireland till 1116, and Gwenllian, a princess of the House of Gwynedd. On the death of Gruffydd in 1137, the succession to the throne of Deheubarth passed to his five sons (Rhys amongst them). Given the Welsh custom of partible inheritance, such an event was usually the prelude to catastrophe. In this case, however, disaster had already struck, for most of Deheubarth had fallen into the hands of the insurgent Norman lords, only Cantref Mawr remaining intact. The brothers, with little to squabble over set about restoring their fortunes with great determination. By 1153, the kingdom was largely rebuilt, and with the reconquest of Ceredigion over the next two years, neared the limits of its greatest extent. By 1155, moreover, four of the brothers had died in the struggle, leaving Rhys to impose his rule unchallenged from within.

The threat from without, however, was very real, and in 1158 Henry II, having humiliated Owain Gwynedd in

the north, turned his attention to Rhys in the south, restoring much of Deheubarth to the Norman lords, and to the Crown. When Rhys rebelled, he was arrested and taken to England, and Henry showed his determination to establish his overlordship in Wales by forcing both Rhys and Owain to pay homage at Woodstock in July 1163. When the Welsh showed further signs of resistance, Henry proceeded to marshall a huge and apparently unstoppable military force. But events took a sudden and dramatic turn. The expedition was defeated, as much by the mountains and the weather as by the Welsh, and this sharp and costly reverse was combined with growing political disunity arising from difficulties with Thomas Becket and new concerns in Ireland, to occasion a reappraisal of English policy.

Rhys's prospects, therefore, suddenly grew brighter, and he was quickly able to reclaim much of the lands lost in 1157. By the end of the 1160s, he was squeezing the Norman Lords of Dyfed. The most powerful of these, Richard, Earl of Pembroke, was busy in Ireland, where he seized the throne of Leinster in 1171, laying claim to suzerainty over the whole island. Henry II, anxious at his growing power, and at other uncontrolled baronial enterprise in Ireland, sought to marshall an expedition. In these matters, the interests of Henry and of Rhys came into a novel alignment. Rhys would have cared little for a drive to curb baronial power across the water, but it fitted with his desire to seize its sources in Dyfed and to overcome the hostility of Henry. Furthermore, the enterprise involved the export of his own rivals and enemies. A phalanx of lesser lords, of Norman and Welsh descent, left for Ireland in 1171, the first English royal expedition to that island, though not the last. Henry and Rhys met in the Forest of Dean; the alliance which issued from the encounter, however, was not of equals: in 1172, Rhys was made justiciar, and hence 'lord', a position roughly analogous to that of viceroy, whilst retaining the allegiance of the lesser lordships around the edges of his own core territory of Deheubarth. Whatever the legal ambiguities of this peculiar arrangement, it made political sense. His new role and title formally recognized the fact of Rhys's predominance in Wales as a whole, unchallengeable after the death in 1170 of Owain Gwynedd and the onset of fraternal strife in the northern kingdom.

The pre-eminence of the Lord Rhys was celebrated at the magnificent eisteddfod at Cardigan castle in 1176. He took care to bind to himself by marriage the most powerful Anglo-Norman families of Wales and the Marches. Under his rule, the new reformed Cistercian monasteries at Whitland and Strata Florida formed the models for others. Rhys granted lands to the Cistercians, he was familiar with the Latin spoken in their houses, and with French. The cult of David, and Celtic symbolism and style, flourished under his patronage, but within the structures of the reformed Anglo-Norman religion. It is probable that Rhys was responsible for the first assemblage in book form of the texts of Welsh law. But hopes of continued juridical and political independence did not last, partly because they depended upon the goodwill of Henry. From 1189, with the accession of Richard I, there was growing tension with the Norman Marcher lords. Rhys chose military offensive as the best means to secure his position, and was able to win some victories in the Marches, notably at Radnor in 1196, but the Normans were already pressing hard at the frontiers of Deheubarth. Rhys died in 1197. Over the next years, control of his kingdom was divided and redivided amongst sons and nephews, amidst continuing scenes of acrimony and chaos. In 1216, Llywelyn I was able to impose order from the outside, but by then Deheubarth had ceased to exist as a kingdom in its own right.

RHYS AP TEWDWR (*d.*1093) laboured from 1078 to establish his rule over Deheubarth after several years of quite exceptional internecine savagery in the kingdom following the death in 1063 of Gruffydd ap Llywelyn of Gwynedd. Each man sought, from opposite ends of the principality, to unify its two most formidable kingdoms under his own personal rule. But Rhys was faced with new opponents, more dangerous than those who had frustrated Gruffydd. William I, following his invasion of England, granted to his barons extensive lands in the Marches, and they also annexed Gwent. The Conqueror himself was too preoccupied with digesting his gains in England to consider a concerted campaign in Wales; by 1081 he was prepared to recognize the legitimacy of Rhys's rule in exchange for the payment of tribute. Under William II, however, the Marcher lords became even more aggressive, overrunning Glamorgan and parts of Powys; in 1093 Rhys was killed whilst resisting their further south-westerly progress into Deheubarth. His death anticipated the temporary reduction of the kingdom to a rump; by 1100, Normans and later insurgents from Powys and Gwynedd occupied its east (Brycheiniog), north (Ceredigion) and much of Dyfed in the west.

RICARDO, DAVID (1772-1823) was a leading authority on economic questions in the generation after Adam Smith. He was a man of versatile ability. Though rightly famous for his masterly work, *Principles of Political Economy and Taxation* (1817), it is perhaps unfair to see him only as the principal propounder of the classical political economy whose laws and logic were treated with such exaggerated respect by his followers and adopted so keenly by manufacturers. Ricardo was primarily an analyst and it was unlucky for his reputation that he was treated as a prophet.

He was the third son of a large family. His father was a Dutch Jew who had come as a young man to England and made money on the stock exchange; he was reputed an able and honest man. David's education was largely practical; from the age of fourteen he was employed in his father's business. He married Priscilla Wilkinson when he was just twenty-one and he upset his father by giving up his Jewish faith. He made a lot of money on the stock exchange at a time when war finance offered great opportunities to an alert speculator. All the same he earned a name for probity and also found time for other interests, notably scientific ones. He fitted up a laboratory, made a collection of minerals and was an original member of the Geological Society (1807).

In 1799, while staying at Bath with his ailing wife, he first encountered *The Wealth of Nations* and became interested in Smith's scientific treatment of economic questions. The depreciation of the currency was causing alarm in 1809 when Ricardo wrote some letters on the subject for James Perry, editor of *The Morning Chronicle*. They were later gathered into a pamphlet. The analysis and proposals of the bullion committee (1810) followed Ricardo closely. It recommended the resumption of cash payments in two years to correct a depreciation which was the result, in the committee's view, of excessive issue by the Bank of England. In the subsequent debate Ricardo added to his reputation. Malthus was among his admirers, though the two men differed on the question of agricultural protection. Malthus wanted some degree of protection, while Ricardo argued that this was inconsistent with the theory of rent which Malthus had himself propounded (it is more usually named after Ricardo). In 1819, after he had become the representative of the twelve voters of the Irish borough of Portarlington, he rose, after being 'loudly called upon from all sides of the house', to support Peel's measure for the resumption of cash payments, which followed his own recommendation of three years before, that banknotes should be exchangeable not for gold coin but for standard bars of gold bullion.

Ricardo was a reluctant speaker, 'frightened by the sound of his own voice', as he confided to McCulloch. He was also but an indifferent writer. His *Principles of Political Economy and Taxation* was influential mainly because of the simple force of his main arguments and the fervent advocacy of his cleverest disciples, James Mill and McCulloch. He was listened to as an oracle by radicals and utilitarians, with whom he usually agreed upon such matters as parliamentary reform and free trade. Politicians were slowly being educated in the principles of the new 'science': men like Parnell, the Whig, who had been a prime mover in the Corn Law of 1815 but explained to the house in 1827 that he had changed his mind on closer acquaintance 'with the science connected with it'. He summarized what was in effect Ricardo's argument: dear corn meant high wages; high wages, low profits; therefore a capital shortage. Less appreciative comment about 'the change-alley people' and their influence comes from Cobbett (*Political Register*, September 1819): 'Faith! They are now become *everything*. Baring assists at the Congress of Sovereigns and Ricardo regulates things at home'. Ricardo's whole outlook was generously liberal: he voted against the Six Acts, the Foreign Enlistment and Alien Acts, and he denounced religious prosecution, notably that of Carlile. He was naturally, however, most cogent in economic questions. He supported a scheme for enabling the poor to buy annuities, opposed every kind of subsidy and tariff, and voted for every reduction in taxation. He grew bolder with age. He convinced himself, if not others, that it would be possible to pay off the national debt, in a year, by an assessment on all the property of every county.

Maria Edgeworth gives a pleasant account of Ricardo at home among his family at Gatcombe: he was ever starting new topics of conversation and arguing urbanely for the fun of it. He enjoyed charades and long walks. Letters describing a family tour to the continent in 1822, to visit some of his Dutch relations and to meet fellow economists, were later privately printed. There was no hint in the strenuous programme of that year of his sudden collapse in health in 1823. He was widely mourned. James Mill displayed what Mrs Grote called an unexpected tenderness of feeling. McCulloch, subsequently his biographer, said that Ricardo had supported nearly every London charity, as well as an alms-house and two schools in Gatcombe. A traditionalist like Lord Grenville could praise him: 'Radical as he was, I consider Ricardo's death as a great loss both to the country and to government.'

The 'iron law of wages' was supposed to be derived from his principles, though it is likely that for Ricardo the law was no more than a postulate for logical purposes of argument. He was often less extreme than has been supposed: on free trade, for example, he never demanded more than 'gradual recurrence to the sound principles of an universally free trade'. What may fairly be laid to Ricardo's door is that he was too abstract. By making assumptions of a quasi-scientific sort about 'economic man', by using impersonal concepts such as 'labour', he and his disciples fostered the idea that there were certain immutable 'laws' which determined the operations of man in his capacity as producer and earner. No wonder that 'the gloomy science' came to be hated as a new weapon in the hands of the employer of labour. There is a certain rough justice in the fact that Ricardo's theory of value – that it is proportionate solely to the labour embodied – was taken up by Karl Marx, with consequences which Ricardo would, of course, have repudiated with horror!

RICCIO or RIZZIO, DAVID (1533?-66), secretary to Mary, Queen of Scots, was born probably in 1533.

Generally reputed in his own day and for centuries since to have been the low-born son of a teacher of music at Turin, David is now thought to have come of a noble and wealthy family in Piedmont, that of Riccio di Solbitro. If this is true, then his poverty may have been a pose and his true status well known to the queen. He is said to have had a pleasing bass voice and to have played the lute (Sir James Melville in his *Memoirs*, 1929 edn, p.103, calls him 'a merry fellow and a good musician'), to have spent some time at the court of the Duke of Savoy, and then at the age of twenty-eight to have arrived in Scotland in the wake of Morette, who was on a mission for the duke (1561). Mary had three *valets de chambre* who sang in her private chapel and she was looking for a fourth to complete the quartet. Riccio applied for the post and was accepted. He held this position for some years and then in 1564 the queen's French Secretary, Raullet, was dismissed for having been corrupted by English gold, and Riccio was appointed in his place. A hostile writer, Randolph, had it that Riccio 'croope in on suspicion gathered against Raulet'. Mary was at this point planning to take the direction of policy entirely into her own hands and she feared that her French Secretary might betray her to her uncle of Lorraine. The new appointment cannot have been a great success, for Melville records that 'advices given by the Queen of England were misconstructed ... partly because David Riccio, lately admitted to be French Secretary, was not very skilful in inditing French letters, which she [Mary] did write over again in her own hand' (ib., p.23). One of the grounds for Riccio's unpopularity was that many looked on him as a Papal agent (Melville called him to Mary 'a known minion of the pope', ib., p.106), but he was never acknowledged as such by the Papacy.

At this point two things are certain – first, 'the extraordinary favour [which Mary] carried to that man' (Melville, ib., p.105); secondly, that it was Riccio who was a chief supporter of the Darnley marriage. Melville again noted that Riccio was Darnley's 'great friend at the queen's hand' (ib., p.107). Darnley and Riccio were at first intimate friends, playing tennis together by day and sharing the same bed by night.

After Mary married Darnley, Riccio virtually became Secretary of State. It did not take Mary long after her marriage to find out what a disastrous mistake she had made. Her hatred for the insufferable Darnley grew, and as it grew Riccio attained the position which should have been that of Mary's husband. He became the queen's adviser on all matters, even in the presence of the Scottish lords. The only road to royal favour was Riccio. Darnley demanded the Crown Matrimonial, but he was refused that and treated with (perhaps well deserved) contumely. The arrogance of Riccio became insupportable to the Scottish lords, as it was insupportable to

Darnley. And his arrogance was encouraged by the queen. Darnley's jealousy at last reached the point where he accused Mary of being Riccio's mistress. Darnley thereby played into the hands of those lords who hated Riccio. The murder of Riccio was the inevitable result.

As so often happens in conspiracies, enemies find themselves on the same side, bound together solely by hatred of a common enemy. Catholic relatives of Darnley resented his treatment by Riccio; Protestant lords saw in Riccio a Papal agent for restoring the Catholic religion in Scotland; many of both parties saw in Riccio the chief proposer for the bill to come before parliament for confiscating the lands of those lords who had rebelled against Mary at the time of her marriage with Darnley. Morton, Moray, Lethington, Argyll, Ruthven combined to slaughter Riccio. All had a common aim, to be rid thereby of Mary. All were determined to make the murder appear the work of Darnley. Thus it was that Darnley's dagger was left in the side of Riccio. The murder took place in the evening of Saturday, 9 March 1566, in the palace of Holyrood. Riccio was dragged from the very presence of the queen when they were at supper and struck down outside with fifty-six dagger strikes. His body was buried at first before the door of the abbey: later, by Mary's orders, it was laid in the royal tomb at Edinburgh, but then it was transferred to another part of the church.

Further Reading

W. A. Gatherer, introduction to G. Buchanan's *The Tyrannous Reign of Mary Stuart*, 1958.

RICH OF ABINGDON, EDMUND (*c*.1170-1240; Archbishop of Canterbury 1234-40; canonized 1246) provides an example of how the best men often made ineffective prelates, political failure nonetheless being a qualification for sainthood. Born near and educated at Oxford, Edmund's intense personal piety was fostered by his forceful mother, Mabel (his father having escaped into Eynsham Abbey). For the rest of his life Edmund wore a particularly painful hair shirt. In 1192, Edmund went to Paris, whence he returned to teach the Quadrivium before turning to theology. At Oxford, Edmund gained a reputation as a popular preacher and teacher famed for the slickness of his expositions, some of which so defied logical explanation that they were ascribed to divine inspiration. Seemingly a model don, Edmund occasionally dozed off while teaching, a result, perhaps, of his inability to lie down to sleep at night because of his hair shirt. In 1222, he abandoned lecturing on theology, allegedly because he found the fashionable disputation method of teaching and learning, by which pupils and masters orally exchanged competing arguments and texts in a combative search for truth, conducive to vanity. As canon and treasurer of Salisbury, Edmund displayed administrative skills. These, with his contacts with the royal family as a spiritual adviser to the king's sister, Eleanor and his achievements as a scholar recommended him as archbishop after Pope Gregory IX had rejected three other candidates. As a spiritual guide, Edmund set an impressive example; as a politician, he was handicapped by a tender conscience without the stomach for confrontation of his colleague Robert Grosseteste of Lincoln. After playing a pivotal eirenic role in the removal of Peter des Roches's government in 1234, Edmund suffered consistent disappointment and rebuff, both from the king and the pope. In 1236, he acquiesced in the decision of the council at Merton on bastardy although it ran counter to canon law; 1238 saw his impotent outrage at the marriage of Simon de Montfort to Princess Eleanor, in contradiction to her oath of chastity he had witnessed; the political crisis of 1238 exposed the loss of episcopal influence in the previous four years. Edmund resisted papal demands for taxation for the war against Frederick II and the scheme to reserve 300 English benefices for papal appointment. This championing of the rights of the indigenous church won him the approval of Matthew Paris who composed a respectful biography of Edmund after his death. But Archbishop Edmund ran aground on the shallows of detail. Unlike Grosseteste he failed to articulate clear principles and strategies. A sympathizer with the reforming attitudes of Langton, Edmund lacked the skill to assert ecclesiastical interests in the secular world or implement change within the church. In 1237, as a recognition of his exposed weakness, a papal legate, Otto, was appointed to pursue both papal interests and church reform. Edmund's position was severely compromised. An unsuccessful appeal to the papacy in 1237 over the rights of Canterbury was followed by continued failure to resolve his conflict with the monks of Canterbury over a clutch of vested interests, including his foundation of a house of secular canons at Maidstone. In 1240, he withdrew again, ostensibly to visit the pope. Seeking the shades of Becket and Langton at Pontigny, he died at nearby Soissy. In death, his personal qualities soon obscuring his public failure, Edmund became an ideal subject for canonization by a papacy eager to claim martyrs for ecclesiastical rights. Miracles of healing soon began to be ascribed to him, his tomb becoming a place of veneration. In 1246 he became the last Archbishop of Canterbury to be canonized. His cult was immediately popular, especially among Englishmen, including those who thwarted him in life such as Henry III, who visited the shrine in 1254. Richard of Cornwall, Edmund's ally in 1238, was especially devoted, visiting Edmund's shrine in 1247 and naming his second son after him. Such was the ubiquitous appeal of the dead archbishop that he was admired by royalists and rebels alike in the 1260s, including Simon de Montfort whose marriage Edmund had so vigorously opposed. His shrine continued to attract English pilgrims, including Edward I in 1286. In England the cult was maintained at Catesby, in Northamptonshire, a house reputedly founded by Edmund for his equally ascetic sisters. Edmund conformed in aspiration to the academic reforming prelates of the age of Innocent III, scholars, administrators, spiritual advisers and statesmen. Although failing to put these ideals into effective practice, Edmund's personality left its mark on contemporaries. He combined scholarship with piety: the mystical *Mirror of the Holy Church* has been ascribed to him. He believed in personal conversion and the supremacy of private conscience: an unlikely archbishop and an unlikely saint. His most lasting memorial is appropriately where he achieved most unalloyed renown, in the community of students and scholars named after him at Oxford, St Edmund Hall.

Further Reading
C. H. Lawrence, *Edmund of Abingdon*, 1960.

RICHARD I (1157-99; King of England 1189-99) was one of the most glamorous of medieval monarchs and, judged by what mattered at the time, one of the greatest. Yet, admired and feared by contemporaries, he has been reviled by modern historians. No English king has had more legends woven about him, by scholars no less than romancers. Until the seventeenth century, he was a hero. Since then, while retaining a popular image as a knight, he has been condemned as an absentee warlord who capriciously milked England of its wealth to fund campaigns in France and the Mediterranean, by implication far away places of which good Englishmen know nothing. Yet for more than a century after his death, his aura lent lustre to his successors. Henry III was proud to dine beneath his uncle's shield and decorated his palaces with murals and titles depicting Richard's heroic exploits on crusade. Edward I's crusading provoked the comparison: 'Behold he shines like a new Richard'. Another observer contrasted the uneasy first six years of Edward II's reign with the drama and success of Richard's first three. Far from being a shameful example of royal neglect and princely self-indulgence, Richard I was the yardstick for admirable English monarchy.

Born in Oxford, the third son of Henry II and Eleanor of Aquitaine, Richard spent most of his early years in England. Whether acquired then or later, in adult life Richard displayed particular affection for the insular saints Alban and Edmund of East Anglia. He had some fond memories of childhood: when king in 1189, he gave estates in Wiltshire to his former wet-nurse, Hodierna, whose reward is recalled in the parish of Knoyle Hodierne. Apart from military training, Richard received an excellent education. Belying his popular image as being little more than an effective killing machine, Richard was a talented linguist. He could tell jokes in Latin and recite poetry in French and Provençal. He exhibited interest and skill in choral music. For all his passion for tournaments, the trappings of chivalry and the reality of fighting, Richard was no mindless thug. He brought his intellect and insight to the conduct of war, initially in consolidating his rule in Aquitaine then, as king, in launching a massive amphibious force on the Third Crusade and subsequently in regaining territory in France. There was more to successful warfare than mastery of riding, holding the lance and sword-play. Raising money, men, ships and supplies for the crusade; building castles; and, above all, leading men and convincing them to fight, demanded skills of a high order. Richard's own family history was littered with those unequal to such tasks: Robert Curthose; Stephen; John.

In 1167, it was decided that Richard should inherit the lands of his mother, the county of Poitou and the duchy of Aquitaine, for which he did homage to the King of France in 1169. From 1172, when he was formally installed as duke, Richard's career was chiefly spent in asserting ducal power over a recalcitrant nobility in a large and diverse province: excellent training for kingship. Politically, Richard faced tensions within his family: he joined his mother and brothers in the Great Rebellion against Henry II in 1173-4 during which he held his first independent command; in 1182-3 his authority was challlenged by his elder brother Henry; finally, in 1187-9, he was heavily engaged in securing inheritance to all the Angevin lands. Throughout, Richard showed himself energetic, single-minded and resourceful. A sign of his self-confidence is shown by his willingness to ally with Philip II of France in order to secure his inheritance. Philip's price was Richard's public acceptance of Capetian overlordship. As king, whatever the political favours, personal obligation or legal status, Richard felt no constraints in dealing with Philip. As ever, the effectiveness of Capetian attempts to exploit their overlordship depended on the behaviour of their vassals rather than their own efforts.

Richard's accession as King of England, for all the uncertainties of 1187-9, was the most harmonious and least challenged of any English king between 1042 and 1272. His coronation at Westminster, the first for which we have a detailed account, was lavish, the feast afterwards even more so. Behind such ceremonies lay atavistic traditions of sacral kingship – the centrepiece of the coronation being the anointing of the king on his head, hands and bare chest – and the assertion of power. Richard had especial need to signal his authority as he had determined to lead an army to the Holy Land to recapture Jerusalem. Richard needed to establish an effective regency and raise vast sums of money. It is no small tribute to Richard as a political leader that Angevin authority survived his absence and his people contributed to his crusade in almost unprecedented amounts.

Few things reveal the absolute gulf between the Middle Ages and our own time more than the crusades. Modern experience of war has stripped away the last vestiges of noble, chivalric veneer. The squalid ends of empires have cast suspicion over stereotypes based upon cultural or racial superiority and antagonism. Religious wars have too often contradicted the faith ostensibly in dispute. Yet, for many of Richard I's contemporaries, few ideals were nobler, for the layman none more meritorious than taking the sign of the Cross to defend or recapture the scene of Man's Redemption, the Holy Sepulchre and the Holy City of Jerusalem. To achieve either required personal commitment of a very high order: many failed to reach their destination; more did not return. Crusading demanded material resources and organization usually beyond an individual. The First Crusade (1096-9), which captured Jerusalem, had attracted only sparse support from Englishmen, although many from the Anglo-Norman aristocracy took part. The second large-scale expedition (1146-9) elicited a more widespread response. Nobles used it as a respectable excuse to escape political dilemmas at home. Contingents from London, East Anglia and the Channel ports made a significant contribution to the crusading fleets which succesfully besieged Lisbon in 1147. By 1187, a tradition of interest in and visits to the Holy Land had become well-established in England. News that the armies of the Christian King of Jerusalem had been annihilated by the Egyptian sultan Saladin at the battle of Hattin (July 1187) and that Jerusalem itself had fallen (October) galvanized the west. The Angevin lands, including England, were swept up in the huge military effort now known as the Third Crusade. In November 1187, Richard was the first prince north of the Alps to take the Cross.

The Third Crusade became a central preoccupation of Angevin government and a major dimension of English politics. Where Henry II had temporized for decades, Richard acted decisively: nine months after his coronation and just under a year after his father's death, Richard set out on crusade from Vézelay in northern Burgundy. On the evidence of his organization and conduct of the crusade alone, Richard is revealed as a most formidable politician and administrator, as well as a commander of stature. An experienced general, Richard realized that there was no limit to the treasure needed for the crusade: its first year cost at least as much as the king's annual income. Roger of Howden, a royal clerk and former justice who himself went on Richard's crusade, recalled that the new king 'put up for sale all he had, offices, lordships, earldoms, sheriffdoms, castles, towns, lands, everything'. Officials of his father, including the justiciar Ranulf Glanvill, were sacked and heavily fined, their offices auctioned to the highest bidder. Episcopal sees, such as London and Ely; forest rights; town charters; even his own demesne lands were all sold off. Richard told his friends that he would have sold London itself if he could have found a buyer.

Richard's preparations were precise, effective and breathtakingly large. He raised and pre-paid a fleet of over 100 ships, carrying perhaps 8,000 men. His own land army, which met the fleet at the prearranged rendezvous ports of Marseilles and Messina, may have totalled as much as 9,000. Having wintered in Sicily, but for a storm which blew his huge fleet off-course (allowing him, with typical aggression, to capture Cyprus) Richard would have arrived in Palestine as he had planned, a year after embarkation. To exert such control over logistics and strategy by land and sea over the length of a continent is a feat unparalleled in previous English history. Although from 1189 significant private contingents departed for the Holy Land, notably from London, the core of the English response to the crusade was very much that of central government, from the hiring of ships from Cinque Port merchants to the ordering of horse-shoes from the Forest of Dean, cheeses from Hampshire and bacon from Warwickshire. The dynamism behind such operations was that of the king himself. Where other crusader princes – the King of France or the Emperor of Germany – relied on leading a coalition of self-financing vassals, Richard made sure that his leadership was supported by a massive force in his direct control and pay. The Third Crusade was a triumph of Angevin organization, in scope, imagination and execution, one of the most remarkable governmental achievements of the Middle Ages.

To medieval observers, Richard's crusading exploits confirmed him as the ideal prince. Modern criticism, by contrast, condemns Richard for leaving his lands dangerously exposed to internal wrangling and external threat. Dynastically, Richard was taking a risk. Like Louis VII of France before him (in 1146), he set out for the east without a male heir. He compounded possible confusion by recognizing, for immediate diplomatic advantage, his infant nephew Arthur of Brittany as his successor at Messina in October 1190, whilst having only recently built up the landed position of his brother John to almost viceregal status in parts of England. However, the regency arrangments worked, with the little local difficulty of the fall of his chosen viceroy Longchamp being smoothly resolved by his replacement with Walter of Coutances, Archbishop of Rouen (1191) and, finally, by the appointment of Hubert Walter as Archbishop of Canterbury and justiciar in 1193. If Richard had returned, as planned, in the spring of 1193, all would have been well. Furthermore, Richard did not cut himself off from problems at home. On rumours of political tensions in England, Walter of Coutances was despatched as royal troubleshooter from Sicily early in 1191. Richard was kept in close touch by a stream of messengers: in return he sent regular newsletters announcing his triumphs, such as the capture of Acre (July 1191) and the defeat of Saladin at Arsuf (September 1191). News from England could have reached the Holy Land in little more than two months: the king knew of Longchamp's deposition in October 1191 by the following January. For England, Richard on crusade was only different from Richard in Aquitaine by degree.

The problem was Richard's failure to return in 1193. He had begun his journey east in July 1190. Having sent an advance guard to the siege of Acre in the autumn of 1190, Richard and the bulk of his army wintered at Messina in Sicily before embarking for Palestine. Having almost casually overrun Cyprus, Richard arrived at Acre in July 1191: the city fell a month later, after a siege of two years. Philip II of France left for the west three weeks later, leaving Richard as the dominant commander. After repulsing Saladin and occupying Jaffa, Richard twice tried an assault on Jerusalem, each time withdrawing a few miles from the Holy City because of the vulnerability of his supply lines and the realization that, even if he could take Jerusalem, he would not be able to hold it. Such careful campaigning and agonizing, but militarily enlightened, decisions mark Richard as an outstanding general. Persuading his followers to obey him, to have the prize of their efforts dashed from them at the last moment, reveals a remarkable leader of men. As 1192 progressed, military stalemate forced a three-year truce to be agreed between Richard and Saladin in August 1192 (they never actually met, *pace* thirteenth-century myth-makers). Although the Holy City remained in Muslim hands, the littoral of Palestine was restored to an attenuated Christian kingdom of Jerusalem. Part of the deal was that crusaders were allowed to fulfil their vows and pray at the church of Holy Sepulchre under Saladin's safe conduct, no doubt the source of his laudatory reputation in the west thereafter. Richard declined the offer, preferring to leave his own vow unfulfilled for future redemption. Richard sailed from Acre in October 1192. So far, so good.

What transformed Richard's crusade from orderly and dignified, if limited, success into potentially fatal personal and political disaster was his capture on his way home in December 1192 by Leopold of Austria, whom Richard had insulted during the siege of Acre. Within a few weeks, Leopold had sold Richard to Henry VI of Germany. Richard stayed in captivity for a year while Henry conducted an auction for the king's release. One side of the bidding was Richard, backed by the resources of the Angevin empire. On the other were Philip of France and Prince John, in 1193-4 allies in a partially successful attempt to dismember Richard's continental possessions. Richard won, offering a ransom of 100,000 marks, the bulk of which was paid before the king's release in February 1194. Such was the importance of Richard's freedom that, on hearing of the deal with Henry VI, Philip II wrote to John: 'Look to yourself: the devil is loose'.

But the damage had already been done. Although the regency in England held firm under Eleanor of Aquitaine, Walter of Coutances and Hubert Walter, strategically important parts of Normandy were lost to the French king in the year of Richard's captivity, the recovery of which dominated the last five years of the reign. Imprisonment of medieval rulers was not unknown, but, as in the cases of Stephen, Henry III, Edward II, Richard II, Henry VI, etc., was usually the result of internal discord. Not all precedents were reassuring. Richard's great-great-uncle, Robert Curthose, Duke of Normandy, spent twenty-eight years in prison. Like him, Richard took to poetry to while away the time, although there is no truth in the legends of his being sought out and discovered by a faithful minstrel Blondel. Observers were impressed at Richard's demeanour. One usually hostile French writer enthused that Richard bore himself in adversity as if 'seated on the throne of his ancestors at Lincoln or Caen'. Even at the nadir of his fortunes, Richard knew how to cut an impressive figure. But part of the blame for his predicament must be his. Alone of the great leaders of the major crusades, he had failed to arrange safe passage home. If the consequences for his power and dominions were limited partly by his own effort, the severity of the threat was no less his responsiblity. The obverse of his self-confidence was a streak of recklessness.

During his brief, and as it transpired final, visit to the land of his birth (March-May 1194), he ostentatiously rededicated his rule to two national saints closely identified with English crusaders, Thomas Becket and Edmund. Like Stephen on his release in 1141, at Winchester in April 1194 he revived the custom of ceremonially wearing his crown. But Richard never fully escaped the repercussions of his captivity. One of the terms of his release was that he had to perform homage to Henry VI for England, technically thus reduced to a fief of the empire. Richard was able to ignore any practical implications of this, helped by the early death of Henry (1197) and subsequent German civil war. His homage had only personal advantage, easing the speed of his freedom. By contrast, when John, in a move much criticized by later commentators, submitted England to the overlordship of the papacy in 1213, he gained practical support from successive popes which proved vital in keeping the Angevin dynasty on the English throne. More seriously, the loss of lands in France, particularly in the Seine valley, significantly weakened the external defences of his lands, as well as showing how continental loyalties, at least, could be swayed away from the Angevins, a lesson repeated more devastatingly a decade later.

Richard's ransom and consequent wars with Philip of France cost his subjects a fortune. The ransom of 1193 necessitated the levy throughout the Angevin lands of a tax on moveables and twenty-five per cent on incomes. A year's wool crop was requisitioned from the great Cistercian sheep ranches of upland England, as well as ecclesiastical gold and silver plate. The speed of collection – at least 70,000 marks were paid in six months before Richard's release – is testimony to the efficiency of royal administration and, more strikingly, the loyalty of taxpayers. Richard's officials could not have coerced such sums from an unwilling populace: the support, particularly, of the baronage was vital, fiscally as it was politically, in resisting the schemes of John. Richard was alert to the political dimension. Even in his German prison, he wanted to know how much each baron had contributed to the ransom 'so that we may judge how far we must return the compliment'. Angevin kings forgot nothing but learnt much.

No less remarkable were the sums raised 1194-9 for Richard's French wars realizing tens of thousands of pounds and necessitating a new land tax – the carucage – in 1194. Typically, Richard's officials, in a manner powerfully reminiscent of his father's reign, took the opportunity of the king's return to launch an extensive general investigation into what they called 'royal pleas', meaning all the king's potentially lucrative rights. Whatever else, Richard's reign saw no slackening of the grip of Angevin government. Apart from the characteristic ploy of extracting protection money from wealthy individuals, towns and the vulnerable Jewish community, those who had bought offices in 1189 were now informed that they had in fact only purchased a short lease and had to pay a further sum to retain possession. Richard understood that success in war, which revolved around sieges and scorched-earth campaigns, went to the general with the most money. Wages, food, siege engines: all were expensive. Castle-building was astronomically so: Château Gaillard, built on the Seine as an offensive bastion against the French, in two years (1196-8) cost £11,500. (The total royal expenditure on English castles for the whole reign was only £7,000.)

The question often posed is whether Richard's military enterprises bled his dominions white, leaving them vulnerable to French attack after his death. Evidence from England and Normandy for the early years of John's reign suggest that these milch cows were by no means exhausted. What differed was the willingness to shoulder the burden which was related directly to the popularity of the ruler and his success or, in John's case, lack of it. Richard's exploitation of his resources depended as much on perceptions of him as a ruler as on the bureaucratic skills of his officials. Thanks to both, Richard's rule went unchallenged despite his extravagant demands on his subjects. By 1199, almost all the

lands lost to Philip II had been recaptured, with some others added. Richard's supreme ability to harness men and materials to specific political objectives continued to pay rich dividends.

Richard died on 6 April 1199 from a crossbow wound suffered during a siege of the castle of Chalus-Chabrol, near Limoges in Aquitaine. He is one of eight post-conquest kings so far who have died violent deaths. This alone makes the event notable. But the manner of it has encapsulated much of the criticism of Richard: foolhardy in pursuit of ephemeral, capricious greed. It was later claimed that Richard believed that Chalus-Chabrol housed hidden treasure. Such claims miss the mark. His death was in keeping with his adult life but not in the way his insular critics imagine. Apart from the years of the crusade, Richard's career was largely spent in maintaining, protecting and extending his inherited lands and jurisdiction, chiefly on the continent where they were most vulnerable. For Richard, England demanded no especial attention. At Chalus he was policing a troublesome rebellion in a strategically vital part of his dominions.

However, Richard received his fatal wound because he exposed himself to enemy fire without the protection of armour. Richard's personal bravery and recklessness in battle was no small part of his reputation. It is also remarkable how many medieval commanders died because they could not bear to wear full armour in the front line (testimony to quite how uncomfortable it all was). Richard's lack of caution may have been part of his political personality. Literary convention urged enjoyment of war, well expressed by Richard's own protégé Bertrand of Born: 'once he has entered the fray let each man of high birth think of nothing but the breaking of heads and arms; for it is better to die than to be vanquished and live'. The reality may have been less gung ho. Henry II, for one, was circumspect about fighting and revolted by casualties in which Bertrand seemed to delight: 'I find no such pleasure in food, wine or sleep as … in seeing men great and small go down on the grass by the ditches; and in seeing the dead, with the pennoned stumps of lances in their sides'. Richard appears a creature inhabiting Bertrand's world. Yet he consistently refused to impose his own foolhardy heroism on his troops. Richard fought in the front line, as when he famously waded ashore at the head of a relief force to save Jaffa falling to Saladin in 1192, because that is where leaders who expected to be obeyed fought. Such behaviour was deliberate. The example was not one to follow but to inspire.

Richard's personality, as opposed to his legend, has left scant trace. Indifferent to personal safety, he was capable of calculated cruelty, as when he had executed 3,000 Muslim captives after the fall of Acre. His crusade testifies to militant piety. A man of few but decisive words, he could be eloquent when occasion demanded, as in his defence of himself at Speyer in 1193. He lacked pettiness and vindictiveness. Many of his father's loyal servants found in him a generous master. He forgave the crossbowman who fired the fatal shot at Chalus. Richard can be considered negligent in failing to produce an heir after eight years of marriage to Berengaria of Navarre, but there is little evidence to support accusations of homosexuality. These reflect misunderstandings of medieval habits, where sharing a bed, which Richard is said to have done with Philip II, was a symbol of brotherhood, of a contractual rather than erotic relationship. In any case, almost nobody suggested Richard was a homosexual until the mid-twentieth century. A maverick hermit in 1195 accused him of 'illicit acts' and reminded him of the fate of Sodom, but other observers criticized his voracious appetite for girls, even on his deathbed. Richard's one acknowledged bastard was sufficiently well-known for Shakespeare to give him the leading role in his *King John*, where Richard – complete with the thirteenth-century story of ripping out and eating the heart of a lion – is held up in heroic contrast to his shifty brother.

Richard ruled England in his own interests, as did all medieval kings. The difference was that, unlike so many of them, he did it rather well. His captivity was partly his fault. The uncertainty about his preference for Arthur or John allowed Philip II to cause trouble after his death. But while he lived he held most of his vast territories together, bequeathing his successor the most extensive inheritance in western Europe. It was hardly Richard's fault that John squandered it. His early death can be counted a blessing, as in the case of Henry V. But Richard achieved a huge amount in a brief decade. Supremely, he won the acquiescence of his subjects and the respect of his enemies. A French chronicler called his performance in captivity 'lionhearted'; a thirteenth-century Muslim observer called him the most remarkable ruler of his times.

Further Reading
J. Gillingham, *Richard the Lionheart*, 1978.

RICHARD II (1367-99), who ascended the throne in 1377, was the son of Edward the Black Prince and Joan of Kent. Few kings have been held more directly responsible for the disasters of their reigns and for their own depositions. A man of mercurial temperament, highly emotional and hot-tempered, Richard was inclined to outbursts of rage, impulsive actions, and violent quarrels with those about him. His lack of self-control helps explain his failure to establish his ascendancy over greater subjects, but it does not explain his deposition, nor does it detract from such good qualities as his loyalty to his servants and his intelligence. If Richard was indeed 'temperamentally unsuited for

kingship', it was because he departed from the accepted pattern of kingship, because of his arbitrary autocracy, and because of his inability to understand where power in England really lay.

It was unfortunate that there was no regency on Richard's accession in 1377 at nine years of age. The only credible regent was John of Gaunt, Duke of Lancaster, eldest surviving son of Edward III, but his controversial role in the crises of 1376-7 ruled him out. Richard therefore had to be allowed the attributes of an adult king, such as a personal seal (signet), whilst government was conducted *at first* on his behalf by his council, ministers and household and he himself remained in the care of his mother. No formal decision was ever made about the date when Richard would take over in person. This proved an unfortunate mistake, for Richard was precocious, assertive and impatient to exercise his own prerogatives. He was still only fourteen in 1382, when his wishes were already an important ingredient in policy and when he dismissed his chancellor for failing to implement his commands. He was still only sixteen when he told parliament that the choice of his councillors was his business alone, and still only nineteen when he refused to dismiss even a scullion from his kitchens at parliament's request! The crises of 1386 and 1388 arose from the misgovernment of a teenager, who should not have been in charge so early. They would not have happened had his authority been postponed to his formal majority in 1389. His early mistakes soured his reign, creating the mutual distrust and resentment that surfaced so dangerously in the last years. His subjects found his assertion of his kingly dignity and prerogatives difficult to stomach in a child and therefore little easier when he was grown.

Richard's exalted sense of royal dignity as a teenager continued into adult life. He consistently regarded his government, policies, choice and conduct of officers and councillors as exclusively his business. To criticize any of these was intolerable: it was not just opposition but treason. The impeachment of his chancellor in 1386 was followed in 1387 by Richard's questions to the judges, who declared the acts of opposition and parliament to be illegal and treasonable. Criticism of household finances in 1397 was also condemned as treason. Opposition could not be brooked and must be destroyed with overwhelming force, as it was in 1397, but the cards were seldom stacked so strongly in Richard's favour. When parliament rejected his objections in 1386, Richard could only prevaricate obstinately and was given an uncomfortable lesson in mixed monarchy. He should have learnt that he must co-operate with his greater subjects and must rule by consent if he wanted to retain his Crown. What he learnt, apparently, was that his subjects did not approve of autocracy. Hence his defensive preoccupation in his last years with his own personal security, which by itself was not enough to keep his throne.

To be an effective medieval king was to take on an arduous office carrying awesome responsibilities for the good of one's subjects. Richard was not a hardworking administrator and did not consistently seek the benefit of his people. Admittedly he was on occasion genuinely compassionate to his lesser subjects, but he was less conscious of his duties and responsibilities towards them than of the rights, prerogatives and personal advantages that kingship held for himself. Such defects were muted in his peaceful middle years, but from 1396 he treated his subjects' property with contempt. Not only did he take loans that he did not repay, not only did he force his subjects to buy pardons, but he compelled individuals and communities to seal so-called 'blank charters' that placed their goods and bodies at his mercy. This was rule by terror. In the last resort Richard preferred to coerce and frighten rather than cultivate support and rule by consent.

Nobody's consent and support was more important to a medieval English Crown than that of the nobility, for no king could withstand their concentrated resources. Hence their accustomed role as friends and natural councillors of kings. Richard, however, never seems to have cultivated the nobility as a class or to have appreciated the enormous resources dispersed in their provincial estates. His council did not consistently contain the greatest and most experienced magnates, even though Richard was a man of uncertain judgement and limited experience, who needed the best advice he could get. He did not like honest councillors, who told him the truth about his government, and preferred those who said what he wanted to hear and deferred to his wishes. He relied on intimates like Vere and Aumarle, who were short on power, experience and competence, but agreeable to him personally. He was the prey of flatterers, who pandered to his wishes rather than speaking out and thus secured immediate access to his patronage. If Richard's councillors were insubstantial and indeed corrupt, his distribution of favours was indefensible, because it favoured the unworthy over the deserving. Contemporaries, for example, objected to the endowment of Vere and Suffolk in preference to his uncle Gloucester and considered that his creation of five dukes in 1397 devalued the title itself. He surrounded himself with rich courtiers with grand titles without realizing that their promotion counted for little in the provinces. The *duketti* of 1397 could not rival John of Gaunt.

Just as Richard deliberately departed from contemporary expectations as a ruler, so too he shrugged off the military responsibilities of kingship. Richard's father and grandfather were both great soldiers, Richard succeeded to their titanic struggle with France, and the unsuccessful war dominated his reign, yet Richard was no soldier. He must have been trained in arms like all young aristocrats, but displayed no prowess or strategic sense. Richard led expeditions only to Ireland, where there were no serious enemies, and to Scotland, where he relied heavily on the experience and advice of others. He never led an army to France, as many thought to be his duty, and left this tougher and more important assignment to his great nobles. He was not without courage, but lacked the inclination – and perhaps the aptitude – to acquire the military competence or fulfil the military role expected of a king.

If Richard failed to conform to the normal pattern of kingship, it was because he arrogated to himself exceptional status and dignity. Probably not a carefully considered policy, it was a habit of mind that set him at odds with his subjects, whom he knew would disapprove. A mixture of injured pride, vengeance, and a desire to vindicate past conduct and assert himself in future help explain his actions in his second tyranny of 1397-9. His political and military incapacity and the unpopularity of himself and his agents explain why it all ended so disastrously. In the last resort Richard was not clever enough to make a success of the unconventional style of kingship that he chose for himself.

Further Reading

N. Saul, *Richard II*, 1997.
C. Given-Wilson, *The Royal Household and the King's Affinity: Service, Politics and Finance in England 1360-1413*, 1986.
J. A. Tuck, *Richard II and the English Nobility*, 1973.
A. Goodman, *The Loyal Conspiracy: The Lords Appellant under Richard II*, 1971.
C. Barron, 'Tyranny of Richard II', *Bulletin of the Institute of Historical Research* xli, 1968.
R. H. Jones, *The Royal Policy of Richard II: Absolutism in the Later Middle Ages*, 1968.
A. B. Steel, *Richard II*, 1941.

RICHARD III (1452-85) who ascended the throne in 1483, was the youngest son of Richard, Duke of York and his duchess, Cecily Neville. The accession of his eldest brother as King Edward IV in 1461 made him into a prince of the blood royal, but the subsequent birth of numerous nephews and nieces shunted him progressively farther down the line of succession. When he took the throne in 1483, he inaugurated what was arguably the most disastrous reign of any English king. It terminated with his defeat, death, and the destruction of the Yorkist dynasty. He has normally been accused of usurping the throne illegally and by force, of murdering his nephews, the two Princes in the Tower, of planning to marry his niece Elizabeth of York, and of reigning tyrannically. Only recently have these charges been vigorously and effectively countered. Richard, it is commonly said, was not guilty of any of these charges and certainly cannot be proved to have been at fault.

More positively, much play has been made of his loyal and devoted services to his brother Edward IV, his benevolent rule of the north before his accession and the whole country thereafter, and of his evident idealism. Richard was potentially the greatest and best of English kings. At the very least, he was more sinned against than sinning.

Richard can never have had much expectation of succeeding to the Crown before 1483. From 1461 he devoted himself instead into making a success of his role as a royal prince and the greatest of subjects. It was during these years that he supported King Edward through all the dynastic vicissitudes of 1469-71, participated in the invasion of France in 1475, implemented the royal will in northern England, and in 1480-3 commanded Edward's war effort against Scotland. King Edward can have had no fears for his loyalty. Such service was a duty. It also served Richard's purpose by advancing his political influence and in enabling him to construct for himself a formidable power-base in the north. This was based on a combination of royal favour and on the inheritance of his wife, Anne Neville, daughter of Warwick the Kingmaker. He exploited each to the full and supplemented them with judicious use of purchase, threats and force. Richard appears to have been unusually clear-sighted in what he wanted to achieve, particularly single-minded and determined in its pursuit, and utterly ruthless in its implementation. If he could be grasping and uncompromising where he possessed the advantage, he could also be flexible and conciliatory, but he did not lose sight of his ultimate ends and was prepared to wait long for his opportunity. In all this, perhaps, he was unexceptional, though the scale of his self-aggrandizement marks him out from his *immediate* contemporaries and raises the question of where his ambitions would ultimately lead. He had a good working knowledge of the law, was an able administrator, and was militarily formidable as a knight, divisional commander, and commander-in-chief. He met the great on equal terms and the gentry as lord, yet was valued by both as a just arbiter of their quarrels and inspired not merely loyalty but also devotion. At least conventionally pious, he was generous as well as grasping and prudish as well as lecherous. Personal stature and magnetism strengthened the influence of birth and landed power, making him much more than merely his brother's agent. Richard was capable of considerable political independence and his priorities were not always those of Edward. Indeed one may argue that his power, like that of the Wydevilles, was constructed by taking advantage of his brother as much as by the latter's encouragement. His power in the north was used on Edward's behalf, but need not always have been so.

That Richard was so successful as Duke of Gloucester could have been a great asset as king. He knew all those who mattered politically and yet was untainted by association with any court faction. He could share fully the interests and values of other great noblemen, until recently his equals, and could command their obedience by compelling their respect. Experience as duke had prepared him for managing royal finances, for diplomacy and warfare, for patronage and law enforcement. He could appeal to mutual ideals of nationality, loyalty, lordship, honour and Christianity. He knew how to command and to reward and could inspire by common ideals and by mutual self-interest. He continued the administrative innovations of his brother, perhaps shared in administrative and legislative reforms, and pursued a foreign policy committed to peace. Such intentions and achievements, however, play only a small part in his activities as king. He merely dabbled in them and did not complete his work, perhaps because his reign was dominated by the struggle for survival, to defeat enemies within and without, and to buy support. He was the king of a narrow faction, that became progressively more restricted as his reign persisted, and lacked the leisure or the consent to make far-reaching changes, if indeed these were ever contemplated. He could never liquidate the opposition that he had created when he became king. Historians cannot disregard this either or confine themselves to what might have been.

Richard became king on 26 June 1483 by setting aside the claims of the sons of his brother Edward IV. Richard justified himself by denying the princes their hereditary right to the Crown: their father Edward IV was a bastard, not the legitimate son of Richard, Duke of York, and he was not legally married to his queen, the prince's mother. Although serious, such charges were for the church court – not Richard – to decide. They cannot now be proved, may indeed have been false, and were actually insufficient to justify his case. Kings were kings not purely by hereditary right but by general consent. Edward V had been universally recognized as king, not least by Richard, and therefore *was* king. Subsequent aspersions on his hereditary title, however accurate, could not make him otherwise. Richard undoubtedly usurped the throne of a generally accepted king.

Richard made himself king by eliminating Earl Rivers and Lord Hastings and driving the queen and her son Dorset into refuge with the backing of a northern army. The threat of overwhelming force could not be constantly maintained and almost as soon as he was crowned he was faced by rebellion by erstwhile supporters of Edward IV and Edward V. The princes were still dangerous to him, for there were certainly many who did not believe them to be bastards and not the rightful successors of Edward IV. Like such other deposed kings as Edward II, Richard II and Henry VI, they were surely too dangerous for Richard to let live. By August 1483 it was widely rumoured that they were dead and no evidence, then or since, has been produced to the contrary. Almost certainly Richard was responsible for their destruction, which could be justified in the interests of peace and order, whether or not he believed them genuinely illegitimate. Rightly or wrongly, Richard took the blame. The proposal to marry their sister, his niece, was designed to strengthen his title and again presumes the deaths of her brothers. That it did not occur was apparently due to opposition by ecclesiastical lawyers and his northern supporters, not because Richard saw anything wrong with such an incestuous union.

Richard made himself king by the support of his northern retinue and maintained himself on his throne with their support. He was essentially a northern king. The rebels, many of them retainers of Edward IV and the Wydevilles, came overwhelmingly from southern England, where Richard had little support. After their defeat in Buckingham's Rebellion in the autumn of 1483, Richard had to replace them as landowners, local government, and coastal defence against Henry Tudor by northerners whom he transferred wholesale into the southern counties, where they were regarded, at least by some, as agents of a northern tyranny. Hence partly Richard's poor press even among immediately contemporary chroniclers. Some northerners continued to support Richard's cause even after Bosworth, but it was the desertion of others *at* Bosworth that precipitated his fall. The ambitious egotism that Richard displayed as duke and which might have served him well as a *legitimate* king was not enough once his integrity and morality were questioned. He lost the propaganda war, then and since, and lost his throne and reputation too. Unjust, perhaps, but historical fact.

Further Reading

J. Gillingham, *Richard III: a Medieval Kingship*, 1993.
M. A. Hicks, *Richard III and his Rivals*, 1991.
R. E. Horrox, *Richard III: A Study in Service*, 1989.
R. A. Griffiths and J. W. Sherborne, eds, *Kings and Nobles 1377-1529*, 1986.
P. Hammond, ed., *Richard III: Loyalty, Lordship and Law*, 1986.
C. D. Ross, *Richard III*, 1981.

RICHARD, DUKE OF YORK (1411-60) turned the crisis of the 1450s into the dynastic contest of Lancaster and York. The son of Richard, Earl of Cambridge by Anne Mortimer, he was descended from Edward III through two lines: via Cambridge's father Edmund, Duke of York (*d*.1402) and via Anne's great-grandfather Lionel, Duke of Clarence (*d*.1368). Lionel was the elder brother of John of Gaunt, ancestor of the Lancastrian kings. Cambridge was executed for treason in 1415 but his brother's death a few weeks later made his son Duke of York. When Anne's brother died in 1425, Richard became Earl of March and Ulster. Though not quite in the class of John of Gaunt, Richard's income of about £6,500 made him the richest nobleman of his age. He was particularly strong in Wales and Ireland. His marriage to a daughter of Ralph Neville, Earl of Westmorland and Joan Beaufort gave him wide family connections and proved a priceless political asset.

York was a knight of the Garter as early as 1433 and king's lieutenant in France (commander-in-chief) in 1436. His terms of reappointment in 1440 withheld only the title of regent, and he was given two counties and three vicomtés in 1444. Like his Mortimer predecessors, he became lieutenant of Ireland in 1446 and 1454. About 1445 his two sons were created earls and he benefited as much as anyone from the fall of the Duke of Gloucester. He was thus treated exceptionally favourably. But York was not satisfied to be the greatest of subjects. The regal scale of his spending outran even his income. He planned to wed his son to a French princess, dreamed of the Crown of Castile, and saw himself as heir to Henry VI in 1447-53. Supreme command was merely his due. He was unduly bitter about arrears in his salary, was insulted by the independent command of one Beaufort in 1443 and his succession in France by another in 1446, and he may even have resented the creation of new dukes. He felt he had not received his due and was being victimized. It was thus a mixture of pride, ambition, and paranoia that prompted him, like Gloucester earlier, to insist that government required his approval.

Yet York was not outstandingly able. Extravagance forced disagreeable expedients on him which, characteristically, he blamed on the government. In France he delegated military operations to others and barring some minor reforms appears inactive. There and in Ireland the support he won may stem partly from misapplication of royal patronage, as he was charged in 1446. Certainly his protectorates won him new partisans. Ten years spent continually abroad preceded his identification in 1450 as the remedy for evil rule, an image he assiduously fostered. He posed as a reformer and presented Somerset as an obstacle to be removed by any means. He would not accept even the king's veto. Most lords initially supported neither duke and gave priority to their loyalty to the king. They thwarted York's coup in 1452, but by preventing his punishment enabled him, more ruthlessly, to eliminate his foes in 1455. Because King Henry could not curb him, York repeated his protests, obstruction, and coups and made effective government impossible. Once acceptable to all, York evolved into a factional leader, forcing a choice first between himself and royal favourites, and then in 1460 between himself and the king, repudiating his allegiance and claiming the Crown by hereditary right. His recognition instead as Henry's heir solved nothing, but precipitated the Wars of the Roses and his own death at the battle of Wakefield in the last day of 1460.

Further Reading
M. K. Jones, 'Somerset, York and the Wars of the Roses', *English Historical Review* civ, 1989.
P. A. Johnson, *Duke Richard of York 1411-60*, 1988.
T. B. Pugh, 'Richard Plantagenet (1411-60), Duke of York, as the King's Lieutenant in France and Ireland' in *Aspects of Late Medieval Government and Society*, J. G. Rowe, ed., 1986.
R. L. Storey, *The End of the House of Lancaster*, 2nd edn, 1986.
J. M. W. Bean, 'The Financial Position of Richard, Duke of York' in *War and Government in the Middle Ages*, J. Gillingham and J. C. Holt, eds, 1984.
R. A. Griffiths, *The Reign of King Henry VI 1422-61*, 1981.

RICHARD, EARL OF ARUNDEL and SURREY

(1346-97) was one of the Lords Appellant of 1388 and was executed in 1397 in Richard II's revenge. Yet the career of his father and namesake had been characterized by distinguished military service, which the son wished to emulate. He served in the royal household in 1368; in France in 1369 and 1380; at sea in 1371, 1377-8, when he took Cherbourg, in 1383, and in 1387, when he won a major victory off Margate; in Scotland in 1385; on the councils of Edward III and Richard II from 1376; on a commission to reform the royal household in 1380; and as one of two trusted councillors about the king in 1381. As councillor and commander he was well-placed to criticize the government's management of the war in France in the 1380s and his actions as Lord Appellant were probably intended to ensure its more effective prosecution. Certainly he did not act to enrich himself or from disloyalty, but used the temporary predominance of the Lords Appellant to command a successful naval raid on the Isle of Oleron, to become captain of Brest, and to secure his reappointment as admiral for a further five years.

King Richard's majority in 1389, however, ended all that. Arundel was supplanted as admiral and received no further commands. A man of action forced into inactivity, hot-tempered and tactless, honest to a fault and lacking in finesse, he was ill-suited for political survival under a hostile king anxious to humiliate him: his unlicensed second marriage resulted in a heavy fine; his charges against Gaunt in parliament in 1394 were dangerously near to the truth, but resulted only in an enforced public apology; probably innocent of involvement in the Cheshire revolt, he was blamed nevertheless; and his disrespect at Queen Anne's funeral, if such it was, resulted in a blow from the king, imprisonment, and binding over to keep the peace on massive sureties – surely a disproportionate punishment for such an offence. Understandably, perhaps, 'Of the former appellants, only Arundel maintained his old attitudes of defiance and suspicion', fuelled Richard's hostility, and thus led directly to his own trial and execution.

Arundel has received a bad press from historians. They have disparaged his weapons and martial pursuits as an obsession with violence and his involvement in the political murders of 1388 as an extension of it. 'Opposition was in his blood' (Steel). Yet it was not. Up to 1387 he was 'devotedly loyal' and his opposition thereafter was compatible with his allegiance and can indeed be seen as public spirited. His criticism of government in 1384, of Gaunt in 1394, and his actions in 1388 all aimed at more effective use of royal resources for prosecution of the war. They were constructive, not destructive. Historians have generally accepted the deficiencies of the government of the 1380s and hence, by implication, that the Lords Appellant were justified in their actions.

Arundel was not merely a soldier and politician. He was certainly literate. He was genuinely affectionate to his brother the archbishop, to his second wife Philippa, Dowager-Countess of Pembroke, after whom he renamed Shrawardine Castle as Castle Philip, and was committed to the advancement by marriage of his children. His father, who did not die until 1376, intended to establish a hospital at Arundel, a project that Arundel fulfilled and indeed expanded, setting up and endowing Holy Trinity College there. His piety emerges also in other benefactions, his will, and his proposed trips abroad on pilgrimage or crusade in 1383 and 1389 that were overtaken by events. To accept him as 'a typical product of late fourteenth-century chivalry' (McKisack) does not make him unintelligent, inhuman or narrow-minded.

Further Reading
A. Tuck, *Richard II and the English Nobility*, 1973.
A. Goodman, *The Loyal Conspiracy: The Lords Appellant under Richard II*, 1971.
M. McKisack, *The Fourteenth Century*, 1959.

RICHARD, EARL OF CORNWALL

(1209-72; King of the Romans 1257-72) was the second son of King John and younger brother of Henry III. His career exemplifies the ambition and reality of Angevin rule in the mid-thirteenth century. Claimant to the county of Poitou (1225), the duchy of Gascony (1242-3) and the Holy Roman Empire (1257-72), and repeatedly refusing to accept the papally-proffered title of King of Sicily, by contrast Richard's material power rested on his estates in the Thames valley and East Anglia, his earldom of Cornwall, his control of the Cornish tin mining industry and his position in the English baronage and court. Angevin dreams remained international: Richard himself was an active crusader. Angevin authority, however, rested on control of England. Richard's failure to give substance to his foreign aspirations underlined this withdrawal to insular, national preoccupations. Few individuals more neatly illustrate how the rulers of England, in spite of themselves, became English monarchs. Richard of Cornwall even notoriously spoke good English.

Richard was a tremendous swell, a lover of ceremonies, titles, pomp, luxury, pretty women and fine clothes: even in prison he insisted on wearing scarlet robes. But he lacked one essential element to complete the perfect image of what he spent his life being, a king-in-waiting. A puny child, Richard's poor physique denied him a proper training in arms. For all his pride and tenacity in defending or asserting his rights, Richard was a talker, not a fighter. Never was this better displayed than on his crusade of 1240-1. No battles were fought, still less victories achieved. The treaty Richard negotiated with the sultan of Cairo was less realistic than that signed the year before with the sultan of Damascus by the Count of Champagne. Yet Richard's reputation soared at what contemporaries saw as his success, hardly surprising as he handled his own publicity. The story of his triumphs depended on his own newsletter and carefully targeted reminiscences with well-placed chroniclers, such as Matthew Paris. The whole exercise was a masterpiece of self-promotion. There was another, equally characteristic side to Richard's crusade. He secured the release of French prisoners and the burial of Christian soldiers killed in a rout at Gaza in 1239. Gestures and diplomacy, rather than blood and iron, won for Richard the admiration of western chivalry, and more. At a very tricky moment at Taillebourg in 1242, Richard managed by negotiation to extricate his brother from an untenable military position because the French were grateful at his having secured the release of their compatriots the year before.

From 1215 until 1223, Richard was educated at Corfe Castle by an obscure royalist backwoodsman, Roger d'Acastre, under the aegis of the influential Poitevin Peter de Mauley. Roger may not have been the ideal gentleman scholar to act as Richard's tutor. Much of the tuition may have been unfashionably in English and Richard never developed an interest in any of the arts, apart from the sartorial, either directly or as a patron. His concern in the construction of his religious foundations, notably at Hailes in Gloucestershire, did not stretch beyond the financial and pious. The contrast with his brother Henry, the refined mastermind of Westminster Abbey, is plain. What Richard's education does seem to have provided – or at least not impeded – was an excellent head for finance and business acumen, what would now be called management skills, i.e. the ability to deal with people, to strike bargains, to achieve through negotiation and personal contact simultaneous public consensus and private advantage.

The position of the king's brother was rarely enviable. Although in the 150 years before Henry III's accession, two out of seven kings had succeeded brothers, the awkward, hand-to-mouth experiences of Henry I or John before ascending the throne were less than encouraging precedents. For more than twenty years, until 1239,

Richard was the heir presumptive during which time his relations with the king were often strained. Ironically, after the birth of the future Edward I, Richard's position at court was increasingly important, his influence more consistent and significant. Before 1239, Richard could be seen by some as a potential leader of disaffected barons and, on more than one occasion, acted as such, in 1233 and 1238, for example. Thereafter, his role was that of a mediator in crises whose loyalties were hardly in doubt. Oddly, and perhaps typical of Henry III, the barometer of Richard's loyalty was the grants he received rather than the services he performed. His loyalty was purchased at a high price, which, however, for the king was worth it.

Richard's public career began in 1225 when he was knighted and sent as figurehead of a successful campaign to secure continued Angevin overlordship, if not much practical control, over Gascony. In 1225, Richard was granted Cornwall, a traditional holding for cadets of the royal line since the Conquest: William I's brother Robert of Mortain; Reginald, bastard son of Henry I; and King John in the 1190s all held Cornwall. Although created Earl of Cornwall in 1227, Richard only received his lands in fee (i.e. with tenure rather than at the king's pleasure) on his marriage in 1231. His first marriage points to Richard's disaffection with his brother, whom he did not consult. Isabel Marshal (d.1240) was the sister of the leader of baronial opposition to the régime of Hubert de Burgh. Richard spent the next decade running with the foxes of magnate discontent opposition and hunting with the hounds of royal favourites. On three occasions, 1227, 1233 and 1238, he challenged his brother, only to be bought off with lavish grants. As Richard's biographer, Denholm-Young put it, 'Richard never quarrelled with Henry without coming away a richer man'.

The years around 1240 were pivotal in Richard's career. The death of his first wife in 1240 loosened ties with the traditional opponents to royal authority, while his crusade won him an international fame and cosmopolitan contacts, a position reinforced by his friendship with the emperor, Frederick II, and his second marriage to Sanchia of Provence (d.1262), sister to Henry III's wife Eleanor. He was provided with an income granted by the pope, from the money paid by those who had taken the Cross but had redeemed their vows for cash rather than actually going on crusade. In England, Richard's importance was increasing. Politically, his contacts with the higher nobility and his proximity and influence over the king made him a ubiquitous arbiter of potentially damaging disputes between nobles and with the Crown. In this capacity Richard acted between Simon de Montfort and Gilbert Marshal, both his brothers-in-law, and the king in 1239; in 1244 he negotiated a treaty with Scotland and sat on the committee to investigate baronial grievances against the Crown in 1244; in the 1250s he acted as ambassador to France and settled disputes between Londoners and Westminster Abbey. In 1252, he determined the amount of Simon de Montfort's expenses when lieutenant in Gascony; in 1260 he mediated between the Earl of Gloucester and the Lord Edward and the king; and in 1267 and 1270 he handed down awards to resolve the grievances of the new Earl of Gloucester, especially with the Lord Edward. As a troubleshooter, Richard clearly set great store by his ability. What evidence we have, for example on the 1270 award, suggests that others did not share his self-esteem, Earl Gilbert forcefully exposing Richard's award as one-sided and short-sighted. Given the repeated difficulties faced by the court during Henry's reign, Richard's political and legal skills may have been exaggerated, but at least they appeared better than Henry's.

Richard was almost a sort of vice-king. He fought for his brother in Brittany in 1230; in Poitou in 1242-3 and against the barons in 1263-4. He was regent in 1253-4, 1264 and, de facto, 1270-2. At other times, in the words of the royalist chronicler Thomas Wykes, 'on his nod hung all the business of the realm'. Richard had little consistent political philosophy, unlike his verbose brother who was forever lauding the power of kingship. Some saw Richard as a trickster, a man who would do anything for the right price. In March 1246, he was strongly opposed to papal demands on the English church. By July he had completely changed his mind, adopting a pro-papal stance. Between these dates he had received the papal grant of crusade vow redemptions. Nonetheless, Richard's influence lent an element of cohesion to English politics and it is perhaps significant that the two major disasters for Henry III's régime, the Sicilian Business and the Provisions of Oxford, did not involve Richard, the first because he opposed the scheme from the start; the latter because he was out of the country. His reaction to the papal invitation to conquer Sicily suggests a man of realism: 'You might as well say: I will sell or give you the moon; go up and take it'.

What set Richard apart from other magnates, besides his birth, was his great wealth and the financial role which that allowed him to play. In addition to his very extensive estates centred on Cornwall, Wallingford, Berkhampstead and Eye, he enjoyed the monopoly on Cornish tin (the Stannaries) which alone brought in between 1,000 and 3,000 marks a year, the cash redemption of crusade vows and tallages from the Jews. Such were his resources that he was able to retain many of his noble followers on crusade. Between 1240 and 1271, he lent the Crown just under £40,000. In 1256-7, he spent 28,000 marks buying the votes of three German electors. Most spectacularly, in 1247, he undertook the farm of the royal Mint for twelve years, during which time coinage worth £1 million was produced, and organized the first complete recoinage since 1180. For a capital outlay of 10,000 marks, Richard made profits of perhaps £20,000. The recoinage was perhaps Richard's most constructive act in government. At times, it appeared that Richard's finances and those of the state were synonymous, recognized in 1271 when his own treasurer, Philip of Eye, became the king's Treasurer.

This Croesus had political ambitions. He wanted to become a king. So, in keeping with the grandeur of his brother's foreign policy, in 1257 Richard bought himself one, the Crown of Germany. For a few years it seemed possible that he would be able to persuade the pope to crown him emperor as well. In the event, although crowned King of the Romans (i.e. emperor-designate) at Aachen in May 1257, he was never more than King of the Rhineland and even that was largely honorific, his four brief visits (1257-9; 1260; 1262-3; 1268-9) having more ceremonial than political significance. It was through his German connections that in 1269 he married his third wife, Beatrice of Falkenburg (d.1277), like the other two a noted beauty.

After 1260, Richard saw that his imperial longings were as chimeric as his brother's Sicilian hopes had been. During the baronial wars of the 1260s, Richard, although again acting as mediator in trying to increase magnate support for the royalists, was a consistent advocate of his brother's cause. By 1264, he pushed for a military solution, although himself no warrior. After the surprise defeat of the royalists at Lewes, he was captured in a nearby windmill attempting to make good his escape. From May 1264 until September 1265 he was held in comfortable captivity. Thereafter, while profiting from grants of land from the disinherited rebels, he worked for compromise, but power had shifted to the next generation, to the Lord Edward and Richard's own son Henry, surnamed 'of Almain' in deference to his father's German Crown. Only when Edward and Henry departed on crusade in 1270, did Richard again emerge as a leading political figure, his brother by then having slid into the shadows of senility. Ironically, Richard predeceased his brother, dying in April 1272 four months after a debilitating stroke. His passing, followed in November by Henry III, marks an epoch in English political history. They were the last of the Angevins, whose ambitions were neither predominantly English nor British.

Further Reading
N. Denholm-Young, *Richard of Cornwall*, 1947.

RICHARD OF CLARE (*d.*1176), nicknamed by some contemporaries 'Strongbow' (a play on one of his titles, Lord of Striguil), was the most prominent of the Anglo-Norman lords who began to colonize Ireland in the reign of Henry II. The son of Gilbert, Earl of Pembroke, he inherited his father's estates in south Wales in 1148. His loyalty to King Stephen cost him his earldom on Henry II's accession. In consequence, as Gerald of Wales commented, 'his pedigree was longer than his purse'. In common with many disinherited noblemen, Richard was open to any proposal likely to restore his fortune. Ireland offered just such an opportunity.

As with England in the 1060s and Scotland in the 1090s, internal Irish political tensions attracted foreign intervention. There had been ecclesiastical pressure on Henry II to consider extending his overlordship to Ireland since the 1150s, but it was only on the invitation of Dermot, King of Leinster, that intervention began. In 1167, Henry II gave Dermot permission to recruit supporters to help him win back control of Dublin from the King of Connaught. A few Marcher lords, led by Robert FitzStephen and Maurice FitzGerald landed at Wexford in 1169. Richard of Clare joined them in August 1170 having reached a very favourable deal with Dermot: Richard was to marry Dermot's daughter and in due course inherit his kingdom.

The Anglo-Normans were immediately effective, using military techniques new to Ireland, such as the motte-and-bailey castle, and mounted knights operating in conjunction with archers and infantry. In September 1170, Dublin was taken and by the time Dermot died in 1171, his power over Leinster had been restored. Richard of Clare now asserted his claim to Leinster. This not only ran counter to Irish law but also aroused the suspicion of Henry II, anxious lest any vassal of his dare establish himself as a ruler independent of his authority. In the autumn of 1171, therefore, Richard was faced by a siege of Dublin by Rory O'Connor, King of Connaught; withdrawal of royal aid from England; and the imminent arrival of Henry himself armed to conquer all, including Richard, who stood against him. Richard defeated King Rory, but had to obey Henry. Paying homage for his Irish lands, Richard was confirmed in control of Leinster, but only received the key towns of Waterford, Wexford and Dublin in 1174. From 1173 to 1176, he seemed to have acted as Henry's viceroy in Ireland, a position he adopted from Henry's initial agent, Hugh de Lacy who was established as Lord of Meath. However, if Henry had hoped that by formally imposing his lordship on Irish and Anglo-Normans alike (Rory O'Connor submitted in 1175) he had solved the problem of his authority in Ireland, he was wrong. But the violence and instability in Ireland, which had attracted Richard of Clare in the first place, cannot be seen in nationalist terms. The Irish kings fought each other; they fought the Anglo-Normans; they allied with the Anglo-Normans against Irish rivals. It is true that beneath this carapace of feuding and flouted legality, Anglo-Norman settlement began, especially in the east, adding yet another fault-line along which Irish society could tear

and break. But it must be remembered, when any facile condemnations about English involvement in Ireland are trotted out, that opportunists like Richard of Clare had been given their chance and their stake in Ireland by indigenous Irish leaders. Henry II reluctantly became involved only when Richard of Clare's success seemed to threaten his interests elsewhere.

RICHARD OF DOVER (*d.*1184: Archbishop of Canterbury 1173-84) was the unlikely choice as Becket's successor. A previously obscure mediocrity, he nevertheless demonstrated, to the anger of the Becketeers, that effective co-operation with the king was possible. Although not glamorous, Richard's credentials were appropriate. He had been a monk at Canterbury and, unusual in a household dominated by secular clerks, one of Archbishop Theobald's chaplains before being promoted as Prior of St Martin's, Dover in 1157. His suitability for the primacy seems to have become apparent on a visit he made to Henry II in 1173 as part of a delegation to discuss the election of a new archbishop. While the form of a free election was preserved, as, in the circumstances of the king's submission to the pope earlier in the year at Avranches, was essential, it represented a deal struck between Henry, his justiciar, Richard de Lucy, and the prior of the Canterbury monks, Odo. Such outward compliance with canonical precept and practical compromise with secular authority set the tone for Richard's tenure of Canterbury. The contrast in style and concerns between Richard and his predecessor could hardly have been greater. Richard was interested in the reform of the clergy. A canonist of some enthusiasm, he collected papal decretals for circulation in England and acted as a papal judge-delegate. But he was also a royalist. In 1173-4, he went along with the appeal against his election by the Young King Henry because he knew that he had the Old King and the bishops on his side: this appeal to Rome looked good but was wholly ineffectual. He consistently defended the king's role in episcopal elections (to the irritation of Pope Alexander III); he allowed the king to sit in on his judgements as papal delegate; he approved of the use of bishops as royal justices; he argued for the trials of murderers of clerics to be held in secular courts; and he specifically repudiated Becket's hostility to what he had called double punishment in cases where clerks were tried by secular as well as ecclesiastical courts. In a letter of 1176, Richard put forward the view that if one court 'supplements the other's insufficiency, that is not a double punishment but a combined punishment'. Such opinions provoked accusations that he lost for the church every point for which Becket had fought. But it was Richard's policies, not Becket's, which charted the relationship between the English church and state for the rest of the Middle Ages.

Further Reading
H. Mayr-Harting, 'Henry II and the Papacy', *Journal of Ecclesiastical History*, 1965.

RICHARD OF FOUNTAINS (*d.*1139), the first abbot of the great Cistercian Abbey of Fountains in Yorkshire, presents a revealing example of how the new wave of spirituality associated with the Order of Cîteaux became established; how it differed from existing practices; and how, equally, it grew from traditional monasticism. Richard was Prior of St Mary's, York, a wealthy Benedictine house, under an aged, easy-going abbot, Geoffrey. In 1132, with the help of his friend the ascetic Archbishop Thurstan, patron of hermits and sponsor of the first Cistercian house in the north at Rievaulx, Richard led a schism, not unlike that from Molesme to Cîteaux in 1098. With the example of the white monks recently settled at Rievaulx, and the encouragement of Bernard of Clairvaux, Richard and a few of his fellow monks established a new monastery in Skeldale on land given them by Thurstan. Soon known as Fountains Abbey, this became the leading Cistercian house in Yorkshire and exerted a profound influence throughout the northern province. Richard's departure from St Mary's was caused by his impatience at the failure there to follow the pristine Rule of St Benedict, in particular over time for prayer, study and work; silence; and diet. He sought a more eremitic existence. Initially he had hoped to find it in reforming St Mary's. Only when this was rejected did the archbishop effectively allow him to break his vow of obedience in order to follow a new vocation. Yet in spite of the inter-order polemic that characterized much of the monastic debate in the twelfth century, relations and exchange between Benedictines and Cistercians continued close and frequent, in both directions. It was the logic of institutional inertia; the ties of custom; the responsibilities of possessions; and the wishes of the majority that prevented reform within established houses as much as any burning radical desire by reformers to secede. Richard and his abbey quickly found that they too became part of a not entirely other-worldly organization. Richard himself died not in Skeldale, but in Rome in 1139 on Archbishop Thurstan's business. His career suggests that the Cistercian *démarche* was far less a rejection of traditional forms of regular religious life than either the hermit movement of the twelfth century or the friars in the thirteenth.

RICHARDSON, SAMUEL (1689-1761), novelist, has recently been revived in critical opinion; his important place in the development of his craft has always been beyond dispute. He was influential and respected in his day, in France and Germany as well as at home, but his personal life was insignificant; there are few details worth recording. He was the son of a carpenter who seems to have hoped that his son would enter the church; but there was little money for his schooling, which was haphazard. Christ's Hospital and Charterhouse claim him, but there is no proof that he went to either school. He became a stationer's apprentice in 1716, set up as a printer in 1719, married in 1721. He prospered in business, becoming for a time printer to the House of Commons, but his private life brought the agony of successive bereavements. Of six children to his first marriage, five died in infancy. His wife died in 1730, but he married again in the following year: more deaths ensued. It was common enough in his day, but the effect upon a sensitive heart may be guessed. Critics who have commented on the obsession of Richardson with sex, the suggestiveness and even sadism of the protracted affairs described in his novels, have neglected this side of his life. In 1739 he took the lease of a pleasant house at Hammersmith; his books were not written under the pressure of financial need.

In November 1740, the first volumes of *Pamela* appeared and were an instant success. Richardson had been asked to compile some 'letters written on such subjects as might be of use to those country readers who were unable to indite for themselves'. One subject of these letters was the dangers that beset a young woman who was engaged as a family servant, especially if she were pretty. This was the genesis of *Pamela, or Virtue Rewarded*, a record, eventually in four volumes, in letters and then in journal form, of the resistance of the virtuous servant to the seductive advances of Mr B. – and her subsequent happy marriage. Richardson seems to have written without difficulty; he said himself that he 'almost slid into the writing of *Pamela*' and the novel took him only three months to write. The heroine, it has been said, is 'precisely the sort to appeal to the bourgeoisie, then and now'. Prudence, artfulness, a hypocritical strain in her seeming innocence, may account for the interest she aroused, both in her readers and in her lover, who described her as 'an artful young baggage', more than the sentimental principles of virtue which the author sought to cultivate 'in the minds of the youth of both sexes'. Readers have variously found *Pamela* tedious, repulsive or gripping. Doctor Johnson declared: 'If you were to read Richardson for the story, your impatience would be so much fretted that you would hang yourself. But you must read him for the sentiment, and consider the story as only giving occasion to the sentiment.' He also pronounced Richardson to be 'the greatest genius that had shed its lustre upon this path of literature'. This may seem an exaggerated verdict, but *Pamela* did point towards a fruitful development in fiction, towards the novel of analysis of feeling. To this, for all his vulgarity and cynicism, he brought an almost feminine intuition and a gift for colloquial speech that makes his characters of the middle and servant class live in their own right.

Clarissa Harlow, which followed in 1747 and 1748, had many of the faults of its predecessor, amongst them its inordinate length. The picture by Leech of a page boy staggering under the weight of its eight volumes (in the first edition there were seven) may be for some readers a suitable comment on a pretentious work. Again his purpose was ostensibly moral: to show that a reformed rake does not necessarily make the best husband. In a time when arranged marriages were common, the refusal of Clarissa to accept her parents' choice of husband touched upon a live issue. She was tricked into putting herself under the protection of Lovelace, a more complex villain that Mr B., but designed primarily to bring out the essential nobility of the heroine. After piling on the agony of her deception and humiliation, Richardson achieves the difficult feat of presenting her death as a relief and a sort of triumph. *Sir Charles Grandison* is supposed to have been Jane Austen's favourite among the novels which influenced her own art. But because Richardson is unable to infuse the same life into an upper-class hero as into a woman of his own class, the novel is hampered from the start. Sir Charles, impeccable in his own disinterested conduct, amounts to an embodiment of eighteenth-century notions of virtue, but feeling is little roused because there is no vital conflict in the book. So the reader has to content himself with the social portraiture and a pleasing delicacy of style, with a tendency towards epigram, which go far to explain Jane Austen's preference.

On the publication of *Pamela*, Richardson became a figure of consequence, at least as large in his own ideas as in those of his admirers. Fashionable ladies made a point of being seen with the book; it was recommended from the pulpit and paid the compliment of satires, the most notable being *Joseph Andrews*. In France, where he was fortunate in his translator, Prévôst, he was received with rapture. Diderot was unrestrained in his eulogy: 'You shall remain on the same shelf as Moses, Euripides and Sophocles and I shall read you by turns'. De Laclos, the author of *Les Liaisons Dangereuses*, acknowledged his debt; more important for the world was the reaction of the young Rousseau, whose *Nouvelle Heloise* was suggested by *Clarissa*. The same appeal of Richardson to those who were beginning to swim in the currents of Romanticism can be seen in his popularity in Germany, where the market was soon full of imitations. It is disappointing to turn from the almost prophetic status of the work, largely dependent though it was upon the contemporary fashion in literature, to the personality of the man. Easily flattered himself, he was absurdly sensitive to criticism. He himself criticized the works of Fielding in a way which showed as much jealousy as lack of comprehension of that virile talent. He told Fielding's sister

that he was concerned for his continued lowness! He continued, however, to edify his admirers with his letters and reflections, in which moral issues loomed large. In his last years he was increasingly subject to nervous disorders and insomnia. In July 1761 he died of a paralytic stroke.

Further Reading
T. C. D. Evans and B. D. Kimpel, *Samuel Richardson*, 1971.
John Carroll, ed., *Selected Letters of Samuel Richardson*, 1964.

RIDLEY, NICHOLAS (*c*.1503-55), Bishop of London, martyr, was born at Willimotiswick Castle, South Tynedale, in Northumberland, in about 1503; he died on 16 October 1555. He was the second son of Christopher Ridley of Unthank Hall, Northumberland, and Ann Blenkinsop, having one brother, Hugh, and two sisters, Elizabeth and Alice. He was educated at Newcastle, but not at the Grammar School, which was not founded until 1525. He then went to Pembroke Hall, Cambridge. His uncle, Dr Robert Ridley, was a Cambridge man, being a fine scholar who collaborated with Polydore Vergil and who taught Greek in the university, and he offered to pay Nicholas's expenses. Nicholas repaid his uncle's generosity by soon becoming an outstanding scholar in both Latin and Greek. He took his BA in 1522 and then turned to study Philosophy and Divinity. He was ordained probably early in 1524 and was offered a fellowship at Oxford which he declined. In that year he was made a Fellow of Pembroke Hall and the next year (1525) he took his MA.

Ridley was said to be a man of small stature, handsome, well built and clean-shaven. He was not a political priest like Wolsey or Gardiner, nor a saintly reformer like Bilney and Latimer: he was a scholar, an intellectual, living among books and disputations and preferring an academic life to any other. It was probably during this period that Ridley met and made friends with Cranmer. From 1527 to 1530 Ridley was abroad studying (again at his uncle's expense) at the Sorbonne in Paris (1527) and at Louvain for some six months in 1529. He was back in Cambridge in 1530.

In 1532 he was made Chaplain to the University, a post which he held for four years together with that of Senior Proctor for part of the time. He resigned probably in 1537 when, having taken his BD, he became private chaplain to Cranmer and left Cambridge to live at Cranmer's manor of Ford in Kent. It was almost certainly during this last period at Cambridge that Ridley changed from an orthodox Catholic into a Protestant. When in 1538 Cranmer presented him with the living of Herne, close to Ford, Ridley still believed in Transubstantiation and probably thought that auricular confession was beneficial and to be encouraged, but not essential to salvation, because he could find no scriptural authority for it.

The passing of the Act of the Six Articles changed the whole situation (1539). This was a conservative measure which put the brake on the trend towards Protestantism. The fall of Thomas Cromwell made the position of the Protestants extremely dangerous. Ridley was by that time the most able debater among the Protestants, even including Cranmer. In 1540 he was elected Master of Pembroke Hall, Cambridge, but he did not reside in the university, because he was helping Cranmer to bring about gradually the Protestant Reformation and this was not a moment when he could leave the archbishop. Cranmer now appointed him to one of the prebendal stalls at Canterbury, but Ridley found life there far from pleasant, owing to the incessant quarrels between the Catholic and Protestant clergy, not only over religious matters, such as church services in English, but over petty questions such as the boundary between his garden and Dean Wotton's.

It was while he was at Herne that Ridley came to his decision on the question of Transubstantiation. He had certainly made up his mind by the end of 1546, although he made no public declaration until December 1548. When the Lutherans and the Zwinglians renewed their controversy in 1544, Ridley sat down to examine the whole question. He read Bertram of Corbie's treatise, which had been written in 840 for the emperor, Charles the Bald, and which was published in 1532. That led him to examine the writings of the early Fathers. As a result he came to the conclusion that no change took place in the inward nature of the bread and wine after the prayer of consecration and that the flesh and blood of Christ were not corporeally present in the bread and wine: but he never denied the spiritual presence of Christ in the bread and wine. Ridley was now a heretic.

In October 1545 Ridley was made the Eighth Prebendary in the cathedral church at Westminster. On 4 September 1547 he was designated Bishop of Rochester and he was consecrated at St Paul's on the 25th. He had also just been given the living of Soham in Cambridgeshire. When he became a bishop, he was allowed to retain all his preferments and to hold them in commendam. He was also chaplain to Edward VI.

From now onwards throughout the reign of the Protestant Edward VI Ridley was engaged with Cranmer in carrying through the English Reformation. The first problem which confronted them was that of images. The more extreme Protestants in London took the law into their own hands and removed the images in St Martin's Church in Ironmonger Lane. Cranmer decided to support this action. On Ash Wednesday, 23 February 1547, in a sermon preached before Edward VI Ridley dealt with the question. The line he took was that as far as he could see it was wrong for images to be displayed in the churches, but he was open to be persuaded that he was wrong in his opinion. He made a cautious and tentative suggestion that both images and holy water should be dispensed with.

The question of the Mass was a far more important and difficult matter and at this moment Cranmer and Ridley had no intention of allowing any attacks to be made on it. The success which the extremists had won over images led them to think they would be as successful, if they tried to force the government's hand, over the Mass, which they now openly denounced as idolatry. In December 1547 Ridley preached at St Paul's Cross and hotly attacked the fanatics. He did not indicate at all what was his own belief about the Real Presence, so that everybody assumed that he believed in it. Ridley was to be reminded of this sermon in 1554/5, when he was in prison and being tried for his life.

In November 1548 Cranmer produced the first draft of his Book of Common Prayer. There is no evidence that Ridley had any direct hand in the drafting, but it is reasonable to suppose that he was much consulted by Cranmer in its composition. It was clear that the Prayer Book struck at the very roots of Transubstantiation and therefore Cranmer and Ridley now came out into the open. A disputation was arranged in the House of Lords for 17 December and it lasted three days. Ridley was said to be at his very best and to have confounded the arguments of Heath and Day. It was just about this time that Ridley also spoke in favour of a bill to allow the clergy to marry.

During March and April 1549 Ridley was mostly in his diocese at Rochester, ensuring that the Book of Common Prayer was being accepted by everybody, but this work was interrupted by his being called on to deal with the ravings of Joan Bocher. He had been put on the Commission of Visitors who were to ensure that the new religious policy was universally enforced in Cambridge. The Visitors arrived in Cambridge in May. Ridley found himself involved in a dispute over a proposal to suppress Clare Hall. Ridley firmly stood out against Protector Somerset, and Clare Hall was saved. In June he presided over three disputations between Catholics and Protestants on the subject of the Mass. This was an academic exercise in the Philosophy Schools involving no political action afterwards. At the end Ridley summed up and decided against the doctrine of Transubstantiation: even the Catholics admitted that his speech was a wonderful performance.

Bonner was deprived of his bishopric in October 1549; in the following February Ridley was appointed to the see of London, but he was not installed until 12 April when he himself was not there and he was installed by proxy. Ridley behaved with notable kindness to Bonner's family, allowing Bonner's mother and sister to reside in his palace at Fulham and frequently inviting them to dine with him, and treating Mistress Bonner with the utmost respect; he would seat her at the head of the table and would not allow her to move lower down, even when a member of the Council was at dinner.

London was a difficult see to administer, for it was the centre of the extreme Protestants and Anabaptists. Ridley was always a strict disciplinarian and he was determined to crush the extremists, and at the same time to see to it that the Reformation was enforced throughout his diocese.

The first problem he tackled was that of the altar – was there to be an altar for the communion service or a communion table? If a table, where was it to stand, at the east end or in the body of the church? Ridley had already in 1549 removed the altar in Rochester Cathedral and substituted for it a movable table which he placed for the time being in the position which the altar had occupied. In May 1550 he made a visitation of his new diocese of London which lasted for seven weeks. At the end of it not a single altar remained. During the visitation Ridley interviewed every vicar and curate in his diocese and insisted on each of them making a written submission to his Injunctions.

The second problem was that of vestments. John Hooper was about to be consecrated Bishop of Gloucester, but he refused to wear vestments. At that moment the wearing of vestments was prescribed by law, therefore Ridley strongly opposed Hooper and also the Council, which was inclined to give way. Ridley's line was that he himself did not care much for vestments, but he did not regard them as being of spiritual importance. On the other hand, the law said they must be worn and the law must be upheld. Hooper became defiant and unreasonable and at last he was put in the Fleet. A royal pardon was granted to Cranmer and Ridley if they consecrated Hooper without vestments. Ridley still stuck out, because he saw in Hooper's obstinate opposition a desire to place individual judgement above ecclesiastical authority; that could only create chaos, that sort of anarchy which was characteristic of the Anabaptists. In the end Ridley carried his point and Hooper was consecrated wearing vestments.

Meanwhile Ridley was employed in various ways: he was frequently examining and disputing with Gardiner, the deprived Bishop of Winchester who was in prison: he was a member of a commission which was sent to inquire into scandals at Eton College (1552): he met John à Lasco to discuss how best to solve the difficulties raised by the church services of the foreign Protestant exiles in London: he paid a visit to the Princess Mary and tried to persuade her to hear him preach, but he failed entirely (1552). In 1553 he preached before Edward VI a sermon on the poverty of the London poor, a sermon which did a great deal to move the king to reopen St Thomas's Hospital, which had been suppressed for its wealth by Henry VIII, to found St Bartholomew's and to grant the revenues of the Savoy to St Thomas's.

The death of Edward VI and the accession of the Catholic Mary left Ridley in a perilous position. He had signed the will of Edward VI by which the succession to the throne was altered so as to cut out Mary and bring in Lady Jane Dudley as queen. On 16 July, not the 9th, Ridley preached at St Paul's Cross to a crowd which was whole-heartedly in favour of Mary. Ridley attacked Mary resolutely and called both her and Elizabeth bastards, an attack which Mary never forgot nor forgave. Northumberland's plot failed; Ridley went towards Framlingham to try to make his peace with the queen, but she had him arrested before he got there and sent him to London to the Tower. He was deprived of his bishopric, and Bonner was reinstated. Wyatt's rebellion made things still more difficult for the Protestant prisoners, but what Mary wanted was for the Protestant leaders to make a public recantation. In 1554 Ridley, Latimer and Cranmer were sent to Oxford for a public disputation. At the close of a noisy and hostile session Ridley was declared a heretic and was excommunicated. Every effort was made to persuade him to recant, but Ridley stood firm. He spent his time in prison writing to his followers to encourage them to remain loyal to the Protestant cause: he wrote a series of treatises on various aspects of Protestantism which he smuggled out of prison and which were sent abroad and there printed and smuggled back into England for distribution. On 15 October he was formally degraded from the priesthood and handed over to the Mayor for execution. The next day, 16 October, he and Latimer were burned 'on the north side of the town in the ditch over against Balliol College'. Whereas Latimer died quickly and in little pain, Ridley's death was prolonged and agonizing. The fire had been badly laid and burned only slowly under the faggots, with the result that the flames did not reach the gunpowder which had been provided to hasten his death. Slowly the lower part of his body was burned away. Ridley screamed in agony: 'I cannot burn. For God's sake let the fire come unto me.' He was not burning at all above his waist, his shirt was not even scorched. At last a soldier hauled a faggot away and let the flames rise: they reached the gunpowder and Ridley's pain was over.

If Bonner may be looked on as the outstanding example of the uncompromising conservative bishop; if Latimer stands for the plain, down-to-earth defender of what he felt to be right; if Hooper may be taken to represent the violent, irrational and extreme reformer; Ridley may well be taken as standing for everything which was best in the English Reformation. He was gentle by nature, devoid of rancour, kind to his opponents, firm in his opinions, bold in opposition, as good a scholar as Cranmer and less timid, a man of independent judgement and with an understanding of genuine statesmanship, of invincible faith and undaunted courage. The

Anglican Reformation probably owes as much to Ridley as to any other single man.

Further Reading
J. G. Ridley, *Nicholas Ridley*, 1957.

ROBERT I, THE BRUCE (1274-1329) was one of the greatest kings in Scottish history, though his earlier career gave little hint of future triumphs. When Bruce became Earl of Carrick on the death of his father (also Robert) in 1304, it was already clear that he harboured greater ambitions. His father's father, another Robert Bruce (*d.*1295), had been one of the losing 'contenders' who in June 1291 had accepted the competence of the court appointed by Edward I to decide which of them was the rightful King of Scotland. The winner, John Balliol, was from the outset dependent on the good offices of the English, and the humiliations which they heaped upon him culminated in an invasion. Balliol's active military resistance was short-lived and, by July 1296, Edward had accepted his abdication. Now, those who wished to resist the imposition of direct English control had to choose the royal banner under which they would fight. Balliol had been chosen with the consent of the Scottish barons and duly crowned at Scone on 30 November 1292: it could be argued that his abdication had been forced upon him and was therefore illegal. But an absent king, politically supine, and repeatedly humiliated by his captors, was scarcely inspiring as a symbol of resistance. The main alternative was Robert Bruce, grandson of the 'contender'.

Bruce, of course, was later identified with the patriotic party, but the Scottishness of his family was of fairly recent vintage. They had come from Brus (now Brix) on the Cotentin peninsula in Normandy, and were granted lands by Henry I in the north-east of England in a period of good relations between the English king and David I of Scotland. David granted the Brus family the lordship of Annandale, a vast territory near the border at the Solway, so that the family held lands in both countries. Since the natural posture for such a family was to work for an accommodation between English and Scots it is not surprising that after Balliol's abdication Robert hoped to be made a vassal king in Scotland and swore fealty to Edward at Berwick in August 1296.

Once Edward returned to England the struggle flared up again. Together with James the Steward, William Lord of Douglas and Bishop Robert Wishart of Glasgow, Bruce raised forces which, though defeated at Irvine in July 1297, were not finished. Cressingham reported that only the eastern border country was in his firm control. Soon, northern forces led by Andrew de Moray joined up with those of William Wallace and inflicted a disastrous defeat upon the English at Stirling. With Edward away in France, they ruled Scotland in the name of John Balliol. But after Wallace's defeat at Falkirk in July 1298, his

place was taken by the two new guardians, Robert Bruce and John Comyn, Lord of Badenoch. Comyn had his own rather distant claim to the throne, but his marriage to Balliol's sister, Allianora, and his family's general alignment, predisposed him to support the Balliol cause. War continued but the magnates were split, and feared Edward's return from France. It is clear that, at this stage, both factions hoped for a negotiated deal, in which their respective claims to the throne would find favour with the English. The attachment of the Comyns to the discredited Balliol may suggest that they did not expect, or wish for, a strong and independent policy. But when Bruce resigned as guardian in 1300, it was not in protest at the failure to pursue such a policy. In 1302, he submitted to the overlordship of Edward I in return for an undertaking to examine the Bruce claim.

The Comyns could still pose as representatives of the nation and its absent king, John Balliol, so long as they defended, or were believed to defend, its territory against complete domination by the invader. In 1300-1 England controlled little outside the Borders and Lothian. But with his new invasion of May 1303, Edward began to make headway, and in March 1304, at a parliament held at St Andrews, most of the nobles, led by the Comyns, pledged allegiance to the English king. Edward's ordinance of September 1305 gave the leading magnates a share in the government of Scotland within a framework of overall English control. Perhaps hoping for influence within the new dispensation, Bruce stayed his hand and even helped in the hunt for William Wallace. But on 10 February 1306 his supporters killed John Comyn in the church at Dumfries; the murder opened Bruce to the charge of sacrilege, and the probable loss of ecclesiastical support. It is hard to think of Comyn's death as a mere accident; perhaps it was intended merely to capture him, perhaps Bruce had already decided on a coup, and had calculated that the leading supporter of his legitimate opponent must be removed swiftly and by surprise, despite the political costs. However that may be, there was no alternative but to fight for the throne.

On 25 March 1306, Robert Bruce was enthroned at Scone by Isabella, sister of the late Duncan, Earl of Fife. Little more than a quarter of the Scottish magnates seem to have supported Bruce at the outset. Only one earl, Atholl, is certainly known to have attended his coronation, and the only bishop present was Robert Wishart, of Glasgow. The English were not idle on the diplomatic front. On 18 May 1306 came Pope Clement V's decision to excommunicate Bruce for sacrilege. Political isolation led to military catastrophe at the hands of the English or the Comyns and their friends. There were defeats, by the Earl of Pembroke at Methven near Perth, then at Atholl and then by the Lords of Argyll and of Lorn, at Dalry in July or August, as Robert was forced westward. Finally he was able to escape the reach of this powerful coalition, taking refuge, probably in Islay, with the Macdonalds. Meanwhile, supporters such as the Countess of Buchan were imprisoned, along with Bruce's wife, and two bishops, Wishart and Lamberton of St Andrews, were clapped in irons. Other allies, including the most prominent, the Earl of Atholl, were hanged. These were desperate times for Robert. He was able to recruit some meagre forces, to make landfall at Arran in January 1307 and to reach his estates in Carrick, but his brothers, Thomas and Alexander, were defeated and executed by the Macdowells of Galloway. Still, Robert did well against English forces under Pembroke at Loudon Hill on 10 May; though almost at the end of his resources, he was able to break out from the south-west, and was beginning to employ the 'hit and run' techniques of guerrilla warfare.

By this time, Edward I had determined to supervise personally the reduction of Scotland. He travelled northwards, but in September 1306, near Carlisle, was forced to a halt by illness and died, just short of the Solway border, on 7 July 1307. From that date, it is now clear, the tide turned. Edward II marched northwards, but failed to find the elusive Robert and withdrew after only a week, taking most of the English field troops with him. Now, in the areas not controlled by the Comyn confederacy, the lesser men who in 1297-8 had formed the backbone of the power of Wallace and Andrew de Moray took new heart. The comparatively prosperous province of Moray had no resident earl; its lairds and lesser men heeded Bruce's call, destroying the Comyn Lords of Badenoch. His strength in the area disrupted communications between the hostile magnates of Buchan, Ross and Argyll who found it hard to co-ordinate their efforts. In 1307-8, Robert won notable victories, at Slioch and Barra, against the Comyn Earl of Buchan, who fled to England, and in the west at the Pass of Brander, against John of Lorn. Success helped to concentrate the minds of waverers; the Earl of Ross came over. More northern castles fell, and in mid-1308 the burgesses of Aberdeen, with Robert's help, succeeded in capturing the castle which overlooked their town. This secured a strategically placed port, and therefore supplies, including weapons, from abroad.

Despite his excommunication, Bruce gained support from many of the bishops and other clergy. Bishop Wishart had absolved Robert of the murder of Comyn, and wrote of his struggle as a crusade. Robert's success, however, was founded upon his uncontested control in the north, which soon extended down to the Forth; progress was slower in Galloway, and Lothian remained in English hands. By March 1309, the king felt secure enough to hold a parliament at St Andrews, where the prelates issued a nationalistic statement in his cause. At that assembly, it was 'discovered' that Balliol had been a usurper all along, ruthlessly imposed by England on the protesting magnates. History was thus employed as the servant of politics, in the cause of establishing Robert's legitimacy. (In the surviving statutes of Robert's reign, his predecessors sometimes appear as 'ancestors'! There is no mention of 'King John', who appears only rarely, as John Balliol.) From St Andrews, a diplomatic appeal was sent to Philip IV, and the French king was persuaded, perhaps by the number of Bruce's noble supporters, to grant him recognition. By October, Robert controlled almost all Scotland north of the Forth except for a few strongholds which could be supplied by sea. He followed a consistent policy of destroying castles, realizing that the English could not occupy the kingdom without them.

Edward II, meanwhile, was increasingly mired in debt and baronial dissension. His invasion of 1310 was so ineffective as to encourage Robert to raid the far north; by 1312, with the execution of Gaveston, it was England that seemed the more likely to discover the delights of civil war. Over the next ten years, Robert was able to extract at least £20,000, as 'protection money' from the northernmost English counties. In October 1313 his opponents were granted one year to submit on pain of forfeit of their lands, though it is not clear how effective this threat was. Most of the remaining castles had fallen, including Roxburgh and Edinburgh; outside Lothian, Stirling alone held out. It was there in October 1313 that Robert obtained from de Mowbray, the constable, a promise that Stirling castle would surrender if no English force had arrived to relieve it by 24 June 1314. Now, any such force could be expected to be large and well-equipped, yet the prize of Stirling might tempt the Scots into a disastrous battle. The agreement with de Mowbray could only be expected to bring forward such a clash, and was therefore a miscalculation. But not by very much.

For it was only on 21 July 1314, that the army of Edward II reached Edinburgh, advancing to the Bannock burn near Stirling on the 23rd, the day before its scheduled capitulation. The English infantry numbered over 15,000, but it was a troop of the 2,500-strong cavalry which spearheaded their advance towards Stirling. Robert's forces, however, were able to parry this thrust. On the following day, 24 June, though heavily outnumbered, Robert ordered his 8,000 men to give battle by means of a frontal attack. His reasoning soon became apparent. The opposing army, though protected on the flanks by marshland, was also cramped by it. Thus, the fabled archers could not fan out, and the armoured cavalry could not manoeuvre; the knights were forced to fight on a narrow front, and could not make their numbers tell. Here, the English suffered a disastrous and historic defeat, with many dead, in the combat and through drowning. His forces scattered, baggage and weapons seized, Edward scuttled away to Dunbar. There is no doubt that the tactical and strategic brilliance of Robert Bruce, and his skill in choosing and deploying his officers, were indispensable in the winning of this justly famous victory.

Other factors, however, were involved. King Edward I had regarded his Scottish opponents as rebels and traitors, and treated them with vindictive savagery, irrespective of status. Through words and deeds, Edward helped inspire in many Scots a patriotic spirit which was not quenched by the feebleness of his son. Bannockburn drew heavily upon, and helped to temper, this spirit. It ended, for a while at least, English pretensions in Scotland, and was pivotal in securing a new dynasty. All but the core of Balliol's support now melted away. On 6 November 1314, the parliament, sitting at Cambuskenneth near the field of Bannockburn, announced that the estates of those who had failed to pledge their loyalty under the terms laid down at Dundee a year earlier now lay under forfeit. The Balliols, the Comyns, the McDougalls of Argyll and the Earl of Atholl (who had deserted on the eve of victory) were deprived, and this involved very large slabs of Scottish territory. Many opponents, however, including the Earls of Fife, Dunbar and Mar were reconciled. Chief lieutenants were well rewarded. James Douglas received several lordships, and Bruce's nephew, Thomas Randolph, was created Earl of Moray. Generally, through patronage, Robert raised to pre-eminence magnates whose interests were bound up with the survival of his dynasty. Royal security was also underpinned by legal measures. The holding by Scots of English lands (which obligated them to pay homage to English monarchs) was outlawed. It was especially important, at this time, to legislate against foreign intervention in the Scottish succession, since Robert had only a daughter, Marjorie, by his first wife, Isabella of Mar. In April 1315 it was agreed that Robert's brother Edward should take precedence over Marjorie and her heirs; elaborate provisions were made for choosing an alternative should both fail. But these proved unnecessary. In 1324 a son David, later David II, was born to Robert by his second wife Elizabeth de Burgh, daughter of the Earl of Ulster whom he had married over twenty years before in about 1302.

The birth of David must have come as a very great relief to Robert, for in 1318 Edward Bruce died, in Ireland, where he was engaged alongside native Irish forces against the English. Robert strongly supported this initiative and may, like his brother, have hoped that if it met with success, the Welsh, chafing under their new rulers, might also be brought into the alliance against them. It is perhaps only with hindsight that this larger celtic alliance seems far-fetched; in the event it was in Ireland that the venture collapsed. Still, Robert was bringing his own kingdom under control: his 1318 parliament made energetic efforts to rebuild external

defences and to strengthen and regularize justice and administration. The king's chief difficulties were in his dealings with the papacy and with Edward II. These were not unconnected.

Pope John XXII was committed to a crusade against Islam, but this depended on the troops of the rulers of Christian Europe, including England and Scotland; to free these he sought in 1317 to broker a peace between them, based on the territorial status quo. Since this would have left Berwick in English hands, Robert rejected it. Strenuous English diplomatic efforts further deepened the odium in which Robert's sacrilege had placed him. His excommunication was confirmed, he and four bishops were summoned to Rome, and Scotland was placed under an interdict. Accordingly, in May 1320 the Scots dispatched three official letters to Rome. These included the 'Declaration of Arbroath', a ringing affirmation by the nobility of Scotland's independence and the legitimacy of its king. This was defended, not on the basis of Robert's birth but because he 'has restored the people's safety and will defend their freedom', for if the king should betray his country to the English, they 'would make another king capable of defending us'. Perhaps some men noted a discrepancy between the baronial commitment to national freedom attested in the heroic prose of Arbroath and the baronial addiction to factional and family advantage evidenced by the war. In summer 1320, five of the Scottish signatories of the Declaration were found to have been involved in a plot to assassinate Robert in the interest of William Soules, a son of one of the less credible of the competitors of 1291. The conspirators seem to have been motivated by little other than jealousy of those who had done better out of the distribution of forfeited lands, and Robert had several hanged. But until 1328, the papacy refused to rescind the measures against him, or to recognize his kingship.

On the southern front, hostilities eventually fizzled out. In 1318, Robert took Berwick. The following year the English failed to retake it, and suffered damaging reverses in Yorkshire; Edward II's retaliatory invasion in December, and his renewed attack in 1322 were equally ineffectual. There was little left for the English king but to end the long period of hostilities. The thirteen-year truce of May 1323 offered little to Robert other than time: it addressed him as 'Sire Robert de Brus'; the English refused recognition of Scottish independence and clearly meant to renew hostilities later. In the meantime Robert sought to strengthen his government, his tactics included some judicious bargains. In the parliament of 1326 at Cambuskenneth, an explicit agreement was made, whereby the lords and burgesses (on behalf of themselves and the freeholders) promised to pay a tenth of their income to the Crown to supplement revenues depleted by war; but in exchange, King Robert agreed to abandon requisitioning for some purposes and to pay the market price.

At Corbeil in 1326, Robert signed a treaty of alliance with Charles IV of France. This provided that if either Scotland or France were involved in a war with England, the other would assist. But the security of Scotland was, as so often, improved most by internal dissension in England. Edward II was forced from the throne by his wife Isabella and her lover Mortimer, and with his deposition, the truce lapsed. Robert took full advantage of this legal loophole, and of the weakness of the English regency, to invade Northumberland, and at last he was able to force his opponents to the negotiating table. The treaty was signed in the presence of the Scottish king at Edinburgh, in Holyrood Abbey, in March 1328. It was the crowning political achievement of Robert's life, not least in its preamble, which announced an accord between two sovereign kings. England renounced all claims to sovereignty over Scotland, agreeing to return all earlier documents which might compromise this. It explicitly recognized Robert as king, and tacitly disavowed his Scottish enemies by remaining silent about their forfeited lands. The peace was signed without prejudice to the Scottish alliance with France. Robert's son David was to marry Joan, the sister of Edward III (and did so in July 1328). On the minus side, the Scots were to pay £20,000 into the bankrupt English treasury, and the Stone of Scone was not returned. But the balance of the treaty was overwhelmingly positive. Furthermore, it opened the road to Robert's rehabilitation in Rome. In October 1328, he was released by Pope John XXII from his excommunication; on 13 June 1329 a bull was issued permitting the annointment as kings of Robert I and his successors. Robert did not live to hear this news. Already gravely ill during the finalization of the Treaty of Edinburgh, he died at Cardross, near Dumbarton, a week before his official legitimation.

During his eventful reign Robert did much to strengthen the Crown against its opponents both within and without; but his most careful preparations could not protect against the immediate consequences when the succession of a five-year-old king combined with the recovery of English political unity and purpose. Indeed, in the 1330s, it may have seemed that Scotland had simply reverted to its earlier factionalism and dependence. But Robert had laid the basis of a polity, in which loyalty to the dynasty and the nation began more consistently to outweigh the lure of immediate advantage, even in the succession of minorities which followed.

ROBERT II (1316-90), the first of the Stewart kings, was born in 1316, the son of Walter Stewart and Marjorie Bruce. Walter was the sixth High Steward of Scotland, an office which had became hereditary in his increasingly prestigious and wealthy family (originally

from Dol in Brittany). It had descended through an unbroken succession from Walter (Fitzalan, d.1177) appointed to his position by David I. Marjorie was the daughter of Robert the Bruce by his first wife, Isabella. For a time, until 1324, Robert Stewart was heir presumptive to the Scottish throne. In that year, however, Bruce's second wife, Elizabeth de Burgh, gave him a son, David, and in 1326 parliament agreed that only if David should die without issue would the throne then pass to Robert Stewart. This was a logical application of the rules of succession which (though breached by Bruce himself) had by now become accepted, but it meant that when David became king in 1329 (as David II) his heir was a nephew eight years older than himself.

Robert's early career is hard to trace, partly because of the chaotic state of Scotland at the time. In late 1333 after Halidon Hill, then aged seventeen, he seems to have been in hiding; there is no evidence that Robert became guardian in 1334. Andrew Murray, whom the king favoured, had been captured early at Roxburgh but was ransomed and resumed his duties as guardian in late 1335. Only after Murray's death in 1338 did Robert take over the leadership, and then not, it seems, very effectively. He is reported to have been of a kindly and pacific disposition, qualities for which the political situation in fourteenth-century Scotland has not become legendary; much later, in 1385, it was reported disapprovingly that Robert (now aged seventy) was 'no valiant man, but one who would rather remain at home than march to the field'. After the capture of David II at Neville's Cross, Robert became lieutenant; he probably owed this to the death at the battle of his rival John Randolph, Earl of Moray, another royal favourite. He acquired the lands of the vacant earldom of Strathearn, and became its earl in 1357. Probably anxious about the succession, Robert launched an abortive coup in 1363, backed by the Earls of Douglas and March, though his sons John and Robert seem to have been keener than him in this cause.

On his accession in 1371, Robert renewed the French alliance. There still remained in English hands Scottish territory relinquished by Edward Balliol in 1334, but Robert did not want to provoke Edward III unduly, so he allowed the provisions for active mutual aid to lapse. However, with the accession of Richard II in 1377, England was much weakened; Robert witheld outstanding ransom payments (for David II) and intensified the pressure on English-held areas. In 1384, when the much violated truce expired, relations with England were already poor. Also, the French needed action, and were prepared to pay for it. In 1385 they sent £8,000 and 1,000 knights under Jean de Vienne. These knights never saw combat; their sense of honour was outraged by the Scottish tactic of refusing battle against superior forces, even as Melrose Abbey burned, and they soon returned to France. Still, Lochmaben and Teviotdale were recaptured, and though the Scots were forced back by Richard's large army which ravaged as far north as Edinburgh, the English forces withdrew within days.

Border fighting continued for the remainder of Robert's reign, though it seems to have been occasioned chiefly by baronial jealousy rather than national policy. In the bloody battle of Otterburn (1388), the second Earl of Douglas met his death in a clash with feudal rivals the Percies. During Robert's reign the Earls of Douglas (the 'Black Douglases', from their heraldic colour), acquired almost the status, and the power, of kings. In 1371 the first earl launched an apparent bid for the throne itself, which may have been intended simply to intimidate the new king. At Threave in Kirkudbrightshire, the third earl, Archibald (the Grim), built a tower house as bleak as his name, from which he ruled the whole of Galloway, as well as the earldom of Mar and the lordship of Bothwell.

With his continuing favour, Robert's three sons also became disproportionately powerful. The youngest was Lord Alexander of Badenoch, 'the Wolf of Badenoch', a career arsonist, apt to treat savagely anyone unwise enough to get in his way. Chided for his peccadilloes by the Bishop of Moray, the Wolf's answer was to burn down the bishop's cathedral at Elgin, and then the burgh. The eldest was John, Earl of Carrick, who in 1384 took over the government from the enfeebled king; in 1388, however, the earl also became ill, and was in his turn displaced by the middle brother Robert, Earl of Fife, later the first Duke of Albany. The Register of Moray reported that towards the end of the reign there was 'no law in Scotland, but the strong oppressed the weak and the whole kingdom was a den of thieves'. But would a new king improve the situation?

There had been no real dispute about Robert's own right to the throne, but questions had arisen about the legitimacy of the children (especially the three sons mentioned above) of his first marriage with Elizabeth Mure, which had infringed canon law concerning matches between blood relatives. Papal dispensation was received, but only in 1347, after the children's birth. Bastards had often been retrospectively legitimized by the marriage of their parents, but could retrospective legitimation of an incestuous relationship confer legitimacy on its offspring? If not, then the rightful heir was the David, the king's eldest son by his second wife, Euphemia, whose marriage was of spotless canonical virtue. Robert was determined to uphold the right of his sons by Elizabeth, of which John, Earl of Carrick, later Robert III, was the eldest. His declaration on this matter was confirmed by the prelates and bishops in 1371, and the resulting order of succession set out by parliament in 1373. By this the principles of legitimation which lay behind the decision were enshrined in Scottish law. Robert II's pioneering role in the change is exceptionally apposite, since he is known to have fathered a total of thirteen children by his two wives, of which several had been born in canonical incest, and at least eight by other women. When Robert died in 1390 he was succeeded by his eldest son John, who took the title Robert III.

ROBERT III (*c*.1337-1406) was the son of Robert II, King of Scots, by his first wife Elizabeth, and christened John. He was crowned Robert III in 1390; the name John had proved unlucky for recent French kings, but probably the main reason for its abandonment was the sensitive issue of John Balliol. Leaving aside the sad record of civil and international war which his reign had brought, Balliol's enforced abdication raised the question, tricky for Crown legitimacy, of whether a new King John would be known as John I or John II. Robert III was the 100th descendant of Erc in the line of Scottish kings, but this was probably the most distinguished aspect of his reign. He seems to have continued the unhappy record of his father, weakening the resources of the Crown by gifts of pensions, some heritable, to retainers. The chief beneficiaries of royal largesse were courtiers and the king's many relations, who, with the Douglases, now dominated the topmost nobility, in a period of economic stagnation and misery. There was continuing war with England, in which the most notable exchange of Robert's reign was the disaster at Homildon Hill in 1402 which had followed a half-hearted invasion of northern England.

The reign has become notorious for baronial anarchy, and even royal jurisprudence was sometimes unorthodox in style. In 1396, in a dispute immortalized by Scott in *The Fair Maid of Perth*, two Highland clans were permitted to try the strength of their legal claims by means of a mortal combat. Exchequer funds were provided for the building of a special enclosure on the Inch of Perth, and there thirty champions chosen by each side set about each other, with Robert himself as referee. At length, evidently concerned to spare his subjects unnecessary suffering, the king is reported to have stopped the contest, which timely intervention may have been welcomed by the twelve survivors. From 1393, Robert seems to have run the country himself, in a manner which aroused widespread complaint. For in 1399, a general council blamed both lawlessness and 'misgovernance' upon 'the king and his officers', and appointed his eldest son David, Duke of Rothesay, as lieutenant.

Rothesay was not an improvement, abusing his powers and resisting attempts by the council to restrain him. He also pursued a rivalry with another and more ruthless politician of the hour, his uncle, now Duke of Albany. In these battles, Robert seems to have wielded very little authority. Finally, in 1401, Robert was persuaded, almost certainly by Albany, to order Rothesay's arrest, and he died in 1402, in suspicious circumstances. This death meant that only Robert's younger son James stood between Albany and the throne. After a delay perhaps occasioned by Robert's age and illness, he arranged for James to be sent to France, but the boy was captured by English pirates on 22 March 1406. This disastrous news may have reached Robert before his death on 4 April. He is reported to have lamented: 'Here lies the worst of kings and the most miserable of men.'

ROBERT, nicknamed **CURTHOSE** (*c.*1053-1134; Duke of Normandy 1087-1106) twice failed to make good his claim to the English throne. The eldest son of William the Conqueror, he had been designated Count of Maine in 1063 and Duke of Normandy in 1077-8. Impatient for power and easily led by dissident Norman barons, from 1078 he persistently rebelled against his father. Nevertheless, on his deathbed, William confirmed Robert's succession in Normandy, leaving England to his more capable son William Rufus. Between 1087 and 1088, Robert and his allies made a concerted but unsuccessful bid to wrest England from his brother. Thereafter, his rule in Normandy was constantly undermined by William and his youngest brother Henry. In 1096, having mortgaged his duchy to William for 10,000 marks, he departed on the First Crusade, during which he won for himself glittering fame. On his return he found William dead and Henry installed in England. Once again, his invasion of England failed, terms being agreed at Alton in 1101. In 1106, Henry exploited his growing political advantage in Normandy, defeating and capturing Robert at the battle of Tinchebrai. Thereafter, Henry held his brother in comfortable but close confinement. It was said that Henry mitigated the harsh treatment usually meted out to his political prisoners in deference to Robert's status as a former crusader. Most of Robert's captivity was spent in Cardiff Castle where, according to tradition, he learnt Welsh and composed at least one poem, on a tree he could see from the window of his cell. His threat to Henry I was maintained by his son, William Clito (*d.*1128). Robert was a poor ruler, vain and malleable. He was, however, a fine warrior, who once wounded his own father in battle at Gerberoi (1079) and earned such fame on crusade that even in his lifetime chroniclers invented improbable deeds of valour and spread the false story that he had been offered the Crown of Jerusalem in 1099. His legendary deeds were enshrined in stained glass by Abbot Suger at St Denis. As an effective, disciplined ruler, Robert was a failure, but as a military leader and companion, he won renown, a paradox central to many political tensions of the period.

Further Reading
C. W. David, *Robert Curthose*, 1920.

ROBERT, EARL OF GLOUCESTER (*c.*1090-1147) had all the kingly attributes except one: legitimacy. The eldest of Henry I's twenty or so bastards, literate, intelligent, brave, adept at the factional politics of court and a patron of both the church and the arts, Robert had to stand back to watch others compete for the throne, literally so in 1127 when he lost his claim to precedence over his cousin Stephen of Blois when doing homage to his half-sister, the Empress Matilda. It was some measure of an increase in orderliness and legal propriety that William the Bastard could inherit a duchy and win a Crown, while his grandson, Robert, whose personal credentials were second to none, had to be content with a supporting role.

Under Henry I, Robert was prominent in a party consistently loyal to the king. In 1119, Robert fought at Brémule against the King of France and in 1123 against the Norman rebels; in 1126, he was given custody of his uncle Robert Curthose. Despite acquiescing in Matilda's succession, he still fought against the Angevins on Henry's behalf in the 1130s. Robert's reward was in lands in south Wales and the west country and the earldom of Gloucester (1122). After Henry's death in 1135, it was not his loyalty to the empress which swayed him so much as his own self-interest: arguably, his hesitation in deciding where that lay allowed Stephen to grab the throne.

Admired by William of Malmesbury, Robert has traditionally been seen as a noble, chivalrous defender of the hereditary rights of his half-sister. His actions between 1135 and 1139 suggest more selfish motives. His unusual conditional homage to Stephen in 1136 signalled his importance to the new king but it may also have been forced on him by his isolation among the English baronage and the threat to his lands in southeast Wales posed by a Welsh revolt, the crushing of which, it has recently been suggested, may have prompted Robert's literary protégé, Geoffrey of Monmouth, to write his *History of the Kings of Britain*. Although Robert co-operated with Stephen at the siege of Exeter in 1136, he soon became alienated from the new régime, not least because of the favours granted to the Beaumont twins, Waleran of Meulan and Robert of Leicester, old rivals from the court of Henry I. Opposition to the Beaumonts provide a leitmotif in the rest of Robert of Gloucester's career, not least in the fighting at Wareham (1138), Worcester (1139) and Tewkesbury (1140).

It was probably the growing influence of Waleran of Meulan in particular that led to Robert distancing himself from the king in Normandy in 1137 and his fears of assassination by the royalist mercenary, William of Ypres. In 1138, the formal break with Stephen occurred, but after the failure of the Angevins to capture Normandy in 1138-9, Robert, perhaps in desperation lest his English estates would be lost, landed at Arundel with Matilda to dispute the English throne. In England,

Robert provided the judicious advice, material support and personal charm that Matilda so conspicuously lacked. That she retained followers at all may in part have been the achievement of her gregarious and generous half-brother with his knack for friendship. Although playing the leading military role on the empress's side, Robert also managed to use the civil war to build an almost impregnable power-base for himself in southwest England, centred on Bristol, a control that the vicissitudes of the wider dynastic struggle did little to challenge. 1141 saw his greatest triumph in the crushing defeat of the king at Lincoln in February, but his victory exposed the vulnerability of his position. Unless he looked after his own interests, he would have no more guarantee of security at an Angevin than at a Blois court. The former suddenly looked a forlorn prospect after the Rout of Winchester in September, where only Robert's personal courage and chivalry secured Matilda's escape at the price of his own capture.

The subsequent exchange of Robert for Stephen inaugurated stalemate, during which Robert consolidated his hold over the south-west (just as his rival Robert of Leicester extended his grip on the Midlands). To the end, Robert was inflexible, not only over the Angevin claim but, more damaging to prospects of civil peace, in harbouring the factional rivalries and grudges of the 1130s. Robert's death in 1147 allowed English magnates to make private accommodations with each other: Robert's own son, William, even married Robert of Leicester's daughter c.1150. It may be no coincidence that only a few months after her faithful defender died, Matilda left England.

If Robert of Gloucester was a vigorous politician, he was also one of the leading literary patrons of his generation. Apparently something of an intellectual himself, eager at quoting biblical analogies, Robert was the focus of a group of writers which included the historian William of Malmesbury and the historical romancer Geoffrey of Monmouth, writers of secular narrative histories whose interest in the epic past of Britain was presumably shared by their patron. William of Malmesbury's revised *Gesta Regum* was dedicated to him, as was his *Historia Novella* which extensively eulogizes the earl. Not only was Robert one of the dedicatees of Geoffrey of Monmouth's *History*, but he circulated copies of it to his monastic foundations and to his friends, including Walter Espec. Inside the nobility's metal helmets and chain mail were men of cultivation and intellectual curiosity. Robert employed mercenaries such as the bestial psychopath Robert FitzHubert; at the same time he fostered a literary genre that captured the imagination of the civilized world.

Further Reading

D. Crouch, 'Robert, Earl of Gloucester and the Daughter of Zelopheliad', *Journal of Medieval History* xi, 1975.

ROBERT, EARL OF LEICESTER (1104-68) was the younger of the twin sons of Robert of Meulan (*d.*1118), Henry I's chief adviser. While his brother, Waleran, was mercurial, even flashy, Robert was renowned for patience and circumspection. Until the 1140s very much under Waleran's shadow, Robert slowly built up one of the largest baronies in England and a major political position through alliances with other magnates and a growing network of vassals whose loyalty was secured by firm discipline. By 1154, Robert was perhaps the most powerful baron in England as well as being a political veteran whose experience embraced over thirty years. He had also gained a reputation as an administrator, negotiator and lawyer, (in the words of Richard FitzNeal who knew him 'a man of sound judgement, well educated and practised in legal affairs'). Something of an intellectual, his views on royal authority and treason were quoted by John of Salisbury in his *Policraticus* and he himself wrote on philosophy and astronomy. In 1155, Henry II harnassed both Robert's territorial power and his personal talents to the new régime by appointing him justiciar, an office which he held, as the senior partner to Richard de Lucy, until his death.

Under his father's will, Robert received the family lands in England, including the earldom of Leicester, but in 1121 his marriage to Amice, heiress of Breteuil brought him a strategically important fief in Normandy. Brought up at Henry I's court, by the early 1130s, Robert shared in the high favour bestowed on his family and their connections; he also witnessed fifteen royal charters between 1130 and 1135, a sign of things to come. With the death of Henry I and the accession of Stephen, Robert shared in the heyday of Beaumont power, taking the opportunity to settle old scores with territorial rivals, such as the Tosnis in Normandy. In 1139 he helped his brother destroy Roger of Salisbury, receiving from Stephen the city and earldom of Hereford the following year. Robert's diplomatic skills were exercised in 1141 when he negotiated the division of the family lands so that he could retain his English estates, as a supporter of Stephen, and his brother Waleran his French lands as an adherent of the Angevins. Although remaining a close associate of King Stephen, Robert spent much of the rest of the reign securing his own position. Independent of the king, he formed treaties with Angevin magnates, such as Ranulf of Chester, in order to reduce the prospects of damage to his landed interests, especially in the Midlands. He was notorious for controlling his tenants over whom he lay the constant threat of disseisin. In 1153, he changed sides, soon becoming one of Henry FitzEmpress's chief counsellors and having his Norman estates restored.

As justiciar, he acted as Henry's main adviser at court and his representative when the king was abroad.

Although prominent in the Becket controversy, he avoided the excommunications of 1166, perhaps because the archbishop saw him as of independent mind, a possible mediator. His duties as justiciar included presiding at the Exchequer; carrying out royal writs; overseeing local royal officials; acting as a judge in hearing major pleas of the Crown; provisioning royal castles and palaces; paying troops and transporting treasure. Robert was a dominant figure in government and aristocracy, with unrivalled royal confidence and estates to match, stretching from Wales to East Anglia. Much of the later prestige attached to the justiciarship derived from Robert's own reputation as a politician of unequalled experience; a royal servant of expertise and a baron of the highest lineage and unsurpassed wealth. Yet sometimes his dual role found him out. In c.1167, he had obtained a special writ of exemption from demands on his lands under the Forest Laws. This caused outrage among the old Exchequer hands led by Nigel of Ely who insisted that anyone who sat at the Exchequer possessed ex officio exemption which did not require specific royal approval. It is one case of many where Earl Robert's first thought was to promote and protect his own property and interests while at the same time serving the king. FitzNeal described Robert as strong-minded and diligent. Henry II recognized his quality and, again in FitzNeal's words, made him 'head not only of the Exchequer, but of the whole kingdom'.

Born to greatness, Robert acquired further greatness by doing well out of the civil war of Stephen's reign and was thus in an unrivalled position to exploit his opportunities when high office was thrust upon him. Robert has been called 'the model of the curial magnate' and his career, taken with those of his father and brother, expose how unrealistic is the historical cliché which pits kings against barons. Medieval realms only operated through intimate co-operation between ruler and the most powerful of the ruled. Such relationships were inevitably at times tense and could degenerate into acrimony and violent confrontation especially if, as under Stephen, the king was a poor manager of men. But such dislocation was the product of mutual dependency not separation of interests. Robert did well out of kings and did well for kings: in him and those like him, we can see how effective medieval government operated to the desired benefit of all involved. Sectional interests as often as not united monarch and magnate as divided them. Twelfth-century kings had no option or desire to base their rule on others than the natural leaders of society of whom few were more effective than Robert of Leicester who combined self-interest and loyalty to the material advantage of master and minister alike.

Further Reading
D. Crouch, *The Beaumont Twins*, 1985.
F. J. West, *The Justiciarship in England*, 1966.

ROBERT OF BELLÊME, EARL OF SHREWSBURY (1052/6-c.1130) was one of the most powerful Anglo-Norman magnates of the second generation after the Conquest. Son of Roger of Montgomery, first Earl of Shrewsbury, he had already acquired large estates in Normandy and Maine before his father's death in 1094 when he received, as the elder surviving son, the patrimonial lands in the duchy. In 1098, on the death of his younger brother Hugh, he received the extensive Marcher earldom of Shrewsbury and the family property in Sussex, to which Robert added the Midland fief of Tickhill by purchase and the county of Ponthieu by marriage. He thus controlled lands stretching from the Somme estuary and northern Maine, through Normandy, southern England to the Midlands and into Wales. He personified a Norman 'Empire' linked rather than divided by the Channel. In Rufus's reign he was notorious for two things: his cruelty and interest in military architecture, both useful attributes for a man in his position. If his power was spectacular, so was his fall. Robert had supported Robert Curthose for the English throne in 1088 and, although he had formally accepted Henry I in 1100, retained this loyalty, possibly calculating that his own power would be the greater under the ineffectual Curthose. In 1102, all his English lands were confiscated after an abortive attempt to resist Henry, who, unable to trust Robert, had determined to destroy him. The rest of Robert's political career was spent in Normandy, his opposition to Henry persisting even after Curthose's defeat in 1106. In 1112 Henry lost patience. Robert was arrested and incarcerated, first in Normandy then, from 1113, at Wareham in Dorset. There he spent the rest of his life, hidden from view except for a reference in the Pipe Roll of 1130 to payments for his maintenance and clothing. The wheel of Fortune had come round. His grandfather had been a minor ducal official in Normandy. Through good marriages, the patronage of William the Conqueror and their own predatory instincts, the family had reached the highest rung of the nobility. Their rise had been spotted with blood, of their opponents and subjects; sometimes their own: Robert's mother, Mabel, had been brutally murdered; his brother Hugh killed by a Viking on a raid to Anglesey. The ascent and destruction of Robert's family provides an object lesson in how Anglo-Norman politics worked away from the sanitized niceties of government bookkeeping.

ROBERT OF MEULAN, LORD OF MEULAN and BEAUMONT, EARL OF LEICESTER (1046-1118) was the leading lay adviser to both William II and Henry I. Although in the course of a long public life he amassed extensive estates in England, Normandy and France, Robert was the nearest thing to a king's minister that contemporary circumstances allowed, the more remarkable as his successors as royal lay advisers – with the exception of his own son Robert of Leicester, justiciar to Henry II – tended to come from less exalted ranks of the nobility, men such as the justiciars Ranulf Glanvill, Geoffrey FitzPeter and Hubert de Burgh. Robert's career made a distinctive impression on contemporaries and affords a rare glimpse into how eleventh-century politics worked.

The son of a prominent Norman magnate, Roger of Beaumont, Robert made his name by his deeds at his first battle, Hastings. Thereafter, during his father's lifetime, Robert sought his fortune in England. By 1087, he had become one of William I's active *curiales* and held land in England worth a significant but not spectacular £254. In the early 1080s he had inherited the county of Meulan from his maternal uncle but, despite succeeding to his father's Norman lordships a decade later, his interests and loyalties remained Anglo-Norman. Unusually, he faithfully supported all of the first three post-Conquest kings. After spending much of 1087-93 in France securing his inheritance, from 1093 he emerged as William Rufus's closest counsellor, playing a prominent role in the dispute with Anselm and the king's French campaigns.

On the sudden death of Rufus in August 1100, Robert smoothly transferred his allegiance to Henry I. For the last eighteen years of his life, Robert appears as the most frequent witness to the new king's charters, a reflection of his influence. By 1107 when, perhaps in reward for his part in Henry's acquisition of Normandy, Robert was given the earldom of Leicester, he had become a major landowner in England as well as northern France, with estates especially extensive in the Midlands. While Roger of Salisbury ran the royal administration, centred upon the Treasury and Exchequer, Robert's influence was in politics, diplomacy and the law. Robert played a crucial role in furthering Henry's cause in Normandy 1103-6 and undermining that of the duke, Robert Curthose, with whom Robert of Meulan had long had strained relations. He continued to be closely involved in the dispute with Archbishop Anselm, his prominence recognized by Pope Paschal II who identified Robert by name for excommunication in 1105. However, Robert was instrumental in securing a compromise with Anselm, finally concluded at Bec in 1106, and in persuading Henry I to stick to the agreement, to moderate church taxes and restore church lands. In 1109, Robert 'with flattery, coaxing and apology' tried to persuade Archbishop Thomas of York to profess obedience to the see of Canterbury, an attempt repeated with Thomas's successor, Thurstan, in 1116.

As a significant Norman lord, wealthy French count and English earl, with experience of public affairs stretching back to the 1060s, Robert was well placed to further his own interests. He established an elaborate, almost quasi-regal administration for his English and continental lands: in England he had his own Exchequer, in imitation of the new royal accounting office. At Leicester, he restored the Anglo-Saxon court of Portmanmote, a tribunal of twenty-four, to replace trial by combat. He insisted that his twin sons, Waleran and Robert, both of whom were to play leading political roles in the next generation, received good educations. He was tenacious of his own rights and lands. In 1111, in revenge for an attack on Meulan, he ravaged the French king's capital at Paris causing so much damage that the Ile de la Cité required extensive rebuilding. Ruthless in manipulating his position and the law to acquire new estates, on his deathbed he characteristically refused to restore any lands he had illegally seized. Robert's private life may not have been untroubled. He had married late (*c.*1096) Isabel of Vermandois who was alleged to have eloped with William of Warenne, whom she subsequently married, before Robert's death. As in contemporary romances, so in life, infidelity and chivalry could be close companions.

Robert's interest in public affairs and desire to influence royal business, although personally enriching, was not solely self-seeking. To Robert was attributed Henry I's less aggressive, less ostentatious and more conciliatory tone of government, notably towards the church and in the delicate handling of the prickly Norman baronage. William of Malmesbury wrote of Robert as 'the persuader of peace, the dissuader of strife … urging his lord the king rigorously to enforce the law; and himself not only abiding by existing laws but proposing new ones'. Not the least of Robert's achievements may have been to temper Henry's notorious personal brutality. Orderic Vitalis, who may well have met Robert, attributed to him a remarkable political testament delivered to Henry I in 1101. This may stand as a blueprint for effective medieval political management which, even if the chronicler's invention, suggests what policies contemporaries associated with Robert.

'We … to whom the common utility is committed by Divine Providence, ought to seek after the safety of the kingdom and of the church of God. Let our chief care be to triumph peacefully without the shedding of Christian blood, and so that our faithful people may live in the serenity of peace … Speak gently to all your knights; caress them all as a father does his children; soothe them with promises; grant whatever they might request and in this manner cleverly draw all to your favour … do not hesitate to make magnificent promises, as is fitting to royal munificence. It is better to give away a small portion of the kingdom than to lose both victory and life to a host of enemies. And when … we have come to the end of this business (withstanding the threat of Robert Curthose), we will suggest useful measures for recovering the demesnes usurped by rash deserters in time of war'.

It is worth noting that the 'useful measures' mentioned included accusations of treason, deprivation of patrimonies and forced exile. As with all successful medieval politicians, Robert of Meulan knew that violence and the threat of violence was the strongest supporter of conciliation.

Further Reading
S. N. Vaughn, *Anselm of Bec and Robert of Meulan*, 1985.

ROBERT OF MORTAIN (*c*.1031-90), half-brother of William the Conqueror, became the wealthiest subject of the English Crown in the generation after the Conquest. The second son of the Conqueror's mother, Herleve and Herluin, Vicomte of Conteville, Robert was appointed by William, Count of Mortain in south-west Normandy around 1055. Robert's elevation was part of William's policy of creating a close network of loyal nobles, often related to the ducal house, with and through whom William controlled his duchy and, later, was to conquer his kingdom (Robert's full brother, Odo, was Bishop of Bayeux). Robert's prominent part in the invasion of England was remembered in his depiction in the Bayeux Tapestry advising William with his brother Odo after the landing at Pevensey. Both at Hastings and during the often difficult pacification of England 1066-9, Robert proved an effective military subordinate to William. His reward was massive. By 1086, with almost 800 manors from Sussex to Yorkshire to Cornwall, as well as valuable castles, such as Pevensey, Robert was the greatest secular landholder after the king and the church. Together, his and Odo's estates were worth £5,000: the next richest lay holdings were valued at *c*.£750. However powerful his grip on his vassals, William preferred to keep power in the family. This presented problems; both his brother Odo of Bayeux and son Robert Curthose openly rebelled. Unlike the restless Odo, Robert of Mortain made little individual mark on events. He spent much time with his half-brother in a career, until 1087, conspicuous by its loyalty. In 1087, Robert persuaded the dying king to release Odo from prison and was probably one of those who insisted that Robert Curthose succeed to Normandy. Although initially accepting William Rufus as king, in 1088 Robert threw in his lot with Odo and Curthose. He held Pevensey for the rebels, withstanding a six-week siege by Rufus in person. After his submission, he was pardoned but withdrew to Normandy to die. Robert emerges dimly from the records, the least colourful or defined of a family of striking personalities. He seems to have been on close terms with both his brothers and to have harboured a soft spot for Robert Curthose. Alternatively, he wished to preside over his lands free from superior exactions, an independence fostered perhaps by his paternal inheritance (it

was in his father's monastery of Grestain that he was buried), and later offered by the policies of Odo and the character of Curthose. Only the accident of his mother's liaison with Duke Robert I elevated this child of provincial aristocracy to the greatest heights of the Anglo-Norman baronage. In the eleventh century at least, nobility could be acquired by favour and fortune, not just by blood.

ROBERTS OF KANDAHAR, FIELD MARSHAL EARL (1832-1914), otherwise known as 'Bobs', Kipling's hero, was a popular figure, which his rival, Lord Wolseley, never was. The streets from Paddington to Buckingham Palace were lined with crowds more than six deep on his return from the Boer War in 1900. The small trim figure, upright on his grey charger, had been a soldiers' soldier, famous for his courage and his courtesy, long before the public took him to its heart. Son of an Anglo-Irish general serving in India, he arrived there himself in 1851, and apart from taking part in the campaign under Napier in Abyssinia, he spent the whole of his military life in the army in India until he retired as its Commander-in-Chief in 1893. In 1859 he was awarded the Victoria Cross for rescuing a standard from two sepoy mutineers, one of whom pressed a musket against his body which failed to go off when the trigger was pulled. To legendary gallantry he added a reputation for caring for the welfare of his men and for training them properly, using field conditions instead of parade-ground drill and teaching them rapid rifle fire at mobile targets.

He first became famous as a successful commander on the North-West Frontier in the Second Afghan War. Afghanistan was border territory between India and Russia. The British government took on full responsibility for India from the East India Company after the suppression of the Mutiny, and in 1878 the Viceroy, Lord Lytton, decided on a forward policy to counteract the growing influence of the Russians in Kabul. Roberts led a column through the mountains, defeating the ever-formidable Afghan tribesmen with bold flanking movements round their positions on the craggy hills above. When the British Mission sent to follow up his victories was massacred by the Afghans, Roberts, after fighting his way back to Kabul, led his force right across the country to rescue the British troops besieged in Kandahar, covering 314 miles across mountains over 8,000 feet high in three weeks, with the midday August temperature at 110 degrees. It became the most famous march in the annals of the Empire. Roberts succeeded where many have failed, including the British in the First Afghan War, and, more recently, the Russians.

Back in England it looked as if honourable retirement would be his fate, though his book *Forty-one Years in India* ran to thirty-five editions, and was notable for the generosity of his judgements of friend and foe alike. Wolseley's ring of 'African' officers dominated the management of the army. Roberts was no enthusiast for some of Cardwell's reforms, especially short-service commissions, and he had no flair for administration. He was the Tory general, a target for Radical journalists, an outspoken opponent of allowing Indian judges to have jurisdiction over Europeans and of commissioning native officers in the Indian army. But, though a year older, he had aged better than Wolseley, keeping fit with hunting, pig-sticking and polo. So, with a Conservative government in power, he was picked to become Commander-in-Chief of the British forces in the Boer War after Buller's defeats. The year he spent out there seemed successful, and he handed over to Kitchener, saying that the war was nearly over. But he had failed to trap the main Boer generals, and left behind him a guerilla enemy who prolonged it for three years, partly thanks to shortcomings of the new system of army transport, for which he had been responsible.

Roberts returned to London to become the last Commander-in-Chief of the British army (the post was abolished in 1904). He had already been described as a 'dangerous dolt' for his warnings about Germany. Now, suggesting prophetically that 'a shot fired in the Balkan Peninsula might produce an explosion which would change the fortunes of every remotest colony in our Empire', he campaigned for compulsory training throughout the country, to provide home defence and free the army for overseas duty. He lived long enough to see his prophecies come true, and died of pneumonia in France in December 1914, visiting British troops in the trenches.

Further Reading
D. Pelham Jones, *Lord Roberts*, 1954.
Earl Roberts, *Forty-one Years in India: from subaltern to commander-in-chief*, 2 vols, 1897.

ROBINS, JOHN (*fl.*1650-2), the Ranter, had been a small farmer, but sold his land and went to London when he came to believe that he had divine powers, notably that of raising the dead; he once said 'I have had nine or ten of them at my house at a time, of those that were said to be raised from the dead'. His followers deified him, and he was known as 'the Ranters' god'. He had a plan to convert the Jews by leading 144,000 men to the Holy Land, and trained his volunteers on a diet of dry bread, water and raw vegetables; it was fatal to some. Arrested in 1651, he spent ten months in prison, in the course of which he was visited by Lodowick Muggleton and John Reeve. According to Muggleton, they used their power to pronounce eternal damnation upon him; whereupon he recanted, wrote to Cromwell, was freed from prison, returned to the country and became a farmer again.

ROBINSON, FREDERICK JOHN, VISCOUNT GODERICH, 1st EARL OF RIPON (1782-1859) was prime minister for five months: 'a transient and embarrassed phantom', Disraeli called him. Unable to master his colleagues or to secure even the semblance of harmony from the reluctant coalition which passed for a Cabinet, he eventually resigned in despair. Financial abilities, a sensitive and philosophic mind, and a pleasant, witty, House of Commons manner had carried 'Prosperity Robinson' too far. In less demanding offices he would have a further useful career.

He was the second son of the second Lord Grantham and of Lady Mary Yorke. At Harrow he was the schoolfellow of two future prime ministers, Aberdeen and Palmerston, and of Lord Althorp. After serving for two years as private secretary to the Lord Lieutenant of Ireland, his kinsman, the third Earl of Hardwicke, he was elected to parliament for Carlow in 1806 and in the following year for Ripon, where he sat for twenty years. He was soon promoted to minor offices in the Tory administrations of 1809 and 1812. In September 1809 he resigned from the first (he was Under-Secretary for the Colonies) in sympathy with Castlereagh. He strengthened this alliance when he accompanied Castlereagh to Vienna in 1814. In March 1815 he introduced the 'Corn Law' which prohibited the importation of corn until the home price had reached eighty shillings a quarter – with 'the greatest reluctance'. He suffered from the bill's unpopularity when a mob attacked his house in Old Burlington Street and destroyed some valuable pictures. In January 1818 he was appointed President of the Board of Trade. In May 1820 he declared in the House of Commons that 'he had always given it as his opinion that the restrictive system of commerce in this country was founded in error, and calculated to defeat the object for which it was adopted'.

In January 1823 Robinson was given a chance to go further in the direction of reform when he became Chancellor of the Exchequer, for his successor at the Board of Trade was Huskisson. The two men worked together under Liverpool's skilful direction in the 'economic Cabinet' in the interest of fiscal liberalism; they were assisted by a general revival of trade and a climate of opinion which was increasingly favourable to the axioms and policies of the classical economists. He was lucky, like any chancellor who is in a position to make reductions of taxation, but he used his position skilfully, combining the lowering of such taxes as the window tax (halved in 1823: there was great rejoicing) with the reduction of the debt, and judicious grants for such objects as the purchase of the Angerstein collection 'to lay the foundation of a national gallery of works of art', the erection of buildings for the British Museum and the restoration of Windsor Castle. In his free trade budget of 1824 he proposed to use his surplus 'as a means of commencing a system of alterations in the fiscal and commercial regulations of his country'. Especially important was the reduction of duties on raw silk and the end of the prohibition of importation of manufactured silk – now subject to a duty of thirty per cent.

Robinson's free trade policy did not lack courage, and it succeeded. His style may be studied in his third budget, of 1825, when he congratulated the House on the prosperity of the country and invited members to 'contemplate with instructive admiration the harmony of its proportions and the solidity of its basis' before reducing duties on iron, hemp, coffee, sugar, wine, spirits and cider. Expansive chancellors have often had to swallow their boasts: before the end of the year a commercial crisis caused primarily by the over-issue of paper money forced Robinson to prevent the issue of notes under £5. Evidence of mounting distress in 1826 did not deter him from a sanguine assessment of the country's situation in his budget of that year. It was indeed remarkable, as Martineau pointed out, what different conclusions 'Prosperity Robinson' (Cobbett's name for him) and 'Adversity Hume' could draw from identical statistics. Robinson wanted Liverpool to promote him to the House of Lords and a less onerous post; when Canning became prime minister he was created Viscount Goderich and Secretary of State for War and the Colonies. His failure to uphold the government's position in the House of Lords against Wellington and his high Tory phalanx should have disqualified him for higher office. But when Canning died George IV chose Goderich to form a Cabinet.

He began badly by yielding to the king, as it appeared to his colleagues, over the appointment of Herries to the Exchequer. Herries quarrelled bitterly with Huskisson over the chairmanship of the finance committee. Robinson was surprisingly defeatist. In Cabinet meetings 'Goody Goderich' was ill at ease, his sudden tearful collapses in odd contrast to the bland face he normally presented. It was perhaps fortunate that he never met parliament. On 8 January 1828, he resigned – but seems to have been surprised that he was offered no place by his successor, Wellington. He supported the Catholic Emancipation Bill, however, and the repeal of the Corporation and Test Acts. 'A good and useful speech' on the national debt (1830) showed him at his best. His appointment to be Secretary of War and the Colonies in Lord Grey's government (1830) and his commitment, after 'a sacrifice of many preconceived opinions, of many predilections, and of many long-cherished notions' to parliamentary reform, probably represented his true position – a mild and guarded liberalism. His proposals for the abolition of slavery were, however, unacceptable; so Stanley succeeded him and he became Lord Privy Seal and Earl of Ripon. With Stanley and Graham he resigned over the appointment of the Irish

Church Commission (May 1834). Peel made him President of the Board of Trade in 1841. In May 1843 young Mr Gladstone succeeded him; he went to the Board of Control. It was fitting that he should move the second reading of the Bill for the abolition of the Corn Laws – and subsequently resign with Peel in June 1846.

Ripon died at his house on Putney Heath in January 1859. He was buried at Nocton in Lincolnshire. He had always seized any chance of escaping to his Lincolnshire estate. The indifferent health of his wife (they married in 1814; she was Albinia Hobart, daughter of the fourth Earl of Buckinghamshire) may have been another inducement. Unfortunately he gave the impression of wanting the fruits of office while shrinking from the toils. Peel described him as 'a perfect master of the arts of commerce' but Gladstone, his vice-president at the Board of Trade, 'came to form a low estimate of the knowledge and information of Lord Ripon'. He had expressed his dread of 'the labour and confinement of the situation' when made chancellor; a friend congratulated him on being promoted to a position 'where *work* you must and *speak* you must'. As a speaker he usually pleased, since he had the art of 'enlivening even dry subjects of finance with classical allusions and pleasant humour' (Le Marchant). 'His political convictions,' said Lord Crewe, 'were limited to those announced by the diverse governments of which he was a member.' His only surviving son inherited his abilities and his liberalism and became Governor-General of India.

Further Reading
W. D. Jones, *Prosperity Robinson*, 1967.

ROBINSON, HENRY CRABB (1775-1867), chronicler of his times, was the son of a tanner of Bury St Edmunds. In his youth he was an attorney's clerk. A small legacy enabled him to go to Germany. He was there for five years, 1800-5, mainly at Jena, Frankfurt and Weimar. Outgoing, friendly, liking the company of interesting people, he met most of the Germans who exercised such an influence at that time, notably Goethe, Schiller and Herder – and the famous émigré, Mme de Stael. From 1807 to 1809 he worked for *The Times*, latterly in Spain: he could be called the first war correspondent. In 1813 he was called to the Bar and worked hard enough to enable him to retire, in 1828, with sufficient income to enable him further to cultivate and record literary life. He was one of the founders of London University (1828) and an early member of the Athenaeum Club.

It was said of Crabb Robinson that he never lost a friend. Only with Hazlitt was there a brief estrangement – and then because that provocative writer criticized both Wordsworth, another friend, and the law – his profession. Robinson certainly never wearied in the pursuit of friendship, nor in the acts of imaginative kindness which secured it. He had a special regard for Coleridge; for Blake the devotion that the critic owes to genius. It is partly through him and through his matchless diaries that we know them, along with Lamb, Wordsworth, Southey, the Flaxmans, Miss Mitford; indeed few among the most interesting, gifted people of the day were outside his acquaintance. The value of his diaries lies in his assiduity, his fairness, in a way the ordinariness, allied to integrity, that inspired trust – and confidences. The attraction lies in the absence of malice, affectation, exhibitionism. 'The best English diaries,' wrote Kate O'Brien, 'have been written by bores.' If this be a rule, he is an exception for which we, like his many friends, may be grateful.

RODNEY, GEORGE, 1st BARON RODNEY (1719-92)

was one of the most enterprising admirals of his time. Although not always popular with the government or men under his command, he rendered great service by his victory of the Saints after a war in which the navy had scant success.

Born in London, of an old Somerset family, and sent to Harrow by his guardian, the Duke of Chandos, he entered the navy in 1732. He was a captain at twenty-four and a rear admiral at forty after brave and notable service. In 1762 he commanded the expedition which captured Martinique, but the next phase of his career was prejudiced by his extravagance and by the admiralty's suspicion that he was liable to be truculent in delicate situations and that he wanted war to provide a chance to redeem his debts. In 1774 he was forced to evacuate to Paris in order to escape his creditors. He was recalled in 1780 to command in the West Indies, with Samuel Hood, a keen young officer, as second-in-command. After the failures of Byron and the resignation of Keppel and Barrington, the government was anxious for some success. 'For God's sake go to sea without delay,' wrote Sandwich; 'You cannot conceive of what importance it is to yourself, to me and to the public.' Rodney was released from his creditors by the generosity of a French nobleman – a pleasantly civilized touch – but he was kept to his cabin by the gout, another enemy, when his fleet chased the Spanish in a night action off Cape St Vincent and took six ships. In April and May he fought three drawn engagements with the French fleet. In February 1781 he seized St Eustatius, with stores valued at £3,000,000. Rodney and the general shared the spoils and dallied on the island, behaving in a way that caused scandal in the fleet and questions in parliament. Hood, complaining of his chief's dilatoriness, added, 'The Lares of St Austatius were so bewitching as not to be withstood by flesh and blood.'

Rodney had already fallen foul of some of his captains. He was evolving, during these campaigns, a new tactical plan based upon breaking the enemy's line. He is said to have outlined the idea with cherry-stones at the dinner table of Lord George Germain. But it is typical of him that he never took the trouble to explain the plan properly to his captains. He was very polite and equable, but an intolerant commander. While his private letters are redolent of his love for his family, his dispatches are often sharply critical of the men who served under him. Nor was he popular with them. Aloof, very much a man of the world, with a keen eye for property and prize-money, a politician who had fought an expensive election for Northampton and could say that 'a man in our country is nothing without being in parliament', Rodney was the opposite of Hood, professional middle-class, a puritan about prize-money.

Rodney had returned to England in August 1781 to face his critics and the planters' lawyers. He went back to the West Indies full of confidence that he could 'restore the empire of the Ocean to Great Britain'. In the heavy rollers of the Saints passage, between Guadeloupe and Dominica, the British squadrons waited to intercept the enemy under de Grasse. Here hurricane was as great a danger as the enemy's guns. When the two fleets were passing in line on opposite courses, suddenly, by the nineteenth of the thirty French battleships, Rodney ordered his captain to put over the helm and break through the French line; two others turned, each followed by a column of ships which in turn, with their broadsides, raked the French vessels at the point of rupture. Thus the French were thrown into confusion and five ships were disabled and taken. As night fell upon the victory, Hood urged that the fleet go in chase of the enemy, but Rodney made no attempt to pursue, saying to his indignant subordinate, 'Come, we have done very handsomely.' Hood exaggerated when he said that they could have taken the whole French fleet. Rodney's was the responsibility of keeping his fleet in being, and the French were fast sailors. Perhaps a few more damaged vessels might have come in as prizes. Ever since there has been controversy about the battle of the Saints: whether Rodney's tactics were deliberate or just improvised; how much he owed to the initiative of Commodore Afflick who led the second squadron to break the French line. Whatever the answers, Rodney had achieved something considerable in breaking away from the grip of the Fighting Instructions. He bequeathed to the admirals who followed him a good example of tactical initiative. He returned home to a peerage and a pension of £2,000 a year. He sailed no more, but there were still battles to fight, in the law courts, in matters arising from the damage to planters' property in the West Indies. He died, in 1792, a relatively poor man.

Further Reading
D. Hanney, *Rodney*, 1903.
A. H. Mahon, *Types of Naval Officers*, 1901.

ROE, SIR THOMAS (1581?-1644), diplomat and explorer, born of merchant stock at Low Leyton in Essex and educated at Magdalen College, Oxford, a young courtier in the last years of Elizabeth's reign, was knighted in 1605. An Elizabethan in his versatility, charm, conversational powers and Protestant nationalism, he was sent by Henry, Prince of Wales, to search for gold between the Amazon and the Orinoco in 1610-11. Roe advocated the formation of a West Indian company; went as ambassador to the Mogul emperor for the East India Company (1615-18) and won leave for Englishmen to travel for trade in his dominions; served as political adviser to Elizabeth, Queen of Bohemia, and as Chancellor of the Order of the Garter; and collected precious manuscripts and coins for the University of Oxford. His embassies on behalf of the Crown took him to Turkey (1621-8), to Poland and Sweden, where Gustavus Adolphus presented him with £2,500 (1629-30), and to Hamburg and the Empire (1638-40). Roe hoped in 1632 to be appointed Secretary of State, and his qualities would have lent distinction to that office. But he stood for an anti-Catholic foreign policy, directed mainly against the Habsburgs, and this old-fashioned attitude did not appeal to his friend Laud, who threw his influence on the side of Windebank instead. Nor did Laud show much sympathy for the project of the Scotsman John Durie, whom Roe backed, advocating the unification of all Protestant churches.

Further Reading
M. J. Brown, *The Life of Sir Thomas Roe, Itinerant Ambassador*, 1970.

ROEBUCK, JOHN (1718-94) was an inventor and entrepreneur who made an important contribution to the spectacular industrial advance of his time. He studied chemistry and medicine at Edinburgh and Leyden but soon abandoned medicine for technology. He established a chemical laboratory in Birmingham and invented some improved methods of refining precious metals and processes for the production of chemicals. Learning from the seventeenth-century chemist Glauber that lead was not attacked by sulphuric acid, he substituted lead for glass; this freed manufacturers from the use of fragile laboratory-scale apparatus and made possible cheap and relatively large-scale production. With Samuel Garbett he founded a vitriol manufactory but he decided that better opportunities existed in Scotland, where the bleaching trade was expanding fast. In 1749 he established a sulphuric acid plant near an old salt works at Prestonpans to provide cheap chemicals for bleaching, but despite secrecy about his methods and material (he imported sulphur from Leghorn and saltpetre through the East India Company), his patent rights were dubious and widely infringed upon. His works remained the largest, but many others sprang up to supply a growing demand in the textile industry. His pioneer work was a big factor in the low cost and massive production of bleached and printed goods.

Roebuck was, however, unfortunate in other fields. In 1760 he founded the Carron iron foundry and in 1762 invented a process of iron manufacture involving the use of pit coal. The Carron works were to become famous, but Roebuck did not benefit from their success, for he lost money heavily in coal mines and salt works in Linlithgowshire, and in 1773 he became bankrupt. He was the friend and patron of James Watt and it was he who suggested that Watt apply for a patent for steam engines, for he anticipated that they would be useful for pumping out his coal mines. His share in the patent was valued by his creditors at a farthing, but Boulton took it over in exchange for the cancellation of Roebuck's debts to him. Roebuck's enterprising career shows that great progress could be achieved by a man who was both scientist and technologist, but also what risks such men had to take to find a profitable way in which to make use of their technical discoveries.

Further Reading
A. and L. N. Clow, *The Chemical Revolution*, 1952.

ROGER OF HOWDEN (*d.*1201/2), a Yorkshireman from the East Riding, was vicar of Howden from 1173/6. A royal clerk by 1174, he was involved in diplomatic missions, led an inquiry into vacant abbeys (1175) and was an itinerant justice 1185-90. In 1190, he accompanied Richard I on crusade. At the siege of Acre he was in close touch with a group of crusaders from his part of Yorkshire. In 1191, Richard sent Roger back to Europe to keep an eye on Philip II of France. One of Roger's patrons was Hugh du Puiset, Bishop of Durham whose fall from power as justiciar in 1190 may have led to Roger's exclusion from office in the 1190s as he retained close links with the bishop, who died in Howden in 1195. Roger wrote two major chronicles, the *Gesta Henrici II et Ricardi (Deeds of Henry II and Richard)*, which covered events to 1192 and a *Chronica*, which revised and edited the *Gesta*, extending it to cover a wider span, 732-1201. The *Gesta* has been attributed to another chronicler, the so-called 'Benedict of Peterborough', but it is now clear that Roger wrote both. For the reigns of Henry II and Richard I, Roger is an indispensible source. Drawing heavily on official records, Roger provides a detailed account of central government, diplomacy, international affairs and high politics, while keeping an eye on local events in south Yorkshire. He preserves a detailed itinerary of Richard I's journey to Sicily and Palestine in 1190-1, and an eye-witness account of the siege of Acre. Reflecting his own career and interests, Roger copied into his text Henry II's assizes, the law book attributed to Ranulf Glanvill, names of Henry's justices, papal letters and diplomatic treaties. Roger set a standard for dispassionate narrative and official history not often met by other chroniclers of the political scene. His private life may have been more turbulent. A story did the rounds in the late 1180s of the parson of Howden's mistress (his *belle amie*) whose immorality was exposed by a miracle at a local shrine which led to her being publicly beaten up. Perhaps Roger's crusade was of penitence or escape.

Further Reading
D. Corner, 'The *Gesta Regis Henrici Sewind* and *Chronica* of Roger, parson of Howden', *Bulletin of the Institute of Historical Research* lvi, 1983.

J. Gillingham, 'Roger of Howden on Crusade', *Medieval Historical Writing*, ed. D. O. Morgan, 1983.

ROGER OF MONTGOMERY (*d.*1094), first Earl of Shrewsbury, created one of the most powerful and strategically important lordships in post-Conquest England. The son of a Norman vicomte, he first appears in the army of Duke William in 1051-2. Probably only a few years younger than the duke, thereafter he enjoyed William's special confidence. In the early 1050s he greatly increased his estates by marrying the forceful Mabel, heiress to the extensive lordship of Bellême. Although closely involved in planning the invasion of 1066, Roger remained in the duchy to help the administration of the Duchess Matilda. It was only the later romances of Wace that put him at Hastings, a tribute to his subsequent fame and reputation. In 1067, however, he accompanied William to England where he received huge estates in Sussex and Shropshire. By the end of 1074, he was titled Earl of Shrewsbury. His administration of his Marcher lands provide an insight in how the Conquest was secured. Roger had a more or less free hand. Before 1066, there had been no Crown lands or royal thegns in Shropshire: by 1086, apart from Roger, there were only five other lay tenants-in-chief in the whole county. To support him, Roger gave out land to men already his vassals in Normandy with whom he set about building castles (as at Shrewsbury and Montgomery) and extending his power into Wales. Orderic Vitalis, whose father, Odelerius, was Roger's chaplain, described the earl as wise and prudent 'a lover of justice, who always enjoyed the company of learned and sober men'. His English subjects were as unimpressed as they were unfavoured. The citizens of Shrewsbury complained that they still had to pay the same level of geld after the castle had been built as before, perhaps because of the loss of houses incurred in its construction, let alone the forced labour. Roger's rule was effective and ruthless; his authority based on ties of personal allegiance; a network of castles; successful protection from the Welsh; and brute force. In many ways he remained a conqueror and exploiter rather than a settler. But he left his mark on the Marches, in his castle mounds and the

perpetuation of his name in the Welsh town and county of Montgomery. As J. Le Patourel wrote, Roger's career 'shows what was possible in Norman society during the eleventh century'.

ROGER OF PONT L'EVEQUE (*d.*1181; Archbishop of York 1154-81) has suffered from being judged by his role in the Becket controversy. Although this perspective aptly reflects the corrosive embrace of the affair, it does not give Roger his due. A well-educated Norman, a good Latinist and able church lawyer, Roger was one of the talented group of erudite secular clerks Archbishop Theobald gathered around him in the 1140s. Later hostile gossip suggested that Roger was condescending and antagonistic to the less academically groomed Thomas Becket. Yet until the parting of the ways in 1162-4, there was no especial antagonism between Roger and Thomas, beyond perhaps inevitable rivalry for preferment and attention in the competitive, self-consciously superior hot-house of Theobald's household, the twelfth century's equivalent of Jowett's Balliol, just as Bayeux was the eleventh's. Roger, indeed, had little to be jealous about. One of Theobald's favourites, in 1148 Roger became Archdeacon of Canterbury and in 1154, largely through Theobald's influence, Archbishop of York.

Theobald may have hoped that in Roger he would have a pliant Archbishop of York who, with his Canterbury background, would forego the usual disputes with the southern metropolitan. In fact Roger turned native, becoming an aggressive and skilful advocate of York's claims to equality with Canterbury and authority over the Scottish episcopacy. In York itself he extended the Minster with the construction of a new choir, east end and lavishly endowed chapel of St Sepulchre, as well as building himself a substantial palace. To his scholarly interests may be attributed surviving twelfth-century manuscripts still in the Minster Library. Perhaps it was because of his benefactions, made possible by the considerable fortune he amassed, or his absences on national business that he retained good relations with his chapter. His household included the renowned Italian canon lawyer Master Vacarius, another old boy of Theobald's entourage. He accompanied Roger north in 1154 and never went back, his presence testimony to Roger's stature and the attractions, under his rule, of the northern province. Roger brought to the province of York a stability not seen for more than a decade before his election and not witnessed again for another thirty-five years after his death.

As Archbishop of York, Roger's finest hour should have been when he crowned Henry II's son king in June 1170. Instead, this formed a prime charge in the indictment levelled at him by the supporters of Becket for whom Roger had been an invader of the rights of his superior metropolitan, a malicious inciter of royal anger and, even, a conspirator and paymaster of the saint's murderers. By 1162, when Becket was appointed Archbishop of Canterbury, Roger was already an experienced prelate. Outside his diocese he served as a papal judge-delegate; he undertook diplomatic missions for the king; he regularly attended the king's court; and, in the Canterbury vacancy after the death of Theobald in 1161, he had acted, with papal approval, as head of the English church. Historically and perhaps personally, tension with the new Archbishop of Canterbury was likely, if not inevitable. After 1163, Roger sided with the king – as in the end did all his brother bishops. Appointed a papal legate in 1164, Roger's connivance at the Young Henry's coronation was unsurprising, but it attracted Becket's especial wrath and his disciples' particular venom. It was Becket's excommunication, on the eve of his return to England in November 1170, of Roger and two colleagues for their part in the coronation that prompted Roger's visit to Henry at Bar-le-Roi over Christmas; the king's outburst of rage at his former chancellor; and the retaliation of the four knights. Some later said that Roger helped plan the knights' attack. This probably owes more to the hysteria of Becket's bereaved followers than truth. Although he was suspended by the pope, by the end of 1171 he had been rehabilitated: the charges of the Becket faction had not stuck.

Throughout the Becket controversy, Roger had played his own game. While Foliot took the polemical lead, Roger exploited the situation to consolidate, where possible, the rights of York. He disagreed with Becket's position; deplored his methods; and had little regard for his powers of argument, but he was motivated not by personal spite or ideological disagreement but institutional advantage. In the aftermath of the martyrdom, such expedient opportunism was damned by hindsight but was more representative of how the church operated than Becket's histrionics. Roger persisted with his attempts to establish York's independence from Canterbury under Becket's successor, Richard of Dover, and continued to assert his claims over Scotland. He played a significant role on the king's side in the rebellion of 1173-4. Looked at from his new palace, his career was neither blighted nor peripheral.

Dangerously for the historian, Roger's opposition to Becket ensured that his personality received close and unflattering scrutiny from the martyr's apologists. Even the high-minded John of Salisbury in 1172 dragged up a twenty-year-old scandal about Roger's sex life. In the early 1150s Roger apparently had a homosexual affair with a beautiful boy, possibly an oblate, called Walter. When Walter later told others about the liaison, Roger, perhaps fearing blackmail and the ruin of a career so promisingly launched, used his authority as archdeacon to have the unfortunate Walter's eyes put out. Then, to silence him for good, Roger persuaded some secular judges to convict Walter as a felon and have him hanged. There followed a cover-up, smoothly orchestrated by Archbishop Theobald, ending with absolution from the pope. As a story, it had much to titillate: illicit sex; the abuse of power; the murky private lives of the great; the establishment closing ranks. How much, if any of it, is true is impossible to estimate. It is hard to credit that Roger, so soon after these events, would have been selected by Theobald as Archbishop of York, nor that he could, as he did, have kept on such civil terms with the rest of Theobald's high-minded, priggish protégés. John of Salisbury's salacious story probably tells us more about him and the sort of scabrous tale popular in twelfth-century educated circles than it does about Roger.

Further Reading
F. Barlow, *Thomas Becket*, 1986.
A. Aylmer and R. Cant, *A History of York Minster*, 1977.

ROGER OF SALISBURY (*c*.1065/70-1139; Bishop of Salisbury 1102-39) was the dominant figure in English royal administration for a generation. As chief financial and judicial minister of Henry I and Stephen for thirty years, he created lasting institutions of central government, notably the Exchequer, and provided a model for the later Chief Justiciars of the Angevin kings. The shadow of 'Roger the Great', as some called him, lies heavy across all descriptions and discussions of the origins of effective departments of state and national bureaucracy. To his admiring great nephew, Richard FitzNeal, in his *Dialogue of the Exchequer* (1179), Roger was 'the chief mover in great matters'; to his modern biographer, he is 'one of England's greatest statesmen'.

Yet the character, mind and motives of this most powerful of ministers of the Crown remain elusive. No minutes of meetings or personal correspondence survive, only a small proportion of the official documents issued or received by him. What exists suggests a man of energy, talent and ruthlessness, but also seriousness and resilience. Like a surprising number of English leaders, he was self-made. In his delight in ostentation and power, he was perhaps more of a Wolsey or a Thatcher than a Thomas Cromwell; in venality more a Lloyd George. As with all these, at his plenitude Roger was both innovative and feared; with them, too, his fall was sudden and complete; but, uniquely in this company, Roger's legacy was incontestably durable.

Roger first came to the notice of the future Henry I as a priest from the Avranchin region in south-west Normandy, probably in 1091. According to legend, Roger recommended himself by the speed with which he said Mass. If this story – written a century later – was designed to cast doubt on Roger's vocation, it may have been wide of the mark. It was unusual for ambitious secular clerks of the time to proceed to full Holy Orders so young. There are signs that Roger's spiritual life, while overlaid with secular employment, was neither assumed nor dormant. The chronicler William of Malmesbury, who knew Roger, mentioned his reluctance to stay in royal service after he became a bishop. Although he amassed an awesome fortune, he was not obviously corrupt and claimed he received no formal salary after becoming a bishop. In 1114, he successfully opposed what he regarded as the king's poor choice of candidate for the archbishopric of Canterbury. A cultured man, with interests in education and the arts, throughout his public career Roger was an active patron of Augustinian canons, a new order with a particular mission to the laity and one popular with some of Roger's contemporaries with unimpeachable spiritual credentials. His most notable benefaction was to St Frideswide's Priory in Oxford. At the end of his life, his contrition for harming the interests of certain religious houses appears focused and genuine. No saint, indeed a notorious sinner with an openly acknowledged mistress, Roger was probably a traditionally committed priest, who saw the separation from secular matters and the imperatives of canon law in a rather more relaxed light than the Gregorian reformers around him. Except to the noisy puritans of his day, this did not make him a hypocrite.

However he caught Henry's eye, by 1100 Roger was a chaplain, possibly steward, in his household in Normandy. After Henry's accession in 1100, as the king's chaplain, he began witnessing charters in England. Early in 1101, Roger became Henry's chancellor, in which capacity he used to dictate charters on the king's behalf. His prominence in the chancery was recognized by his appointment as Bishop of Salisbury in 1102 (although consecration by Archbishop Anselm had to await the resolution of the dispute over investiture in 1107). His status within the régime as a whole was clearly signalled by a succession of lucrative grants of castles, estates and benefices beyond those attached to his see. Soon his interests stretched across southern England, from London to Wiltshire. Roger's political prominence was notably confirmed in 1106 by the commital to him of the captive Richard Curthose, the king's elder brother, who remained imprisoned in Roger's castle of Devizes for the next twenty years. The bishop's ménage at Devizes was bizarre, the eldest son of the Conqueror rubbing shoulders with the bishop's articulate mistress, Matilda of Ramsbury, and their children. Whether they conversed and, if so, what they had to say to each other, is matter for speculation.

By 1109, Roger had advanced to the forefront of royal administration acting in concert with the regent, Queen Matilda, during the king's absences in France. His activities had become primarily judicial (he had acted as a local justiciar at least since 1106) and financial. Here, at the centre of government, Roger established his authority and wielded power, in the phrase of more than one observer, 'second only to the king'. Here, too, he laid the foundations of a system of central fiscal scrutiny and control that survived for centuries.

The pre-Conquest English kings had apparently kept track of what was owed and paid them by means of tallies, sticks notched according to the amounts received and split into two, so that each party held a record. It seems that this system, operated by 1066 at the main royal treasury at Winchester, was ad hoc, there being no regular, central audit to scrutinize revenue. After the Conquest, a larger royal demesne; higher demands on expenditure; the introduction of sheriffs' farms; the perceived necessity for accurate accounts of revenue paid and owing; and even, perhaps, the Domesday Survey, prompted the establishment in the 1090s of regular meetings of royal officials to audit receipts, identify debts and settle disputes. It was this central audit that Bishop Roger reorganized and transformed, almost certainly in response to raising the marriage aid for Princess Matilda in 1110. From that year, at the latest, the office of the household which collected levies, assayed receipts, adjudicated complaints and recorded payments, debts and pleas, was known as the Exchequer.

The Exchequer derived its name from the five foot by ten foot cloth marked with white columns of an abacus against a black background (so not actually chequered) which covered the table at which the audit was conducted. The use of this visual computer was, with the various methods of checking the number, weight and content of the coins received, designed to establish the Exchequer calculations beyond doubt. It also speeded up the process of demonstrating to the sheriffs whose accounts were being audited the sums, especially deficits, involved. The unimpeachable accuracy of the Exchequer's accounting was essential as much of its business, and most of its importance, depended on its role as a court, where judgements were delivered on the whole range of the king's fiscal affairs, including fines and profits of justice. In a similar move to secure acceptance of decisions, records of the annual audit held at Winchester each Michaelmas were committed to rolls of parchment and stored. The first mention of these so-called Pipe Rolls was in 1114, although only one survives from Roger's career, that of 1130. As in earlier centuries and across Europe, officials were almost automatically suspect, the distinguished contemporary Arabist and astrologer Adelard of Bath accusing England's chief men of violence, 'the magistrates wine lovers and the judges mercenary'. Given this ritualized suspicion, openness and accuracy were at a political as well as financial premium.

The adoption of the abacus as a tool of bureaucracy was no accident. In and around the English court *c.*1100 there was considerable interest in mathematics and computing. Adelard of Bath himself translated Euclid, studied the abacus and computed horoscopes. The Lorrainer, Robert Losinga, Bishop of Hereford (1079-95) may have introduced the abacus into England. One of Henry I's prominent sheriffs, Hugh of Buckland (*d.c.*1115), provided administrative information to the author of a treatise on the abacus, Turchil: either of them may have helped devise the Exchequer itself. Another influence was the school where Adelard had taught at Laon in northern France, with its leading *magister*, Anselm, and his brother, the mathematician Ralph, who also wrote on the abacus. To Laon, Roger sent his nephews, Alexander and Nigel, and employed a Laon graduate, Guy of Etampes as master of the school at Salisbury. Whatever else, the Exchequer was introduced by a circle of clerical administrators well abreast of the most recent developments in scholarship. It needed the practical skills of Roger to translate theory of such as Turchil's into a durable instrument of government.

By the early 1120s, Roger's ascendancy was complete. As early as 1113, his authority was described by a suppliant bishop as 'procuration' (*vestra procuratio*) implying control and management. This Roger particularly displayed in matters fiscal and judicial, but his wider political role steadily grew. The deaths of Queen Matilda (1118) and Prince William (1120) left him the sole viceroy in name as he had been before in action. During Henry's absence 1123-6 Roger ruled England, described by one witness as 'guardian' (*provisor*), by himself as procurator of the realm. As viceroy, Roger oversaw all aspects of government and issued writs in his own name authorizing expenditure or fiscal pardons. In 1124/5 he organized a major reform of the coinage after Henry's troops had complained of the debased content of the money with which they were being paid. Roger's tactics give an insight into the rougher side of twelfth-century administration. Ninety-two minters were summoned to Winchester where most were blinded and castrated. By 1124, Roger had also instituted a system of ad hoc itinerant justices to hear royal pleas and supervise the activities of sheriffs. In this period Roger demonstrated the efficacy of a more impersonal rule, a model exploited fully after 1154 when the King of England held more extensive lands and interests overseas. Under the Angevins the Exchequer consolidated its position as the pivotal fiscal and judicial institution of royal control over his subjects and provinces; the tactic of itinerant justices was formalized, after 1168, into regular circuits by justices-in-eyre; and the post of viceroy and king's alter ego was vested in the office of Chief Justiciar.

In fact Roger's years of power did not win him total security of royal favour. In 1126, on the king's return,

Robert Curthose was transferred into the keeping of Robert, Earl of Gloucester, Henry's illegitimate son. In 1128-9, a special audit was held by Robert of Gloucester and Brian FitzCount, which uncovered extensive indebtedness among the sheriffs, many of whom had been appointed by Roger a few years earlier. This audit produced a thorough reorganization of administration, revealed by the unusually full Pipe Roll of 1130. Not only were some of Roger's associates, such as Geoffrey de Clinton, attacked, but the use of Earl Robert and Brian FitzCount to scrutinize administration as well as their findings implied criticism of Roger's management. Roger never again acted as regent.

One explanation for this apparent decline in royal confidence may have lain in Henry's plan to secure the succession for his daughter Matilda and his son-in-law Geoffrey of Anjou. Although Roger swore to uphold this succession in 1127 and 1131, he may have had misgivings: in 1135 he quickly embraced the claim of Henry's nephew Stephen of Blois. Henry's schemes for the succession had been worked out among intimates outside Roger's circle, two of whom, Earl Robert and Brian Fitz-Count, both strong Matildine partisans, conducted the 1128-9 investigation. Alternatively, this apparent reining in of his authority may have reflected royal unease at Roger's pre-eminence: in 1129 one royal clerk put Roger's name on a charter instead of the king's.

If Roger's power was restricted, he remained administratively indispensible. Throughout his long tenure of high office, he attracted no whiff of scandal or charges of corruption in his conduct of business. Yet, unafraid to enjoy the fruits of office and the patronage of a grateful monarch, Roger built up a powerful temporal position and, with two nephews installed as councillors and bishops (Alexander at Lincoln 1123 and Nigel at Ely 1133), established a unique dynastic influence. He also found time to be an energetic and effective diocesan. His capacity for work was evidently considerable.

If anything, the death of Henry I in 1135 temporarily restored Roger's position. As guardian of the treasury at Winchester and head of the Exchequer, he played a crucial role in supporting Stephen's successful coup. His son, Roger, became chancellor and Adelelm, probably another son, acted as the king's Treasurer. Yet the appearance of government as a family firm was deceptive. Roger retained his grip on administration, his style as peremptory as ever, as in a writ of 1138: 'On behalf of the king and myself, I order ...' But politically, his star was waning. Roger, now ageing, was unable to control the new king's expenditure, the treasure amassed by Henry I being rapidly and disastrously dissipated. This financial failure, over which Roger presided perhaps helplessly, revealed that the main political decisions were being taken by the king and his own close advisers, notably Waleran of Meulan.

It may have been fears of Roger's entrenched power combined with his possible disapproval of the management of affairs that led to Stephen succumbing to Waleran's determination to destroy Roger and his family. It was rumoured that the bishop harboured sympathy for Matilda, although this is circumstantially unlikely. The fall of Roger was encompassed at Oxford in June 1139, when his men were embroiled in a contrived affray, the bishop then being charged with a breach of the king's peace. Roger was personally treated very badly, at one point being committed to a cowshed. His castle of Devizes, defended by his mistress and nephew, Nigel of Ely, surrendered to the king after Stephen had threatened to execute one of Roger's sons. Although Roger and his episcopal nephews were allowed to retain their sees, their goods and property were confiscated. Such was the gigantic size of Roger's treasure, that this may have been one motive for the bankrupt king's actions. To signal the change of ministry, a new royal seal was made.

The charges against Roger were heard in a church council at Winchester, when the king's breach of clerical privilege was also challenged. In the event Roger was neither convicted nor exonerated; he kept his see but the bulk of his possessions and wealth were lost. Out of office, the ailing bishop spent his last months organizing restitution for those he had harmed or neglected, especially in the church. It is said that all political careers end in failure; there are few for whom that failure was seemingly so complete. When Roger died in December 1139, his and his family's fortunes were in ruins; the treasury over which he had presided was empty, except for his own wealth which had been pillaged; his country was embarked on civil war, the administration which he had created was disrupted to the point of extinction. Yet for all that, his method of rule and his institutions of government survived to ensure that Roger's legacy was the most constructive of any single royal official in the early Middle Ages.

Further Reading
E. J. Kealey, *Roger of Salisbury*, 1972.

ROGER OF WENDOVER (*d.*1236) was a monk of St Albans. He rose to be prior of the dependent cell at Belvoir but had to be removed in 1219 for financial mismanagement. Sometime after 1202, perhaps as late as 1231, he began writing a history from the Creation to his own day, the *Flores Historiarum (Flowers of History)*. Unoriginal to 1202, from then until he finished writing in 1234 Roger used no surviving chronicle. Unfortunately, he seemed to have relied heavily on his own imagination or gossip to fill the gap. The black reputation, almost gothic horror that surrounds the posthumous reputation of King John derives largely from Roger's account written a decade or so after the king's death. His

anecdotes establishing the image of John as lecherous, idle and sadistic, as far as they can be checked, appear to have been invented. His picture of the young Henry III is more sympathetic, perhaps because royal policy was less destructive of church interests; perhaps because, in retrospect, anyone was better than John. Roger has Henry declare 'I prefer to be considered a stupid king rather than a cruel or tyrannical one'. Roger took his stand with the barons, and was virulent in opposition both to royal exactions and the intrusive authority of the pope (who had in 1215 supported the royalists). Roger's attitudes were partisan. His portrait of John, however, may accurately reflect what was said of the late king in the years after the civil war and the often uneasy minority of Henry III. Roger was, in fact, a dull storyteller, loading his tales with circumstantial evidence in a pedestrian literary style. His fame, and the currency of his stories, depend largely on his successor as chief historiographer at St Albans, Matthew Paris, who incorporated, edited and 'improved' Roger's account in his *Chronica majora*.

Further Reading
A. Gransden, *Historical Writing in England c.550-c.1307*, 1979.

ROGERS, JOHN (*c.*1500-55), first Protestant martyr in the Marian persecution, was the son of John Rogers of Deritend, in the parish of Aston, near Birmingham. He was educated at Pembroke Hall, Cambridge, where he took his BA in 1525, and in 1532 was appointed Rector of Holy Trinity in the City of London. He resigned this living in 1534 and became chaplain to the Company of the Merchant Adventurers in Antwerp. At that time he was an orthodox Catholic priest, but he now fell in with Tyndale and was soon converted to Protestantism. Before he was arrested in 1535, Tyndale handed over to Rogers his incompleted translation of the Old Testament. Tyndale was burned in October 1535; during 1536 Rogers devoted himself to completing the Old Testament by adding to it Miles Coverdale's renderings (published in 1535) of the untranslated books and of the Apocrypha, and Tyndale's own translation of the New Testament (published 1526). Rogers's only original contribution was the Song of Manasses in the Apocrypha which he found in a French Bible printed in 1535. Rogers was also responsible for the preface, the marginal notes (the first English commentary on the Bible), and a calendar and almanack and other additional matter. Rogers signed the title-page with the name 'Thomas Matthew' and the book came to be known as Matthew's Bible. This was the book largely drawn upon for the Great Bible of 1539.

While at Antwerp Rogers married, probably in 1537, Adriana de Weyden: Weyden means 'meadows' and when in 1552 he naturalized his wife and children by a special act of parliament, the name was anglicized into Pratt from the Latin form 'prata'.

When Edward VI came to the throne, Rogers returned to England (1548). He was given three livings in London and in 1551 he was appointed to a prebend of St Paul's by Nicholas Ridley and shortly afterwards became divinity lecturer at St Paul's.

With his Protestant views Rogers naturally sympathized with Lady Jane Grey rather than with Mary Tudor. He preached two sermons for which he was had up before the Council, and in 1554 he was sent to Newgate. Here, in conjunction with Hooper, Bradford and others, he drew up a confession of faith of the most extreme Protestant type. He was again examined by Gardiner with much rudeness and even brutality and was condemned to death as a heretic. When he asked to be allowed to see his wife, he was refused, and it is said that he met her and his eleven children on the way to the stake. At the stake he was offered a pardon, if he would recant, but he refused and he was burned just outside the entrance to the church of St Bartholomew in Smithfield. He was the first of the Protestant martyrs, and his example had a widespread effect in encouraging others. Ridley confessed that the news of Rogers's death had destroyed 'a lumpish heaviness' in his heart.

Further Reading

M. L. Loane, *Pioneers of the Reformation in England*, 1964.
J. F. Mozley, *Coverdale and his Bibles*, 1953.
J. L. Chester, *Life of John Rogers*, 1861.

ROGERS, SAMUEL (1763-1855), poet, seemed to live for his craft, but did not need his craft to live. 'The Banker Bard' was a wealthy man. He was also generous in hospitality, patronage and support of friends: in his way, a significant figure in the circles where aristocracy met talent.

He grew up in Stoke Newington, near London. His father was a banker, and a Dissenter. Samuel's taste for poetry was first roused by admiration for a local hymn writer, Dr Watts. His early poems were praised. Through *The Pleasures of Memory*, he came to the notice of Charles James Fox, whom Rogers idolized, and of Byron, better poet than critic, who thought it one of the 'most beautiful didactic poems in our language'. He was content, moreover, to share a volume with 'the melodious Rogers'. In 1814 Murrays published *Lara, A Tale* (Byron's) with *Jacqueline, A Tale* (Rogers's). By then Rogers had retired from active banking.

Napoleon's downfall enabled Rogers to travel extensively. Its product was two works, *Human Life* and *Italy*. Thereafter, writing little, he dedicated himself to producing his existing work in the finest possible style. Indeed there have never been finer editions of poetry. He spent £10,000 on *Italy* and *Poems*, commissioning Turner and other famous artists to embellish them. His view of Italy was far from the romantic and revolutionary spirit that excited Shelley: it provided for the tourist, cultivated, or seeking culture. Rogers was offered the Poet Laureateship in 1850; perhaps wisely he refused. In eccentric old age he kept up his famous literary breakfasts. He would walk everywhere, in all weathers. His last few years were spent in an invalid chair after he had been run over by a carriage. With Rogers, his fine bindings and tasteful verse, his purposeful travelling anticipating Augustus Hare, his celebrated table talk and cultivation of good company, we enter the Victorian world.

ROLLE, RICHARD (*c.*1290-1349) of Hampole was one of the greatest mystics in medieval England and is certainly the one about whom most is known. Mystics meditated on Christianity and experienced divine revelations that gave them greater understanding of God and Christ. The centre of late medieval mysticism lay in the Low Countries, where Ruysbroeck, St Thomas à Kempis and other great mystics lived, but another centre was England. Four important English mystics of the fourteenth century are known by their writings: Walter Hilton (*d.*1396), an Augustinian canon from Nottinghamshire; Juliana Norwich (*d.*1373); Rolle; and the anonymous author of the *Cloud of Unknowing*. Other minor mystics are also known, such as Margery Kempe, and many others read and were influenced by mystical works in the next century, such as Henry VI, Cecily, Duchess of York and John Blacman. To judge by surviving manuscripts, mystical writing was widely read both among the clergy and the laity, which is striking evidence for a high standard of religious knowledge among at least some ordinary people.

Richard Rolle has the best documented career of any English mystic. The son of William Rolle of Thornton in Richmondshire (Yorks.), he attended school and was then sent by an archdeacon to Oxford University. He did not take a degree but left prematurely, preferring the spiritual knowledge revealed by his meditations to the abstract learning derived from the speculative theology of the schools. He then became a hermit in a wood, in spite of opposition from his family, who thought him mad and tried to restrain him. He escaped and led a wandering life, until settled at Rotherham by a patron, who met his material needs and enabled him to live a life of contemplation. Subsequently he moved on to Anderby and eventually Hampole by Doncaster near a Cistercian nunnery, where he died, presumably of plague. Although living very simply and ascetically and revered as a saint, at whose grave miracles were supposedly performed, Rolle retained an interest in practical teaching and wrote extensively on a variety of religious subjects.

Rolle is best known from his books, which are numerous and varied in character. He wrote Latin prose and verse *and* English prose and verse. The most popular of his books were apparently the Latin works on immediately useful topics, e.g. commentaries on parts of the Bible, which were presumably read initially only by the ordained clergy. One work indeed was concerned to instruct a parish priest in the basic duties of his post. His English works were apparently less popular and his English lyrics were read least of all. There are almost 100 surviving manuscripts of his *Amendment of Life* in Latin and fifty-eight surviving commentaries on the Psalms. It was actually in his vernacular works that Rolle developed his more emotional and individualistic interests and in them that he developed his devotion to Christ's Passion and his Holy Name, topics that achieved much greater popularity later in the Middle Ages. It was even worthwhile for the Lollards to produce pirate editions of Rolle's works to impart heresy unconsciously to the unsuspecting. Rolle's own work was quite orthodox.

Further Reading

A. Bancroft, *The Luminous Vision: Six Medieval Mystics*, 1982.

W. A. Pantin, *The English Church in the Fourteenth Century*, 1955.

ROMILLY, SIR SAMUEL (1757-1818), law reformer, was born in Frith Street, Soho, the son of Huguenot parents. His father, a jeweller, had emigrated from Montpellier; his mother brought some wealth into the family. With the help of his autobiography we can trace the melancholy of his later life to a lonely childhood. Left largely to a nurse who read to him from Fox's *Book of Martyrs* and the *Newgate Calendar*, taught the strictest tenets and traditions of Calvinism, Romilly might well, when he came to lose his faith, have lapsed into a nervous prostration. From this state and from the drab life of his father's shop he was saved by a legacy from a relative of his mother, which enabled him to read at the Bar. He made there a great reputation and an income, at his prime, of £15,000 a year. He also acquired an unequalled knowledge of the criminal law both of England and the continent. He studied the work of Beccaria, the Italian jurist, and Bentham, another reformer who preached the principle of 'equal punishment for the same crime'. The importance of Romilly in the history of legal reform is that he was a passionate idealist, but a profound lawyer and a working politician as well. He became Solicitor-General in the 'ministry of all the talents' in 1806, though he was not then a Member of Parliament. That year saw his Bankruptcy Law, a valuable civil law reform. He remained in the House of Commons after the fall of the Ministry in 1807 and began, in the following year, his campaign to bring some reason and humanity into the penal code.

To his work he brought a reputation for high-mindedness and a manner that was severe, but sincere enough to impress his most obdurate opponents. We may be shocked at the arguments of those who defended a situation in which children of twelve could be executed for stealing twenty-five pence (like Lord Ellenborough who opposed an amendment to raise the amount to fifty pence), but we should recall that they were prisoners themselves of conventional thinking, the love of liberty and the desire to protect property, at a time when there was no adequate police force, no proper prisons, no deterrent except the awesome ceremony of the Black Cap and the public horror of execution. That Romilly achieved anything at all at a time when all change was suspect as tending to Jacobinism and when he was known to have been an admirer of Napoleon, was because he was practical in his objectives, argued as a lawyer before lawyers, and never let himself be branded as a mere doctrinaire. At the height of the excitement of 1789 he, who had travelled in France and knew the country so well, had sent to Mirabeau an abstract of the Rules of Procedure of the British House of Commons for the use of the States-General! How unfortunate, we may think, that they were never adopted – but how typical of Romilly that he should have seen in the constitution of England the salvation of France. He was indeed no democrat. He sat for a succession of boroughs, but resolutely refused to commit himself to his electors upon anything 'calculated to court political favour'. He was appalled by the business of electioneering, even by celebrations of victory, and would have preferred, as he admitted, to have purchased a seat with cash. He may thus be seen as a Whig of the Whigs, an extreme case of the gulf between enlightened opinion in parliament and people in the constituencies.

Successive bills presented by Romilly were rejected by the Commons or the Lords. The fourth time he moved his Bill to repeal the Shop-Lifting Act, in 1816, he was able to tell the House that, even as he spoke, a boy convicted of shop-stealing was awaiting execution in Newgate gaol. He managed to secure the abolition of the death penalty for the crime of stealing from bleaching grounds, in England and Ireland, on petition of the manufacturers themselves who said that the severity of the sentence made the Act ineffective, prosecutions being rare and convictions rarer still. He also secured the repeal of an old statute making it a capital offence for a soldier or sailor to beg without a pass. In 1818, however, the Lords threw out yet again his Bill to repeal the Shop-Lifting Act; shortly afterwards his wife died, and Romilly killed himself in a sudden fit of despair. Lord Eldon came into court the next morning and saw the empty place in court where Romilly had been accustomed to sit. 'His eyes filled with tears: "I cannot stay here," he exclaimed; and rising in great agitation, he broke up his court.' Peers, bishops, judges might vote against him, his achievement might seem barren, but his career saw the tide turn. Legislation such as that of 1817, reintroducing the death-penalty for the destruction of lace-frames, would henceforward be impossible. The month after Romilly's death, petitions began to flow in, demanding a revision of the Criminal Code. In 1819 a Committee of Inquiry was set up. Subsequently Peel, the practical, conservative statesman, put Romilly's hopes and ideas into effect and hacked through the jungle of penal laws.

Fastidious, fair-minded, humane, patient in the face of disappointment, Romilly was one of the men who kept alive the conscience of the nation at a time of peril. It is easy to forget that his decade as a reformer coincided with a crisis of the Napoleonic Wars and unnerving disorders at home. In these years he managed to persuade moderate politicians that his cause was right.

Further Reading
C. G. Oakes, *Sir Samuel Romilly*, 1935.

ROMNEY, GEORGE (1734-1802),

portrait painter, was born in Lancashire, was apprenticed to a local artist and, shortly after his marriage to Mary Abbott in 1756, established himself in Kendal and invited clients. In 1762 he removed himself, but not his wife or children, to London, where he had some preliminary success with history paintings submitted to the Society of Arts. He travelled abroad to France and Italy, and when he finally returned to England in 1775, he was in a fair way to engage a public somewhat tired of the pomp of Reynolds and the subtlety of Gainsborough. Although he remained a shy, vulnerable, solitary man, who refused to send his pictures to the Academy, he attracted a wide patronage and not least – for it was worth a legion of flatterers – that of the Duchess of Devonshire. Soon he was the professional rival of Reynolds himself, who, being nettled that fashion was thus preferred to art, spoke coldly of 'the man in Cavendish Square'. Romney might have been expected now to call his wife to share in his success; but, whether at her own wish or not, she continued lonely in Lancashire for twenty years, during which her husband passed through prosperity to the sole eminence to which Reynolds's death raised him; only then, with the sense upon him that the night was coming when he could not work, did Romney return to his wife. To her credit, and perhaps a little to the credit of Romney's charm, she gladly received him until his death in imbecility in 1802.

The parents of Miss Bowles were for having her painted by Romney, fearing the tendency of Reynold's portraits to fade. 'Never mind,' they were told, 'a faded picture by Reynolds is better than the best of Romney's.' What Reynolds made of the girl and her dog is there in the Wallace Collection for anyone to delight in; but in any case the comparison was just. Romney's pictures do not glow like Reynolds's, they do not explore the mysteries which Gainsborough's do. But Romney was always elegant. In him a masterly hand supported a strong and simple sense of style. He could realize the visionary prospects of an aristocratic youth on the verge of manhood (*William Pitt*, *Richard Newman Harding* and some of the Eton leaving portraits); he could figure the maturity of an interesting man (*Joseph Allan*, *Warren Hastings*; and the portraits of *Cowper*). Unfortunately he fell for the space of four years from 1781 into a sort of infatuation with Emma Lyon or Hart, soon to be Lady Hamilton, who appears now 'in a straw hat', now 'in a turban', now surprisingly as 'Innocence'. He painted about fifty pictures of her. Lady Hamilton (however lovely) was a shallow woman, as unworthy perhaps of Romney's attentions as of Nelson's. Yet Romney seems to have taken her as the type of womanhood, and thereafter could hardly paint a woman in depth: an easy sentimentality, a failure in taste amounting to the banal, pervades his work, and intrudes even into the Eton portraits.

Romney's freshness was always attractive; it is due in part to his temperamental dislike of finishing a picture once the heat of invention had cooled. Cartloads of paintings just begun were removed from his house at Hampstead after his death, and even in his finest work the details are often only sketched in.

Further Reading
Leger Galleries, *George Romney as a Painter of Children*, 1984.
Ellis Waterhouse, *Painting in Britain 1530-1790*, 1969.

ROOKE, ADMIRAL SIR GEORGE (1650-1709),

the captor of Gibraltar, had fought at Beachy Head and La Hogue; he had been Commander-in-Chief both in the Mediterranean and in the Channel; and in 1700 he had been in command of a fleet supporting Charles XII of Sweden against the Danes in the Sound. Loyal, honest, cantankerous, Rooke was a capable rather than an imaginative admiral. He has been described as 'a sluggish, wary man whose imagination had no room for great designs'*; he was certainly very hostile to the policy of British naval control of the Mediterranean. In 1702 he had put to sea, with a force of soldiers under Ormonde, to take Cadiz. The expedition had been a fiasco, redeemed only by the chance discovery on the way home that a Spanish treasure-fleet, guarded by fifteen French ships of the line, was sheltering in Vigo Bay. Rooke's force sailed up the narrow inlet and destroyed the warships, although most of the treasure seems to have been removed before the battle. Two years later, in 1704, Rooke entered the Mediterranean with the object of combining with the Duke of Savoy's army in an attack upon Toulon. This proved impossible. Nor did the

*W. S. Churchill, *Marlborough*, 1967 edn, vol. II, p.84.

landing of 1,600 marines near Barcelona, then under French control, provoke the Catalans to rise in revolt. The marines were re-embarked, and the fleet sailed off in search of other prey. At a council of war Gibraltar was decided upon, perhaps because Byng, whom Rooke disliked, spoke against it. It was not a new idea, but the Rock in 1704 was remarkably ill-fortified, and it fell comparatively easily. British possession was challenged within less than a month, by a French fleet under Admiral Toulouse, and, in a battle off Malaga, Rooke's force drove off the French, who made no further challenge for control of the Mediterranean during the war. 1704 was a year of decisive victories. Blenheim had been fought in the interval between the taking of Gibraltar and the action off Malaga. George Rooke, who had been a Tory MP since 1698, was acclaimed when he got home as a victor at least equal to Marlborough, whom the Whigs had adopted as their own. This flattered the admiral a good deal.

ROSSETTI, CHRISTINA (1830-94) was acclaimed by Edmund Gosse as 'a wonderful woman who stands almost alone in the forefront of the world's female poets'. After her death her work suffered a neglect out of proportion to that of Victorian poetry in general. Recently, however, she has been the subject of much attention. Critics now, not only those of feminist inclination, tend to endorse Gosse's verdict.

Her father, exile for the Italian liberal cause, poet, student of Dante, had lived in London since 1824. Latterly almost blind, querulously demanding, he came to rely excessively on Christina. Her mother, Lavinia Polidori was devout and fond. Her brother, Dante Gabriel, especially through his painting, exhibited the family genius in its most extrovert form; Maria, her eldest sister, governess by necessity, scholar by inclination, 'throve on ritual' (Edmund Gosse): she eventually became a nun. Christina's childhood, precociously literary, suggests a personality closer to Gabriel's: she would be 'a woman of expansive heart, fond of society' predicted William, her other brother. At the age of fourteen, however, she suffered a nervous breakdown. She emerged after several years, introverted, ultra-cautious in relationships; did she fear relapse into mental illness? She was strong mainly in her Anglo-Catholic faith and in her poetic vocation. The relentless self-examination of her poems, the painful awareness of sin, the particular interest in death, the pervading sense of life curtailed, of a heart frozen, 'hard and cold and small, of all hearts the worst of all': all suggests the claustrophobia of a small town house and a personal development under a kind of house-arrest – with which she seems, by her own account, to have concurred; living 'in my shady crevice, that being to my certain knowledge the place assigned to me'.

'When real life introduced upon Christina's "hushed life drama", the effects could be a violent collision.' Frances Thomas goes on to argue that her loneliness enabled her to create at white heat. What might have been lost in breadth of experience was gained in concentration of feeling, the commitment of a keen intelligence and powerful sense of duty, to her vocation and her craft. *Goblin Market* (1862), a moral tale for children, with its variety of metre and rhythm, and its sinister subterranean echoes, illustrates the interaction between her poetic sensibility and her faith. The goblin vendors of magic fruit are symbols of temptation: add a sensuous feast of words and images, 'the odd freakishness' (William), the enveloping sense of magic – and it will be seen why it is regarded as her masterpiece. But there is so much more. In the poems that appeared from time to time in collections like *The Prince's Progress and Other Poems* (1866) and *A Pageant and Other Poems* (1881) there are sad thoughts and sombre hues. Her famous carol suggests the landscape of her mind: 'In the bleak midwinter/Frosty wind made moan.' Lyricism, humour and, always, that serious concern for clarity in image and thought links her to the Pre-Raphaelite Brotherhood.

Her renunciation of marriage (she rejected two suitors) was voluntary: some other Victorian women might have envied the freedom to remain single that she earned from her poetry. She became an Associate of St Mary Magdalene's Home at Highgate for the reclamation of prostitutes. Her church visiting gave her insights into the rough and brutal side of life. Her mysticism was channelled through and nourished by the high Anglican ideals and practices she valued so much. Hers was an active, absorbed, purposeful life. The older Christina Rossetti, the little dumpy figure, invariably in black, reminded a friend of an Italian nun. A pale, set face, looking shyly at the world through heavy lidded eyes, might tell strangers to keep their distance. But friends were still entranced by her voice, 'made up of strange, sweet inflexions'. She guarded her inner life to the end. So it is mainly through her poems that we can know her – and then through a glass darkly. 'My heart is like a singing bird.' Taking our cue from that joyous first line, dare we hope that she was sometimes happy?

Further Reading
Frances Thomas, *Christina Rossetti*, 1992.

ROSSETTI, DANTE GABRIEL (1828-82), painter, poet and decorative designer, was the son of a political refugee from Italy and a thoroughly-anglicized Italian mother. Although he was three-quarters Italian, he became *plus Anglais que les Anglais*, and never in fact visited Italy. The 'tension' between the two sides of his nature – between a Mediterranean sensuality which easily ran over into passion, and the normative, Protestant Englishness which frowned upon those passions –

was for a long time fruitful in his artistic life, but ultimately destructive.

To begin with, he vacillated between poetry and painting. It seemed he could distinguish himself in either. 'If any man has any poetry in him,' he said later to Burne-Jones, 'he should paint, for it has all been said and written, and they have scarcely begun to paint it.' Nevertheless, like William Morris, Rossetti ran his poetry and his painting in tandem: writing poems to accompany his pictures, to be incorporated even within the frame; and quarrying literature for material for his paintings.

Rossetti's art – though refreshingly 'new' and colourful and brilliant – was probably overpraised by contemporaries. But his influence was out of proportion to his achievement. His was the inspiration in both the first and the second stage of the Pre-Raphaelite Movement. He gave that Movement its medieval character. It was he who, by his example, induced Burne-Jones and William Morris to become professional artists, and led the revolution in decorative design which they carried further. He was credited, indeed, with being responsible for the rebirth of the Romantic School in England. For all this it is hard to account, except by realizing the power of his personality. His appearance – the sensual underlip, and the steady brooding, blue-grey eyes, expressed in physical terms the two aspects of his nature; while the intensity and single-mindedness which he gave to the pursuit of beauty through art, were instantly attractive, and then infectious, to fellow travellers on that road.

For him, the Pre-Raphaelite Movement was as much as anything a rebellion against the formalism (as he saw it) of the Royal Academy, whose Antique School he had attended for a reluctant year. But he quickly became the Movement's apologist, its theoretician, through the medium of a periodical, *The Germ*, which his brother William edited. The first painting he exhibited as a Pre-Raphaelite was *The Girlhood of Mary Virgin* (1849, Tate Gallery). This has a purity of sentiment, and a simplicity of style, which recall the art of the early Renaissance. It teaches morality by example. All of that was typical of the Pre-Raphaelite 'programme'. Rossetti's unsophisticated view of the Annunciation, *Ecce Ancilla Domini!* (also in the Tate) appeared in the following year. But Rossetti was never happy with oils. He evolved a technique of watercolour painting which suited his purposes: hatching brilliant colours over a pure white ground with a nearly-dry brush. His subjects are taken mostly from the Bible, Dante, Malory's *Le Morte d'Arthur*. The mood is often that of *The Lady of Shalott* or Keats's *Eve of St Agnes*. His preparatory drawings are wonderfully free; but his finished compositions are crowded and awkward – as though he had set himself the task of fitting his angular figures into as small a space as possible (e.g. *The Wedding of St George and the Princess Sabra*,

1857, Tate). Nevertheless, the vision is splendid: and the religious or spiritual tone seems genuine enough in these earlier pictures.

In 1857, Rossetti persuaded some of his friends – including Burne-Jones and Morris – to join him in decorating the walls of the Hall in the new Oxford Union with illustrations of *Le Morte d'Arthur* done in fresco. The work, undertaken lightheartedly and without knowledge of fresco technique, was radiant – for a few months; whereupon it sank into the darkness in which it still reposes. But the adventure illustrates the hold that Rossetti had over his 'disciples'; one of whom (Val Prinsep) remembered how Rossetti had been 'the planet round which we revolved. We copied his way of speaking. All beautiful women were "stunners" with us … Medievalism was our *beau idéal*, and we sank our own individuality into the strong personality of our adored Gabriel.'

One such 'stunner' was Jane Burden, daughter of a livery-stable keeper, and a great beauty. Rossetti met her in Oxford, fell in love with her, persuaded her to model for one panel of the Union frescoes. Then, because he was still deeply involved with another woman, he encouraged William Morris into marrying Jane. The 'other woman' was Elizabeth Siddal, who had modelled for Ophelia in Millais's painting, before settling into a long affair, delectable and painful by turns, with Rossetti. He drew and painted her scores of times: perhaps the best of all his work. He saw her as Beatrice to his Dante. It is clear she was unusually beautiful – and herself an artist. When Morris married Jane Burden, Rossetti finally married Siddal. The marriage lasted only two years. She became increasingly depressed, and died in 1862 – perhaps by design – of an overdose of laudanum.

Rossetti, in an agony of remorse, deposited the manuscript book of his poems, never yet published, in the coffin alongside the woman who had inspired them. But his friends, who had heard them read and had prized them in manuscript, prevailed on him in 1869 to disinter the poems, and they were published in 1870. Other collections followed. Welcomed as truly romantic after the drawing-room chivalry of Tennyson's *Idylls of The King* (1859), Rossetti's poems have not in fact endured in popularity as those of his sister Christina. He is the poetical heir of Keats and (on the mystical side) of Blake; but his language falls short of Keats's, and is too luscious for Blake. His sonnets, especially those of *The House Of Life*, have been rightly praised, but they lack the force of Milton's, Wordsworth's, or even Elizabeth Browning's. It is the striking imagery, and the 'tension' between sensuality and mysticism, which still draw the reader. In poetry, then, Rossetti's principal heir was Swinburne. But perhaps his most valuable legacy to literature was his exquisite translations of Dante and the best of other Italian poets.

Meanwhile, his painting had changed radically. From about 1859 (*Bocca Baciata* – 'Kissed Mouth') he begins to leave behind the small, dense watercolours which share the spirit of his poetry, and embarks on a series of oils, mostly full-front 'portraits' of women, and growing in size from the mid 1860s. They have allusive titles, but the allusions do not veil the frank sensuality of these later paintings. The model for many of them is Jane Burden, now Jane Morris – to whom Rossetti began again to pay court not long after the death of his wife. She returned his advances. The affair lasted for years. Her husband was complaisant, though it finished his affection for Rossetti.

In fact, Rossetti became increasingly isolated, driven in on himself by a kind of paranoia which acted to exclude even his intimate friends. Burne-Jones was deeply shocked by Rossetti's decline: 'It has been the saddest sight I have had in my days … He is the beginning of everything in me that I care for.' In an attempt to relieve his insomnia, and kindle again and again the embers of a dying fire, Rossetti became addicted to a drug similar to that which had killed his wife. A public attack – foolish but not quite unfounded – on the morality of his poetry depressed him further. He seems to have felt that he had 'sold the pass', had betrayed ideals which he himself had proposed in the palmy days of the Pre-Raphaelites, and within the bright circle of his disciples. He died of a mixture of drug abuse and disenchantment. Some people remembered that he could be cruel towards those he disliked, or that he could be financially unscrupulous. They recalled the darkness of his last years. But his friend Watts-Dunton, writing soon afterwards in the *Encyclopaedia Britannica*, gave him a happier epitaph: 'In all matters of taste Rossetti's influence has been immense … One of the most wonderful of [his] endowments, however, was neither of a literary nor an artistic kind: it was that of a rare and most winning personality which attracted towards itself, as if by an unconscious magnetism, the love of all his friends, the love, indeed, of all who knew him.'

Further Reading
Alicia Craig Faxon, *Dante Gabriel Rossetti*, 1989.
Virginia Surtees, *The Paintings and Drawings of Dante Gabriel Rossetti, A Catalogue Raisonné*, 1971.

ROUBILIAC, LOUIS FRANÇOIS (1695-1762), one of the greatest English sculptors – if he can be called English – was born at Lyons and came to England only in his thirties. But he was the greatest of the immigrant artists who transfigured English sculpture in the first half of the eighteenth century – greater than Scheemakers and Delvaux, greater even than Rysbrack – and all his mature work was done in the country of his adoption.

Born therefore in the city which had bred Coysevox, trained by Permoser, the German sculptor who had learnt the baroque from Bernini himself, working in a Paris indelibly marked by the artistic hegemony of Le Brun – a variety of influences went to the making of Roubiliac's style. What emerged was something relatively simple and composite and very much in tune with the France of Louis XV: Roubiliac was a rococo sculptor, by which we understand that he accelerated the broad emphatic andante of baroque into something more mercurial and more elegant – like a musical change into semiquaver time. Rococo sculpture is particular about details; it rejoices in density of rhythms, in a multiplicity of surface planes; it would rather record a transitory mood than an immortal longing; it finds the real physiognomy – 'warts and everything' – more to the taste than the ideal. Rapid movement is of the essence of such sculpture; and drapery is no longer suffered to fall in patterns of its own, but is sought in aid to accentuate the movement of the figure below it. Take, for example, Roubiliac's statue of Forbes of Culloden in the Parliament Hall in Edinburgh: see here how multiplied detail can avoid confusion: the features are unflattering, the veins stand up in the hands and stockinged legs; the deep curls of the wig, the stiff creases in the satin robes, make a hundred little rhythms; beam light on the statue, and the light disintegrates on 1,000 angled planes; yet all these particulars are drilled into informing the single, superb gesture of pacification. Or compare one of Roubiliac's busts of Pope with Rysbrack's: the one explores the lines of pain, in pity it portrays the magnificent cripple; the other forgoes the pathos in its eagerness to declare the nobility of the poet. Each is a masterpiece; only the point of view is different.

On his arrival in England in the early 1730s, chance gave Roubiliac a patron in Edward Walpole, the natural son of the prime minister. Through Walpole he met the sculptor Sir Henry Cheere, who obtained for him his first commission, a statue of Handel for the Vauxhall Gardens. Tyers, promoter of the Gardens, pleased with Roubiliac's skill, found him sitters for busts. His advancement, as it was made in the shadow of his predecessors, was a little slow; but by 1745 he was teaching sculpture at Hogarth's Academy in St Martin's Lane, a popular and respected figure. Already he had done some distinguished work: the busts of Pope which have been mentioned, and a bust of Hogarth (National Portrait Gallery) which is that pugnacious humorist to the letter; and he was to go from strength to strength in this vein, showing special aptitude for the portrayal of ugly men, but also (in 1751-7) creating, from painted portraits and from his own imaginative genius, the series of past celebrities of Trinity College, Cambridge.

In the 1740s he began on his great series of funerary monuments, of which it is to be noticed as an innovation that the central figure, the commemorated, no longer reclines in an attitude of post-mortal calm, but regularly takes a part in the action of the group. And such action is often most vigorous and dramatic. The Duke of Argyll, cast as the dying hero, is certainly calm enough amid a scene of activity (1745, Westminster Abbey); but Bishop Hough (1746, Worcester Cathedral) starts up like a latter-day St Paul, blinded by heavenly light; while Captain Hargrave in the Abbey (1757) is trapped between the toppling pyramid of Time and the discomfiture of Time himself and Death. As for the Abbey monument to Lady Elizabeth Nightingale (1761), where Death, again a skeleton, emerges from below the tomb and stabs at the unfortunate lady – well, that is a byword for the dramatic monument and is certainly a trifle grotesque. By way of contrast, to see what Roubiliac could achieve in a mood of serenity and grace, one should go to the monuments of the Duke and Duchess of Montagu in Warkton Church (Northamptonshire) or, better still, to the ante-chapel of Trinity College, to the perfectly noble statue, that of Sir Isaac Newton,

> ... with his prism and silent face,
> The marble index of a mind for ever
> Voyaging through strange seas of thought, alone.

ROUS, JOHN (c.1411-91), antiquary of Warwick, was chantry chaplain of Guy's Cliff. He is thus one of the few members of the late medieval clerical proletariat to be more than a name. He took his MA at Oxford University by 1445 and worked the rest of his life at Guy's Cliff. That he rose no further suggests a lack of ambition and contentment with his lot. A plump, clean-shaven, gentle man, he was no dynamic thruster and his job left him plenty of time for his literary pursuits.

Cantarists were required to celebrate mass daily and thus had little time for travel, but Rous managed some prolonged journeys, borrowed and bought books – including some surprisingly up-to-date ones – and built up a considerable library. If in touch with the wider world, his horizons were intensely local. The chantry was for two priests and was idyllically located on the River Avon on the reputed site of the hermitage of the legendary giant Guy of Warwick, who was supposed, mistakenly, to be ancestor of the Earls of Warwick. Rous's situation explains why he wrote his lost works on giants, Guy's Cliff and Warwick, and the two surviving versions of his *Rous Roll* about the earls themselves. Only his *History of the Kings of England* departs from this pattern. Rous identified himself so much with the earls that his work represents the

culmination of all previous essays in propaganda on the past of the various families whose estates had merged with those of the Beauchamps to form the powerful earldom of the later Middle Ages. His yardstick of measurement of the achievements of the earls and their countesses is the extent of their benefactions to the town of Warwick, its churches, priories, hospitals, and chantries.

Valuable though the *Rous Roll* is 'as an indication of how contemporaries saw their own history', its importance 'lies less in the information which it provides than in its evocation of the outlook and interests – the mental climate – of the age when it was written', for which it is indispensable.

Rous has been criticized both as a time-server and historian. Having praised the Warwick heiress Anne Neville and her husband Richard III in 1483, after Bosworth he portrayed his erstwhile patron as a deformed tyrant. If political expediency took priority over historical accuracy, it is hardly surprising given Rous's age and vulnerability. As for his historical stature, all his writings – as Professor Ross scathingly said – are undiscriminating in their use of evidence, credulous of myth and miracles, hopelessly inaccurate, and almost negligible in their achievements. Such charges, however, are strangely reminiscent of those levelled at the indispensable Froissart and moreover ignore Rous's antiquarian significance. He was an enthusiastic and energetic antiquary, who did much more than credulously accept existing written and oral traditions. That he could portray past Earls and Countesses of Warwick in appropriate clothes and armour is testimony to meticulous research on monuments, seals, and therefore documents. He knew how the past differed from the present. His moral outrage and concerned humanitarianism about enclosure and depopulation does not conceal careful fieldwork and a capacity to analyse changes occurring around him. Ironically it is his flawed published works that have so damaged his reputation. Had we more of his notebooks, like William Worcester's, we *might* hold him in higher estimation. But his notebooks, like his library, are irretrievably lost.

Further Reading
E. Mason, 'Legends of the Beauchamps' ancestors: the use of baronial propaganda in medieval England', *Journal of Medieval History* x, 1984.
A. Gransden, *Historical Writing in England* ii, 1982.
W. H. Courthope, ed., *The Rous Roll*, 2nd edn, 1980.

ROWLANDSON, THOMAS (1756-1827), artist and satirist, was born in comfortable circumstances, studied at the Royal Academy Schools and in Paris while still a boy, and exhibited drawings at the Academy from the age of nineteen. Having squandered a small fortune, he supplied his needs by prodigal use of reed-pen and brush. He settled in London, from which, to refresh his experience, he travelled abroad as often as wars permitted. His huge and various oeuvre has been described by a modern critic as an English equivalent to Balzac's *Comédie Humaine*; but the inspiration is Rabelaisian. He drew with tremendous brio, startling humour and a total absence of modesty. In his work (the items of which were multiplied by engravings) we find tableaux of theatres and ballrooms, amusement parks, fairs and race-meetings; views of town and country, thickly peopled, shaded by stylized trees, extracts of Merry England; scenes of rustic gatherings at inn or stable in the vein of his friend Morland; and book illustrations, as those for William Combe's *Tours of Dr Syntax* – not to mention the great number of drawings (today we should call them cartoons) which are simply humorous commentaries on the life of his day.

In the kingdom of satire, he divides the honours of the time with Gillray. Gillray was the political, Rowlandson the social, satirist. Rowlandson's blows are aimed at general anomalies, at the scandals of electioneering, at horse-trading in high places, at the hypocrisy of the rich and the fecklessness of the poor. Here he is heir to Hogarth; but he caricatures more savagely than Hogarth and sacrifices truth of observation to a hunger for the grotesque. We do not recognize his creatures as we do Hogarth's, but we laugh at them more. Thus, since he satirized to amuse, not to convert, he was not the preacher that Hogarth was.

He is called a watercolourist, but he harked back to the older practice, and used watercolour only to tint his line-drawings. It is with line that he is the master: however complex the organization of his picture, however widespread the action, Rowlandson's fluent rhythmic line defines the parts, weaves in and out of them, and draws them into a coherent and satisfying composition.

Further Reading
Ronald Paulson, *Rowlandson, a new interpretation*, 1972.

RUPERT, PRINCE (1619-82) was born in Prague, the third son of Frederick of the Palatinate and James I's daughter, Elizabeth. His parents were driven out of both Bohemia and the Palatinate soon after his birth, and Rupert spent nearly all his boyhood in Holland, growing into a tall and powerful young man, as impulsive as he was athletic, earning the nickname of Rupert-le-diable. A visit of six months to England in 1636-7 won him the favour of Henrietta Maria and a dashing reputation at court. Inevitably he joined the Dutch army fighting in the Netherlands and took part in the siege of Breda in 1637. Next year he was captured by the imperialists at Vlotho, and until 1641 he remained a prisoner in Austria. When his release had been negotiated he came to England early in 1642, scenting the prospect of war; and after escorting Henrietta Maria to Holland he returned, to be commissioned in August as General of the Horse in the Royal Army. It was an extraordinary appointment for a man of twenty-three who had spent more years in captivity than on campaign, even though he had put his time to use in studying the theory of war.

Rupert served Charles I with complete loyalty and boundless courage throughout the First Civil War, and he was undoubtedly the ablest soldier in the royalist armies in England. As a leader of cavalry he was superb, whether in the raids like that round Chalgrove in 1643 or in the charges in battle as at Edgehill and Naseby. He had learned from Gustavus, and Cromwell was in some measure his pupil. Moreover, he brought to the conduct of the king's war a swiftness of action – as, for example, round Oxford in the autumn of 1642 and on the eve of Marston Moor in 1644 – which was tactically invaluable and which could have served as a tonic and model to a command less rent by faction. How well he mastered the arts of siege and storm he showed in Lancashire in 1644 and at Leicester in 1645. Nevertheless, for all his qualities he was in some ways disastrously deficient in generalship. Despite his devotion to the royalist cause, his concentration upon the needs of his own troops was too great. Even as a cavalry commander he failed, as Oliver did not, to retain control of his troops after the charge. Above all, he lacked the comprehensive vision of the great commander, and neither in campaign nor in battle did his grasp compare with that of Fairfax or of Cromwell. He was much handicapped by the indecisiveness of the king and by the chronic obstructionism of such men as Goring, Digby and Wilmot. Yet not all the faults were theirs. Rupert had more than his share of the impatience of youth, and his impatience quickly became contempt. He was a man of prejudices, and he had plenty of charm but very little tact. In the intensely personal structure of the royalist high command, Rupert's characteristics were more likely to irritate than to inspire, especially since from the very beginning he appeared to owe his high rank to his relationship with the king.

His first encounter in the Civil War was the skirmish at Powicke Bridge in September 1642. Next month after Edgehill he was for driving on to London, and at Brentford on the outskirts we find him leading an infantry charge in an attempt to force a way into the capital. During the first half of 1643 he spent much time extending royalist control from Oxford over the south and west Midlands, and in July he took Bristol for the king. But that September at Newbury – in the first major battle of the war and a decisive turning point in royalist fortunes – Essex and the trained bands of London apprentices withstood Rupert's cavalry. Moreover, he was already involved in serious quarrels with the queen as well as with courtier-soldiers like Wilmot. Yet the early months of 1644 brought royalist successes and showed Rupert at his most brilliant. Moving northwards towards the challenge of the invading Scots, he relieved Newark in March by rapid and masterly manoeuvre, and in early summer he overran Lancashire, slaughtering the defenders of Bolton in one of the few conflicts of the English wars which had the savage flavour of the Thirty Years' War.

His career had reached its peak. In June he moved east and relieved York, surprising his enemies by moving swiftly in from the north. But on 2 July, outnumbered three to two, his army was shattered at Marston Moor. Thereafter the final defeat of the royalists was delayed more by the mistakes of the parliamentarians than by the skill of their own generals. Rupert withdrew southwards with the remains of his army. In November he was appointed Commander-in-Chief of the Royal Armies, a post which quickly involved him in disputes with Goring and Digby. The spring campaign which he planned for 1645 from his base in the Welsh Marches came to nothing, while the enemy was organizing the instrument of final victory, the New Model Army. At the end of May the prince won his last victory, compelling the surrender of Leicester; in mid-June came his utter defeat at Naseby. His opponents among the royalists were ready to make him the scapegoat of the king's disasters, the more so when he argued at this stage for a treaty which might have saved much for Charles. In September, for sound military reasons, he surrendered Bristol. Charles, characteristically, dismissed him from command without even seeing him. Although a reconciliation was patched up after Rupert had compelled the king to face him and obtained a court-martial which acquitted him of all charges of treachery and neglect of duty, his career as a royalist soldier was over.

After the surrender of Oxford in 1646 Rupert was permitted to go abroad. He fought briefly for the French against the Spaniards in Flanders. Then in 1648, taking advantage of mutinous feelings in the parliamentarian fleet, he got command of a small squadron of English ships. From 1649 to 1652 he was part royalist admiral, part buccaneer – running supplies to the Scillies so long as they resisted, capturing English merchantmen in the Mediterranean, taking prizes off Gambia and in the Caribbean where in 1652 his brother Maurice was lost. His exploits can be overrated, and he was never a serious threat to the English Republic: Blake destroyed many of his ships in the Mediterranean. After his return to his cousin Charles II's court in France in 1652, Rupert exercised little influence in the royalist cause. He spent most of the interregnum in Germany, at his brother the Elector Charles Louis's court at Heidelberg, with the emperor in Vienna, or fighting for the King of Hungary; he settled finally at Mainz, turning his energies to chemical experiments and to develop the art of the mezzotint.

Charles II invited him back to England at the Restoration and settled upon him a pension of £6,000 per annum. Rupert belonged to the generation of elder statesmen, but he had never been a statesman. His contribution to the world of Restoration England, a world very different from that of the 1630s, was inevitably that of the fighting man. He commanded at sea in the Second Dutch War (1664-7), leading the van at Southwold Bay in 1665, joining with Monck in the celebrated 'Fighting Instructions' of 1666, suffering defeat in the Four Days'

Battle of 1667 and winning victory off the North Foreland in the same year. During the Third Dutch War he was appointed (1673) to the Board of Admiralty. Yet his concerns were not merely naval. He served on the Tangier Board, and, as the map of Canada shows, he was a leading figure in the early activities of the Hudson Bay Company. He was one of the founders of the Royal Society, and during this time as Governor of Windsor (from 1668) he experimented, particularly with firearms, in his own laboratory there. He continued to produce mezzotints and left to posterity some very beautiful examples of the craft. He hunted, and he played tennis with great skill. He died a bachelor, but from 1667 onwards the young actress Peg Hughes was his cherished mistress. Pepys was no doubt right in finding Rupert, with whom he clearly had an occasional brush, irascible and rather old-fashioned.

Further Reading
P. Morrah, *Prince Rupert of the Rhine*, 1976.
Austin Woolrych, *Battles of the English Civil War*, 1961.

RUSKIN, JOHN (1819-1900), polymath, poet, artist, writer, prophet and social reformer, was above all the most influential art critic of nineteenth-century Britain. Before his time, there was no art criticism to speak of; the purpose and the status of art in Britain were ill-defined and largely conventional; aesthetic philosophy was in its infancy. Since Ruskin's time, however, it is not too much to say that no art critic has escaped his influence.

But that was only one aspect of his achievement. The mass of the thirty-nine volumes of the posthumous edition of his works (1903-12) buried him from the eyes of the general public. These volumes can still be found – with pages uncut. But, during his lifetime, his intellectual authority was so conspicuous, and the empire of his disciples so wide and numerous, that it is probable that he – along with Carlyle – did more than anyone else to shape the culture of Britain in the nineteenth century. It was therefore a piece of great good luck that both these giants were men of high moral purpose, who were deeply at odds with the materialism of their time, and had no use for theories or practices which did not help people to live better and happier lives. Indeed it was partly due to the example of Carlyle and Ruskin that very many artists and writers of that century were principally concerned with the *moral* effect of their work. 'Righteousness' was a word much on Ruskin's lips; and, righteousness being out of fashion, Ruskin and his persuasions have followed. But Tolstoy, Bernard Shaw and Gandhi claimed to have been inspired by Ruskin the social reformer. William Morris was an early disciple. A college in Oxford for working men and women from the Trade Unions was named after him (1899). And, when the parliamentary Labour party first met, and members were asked what had been the decisive influence on their lives, almost every one answered: 'the works of Ruskin'.

By descent, he was three-quarters Scottish, but born in London, in 1819, the only child of middle-aged parents. Frederic Harrison, who was one of Ruskin's many biographers, describes how 'the child was brought up under a rigid system of nursing, physical, moral and intellectual; kept without toys, not seldom whipped, watched day and night, but trained from infancy in music, drawing, reading aloud and observation of natural objects' – and, it should be said, treated by his parents with an obsessive love and indulgence.

From a very early age, he wrote prose and poetry which went some way to justifying the view that he was a genius. His first sermon, delivered at the age of five, began, 'People, be good' – an important clue to all his later writing. His mother, a strict Calvinist, obliged him to read aloud from the Bible every day, with the result that all his life he had large portions of it by heart, and that his written style was (especially in his youth) deeply coloured by the gorgeous, but often indistinct, language of the Authorized Version.

He received an eclectic education, chiefly from private tutors. His father, a successful wine-merchant and a man of excellent taste in other fields, encouraged the boy to read the best of English literature. He also took him on the long annual expeditions he made (with his wife) to visit clients, both in Britain and on the continent. As the secondary aim of these journeys was to see everything beautiful in nature and in art which lay along the route, they may be said to have formed the most important part of his education. While still in his teens, he was attracted to certain places with a passion that lasted all his life: to the mountains and lakes of Cumberland, to the cathedral-towns of northern France, above all to the Alps. Later he was to make such journeys on his own – through France and Switzerland to Italy – staying away for months at a time: drawing, writing, thinking, but above all *observing*; and then analysing and describing, with accuracy as minute as Robert Browning's, and with a glorious eloquence, why it was that some of what he observed gave him intense pleasure.

In January 1837 he went up as a gentleman-commoner to Christ Church, Oxford. The young bloods who were his companions treated him pleasantly, but the financial cost of the enterprise weighed on him, and his mother (amazingly) came to live in the High Street during term, so that she could supervise her son's health. Then, being rejected in love by the daughter of M. Domecq, his father's Spanish partner in the sherry business, Ruskin experienced a kind of breakdown, with symptoms of tuberculosis, which took him away from Oxford for two years (though not before he had won the Newdigate Prize for Poetry. Gladstone later wished to make him Poet Laureate in succession to Tennyson, but poetry was

never his strongest suit). Finally, in 1842, he was awarded an honorary Fourth, and so was able to publish his first major work as 'A Graduate of Oxford'.

In passing, it should be made clear that Ruskin was a manic depressive most of his adult life. The depressions set in on deeper and longer tides, until (from 1878) they turned into periods of madness. When he was depressed, nature and art presented him with 'a universal blank', and the sun turned dark in the sky. But usually he was very different. His lonely upbringing had made him reserved, but in most circles he commanded attention. Sir Sidney Colvin saw him from the stance of the next generation: 'No man had about him more – few can ever have had so much – of the atmosphere and effluence of genius, and when he came into the room I used consciously to thrill to his presence.' Slender and slightly bowed, in dark-blue frock-coat, bright-blue stock – his invariable dress; and, below sweep of soft brown hair and bushy eyebrows, eyes of an intense blue, which fixed and penetrated yours: that was how he struck people.

The book by 'A Graduate of Oxford' was *Modern Painters* (1843). Further volumes followed at intervals, the fifth and last in 1860. This first volume was principally concerned with proving the superiority of Turner and other 'modern' landscape-artists to 'all the Ancient Masters'. The second volume (1846) was the fruit of an extended visit to Italy, which enabled him to write with new authority about Italian art and architecture. But the work developed into a majestic exposition of the relationship of art to natural phenomena, and of both to God and man. Indeed *Modern Painters* became so ambitious in its aims, so discursive, that the Index took up a whole sixth volume. In the fifth volume, for example, we pass through an exhaustive study of the function of leaves and branches, a marvellous analysis of the formation of clouds (no-one ever wrote so well about clouds), an amusing account of the role of the dog in Veronese's paintings, a curious interlude on Vulgarity and the nature of a gentleman, to the famous chapter on *The Two Boyhoods*, the comparison of the youth of Giorgione with that of Turner, in which Ruskin explores the effects of environment on the artistic nature. He himself describes *Modern Painters* as 'the work through which we have passed together in the investigation of the beauty of the visible world'.

Three things are to be noticed. First, because *Modern Painters* developed over twenty years, Ruskin often contradicts himself, as fresh experience modifies previous conclusions. Secondly, although his descriptions are usually based upon close and lively observation, their meaning is liable to be obscured by the sheer magnificence of the language, and the hypnotic music of the march of his sentences. He is one of the greatest writers of English prose. His contemporary popularity was largely due to that. But the twentieth-century distrust of eloquence as the cloak of so many crimes, is one of the reasons why he is little read today. Thirdly, although he did recognize the dangers of being read mainly for his 'purple passages', and began to economize with language, his discursiveness increased hand over fist – until, in his late works, when his mind was clouded, every sentence started a new line of thought.

In 1848, he married Euphemia (Effie) Gray, another Scot and a remote cousin. The marriage was typical of many Victorian marriages: engineered by the parents, and entered into by the parties, upon expectations which were disappointed by experience. A decree of nullity was granted in 1855, and Effie married the painter Millais, to whom Ruskin had (rather pointedly) introduced her. But this was not his last love. The wretched affair of Rose La Touche dragged on for fifteen years from 1859, and was a principal cause of his increasing instability.

In *The Seven Lamps of Architecture* (1849) and *The Stones of Venice* (1851-3), published between volumes 2 and 3 of *Modern Painters*, Ruskin attempted to give a moral, even a religious, character to Gothic architecture. He later regretted the success he had had in virtually *dictating* a style for public and private buildings: 'There is scarcely a public house near the Crystal Palace but sells its gin and bitters under pseudo-Venetian capitals ...' He was as responsible as Pugin for the excessive 'Gothicization' of Victorian architecture – of which the University Museum in Oxford (built under Ruskin's supervision) is an example.

He had already – in letters to *The Times* whose effect was a convincing measure of his ascendancy – come out in defence of the Pre-Raphaelites: 'They may, as they gain experience, lay in our England the foundations of a school of art nobler than the world has seen for 300 years.' Now, as the fifties drew to a close, and *Modern Painters* likewise, he felt he had had enough of art criticism. His experience of teaching at the new Working Men's College had opened his eyes to social problems which had been invisible from the insulated comfort of his parents' villa at Denmark Hill. He began to see poverty and social dislocation at first hand; and, as usual, he immediately wished to correct it. This obliged him to explain why he greatly disliked the 'civilization' of his day, and to expose the wicked injustices of laissez faire economics. He had simply to change his clothes, he thought, to become the prophet of social regeneration. But the essays which he sent to *The Cornhill Magazine* in 1860 aroused a storm of abuse, as property-owners everywhere caught more than a whiff of socialism in such a sentence as: 'Government and co-operation are in all things the Laws of Life; Anarchy and competition the laws of Death.' Thackeray, editor of *The Cornhill*, was obliged to silence his distinguished contributor. The letters were published with others in 1862, as *Unto This Last*. Ruskin himself thought the book his best; and there is no doubt that this gentle, humane exposé of classical economics is one of the cardinal, even revolutionary, books of the nineteenth century. Other works followed, of a radical tone: *The Crown of Wild Olive* (1866) and *Time and Tide* (1867). From 1871, he wrote and published a series of letters addressed 'To the Workmen and Labourers of Great Britain'. He called them *Fors Clavigera* (Ruskin's titles were mostly obscure). The letters are, in Frederic Harrison's words, 'a desultory exposition of the Ruskinian ideal of life, manners and society, full of wit, play, invective and sermons on things in general'. The rancorous opposition which he had experienced, caused Ruskin to express in these letters an increased bitterness and pessimism. There are also premonitions of his mental breakdown.

Meanwhile, in 1864, his father died. The son's political attitudes had made a breach between them which was never closed; but he inherited a large fortune, which his habitual generosity, and his objection on principle to investing for interest, quickly absorbed. Not content with expounding theory, he put some of his ideas into practice: he founded a lay community called St George's Guild; persuaded leading intellectuals (including Oscar Wilde, Andrew Lang, Alfred Milner, and Arnold Toynbee as foreman) to work on building a road at the village of Hinksey; worked himself with a stone-breaker; opened a model shop; started a museum at Sheffield. The last was soon the only survivor of these philanthropic schemes. But those who laugh at Ruskin have not considered how many real benefits that are taken for granted today were advocated by him: free schools, free libraries, garden cities and green belts and a National Trust, smokeless zones, the old-age pension, the living wage and a graduated income-tax.

In 1869 he was elected Slade Professor of Art at Oxford University. For several years he lectured regularly to a packed Sheldonian Theatre. But his message became more incoherent as his mental powers relaxed. On his mothers death at ninety, in 1871, he broke with the past, decided to have a home of his own, and bought (unseen) a property called Brantwood on Coniston Water. In 1878 he went (in his own words) 'heartily and headily mad' for about six weeks. Later that year he had to face a libel action brought against him by Whistler, but was too ill to appear. He resigned his professorship. The attacks of insanity increased in number: and, though he was reinstated as Slade Professor in 1883, he was demonstrably losing his reason. In 1885 he left Oxford for good, and retired to Brantwood. He was still able to write the eminently sane pages of the genial, sunset autobiography he called *Praeterita* ('Things Past') – though it was not quite finished when he relapsed (for his last eleven years) into a daydream, silent and unresponsive, much photographed as if he were a breathing statue. He is buried at Coniston, where a museum is established in his memory.

But his true memorial is of course in the minds and deeds of the countless men and women whose lives were better because of him. A. C. Benson has written that what Ruskin did was 'to break utterly to pieces the old leisurely feeling about art as a pleasant and dignified adjunct to life. He taught men and women to look close, to compare, to discriminate, to wonder, and above all to care for art as the most passionate expression of one of the deepest and strongest of human qualities, the love and worship of beauty'. And *The Westminster Gazette* of 23 March 1915 carried the account of a desperately-wounded soldier – 'a man of the Lancashire Fusiliers' – who, as he lay dying, would not be separated from his copy of *The Crown of Wild Olive*, and asked that it should be buried with him.

Further Reading
Sir Kenneth Clark, *Ruskin Today*, 1964.
John Ruskin, *Praeterita*, 1885 onwards.

RUSSELL, EDWARD, EARL OF ORFORD (1653-1727), admiral, a member of the great Whig family, was commissioned in Charles II's navy. The persecution of the Whigs in the early 1680s drove him to support William of Orange, with whom he kept in touch during James II's reign. In 1688 he was one of the seven signatories of the famous invitation, and after the Revolution he was in the inner circle of Whig leaders, the Junto. When Torrington was defeated off Beachy Head in 1690 and withdrew to the Thames, it was Russell who was sent to arrest and supersede him. Two years later he defeated the French fleet off Barfleur in the battle of La Hogue. The victory saved Britain from invasion and broke French naval strength for the remainder of the war. Much of the credit for the destruction of the French warships belongs to Rooke, and Russell was strongly, though probably unjustly, criticized at home for his failure to follow up his success by landing on the enemy coast. The government, predominantly Tory at the time, dismissed him, but he was recalled to employment in 1694, serving both as First Lord and at sea. In 1694-5 he commanded the first major English fleet to winter abroad when, most reluctantly and at William's insistence, he remained in the Mediterranean. Created Earl of Orford in 1697, he was dismissed from office in 1699, and later unsuccessfully impeached for his part in the Partition Treaty. An obstinate and truculent man, Orford was the least effective of the Junto in Anne's reign, though he was briefly First Lord again in 1709-10. George I recognized his Whiggery rather than his esteem by appointing him one of the Lords Justices in 1714.

Further Reading
J. Ehrman, *The Navy in the War of William III*, 1953.

RUSSELL, LORD JOHN, 1st EARL RUSSELL (1792-1878), third son of the sixth Duke of Bedford, was brought up at Woburn and remained close to his brothers. He was intellectually a true Whig. His first work was a life of William, Lord Russell, the Whig martyr of 1683: 'portrait of a man who, heir to wealth and title, was foremost in defending the privileges of the people.' But he lacked the easy confidence of the aristocrat. This had much to do with his size, for he was only five foot four-and-threequarter inches tall and never weighed more than eight stone. Grey, his leader, called him 'a little animal engrossed by an inordinate ambition', though others spoke more affectionately of 'little Johnny'. He was turned down more than once before he married, aged forty-three, a young widow who died three years later; and his second wife was even shyer than he, a bad hostess, but dominant in the home. He was also dogged by poverty. His brother, the seventh duke, made retrenchment his priority, and Lord John eventually had to rely on the queen to provide him with a house appropriate to his position as prime minister, Pembroke Lodge in Petersham.

He made his way to the top through his ability and energy, and through his determination to express and carry through high Whig principles. His mind was exploratory, quick and restless, and he commanded the respect of intellectuals such as Mill and Jowett, as befitted the grandfather of Bertrand Russell. He was one of the first Englishmen to take a bath every day. It has to be said that there was also a surprising lack of talent amongst the younger Whigs, partly because of their long spell in opposition. An MP aged twenty-one, he early established his reputation as an enthusiast for parliamentary reform by introducing four motions between 1819 and 1826, claiming that 'the votes of the House of Commons no longer imply the general assent of the Nation'. He was one of the four who drafted the First Reform Bill, and his name was made when Grey asked him to introduce it in the Commons (1831). He was in the forefront of the struggle to get it through, he and Althorp being described as the vinegar and the oil in the Committee stages, and he earned the reputation of a dangerous Radical, when he told the Birmingham Political Union that it was 'impossible that the whisper of a faction should prevail against the voice of a nation'. From 1832 onwards there was an unavoidable strain in the relationship between this aristocratic Whig reformer and the House of Lords, and Lord John's subsequent political achievements were disastrously diminished by the Peers. But his triumphant success in the passing of the Great Reform Bill led to his promotion to the Cabinet, and Melbourne made him Leader of the House of Commons in 1834.

Throughout Melbourne's ministry (1835-41), his was the driving force. 'No man,' wrote Gladstone, 'ever led the House of Commons with a more many-sided activity or more indomitable pluck.' Yet he did not get much legislation through parliament. He championed justice for Ireland, and after the Lichfield House Compact between the Whigs and O'Connell the way seemed clear for church and land reform there. But when he commuted the tithes paid to the Anglican Church of Ireland by a nine-tenths Catholic population, Tory majorities in the Lords blocked the appropriation of any money thus raised for uses outside the church, so the injustice went on. Land reforms, whether to change the landowners or protect the tenants, ran up against the vested interests of English absentee landlords. An Irish Poor Law got through, but the Municipal Corporation Act did not. 'The Statute Book is full of Insurrection Acts,' he said, 'but … I can find none admitting the Irish Catholics to be treated as the free subjects of a free country.' It was one of his life's themes, but it was left to Gladstone to carry through the measures which he often but unsuccessfully introduced over thirty years.

He was also concerned with educational improvements. Again, his idea of education boards throughout the country had to wait for Gladstone, but his Education Act of 1839 laid the basis for the future development of state education by setting up a Privy Council Committee to appoint inspectors. He handled the Chartist upheavals of 1839 by an effective blend of firmness and moderation, appointing Charles Napier, a good soldier but a Chartist sympathizer, to command the troops; and he took Peel's criminal law reforms further, establishing a separate juvenile prison and a prison inspectorate. As Colonial Secretary from 1839, he carried through the recommendations of the Durham Report, thus ensuring the survival of a united Canada within the Empire. Considering Melbourne's indolent and conservative temperament, it was not a bad record. It earned him the natural succession as Whig leader.

He was to be prime minister when Peel fell, from 1846 until 1852. As such, he was not highly regarded. His task was not easy. In opposition the Whigs had shown their old weaknesses, attending debates in parliament irregularly and voting independently, while the allegiance of the Radicals and the Irish was uncertain. He was not able to form a ministry to repeal the Corn Laws, even after he had declared his conversion to free trade in his Edinburgh letter, and so he passed 'the poisoned chalice' back to Peel. After the split between the Peelite and Protectionist groupings of the old Conservative Party, the political scene became still more unstable, and only Palmerston was able to lead a strong ministry between 1846 and 1868. But Lord John would have been an inadequate leader even in simpler times. He was so unbusinesslike that he would put the wrong letter in the wrong envelope, leave out enclosures, mislay papers and forget to give official boxes to the messenger. He was a short-term thinker, who started hares but did not chase them. When in 1851 he exclaimed in frustration to his Cabinet that 'a government ought not to be the only body of politicians in the country who proposed nothing', a minister replied: 'Good heavens, I am sure you are always bringing forward something new about everything.' Unlike Peel, he did not think through his policies before presenting them. In particular he never had a firm grasp of finance: in 1848 his first budget had to be withdrawn after ten days. Twice he made speeches on issues close to his heart which got him into a disastrously false position. The first earned him the nickname 'Finality Jack', when in 1835 he committed himself against a further extension of the franchise, which later embarrassed him, as the renewed champion of Reform. The second was on the burning religious topic of the day. In 1850 Pope Pius IX created twelve Roman Catholic sees in England and made Wiseman Archbishop of Westminster. Protestants were already on the boil after the explosive excitement within the Church of England caused by the Oxford Movement and the conversion of Newman to Rome. Lord John had early shown his Whiggery by supporting the dissenters and successfully moving the repeal of the Test and Corporation Acts. Now he wrote to the Bishop of Durham, blaming the pope for his aggression, and Puseyite spies within the gates for reintroducing 'the mummeries of superstition'. Though it won him some cheap applause, it cost him the support of the Irish and of the Peelites, who were tolerant or High Church. His Ecclesiastical Titles Act, banning the use of Roman Catholic titles in Britain, was never enforced.

Palmerston brought him down in 1852, allying with the Protectionists in his 'tit-for-tat with Johnny Russell'. He joined Aberdeen's Peelite-Whig ministry, but behaved like a prima donna, constantly threatening resignation and finally timing it so as to bring down the government, in a conspicuously disloyal way, when it was under attack for its handling of the Crimean War. Few Whigs were ready to serve under him again. He was thus unable to collect a Cabinet to succeed it, and had to watch Palmerston take over. He went to Vienna to negotiate a peace with Russia which the Allies never intended to accept, and earned further unpopularity for his efforts.

His closing years were happier, but not much more successful. Palmerston asked him to be Foreign Secretary, and he held the office throughout the 1859-65 ministry. They worked closely together – the queen called them 'those two dreadful old men'. It was partly Earl Russell's (as he had now become) dilatoriness that allowed the *Alabama*, commissioned by the Confederates, to sail from Liverpool during the American Civil War, and wreak havoc among northern shipping, for which the British later had to pay handsomely. Their efforts to stop Bismarck and the Austrians expelling the Danes from Schleswig failed humiliatingly.

Nonetheless, when Palmerston eventually died the queen sent for Russell and he became prime minister once more. The Whig-Peelite coalition had been consolidated under Palmerston, and Russell had Gladstone to lead the Commons. He had had a Reform Bill ready when he lost power in 1852, and had come up with another in 1860. Now he looked to round off his political life as he had begun it. There was a sense that a further extension of the franchise was inevitable after Palmerston's death. But he was to have one last frustration. There were enough Palmerstonians left among the Whigs, led by a powerful orator, Robert Lowe, to defeat the modest extension and redistribution which he and Gladstone proposed. So he resigned. It was left to Disraeli to out-manoeuvre the Liberals and carry through the far more radical changes of the Second Reform Act of 1867.

When the Liberals won the subsequent election under the new franchise, everyone, including Russell, accepted Gladstone as the proper prime minister, and many of the reforms which Russell had suggested, in Ireland, education and the army, were carried through by a party with a cohesive majority and a strong leader. His ideas had been the right ones for his times, but in a period of political instability he had lacked the personal qualities to get them onto the Statute Book, and was overshadowed by Peel and by Palmerston. He was 'little Johnny Russell' to the end.

Further Reading
J. Prest, *Lord John Russell*, 1972.

RUSSELL, LORD WILLIAM

RUSSELL, LORD WILLIAM (1639-83), Whig martyr, son of that fifth Earl of Bedford who changed sides twice in the Civil Wars sat in Charles II's parliaments for Tavistock and for Bedfordshire. He was one of the pro-Protestant and anti-French MPs who helped to form the 'Country Party', attacking first Buckingham and then Danby. After the Popish Plot revelations had begun, it was Russell who moved in the Commons for the withdrawal of the Duke of York from the king's presence and councils, and before long he was one of the leading supporters of Exclusion. After the Oxford Parliament of 1681, the collapse of the Whig plans for a legal change in the succession, and the death of Shaftesbury, Russell became one of the so-called 'Council of Six'. His eminence in Whig counsels made him an obvious target for royal revenge, and the obscure association of the Council of Six with the shady group who hatched what came to be known as the Rye House Plot gave the king his opportunity. In the summer of 1683 Russell and the other Whig chiefs were arrested. Charged with treason, he was condemned on hearsay evidence and beheaded in Lincoln's Inn Fields. Charles, characteristically, showed no mercy when he could afford not to do so, saying 'If I do not take his life, he will soon have mine'. High-minded, courteous, ill-advised, naive,

Russell may have been guilty of treason and was certainly guilty of misprision of treason. In his death he became the proto-martyr of the Whig cause, not least because he firmly refused at his trial to abandon the belief that there are times when it is right to resist a government by force.

RUSSELL, WILLIAM HOWARD

RUSSELL, WILLIAM HOWARD (1820-1907), war correspondent, was born into an impoverished middle-class Irish family, with a Protestant father and a Catholic mother. He caught the attention of Delane, editor of *The Times*, by his reporting of an Irish election, was used to describe the funeral of the Duke of Wellington and to investigate the railway boom, and was then sent off to the Black Sea at the start of the Crimean War. That was where he became famous. He went on to report on the Indian Mutiny, the American Civil War, the Prussian wars against Austria and France, and, for *The Telegraph*, the Zulu War. He was editor, and for some time proprietor, of the *Army and Navy Gazette*. But most of his work was for *The Times*, and it was as Russell of *The Times* that he made his name.

The Times in his early days was under the management of a formidable trio, John Delane, John Walter III and Mowbray Morris. Billy Russell became as well known to the reading public as any of them. He was a bon viveur and raconteur, a regular diner at the Garrick, with a rich repertoire of Irish songs. He became friendly with the Prince of Wales. His charm opened many doors to valuable information. Sir Colin Campbell, who had initially had him thrown out of his headquarters in the Crimea, was won over and chatted regularly with him about his plans during the Indian Mutiny. He got to see President Lincoln ten days after his arrival in America. He watched the battle of Königgrätz (1866) from a tower in the heart of the village, thanks to the Austrian commander, Benedek: and the battle of Sedan (1870) alongside the King of Prussia, Bismarck and Moltke from a hilltop above the scene. But he was essentially a front-line correspondent, no stranger to physical danger. In India, recovering from an injury, he was overrun by hostile cavalry while trying to escape on horseback, naked save for a shirt, to be rescued by a Highlander as he lay helpless on the ground. A Yankee, fleeing from Bulls Run, pulled a trigger on him, but the gun did not go off: the Yankees disliked him so much for his reporting of their retreat that he eventually left the country halfway through the war.

Russell's overblown style was very different from modern journalism. But he aimed for factual accuracy and honest reporting and, with a readership unused to news from the front line, his influence was unprecedented: some have compared it to the effects of television on public opinion in the USA during the Vietnam War. From the Crimea he sent two packages a week,

1088 / Russell, William Howard

each of 6,000 words: they took about ten days to reach England by sea. His description of the shortage of medical supplies, the breakdown of the commissariat, the red tape and anachronisms of the British command structure, and the superiority of the French in all these departments, led to the fall of Aberdeen's government. 'You were the true soldiers' friend, Mr Russell', said a corporal of the Black Watch. His reports on the savagery of the treatment of Indians after the Mutiny did much to make the Viceroy's policy of clemency more acceptable to the British public. The War Office paid attention to his comments on the superiority of the Prussians' needle gun. As an Irishman he was never an imperial jingoist, and as an observer he came to hate the beastliness of war. Towards the end of his life, he found himself ill at ease with the selective reporting and low regard for accuracy of the popular press. The inscription on his bust in the crypt of St Paul's Cathedral reads: 'The first and greatest of war correspondents'.

Further Reading
A. Hankinson, *Man of Wars: William Howard Russell of* The Times, 1982.

RYSBRACK, JOHN MICHAEL (1693-1770), sculptor, a Fleming of an artistic family, came to England in 1720 as not the earliest, but (bar Roubiliac) the most distinguished, of that irruption of foreign sculptors which dominated English sculpture in the first half of the eighteenth century and breathed new life into the native school. He came with an introduction to James Gibbs, the architect, and was at once engaged in carving, from Gibbs's designs, a series of works which included a bust of the Earl of Nottingham. The bust is significantly a portrait in the Roman manner – not that veneration of the antique was anything very new, but that it was more closely observed in the days when victorious Englishmen were first making the Grand Tour, building houses in the Palladian style and really thought themselves a Rome revived. By the time of Flaxman, the attitude had become regnant in English sculpture. But it is the blending of the antique with the late baroque which made, and makes, the particular attraction of Rysbrack's work.

To which it must be added that he was a supreme portrait sculptor in the years falling between the death of Kneller (1723) and the return of Reynolds from Rome in 1753, when much of the finest portraiture in England was done in terracotta and marble. Indeed portrait sculpture, which had too often been simply the perquisite of funeral monuments, came of age in the hands of Rysbrack and Roubiliac, as an autonomous class of English art, that of the portrait bust, greatly prized for its heroic associations. By 1732, Rysbrack had done sixty or more busts, often in two versions (terracotta, then marble). Among the contemporary portraits were Gibbs himself and Alexander Pope, both brilliantly figured; but there were also heroes of the past, the Black Prince and Oliver Cromwell, Spenser and Milton, emblems of England's glory, busts of a sort which went to honour the libraries and grottoes of the new palaces, and fill the Temple of British Worthies at Stowe. Rysbrack went on to do busts of the royal family (e.g. the tender *Queen Caroline*, *c.*1739, in the Wallace Collection), the prime minister (Walpole, 1738, National Portrait Gallery), and a long list of aristocrats, writers, artists and professional men.

Not that, in giving currency to the bust, he neglected the funeral monument, the traditional forum of English sculpture: in 1731 his monument to Sir Isaac Newton was revealed, perhaps the finest post-medieval tomb in Westminster Abbey, and in about 1732 the monument to the first Duke of Marlborough at Blenheim. To say that in both of these he worked partly from designs by the architect William Kent is not to depreciate the large contribution of the sculptor: the animated figures are carved in perfect equilibrium within the formal pyramid, the expression is restrained and very moving. Rysbrack had always more restraint than Roubiliac: he tended to prefer the ideal above the real, and what is taken from naturalism is given to nobility. After 1750 – perhaps owing to the rise of Reynolds and Gainsborough – the number of his portrait commissions fell off, but he kept his freshness, even modified his style, and continued to create monuments which are the treasures of our churches.

S

SACHEVERELL DR HENRY (1674?-1724) was the grandson of a Nonconformist minister ejected in 1662. A Fellow of Magdalen, Oxford, he became notorious as a rabble-rousing preacher of High Church opinions. Impressive in appearance but superficial in mind, intemperate in language, with a flair for slightly pompous Billingsgate, 'the Doctor' was an unattractive and foolish character, the mouthpiece of the 'high-flying' Tories of Oxford. In 1702 he had celebrated the accession of Queen Anne by a sermon on the alliance of throne and altar. In it he provided a Tory catchword by hanging out 'the bloody flag of defiance' against Dissenters, and he denounced occasional conformists, those 'insidious persons who can creep to our altars' with the purpose of undermining them. In 1709, on the anniversary of William III's landing in Torbay, Sacheverell delivered before the Lord Mayor of London at St Paul's a sermon on the text, 'In perils among false brethren'. It was printed and sold 40,000 copies. In effect it was an inflammatory attack both upon the Glorious Revolution and upon the predominantly Whig government of the day. Sacheverell defended non-resistance, assailed toleration as well as occasional conformity, condemned the dissenting academies for teaching 'all the hellish principles of Fanaticism, Regicide, and Anarchy', and denounced Lord Treasurer Godolphin as the 'wily Volpone' who had betrayed his party. The Lords condemned the sermon as a seditious libel, and the government decided to impeach its author. This decision was a political blunder, and opened the way to the fall of the government. Public opinion, tired of the expensive and apparently endless war, was ready to take up any cause against Godolphin and the Whigs, and Sacheverell and 'the church in danger' were – for the time being – an excellent one.

The impeachment opened in February 1710. Westminster Hall was packed; like the early stages of Warren Hastings's trial, that of Sacheverell was an event of the London season, with Whig and Tory ladies going at seven in the morning to secure their seats. The doctor himself travelled to and fro in a glass coach, with a retinue armed with bludgeons and drawn swords and a vast mob roaring for 'High Church and Sacheverell'. Queen Anne's sympathies were as evident as those of the crowds, and her Chaplains supported Sacheverell as he faced his opponents. The Whig accusers of Sacheverell had little difficulty in demonstrating that the Revolution was an act of just resistance, and his Tory champions, not daring to deny this, were driven to considerable sophistry in order to square Sacheverell's words with the events of 1688. The doctor himself ingeniously maintained that there had in fact been no resistance in that year, for William of Orange had himself proclaimed that he did not come to conquer England. Whatever the merits of these arguments, the votes of the Peers revealed how the political tide was flowing in 1710. By sixty-nine to fifty-two they found him guilty; by a majority of six votes only they suspended him from preaching for three years, in effect the lightest possible sentence.

Sacheverell was, briefly, a national hero. A Tory admirer had presented him with a living in Shropshire, and his journey thither was a triumphal progress, with banquets and peals of bells, the local gentry providing guards of honour as he passed through the countryside and the towns welcoming him with speeches. Five months later, in August 1710, Anne dismissed Godolphin. In October a general election was held in which 'Sacheverell' was a password to victory. The Tories and High Churchmen, backed by the queen, won a handsome triumph, and in the four years of power which followed they placed on the statute book two of the doctor's favourite measures, the Occasional Conformity Act (1711) and the Schism Act (1714), the latter aimed at closing down dissenting academies. Sacheverell himself meanwhile was presented (1713) to a London living, St Andrew's, Holborn. But this was the limit of his promotion. If ever a man had, in purely political terms, earned a bishopric, it was Sacheverell. Yet none came his way, even though he courted St John with some care, and Anne's death in 1714 extinguished his hopes as well as those of more eminent men. There were some, like the Oxford Jacobite Thomas Hearne, who thought that Sacheverell ought at the least, if he really believed what he preached, to have become a Non-juror; Hearne considered him 'conceited, ignorant, imprudent'. He died in 1724, it is said from the results of an accident.

Further Reading
Geoffrey Holmes, *The Trial of Dr Sacheverell*, 1973.

SACKVILLE GERMAIN, LORD GEORGE, 1st VISCOUNT SACKVILLE (1716-85), soldier and politician, has left a notorious name because of the events of a few hours on the battlefield of Minden in 1759. Moreover he had a second career in politics less well-known than the first, more meritorious but equally unfortunate; for the military failures of the American War he must be held in some measure responsible.

Sackville, whose father was the first Duke of Dorset, was educated at Westminster and Trinity College, Dublin; he entered the army and parliament. He served with credit at Fontenoy, where he was wounded, and in Scotland, during the 'pacification' of the Highlands. From 1750 to 1758 he was chief secretary to his father, when Dorset was for the second time Lord Lieutenant of Ireland. His reputation was good, though he was held to be arrogant. By 1757 he was lieutenant-general of the Ordnance and colonel of the Second Dragoon Guards. In 1757 his friend Pitt offered him command of the Rochefort expedition which, believing the plan to be misconceived, he refused. After its failure he sat on the Commission which examined Mordaunt, the unsuccessful commander. He was second in command, in 1758, in Marlborough's abortive attack upon St Malo. This failure may have affected his nerve or judgement. No adequate reason can, however, be offered for his lapse at the Battle of Minden, where he was in command, under Prince Ferdinand of Brunswick, of all the allied cavalry. The infantry had broken the French line, six British regiments bearing the brunt of fierce fighting. Ferdinand ordered Sackville to advance and, when he took no action, repeated the order several times. Sackville would not give the order and the French were allowed to escape from what could have been a complete disaster. Furthermore he specifically ordered Granby, his fiery second in command, to stand still. He was 'disobliged' with both Granby and Ferdinand. Was he a coward, as Fortescue thought? Did he, as seems more likely, make a sulky stand upon what he may have realized was an initial error of judgement? He suffered for it, for he was shunned in camp and drawing room, court-martialled and disgraced. The sentence that he was 'unfit to serve the king in any capacity' was read out, by express order of Pitt, at the head of every regiment 'so that officers might be convinced that neither high birth nor great employment can shelter offences of such a nature'.

Yet Sackville was brought forward again by George III (who saw him as an injured man) because of his dislike of his father's ministers. In 1765 he became Vice-Treasurer of Ireland in Rockingham's administration – an appointment which caused Pitt to refuse to join the ministry. In 1770 he took the name of Germain, with the property of the widowed Lady Betty Germain, and fought a duel with one of his traducers. He adhered to Lord North's ministry in 1770 and was rewarded by appointment to be Secretary for the American colonies in 1775 (and Board of Trade). He now became imaginatively bellicose, urging decisive military action upon cautious colleagues. For 1777 he produced a Pitt-like plan to end the war. That it failed was no more Germain's fault than Burgoyne's or Howe's. Had it succeeded, as with closer co-operation between Howe and Burgoyne it might have done, Germain's reputation would have been recovered. As it was, in increasingly difficult circumstances after Burgoyne's surrender and the development of a full-scale European war, he showed at least more energy and resource than his prime minister, Lord North.

Further Reading
G. Saxon Brown, *The American Secretary: the Colonial Policy of Lord George Germain*, 1963.

SADLER, SIR RALPH (the usual spelling is nowadays SADLEIR, but Sir Ralph himself usually dropped the 'i': the form SADLEYER is also found) (1507-87), diplomatist and statesman, was born in 1507 and died in 1587. His father was a steward or minor official in the service of the Marquis of Dorset and of Sir Edward Belknap. While still young, Ralph was taken into the household of Thomas Cromwell, later Henry VIII's great minister and Earl of Essex. Probably in 1536 Sadler was made a gentleman of the king's privy chamber, and he at once made so good an impression on the king that Henry VIII sent him in 1537 on a most delicate and important mission to Scotland, to try to find out how much truth there was in the complaints made by his sister Margaret, the queen-dowager, against her third husband, Lord Methven, and to investigate the relations between the King of Scotland and the French. He succeeded in helping Margaret, and after a visit to James V, who was in France, he improved Anglo-Scottish relations. Until his death, Sadler was to be the foremost expert in English political life on the Scots.

So pleased was Henry VIII with Sadler's work that in 1540 he sent him again to Scotland to try to separate the king from the advice and policies of Cardinal Beaton, who was wedded to a Franco-Scottish alliance. Sadler was to advise James V to take to himself the wealth of the Scottish church, as Henry had done in England. The mission was a failure, but Sadler had done his best. Henry was so satisfied with Sadler's work that in 1540 he made him one of his two secretaries. He was also knighted and made a privy councillor and he entered parliament as MP for Hertford (1541).

After the battle of Solway Moss, which was immediately followed by the death of James V, Sadler was sent to Scotland again. He was specially charged to arrange a marriage alliance between the new queen, the baby Mary, and Henry's son Edward, Prince of Wales, in order to prevent any recovery of influence by the Cardinal Beaton, who had been imprisoned by the Protestant regent, Arran. The treaty was made, one clause of which provided that the queen should be brought up in Scotland under the care of 'an honourable knight and lady of England'. Henry proposed that Sadler and his wife should undertake this charge, but Sadler succeeded in avoiding this task. Party feelings broke out again in Scotland, and at one point Sadler's house in Edinburgh was besieged by the mob, and he narrowly escaped death from a musket bullet as he was walking in the garden. Sadler retired to Tantallon Castle (1543), an episode which Sir Walter Scott commemorated in *Marmion*, Canto 5. Sadler soon returned to England, but all his work was undone when war between England and Scotland broke out (1543). Sadler accompanied the Earl of Hertford on his campaign as treasurer to the army, an office which he filled again in the 1545 campaign.

Owing to his frequent absences on diplomatic missions, Sadler was not able to carry out his duties as Secretary of State and he was replaced by Paget (1543), but he himself was given the post of Master of the Great Wardrobe. When Henry died in 1547, he left Sadler a legacy of 200 gold marks and appointed him a member of the council to which the government of the country was entrusted during Edward VI's minority. When Somerset set out for the Pinkie campaign (1547), Sadler again went with him as High Treasurer of the army. After the battle, in recognition of his outstanding services during the fighting, Sadler was raised to the rank of knight-banneret, a dignity which Holinshed calls 'above a knight and next to a baron'. Sadler was present when Bishop Gardiner was arrested (1548) and he was also with the force which put down Ket's rebellion (1549). During Mary's reign Sadler remained in retirement at his home at Standon, near Ware in Hertfordshire.

In Elizabeth's reign Sadler, as a sound Protestant, became one of Cecil's most trusted servants. He was sent once more to Scotland with secret orders to arrange an alliance with the Protestant party. When hostilities broke out at Leith, he was at the camp and had a chief share in making the treaty of Leith (1560). In 1568 he was appointed Chancellor of the Duchy of Lancaster, a highly lucrative office. When Mary, Queen of Scots, fled to England, Sadler, very much against his will, was one of the commissioners appointed to meet the Scotch commissioners to deal with the problem of the Scots' queen. He it was who made the précis of the Casket Letters for Cecil. He it was also who was sent to arrest the Duke of Norfolk at the time of the Rising of the Northern Earls.

And Sadler it was who twice found himself warder over the Queen of Scots, at Sheffield in 1572 and at Wingfield in 1584. He hated these appointments and never ceased applying for release, but before it came he had had to transfer the queen from Wingfield to Tutbury. He was relieved in 1585. The next year, after the Babington Plot, Sadler was one of the commission which condemned Mary to death.

Sadler was a man of much importance in his own day. He was loyal, courageous and shrewd; his abilities were indeed greater than the offices which he held suggest. Everybody trusted him and he was well rewarded by the sovereigns whom he served. When he died on 30 March 1587, he was said to be the richest commoner in England. He had sat in eight parliaments; he was a privy councillor under three sovereigns for close on fifty years; he knew more about Scotland than any other Englishman; he was a brave soldier; he was also 'a most exquisite writer' (Lloyd, *State of Worthies*), and his state papers are now invaluable historical sources. He was a little man, devoted to field sports, especially to hawking. He was married and had three sons and four daughters.

Further Reading
A. J. Slavin, *Politics and Profit*, 1966.
T. U. Sadleir, *A Brief Memoir of the Rt. Hon. Sir Ralph Sadleir*, 1907.
A. Clifford, ed., *The State Papers and Letters of Sir Ralph Sadler*, with a memoir by Sir Walter Scott, 1809.

SALESBURY, WILLIAM (*c.*1517-*c.*1600), translator of the Scriptures into Welsh, came of an old and distinguished Norman-Welsh family and was educated at Oxford, where he became a strenuous supporter of the reforming movement in religion. He published many books to further the Reformation. In 1547 he published his English-Welsh dictionary, and in 1567 he collaborated with Bishop Davies in translating the New Testament and the Prayer Book into Welsh, he himself translating all the New Testament except the pastoral epistles and the Revelation. His printed Welsh had a very odd appearance owing to his theory that the Welsh words should be spelt as nearly like their supposed Latin originals as he could make them. He is said to have pursued his studies in a secret room which could be entered only by climbing up the chimney.

SALT, SIR TITUS (1803-76) was an industrial tycoon and a philanthropist. The combination of natural resources and technological revolutions; low taxation and free trade; victory over Napoleon, and a reformed parliament in which the voice of industry could be heard alongside those of land and commerce; together these created unique opportunities for enterprising entrepreneurs in mid-Victorian Britain. Many of them, brought up in families with clear and simple Christian beliefs, used the fortunes they made for the benefit of the communities in which they worked. Sir Titus Salt was one. His father, a West Yorkshire farmer, set up as a woolstapler in Bradford in 1822, got his son apprenticed and then employed him as a buyer. In 1834, on one of his buying trips, young Titus spotted some dirty bales from Peru in a Liverpool warehouse, took a sample of the evil-smelling wool off with him and experimented with spinning the long straight fibres. They produced a high-quality, glossy yarn. This was alpaca. He developed the techniques and built the machinery to turn it into cloth; and introduced Alpaca Orleans, the mixture of alpaca and cotton in which Victorian ladies were to dress themselves for the next fifty years. He then did the same for mohair, from the fleece of the Turkish angora goat. Together these made him the leader of the West Yorkshire worsted industry, itself the leader of the world.

Bradford's population grew from 43,527 in 1831 to 103,778 in 1851. Salt saw the running of his business and the creation of decent living conditions for his workers as part of the same task. As Mayor of Bradford in 1849 he started proper drainage, fitted anti-pollution devices to his factory chimneys, built mechanics' institutes and music halls as alternatives to the ubiquitous pubs, and gave a sixty-one-acre park to the town. Next year he started the planning of Saltaire. He decided to put his fortune and his energies into this, rather than buying a country estate and becoming a landowner. He concentrated his five factories on a site three miles out of Bradford, in one palatial Italianate building, its chimney disguised as a campanile, its noisy machinery underground. Round it during the next twenty years he built 850 houses for the work force, with public baths, hospital, library, and a Congregational church with room for 600. There were cricket pitches and a boathouse: but no public house, pawn shop or police station. It was all done before he died, and built so sturdily that it survives today, though mostly as a tourist attraction. He was in some ways a true man of his time, an employer of child labour and a stern opponent of trade unions. Yet he was the local hero. When he died, work stopped in all the mills for miles around and 120,000 people turned out to witness his last journey.

SAMSON OF BURY (1135-1211; Abbot of Bury St Edmunds 1182-1211) was perhaps a more typical abbot than the saints and scholars who are so often taken to represent twelfth- and thirteenth-century religious and monastic life. Unusual for his time in having an intimate biography written of him which is far from unthinkingly or consistently laudatory, Samson's spirituality, whatever it was, is hidden behind practical affairs. Yet such mundane matters as balancing accounts and managing estates were fundamental to contemporary monasticism. Without the sometimes predatory acquisitive instinct

none of the great monastic revivals would have been possible, nor would the exercise of learning or holiness. The successful man of God had to be adept in dealing with Mammon. Few were more energetic or notorious in their pursuit of the essential material basis for the spiritual life than Samson of Bury.

The chronicle written by another monk at Bury, Jocelin of Brakelond, presents a uniquely rounded portrait of Samson; its richness of texture prompted Thomas Carlyle to celebrate Samson's life in his popular *Past and Present* (1843). Jocelin's biography reflects the author's own changing relationship with his subject. From Samson's election as abbot in 1182 until 1187 Jocelin was his chaplain and acted as his secretary; thereafter he became more closely involved in other areas of the abbey's life, becoming guestmaster in 1200. As Samson spent much of his time trying to restrict the monks' administrative freedom, control of property and independence of action, Jocelin's tone became increasingly critical, at times even hostile towards his former hero. Although his *Chronicle* ends in 1202, Jocelin's picture of Bury and its abbot is one of the most vivid medieval accounts of monastic life.

Samson, like a number of twelfth-century abbots (e.g. Baldwin of Ford), began his career as a secular clerk. A Norfolk man, he followed the fashion of studying in Paris. He first served the great local Benedictine house of Bury St Edmunds in 1160, ironically as spokesman for the monks in an appeal to Rome against the abbot: this earned him a spell in the abbatial prison at Castle Acre. Seeing, perhaps, the opportunity for advancement within a protected corporate structure, Samson took monastic vows at Bury in 1166. He soon proved himself an effective administrator, holding a series of offices, including, in the 1170s, that of novice master. Jocelin of Brakelond was one of his charges. This wide experience of how the abbey was organized not only helped build for Samson support among the monks, in whose interests he had once more been confined briefly to Castle Acre, but was also ideal preparation for his period as abbot. He knew, none better, where lay the monks' interests, weaknesses and inefficiencies.

On his election as a compromise candidate in 1182, Samson's objectives were clear: the restoration of the abbey's finances through a recovery of temporal rights and vigorous management of property. A thorough investigation of abbey estates was conducted. Within two years, all debts had been paid off and by 1186 a book, known as *Abbot Samson's Kalendar*, had been completed listing all the rights and revenues owed to the monastery from each of its holdings. The increased revenues that ensued were used by Samson to pursue contested rights, for instance in the 1190s over the number of knights' fees attached to the monastery, and to rebuilding the abbey church and other monastic quarters (he had been master of the workmen 1180-2 when the choir of the church was rebuilt). Although vigilant in protecting the abbey's privileges and immunities, Samson also encouraged the liberties of the town of Bury, not least as a counterweight to the pretensions of his monks. Similarly, as had his predecessors, he allied with the king to control the aspirations of the Bury monks. It was little wonder that their resentment at his autocratic manner and behaviour, as well as to the detail of his policy, grew. At one stage, in 1199, Samson feared for his life. The sustained opposition was based on legitimate anxieties as well as corporate self-interest. Samson saw his responsibility in running Bury as that of a royal tenant-in-chief accountable to the king for his barony: hence his determination to control as much of the community's property as possible. The monks, on the other hand, feared that, during any protracted abbatial vacancy (as occurred in 1180-2 and 1211-15) the lands that the abbot had taken from the community would be dealt with by the king as part of the abbot's barony and controlled by the Crown. However, it is also clear from Jocelin's politically alert account that the monastic body itself was a network of disputing factions, based on age and personal loyalties. Where other writers give only the merest hint of such institutional discord, Jocelin exposes in detail what must, nevertheless, have been a commonplace of life in such wealthy, cloistered communities of men or women, where pettiness could be interpreted as principle and prejudice as piety.

Inevitably, by taste and position, Samson was heavily engaged in national secular as well as local ecclesiastical politics. Perhaps his most memorable intervention was in the 1190s when he defended Richard I's administration from John's attempted coup. In 1193 he excommunicated John and the other rebels and, with his military retinue, besieged John at Windsor. Later he visited Richard in Germany. As with his policies towards his abbey, Samson's characteristically firm stand suggests not only a strong personality but a substratum of principle and conviction beneath his actions. However, Samson realized the importance of royal favour and was reconciled to John after he became king in 1199.

Samson was no saint. An effective administrator, he was more at home with the intricacies of politics and estate management than with ascetic rigour or spiritual endeavour. Jocelin describes him as disliking introverted scholarly monks, preferring good organizers. Apparently he harboured the unfulfilled wish to have been the abbey's accountant. Although adequately versed in Latin, he preached in French and English, the latter with a Norfolk dialect, a habit he shared with another expert administrator, Robert Walpole. Something approaching local pride may be deduced from his devotion to St Edmund, on whose miracles he compiled a largely derivative treatise between 1166 and 1182 and whose body he examined in 1198 while constructing a new shrine for the saint. Although, on hearing of the loss of Jerusalem and the True Cross in 1187, he took to wearing hair shirts and drawers and abandoned eating meat, he was not noted for personal privation, and, in any case, he preferred 'fresh milk and honey and such like to any other food'. Energetic, at times almost frenetic, he could be impulsive or showy, as when he appeared in front of his guest Henry II in 1188 carrying a needle, thread and a cloth cross and demanding to be allowed to go on crusade. The king refused.

Jocelin's detailed physical description of Samson is a mirror of his personality:

Abbot Samson was of middle height, and almost entirely bald; his face was neither round nor long, his nose prominent, his lips thick, his eyes clear as crystal and of penetrating glance; his hearing of the sharpest; his eyebrows grew long and were often clipped; a slight cold made him soon hoarse. He had a few white hairs in a red beard and a very few in the hair on his head, which was black and rather curly; but within fourteen years of his election he was white as snow. He was a man of extreme sobriety, never given to sloth, extremely strong and ever ready to go either on horseback or on foot, until old age prevailed and tempered his eagerness.

Further Reading
Jocelin of Brakelond, *Chronicle*, ed. and trans. H. E. Butler, 1949.

SAMSON OF WORCESTER (*d.*1112: Bishop of Worcester 1096-1112), a chaplain to William I and William II, was claimed by V. H. Galbraith in 1967 as the compiler and scribe of the so-called Great Domesday Book, the surviving fair copy of the survey of 1086. A Norman of noble origins, son of Osbert, a priest, like so many administrators of the first and second generations after 1066, Samson was a protégé of Odo of Bayeux, becoming a canon and treasurer of Bayeux Cathedral. In royal service by 1074, he apparently declined the see of Le Mans in 1081 saying that he was a man of this world not the next. Although having been married and still only in minor orders, Samson was appointed by William II to the bishopric of Worcester in 1096: a striking, and possibly deliberate, contrast to his saintly predecessor Wulfstan. Samson was at the centre of a remarkable ecclesiastical dynasty: his brother Thomas of Bayeux was Archbishop of York (1070-1100), as was one of his sons, Thomas, (Archbishop of York 1109-14); another son, Richard, was Bishop of Bayeux (1108-33). This scale of preferment for one clerical-administrative family is impressive but not unique; it was matched if not surpassed by the rise of Roger of Salisbury and the Le Poers under Henry I. Samson was one of those secular minded ecclesiastics so mistrusted and vilified by the reformers clustered around the late eleventh-century papacy. According to William of Malmesbury, Samson was an '*antiquorum homo morum*' a man of the old school. Although personally given to the pleasures of the flesh, particularly food ('a veritable sink of eatables' in William of Malmesbury's phrase) Samson does not seem to have been a bad bishop. However, recent scholarly opinion denies his authorship of Domesday, not least because there are inconsistencies and errors in the valuation attached to one of Samson's own estates, Templecomb (Somerset), by the scribe Galbraith sought to identify as Samson himself. Whatever their other shortcomings, Norman curial officials and landowners were unlikely to make mistakes of that sort.

Further Reading
J. C. Holt, *Domesday Studies*, 1987.
F. Barlow, *The English Church 1066-1154*, 1979.

SANCROFT, WILLIAM (1617-93), Archbishop of Canterbury, was born of yeoman stock at Fressingfield, in Suffolk, and educated at Bury St Edmunds Grammar School and Emmanuel College, Cambridge, of which he became a Fellow. Turned out of his fellowship in 1651, he wrote against Calvinism and against the Commonwealth, but remained in England until 1657. Returning from abroad at the Restoration, he was appointed a royal Chaplain in 1661 and Dean of St Paul's in 1664. He held this benefice until he was elected to Canterbury in 1677, and gave much of his energy to the rebuilding of St Paul's. As archbishop he tried in vain to reconvert James, Duke of York, to Anglicanism, and when the latter came to the throne in 1685 Sancroft inevitably found himself in an equivocal position. He served, but only for a short time, on the Ecclesiastical Commission created in 1686, and in 1688 he was in name at least the leader of the Seven Bishops in their refusal to read the Declaration of Indulgence. After their acquittal he urged the king to retract his illegal steps, he declined to condemn William's Declaration, and he was one of those who at the eleventh hour advised James to call a free parliament. But after James's flight Sancroft retired to his palace at Lambeth and withdrew from public action, maintaining that William was a usurper and that nobody who had taken an oath of allegiance to James could honestly swear loyalty to him. Thus he had no part in welcoming William to London, nor was he present when the Convention of 1689 declared the throne vacant. His inaction helped to make futile the project of a Regency of William and Mary in James's name, a policy which he was prepared to accept. He was deprived in 1690, and evicted from Lambeth by process of law in 1691, retiring to Fressingfield. By executing in the same year a deed conveying the exercise of his authority as archbishop to the Non-juring Bishop Lloyd of Norwich, he did his best to perpetuate the schism in the Church of England, and to the day of his death in 1693 he continued to pray for James II as King of England, and declined to take communion with those who had sworn allegiance to William. Burnet, who disliked Sancroft, calling him a 'dry, cold man, reserved and peevish', thought he had played 'a very mean part in all the great transaction' of the Revolution; and it is easy, with Macaulay, to condemn his behaviour as ineffectual and even uncharitable. Certainly Sancroft was an embittered old man, and there were other Non-jurors, notably Ken, who declined to prolong schism. In defence of Sancroft it can be said that he was notable for his personal sanctity; that the Non-jurors, some 400 in all, included many of the most upright and learned Anglicans of the time; and that, whatever the political implications of their protest, they were contending for the spiritual independence of the church.

SANDBY, PAUL (1725-1809), watercolour artist, is called 'the father of English watercolour' – which needs explaining. Watercolour painting, whether done opaquely after the manner of tempera or transparently over a light ground, had been known for several centuries. The medieval missalists had used it; the portrait miniaturists of the seventeenth century had used it; and the Dutch, as usual, had perfected it. But the fashion for tinted topographical drawings (intended to be multiplied by engravings) grew apace among the estate-proud English squirearchy of the eighteenth century; and Sandby was the first to add to these the ingredient of *art*, to make (in other words) pictures out of pictorial records. Thus he was the founder of the English School of watercolourists, for there succeeded him all those artists who have made of English watercolour a unique contribution to the sum of pictorial art.

He drew employment chiefly from the army: first in the department of military drawing at the Tower of London; then as draughtsman to the Survey of the Highlands which was carried through after the '45; and later as chief drawing-master to the RMA, Woolwich. He was a public figure, being Director of the Society of Arts, a founder-member of the Royal Academy (1768), and an exhibitor at the Foundling Hospital. He demeaned himself by burlesquing Hogarth, but bought paintings secretly from Wilson to save him from starving. A collection of his work may be seen at Windsor Castle.

SAUNDERS, SIR CHARLES (1713-75), admiral, may be a name known to only one for every ten who can relate the story of Wolfe and the capture of the Heights of Abraham. Yet the naval commander in the intricate operation which was completed by Wolfe's brilliant assault must share the credit for the winning of Quebec and consequently of Canada, not only for his competent navigation but also for his loyal co-operation, rare between sailor and soldier at any time. In Saunders the genius of Wolfe found its perfect complement.

He was with Anson in his voyage round the world, an experience which, for the survivors, was uniquely valuable. Not only had men like Saumarez, Hyde Parker and Saunders shared in a sustained test of seamanship and endurance; they also enjoyed for the future the patronage of the man who was First Lord of the Admiralty for a vital decade. Anson was a good judge of men and Saunders was one of his special protégés. He served with distinction in the rest of the War of the Austrian Succession, being with Hawke in his victory of October 1747. He became an MP in 1750 and remained so for most of his life, and he became Controller of the Navy in 1755, but he was happiest at sea. In 1756 he went to the Mediterranean as rear-admiral and did useful service, with Osborne, against the Toulon fleet. When Pitt and Anson worked out the ambitious plan to secure Canada by threefold attack, it was Saunders who was chosen to sail up the St Lawrence, a long and notoriously hazardous passage. With him was Holmes, a man of cool nerve, and a young navigator, James Cook, whose survey of the St Lawrence is a classic of its kind. Saunders and Holmes both thought that Wolfe was rash to attempt a landing below, and the ascent of the Heights of Abraham, but gave him whole-hearted co-operation. Saunders held the reach below Quebec and made feint attacks to distract the attention of the French, while Holmes looked after the landing. After the fall of the city, Saunders sailed home, making all sail to join Hawke when he heard of his engagement, but arriving too late to share in the victory of Quiberon Bay. He returned to the Mediterranean for a time, but had little more active service. Knighted in 1761, he became First Lord of the Admiralty for a short time in 1766.

Further Reading
C. P. Stacey, *Quebec*, 1959.

SAVERNAKE, WILLIAM (*c.*1380-1460) illustrates the lifestyle of the lower clergy and perhaps also of the urban tradesman of the later Middle Ages. Presumably a Wiltshireman, he was ordained in 1409, was appointed vicar of Ibberton (Dorset) in 1441, and in 1452 became chaplain of Munden's chantry, Bridport. This was a less arduous post than that of vicar for an old man, for cantarists had no parochial responsibilities and had only to celebrate mass (Holy Communion) and hold other services daily for the good of the soul of the founder. Most founders of chantries provided for only one priest, who held services at an altar or chapel within an existing church. The chantry founded by John Munden in 1349, somewhat unusually, employed two chaplains, used a separate building for services (St Michael's Chapel), and paid them £5 each, which was quite a generous salary and was actually exceeded in practice. Many chantries failed, sometimes through lack of income, but often because the chaplains neglected or embezzled the endowment. It was to prevent this and to ensure that masses were said for their benefit forever that founders often made monasteries or town corporations responsible for supervision of their chantries. Bridport corporation took its responsibilities seriously, inspecting the accounts and property each year. It was probably for this reason that Savernake as warden compiled accounts in 1453-60, though he certainly kept them in much more detail than was needed. It is this detail that is of such value, as such relatively poor and small households normally could not keep accounts and had no need for them anyway.

John Munden had been a wealthy and important man – MP and JP for Dorset – and his house, in which the chaplains lived, was a substantial structure containing hall, kitchen, pantry, separate bedrooms, and probably other rooms too. It was quite well-furnished with tables, chairs, pots and pans, and even silver spoons. There was a walled garden, a dovecot, which provided fresh meat, and an orchard, where the chaplains grew fruit. It must have been one of the better residences in Bridport. The chaplains were responsible for keeping up these premises, the chapel, and the properties that formed the endowment, all of which were repaired from time to time by workmen, who took lunch with them. They also provided candles, wine, etc. for the chapel. They were able to afford a servant paid not more than £1.10s. a year and a laundress at 4d. a quarter, and were also able to entertain guests, mainly ecclesiastics and some for weeks at a time. Evidently they were quite comfortably off, though life for two old priests was extremely quiet.

The accounts are most valuable for what they tell us about the diet of ordinary people in the later Middle Ages. The basic foodstuffs were bread and second-best ale, though best ale or wine was consumed on occasion. They ate a lot of meat: normally beef, pork *and* mutton each week, sometimes veal, lamb or chickens, once each woodcock and goose. The fish and other seafood they ate one day each week and daily in Lent was often fresh rather than salted and was surprisingly varied: stockfish, mackerel, oysters, ling, haddock, cod, whiting, conger eel, hake, herrings, mussels, whelks and cockles. They made the Lenten diet slightly more interesting with almonds, figs and raisins. After Lent, understandably fed up with fish and figs, they cut them to the minimum and instead ate more eggs and butter. Like most medieval people, they consumed a lot of peas, spices like pepper, ginger and cinnamon, and used honey as a sweetener. They bought only a little fruit, perhaps because they grew it themselves. It is surprising how varied their diet was and that they could buy fresh meat and fish in such small quantities throughout the year. It is also amazing how well the two of them could live on a combined income of about £12.

Further eading

K. L. Wood-Legh, ed., *A Small Household in the XVth Century*, 1956.

SAVILE, GEORGE, 1st MARQUIS OF HALIFAX

(1633-95), statesman and essayist, was born at Thornhill, near Wakefield, heir to one of Yorkshire's great county families. Educated at Shrewsbury and in France and Italy, he inherited his father's baronetcy in 1644. His background was royalist, and he sat for Pontefract in the Convention of 1660. Charles II gave him a barony in 1668 and admitted him to the Privy Council in 1672. He was a man of superb mind, urbane and witty, wealthy and incorruptible, a fine orator, one of the outstanding figures of the century: in the famous words of Dryden's *Absalom and Achitophel*:

> Jotham of piercing wit and pregnant thought,
> Endued by nature and by learning taught
> To move assemblies.

But he was oddly ineffective as a politician, partly because of the strain of criticism and flippancy in him that gave frequent offence, yet more because he was a patrician intellectual who liked to be, and could usually afford to be, aloof from decision. Independent in judgement, a mediator by instinct, Halifax was ill-suited for political action. The results of this were unfortunate for him. Burnet, in a severe yet sympathetic sketch, recognizes that 'the liveliness of his imagination was always too hard for his judgement'; but he points out that 'with relation to the public, he went backwards and forwards, and changed sides so often, that in conclusion no side trusted him'. So we find him in the 1660s a member of the 'Country' group, a progressive younger royalist hostile to Clarendon; then a stern critic of the Cabal, yet also an opponent of the Test Act; next quarrelling with Danby, who had him removed from the Council after Halifax had commented that Danby's refusal of a bribe from a potential tax-farmer had been like that of 'a man, who, being asked to give another the use of his wife, declined in terms of great civility'.

In 1679 he returned as a member of 'Temple's' Privy Council. The step marked a kind of *rapprochement* with the king, with whom he had a good deal in common: his *Character of King Charles the Second*, written soon after Charles's death but not published until the next century, is much the best character study of a monarch in the English language. The agreement was clinched by an earldom. Scarcely surprisingly, Halifax, though concerned for the Protestant supremacy, did not follow Shaftesbury, with his mob politics and his support of the shallow Monmouth, in the exclusion episode. Instead he backed the scheme for imposing limitations upon James, and, fighting almost alone, used the full powers of his oratory to defeat exclusion in the Lords in 1680. As men's tempers cooled after the crisis Halifax enjoyed

more political authority than at any other time, and in 1682 he became a Marquis. But the return to England in that year of the Duke of York, who was little given to gratitude and found Halifax too clever for comfort, changed the situation. Halifax, though appointed Lord Privy Seal, in effect took up his customary role of detached critic. The politics of 'high' Tories like Rochester were no more to his taste than the proceedings of Shaftesbury's Whigs had been. He opposed the execution of the Rye House 'plotter', Russell, just as he had opposed that of the Popish 'plotter', Stafford. Significantly, it was at this time that he wrote, and circulated privately (it was not published until 1688) the most revealing of all his political pieces, *The Character of a Trimmer*, with its defence of the middle path in politics. 'Why', says Halifax in his preface, 'after we have played the fool with throwing Whig and Tory at one another, as boys do snowballs, do we grow angry at a new name, which by its true signification might do as much to put us into our wits, as the other hath done to put us out of them?'

The accession of James II in 1685 soon brought Halifax's dismissal, because of his refusal to support the repeal of the Test and Habeas Corpus Acts. He returned to his great mansion at Rufford, more a critic than an opponent of James II's Catholic despotism. In *A Letter to a Dissenter*, not printed but circulated widely through the post, he warned Nonconformists not to be taken in by the Declaration of Indulgence of 1687: 'You are therefore to be hugged now, only that you may be the better squeezed at another time'. Sheering away from the prospect of revolution, he replied non-committally to Dykveld's inquiries in 1687, and declined to sign the invitation to William in 1688. He preserved his neutrality into the crisis itself, asking James to call a free parliament even after the invasion, and acting as his 'ambassador' to William at Hungerford. Only after James's first attempt at flight did Halifax abandon his neutrality. He then went over wholeheartedly. He accepted William's commission to persuade James to flee a second time, and did his task harshly. He became Speaker of the Lords in the Convention, opposed the regency plan, and led the Whig peers to offer the Crown to William. In February 1689 it was Halifax who formally invited William and Mary to become king and queen. Once again he took office as Lord Privy Seal.

Yet once again he held power for a short time only. In February 1690 he was forced to resign, ostensibly as a scapegoat for the disastrous Irish campaign of the previous autumn, in fact because he could not shake off his past. The Whigs had not forgotten his 'desertion' over exclusion; Danby, now once more becoming the leading minister, had not forgiven him. He lived on for five more years. Like most of his contemporaries of equal rank, he kept in touch with the exiled Jacobite court. He took part in the Lords' debates from time to time, as for example when in 1694 he opposed the creation of the Bank of England as a privileged corporation. And he devoted some of his energies to pamphleteering in the prose style, compounded of irony and direct statement, of which he was the finest exemplar of his time. He died in 1695 and was buried in Westminster Abbey.

Further Reading
J. P. Kenyon, ed., *Halifax: the Complete Works*, 1969.
H. C. Foxcroft, *A Character of the Trimmer*, 1946.

SAYERS, TOM (1826-65), prize fighter, was the last famous figure in the old bare-fisted ring: two years after his death the Marquis of Queensberry devised rules which transformed boxing. PR, or 'the fancy' as it was generally known, was the favourite sport of the early Victorian underworld. Earlier it had attracted the patronage of the regent and his friends at the ringside. The crowds around the fights in which Sayers won and defended his Champion Belt included peers of the realm, army officers, MPs and JPs, and even clergy. But the atmosphere was rowdy and chaotic, and the fights themselves were illegal, and liable to be interrupted by 'the boys in blue'. The rules were very different from those introduced by Lord Queensberry. The open-air ring was put up where the fight was least likely to be disturbed. Rounds would end only when a boxer fell, and there was no limit to the number of them. Boxers could wrestle each other to the ground. Nine fights out of ten were lost through exhaustion.

Sayers, at between 10.2 and 10.12 stone, was a middleweight, and, measuring only 5' 8½", was normally outreached. But he carried much of his weight around his shoulders and neck, had a tough face which did not cut easily, and was patient and determined. As the 'good little 'un', and with a big smile which was not often shifted, he became a sporting hero. Between 1849 and 1860 he fought sixteen 'mills', losing only one of them, to Nat Langham in sixty-one rounds. His longest mill went through 109 rounds. He won the Champion Belt in 1857 from the Tipton Slasher, who was more than three stone heavier and four inches taller than him. His most famous fight was against an American, John Heenan, the Bernicia Boy, who came to try to take the Belt across the Atlantic in 1860. Two trains, one with thirty-three carriages, took spectators from London Bridge to Farnborough, then remote enough for authority to turn a blind eye. Each side was backed for £200, and the betting was huge. Sayers was pitted against a much heavier, taller and this time younger man (Heenan was 6' 2", and weighed nearly fourteen stone). They fought to a standstill in thirty-seven rounds: Sayers had lost the use of his right arm early in the contest, and 'the Boy's' eyes were so closed that he started one round by attacking Sayers's second by mistake. The fight was declared a draw after

the crowd had invaded the ring. *The Times* gave it 6,000 words. Thereafter £3,000 was raised for Sayers by public subscription. He never fought again, and died five years later: the mastiff who followed his hearse in an open carriage to Highgate Cemetery now adorns his tomb there.

SCOTT, SIR GEORGE GILBERT (1811-78), Gothic architect, was educated at home in a somewhat haphazard manner by his father, who was a low church parson in north Buckinghamshire. Scott was later to write: 'The defects of my education have been like a millstone about my neck and have made me almost dread superior society.' Lacking companionship, he became a solitary wanderer in woods, fields and old churches: the nearby church at Hillesden first inspired his interest in Gothic design. This, together with some enjoyable lessons from a local drawing master and mathematical instruction from his uncle in London, encouraged him to embark on training to become an architect.

Most of his earliest buildings were workhouses. Modest by nature, he owed much at the beginning of his career to W. B. Moffatt, an energetic and well-organized colleague who had trained with him. Together they worked hard and quickly built up a busy practice. Churches came next. Scott read the *Ecclesiologist* and came under the influence of Pugin's writings – 'Pugin's articles excited me almost to fury ...' His churches were large and in the middle pointed style. The first important one, St Giles in Camberwell, built in 1843, received comments of approval from the Cambridge Camden Group. Next he gained international recognition by winning a competition to rebuild St Nicholas in Hamburg. Scott had become a well-established architect. His office grew large, with numerous assistants and so much work that for some jobs he could only have had overall supervision. It is estimated that in the last thirty years of his life over 700 buildings were designed or restored from his office, including many of the cathedrals of England. In 1849 he was appointed surveyor of Westminster Abbey.

His many buildings also included secular ones. Some of them are still well-known landmarks. In London he was responsible for the building of the Foreign Office – in a Renaissance style on the insistence of Lord Palmerston. His original design for this government building (in a Gothic style) he adapted for the Midland Grand Hotel beside St Pancras Station. He was chosen to build the Albert Memorial in Hyde Park. He designed the central building of Glasgow University and, very early in his career, the Martyrs' Memorial in Oxford.

Scott was knighted in 1872 and died a rich and successful man. In his day he was considered to be the greatest architect of the Gothic Revival. Now he is less revered, being regarded as highly competent but not a genius. There has always been criticism of his restoration work, which is seen as too complete and uniform. It was in response to it that William Morris founded the 'Anti-Scrape Society' (the Society for the Protection of Ancient Buildings). But it should not be forgotten that in Scott's day many cathedrals and churches were in a desperate state of repair. As a committed Gothicist, Scott always claimed that he was only returning churches to how they had been in medieval times. A less efficient man might not have been so thorough in what he swept away.

Further Reading
Kenneth Clark, *The Gothic Revival*, 1950.

SCOTT, JOHN, 1st EARL OF ELDON (1751-1838) was the younger of two brothers, sons of William Scott, a Newcastle coal merchant, and Jane Atkinson; both brothers became famous lawyers. The elder, William, was the finer scholar and an equally good lawyer in his own sphere, the admiralty and ecclesiastical courts. He is commemorated by Oxford in the Stowell law fellowship, from the title that he acquired in 1821. He also represented the university in parliament for twenty years. The friend of Dr Johnson in his old age and a member of 'the Club', he was a stout Tory all his life though he played little active part in politics. John Eldon, by contrast, was drawn early into high politics. He became Solicitor-General when he was thirty-seven. He was Lord Chancellor, with only a year's break, for twenty-six years. During that time, as Sydney Smith put it: 'Lord Eldon and the Court of Chancery sat heavy on mankind.'

He was an enterprising young man. From Newcastle grammar school he went to University College, Oxford. At the age of twenty-one he eloped with Bessy Surtees, daughter of a rich banker: a wild start to a sedate and happy marriage of nearly sixty years' duration. Called in 1776, he acquired a large practice in the equity court. In 1783 he took silk and entered parliament, under the wing of Lord Thurlow, as member for Weobley, a decayed borough in Herefordshire. He conceived himself to be a Pittite for life. But it was only in his hatred for the Revolution and Napoleon that he resembled Pitt. Solicitor-General in 1788, he became Attorney-General in 1793 and took a leading part in the measures of those years against sedition and conspiracy. This part was not disagreeable to him. But he was scrupulous in his concern for precedents and points of law. He inclined to hold strictly to the letter of the law and he was willing to see it reinforced by statute, but he was always impartial. In 1799 he became Chief Justice of the Common Pleas and a peer; in 1801, under Addington, he first sat upon the woolsack.

If Eldon's conservatism is to be judged from his more extreme statements, it appears to be almost grotesque. About Russell's bill of 1828, for instance, to repeal the

seventeenth-century Test and Corporation Acts: 'Bad, as mischievous and as revolutionary as the most captious Dissenter would wish it to be.' Of the growth of societies for the education of working people, the 'march of intellect' movement, he declared that it would direct 'a hundred thousand tall fellows with clubs and pikes against Whitehall'. On the question of parliamentary reform he was predictably adamant. Writing to his brother in April 1830 he declared that the reform agitation was of 'a more frightful kind than the prospect of 1791': at least the republican and treasonous language then employed had made it possible for the government to act with the sanctions of law. Furthermore 'the sacrifice of the Test Act, and the passing of the Roman Catholic Emancipation Bill have established a precedent so encouraging to the present attempts at revolution under name of Reform, that he must be a very bold fool who does not tremble at what seems to be fast approaching'. 'My Lords,' cried the old man in a House of Lords debate, 'sacrifice one atom of our glorious constitution, and all the rest is gone.' His rigorism could have far-reaching consequences. A judgement of 1805, for instance, declared that the statutory limitation of subjects (usually defined in the sixteenth and seventeenth centuries) in grammar schools was binding. Until an act of 1840 empowered courts to change the statutes, some Elizabethan grammar schools could teach nothing but Latin and Greek.

Obscurantist, alarmist and immovable in the face of argument, Eldon was in high favour with George III, who came to regard him as indispensable. He acquired a similar ascendancy over George IV. The tough, industrious lawyer and the self-indulgent prince shedding tears together over the prospect of Catholic emancipation make an affecting scene. When George had to read the speech from the throne announcing recognition by Great Britain of the republics of Buenos Aires, Mexico and Colombia he protested that he had the gout and had lost his false teeth. Eldon, who detested Canning and had opposed the measure, read it for him – with reluctance. Lord Sidmouth, his brother's son-in-law, was his natural ally and in the years from Waterloo to 'Peterloo' Eldon joined with the Home Secretary in a firm alliance against new ideas and popular movements. They liked to refer to themselves as 'the last of the old school'.

He was not, of course, unique. His power came partly from the fact that he voiced and lent prestigious authority to the views of numerous squires and parsons. His own career commended his outlook to the new rich as to the old. 'Pompously patrician as only a self-made man can be' (Steven Watson), he also represented the conservatism which was then to be found in its richest and most eccentric forms in clerical, unreformed Oxford (which venerated Eldon as its high steward), and in law courts where the name of Blackstone was still more important than that of Bentham. The courts were Eldon's life. He acquired a deep and subtle knowledge of the law and with it that backward-looking tendency which is the vice as well as the virtue of the English lawyer bred on precedents. The anonymous author of his *Life* (1827) wrote that Lord Eldon 'had no acquaintance with the state of the institutions of other countries, and he had no notion of the rapid improvements that were going forward in his own. His studies in modern literature were confined to the Gentleman's Magazine.' In short, we see supreme professional competence and a closed mind in formidable combination. Lord Eldon's staunchness had its admirable side. 'He never ratted', an Oxford man called out on one of his visits to that city. There was a sort of oaken consistency about the man. It is a quality that emerges more attractively from his legal work than from his political career, which was devoted to 'dishing the Whigs', keeping men whom he regarded simply as traitors out of office, even as in 1812, in a coalition; to preventing the removal of religious restrictions and, most harmfully perhaps, against the Tory Peel as against the radical Romilly, to defending every detail of the criminal law from rationalization of its often barbaric punishments and procedures.

The delays of the chancery court in Eldon's time were the subject of constant complaints. Dickens has immortalized the delays and vexations of litigation about wills and property that were its principal business. It was essentially of Eldon's court that he was writing. It was during his time that the delays became intolerable. This man, who was so decisive in his ordinary judgements, balanced legal points in a way that critics found unfeeling and pedantic. But there was a good side to Eldon's long deliberations, his reserved judgements and his not infrequent reversals of his deputy's decisions. No-one knew better than he that his judgements would become part of the fabric of the law, to be treated with the same respect that he accorded to past judgements. He was therefore determined not to be rushed. The judgements he made were hardly ever reversed. A parliamentary commission on the delays of Chancery could do little about it, for Eldon himself presided and, in the words of *The Times*, its report was 'an apology for all the abuses of the court'. What was required, and what Eldon was unlikely to countenance, was several vice-chancellors and several courts of equity.

Eldon was prepared to work like a horse but it was not enough. What he did achieve, however, was more important than the improvement of the machinery. He crowned the work of Lord Hardwicke, to whom alone among chancellors he can be compared in this respect, by giving permanent form to the principles of his science. In his time Equity became 'a fixed body of legal doctrine'. In the case of *Gee v. Pritchard* (1818) he defined his view thus: 'The doctrines of this court ought to be as well settled and made as uniform, almost, as those of the Common Law, laying down fixed principles, but taking care that they are to be applied according to the circumstances of each case'. Equity after Eldon was much more than a miscellany of remedies more elastic than the Common Law allowed; it was part of the law of the land, in its administration and protective functions, and thus complementary to the Common Law. It is for this that Eldon should be remembered – as a great public servant.

In his private life Eldon was kind, cheerful, and not abstemious. He confided to Brougham that he would have been dead had he left off his wine, 'viz, nearer two than one bottle of port a day'. Greville, who thought him 'a contemptible statesman', describes him 'beguiling the tedious hours' during which the prince regent used to keep the Lords in Council waiting at Carlton House, with amusing stories of his early professional life and well-told anecdotes of celebrated lawyers. Perhaps there was a salty, saving touch of realism about the man, a human being beneath the wig of justice. He could view his own career with detachment – and he knew that times were changing. 'If I were to begin life again,' he said once, 'Damn my eyes but I would begin as an agitator'. But it is slightly forbidding to be told that his idea of humour was to translate *Chevy Chase* into the style of a bill in chancery.

Further Reading

Lord Campbell, *Lives of the Lord Chancellors*, 1847.
Lord Brougham, *Historical Sketches of Statesmen*, 1839.

SCOTT, SIR WALTER, BARONET (1771-1832), poet and novelist, was the son of Walter Scott, Writer to the Signet, and of Anne Rutherford, daughter of Professor Rutherford of Edinburgh. On his father's side he was descended from one of the many branches of the Buccleuch family. Edinburgh and the abrasive but cultured life of its lawyers and academics, the Borders and the traditional life of the laird, provided the background of his life and writing. He was born in a wynd in the Old Town – such a one, perhaps, as is described by Stevenson in his essay. When a baby he became crippled in the right leg and he walked with a limp all his life. With his friend John Irving he composed romances. Following what he called the 'principle of romantic research' he read Dante and fastened 'like a tiger, upon every collection of old songs and romances which chance threw in my way'. He went for long country walks 'for the pleasure of seeing romantic scenery'. The spirit of story-telling possessed him as he stood on the field of Bannockburn or tramped across the Pentland Hills. 'In crossing Magus Moor, near St Andrews, the spirit moved me to give a picture of the assassination of the Archbishop of St Andrews to some fellow travellers … and one of them, though well acquainted with the story, protested my narrative had frightened away his night's sleep.'

Many childhood months were spent on his grandfather's farm in Teviotdale. The delicate child grew up a tall man, strong, a great walker and a tireless horseman. 'The de'il's in ye, Sherra,' Archibald Park would say; 'Ye'll never halt till they bring ye hame with your feet foremost.' From Edinburgh High School, in 1783, he went to the university. At first he worked as writer under his father, but soon decided to become an advocate. In 1792 he was called to the Scottish Bar. As readers of Cockburn will know, this was a brilliant period in Edinburgh's history. There were giants on the bench and in the university. Young men disputed and philosophized and pursued their own forensic or literary ambitions; it was a prolific, slightly arrogant society. With the intellectual side of his professional community Scott was out of sympathy. The prevailing mood was Presbyterian, if not free-thinking, while his sympathies were Episcopalian and Jacobite. As a political movement Jacobitism was dead, but Scott's romantic imagination fed upon the stories of those who had been out in the '45. As he reacted against the rationalism of the urban patriciate, so he dwelt more fondly on the ballads, songs and tales of Old Scotland. He dwelt securely, however, in both worlds and his attitude was ambiguous. The conflict of Jacobite and Hanoverian is the theme of three of his greatest novels, *Waverley*, *Rob Roy* and *Redgauntlet*, and inspires some of his finest writing. His treatment of this subject gains by his being able to see, feel and present both sides of the embittered question of loyalty. The Augustan, Johnsonian side of him was as strong as the sentimental. There was nothing sham or make-believe about his espousal of the dying Gaelic civilization. His was a true sympathy founded upon massive reading amongst chronicles and plays, deepened throughout his life by the observations of a countryman and by his acquaintance with ordinary folk.

Scott's view of history was a fanciful one: intuition, knowledge and imaginative sympathy operated in a creative harmony. He ever preferred the particular to the abstract. As he said in a letter of 1808, he had been 'an antiquary many years before (he) thought of being a poet'. The reading of Percy's *Reliques*, together with his own love of Scottish stories, led him to collect and improve upon old ballads. In *The Border Minstrelsy* (1802) he could be antiquarian, scholar, historian, critic and poet. He went on naturally to composing poems and then prose stories of his own. So close are Scott's writings to his own nature that they may justly be called a labour of love. He early practised his pen with translations from German authors. He acquired enough of this and other languages – French, Italian, Gaelic – to enrich his store of tales. His remarkable memory ensured that he would forget little of what he learned. The novelist grew out of the poet, the poet out of the 'sentiments, manners and habits' of the past.

Scott responded, as a stout Tory, to the challenge of the French war and became quartermaster of a volunteer regiment of Edinburgh dragoons. In 1797 he married Charlotte Carpenter, daughter of a French widow who had taken refuge in Britain, and settled in Castle Street. In 1799 his father died; in the same year Scott became sheriff-deputy of Selkirkshire. His extensive rambles along the Marches, his 'Liddesdale raids', bore fruit in the *Border Minstrelsy*, then (1805) in his first and best long poem, *The Lay of the Last Minstrel*.

The *Lay* was a mighty success. Scott reached the public which later lionized Byron. The *Lay* was followed by *Marmion* (1808) and *The Lady of the Lake* (1810). Later poems, *Rokeby*, *The Bridal of Trierman*, *The Lord of the Isles* and *Harold the Dauntless* were less well received. The epic is a heavy diet and readers were sated. Those who read them may still be stirred by passages of *Marmion* and the *Lay*, as by the light and noise of a thunderstorm. Scott was a born minstrel; he caught the elemental moods. Significantly, a great admirer was to be Thomas Hardy. He composed swiftly, much of it on horseback. The insight of, for instance, the speech of Rhoderick Dhu in *The Lady of the Lake* is rare. Too much of the verse has an air of false melodrama today: sham-Gothick. The stories are diffuse, the language conventional; above all Scott was inhibited by polite usage from using the dialect or depicting the habits of ordinary Scots. He was not so inhibited in his Scottish novels and it is this closeness to nature and to his own experience that makes them, especially the early ones, when his vision was fresh and his intellectual strength unimpaired, so far superior to the rest.

In 1805 he settled at Ashiestiel on the Tweed but he kept up his legal work; in 1806 he got the reversion of a clerkship to the Court of Session. To help an old school-friend, and to further his own literary career, he became a partner in James Ballantyne's printing business. He edited Dryden, wrote for the *Edinburgh Review*; then, with more enthusiasm, for the Tory *Quarterly Review*, started by Murray in 1808. With capital, and pledges beyond his means, he backed Ballantyne's publishing ventures. Naive in money matters, Scott was involved in speculation and capital liabilities greater than he realized. Meantime his affairs prospered. In 1812 the clerk died and he came by a larger salary. Money flowed in from his verse romances and he invested it in a dream: he bought the estate of Abbotsford on the Tweed and set about improving it. Readers of Lockhart will recall the place which house and estate occupied in Scott's affections. Abbotsford, with its walls of old suits of armour and its library of 20,000 volumes, reveals the complex personality of the man as well as anything that he wrote. He longed for a great estate: to be an improver and benefactor, to keep open house. He insisted upon having the house lit with gas: he loved a bright light, because it was gay and exciting, and ignored the immense cost of installation. At the same time he hankered after simple ways and his entertainment was homely as well as splendid.

His literary life, too, is full of contradictions. A first impression is one of stamina, *Old Mortality*, *The Black Dwarf*, *Rob Roy*, *The Heart of Midlothian*, *A Legend of Montrose*, *The Bride of Lammermoor* and *Ivanhoe* were all written between 1817 and 1820, when he was involved in much legal business, suffering crippling pain from gall-stones and rheumatism; also writing essays and reviews – and planning developments at Abbotsford. It is an example of artistic fertility, A. N. Wilson suggests, comparable to Michelangelo's ceiling in the Sistine Chapel, or Mozart's symphonies.

'They cannot say but what I had the crown,' he wrote in his journal in 1827: he composed in different veins with extraordinary self-confidence. At the same time he persisted in an amateurish, anti-intellectual, casual tone: 'amusing myself with composition, which I felt a delightful occupation, I could also give pleasure to others' (Introduction to *The Chronicles of the Canongate*). This ambivalence surely came from a personality of many sides. The wordy antiquary of his ponderous introductions, the eighteenth-century gentleman, the sharp lawyer, the traditionalist are all to be found in his novels, sometimes in startling juxtaposition. In his worst books (the reader may choose among several notable examples!) there is artificial writing and weary reading. In the best he is sufficiently detached as an artist, sufficiently involved as a man, to present living studies in depth – a Meg Merrilies, a Bailie Nicol Jarvie, or, both containing a good deal of himself, a Frank Osbaldistone, an Alan Fairford: all in a convincing frame. Indeed Scott presents the greatest diversity of realistic human characters outside Shakespeare.

Scott's edition of Swift came out in 1814. But this year was notable for a more seminal event. Hunting for fishing tackle in a drawer he came across the unfinished manuscript of a story he had written in 1805, but put away when he had shown it to a friend who was cool about it. Now he completed it. On 7 July *Waverley* was published, anonymously. Scott despised literary fame just as he disliked literary conversation: to 'talk book' was no substitute for life and the novel was not, in his eyes, a high form of composition. Few men have written so well, with such a modest opinion of what they were writing. Yet he found in *Waverley* and some of the romances that followed by 'the author of *Waverley*' (his identity was readily guessed at by his friends but not avowed by him until 1827) a richer vein than in his poems. *Guy Mannering*, *The Antiquary*, *Old Mortality*, *Rob Roy*, *The Heart of Midlothian*, *The Bride of*

Lammermoor and *A Legend of Montrose* are drawn from the century between the Civil War and the '45; from a turbulent century as well known and described, albeit from the standpoint of the Scottish laird, as if he had lived amongst the Covenanters, Jacobites and the ordinary men he describes so well. 'The unexpected newness of the thing, the profusion of original characters, the Scotch language, Scotch scenery, Scotch men and women, the simplicity of the writing, and the graphic force of the descriptions – all struck us with a shock of delight'.

What Scott did was to put life into history by showing history as life. When he left Scotland, still more when he left recent history for the Middle Ages, the story-teller was still effective. But to the lover of Scott, *Ivanhoe*, *Quentin Durward*, *Peveril of the Peak*, to name the best known, perhaps, of the non-Scottish novels, may seem false coin. Scott, spurred on by his wretched publishers, was writing outside his province. When he returned, in 1824, in *Redgauntlet*, to Scotland and to his own life – for this book is written around his memory of his father and scenes of his boyhood – he wrote another novel of genius. It is full of the tense and tragic conflict of his best work. He is dealing with a practised hand with two worlds he knew well: lawyer and Jacobite laird in a balance of opposites. For good measure, in 'Wandering Willie's Tale', there is thrown in one of the finest short stories in the language.

He worked according to a strict regimen, writing much before breakfast, completing a novel sometimes in about three months. His writing tended to be planless, his plot developing as he went along. He found time, too, for the life of the laird, supervising the planting of trees and the clearing of rides; he was busy in Edinburgh affairs, a firm Tory, more trusting than discreet in his choice of friends and support of local factions. No man had trained so hard to beat the French, practising with his troop for hours at sabring turnips on sticks: 'Cut them down, the villains, cut them down!' When George IV made his memorable visit to Edinburgh in 1822 and put new life into Highland traditions by parading in Royal Stuart tartan, Scott, who had become a baronet in 1820, invited caricature by the fervour of his welcome. But George, for all his follies, was an admirer of Scott's novels. The unreformed constitution became objectionable to most Scots before 1832 because the burghs were notoriously at the disposal of the ministry, but Scott defended the status quo with ardour.

More damaging to him were errors of judgement in his private life. He was fleeced by the local farmers, who understood his ambition to make a large estate. When his publishers were ruined in the financial panic of 1825 and he became liable for debts of £130,000, he had few resources to meet his creditors. With heroic confidence he set himself to pay all by his writing, refusing all offers of help: 'This right hand shall pay it off.' *Woodstock*, the work on which he was engaged, fetched £8,000, the monumental *Life of Napoleon*, his greatest incursion into history, in nine volumes, £18,000. Within a few years his creditors had received a dividend of six shillings in the pound. But the art of his novels, and his health, failed under the strain. He earned vast sums, too much for the good of his art – for facility was his enemy – but always too little for his creditors. His delicate sense of honour ruined his last years. The man emerges a hero, but the wastage of a great art remains a tragedy of literature. There is more of the antiquarian, less of the natural story-teller, in *The Chronicles of the Canongate*, *The Fair Maid of Perth*, *Anne of Geierstein*. His wife died; then in 1831 the beloved grandson Johnnie Lockhart, for whom he had written a boy's history of Scotland, *Tales of a Grandfather*. From a voyage to the Mediterranean he came home a broken man to die at Abbotsford in September 1832.

The event was received as a public calamity. No author has left a stronger impress of integrity and goodness. In his fine essay on Scott, Hazlitt, a stern critic of his political views, wrote of the essence of his genius: 'Our author has conjured up the actual people he has to deal with … in their habits as they lived; he has ransacked old chronicles, and poured the contents upon his page; he has squeezed out musty records; he has consulted way-faring pilgrims, bed-rid sybils. He has invoked the spirits of the air; he has conversed with the living and the dead, and let them tell their story in their own way; and by borrowing of others has enriched his own genius with everlasting variety, truth and freedom.' The virtues of the man are inseparable from those of the writing: simplicity, unpretentious humour, fortitude and a pleasing absence of guile. After death he received his due in one of the most readable of literary biographies. Let the sceptical reader who wishes to be introduced to the author of *Waverley* read Lockhart's account: 'Scott's Den', 'Scott at Breakfast', 'Scott's Raid into Liddesdale' – these are descriptive essays worthy of the master. They should, however, be treated only as a beginning, for Lockhart was often inaccurate and sometimes unfair. Buchan and Lang are also entertaining but they follow the master very closely. If one wants an appreciation of Scott's greatness as a novelist one should turn to Cockshut's critical appreciation: or to that of a fellow novelist, A. N. Wilson. Then one may read or reread *Waverley* and its peers and discover for oneself what the world has largely forgotten, that Sir Walter Scott is one of the select company of the world's great novelists.

Further Reading
A. N. Wilson, *The Laird of Abbotsford*, 1980.
E. Johnson, *Sir Walter Scott, the Great Unknown*, 2 vols, 1970.
A. O. J. Cockshut, *The Achievement of Walter Scott*, 1969.
J. G. Lockhart, *The Life of Sir Walter Scott*, 1848, Everyman edn, 1906.

SCROGGS, SIR WILLIAM (1623?-83), judge, came from Deddington, in Oxfordshire. According to Dugdale, his father was a Smithfield butcher; yet Scroggs went to Oxford, first to Oriel and then to Pembroke. He fought for the king in the Civil War, was called to the bar from Gray's Inn in 1653, and was knighted at the Restoration. Handsome and able, though brutal, foulmouthed and a notorious debauchee, Scroggs was a successful counsel. Danby promoted him to the bench, and in 1678 he became Lord Chief Justice, just in time to preside over the Popish Plot trials. At first he accepted the tales of Oates and the informers and browbeat the defendants in his customary coarse manner. But in the trial of Wakeman, the queen's physician, in 1679, when Oates was exposed as a liar, Scroggs instructed the jury not to believe the evidence for the prosecution, and the defendant was acquitted. Whether Scroggs's charge represented genuine devotion to justice or whether, as Roger North suggests, he sensed that royal favour was not so much on the side of the Whigs as he had supposed, the decision slowed the pace of persecution. But Scroggs himself, 'the Mouth' as he was nicknamed, was grossly assailed, by lampoons, by personal assault, by charges of encouraging popery, and finally (1681) by impeachment. This failed, but Charles removed him from office and gave him a pension of £1,500 a year. Scroggs retired to his Essex estate and died in 1683.

SCROPE, SIR GEOFFREY (*c*.1285-1340), Chief Justice of King's Bench, is a 'notable instance of the way in which a medieval common lawyer … could acquire great wealth and attain an influential position within the most exclusive circles of society'. The younger son of an established North Riding gentry family, Geoffrey married into the same circle and expressed his aristocratic tastes in his coat of arms, his jousting, the crenellation of his principal seat, and above all his acquisition of land. Starting apparently with nothing, Geoffrey built up a substantial estate in thirteen counties, the basis of the barony of Scrope of Masham created for his son, and was a generous benefactor to Coverham and Jervaulx abbeys. Legitimate fees of office and occasional royal bounty alone cannot explain his wealth. He enjoyed retaining fees (latterly perhaps illegally) and payments for legal services from third parties, lent money to embarrassed neighbours, and twice abused his position to seize land and to prevent a legal inquiry into his activities. His behaviour however was never notorious and compared with predecessors like Weyland, Hengham, Stratton and Langton his career suggests that corruption in office and hence the rewards of such office had diminished. Success in the legal profession henceforth raised men only into the ranks of the county gentry and other means were needed to raise even the Scropes of Bolton and Masham into the lowest ranks of the peerage.

It is not clear what was needed to succeed at law. Clerical status was no longer necessary as it had been a generation earlier. An obvious advantage for Geoffrey was that his elder brother Henry (d.1336), ancestor of the Scropes of Bolton, had already made his mark in legal circles. Henry was a royal justice by 1308 and subsequently became both Chief Justice of King's Bench, the most senior court, and Chief Baron of the Exchequer. Geoffrey was a pleader in 1304, when the lawcourts were at York, a serjeant-at-law in 1316, justice of Common Pleas in 1324, and Chief Justice of King's Bench from 1324. No penalty was exacted for his partisan conduct in the crises of the 1320s. Prominent though he was as a lawyer, overshadowing his brother, Geoffrey was much more than this, with distinguished military, financial, and above all diplomatic service to his credit. From 1319 on he served on twenty missions, securing exemption in 1334 from future embassies except when the king went himself, and was indeed with the king at Ghent at his death. Geoffrey had become one of Edward III's most trusted advisers. His career again shows that ability and royal confidence rather than the particular office held was the key to political importance and hence to the rewards of office and self-advancement.

Further Reading
B. Vale, 'The Profits of Law: The "Rise" of the Scrope Family in the Early Fourteenth Century' in *Profit, Piety, and the Professions in Later Medieval England*, ed. M. A. Hicks, 1990.
E. L. G. Stones, 'Sir Geoffrey le Scrope, c.1280-1340, Chief Justice of the King's Bench', *English Historical Review* lxix, 1954.

SCROPE, RICHARD (c.1346-1405), Bishop of Lichfield (1386-98) and Archbishop of York (1398-1405), was the only English archbishop to be executed for treason in the Middle Ages. Up till then, he was 'an obscure and colourless figure' with no distinguishable political affiliations and was indeed the 'very antithesis of the ambitious, worldly prelate'. Although a younger son of Henry, Lord Scrope of Masham, he did not rise with the rapidity of such aristocratic clergymen as Courtenay and Arundel. He studied at both Oxford and Cambridge Universities. By 1375 he was a bachelor of arts reading civil law and was the official principal (judge) of the Bishop of Ely and by 1379 he was doctor of both laws. He had received his first benefice in 1368 and was ordained in 1377. Birth and education did not lead however to administrative service to the Crown, but to the Papacy: he was a papal chaplain and auditor of the sacred palace in 1381 and an apostolic notary in 1386. Hence, apparently, his appointment as Dean of Chichester in 1382, his abortive election as bishop there in 1385, and his appointment as Bishop of Coventry and

Lichfield. He was consecrated by Pope Urban VI himself at Genoa in 1386. Returning home, he may have become an unusually conscientious bishop and was certainly regarded by the chroniclers as 'primarily a churchman and a scholar'. He became a royal councillor and served on diplomatic missions to Scotland and the Curia. In 1398 he was rewarded by elevation to the archbishopric of York.

No archbishop could entirely escape involvement in politics and inevitably Scrope was involved in the formalities of Henry IV's succession to Richard II in 1399. Neither then nor in 1403, however, did Scrope reveal clear political loyalties and he does not seem to have taken a distinctive line in convocation either. It was therefore probably as great a surprise to Henry IV as to modern historians that Scrope should have rebelled in 1405. His immediate accomplice was the young Earl Marshal, with whom he raised the city of York, but he must have been in league with the Earl of Northumberland as well. Northumberland certainly hoped to depose Henry IV and this may also have been Scrope's aim, for he denounced Henry IV's perjury in taking the Crown. His other charges, however, concerned misgovernment that could have been remedied: excessive taxation of clergy and laity – which had some justification – and evil counsel and other abuses, which may not have done. Whatever his intentions, Scrope was unable to join forces with Northumberland and was forced to negotiate. Promised that his grievances would be remedied, he disbanded his forces – the alternative being certain defeat – and once defenceless was arrested. In spite of the desperate intervention of Archbishop Arundel, the king organized his summary and illegal trial, in which Chief Justice Gascoigne refused to participate, and he was executed in his own cathedral city of York.

He died as a dignified spiritual leader. Conveyed to execution in humiliating style on a 'collier's sorry mare ... bareback with a halter for a bridle', he sang psalms as he went, and was beheaded with five blows in commemoration of the five wounds of Christ. His claim to have rebelled for the liberties of the church, his illegal execution, his local popularity, and the manner of his death all enabled him to be presented as a martyr and help explain his immediate veneration as such. In 1070 Becket's violent death forced Henry II into humiliating penance, but times had changed. Archbishop Scrope's death gave Henry IV a guilty conscience that lasted until his own death, but no immediate political repercussions – such as papal hostility – counterbalanced the deterrent effect on other potential rebels. It is highly debatable whether Scrope's execution was indeed King Henry's 'biggest mistake' (Kirby).

Further Reading
P. McNiven, 'The Betrayal of Archbishop Scrope', *Bulletin of the John Rylands Library* liv, 1971.

SCROPE OF BOLTON, LORD RICHARD (1327-1403) raised his family to the peerage by a career of unremitting service on the battlefield and in administration. The eldest surviving son of Chief Justice Henry Scrope (*d*.1336) and occasionally denigrated for his lowly origins, he inherited his father's military interests and his sense of honour, successfully defending his right to the crest of a crab (1347) and his arms against the Carminowes (1360) and in the celebrated Scrope and Grosvenor controversy (1385). His military career was remarkable for its length, almost forty years, and for its variety, as he fought at sea and on land, in France, Scotland and Spain, including Crécy and Nevilles Cross in 1346, Espagnols-sur-Mer (1350), and Najera (1367) among his battle honours. He was never in command in France, for he was neither a front rank landowner nor a member of the royal house, but he served repeatedly from 1367 in the retinue of John of Gaunt, Duke of Lancaster, whose retainer he was. As a northerner active in border conflict from his teens, however, he was highly suitable as warden of the West March in 1375 and frequently engaged in negotiations with the Scots. Distinguished military service, local commissions in Yorkshire, and election as knight of the shire for the county led naturally to a series of front-rank ministerial appointments: Treasurer of England in 1371-5, Steward of the Household in 1377-8, and Chancellor of England in 1378-80, and again in 1381-2. Hence his individual summons to parliament from 1371 as a baron and hence perhaps also Henry IV's remission at his request of the forfeiture due on the death of his son William, Earl of Wiltshire. Richard had been loyal to the Crown and the House of Lancaster, both then represented by Henry IV. But such advancement and national exposure left him still a Yorkshireman with predominantly local interests, who sealed his social arrival with a new castle at Bolton in Wensleydale – a status symbol rather than military necessity – and generous patronage of the church, some of which – such as Wensley College – were never fulfilled, but which illustrate his assiduous cultivation of local contacts.

Richard's combination of service to both Crown and Duke of Lancaster went with a reputation for complete integrity: a warning to those of us who suppose such ties to be incompatible or to be evidence of self-interest and infirmity of commitment. His appointment as lay treasurer in 1371, itself a remarkable departure from precedent, took place with parliamentary approval on dismissal of his predecessor. The impeachment of his successor in 1376 again left him personally unsullied. Indeed he then agreed to testify – but only if released from his oath of confidentiality as a councillor – and promised not 'to spare any living man but will say the truth entirely to my knowledge'. He presided at the trial of Alice Perrers in 1377. As chancellor in 1381-2 he refused to seal certain extravagant grants made by the young Richard II, resigned his seal only into the hands of the boy king, and declared that he would not take up office under him again. He again spoke up boldly for his brother-in-law Suffolk at his impeachment in 1386 and supported the Appellants in 1386-9. This is the picture not of a weathercock but of a man of independence and principle, who was not afraid of speaking out in defiance of the king, or of popular or parliamentary opinion. He epitomized the contemporary ideal of the forthright and truthful councillor. Such a model was preferable to kings in theory rather than practice, and several times could have led Scrope to disaster, most notably in 1397, when King Richard chose instead to pardon him for supporting the Appellants. Fortunately he escaped the disgrace experienced by Lord Latimer, whose career otherwise so closely parallels his own.

Further Reading

G. A. Holmes, *The Good Parliament*, 1975.

SCROPE OF BOLTON, WILLIAM, EARL OF WILTSHIRE (*c*.1351-99) was the brains behind Richard II's second tyranny of 1397-9. He was the eldest son of Richard, Lord Scrope of Bolton (*d*.1403) and his early career rivalled his father's for military and administrative distinction. He served in France with John of Gaunt in 1369 and 1373, assisted in a Neapolitan blockade of Venice, and went crusading in Prussia. From 1383-92 he was seneschal of Gascony, in 1386-9 captain of Cherbourg, and from 1389 captain of Brest. National recognition came in the 1390s with his election as knight of the Garter (1394) and appointments in turn as chamberlain of the royal household (1393-8) and treasurer of England (1398-9), his brother Stephen succeeding as chamberlain. He was nominated executor by the king in 1399. His creation as Earl of Wiltshire completed his family's rise from obscurity to comital rank in only three generations.

Scrope's personal promotion was not exceptionally rapid. Like Montagu, he was already in his forties when he became chamberlain of the household, the key political position that brought him, like Latimer and Burley somewhat earlier, the dominance of the royal household, control of access to the king, and the king's friendship and trust. He became Richard's indispensable agent everywhere. Constable of Beaumaris in 1394 and of Caernarvon and Pembroke in 1395, he became justice of Chester and north Wales, and in 1397 was granted the 'whole county and lordship of Anglesey'. He accompanied Richard to Ireland in 1394 and became justiciar there from 1395. He commanded the important castle of Queenborough. He was a Lord Appellant in 1397. His councillorship led ultimately to his dominance of the council, of which he was an assiduous attender with a wide brief. Of all Richard's favourites, only the Duke of

Aumarle received more honours and rewards, but he lacked the ability, industry, and willingness to shoulder the daily routine of government that enabled Scrope to dominate the central administration. It was Scrope, not the Duke of York as figurehead, who was really in charge in England during Richard's second invasion of Ireland. 'Modern historians have not fully recognized the pervasiveness of his powers, but it was all too apparent to his contemporaries', who regarded him, Bushy and Green as 'the king's most evil councillors and the fosterers of his malice'.

Scrope, like Montagu, was long denied his baronial inheritance by the longevity of his father and provided for himself by marrying an heiress. His wealth emerges from his purchase of lands in Wiltshire and the Isle of Man, whose arms he quartered with his own. He was greedy for wealth and prestige and was not scrupulous how he acquired it. Royal favour was exploited to accumulate offices, which he exercised by deputy and thus less effectively than Richard hoped. Each office brought a salary and from 1397 he secured a stream of outright grants: in 1397 Anglesey and Warwick's lordships of Barnard Castle, County Durham, and Pains Castle in Wales; in 1398 the Lancaster honour of Pickering in Yorkshire; and in 1399, so it was rumoured, he planned the ruin of further magnates to secure their lands. Already he was great in Wales, Wiltshire and the north: what would satisfy him? Acquisitive and underhand, socially inferior to the other *duketti*, he was detested, despised, but also feared as the ablest and most dangerous of Richard's favourites. Hence his summary execution with Bushy and Green at Bristol in 1399: the only one of Richard's favourites of noble birth to be executed, whilst Surrey, Salisbury, and even Exeter and Aumarle, were spared. He died childless and his earldom died with him, but his brother was allowed to keep their father's barony.

Further Reading
C. Given-Wilson, *The Royal Household and the King's Affinity: Service, Politics and Finance in England 1360-1413*, 1986.
J. A. Tuck, *Richard II and the Nobility*, 1973.

SEGRAVE, SIR JOHN (*c.*1256-1325) of Segrave (Leics.) was retained in 1297 by the Earl Marshal, Roger Bigod, Earl of Norfolk. Although it is the first indenture of retainer for life to survive, it was not the first one to be made. It is so like other early indentures that it can be taken as typical of the contracts made between lords and their retainers under Edward I and indeed for the rest of the Middle Ages. Whereas feudalism, by now obsolete, involved permanent contracts sealed by permanent grants of land, the indenture system involved temporary payment in land or money and has been named bastard feudalism. Segrave promised to serve the earl in person

with five knights and ten men-at-arms in peace and in war against all-comers except the king for the earl's lifetime. In peacetime he would bring sixteen lances whenever summoned and would receive keep for his men (bouche of court) and his horses and wages for his grooms. If the king fought in Gascony, France or Flanders, then Segrave would bring twenty horsemen, receiving a fodder allowance, but nothing for the men except a lump sum of £80. If the earl did not go, Segrave would serve on the same terms. In return, Segrave received the manor of Lodden in Norfolk for life, two robes annually as the earl's senior banneret and robes for his five knights like those of the earl's own knights. Also implied was support from the earl in his own lawful business. In addition to his own men, the earl recruited unattached bannerets, knights and their retinues, often, like Segrave, from other parts of England. Almost at once Segrave accompanied his lord to the Exchequer to stop collection of a tax and soon after he excused the earl's absence from campaign to the king. He was one of the earl's household and he deputized as marshal in the campaign of 1301. Such contracts were normally for the life of the retainer, but as Bigod had no heirs Segrave was retained only for the life of the earl, who died in 1306. Segrave's son Stephen was retained by the Earl of Lancaster by 1308 and Segrave's own contract with that earl may date from then too. He was to serve with thirty men-at-arms for fifty marks (£33.66) and in 1322 was third in Lancaster's list of bannerets, after the Earl of Surrey and another banneret. His brother Nicholas, however, was much more prominent in the earl's service.

Bastard feudal contracts almost invariably reserved the retainer's allegiance to the king. Thus Segrave was entitled to withdraw his service during Lancaster's rebellion in 1321-2. Moreover such contracts were compatible with continued service to the Crown. Segrave had served in Wales (1277, 1282, 1285), Ireland (1287) and Scotland (1291), was again in Scotland each year from 1297-1307, and was keeper of Scotland in 1302-5, when he captured Wallace and did much to restore orderly English government. Again keeper of Scotland from 1309 and Keeper of the Cumberland Marches in 1313, he was captured at Bothwell after Bannockburn in 1314 and was ransomed with royal help. Back in the north in 1318-19, he was in Gascony at his death in 1325.

Segrave attended parliament as a baron from 1296 and was on the continual council set up in 1318. His principal reward from the Crown was a grant of lands worth £100 a year or £1,000 to buy lands in 1312. In 1308 he had been appointed justice of the forests beyond the Trent and custodian of Nottingham castle, offices he briefly lost in 1310-12 due to opposition to Gaveston, and in 1314 the custody of Derby was added. Complaints of extortion provoked a commission of inquiry in 1314-15 and presumably also explain why the townsmen of Nottingham besieged him in the castle in 1315. By his death he had extended his estates into Norfolk, Oxfordshire, and other counties, and had improved them by crenellating his houses, creating parks, founding markets, and securing grants of hunting rights.

Further Reading

M. Prestwich, *War, Politics and Finance under Edward I*, 1972.

N. Denholm-Young, *Seignorial Administration in England*, 1937.

SELDEN, JOHN (1584-1654), antiquary and conversationalist, came of Sussex yeoman stock and was educated at Chichester Free School, Hart Hall, Oxford, and the Inner Temple. Called to the Bar in 1612, he won even as a young man an immense reputation for his knowledge of legal records and history, but he practised little. If Aubrey is to be believed, he found it more profitable to be steward to the Earl of Kent, whose countess was his mistress. He took the Puritan side in politics. In 1617 he was in trouble with the High Commission for his *History of Tithes*, in which he doubted their divine sanction. He was an anti-Buckingham MP in the 1620s and was imprisoned in 1629 after the attack on the Speaker. As member for Oxford University in the Long Parliament he remained in London after 1642. But it is difficult to discern revolutionary enthusiasm in Selden, and certainly after the outbreak of civil war he played little part in politics. To the Assembly of Divines of the 1640s he brought a cool and somewhat cynical scholarship which can scarcely have pleased zealots of any persuasion: in Aubrey's phrase, 'he was able to run them all down with his Greek and Antiquities'. Clarendon speaks of his 'stupendous' learning, and certainly his range was vast. He wrote authoritatively on duels and titles, on problems of inheritance and of sea-power. His *Mare Clausum*, claiming English control of the narrow seas, was published by royal order in 1635. His edition of Eadmer's *Historia Novorum* (1623) included the first critical essay on Domesday Book and has remained of value to scholars. He won a European reputation as an orientalist by his treatise *De Deis Syriis* (1617). Yet Selden was no pedant. His most celebrated memorial is his *Table Talk*, first published in 1689, for he was an engaging conversationalist, with a dry and agreeable irony, whose intimate friends ranged from Ben Jonson to Clarendon. The latter 'valued himself upon nothing more than upon having had Mr Selden's acquaintance from the time he was very young'.

SELINA, COUNTESS OF HUNTINGDON (1707-91), 'Queen of the Methodists', as Horace Walpole called her, was a formidable patron of the evangelical revival of the eighteenth century. Her fame has been obscured by the achievements of the Wesleys; theirs became the central movement while her puritan connection was rejected alike by church and Methodists. But the impact of her personality and the scale of her achievement were both immense. She may be seen as one of the greatest of female eccentrics, 'Pope Joan', or as a noble 'Mother in Israel' (Whitefield's description). Either way her sincerity and power are undeniable.

Second daughter and co-heiress of the second Earl Ferrers, she was lucky in her husband, Theophilus, ninth Earl of Huntingdon, who accepted without fuss the enthusiasms of his wife, embarrassing though they must sometimes have been. His own sisters, who were notably pious, contributed to the evolution of a proud woman with a strong sense of duty into a single-minded missionary. 'Since I have known and believed on the Lord Jesus Christ for life and salvation,' she declared, 'I have been as happy as an angel'. She turned her house in Leicestershire, Donington Park, into a centre of religious life where, said Whitefield, 'We have the sacrament every morning, heavenly conversation all day, and preach at night'. Maids and gardeners were examined about the state of their souls and two schools were set up for the religious teaching of local children. But her main effort was directed towards the improvement of the upper classes where, as she saw, cynicism and loose morals stemmed from the decline of personal religion and the increase of wealth, without a corresponding sense of duty. In her drawing room the luminaries of society were exposed to the preaching and prayers of her evangelists. Polite acquiescence was the most she could get from men like Chesterfield or Bolingbroke. The Duchess of Suffolk, George II's mistress, thought that Whitefield's remarks were aimed at her. The Duchess of Buckingham thought it 'monstrous to be told that you have a heart as sinful as the common wretches that crawl upon the earth' and could not 'but wonder that your Ladyship should relish sentiments so much at variance with high rank and good breeding'. Some, however, were converted: Lady Frances Gardner; two sisters of Lord Chesterfield and his ex-mistress who, as Horace Walpole said, bestowed 'the dregs of her beauty on Jesus Christ' and Lord and Lady Dartmouth. Elegant chapels were built or restored in London and the fashionable spas. The chapel at Bath, with its comfortable red cushions and air of sober luxury – a balcony for elect ladies and a special pew, with its separate mahogany entrance, for visiting clergy who might want discreetly to hear the Word – expresses the flavour of Lady Huntingdon's work.

Lord Huntingdon died in 1746 leaving her in control of family and fortune. She assumed the leadership of the Calvinist element among the Methodists. She gave money to many causes, Whitefield's mission to Georgia and his tabernacle in England, to deserving preachers and not always deserving beggars. Besides her own personal following of enthusiastic men in and outside the church, she controlled a connection that grew to include over seventy chapels. Despite uncertain health she worked intensely, corresponding, lobbying, organizing at every level. Preachers were saved from being pressed into the army; Garrick was persuaded to take off a play which contained a skit on Whitefield, her homicidal cousin, urged to repent (and prevented from seeing his mistress) in his last hours before being executed for murdering his steward. George III admired her and, on her prompting, delivered Archbishop Cornwallis a strong rebuke for holding unseemly routs at Lambeth on Sundays. 'I wish there was a Lady Huntingdon in every diocese,' he said to a bishop who complained of her interference. Her work was aided by a growing reaction against what she called the 'system of heathen ethics, varnished over with the name of Christian morality', but she also helped to foster the new puritanism in a section of the ruling class.

In 1779 the Consistory Court of London disallowed her claim to appoint as chaplains as many Anglican priests as she wanted; she therefore registered her chapels as dissenting meeting houses. On the other flank she broke with Wesley when he and his followers rejected predestination; he also resented the intrusion of the countess and 'my lady's preacher'. After her death the connection did not grow. But the college which she founded at Trevecca, already the centre of Howell Harris's crusading Methodism in Wales, produced trained, godly pastors eager to preach the gospel of salvation to a selected few. Today there are only thirty-odd chapels left, mostly in the south. The college is now at Cambridge. Abroad there is an active mission in Sierra Leone that was founded in the year after her death. Dogmatic, humourless, narrow – these traits can be discerned perhaps in the lines of her long face, wearing what Edith Sitwell called a 'sunken look of piety', thin-lipped and severe. She was also very brave. She nursed a friend through an attack of smallpox and she bore stoically the loss of two sons from smallpox.

Further Reading
S. Tytler, *The Countess of Huntingdon and her Circle*, 1967.

SEVERUS, LUCIUS SEPTIMIUS (*d*.211) ruled as Roman emperor from 193 to 211. He spent the years 208-11 in Britain campaigning against the tribes beyond the northern frontier and died at York in February 211. It was possibly during this imperial visit that Alban, the first British Christian martyr, was executed on the orders of Severus's son Geta, who had been left in charge of the administration of Britain while his father was absent on campaign.

SEXBY, EDWARD (*d*.1658), a Suffolk man, fought in the Civil War in Cromwell's regiment of horse, and was one of the first of the army's 'Agitators', appearing before the Commons in 1647 and opening the case for the rank and file in the Putney Debates later that year. Commissioned and appointed Governor of Portland in 1649, he commanded a regiment of foot in Scotland in 1650. A Lieutenant-Colonel in 1651, he was cashiered in that year for using too much pressure to make soldiers re-enlist. Nevertheless, from 1651-3 he was sent on a mission to Bordeaux to make trouble for the French government, then involved in the Fronde; he was in close touch with L'Ormée, the republican group in the city, and had *The Agreement of the People* translated into French for his purposes. But after his return he became a violent opponent of the Protectorate, with a variety of plans for uniting Levellers and royalists against Cromwell. Involved in Wildman's plot of 1655, he was arrested but allowed to escape. He went to Amsterdam and employed his ready tongue and considerable self-confidence to win support from royalist exiles for his schemes, and when their leaders began to see through his lies he turned to negotiations with the authorities in the Spanish Netherlands. In 1656 he and Wildman devised a plot in which a group of ex-soldiers headed by Miles Sindercombe were to assassinate Cromwell; this was eventually betrayed early in 1657 after gunpowder had been smuggled into Whitehall Palace, and Sindercombe poisoned himself in prison. At this time Sexby wrote with the help of the royalist Captain Titus a notorious pamphlet in justification of assassination, *Killing No Murder*, which he dedicated ironically to Cromwell. Later in 1657 he came to England, and was arrested and sent to the Tower, where he died in 1658.

SEYMOUR, SIR EDWARD (1633-1708) (baronet in 1685), a prominent member of every House of Commons from the Restoration to the middle years of Anne's reign, was 'descended', as a unanimous testimony of the Commons put it in 1701, 'from ancestors who have been successful in commanding armies and fleets of this kingdom and from a Protector of the realm'. A grandee with his family mansion of Berry Pomeroy, near Totnes, in Devon, proud of his lineage and insolent in speech (Sir Keith Feiling notes the story of Seymour as Speaker of the Commons telling Colonel Birch that it was indecent for him to brush his beard without a looking-glass), Seymour was by temperament a loyalist and thus became 'High Tory' in outlook in the reigns of William and Anne. Yet he was above all a 'country' politician, electoral master of a 'western empire' which included seats in Cornwall and Devon, and the natural leader of the west country MPs of his day. Seymour had no doubts about the supremacy of the landed interest. He once said 'I am one of those that welcome all propositions that have a tendency to ease Lands', and in Anne's reign he walked out of the Commons when a tax on malt was proposed. Ambitious, vain, insular, full of prejudices, against 'fanatics', popery, the Dutch and the Scots, Seymour was not an easy colleague, nor was his financial integrity above reproach, as the attack on him in 1694 indicated; his patriotism was far from selfless. But he was a man of ability and courage whose beliefs and prejudices reflected much that was generally accepted by Englishmen of his day.

MP for Hindon in 1661, he led the Commons in demanding the impeachment of Clarendon (1667). Twice chosen as Speaker in Charles II's reign, a country gentleman interrupting the succession of lawyers who had established a monopoly of the office, he was rejected the second time (1679) by the king. Strongly anti-Catholic, he was, nevertheless, hostile to Exclusion, one of the relatively few MPs of the years 1678-81 who were; characteristically his opposition rested not on theories of hereditary right but upon the practical difficulties of enforcing the policy, and he was a leading advocate of 'limitations' or a 'regency'. He enjoyed royal favour at the crisis of Exclusion, but lost it in the last years of Charles's reign – perhaps because he did not get the office to which he felt entitled, yet perhaps also because he read the signs of approaching Catholicism.

Certainly in James's reign his attitude was clear from start to finish. He once claimed 'My family were instrumental in the Reformation, and not any have been pointed out for popery', and almost alone he upset the brief honeymoon of the first session of James's only parliament by a violent attack on the government for its intrigue and corruption in the elections, in which Seymour's west country influence had been somewhat diminished. In the course of this he stressed the need for MPs 'attached to the laws of England' at a time when 'there is already talk about the repeal of the Test Act and the Habeas Corpus Act, the one a bulwark against the establishment of popery at the expense of Protestantism, the other the firmest foundation of English liberties'. Thus Seymour had nailed his colours to the mast at once, and it is not surprising to find him leading west country opposition to James's pressure on the JPs in 1687. When William landed next year at Torbay and advanced to Exeter, it was appropriate that Seymour should be one of the first leading Englishmen to join him, and characteristic that he should do so in a carriage drawn by seven horses. His reason for rebellion was the need to defend Protestantism, and thus it was not necessarily illogical of him to oppose the offer of the crown to William. He took the oaths to William and Mary, and demonstrated his loyalty to the Revolution by never dabbling in Jacobitism.

There were still nearly twenty years of his political career ahead, years spent partly in jealousy and sheer obstreperousness, partly in the maintenance of high-flying Toryism of an independent kind. He held office as a Treasury Commissioner from 1691 to 1694; lost his seat at Exeter in the Whiggish election of 1695, regained it in the Tory swing of 1698, and thenceforward for the rest of William's reign pursued a savage vendetta against the Whigs. Nevertheless, it was in keeping with his general attitude that it should be Seymour who in the last months of William's reign moved in the Commons for no peace with France while Louis XIV continued to recognize the Old Pretender as James III. Under Anne he held office as Comptroller of the Household from 1702-4. His views on the conduct of the war were Tory ones, opposed to the costly land campaigns in the Netherlands, and they did not please Marlborough, who wrote to Sarah in June 1703: 'We are bound not to wish for anybody's death, but should Sir Edward Seymour die it would be no great loss to the queen nor the nation.' Seymour for his part thought Marlborough should be impeached. Inevitably with the development of the war Seymour was dismissed, in 1704. He died in 1708, in some ways much more a prototype of later 'Toryism' than either Harley or St John.

Further Reading
Keith Feiling, *A History of the Tory Party, 1640-1714*, 1924.

SEYMOUR, EDWARD, 1st EARL OF HERTFORD, DUKE OF SOMERSET (1506?-52), Protector, was born probably in 1506. He was executed on Tower Hill on 22 January 1552. He was the brother of Jane Seymour, Henry VIII's third wife. He led the normal life of a sixteenth-century courtier who had secured the good opinion of the king, holding various minor offices and amassing a very large number of estates, steadily advancing in the peerage, but for some time having little influence in politics. On the fall of Thomas Cromwell, Hertford (as he became in 1537) continued to rise in the king's favour. In 1542 he became Lord High Admiral, but he relinquished the post almost at once. In March 1544, he was in command of the force sent to Scotland which pillaged Edinburgh, and in 1545 and 1546 he saw further military service in France, where he won a brilliant military success over de Briez at Boulogne in 1545. Signs of his increasing importance were his appointment in 1544 as Lieutenant of the Kingdom during the king's absence in France and his diplomatic missions to the emperor, Charles V.

The jealousies between Hertford and the powerful Howard family (Norfolk and his son Surrey) came to a head in 1546. It is not possible to say that the dramatic fall of the Howards in January 1547 was Hertford's work, but when on 28 January the king died, Hertford was by far the most important man in the kingdom. He succeeded in keeping the news of Henry's death secret until he had got possession of Edward VI; then the news was published, but the most inconvenient clauses of Henry's will were suppressed. In spite of some opposition in the Council, Hertford was made Protector, and on 16 February he became Duke of Somerset. For the next two years he exercised virtual royal authority. In one prayer used by him he speaks of himself as 'caused by Providence to rule', and he even wrote to the King of France as 'brother'.

The great historian of the early part of this century, A. F. Pollard, saw Somerset as the 'Good Duke', a big-hearted liberal in his government of England, whose aim was to help the poor commons and to advance the Protestant cause. According to Pollard, Somerset was too good for his age and his efforts to please the people led instead to rebellion in 1549, as a result of which he was overthrown by the unscrupulous Earl of Northumberland and the hard-nosed realists of the Council. Such an interpretation of Somerset has been emphatically rejected by Dr M. L. Bush in a recent study. Bush argues that the key to Somerset's policy is to be found in his desire to conquer Scotland, a goal he pursued with 'obsessive stubbornness'.

When Henry VIII died, the problem of Scotland, in which Somerset had been deeply involved already, was unresolved. The Protector decided, like a good soldier, to finish the job. He won the battle of Pinkie (September 1547), and then decided to conquer the Scots completely by establishing a series of fortresses to hold the country in a state of military occupation. He did so out of no idealistic desire for the union of the two countries, although he did plan to marry Edward VI to the infant Queen of Scots, Mary, to complete the English conquest. It turned out that he could not achieve his aim: England did not have the money to build and man the strongholds he contemplated. In the end, the Scots remained independent and sent their queen to safe-keeping in France, where she was betrothed to the Dauphin. While he fought Scotland, the French predictably enough attacked him in the rear. Somerset was forced to surrender Boulogne (1548).

To pay for the Scottish campaigns, heavy taxation was imposed on the people, the money gained from the dissolution of the chantries was squandered, and the currency was debased still further. The results were inflation and social discontent. In response to the complaints of the people, Somerset sought to regain popularity by supporting the reforming efforts of John Hales, one of the so-called 'commonwealth men'. Hales was responsible for setting up a commission in 1548 to enforce legislation against enclosure, and for the passage of Acts of Parliament to prevent enclosure and to relieve the poor. Somerset encouraged Hales so that the people would blame their ills not on government policy but on sheep-farming. It was as a result of this desire for support and popularity rather than for any really genuine liberalism that Somerset repealed the Treason Act of 1534 and the Act of Six Articles of 1539. Somerset's

disastrous foreign policy also helped to determine the pace of his religious policy. He was a committed Protestant, but found it necessary to proceed slowly with the religious changes he favoured because of the need to keep on friendly terms with Charles V while he fought the French. At the beginning of the reign, therefore, all that was done was to allow communion in both kinds (1547) and to bring an end to traditional Catholic ceremonies like using palms on Palm Sunday, ashes on Ash Wednesday and to have the beautiful wall-paintings in the churches of England obliterated with lime (1548). By 1549, when his foreign policy had failed, he allowed the publication of an English prayer book, known as the Book of Common Prayer because unlike the Latin missals it was to be used commonly all over England, not in different forms in different dioceses. This was to be enforced by the Act of Uniformity, imposing a uniform service everywhere.

On the whole, Somerset carried the Council with him in his policies. He issued many proclamations in his brief reign, but this does not show a dictatorial spirit, merely that his period in office was a time of crisis, when urgent measures were often needed. However, in 1549 there occurred a series of rebellions which convinced many of the other councillors that Somerset was more trouble than he was worth. His position had already been shaken when he sent his own brother, Thomas Seymour, to the block. The revolts of 1549 were centred mainly on Norfolk and Cornwall, although there was trouble in many other parts of the country. Government policy, religious, fiscal and military, played its part in the causes of those uprisings. Somerset could not deal immediately with the rebels, largely because he needed all his troops for the Scottish wars and also because it was good policy in such circumstances to play for time, in the expectation that the rebels would soon get tired of rebellion and disperse. In the end, action was taken and the rebels were brutally suppressed. The entire council now turned against Somerset, both the more conservative councillors like Arundel and Southampton and the radicals like Warwick. In October 1549 he was dismissed from his offices and imprisoned. It was not thought wise, however, to execute him immediately, and he was released and lived on until January 1552, when Northumberland felt secure enough to have him tried and executed.

Somerset was a failure: he did not conquer Scotland, and what had seemed a strong position as Lord Protector in 1547 had completely disappeared two years later. He misused his position, enriching himself and his supporters, and demolishing part of St Paul's Cathedral to build Somerset House, his great London mansion. But it could have been worse. A monarchy is at its weakest when the ruler is a minor, and Somerset at least protected his nephew's life: he was no Richard of Gloucester. Nor, of course, was he a Duke of Northumberland; he did not seek to subvert the succession. He was careful to begin the political education of his charge, and to prepare him for the burdens of kingship which awaited him. It must say something of Somerset that while he held sway there were no religious executions in England, and also that, however muddle-headed he was as a politician, there were some poor people who did regard him as a 'Good Duke'.

Further Reading

J. Loach, *Somerset: a Reassessment*, 1994.

M. L. Bush, *The Government Policy of Protector Somerset*, 1975.

SEYMOUR, JANE (1509?-37), Henry VIII's third wife, was born probably in 1509 and died on 24 October 1537. She was the eldest of eight children born to Sir John Seymour of Wolf Hall, Savernake, Wiltshire, and his wife, Margaret, daughter of Sir John Wentworth, who claimed distant relationship with the royal family. She was the sister of Edward Seymour, later Duke of Somerset and Protector in the reign of Jane's son, Edward VI, and of Sir Thomas Seymour, Lord High Admiral, who was executed in 1549 by the reluctant command of his brother.

Little is known for certain of Jane's life, especially of her early life. Before Catherine of Aragon ceased to be queen, she was one of her ladies-in-waiting, and after Anne Boleyn married Henry VIII, she was in the service of the new queen. Probably it was in 1534 that Henry fell in love with her, and from that moment he paid much attention to her, to the fury of Anne Boleyn. Jane behaved with the greatest discretion and propriety, refusing all the king's advances until he was able to marry her. While the trial of Anne was pending, Jane lived with her brother and his wife, and Henry undertook to see her only in the presence of her friends. Two days before Anne's execution Cranmer declared his marriage with Anne null and void and on the day of execution (19 May) he issued a dispensation for Henry to marry Jane without publication of banns. They were married on 30 May 1536.

Her married life lasted a little more than a year. During that time she was able to reconcile Henry with his daughter, Mary, and to win golden opinions from all who came in contact with her. She seems to have had no sympathy with the Reformation: Luther called her 'an enemy of the gospel'; Cardinal Pole declared that she was 'full of goodness'. It is said that during the Pilgrimage of Grace she pleaded with Henry to restore the monasteries, but that he warned her not to meddle in affairs of state, if she wanted to avoid Anne Boleyn's fate. On 12 October 1537, she gave birth to a son, Edward, later Edward VI, but she herself died on 24 October.

Jane Seymour appears to have been the best loved of Henry's wives. He went into mourning for her, which he did for none of his other wives, and he ordered that his own body should be buried beside hers in St George's Chapel, Windsor. Owing to her frail health she was never crowned queen.

SHAKESPEARE, WILLIAM (1564-1616), poet and dramatist: modern research has greatly increased the evidence for the life of Shakespeare and reasonable deductions from that evidence have further enlarged our knowledge. The following account assumes the truth of both evidence and deductions, but references are given to books which discuss fully the problems involved.

William Shakespeare was baptized in Holy Trinity church at Stratford-upon-Avon on 26 April 1564. It was usual to hurry children to baptism, because the rate of mortality among babies was so high in the sixteenth century: by convention Shakespeare's birthday is now celebrated on 23 April, but there is no evidence to justify the choice of that date or of the room now shown to the public as the birthplace (M. M. Reese, *Shakespeare, his world and his work*, p.9, Chambers and Williams, *A Short Life of Shakespeare*, pp.11 and 133). He was the third child in the family of eight and the eldest of four sons born to John Shakespeare and Mary Arden. John was a well-to-do yeoman, a glover and curer of soft skins for gloves, at Stratford-upon-Avon, himself a native of Snitterfield who came to Stratford halfway through the sixteenth century. He became a man of much importance: he bought two houses in 1556, two more in 1575 and by 1590 he owned two contiguous houses in Henley Street. Between 1557 and 1568 he held all the chief municipal offices and reached that of Bailiff. Later he fell on evil days and declined in importance, but all the same in 1596 he was granted a coat of arms. He died in September 1601. There is no evidence to prove that the Shakespeares were either Protestant or Catholic 'recusants', but we know that William became godfather to William Walker in 1608 (and godfathers had to be sound Anglicans) and remembered him in his will ('to my godson William Walker xxs in gold'). The significance of this is discussed in a chapter entitled 'William Shakespeare, Anglican' in T. W. Baldwin's *William Shakespeare's Petty School*, 1943 (M. M. Reese, ib., pp.16 ff.).

William's mother was Mary Arden, the youngest of eight daughters of Robert Arden of Wilmcote. She was connected with the Ardens of Park Hall; she married John in 1557 or 1558 and outlived him by seven years.

Of William's education we know nothing for certain, but the probability is that he went to the King's New School in Stratford, but there are no lists existing of these early years. Certainly at some time or other he acquired a knowledge of the usual subjects taught in the grammar schools of his day. Ben Jonson's famous tag, 'Small Latin and less Greek' means no more than that.

Judged by Jonson's own high standard of scholarship, Shakespeare was no scholar, but he was as well educated as any other boy of his standing: he learned and loved Ovid, but he does seem to have disliked the formal education of his time (M. M. Reese, ib., pp.10, 389 ff.). It is possible, however, that he himself was a teacher in the years before he took to the theatre.

In 1582 Shakespeare was granted a licence by the Bishop of Worcester to marry Anne Whateley of Temple Grafton. Here lies a problem which has never been solved. Certain it is that William Shakespeare married 'Anne Hathwey of Stratford', though nobody knows when or where. Who then was Anne Whateley? Was she merely a clerical error in the licence? Yet, if it is easy to write Whateley for Hathwey, it is more than difficult to write Temple Grafton for Stratford (Chambers and Williams, *Short Life of Shakespeare*, pp.16-17, 140-2).

Anne Hathaway of Shottery was twenty-six when she married Shakespeare, eight years older than her husband, and she was already pregnant. A daughter, Susanna, was baptized on 26 May 1583, and on 2 February 1585 were baptized the twins, Hamnet and Judith. There is no convincing evidence that the marriage was an unhappy one, but if we may judge from the frequent allusions throughout his plays, Shakespeare seems to have held strongly that wedlock must be sanctioned by the church (M. M. Reese, ib., pp.28-31).

By 1592 Shakespeare was in London. We do not know why he left Stratford. The legend, as now presented, that he made Stratford too hot to hold him by poaching Sir Thomas Lucy's deer in Charlecote Park will not stand up to detailed examination, even if there may be a grain of truth in the episode (M. M. Reese, ib., pp.31-4). The fact remains that Shakespeare was in London by 1592, and he was a professional actor with one, but we know not which, of the 'Companies' of actors. It is possible that he may have begun his theatrical life with Alleyn's company, if the story is true that he started his career by holding gentlemen's horses at the playhouse door, for the only theatres to be reached by horseback were The Theatre and The Curtain, both of which were in the hands of Alleyn in 1590-1. By 1592 Shakespeare was successful enough to arouse the jealousy and anger of Greene, who attacked him as 'an upstart Crow, beautified with our feathers'. It is possible that Shakespeare was writing plays for more than one company between 1592 and 1594, but by 1594 he was a full member of the Lord Chamberlain's Men, with whom he was to spend the rest of his professional life.

Shakespeare was living in London in St Helen's, Bishopsgate, and the probability is that he had his wife and family with him. In 1596 one of the twins, Hamnet, died and Shakespeare may well have thought that he would move his family to Stratford to avoid the dangers to health in London. Certainly the next year he bought New Place, the best house in Stratford, to provide a home for his wife and daughters. He himself moved from Bishopsgate to Bankside. At this time he was closely associated with Francis Langley, owner of the new Swan theatre in Paris Garden in Southwark, and it is possible that his company was then playing at the Swan. Shakespeare and Langley became involved in a violent quarrel with the notorious Justice of the Peace, William Gardiner, a Puritan who was opposed to play-acting, and Shakespeare was bound over to keep the peace (Hotson, *Shakespeare versus Shallow*). From 1596 onwards Shakespeare visited Stratford more frequently and for longer periods, nor was New Place the only property he bought. It is clear that Shakespeare was making a good deal of money and he gradually became the largest property holder in Stratford.

In 1601 his father died and left Shakespeare the houses in Henley Street, which he let. He bought 107 acres of land and a cottage and garden in Chapel Lane. In 1605 he bought for £440 a thirty-two-year lease of tithes in Stratford and nearby villages, and for the last ten years of his life Shakespeare was the outstanding citizen in Stratford.

He was in London in 1612, 1613 and 1614, and at some point he moved his London lodgings to Silver Street in Cripplegate. In 1613 he bought the gatehouse of the Blackfriars Priory for £140 as an investment. In that year his last play, *Henry VIII*, was produced at the Globe Theatre in June. Tradition has it that he himself spoke the Prologue, so that he would have been present at the fire which destroyed the Globe during that first performance. There is no one moment when Shakespeare retired from the theatre: rather he spent more and more time at Stratford and gradually gave up his theatrical work in London.

In 1608 Shakespeare's mother died. The year before his daughter, Susanna, had married Dr John Hall, but unhappily there was only one child, a daughter. He made his will in either 1615 or 1616, and that will has become famous for the clause in it by which he left to his wife Anne 'my second-best bed with furniture' – the only mention of his wife in his will. This is no proof of a lack of affection on Shakespeare's part: rather it suggests that he knew that in his happy and united family he could take it for granted that Anne would be properly looked after at New Place to the end of her life. The greater part of his estate went to Susanna, for it is clear that Shakespeare wanted most of his property to pass undivided and to remain within the family. Wealthy widows did not long remain widows in the sixteenth century. Their new husbands saw that they took their wealth with them.

Shakespeare died (tradition has it) on his birthday, 23 April 1616. He lies buried in the chancel in front of the altar in Holy Trinity Church, Stratford-upon-Avon.

Lack of space forbids any discussion here of the many

problems which surround the dates of composition of the plays.

The generally accepted chronology of his plays is as follows: 1590-1, *2 Henry VI* and *3 Henry VI*; 1591-2, *1 Henry VI*; 1592-3, *Richard III* and *The Comedy of Errors*; 1593-4, *Titus Andronicus* and *The Taming of the Shrew*; 1594-5, *Two Gentlemen of Verona*, *Love's Labour's Lost* and *Romeo and Juliet*; 1595-6, *Richard II* and *A Midsummer Night's Dream*; 1596-7, *King John* and *The Merchant of Venice*; 1597-8, *1 Henry IV* and *2 Henry IV*; 1598-9, *Much Ado about Nothing* and *Henry V*; 1599-1600, *Julius Caesar*, *As You Like It* and *Twelfth Night*; 1600-1, *Hamlet* and *The Merry Wives of Windsor*; 1601-2, *Troilus and Cressida*; 1602-3, *All's Well That Ends Well*; 1604-5, *Measure for Measure* and *Othello*; 1605-6, *King Lear* and *Macbeth*; 1606-7, *Antony and Cleopatra*; 1607-8, *Coriolanus* and *Timon of Athens*; 1608-9, *Pericles*; 1609-10, *Cymbeline*; 1610-11, *The Winter's Tale*; 1611-12, *The Tempest*; 1612-13, *Henry VIII*, perhaps part of *The Two Noble Kinsmen*.

Shakespeare also wrote the poems *Venus and Adonis* (1592-3); *The Rape of Lucrece* (1593-4); *The Sonnets* (1595-9); *The Phoenix* and *The Turtle* (1600).

Equally, it is not possible here to discuss the problem of the *Sonnets*, which were published by a piratical printer in 1609. Who was the 'Mr W. H.' to whom the sonnets were dedicated? Was it Shakespeare's patron, the Earl of Southampton? Was it William Herbert, son and heir of the Earl of Pembroke? Was it the printer, William Hall? Who was the Dark Lady?

Many thorny problems surround the dates when the plays were published. By the end of Elizabeth's reign fifteen Shakespearean texts had appeared, of which six (perhaps seven) were 'bad' quartos: of eight the original texts were 'good' quartos. Not much more printing was done before the issue of the First Folio in 1623 by Heminges and Condell, which covered eighteen of the nineteen plays already issued in quarto. *Pericles* was omitted. The Second Folio was printed in 1632, the Third Folio in 1663 (a second issue of 1664 included *Pericles* and one or two plays not by Shakespeare). The Fourth Folio was printed in 1685. It is one of the tragedies of English literature that not a single manuscript of Shakespeare's work remains to us. The only handwriting of his which we possess is to be found in six signatures (to one are appended the words 'by me'), three of which are on his will. It is possible that in the manuscript play, *Sir Thomas More*, one page is in the handwriting of Shakespeare.

Shakespeare's tremendous success arose from the fact that he combined in himself three roles – he was a poet, a playwright and an actor: up to his time the theatre had never known such a trinity in unity. Shakespeare created the theatre as we understand that word. But Shakespeare was first and foremost a poet, before he was a playwright

or an actor. We know nothing about his ability as an actor, but he understood the professional needs of the theatre, because he lived with, acted with and wrote for actors – not actresses, because feminine parts were then played by boys. His dramatic work was at first conditioned by the literary conventions of his times – the classical imagery, the use of the soliloquy, the affectations of speech which appear, notably, in the verbal agility in punning. He was also governed by the general views of his time on the nature and purpose of Man, the supernatural, etc. What raises Shakespeare far above all his contemporaries is his ability to emancipate himself from these conventions and yet to transmute them by his own genius to his own use. Shakespeare was a poet who for his living had to write plays. Because he was a poet, and one of the greatest, he could not but produce dramatic poetry: his triumph was that he gave to the theatre poetic drama – every dramatic thought, every dramatic situation was to be presented in the imagery of poetry (Spurgeon, *Shakespeare's Imagery*; H. Morris, *Elizabethan Literature*, pp.205 ff.).

Two other points have to be remembered: Shakespeare was never an entirely free agent, for he had to provide suitable parts for the actors in the company, and also he had to provide the right sort of play for the audience which was going to hear it. A play which would score a success at The Theatre in Finsbury Fields might offend the public at the Globe on the South Bank: a royal command to perform in front of the queen or a private performance at a nobleman's house would demand a totally different sort of play (Milton Holmes, *Shakespeare's Public*).

What sort of a man was this William Shakespeare? 'Without a single dissentient voice his contemporaries testify to his sweetness, gentleness, honesty and "civil demeanour": no famous man has had so little evil spoken of him' (M.M.R. ib., pp.381, ff.). And, indeed, the width of his sympathy with every sort of human being stands out in all his writings. To him evil is detestable, but the evil-doer is an object of compassion, except where the criminal has given himself over to evil, as in Iago. Nothing is more moving in Shakespeare's plays than the defence by Costard of Sir Nathaniel in *Love's Labour's Lost* (Act. V, sc. ii, 569) – and Sir Nathaniel was a schoolmaster. Shakespeare is the most merciful of all the great men. Ben Jonson called him 'my gentle Shakespeare' and 'my beloved author'; 'I lov'd the man, and do honour his memory (on this side Idolatry) as much as any. He was indeed honest and of an open and free nature: had an excellent Phantasy: brave notions and gentle expressions.' In his last years Shakespeare became the best known figure and the most popular in Stratford, so that he was welcome in many homes and welcomed many to his own New Place. Down the centuries and across the continents his name glows ever brighter, so that perhaps Carlyle's claim is no empty boast, 'he is the grandest thing we have yet done'.

There is no authentic portrait of Shakespeare. On the chancel wall in the Stratford church stands a bust, the work of Gheerart Janssen, commissioned and completed a few years after Shakespeare's death, but it is to be hoped that this dull and heavy work reinforces Shakespeare's own verdict, 'there's no art To find the mind's construction in the face'. In the First Folio there was printed a drawing by Martin Droeshout, a Dutch engraver, but as he was only fifteen years old when Shakespeare died he must have copied another picture. The painting now at Stratford was copied from the engraving.

Further Reading

S. Schoenbaum, *Shakespeare: a Compact Documentary Life*, 1987.
M. C. Bradbrook, *Shakespeare: The Poet in his World*, 1978.
Milton Holmes, *Shakespeare's Public*, 1960.
M. M. Reese, *Shakespeare, His World and his Work*, 1953.
Ivor Brown, *Shakespeare*, 1949.
E. K. Chambers and C. Williams, *A Short Life of Shakespeare*, 1933.
Lamborn and Harrison, *Shakespeare, the Man and His Stage*, 1924.

SHARP, GRANVILLE (1735-1813), philanthropist, was a leading personality in the anti-slavery movement. He was a scholar who acquired most of his extensive knowledge in his scanty spare time, a man of strong principles who fought for what he believed right with extraordinary tenacity. His enthusiasms sometimes led him into eccentric paths. He was unwise to try to persuade Charles Fox that Napoleon was the 'Little Horn' of Daniel's prophecy or to suggest at a public meeting that soldiers of the Peninsula should be provided with bales of wool to make a rampart against enemy attack. He had done so many good and generous things that he might be forgiven for tilting at a few unlikely windmills in his old age. In the words of James Stephen, 'As long as Granville Sharp survived it was too soon to proclaim that the age of chivalry was gone.'

He was born at Durham, the ninth son of Thomas Sharp, prebendary of Durham and a theological writer of some note, and the grandson of John Sharp, Archbishop of York. His father's family being larger than his means, Granville was sent to London at the age of fifteen to be apprenticed to a linen draper. Since successive masters were Quaker, Presbyterian, Irish Roman Catholic, and atheist, it is not surprising that he followed his father's inclination to theology and taught himself Greek and Hebrew. In 1758 he obtained a post in the Ordnance Department. He wrote two Old Testament studies and *A Short Treatise on the English Tongue* (1767). He never became a Quaker, though his work brought him into contact with them. He was never ordained – but showed where his sympathies lay when, after the American war, he started a successful movement for the consecration of bishops in New York and Pennsylvania.

In 1765 Sharp befriended a negro, Jonathan Strong, whom he found wandering destitute, having been deserted by his master, James Lisle. Later Lisle had Strong imprisoned as a runaway slave, but Sharp secured his release and prosecuted Lisle for assault. A counter-action was brought against Sharp for detaining another man's property. Sharp found that he had no legal case: masters had property in their slaves even when in England. He wrote about and researched into the law of personal liberty and interested himself in similar cases. Eventually, in the case of James Sommersett (1772), the judges laid down the great principle that 'as soon as a slave sets foot upon English territory he becomes free'. A first step had been taken towards the suppression of the trade and it was the work of Sharp who, 'though poor and dependent and immersed in the duties of a toilsome calling, supplied the money, the leisure, the perseverance and the learning required for this great controversy'.

Beyond doubt Sharp enjoyed litigation. He defended, with success, the claim of the Duke of Portland to the forest of Inglewood and the castle of Carlisle (against the rival claim of the Lowthers). He agitated on behalf of the Caribbees, the original West Indians, when it was reported that the government planned to eliminate them. He supported the American colonists and resigned his ordnance post when war began (1776). He joined Oglethorpe in his crusade against the press-gang. But slavery remained his main interest. Tracts flowed from his pen, five in 1776 alone. In 1787 he was appointed chairman of the largely Quaker committee set up to gather 'such information as may tend to the abolition of the Slave Trade'. One difficulty was the number of liberated slaves in England. From 1783 he was planning for the settlement of a colony at Sierra Leone. The first shipload sailed in 1787; the freed slaves were accompanied by a number of 'whites, chiefly women of the lowest sort'. Four years later the Sierra Leone Company was set up to run the enterprise. There were immense problems; eventually the Crown took over the colony (1808). The affair provides a good example of the way in which the state was saddled with territorial concerns after private enterprises, commercial and philanthropic, had failed to solve problems of their own making.

Sharp had the happiness of seeing the slave trade abolished (1807). His approach to this evil was always that of an evangelical Christian. In 1804 he was chosen first chairman of the British and Foreign Bible Society, which he had helped to found. He helped to start the African Institution in 1807 and the Society for the Conversion of the Jews in 1808. There was a narrow, prejudiced side to his zeal. In 1813 he was first chairman of the Protestant Union, founded to fight against Catholic Emancipation.

Perhaps the greatest work of his later years was the enunciation of 'Granville Sharp's canon' – a vital linguistic contribution to the orthodox trinitarian case against the Unitarians. Sharp never married and lived usually in rooms in the Temple. He died at Fulham at the home of his sister-in-law. His good and useful life is well summarized by James Stephen: he had 'the most inflexible of human wills united to the gentlest of human hearts'.

Further Reading

Roger Ansley, *The Atlantic Slave Trade and British Abolition, 1760-1810*, 1975.

Sir James Stephen, *Essays in Ecclesiastical Biography*, 1860.

Prince Hoare, *Memoirs of Granville Sharp, Esq.*, 1828.

SHAW, RICHARD NORMAN (1831-1912) was a leading architect in the second half of the century, well known for the eclecticism of his style.

Born in Scotland, he was trained in the Gothic trad_ition, having been a pupil of William Burn. He travelled in France, Germany and Italy, worked as chief draughtsman to G. E. Street, and in 1866 set up in practice with a friend from Burn's office, Eden Nesfield. By then times were changing. Architects of their generation were moving away from the strict principles of Gothic design and looking at other aspects of traditional English building. As industrialization spread its ugly face across the British countryside, Shaw realized how many old houses and building traditions were in danger of being swept away. With Nesfield, he studied picturesque old farmhouses and cottages in Kent and Sussex. Shaw wanted to keep these vernacular styles alive. So he used details from them in the new houses which he designed, for example gables, tall chimneys, half-timbering, tile-hanging and mullioned windows. Eastlake termed the style 'Old English'.

Within a few years both architects had refined their work and based their designs more specifically on seventeenth-century brick buildings – the 'Queen Anne' style as it was known. At this time (the late 1870s) Shaw had some involvement with the building of Bedford Park in London, a speculative venture which was the first ever garden suburb.

Shaw also built large country houses, important commissions which received much publicity. He built these houses in his own eclectic style. Much depended on the site. The buildings were usually extensive, often sprawling, with highly original lay-outs and features. Cragside in Northumberland, built for Lord Armstrong between 1870 and 1885, is probably the best known of his country houses.

By the 1890s Shaw was regarded by many as the country's pre-eminent architect. His numerous assistants and pupils were devoted to him. Several of them went on to become well-known themselves – in particular Lethaby, Newton and Prior. Lutyens was not a pupil but was much influenced by him. The creation of the Arts and Crafts Movement had several sources, but a group of Shaw's pupils were notably influential in setting up the organization.

Shaw's later years were less happy. He continued to receive commissions, now more for public than domestic buildings (for example New Scotland Yard in London in 1890). His style changed yet again, becoming more classical with baroque details. With ailing health he stayed at home in London and became involved in the LCC's plans for the development of the city. Schemes for the rebuilding of the Regent Street Quadrant at Piccadilly Circus were long drawn out and controversial. Shaw played an important part in the discussions, but died before they were resolved. His reputation by now was sadly diminished. It was not until the second half of the twentieth century that his buildings were once more admired.

Further Reading

Andrew Saint, *Richard Norman Shaw*, 1976.

SHELDON, GILBERT (1598-1677), born at Stanton in Staffordshire, the son of a servant of the Earls of Shrewsbury, was educated at Trinity College, Oxford. In 1622 he became Fellow and in 1626 Warden of All Souls. Oxford don, royal chaplain, friend of Edward Hyde, Sheldon was a member of Falkland's circle at Great Tew, not one of those who favoured or was favoured by Laud. When the Long Parliament met, his views were those of Hyde, with whom he kept in touch through the war years. In 1648 he was turned out of All Souls and briefly imprisoned, and during the Commonwealth he lived in retirement in his native midlands. Reinstalled at All Souls in 1659, he was appointed Bishop of London at the Restoration, and he was the dominant Anglican figure in the Savoy Conference and in the religious settlement that followed, although he did not go to Canterbury until Juxon's death in 1663. Sheldon was a subtle negotiator as well as a capable administrator. He was more responsible than any other man for the re-establishment of the Anglican church and, more particularly, for the form that re-establishment took – with a supremacy clear and buttressed by law, yet free from the prerogative courts and from the other objectionable extremities of Laudianism. He was firm for the Act of Uniformity and for the resultant expulsion of Nonconformist clergy. An ecclesiastical statesman, courtly in manner, strong in judgement, one who in Burnet's unfavourable verdict regarded the church as 'a matter of policy [rather] than of conscience', he was, as Burnet admits, generous and charitable, an archbishop who stayed at Lambeth throughout the plague of 1665 while the court fled from London, and who reproved Charles II for adultery. The University of Oxford owes more to Sheldon than to most of the archbishops who have been her sons, for he encouraged the antiquarian activities of Anthony à Wood, and he employed Wren to build at his expense the Sheldonian Theatre, opened in 1669.

Further Reading
V. D. Sutch, *Gilbert Sheldon, Architect of Anglican Revival, 1640-75*, 1973.

SHELLEY, MARY WOLLSTONECRAFT (1798-1851)

wrote *Frankenstein*. In play and film its story has so caught and held the imagination of successive generations that the single fact might be held sufficient to justify her inclusion among the famous. Indeed she might otherwise chiefly be known as the poet's second wife: no mean qualification either, since William Godwin's daughter came as near as any woman could to meeting Shelley's requirement for life partnership: 'one who can feel poetry and understand philosophy'. Aged sixteen she eloped with Shelley to form the notorious *ménage à trois*, with Claire Clairmont, through whom their fortunes became intertwined with those of Byron. After two suicides, those of Mary's half sister, Fanny, and Shelley's deserted wife, Harriet, in December 1816, her relationship was formalized by marriage. Already she had borne a son, William. There would follow Clara and Percy: the latter would inherit the Shelley baronetcy. From 1818 the Shelleys lived in Italy: Venice, Rome, Naples, finally Pisa. In June 1819 William died. In July 1822 Shelley was drowned. Thereafter Mary lived mainly in England, reconciled to her father, giving her time mainly to editing and publicizing her husband's poems, educating her son, writing more novels. *The Last Man* (1826) is usually held to be the best of them: it describes the future destruction of the human race by a plague. Her *Journal* is a rich source for those seeking to track Shelley's life and enter his mind. She did not marry again.

Frankenstein had been published in 1818. Subtitled *The Modern Prometheus* it narrates the dire consequences that arise after a scientist has artificially created a human being. There is much of Godwin in the manner and matter of the book: chains of the mind, the power of truth, the virtues of republicanism. More generally it is of its age: Rousseau would recognize Frankenstein's creation, archetypal man in the state of nature, virtuous until corrupted by his treatment by other people. It is redolent of the darker side of Romanticism. Within the Gothic genre, it offered a sustained metaphor for the upheavals of the age. Shelley contributed much. The intense household, at once idealistic and self-absorbed, reading adventurously, revelling in speculation and story-telling, provided the perfect ambience. *Frankenstein* remains Mary's creation, its unique character her incontestable achievement.

Further Reading
Muriel Spark, *Mary Shelley*, 1987.

SHELLEY, PERCY BYSSHE (1792-1822),

poet, was the son of a Sussex baronet, Sir Timothy Shelley, of Field Place, Horsham, and of Elizabeth Pilfold. Timothy's father, Bysshe, the first baronet, had married heiresses, Mary Michell and Elizabeth Perry, and had large estates. Timothy was briefly in parliament. His wife was handsome in a rather stately way, a good letter-writer and a lover of the countryside. They married in October 1791. Field Place was a delightful old house for an imaginative child: 'very rambling, with long passages and odd corners, turnings and recesses, floors on different levels', set in a park, with fine trees and large gardens. Percy, a beautiful child, was the eldest of seven. His father 'read the Classics and other Books with him in the full hopes of making him a good and Gentlemanly Scholar'.

As a child Percy displayed a precocious inventiveness: he told his family and the servants fabulous stories about dragons and spirits. In his holidays he would divert himself, between shooting, riding and inspecting sheep, by writing poems. Elizabeth, his sister, contributed to one collection lines which put the case plainly:

> For they're all alike, take them one with another,
> Begging pardon – with the exception of my brother.

He had a good memory and ear: Gray's *Ode on a Favourite Cat* he reproduced entire after one reading. Two other traits hinted at a future less conventional than that of scholar-squire. He noticed the poverty of country people and planned to do something about it. One boyish scheme was to educate an orphan girl. He once made a stir at a dance by selecting for his partner a girl who was sitting out: she had been seduced and was being ignored – and that was enough for him. The miniature painted by the émigré Duc de Montpensier, in 1802, depicts a sensitive but confident face. In the same year he was sent to his private school, Sion House Academy. He suffered the shocks that other boys from spacious, cherished homes, unacquainted with school, have endured at the hands of boarding school bullies. He retreated into solitude and books – preferably thrillers, strong stuff in that heyday of vampires and spectres. 'While yet a boy I sought for ghosts', he wrote in the first line of *Hymn to Intellectual Beauty*, and 'called on poisonous names'. He dreamed dreams that transcended mere schoolboy curiosity about the unknown. These lines from the dedication of *The Revolt of Islam* describe an intense experience which may belong to the years of Sion. He was crying, one 'fresh May-dawn', outside the schoolroom with its 'harsh and grating strife of tyrants and of foes':

> So without shame I spake: 'I will be wise,
> And just, and free, and mild, if in me lies
> Such power.'

Eton in 1804 began a time of liberation, despite the

temporary constraints of fagging, the 'Shelley-baiting' and later the 'fierce dominion' of Dr Keate, who taught Shelley in the sixth form. In July 1810 he translated half of thirty-seven books of Pliny's *Natural History*! Keate noticed that he fell into metrical rhythms even in his Latin prose. He gave his housemaster a shock with an electrical machine. Astronomy also fascinated him. 'His jubilee was night. His spirit bounded on the shadow of darkness, and flew to the countless worlds beyond', wrote one contemporary. One friend, Halliday, recalls of Shelley 'the sparkling poetry of his mind', which 'shone out of his speaking eye, when he was dwelling on anything good or great'. As later at Oxford he threw a romantic haze over the countryside, transforming what he saw into a land of enchantment. What great walkers those romantics were – even Coleridge! Shelley was 'strong, light and active', Hogg wrote of him at eighteen, and well-suited 'to perform, as it were, a pedestrian steeplechase'.

Shelley went up to University College, Oxford. Imagine the clerical university, the factiousness of an inbred society, tutors who were aggravated by his civil rejections of their views, and the young scholar, idealist and egotist in a combination which would not have been so unusual if he had not also been so strong-willed: conflict was inevitable. Shelley read a lot: Plato, the Greek dramatists, historians, Shakespeare; he studied logic and science; above all, encouraged by his father, who urged him to compete for a poetry prize, he plied his pen. Of his interests at this time *A Poetical Essay on the Existing State of Things* – an early form of *Queen Mab* – may have been typical: the profits were intended for Peter Finnerty, who was in gaol for writing a 'libellous' letter against Lord Castlereagh. He also wrote *The Necessity of Atheism*, prepared with his friend Thomas Hogg and published by Philadelphia Phillips at Worthing. Written a stone's throw from the college chapel which symbolized the Anglican supremacy, this anonymous tract argued logically from the premise that 'The senses are the source of all knowledge to the mind'. It was sold at his printers and sent out to heads of colleges and bishops. Shelley and Hogg were expelled. Shelley had been a peacock in dress and pursuits. He went for country walks armed with a pair of duelling pistols. He played all the parts as though he had never expected to stay long. But he was 'good-natured and kind' – and he was only eighteen. And he, of all people, never knew an Oxford summer! A pleasant Oxford story may be his memorial, to go perhaps with the effigy by which the college made amends. Hogg tells of the young philosopher on Magdalen Bridge, grasping a baby from his mother's arms, inquiring 'in a piercing voice, and with a wistful look, "Will your baby tell us anything about pre-existence, madam?"'. So Shelley went to London to continue the partnership of minds with Hogg; he chose

15 Poland Street, since the name 'reminded him of Thaddeus, of Warsaw, and of freedom'.

Timothy offered his son a voyage to the Greek islands on condition that he parted from Hogg. Shelley refused: he also rejected a generous offer by the Duke of Norfolk to accommodate him in due course with a parliamentary seat at Horsham. Only the good offices of an uncle secured him an allowance. Shelley stayed in London, wrote satires of the prince regent, even threw them into carriages attending a Carlton House banquet. He attended anatomical lectures at Bart's, and visited Cwm Elan in Radnorshire, the estate of Mr Thomas Grove, father of the girl whom Shelley had wanted to marry. He then married another, Harriet Westbrook. Sixteen years old, a school friend of his sisters at Clapham, brought up to strict principles, she had met Shelley, been disturbed by his atheism and fallen in love with him. 'He was endowed by Nature with an aspect truly angelic', said Leigh Hunt. On 28 August 1811 they married in Edinburgh. He inscribed the register: 'Percy Bysshe Shelley, farmer, Sussex'.

Shelley returned from a stormy visit to his father to rescue his wife from Hogg, who had taken too literally Shelley's views on the sharing of property, and in November 1811 settled in a cottage near Keswick. There he met Southey whose reaction was amused: 'Here is a man who acts upon me as my own ghost would do. He is just what I was in 1794.' Shelley was predictably disappointed. He dashed off to Dublin with a stirring *Address to the Irish People*. He suggested religious toleration for all at a Catholic emancipation rally, and was hissed out, enemies put it about that he was only fifteen. The autumn of 1812 saw the Shelleys at Tremadoc helping William Madocks to reclaim marshland behind a sea-wall and build the town of Portmadoc. An attempt was made, one February night, to murder the poet. By whom, or why, has never transpired. Out of such experiences a more mature person and a greater poet was made. He intended to measure the quality of life by 'enthusiast feeling' in 'actual living', rather than by 'some grey veteran's of the world's cold school'. He remained true to this: the Shelley who was drowned in Italy was little different from the Shelley, self-deluding, quixotic, impulsive, who sent off copies of his *Letter to Ellenborough*, some by balloon and some in bottles down the Bristol Channel, and who, in 1813, brought out his private edition of *Queen Mab*. His friend Hookham had declined to publish this 'philosophical poem', which employs an un-Shakespearean fairy queen to utter lectures on politics and religion. Godwinist in anticipation of human growth toward justice and perfection by the operation of free minds, vehement in denunciation of kings, priests, statesmen, commerce and war, it is diffuse but not vague. This least indolent of romantics had acquired experience through wide reading – and his notes to the poem, on such matters as vegetarianism, indicate a bold intelligence.

Shelley's domestic life was one of constant motion. In June 1813 Harriet had a baby girl. He collected a coterie in London, centring upon J. F. Newton, a vegetarian, mystic and student of the zodiac. Amidst debts, borrowings, poems and hypochondria (he believed for a time that he had contracted elephantiasis), such relationships kept him stable. The strain on Harriet was immense. In March 1814 they were remarried, with proper formality, at St George's, Hanover Square. In the summer of 1815 they separated: his mind suffered, 'like a little kingdom, the nature of an insurrection' for he had fallen in love with Mary Godwin, the daughter of William Godwin and Mary Wollstonecraft. Mary proposed that they live together – Mary as sister, Harriet as wife! Shelley felt that Harriet could not be a partner of his life: she could not feel poetry nor understand philosophy. She resented the false gods and demanding friends – Godwin above all. Shelley also wished to escape from Harriet's intrusive sister Elizabeth.

In the summer of Waterloo Shelley lived at Bishopsgate, near Windsor: to this period belong *Summer Evening Churchyard* and (December) *Alastor or the Spirit of Solitude*. The latter's theme is that self-centred seclusion is punished by a daemon of ruin – but it may also be read as an elegy for the lost dreams of youth. In May 1816 Shelley and Mary went to Geneva. There they met Byron, and Claire Clairemont. The poets' encounter was mutually inspiring: they boated together, recited and made poetry, and told stories. Mary's story, *Frankenstein*, was the most successful. Shelley returned in September with the third canto of Byron's *Childe Harold* for the printer, and Claire, carrying Byron's child, the future Allegra. In October 1816, Fanny Imlay, the daughter of Mary Wollstonecraft by her first marriage, committed suicide: neglected by Godwin, she had adored Shelley. Then Harriet was found drowned in the Serpentine (December 1816). Suicide is most probable, since she seems to have been rejected by her family. Well might Shelley now 'stare aghast'. Was he doomed to destroy those who loved him? At the end of the month he married Mary at St Mildred's, Bread Street, for form's sake, on Godwin's insistence. But he was sick at heart. He offered a home to Claire and Allegra (born in January) and filed a suit in Chancery for custody of Harriet's children which was refused by Lord Eldon.

In December 1816 Leigh Hunt honoured Shelley, Keats, Reynolds and Byron, in his manifesto *Young Poets*, as the men who would reanimate English poetry. It was at Hunt's cottage in Hampstead that Shelley met Keats. Keats was lost in Shelley's 'daedal round with nature, and his Archimedean endeavours to move the globe with his own hands'. It was at Hampstead that Shelley rescued a woman having a fit: this was one of his 'most ordinary actions'. Among those whom he met were Hazlitt, Haydon, Severn and Horace Smith, a city man. They all left descriptions from which a composite picture may be formed. Fair, freckled, light-brown hair, delicate-looking, a gentle expression, a light voice (Haydon thought it 'feminine', Hazlitt 'shrill'), intensely blue eyes which seemed (Severn) 'to dwell more on the inward than the outward aspect of nature', slender, slightly drooping figure, unmistakably 'a *gentleman* … one that is gentle, accomplished and brave' (Smith). Hazlitt wrote of his 'flexible form' that 'appears to take no strong hold of things, does not grapple with the world about him but slides from it like a river'.

Albion House, Marlow, was to be his Dove Cottage: here he could husband his resources and observe nature. He lived sparingly; his diet was largely vegetarian; he walked a great deal and rowed on the Thames. Here he was seen 'with his hat wreathed with briony, or wild convolvulus; his hand filled with bunches of wildflowers plucked from the hedges as he passed …' The abstracted poet was also the warm-hearted squire: there were coins and blankets for the poor, visits to cottages, amateur medical advice: some of the country people liked the man whom their betters declared to be an atheist and seducer. At Marlow he wrote *Laon and Cynthia* (later published as *The Revolt of Islam*), with the revealing subtitle *The Revolution of the Golden City: A Vision of the Nineteenth Century*; its preface announced that the poem was written 'in the cause of a liberal and comprehensive morality'. Cynthia has been called the first 'new woman' in our poetry; she is as intelligent as she is passionate. But Hunt's judgement, 'The work cannot possibly become popular', was an understatement. Shelley wrote as if he had never met any real people, because he deliberately set out to be universal and abstract. In *Prometheus Unbound*, a greater poem in three Acts (a fourth was added, more lyrical but obscure and not obviously related), *Prometheus* embodies his Platonic idea that 'reasoned principles of moral conduct' are useless unless man can learn what is beautiful and virtuous.

Suffering from ill-health for which a damp house and his importunate father-in-law may be held to blame, Shelley was persuaded to go to Italy. He and Mary left in March 1818 after a hasty christening of their son and daughter and Allegra. Harriet's children had to be left behind, of course: when Charles Bysshe died of consumption in 1826 his old grandfather, who had brought him up fondly, simply described him on his memorial as 'grandson of Sir Timothy and Lady Elizabeth Shelley'. The Shelleys enjoyed a leisurely journey, taking in the sights while Shelley gathered inspiration for the glorious poetry of his last period. Some of the shorter poems, such as *Stanzas written in Dejection near Naples*, witness, however, to distress. His infant daughter Claire died in September 1818 at Venice, where Shelley stayed with Byron. In June 1819 his son William died at Rome. Then his servant Paolo attempted to blackmail him over the parentage of a mysterious infant. When 'my poor Neapolitan', as Shelley called the supposed mother, died in the summer of 1820, he wrote: 'It seems as if the destruction that is consuming me were as an atmosphere which wrapt and *infected* everything connected with me'. Shelley was burdened by his past and by present griefs. He also felt uprooted. He found Italy exquisitely beautiful, but he remained very English.

He sought solace in intense writing. In 1819 he wrote most of *Prometheus* (at about the same time Beethoven was composing his *Choral Symphony*) and the *Cenci*, a Webster-like drama, regarded by St John Ervine as proof that Shelley 'knew the tricks of the theatre trade by instinct'. *The Mask of Anarchy*, a manifesto directed to the working men of England, was composed in generous rage after he heard of Peterloo (August 1819). Some of his noblest lyrical poems also belong to this year, notably the *Ode to the West Wind*. In 1820 the Shelleys settled in Pisa with their baby son Percy, who had been born the previous November, and Shelley wrote the *Letter to Mary Gisborne*, the translation of the Homeric *Hymn to Mercy*, the fantasy of *The Witch of Atlas* and the satirical drama of *Oedipus Tyrannus* or *Swellfoot the Tyrant* (King George IV).

The romantic Skythrop in Peacock's satirical novel, *Nightmare Abbey*, sold but seven copies of his treatise 'upon reforming the world' but he was undaunted. Shelley recognized and enjoyed his friend's caricature of himself: he, too, sold but seven copies of *Oedipus*. The *Epipsychidion*, 'an idealized history of my life and feelings', originated with his meeting with Emilia Viviani in a convent near Pisa. He had fallen briefly in love with her – and may have wanted her to elope. Very different is the *Adonais*, an elegy suggested by the death of Keats – more about Shelley than about Keats, and most about the condition of mankind.

> Life, like a dome of many-coloured glass,
> Stains the white radiance of Eternity,
> Until Death tramples it to fragments.

In this incomparable poem Shelley indeed obeyed Keats's injunction to him 'to be more of an artist'.

In prefaces to his works Shelley expounded political and moral views. As he told Peacock, he considered poetry 'very subordinate to moral and political science'. When, however, Peacock wrote his *Four Ages of Poetry*, arguing that poetry was a primitive thing, Shelley accepted the challenge. Philip Sidney, author of *Apologie for Poetrie*, was one of his idols. He wrote his great essay, the *Defence of Poetry*, in the vein of Sidney. Poetry, he affirms, 'lifts the veil from the hidden beauty of the world, and makes familiar objects be as if they were not familiar'. Shelley also draws upon his own

experience: 'When composition begins, inspiration is already in the decline, and the most glorious poetry that has ever been communicated to the world is probably a feeble shadow of the original conceptions of the poet.'

Shelley's last poem, aptly called *The Triumph of Life*, shows that he was at the height of his powers. In his insistence upon 'the contagion of the world's slow stain', Shelley seems to be giving up the idea that earthly happiness is possible: the word 'triumph' is surely intended ironically. The poem, which Eliot held to be his wisest and best, ends abruptly with the line: 'Then, what is life? I cried'. There is an urgency about the verse, as if Shelley has much to say in a hurry: he is looking on in a vision at a crowd of people hastening blindly along a dusty road. The poem was written in a lonely house on the Bay of Spezia. In June Shelley heard of the arrival of Leigh Hunt in Italy: he and his friend Williams set sail for Leghorn. The meeting with Hunt was a happy one: they planned a new journal.

On 8 July Shelley and Williams left Leghorn for Lerici; they sailed into the haze of a coming storm; the boat was swamped by a heavy sea – she appears to have been rammed by a felucca. Some Italian fishermen knew that they had money on board. The bodies were washed up near Viareggio. In Shelley's pocket was a volume of Keats's poems 'doubled back, as if the reader, in the act of reading, had hastily thrown it away'. On 15 August 1822, in the presence of the quarantine officers, Italian soldiers, Trelawney, Hunt and Byron, Shelley's corpse was burned, on a funeral pyre. The flame looked 'as tho' it contained the glassy essence of vitality'. Byron turned away from the Virgilian scene and swam out to his ship. The heart was sent to Mary; the ashes to the Protestant cemetery at Rome.

The world has seen many faults in Shelley. We may feel with his friend Williams: 'His greatest fault is ignorance of his own worth.' After years when he had believed himself to be a saviour, he had come to doubt his own capabilities – precisely at the time when he was realizing them, not as a philosopher but as a poet, a worthy contributor 'to that great poem, which all poets, like the co-operating thoughts of one great mind, have built up since the beginning of the world'.

Further Reading
N. Rogers, *Shelley at Work*, 1956.
N. I. White, *Shelley*, 2 vols, 1947.
Edmund Blunden, *Shelley*, 1946.

SHERIDAN, RICHARD BRINSLEY (1751-1816), dramatist and politician, was the grandson of an Irish clergyman, a Jacobite and a friend of Swift, who lost his living with a sermon, on the anniversary of George I's succession, on the text 'Sufficient unto the day is the evil thereof'. His father earned some fame as actor, dramatist and manager of plays, and as author of a pronouncing dictionary. His mother, Frances, was no mean actress. Sheridan inherited his parents' talents and interest in the world of theatre. He went to Harrow School (1762-8). He subsequently lived on the hill in a house which is, today, one of the school's boarding houses. Meanwhile the family lived in Bath, where he met Elizabeth Linley. He eloped with her to France, fought two duels with the Welsh beau whom she had thus escaped, and came home, not to the intended career at the bar, but to marriage and the precarious life of writing for the theatre.

Beaux and Bath, courtships, elopements and duels – these were good ingredients for a comedy. Throw in a bumpkin or two, an irascible father, a disreputable Irishman, Sir Lucius O'Trigger, and a lot of the verbal rapier work of the sort that audiences delight in – and there is *The Rivals*. Produced at the beginning of 1775, it was not at first well received; revised and recast, it won acclaim. He had given familiar situations and characters new freshness. Its brittle elegance and exuberant spirits have won playgoers ever since. Mrs Malaprop's verbal misfortunes still amuse but his Faulkland, an introspective sentimentalist, is a subtler study.

Looking for someone to succeed him as manager and proprietor of Drury Lane Theatre, Garrick saw in the young Sheridan a man with a rare sense of theatre. He became a partner, with two wealthier backers. One of them, Thomas Linley, provided the music for *The Duenna* (1776), whose charming lyrics and intriguing plot earned great popularity. Its seventy-five performances exceeded the sixty-two credited to *The Beggar's Opera*, the previous record. *St Patrick's Day* and *A Trip to Scarborough* are pleasant pieces, but better known today are *The School for Scandal* and *The Critic*. The former earned him the title of 'The modern Congreve'. Combining innocence and sophistication, Lady Teazle, country girl amazed and pleased by the sexual licence of high society, gives the actress glorious opportunities. Insincere specimen of 'the man of feeling', Joseph Surface stands out among other parts, each cleverly matched to the skills of his cast. With its lively ridicule of affectation and pretentiousness, it may be considered the greatest comedy of manners in the language. *The Critic*, first performed in 1779, again showed how Sheridan could improve on an earlier model: in this case Villiers's *The Rehearsal*. Puff is a type, Sir Fretful Plagiary has more individuality: unkindly modelled on the dramatist Richard Cumberledge he epitomizes the vanity of authors.

Unfortunately for the theatre, Sheridan's career as playwright virtually ended when he entered politics in 1780. *Pizarro* (1799) would be found derivative and mediocre. He was already a luminary of society, upon Dr Johnson's instance a member of 'the Club'. Now as a Foxite Whig he displayed wonderful powers of oratory. In 1782 he became an Under-Secretary; then in the

coalition of Fox and North Secretary to the Treasury. His unfailing good nature and ready wit made him many friends, notably the Prince of Wales, now aspiring to a political role; but this association did Sheridan little good. With Fox and the prince he gambled and drank of nights, was encouraged to think of political questions in personal terms, and became implicated in the unfortunate regency issue. In 1788 he championed the prince's claim to be regent during the insanity of George III. It was Fox rather than Sheridan who put the regent's claims in such an uncompromising way that they seemed to flout the constitutional right of parliament, but Sheridan's prospects were blighted by the debacle which ensued when George III recovered his wits. The impeachment of Warren Hastings in Westminster Hall did not improve the position of the Whigs, even though the subject of Sheridan's first speech, the Begums of Oudh, gave him the material for a masterpiece of rhetoric, for Pitt's neutrality deprived the trial of political significance. Before Sheridan had finished his peroration and collapsed melodramatically into the arms of Burke, experienced politicians were overcome by emotion and fashionable ladies fainted in the galleries. Sheridan soon tired of the trial, however, and began, with the other friends of Fox, to experience the frustration of opposition. He made his mark from time to time, in defence of the Revolution and in attacks on Pitt, notably upon his policy of coercion and the infamous Scottish trials.

Sheridan was ever a friend of liberty but he was also a patriot. As a good Irishman he strove to prevent the Act of Union but when invasion of England threatened he raised his own regiment of volunteers. Later he supported the Peninsular War. He had little talent for administration and it may be that his political achievement would have been superficial, even if he had been luckier, or less steadfast, in his political connections. In his last years he drank heavily and became a figure of derision in the House of Commons which he had once adorned. Yet he could argue well on occasion. The speech he made when moving that there be an inquiry into Irish affairs, in August 1807, showed him at his best. To the end of his life he could rise above party considerations to humane and patriotic statesmanship. He held office once again, as Treasurer for the navy, in the coalition of 1806, but soon thereafter resigned. After Fox's death he was treated coolly by the Whig leaders, as if he were a castoff entertainer. He lost credit further during the complicated negotiations of May-June 1812 over the formation of an administration to follow Perceval's because he was thought to have deliberately withheld information that he had received from Lord Yarmouth, the regent's friend, and so materially damaged Whig changes of office. He embarrassed the House by his faltering explanation of his conduct. At worst he was guilty of misjudgement. But clear thinking was now beyond him. He looked as debauched as he was. His once expressively handsome face was swollen, his nose scarlet; only the brilliant eyes recalled his youthful charm.

Recklessly generous when he had any money, Sheridan was unlucky in business ventures. In 1791 old Drury Lane was burned down and had to be rebuilt at great expense; it was burned down again in 1809. He had always been altruistic about office and he had only one small place, Receiver of the Duchy of Cornwall.

He died deeply in debt. We may regret that the man whose plays gave such delight, whose speeches had improved so many parliamentary hours, should have found so little fulfilment in his political career. When the Whigs had no man that was 'at all a match for little Perceval', the eclipse of Sheridan was sad. He does not seem, however, to have become bitter or depressed. Of all the great Whigs he is in some ways the most likeable personality.

Further Reading
J. H. W. Morwood, *Sheridan*, 1985.
W. S. Sichel, *Sheridan*, 2 vols, 1909.

SHIPPEN, WILLIAM (1673-1743), Tory and Jacobite, was the son of the rector of Stockport in Cheshire and was educated at Stockport Grammar School and at Trinity College, Cambridge. After practising law he entered parliament for Bramber, a borough of Lord Plymouth, but was then unseated on petition. In 1710, however, he returned upon the High Church cry 'Huzzah for Queen and Church'. He was prominent in the October Club, strong for Anglican measures and for the charges against Marlborough. After 1714, the debacle of the Tories and the exile of Bolingbroke, he emerged as a leading spokesman for a loose grouping of some fifty independent-minded members, united only in their detestation of court and palace. Shippen's own position was precarious: he was an avowed Jacobite but committed to working by constitutional ways. He spent a few months in the Tower for his speech at the opening of parliament in 1717, when he said that ''twas a great misfortune that the king was stranger to our language and constitution', but thereafter he enjoyed a certain immunity, as the ministry grew more stable and the Jacobite threat receded. From Walpole he got a gruff appreciation; politics apart, they were friends. 'Whoever is corrupt', said Walpole, 'Shippen is not'. When the vote of the Tories could have been fatal to Walpole in 1741, Shippen and his friends abstained, for he preferred Walpole to any conceivable alternative.

Sometimes Shippen's opposition was more effective. In 1716 he made a stout resistance to the Septennial Bill, declaring that 'Long Parliaments would grow either formidable or contemptible' and he was prominent in the attack upon the excise scheme of 1733 which Walpole was eventually forced to withdraw. He was predictably

hot about the South Sea Company and was attacking ministerial participation in the affairs of the company several years before the crash. The Civil List and the king's frequent journeys to Hanover were regular targets and for 'the bottomless pit of the secret service' he had an exaggerated horror. Shippen was not a great orator; indeed Horace Walpole tells us that he habitually spoke with his glove in his mouth. But the disinterested and bold critic who is known to have no ambitions for himself, who can speak to the minds and moods of the independent gentleman, has seldom wanted a hearing in the House. Shippen's wife reflected his prejudice admirably: she would never attend the court of the Hanoverian king. Shippen's own outlook was limited. But his character and actions may have had more effect than the bibulous toasts of stay-at-home Jacobite squires. In an age of placemen and faction Shippen helped to preserve, if not greatly to enrich, the Tory tradition.

Further Reading
J. Biggs-Davison, *Tory Lives*, 1952.
K. G. Feiling, *The Second Tory Party, 1742-1832*, 1938.

SHORE, JOHN, 1st BARON TEIGNMOUTH (1751-1834) was a great Indian administrator, a man of strong Christian faith who helped to establish high standards for the British rulers of India. His father was a company man; his mother was the daughter of Captain Shepherd, a captain in the company's naval service. India was in his blood. He went to Bengal from Harrow, where William Jones, the great orientalist, was among his friends.

In the company's service he rose steadily by a stoical devotion to duty. The year after he arrived at least a fifth of the population of Bengal died in a famine. He could be under no illusions as to the size of the administrative and social problems. By nature a cool, mild man, Shore stuck to duties which he found distasteful, in a climate that was barely tolerable, for a salary which he steadily refused to augment by the customary sweets of office. 'Poor I am and may remain so', he wrote to his mother, 'but conscious rectitude shall never suffer me to blush at being so.'

At the age of nineteen he became Assistant of the Revenue Council of Bengal at Murshidabad and, having an idle superior, took on most of the work. Rarely have men so young been given such huge responsibility. From 1775 to 1780 he was on the Revenue Council of Calcutta, and later on the committee of revenue. He drew up the minute which formed the basis of Bengal's zemindari system of revenue collection. (The zemindar was a hereditary revenue collector: Shore wanted his lease to last for ten years. In 1793 Cornwallis – against his wishes – fixed the settlement in perpetuity.) From 1787 to 1793 Shore was on the Supreme Council of Bengal. Like many dutiful men he was prone to think himself a martyr. 'The life of a man in Bengal who does his duty is really that of a galley-slave', he wrote. 'He is in constant warfare with innumerable opponents and must submit to the common tax of censure and calumny.' But there was a lighter side. As a good Harrovian he played cricket. He found time to translate into English in three volumes a Persian form of the *Jog Bashust*, a Sanskrit exposition of the doctrines of Vedanta. Letters to his friends contained verse translations from the Arabic. Foremost among his early friends was Augustus Cleveland, a local magistrate who died at twenty-nine and left a legendary name behind him. He also spoke of his love for Cornwallis, the Governor-General before him. It was Shore's brief to supply sound administration, to preside over a period of consolidation after the great advances made by Cornwallis.

Appointed Governor-General in 1792 (despite Burke's protest) he accepted the baronetcy which he had earlier refused. When after four years a mutiny in the Bengal army and the serious turn taken by the French war led to the appointment of a man of action, Shore may not have been sorry to leave. His solemn, cautious paternalism was a far cry from Wellesley's imperious pride. One cannot imagine that great pro-consul writing as did Shore: 'When I consider myself the Ruler of twenty-five millions of people ... I tremble at the greatness of the charge ... I consider every native of India, whatever his situation may be, as having some claim upon me.' 'Has not Providence', he asked himself, 'imposed upon you the care of millions?' He could be criticized for allowing the Marathas to invade the lands of the Nizam, and the French to penetrate with 'advisers' into several other states. In the north the Sikhs, in the south Tipu Sahib, prepared for war. Yet on occasion he could act with courage – as over the Oudh succession. The words in which he affirmed his belief in moderation deserve to be recalled: 'Our reputation for justice and good faith stands high in India and if I were disposed to depart from them, I could form alliances that would shake the Maratha empire to its very foundations. I will rather trust the permanency of our dominion to a perseverance in true principles.'

He came home to an Irish peerage. He became a privy councillor and a member of the board of control. He was closely associated with the Clapham sect of evangelicals and became the first president of the British and Foreign Bible Society. His *Memoirs of Sir William Jones* (1804) provided a solid memorial to his old school friend. He lived to a great age. Lord Macaulay wrote of him: 'Of his integrity, humanity and honour it is impossible to speak too highly.'

Further Reading
P. Woodruff, *The Men Who Ruled India*, vol. 1, 1953.
Lord Teignmouth (son), *Memoir of the Life ... of Lord Teignmouth*, 1843.

SHOVELL, ADMIRAL SIR CLOWDISLEY (1650-1707), from Cockthorpe in Norfolk, was perhaps the most noteworthy British admiral of the period between Blake and Anson. Legend says that he began his career as a cabin-boy, and there was a family tradition of him swimming under fire with dispatches in his mouth. His most distinguished fighting achievements were at Barfleur, where he broke the French line of battle in 1692, and in the Mediterranean during the early years of Anne's reign. He took part with Rooke in the capture of Gibraltar and the battle off Malaga (1704), and commanded the naval forces which assisted Peterborough to capture Barcelona (1705). But returning to England after the unsuccessful attack on Toulon in 1707, Shovell's flagship *The Association* was wrecked with three others of his fleet on the Western Rocks of the Scilly Isles. Nearly 2,000 men were lost, and Shovell was one of them: cast ashore alive but unconscious, he was murdered, so the story goes, by a woman for the sake of his emerald ring. Buried first in the sands of Porth Hellick, his body was later taken to Westminster Abbey, where it lies beneath a monument which, as Addison pointed out, is peculiarly inappropriate to a man who seems to have been very much a blunt and rough sea-captain.

Peterborough, commander of the land forces at Barcelona in 1705, described Shovell at the time as 'brave if I may say to a fault ... and thinks that whatever is directed first must be begun, and when begun must be carried on what accidents soever occur, or whatsoever improbabilities come in the way'. Five years later Prince Eugene, leading the allied armies attacking Toulon, underlined this comment when he wrote of the two British admirals Shovell and Norris that 'they refuse to listen to facts, and adhere obstinately to their opinion that for good or ill everything must be staked on the siege of Toulon. Yet the pure impossibility of this is clearly before their eyes.' Shovell was, for whatever reason, an unlucky commander, whose achievements in battle were limited. His importance in the history of the British navy rests more upon the standards of discipline and skill which the evidence shows him exacting from his officers. In this sense Shovell was one of those who laid essential foundations for the naval triumphs of the middle years of the eighteenth century.

SIDDONS, SARAH (1756-1831), actress, was 'born in the Shoulder of Mutton inn at Brecon, the eldest daughter of Roger and Sarah Kemble: Roger was actor-manager of a travelling troupe. At first a lady's maid, she was soon being called on for recitations in the servants' hall. Like her sister, Fanny, she became an actress. At eighteen she married William Siddons, an indifferent player and personality, but a fair judge of his wife's talent. Her first success seems to have come at Cheltenham with a performance in *Venice Preserved*. From Worcester a clergyman wrote to tell Garrick that she had a fine figure and would do especially well 'in breeches parts'. (She was in fact prudish in such matters; when she played Rosalind she insisted upon appearing in a costume that was not recognizably either masculine or feminine – and somewhat ridiculous!) At Drury Lane in 1775-6, the then ageing Garrick gave her promising parts, including Lady Anne against his Richard III, but she did not excel and was not re-engaged. Never a modest critic of her own work, she blamed Garrick for her failure; in truth she was inhibited and had not developed the grand and passionate style of her maturity. In the provinces again she was coached by Mr Pratt, bookseller of Bath, and acquired the poise which she never thereafter lost.

The Duchess of Devonshire found her another opening in London; in 1782 she returned to Drury Lane and enraptured her audience in Southerne's *Fatal Marriage*. The theatre was packed for every performance of *Measure for Measure*, in which she played Isabella. Her true métier she found when she played Lady Macbeth. She refused, to the consternation of the management, to carry a candle in the sleep-walking scene, as Mrs Pritchard had done. But the audience were so engrossed by her performance that they did not notice. Now she could make her own rules and terms. Several of her brothers and sisters, notably John Kemble, followed in her wake, and with them arrived a new style of acting. Less natural than Garrick and his contemporaries, less vivacious than Edmund Kean in his heyday, theirs was a stately, declamatory manner, 'high tragedy', suited to Sarah's Junoesque figure. 'If you ask me, "What is a queen?",' said Tate Wilkinson, 'I should say, Mrs Siddons.' Yet Haydon said that 'she always seemed to throw herself on nature as a guide', while she told Dr Johnson: 'Sir, on the stage art does not adorn; nature adorns her there and glorifies her.'

She was a striking woman, with high-bridged nose and imperious mouth, the delight of painters and symbol of fashionable society. Reynolds and Gainsborough immortalized her on canvas. Playwrights and politicians were at her feet, among them Burke, Windham, Goldsmith and Sheridan – though the last found difficulty in paying her salary. Dr Johnson, whom she visited at Bolt Court, pronounced her 'one of the few persons whom neither praise nor money ... had depraved'. 'One would as soon think of making love to the Archbishop of Canterbury as to Mrs Siddons,' people said. She lived mostly apart from her husband and quarrelled bitterly with her sister Fanny. She was sharp in money matters and haughty back-stage: managers winced before her demands. She had children to support, seven altogether, though four of her daughters died young. By all accounts she was a

devoted mother, and would turn down invitations to dinners to be with them.

After the '80s she began to appear less regularly. Volumnia, Cordelia and Desdemona remained among the parts which she invested with that special character of which Hazlitt wrote: 'Power was seated on her brow; passion emanated from her breast as from a shrine. She was tragedy personified.' In 1802 she and her brother John took a share in Convent Garden Theatre. It was burned down and rebuilt, but the seats were more expensive; after reopening there were riots for nights and a clamour for the 'OP' (old price). In 1812 Mrs Siddons took her final bow as Lady Macbeth. She had grown somewhat stout, but still appeared occasionally in 'benefits'. When she died in 1831, over 5,000 people attended her funeral in Paddington church, a tribute to the years when 'to have seen Mrs Siddons was an event in everyone's life'.

Further Reading
Y. Ffrench, *Mrs Siddons*, 1936.

SIDNEY, ALGERNON (1622-83), great-nephew of Sir Philip Sidney, fought for parliament in the Civil War and was wounded at Marston Moor. He declined to take part in the trial of Charles I, and withdrew from politics after Cromwell expelled the Rump. In 1659 he returned to the Council of State. A sincere Republican, he refused to accept the Restoration, and remained in exile until 1677, engaging in a good deal of intrigue with Louis XIV and others against Charles II. After his return he was still viewed with some suspicion; his influence among opponents of the monarchy was considerable, and Louis XIV thought it worthwhile to include him among his pensioners. After the dissolution of the Oxford Parliament and the collapse of constitutional opposition (1681) a number of the leading Whigs turned to conspiracy against Charles II and in 1683 formed the Council of Six, of which Sidney was a member. He was among those arrested that summer in connection with the Rye House affair, and was tried before Jeffreys in November on a charge of high treason. Despite his able conduct of his own defence he was found guilty and beheaded on Tower Hill. Parts of his *Discourses Concerning Government* (published in 1696) which defended the right of rebellion were found in manuscript in his rooms and put in evidence against him. It remains uncertain whether Sidney was guilty either of the Rye House Plot or of the more general conspiracy to stage a widespread revolt of which that was a part. What is certain is that he became the most celebrated of Whig martyrs, with a reputation for a lofty and incorruptible Republicanism. The historian who a century later discovered in the French documents that Algernon Sidney had taken bribes from Louis XIV said 'I felt very near the same shock as if I had seen a son turn his back in the day of battle'.

SIDNEY, HENRY, EARL OF ROMNEY (1641-1704), supporter of William of Orange, came of a noble family whose loyalty to the Stuarts was notoriously limited: of his elder brothers, Philip, third Earl of Leicester, was a prominent Cromwellian, and Algernon was a Republican executed after the Rye House Plot. Henry, the youngest of the family, was more celebrated in Charles II's reign for his looks than for his principles. He was outstandingly handsome, and known as 'a terror to husbands'. A courtier in the middle years of the reign and appointed Master of the Robes in 1677, he entered the Commons in 1679 and supported the Exclusion policy. Charles sent him as envoy to The Hague, where he won the regard of William of Orange, and from 1681 to 1685 he commanded the British regiments in Dutch service. For most of James II's reign he kept out of England, but he was in close touch with affairs at home, notably through the wife of his nephew Sunderland. Early in 1688 he returned and sounded opinion for William. His rakish indolence veiled a talent for intrigue, and Macaulay's comment on him at this point – 'Incapable, ignorant, and dissipated as he seemed to be, he understood, or rather felt, with whom it was necessary to be reserved, and with whom he might safely venture to be communicative' – may be peculiarly apt. Certainly Burnet, who was in a position to know, implied that Sidney was the prime organizer of the invitation to William, as well as one of its seven signatories.

He returned to Holland in time to take part in the invasion, but he played an undistinguished role in public affairs outside the court during William's reign. He fought at the Boyne, and received Irish land grants, most of which were later resumed. During 1690-1 he was Secretary of State, with little influence on policy, and for a few months in 1692-3 he was a totally unsuccessful Lord Lieutenant of Ireland. He was created Earl of Romney in 1694, and was Groom of the Stole during the last two years of William's reign, dying of smallpox in 1704.

SIDNEY, SIR PHILIP (1554-86), poet, statesman and soldier, was the eldest son of Sir Henry Sidney and his wife, Mary, daughter of John Dudley, Duke of Northumberland. To his contemporaries he clearly resembled one of those heroes of Greek antiquity in whom all gifts and graces were congruously blended. Educated at Shrewsbury and Christ Church, and then travelling abroad for two years (when he was in Paris on the day of the St Bartholomew massacre), he was soon employed about the court and sent on missions to more than one foreign potentate. To us his public career must seem one of promise rather than achievement, but there is no gainsaying the extraordinary love and admiration which he won from all who knew him. His biographer, Fulke Greville, had 'friend to Philip Sidney' inscribed on his own tombstone, and Thomas Thornton wanted it similarly recorded that he was Sidney's tutor.

Sidney's heroic death was brought about by his refusal to wear armour on his thighs, out of bravado at the siege of Zutphen, fighting against Catholic Spain. Dying himself, he gave his bottle of water to a dying soldier. His death was followed by an astonishing outburst of grief from all, including the queen. Over 200 poetic elegies (one of which came from his devoted friend Spenser) mourned the irreparable loss of one who combined in his own life and character the qualities of the ideal Englishman.

Sidney was not only a man of diplomacy and action. His enormous pastoral romance *Arcadia* was written for the benefit of his sister in 1580-1, when his courageous protest against the queen's projected marriage with the Duke of Anjou temporarily estranged him from her court. He did not mean the work to be published (nothing of his was published till the 1590s), and on his deathbed he desired that it should be burnt.

The *Arcadia* is not now easy reading, being, as Horace Walpole harshly but not untruly called it, a jungle of pastoral, sentimental and heroical adventures, full of digressions and improbabilities, with much prose-poetry and tortuous convolutions. There are a few passages of rich beauty, but the main cause of the book's enormous popularity for a century and more was the newness of such a feast of romance and sentiment. Scattered among these letters – together with some disastrous experiments in classical metres – are some of Sidney's best poems, but his main contribution to English poetry was undoubtedly the sonnets which he wrote to Penelope Devereux, daughter of the Earl of Essex, entitled 'Astrophel and Stella'. Not all judges are agreed on the merits of these sonnets. Hazlitt, to the astonishment of Lamb, thought them 'jejune and frigid'; Saintsbury called the one beginning

With how sad steps O moon, thou climb'st the skies

the first perfectly charming sonnet in the English language.

The third work for which Sidney is known is his *Apologie for Poetrie* in reply to an abusive attack on the theatre by Stephen Gosson, an ex-playwright turned Puritan, who hoped to find Sidney on his side. Sidney replied with an eloquent exposition of his conviction of poetry's supremacy over all other studies, both for edification and delight. It is a work of much charm and considerable humour. The limitations of his judgement are shown by what he says of the theatre, where he insists on the rigid dramatic formalities which were shortly to be blown sky-high by Shakespeare and his fellows. But much may be forgiven the author of the famous and disarming declaration, 'I never heard the old song of Percy and Douglas that I found not my heart moved more than with a trumpet.' A critic who writes like that about poetry has the root of the matter in him.

Further Reading
J. Buxton, *Sir Philip Sidney and the English Renaissance*, 1987.
H. Morris, *Elizabethan Literature*, 1958, pp.58-66.
F. S. Boas, *Sir Philip Sidney*, 1955.
Mona Wilson, *Sir Philip Sidney*, 1931.
M. W. Wallace, *The life of Sir Philip Sidney*, 1915.

SIGURDSSON, HARALD, commonly called **HARDRADA**, 'the Ruthless' (1016-66) was King of Norway from 1047 until his death in battle at Stamford Bridge in 1066. He was a descendant of Harald Fairhair (the father of Eric Bloodaxe) and a half-brother of King Olaf Haraldson, better known as St Olaf. Olaf was defeated and killed by his rebellious subjects at the battle of Stiklestad in 1030. Harald, who was fighting alongside his half-brother, was wounded but managed to escape. He spent the following fifteen years in exile as a soldier of fortune, partly in the service of the Princes of Russia, partly in the famous Varangian regiment of the Byzantine emperors: in the latter employment he saw service in Bulgaria, Sicily, Asia Minor and Syria. During these years he amassed a fortune from booty, enjoyed all sorts of exotic adventures, earned a reputation as a commander famed for his bravery and ruthlessness and acquired a loyal band of followers. Accompanied by them he returned to Scandinavia in 1045 to lay claim to Norway. His nephew Magnus, who had been ruling Norway since 1035, was overawed and agreed to share the kingdom with Harald. The death of Magnus in 1047 left Harald as sole king. His reign in Norway was largely taken up with long-drawn-out warfare against King Sweyn Estrithson of Denmark, which came to an end in 1064.

The peace made in 1064 freed Harald for a project he had long been meditating: an invasion of England. In 1038 Magnus of Norway and Harthacnut, the son of Canute who was at that time King of Denmark and claimant to the throne of England, had made a treaty which stipulated that if either party should die without an heir his kingdom should pass to the other. Harthacnut had died childless in 1042. Magnus claimed both Denmark and England under the terms of the treaty and until his death in 1047 was regarded with apprehension by the English government of Edward the Confessor. Harald Hardrada persuaded himself that he had inherited Magnus's claim to England. In 1058 his son had raided England. Once peace had been made with Denmark Harald began to prepare a great invasion fleet which he proposed to lead in person. It was just a question of when the blow would fall.

In the event it fell in the late summer of 1066. Harald, his forces enlarged by the adhesion of Tostig who had been sent into exile in the previous year, crossed the North Sea and after ravaging the coast of Yorkshire sailed up the Humber and the Ouse. The ships were left at Riccall and the Norwegian army advanced overland the remaining nine miles to York. A Northumbrian army which attempted to block the way was shattered at Fulford, just south of York, on 20 September. Harald and Tostig received the submission of York and then withdrew a few miles to the east, to Stamford Bridge at the crossing of the river Derwent, to await the delivery of hostages. There they were surprised on the following day by King Harold of England, who had dashed up from the south with astonishing speed after hearing of the invasion. The battle of Stamford Bridge was hard fought but ended in an overwhelming English victory. Both Harald Hardrada and his ally Tostig were killed. Of the 300 or more ships which had brought the invaders a mere twenty-four sufficed to carry the survivors home to Norway.

Further Reading
M. Magnusson and H. Palsson, *King Harald's Saga*, 1966.

SIMEON, CHARLES (1759-1836), was one of the most influential evangelical churchmen of his day. His territory was a small one. In all his life he was but Fellow of King's, and Vicar of Holy Trinity, Cambridge which became a mission centre for the conversion of Englishmen to the Evangelical idea: intense belief in the saving force of the Gospel, in the necessity of personal conversion. The moral earnestness, the ordered lives of men who lived hourly under 'the great taskmaster's eye', the prayerful, regulated charity of the men who came under Simeon's spell, were to have a bracing effect upon English society.

Simeon's was only one voice among several. But his own standing and personality, the consistency of his preaching over a period of fifty-three years at Holy Trinity, the strategic importance of Cambridge, home of an earlier reformation, all contributed to his unique fame. His sermons are almost unreadable today, his church was sometimes the scene of crude riots, his efforts met with apathy and hostility. His style would seem odd to us and lent itself, in lesser imitators, to caricature. 'Mama, what is the gentleman in a passion about?' said the small girl who was taken to hear him. Not many of his disciples could obtain preferment, for Low Church and 'High and Dry' alike mistrusted their zeal. Bishop Marsh of Peterborough even invented a 'trap', eighty-seven carefully worded questions, for all who sought a living in his diocese. They could usually hope to impart their message only through proprietary chapels and afternoon lectures. But they won disciples and touched the moral life of the nation at every point.

'The deepest and most fervid religion in England,' said Liddon, 'during the first three decades of this century was that of the Evangelicals.' Some of the best of these, like Henry Martyn, 'the pious chaplain', and Daniel Corrie, first Bishop of Madras, acknowledged Simeon to be their inspiration and accepted his guidance. Simeon founded a trust to secure benefices for evangelicals and helped to found the Church Missionary Society. Without his preaching and example evangelical religion might not have been the force it was inside the framework of the Church of England.

Further Reading
H. C. G. Moule, *Charles Simeon*, 1948.
C. H. Smyth, *Simeon and Church Order*, 1940.

SIMEON OF DURHAM (*fl.*1100-50), precentor and monk of Durham Cathedral in the early twelfth century, has had ascribed to him some important historical works. The *Historia Regum*, a compilation of annals, legends and extracts from other historians covering the period from the seventh century to 1129, contains original material for the years 1119-29. It also preserves much of value from earlier sources, including, it has been argued, material collected in the tenth century of especial interest for the history of Northumbria and the claims of the church of York to ecclesiastical independence from Canterbury. The *Historia* is, therefore, potentially a text of great interest and originality for Anglo-Saxon history. Simeon's attribution as author depends on a reference in a later twelfth-century manuscript of the *Historia* by which time, in any case, several modifications had been made. To Simeon has also been ascribed, with no more certainty, the *Historia Dunelmensis Ecclesiae (History of the Church of Durham)*, a history of his diocese down to 1096. Even if the authorship of either book cannot be definitively ascertained, they both point to the growing interest in the past in twelfth-century monastic communities. Both try to demonstrate the continuity of the traditions and privileges of the community of St Cuthbert at Durham, despite the reality that monks were only reintroduced there in the late eleventh century after a gap of three centuries or more. In such works the past was pressed into service of the present. Simeon has also been linked, appropriately perhaps, with an account of the translation of St Cuthbert in 1104.

Further Reading
A. Gransden, *Historical Writing in England c.550-c.1307*, 1974.

SIMNEL, LAMBERT (1475?-1525), impostor, was the son of Thomas Simnel of Oxford, variously described as a joiner, an organ builder, a shoemaker or a baker.

Polydore Vergil records that Simnel was a 'comely youth and well-favoured, not without some extraordinary dignity and grace of aspect'. An Oxford priest, Richard Symonds, conceived the idea of setting up Simnel as Richard, Duke of York, the younger of the two princes murdered in the Tower. Later, Symonds decided it would be better to pass Simnel off as the Earl of Warwick, son of 'false, fleeting perjured Clarence', and hence nephew to Edward IV. This was a more difficult task because the Earl of Warwick was alive and in the Tower of London. It seems likely that Symonds was acting from the beginning with the support of the Yorkist leaders, and it may be that the plot is indicative of Yorkist sympathies in Oxford University, 'the home of lost causes'.

Simnel was sent to Ireland early in 1487 where the Yorkists were strong and where his alleged father (the Duke of Clarence) had been born. The Earl of Kildare, the uncrowned King of Ireland, welcomed him and he was crowned king in Dublin Cathedral, taking the title Edward VI and using as a crown a circlet of gold filched from a statue of the Virgin Mary. By now a full-scale plot against Henry VII was taking shape: Margaret, Dowager-Duchess of Burgundy, sister of Edward IV and implacable enemy of Henry VII, sent 2,000 mercenaries under Martin Schwartz to Ireland, where they were joined by the Earl of Lincoln (a genuine nephew of Edward IV) and Lord Lovell, a Yorkist noble who had led a rebellion against the king the previous year.

To meet the emergency, Henry VII had called a Great Council in February and had paraded the real Earl of Warwick in London in an attempt to show that Simnel was an impostor. He then marched out from London, unclear at first whether to expect an attack from the Netherlands, where Margaret was, or from Ireland.

Simnel's forces crossed from Ireland and landed at Furness (Lancs.) on 4 June 1487, marching across the Pennines and down the Fosse Way. They met the king's army at Stoke, a village near Newark and after a battle of three hours the king was victorious. This was the last battle of the Wars of the Roses. Schwarz was killed, as was Lincoln. Lovell escaped but then disappeared, perhaps drowned fording the River Trent in his armour, perhaps starved to death when hiding from his pursuers in the walled-up cellar of his house at Minster Lovell. Most authorities claim that Symonds was also taken prisoner at Stoke, but Cardinal Morton's register (in Lambeth Library) makes it clear that he was committed to prison in February 1487 and hence did not even go to Ireland with Simnel. Symonds apparently stayed a prisoner for the rest of his life. It seems likely that if Simnel had succeeded in defeating Henry – as well he might – the Earl of Lincoln would have been the chief beneficiary and have made himself king.

Henry VII behaved with much politic leniency towards the young and gentle Simnel. He turned him into his scullion, and Simnel later rose to be his falconer. When the Earl of Kildare and a number of Irish nobles visited Henry a few years later, Henry had Simnel serve them wine after a feast, an experience which brought a momentary pause to the jollity of the occasion, but which was soon passed off as a good joke. Later, Simnel was transferred to the household of Sir Thomas Lovell, where he died in 1525.

Further Reading
D. Scott Daniell, *The Boy They Made King*, 1959.
Polydore Vergil, *Anglica Historia*.

SIMON STOCK (*d.* 1265), an Englishman who became sixth Prior-General of the Carmelite Order of mendicants, embodies the twelfth-century tradition of anchorites, eremitic holy men and women, with the thirteenth-century's passion for corporate organization. Unlike St Francis, however, his vocation was dictated by a physical as well as emotional return to biblical precept. His life coincided with a brief moment when western Christendom encompassed the Near East and whose horizons were set at a distance only imagined in the two subsequent centuries. Yet his career also exemplified the retreat from that eastern dimension as the Order was transformed under his leadership.

Simon's origins are obscure. Possibly born as early as 1166, later legends attribute to him a noble lineage to compare, presumably deliberately, with the archetype of thirteenth-century Christ-like holy men, Francis of Assisi. Hagiographic etymology relates his cognomen, 'Stock', to his having spent twenty years in a tree trunk. What is more certain is that at some time in the first half of the thirteenth century Simon went to Palestine and joined a congregation of hermits on Mt Carmel. There existed a long tradition of Christian hermits and monks on the biblical site of Elijah's cell and his confrontation with the priests of Baal. In the early thirteenth century, one group of Latin hermits organized themselves under a simple Rule, dedicated to the Virgin Mary. Originally designed for the holy men living on Mt Carmel itself, after the Crusade of Richard of Cornwall (1240-1) the Order was taken up by patrons in the west, not least in England where land grants to members of the Order began in the early 1240s. It was at one of these estates, Aylesford in Kent, that the first General Chapter of the Order was held in 1245 and where, at another Chapter two years later, Simon was elected prior.

As prior, Simon confirmed the translation of the Carmelites from a group of hermits wedded to their eremitic tradition in the Holy Land into an international Mendicant Order. Symbolic of the change was the substitution (only finally accepted in 1286-7) of a simple white habit for the original, somewhat bizarre multicoloured habit, which, unsurprisingly, had caused some less than flattering comment. In 1248, Simon secured the approval of Pope Innocent IV for a new constitution for the Order and permission for brothers to settle in the west. Almost immediately, the nature and focus of the Carmelites shifted: they became extensive landowners in the west and significant members of the ecclesiastical community; and they began to attend the schools and universities at Oxford, Cambridge, Paris and Bologna. Such innovation met with resistance from traditionalists within the Order and from existing vested interests outside. But it conformed to similar developments in, for example, the Franciscans. To survive and to answer the demand of laymen for fresh outlets for religious patronage and spiritual vocations, simplicity, other-worldly idealism and intimacy with the sites of Holy Geography had to give way to more institutionalized and accessible temporal structures. This Simon's priorship largely set in motion.

SINCLAIR, SIR JOHN (1754-1835), first baronet, was the first president of the Board of Agriculture and the author of a great survey of Scotland. Learned, versatile, energetic and public-spirited, he typifies the 'improving' spirit of the age and adds a distinctive Scottish flavour. All his life he combined real and good achievements with a humourlessness and complacency – and a love of the grandiose – which invite ridicule. Walter Scott dubbed this benefactor of his country 'Cavaleiro Jackasso'. One of his first acts on inheriting, at the age of sixteen, a great Caithness estate, was to build a mountain road across Ben Cheilt. It was to be the first of many enterprises on behalf of people who lacked the spirit or means of self-help.

Sinclair was educated at Edinburgh, Glasgow and Oxford Universities. He read for the bar and entered parliament, first for Caithness, then for Lostwithiel. He was able to make good use of his position as an independent member at a time when Lord North needed all the votes he could muster – and secured the grant of £15,000 for famine relief in the north of Scotland. In 1785 his first wife, Sarah Maitland, died after nine years of marriage and he went on a prolonged tour of northern Europe. In 1788 he married again, to the daughter of Lord Macdonald; they had a large family. Pitt gave him a baronetcy, found him an awkward man to deal with but, in 1793, appointed him to be President of the Board of Agriculture. His *Statistical Account of Scotland* began to come out in 1790 and ran to twenty-one volumes. It was compiled from reports furnished by parish ministers and not its least interest is the picture it gives of this useful and versatile class of men. Sinclair first introduced the word 'statistical' into the language. The *Account* is a rich quarry for historians of Scotland; in its time it provided the material facts, local and often expert comment, for constructive measures of government. Anyone who wants to understand the entrepreneurial mood of the time could do worse than read Sinclair on the benefits of the steam engine or the potato. For him the industrial revolution was the moving of a new spirit. He rejoiced over the spectacle of 'a people naturally possessed of but few material resources, and living in a bleak and unpropitious climate, employing their activity, their constancy and their genius in triumphing over a sterile soil …'

Large areas of Caithness were cultivated on a 'rig and rennel' (or open field) system of a primitive sort. Feudal services survived, including 'thirlage' (thraldom). Sinclair encouraged the rotation of crops and sowing of rye-grass and clover. He introduced the Cheviot sheep which were to come to the aid of the landowner in many parts of the Highlands, with consequences which have been seen as unmitigated tragedy, or as a sad, but inevitable and even healthy change. For Sinclair sheep were only part of a larger scheme. He planted trees, founded a herring fishery at Wick, began to rebuild Thurso and established manufactures in those towns.

In 1798 he lost his office to Lord Somerville, who was put forward by Pitt after Sinclair, as the story goes, had suggested that the president would be a peer! There was much criticism of the way he had handled the county reports in England. But he returned in 1806 and remained president until 1813. By then he had accepted a lucrative sinecure, and left parliament. 'Sir John Sinclair has gotten the golden fleece at last', wrote Scott. Perhaps he deserved it. He was, in one foreign observer's view, 'Britain's most indefatigable man'. One of Raeburn's portraits depicts an upstanding, noble-looking laird in the uniform of his own regiment of 'Rothesay and Caithness Fencibles'. In later life he dwelt mainly in Edinburgh, proving, to his own great satisfaction, that the pen was mightier than the sword. The *Quarterly Review* struck a fair balance. 'While we smile at his harmless egoism, we are free to acknowledge the debt of gratitude we owe him'.

SIWARD (*d.*1055) was a Danish follower of Canute who was rewarded with an earldom in Northumbria. From about 1032-3 he was Earl of Deira (Yorkshire); to this was added Bernicia (the northern half of Northumbria) in about 1042. Very little is known of his tenure of office. He seems to have governed a restive province with fair success. He may have been responsible for extending English rule across the Pennines into Cumbria, where British, Norwegian and Scottish princelings had been ruling and squabbling since the early tenth century. Siward is best remembered – thanks to Holinshed and Shakespeare – for his exploits against the Scots. The most famous of these occurred in 1054 when he led an army into Scotland, defeated Macbeth and replaced him as King of Scots with Malcolm Canmore. In the following year Siward died and was buried at York in the church he had founded and dedicated to St Olaf (now St Olave's). He was succeeded as Earl of Northumbria by Tostig Godwinson.

Further Reading
W. E. Kapelle, *The Norman Conquest of the North*, 1979, may be used, with caution, for all that relates to the north of England in the eleventh century.

SKIPPON, PHILIP (*d.*1660), parliamentarian Commander, was a soldier by profession. Clarendon sourly put it that 'the man had served very long in Holland and from a common soldier had raised himself to the degree of a captain, and to the reputation of a good officer'. In fact, he was the son of a Norfolk gentleman, and had served as a volunteer with Sir Horace Vere's force, first in Germany on behalf of the Elector Palatine and then for thirteen years with the Dutch against the Spaniards. This experience was put to good use, for Skippon's principal role in the parliamentary army was as a trainer of troops. In 1642 he was put in charge of the trained bands of the City of London, and it was these men who turned back the king's army after Edgehill and bore the brunt of the fighting at the first battle of Newbury. Appointed Major-General of infantry in the New Model, Skippon contributed greatly to the training of the army which triumphed at Naseby (1645), where he was severely wounded. Yet the battle with which his name is most closely linked was the parliamentary defeat at Lostwithiel (1644), where he commanded the rearguard in the desperate retreat through the Cornish lanes to Fowey. Deserted by his superior, Essex, Skippon was forced to surrender, although, characteristically, he wanted the army to cut its way out. A parliamentary captain wrote of Skippon in this campaign 'never did I see any man so patient, so humble and so truly wise and valiant in all his actions as he'.

In the Second Civil War he was in command of London. Although he declined, like Fairfax, to have anything to do with the execution of the king, he served the Commonwealth loyally in various ways – as MP and one of the Cromwellian lords, as Councillor of State, as the Major-General in charge of London in the scheme of 1655; and he seems to have been one of the few soldiers who wanted Oliver to take the crown. He supported Richard Cromwell, but after his fall Skippon for the last time was reappointed Commander of the London Militia. He died some months before the Restoration. 'Stout Skippon' or 'Honest Skippon', as he was known, was a deeply religious man of no great subtlety of mind, yet of practical ability and outstanding integrity. He wrote several books of devotions for the use of soldiers: one of them was *The Christian Centurion's Observations, Advices and Resolutions*. After he was taken prisoner at Lostwithiel, the king urged him to change sides. Skippon replied that 'he was fully resolved of those Principles to which he stood to be for God and His Glory in which by God's assistance he would live and die'. The words are a commentary on the career of a man who exemplified the best sort of Puritan soldier.

Further Reading
C. E. Lucas Phillips, *Cromwell's Captains*, 1938.

SMEATON, JOHN (1724-92), engineer, was born in June 1724 at Austhorpe, near Leeds. His father, a successful attorney, sent him to the grammar school at Leeds; at sixteen he started work in his office, copying legal documents. Smeaton, who had shown interest at school in mathematical problems and worked at ambitious projects in his workshop at home, even forging his own iron and steel, soon abandoned the law. He was apprenticed to an instrument-maker and set himself up in the trade. In 1750 he read a paper on the mariner's compass to the Royal Society. Three years later he was elected a Fellow. In 1755 a visit to the Low Countries introduced him to advanced problems of canal, harbour and drainage works; he already had a large theoretical knowledge of hydraulic engineering.

Later in the same year he was commissioned, on Lord Macclesfield's recommendation, to build a new lighthouse on the Eddystone Rock in place of the wooden one destroyed by fire. Built in large blocks of dovetailed stone, rooted in the rock, Smeaton's lighthouse became famous and the engineer with it. It was a fine piece of engineering, only to be replaced in the late nineteenth century after dislodgement of rock.

In Smeaton's time, the specialized engineer was unknown. Like James Watt, his contemporary, Smeaton's field was necessarily wide. He was a practical man who tended to fight shy of theory. Thus, although he played some part in the development of the steam engine, modifying the valves of Newcomen's engine and providing it with a larger cylinder to give greater power to the atmospheric steam pump, he was sceptical about the idea of reliable circular motion from steam power. In November 1781 he told the Commissioners of His Majesty's Victualling Office that 'no motion communicated from the reciprocating beam of a fire engine can ever act perfectly equal and steady in producing a circular motion, like the regular efflux of water in turning a mill-wheel'. His waterwheels were, however, ingenious and provided a useful service to Roebuck's Carron Ironworks in Scotland.

He might have been better known as a canal builder had he enjoyed the patronage of a rich man – such as the Duke of Bridgewater. He built the Calder and Hebble Navigation, from Wakefield to Sowerby Bridge (1758-65): a river improvement in difficult country. His greatest work was, however, the Forth-Clyde canal. Despite the patronage of Lord Dundas, his comprehensive scheme (December 1764), involving an expenditure of £79,000, met with procrastination and criticism and involved him in quarrels with other engineers whose views were consulted – notably Brindley, who wanted a narrower canal. In the end Smeaton's plan was adopted, but work on the canal was suspended owing to financial difficulties and completed later by Whitworth. He also built several fine bridges, comparable with those of Telford in England, notable examples being at Perth and Coldstream. But his bridge over the Tyne at Hexham collapsed during a flood in 1782, his only certain failure.

Smeaton was the first man to style himself 'civil engineer', not merely as opposed to a military engineer, but also as a member of a distinct profession. He insisted upon high standards of ethical behaviour, was cautious, for instance, about accepting commissions, and took an active interest in the development of his pupils. In 1771 he formed a society, with a group of followers, to discuss engineering problems – the forerunner of the Institute of Civil Engineers.

Smeaton died at Austhorpe in 1792. He had spent much of his last years there, in the study and workshops in the tower which he had added to his father's house. Straight and plain in his manner, a Yorkshireman who spoke his mind, in some ways he seems to anticipate the virtues of the Victorians in his public spirit and strong integrity. Though an engineer rather than an inventor, it was well said of him that he could touch nothing without improving it.

Further Reading
L. T. C. Rolt, *Great Engineers*, 1962.

SMILES, SAMUEL (1812-1904), author of *Self-Help*, was the embodiment of Victorian middle-class values. He was brought up in Scotland, came south to Yorkshire, thence to London. He was an enthusiast for free trade, railways, state education and public libraries. Doctor, town councillor, editor of the radical *Leeds Times*, secretary in turn to the Leeds/Thirsk Railway, Leeds Central Station and the South-Eastern Railway, and thereafter to the National Provincial Assurance Company, he worked so hard that he gave himself a stroke. With characteristic determination he recovered the full use of his limbs, and found all the more time for his writing. This brought him fame. For Victoria's Golden Jubilee he was a guest at the Mansion House Dinner and in the front row of the gallery at the Westminster Abbey Service. On holiday in Italy he was greeted by Garibaldi. His books were translated into Arabic and Japanese, as well as the main European languages, and were extensively pirated in America.

He specialized in writing biographies of those whose achievements were the result of the virtues he extolled. Starting with George Stephenson, he went on to publish his *Lives of the Engineers*; but his subjects also ranged from a warehouseman who had become a millionaire to a baker in Thurso. All his heroes had pulled themselves up by their own bootstrings. The titles of some of his other books tell their own story: *Character, Thrift, Duty.* He had already proclaimed the message which stirred the Victorian public in *Self-Help,* published in the same year as Darwin's *Origin of Species,* 1859. 'The prosperity of a people must depend eventually on individual exertion.' 'The capitalist is a man who does not spend all that is earned by his work.' 'Convicted criminals have now had every consideration shown to them, but the question arises whether some consideration is not also due to those who are robbed.' Smiles hit out at the idle aristocrats and the idle poor alike. Those who lived on the labour of others were the enemies of society. Poverty was normally the result of improvidence. The Victorian middle classes agreed, and bought his books, 270,000 copies of *Self-Help* before his death.

Further Reading
Asa Briggs, *Victorian People,* 1954.

SMITH, ADAM (1723-90), the Scottish economist whose work was extremely influential in the nineteenth century, and who counted the younger Pitt among his disciples, was born in Kirkcaldy in 1723, a few months after the death of his father. As an infant of three he was playing on the doorstep of his uncle's house when he was carried off by a party of tinkers who might have destroyed or abandoned him, had they not been overtaken by the uncle and his friends. At Kirkcaldy school he was taught by a Mr David Miller, a fine type of the Scottish schoolmaster who teaches his pupils the supreme value of sound learning. After a period at Glasgow University from 1737 to 1740, Adam Smith won an Exhibition to Balliol College, Oxford. As a boy he was remarkable for his passion for reading and for the habit of talking to himself which remained with him all his life. At Oxford he spent a great deal of time translating famous French books in order to improve his own prose style. He showed, however, no marked enthusiasm for any one vocation or employment and he turned away stubbornly from entering the Church of England.

This was an interesting period in the history of Scotland. The ending of religious war and the pacification of the Highlands produced an age of prosperity and culture which made Scotland one of the leading centres of learning in Europe. In Edinburgh, where he went to live in 1748, Smith made the acquaintance of the great philosopher, David Hume. In 1751 he was elected Professor of Logic at Glasgow University and in the following year succeeded to the Professorship of Moral Philosophy. Like Montesquieu he was preoccupied with the growth of societies and institutions and observed the relationship between economic conditions and political changes. The means of producing a prosperous and powerful state absorbed his attention and much of the exploration which he did in economics and political science at Glasgow found subsequent expression in the 'Wealth of Nations'. He had a high reputation as a lecturer. He spoke without any great apparatus of notes and put forward his propositions rather hesitantly; then, imagining possibly some disbelief and criticism among his hearers, he lost his diffidence and argued with animation and force. His opinions were discussed widely in literary clubs and among the students, and his turns of speech and mannerisms were much imitated.

In 1759 he published *The Theory of the Moral Sentiments.* David Hume, who despised popularity, was appalled to see how universally well-received it was. Three bishops came to the publishers in one day to buy it. Charles Townshend, of whom Hume drily observed, 'he passes for the cleverest fellow in England', was impressed with Smith's writing and made plans for him to accompany the young Duke of Buccleuch on the Grand Tour of the continent. In 1764 began the Grand Tour which was to last three years. They visited Paris, Toulouse (where the working of the French system of provincial government was carefully observed) and Geneva. They returned through Paris and Smith was introduced to many of the leading thinkers of France, such as Turgot, Necker and Helvetius. Unfortunately he kept no journal, wrote few letters and destroyed before his death many of the materials which would have entertained future biographers. Turgot and the French writers of the period were, like Smith, concerned with discovering the basis of a happy human society and a way of improving it by regulation. Adam Smith was also fascinated by the French theatre and its lively comedies. He was always interested in the art of drama and once began an essay on the subject.

Having returned to Scotland, he lived quietly for almost ten years with his mother in Kirkcaldy. Hume thought a town the best place for a man of letters: 'You will cut yourself off from human society to the great loss of both parties,' he wrote. The fruit of Smith's withdrawn existence was seen in 1776 when he published the *Inquiry into the Nature and Causes of the Wealth of Nations.* In this book he advocated the benefits of mutual trading between nations and attacked the old 'mercantilist' theory that in trading matters all should be competitive and one country could only gain by another's loss. He was thus instrumental in persuading future statesmen such as Pitt and Huskisson to remove many of the old restrictions on trade. 'Free Trade' such as he advocated suited England admirably in the Industrial Revolution, when no country could compete with her rapid output of goods. He also criticized the old belief that the only valuable form of wealth was gold and argued that bullion was merely a token of exchange and that intercourse with other countries should not suffer because one country wished to keep its gold tightly locked up in a national money box. Each part of the world performs certain economic functions more happily than others. It is easy to make wine in France, difficult in Great Britain: Britain should not therefore try to make wine, but should concentrate on her metal industries and exchange hardware for wine. Both countries will then benefit. Underneath the economic argument lies a basic belief, which Adam Smith shared with his French contemporaries, that human nature is capable of choosing a good and unselfish course and that it is wrong for governments to interfere too rigidly in social affairs. Men, if left to themselves, pursue their own good; but they will add greatly to the common happiness by diffusing their prosperity. Just so a millionaire will give employment and prosperity to others if he takes up residence in a poor and derelict village. The arguments of Adam Smith were later quoted by unscrupulous employees and business men against governmental control and inspection in industry, but they distorted his views by using them in this way, just as the French revolutionaries distorted the views of the French thinkers with whom Smith had been in sympathy.

The Wealth of Nations is not merely a staid statistical study. It has a dry Scottish humour and an elegance that has something in common with those other two products of the age of grace and good sense which also appeared in 1776: Gibbon's *Decline and Fall* and the American Declaration of Independence. For two years after its initial appearance Smith lived in London, but in 1778 the Duke of Buccleuch, grateful to his old tutor-companion, procured for him a position in the Scottish Customs Board and he returned to Edinburgh where he spent the last twelve years of his life. His mother, though of very advanced age, came to live with him in town and his cousin, a Miss Jane Douglas, kept house. He collected a small library and lived the life of a retired scholar, always putting off the collection and publication of his papers. His mother's and cousin's deaths left him very isolated; his own death came in 1790 after a painful illness. A few days before he died he gave orders for the destruction of most of his incomplete work and his early lectures.

In 1787 he had been made Rector of Glasgow University. 'No man can owe greater obligations to a society than I do to the University of Glasgow', he wrote in his letter of thanks. 'They educated me, they sent me to Oxford. Soon after my return to Scotland they elected me one of their own members ... The period of thirteen years which I spent as a member of that society I remember as by far the happiest and most honourable period of my life, and now after three and twenty years' absence to be remembered in so very agreeable manner by my old friends and protectors gives me a heartfelt joy which I cannot easily express to you.'

Further Reading

I. S. Ross, *The Life of Adam Smith*, 1995.

I. Hont and M. Ignatieff, *Wealth and Virtue: the shaping of Political Economy in the Scottish Enlightenment*, 1983.
R. Koebner, 'Adam Smith and the Industrial Revolution', *Ec. H.R.*, 1959.
C. R. Fay, *Adam Smith and the Scotland of his Day*, 1956.

SMITH, JOHN (1580-1631), effective founder of Virginia, was the son of a tenant-farmer of Willoughby in Lincolnshire. He was twenty-seven when he sailed to Virginia, and before that date he had already had a lifetime's adventures, even if we may trust only parts of his own account. According to this, he had sailed to Italy with a party of pilgrims from France, been thrown overboard as a Huguenot and rescued by a pirate; fought for the emperor in Styria and killed three Turkish champions in single combat; been captured, sold into slavery and taken to Constantinople and Varna; killed his cruel master, made his way to Morocco, and reached home on an English naval vessel. By 1606 he was active in forming the Virginia Company, and in 1607 he was one of the 120 men who set out to the promised land. Arrested during the voyage on a charge of conspiracy, he was found to be one of the councillors named in sealed orders to manage the affairs of the colony, and was soon released. This was as well, for the evidence suggests that without Smith's leadership the colony would have collapsed through the idleness and faction of many of the settlers. By his resourceful direction and personal exertions, in building Jamestown, farming, dealing with the Indians and exploring, John Smith set Virginia on its feet during the rather over two years that he spent there as a young man. The most famous tale about him – that he was captured by hostile Indians and condemned to have his brains beaten out with clubs, but released on the intervention of Pocohontas, the young daughter of the chief Powhatan – is not well-authenticated, yet it is not inherently improbable. In two voyages in 1608 he explored the coasts of Chesapeake Bay and sailed up the Potomac and Rappahannock rivers. For the best part of a year (1608-9) Smith was president of the colony, and conditions improved substantially. His *A True Relation*, the first printed description of Virginia, was taken to England in manuscript in 1608, and its publication was of propagandist value; while his *Map of Virginia with a Description of the Country*, published at Oxford in 1612, was remarkably accurate and was still in use in the late nineteenth century. Smith himself set sail for England in 1609 after being injured in an accident. Although he actively encouraged colonization and took part in voyages to New England, he never returned to Virginia.

Further Reading

Philip L. Barbour, *The Three Worlds of Captain John Smith*, 1964.

SMITH, SYDNEY (1771-1845) was a country clergyman and liberal journalist, 'the Smith of Smiths' in

Macaulay's words; 'a diner-out, a wit, and a popular favourite' in his own words. Smith's life and letters offer valuable insights into the Whig spirit of his day. His honourable sense of duty redeems the coolness of a reluctant clergyman; his kindness and common sense improves the complacent doctrines of the Whig.

Smith was born at Woodford, the son of Robert Smith, a handsome, clever but restless man; his mother was of Huguenot extraction, her father having been a wine merchant in Languedoc. Sydney was unhappy at Winchester, though he became Prefect of Hall, but found New College, Oxford, where he was successively Scholar and Fellow, more congenial. He wished to be called to the Bar, but lacking private means, he entered the church instead and accepted the curacy of Netheravon on the Salisbury Plain (1794). The isolation of the place depressed him but he worked hard for his poor parishioners and earned the friendship of a sympathetic squire, Michael Hicks Beach. As tutor to the squire's son he went to Edinburgh where, 'amidst odious smells, barbarous sounds, bad suppers, excellent hearts, and most enlightened and cultivated understandings' he found what he needed. To the wit, assurance but essential seriousness characteristic of the best minds of their society, the Scottish Whigs added an earnest desire for liberal reform. Their critics saw also intolerance and dogmatism. Indeed the impact of the French Revolution, the Scottish love of debate, and the personal and professional rivalries of the 'Athens of the North' all helped to put an edge on political argument. Out of this ferment was born the *Edinburgh Review* (1802) when Smith, Jeffrey and Brougham decided to give voice and coherence to liberal views. Its explicit objective was reform at a time when, as Smith later wrote, 'the Catholics were not emancipated, the game laws were horribly oppressive, steel traps and spring guns were set all over the country ... Lord Eldon and the Court of Chancery pressed heavily upon mankind – libel was punished by the most cruel and vindictive imprisonments – the principles of political economy were little understood ... the enormous wickedness of the slave trade was tolerated'.

Smith wrote for the *Edinburgh* for twenty-eight years. Upon subjects as diverse as the game laws, the abuses of colonial administration, the spirit of 'fanaticism' in the church, and the woes of Ireland, he compelled attention. Criticism was all the more effective when it was rendered with grace and irony. The first paragraph, for example, of his article upon a report of the necessity for 'climbing boys' offers the reader the heart-warming picture of 'an excellent and well-arranged dinner ... the most pleasing occurrence, and a great triumph of civilized life'. We see 'the descending morsel and the enveloping sauce ... the rank, wealth, wit and beauty which surrounds the meats' and 'the smiling and sedulous host, proffering gusts and relishes – the exotic

bottles – the embossed plate – the pleasant remarks – the handsome dresses ...' The transition is abrupt. 'In the midst of all this who knows that the kitchen chimney caught fire half an hour before dinner – and that a poor little wretch, of six or seven years old, was put up in the midst of the flames to put it out?'

In 1800 Smith married Catherine Pybus; their match was to prove ideally happy. In 1803 they came south to London. Smith preached in fashionable chapels, lectured to appreciative audiences at the Royal Institution, and became a sought-after guest at dinners. Notably he was to be found at Holland House, the brilliant centre of Whig hospitality, where the memory of Charles James Fox was kept alive and his ideals and causes cherished for the day when a younger generation of Whigs could once more find means of expressing them in political reforms. Smith was devoted to Lady Holland, she, in her somewhat demanding fashion, to him. Lord Holland, as Smith's daughter later wrote, was 'able and willing to appreciate' Smith, whose 'society it is impossible to enjoy without loving as well as admiring him'. Smith fitted, shyly at first, but soon with confidence, into the world of aristocratic politicians. But he was not rich. He could not refuse the living of Foston-le-Clay which Lord Chancellor Erskine contrived to provide for him (1806).

The arrival of the celebrated wit and writer, 'fresh from London, not knowing a turnip from a carrot', at a Yorkshire village where there had been no resident clergyman for 150 years, was quaint enough. What makes the story pleasant and touching is the way in which Smith took to the country life and gave himself to the people. He resolved 'not to smite the partridge; for if I fed the poor, and comforted the sick, and instructed the ignorant, yet I should be nothing worth if I smote the partridge'. He made it his practice to visit London for two months a year. He farmed 200 acres at Foston, but continued to write. In 1807 the letters of 'Peter Plymley' attracted attention. Written ostensibly to his brother, a country parson, Plymley's vividly satirical letters exposed current views of Protestants towards Catholic Emancipation. Friends recognized Smith behind the pseudonym. Meanwhile he was starting allotments for the poor, befriending farmers and labourers and building himself a parsonage 'equal to any inn on the North Road'. His isolation gave him time to think. His contacts with humble folk enriched the humanity which seldom fails to shine through his most caustic writing. He confessed however to feeling lonely in the countryside. 'Flowers, green turf, and birds: they all afford slight gratification, but are not worth an hour of rational conversation; and rational conversation in sufficient quantities is only to be had from the congregation of some million people in one spot.' From Foston, in 1829, Smith moved to Combe Florey; he was already a canon of Bristol. In 1830 the Whigs gained office and Smith preferment. He was too unconventional to be made a bishop – even by Lord Melbourne. Instead he went to a canonry of St Paul's. There he preached sound sermons and diffused a spirit of benevolence.

Smith's religion of common sense and kindness had its limitations. It is hard to admire his scornful attitude towards missions. One may look in vain for any understanding of the finer motives of the clerical enthusiasts, high and low, whom he professed to despise. But much may be forgiven a man who, when asked his opinion upon a plan for laying a wooden pavement around St Paul's, observed, 'Let the dean and canons lay their heads together and the thing will be done'; or who said of Macaulay that he was like 'a book in breeches'. Greville said of Smith, on his death, 'he had the true religion of benevolence and charity'. Many of his friends must have hoped that he found his reward, 'eating pâtés de foie gras to the sound of trumpets' – for that, it was reported, was Smith's idea of heaven.

Further Reading
Nowell C. Smith, ed., *The Letters of Sydney Smith*, 2 vols, 1953.
Hesketh Pearson, *The Smith of Smiths*, 1934.

SMITH, W. H. (1825-91) was a successful politician, as well as the owner of a retail chain. This he developed into a national institution, by obtaining exclusive rights to sell papers and books in Euston Station (1848), and then gaining similar monopolies on most of the new railway lines. To fill his stalls with popular respectable books he went into publishing, and Smith's 'yellowbacks' spread through the land. All this made him a very rich man. Entering politics, he won John Stuart Mill's seat at Westminster as a Conservative (1868). He was no speaker – 'a good country rector reading a prosy sermon', commented a fellow Member – and many in his party condescended to 'the Bookstall Man'. But he was an excellent man of business. He saved the land along the new Thames Embankment from property developers; after a five-year struggle with the Treasury it was turned into public gardens. Disraeli made him Financial Secretary to the Treasury and in 1877 First Lord of the Admiralty. Audiences laughed at 'The Ruler of the Queen's Navee' in *HMS Pinafore*, but he won respect for his efficient management of the fleet during the crisis leading to the Congress of Berlin in 1878. He learnt to wear knee breeches at Windsor with the best of them. When he became leader of the House of Commons under Lord Salisbury in 1887, he had to endure the Irish at their most rampant: he died on the same day as Parnell. He was the first to use the guillotine in debates, which has made it possible for subsequent governments to get through their business. Yet the Pall Mall Gazette saw him as 'the most popular man that has led the House of Commons for the last twenty years'. This owed

something to his wealth, for he and his wife Emily, to whom he wrote every day when they were apart, entertained handsomely on their steam yacht, *Pandora*: but more to his kindly manner, warm heart, practical efficiency and persistent sense of duty.

SMITH, WILLIAM (1769-1839), geologist, a self-educated surveyor, engineer and collector of fossils, first obtained an insight into the nature of strata while cutting canals. He discovered distinctive groups of fossils in different stratas. 132 years after the zoologist Martin Lister had proposed to the Royal Society a map showing the different kinds of British 'soiles', in 1815, Smith published the first coloured geological map. On a scale of five miles to an inch, his map shows twenty different rock formations for which he used the familiar local names, like London clay. His companion work, *Strata Identified by Organized Fossils* (1817), illustrated the organic remains characteristic of each rock unit. His general conclusion, 'that each formation is possessed of properties peculiar to itself [and] has the same organized fossils throughout its course' was the first clear statement of the principal of faunal sequence: the basis for worldwide correlation of fossiliferous strata into a coherent system. He showed that there are two different kinds of order in nature: one, in spatial arrangement of rock units; two, in succession of ancient forms of life.

Smith's pioneering map-making was followed up by George Greenough, who gave up his seat in parliament (1812) to devote himself to geology, formed a Geological Society and produced geological maps of England and Wales, and, later, of India. Whether Smith's influence is gauged by the scholars and scientists who thronged his soirées, by the fashion for fossil hunting that made the specimen bag, with pick and hammer, near-essential accoutrements for a Victorian gentleman's country holiday, or by the steady erosion, long before Darwin wrote, of belief in biblical accounts of the creation, it can be seen to be immense. Not for nothing has he been called 'the father of British geology'.

SMITH, SIR WILLIAM SIDNEY (1764-1840), known always by his second name, was one of the more unconventional seamen of his time. He was a less stable character than the fictional Hornblower, but if Mr C. S. Forester had ever found himself short of material for his stories of the sea he need only to have borrowed from the career of Sidney Smith.

He joined the navy at the age of thirteen and served in the American war under Rodney. In 1793 he joined Lord Hood's fleet at Toulon, without appointment and in his own ship. When Hood was forced to evacuate the town Smith was entrusted with the demolition of the French fleet; the operation was botched and only half the ships were sunk, for which the blame was placed on the Spanish sailors who carried it out. Smith is next to be found operating off the Dutch coast in support of the Duke of York's expedition, 'turning every vessel he saw into an imaginary gunboat' (Bryant). His approach to war was that of an Elizabethan buccaneer with a taste for fighting against odds. In 1796 he was captured during a raid on Le Havre and imprisoned. The French would not allow exchange to a man who had so damaged their shipping. From his prison in Paris he managed to supply the British government with important information. In 1798 he escaped and secured himself a command of an eighty-gun ship, the *Tigre*. He quarrelled with most commanders, for he was an incorrigible individualist, quarrelsome and vain. But in 1799 he was sent with a small squadron and a roving commission to the Mediterranean. There he earned the fame he craved by his defence of Acre.

Napoleon underestimated the strength of the crusader fortress when he began its siege in March 1799. It was brilliantly defended by the émigré officer Phélypeaux and 3,000 Turks. But it would have fallen without the efforts of Smith and his squadron of three ships. He cut off Napoleon's small boats laden with siege stores and maintained the garrison's own supplies. At the critical point, as the desperate French launched their last assault, British sailors helped to man the breach. Napoleon, who had announced that the whole fate of the east hung on it, now abandoned the siege, leaving a third of his force dead. 'If it had not been for you English,' he was later to say, 'I should have been emperor of the east. But wherever there is water to float a ship we are sure to find you in the way.'

Without orders, on his own ship, Smith concluded a treaty providing for the evacuation of Egypt which his government had to repudiate. But his will to win could not be neglected by the admiralty: in 1805 he was promoted to admiral's rank. He was to be found wherever there was danger or service of an unusual sort. In 1807 he organized the timely evacuation of the Portuguese royal family from Lisbon. Later he served mainly in South American waters. He never experienced again the glory of his defence of Acre. His boastful panache – for a time he affected long mustachios – came perilously near to buffoonery. His greatest asset was imagination. He was an early advocate of the use of torpedoes against the French invasion flotillas at Boulogne. Fittingly, and typically, he was present as an interested spectator at the battle of Waterloo. In his later years he lived mainly in Paris, amusing himself with a fictitious order of 'Knights Liberators', whose aim was to liberate Christian slaves from Barbary, but who seem to have existed mainly in his correspondence.

Further Reading
J. Barrow, *Life of Sir William Sidney Smith*, 2 vols, 1848.

SMOLLETT, TOBIAS (1721-71), novelist, was born at Dalquhurn, Cardross, Dunbartonshire. His father died soon after and Tobias was brought up by his mother, aided by a small allowance from his grandfather, Sir James Smollett, a Scottish judge, MP and commissioner for the drafting of the Union. He was educated at Dumbarton School and at Glasgow University. He was then apprenticed to a Glasgow surgeon but at the age of eighteen he took the road to London, with a play in his pocket and a fervent belief in his own talents. Failure to secure the production of *The Regicide* put his hackles up. Garrick and Lyttelton were among the early targets of his sarcasm; in the course of his life he quarrelled with most of the literary figures in London. Touchy and opinionated, he could yet be affectionate and generous at times. He took a commission aboard the *Cumberland*, bound for the West Indies with Admiral Vernon, but after the failure of the attack upon Cartagena he went for a short time to Jamaica; he returned, in 1744, with Anne Lascelles, a planter's daughter whom he subsequently married, and a store of naval experience.

He combined a surgeon's practice in Downing Street with occasional writing, but without notice until the publication of *Roderick Random*, in 1748. Its deft loose framework, upon the plan of Le Sage's *Gil Blas*, gave him scope for characterization, and a brisk narrative, abounding in violence, earthy detail and rough humour. Dickens liked *Roderick Random*, but he is a shameless fellow who seems to exist primarily for the purpose of describing his adventures. Smollett lacked any discernible view of life and conduct; furthermore he sees men and women from the outside. But within the limits of the picaresque tradition the novel has great verve and one special feature, the English sailor. In the Hanoverian navy, Smollett found a rich field for the study of human nature; in such men as Oakum and Jack Rattlin he started the literary tradition of the British tar, just at the time when the navy was about to acquire its special place in English hearts. In 1750 Smollett travelled to Paris to find material for a new novel; the fruit of this was *The Adventures of Peregrine Pickle* (1751). Pickle himself cannot be admired: he is a bully, amoral, witty mostly at the expense of others. But in Commodore Trunnion, for all his prolixity, Smollett created a character of the first order. The simple, salty sea-dog shows that for all his faults, clumsiness of construction, prurience, the 'Smelfungus' side of him that Sterne so aptly hit off, there was more than knockabout in Smollett's art. He had a vein of comic genius. After failing to make his way as a physician at Bath, it is typical that he should write a pamphlet to show that Bath water was no more efficacious than any other – but equally typical that he should utilize his experiences for some of the best scenes in *Humphrey Clinker*.

After 1751 Smollet abandoned medicine and, settling

in Chelsea, at Monmouth House, devoted himself to a literary career. Here he was visited by Johnson, Garrick, Sterne and the hacks whom he installed in his 'literary factory', an enterprise for the publication of large works, in which he was to do the lion's share of the writing. This produced over £600 a year, but he was a large spender and debt and ambition drove him on. The *History of England*, ultimately in nine volumes, for which he said that he had read more than 300 works, was written in haste, in order to anticipate Hume, who was also engaged upon a history. That he could be generous is shown by the praise that he gave in his volume to Fielding, with whom he had quarrelled bitterly, and to Hume. As he became established, he mellowed somewhat. But he played little part in the social life of literary London. The preparation of Dodsley's *Compendium of English Voyages*, including Smollett's own account of the Cartagena expedition, the compiling of a universal history, a series of excursions into journalism, the editorship successively of the *Critical Review* (1756), the *British Magazine* (1760), and the *Briton* (1762) (the latter fated to become the chopping-block for Wilkes's *North Briton*) – all taxed Smollett's nervous energy. Meanwhile he did not abandon fiction. *The Adventures of Ferdinand, Count Fathom* (1757) is among the less successful of his efforts, but *Lancelot Greaves* (1760) has its admirers. Sir Lancelot and Sir Timothy Crabshaw are pale imitations of their great originals in Cervantes, and the fun is largely horseplay, but there are several good minor characters. There is no better guide than Smollett to Georgian England, not only in the caricatures that enrich his novels but in the description of places – a country estate in *Lancelot Greaves* or Bath in the period of its hectic building in *Humphrey Clinker*.

Smollett's life was not unadventurous. In 1759 he was imprisoned in the King's Bench prison for three months for impugning the courage of Admiral Knowles in the *Critical Review*. His health was broken by overwork and fretting. He had some of Matthew Bramble's crossness with the world, and perhaps, too, his essential good nature. It was a great blow to him when in April 1763 his only child, Elizabeth, died at the age of fifteen. With his disconsolate wife he embarked upon a long tour of France and Italy. In 1765 he published the account, carping in tone, but for all that a mine of interesting and entertaining information. His spleen may be contrasted with the more serene temper of the journal of the last voyage of the dying Fielding. He saw everything – inns, Roman Catholicism, pictures – with jaundiced eye. On his return he made a visit to Edinburgh, where he was received with acclaim. Revisiting Scotland, and Bath again, now as a patient, he gathered material for his next novel. But before this he delivered himself of a Rabelaisian commentary upon the political scene, as seen by an atom while in the body of a Japanese. The

Adventures of an Atom may reflect his disappointment at what he regarded as the neglect of his talents by successive ministries; it is Smollett at his most gross and unpleasing. In the same year, 1769, he left England to reside in a villa at Leghorn; here, in 1771, he died, but here, too, he wrote *Humphrey Clinker*. This work, conceived in a gentle mood of recollection, without the rancour and with less of the crudity of earlier works, is written in the form of letters; the story is straightforward and not overlong. The characters are more rounded than most of Smollett's. Matthew Bramble, his sister Tabitha, Winifred Jenkins, the Welsh maid, and Lismahago (original of Scott's Dugald Dalgetty?), are memorable. Smollett could, in few lines, create a type with a skill in which only Dickens, an admirer of his work, excelled him. The evidence of *Humphrey Clinker* is that Smollett died at the height of his powers. After his death there was published an *Ode to Independence*. The work is no greater than other poems that he wrote, but the subject is typical of his defiant temperament; its title makes a fitting epilogue to his truculent life.

Further Reading
Lewis M. Knapp, *Tobias Smollett, Doctor of Men and Manners*, 1949.

SOANE, SIR JOHN (1753-1837), architect, was probably the most promising figure in architecture at the turn of the century; after which he has to bear comparison with Nash, whose work was about as different from his as it could have been. Nash was an architect of enormous versatility, who preferred to work in the grand manner, to immerse detail in the over-all effect of mighty schemes. Soane by contrast was an artist of limited range – which, broadly stated, was the neo-classical – who nevertheless went to the furthest limits of that range, and, in so doing, produced some work of surprising originality and an almost twentieth-century timbre. It must be added that, although he was sparing in detail, it is the accumulation of clever effects of detail that makes the success of his best buildings.

Having an ambitious frame of mind, he advanced from being the son of a mason to being a pupil of George Dance II and Henry Holland, leading architects of the neo-classical school. He won medals at the Royal Academy, went to Italy on a travelling scholarship, and returned to England in 1780 to a modest diet of country-house design; from which he was rescued by his appointment in 1788 (on Pitt's recommendation) to take over from Sir Robert Taylor, who had died in office, the work of constructing the Bank of England. Now Soane seems to reach maturity in a step. The Bank Stock Office goes up. There is a whiff of Byzantine influence about it, but it breathes on the whole a spirit older than classical antiquity: in such a building Agamemnon might have dwelt. It shows the influence of the theories of the Abbé

Laugier, prophet of neo-classicism, who, writing in 1753, had recommended to architects the simple logic of the hut of primitive man, 'the model upon which all the magnificences of architecture have been imagined', and advised that 'one would never put anything in a building for which one cannot give a solid reason'. This plea for economy of means serves also as a comment on much of twentieth-century architecture – from which we deduce Soane's apparent modernity.

There followed the Rotunda in 1796: the unusual grooved ornamentation was perhaps borrowed from Piranesi's Egyptian patterns – Soane was to use it frequently. Much of his building at the Bank has been obscured by late additions, but the fine screen-wall, which is of a decidedly classical design, is largely intact, and the variety of his work on the Bank illustrates his eclectic taste.

Thereafter he built some exquisite country-houses: Moggerhanger, with its curved Doric portico (a dash of Regency), and Pitzhanger (now the Ealing Public Library), fronted by Ionic columns, each with an individual entablature and a figure atop. But his two most interesting buildings are the Dulwich College Art Gallery and Mausoleum, built with a bequest, and his own house at 13 Lincoln's Inn Fields. The Dulwich building, which has been reconstructed after wartime damage, is again primitive in concept; again it bears the grooved patterns; the mausoleum is central, flanked by alms-houses, the picture gallery behind; the proportions are striking, and the whole work is restrained and economical (and not only because there was little money to spend). Of the interior of his own house, of the ingenious methods of lighting and use of mirrors, of the highly personal decoration, much could be said; on the exterior, the pilasters grow out of the top of each other, and their capitals do not support entablatures, but mark the stages of vertical proportion. In this house the fastidious old man assembled the sculptures, the Hogarth paintings, the thousands of architectural drawings, the sarcophagus of Seti I, and the other *personalia* which he presented to the nation before his death and which can still be seen there.

He was Professor of Architecture at the Royal Academy from 1806 and was knighted in 1831. But he remained a retiring man. The uneasiness he felt in society is mirrored in his work – he often seems uncertain how far he can safely go; sometimes his proportions make the architectural equivalent of a social gaffe. He was not 'safe', but that was the price of his originality.

Further Reading
Dorothy Stroud, *Sir John Soane, Architect*, 1984.

SOMERS, BARON JOHN (1651-1716), lawyer and Whig, born at Whiteladies, near Worcester, the son of an attorney, was educated at Worcester Cathedral School, Trinity College, Oxford, and the Middle Temple, and called to the bar in 1676. His first big case, which opened his way to political as well as legal eminence, was the Trial of the Seven Bishops (1688), in which as junior counsel for the defence he put the constitutional argument against James with lucid force; and he seems to have been the leading draftsman of the Declaration of Right. William III rewarded Somers's services by making him Solicitor-General (1689), Attorney-General (1692), Lord Keeper (1693) and finally Lord Chancellor (1697). Throughout the period from the Revolution to the death of Anne, Somers was a consistent and energetic Whig, becoming one of the five Lords of the Whig Junto. Able, cautious, and eloquent, Somers was one of the few Englishmen to whom William III gave his confidence; it was Somers who persuaded the king not to return to Holland after the Commons voted in 1698 to disband the Dutch guards. Yet his intimacy with the king increased Tory rancour against him, and in 1700 William dismissed him from office because of the Commons' lack of trust. In 1701 the Tory majority in the Commons proposed his impeachment, mainly on the ground that in 1698 he had affixed the Great Seal to a blank commission authorizing unnamed plenipotentiaries to sign the Partition Treaty of that year, but the Lords declined to proceed.

In Anne's reign Somers was long out of favour: the queen was prejudiced, and in 1702 declined to have him sworn of her Council. No doubt it was prudence which led him in 1703 to make insincere offers of service at St Germain; like Marlborough, he was ready to insure. Meanwhile with Wharton he led the Whigs in the Lords, and he played a prominent and statesmanlike part in forming and passing both the Regency Act (1706) and the Act of Union with Scotland (1707). After the Whig triumph of 1708 Anne accepted him as Lord President of the Council and his courteous and grave manner soon led her to revise her opinion of him. As a member of the ministry Somers was a leading advocate of the policy of 'No peace without Spain' which prolonged the war with Louis XIV. He fell with his colleagues in 1710, not before he had indulged in intrigue to secure his own succession to Godolphin's place as Treasurer, and he did not reappear at the Privy Council until the day before Anne's death in 1714. Like all the Whigs, Somers welcomed the Hanoverian Succession, but George I did not name him among the Lords Justices who were to rule until his own arrival. Somers died in 1716. Macaulay described him as 'the greatest man among the members of the Junto, and, in some respects, the greatest man of that age'. This may be a Whiggish verdict. Nevertheless, he was unquestionably a man of outstanding mind who won his way by ability into the topmost ranks of the Whig aristocracy, a superb lawyer, a great constructive statesman, and a judicious patron of such writers as Addison and the historiographers Rymer and Madox.

Further Reading
W. L. Sachse, *Lord Somers: A Political Portrait*, 1975.

SOMERSET, MASTER JOHN (*c*.1395-*c*.1455) was one of the most successful doctors in late medieval England. Having studied in the arts faculty at Oxford University, he migrated to Cambridge to escape the plague and was Fellow of Pembroke Hall from 1416. He was Master of Arts and grammar by 1418, when he was schoolmaster at Bury St Edmunds grammar school and was already skilled in medicine. In 1423 he was practising medicine and surgery in London and by 1428 had graduated as doctor of medicine, probably at Cambridge. Before then he served Thomas Beaufort, Duke of Exeter (*d*.1426), whose executor he was, and it was probably as nominee of Humphrey, Duke of Gloucester that he became physician to Henry VI in 1427, accompanying him to France in 1430 and remaining with him until at least 1451. Somerset's other skills were quickly pressed into use as one of King Henry's teachers and he was sometimes described as the king's master from 1429, becoming one of the formative influences on the young monarch. Their intimacy outlasted the royal minority. In 1440 he was trustee of lands that King Henry intended for his new colleges at Eton and King's, Cambridge. He supervised the building operations for Henry VI's new foundations of Eton and King's Colleges and may indeed have helped shape them. In 1450 he was one of twenty-nine individuals that Cade's rebels wanted removed as a harmful influence from the royal entourage. He was alive in 1453 but dead by 1455.

Somerset's influence emerges in his rewards, which were quite exceptional for a royal physician and teacher. As he was married twice and not ordained, he could not be rewarded at no direct cost to the Crown with benefices or even a bishopric like William Waynflete, but received instead annuities and offices. His original annuity of £40 in 1428 was increased by £60 in 1432 and by £40 in 1439, making a total of £140 a year, but this was not all. He was appointed Chancellor of the Exchequer in 1434, Warden of the King's Exchange and Mint in the Tower in 1439, and in 1442 Surveyor of the King's Works at Sheen and Westminster palaces, the Tower, and Eton College. From 1439 he received £40 a year from Bury Abbey, from 1441 a pension from Merton Priory, and no doubt other sums from other bodies. Not surprisingly, he became rich – his pleas of poverty in 1449 lack conviction – and he acquired a house at Osterley in Isleworth and sufficient land nearby to qualify as JP for Middlesex from 1439 and MP in 1442. He built up a considerable library, had a reputation for charity, and founded a hospital for nine poor men, a chapel, and a gild of St Raphael, St Gabriel, St Michael and All Angels at Brentford End, Middlesex, for which he was licensed to grant endowments in 1446. There were no children from his two marriages.

Somerset was 'immensely learned and a polymath of his day' with interests embracing medicine, the arts and grammar. He reputedly wrote medical treatises, though none can certainly be identified today. His closeness to the king made him an obvious intercessor for learned people and individuals seeking royal favours. Hence, perhaps, the dedication to him in 1428/32 of a historical work, the second recension of the pseudo-Elmham, and hence too the fees paid him by ecclesiastical corporations. He was an executor of Duke Humphrey and was asked by Oxford University to secure the books promised by the duke. If he did anything about this, he was unsuccessful, but he gave the university a book and vestments on his own behalf. He gave substantial collections of books both to Peterhouse and Pembroke College, Cambridge. His was a unique career.

Further Reading
A. Gransden, *Historical Writing in England* ii, 1982.
R. A. Griffiths, *The Reign of King Henry VI 1422-61*, 1981.

SOPER, WILLIAM (*d*.1459), Keeper of the King's Ships, was already an established merchant of Southampton, when first recorded in 1410. What he was trading in then is not known, but later he had commercial contacts in Spain and dealt in wool with Italy, which he may even have visited. He owned at least one ship and was engaged in piracy or privateering. From the mid-1420s his trading activities declined, perhaps because he became a financier: certainly he employed sophisticated Italian banking techniques and mixed freely with the Italians. He also dealt extensively in property, driving a particularly shrewd bargain with the Southampton Franciscans, and improved his sites by building. He even leased the Southampton Watergate. However he made his money, he certainly became rich, acquiring lands in and around Southampton and leaving hundreds of pounds in cash in his will. Perhaps second in wealth among citizens of Southampton, he became a member of the ruling oligarchy, becoming steward (1410), twelve times MP from 1413-49, and mayor in 1416 and 1424.

In 1413 Soper was appointed collector of both the customs and subsidy and held office for thirty years. From 1418 he was surveyor, from 1420 keeper, and from 1441 Controller of the King's Ships. Soper's keepership coincided with Henry V's massive naval build up and Henry VI's shameful neglect. As the chief royal agent in Southampton, Soper served on commissions of all kinds and was appointed a verderer of the New Forest. Already old and unable to ride, Soper relinquished his offices in the 1440s and spent his last years in comfortable retirement.

If the extent of Soper's royal service was unusual, his

financial expertise and head for business were not, yet he was no merchant stereotype. He may have married Isabel for convenience, but before her death he was lover of her kinswoman Joan Chamberlain, whom he married on Isabel's death. Although their marriage was technically null, their adultery and its invalidity were not generally known. Soper's conscience, however, was troubled and he went to the considerable trouble and expense of securing papal absolution and a dispensation to remain married. Not surprisingly he provided carefully for his widow. He also sought the salvation of his soul. Before his death he built a marble tomb in Southampton Friary, reroofed and adorned the friary, and endowed a chantry and obit there. While his benefactions to the poor were unusually extensive, he was quite conventional in his desire that his obit should be marked by sounding Southampton's assembly bell and by the attendance of friars, mayor and other city fathers. His concern for status in death is paralleled by his lifestyle. 'Soper certainly seems to have used his wealth in what might be called the classic English manner – to build up his social position by obtaining the status that attached at the time to the ownership of land'.

He resided from choice at his country house at Newton Bery, where he maintained a substantial staff, a private chapel and chaplain, and horses and hounds for hunting in the New Forest. It was there in 1430 that he entertained the captain of the Florentine galleys so courteously that he did not wish to leave and there apparently that Soper retired, dying an esquire: a remarkable distinction at a time when it was normally businessmen's sons, not businessmen themselves, who achieved acceptance as gentlemen.

Further Reading
C. Platt, *Medieval Southampton: The Port and the Trading Community AD1000-1600*, 1973.
S. Rose, ed., *The Navy of the Lancastrian Kings: Accounts and Inventories of William Soper, Keeper of the King's Ships 1422-27*, Navy Records Society 123, 1972.

SOPHIA, DOWAGER ELECTRESS OF HANOVER

(1630-1714), who almost became Queen Sophy of Great Britain, was the youngest daughter of James I's daughter, Elizabeth, and Frederick the Elector Palatine. In 1649 it was rumoured that she would marry Charles II, but nothing came of it; instead she married Ernest Augustus, first Elector of Hanover. By the time of the Glorious Revolution she was the last surviving grandchild of James I, and the nearest Protestant heir to the English throne after Mary, Anne and their descendants, and the proposal to fix the succession upon her and upon the Hanoverian line was discussed at that time. In 1701, after the deaths of Mary and of Anne's children, Sophia was named in the Act of Settlement as the heir. She was a clever, witty and lively old woman, broad in her interests, international in outlook, a friend of the philosopher Leibniz; abler and less parochial than her son George, she much enjoyed her position as heir-apparent and had no hesitation about playing English politicians off against each other. Knowing that the Whigs on the whole were firmly tied to the Hanoverians anyway, she was ready to be cool to them and to encourage the Tories. She welcomed the project of a visit to England which English politicians out of office canvassed from time to time in order to embarrass the government; Anne regarded it with horror and contrived to prevent it. Although Sophia was thirty-five years Anne's senior, she died, aged eighty-four, only some three months before her in 1714.

Further Reading
A. W. Ward, *The Electress Sophia and the Hanoverian Succession*, 1909.

SOUTHEY, ROBERT (1774-1843), poet, biographer

and historian, was the son of Robert Southey, a Bristol draper unsuccessful in his business. He was brought up by an aunt, Miss Tyler, a haughty but not ungenerous person, who intended to adopt him but gave up the idea when he took an unorthodox path. A solitary child, he was discouraged from playing lest he should make himself dirty. He was four years at Westminster but was expelled in 1792 for an article in the school magazine in which he attributed the invention of flogging to the devil. At Balliol he read voraciously but left without taking a degree. At this stage he was a rebel of a not unfamiliar sort. He protested against the college rule forbidding the wearing of boots: 'To me it is a matter of indifference, but folly so ridiculous puts me out of conceit with the whole.' He wore his hair unpowdered to show what he thought of Pitt's powder tax. In a slightly aquiline way he was unusually handsome. All portraits catch his proud look, but his manner was gentle: 'An eye piercing with a countenance full of genius, kindliness and intelligence' was how his friend Cottle saw him.

At Balliol he was visited by Coleridge; together in 1794 they sketched out plans for a 'pantisocracy' beside the Susquehanna where men should find regeneration in the communal pursuit of farming. In the event Southey did not travel to utopia in America but to Lisbon, where an uncle was chaplain. There he learned 'to thank God he was an Englishman'. There seems to have been an idea that Southey would be ordained, but his inclination was at this time towards Stoic philosophy and republicanism. Since boyhood he had been writing. His aunt had been interested in the theatre and Southey often went to plays. The great epics of literature stimulated his romantic imagination: 'No-one,' he later wrote, 'had ever a more decided turn for music or for numbers than I had for romance.' Before he went to Westminster he was writing epics of his own, in blank verse. He now wrote in democratic vein. *Wat Tyler* was unpublished for twenty years and a great embarrassment to Southey when it did appear, unsanctioned by the author. *Joan of Arc*, an epic, was published in 1796 by Cottle.

Before going to Portugal he married Edith Fricker, sister of Coleridge's wife Sarah; on return in 1797 he settled to read law in London and to write for a living. His *Letters from Spain and Portugal*, lively accounts, encouraged Charles Wynn, his Westminister and lifelong friend, to support him with a small annuity. Southey repaid him by assiduous work. Two themes predominate in his literary life: epic and history. The former he hoped would ensure him a place with posterity, but he was rarely more than a commonplace poet, exceptionally fluent in the Augustan manner. 'Joan of Arc' won many admirers, however. Lamb enthused: 'On the whole I expect Southey one day to rival Milton. I already deem him equal to Cowper and superior to all living poets besides'. Poems like 'Thalabar' (1801), 'Madoc' (1805) (whose relative failure much saddened him), 'The Curse of Kehama' (1810), 'Roderick' (1814) and 'A Tale of Paraguay' (1825) have their merits. Coleridge referred to the 'pastoral charms and wild, streaming lights' of 'Thalabar'. A modern critic has said of Southey that if he had only 'written more of England, which he knew and loved devotedly, instead of dealing with remote subjects ... he might have been a major poet' (Simmons). These poems, as Jeffrey justly observed, depended too much on their colouring. They find few readers today.

Southey never lost his writer's soul or stooped to literary drudgery. His own enthusiasm dictated his choice of subject. He began his *History of Portugal* before his second visit to that country in 1800; only the *History of Brazil*, one section of the larger work, was ever published. He had accumulated too much material for even his busy pen. When he chose a manageable subject, however, he revealed himself a gifted writer of prose. Of his *Portugal* he wrote to Wynn in 1801: 'My heart and soul are in the work. I hope you will like the plain, compressed, unornamented style, in which I endeavour to write strength and perspicuity.' One may regret that he could not have chiselled from his vast quarry some monolith – a life of Henry the Navigator, for example. For when he did match style and subject successfully he was very fine. His *History of the Peninsular War* might have been a classic had it not been trumped by Napier's. His lives of Nelson and Wesley were among the best biographies of their day: brisk, well-proportioned and fair. Methodical and confident in his ability, inexhaustible apparently in his self-appointed discipline of writing, he stands out among his circle for his sense of purpose.

After a brief period as secretary to a Chancellor of the Irish Exchequer (1801-2) he went to live at Greta Hall, Keswick, where the Coleridges were already established. Here he supported Coleridge's family as well as his own. It was to find a way of describing Southey's steadfast presence that Coleridge conceived the word 'reliability'. Others had harsher things to say about him as the tame government bard, Peacock's 'Mr Feathernest'. He received from 1806 a small government pension and in 1813 he became Poet Laureate. In that capacity he made himself ridiculous by writing 'A Vision of Judgement' (1821) which described the reception of George III into celestial bliss and had the ill-luck to attract the sardonic wit of Byron. Byron said to Moore: 'To have that poet's head and shoulders, I would almost have written his Sapphics.' But in his journal he wrote more sympathetically: 'His appearance is *Epic*; and he is the only existing entire man of letters ... His manners are mild but not those of a man of the world, and his talents of the first order. His prose is perfect.'

Southey's conservatism was more rational and sympathetic than that of Eldon or Sidmouth. He denounced Malthus, exposed the abuses of the Poor Law. Indeed this high Tory, who was so upset by the 'madness' of the Reform Bill that he believed an outbreak of cholera to be a divine visitation on a wicked people, was also a strong and practical advocate of the rights of the poor. 'I incline to think there will come a time when public opinion will no more tolerate the extreme of poverty in a large class of the community than it now tolerates slavery in Europe.' He attacked passionately the 'new sort of slave-trade' by which workhouse children were sent off in wagon-loads to supply the new manufactories with cheap labour. It was sad that his political jeremiads invited – as they deserved – such ridicule, but his social policies were imaginative and fruitful. They influenced profoundly both 'young England' and the Christian socialists. Newman was one of his most ardent admirers. Shelley, the opposite to him in personality and ideas, found him a sympathetic friend.

He was devoted to his family but he could always find time for friends and visitors. This was real generosity, for time is the wealth of such a writer. He was a sympathetic reviewer and took care to help new authors; not for him the ruthlessness of a Jeffrey or a Macaulay. Even in controversy, as with Byron, he was more self-righteous than vicious. He accumulated a wonderful library and he liked to play with his numerous cats (his correspondence is much concerned with them). There are some delightful things in his occasional writings: *The Cattery of Cat's Eden* and his children's story, *The Three Bears*. He was only a spectator amongst the wild scenes of the Lakes, not essentially a Laker. 'You have been reading the great book of Nature', he said to John Wilson as he stood by the window admiring the view. 'Here' – he pointed to his library – 'are the volumes of men.' He described himself as 'one, at the foot of Skiddaw, who is never more contentedly employed than when learning from the living minds of other ages'. His knowledge was indeed vast: witness the contributions, from 1808 to his death, to the *Quarterly Review*. Faced with such an admirable life we are still left with regret that he spent so much time outside his best field. He excelled, biographies apart, in comment on the contemporary scene. His letter describing the ancient and beautiful Portuguese university town of Coimbra is as evocative as anything of its sort. His *Letters from England* (1807), purporting to be the translation of a Spaniard's account of travel in England, is a witty, observant, sometimes startlingly sharp documentary on English life and manners. It reveals a sensitive person with a gift for irony.

He had need of stoicism before he died. Three children died; his wife went mad in 1834, died in 1837. His own faculties were clouded thereafter. He married the poetess Caroline Bowles in 1839 for companionship and he toiled on to the end at his books, greeting his friends without knowing them. He died among shadows and there his reputation has remained. And yet where light has been shed there is revealed a good man and a fine writer of English prose.

Further Reading
G. Carnall, *Robert Southey and His Age*, 1960.
J. Simmons, ed., *Letters from England*, 1951.
J. Simmons, *Southey*, 1945.

SOUTHWELL, ROBERT (1561-95), Jesuit martyr and poet, was born towards the end of 1561. He was the third son of Richard Southwell of Horsham St Faith, near Norwich. His father was the illegitimate son of that Sir Richard Southwell who took a leading part in the destruction of the monasteries and whose unscrupulous and hard-bitten character is clearly revealed in the drawing by Holbein at Windsor Castle. The Southwells were cousins of the Cecils and the Bacons.

Robert's life began excitingly with his being kidnapped when he was an infant by a gypsy woman who was captivated by the baby's beauty in his cradle. The child was soon recovered and lived an uneventful life, the youngest in a family of three boys and five girls. In 1576 at the age of sixteen he left England with his cousin, John Cotton, and went to live at the English college at Douai, with the object of attending the Jesuit school nearby. Robert was at once attracted by the Jesuit order and applied for admission, which was refused him. He then moved to Rome and on 17 October 1578 he was accepted as a candidate for the order of the Jesuits. His two years as a novice were spent chiefly at Tournai; he became a full-fledged Jesuit in 1580, returned to Rome, took holy orders and became Prefect of Studies at the English college in Rome. From this moment his heart was set on one thing – to be sent on the English mission to minister to the persecuted Catholics in England. This

was certain to end in martyrdom, for the penal laws against Jesuits were appallingly severe. On 8 May 1586 Southwell set out for England with Henry Garnett. They landed on the east coast in July, but Walsingham was well aware that they had arrived and from that moment Southwell was closely watched. Under the assumed name of Cotton he lived for the most part in hiding in London, but he moved about secretly into Sussex and the north country, comforting the persecuted, celebrating the Mass and making new converts to the Catholic religion, besides strengthening the weak and the relapsed. He soon won the reputation of being 'the chief dealer in the affairs of England for the papists'.

In 1589 he became chaplain to the Countess of Arundel, with whom he had rooms in her house at the Strand. Much of his time was spent in writing treatises to encourage his fellow Catholics or protests against the policy of the government, which he managed to have printed and distributed, of course anonymously, but Cecil and Walsingham were highly suspicious. Robert continued this dangerous and courageous life up to 1592, but on 20 June of that year he was arrested at the house of a Catholic friend, Richard Bellamy, who lived at Uxenden Hall, near Harrow-on-the-Hill. The Bellamy family were staunch Catholics and had been put under arrest as recusants. Southwell used to celebrate Mass there and instruct the sons and daughters. One daughter, Anne, was the first to be made prisoner and she was examined by Topcliffe. She gave away the means by which the Catholic priests were hidden in the house. Topcliffe made all arrangements to catch the next priest who arrived: that proved to be Southwell and he was easily taken. Topcliffe wrote to the queen, 'I never did take so weighty a man, if he be rightly used.' He was imprisoned first in Topcliffe's house in Westminster, where he was brutally tortured. He was then moved to the Gatehouse where he lived in such filth and misery that his father begged the queen either to release him or let him be imprisoned in better quarters. The queen ordered him to be sent to the Tower, where he was allowed books and clothes and some friends to visit him. But he was thirteen times examined by members of the Council and he was tortured ten times, not by the rack, but by new forms 'each one worse than death'.

In February 1595 he was put on trial for treason, condemned to death, and on the 21st he was drawn to Tyburn, where he was hanged. He was saved from the final agonies of quartering by Lord Mountjoy, who refused to allow the hangman to cut the rope before Southwell was dead.

Robert Southwell was a man of singular beauty both of face and of mind. Strong in his religious faith, free of all rancour, with his eyes set always on the heavenly crown which he felt assured would be his, gentle yet firm, a poet, yet also a man of action, endowed with almost superhuman courage, he remains for posterity probably the most beautiful of the Catholic martyrs – only Campion can rank with him. He was a great Elizabethan poet and an excellent writer of prose.

Further Reading
H. Morris, *Elizabethan Literature*, pp.78-9, 1958.
Christopher Devlin, *The Life of Robert Southwell*, 1956.
R. Southwell, *An Humble Supplication to Her Majesty*, ed. R. C. Bold, 1953.
Pierre Janelle, *Robert Southwell the Writer*, 1936.
Dom Hilary Steuert, *Downside Review* LIV, 1936.

SPENCE, THOMAS (1750-1814) has been variously described as a forerunner of Communism, the Babeuf of England, or as a crank, a harmless and peripheral figure in the radicalism of his time. Babeuf plotted in 1796 the overthrow of the existing régime in France and the creation of a new society with community of property and absolute equality among citizens. The outlines of the conspiracy were revealed to English readers of the *New Annual Register* in 1796. Thomas Spence, an impoverished schoolmaster from Newcastle upon Tyne, had come to London in 1792. He was at once arrested for selling Paine's *Rights of Man*, but acquitted. He made a meagre living by publishing and selling tracts from a series of shops and, in the end, from a barrow. With his tracts he might sell saloop (a popular coffee-like drink made from medicinal bark) and, for a time, political token dies of halfpenny and farthing size. Place gives us a delightful description of this resourceful man: 'Not more than five foot high, very honest, simple, single-minded, who loved mankind, and firmly believed that a time would come when men would be virtuous, wise and happy. He was unpractical in the ways of the world to an extent hardly imaginable.' He invented a phonetic alphabet and used it for an account of his own trial in 1801. But, with his hand-bills and slogans – SPENCE'S SYSTEM was a familiar message on London walls – and his periodical *Pig's Meat* (1793-6), he did not appear to ministers to be as 'harmless and simple' as he did to Place. He was imprisoned for the second half of 1794 under the suspension of Habeas Corpus and again in 1801, after trial for writing seditious publications. Ministers saw him as one of the 'hidden hands' behind the popular agitations. What was his true role?

He seems to have developed his own distinctive theories of land nationalization as a young man at Newcastle. He regarded landlords as beneficiaries of the conquerors and robbers of the past. He urged social revolution. Parish by parish, the ownership of land must be resumed into the hands of the inhabitants. A quotation from his *Restorer of Society to its Natural State* (1800) goes far to explain why a wartime government was concerned about the activities of Spence and his friends of the Cock and the Mulberry Tree. 'The public mind being

suitably prepared by reading my little Tracts and conversing on the subject, a few Contingent Parishes have only to declare the land to be theirs and form a convention of Parochial Delegates. Other adjacent Parishes would immediately on being invited follow the example and send also their Delegates and thus would a beautiful and powerful New Republic instantaneously arise in full vigour.' Not only in the countryside, but also in the teeming back-streets of London there was distress enough to commend desperate measures. Spence had no large following in towns, and in the villages, of which he spoke so hopefully, his name was unknown. But he and his Spenceans provoked and sustained discontent with their chalk and charcoal. They agreed to organize themselves as loosely as possible, with 'field preachers', which made it hard for the government, as later for the historian, to detect them.

Spence's death was not the end of his ideas. He was buried with ceremony by 'a numerous throng of political admirers' according to a contemporary newspaper. 'Appropriate medallions were distributed, and a pair of scales preceded his body, indicative of the justice of his views … Upon Mr Spence's principles, a sect was founded called the "Spenceans".' After the Watsons, Thistlewood and their group had tried to turn Hunt's Spa Fields meeting into a rising of London, the Spenceans were given official recognition. One of the 'Gag Acts' of 1817 suppressed 'all societies or clubs calling themselves Spenceans or Spencean Philanthropists'. But when Thistlewood and his gang planned to assassinate the Cabinet (1819) we may be sure that they went beyond what the master would have approved. This was not how the millennium would come about, the Spencean dream:

> No more distress, all happiness,
> From landlords once set free,
> The bells shall ring, we'll dance and sing
> On Spence's jubilee.

Further Reading
D. Rudkin, *Thomas Spence and his Connections*, 1927.
Arthur W. Waters, ed., *Spence and his Political Works*, 1917.

SPENCER, CHARLES, 3rd EARL OF SUNDERLAND (1674-1722), politician, unlike his father, the second earl, who made himself indispensable to William III within months of deserting James II, was a man of fixed principles, the embodiment of the stiff Whiggery of the Glorious Revolution. With this went, however, a restless ambition and capacity for intrigue that made him distrusted by many of his colleagues. Few great political figures have inspired less affection than he.

His father's fame and knowledge of the business of politics ensured the intelligent son a good start. He entered parliament for Tiverton in 1695. By his first marriage he entered the Newcastle circle. It was his second marriage, however, to Anne Churchill, that did most to promote him. Although a member of the Junto and one of the inner group of Whigs, he might not have become Secretary of State if he had not been Marlborough's son-in-law. In 1705 he had done good service as envoy at Vienna with the task of mediating between the emperor and the Hungarian insurgents; in the following year the Churchills, who wished to be assured of solid support at home, pressed Anne to accept him. She had reason to dislike him for his avowed republicanism and frigid manners, and feared that she was 'throwing herself into the hands of a party'. Sunderland, awkward and proud, did not even try to please Marlborough: as Vryberg said, 'he does not hesitate even to gainsay his father-in-law's opinions when he thinks they are not right'. His dismissal in June 1710 was the prelude to the defeat of the Whigs in the general election of that year. He was rightly thought to be associated with the policy of all-out war and 'No peace without Spain' and the more extreme Tories wanted to prosecute him. He trimmed his sails a little and even voted for the Occasional Conformity Bill (1711) which he was only too pleased to see repealed in the next reign. He could afford to wait, however, for the accession of George I, upon whom his prospects depended. When George formed his first ministry he thought himself slighted by the office of Lord Lieutenant of Ireland. In August 1715 he slipped into Wharton's office of Lord Privy Seal, on the latter's death, and addressed himself to the interests of the king and Stanhope. During the crisis of George I's relations with Townshend he was conveniently in Hanover and able to misrepresent the actions of the ministers at home. Townshend was dismissed in December 1716. In April 1717 the ministry was reconstituted with Stanhope, First Lord of the Treasury and Sunderland, Secretary of State. In the following year he exchanged offices with Stanhope. He made little effort to dispute Stanhope's primacy, accepting the fact that he directed foreign affairs. He had plenty of scope, however, and enjoyed the confidence of the king, who had earlier mistrusted him as a covert republican, but came to appreciate his savoir-faire, fluent French, and the attention to the king's interests. The Peerage Bill of 1719, which sought to limit new creations – and failed – reflected his oligarchic attitude. He welcomed the scheme of the South Sea Company to take over, on favourable terms, the greater part of the National Debt, and shared therefore the odium which fell upon ministers when the speculative bubble collapsed in August 1720. Though he received an allocation of company stock there is no evidence that he was particularly corrupt in his dealings with the company, but he fell with those who were. Aislabie, Chancellor of the Exchequer, was expelled from the House of Commons in March 1721; Sunderland resigned office in the same month and Walpole replaced him. Sunderland

still had the ability and will to come back, though Walpole earned the gratitude of the king by the stout way in which he defended the court and screened the ministers (Sunderland himself was acquitted by 233 votes to 172).

Had Sunderland lived he, not Walpole, might have dominated the next twenty years; at least there would have been a battle of giants. But in April 1722 he suddenly died, of pleurisy, leaving behind the superb library that he had amassed at Althorp and an heir to carry on the titles of the Churchill family. He was not widely mourned for most thought him selfish and arrogant. His habitual expression was, in later years, glum and sour. Yet he was capable of deep feeling. He loved his wives passionately; he wrote to Anne, his second wife, wherever he was, by every post. Foreign diplomats, says Ranke, trusted him. He was a man of cultivated tastes, fastidious by the side of a Walpole or a Townshend. Of his talent there is little doubt. Hardwicke wrote later of his ability to 'remove from one office to another still retaining the character and influence of prime minister'. But he lacked that warmth of personality which makes political friendships live. To contemporaries he was remote, Jesuitical. To us there is something objectionable in his patrician insolence. He is the least appealing of the Venetian oligarchs.

Further Reading
J. J. Murray, *George I, the Baltic and the Whig Split of 1717*, 1969.
J. H. Plumb, *The Growth of Political Stability in England, 1675-1725*, 1967.
W. S. Churchill, *Marlborough: His Life and Times*, vols III and IV, 1933-8.

SPENCER, HERBERT (1820-1903) was hailed by Darwin as 'our great philosopher'. Today his heroic design and life's work, the creation of a synthesis of existing knowledge, is likely to be praised more for its sheer audacity, and its influence on contemporaries, than for its intrinsic value or relevance to the problems he confronted.

His father was a nonconformist schoolmaster in Derby. A boyhood episode is recounted in his *Autobiography* (1904). Aged thirteen, overcome by homesickness while staying near Bath, Herbert walked home, sustained only by bread and water, without sleep for two nights: 115 miles between 6 p.m. on Thursday and 3 p.m. on Saturday. It suggests the individualism, verging on the eccentric, that he was to advocate as system and express in personality. Offered by an uncle a place at Cambridge, he turned it down and embarked instead on a career as a railway engineer. With the radical tradition of 'a family essentially dissenting' and a tincture of German idealism, natural science would be his chief inspiration. Largely self-taught, he was so captivated that he saw its principles as the key to understanding society and charting its course. At twenty-four he turned to journalism. Keen to operate on the frontiers of knowledge and social action he tackled subjects like Mesmerism and universal suffrage. His main interest however, during five years (1848-53) as sub-editor of *The Economist*, and in his first book, *Social Statics* (1851), was the advocacy of an extreme form of laissez faire. He would allow the state no role beyond the protection of citizens' natural rights.

Friends at this time included J. S. Mill, G. H. Lewes and, famously, Mary Anne Evans (George Eliot). 'I have known but few men with whom I could discuss a question in philosophy with more satisfaction': his cool, not to say patronizing assessment of her rare mind answered those who expected them to marry. His own mind was committed, with the enthusiasm and approach of an engineer designing a great bridge, to the grand project for which *First Principles* (1863) laid the base. It did not exclude parallel work. His articles on the value of scientific education, reissued in 1861 as a book, *Education, Intellectual, Moral and Physical*, addressed an urgent need: they were translated into thirteen languages, including Arabic and Japanese. His main interest initially, however, was in evolution. He had worked out his own theory, that it was caused by the inheritance of acquired characteristics, when Darwin published *The Origin of the Species* (1859). Now he accepted the Darwinian thesis of natural selection, even coined the phrase by which it was most widely understood: 'the survival of the fittest'. The use he made of it, identifying the fittest with the best, adapting it to social theory, is significant. It underpinned his argument that all aspects of thought could be shown to form a coherent, closely ordered system, that progress could be relied to come through the application of science, tempered by philosophy. Evolution proceeded from the simple to the complex, its goal was individualism: progress was not an accident but a necessity. 'What we call evil and immorality must disappear. It is certain that man must become perfect.'

In 1860 Spencer received subscriptions for a comprehensive work, *The Synthetic Philosophy*. It would take thirty-six years to complete. Within the main structure, ambitious undertakings in themselves, were volumes devoted to first principles, and to biology, sociology and morality. To prepare the ground for *The Principles of Sociology*, from 1873, Spencer was writing a series, *Descriptive Sociology*. By his will, trustees were appointed to see it published. It was completed by 1934. By then others, like Bergson and Durkheim, had sought to follow him in the construction of grandiose intellectual systems. But the very specialization that he had anticipated, with intensive research, in the field, for example, of social anthropology, was undermining vital parts of his system. He had never won credence in academic circles. Nor has he since. Ernest Barker saw him as

'a brilliant generalizer from imperfect data which he had never really thought out'. T. H. Huxley said that Spencer's idea of a tragedy was 'a deduction killed by a fact', pointing lethally to the tendency of Spencer, as of other system-builders, to seek and select only what confirmed his theories. With his dome-like, bald head, fringed with iron-grey hair, and his rough, old-fashioned tweeds, talking to himself in abstracted state, as he appears in the memoirs of Beatrice Webb, ever pursuing what could not be caught, the elderly sage invites caricature. But she acknowledged his influence on her ideas of social reform and saw him as sad – not pathetic. His writings were voluminous and graceless. The fact that they were so widely studied is impressive evidence of the intellectual energy of the Victorian public. Even if he did not provide complete answers he tackled questions of critical importance and challenged his readers to think about the proper relationship between the individual and the state, and the role of science in determining social policy.

SPENCER, JOHN CHARLES, VISCOUNT ALTHORP, 3rd EARL SPENCER (1782-1845) is better known by the first title. He had it until the death of his father, who had been Pitt's First Lord of the Admiralty. His mother was Lavinia Bingham. He was Chancellor of the Exchequer in Grey's reform ministry and leader of the House of Commons during that momentous time. He was educated at Harrow, where Byron and Peel were among his schoolfellows, and at Trinity College, Cambridge. He used to talk modestly about his attainments at school and university, but he was notably conscientious, as in everything he tackled in life. At Cambridge he took a degree, which was not then obligatory upon a nobleman. He also incurred debts at Newmarket which encumbered his purse and property for the rest of his life. His fervent devotion to hunting and his rustic manners dismayed his parents. His father spent his years of retirement amidst the splendid paintings of Althorp and a library which he made among the greatest in the land (created by the second Lord Sunderland, in 1892 it went to form the nucleus of the Rylands Library in Manchester). He could not understand his son's reluctance to travel abroad or look at pictures.

Althorp began his political career conventionally enough, becoming member for Okehampton as supporter of Mr Pitt. From 1806 to his elevation to the earldom he was member for Northamptonshire. In that year he was given a junior lordship of the Treasury under Grenville and became devoted to Fox, then in his last year of life but still able to fascinate a young man of simple idealism. He attached himself to 'the Mountain', as Romilly, Whitbread and the advanced Whigs were called, and traces of the radicalism of this period remained for the rest of his life. In these early days, however, he took his hunting more seriously than his politics and he was a renowned master of the Pytchley. He made the happiest of marriages in 1814 to Esther Acklom; four years later he was left broken-hearted by his wife's death in childbirth. He remained thereafter lonely and unconsoled. It was typical of him and of feelings deep beyond expression that he at once gave up hunting. The squires of Northamptonshire thought he would never be so famous again.

Thereafter he buried himself in the study of contemporary social and economic problems to make himself a more useful politician. The knowledge he gained was to prove useful to him at the time of the Factory Act of 1833. It was he who proposed the amendment to that act providing for regular inspection of factories employing child labour – and making the act therefore a genuine protection to those for whom it was designed. Meanwhile he maintained a steady opposition to Liverpool's administration, though he gave qualified support to Canning. Well-informed and practical, this 'very model and type of an English gentleman', in Greville's phrase, Althorp was surprisingly Benthamite in some of his views. He was early a free-trader and always a champion of economy. His mind worked slowly, but his deficiencies as a speaker did not displease the House, since he made a point of being brief and direct. 'There is a better speaker than Althorp in every vestry in England,' wrote Campbell. When he was chancellor he rose to answer the Tory Croker's spirited attack, saying that he had made some calculations, which he considered as entirely refuting Croker's arguments, but had unfortunately mislaid his notes; but if the House would be guided by his advice, it would reject Croker's amendment. That they did so as a matter of course suggests respect for scrupulous honesty and sound judgement.

Althorp read his Bible regularly for strength and guidance as to his duty and policy. Out of struggle, solitary reflection and a conscientious habit of puzzling things out came a stock of wisdom on which his colleagues came to rely. He preserved links with radicals and liberals of the younger generation, men like Russell, Buller and Macaulay, whom proud Grey hardly reached. His radical affiliations, liberal sympathies and impeccable Whig pedigree combined to make him the central figure: after 1830 he was the man, above all, who preserved party unity in the hectic manoeuvres of the Reform crisis. As Chancellor of the Exchequer he was sound if unimaginative. As leader of the Whigs in the House he acquired a unique authority. Early in 1830, in a room in Albany, a group of about forty Whigs had asked Althorp to take the leadership, nominally but ineffectually exercised by Tierney, who had died in January. Peel suddenly noticed in the Commons that Whigs referred to themselves as 'we'. Althorp was more than a figurehead in this new-found unity of purpose and planning. His

kindness and accessibility made him the man in whom all could confide. Durham, Macaulay, even Brougham had to bow to his easy supremacy.

During the tense, hot, reform debates in 'the ill-ventilated, ill-lit, uncomfortable, sacred room' (Trevelyan), Althorp was a rock of steadiness and cheerfulness. It was in July and August of 1831, when the bill was being fought over in committee, that stamina and nerve were really tested. Of this session Macaulay wrote that he believed there were 'fifty members of the House of Commons who have done irreparable injury to their health by attendance in the discussions'. Russell was keen and game – but 'done up with fatigue'. The opposition was repetitive, pedantic, violent and obstructive, epitomized and led by the able but reckless Wetherell. Althorp remained so unruffled and good-tempered that even his opponents could not be angry with him. It was common knowledge that he was not in this business, 'where so much property, such great principles were at stake', for his own gain. He had no personal reason to be dismayed at the first defeat of the ministry. When a messenger brought news of Wellington's failure to form a ministry, Althorp was found 'in a closet with a groom, busy oiling the locks of his fowling pieces and lamenting the decay into which they had fallen during his ministry' (Lord Cockburn).

With people Althorp was usually conciliatory; on issues he could be obstinate. Against strong pressure and the temptation of a popular gesture he stood out for the maintenance of pensions to those who already had them, although he admitted that he had not the support of 'the great majority out of doors'. There was a principle at stake; contracts had been entered into. In Cabinet he was sometimes overruled by less liberal colleagues. But when Cabinet differences came to a head over Ireland, where he opposed the policy of coercion and believed that it was essential to try to work with O'Connell, he insisted upon resigning. Grey also resigned: he wanted to retreat to Howick. He persuaded Althorp to stay for a few months more to help Melbourne. In the autumn of 1834 Althorp took up his earldom and Melbourne at once went to the country.

'He came out of the fields and woods and to the fields and woods he returned.' The new Earl Spencer gave up politics for good and devoted himself to the nurture of his neglected estate, to stockbreeding and the general encouragement of agriculture. He became the first president of the Royal Agricultural Society and founded the agricultural college at Cirencester. The man who always opened his bailiff's letters before his political correspondence, Melbourne's 'tortoise on whom the world rests', had no qualms about refusing the lord lieutenancy of Ireland and the governor-generalship of Canada. He had once described his entry into politics as the great fault of his life. Yet there, for a few critical years, he achieved greatness. Macaulay said of him that he had 'the temper of Lord North with the principles of Romilly'. 'No-one', said Greville, 'neither of the Pitts, nor Canning nor Castlereagh, could govern with the same sway the most unruly and fastidious assembly which the world ever saw'.

Further Reading
H. W. C. Davis, *The Age of Grey and Peel*, 1929.
Sir D. le Marchant, *Memoir of Lord Althorp*, 1879.

SPENCER, ROBERT, 2nd EARL OF SUNDERLAND (1641-1702),

was a politician notorious for his pliancy even in an age when few men found it easy to be consistent in their political principles. Owing something in his early career to the backing of Charles II's mistress, Louise de Kéroualle, Duchess of Portsmouth, he first reached high office at the time of the Exclusion (favouring William of Orange, not Monmouth), and the king dismissed him in 1681. But he returned to favour and to office in 1682, and for the next six years was the chief figure in English government, and the leading proponent of a pro-French foreign policy. Somehow he persuaded James II to forget his support of Exclusion. As Lord President of the Council from 1685, manager of Crown patronage and of parliamentary business, and leader of the attack on the Church of England (for example, in the expulsion of the Fellows of Magdalen College, Oxford), Sunderland appeared to be the chief instrument of James's Catholic despotism; and in June 1688 he announced his own conversion to Rome. Yet he remained more realistic than his master, pressed for the summons of a parliament in 1687-8, and advocated clemency for the Seven Bishops. When William's invasion came, Sunderland fell into utter panic, and demanded the total reversal of James's policy, whereupon the latter dismissed him; and in December, when William's success was evident, Sunderland fled to Rotterdam. He turned at once, with a blend of great dexterity and boot-licking hypocrisy, to making his peace with William and to rebuilding his career. Lady Sunderland returned to England to mobilize influence; he announced his reconversion to Anglicanism, and wrote an anti-Catholic apologia, *The Letter to a Friend*; and although he was one of the few men exempted from the Bill of Indemnity and Act of Grace of 1689, by May of that year he felt it safe to return to England. Speaking of himself as having 'nothing to fear, little to hope for', regarded by others as 'the great apostate', he was wisely slow in attempting to re-enter public life. Not until 1691 did he take the oath in the Lords, nor until November of 1692 his seat. Yet earlier that year he was beginning to act as a confidential adviser to William III; and from 1693 to 1698, although he held no major office, he was 'the Minister behind the curtain' who organized ministries, managed parliament and dispensed patronage. In

1698 he resigned the Lord Chamberlainship following an attack on him in the Commons, and henceforward until his death in 1702, soon after that of William III, Sunderland's role was that of the elder statesman.

It was a strange career. The eighteenth-century writer Oldmixon observed that 'Lord Sunderland had a vast genius, but his conscience was of a like extent'; in 1688 the Princess Anne had described him as 'the subtillest, workingest villain that is on the face of the earth'. Insolent and impetuous as a young man, Sunderland over the years grew into a *grand seigneur*, self-confident, suave and urbane, occasionally breaking his smooth cynicism with savage sarcasm; a modern historian has spoken of 'the sinister charm of his middle years'. He was a great deal more than a time-server. His strength lay in his quick grasp and detailed knowledge of foreign affairs, and – as three such different kings as Charles II, James II and William III all found – in his readiness to take responsibility and in his skill as a man of business; Sunderland, it has been suggested, was the first of the great 'undertakers', the intermediaries between court and 'faction' who were essential to post-Revolution politics. No doubt he was fortunate, like others, in that William III was so little vindictive by nature; and that the political ferocities of the previous generation had died away. One of the greatest achievements of the Revolution of 1688-9 was that it was not followed by an orgy of revenge. Sunderland was a major beneficiary of this; yet it may perhaps be claimed that his own political attitude had done something to calm the violence of seventeenth-century English politics. For the rest, this highly intelligent man has a secure place in the artistic history of England, as a patron of literature, a collector of Italian paintings, and above all, the rebuilder (*c*.1667-8) in elegant fashion of the Elizabethan mansion of Althorp, the Spencer family seat in Northamptonshire.

Further Reading
J. P. Kenyon, *Robert Spencer, Earl of Sunderland*, 1958.

SPENSER, EDMUND (1552-99),

poet, was born in London, the son of a merchant. He was educated at the Merchant Taylors' School under Richard Mulcaster. At the age of seventeen he contributed a number of verse translations from Dutch, French and Latin, to an anti-Catholic work by Jan van der Noot entitled *A Theatre for Worldlings*. He went up to Pembroke Hall, Cambridge, in 1569 and took his BA in 1573 and MA in 1576. He may have visited Ireland or Lancashire on going down, but certainly by 1578 was secretary to Dr John Young, Bishop of Rochester, who was also Master of his Cambridge college.

In 1579 he obtained a place in the Earl of Leicester's household, where he became acquainted with Sir Philip Sidney. In that year he published his first major work, *The Shepherd's Calendar*, which he dedicated to Sidney.

This was a poem of twelve eclogues, one for each month, and each written in a different metre. A number of shepherds conduct philosophical and aesthetic discussions in the poem, which idealizes the pastoral, rural life. One of the eclogues was dedicated to the praise of Eliza or Queen Elizabeth. This work was a success and established Spenser's reputation as the great poet of his age. At about this time he married Machabyas Chylde.

In 1580 Spenser went to Ireland as the secretary to the Governor, Lord Grey de Wilton. For the next eighteen years, Spenser held a series of offices in Ireland. In 1582 he became deputy to Ludowick Bryskett, clerk in Dublin to the Council of Munster. In Ireland, Spenser bought and was granted land, becoming one of the 'undertakers', or colonizers, of Munster. From his Irish experiences grew a work which he published in 1596, *A View of the Present State of Ireland*. In this book, written as a dialogue, he advocated taking drastic steps to solve the Irish Question, spending money and sending troops to make Ireland a true English colony. Within a short time of writing the book, Spenser's diagnosis was to be proved correct.

While working as an Irish civil servant, or colonial administrator, Spenser was writing poetry at a furious rate, returning every so often to London to see his compositions through the press. His greatest work was the *Faerie Queen*, published in two stages in 1589 and 1596. This is an epic poem of six books, although the original plan was for twelve. It is allegorical almost to a fault, each character representing an historical figure or an abstract concept, or both. The Faerie Queen herself is Elizabeth I or the personification of glory. A representation of the Anglican church (Redcross Knight of Holiness) also features in the First Book, while in Book Five the defeat of the Spanish Armada and the execution of Mary, Queen of Scots are dealt with, along with the work of Lord Grey de Wilton in Ireland. It is unlikely that this poem is much read these days, except for examination purposes, but in Elizabeth's reign it was widely popular. It earned from the queen a richly deserved pension of fifty pounds a year: Elizabeth was a ruler who recognized talent, and also flattery, when she saw it.

Spenser found time for other verse compositions. In 1591 he completed *Colin Clout's Come Home Again*, in which rural and urban life were contrasted. This great classical theme was one of Spenser's obsessions. In 1591 he published a number of shorter verses, including *Prosopopoeia or Mother Hubbard's Tale*, which referred to Lord Burghley in unflattering terms. In 1595 he printed a number of love poems, *Amoretti and Epithalamion*, inspired by his second wife, Elizabeth Boyle, whom he married in about 1594, his first wife having died.

After seeing the second part of *The Faerie Queen* through the press, Spenser returned to Ireland, but was soon caught up there in the tragic events of the great rebellion of 1598. His castle at Kilcolman, County Cork, was destroyed and Spenser was forced to flee first to Cork and then, destitute, to London. Along with all his possessions, he had lost a number of newly composed poems when his castle was burned down by the rebels.

Within a few months he was dead, and buried at the expense of the Earl of Essex in Westminster Abbey. A later monument describes him as 'the prince of poets in his time', a claim which none would challenge. Dryden claimed that 'no man was ever born with so great a genius' and C. S. Lewis says that pope imitated him as if he were an ancient. Within the classical tradition, says Lewis, he is as secure as Milton, but 'his world has ended and his fame may end with it'.

Further Reading
H. Shire, *A Preface to Spenser*, 1978.
C. S. Lewis, *English Literature in the Sixteenth Century*, 1954.
A. C. Judson, *The Life of Edmund Spenser*, 1945.

SPURGEON, CHARLES (1834-92) was a famous preacher. Victoria's reign was one of the great eras of the sermon. Sundays were still days for home or church. The cities were growing larger, transport was improving, more people were educated, and conscience was stirring deeply as the squalor of the industrial world became more obvious. There were many fine preachers to draw the crowds, and Charles Spurgeon was perhaps the most remarkable of them. He was an infant prodigy. Chosen as Pastor of a small, thatched Baptist chapel at Waterbeach, near Cambridge, when he was only eighteen, he was invited to the pulpit at the Park Street chapel in Southwark, and despite his bumpkin accent and clothes, he soon became resident there. The congregation of eighty grew apace. Twice a day the roads nearby were filled with carriages and the pavements crowded with walkers; and the conductors of the buses north of the Thames were crying out: 'Over the water to Charlie.' When the chapel, which held 1,200, needed enlarging, Spurgeon moved to Exeter Hall, and thence, when even its capacity of 5,000 proved too small, to the Music Hall in Surrey Gardens. There he met with disaster, for on 19 October 1858, with 10,000 inside and as many outside, there was a shout of 'Fire', and a stampede followed which cost seven lives. Yet this gave him fame nationwide. For three years he went on using the Surrey Hall. He also addressed huge crowds out of doors, the largest being at the Day of National Humiliation after the Indian Mutiny, when 23,584 people came to hear him at the newly re-erected Crystal Palace. Then he raised the money to build the Metropolitan Tabernacle near the Elephant and Castle, where he preached to congregations of often 5,000 for the rest of his life. His sermons were published weekly from 1854 until 1917, and there must have been many like the farmer's wife at Blairgowrie, who sent her husband to market with a shopping list: 'And John, dinna forget Spurgeon.'

Spurgeon was short and podgy, and often dogmatically quarrelsome with his fellow Baptists. He lived in a large house, and his horses were so good that an Archbishop of Canterbury borrowed them for his carriage. But he never lost his preaching power. This was partly because of his skill as an orator. He had a lovely voice, used homely examples and could move audiences in a moment from laughter to tears, from joy to pathos, from heaven to hell. But it was also because his message was always Christ-centred, and came straight from his heart to the hearts of his listeners. With him, it was said: 'Dissent stepped out of the back streets and spoke to the nation.'

Further Reading
C. H. Spurgeon, *The Metropolitan Tabernacle, its history and work*, 1876.

ST GEORGE, MASTER JAMES (*fl.* 1261-1309), the master mason responsible for Edward I's Welsh castles, 'stands without a rival … as a military designer of the late thirteenth century' (Harvey) and was 'amongst the greatest architects in English history'.

Edward I's conquest of Wales was consolidated by the construction of fourteen castles, eleven of them royal, that ringed Gwynedd in north Wales with impregnable fortresses that were easily supplied and reinforced from the sea. Built regardless of expense in labour and money, these castles were of the largest size and most advanced design. They brought together three innovations hitherto found singly in Palestine and elsewhere: instead of keeps, they possessed curtain walls with massive towers of bold projection designed to enfilade attackers; their concentric rings of fortification enabled defenders on both walls to fire on the enemy, whilst the inner ward remained a defence of last resort; and their massive gatehouses were points of strength rather than weakness. In four cases they were associated with new walled towns like the *bastides* of southern France. These innovations first appear at the Tower of London in 1274 and at Caerphilly, under construction for many years from 1271, both of which may also be the work of James St George.

Master James St George originated at St-Georges d'Esperanche, a favourite residence of the Counts of Savoy, and was employed from about 1261 by Count Peter on his castle of Yverdon, which resembles the Edwardian castles in Wales. In 1273, following his crusade in the Holy Land, where the finest existing castles were to be found, Edward I visited the count at St-Georges, where he presumably met James St George. However that may be, James is generally credited with the overall design of all the Edwardian castles in Wales, although other masons on site implemented the plans

and devised the details. From the end of the first Welsh war in 1277, James was employed with Master Richard Lenginour on constructing new castles at Flint and Rhuddlan, where he made his headquarters, and may also have been involved in work at Builth and Aberystwyth. After the second Welsh war of 1282-3, he was responsible for building castles at Conway and Harlech and for the design for Caernarvon that was actually executed by Master Walter Hereford. The rebellion of 1294 resulted in the construction of his masterpiece, Beaumaris in Anglesey, which was completed only after 1316 to his original plans. From 1302 he was responsible for work on Linlithgow Peel in Scotland, perhaps also working at Kildmay Castle, in 1304 he was present at the siege of Stirling, and by 1309 he was dead.

As an indispensable expert, James was well-rewarded for his services. From 1284 he was paid at the high rate of 3*s.* a day, a pension of 1*s.*6*d.* being promised to Ambrosia his wife should she survive him, in 1290-3 he was constable of Harlech with total emoluments of 100 marks (£66.66), and in 1295 he was granted a manor worth £25 a year. Such rewards far exceeded the normal expectations of master masons.

Further Reading
M. Prestwich, *Edward I*, 1988.
R. A. Brown, H. M. Colvin and A. J. Taylor, eds, *History of the King's Works* i, 1963.

ST JOHN, HENRY, 1st VISCOUNT BOLINGBROKE (1678-1751), Tory politician, born at Battersea, son of a Whig rake and grandson of a Puritan admiral, was educated at Eton, where Robert Walpole was his contemporary. He entered the Commons as member for Wootton Bassett in 1701, and no politician in our history has risen so swiftly to eminence merely by his own abilities. Within twelve months he was a leader of the 'high-flying' Tories, and from 1704-8 he was Secretary at War. St John dazzled many of his contemporaries by his grace and eloquence, his wit and resource, and at this stage he was ready to learn from Harley in the Commons and from Marlborough, for whom he showed a genuine hero-worship in the years of Blenheim and Ramillies. But his views, alike of principles and of men, were never fixed. In 1710 he joined Harley in the task of destroying Marlborough and of ending the Spanish Succession War. Created Viscount Bolingbroke in 1712, he was the chief English architect of the Treaty of Utrecht in 1713. He was already on bad terms with Harley, now Earl of Oxford, and in 1714 he became the head of the ministry by persuading Anne to dismiss the older man. It was too late. In the famous words of his letter to Swift, 'The Earl of Oxford was removed on Tuesday; the queen died on Sunday. What a world is this and how does fortune banter us!'

George I dismissed Bolingbroke from the secretaryship even before he landed in England. Facing the certainty of impeachment, Bolingbroke fled to France, and in 1715 became Secretary of State to the Old Pretender, who in his turn dismissed him in 1716. Seven years later, by dint of supplicating English politicians and of bribing George I's mistress, the Duchess of Kendal, he was allowed to return to England but not to resume his seat in the Lords. His house at Dawley became for some ten years the centre of opposition, an opposition stimulated by his writings in *The Craftsman* from 1726 onwards. Completely failing to break Walpole, Bolingbroke gave up the struggle and withdrew to France in 1736. He devoted the remaining fifteen years of his life to writing, his most celebrated piece being his political essay, *The Idea of a Patriot King*.

Bolingbroke has one substantial political achievement to his credit, the Treaty of Utrecht. He recognized that the country needed peace, and he initiated and carried through the negotiations to obtain it. Yet even this was marred by the methods he used, above all by the 'Restraining Orders' to Ormonde and by the desertion of the Catalans; and his secret negotiations with the French and Britain's cavalier treatment, to put it in modern terms, of her allies contributed powerfully to the legend of 'perfidious Albion'. Bolingbroke himself paid the penalty of these methods, for they convinced the Elector of Hanover that he was a Jacobite and could not be trusted. The treaty apart, Bolingbroke's career was that of an unscrupulous politician whose lack of principle was not even excused by success. He used Marlborough and Harley to promote his own rise to power and turned against them when they had served his purpose. A freethinker and a notorious profligate who treated his first wife with harsh infidelity, he used his gifts to play up to the prejudices of the Anglican High Tories, and then abandoned them to the political wilderness by his flight to the Pretender in 1715. The real criticism of his conduct at the death of Anne lies not so much in the folly of his flirtation with Jacobitism as in the complete absence of preparation for a foreseeable crisis. The brilliant realist had no plan ready. Just before Anne's death he had even invited the Whig chiefs to dinner and sounded their support. When the crisis came his nerve failed completely, and he fled disguised as a valet.

He soon despaired of Jacobitism, for he was never allowed real power at St Germain. But his rash action overshadowed the remainder of his career. Besides keeping him out of the political fighting-line, it left him always vulnerable, and in particular it gravely weakened his efforts to destroy Walpole. He claimed after his return to be above party, to wish to set the nation free from the Whigs and from the 'Robinocracy'. But his only way of doing this was to fuse the various opponents of Walpole into another party, and in this he did not succeed, despite his victory over the Excise Bill in 1733. In practice there was nothing to suggest that the opposition was more than factious. Moreover, Walpole was a far shrewder politician than Marlborough and far tougher than the ageing Harley. So Bolingbroke's second political career was less successful than his first.

His reputation has depended as much upon his writings as upon his political practice, and with even less real justification. *The Idea of a Patriot King*, with its doctrine of the abolition of party and its emphasis upon service to an idealized Crown above all faction, was not original, nor was it notably influential. It is no longer possible to maintain that George III as Prince of Wales was brought up on it. The cult of Bolingbroke – of a highly-idealized Bolingbroke – was the creation of a nineteenth-century Tory, Disraeli. Further, his teachings were fundamentally out of touch with the political and constitutional evolution of his time. As a political philosopher Bolingbroke was shallow. It is unfair to maintain that he was also bogus, merely because the principles he developed in his writings were different from the practice which he followed when he was in parliament; the conditions of the 1730s were very different from those of Anne's reign. Nevertheless, the contrast between the two is extraordinarily sharp. We may perhaps defend the earlier Bolingbroke as a superb political tactician, or the later one by saying with Keith Feiling that he 'Harleysized, that is to say modernized, the whole basis of Tory thought'.* Both lines of defence are generous. He has remained something of an enigma to historians, yet it seems impossible to escape the truth of the much-quoted words of Swift's friend, Erasmus Lewis, when he wrote 'His character is too bad to carry the great ensigns; for the man of Mercury's bottom is too narrow, his faults are of the first magnitude'.

Further Reading
I. Kramnick, *Bolingbroke and his Circle*, 1992.
Sheila Biddle, *Bolingbroke and Harley*, 1975.
H. T. Dickinson, *Bolingbroke*, 1970.
Jeffrey Hart, *Viscount Bolingbroke, Tory Humanist*, 1965.

ST JOHN, OLIVER (1598?-1673), parliamentarian, came from the Bedfordshire gentry and was educated at Queens' College, Cambridge and Lincoln's Inn. He was imprisoned for a short time in 1629 on suspicion of sedition, and Clarendon, who describes him as 'a man reserved, and of a dark and clouded countenance, very proud', says that this embittered him against the court. Other factors brought him into the ranks of the king's enemies: he was a Puritan, he was in the Providence Island Company, and he was connected with Cromwell by marriage. As counsel for Hampden he won fame by his speech in the Ship Money case, and as MP for Totnes he was second only to Pym in the opposition in the Long Parliament. His appointment as Solicitor-General in

---

*Keith Feiling, *History of the Tory Party, 1640-1714*, 1959 edn, p.482.

1641 made no difference. He led the attack on Ship Money and was prominent in the onslaught on Strafford; arguing for attainder, he advocated the overriding of the normal process of law, 'for it was never accounted either cruelty or foul play to knock foxes and wolves on the head … because they be beasts of prey'. After Pym's death St John and Vane were the joint leaders of the war party in parliament, successfully plotting against Essex in 1644 and backing Cromwell and the army in 1647. In 1648 St John was appointed Chief Justice of the Common Pleas, and from this time onwards he was much less prominent. Whether this was because he disapproved of the proceedings of the Commonwealth or because he was genuinely more concerned about the law than about politics is not wholly clear. Certainly he took no part in the trial of Charles I. Although he approved the expulsion of the Rump, he opposed the Instrument of Government, and in 1657 he tried to persuade Oliver to take the crown as a constitutional monarch. A hard and fanatical Puritan, yet a lawyer who feared the perils of disorder, he backed Monck in 1660 and accepted the Restoration. Excluded from the Act of Indemnity, he lived in retirement until he went into exile in 1662, dying abroad in 1673.

Further Reading
The *Dictionary of National Biography* article is by C. H. Firth.

STAFFORD, HENRY, DUKE OF BUCKINGHAM

(*c*.1457-83) made Richard III king. He probably resented Edward IV's denial to him of the respect and authority due to his birth, rank and power. A royal prince as senior representative of Thomas of Woodstock, youngest son of Edward III, he was 'head of the wealthiest and most long established of the English magnate families'. Succeeding as a toddler, his marriage to the queen's sister included him in the Yorkist royal family. Hence his early majority in 1473 and his election as KG next year. Unfortunately an exaggerated notion of his own importance prompted his assumption of Woodstock's arms and his claim to the Lancastrian half of the Bohun inheritance. Edward's reluctance to lose £1,000 a year to his wealthiest subject was fed by the suspicion that the adolescent duke had designs on his Crown. Royal disfavour was only momentarily dispelled in 1477-8, when Edward acted as godfather to Buckingham's son and the duke as high steward sentenced Clarence to death. Lord Hastings's indentured retainers kept Buckingham out of the Midlands – he was not even JP in his home county of Stafford – and although the greatest Marcher lord he was excluded from the Council of Wales, which his Wydeville kinsfolk used to enhance their power at Marcher lords' expense. Blaming the Wydevilles and lamenting his marriage to one of them, he feared Edward V's accession would consolidate and increase their influence. He therefore wanted change at the top and had exorbitant demands of his own, which only Richard could satisfy.

Buckingham's role in Richard's revolution was crucial. He shared in the seizure of the young king, dominated the council, and organized Edward V's replacement by Richard III. Clever, eloquent and persuasive, he was in turns shrewd manipulator and honest broker, skilful committee-man and popular demagogue. He revelled in the panoply of power, presiding over the coronation and making himself high steward and constable of England, but the realities of power did not escape him. The coup was risky, took courage and involved bloodshed. Buckingham accepted the necessity for his erstwhile kinsmen to die. Besides honours, he received his Bohun inheritance and the rule of Wales, where he became chief justice and chamberlain of north and south Wales, steward of all the Marcher lordships and constable of fifty-three castles, and military commander of adjacent shires. It was a 'spectacular delegation of royal authority, entirely without precedent in the entire annals of the medieval English monarchy – and was never to be repeated'. Besides such greed and ambition even Warwick the Kingmaker does not compare.

Viceroy in Wales and the king's right-hand man, Buckingham had achieved all he could possibly expect. What next? Later in 1483 he rebelled, ostensibly in support of Henry Tudor, was defeated and executed. Modern historians find this almost inexplicable. For Thomas More the duke wanted the Crown for himself, but was persuaded to support Tudor instead. He had known Tudor as a boy, but it is hard to see why he should prefer him to Richard, unless he thought him easier to manage or hoped for the throne himself later. The risks surely outweighed any gains. If Richard had denied any requests, he was unaware of any rift, and anything he denied could hardly match what he had already given. Perhaps Buckingham feared a successful Wydeville-Tudor coup. In any case Buckingham disastrously miscalculated his support, for few followed him and Brecon Castle was sacked behind him, but it was the flooded Severn that isolated him. The main uprising of Yorkist and Wydeville gentry in the southern counties was too poorly coordinated and Henry Tudor arrived too late to succeed. Buckingham's overmighty phase was brief indeed.

Further Reading
C. D. Ross, *Richard III*, 1981.
M. A. Hicks, 'The Changing Role of the Wydevilles in Yorkist Politics to 1483' in *Patronage, Pedigree and Power in Later Medieval England*, C. D. Ross, ed., 1979.
C. Rawcliffe, *The Staffords, Earls of Stafford and Dukes of Buckingham 1394-1521*, 1978.

STAFFORD, HUMPHREY, DUKE OF BUCKINGHAM

(1402-60) strove to moderate the personal antagonisms that escalated into the Wars of the Roses. He was only a baby when he succeeded his father Edmund, Earl of Stafford (*d.*1403), a Midland magnate with a long tradition of service to the Crown. His mother Anne (*d.*1438), daughter of Thomas of Woodstock (*d.*1397) and granddaughter of Edward III, brought him half the great Bohun inheritance mainly in Wales, the earldoms of Buckingham, Hereford and Northampton, and four Bourchier half-brothers. He was a prince of the blood royal and with £6,000 a year 'among the richest and most powerful landowners in England', scarcely second to Richard, Duke of York. He married Anne, daughter of Ralph, Earl of Westmorland and Joan Beaufort, legitimated bastard of John of Gaunt and half-sister of Henry IV. Such wealth, power and connections explain his election as KG in 1429 and his creation in 1444 as Duke of Buckingham with precedence over all future dukes not the sons of kings. Charles VII of France seriously considered a match between his daughter and Buckingham's son.

The duke's exceptional services during the 1450s built on those of preceding decades. Already in France in 1420, he accompanied Henry VI there in 1430, contributing to English consolidation as lieutenant-general of Normandy, governor of Paris, and constable of France. He went on embassies and was captain of Calais in 1442-51. He was a royal councillor in England from 1424 and attended fairly assiduously. In reward for such services he was created Count of Perche in 1431, controlled Tutbury honour from 1435, was granted Penshurst from 1447 and was appointed warden of the Cinque Ports from 1450. Perche brought in an estimated £533.66 'in time of peace', but he was owed £19,395 for Calais in 1449, a time when his Welsh income was declining. Unlike the Duke of York, who faced similar problems, Buckingham surmounted them without resort to crisis measures. His high regard amongst contemporaries reflects the industry and capacity he brought to his military and administrative responsibilities, even if he did lack the 'necessary qualities ever to become a great statesman and leader'. If he avoided commitment to Beaufort or Gloucester in the 1420s and '30s, he shared in the trials of Joan of Arc and Eleanor Cobham and the arrest of Gloucester. He quarrelled with other noblemen and arbitrarily imprisoned and despoiled the Montford family. His reputation was not without blemish.

Buckingham was related to all important parties in the 1450s – the king and queen, York and Somerset, the Nevilles and Bourchiers – but refused to join any faction. In 1455, on the eve of the first battle of St Albans, he gave priority to his allegiance and the maintenance of royal authority:

> We wish the whole world to know that we have not come here to support any one person or for any other cause but only to be in company with the king our sovereign lord, as by right we are bound to do.

His refusal to surrender the Duke of Somerset did not mean he thought him right. He stood by the king during Cade's rebellion and the Dartford fiasco, but he sought to prevent extreme measures against York. When the king was mad, Buckingham backed York and his Bourchier half-brothers held ministerial office. He acted as surety for both parties. Loyalty and even-handedness, however, became ever more difficult. In 1459 he stood by the court both at Ludford and the ensuing Coventry parliament, when York was defeated and condemned. In 1460 he was one of those deliberately eliminated by the Yorkists at the Battle of Northampton. The time for principled moderation and reconciliation had passed.

Further Reading
R. A. Griffiths, *The Reign of King Henry VI 1422-61*, 1981.
C. Rawcliffe, *The Staffords, Earls of Stafford and Dukes of Buckingham 1394-1521*, 1978.

STANDISH, HENRY (*d.*1535), Bishop of St Asaph, died in 1535; the date of his birth is unknown. Very little is known of his early life except that he studied at both Oxford and Cambridge. He became warden of the Franciscan house, Greyfriars, in London. Somehow he won the favour of Henry VIII and became a frequent preacher at court. In 1515 he suddenly leaped into fame as the most popular man in London.

The arrest of Dr Horsey, the Bishop of London's chancellor, on a charge of murdering Richard Hunne put the bishop and the ecclesiastics in a difficult position. If Horsey were brought to trial, he would almost certainly be found guilty. It was of paramount importance to prevent his being tried. FitzJames, the bishop, very rashly determined to try to save him by confusing the issue. Parliament was just about to assemble and would be very anti-clerical. The bishop appointed Richard Kidderminster, Abbot of Winchcombe, to preach at St Paul's, and he instructed him to defend the thesis that no cleric could be cited in any secular court. The sermon raised violent passions; it was criticized in parliament, where the Commons were engaged in trying to re-enact a temporary law of 1512 which subjected criminous clerks in minor orders to the secular courts. An appeal was made to the king, who agreed to a debate at Blackfriars at which he would be present (10 March 1515). Henry Standish defended the secular view with much success. The City of London showed its gratitude by repaving the church of the Greyfriars. Standish was summoned before Convocation and he appealed to the king for protection. A second debate at Blackfriars was held, in the presence of Henry VIII, where Standish again defended his point of view. The judges asserted that in citing Standish before them, Convocation was guilty of Praemunire.

A final meeting was held at Baynard's Castle at which the king arranged a compromise; charges against both Standish and Horsey were dropped; the king's dominance over the church in England was asserted and the parliamentary attack on clerical privileges was withdrawn.

Standish was soon rewarded by the king with the bishopric of St Asaph (1518). He remained popular at court and was employed on several less important diplomatic missions, although Wolsey blocked his promotion in the church. At one point he quarrelled with Erasmus, of whose translation of the New Testament he disapproved. He was one of Catherine of Aragon's counsellors in the matter of the divorce, but she never trusted him, not unnaturally thinking that he was really on the king's side. He took part in the coronation of Anne Boleyn and he was one of the three bishops who consecrated Cranmer Archbishop of Canterbury. He died on 9 June 1535, at an advanced but unknown age.

Further Reading
H. Maynard Smith, *Pre-Reformation England*, 1938.
A. F. Pollard, *Wolsey*, 1929.

STANDISH, CHARLES, 3rd EARL STANHOPE

(1753-1816), politician and scientist, was a man of diverse talents and interests who could be relied upon to be original in any situation. Egocentric, sometimes ridiculous, callous in his private life, in public affairs ranging from the perceptive to the perverse, his inventive talents amounted to genius, even if they were often misapplied. Educated largely at Geneva, where his parents moved when he was ten, Lord Mahon, as he was styled until he inherited the earldom in 1786, early displayed radical inclinations. In 1780 he harangued the Gordon rioters and advocated the end of hostilities in America. Although he sat for the rotten borough of Chipping Wycombe, by the patronage of Shelburne, he persistently advocated parliamentary reform. He attacked Pitt's Sinking Fund with sound reasoning. He was married to Pitt's aunt, but became permanently estranged from the family after the French Revolution. 'Citizen Stanhope' had an excessive zeal for the principles of the revolution and imposed them upon his unhappy family. Lady Hester, his daughter, like the others was disinherited: she became housekeeper to Pitt until his death; later she displayed all her father's pride and eccentricity, settling eventually to the life of an Arab sovereign among the Druses of Mount Lebanon.

It is easy to conclude that Stanhope was a little mad. He lent himself to caricature and was a favourite subject of Gillray. He undoubtedly enjoyed the notoriety he acquired through his advocacy of friendship with the French republic and the speeches that he made in the House of Commons upon this theme. His London house was fired by rioters in 1794. But his inventions were remarkable. Around 1777 he had constructed two calculating machines. He patented steam vessels, in 1790 and 1807, which were adopted by the admiralty. He invented

a microscope lens and his process of stereotyping was acquired by the Clarendon Press in 1805. In 1811, after some years in which he had retired from parliament in dudgeon, he had a success with his Gold Coin and Banknote Bill. He was interested in canals and projected one from Holsworthy to the Bristol Channel. He wrote upon many subjects from electricity to musical tones. In the year of his death he was pressing for a committee of parliament to reform weights and measures. Political life would have been duller without him, society the poorer.

Further Reading
A. Newman, *The Stanhopes of Chevening*, 1969.
G. Stanhope and G. P. Gooch, *The Life of Charles, Third Earl Stanhope*, 1914.

STANHOPE, PHILIP DORMER, 4th EARL OF CHESTERFIELD

(1694-1773), a man who embodied many of the characteristic virtues and failings of the time, is deservedly known for his *Letters to his Son*, an epistolary code of conduct in polite society. He was also a statesman of higher repute in his day than may be inferred from the bare record of his achievement.

The grandson of Halifax the Trimmer, whom he resembled in his 'large and cautious mind' (Macaulay on Halifax), the son of the morose Jacobite third earl, he was brought up under the wing of his grandmother, Lady Halifax, herself a woman of wit and sense. His tutors and Cambridge produced a finished classical scholar, although he looked back upon that 'illiberal seminary' with some scorn for his own pedantry: 'when I talked my best, I quoted Horace; when I aimed at being facetious, I quoted Martial; and when I had a mind to be a fine gentleman, I talked Ovid'. His connections led him naturally into politics and at the age of twenty he represented the negligible electorate of St Germans. Disqualified for sitting under age, he found a congenial retreat in Paris, where he found the modes of the Regency much to his taste. Upon the death of his father he took his place in the Upper House, where his oratory shone all the brighter for having few rivals of his scholarship or taste. His detached and fastidious spirit did not commend itself to Walpole, who would have liked to bind him to his interest. In 1720 he accepted the post of Captain of the Yeomen of the Guard but made no use of its opportunities for gain. In 1723 he refused Walpole's offer for the garter, 'one of the tags Bob gave his boys', and his support of the Prince of Wales's interests earned him the dislike of George II and Queen Caroline. His embassy at the Hague enabled him to gratify his taste for gambling, the only vice to which he was immoderately addicted; there he 'courted the good opinions of the Dutch by losing great sums at play'. He also conducted his more serious business with skill and played a large part in the negotiations of the Second Treaty of Vienna, in 1731, when the emperor agreed to abolish the Ostend

Company and England guaranteed the Pragmatic Sanction. Any credit he gained with the administration was lost, however, when he opposed the Excise Bill in 1733. His greatest parliamentary performance was his attack upon Walpole's bill of 1737 to compel theatrical managers to submit plays for licence to the Lord Chamberlain. The measure found its place in the statute book and stayed there, the despair of producers and the butt of satirists, until 1968. But Chesterfield made his point in a speech 'full of wit of the genteelist satire and in the most polished classical style'.

Governors-General of Ireland were not always conscientious and appointment to Dublin was regarded at Westminster as notice of dismissal. Chesterfield was appointed Governor-General in January 1745, after the fall of Carteret on the insistence of the Pelhams. George II may have been pleased to see him removed to Dublin, but Chesterfield also served his interests well. He earned respect by his tact, courtesy and strength of purpose, and his efforts ensured that Ireland was quiet during the dangerous crisis of the '45. His informal entertainments at the castle pleased Dublin society, but he showed sympathy too with the plight of the peasantry: 'the poor people in Ireland are worse used than negroes by their lords and masters'. He returned in April 1746, leaving his new plantations in Phoenix Park as his memorial, and became Secretary of State for the Northern Department in place of Harrington. Like his predecessor he found it hard to 'tug at the oar with one who cannot row, and yet will be paddling so as to hinder you from rowing'. He was not prepared, as he said, to act as a mere 'commis' to forward Newcastle's instructions, and so resigned in February 1748. Newcastle found in Holderness a more complacent colleague and Chesterfield found compensations in what he termed 'philosophical quiet', the pleasures of gaming at White's, building a fine house in what is now South Audley Street, cultivating pineapples and collecting works for his library. He did not again take office but played the leading part in the Reform of the Calendar in 1751. Newcastle urged him 'not to stir matters that had long been quiet' and may have thought himself justified in the ignorant clamour of the mob who thought they had been cheated of their 'eleven days'. But Chesterfield could afford to be more detached and his speech was luminous; even if he did not understand the astronomical arguments with which he was supplied by Bradley, Astronomer Royal, and Lord Macclesfield, he was proud of the harmonious periods of his speech. It was a minor triumph of the age of reason, and suitable that Chesterfield was the man to promote it.

His letters to his son convey the best and worst of the polite values of the time. *Suaviter in modo*, a phrase which he liked, might have been his motto. The general tone is not elevated: enthusiasm is to be abhorred and moral values take second place to graceful manners. It should be recalled, in his defence, that he was penning advice to his illegitimate son about the ways of the world, not a text-book of morals. His detached and witty appraisals may command our admiration: 'In my mind, there is nothing so illiberal and so ill-bred as audible laughter'; his attitude to women is, however, displeasing: 'They have in truth but two passions, vanity and love; these are their universal characteristics'. He seems to have been consistent in this respect. In 1733 he married Petronilla von der Schulenberg, natural daughter of George I by the Duchess of Kendal: a political and financial arrangement which did not prevent his taking a new mistress to his house while his wife retired to occupy a house next door.

Further Reading
B. Willey, *The English Moralists*, 1964.
S. Shellabarger, *Lord Chesterfield*, 1935.
B. Dobrée, *Chesterfield's Letters*, 6 vols, 1932.

STANHOPE, WILLIAM, 1st EARL OF HARRINGTON (1690-1756) was Secretary of State in all for fourteen years and in office almost continuously for twenty-one years. Yet he has left but a small mark on the history of his time and one wonders if he has been underrated. It seems probable that his talents, like his training, were largely diplomatic, and that he was quiet, competent and diligent, a man for the routines of office rather than for big initiatives and flights of policy.

Stanhope served in Spain as a colonel of Dragoons; after the Spanish Succession War he became a Member of Parliament for Derby. He was much employed abroad in diplomatic missions, as a special envoy in Madrid (1717-18) and at Turin (1718-19). He was ambassador in Spain (1719-27) and in 1726 obtained from Ripperda the revelation of the articles of the secret Treaty of Vienna. He did not give, in return, Gibraltar, so ardently wanted by the Spanish, but successfully negotiated the Treaty of Seville whereby the English received trading privileges in return for acceptance of Parma and Piacenza being garrisoned by Spanish troops (1729). This was the climax of two years of negotiation at Aix-la-Chapelle and Soissons. In 1730 he was rewarded with the post of Secretary of State for the Northern Department, in succession to Townshend whom Walpole had managed to oust. He was a suitable man to be under Walpole and in partnership with Newcastle, but he was not entirely happy about all aspects of Walpole's policy. He was George II's man and could take a discreetly independent line, for instance, in 1741 when he negotiated a treaty of neutrality for Hanover without Walpole's knowledge. He did not share Walpole's faith in France – and he took care not to share in his fall after two years of war against France. In 1741 he became Lord President of the Council, in 1742 he was created earl. In December 1744 he succeeded Carteret as Secretary of State, though by now he seems to have been regarded without enthusiasm by king or fellow ministers.

Queen Caroline once remarked of him that he needed 'six hours to dress, six hours to eat, six hours with his mistress and six for sleep'. He was complaisant enough but not to be treated with such contempt as this might seem to imply. He may have seemed indolent when he failed to see ambassadors because he was laid up with gout. His written instructions were however invariably clear. He lost favour with George II, whose Hanoverian interests he had assiduously studied, by taking part with the Pelhams in the collective resignation of February 1746. In November of that year he resigned by himself, in protest against Newcastle's interference with the affairs of his department, and was replaced by Chesterfield, but he was promptly sent to Ireland as Lord Lieutenant. It was the usual shelf in the eighteenth century for ministers thought to be too important for mere dismissal.

Further Reading
J. Black, *British Foreign Policy in the Age of Walpole*, 1985.

STANLEY, EDWARD, 14th EARL OF DERBY

(1799-1869) was every inch an aristocrat. With thick brown wavy hair, strong mouth, firm chin and aquiline nose, he looked a young man for much of his life, until the pain of gout drew his skin tight and pale. His casual, off-hand manners were what people expected from the scion of a long line. So was his love of sport. He spent as much of his life as he could at Knowsley, shooting his birds and his rabbits, 'a lively rattling sportsman', drawing his political metaphors from the field: so Peel, clinging to office in 1835, was 'a hunted fox, who, instead of dying gallantly before the hounds in the open, skulks along the hedgerows and at last turns up his legs in the ditch'. At Newmarket he could be seen joking, laughing and shouting amongst the crowds round the bookies. He was elected Steward of the Jockey Club in 1848. He ran his estates effectively, and in Lancashire, where most of them were to be found, he played the part of the *grand seigneur* to such effect that his family's fame has been secure there ever since. He commanded the respect of the whole county when he chaired the Central Committee of the Relief Fund set up for the cotton workers made unemployed by the American Civil War, and led the donations with the largest single gift ever made up till then to a charity.

His political standpoint was aristocratic, too. He was the champion of the landowners. He saw them as 'men ... who for generation after generation have been the centre each of his respective locality; ... who conduct the business of their respective counties; ... who exercise a modest and decent hospitality, and preside over a tenantry who have hereditary claims upon their consideration and affections'. He was also the champion of the

established church, and made his last speech in the House of Lords in its defence. His often light-hearted style made some regard him as cavalier to the point of being casual. 'What fun we shall have now that you have come', he said when his old adversary Russell joined him in the House of Lords. But it was a sense of obligation as well as an enjoyment of politics which kept him there through long periods of painful illness.

The young Stanley had one outstanding gift among many. His voice, his looks, his manner and his intellectual wit made him the most highly regarded orator of his generation, in an age when oratory was the making of political giants. Daniel Webster, visiting the Commons from America in 1839, wrote that Stanley had made the best speech he had ever heard; an opponent said: 'Stanley is a host in himself.' He was 'the Rupert of debate'. Melbourne thought he would be the next prime minister after him through 'the mere force of superior will and eloquence ... like a young eagle above them all'. Indeed, he was to be prime minister, three times. Yet there was a wicked fairy present at his birth, for he never had the good fortune to lead a government with a majority in the House of Commons.

In his early career he changed parties often. Brought up a Whig, he moved over to the Tories as a Canningite, and then back with them to join Grey's Whig government as Chief Secretary for Ireland. There he set up a non-denominational Board for National Education; but his main measures were conservative; preserving tithes for the Church of Ireland by getting them permanently commuted from kind into cash, and redistributing the church's income to make more equitable its spread between rich and poor benefices and bishoprics. But he resigned in 1834 when Russell proposed to appropriate this income for purposes outside the church. Meanwhile he had made an enemy of O'Connell by his policy of vigorous coercion to enforce order in Ireland, and he was a determined upholder of the Union between England and Ireland. The continued Whig alliance with the Irish in the Commons drove him back to the Tories again, and he became Secretary for War and the Colonies in Peel's government in 1841. He had already held this post briefly under Grey, and had been responsible for the Act which finally abolished slavery. Now he sympathized with Aberdeen's conciliatory foreign policy, and helped in the peaceful solution of the conflicts with the United States which had brewed up under Palmerston, stopping a scheme for a British settlement in northern California, and achieving a satisfactory eastern frontier between the USA and Canada. The war with China was ended, and it was Derby who arranged for the new British acquisition, Hong Kong, to become a free port, thus laying the foundation of its future wealth. He became involved in a row with the New Zealand Company, by backing the Maoris and the missionaries in land disputes. Here he failed to keep his Governor under control, and the Maori war which broke out was a blot on his otherwise good record. His anti-colonialist instincts, however, command sympathy now as they did then.

But one more resignation lay ahead, the most significant in his career. When Peel decided to repeal the Corn Laws in 1846, Stanley was the only important minister to leave the Cabinet. It was a bitter break, for although he was never close to Peel, he had become friendly with Graham, Aberdeen and other 'Peelites'. But he put loyalty to the landed class first, and soon found himself at the head of the party of Protectionists, strong in numbers but without any other recognizable leaders. For the rest of his life this group was the largest in the Commons, but never in a majority, or with enough allies to rule confidently. Derby, as he became in 1851, formed governments in 1852, 1858 and 1866, but the inexperience of the ministers in the first was such that it was nicknamed the 'Who? Who?' government, after the Duke of Wellington's deaf inquiries as the names were read out to him. Only in 1866 did young men of ability emerge, such as the future Lord Salisbury. In the Commons all through this frustrating time Derby relied on Disraeli, who had made his name by leading the onslaught on Peel, but whose flamboyant style and Jewish background, let alone his swift abandonment of Protection once he saw that it was a political incubus, aroused in his followers suspicions which took twenty years to fade.

Derby's aim was to keep the Conservative party in being after the split over the Corn Laws, and he succeeded. He kept the name, and he turned what had been just a large rump of Protectionists into the natural protectors of the traditional British constitution as well as of the landed interest. But he failed to win over the Peelites, who nearly all went to the Whigs with Gladstone, to form the nucleus of the future Liberal party. He also failed to build up any sort of party organization or to gain a foothold in the new Penny Press – indeed he opposed the abolition of the duty on paper which made that style of journalism possible. His main achievement in government was the Government of India Act, transferring control from the East India Company to the Crown. His foreign policy was pacific and traditional. He looked back to the Concert of Europe, when the great powers held together to keep the peace: his support for Austria in Italy won the favour of the queen.

But the item on every government's agenda was parliamentary reform, and though it was Russell who kept on bringing the subject up, it was Derby and Disraeli who eventually carried through the Second Reform Bill. 'There is more danger,' wrote the Tory Greville in his *Diary*, 'in conferring political power on the middle classes than in extending it far beneath them.' Derby had been impressed by the responsible behaviour of the unemployed cotton workers of Lancashire. He was also disturbed by the Reform riots in Hyde Park. He thought that the right extension and redistribution of the franchise might help the Conservatives to the overall majority which they could not get within the existing electorate. So when Whig rebels defeated Russell's Reform Bill and the Conservatives took office in 1866, Derby urged Disraeli to frame a bill which would suit them, and which Gladstone, now the Liberal leader, could not oppose without being inconsistent. They went for household suffrage in the boroughs, but only for those who paid their own rates and had a two-year residential qualification. Household suffrage was 'a leap in the dark', and it became a bigger leap when the Liberals carried an amendment giving the vote to all householders, and another reducing the period of residence required to one year. But Derby was all out to 'dish the Whigs'. His influence and Disraeli's oratory kept their party together, and the Bill succeeded where several earlier attempts had failed. 'I have the greatest confidence in my fellow countrymen,' he said, 'and I entertain a strong hope that the extended franchise … will be the means of placing the institutions of this country on a firmer basis.'

This was Derby's own epilogue to his career. The gout which had attacked him over the last thirty years overwhelmed him: and in the same year (1868) he handed the leadership over to Disraeli, whom he had loyally backed through some rough water, even against those who supported his own son. He left him to face disastrous defeat at the polls later in the year, but to gain in 1874, with better party organization, the Conservative majority in the Commons which he himself had never had.

Further Reading
W. D. Jones, *Lord Derby and Victorian Conservatism*, 1956.

STANLEY, SIR HENRY (1841-1904) is better known as H. M. Stanley, the journalist turned explorer. But even that was not his real name. He was born in Denbigh, in north Wales, to Elizabeth Parry, but named Rowlands after the man who was believed to be his father. Neither parent played much part in his life, for by the age of seven he was in the St Asaph workhouse, whence he escaped after seizing the birch from his sadistic teacher and thrashing him with it. He crossed the Atlantic as a cabin boy, and got his new name from a benevolent New Orleans cotton broker, who adopted him. Life continued to deal him hard blows, for Mr Stanley died suddenly. Henry was caught up in the Civil War, was captured, changed sides, and, becoming a merchant seaman, was the only person to escape when his ship went down. He joined the US Navy, deserted, and became a roving freelance reporter. He had learnt to survive.

The lucky break which opened up the future for him came in Abyssinia, where he had gone to report for the *New York Herald* on the British expedition sent to punish Emperor Theodore for maltreating prisoners. As soon as he had got his description of Napier's victory at Magdala despatched, the cable line broke, so London first heard the story via New York. His next scoop made him world famous. In 1871, financed again by the *Herald*, he met Livingstone, who had been missing for three years and reported dead, at Ujiji on Lake Tanganyika. He celebrated his success with the first of his vivid books. Its title, *How I Found Livingstone*, conveys its flavour. The British were stung by having had their hero discovered by a brash American journalist, especially as the *Herald* had concealed the purpose of Stanley's expedition for as long as they could. For twenty years thereafter Stanley got a bad press in Britain. But Livingstone had inspired him. Especially, he wanted to go on with his exploration northwards down the River Lualaba, to discover whether it was the headwater of the Nile. In 1874 he was back in Zanzibar, assembling a heavyweight expedition, with 358 people and eight tons of supplies, presents and weapons. He circumnavigated Lake Victoria and Lake Tanganyika, persuaded Mtesa, the powerful chieftain of Uganda, to convert from Islam to Christianity, and then joined forces with Tippoo Tib (so called because of his habit of blinking rapidly), who was the dominant Arab slave trader in Central Africa. This made it possible for him to follow the Lualaba to the point where it turns westward as the Congo River, and then to pursue its course until he reached the Atlantic Ocean. Through forests they went, where pythons and puff adders threatened along the interlaced boughs which shut out the daylight. The natives were cannibals. Tippoo Tib abandoned him, but Stanley pressed on down seven huge cataracts, stretching over 150 miles, which he named the Stanley Falls, dragging the boats where they could not clear the rocks. Only 115 emaciated survivors emerged in 1877, but Stanley was one of them, full of tales of riches, especially ivory, awaiting European traders.

The 'Scramble for Africa' began. Stanley fell in with a rich new sponsor, Leopold II, King of the Belgians. Under the cloak of creating a free trade area in Central Africa, Leopold planned a new empire of his own, and in 1879 he sent Stanley back to build a highway and trading stations there. This took five years. The natives dubbed Stanley 'Bula Matari', the Breaker of Rocks, and the work was so strenuous that he nearly died. But at the end he had made treaties with 450 chiefs, and claimed 800,000 square miles and 15,000,000 people for Leopold's Association Internationale Africaine, later to be transformed into the Belgian Congo.

His last expedition (1887) was to rescue Emin Pasha, the German governor of Equatoria, south of the Sudan. Emin had been left there when Gordon was killed in Khartoum. Leopold saw the proposed relief expedition as a chance to extend his empire to the Nile, and persuaded Stanley to lead it to Equatoria from the west rather than the east. The forests proved the worst he had encountered – no paths; hornets and ticks to add to the snakes and spiders; poisoned arrows from the natives. His rearguard, left to protect the stores, was destroyed. When he finally got to Equatoria he had to bully Emin Pasha, who did not want to be rescued, into accompanying him over the 1,200 miles to Zanzibar. Strangely, this, his least successful enterprise, earned him the plaudits back in England which his earlier successes had not. He wrote a bestseller, *In Darkest Africa*, married the cultured and beautiful Dorothy Tennant, who had previously turned him down, and became an MP and a Knight.

Stanley's was a 'rags to riches' story, and he arguably covered more new ground as an African explorer than any of his predecessors, surviving the toughest journeys of them all. But he never won the hearts of the public, or of the Geographical Establishment, in Britain. He was too brash, wore polished boots, used his Schneider rifles to deal with native attacks, worked for an American paper and a Belgian king. When he died, the dean refused to allow him to be buried alongside his hero, Livingstone, in Westminster Abbey.

Further Reading
Thomas Pakenham, *The Scramble for Africa*, 1991.
Byron Farwell, *The Man who Presumed*, 1958.

STAPLEDON, WALTER (*d*.1326), Bishop of Exeter 1308-26, was a younger son of a minor Devonshire gentleman. After studying at Oxford, where he became a doctor of both canon and civil law, he returned to his native west country. Rector of Aveton-Giffard from 1295 and a freeman of the city of Exeter from 1300, he entered the service of Bishop Bytton, becoming his official principal (judge of the Consistory Court), canon (1301) and precentor (1305) of Exeter Cathedral. On Bytton's death, he was surprisingly elected bishop, perhaps because of his learning and local connections.

Initially ill-prepared for his new office, Walter proved in time an indefatigable diocesan. He spent forty per cent of his time in the diocese until ministerial office forced him to employ a suffragan bishop. He visited the archdeaconries of Totnes and Cornwall on six occasions and that of Barnstaple four times, defended his rights of patronage against the Crown, and gave generously to the rebuilding of the choir of Exeter Cathedral. As befitted a university man, he wished to raise the quality of the parish clergy, granting 439 licences for non-residence to potential university students, endowing scholarships for twelve students of grammar in Exeter, and founding Stapledon Hall (later Exeter College) Oxford for thirteen poor scholars from the diocese, twelve in the faculty of arts and another reading for a higher degree. No special rights were reserved for founder's kin, but they played an important role in his foundation, assisted him in his episcopate, and benefited substantially from his elevation. Two clerical brothers and two nephews were advanced in the church, his eldest brother Richard – like Archbishop Melton's nephew – became a substantial landowner, and favourable marriages were arranged for his nieces and other kinsfolk.

As a bishop, Stapledon was inevitably involved in politics. Court connections are suggested by his royal favours and regular diplomatic employment, but he deliberately avoided political commitment until 1320, when he was appointed suddenly – and without appropriate experience – as treasurer of England. Apparently the Despensers' candidate, he resigned on the eve of the Despenser War in 1321, declined to support Edward II's decision to recall them, yet was again treasurer from 1322-5. At the Exchequer he calendared and sorted the records, enlarged the staff, and systematically exploited traditional revenues, notably by levying harshly and unreasonably long-forgotten royal debts. Later petitions and his own transactions indicate that he also exploited his office to his personal advantage, admittedly on a much lesser scale than the Despensers themselves. Justly or unjustly, he was blamed for the confiscation of the estates of Queen Isabella, who became his enemy, and for the London eyre of 1321. Although evidently of secondary significance, he thus acquired a reputation for rapacity and covetousness, which explains his murder by the London mob in Cheapside in the revolution of 1326 and his subsequent condemnation in the first parliament of Edward III. Stapledon's fate foreshadows the later murders of Archbishop Sudbury (1381) and Bishops Moleyns and Aiscough (1450), who were also too closely associated with unpopular political régimes.

Further Reading
M. Buck, *Politics, Finance and the Church in the Reign of Edward II: Walter Stapledon, Treasurer of England*, 1983.

STEAD, WILLIAM THOMAS (1849-1912) shares with his schoolfriend from Silcoates, George Newnes, the claim to be the founder of what Matthew Arnold dubbed 'The New Journalism'. But he was the more remarkable of the two, both in style and ambition. Wearing a sealskin cap and a garment like a pyjama top instead of a shirt, and sporting a shaggy red beard, he challenged the high society in which he often moved. He enjoyed catching, cooking and eating mice, having read of this being done during the siege of Paris, and recommended them to his friends as a tasty dish on a piece of toast. He was as explicit as Rabelais about sex, and proud of his self-control in having no more children after he and his wife had bred six in six years. He became obsessed by spiritualism, and his 'spooks', as he called them, included Tennyson and Catherine the Great.

But while Newnes aimed to entertain, Stead was determined to influence. As an office boy in a Newcastle counting house he wrote such striking contributions to the *Northern Echo*, the first English halfpenny paper, that he was made its editor when he was only twenty-two. From this provincial base he made world history by blazing abroad the stories of the Bulgarian atrocities and getting Gladstone to take up the cause. Moving to the *Pall Mall Gazette* in London in 1880, he succeeded Morley as its editor three years later. He transformed it, from a paper written by gentlemen for gentlemen to the prototype for the popular press of the twentieth century. Strong cross-headlines, maps and diagrams, the interview, the gossip column and the stop press were all techniques which he introduced. The balance of the content was transformed: more news and less comment.

In this strident tone, Stead launched his crusades. The most notorious of them was against juvenile prostitution. In a series of articles he exposed the traffic in young girls. To prove his point he bought Eliza, aged thirteen, from her mother – though instead of selling her, he placed her, still a virgin, in the care of the Salvation Army. Found guilty of abducting her, he spent three months in Holloway Gaol. The *Gazette* sold out for months. He also campaigned against London's slums, persecuted Dilke and Parnell, urged Gladstone to send Gordon to Khartoum, and stirred up public anxiety about the navy's shortages so successfully that he pushed the government into building the Dreadnoughts. No pen in England, it was said, wielded ascendancy comparable to his.

Stead had an exalted view of the importance of the editor. While in gaol he wrote *Government by Journalism*. The Press was to be the 'Great Inspector', and he proposed a scheme, modelled on the Major Generals of his hero Oliver Cromwell, to divide the country into regions, in which groups of journalists would act as pollsters, 'interrogators of democracy'. Driven by strong Puritan faith (he referred to God as his Senior Partner), he hoped to be 'the Moses of our nineteenth century ... the Captain of our Exodus into the Canaan of a truer social order'. He could have become a dangerous man. But he had many likeable sides to him which prevented this. His enthusiasms were diffuse: Esperanto, a cure for cancer, a process for distilling gold out of sea water, as well as his spooks. He lost influence by opposing the Boer War and pushing for a system of arbitration to prevent wars in the future. He resigned from the *Pall Mall Gazette* in 1890, to start the *Review of Reviews*. This soon had Australian and American editions, and Stead saw it as the vehicle for creating 'a world-wide journalistic civil church', with its capital in Chicago. He was on his way to America when he went down with the *Titanic*. He was last seen helping women and children into the lifeboats, as the bandsmen played, at his request, 'Nearer My God to Thee'.

STEELE, SIR RICHARD (1672-1729), journalist and Whig, was an Irishman from Dublin, the son of a well-to-do attorney. He was educated at Charterhouse, with Addison as his contemporary, and at Merton College, Oxford. After serving in the Life Guards and living a somewhat dissipated life he turned to writing plays, and in 1707 Harley gave him the post of official gazetteer. In 1709 he started the *Tatler*, published every other week-day, and ran it with Addison's help until 1711; and during 1711-12 he and Addison produced the *Spectator*. Their aim, in which they attained a real measure of success, was to civilize public taste, to make the middle class in particular more moral and more polite – 'to enliven morality with wit, and to temper wit with morality'. Hence came, for example, Steele's famous attack upon duelling. These two papers were very largely non-political. But Steele was an ardent Whig and also used his pen on behalf of Godolphin's ministry, which rewarded him with a second official post, in the Stamp Office. When the Whig's were turned out in 1710 Steele lost his gazetteership, yet not until 1713 did he resign his second office, become an MP, and attack the Harley-St John ministry over the question of the French delay in dismantling the fortifications of Dunkirk. In 1714 he wrote *The Crisis*, a pamphlet in which he declared that the Protestant succession was in peril under the Tory ministry, and this caused his expulsion from the Commons. The accession of George I brought Steele into favour. He was knighted in 1715 and obtained a number of government posts. In 1718 he quarrelled with Addison when the Whig groups in parliament split over the Peerage Bill. His last play, *The Conscious Lovers*, was produced at Drury Lane in 1722.

Further Reading
W. Connely, *Sir Richard Steele*, 1934.
G. A. Aitken, *Sir Richard Steele*, 1889.

STEPHEN, SIR LESLIE (1832-1904), literary critic and agnostic, was the first editor of the *Dictionary of National Biography*. Though his lifespan was little above the ordinary, his cultural span was exceptional: at one end the grandson of John Venn, Rector of the famous Evangelical church of Clapham, at the other the father of Vanessa Bell and Virginia Woolf, the sisters at the heart of the Bloomsbury set. He took Orders at Cambridge, but resigned them when he examined for himself the historical truth of the Gospels. He left Cambridge for London in 1867, with regret for its libraries, heady debates and satisfying afternoon hours of coaching on the Cam: grew a straggly red beard, and married, first Thackeray's daughter, and, after her early death, Julia, daughter of one of the Pattle sisters who permeated the Pre-Raphaelite world, who was already a widow.

He made his name, and many friends, as a literary and philosophical journalist, writing chiefly for the *Fortnightly Review* and for *Cornhill*, of which he was editor from 1871 to 1882. There he commissioned distinguished writers, Hardy, Stevenson and James amongst them, and wrote many essays himself, subsequently reprinted in the three volumes of *Hours in a Library*. He found his métier in the world of ideas, and in 1876 published his magisterial *History of English Thought in the Eighteenth Century*. As a literary critic he looked for the author behind the writing. 'The Waverley novels bring me a greeting from Scott.'

Huxley coined the word 'agnostic', but Stephen spread it. With his logical and somewhat puritanical mind, he rejected any doctrine which was incompatible with observable evidence. Evidence did not support the existence of God. Theology was speculation about the unknowable. If one faced these truths honestly one could not remain a 'believer'. Stephen aimed his sharpest barbs at Broad Churchmen who compromised and fudged, and he moved the Victorian debate about religion onto different ground.

Although he was an uncompromising thinker, Stephen had a hypersensitive personality, and sought to shake himself free from self-doubt by hard work and energetic exercise. He was a fanatical oarsman at Cambridge, and then took to climbing, becoming President of the Alpine Club. For *Cornhill* he would write an 8,000 word article in a single session. From 1882 his main and titanic work was *The Dictionary of National Biography*. He owed much to a far-sighted and generous publisher, George Smith, and after nine years he handed over as editor to his collaborator, Sydney Lee. But by then he had set standards of factual accuracy, balance, and freedom from verbosity and excessive eulogy, which made it the best of its sort in the world. Three hundred and seventy-eight of the entries are his.

Stephen was not a clubbable man: he was famous for his silences. Marriage and home were important to him. He was twice blessed with a happy union, twice shattered by its sudden end. He wore his agnosticism like a badge, holding it to be his duty to show that a virtuous life could be led without religion. As a friend, particularly to English and American writers, he commanded affection, but as paterfamilias to his teenage children late in life, he cut the tyrannical, self-pitying figure of Mr Ramsay in Virgina Woolf's novel *To the Lighthouse*. Yet it is Leslie Stephen's whole career, as one of the most influential literary figures of late Victorian England, which deserves to be remembered, rather than the mean, self-centred father of his daughter's recollection.

Further Reading
Noel Annan, *Leslie Stephen, the Godless Victorian*, 1984.

STEPHEN OF BLOIS (*c*.1096-1154; King of England 1135-54) is chiefly remembered as an unsuccessful king whose reign formed a chaotic interlude between the masterful rule of Henry I and Henry II. The damning verdict of the Peterborough version of the *Anglo-Saxon Chronicle* has stuck: 'People said openly that Christ and his saints slept'. English historians and their audience prefer strong kings, whatever their cost in terms of misery. For eight and a half centuries Stephen, who eminently failed to control events, has received short shrift. Yet it is not entirely obvious that conditions in England, when viewed from a perspective other than that of royal government or hostile and judgemental monastic chroniclers, were markedly worse than under more effective monarchs. Devastation was local, confined to areas most affected by civil war, such as parts of the west country, or temporary, as in East Anglia during Geoffrey de Mandeville's ravaging of 1144 or the areas affected by Henry FitzEmpress's destructive campaign of 1153. When compared to other parts of Europe, for example Stephen's native northern France where baronial banditry and terrorism were endemic in the early twelfth century, the contrast is less apparent. Stephen was faced with identical problems to those which confronted all new kings in this period: how to secure his position and to manage his kingdom and magnates. His lack of success speaks loudly of the scale of his difficulties and his personal and political incapacity to deal with them. It is less clear that his reign witnessed particular social or political disintegration. What his accession did reinforce was the tradition that the kingdom of the English was reigned over by foreigners: Danes and Norman French in the eleventh century; French in the twelfth and thirteenth; Welsh (of a sort) in the late fifteenth and early sixteenth; Scots in the seventeenth; and varying sorts of Germans ever since. England's place in Europe was never more underlined than in its rule by King Stephen whose previous interest in the realm had been purely tenurial. That he became king at all demonstrates that modern concepts of nationalism, so intrinsic to the medievalists of three and four generations ago, cannot be applied to English politics of the twelfth century.

Stephen was the third son of Stephen, Count of Blois and Adela, daughter of William the Conqueror. His forceful mother, widowed in 1102, sent him to be educated at the court of her brother, Henry I of England. Stephen soon became the recipient of regular and lavish grants of titles and lands from his uncle in Normandy and England. By 1113, he was Count of Mortain and received the extensive honour of Eye in Suffolk. The following decade saw his holdings extend into at least twenty-one counties. In 1125, he was given the valuable and strategically important county of Boulogne on marrying its heiress. By 1130, his demesne property in England alone amounted to at least 1,339 hides making him one of the richest magnates in the realm.

Although, with the other barons, Stephen had sworn to uphold the rights to Normandy and England of Henry I's sole surviving legitimate child, the Empress Matilda, as the king's nephew and favourite, and supported by an influential faction of barons, he retained a keen interest in the succession. Henry I died on 1 December 1135 at Lyon-la-Forêt in Normandy. Immediately on hearing the news, Stephen crossed from Boulogne to England and, within three weeks, had secured the support of London, Henry's government officials and the church. Recognition by the royal administration based at Winchester under Roger, Bishop of Salisbury was crucial as it gave Stephen access to the royal treasure. Stephen was crowned by the Archbishop of Canterbury, William of Corbeil, on 22 December 1135.

The speed of Stephen's coup took his rivals – Matilda and her husband, Geoffrey of Anjou; Stephen's elder brother, Theobald; and Henry's illegitmate son Robert of Gloucester – off-guard. News of Stephen's coronation ended plans of the Norman barons to offer the duchy to Theobald. Stephen's quick action was reminiscent of Henry I's seizure of the throne in 1100: once the king was crowned the only alternative to acceptance was rebellion and civil war. By May 1136, all the English barons, including Robert of Gloucester, had recognized the *fait accompli*; the church had been granted a Charter of Liberties as the price for its support; and the hostile King David of Scotland, who himself could have constructed a claim from his direct descent from Ethelred the Unready, had been bought off. But Stephen's success had not been achieved without cost. Whatever he and his ally Hugh Bigod implausibly claimed, he had not been designated king by his uncle, and he did not have the best hereditary right. Internally, his position depended on the forbearance and co-operation of those who had acquiesced in his 'election', even though, as the contemporary chronicler Henry of Huntingdon gloatingly pointed out, such approval meant breaking their oaths to Matilda. Externally, he could hardly expect his cousin and the Angevins to surrender their expectations without a fight. To combat possible disaffection, Stephen was precariously dependent on the support of a few powerful individuals, such as Robert of Gloucester or Stephen's brother, Henry, Bishop of Winchester, who had been energetic on his behalf in December 1135.

The new king's vulnerability was emphasized by his inability to prosecute the siege of Exeter (1136) against Baldwin de Redvers because of his troops' lukewarm support and the fiasco of his campaign against Geoffrey of Anjou in Normandy (1137), when his army disintegrated into rival fighting groups of Normans and Flemish mercenaries. The massive treasure left by Henry I was dissipated for little tangible gain. Stephen tried to build a faction of his own to control government centred on the glamorous but feckless Waleran, Count of Meulan. Experienced sheriffs were replaced and, in 1139, Roger of Salisbury and his nephews, who had run the royal financial administration for a generation, were crudely ousted from power, and their castles seized. Henry of Winchester, who, as papal legate (1139-43), was effectively head of the English church, was alienated by the appointment of Theobald of Bec as Archbishop of Canterbury in 1138. Disenchantment and self-interest in the face of a king who seemed alternately aggressive and inept, led to defections, notably Robert of Gloucester's in 1138. In an attempt to exploit this dissatisfaction, in 1139 Matilda landed at Arundel opening the way to civil war.

Matilda's support came less from those wedded to her hereditary claim than from those who had felt cheated of lands by Henry I or preferment under Stephen, and those whose allegiances were determined by local rivalries or the need to protect their lands. Although enjoying military superiority, Stephen appeared to lack adequate resources or resolve to crush his opponents, whose strength was based around Robert of Gloucester's estates in the west country. Increasingly the conflict turned on the control of strategic towns and castles, such as Wallingford, Cricklade and Oxford in the Thames valley. The only prospect of a decisive end to the struggle came in 1141. On 2 February, Stephen himself was captured at the battle of Lincoln and imprisoned at Bristol. For a brief moment, the accession of Matilda looked possible, especially when both Henry of Winchester and Waleran of Meulan came over to her side, although the latter only did so to protect his continental possessions from Angevin attack and the former was soon alienated. Matilda's victory was clouded by her boorishness, especially her off-hand treatment of the Londoners which prevented her consecration. Her support remained tentative, and crumbled in the face of a vigorous offensive by Stephen's wife (also called Matilda) and his mercenary commander William of Ypres. In September 1141, Robert of Gloucester was captured at the so-called Rout of Winchester, from which the empress only narrowly escaped, and was promptly exchanged for Stephen. To signal his rehabilitation (and emphasize a crucial distinction with Matilda), the king attended a legatine council at Westminster in December 1141 at which the legate, Henry of Winchester, and the clergy reaffirmed support for Stephen as the anointed king. Thereafter, neither side established a clear military advantage in England. Matilda's partisans held important castles in the southwest and East Anglia, but Stephen secured London, Winchester and the Midlands, improving his position in 1142 by capturing Oxford whence Matilda had to flee by night through the enemy lines across the snow and frozen Thames camouflaged in a white cloak. On the continent, however, Stephen lost ground decisively between 1141 and 1145 as Geoffrey of Anjou completed the conquest of Normandy. This further strained loyalty to Stephen as some, like Waleran of Meulan, were forced to submit to the Angevins to protect their Norman patrimonies.

Relations with the church, since the arrest of the bishops in 1139, were soured. Personally conventional in his patronage of religious orders such as those of Savigny and Cluny, Stephen was the first English king for centuries to lose control over some major ecclesiastical appointments, such as the election to the archbishopric of York after 1140. He was further undermined by the consistent opposition of Bernard of Clairvaux, the self-appointed and widely acknowledged keeper of the public conscience of Christendom, and his pupil, Pope Eugenius III (1145-53), both members of the increasingly influential Cistercian order which in 1147 swallowed up the Savigny order. Archbishop Theobald's flight to the council of Rheims (1148), in defiance of a royal prohibition, and his later sympathy for the Angevins confirmed Stephen's weakness. After failing to retain his legateship, Henry of Winchester's authority and ability to deliver ecclesiastical support faded. One damaging political result of the coolness between king and church was the latter's refusal to crown Stephen's eldest son, Eustace, in his father's lifetime. Stephen and James II are the only post-Conquest monarchs of England to fail to secure the succession of living legitimate sons. Perhaps that is the true measure of Stephen's failure. Even King John did better.

In England, Stephen pursued an erratic course. Anxiously eager to win quick advantage, he cast an essential prerequisite of good lordship, trustworthiness, into doubt. He spectacularly broke his own safe-conducts when he arrested at court the powerful and potentially dangerous magnates Geoffrey de Mandeville (1143) and Ranulf of Chester (1146) at times when they were professing loyalty to him. Hardly surprisingly they both rebelled as soon as they were released. If Stephen could not be trusted, neither could he be feared as his uncle had been. Although a vigorous campaigner, Stephen lacked ruthlessness: withdrawing from Bristol in 1138; allowing Matilda safe-passage from Arundel to Bristol in 1139; releasing Geoffrey and Ranulf; paying for Matilda's son Henry's withdrawal from England in 1149. A typical incident occurred in 1152 when Stephen was besieging John Marshal's castle at Newbury. To allow time for a parley, John sent his son William to Stephen's camp as a hostage promising that, during the lull in hostilities, the garrison would not be reinforced. John broke the conditions, but Stephen failed to execute the five-year-old William, who thought the whole thing a game, especially as he and the king had played 'knights' (a tournament game played with straw figures) in the royal pavilion. The future Regent of England was unlikely to have learnt much statecraft from this encounter, but he later recalled the old king with some affection. Yet in the twelfth as in other centuries, nice people rarely make effective rulers.

By the late 1140s, the civil war had reached stalemate. Despite the death of Robert of Gloucester (1147), the final withdrawal to Normandy of Matilda (1148) and the failure of Henry FitzEmpress's invasion of 1149, final military victory eluded Stephen. However, his grip on most of England seemed secure. Central government continued to work. The chancery seems to have been little affected by the troubles although, with a number of counties outside royal authority, the Exchequer operated on a reduced scale. To combat local insecurity and to try to prevent a collapse of law and order, Stephen appointed earls in many counties whose office supplemented existing royal agents, such as the sheriff. However, the weakness of royal power was obvious. Between 1149 and 1153 a series of private treaties were agreed between magnates on opposing sides designed to limit mutual hostility in case of a renewal of the civil war, the most famous being the 'final peace and concord' arranged by Robert of Leicester and Ranulf of Chester. Although these treaties were not, in fact, very effective in keeping the peace, they signal the king's inability to provide justice and a common desire among the barons to protect themselves from unnecessary or excessive damage in the protracted struggle for the throne.

Increasingly this struggle was one Stephen could not win. After 1150, the rival candidate was Matilda's son, Henry, who held unchallenged control of Normandy and, after his father's death in 1151, Anjou and enjoyed the tacit approval of the papacy. In 1153, Henry invaded again and after a deliberately violent campaign in the south and Midlands, the magnates, fearful of the destruction promised by the Angevin's scorched earth tactics, forced each side to negotiate for peace at Wallingford. During the subsequent negotiations, Stephen's son Eustace conveniently died. The final treaty of 1153, accepted in principle at Winchester (in November) and promulgated at Westminster (in December) provided for Stephen to remain king for his lifetime then for Henry to succeed as the hereditary heir of Henry I. Stephen remained active, but king only on sufferance of his successor. He died on 25 October 1154.

The events of Stephen's reign have proved fertile for historical debate and have been interpreted variously as 'feudal' anarchy; a war of succession; and a struggle by the baronage to establish recognized hereditary succession to their fiefs. The causes of the collapse of royal control have been attributed to Stephen's lack of financial resources by 1138; to a baronial desire to maintain or recreate Anglo-Norman unity; to a noble reaction against weak kingship; and to accident. The circumstances of 1135 made civil war almost inevitable and Stephen, his coup achieved, failed to master the problems of faction and local baronial disputes. So soft-spoken that, it was alleged, he had a spokesman to address his troops before battle; chivalrous; energetic; by turns foolhardy and indecisive, Stephen, for all his lineage, opportunities and position, appears as rather colourless, unimpressive in an age when personal impressions counted for much. He was no match for the forces which, in order to succeed, he needed to dominate.

Further Reading
R. H. C. Davis, *King Stephen*, 1967.

STEPHENSON, GEORGE (1781-1848), the first of the railway-builders, was born in 1781 at Wylam, a colliery village in Northumberland. His father was employed as an engineer in charge of the steam engines used for pumping and winding at the pits. From the start the steam engine and the wooden tracks of the wagon-way were familiar features of his world. His family was poor and George was illiterate until the age of eighteen.

The story of his education is one of the finest sagas of 'self-help'. At night-school, after his day's work, he learned to read and write and to do arithmetic. At the age of twenty-one he was appointed engine man at the Willington colliery; in the same year he married. He worked furiously to keep his family and to educate his only son, Robert: cobbling shoes, mending watches, or stevedoring in the Newcastle docks. At length he was able to send Robert to school at Newcastle. Throughout their lives they were partners and Robert became a celebrated engineer before his father's death.

Stephenson had many interests – at about the same time as Davy he invented a miner's safety lamp – but he was concerned chiefly with the steam locomotive. The practical need for this was plain, since horsepower was inadequate and laborious; the technical problems also appealed to his inventive mind. Other attempts had been made, such as those of Cugnot (1770), Symington (1786) and Murdoch (1786) to make road locomotives, but without success because existing road surfaces would not bear their weight. But Trevithick in south Wales and Blenkinsop at Leeds had more recently been successful with tram engines for colliery working.

Stephenson's first engine, the *Blucher*, was made for the proprietors of Killingworth colliery in 1814; it incorporated Trevithick's device, since neglected, for piping back the steam into the chimney of the engine, increasing in this way the draught and power of the engines. When Edward Pease, a Quaker coal-owner, secured the passage of a bill, in 1821, for the construction of a railway between Stockton and Darlington, Stephenson persuaded him to use steam locomotives and was appointed engineer of the project. Stephenson's greatness was not as a technical innovator; here he was one among several. But as a civil engineer, an organizer of technical resources, he was superlative. He conceived of the railway as a whole enterprise. Something in the way that he had risen, by overcoming one difficulty after another, gave him a rugged confidence in his own judgement; indeed few men's decisions have been so crucial for the future. He showed by the success of his Stockton and Darlington railway, 4ft. 8½in. gauge (still the standard), that goods and passengers could be carried efficiently along the line.

The project for a tramroad between Liverpool and Manchester was mooted independently; it arose primarily from the need to break the canal's monopoly in communications between the fast-growing towns and was opposed by canal companies as well as by landowners. The minutes of evidence on the bill that eventually became law in 1825 show how the Tyneside mechanic often got the better of the professional lawyers ranged against him. 'Suppose, now, that a cow were to stray upon the line and get in the way of the engine, would not that, think you, be a very awkward circumstance?' 'Yes,' replied Stephenson, 'Very awkward – for the coo.' His work upon the construction of the thirty-one-mile line which traversed the notorious Chat Moss showed that his confidence was not misplaced. A complex organization had to be created for the flow of materials and the handling of labour. When completed, the line had the first railway cutting in England, at Olive Mount, sixty-three bridges and the great Sankey viaduct, built mainly of brick. It was the first of those viaducts, usually graceful, even adding to the beauty of the valley they crossed, which were to become a feature of the landscape. Stephenson also won the competition for the best locomotive with the *Rocket*, capable of nearly thirty miles an hour although the directors only stipulated ten. In the same year, 1829, the Liverpool tunnel was opened. In the following year the line was opened. When Huskisson was knocked down and fatally injured, Stephenson himself drove the dying man to Manchester at full speed.

Swiftly Stephenson became one of the leading engineers in the country. He built the Manchester and Leeds, the North Midland and the Grand Junction railways. His son established his reputation by the construction of the London and Birmingham and became a central figure in the railway age which his father had pioneered. Stephenson retired from active work in the forties but continued to advise and influence. He was consulted in Belgium and he surveyed in Spain. He took an interest in the education of working men and in pursuits less serious. He birds-nested in spring and grew melons in summer in his delightful garden at Tapton near Chesterfield. It is pleasant to record one of the more eccentric of his achievements. By encasing cucumbers in glass tubes he at last persuaded them to grow straight – a matter which had long occupied his attention.

Further Reading
L. T. C. Rolt, *George and Robert Stephenson*, 1960.
S. Smiles, *George and Robert Stephenson*, new edn 1904.

STEPHENSON, ROBERT (1803-59), engineer, was the remarkable only son of his remarkable father, George. Working as close partners, and with complementary strengths, they are justly considered the founders of the railways in Britain, the first in the world to be built. Only Brunel could match them.

George, whose wife died when Robert was only three, saw to it that his son had the formal education which he had missed, sending him to school in Newcastle and to Edinburgh University. Robert was a precocious boy. When he was only seventeen he helped his father to survey the Stockton-Darlington line, and at twenty-one he not only surveyed a branch of it himself, but steered through parliament the Bill to authorize its building. When George and two Durham industrialists, depressed by the quality of engineering to back their railway schemes, decided to build their own locomotive workshop on Forth Street in Newcastle in 1823, they made Robert its Managing Director, and called the firm 'Robert Stephenson & Company'. Next year he took himself off to Colombia to supervise mining there: but in his absence, things soon went wrong at the works, and in 1827 he returned to take charge.

There followed the great creative period in the history of the railways. In 1829 the Directors of the Liverpool and Manchester Railway Board decided to stage a competition for the best locomotive for their proposed line. Four competitors made it to the course (a one-and-a-half mile track, over which the engine was to run twenty times each way), but one of the engines was disqualified, as it was propelled by a horse running on a treadmill. Robert Stephenson, acting on an idea of the Board's Treasurer, Henry Booth, had built a boiler with twenty-five small copper flue tubes instead of two big ones, thus dramatically increasing the heating surface, and enabling the engine to raise steam over long distances. He called it *The Rocket*. In front of an audience of 10,000 excited people, it covered the sixty miles at an average speed of fourteen m.p.h., showing off in front of the grandstand over the final run by accelerating to twenty-nine m.p.h. Its nearest rival 'mumbles and roars and rolls about like an Empty Beer Butt', wrote a spectator. *The Rocket* had triumphed in style. Robert Stephenson was soon improving on it. By 1830 he had built *The Planet*, which incorporated the engine beneath the boiler, and drove the rear wheels through a cranked axle. A larger version, *The Samson*, pulled eighty tons up a 1:96 gradient. From the primitive standing steam engine, the prototype of the modern locomotive had been achieved. By 1840 the Stephensons were supplying engines to France, Berlin, Milan and St Petersburg, and up and down the east coast of the USA. Robert Stephenson was proudest of his work as a designer and builder of steam locomotives. In assessing his greatness as a mechanical engineer, we must realize that most of what was made in the Forth

Street workshops at this stage was done by hand. There was only one small engine to drive the lathes, and no crane.

But he was also to become a famous civil engineer, as the Engineer-in-Chief in charge of the creation of the London and Birmingham Railway. He walked the route six times while surveying it, and his mastery of its details enabled him to survive fierce cross-questioning in the House of Commons by counsel for the road-coach and canal proprietors. Unlike his father, he organized thoroughly: unlike Brunel, he delegated effectively. This was just as well, for the task was a huge one, employing 20,000 men. He divided the line into six-mile contracts, and only ran the work directly himself when the difficulties were proving too great for the man on the spot. There was treacherous, crumbling rock, with powerful water springs, at Blisworth, and an epic engineering saga at Kilsby, where Stephenson was forced by the intransigence of local landowners to drive a tunnel 2,400 yards long through underground quicksands. He pushed his navvies ruthlessly, and many died. The first train steamed into Euston in 1838 six months late, and the line cost £50,000 per mile instead of the estimated £21,736. But this was the first railway into London, its importance fittingly proclaimed by the huge Doric portico at the entrance to its terminus at Euston Station.

Stephenson went on to build some remarkable bridges for his railways, the High Level Bridge over the Tyne at Newcastle, the Royal Border Bridge across the Tweed at Berwick, and the tubular bridges over the Conway and the Menai Strait onto Anglesey. He designed these last ones differently, because of the disaster when his Dee bridge near Chester collapsed beneath a train in 1847, seven months after it was opened, the result of stress on the cast iron girders. The Menai bridges were made of wrought iron tubes, which had to be floated out from the shore where they were constructed, and raised from the sea into position. The climax of this until then unique engineering feat, witnessed by Stephenson, Brunel, other leading engineers and a huge crowd, with bands and guns to celebrate, was dramatically interrupted when the hawser controlling one end of a 1,500 ton tube spun off its capstan. The foreman grabbed it, the crowd rushed to help him, and together they won a mighty tug-of-war and heaved the tube into its proper place.

Such an episode gives the flavour of the human scale of these sensational Victorian engineering achievements. Stephenson wore himself down. His wife died young, and they had no children. Driven by nervous energy, often chain-smoking cigars, he gave little time to his private affairs, and nearly went bankrupt through taking shares in one of the firms for which he worked, which failed. Even when his father's wealth became his, he found his home an empty place, relaxing only on his steam yachts. He filled his time with work. In 1847 he

became Tory MP for Whitby, and held the seat until he died. As such, he showed little foresight, supporting agricultural protection and discouraging Palmerston from getting involved in the Suez canal project, which he said would run into the sand. He and Brunel died in their fifties within a month of each other, both burnt out.

Robert Stephenson was a modest man, less visionary and more conservative than his father. But he was more patiently thorough, too. Through his mastery of the technical problems of the civil and mechanical engineering involved, Robert Stephenson & Co turned the ideas of George into the railways which, more than anything else, underpinned the Victorian Age.

Further Reading
L. T. C. Rolt, *George and Robert Stephenson: the railway revolution*, 1960.

STERNE, LAURENCE (1713-68), author, who achieved fame largely upon the basis of one novel, was born at Clonmel in Ireland where his father, an army officer, was then stationed. His mother was the daughter of a regimental sutler. He followed the regiment around but at the age of ten was sent to Halifax school where he stayed for eight years. Then his father died and his mother was left penniless, but he was helped by a cousin to go as a sizar to Jesus College, Cambridge, where he made the friendship of Hall-Stevenson, Eugenius in *Tristram Shandy*. In 1736 he took his degree and Holy Orders. In 1738 he acquired the Yorkshire living of Sutton, to which he soon added a second parish and a prebend of York, where his great-grandfather had been archbishop. In 1741 he married Eliza Lumley, though he did not for long remain satisfied by her companionship. They had one child, Lydia, to whom he was attached with a consistency of feeling which was rare in him.

Sterne's habit of shirking his responsibilities made him unpopular with his parishioners, although he was welcome in houses where a keen, none too fastidious wit was appreciated. In 1758 Mrs Sterne went out of her mind and was removed to an asylum; Sterne started the composition of *Tristram Shandy*. In 1760, after the publication of two volumes of his masterpiece, he came to London to savour its success. He was adopted by such influential patrons as Lord Bathurst but he did not lack critics. Goldsmith attacked him, Dr Johnson predictably detested him, and he drew the wrath of Whitefield: 'O Sterne, thou art scabby, and such is the leprosy of thy mind that it is not to be cured like the leprosy of thy body, by dipping nine times in the river Jordan.' Sterne invited abuse by impersonating the character of his hero. On the success of *Tristram Shandy* he hoped that he would climb from provincial obscurity to preferment in the church. He hoped that his book would advertise his talents; meanwhile he puffed it by his ostentatious behaviour. 'I wrote,' he said, 'not to be fed but to be famous.'

Tristram Shandy may be enjoyed at different levels and critics disagree, inevitably, about its author's intentions and skill. But there is no dispute about the importance of the work in the development of the novel. The popularity of the work of Fielding and Smollett carried with it the danger that the novel might stay upon the level of everyday life. A film can be made of *Tom Jones* because it reproduces scenes of contemporary life round an organized narrative. It would be hard to make a film of *Tristram Shandy*, because Sterne deliberately departed from the 'Life and Adventures' scheme and set out to make a channel for the opinions and whims of his characters. In asserting his own liberty, he cleared the field for those who followed him. Goethe found the characteristic quality of Sterne's genius to lie in his freedom of spirit and his readiness to withdraw into the citadel of his inner self; what was unsatisfactory in his character as priest and friend was part of his quality as a writer. 'Sterne,' he said, 'is a free spirit, a model in nothing, in everything an awakener and suggester.' E. M. Forster discovers a 'charmed stagnation about the whole epic – a god is hidden in Tristram Shandy and his name is muddle, and some readers cannot accept him'. But if there is an appearance of anarchy, it is not for want of scheme or of a rational approach in the writer. Even his sentimentalism, which some detest, is deliberately cultivated and highly wrought. His wit is learned, legalistic, logic-chopping, physical, the last child of the age of reason rather than the first effusion of the romantics. Thus he states his Shandean philosophy: 'True Shandeism opens the lungs and forces the blood and other vital fluids of the body to run freely through its channels, makes the wheel of life run long and cheerfully round'. Not all find Sterne's humour satisfying. 'The man is not a great humourist', said Thackeray, 'he is only a great jester'. Many have found his prurience, his peep-hole suggestiveness offensive. Indeed no great novelist has to have so much forgiven him. If his reputation survives, despite all the obvious blemishes, it must be primarily because of a psychological subtlety which transcends mere oddity and foible. His caricatures have recognizable life. Walter Shandy, Uncle Toby, Corporal Trim, each have their own hobby-horse. They pursue their delusions with a fervour that is lovable and just credible. All is rooted in Sterne's theory that when man becomes deeply attached to a favourite occupation, his character takes shape and colouring from the materials belonging to it.

Sterne's life, after his arrival in London, seems to have been dominated by his desire to cut a comic figure. But it should be recalled that in 1762 he suffered a breakdown in health; for some time he had suffered from a weakness of the lungs; ultimately he died of pleurisy.

His flirtations were primarily affairs of sentiment which subsequently he could regard with ironic detachment. In 1760 he acquired the living of Coxwold, and his wife recovered, but he did not reside there long. He published his sermons and produced from time to time further instalments of *Tristram*, finally completed in 1767. In 1762, with his wife and daughter, he went to France. He was received with rapture in France where his way of thinking was in tune with the mood of the salons: there ensued two years in the south of France. In 1764 he divided his time between London, Bath and York. In 1765 he embarked upon a tour of Italy from which was born the *Sentimental Journey*. Yorick's voyage of sensibility is a catalogue of incidents, preposterous, touching, base. If Yorick is betrayed by a hopeless instability of purpose and feeling, then he is partly Sterne himself. Sterne, in London, in 1767, enjoyed the last of his sentimental treats in a prolonged affair with Mrs Draper; when she was recalled to India by her husband, Sterne set down the record of his feelings in his *Journal to Eliza*. 'It had ever,' he made Yorick say, 'been one of the singular blessings of my life, to be almost every hour of it miserably in love with some one.'

Further Reading

A. H. Cash, *Laurence Sterne*, 2 vols, 1975 and 1992.
Peter Quennell, *Four Portraits*, 1945.
T. Yoseloff, *Laurence Sterne*, 1945.
W. Sichel, *Sterne*, 1910.

STEVENSON, ROBERT LOUIS (1850-94) is one of the few writers instantly known by his initials. RLS brings to mind *Treasure Island* and *Kidnapped*, tales of adventure for the young – and young at heart; *The Strange Case of Dr Jekyll and Mr Hyde*, mysterious and macabre; the tender sensibility of *A Child's Garden of Verses*. They are part of a larger output: other novels, short stories, essays, and tales of travel that portray a vivid personality. In certain ingrained ways he was a true Scotsman, yet spent much of his creative life abroad. He could have lived the life of an invalid; yet he was bold to the point of recklessness. Boy and man he expected attention; yet he won friends wherever he went. He scoffed at 'busyness' as 'a symptom of deficient vitality' – but studied untiringly to improve his style and turned each experience to literary effect. His own story is as unusual as anything that he wrote. Living or writing he was an adventurer of genius.

Formative years were spent in Edinburgh. The family was prosperous. His mother, a Balfour (he gave the name to the hero of *Kidnapped*), came from a line of ministers. Hers was the raven hair and dark complexion that made him look foreign and southern. His father and grandfather were noted engineers, responsible for Scotland's northern lighthouses: the hazards of storm and wreck, his father's tales of mystery and murder, of lonely inns and pirates, seized his young imagination. The sea would always be important: it was power, health and peace of mind. Weak-chested, prone to bouts of bronchitis, this only son was cherished by his nurse, Alison Cunningham, to whom, 'angel of my infant life', he dedicated *A Child's Garden*. Staunch Presbyterian by the rules of catechism and 'gude book', her stories told much of sin and punishment. The eerie and ghastly would always fascinate. He would react flamboyantly to his Calvinist upbringing and reject its theology, but the Calvinist spirit survived. It inspired the idea of Dr Jekyll's shrunken alter ego, pure evil; also the grim minister, Murdoch Soulis, in *Thrawn Janet*. Stevenson grew up a bundle of nerves, whims and fancies. He accompanied his father to lighthouses, for instance to the Isle of Eraid, off Mull: David Balfour would be stranded there. Turbulent seas and bare moors would enter his idea of Scotland, along with the grey towns of Fife, the Covenanters' graves, the wynds of Edinburgh, and its lamps 'no stars as lovely'.

'My style is from the Covenanting writers,' he would tell James Barrie. At sixteen he wrote a pamphlet on the Pentland Rising. After desultory studies at Edinburgh University, between, first, engineering, then law, eight years altogether, his anxious parents had to fall in with his intense desire to be a writer. The young Bohemian, another Villon as he envisaged himself, with his shoulder length hair, lustrous eyes, velvet jacket, dark blue flannel shirt, and smoking cap, haunted Edinburgh taverns. He disdained 'the great handicap race for six-penny pieces'. He loved to be in company and was usually its star: his fellow student, Charles Baxter, would be a life-long friend. The poet, W. E. Henley (model for Long John Silver) loved 'the old riotous, intrepid, scornful Bohemian', and would resent the wife who sought to domesticate him. 'What a famous preacher I would have made!', Stevenson declared – as he proclaimed his atheism. Edmund Gosse wrote of his 'child-like mirth … bubbling with quips and jests … silly with the silliness of the inspired schoolboy'.

Stevenson set out to learn the writer's craft by imitating models in prose and verse. Favoured writers were Scott, Wordsworth, Borrow, Whitman; among contemporaries Meredith – he read *The Egoist* 'five or six times'; an early essay, 'Roads', bears Hazlitt's imprint. Four factors were at work at this stage: his alienation from his family, a stay in Suffolk, winning the friendship of Sidney Colvin, which gave him an entrée to English literary society, and love: in Suffolk he met Fanny Sitwell, Colvin's future wife. For all his flow of words, and 'frenchified flourishing hands', he found English society daunting: 'The first shock … like a cold plunge.' He could worship this older, worldly woman without commitment; she encouraged his aspirations. Early essays, mostly for *Cornhill*, attracted notice. Travel was

involuntary, for his health, but enjoyed. 'Ordered South' celebrates the passion for France that he expressed so exhilaratingly in *Travels with a Donkey in the Cevennes* (1879).

In 1876 Stevenson met and fell in love with Fanny Osbourne, another older woman, American and married. She returned to California in 1878, he followed her there in the following year. *Across the Plains* and *The Amateur Emigrant* record memorably the pains of the journey. He could hold his own, in any company: hobos, gold-diggers, ranchers, sailors, gamblers, emigrants from different lands, all found their way to his pages. Now the prose was muscular, unadorned, without affection; interest comes from what he saw, felt and survived. He nearly died. Fanny nursed him devotedly; she obtained a divorce in the following year, they married, had the honeymoon by an abandoned silver mine that is recorded in *The Silverado Squatters*, then returned to Scotland and to forgiving parents.

After a wet Scottish summer, tuberculosis threatened, and Stevenson went to Davos and there completed the story he had been working on with his stepson Lloyd Osbourne. *Treasure Island* reflects his contentment: his writing flowed, Gladstone sat up all night reading it. *Prince Otto*, which followed, was more studied, less successful. A collection of essays, *Virginibus Puerisque* (1881) extended his reputation. Stevenson always found it hard to develop a story. In Gosse's judgement he was 'an essayist writing stories, rather than a born novelist'. Wherever he settled, he would continue to write. He spent a happy time at Hyères, near Toulon: there he worked on his verses and began *The Black Arrow*, before a cholera epidemic drove them back to England (1884) and to Bournemouth. It would not do. He was often ill, but finished *A Child's Garden*, wrote *Kidnapped* and – illustrating his versatility – *The Strange Case of Dr Jekyll and Mr Hyde*.

In 1887, with his wife, stepson and mother he went again to America, found himself famous, received lucrative contracts, collaborated with Lloyd on *The Wrong Box* and *The Ebb Tide*, and began that study in moral ambiguity, *The Master of Ballantrae*. In 1888 the family sailed from San Francisco in a hired schooner. He was to spend the rest of his life in the South Seas. He studied and observed intently, wrote evocative prose. There are few better things in the literature of travel than his description of first landfall in the Marquesas. In 1890 he returned to Samoa from a voyage to Sydney and established himself, and family at Vailima. Is there anything more extraordinary in the history of literature than this ménage? His mother, adapting remarkably; Fanny, strong-visaged, watchdog, critic and collaborator; RLS in his balcony room, always elegant, entirely self-confident, writing the stories that reflected his 'blessed, beastly memories of Scotland': *Catriona, St Ives* with much of Edinburgh in it and *Weir of Hermiston*; the very best of him was the last, its style stripped of superfluities, graphic, terse, compelling. He was working on it on the day he died of a cerebral haemorrhage. Everywhere people mourned the man who had been 'always for the joy, the colour, the adventure in life'. Forty Samoans carried his body to his grave at the top of Mount Vaen. On his grave a plaque was set, with his lines:

> Here he lies where he longed to be
> Home is the sailor home from sea
> And the hunter home from the hill.

Further Reading

M. de Bois, *Robert Louis Stevenson*, 1994.
F. J. McLynn, *Robert Louis Stevenson: a Biography*, 1993.

STEWART, ROBERT, 1st DUKE OF ALBANY
(*c*.1340-1420), Earl of Fife and Menteith and Keeper of Stirling Castle, was the second surviving son of Robert II of Scotland by Elizabeth Mure, and the younger brother of John, later King Robert III. In 1388, he was made guardian, because of the frailty of the ageing Robert II. Upon the accession of Robert III he continued to hold this position, relinquishing it in 1393, when the king himself took over. In 1398 he and his nephew, David, son of Robert III, were created Dukes of Alba and Rothesay respectively, the first two Scottish dukedoms. In 1399, a general council complained against the king's misgovernance, but the Duke of Rothesay was chosen as lieutenant in preference to Albany. This certainly intensified the rivalry between the two.

Rothesay behaved scandalously to the daughters of the Earls of March and Douglas, he abused his own power and refused to consult with the council. All this gave Albany powerful weapons against him. When Rothesay refused to give up his lieutenancy at the end of the three-year term, Robert was persuaded to approve his arrest. Albany was surely instrumental in this. Rothesay was incarcerated in his castle of Falkland, meeting his end there in March 1402 and leaving his captor as heir presumptive. The death was suspicious, to say the least, but Albany's influence was such that in May the general council found that Rothesay had died 'by divine providence and not otherwise'. Albany was made lieutenant for two years, in the first instance, and held the post until the king's death, when a novel situation arose. After the death of Rothesay, only the seven-year-old James, the younger son of Robert III, stood between Albany and the throne. The king ordered that James be conveyed to France for his own safety, but in March 1606 the boy was captured at sea and taken to London. Within days, Robert III died.

No-one disputed that James was the rightful king, but he could not be crowned or take the coronation oath. In April 1406, the general council at Perth made Albany

governor, with powers exceeding those which had at other times been wielded on behalf of crowned heads. The novel legal situation helps explain why, despite the existence of King James, the royal pretensions of Albany's reign could be tolerated. In legal terms, a case could be made for the new great seal, which was struck in his name, for the issue of charters dated by the years of his regency, and even for an Exchequer reference (1409) to the uncrowned king as 'the prince, son of the king, now in England'. Without such royal trappings, it could be argued, how could the governor deal with the lawlessness of the kingdom?

Albany was more than firm in his treatment of heretics, burning the Lollards James Resby, at Perth in 1407, and Quentin Flockhart a little later. But he did not always uphold the law with quite such resolution. In 1409 Albany made a mutual support pact with the powerful Archibald, fourth Earl of Douglas, who was able to help himself to over £5,000 of customs revenues over the next ten years. Albany continued the policy of granting pensions, some heritable, from the Crown revenues. In 1411, Donald, Lord of the Isles, a nephew of Albany, claimed the earldom of Ross against John, Earl of Buchan, who had been awarded it by his father – the Duke of Albany. Donald seized Dingwall and burned Inverness, but at the bloody battle of Harlaw Buchan, with the aid of the Earl of Mar, bastard son of the Wolf of Badenoch – and another nephew of governor Albany – marshalled the burgesses of Aberdeen and local lairds in a successful defence of the town.

Albany made no hurry to secure the return to Scotland of James I. He was more successful in the case of his own son Murdoch, who had been captured at Homildon Hill but ransomed in 1416. Albany was astute enough to counter James's detention by Henry IV by recognizing as King of England a man who attached himself to the Scottish court pretending to be Richard II, the usurped King of England imprisoned and probably murdered by Henry. Albany died in 1420, having attained the extraordinary age of eighty, and was briefly succeeded in the governorship by his son.

STEWART, ROBERT, VISCOUNT CASTLEREAGH, 2nd MARQUIS OF LONDONDERRY
(1769-1822) was born in the same year as Napoleon and Wellington. A statesman of exceptional ability, Castlereagh helped to bring about the final defeat of Napoleon in the world war and to create the durable order which followed his fall. For 100 years his reputation has suffered at the hands of historians who lived in an age of relative stability and could hardly understand the alarming international environment of Castlereagh's time; who could not therefore respect, in Morley's words, 'a European settlement, that set nationality at defiance'. In the light of the two world wars of this

century his principles and politics can be more fairly appraised. He brought his country's authority, and his diplomatic skills, to the first great experiment in international peacetime co-operation.

His father was Robert, later first Marquis; his mother Sarah Seymour-Conway. His family was of Scottish origin but settled since James I's day at Ballylawn in County Donegal; they also possessed the estate of Mount Stewart in County Down. His half-brother, General William Stewart, a notable soldier and diplomat, later succeeded to the marquisate since Robert died childless. Robert was educated at the Royal School at Armagh and at St John's College, Cambridge. He travelled abroad for a year or so and took the chance of hearing a debate in the Constituent Assembly in Paris. From 1790 to its decease he had a seat in the Irish parliament, and in the British House of Commons, for the pocket boroughs of Tregony and Orford, from 1794-7. From 1801 he sat in the united parliament for County Down, always refusing the English peerage which would have compelled him to transfer to the House of Lords. He married in 1794 the daughter of Lord Buckinghamshire; she was beautiful and he remained devoted to her; they had no children. Castlereagh was extraordinarily handsome in the patrician manner so well caught by Lawrence.

In 1798 he was made Chief Secretary on the demand of Lord Cornwallis, the new Lord Lieutenant. His task was to suppress a dangerous rebellion and to conduct through the Irish parliament the legislation for the Act of Union which he knew to be essential. The crushing of the rebellion led to brutal atrocities, while persuading Irish members to accept the Union involved systematic jobbery in titles and money. Castlereagh denounced the way in which the rebellion was crushed; in fact it was outside his control. He may have disliked the methods necessary to carry out the Union, but it should be remembered that parliamentary seats were regarded as a species of property; like Pitt, Castlereagh would have thought it wrong to abolish them without compensation. He was a firm advocate of the emancipation of the Catholics and he resigned, with Pitt, when this was refused by the king. He did not have a strong feeling of party obligation, however, and took office under Addington when he was offered the Presidency of the Board of Control. When Wellesley wanted support for his forward policies, Castlereagh provided it, in parliament and with the directors of the East India Company. Nor did he ever, for political or personal purposes, utilize the vast patronage of the Indian empire. He did, however, urge caution upon Wellesley. His belief that it would be dangerous to be too closely involved in the affairs of 'that turbulent (Maratha) Empire' was proved to be well-grounded.

In July 1805 Castlereagh was made Secretary of State for War and the Colonies. He was Pitt's chief lieutenant in the Commons; the rest of the Cabinet were all in the Lords. In the months when England faced invasion he showed a great composure and an ability to plan operations with meticulous care. Unfortunately the expedition which was to have gone to north Germany to support Prussia had to be recalled to England when Napoleon's too rapid moves and his victory at Austerlitz made it plain that there was nothing for them to do. Of greater significance, though not realized at the time, was Home Popham's capture of Cape Colony in January 1806. In that month Pitt died and Castlereagh was left without office by the oddly-named 'Ministry of All the Talents'. When the Portland ministry was formed, however, in 1807, Castlereagh returned to the War Office. The new administration contained five future prime ministers; Castlereagh was never to hold that office, but he was for many years, with Metternich, the most influential statesman in Europe.

He made intelligent preparations for a new and greater army. Behind the regular army of 200,000 there was to be a regular militia of 120,000 which was intended to supply gaps in the army and take home service off its shoulders. Beyond these forces stood the 'sedentary militia', based upon the counties, another 200,000; 'volunteers of the best description', 180,000, and finally a body of trained men, not yet organized in battalions but available to fill the gaps in the militia. The entire scheme gave the country a military force far better than anything that had existed before. Was it properly used? In the long run success in the Peninsula justified Castlereagh's work but at first there were cruel disappointments. Wellesley's victory at Vimiero was undone by the dilatory conduct of his seniors, Burrard and Dalrymple. Sir John Moore was compelled to retreat precipitately before the French. He won a splendid victory before the evacuation of his force, but he was killed in January 1809. Canning wished to blame Moore for this; Castlereagh, with that magnanimity which seldom failed him, accepted responsibility for the operation. In Moore, Castlereagh had picked a fine professional soldier; it was unfortunate that Napoleon had been enabled by the Convention of Erfurt with Alexander I to concentrate his troops in Spain. In 1809, however, it seemed that he was in trouble with the Austrians. Castlereagh's plan to land a large force at Walcheren to destroy the French invasion flotilla at Antwerp and to exploit any further reverses the emperor might receive was therefore sensible. This time his choice of commander was at fault. Chatham was dilatory and the expedition accomplished nothing beyond the capture of Flushing, having lost half its 40,000 men.

Castlereagh had to cope with all the problems that came with the leadership of the government in the Commons under an ailing prime minister. He was undermined by the ambitious rivalry of Canning. When he discovered that Canning had been making his own membership of the government conditional upon Castlereagh's dismissal, he called him out to a duel. Canning's punishment for months of intrigue was a light wound in the thigh – and exclusion from high office again until after the war. Castlereagh was able to continue in active support of Perceval's administration and before the latter's assassination in 1812 he was recalled to office. From February 1812 until his death he was foreign minister, for all but a few months of that time under Liverpool. These years which saw the defeat of Napoleon, the peace settlement of Vienna and the operations of the Quadruple Alliance tested to the full his diplomatic gifts. He proved himself a statesman of a high order, perhaps the greatest foreign minister that this country has ever had. A modern authority, Lord Strang, has seen him as the founder of the British tradition of firm but conciliatory diplomacy.

Almost alone he had to speak for the government in the Commons, against a captious opposition, and upon a wide range of questions. He showed a mastery on different occasions of constitutional law and monetary policy. He was formidable in argument but more matter-of-fact than eloquent. He was not usually able to inspire the house but he seldom failed to convince it. Hobhouse thought he spoke best when under sharp attack, like a top 'which spins best when it is most whipped'. But he must often have been very tired. It should be remembered that his staff was ludicrously small and amateurish by modern standards; most memoranda, dispatches and letters he penned himself. Government then was personal in a way that is hard for us to grasp. The physical and emotional strain was immense. He had little leisure for the enjoyments of private life. Instead he was immersed in great events. They were exciting enough. He grasped the significance of Napoleon's defeat in Russia and played a big part in the formation of the new alliance, encouraging the Russians and Prussians, on whom its success depended, to come to a closer understanding. When the forces of the great powers had defeated Napoleon at Leipzig, Castlereagh had to prevent the alliance falling apart as others had done; after weeks of personal negotiation at allied headquarters he persuaded them to sign the Treaty of Chaumont, by which they bound themselves to make no separate peace, and to remain in alliance for twenty years after the end of the war. He promised that Britain would pay twice as much for the final efforts of the war as any other power. Castlereagh's personality weighed more, however, than British gold. Metternich was impressed. In his memoirs he later recorded his considered view: 'Absolutely straight, a stranger to all prejudice, as just as he is kind, Lord Castlereagh knew at a glance how to distinguish the truth in everything.' In the opinion of Lord Ripon, who was

with him on mission, his energy at this crisis decided the fate of the campaign.

Castlereagh's initiative and resolve were rewarded. In April Napoleon was expelled to Elba. For Castlereagh the 'Hundred Days' was but an interval, anxious enough, in the complex work of peace-making. The terms of the settlement of Vienna provide the framework for the history of the century that followed. Suffice it to say that a redrawing of the map which was in many ways generous and far-seeing, which produced an order of things more stable than the peace of 1919, was to a large extent his work. At no time in our history has the influence of Britain in Europe been more impressive. It came partly because it was seen to be disinterested, partly because of Castlereagh's moral ascendancy. A clause upon which England insisted was the guarantee of France to abolish the slave trade within five years. The mild treatment of France, even after the Hundred Days, by which that country was able so soon to re-enter the concert of the great powers, reflected Castlereagh's temper. 'Equilibrium' was one of his favourite words. He believed that as a result of the peace settlement 'calculations of prudence' had been simplified for there remained 'but few Pieces on the board to complicate the Game of Publick safety'. He once explained his hopes of a system which would give 'the counsels of the Great Powers the efficiency and almost the simplicity of a single State'. He condemned a French intrigue in Buenos Aires as 'flowing from some of the dregs of that old diplomacy which so long poisoned the body politic of Europe ...' England's duty was to prevent the revival of 'a more contentious order of things', since 'our insular situation places us sufficiently out of reach of danger to admit of our pursuing a more generous and confiding policy'. The treaty, for all its faults (one, the union of Belgium and Holland, was soon to be exposed), embodied these principles and produced a remarkably stable order. But he did not sympathize entirely with the use that the other powers intended to make of that order.

At home, where he was associated with the government's resistance to all suggestions of radical reform and where he played a large part in enacting the Six Acts of 1819, Castlereagh was generally regarded as the embodiment of blind reaction, the willing accomplice of the legitimists. He adhered loyally to the principle that the powers must act together and supported the congresses that met from time to time to put their co-operation into effect. He was, however, temperamentally opposed to what he privately called 'the sublime mysticism and nonsense' of the Tsar Alexander's Holy Alliance and regretted the confusion that ensued between the repressive aims of the *exaltés* and the more negative intentions of the Quadruple Alliance. He was also sensitive to the isolationist spirit that always takes Englishmen after a great war: as danger recedes it becomes once more indecent to be a European! His view was that England should use her influence to restrain the monarchs from unwarranted interference, as in 1820, in the case of the Spanish insurrection and Russia. He later denounced the principle of Troppau, that the powers had a right to act together to suppress revolution, in a way that gave much encouragement to nationalist feeling. Over the Greek question that occupied the last months of his life he laid down principles from which Canning did not deviate. Indeed it may be guessed that if he had lived Castlereagh would have acted much as did the supposedly more liberal Canning. Sure in his own judgement, knowing that he had steady support from the majority of ordinary Members of Parliament, Castlereagh did not care about public opinion. He cultivated an air of aloofness and even said that it was more gentlemanly to be unpopular. There was also a natural shyness: Princess Lieven found him short of words at dinner parties except when he could talk of his sheepbreeding at North Cray. There he was a charming host. In public he was imposing – like Mont Blanc, said Croker. 'He is *better* than ever; that is, colder, steadier, more pococurante, and withal more amiable and respected. It is a splendid summit of bright and polished frost which, like the travellers in Switzerland, we all admire; but no-one can hope and few would wish to reach.' His real forte lay in private negotiation. Wilberforce found him so persuasive in such meetings that he tried always to deal with him by letter. He could wear down an opponent by persistence, knowledge and charm. In 1818 he produced forty-three objections to European proposals that the Quadruple Alliance should intervene in troubles between Spain and her South American colonies. His moral and intellectual ascendancy was better known to the Tsar Alexander and to Talleyrand than it was to the mass of his own countrymen. Metternich thought him to be the only Englishman to understand Europe.

In the summer of 1822 Castlereagh began to show signs of the strain of continuous high office. Besides his supervision of foreign affairs he had to bear much of the brunt of the depression and unrest at home. The unpopularity of George IV made matters worse for his harassed ministers; the ludicrous crisis caused by the queen at the time of the coronation strained loyalty and patience. Castlereagh was a solitary worker and he had few confidants. To the end all this official correspondence was in his own handwriting. He became the victim of an obsession that he was threatened by the exposure of some charge of immorality – probably groundless – though the blackmail may have been real enough. His intense unpopularity with certain radical and popular elements of the public may have worn down his resistance to such insinuations. The king, noticing Castlereagh's uncharacteristically hysterical manner, warned Liverpool and medical precautions were taken.

Lady Castlereagh refused to give him the key of his pistol case but he found a small penknife and stabbed himself to death on the morning of 12 August. It has been conjectured that he was suffering from paraproteinaemia, an imbalance in the blood that could damage the brain, so giving rise to delusions.

He was buried in Westminster Abbey. A few ruffians jeered at his coffin but there was no large demonstration of hostility. That he was universally execrated was a crude Whig myth, promulgated by men such as Byron: his epigrams are too well known. The appreciation of a parliamentary opponent is better worth quoting. Brougham wrote to Creevey: 'Put all their men together in one scale, and poor Castlereagh in the other – single, he plainly weighed them down.' Friends and foes alike recognized his courage, straightness and coolness. Had he lived a year or so more, had he been more articulate, more of a phrasemaker, he might have been able to prove that, as the French historian, Albert Sorel, recognized, his principles 'to which he adhered with unshakeable constancy … were all comprehended in one, the supremacy of English interests; they all proceeded from this high reason of state'. Castlereagh, impassive, lofty, energetic without false display, practical in everything, succeeded, as few English ministers have succeeded since, in being a good European while remaining a steadfast patriot.

Further Reading
C. J. Bartlett, *Castlereagh*, 1966.
J. A. R. Marriott, *Castlereagh*, 1936.
C. K. Webster, *The Foreign Policy of Castlereagh*, vol. i, *1812-15*, 1930 and vol. ii, *1815-22*, 2nd edn, 1934.

STIGAND (*d.c.*1072) achieved notoriety as the last Anglo-Saxon Archbishop of Canterbury. His name was Old Norse rather than Old English, and he was probably a native of Norwich; it is therefore likely that he was of Anglo-Scandinavian descent. He must have been born about 990, for he was already a priest by 1020. (According to the law of the church, not always observed in practice, a man might not be ordained to the priesthood before the age of thirty.) It is in the latter year that he first comes into view, as the king's priest who was granted the newly-founded royal minster at Ashingdon in Essex. In other words, he had ingratiated himself rapidly with the new régime of the conqueror Canute and was doing well out of it. (The parallel with the secular career of Earl Godwin is striking.) His progress during the remainder of Canute's reign was unspectacular, though his subscriptions of royal charters suggest that he remained close to the centre of public affairs. Thereafter his rise was meteoric. King Edward promoted him to the bishopric of Elmham in 1043, onward and upward to Winchester in 1047 and finally to the pinnacle of Canterbury in 1052.

However, there were flaws in his position. First, he had been uncanonically intruded into Canterbury following the expulsion of the previous incumbent, Robert Champart. Second, he was a pluralist: he retained the see of Winchester after his move to Canterbury. Third, when in 1058 he acquired his pallium, the symbol of archiepiscopal authority, it was from the anti-pope, Benedict X, himself in uncanonical possession of the see of Rome. These irregularities were ably exploited by William of Normandy who received papal support for his invasion in 1066 on the grounds that he would purge the church in England of its corrupt head.

It does not appear that Stigand himself was troubled by his neglect of proper form. He comes across from the records that have survived as an extremely worldly prelate. Canterbury and Winchester were the two wealthiest sees in England. He had jobbed his brother Ethelmaer into the bishopric of Elmham on his departure for Winchester in 1047. He was accused of prolonging vacancies in some of the richer abbeys such as Ely in order to divert their revenues into his own pocket. He acquired extensive estates, especially in East Anglia and Gloucestershire, not always by reputable means.

Stigand was immensely powerful as well as immensely rich. The Archbishop of Canterbury was a key figure in the life of the state as well as of the church. Stigand was an able administrator who was one of the first ministers of Edward throughout his reign. By 1066 he had been at the centre of English public life for nearly half a century. He knew everybody who mattered; he knew how everything worked. He was indispensable.

Perhaps it was for this reason that William the Conqueror was so slow to move against him. Stigand had crowned Harold in January 1066. After the battle of Hastings he had toyed with loyalty to Edgar Atheling, but like Archbishop Ealdred of York and others he had come round to William. In March 1067 Stigand was taken in honourable captivity to Normandy. On his return to England he was permitted to resume his archiepiscopal functions. But he must have known that the game was up. In the spring of 1070 a papal legate visited England and held a church council at Winchester at which Stigand was deposed. He must by then have been a very old man. He was permitted to live out the remainder of his days unmolested. He is said to have died in 1072.

Further Reading
F. Barlow, *The English Church 1000-1066*, 1963.

STONOR, SIR WILLIAM (c.1449-94), the central figure of the Stonor Letters, represents the normal lifestyle and aspirations of a country gentleman. The family fortunes had been established by Chief Justice Sir John Stonor (d.1354) and had not changed much thereafter. William was the eldest of seven offspring of Thomas Stonor (d.1474) by Jane (d.1494), apparently a French-born bastard of the Duke of Suffolk. Although strict parents, who kept a strict rein on William's initiative, they provided generously for all their children. Personal profit rather than social advancement explains William's first two marriages to well-endowed widows of mercantile stock, but it was social climbing and the need for an heir that prompted his third marriage to Anne Neville, niece of Warwick the Kingmaker and sister of a former duke. Yet all three marriages offered affection and mutual support through the childbirth, disease and mortality that were constantly recurring themes. William himself lost three wives in seven years. An unusual, but not unique, experience.

The letters illuminate William's management of his affairs: everyday estate administration, his involvement in the wool-trade, ecclesiastical patronage, litigation and legal correspondence. Although he employed a receiver, steward, lawyers and bailiffs, William was certainly the directing influence. Like previous generations of Stonors, William 'took an active share in such public work as fell normally to country gentlemen of rank and favour' as sheriff, knight of the shire (MP) and justice of the peace for Oxfordshire. On one occasion, for example, he exceeded his powers by seizing corn bought privately before going to the market. He sought to increase his local authority and perhaps his income too by taking on stewardships from the Bishop of Lincoln, St Albans Abbey, and St George's Chapel, Windsor. He may have held a forest appointment under Lord Lovell, who asked him to care for his deer, whilst the queen, ironically, accused him of poaching her game. The principal lordly influence was probably initially the de la Poles, of whom both duchesses – Alice Chaucer of Ewelme (d.1475) and Elizabeth of York – feature prominently. After 1480 his main lord was most likely the queen's son, Thomas, Marquis of Dorset, for William was told – surely an exaggeration – that 'you be the greatest man with my lord (of Dorset) and in his conceit'. Richard, Duke of Gloucester also has a walk-on part. Whilst mixing with such people and interesting himself in local politics, William does not actually seem to have been retained by anyone.

Since the days of the chief justice, no Stonor had enjoyed a public career of more than local importance, but in 1478 Stonor was knighted and soon after became a knight of the body. One factor may be his first wife's taste for court-life, another that he was 'the most courteous knight that ever was', but he also needed a patron and we do not know for certain who it was. Court life was costly, as William duly found, but it brought influence. He could not have become steward of Oxford University without court contacts, however generous he had been to impoverished scholars. Although his household office gave him a role at Richard III's coronation, prior loyalties to Edward IV's children and the Wydevilles must explain his participation with so many southern gentry in Buckingham's disastrous rebellion in 1483. Although William escaped alive, his estates were confiscated, but they were restored on Henry VII's accession. William recovered his household office and was made a banneret on the field of Stoke in 1487, without however significantly improving the family's wealth or standing. That pattern was more common than radical transformation in a single generation.

Further Reading
C. L. Kingsford, ed., *Stonor Letters and Papers of the Fifteenth Century*, 2 vols, Camden Society, 3rd series xxix xxx, 1919.

STRATFORD, JOHN (*c.*1280-1348), Bishop of Winchester (1323-3) and Archbishop of Canterbury (1333-48), was 'something of a statesman'. From Stratford-on-Avon and educated at Oxford University, he attended Merton College, and was doctor of canon and civil law by 1311 and assured of rapid employment. The university's proctor at the Curia in 1311, official of the Bishop of Lincoln in 1317, and Dean of Arches by 1321, he was a royal clerk by 1320 and frequently ambassador thereafter. In 1323 he was promoted Bishop of Winchester while at the Curia rather than Edward II's nominee Robert Baldock. The king furiously accused him of 'acting fraudulently in the affairs committed to him by the king for the profit of himself and his friends and not without the vice of ambition'. Forced to answer for his embassy, Stratford's lands were withheld, he had to buy the stock back, and was bound to pay £12,000. Expertise, not reconciliation, explain further diplomacy and his capacity to advise – fatally – that Queen Isabella should negotiate in France. From 1326 he supported the Earl of Lancaster and thus shared his disgrace in 1329. The fall of Isabella and Mortimer ushered in ten years when Stratford was chief minister and thrice chancellor. His brother Robert, Bishop of Chichester 1337-62, was chancellor twice.

As a minister, Stratford supported the French war, but as a cleric, he was under papal pressure to seek peace and opposed infringements of ecclesiastical and lay liberties. A highly popular stance. Edward III's war effort was crippled by lack of money and so in 1339 he made Stratford head of government with responsibility for providing adequate supply. Stratford satisfied certain popular grievances in return for new taxes, but these proved too little too late and compelled a truce in 1340. Regrettably 'the state lacked the mechanism to control the fiscal arrangements which would ensure the very high receipts from taxation which the king needed', but Edward blamed Stratford, accused him of malice and neglect, and brought him to trial. Edward's attack on the concessions Stratford had made gave the archbishop support in council and parliament, made the clash into a crisis for himself, and turned Stratford into a constitutional hero. The archbishop resisted and escaped unscathed, but his career in government was over.

In 1323 John XXII was impressed by Stratford's 'watchful zeal and careful diligence, his persistent labour and the loyal and skilful way he conducted the royal business'. He was: 'sufficiently endowed with the highest gifts, of a conspicuous fairness of manner and refined elegance of life, adorned with honourable behaviour, prudent in spiritual matters and circumspect in temporal business. One who will understand the church, rule it usefully and govern it wisely.' He was a devotee of St Thomas Becket. Yet Stratford's biographer remarks on his worldliness, he was capable of remarkable arrogance and virulence, and he made irreconcilable enemies of two kings and Bishop Orleton.

The archbishop never lost interest in his roots at Stratford, where his parents had founded the chapel of the Guild of Holy Cross and the associated almshouse. John largely rebuilt Holy Trinity Church, established a chantry to Becket there, added a college of priests, and endowed it with the parish church. His brother Robert helped pave the streets and their kinsman Ralph Stratford, Bishop of London 1340-54, built a house for the priests. Locality, family and piety coincided.

Further Reading
W. M. Ormrod, *The Reign of Edward III*, 1990.
P. Heath, *Church and Realm 1272-1461*, 1988.
N. M. Fryde, 'Edward III's removal of his ministers and judges 1340-1', *Bulletin of the Institute of Historical Research* xlviii, 1975.
G. L. Harriss, *King, Parliament and Public Finance in Medieval England to 1369*, 1975.
N. M. Fryde, 'John Stratford, Bishop of Winchester and the Crown 1323-30', *Bulletin of the Institute of Historical Research* xliv, 1971.

STRATFORD DE REDCLIFFE, 1st VISCOUNT (1786-1880), better known as **STRATFORD CANNING**, is the only diplomat to be commemorated in Westminster Abbey, and he may well keep that record, for his fame rests on circumstances which will not be repeated. The electric telegraph did not reach Constantinople during his time there. When Palmerston needed to send an urgent message to him, he despatched three Queen's Messengers by different routes, and the fastest took nine days to reach Belgrade. Stratford grew accustomed to acting on his own: all the more so because he spent most of his fifty working years in the same place. Blessed with distinguished good looks ('a broad and massive overhanging brow gave him an air of profound wisdom and sagacity', commented Layard), and a wife who softened the rough edges of his explosive temper, he was held in awe by the Turks, who called him 'Buyuck Elchi', the Great Ambassador. He himself did not have the same respect for the Turk, whom he described to Wellesley as 'cringing to his superiors, quarreling with his equals, preying upon his dependants and indiscriminately cheating them all'. Indeed, he came to regard their reform as his mission in life. He developed a close 'uncle-nephew' bond with the weak, well-meaning Sultan Abdul Medjid, and found an ally in his minister Reschid Pasha, but his efforts to push through agricultural, administrative, military and tax reforms came to little. Turkey remained 'the sick man of Europe'.

But for a long time he was successful in his other main aim, to keep the Russians out. Behind the personal vendetta between him and Tsar Nicholas I, who had refused to accept him as ambassador to St Petersburg, lay the tsar's Balkan ambitions, nurtured since the Treaty of Unkiar Skelessi (1833) had opened the Straits between the Black Sea and the Mediterranean to Russian ships only. From 1848 Nicholas looked further. The Balkans under Turkey threatened to become hotbeds of dangerous nationalists. They must be occupied and partitioned by stronger powers, with Russia in the lead. Stratford set himself to prevent this. He believed that a firm stand would do so without war, but could not get it from Aberdeen and Russell. 'Shilly-shallying will spoil all', he wrote. 'The extreme desire for peace may bring on the danger of war.' With a government striving for compromise and Stratford encouraging the Turks to take a strong line, misunderstandings were likely. Many back in Britain, the court, the government and *The Times* among them, blamed him for the outbreak of the Crimean War. But most historians have agreed that Stratford had a clearer idea of what was needed to hold off the Russians than Aberdeen did.

He left no lasting legacy. The Peace of Paris which ended the war gave the Turks breathing space, but before Stratford's long life was over the Russians were hovering round the Balkans again. His most enduring achievement had happened earlier, when he helped the Greeks to gain their independence in 1830, and won for them a defensible northern frontier. To his influence over the Sultan we also owe the presence in the British Museum of the frieze from the Mausoleum of Halicarnassus, one of the Seven Wonders of the World.

Further Reading
E. F. Malcolm Smith, *The Life of Stratford Canning*, 1933.

STRATTON, ADAM (d.1294), alias Adam Argoyles, the notorious moneylender and forger, was one of several brothers from Stretton St Margaret in Wiltshire. A clerk, perhaps even a Master of Arts, he became a pluralist to rival Bogo Clare, ultimately holding twenty-three rectories in the province of Canterbury. An executor and therefore presumably a trusted servant of Baldwin, Earl of Devon (d.1262), he entered the service of the earl's sister, Isabella Forz, Countess of Aumale by

1263 and controlled all her financial affairs from 1278-88. She gave him annuities and livings, the deputy-chamberlainship of the Royal Exchequer, in 1276 the chamberlainship itself and its valuable appurtenant lands, and, not least, access to her funds. Henry III and Edward I were satisfied with his service. The chamberlainship involved custody of the Royal Treasury and of Exchequer records and thus offered means to misappropriate royal funds, use royal justice to pursue private debtors, register forged deeds, and generally to coerce and intimidate. From 1260 Adam was buying up the debts of Jews. Henceforth his moneylending and extortion betray not just blatant dishonesty, but also a mastery of financial and legal technicalities that made him very difficult to bring to book. From his headquarters in London's Smale Lane he used the countess's and king's officials and Italian bankers to handle his affairs elsewhere. His success emerges in £12,666 *in coin* alone seized in his possession in 1289, equivalent to half the annual income of the Crown, and his payment of a further 500 mark (£333) fine by 1292.

Adam's fall came in three stages. On behalf of the Countess Isabella, he had cut the seal off a charter to Quarr Abbey, but even his conviction in 1278 and other complaints in 1279 did not interrupt his service to her or the Crown. Complaints of misgovernment in 1289 brought Stratton as well as the judges to trial. Charged with offences reputedly ranging from homicide to sorcery, Stratton abandoned what the king had seized and paid a fine from what remained. Only his conviction for forgery in 1292 ended his service to the Crown, yet although disgraced he retained his livings until his death two years later.

Stratton's career blurs the lines between private and public service and indicates the immense scope for corruption and self-enrichment in the royal administration. Behind the orderly processes and records of government, apparently diligent and devoted officers could oppress and cheat the king's subjects. Contemporaries could not determine whether Adam also defrauded the Crown and found it almost impossible to prove even the most blatant crimes.

Further Reading
M. W. Farr, ed., *Accounts and Surveys of the Wiltshire Estates of Adam de Stratton*, Wiltshire Archaeological Society Record Branch xii, 1958.
N. Denholm-Young, *Seignorial Administration in England*, 1937.
T. F. Tout and H. Johnstone, eds, *State Trials of the Reign of Edward the First 1289-93*, Camden Society, 3rd series ix, 1906.

STREET, GEORGE EDMUND (1824-81), architect, is best known as the designer of the law courts in the Strand in London. Apart from this, almost all his buildings were church commissions – schools and vicarages as well as churches. A devoted High Churchman, who enjoyed singing in choirs, he met Benjamin Webb, secretary of the Ecclesiological Society, soon after finishing his training in Gilbert Scott's office. Webb introduced him to Samuel Wilberforce, Bishop of Oxford, who appointed him his diocesan architect in 1852. Four years later he moved to London and set up his own practice, keeping his Oxford job and later holding the same position in the dioceses of York, Winchester and Ripon. He was responsible for rebuilding the nave of Bristol Cathedral and carrying out extensive renovations to Salisbury and Carlisle Cathedrals.

Street had, it seems, an inexhaustible capacity for hard work. As a young man, most of his leisure time was spent on excursions, making detailed sketches of churches, first in England and then in France, Germany, Italy and Spain. Many of his designs were influenced by what he had seen on the continent. He built in a strong and massive style, designing all the details himself. Often his commissions were in rapidly developing urban areas. One of his most famous churches, St James the Less in Pimlico, built to tower over the surrounding tenements, was described in the *Illustrated London News* in 1861 as 'a lily among the weeds'.

He was Professor of Architecture at the Royal Academy and, just before he died, President of the Institute of British Architects. Street inspired great loyalty and affection among those who worked for him, many of whom went on to become famous – William Morris, Philip Webb and Norman Shaw for example. He was also a friend of the Pre-Raphaelite painters, and took a keen interest in the developing arts and crafts movement.

STUART, ARABELLA (1575-1615) was in the last years of Elizabeth I's reign next after James VI of Scotland in succession to the English throne. Her father, the Earl of Lennox, younger brother of James's father, Darnley, was, through the female line, grandson of Margaret Tudor by her second husband the Earl of Angus. Her claim was slight by comparison with that of James, but his apprehensiveness, always exaggerated, was stimulated by the facts that Arabella was English-born and that the common law forbade aliens, Scots included, to inherit land in England. To make matters worse, Arabella fell in love with William Seymour, grandson of Lady Catherine Grey, heiress to the throne through the Suffolk line under Henry VIII's will, which had disinherited Margaret Tudor. Arabella herself was harmless enough, and James in the early months of his reign sensibly ignored the talk which linked her name with the alleged plotting of Cobham and Ralegh. Until 1609 he treated her kindly, though parsimoniously. Then he imprisoned her when it was rumoured that she was about to marry Seymour. Early in 1610 the couple declared solemnly to the Council that they would not marry without James's

consent, and they were restored to favour. But that July their long patience snapped, and they married secretly. Inevitably the news reached the king, and they were imprisoned separately. Seymour escaped and got away to Ostend. Arabella, too, escaped, but was recaptured off a French ship in the Channel. James locked her in the Tower, where the unhappy woman went out of her mind and died in 1615.

STUART, CHARLES (1753-1801), general, was the fourth son of the third Earl of Bute, George III's prime minister. He was a successful commander in the Revolutionary wars. But for his early death, in Fortescue's opinion, he might have earned the name of a Marlborough or a Wellington. He saw active service first in America. 'Exceedingly intelligent, takes great pains and is as bold as a lion', ran a superior's report. For two years he was in command of a battalion of Cameronians. After his return from America he could find little employment. The name of Bute still aroused prejudice. He travelled, however, a great deal and acquired a knowledge of languages, especially Italian. In 1794, acting in conjunction with Nelson, he executed a masterly attack upon Calvi, the formidable French stronghold in Sicily. Roads had to be made and guns hauled over rocky hills to a height of 900 feet. The town, with its numerically superior garrison, surrendered in August.

In 1798 Stuart was given the assignment of capturing Minorca. 'No-one,' wrote Admiral St Vincent, recommending him, 'can manage Frenchmen as him, and the English will go to hell for him.' Dundas, the Secretary of State, may have had misgivings for Stuart was proud, a true son of the Butes, and held politicians in contempt (though he was himself Member of Parliament for Bossiney). When he had been sent to Portugal to stiffen that country's resistance he had written to Dundas, 'I am determined to be guided by your instructions so long as they are within the reach of my comprehension'! In the view of ministers he was a cantankerous fellow who delighted to scorn orders and to argue with his superiors.

As a commander of men Stuart was inspiring: fiery, strikingly handsome in a thoroughbred way, pleasant-mannered, but a furious worker. He had turned a rabble of French loyalists into a well-disciplined force. With the staunch aid of Graham he secured Minorca without losing a man. He had no field guns, since their carriages fell to pieces on the roads, but by sound planning and a marvellous piece of bluff he brought the French garrison to surrender to a smaller force. He refused (and was surely right in doing so) the pleas of Dundas for a raid on the fortress of Cartagena: 'Let no persuasion of the navy,' he said, 'lead you to conceive its reduction could be accomplished by a handful of men.' He used his time better by fortifying Minorca: every landing place was made an impregnable maze of earthworks. When Nelson appealed for troops to help hold Sicily, however, he responded at once and went there himself with two regiments. He drafted a masterly plan for the island's defence. 'Essential military operations,' he wrote, in words which anticipate the events of the Peninsular wars, 'are too often avoided, neglected and misarranged from the false idea that they can only be effected by disciplined troops, whereas in many cases, in many countries and particularly in Sicily, the joint efforts and exertions of armed peasants are more likely to prove effectual.' How many regular soldiers have been so imaginative? Somehow this unusual man made patriots and soldiers out of suspicious Sicilian peasants. Graham, another Scotsman, equally dedicated and resourceful, completed his work; Stuart had to return to England, sick, worn out by his endeavours.

After his Minorca triumph Stuart had proposed forming a Mediterranean force to operate against the French flank. Attacking extended communications on the Italian Riviera in the summer of 1799 it might have brought disaster upon the extended French armies. The government preferred to mount an invasion of the Netherlands in conjunction with the Russians. When eventually the Cabinet came round to Stuart's Mediterranean plan, ministers had been shaken by the failure of the Helder expedition. Dundas supported Stuart, but the Cabinet was divided and half an already small force was sent to Brittany to aid the royalist insurgents. General Pigott brought 5,000 men to Minorca in April 1800. By then Stuart had resigned. He had refused to implement the decision of the Cabinet to hand Malta over to Russia. Dundas, defending a bad decision – for the Russians were already planning to leave the coalition – was at least right to say 'If officers are to control our councils there is an end to all governments.'

It is hard to resist the conclusion that his country had wasted his talents. As an administrator he was recognized by the Duke of York, an authority at least in that field. He asked for information about Stuart's system of regulation of commissariat, pay and medical departments, 'a system that everyone is loud in praise of'. As a strategist he offered analysis and planning of a high order. He understood the need for naval and military co-operation and his friendly association with Nelson showed what could be done in this way. His Italian plan could have made a decisive difference by giving the Austrians support at the point at which the French were, at that stage, most vulnerable. Napoleon might then have lost the battle of Marengo. Fortescue accepts his failings, his 'imperfect sense of discipline', his lack of physical strength and of that 'divine patience which characterized Marlborough'. And yet he was the soldier who came nearest to Marlborough in the combination of 'personal charm, ascendancy over men, diplomatic skill, bodily courage, resolute will, administrative ability and strategic insight'.

Further Reading
John Fortescue, *Six British Soldiers*, 1928.

STUART, PRINCE CHARLES EDWARD (1720-88) was born at the Palazzo Muti, in Rome, in December 1720. At this time his father, the Old Pretender, or James III as he might be called, according to allegiance, was a disappointed man of thirty-one, melancholy and resigned to a life of exile. His mother, Maria-Clementina Sobieska, was devout, intense and somewhat delicate; she gave birth to a second son, Henry, and then retired temporarily to a nunnery. The cause of her estrangement from her husband was religious: she objected to the appointment of a Protestant tutor, James Murray, for her elder son. James III, who was not prepared to alter his own religion for the sake of a throne, was tolerant nonetheless, and allowed Charles to grow up without settled religious convictions. He was fairly clever and learned Italian, French and English without difficulty, but his education was as haphazard as his family background was unsettled. He grew up a restless boy, agile, active, a good rider and a good shot; tall but slight, with the colouring of his ancestress, Mary Queen of Scots: light brown hair and chestnut eyes (though the iconography of this prince is controversial; some paintings give him fair hair and blue eyes; when he grew a beard it was red).

Charles Edward came to be regarded by Jacobites at home as the hopeful prospect, while he himself became absorbed by the Cause. He made plans for fortifications and hardened himself by long walks and other feats of endurance. In January 1744, in secret and in disguise, he left Rome for France, where an expedition was being prepared. Unfortunately the Brest fleet which was to have escorted the transports to England was scattered by a storm and Marshal Saxe turned to other plans. For over a year Charles dallied incognito, impatient and frustrated by the half-hearted attitude of the French government. Then he decided to cross alone. For this single act of courage and initiative Charles deserves his place in legend. He raised a small loan from Waters, the Jacobite banker in Paris, bought some arms, ammunition and brandy, hired a brig and a man-of-war and set sail for the Western Isles.

After a running fight with an English ship, leaving the brig to put back to France, the *du Teillay* landed the prince with six companions at Eriska at the end of July. On 4 August, Charles dismissed the ship where he had held his first hopeful audiences. On the 19th he raised his standard at Glenfinnan: by his side was Murray of Broughton, a Lowlander, appointed to be his secretary and suspect to the Highlanders from the start. After an agonizing wait, the pipes of the Camerons announced the arrival of his most substantial aid. With 700 of this wild clan were some Macdonalds, Stewarts of Appin, MacDonnells, Clanranalds and MacLeods. Like some other August crises, this venture found the English government unprepared. In Duncan Forbes of Culloden they had a shrewd Lord President whose influence helped to damp down support for the Pretender. But Sir John Cope had neither troops nor talent enough to hold the Highlanders. On 17 September they entered Edinburgh unopposed, now under the command of Lord George Murray, a veteran of the '15. There Charles accepted the huzzas of the people in the courtyard below Holyrood, while his father was proclaimed James VIII of Scotland at the Mercat Cross. Four days later he met Cope, who had shipped his troops south from Aberdeen, at Prestonpans. The two forces, at about 2,500, were equal but Cope's troops were panicky and handicapped further by a morning mist. 'They escaped like rabets,' the prince wrote to his father, after an action that lasted for a bare ten minutes. Cope himself brought to Berwick the news of a defeat which had exposed England to the rebel army. Charles wanted to march direct upon England. Still a somewhat detached figure in all the excitement and the intrigues of his counsellors, he was overruled, stayed in Edinburgh for five weeks and did little more than to declare the Union with England at an end. Edinburgh Castle held out and the bankers whose money was so important took shelter within its walls.

On 1 November the army marched southward, not towards Newcastle where Wade lay, as Charles wanted, but towards Carlisle and the west, where Murray hoped that they would find recruits. On the 15th, Carlisle Castle surrendered. At Lancaster, Preston and Manchester, there was enthusiasm but a scarcity of recruits. They reached Derby, 130 miles from London, on 6 December. There were about 5,000 men but the attitude of the local gentry did not encourage them to expect much response farther south. Wade at Wetherby, Cumberland at Lichfield, another army assembling at Finchley Common – some 30,000 in all were waiting to resist them. Not knowing the full extent of the panic in London, it is not surprising that Charles 'could not prevail upon a single person' to carry on with the march. So the Highlanders turned back, losing the advantage of surprise and morale. The decision must have been wrong: if the Cause had slight hope before, it had no hope thereafter. Indeed, it is hard to resist the view that it was forlorn from the start. But all that Charles achieved had been by bluff and audacity; now he was reduced to campaigning under the conventional conditions in which he was bound to be at a disadvantage. On 17 January his men won a small victory at Falkirk. But at Culloden on 13 April only a miracle, such as the success of his projected night attack, could have saved his starving, ragged men from defeat at the hands of Cumberland's

drilled professionals, supported by artillery and by faith in their cool commander. Charles, who had grown steadily more moody amidst the quarrels of his followers and who had been seriously ill with pneumonia in February, had to watch the battle develop in ground wholly unsuited to the Highlanders' tactics and he did not stay to see their final rout.

When Lord Lovat discussed plans of further resistance, he showed no enthusiasm. He was worn out, broken *au fond* by disappointment as much as by the hardships of the campaign and bitter with his commanders, notably Murray, who had crossed him upon several vital occasions, though with valid military arguments. The cheerfulness and toughness which had so impressed the Highlanders did not wholly desert him. He may even have enjoyed some of his adventures during the months of danger, April to September, when he was being sought by the troops with a price of £30,000 upon his head. With his gallant companions – among them, for a time, Flora Macdonald – in the bothies and hills of Stornoway and Scalpay, Corrodale and Skye, the legend of Prince Charlie received its final touches. After he had eventually departed, with Cameron of Lochiel, Lochgarry and about 100 others, he left behind some brave and affecting memories. But with hundreds of wretched prisoners rotting in the prison hulks of the Thames, crofts burned, the clans broken up, the Jacobite chieftains dead, proscribed or in exile, the Cause was dead. Its ghosts lingered on. Charles Edward did not at once give up hope. For years he wandered, so successfully disguised that historians today cannot trace his movements. In 1748, with peace, came orders to leave France. In January 1755 his father wrote that he had not known of his whereabouts for six years – though the English government might have been able to tell him. But 'James Douglas' occasionally wrote to Waters, in Paris: once he scribbled, 'What can a bird do that has not found a right nest? He must flit from bough to bough.' There is evidence that he lived in Lorraine, in Paris, that he visited Spain, Russia, Sweden, Scotland again. A typical rumour was that he had been complaining of being badly shaved in an Oxfordshire village. Certainly he visited London, in the spring of 1750, met Jacobite sympathizers, inspected the Tower and St James and was received, at St Mary le Strand, into the Anglican church. In 1753, the Elibank plot was unearthed: its object was the capture of the entire reigning house, its principal casualty Dr Cameron, Lochiel's brother. About this time he took a mistress, Clementina Walkenshaw, whom he had briefly met in England in '45, and by her had a daughter. It is possible that she was a spy; she left him in 1760. He had never been much in the company of women; he had long been a heavy drinker and by now was consuming a bottle of brandy a day.

Early in 1766 his father died and Charles awaited his

recognition as Charles III. Neither the pope nor any European power would do this. It was convenient, however, for France to have another 'Young Pretender' and in 1772, for marrying the eighteen-year-old Princess Louisa of Stolberg, he received the promise of a small pension from Louis XV. There was no child and before his death the 'Compte d'Albanie' recognized his daughter by Clementina as his heir. In his last years, in Florence and in Rome where he died on 30 January 1788, she was a sympathetic companion. His wife had left him for a convent in 1780, after a scene when he actually hit her, and then became the mistress of an Italian poet. Charles was probably not such a degraded figure as hostile rumour depicted him, but it would have been better for his fame if he had been killed in 1746. What the few Jacobites, faithful or curious visitors, saw was a dreary and somewhat incoherent old man; the contrast between this shambling figure and the young adventurer of the '45 must have been poignant indeed.

Further Reading
F. McLynn, *Charles Edward Stuart*, 1988.
C. H. Hartmann, *The Quest Forlorn*, 1952.

STUART, HENRY, LORD DARNLEY (1546-67), second husband of Mary, Queen of Scots, was born at Temple Newsam in Yorkshire in 1546. He was the second but eldest surviving son of Matthew Stuart, Earl of Lennox, and his wife, Lady Margaret Douglas, Countess of Lennox, daughter of Margaret Tudor, widow of James IV of Scotland, by her second husband, the Earl of Angus: Margaret Tudor was the aunt of Elizabeth I, therefore Darnley, who had been born in England and was an English subject, was next legal heir to the English throne after Mary, Queen of Scots, if Elizabeth were to die childless. In 1560 de Quadra, the Spanish ambassador, reported to Philip II that if that were to happen the English Catholics would put Darnley on to the English throne. The Countess of Lennox – 'a very wise and discreet matron' (Sir James Melville's *Memoirs*, 1929 edn, p.99) – was at that time corresponding with the Scottish Catholic lords about marrying Darnley to Mary, Queen of Scots. The countess and Darnley, therefore, found themselves shut up in the Tower for a time by Elizabeth, who thought it worth while to deny the legitimacy of the countess on the grounds that her mother had got a Papal divorce from Angus (1527) and that the Scottish estates had declared her to be a bastard. Mother and son were soon released, and Darnley was daily at Elizabeth's court.

In 1564 Sir James Melville was sent by Mary to Elizabeth to get permission for Darnley to visit Scotland in order to 'see the country'. At that moment Elizabeth was suggesting that Mary should marry Robert Dudley, Earl of Leicester, but she very well knew the real purpose of the visit, for she said to Melville, 'ye like better of yon long lad, pointing towards my Lord Darnley ... My answer was that no woman of spirit would make choice of such a man, who resembled more a woman than a man. For he was handsome, beardless and lady-faced' (Melville, ib., p.92). All the same, probably because she feared that Mary might in fact marry Leicester, Elizabeth sent Darnley to Scotland, 'in hope that he being a handsome, lusty youth, should rather prevail, being present, than Leicester who was absent' (ib., p.101).

Darnley arrived at Wemyss Castle on 17 February 1565, where he stayed with Mary for two or three days. It is probable, though disputable, that Mary at once fell desperately in love with 'the properest, and best proportioned long man that ever she had seen: for he was of a high stature, long and tall, even and straight' (Melville, ib., p.107). Darnley was indeed handsome and notably athletic, by repute a good musician on the lute; but his intelligence was of the meanest and he was vain, arrogant, irritable and vicious by the time he was twenty years of age.

The marriage between Darnley and Mary was greatly encouraged by Riccio, who was by this time rapidly advancing in the queen's favour and confidence. In April Darnley fell ill of the measles, and Mary was assiduous in her attentions to him. She knighted him and created him Earl of Ross and later Duke of Albany. On 29 July their public marriage took place in the chapel of Holyrood (1565).

From the moment that he arrived in Scotland Darnley was hated by the Protestant lords, because he was a Catholic. In next to no time he was universally hated for his extreme unwisdom. He chose as his friends the most disreputable of the Scottish nobles, his pride was 'intolerable' and 'his words not to be borne'. Politically he was a menace, for he could not keep his tongue quiet – 'few durst advertise him, ... because he told all again to some of his own servants, who were not all honest' (Melville, ib., p.145). Then he took to drink and treated the queen so shamefully in public that she 'left the house in tears'. Mary knew now what a fatal marriage she had made. She refused Darnley the Crown Matrimonial and she began to advance Riccio to the political importance which should have been Darnley's. Darnley's position was becoming increasingly difficult and there were some of his relations who were offended by his humiliation.

Hated as Darnley was, Riccio was soon even more hated, as a Catholic, as a foreigner, and for his arrogant behaviour. He was virtually the queen's prime minister and all business was conducted by him. Darnley's Catholic friends and Protestant enemies now combined for a moment to murder Riccio. Darnley was not only privy to the plot, but he insisted on being present at the murder, because so great had his hatred for his wife become that he accused her of being Riccio's mistress. Riccio had done him 'the most dishonour that could be to any man'. On Saturday evening, 9 March 1565, Darnley admitted the conspirators – Moray, Morton, Ruthven and others – into Holyrood and led them up by the private staircase into the room where Mary was dining with Riccio. After the murder was committed, it was Darnley's dagger which was left in Riccio's side – borrowed for the purpose by the nobles, who were determined to make him appear as the instigator of and sharer in the deed.

For political reasons Mary could not at once break with Darnley. She promised him his proper position as her husband. Darnley told her 'all that he knew of any man' in the conspiracy. There was a brief reconciliation, but almost at once Mary discovered Darnley's share in the plot. She never forgave him, but she was pregnant and she would do nothing to jeopardize the legitimacy of her child. She began to favour Moray, Maitland and others who hated Darnley. His position was impossible and he determined to leave the country. The nobles met at Craigmillar and determined to be rid of Darnley. Darnley refused to attend the christening of his son at Stirling, left for Glasgow to find a ship to take him abroad, but he fell ill, almost certainly of syphilis, and could not go. Mary was now in love with Bothwell, but she brought about a reconciliation with Darnley and persuaded him, when he was convalescent, to go with her to Edinburgh. She took him to an isolated house at Kirk o' Field, outside Edinburgh, left him there on the evening of 9 February 1566 and went to Edinburgh with Bothwell. Early in the morning of the 10th the house was blown up. Darnley's body and that of his page were found under a tree, unmarked by the explosion: they had been strangled before the house was blown up.

Darnley's body was buried in the tomb of James V in the chapel of Holyrood.

STUART, JAMES FRANCIS EDWARD (1688-1766), Prince of Wales, Chevalier de St George, the Old Pretender, was born to Mary of Modena and James II in St James's Palace. Few men of rank in modern English history have had a more infelicitous inheritance. Popularly believed to be an imposter smuggled into the palace in a warming-pan, certainly when less than six months old smuggled out of the country where he had been born heir to the throne, James Edward was in Macaulay's words 'the most unfortunate of princes, destined to seventy-seven years of exile and wandering, of vain projects, of honours more galling than insults, and of hopes such as make the heart sick'. By his own virtues and weaknesses alike he contributed substantially to his misfortunes. His devotion to Catholicism almost certainly cost him the succession in 1714, yet his tame and flabby personality did nothing to encourage his supporters to lay down their lives, or would-be sympathizers to risk their property, for him.

Proclaimed King of England by Louis XIV in 1701, with his father's deathbed injunction to die rather than abandon Romanism sounding in his ears, he began his political career at thirteen, a helpless tool of his country's enemy. In the futile Jacobite 'invasion' of 1708 he fell ill with measles at Dunkirk, and then sailed all round Scotland and Ireland and back to Dunkirk without landing, showing great courage when the French flagship which was carrying him was bombarded by the pursuing Admiral Byng. He fought at Oudenarde and at Malplaquet; driven from France by the Treaty of Utrecht, he took refuge in Lorraine. In the '15 he arrived on a French ship at Peterhead too late to be of effective help, yet not too late to discourage his supporters by his 'heavy' countenance, his lack of vitality, and his sedate comment that 'for myself it is no new thing to be unfortunate'. After six weeks in Scotland he took ship at Montrose to escape Argyll's pursuing forces, and returned to Lorraine.

His court was riddled with faction, intrigue, and spies; and Bolingbroke, for a short time its ablest member and the Pretender's secretary, was dismissed in 1716. By way of Avignon and Rome he went to Madrid, whence Alberoni organized the futile Jacobite expedition of 1719, and thence back to Rome, where he settled for the long remainder of his days. In that same year he married the Polish princess, Maria Clementina Sobieski, who in 1724 deserted him and went into a nunnery. The pope rewarded him for his loyalty to his faith by giving him a pension. Gray, visiting Rome in 1740, left a gloomy description of him as 'a thin, ill-made man, extremely tall and awkward, of a most unpromising countenance, a good deal resembling King James the Second, and has extremely the air and look of an idiot, particularly when he laughs or prays. The first he does not often, the latter continually.' He showed little enthusiasm for the '45, saying sensibly but unheroically to Charles Edward, 'Be careful, my boy, for I would not lose you for all the crowns in the world.' He died in 1766 and was buried in St Peter's.

Further Reading
J. P. Kenyon, 'The Birth of the Old Pretender', *History Today*, June 1963.
Sir Charles Petrie, *The Jacobite Movement, the first phase, 1698-1716*, 1948, and *The Jacobite Movement, the second phase, 1716-1807*, 1950.

STUBBS, GEORGE (1724-1806), painter, was as considerable a figure in his own field of animal-painting as Gainsborough or Reynolds in theirs. He was born in Liverpool in 1724, the son of a currier; painted portraits in his youth; studied and lectured on anatomy at York; and at the age of thirty travelled to Rome 'to convince himself' (he said) 'that nature was and is always superior to art, whether Greek or Roman'. Such a viewpoint was scarcely intelligible to the partisans of the neo-classical, who were the patrons of England, and Stubbs's originality might have brought him no fortune had he not exerted it in a field of art comparatively untilled but very fertile. For this was the age of the apotheosis of the horse; and Stubbs was high priest.

Not that he courted popularity; he was too solitary and strong. But it happened that he was a scientist, and he loved horses; so he painted horses which are not only real horses – more real in particulars than any painted before or since – but are endowed with a character almost heroic.

> The horses show him nobler powers: –
> O patient eyes, courageous hearts!

By carefully declining, however, to ascribe to his horses *rational* powers, Stubbs both emphasized the dignity of their animal nature and avoided that sentimentality which has been the bane of so many animal-painters. The life-size portrait of *The Hambletonian Rubbing Down* (*c*.1790) is that of the essential thoroughbred, equine from teeth to tail; there are no spurious attributes, no suggestion that the creature is more than the best of its kind. Nor did Stubbs excel at painting horses only: his scientific bent led him to share in that contemporary curiosity about rare animals which has raised a rash of menageries over Europe. Thus he painted for Lord Pigot a cheetah sent by his lordship to George III; for John Hunter (who kept a private menagerie at Earl's Court and formed the Hunterian Collection of anatomical specimens) a yak, an orang-outang and an Indian rhinoceros; and for his brother William Hunter's collection at Glasgow University, a nilgai and a moose. Stubbs seemed equipped to distinguish every prodigy of the animal kingdom.

Much of his anatomical experience he owed to having in his youth, in a lonely farmhouse in Lincolnshire, laboured to compile over eighteen months the wonderful work of science and art called *The Anatomy of the Horse*. Stubbs's models were the very carcasses of horses, which he suspended, flayed and dissected, injecting tallow into the veins, ignoring the offence of the decaying meat in his ardour to record what he saw. Then, as if that had not been enough, he engraved his own drawings because no-one would do it for him. The book, deservedly, won European praise; and Stubbs was henceforth the prey of every gentleman with a thoroughbred to immortalize.

The patient discipline which had furnished *The Anatomy* revealed itself also, not only in the botanical accuracy of Stubbs's trees and plants, but in his faultless composition and use of perspective. *Phaeton and Pair*, for example, is an essay in balance; and the splendid series of *Brood Mares and Foals*, set both in landscapes and against plain backgrounds, have (for all Stubbs's disregard for the classical) the rhythm of a frieze. There are those who hold it against Stubbs that he does not give us enough of wind and weather (as Munnings has done) for his superb creatures to move in; but it is this very understatement which marks Stubbs's pictures with one of the signs of great art, the sign of mystery.

Stubbs was over six feet tall, of great physical strength; yet he who could manhandle a horse's carcass could also conduct minute dissections, make the finest anatomical drawings, and paint with an exquisite sense of texture the scales of a rhinoceros, the pelt of a foxhound, the whiskers of a tigress. And when he turns to give a picture of *human* life in the country, as in 'Reaping', he can make even Gainsborough's pastorals smell a little of the studio. The high gloss of his paintings may be due to his having at one time made some enamel paintings on stoneware plaques for Josiah Wedgwood. He died in 1806, aged eighty-two.

Further Reading
Basil Taylor, *Stubbs*, 1960.

STUBBS, WILLIAM (1825-1901), historian and Bishop of Chester and Oxford, initiated the serious study of history in English universities. He learnt how to read old charters and deeds from his father, a Knaresborough solicitor, and attracted the attention of Longley, then Bishop of Ripon, who became his patron, helped him to a Servitor's place at Christ Church, Oxford, and later persuaded the prime minister, Lord Derby, to make him Regius Professor of that university in 1866. By then he had already, in his spare time from conscientious work as Vicar of Navestock ('I suppose I knew every toe of every baby in the parish'), built up a unique knowledge of the sources of medieval English history. This subject, despised by historians of the Enlightenment, was starting to arouse interest. The novels of Scott, the thunderings of Carlyle, the buildings of Pugin and the churchmanship of Newman, all exalted the Middle Ages. Parliamentary Commissioners began to publish Records in 1802, and the process gathered pace through the Camden Society and others. In 1857 the Master of the Rolls sponsored a new series of publications, mainly of Chronicles. Stubbs produced fifteen large volumes of these, from Dunstan through to Edward II. He went on to publish his *Select Charters*, and to write a *Constitutional History of England*, which was a synthesis of his learning. He saw English liberty emerging from the Anglo-Saxons, and English law from the reforms of Henry II, themselves the product of a creative tension between Saxon local liberties and Norman centralization. His approach was convincing, partly because of the quality of his scholarship, but also because it was what the Victorians liked to believe, and it has permeated British political pride ever since.

Stubbs had to make all the running himself, for no-one else knew half as much. But he was not bowed down by the weight of his knowledge. As an Oxford lecturer he aimed to 'attract an idle audience without seeming to trifle with a deeply loved study', and as a bishop he had to be warned against allowing his wry humour to upset earnest clergy.

Further Reading
John Kenyon, *The History Men*, 1983.

STUCLEY, SIR THOMAS (there are many variations in the spelling of his name) (*c.*1520-78), adventurer, was born probably some time before 1520. He was the third of the four sons of Sir Hugh Stucley and his wife, Jane, daughter of Sir Lewis Pollard, a Judge of the Common Pleas. There is no reason for accepting the rumour that he was the illegitimate son of Henry VIII. Nothing is known of his education, but he was probably a retainer of the Duke of Suffolk until the duke's death in 1545. He was present at the siege of Boulogne (1544-5) and on the death of Suffolk he attached himself to the Earl of Hertford, afterwards Protector Somerset. He then returned to Boulogne, where he held the post of King's Standard-bearer at a wage of 6*s*.8*d*. per day.

Boulogne was surrendered to the French in 1550 and Stucley returned to England to the court of Edward VI and to the service of Protector Somerset. In May of that year he conducted the French Marquis de Maine to Scotland and back on a visit of condolence to Mary of Guise, the Scottish queen, on the death of the Duke of Guise. In April 1551 Stucley was in France at the court of Henry II, where he made an excellent impression. It was characteristic of Stucley that he always succeeded in making a good impression at the first meeting, but he never succeeded in retaining the favour which he acquired. This may be seen in his relations with Queen Elizabeth, Burghley, Pope Pius V, Pope Gregory XIII, Philip II of Spain and many other people. He came back to England as a supporter of Somerset, but the arrest of Somerset foiled his plans, and Stucley fled back to France and entered the service of Henry II, whose confidence he at once won. Henry sent him home to England with a letter to Edward VI strongly recommending him to the king. Henry's real purpose was to obtain information which would help him in his projected attack on Calais, but Stucley used the opportunity to reconcile himself with the English government by betraying the true purpose of his mission. Northumberland, however, thought to win Henry's friendship by betraying to him Stucley's disloyalty, and he threw Stucley into prison and cancelled the previous promise to pay his many debts.

Stucley seems to have been released about 1553, but his debts drove him abroad again. Unable to return to France, he now went to the emperor, Charles V, to whom Queen Mary had written a letter of commendation. He served under the Duke of Savoy until October 1554,

when he came home with the duke, who was paying a visit to England. Stucley was given a guarantee of freedom from arrest for his debts for six months, which enabled him to be at court until 1555, but by then his debts had not been paid. It was essential to him that his fortunes should be repaired; therefore in that year he married an heiress, Anne, daughter of Sir Thomas Curtis, a rich city alderman. On 13 May a warrant for his arrest was issued on a charge of uttering false money. Stucley escaped overseas and again took service under the Duke of Savoy in the English force led by the Earl of Pembroke. He took part in the Duke of Egmont's victory over Henry II of France at St Quentin in 1557.

Being still in financial difficulties and in search of quick wealth, Stucley now took to buccaneering and preyed on the French ships. Complaints against him were soon lodged with the Lord High Admiral, but Stucley's luck held and on 17 July 1558, the admiral reported that he did not 'find the matter sufficient to charge Stucley withal'.

In 1561 Stucley was given a captaincy in Berwick where, in spite of his few resources, he lived sumptuously and gained a reputation for his 'royalty to men at arms'. In the same year he entertained lavishly and made great friends with Shane O'Neill, a friendship which was to have important results later. As a result of his extravagance Stucley had soon exhausted all the wealth of his wife and it was necessary to find a fresh source of income. Stucley therefore embarked on his famous plan for founding a colony in Florida. Once again his power to create a good impression helped him: he was able to persuade Queen Elizabeth to supply one of the ships. The plan to plant a colony was a mere blind to cover Stucley's return to piracy. For two years his exploits at sea 'were a scandal to Europe' (*Dictionary of National Biography*), so that Elizabeth was compelled to disown Stucley and to send some ships for his arrest. Once again he was acquitted, but he had lost the queen money and thus he also lost her good opinion. She never forgave him.

The year 1566 was the turning point in Stucley's turbulent career. Shane O'Neill in that year asked the English government to send Stucley to him to be employed against the Scots in Ulster. Stucley went, with disastrous results. The queen knew that Stucley hated her religious policy and that he had been carrying on treasonable correspondence for at least three years with the Spanish ambassador and that he had accepted a pension from Philip II. She strongly suspected that Stucley's motives in going to Ireland were also treasonable. In June 1569 Stucley was accused of high treason and was shut in Dublin Castle (June to October). He had certainly proposed to Spain an invasion of Ireland, but once more the evidence was not enough to convict him and he was released. From this moment Stucley became a whole-hearted traitor.

Already he was in touch with Richard Creagh, Roman Catholic Archbishop of Armagh, and with Guereau de Spes, Spanish ambassador in London. As soon as he was released, Stucley went to London and offered his services to Fenelon, the French ambassador, but he soon discovered that he could make a better bargain with Spain. He returned to Ireland, fitted out a ship and sailed for Vimiero on 17 April 1570, arriving there on the 24th. Stucley was received with extraordinary favour by the king, who gave him 3,000 ducats, all his daily expenses, and then a further 6,000 ducats and an establishment which was reckoned to cost the king thirty ducats a day. Stucley now lived in the most sumptuous style: he was known as the Duke of Ireland and he asked Philip to create him Duke of Leinster and his son a Marquis. It is a disputable point whether Philip did in fact knight Stucley. Some months later Stucley left Spain and moved to Rome. It is pretty certain that Philip had now become aware of Stucley's real character, partly through letters from Maurice Gibbon, Archbishop of Cashel, who wrote frequently to undermine Stucley's position. Stucley had been trying to intervene in the Ridolfi Plot, but his plan misfired. On his way to Rome, by some means or other, he commanded three galleys at Don John of Austria's great victory over the Turks at Lepanto (1571) and he won great praise for his courageous behaviour in the battle. The kudos he thus gained did something to reinstate him in Philip's favour, to whose court he returned after Lepanto in 1572.

Between 1572 and 1578 Stucley was here, there and everywhere – in Spain, the Netherlands, in Paris, in Rome – trying to persuade the pope and Philip II to embark on an invasion of Ireland. At last, in 1578, Stucley's efforts succeeded, largely through the help of James Fitzmaurice, a Geraldine who was violently opposed to Elizabeth's government in Ireland. Stucley won the favour first of Pope Pius V, then of Pope Gregory XIII, of the Cardinal of Como, who was Secretary of State, and of the English clergy in Rome, notably Dr Maurice Clenog, the Provost of the English Hospital in Rome, who wrote to assure the pope that Stucley was 'a man sent from heaven' (*divinitus*) for the English enterprise. The pope provided 600 Papal infantry which were conveyed to the port of embarkation, the Fortezza del Re Catholico at Port'ercole. Stucley was leader of the expedition and he sailed in the *San Giovanni Battista* (possibly a Spanish ship) early in January 1578.

It was not until 4 April that he reached Cadiz. His ships were so rotten that it was necessary to refit, but Philip refused to allow him to do this at Cadiz. Stucley stayed there from 4 April to the 14th; then he sailed for San Lucar and went on to Lisbon, where he arrived probably on 17 April. Here he found that King Sebastian had no

ships to offer him: instead he offered Stucley a command in his Portuguese army which was about to invade Morocco. Stucley accepted and diverted the Papal troops from the invasion of Ireland to the invasion of Morocco. He declared that he knew Ireland as well as the best, and there were only to be got there hunger and lice. He fought with great courage at the battle of Alcazar, but he was killed early in the day after a cannon-ball had cut off both his legs (4 August 1578).

'Of this man,' wrote Burghley, 'might be written whole volumes to paint out the life of a man in the highest degree of vain-glory, prodigality, falsehood and vile and filthy conversation of life, and altogether without faith, conscience or religion.' Yet Stucley impressed many other people more favourably, even if wrongly and only for a time. He became the hero of more than one play and of several ballads and he appears in Chapter 5 of Kingsley's *Westward Ho!*

Further Reading
Z. N. Brooke, *English Historical Review*, 1913.
J. H. Pollen, *The Month*, 1903.

STURRY, SIR RICHARD (*c.*1330-95) rose from the bottom rungs of the royal household at a time when promotion of any kind was rare, let alone elevation from obscurity to high favour. He was only a valet in the 1340s, still only king's yeoman in 1353, an esquire of the chamber in 1359, and a knight of the body from 1365 until death. He became a trusted councillor both of Edward III and his grandson Richard II. By the 1370s 'he was clearly a favourite of the old king's', his 'familiar servant', and continuously in his company. He has recently been identified with the chamberlain Lord Latimer and mistress Alice Perrers as one of the five individuals most influential with Edward III in his last years. He shared in the defeat and disgrace of this group in the Good Parliament of 1376, when he was dismissed from the council but not impeached, yet remained powerful at court and returned from 1389 as a royal councillor, attending council on 159 days in 1392-3 alone.

No layman could rise in this way without sharing the king's aristocratic and military outlook. Sturry must have been of gentle birth and upbringing, although his origins are obscure. Any connection with the Kentish knight Sir William Sturry, Marshal of the Household, must be distant. His military career lasted from at least 1347, when he displayed great courage in a sea battle, to 1378. He was companion at arms both to the king and Black Prince. He was captured in 1359-60 and received £50 from Edward towards his ransom. His real forte proved to be diplomacy, however, and he became an expert in treating with the French. He was engaged in negotiations almost every year from 1368 to 1394. This 'ancient and valiant knight' owned a *Romance of the Rose*, knew both Froissart and Chaucer, and is one of the circle of reputed Lollard knights supposed – like Clanvowe and Montagu – to have used his position at court to protect heretics from persecution. This Sturry could certainly have done. The precise nature of his Lollardy and indeed his literary interests remain obscure.

Sturry's lack of inherited wealth made him particularly dependent on royal bounty. The most important expression of this was apparently his marriage in middle age *c.*1374 to Alice Blount, an heiress in her own right, widow of an heir to a barony, and a connection through the Staffords with the royal house itself. His fee of a mere ten marks (£6.66) increased tenfold by 1370; a further £60 came from John IV of Brittany from Richmond honour, probably from 1372 following a mission to Brittany in 1371; in 1384 he received a further £66 from the king's mother, Joan of Kent; and he was paid 10*s.* a day as royal councillor from 1389. Besides these he received a series of other rewards, particularly – and probably deliberately – in Wales. Most important perhaps was the custody of the great Marcher lordship of Glamorgan in the minority of its lord from 1376-94 with a fee of £66 with full power of administration and appointment to offices. He was keeper of Aberystwyth from 1385, justice of Cardigan in 1387, and justice of the whole of south Wales in 1391. He showed a sharp eye for profit, securing grants of the escheatorship of Ireland both in 1363 and 1372, only to swop them for opportunities elsewhere, exchanging both his custody of Bamburgh castle and his annuities for lands, and in 1373 and 1388 acquiring custody of two Kentish alien priories. Certainly he used his influence at court to advance himself and presumably enrich himself. Equally he has left more concrete evidence of calculated self-advancement than his associate, the more notorious Lord Latimer.

Further Reading

C. Given-Wilson, *The Royal Household and the King's Affinity: Service, Politics and Finance in England 1360-1413*, 1986.

K. B. McFarlane, *Lancastrian Kings and Lollard Knights*, 1971.

SUCKLING, SIR JOHN (1609-41), Cavalier poet, born at Twickenham in Middlesex, son of James I's future Secretary of State was educated at Trinity College, Cambridge. Inheriting his father's considerable estates in 1627, he travelled abroad and fought for Gustavus Adolphus. In the 1630s he was prominent among the younger courtiers. Aubrey describes him as 'famous at court for his ready sparkling wit' and as 'the greatest gallant of his time, and the greatest Gamester'; credits him with the invention of cribbage; but adds, 'he sent his cards to all Gameing places in the country, which were marked with private marks of his; he got twenty thousand pounds by this way'. Suckling wrote several plays which were performed at court, a good deal of facile,

cynical and licentious verse, and a savage piece of satire about his contemporaries, *The Session of the Poets*. When the Bishops' Wars broke out Suckling used the remnants of his fortune to raise a troop of horse for the king. He dressed them splendidly in white doublets and scarlet breeches, coats, hats, and feathers and gave them battle-axes, but they did not distinguish themselves in any other way. In 1641 he was involved in the Army Plot and fled to Paris, where he soon died in poverty, either of the pox or, according to Aubrey, by poisoning himself.

SULLIVAN, SIR ARTHUR (1842-1900), composer, was the best known English musician of his day. Like Gilbert, he wished that he could have achieved success in a more exalted field than the operetta. But whereas scarcely any of his serious works are now performed, the surviving popularity of 'Gilbert and Sullivan' owes more to his music than to Gilbert's writing, which, being contemporary satire, has dated badly.

Sullivan was a young prodigy. He learnt how instruments worked at Sandhurst, where his father was Bandmaster. At twelve he became a treble in the Chapel Royal at St James's; at fourteen he was selected as the first Mendelssohn Scholar, and studied at Leipzig. In 1862 his music for *The Tempest*, mostly written for his last examination there, was performed at a Crystal Palace concert, and was felt to herald a new epoch. Four years later his first symphony received similar acclaim. But he never wrote another. When he died, after composing a grand opera, orchestral works, odes, oratorios, anthems, many marches, seventy hymn tunes and 114 songs, one critic described him as 'the idle singer of an empty evening'. Posterity has by and large accepted this verdict. The dawn that followed him, heralded by Parry and Stanford, was to reveal the glories of Elgar and Vaughan Williams. Against these, Sullivan's reputation rapidly faded. The two flaws in his make-up as a composer were conservatism and indolence. Lacking curiosity, he became stuck in the traditions of his youth, skilful in pastiche, but never original. Enjoying the life of high society, he often wrote hastily. Though his cantata *The Golden Legend* was performed seventeen times in 1886, it is almost unknown now. *Ivanhoe* opened the new Royal English Opera House and ran for 160 nights. But the Opera House soon turned into the Palace Theatre, and *Ivanhoe* has no place in any repertoire. As the Sullivan without the Gilbert, he is cruelly remembered for one of his most stolid hymn tunes, to 'Onward Christian Soldiers', and one of his most sentimental songs, 'The Lost Chord'.

But through the Savoy Operas his genius sparkled. 'They trained him to make Europe yawn,' wrote Shaw, 'and he took advantage of their teaching to make London laugh and whistle.' His gift for parody matched Gilbert's wit: of Mendelssohn in the fairy music in *Iolanthe*; of

Rossini at the start of *The Gondoliers*; of traditional English songs when Nanki-Poo, disguised son of the Emperor of Japan, opens *The Mikado* with a sentimental ballad followed by a patriotic march and a sea shanty. With skilful orchestration, and a stream of tunes and modulations worthy of Schubert, he outshone Offenbach in the Anglo-Saxon world. Together, Gilbert and Sullivan achieved the originality which apart they could not discover, creating a new art form springing from the culture of their time.

Sullivan composed much of this music by working through the night before it was due, in the middle of a whirl of dinners, race meetings and gambling sessions. He grew up a good-looking young man, with thick black curly hair and an oval, olive-tinted face. He was sensitive, courteous and excellent company. So he was taken up by Society, including two of the queen's liveliest sons, the Prince of Wales and the Duke of Edinburgh. Although he never married, he had a long-standing mistress, Fanny Ronalds, a rich American widow who had taken European high society by storm with Jennie Jerome, later Winston Churchill's mother. Through the later part of his life, including the years of his Savoy triumphs, he was often in sharp pain from kidney stones, but only near the end did his zest for living falter. After his death, two months before the queen's, he was placed firmly on the Victorian shelf by historians of music.

Further Reading

G. Hughes, *The Music of Arthur Sullivan*, 1960.

H. S. Wyndham, *Arthur Seymour Sullivan, 1842-1900*, 1926.

SUTTON, CHARLES MANNERS, VISCOUNT CANTERBURY (1780-1845), was Speaker of the House of Commons from 1817 to 1835, when he was defeated by a Whig candidate and raised to the peerage. The office requires sound judgement, integrity, a commanding personality and, not least, strong physique. Thirteen years' tenure, unchallenged by the Whig opposition, followed by two during the intense and dramatic debates over the Reform Bill, and two more of Whig government, speak volumes for his character. The Whigs only opposed him in 1835 because he was mentioned seriously as a possible premier at a time when the Tories had a chance to defeat the Whigs.

His father, also Charles, was Archbishop of Canterbury; he was educated at Eton and Trinity College, Cambridge. Elected to parliament in 1807, he held office for many years as Judge Advocate General. The experience was invaluable when it came to presiding in the Commons at a time when an unprecedented flood of private bills called for great skill and patience. His end may be held to symbolize the revolutionary change which his career had spanned. He was travelling on a night mail of the Great Western railway. Near Slough he had the apoplectic seizure from which he subsequently died.

SWEYN FORKBEARD (*d.*1014) was successively King of Denmark and, by conquest, of England. Sweyn (properly Swegen) displaced his father Harold Bluetooth and made himself King of the Danes in about 988. He devoted much of his reign to attacking England and exacting tribute, the famous Danegeld, until he finally turned to conquest in 1013. Very little is known of the institutions of tenth-century Denmark, but it is clear that her kings were able to execute large-scale public works such as the great military camps at Fyrkat, Trelleborg and elsewhere, or the causeway at Ravning, and it is likely that some means of raising fleets by means of a royal ship-levy existed. Sweyn's forces were big and well-equipped, bent on the systematic exploitation of the vulnerable England of King Ethelred II.

Sweyn's own part in the campaigns of the years 991-1013 is difficult to elucidate owing to the meagreness of our sources. It is probable that he campaigned in England before his first recorded appearance there in 994, and it is just possible that he was one of the Danish leaders at the battle of Maldon, where Byrhtnoth fell, in 991. In 994 he attacked London unsuccessfully, ravaged in south-east England and wintered at Southampton, exacting a geld of £16,000. He returned to Scandinavia in 995 by way of the Irish Sea. During the years 995-1000 he was apparently detained in the north by troubles about which we are ill-informed with the Swedes and the Poles. It is likely that his marriage to a sister of Duke Boleslav of Poland was connected with these obscure goings-on. The child of this union was Canute (or Cnut), born in about 996. Sweyn may have been back in England in 1001-2, when a geld of £24,000 was levied. He was certainly there in 1003, when he sacked Exeter and ravaged Wiltshire, and in 1004, when East Anglia was the target: Norwich and Thetford were sacked and a fierce but indecisive battle was fought against Ulfcetel of East Anglia. The year 1005 found Sweyn back in Denmark, but he probably returned to England in 1006 when the Danes ravaged in Kent and Sussex and settled on the Isle of Wight for the winter: about Christmas they raided through Hampshire into Berkshire and defeated an English army; £36,000 was forthcoming as geld in 1007. We lose sight of Sweyn again in 1008. It is likely that he was the commander of one of the several Danish armies which were operating in England during the years 1009-12, which exacted a geld of £48,000 and murdered Archbishop Aelfheah. After this he seems to have returned to Denmark by way of the Irish Sea, as in 995, surviving shipwreck off the coast of Pembrokeshire on the voyage home.

In 1013 he came intent upon conquest and his tactics were different. He landed at Gainsborough on the Trent, in the northern Danelaw where he could count on the sympathy of the Anglo-Danish aristocracy. He then systematically laid waste the country in a wide arc through Oxford and Winchester to London. After this display of force, as the *Anglo-Saxon Chronicle* records, 'all the nation regarded him as full king'. Ethelred fled to Normandy and Sweyn returned in triumph to his fleet at Gainsborough. But disaster struck in his moment of glory. He died suddenly on 3 February 1014, bequeathing his ambitions to his son Canute.

SWIFT, JONATHAN (1677-1745), political journalist and satirist, was born in Dublin of English parents and sent to school in Kilkenny. Then he went on to Trinity College, Dublin, where his career was distinguished by his neglect of all studies save history and poetry, so that he eventually only obtained a degree *speciali gratia*. In 1689 he joined Sir William Temple's household, and he spent much of the 1690s with Temple, either at Sheen or at Moor Park, writing *A Tale of a Tub* and *The Battle of the Books* at this time (although they were not published until 1704). Ordained in Ireland in 1694, he held a small prebend there in 1695-6; in 1699 he obtained the living of Laracor, a hamlet near Dublin, and in 1700 a stall in St Patrick's Cathedral in Dublin. Ambitious, conscious of his literary powers, morose and bitter even as a young man, Swift was never content with Ireland, and during the first half of Anne's reign he spent a good deal of time in England, hoping always for preferment and making the friendship of writers like Addison and Steele and of patrons like Halifax. Politically he tended to call himself a Whig, but the Whigs disappointed him, particularly by failing to give him the post of Queen's secretary in Vienna in 1708. The power and fame Swift needed were to come through his pen, yet his writings of these years – although they revealed his ferocious strength – were not entirely discreet. Queen Anne did not approve of *A Tale of a Tub*. *The Argument to Prove that the Abolishing of Christianity may … be attended with Some Inconveniences* (1708) was perhaps too ironic, while his pamphlet of that same year against the abolition of the sacramental test for offices in Ireland was certainly too honest.

Swift's chance came in 1710, with the change of ministry, for Harley was shrewd enough to see his political possibilities. Within a few months this obscure and sour Irish clergyman was sharing the secrets of the Tory government and dining *à trois* with Harley and St John. In 1711 he was a leading member of the Tory 'Brothers' Club' formed to rival the Whig 'Kit-Cat'. For the better part of four years Swift was a major figure in English political life, and he did more than any man to make this period a golden age of political journalism. In 1710-11 he denounced the Whigs with peculiar savagery in the Tory journal *The Examiner*, and in 1711 he demonstrated his crushing controversial powers in *The Conduct of the Allies*, one of the greatest of all political pamphlets. It sold 11,000 copies in a month and, by shattering the

Whig argument for 'No peace without Spain', won English public opinion to accept St John's policy and thus, in Trevelyan's words, 'materially helped to obtain peace for Europe on the only possible terms'.*

In 1713 Anne made Swift Dean of St Patrick's Cathedral in Dublin. It was not what he wanted; as he said, 'all that the court or ministry did for me was to let me choose my station in the country where I am banished'. And banishment came suddenly upon him. In 1713-14 he did his best, in vain, to patch up the widening quarrel between the two Tory leaders. He was quite unaware of the negotiations of St John with the French for the restoration of the Old Pretender, and in his last pamphlet for the Tories, *The Public Spirit of the Whigs* (March 1714), he answered Steele's pamphlet alleging that the Protestant succession was in danger. Four months later Anne died, the Tory ministry was dismissed, and Swift's day of power in English politics was done.

He returned to Ireland and apart from two visits to England spent the remainder of his days there. No minister in the years of Whig supremacy was likely to give him employment or preferment in England. In Lord Orrery's opinion, he made a virtue out of this necessity: 'his chief aim was to be removed into England; but when he found himself entirely disappointed, he turned his thoughts to opposition, and became the patron of Ireland'. In 1724 he wrote the *Drapier's Letters* in successful opposition to Walpole's project of 'Wood's Halfpence', and for a time he was the hero of all Ireland. Two years later the most famous of all his works, *Gulliver's Travels*, was published. As Dean of St Patrick's he was a bitter opponent of the Nonconformists and a generous donor to charity. From about 1738 he was increasingly ill, and in his last years out of his mind. He died in 1745 and was buried in St Patrick's with his own inscription, '*ubi saeva indignatio ulterius cor lacerare nequit*', carved on his tomb.

'Swift shares with Bunyan and Defoe the distinction of having given pleasure to a greater number of people in the last 200 years than any other English author'.† If this statement is true, the irony of such a distinction would have pleased Swift, who so commonly appeared bitter and misanthropic. A frustrated man, whose relations with Stella and 'Vanessa' remain baffling under any kind of analysis; a brooding man who was always ready to impute malice and ingratitude, and whose hatreds – of Whigs and Jacobites, of Low Churchmen, Dissenters and free-thinkers, of Marlborough and Wharton, of the Scots and the Dutch – were corrosive of truth and decency in his language; deeply susceptible to flattery,

---

*G. M. Trevelyan, *England under Queen Anne*, vol. III, 1934, p.192.
†John Hayward, *Swift: Gulliver's Travels and Selected Writings*, 1934, p.xiii.

for all his harshness; yielding to a self-pity unworthy of his magnificent abilities – Swift, at best, remains an unattractive figure. Part of the truth no doubt lies in his remark in a letter of 1725 that 'principally I hate and detest that animal called man; although I heartily love John, Peter, Thomas and so forth'. Both the *Journal to Stella* and *Gulliver's Travels* throw shadow as well as light, and his political career is oddly incidental to any understanding of the man. Yet of two things there can be no doubt. Swift was a man of superb force of mind, a fit peer of Newton and Bentley; and as controversialist and journalist he has no superior in modern English history.

Further Reading
J. A. Downie, *Jonathan Swift, Political Writer*, 1984.
Michael Foot, *The Pen and the Sword*, 1957.
J. Middleton Murry, *Swift*, 1954.

SWINBURNE, ALGERNON CHARLES (1837-1909), poet and critic, was born in the year of the queen's accession and the start of the Victorian age: he represented the extremes of revolt against its rules and values. He lived to see the ascendancy of the 'Georgian' poets: their quiet lines and exact accounts so far removed from his fevered rhetoric, his hectic assertions and the galloping rhythms of his verse. Since, this remarkable lyric poet has had parodists, imitators, but no equals in the style he made his own.

Son of an admiral and grandson of a Northumberland landowner, he was educated at Eton and Balliol College, Oxford. Against such a background and expectations he cut an odd figure. He was short, with narrow sloping shoulders, a long and slender neck and a large head surmounted by a shock of red hair. Henry Adams met him and described 'a tropical bird, high-crested, long-beaked, quick moving, with rapid utterance and screams of humour ... a crimson macaw among owls'. By then (1862) he had left Oxford, without a degree, fallen in with the Pre-Raphaelites, and started to write poems. His father's allowance gave him leisure to be a poet. From old Walter Savage Landor, he received support; one of his finest later works was an elegy on that poet. From Richard Monckton Milnes came more active patronage and, incidentally, an introduction to the writing of the Marquis de Sade: a bibliophile's curiosity perhaps – but to Swinburne fatally attractive, a menu of perversions. He was to be 'more productively abnormal than any other English writer' (Peter Quennell).

In 1865 *Atalanta in Calydon* took readers by storm. With *Poems and Ballads* (1866) he enhanced his reputation. Here was an eloquence in verse that recalled Shelley, a rhythmic energy pulsating through word-music that asked to be chanted aloud. A flavour that appealed to the young was what *Punch*'s reviewer called 'its feverish carnality'. Disapproving, he went, nonetheless,

to the heart of the matter. 'The poet's extravagances of conduct were an inseparable part of his creative evolution' (Peter Quennell). He was possessed by a self-punishing spirit. He loved the sea – the Northumbrian shore of childhood holidays; its imagery runs through his poems. Disregarding storms, he would swim beyond strength and safety. His only known relationship with a woman was with a circus equestrienne; it had a sado-masochistic side to it. He drank much brandy and lapsed into epileptic rages. He slept little and wrote furiously, always driving himself. Since images of cruelty colour his early verse, since he rhapsodized over paganism and sneered mellifluously at Christianity, there is seen a kind of unity between writer, style and message that accounts for the poetry's intoxicating power.

If there is a central and worthy theme it is that of liberty. In 1867 Swinburne met Mazzini and *Songs Before Sunrise* shows the influence of the Italian patriot whom he revered. He needed such a hero, preferably a distant one, associated with a potent, but abstract ideal. (Typically a later heroine, representing past suffering and heroic failure, would be Mary, Queen of Scots, subject of a trilogy of plays.) Mazzini's death, in 1872, left him 'rudderless upon the sombre and chaotic seas of his own perverse and fluid temperament'. Already the fire was dying down. A second series of *Poems and Ballads* (1878) was less stirring than the first, therefore – since there was little thought behind Swinburne's poetry – less interesting. In 1879 he collapsed.

Theodore Watts-Dunton, no mean writer himself but content to be handmaid to genius, took him into his Putney home and placed him under a strict régime. Forty years of sedulously guarded domesticity would see the publication of twenty-three volumes of poetry, prose and drama. The music was quieter, the colours less striking, the ideas less radical. There was little in the timid old gentleman to be seen toddling around Putney Heath to suggest the *enfant terrible* of younger days – but all was not lost. *Essays and Studies* (1875) had already revealed his talent for criticism. His monographs on Shakespeare (1880), Victor Hugo (1886) and Ben Jonson (1889) have still much to tell us. But for the excitement which, if only one is willing to forego analysis, can still affect the reader, we should turn back to those early poems. Then, perhaps fancying ourselves on Bamburgh sands, we should listen as well as read, as wave follows wave, as the foaming chaos of waters ebbs before the new roller comes tumbling along. Then we may appreciate the judgement of Ruskin. 'Atalanta, in power of imagination and understanding, simply sweeps me away ... as a torrent does a pebble. I'm *righter* than he is – so are the lambs and swallows, but they're not his match.'

Further Reading
Humphrey Hare, *Swinburne, a Biographical Approach*, 1949.

SWINDERBY, WILLIAM (*d.* after 1392) is representative of the humble missionaries, who spread a popular form of Lollardy among ordinary people. Little is known about Swinderby's early life. It cannot even be demonstrated that he was ordained, although he claimed to have been, and certainly he had no licence to preach. Like John Ball, he was an unbeneficed and nonconforming chaplain before Lollardy began, but unlike Ball he advocated moral rather than social reform. He was evidently intelligent and literate, an impressive preacher, and possessed of a pragmatic but not foolhardy courage. He occurs first at Leicester, where he denounced the pride and wantonness of women and subsequently the trade and wealth by which the townsmen lived. Understandably such teachings made him unpopular, so he became a hermit in the woods, perhaps supported by John of Gaunt, Lord of Leicester. Meantime Lollardy was introduced, perhaps by Philip Repingdon, a canon of Leicester Abbey, and a Lollard congregation was formed by the layman William Smith and another chaplain in a disused chapel. There Swinderby joined them, helped them to organize Lollard services and schools, and from thence he embarked on teaching tours to neighbouring towns and villages. Thus Leicester became one of the strongest centres of Lollardy.

Inevitably such activities came to the attention of the Bishop of Lincoln, who followed up Archbishop Courtenay's Earthquake Council and attack on academic Lollardy by citing Swinderby to appear before him in 1382. Swinderby was contumacious but eventually appeared, probably under coercion. He was examined, found guilty of heresy, recanted and did penance. His recantation however was insincere and he resumed preaching as soon as he was at liberty, proceeding westwards to Coventry, to the dioceses of Worcester (1387) and Hereford (1390). All the time he was winning influential friends, so that in 1392 local gentry insisted on a safeconduct for him before his examination by Bishop Trefnant. The bishop found him a relapsed heretic, but Swinderby escaped into Wales, where he disappeared from history.

Such men spread Lollardy too widely to be eradicated when the church authorities organized their counterattack. Swinderby's career demonstrates the scope for a determined subversive to exploit diocesan boundaries, the slow and formal procedures of ecclesiastical justice, and the lack of an ecclesiastical police force at parish level. Although Swinderby feared burning as a heretic, deprivation or lack of promotion could not deter him. Penance and prison were the only penalties available against him. The act of 1401 that permitted heretics to be burnt was thus an important deterrent even though seldom invoked, for Swinderby was typical in his distaste for martyrdom. The thirty years up to 1414 were crucial in establishing Lollardy before it was driven underground.

Swinderby is typical also in the debased form of Lollardy that he preached. Here is none of the profundity, complexity, or subtlety of Wyclif's theology, which emerges in only a few crude simplifications – for example, that the communion bread remained bread after consecration. Other beliefs, such as the right to withhold tithes from a lecherous priest and the nullity of sacraments performed by a sinful one, may have been Wycliffite in origin, but need not have been. They were directly relevant to contemporary laymen and came to distinguish popular Lollards from the orthodox, right up to the Reformation. They were dangerous to the church because they made obvious sense and appealed to the prejudices and interests of those humble laymen with whom Swinderby was genuinely concerned.

Further Reading
P. McNiven, *Heresy and Politics in the Reign of Henry IV. The Burning of John Badby*, 1987.
K. B. McFarlane, *John Wycliffe and the Beginnings of English Nonconformity*, 1952.

SWITHUN, ST (*d.*862) was Bishop of Winchester from 852 to 862. Very little is known for certain of Swithun beyond the dates of his episcopate. His holding the important see of Winchester would indicate close connections with the royal family of Wessex. Later tradition held that he had been the tutor of King Ethelwulf, which is not impossible, and that he was prominent among that king's counsellors. In a poem composed within a century of his death he was credited with the construction of a stone bridge over the river Itchen just outside Winchester. The only other event of local importance during his episcopate of which we know was a Danish attack on Winchester in 860. All that may reasonably be said of Swithun is that he conducted himself with credit in difficult times.

A small-scale and local cult of Swithun as a saint may have flourished at Winchester from soon after his death. But the man really responsible for Swithun's posthumous fame was his tenth-century successor, Bishop Ethelwold of Winchester. In 971 Ethelwold removed Swithun's remains to a new and splendid shrine, apparently commissioned by King Edgar, in Winchester Cathedral. Miracles were worked there, pilgrims came not only from distant parts of England but also from northern France. In the 990s Swithun's sanctity and miracles were celebrated by two Winchester writers, Wulfstan and Lantfrid, in Latin verse and prose; also by Aelfric in his Old English *Lives of the Saints*. This vigorous promotion of the cult of Swithun was part of the process by which Edgar and Ethelwold sought to enhance the glory and dignity of Winchester as the main seat of English royal power and an important focus of English piety.

Swithun's cult continued to flourish throughout the Middle Ages. He is mainly remembered today in a jingle about the weather, 'Rain on St Swithun's day (15 July), rain for forty days' (and variants), first attested in the sixteenth century. Like other proverbial attempts to impose order on that elusive element, the English climate, it is more often than not inaccurate.

SYDENHAM, THOMAS (1624-89), physician, came from an old yet Puritan family in Dorset. He entered Magdalen Hall, Oxford, in 1642, went on to Wadham and thence to a fellowship at All Souls in 1648, and did not finally leave Oxford until he went to practise in London in 1655. But his career was much interrupted, for he served in the parliamentarian cavalry in the First Civil War, and fought again for the Commonwealth in 1651. Moreover, although he spent much of his time at Oxford in the study of medicine, it seems probable that he got the most valuable part of his training under the famous Huguenot doctor Barbeyrac at Montpellier. The established physicians disliked the novelty of his professional opinions and perhaps also his Puritanism, so that the College of Physicians did not grant him a licentiate until 1663 and never elected him a Fellow. Nevertheless, Sydenham became a successful and respected practitioner. The friend of Boyle and of Locke, who collaborated with him for some years after 1667, consulted him about the famous operation on Shaftesbury, and

helped him collect data on infectious diseases, Sydenham, even though he was not in close touch with the scientific movement of his time, was the best contemporary exemplar in medicine of the new spirit of rationalism. Saying that 'true practice consists in the observations of nature', he founded all his work, in diagnosis and in treatment, upon accurate and carefully-recorded clinical observation of the patient and of the disease. Such an approach has become the commonplace of modern medicine; in Sydenham's time, when doctors bound themselves to authority and dogma or to magic and quackery, it was revolutionary. Sydenham wished to classify diseases just as his contemporary John Ray was beginning to classify plants, and to this end he recorded his observations upon epidemic diseases in London over a series of years. His greatest written work, *Observationes Medicae* (first published in 1676), which came to be regarded with great respect on the continent, contained careful descriptions founded solely upon experience. It was Sydenham who first recognized hysteria as a distinct ailment; he differentiated measles from scarlet fever; and the gout from which he suffered enabled him to write an authoritative treatise on that complaint. He believed in fresh air and light diet, he was often sceptical about bleeding, he used quinine and opium. A zealous and independent physician, he is commemorated by the London district which bears his name.

Further Reading
G. F. Sydenham, *The History of the Sydenham Family*, ed. A. T. Cameron, 1928.

T

TAIT, ARCHIBALD CAMPBELL (1811-82), a handsome, curly headed, practical Scot, was Victoria's favourite Archbishop of Canterbury. She overrode Disraeli to get him nominated, and when he died asked for a lock of his hair. This was partly because they shared the sufferings of bereavement: Tait lost five children in six weeks in a scarlet fever epidemic. But it was also because he was a Broad Churchman, of whom Albert would undoubtedly have approved. Most of all she liked his strong sense of the Church of England as a national institution with the queen as its head. 'Take the Church of England out of the history of England, and the history of England becomes a chaos, without order, without life, without meaning', he said.

Tait was brought up as a Presbyterian. But he migrated to Oxford, where he took a First from Balliol, succeeded Arnold as headmaster of Rugby, and went on to be Dean of Carlisle and Bishop of London, before becoming archbishop in 1868. As Primate of All England he was more prominent in the political life of the nation than any of his predecessors since Laud. An instinctive moderate and a capable manager, he was respected by intelligent laymen, but mistrusted by the extremists among the evangelical and the Tractarian clergy. The House of Lords was his natural forum: important church business was done in his robing room there. He used his influence to stop the diehards from throwing out Gladstone's Act disestablishing the Church of Ireland, and focused on keeping its endowments. His interest in education went back as far as 1839, to a visit to Prussia, pioneer in compulsory education, and he backed Forster's Education Act in 1870. He supported the repeal of religious tests for university entrance, and his was the Burial Act which allowed dissenters to be buried in churchyards – which led to a protest from 15,000 clergy. He was at best luke-warm about the recently revived Convocation, where High Churchmen dominated the Lower House, and suggested that the cost of printing the Chronicles of its sessions should be shared by its members in proportion to the length of their speeches.

His one disaster was the Public Worship Regulation Act of 1874. This was designed to keep leading laymen in the church happy, by preventing parish priests from introducing elaborate ritual. At a time when the parish church was at the centre of community life, conservative churchgoers did not like their parsons to monkey about with their services. The queen was all for disciplining high churchmen, and Disraeli went along with it as he had little other legislation prepared at the start of his ministry. But the Act led to the imprisonment of the clergy who disobeyed it. They started to acquire the halo of martyrdom, and the embarrassed Tait advised bishops to veto prosecutions based on it. This was an uncharacteristic mistake. Normally Tait was the right man in the right job at the right time. He overflowed with energy, collecting money, building churches, raising the profile of the church in this, the age of its highest prestige. He welcomed the widening horizons of the railways and the new science, and looked forward 'to the time when the whole world shall have been so improved by the blessing of Almighty God that it will be ready for the coming of the Lord'.

Further Reading
E. F. Carpenter, *Cantuar: the Archbishops in the Office*, 1971.

TALBOT, CHARLES, 12th EARL and only DUKE OF SHREWSBURY (1660-1718), most singular of all politicians of the days of William III and Anne, was born at Grafton, in Worcestershire, heir to great estates, a divided home and the Roman Catholic faith. He inherited the earldom in 1667 when his father was killed in a duel by the Duke of Buckingham, Lady Shrewsbury's lover. Brought up by dreary and parsimonious relatives, he was sent in 1674 to study at Navarre College in Paris and at the military academy there, and after a brief taste of campaigning in the Netherlands came home in 1678, the year of the Popish Plot. Excluded from political life by the Parliamentary Test Act of that November, the young peer seems to have been deeply sensitive to the indignities and dangers to which prominent Catholics were exposed. In 1679, apparently under the influence of Dean (later Archbishop) Tillotson, he was converted to Anglicanism. There is no sign that he ever wavered from Protestantism for the rest of his days. Yet the fact that he had once been a Catholic, and the Catholicism of many of his Talbot relations, always encouraged hopes of his return to Rome – and strengthened Jacobite illusions about him.

Shrewsbury was a man of rare quality – deeply humane, individual in outlook, politically courageous in times of crisis, the least vindictive of men. With an able and cultured mind and a sincere charm of manner which rarely failed, he was, with his lands and wealth and rank, certain of an important part in the politics of his day. Yet he was cursed throughout life by an excessive sensitivity and by a lack of confidence which stemmed no doubt from the bitter uncertainties of his childhood. Nicknamed 'the King of Hearts', this attractive young man did not marry until he was forty-five. Politically, his self-distrust encouraged the lack of stamina which made him want to give up high office almost as soon as he was appointed. He was frequently ill, or believed himself ill; the records tell of fits, gout, spitting of blood, shortness of breath. Some of this was doubtless psychosomatic, but not all of it: a hunting accident of 1696 left a persistent legacy of chest trouble. Pride, diffidence, hypochondria, and ill-health made him always a tiresome and unreliable colleague. And in 1700, weary of politics, he left England on a belated Grand Tour and then settled in Rome for some three years. He returned early in 1706, bringing with him as his wife a witty, intelligent and somewhat eccentric Italian widow whose manners infuriated the Duchess of Marlborough and diverted English aristocratic society.

In some measure Shrewsbury's fine gifts appear wasted. He served William III, who thought better of him than of nearly all Englishmen, as Secretary of State (1689-90 and 1693-8); yet despite the dukedom conferred on him in 1694 he spent much effort trying to resign, particularly after Sir John Fenwick falsely accused him of complicity in Jacobite conspiracy. In Anne's reign, between his return in 1706 and his appointment as Lord Treasurer in 1714, he held the second-rank posts of Lord Chamberlain (1710-14) and Lord Lieutenant of Ireland (1713-14). He did not lead, in the sense that Marlborough, Bolingbroke or Wharton led; he did not organize, as Godolphin and Harley did. Nevertheless, on three occasions in his political career his character and actions were of immense significance to his country. The first was when as a young aristocrat of Whig sympathies he was a central figure in the conspiracy which turned James II off the throne and placed William III on it. Shrewsbury was one of the Seven who signed the invitation to William; he joined William in Holland and sailed to Torbay with him; he carried to James the message which finally sent him to France; and he was from the start one of those who wanted William as king. The second occasion came in the middle years of Anne's reign when Shrewsbury, now middle-aged, a

moderate rather than a Whig, the great magnate committed to neither party, joined with Harley to make it possible for Anne to get rid of the Whigs and their dependants Godolphin and Marlborough; and thus to enable the costly war of the Spanish Succession to be brought to an end. The third came in the last hours of Anne's reign when, by common consent of the dying queen's Council, Shrewsbury was given the White Staff of the Lord Treasurer. It was a tribute to him and it was Shrewsbury who presided over the Hanoverian Succession, and thus confirmed by his actions the decision which both he and the English people had taken in 1688.

George I, who had named him as one of his regents to govern the realm until his arrival, thought well of Shrewsbury; but the Whigs could not forgive him his activities in 1708-10. He did not long retain his offices, and he died in 1718. A patron of the arts, he built a classical mansion in Italian style for himself at Heythrop in Oxfordshire. It was burned down in later years and became the site of a Jesuit college.

Further Reading
Dorothy H. Somerville, *The King of Hearts*, 1962.
A. S. Turberville, *Shrewsbury*, 1930.

TALBOT, JOHN, EARL OF SHREWSBURY and WATERFORD (*c*.1387-1453) and Count of Clermont was the outstanding English commander in France after 1429. His death marks the end of the Hundred Years' War. His name of Talbot spread terror among the French and children were scared into obedience for fear that 'the Talbot cometh'. To celebrate his death the church of Notre-Dame-de-Talbot marks where he fell. In 1421 he added his niece's two Shropshire baronies of Talbot of Goodrich Castle and Strange of Blackmere to that of Furnivall, Lord of Sheffield and Hallamshire, which he had held by his first marriage since 1409. John was thus no parvenu, but a nobleman of long lineage and extensive property both in England and Ireland. His income of £1,205 in 1436 was itself more than sufficient endowment for the earldom he received in 1442. 'A deep and genuine commitment to the code of chivalry as he understood it offers the most convincing key to Talbot's character and career'. He was conventionally pious, hearing mass before battle, founding a chantry, and going on pilgrimage to Rome. His commitment to the advancement of the Talbots, the dictates of honour and prestige, and above all his hot temper and ready resort to force explain the many quarrels in which he became embroiled: his quarrel with the Earl of Arundel in 1413, which earned him a spell in the Tower; the thirty-year Talbot-Ormond feud in Ireland, which parliament tried – unavailingly – to end in 1423; his disputes with a former estate officer in Herefordshire, with Joan Lady Abergavenny, and, over parliamentary precedence, with Lord Grey of Ruthin; his unfounded charge of cowardice at Pataye against Sir John Fastolf; his involvement in the Berkeley-Lisle dispute on behalf of his second wife Margaret, and the Talbot-Lisle feud he created by diverting property from his heir to Margaret's own son. As lieutenant of Ireland he was charged with misgovernment and abuse of power. He was an aggressive and combative nobleman, whose energies were best employed abroad if domestic peace was to be preserved.

Talbot's first campaign was against Glendower in Wales in 1404 and he fought in Ireland as lieutenant in 1414-19, missing the Agincourt and first Norman campaigns. He was lieutenant of Ireland twice more. He first served in France in 1419, but returned continuously, sharing in almost every campaign and battle. The ransom he paid in 1429-33 probably prevented any financial profit, but he gained greatly in prestige. Surprise attacks repeatedly captured what he could not formally besiege. He regularly appeared where least expected and his vengeance was fearsome and immediate. Intrepid and dashing, he was the 'most strenuous and most audacious leader of all the battles'. Hard and cruel, 'there was not from the time of Herod anyone so wicked'. For most of his career he was in retreat, suppressing revolts, repeatedly resisting attacks and relieving sieges. One of several generals before Salisbury's death in 1428, he was the favoured field commander of successive lieutenants and accumulated many town captaincies. It was largely due to him that the English remained fifteen years after the Congress of Arras (1435). He was not responsible for the loss of Normandy and was the obvious choice to recover Aquitaine. 'Selfless service in a dying cause' earned promotion as KG (1425), count (1434), Marshal of France (1436), Constable of France (1442) and Ireland (1446).

Except in 1441, under York, and in Aquitaine in 1452-3 Talbot was never commander-in-chief. He 'was primarily an executant, not a planner, of military operations'. This was his appropriate role. He was not a strategist and was defeated in both his battles. Neither should have been fought. His suicidal frontal assault made Châtillon the first battle decided by artillery. He was not the great general suggested by his legend, but the best of those who remained.

Further Reading
A. J. Pollard, *John Talbot and the War in France 1427-1453*, 1983.
E. C. Williams, *My Lord of Bedford 1389-1435*, 1963.

TALBOT, RICHARD, EARL OF TYRCONNEL (1630-91), James II's Lord Deputy in Ireland, was the eighth son of an Irish baronet. A big, handsome, blustering, quarrelsome, rather inept man, 'lying Dick Talbot' had been left for dead at Drogheda in 1649 and made his escape in women's clothes. He had an equivocal career in the 1650s – he said he was willing to murder

Cromwell but Clarendon believed he was in Oliver's pay, and when he was arrested in England in 1655 he got away surprisingly easily by making his guards drunk – and he was the companion of James, Duke of York, in his amours after the Restoration. Twice he was sent to the Tower for insulting the Duke of Ormonde, and he was again imprisoned on suspicion at the time of the Popish Plot. Tyrconnel was devoted both to Ireland and to his Catholic faith, and was the leader of those Irishmen who wished to destroy the existing settlement of Irish land, with its gross favouritism to the Protestant minority. The accession of James II in 1685 gave Tyrconnel his opportunity. As commander of the army in Ireland he disarmed the Protestants, filled the ranks illegally with Catholics, and undermined – with the king's approval – one of the advisers who urged James on to more extreme pro-Catholic steps in England. Appointed Lord Deputy in 1687, he packed Irish law courts and town corporations with Catholics; and when James came to Ireland in 1689 Tyrconnel was to the fore in the parliamentary attack on Protestant privileges and lands. He fought courageously when his cause was shattered at the Boyne, and returned to Ireland to continue the struggle in 1691, dying suddenly of apoplexy.

TALLIS, THOMAS (*c.*1505-85), composer, was born probably in Leicestershire, although neither the place nor the date of his birth is certain. He is first known to history as one of the musicians who were pensioned in 1540 when Waltham Abbey in Essex was dissolved. He was either a chorister or organist there. Between 1540 and 1542 he held a musical post at Canterbury and was then made one of the gentlemen of the Chapel Royal. Until his death he served the next three rulers of England, latterly as chief organist. Mary considered him her principal composer, and he was, until his death, the doyen of Elizabeth's Chapel Royal.

He received various rewards from grateful sovereigns, and bought property in Greenwich. He married a woman called Joan in 1552 – her maiden name is not known. In his later years he was associated with his much younger and subsequently more famous contemporary, William Byrd, who worked with him in the Chapel and also published with him in 1575 a collection of motets, *Cantiones quae ab arqumento sacrae vocantur*. Byrd and Tallis were jointly granted by the queen in the same year the monopoly of printing music, which was surprisingly worth almost nothing because so little music was printed at that time.

As a composer, Tallis's first works were pieces of Latin church music, composed for Catholic ritual in the reigns of Henry VIII and Mary I. Five antiphons of his survive, and three masses, all in different styles. One of his masses was probably written to be performed before Philip II in St Paul's Cathedral at Christmas 1554, containing the Introit '*Puer natus est nobis*', which was doubtless intended to be prophetic as well as seasonal.

Tallis's Latin church music did not cease with the accession of Elizabeth I, although he had to confine himself to composing shorter pieces. It was probably to celebrate Elizabeth I's fortieth birthday in 1573 (although conceivably for Mary I's in 1556) that Tallis composed what some consider his greatest work, the Motet 'Spem in alium', written for forty voices.

Tallis was adaptable and responded to the new demand for English church music which resulted from the English Reformation. He has been called 'the father of English cathedral music'. He used a great variety of styles, both simple and grand, in his settings of the English Service, while abiding by Cranmer's famous insistence on lucidity. He introduced polyphonic English psalms where before there had only been plainsong. The hymn tune 'Tallis', based on the ninth of his works written for Parker's Psalter of 1567 is still used, while Vaughan Williams's 'Fantasia on a Theme of Tallis' is also drawn from this collection. He composed many memorable English anthems.

Tallis also composed a certain number of keyboard works, with a religious theme but for recreational purposes. He wrote for organ and virginals. He himself was an organist while both Mary I and Elizabeth I were virginal players, the former better than the latter.

Tallis was one of the great composers of his century, although it is generally agreed that his achievement is overshadowed by that of his pupil, Byrd. He developed very considerably as a musician, responding to the challenges presented by the religious changes of his age, although his compositions still kept the restrained, undemonstrative, medieval air which is their great charm.

Further Reading
P. Doe, *Tallis*, 1976.

TAYLOR, JEREMY (1613-67), preacher, the son of a Cambridge barber, became a Fellow of Caius. His reputation as an exponent of Anglican orthodoxy in a university where Puritanism was strong attracted Laud's attention, and he became a Fellow of All Souls and a Chaplain to the king. The Civil War years brought difficulties upon him. For a time he found a safe retreat in Carmarthenshire, as Chaplain to the Earl of Carbery at Golden Grove, and it was here that he wrote the works that have preserved his fame – notably the pieces of devotional literature, *Holy Living* and *Holy Dying*, and his *Discourse of the Liberty of Prophesying*, a defence of toleration from the Anglican side comparable with the writing of Chillingworth. During the Republican period Taylor was imprisoned for a time. In 1658 he took a living in Ireland, and in 1661 he became Bishop of Down and Connor, dying in Ireland in 1667.

Further Reading
C. J. Stranks, *The Life and Writings of Jeremy Taylor*, 1952.

TELFORD, THOMAS (1757-1834) was born at Glendinning in Eskdale. His father was an 'unblameable shepherd', in the phrase of his son's epitaph – and his upbringing in the little thatched cottage was simple. He received a sound education, however, at the parish school, left at fourteen and learned to be a mason. For some time he worked on the fast-growing New Town of Edinburgh; to this we may trace his admiration for the severe formality which characterized Scotland's late Georgian architecture. He also planned for himself the life of a poet; at least one of his poems, 'Eskdale', has a certain conventional charm – but he was to find another outlet for creative energy. In 1782 he took the high road to England and found work on Somerset House, then on Portsmouth Dockyard, where he was foreman mason. In 1786 he was appointed Surveyor of Public Works for Shropshire, a fortunate appointment for the man and the county. The north of Shropshire, on the border of Worcestershire and Staffordshire, was being enriched at this time by industrial development; the very names Coalbrookdale and Coalport, with their associations with iron and china, suggest the source of this activity.

Telford was nothing if not versatile. He was the first to excavate Roman Uriconium (Wroxeter). At Buildwas, near the original iron bridge at Coalbrookdale, which had merely imitated in iron the conventional structure of a stone bridge, he built a second – lighter, flatter and with single span arch. He built and improved roads, dressing the roads with small fragments which made the surface impervious to water. He built churches: at Bridgnorth a grave, handsome design which takes full advantage of its site at the end of East Castle Street; two octagonal churches at Malinslee and Madeley. He supervised the restoration of Shrewsbury Castle for Sir William Pulteney and built a pleasant gazebo, red sandstone and again his favourite octagonal shape, on top of the mound. Enough survives of his work in this field to show that he could have become a notable architect, but he was caught up in the intense activity of the industrial revolution.

Telford's Ellesmere canal was the first of some twenty projects on which he was employed. This one is notable for its two aqueducts. The greater one, Pont Cysylte, carries the canal 127 feet over the river Dee, in an iron trough fifteen feet wide, on iron arches mounted on eighteen piers of stone across a valley which, by means of a vast embankment, he narrowed to 1,000 feet. The aqueduct, which took eight years to build, can be seen today, a remarkably impressive record of the confidence and energy of this time. Between 1803 and 1822 he was engaged upon the building of the Caledonian Canal which proved to be more formidable than expected; locks and cuttings had to be made through solid rock in some places. He was less disappointed, however, in his Swedish enterprise, the Gotha canal, for which he designed the locks and bridges between 1808 and 1810. For his work on this great waterway, joining the North Sea and the Baltic, he was rewarded by a Swedish knighthood; he also made a lasting friendship with the intelligent statesman who patronized the work, Count von Platen.

In 1803 Telford had been put in charge of Highland works, the start of a connection with his native country which transformed the wild and inaccessible north. In the course of his labours, in romantic country but often in very simple constructions, he built over 1,000 bridges and about 1,000 miles of road. His iron bridges are not all to the taste of those who look for the picturesque and like lichened stone and mossy humps. Telford is essentially a practical man of the iron age. But he did not lack a sense of style and he had a strong awareness of the need for works to be in harmony with their surroundings. Some of the bridges of Pontifex Maximus, as his friend Southey called him, are beautiful; notable examples are Craig Ellachie and Cartland Crags. Telford also worked on some forty harbours. No single man did more to improve the economic potential of the Highlands.

Meanwhile Telford was also responsible for the improvement of the Holyhead road, from Shropshire, through Wales to Anglesey. It culminated in what is perhaps his most famous work, the suspension bridge over the Menai Straits, with a span of 550 feet, utilizing Captain Brown's new principle, the flat link iron chain. It was opened, at Telford's request without special ceremony, in 1825. In the same year he was appointed engineer to the new project of St Katherine's Dock in London. For five years more after the completion of this scheme in 1829, Telford was continually busy, on projects of many sorts, building up a large staff of pupils who were to carry on his work into a more scientific age. Men who were trained by him had an unbounded admiration for his genius; his pre-eminence is marked by the fact that he became President of the new Institution of Civil Engineers in 1820. He was a reserved man, who could be stern at times, and he never married, but he inspired great devotion. That admirers included Southey and Campbell, the poets, need not surprise us, for the heroic creativeness of his work is in tune with the romantic spirit of the time. He was indifferent about money and prestige. He was buried however, in Westminster Abbey, a fitting honour for one of the finest men of his time.

Further Reading
A. R. B. Haldane, *New Ways through the Glens*, 1962.
L. T. C. Rolt, *Thomas Telford*, 1958.

TEMPLE, FREDERICK (1821-1902), eventually Archbishop of Canterbury, was, at seventy-five, the oldest to be elected to the Chair of St Augustine in Victoria's reign. He was a man of craggy vigour. When he accepted nomination, he said that he felt he had five good working years ahead. He actually had six. His youthful spirit had been refreshed by a late and happy marriage, which produced two sons, one of whom, William, was to become Archbishop of Canterbury himself. But by 1896 his creative energy was, not surprisingly, on the wane.

He was the thirteenth child of a major, but had got to Balliol and flourished there. His concern for education was lifelong. First a lecturer at Balliol, then principal of the training college Kneller Hall, and in 1857 headmaster of Rugby, he had plenty of practical experience in it before he became Bishop of Exeter in 1869. At Rugby he modernized Arnold's curriculum (at the same time, Benson was doing the opposite to the prince consort's at Wellington), spreading history and English throughout the school and introducing science, music and drawing. Increasingly he focused on national education, as a means of opening opportunities for the poor. He believed that education should be for the whole man, and that religion must therefore be at the heart of it. Most primary schools were church schools. In a period in which primary education became compulsory, Temple wanted the church to play its full part alongside the state. He managed to keep the independence of church schools to appoint their own managers and heads, by agreeing that the church should keep up the buildings while the state paid the teachers.

Temple was for a long time suspected of liberalism in the circles of the church establishment. He was a fearless thinker, who believed that all truth came from God and that it was blasphemy to shirk the consequences of scientific or historical discovery. He contributed to *Essays and Reviews* (see F. D. Maurice) and in his 1884 Bampton Lectures took the full doctrine of evolution as axiomatic. Open-minded about historical criticism of biblical texts, he even accepted for ordination a candidate who suspended judgement about all physical miracles in the Bible. Little wonder that his nomination to Exeter had aroused protests. But by 1896 mid-Victorian doubts had become acceptable, even orthodox.

Temple's record as a social reformer was notable. As Bishop of London from 1885, he conciliated successfully in the dock strike in 1889. As archbishop, he advocated state pensions for all and business partnerships for labourers. But he was still a man of his age, and believed that social progress could only come through self help. He campaigned fearlessly for Temperance in rough areas: on one platform he got a blow from a bag of flour which took the wind out of him. He never minced his words. 'Bishop,' he said to one of the speakers at the

Lambeth Conference over which he presided, 'what you mean is all right, but what you say isn't what you mean.' He lived to crown Edward VII. Delegating little, he led from the front: a doughty warrior and a man of stature.

Further Reading
E. F. Carpenter, *Cantuar: the Archbishop in the Office*, 1971.

TEMPLE, HENRY, 3rd VISCOUNT PALMERSTON (1784-1865), Foreign Secretary and prime minister, was the son of an Irish peer, who owned 10,000 acres around Sligo, some Welsh slate quarries, and land in England worth £2,000 a year in rents, with Broadlands, near Romsey, as his main seat. It was a substantial inheritance, but he never cleared the debts which his father passed on, and was a notoriously bad payer himself. Aged eight, he was taken on a tour of France and Italy. The family escaped from Paris only four days before the mob stormed the Tuileries, and young Harry became suspicious of all democratic movements. Italy was more congenial. An Italian tutor left him fluent in the language, and for him the concept of Italy was much more than the 'geographical expression' that it was to Metternich. At Harrow, where he was at school with Aberdeen and four years senior to Peel, old men remembered him as a tough little fighter. More contemporary evidence shows him to have been a hard-working undergraduate at Edinburgh (where he imbibed Free Trade doctrines), and at Cambridge. He fought the strongly Whig Cambridge University seat as a Tory candidate when he was only twenty-one. By then his father was dead, but he had an influential patron in Lord Malmesbury, and was starting to catch the eye of society hostesses as a 'dapper lord'. The Duke of Portland asked him to be a Junior Lord of the Admiralty in 1807, and he became an MP for the pocket borough of Newport. With one interval of six months he remained in the House of Commons until his death fifty-eight years later.

Palmerston's expertise was to be in foreign affairs, and his maiden speech was a defence of Canning's action in sending the navy into Copenhagen to sink the Danish fleet. He justified this on the grounds that national security should override moral considerations, and he stuck to this approach all through his life. But foreign affairs were not his main concern until well into middle age. For nineteen years, from 1809, he was a pertinacious Secretary at War, a junior man alongside the Commander-in-Chief, responsible for the finances and administration of the army, but not for discipline or promotion. He stayed there by choice, refusing several more senior positions. He worked zestfully at the details: widows' pensions, schools for army orphans, a new process for waterproofing greatcoats. He defended flogging – and later, duelling – in the army. He cut the estimates, and he drove his staff hard, making them work long hours, and forbidding smoking in the office. In the heroic events of the last years of the Napoleonic Wars, his role was humdrum.

He was best known on the social scene. 'I suppose we may be glad of it,' wrote young Lady Lyttleton when she heard of his appointment to the War Office, 'as it may divert his lordship from flirting.' It did not. He was elected to Almack's Club in St James's. This was a mixed club, for which you had to be proposed by a member of the opposite sex, and approved by the seven patronesses. Palmerston – 'Lord Cupid' – was believed to have enjoyed the favours of three of these as his mistresses, including Madam de Lieven, wife of the Russian ambassador, and Lady Cowper, whom he was to marry in 1839 after her husband's death. He danced a lively waltz. The flirting went on all through his life, and it earned him a bad name with Victoria, especially when he tried to seduce a lady-in-waiting in Windsor Castle. But the public came to admire his aplomb, and chuckled when, aged seventy-eight and prime minister, he was cited as co-respondent by O'Kane, an Irish MP. 'We know she's Kane, but is he Abel?'

In 1830 he stepped into the part which made him famous, when Grey appointed him Foreign Secretary in his Whig ministry. It was a surprising choice. Palmerston had lined himself up behind Canning, and had resigned from Wellington's ministry with the other Canningites in 1828. Grey felt that an ex-Tory would reassure Russia, Austria and Prussia, all suspicious of his reforming government. No-one anticipated that this second choice for the post (Lansdowne having refused it) would be Foreign Secretary for fifteen of the next twenty-one years, and become the hero of the British public, including the patriotic radicals, and a villain to nearly all the rulers of Europe, including his own sovereign.

For his reputation, his style was as responsible as his policies. His blunt despatches and his 'rollicking air' (Disraeli's description) had a flavour unusual in diplomatic circles. To our minister in Washington, when a British citizen was threatened with the death sentence, he wrote: 'Mcleod's execution would produce war, immediate and frightful in its character because it would be a war of retaliation and revenge.' During the Indian Mutiny, Clarendon's comment, 'he has a jolly way of looking at disasters', was less than admiring. His rudeness in keeping diplomats waiting was notorious: the Belgian minister read the whole of Richardson's *Clarissa* in Palmerston's anteroom. Lord Cupid became the abrasive 'Lord Pumicestone' to Albert and Victoria. He liked to fly solo, sending off important despatches without showing them to the queen, sometimes not even consulting the Cabinet, always unwilling to explain policy to the House of Commons. His survival depended on his professional mastery of the details of foreign affairs, his cheerful optimism, his growing skill as a user of the Press; but above all on the nature of his policies.

'We have no eternal allies and we have no perpetual enemies. Our interests are eternal and perpetual, and those interests it is our duty to follow': thus Palmerston defended himself when accused in the Commons of being unexpectedly pro-Russian. He believed that British interests were normally to be served by allying with constitutional monarchies, and he did not like democratic America any better than the autocratic tsar. He had also grown up in the age of Napoleon, and the threats posed by an aggressive France were never far from his mind. So he backed the monarchy in Belgium: wanted Austria out of her Italian provinces of Lombardy and Venetia, but not at the expense of a spread of French influence there: yet supported a strong Austria north of the Alps, as a balance against both France and Russia. Worldwide, he looked to defend and advance British trade, and a concern for national prestige became his hallmark. In 1856, when he was prime minister, the *Arrow*, a ship manned by Chinese and engaged on piracy, but registered as British in Hong Kong, was boarded by Chinese coastguards. Palmerston ordered the bombardment of Canton by the navy. A vote of censure was passed against him in the Commons, but he won the subsequent election on the theme: 'an insolent barbarian wielding authority at Canton has violated the British flag'.

Whenever diplomacy was concerned with areas within range of the British fleet, he tended to be successful. Thus he was able to get the new Belgian kingdom set up in 1831, with Leopold of Saxe-Coburg, widower of George IV's daughter, as king, instead of Louis Philippe's son. In Portugal he helped the constitutional queen to defeat reactionary challenges, and when she then abolished the constitution, he persuaded her to restore it. The Eastern Question also lent itself to influence through sea-power. Problems were caused all through the nineteenth century in the Balkans and the near east by the weakness of the Turkish Empire and the threat of Russian expansion. During the 1830s Mehemet Ali, the powerful Pasha of Egypt, provoked two crises. The first, when he attacked his nominal overlord the Sultan in 1831, led to a spread of Russian influence when Tsar Nicholas I came to the rescue of the Turks. Palmerston failed to persuade the Cabinet to let him intervene. But by 1839, when the Sultan rashly attacked Mehemet and was routed, he was more his own master. He scored a diplomatic triumph by getting together with Austria, Prussia and Russia to impose a settlement on Mehemet, thus containing Russia, and isolating France, who backed Mehemet. The next crisis led, disastrously, to the Crimean War. But by then Palmerston was no longer Foreign Secretary, and many felt that his forceful approach would have stopped the tsar before he got into a position from which he could not withdraw.

His style had its disadvantages. The French, stung by it, sought revenge, and Louis Philippe and Guizot got it over the Spanish marriages. His relations with Victoria and Albert were very bad for many years. Melbourne, his brother-in-law, protected him after the episode at Windsor, but he was out of place in the new court after Albert's arrival. His apologies, even with tears in his eyes, for sending off despatches without showing them to the queen made the prompt repeat of the offence outrageous to them. His brinkmanship alarmed them. They disliked his sympathetic reactions to the revolutions of 1848, his anti-Austrian policy in Italy, his open contempt for 'petty German princelings' – Albert was one –, and above all his hostility to Louis Philippe, 'the dear king', followed by his support for the emerging Louis Napoleon. They wanted him dismissed. Russell, the prime minister, hesitated to drop him, fearing his popularity with the Radicals, on whose support Russell depended. An opportunity seemed to arise in 1850. Don Pacifico, a Portuguese Jew who held British citizenship by virtue of his birth in Gibraltar, claimed compensation from the Greek government after his house was attacked by a mob. Palmerston ordered the British fleet to act against Greek shipping if the claims were not paid in full. He had gone too far. Don Pacifico's demands were excessive: France and Russia, joint protectors of Greece with Britain, objected to his unilateral action: he misled the House of Commons. His enemies waited to pounce. But he won a surprise victory in one of the most famous parliamentary debates of the century, after a speech in which he claimed that a British subject should expect the protection which a Roman had commanded when he announced: 'Civis Romanus sum'.

Triumphant, he went his merry way. He showed sympathy towards the workmen who attacked the unpopular Austrian General Haynau ('Hyena') when he visited a London brewery, and he held a private meeting with Kossuth, the Hungarian leader of the 1848 rebellion. Next year, 1851, without consultation, he congratulated Louis Napoleon on his coup d'état against the Second Republic. Here was an issue on which he would get no support from the Radicals, and Russell peremptorily dismissed him. It took him only two months to achieve his 'tit-for-tat with Johnny Russell', bringing down the government with a Radical-Conservative alliance against the Militia Bill. By the end of 1852 he was back in office, this time as Aberdeen's Home Secretary. Like Churchill under Chamberlain, he was not associated in public opinion with the shortcomings of the ministry in the entry to and running of the Crimean War. It was this opinion, with *Punch* cartoons of little Pam the Pugilist rolling up his sleeves, that forced the queen to invite him to succeed Aberdeen in 1855. He was her fourth choice.

He was to be prime minister for the remaining ten years of his life, with one fifteen-month interlude. It was a fallow period in parliament, with few legislative achievements. Palmerston was instinctively conservative, and kept parliamentary reform firmly off the agenda. His Cabinet was the oldest in British history. He made no attempt to change the structure of the army after the Crimean War, though his energy and optimism gave new heart to its prosecution. Religious dogma troubled him little (he features, for Trollope, as the head of the incoming ministry who made Dr Proudie Bishop of Barchester), but he was a good Protestant in his dislike for the new Roman Catholic hierarchy in Britain. In Ireland, he saw 'tenant's right as landlord's wrong', and resisted change to the Land Laws. During the American Civil War his sympathies were on the side of the southern gentry. He wrote rasping letters to Lincoln's Minister in London, and allowed the *Alabama*, a Confederate ship built in Birkenhead, to set sail into the Atlantic, where she inflicted heavy damage on Federal shipping. His relations with Gladstone, his reforming Chancellor of the Exchequer, were uncomfortable. During Cabinet discussions, he would draw up two lists of names on scraps of paper. Gladstone he invariably put on the list supporting change: at the foot of those opposing it he always wrote 'Palmerston'.

Yet he became the leader of the first Liberal government. In 1858 he had resigned, blamed for uncharacteristically kow-towing to Napoleon III after the discovery that Orsini, Napoleon's would-be assassin, had made his bombs in England. When he regained office in 1859, he formed a ministry which combined Whigs, Peelites and Radicals in a grouping which held together until Irish Home Rule broke it in 1886 – the Liberal Party. His last years were golden ones. They coincided with a period of economic prosperity, and the most optimistic mood of the Victorian era. Palmerston caught the spirit of the nation. Age had mellowed Lord Pumicestone. He had always been good in the Smoking Room, and Lady Palmerston gave sparkling parties at Cambridge House. His physical energy, famous since he used to swim in the Thames before breakfast, was part of the Palmerston legend. In 1864 he rode to the Harrow School Speech Day from Piccadilly in under an hour, and a month before he died he climbed over the railings at Brocket when he thought no-one was looking, to prove to himself that he could still do it. Although he was losing his diplomatic skill, underestimating the emerging Prussia and blustering to no avail when Bismarck pushed the Danes out of Schleswig Holstein, he won the 1865 election with an increased majority. He died soon after it, two days before his eighty-first birthday, having discovered less than a week earlier the pleasure of mutton chops and port for breakfast. Ironically, his heir as Liberal leader was to be Gladstone, and it was left to Disraeli and the Conservatives to carry on the tradition of Palmerstonian diplomacy.

Further Reading

M. E. Chamberlain, *Lord Palmerston*, 1987.
J. Ridley, *Palmerston*, 1970.
D. G. Southgate, *'The most English minister ...' The policies and politics of Palmerston*, 1966.

TEMPLE, SIR WILLIAM (1628-99), diplomatist, born at Blackfriars, was educated at Bishop's Stortford School and Emmanuel College, Cambridge. His diplomatic career began in 1665 with missions to Munster and Brussels, and in 1667-8 he negotiated the Triple Alliance with Holland and Sweden. Appointed ambassador to the Hague in 1668, Temple was in Charles II's reign the chief English protagonist of friendship with the Dutch. So during the Third Dutch War of 1672-4 he withdrew from political life, but in 1674 he was recalled to negotiate the Treaty of Westminster. Three years later came his most significant diplomatic achievement, the marriage of the Princess Mary to William III of Orange. In 1679 Temple was the principal author of a scheme to reorganize and make more efficient the Privy Council, which Charles for a short time adopted. But it broke down in face of the partisan passions of the Popish Plot period. At the Revolution, Temple remained loyal to James until William's triumph was clear; he declined office under the new régime, although his son became Secretary for War, and he spent the rest of his days in retirement.

Cautious and honourable, Temple enjoyed eminence rather than influence in the politics of his day. Moreover, he was comfortably off, and he preferred the pleasures and safety of private life. His wife, Dorothy Osborne, was a woman of ability as well as of beauty and a natural letter-writer of great charm; it took him seven years to win her, for her father was a royalist commander and his a parliamentarian MP, and by the time of their marriage (1655) her beauty had been ruined by smallpox. Temple spent much time in literary pursuits and Jonathan Swift was for several years his amanuensis. He had a solid and direct prose style, and his writings on international affairs have commanded respect in the twentieth century, most notably his *Observations upon the United Provinces of the Netherlands* (1673). Ironically, he is best known for his essay on *Ancient and Modern Learning*, which accepted the *Letters of Phalaris* as genuine and laid him open to the massive attack of Bentley. He was also a horticulturist and especially a fruit-grower of distinction, both at his earlier estate of Sheen and at Moor Park, near Farnham, which he laid out in the Dutch style.

Further Reading

T. B. Macaulay, 'Sir William Temple' (1838) in *Critical and Historical Essays*.

TENISON, THOMAS (1636-1715), Archbishop of Canterbury, was born at Cottenham, in Cambridgeshire, the son of a Norfolk rector. Educated at Corpus Christi

College, Cambridge, of which he became a Fellow, he was ordained in 1659. From 1680 to 1691 he was Rector of St Martin's in the Fields. Here he won a reputation as preacher and pamphleteer. Moreover, in Burnet's words, 'Whitehall lying within that parish, he stood as in the front of the battle all King James's reign'. For Tenison was strongly anti-Catholic, and enjoyed a vigorous controversy with the Jesuits. In 1688 he was a prominent supporter of the Seven Bishops, and he was well-informed about the projected invasion of that year: his close friend Evelyn recorded under 10 August that 'Dr Tenison now told me there would suddenly be some great thing discovered'. His promotion after the Revolution was rapid, for he was Bishop of Lincoln in 1691 and he succeeded Tillotson at Canterbury in 1694. He owed advancement undoubtedly to his latitudinarian views and to his moderation towards Dissenters, reflecting an outlook with which William III was in close accord. Politically he was a Whig, and his appointment sharpened the divisions which already existed between a bench of bishops who were mainly 'Low Church' and the 'High Church' majority of the lesser clergy. Moreover, the confidence of William meant the hostility of Anne, who took advice on ecclesiastical questions from Sharp of York rather than from Tenison. It was one of the ironies of the reign of a queen whose main interest was the Church of England that she was on bad terms with the Archbishop of Canterbury – and he outlived her. Tenison compounded his disfavour by opposing the Occasional Conformity Bill and by keeping in steady contact with Hanover. He was an active supporter of the Scottish Union of 1707, defending it by arguments showing a broad clarity towards Presbyterianism. He was at the head of the list of Lords Justices appointed by the Hanoverian successor in 1714, and lived long enough to see George I installed in 1715. As in doctrine, so in the range of his social concern Tenison foreshadowed the eighteenth century. While he was at St Martin's he opened the first public library in London; he endowed a school; he played a central part in the foundation of the Society for the Propagation of the Gospel in Foreign Parts (1701); and he was also prominent in the movement in Anne's reign for the reformation of manners.

Further Reading
E. F. Carpenter, *Thomas Tenison, Archbishop of Canterbury*, 1948.

TENNYSON, LORD ALFRED (1809-92), is commonly regarded as the prime representative of poetry in the Victorian age. His becoming Poet Laureate in 1850 was seen to be fitting; he had already accomplished much of his best work. In 1855 *The National Review* applauded him for 'throwing divine grace over the happier emotions'. His peerage, in 1884, crowned a dedicated career. By then the critical tide had turned. The

rediscovery of earlier poets like Donne, less mellifluous but challenging to heart and mind, the work of contemporaries like Browning and Swinburne, together with a growing impatience with typical Tennysonian themes, were helping to create a new climate. The discovery of Hopkins, little known in his time, and the venturesome work of poets like Yeats, Eliot and Pound, would open ears to a different poetic music. It is only recently that a balanced estimate of Tennyson's achievement has become possible, so that the sustained power of poems like 'Ulysses', the awed feeling for the mystery of life that permeates so much of his work, and the sharp poignancy of his finest lyrics, can unite present admirers with those of his day.

Tennyson was the fourth of twelve children, born into an old Lincolnshire family. His father, George, was a clergyman by default. Disinherited by his father, required to enter the living found by family influence, his subsequent behaviour, resentful, glum, sometimes violent, bore heavily on the family in Somersby rectory. A common sense of injustice, concern about the treatment of their mother, uneasiness about themselves and their common inheritance, 'the black blood of the Tennysons', all contributed to an introspective sense of being a family apart. Two of Alfred's brothers descended into madness. Instability marked the conduct of the others. Frederick, the eldest, was recklessly extravagant; even Charles, second, and most 'normal', became addicted to laudanum.

Alfred was sent, in 1815, to Louth Grammar School: he was miserable. From 1820 he was at home, taught by his father with intermittent zeal. Left much to his own resources, he read widely, wrote ambitiously and roamed about the countryside which left so powerful an impression on his poetic sensibility: the leafy hollow of Somersby, providing shelter from the winds that swept across fen and wold; below and beyond the drainage dykes of 'the waste enormous marsh' and line of low dunes, the North Sea and the 'cold grey stones' of its shore. Odd, awkward, much given to mooning about or peering myopically at plants and insects, there was much in the shambling boy that would remain in the man. But the boy was not purposeless. Before he was thirteen he had composed in the style of Pope, Scott and Milton. The 'Devil and the Lady' (not published till 1930) shows a precocious grasp of the techniques of Elizabethan dramatic verse. Byron became the dominant influence. In 1824, when told of his death, Alfred flung himself to the ground and wept; then carved on sandstone, 'Byron is dead'. His fate only strengthened the young follower's sense of destiny. His father encouraged him in the belief that he would be a great poet. In 1827, a Louth bookseller printed his poems, with Frederick's, in 'Poems by Two Brothers'. Alfred's contributions were mostly in the fashionable styles of the time. Shocked by his father's decline into drunken gloom, he would find a more distinctive voice.

Tennyson joined his brothers George and Charles at Trinity College, Cambridge. A subsidy from a generous aunt made it possible. She was more helpful than that other aunt who once said to him: 'Alfred, when I look on you I think of the words of Holy Scripture: "Depart from me, ye cursed, into everlasting fire".' Cambridge was both intimidating and liberating – eventually more the latter, due to the interest aroused by his poetry, his resulting election to The Apostles, to his friendships, with men like Spedding and Fitzgerald and – the deepest of his life – with Arthur Hallam. Hallam helped Tennyson find his voice in that high-spirited society, and saw to the publication of his poems. In 1829 Tennyson won the Chancellor's Gold Medal with a poem called 'Timbuctoo'. In 1830, *Poems, Chiefly Lyrical*, appeared. A journey, ostensibly to support Spanish liberals, was a fiasco, but the austere Pyrenean landscape provided a new range of images. In the same year Hallam, visiting the rectory, fell in love with Tennyson's sister, Emily; two years later, he was her accepted suitor.

The Apostles, predisposed to see genius in any member of their club, needed no prompting to enthuse about Tennyson's poems. With those critics in the *Quarterly Review* and *Blackwoods*, self-appointed arbiters of taste, it was a different matter. In his article about *Poems, Chiefly Lyrical*, Hallam praised too generously. Contemptuously, John Wilson attacked the poems. In his next collection (1832), Tennyson included a satirical epigram on the surly critic. Inevitably it prompted a fiercely hostile review; yet this collection contained 'The Lotus Eaters' and 'The Lady of Shalott'. Wilson hit home when he charged Tennyson with mistaking passing fancies for the poetic mood, with results embarrassingly trivial. Torn between compulsion to write (and earn) and reluctance to bare his soul, Tennyson was vulnerable. He was poorer than ever since his father's death, in 1831. To his wealthy grandfather, the Somersby family were a tiresome brood and he made but modest provision for them. But Tennyson would think of no other career but that of poet. There was an underlying toughness, and it was as well. In September 1833 came a terrible shock. Visiting Vienna, Hallam died, suddenly. A trusted friend now became the poet's muse, the poet's memories a copious source of inspiration.

In 1834, Tennyson fell in love with Rosa Baring. Her family disapproved; she hid her feelings beneath conventional coquetry. It came to nothing. His emotions would be recollected in verse – but not in tranquillity. Three of his brothers were suffering from mental illness. The Tennysons had to leave Somersby, in 1837, for the first of several unsatisfactory homes, in Epping. Meanwhile, out of grief, anxiety, love and pain, Tennyson had found the purging spirit to write some of his finest

verses. 'Two Voices' belongs to this period: the first title was 'Thoughts of a Suicide'. So do the splendid 'Ulysses', 'St Simeon Stylites', poems that were to become parts of *In Memoriam*, and lyrics later woven into *Maud*. Nature and circumstance had given him much: a brooding imagination, a fine ear, a naturalist's curiosity, an artist's eye. No poet has so many precise references to the natural world: the waves breaking on Mablethorpe sands, the pines and waterfalls of Cauteretz, thrift carpeting the rocks of Tintagel. And always he was experimenting, seeking to improve, his guiding principle always appropriateness of verse to mood. 'Let the Great World spin for ever down the ringing grooves of change': an image as powerful as it is inexact.

If Tennyson had died in 1842, the year which saw the publication of *Poems* in two volumes with some new poems, including 'Morte d'Arthur' and 'Locksley Hall', he would have done enough for fame. Though the volume was not rapturously received, the poet had arrived. But the man appeared to drift, 'solitary and sad', as Carlyle described him, 'carrying a bit of Chaos about him, which he is manufacturing into Cosmos'. Half gypsy, half patriarch, he fitted, indeed helped fix, the popular idea of the Bohemian poet. Carlyle again: 'He is one of the finest-looking men in the world. A great shock of rough, dusky, dark hair; bright, laughing hazel eyes; massive aquiline face … sallow brown complexion, almost Indian looking, clothes cynically loose, free-and-easy, smokes infinite tobacco. His voice is musically loose, fit for loud laughter and piercing wail … I do not meet in these last decades such company over a pipe!'

Tobacco – and port: a bottle an evening would be his lifetime habit. It suggests an aching void in a man not suited to a single life. In 1836 his brother Charles had married Louisa Sellwood and Alfred began to correspond with her sister Emily, looking, apparently, towards marriage until, in 1840, her father forbade further letters. In 1850 – mark the interval – Tennyson resumed writing: engagement and marriage followed. He was forty-one, she thirty-seven: they would have two children. In the same year he was appointed Poet Laureate and he published *In Memoriam*. Compiled over the years since Hallam's death, much revised, representing his deepest feelings and most consummate art, it wrote finis to the most creative phase of his poetic life. With a contented marriage, an adoring and capable wife, royal approval and national status, he would respond heartily – but not always as readers expected. *The Edinburgh Review* called on him 'to do the duty which England has long expected of him, and to give us a great poem on a great subject'. With the sombre notes of his ode on the death of Wellington (1852) and his account of the charge of the Light Brigade at Balaclava (1855), he showed that he could do that. Meanwhile he sought to express the ideas of the age.

The Princess (1847) had been his first attempt at a long poem: loose strung, a fantastic medley, with its anti-feminist theme, it is fine in parts, perversely strange overall. Now appeared *Maud*, a 'monodrama' from which many readers recoiled in dismay, from passages suggestive of hysteria and from the poem's morbid, angry hero: was he speaking for Tennyson, another Hamlet, exorcizing fears of 'black blood'? *Maud* was the favourite of all his poems, constantly reread. A peak of another kind was attained with the publication of his Arthurian saga, *Idylls of the King*, in 1859. It was successful, as was his *Enoch Arden* volume (1864). New Arthurian idylls were published in the *Holy Grail and Other Poems* (1870). With them the epic Homeric character of earlier Arthurian essays gives way to more polished, fine-chiselled art.

Reader-fatigue was to be expected; more ominous were the rumbles of discontent. There had always been critics of 'school-room miss' in Bulwer-Lytton's cruel phrase, with the mawkish tendencies and emptily decorative lines of some early poems. Now there was criticism of the moral values that he appeared to be importing into Malory's Arthurian texts. Tennyson turned to poetic drama, with *Queen Mary, Harold, Becket* and, his only prose work, *The Promise of May* (1882), of interest chiefly because of what it reveals of Tennyson's overt pessimism. Like Dickens and Trollope in their later novels, the ageing Tennyson saw little to admire or please in the moral tendencies of his age. When he expressed his mood in the poem 'Despair', in *The Nineteenth Century* (1881), Swinburne parodies him. But Tennyson was not invariably negative. 'The Ancient Sage', appearing in *Tiresias and Other Poems*, tells of his intimations of heaven.

Tennyson accepted his peerage, in 1884, with reluctance. He was ambivalent towards publicity. 'I can't be anonymous by reason of your confounded photographs,' he wrote to Julia Margaret Cameron, his photographer neighbour. Yet one of her images, which he christened 'the dirty monk', was one of his favourite portraits. He remained a seeker, aspired to be a seer. Ever sensitive to current ideas, Christian in sentiment but disrespectful towards dogma, he was, essentially, the poet for the fast-growing middle class. In a new volume (1886), he challenged current ideas about progress and denounced modern decadence with a vehemence that drew a reply from Gladstone. One of the offending poems was entitled 'Locksley Hall Sixty Years After'. The time-span emphasizes the astonishing fact. Creative to the end, sternly true to his vocation, he gave precious time to revising. His last year saw the successful production of his play, *The Foresters*, in New York. He could still write beautifully. 'To Mary Boyle' in *Demeter and Other*

Poems (1889) recalled the tenderness of young love.

A feeling for place permeates some of his best work. Since 1868 he had lived in Aldworth in Surrey in the summer, but continued to winter in his beloved Farringford, scene since 1853 of his happiest days. It was crossing to the Isle of Wight, in 1889, that he wrote 'The Crossing of the Bar'. Characteristic, in its awed sense of the mystery of life, wedding poignantly scene and occasion to a universal human concern, it provides a fitting epitaph to its author's life and work. His funeral was at Westminster Abbey and he was buried in Poets' Corner. The Abbey was packed; the nave lined with veterans of the Light Brigade.

Further Reading
R. B. Martin, *Tennyson, The Unquiet Heart*, 1980.
Christopher Ricks, *Tennyson*, 1972.

TERRY, DAME ELLEN (1847-1928), actress, cast her spell over a range of famous Victorians, from Tennyson to Oscar Wilde, from Lewis Carroll to Gladstone. Shaw and Barrie wrote plays for her. Irving picked her as his leading lady, and in the Lyceum Company they acted opposite each other for nearly twenty-five years. Her eight tours in America spread her fame round the world.

Her private life cannot be accounted an unqualified success. None of her three marriages lasted more than three years, and the father of her two children was not her husband. She was sixteen when the painter G. F. Watts married her, and so innocent that she believed that a kiss from him had made her pregnant. Watts, thirty years older, set out to give her the education and the manners to match her beauty; but she was not made to be a child bride, and when she danced into the middle of one of their grand dinner parties in pink tights as Cupid, he sent her back to her parents. Three years later, still married to him, she went off with Edward Godwin, a thirty-five-year-old architect with many theatrical and literary friends. They stayed together long enough for her to give birth to two children. Then, getting Watts to divorce her, she married a hard-drinking actor, so that he could adopt the children and legitimize them. Her final wedding was to another actor, much younger than her, when she was sixty. She was a devoted mother, and though she spoilt her son, Edward Craig, by paying many of his debts and befriending several of the women he abandoned (including the dancer Isidora Duncan), she made possible his career as a pioneer of uncluttered stage design.

From first to last she was a theatrical trouper. With acting parents, and an elder sister who initially outshone her, she played Puck aged nine, and showed herself a professional even then, by successfully delivering the Epilogue while in great pain, with her foot caught in the trap door which a stage hand had slammed on it. She was taken up by the aesthetes when she played Portia in

1875; and in 1877 by the broader public, for her rendering of a romantic heroine Olivia, who plans to rescue her bankrupt father by marrying a rich and debauched squire. Olivia scarves, caps and postcards became all the rage. Next year began her famous partnership with Henry Irving, with its mixture of Shakespeare and High Victorian dramas, and its caravanserai tours of America, which Ellen Terry loved: 'Heavens, they are a marvellous people!' Much of what they acted suited Irving better than her, for strident melodrama was outside her range. She excelled as Portia, Desdemona and Ophelia; wrestled with Lady Macbeth, whom she tried to play sympathetically; and was too old for Juliet. The part which suited her best was Beatrice, playful and free-spirited. She remained a gamine even when she became famous, sliding down the banisters from her dressing room en route for her entry as Ophelia.

Bernard Shaw was captivated by her, and though they seldom met, they exchanged some 400 letters, mostly during the last three years of the century. He wrote *Captain Brassbound's Conversion* for her, round the part of Lady Cicely, to whom he gave all the warmth, generosity and interest in other people which were Ellen Terry's hallmarks. She lived long enough to become the grand old lady of the stage. At her jubilee Drury Lane matinée in 1906, Caruso sang, Mrs Patrick Campbell recited, Lillie Langtry posed as Cleopatra, and Beerbohm Tree played Benedick to her Beatrice. Fifteen years after that, she was still taking a one-woman show round the world. The family acting tradition has been carried on through the twentieth century by her great-nephew, Sir John Gielgud.

Further Reading
E. Craig and C. St John, eds, *Ellen Terry and Bernard Shaw: a Correspondence*, new edn, 1949.
E. Craig and C. St John, eds, *Ellen Terry's Memoirs*, 1933.

THACKERAY, WILLIAM MAKEPEACE (1811-63), novelist, did not hold with adulatory memoirs: tapping the cover of one such, he told his daughter: 'None of this nonsense about me after my death.' His reputation has since been endangered less by excessive praise than by readers' neglect of all but his acknowledged masterpieces. A clumsy, shambling figure, six foot three, with a massive head, and a schoolboy fight recorded in the flattened bridge of his nose, Thackeray was a big man in other respects: high-spirited, warm-hearted; self-indulgent perhaps, setting much store by fine cooking and old port, but a much suffering man too. He was quick to take offence: it reflected early struggles. A certain diffidence seemed to rein him in, as if he cared more to appear the worldly-wise gentleman than to apply what Trollope called 'the novelist's elbow-grease'. The preparatory work and control of material which Trollope recommended might have made him an even

finer writer; he would then have been another man. Frank Swinnerton envisaged Thackeray, like his Major Pendennis, as a born clubman: but, he adds, 'a clubman of genius'. Looking at the world through Pall Mall windows, the writer who took upon himself to be 'the weekday preacher', might not have disclaimed the description.

Thackeray was a child of Anglo-India: one of those little sacrifices to imperial necessity, with lonely childhoods and early experience of boarding schools; even if not orphaned, generally brought up by English relations. All was conducive to an ambivalent attitude to India and to parents whom the child might hardly know; very likely compounded of vicarious pride, and of a sense of loss – as if paradise were irrecoverably elsewhere. William's father, Richmond Thackeray, died of lingering fever, in Calcutta, in 1815 – the Waterloo year that his son was to recapture in *Vanity Fair*. William was sent back to England. He could never afterwards hear of children being parted from parents without 'his spectacles getting very dim'. He went to awful little schools, in Southampton, then Chiswick. He was reunited, after nearly four years, to his mother, now remarried, to Henry Carmichael-Smith, the upright soldier he would recreate as Colonel Newcome. At the Charterhouse, in *Pendennis* 'Greyfriars', otherwise 'the slaughterhouse', he escaped the tedium of regular study through drawing, and reading anything but set work – most influentially, Fielding and Scott. 'I was abused into sulkiness and bullied into despair.' Yet somehow he received the classical grounding for his felicitous style.

The young Thackeray might have been modelling for Caspar Friederich's portrait of romantic youth. With her beauty and religious zeal, his mother was a strong influence: 'so tender,' he wrote, 'so loving, so cruel.' He anticipated a fortune, but found, at twenty-one, that it had vanished, seemingly through trustees' neglect. At Trinity College, Cambridge, for sixteen months, he enjoyed, but afterwards thought he was ruined by, 'that accursed system which is called in England "the education of a gentleman"'. Visiting Paris, he wrote loftily about people akin to their furniture: 'plenty of varnish with but little bottom'. From mentors like his fictional Bloundell he acquired a dangerous gambling habit. He was indeed a willing gull, vulnerable, like his Pendennis, 'to flashy grace and rakish airs of fashion'. Cambridge, where his set enjoyed 'high fooling' and, like Tennyson, 'went about their gravest deeds/ As noble boys at play', saw also the forming of a great friendship with Edward Fitzgerald: uninhibited letters convey a decided rapport in taste and feeling. Their exchange of views was seminal for 'old Thack'.

At the Middle Temple (1831-2), Thackeray learned something about law, much about London life. Putting his wit and inventive energy into the congenial world of the arts, he illustrated his first articles and stories – but progress was slow and funds failed. His stepfather bought a newspaper so that he could live in Paris as its correspondent. Only when the paper failed (1837) did he return to London. He would remember Bohemian days in Paris, as a happy time. There, in 1836, he met, loved and married Isabella Shawe, a diminutive, red-headed Irish army widow. The outcome was briefly happy; thereafter tragic. After the birth of her third daughter, in 1840, she succumbed to mental illness. There were swings of mood to arouse, then destroy, hope, and harrowing visits to asylums, before she went to live with friends. Thereafter Thackeray led a bachelor's life, reliant on friends to sustain him. He showed that he could cope with the traffic of Grub Street, where apprentice-scribblers fell between large designs and low adventures. He secured patrons, men like the Irish scholar and reprobate, William McGinn, editor of *Frazer's Magazine*. To Carlyle he was 'a half-monstrous Cornish giant, kind of painter, Cambridge man and Paris newspaper correspondent who is now writing for his life ...'

The range of Thackeray's early writing can be judged from the publication of its best, in four volumes, as *The Miscellanies* (1855-7). Written for magazines, notably *Frazer's*, *The New Monthly* and *Punch* (whose focus he helped turn from political radicalism to social satire), under such pseudonyms as Michael Angelo Titmarsh and Fitzboodle, they include *The Yellowplush Correspondence*, the imagined memoirs of a cockney footman; *Major Gahagan*, fantasizing about soldiering in India; the more ambitious *Catherine*, a burlesque of modish 'Newgate' novels romanticizing crime; also a first full-length novel, *The Luck of Barry Lyndon*, racy, uneven, satirical, it anticipates the great novel to come.

Vanity Fair (1847-8) was the first to be published under Thackeray's name and to earn him fame. Imitating Dickens and now appearing to be his rival, it appeared in monthly parts. Already a veteran in the genre, writing his sixth major novel, Dickens would enjoy a more general esteem. It was Thackeray's misfortune to be writing alongside a phenomenon: in his fiction and a very public life, a giant. Thackeray's range was narrower, but he could do some things better than Dickens. He should be treated on his own merits. One is that he is a beautiful writer. His secret lies, according to Quiller-Couch, 'in a curious haunting music, as of a stream; a music of which scarce any other writer of English prose [he was writing in 1925] has quite the natural, effortless command'.

In 1857 Thackeray would stand for parliament in a bye-election at Oxford: he failed, but narrowly. By then he had consolidated his position as leading novelist and popular lecturer. He had won the affection of parents through his enchanting Christmas 'folly': *The Rose and the Ring*. He would still manage, despite sometimes disabling illness, to write three further novels, each having

some merit: *The Virginians*, progeny in style and conception of *Henry Esmond Esquire*; *Lovel the Widower* (1860), *The Adventures of Philip* (1861-2); also promising instalments of a fourth, *Denis Duval*. But these works testify more to facility than to genius. His reputation rests on the work of his prime: *Vanity Fair*, *The History of Pendennis* (1848-50), *Henry Esmond* (1852) and *The Newcomes* (1854-5).

Set in the second decade of the nineteenth century, *Vanity Fair* can be enjoyed as a portrayal of upper-class society. This child of the Raj was, however, too much the outsider to be quite at home with upper-class people. Jos Sedley, the gross nabob, Colonel Dobbin, the straight, worthy soldier, are flesh and blood; the Crawleys, mere types. Thackeray's Lord Steyne is less credible than Disraeli's Monmouth (modelled, in *Coningsby*, on the same man). Yet people of fashion, and those who aspired to it, could enjoy this civilized exposure: spiced and barbed – but a generation distant, therefore comfortably enjoyable. It is Thackeray's descriptions of feeling and motive which lift the novel into the highest class, to keep company with Tolstoy's *War and Peace*. 'Your sensibility is your livelihood': his imagined words to Lawrence Sterne could have been addressed to himself. Interwoven through the story are the fortunes of Amelia Sedley, wealthy, amiable, passive, and Becky Sharp, archetype of the adventuress. Her consistent aim was to escape poverty by advantageous marriage. Unscrupulous, after marriage to Rawdon Crawley, unfaithful – yet one senses Thackeray's sympathy for her spirit. Amelia's husband George was killed at Waterloo; so she did not know of his intended elopement with Becky. She then marries the steadfast Dobbin: virtue has apparently won. But the abiding impression is of ambivalence in behaviour. 'Which of us,' Thackeray concludes, 'is happy in this world? Which of us has his desire, or having it, is satisfied?'

The History of Pendennis (1848-50) is Thackeray's own story. His avowed intention, following in the steps of Fielding, was 'to depict to his utmost power a real man'. He wanted ladies to know 'what is the life and talk of their sons'. From Pendennis's adventures one learns much about the author. Already he is contemplating his life like a rider, amazed at the jumps he has taken in the heat of the chase, confiding, as it were in conversation, with the reader. His daughter Annie said that *Pendennis*, more than any other of his works, was like hearing him talk. His public was therefore unprepared for *Henry Esmond Esquire*, Thackeray's answer to critics who accused him of sloppy construction, and the only one of his novels to come out entire. It was deliberately written in high Augustan style. Esmond tells his own story, from 1691, when he is twelve, and appears as an orphan, adopted by Lord and Lady Castlewood, to 1718, when, Lord Castlewood having died, he marries his widow.

Some were upset by the emotional charge of the story, its 'lowering air of near-incest' (Ann Montsarrat); others by its unlikely dénouement – 'an uncomfortable book' George Eliot called it – but its incidents gain unity and power from Esmond's passion for Beatrix, the Castlewood's daughter. He is brave and sensitive; she is complex. Into her progress, from charming girl to radiant beauty, Thackeray surely put much of his feeling for Jane Brookfield.

Strains in her marriage to his Cambridge friend, William Brookfield, and her confidences, evoked Thackeray's devotion. She seemed to respond. For years – chivalrously, chastely, periodically consumed with jealousy, Thackeray hung about, with a self-inflicted watching brief, until Jane herself lost patience, leaving him in the role of faithful fool – to put his pain into his portrait of Beatrix: like Jane, tall, stately, a cool, vain beauty. The author's suffering became the reader's gain. 'Here is the very best I can do,' he said to a friend in Boston. 'I stand by this book and am willing to leave it when I go, as my card.'

'There's no-one now to share my cup.' With his daughters, to whom he was an assiduous, adoring father, he lived in fine houses: none was ever really a home. *The Newcomes* (1853-5), his study of prosperous middle-class life, was written on club paper, or at a hotel, for he was now often on the move, 'barking' about the country, having overcome earlier awkwardness to become a popular lecturer. Less autobiographical than *Pendennis*, it says more about its author's vision of life. It centres on Colonel Newcombe, an old India hand, and his son Clive, who first loves his cousin Ethel, then, for worldly considerations, marries Rose Mackenzie. Barnes Newcombe, Ethel's father, seeks to avenge his daughter by trapping the colonel into unwise investments. Rose dies in childbirth; the colonel, an almshouse pensioner, with touching grace. No other writer could have handled tragedy with such economy of sentiment.

Twice Thackeray went to America, a golden trail but exhausting. *The Four Georges*, light history but good fun, grew out of one sequence; *The English Humorists* out of another. He had always been imaginatively generous. His position at the summit of the literary world, confirmed latterly by his editorship of the new *Cornhill*, enabled him to help other writers, Charlotte Brontë, Anthony Trollope. His earnings soared. It was not done easily. If 'he was ever too conscious of a footman behind his chair' (W. E. Henley), it was also true that he usually had the printer's devil at his elbow. He had always had an old head on young shoulders, keen to point out the follies of the world. In middle age his health became precarious; some saw a sad man, much pained: 'a big, fierce, weeping, hungry man; not a strong one' (Carlyle). There are signs of tiredness in his later writing. Though there is much to admire in *The Virginians*, and in *The Roundabout Papers*, the perceptive essays of this period, the impression is of a committed writer, sometimes finding solace at his desk, sometimes struggling to fill the page. Did he know that his tenure of life was short? Tours, dinners and work: the pace was hectic, the outward show boisterous. He brought infectious enthusiasm to the building of his *palazzo* on Palace Green, absurdly grandiose for any purpose but display – and who had less need than Thackeray to show that he had 'arrived'?

That brittle pride could still betray him. 'The Yates Affair' exposed raw nerves and split the literary world, as men sided with Thackeray, who secured the expulsion of the young journalist Yates from the Garrick Club, or Dickens, who deplored it. His career had been punctuated by quarrels. The more successful he became, the broader the front he bared to attack. The great exposer of pretence, who helped, in his *Book of Snobs*, to give its present meaning to the word, was vulnerable to the very charges he had so deftly mounted. The strong sense of reality that he so admired in Walter Scott could degenerate into an apparently heartless cynicism. Yet that was not the abiding impression. When the end came there was a sense of calamitous loss. No more would 'Mr Thackeray's New Monthly Work' speed in its yellow covers to homes around the land. It was as much the man as the writer, 'the great loose baggy monster' of Henry James's phrase, that was mourned by the 2,000 who saw him buried at Kensal Green.

Further Reading

Ann Monsarrat, *Thackeray, An Uneasy Victorian*, 1980.
Anne Thackeray Ritchie (daughter), *Chapters from Some Memoirs*, 1894.

THELWALL, JOHN (1764-1834), political reformer and pioneer in speech therapy, was the son of Joseph Thelwall, a silk mercer of London who died when his son was eight. He was sent to school at Highgate, but he was removed at thirteen and put into business. Independent opinions and an addiction to books prevented him from progressing as a tailor. He studied law for a time, but he preferred philosophy to copying 'the trash of an office'. He also had a strong objection to the taking of oaths. He became entirely dependent on the pen for his living. 1789 found him a natural subject for revolutionary propaganda.

He joined in turn the Society of Friends of the People and Hardy's Corresponding Society. Despite a hesitation of speech and a slight lisp he became an effective speaker. His radical diatribes at the Coachmakers' Hall attracted the attention of ministers. In 1793 his pamphlet *Politics for the People, or Hogswash* led to the prosecution of the printer, Eaton – an unwise and unsuccessful move, which did not deter ministers from charging Thelwall and eleven others with treason in the following year. When Thelwall's turn came, in December 1794, Hardy and Tooke had already been acquitted and the government's case torn to shreds. Thelwall might have proved an easier victim, or the jury might have been less sympathetic to a man who made his living by lectures largely devoted to passionate attacks upon the constitution. It was possible to conceive of Thelwall, this stocky, muscular figure with the tastes and talents of a demagogue, as an English Danton. He was brave, original and uncompromising; he was also a poet and philosopher, with a lot of his friend Coleridge in him. 'The minds that really govern the machine of society are at all times few', said Coleridge. Thelwall, an *exalté* among the radicals of his time, would not make a promise lest he should be unable to keep it. He dealt in absolutes. He believed that he had a mission.

He can appear in a somewhat ridiculous light, as in this description retailed by Walsh, the spy, of his appearance at a dinner in Somerset: 'The little stout man with dark, cropt hair ... wore a white hat and glasses ... talked in a great passion.' Yet at the height of the terror in France and in the first year of an ideological war, Thelwall's activities alarmed the government; their mistake was to pitch the charge too high. 'Seditious conspiracy' might have secured a conviction, but even Thelwall's record could hardly sustain a charge of treason. He was defended by Erskine. Thelwall had wanted to defend himself. 'If you do, you will be hanged', wrote Erskine. 'Then I'll be hanged if I do', replied Thelwall. He was acquitted.

Fortunately for Thelwall he had another life besides political agitation. In 1791 he married Susan Vallum of Rutland, his 'good angel'. She bore him four children. He had begun to study medicine and wrote, in 1793, an essay, *Animal Vitality. Poems written in close confinement in the Tower and Newgate* were of modest quality, but they provided an outlet for his romantic yearnings. From 1796 to 1798 he travelled about the country denouncing the government through the medium of 'Lectures upon Roman History'. Sometimes his meetings were broken up by hired mobs. When he stayed with the Coleridges he was being watched by a government spy – but this may have been because of the odd conduct of Coleridge and Wordsworth. In 1798 he went for a rest to a small farm near Brecon and when he returned to London two years later he discarded politics for elocution. His cure for stammering was original, effective and popular. He saw speech impediments as a part of the whole personality of the sufferer. Crabb Robinson describes how he went to hear *Comus* recited by a group of Thelwall's 'stammerers'; he went to be amused, but he stayed to praise. In 1818 Thelwall made another incursion into reform with a new journal, *The Champion*. His rhetorical style was out of date and inappropriate to a publication that was ostensibly aimed at the thinking classes. *The Champion* lost money and Thelwall returned to lecturing.

In 1818 his wife died and three years later he married Cecil Boyle, much younger than he, a woman of social charm and literary ability. He lived to see the reform of parliament. He had then long ceased to be a fire-eater and his friends testified to his integrity and good nature. He had been, however, one of the most effective of the 'English jacobins'. He had helped to keep alive the spirit of radical protest in unpropitious times.

Further Reading
C. B. Crone, *The English Jacobins: Reformers in the Late Eighteenth Century*, 1968.
Charles Cestre, *John Thelwall*, 1906.

THEOBALD (*d.*1161; Archbishop of Canterbury 1138-61) was one of the most effective medieval Archbishops of Canterbury, although by no means one of the most colourful. He came to Canterbury with the classic credentials of an Abbot of Bec, but, unlike his illustrious predecessors Lanfranc and Anselm, his elevation was unexpected and controversial. In 1138, Theobald, a native of Lower Normandy, was unknown in England, a political nonentity who had only become an abbot two years previously. Perhaps his inexperience and lack of involvement in the factional manoeuvring of the early years of Stephen's reign actually commended Theobald in preference to the obvious candidate, Stephen's brother, Henry, Bishop of Winchester. In the event, his abbacy proved of less importance than the influence of Bec's lay patron, and Stephen's closest lay adviser, Waleran, Count of Meulan. However, as with so many of Stephen's political calculations, the appointment of Theobald, rushed through on 24 December 1138, failed to bring the expected benefits. The king had alienated his powerful brother, while, initially, the *ingénu* archbishop was unable to provide any balancing weighty support. Once Theobald did establish his political bearings, although whenever possible observing public loyalty to Stephen, he proved a closet Angevin, resistant to royal control and the king's increasingly urgent demands for the coronation of his son.

Overshadowed between 1139 and 1143 by Henry of Winchester's appointment as papal legate in England, Theobald was content to follow events. In December 1141 he recrowned Stephen and his queen in Canterbury, but after the Angevin conquest of Normandy (1141-4) Theobald pursued an increasingly independent role. In this he was aided by the Angevin sympathies of Popes Celestine II (1143-4) and Eugenius III (1145-53) and Stephen's enfeebled control over the English church. Henry of Winchester's legateship expired with Innocent II in 1143 and Stephen's failure to impose his candidate as Archbishop of York led to a schism in the northern province which left Theobald unchallenged in leadership of the church, a dominance confirmed in 1149/50 by his own appointment as papal legate.

In 1147 he visited Paris at the same time as Geoffrey of Anjou. The following year he defied a royal ban and travelled, at some personal risk, to the papal Council of Rheims. Once there, he characteristically interceded to prevent Pope Eugenius from excommunicating King Stephen. During this exile, he and the young Henry FitzEmpress persuaded the pope to create Gilbert Foliot Bishop of Hereford: securing jobs for people was one of Theobald's chief attainments. Theobald wished to establish the firm authority of both church and state. A weak king meant a threatened church. For the remainder of Stephen's reign, Theobald sought political compromise with his ultimate objective being an Angevin succession. Thus he attempted mediation in 1148 and played a central role in the final agreement of 1153 between Stephen and Henry FitzEmpress, but he refused point blank to crown Stephen's son Eustace in 1152, preferring another brief exile. Seeing royal and ecclesiastical authority as complementary, Theobald was nevertheless concerned to assert his rights as Archbishop of Canterbury, not least against unnecessary papal interference. He regarded Henry of Blois's legateship as doubly threatening in its reliance on papal power and usurpation of Canterbury's primacy. Even the crisis of 1148 can be seen not so much as an assertion of papal authority, more a vindication of Canterbury's right to represent the English church at the Council. This view may have rubbed off on one of Theobald's companions in the open boat which took the archbishop across the perilous Channel on the way to Rheims: Thomas Becket.

Under Henry II, Theobald continued to promote ecclesiastical authority, particularly his own in harmony with the king. It must be uncertain how Theobald would have reacted if Henry had insisted on defining the jurisdictional parameters of church and state as he was to do at Clarendon in 1164. He certainly desired a demarcation of the spiritual and temporal spheres in justice as elsewhere. But his response to the papal Schism of 1159 is perhaps typical. Two popes had been elected, Alexander III and Victor IV. Theobald adhered to the former, but he wrote to Henry: 'while the matter is in suspense we think that it is unlawful in your realm to accept either of them without your approval', although he urged the king to take the advice of the clergy, which the king did.

As archbishop, Theobald maintained the traditional hostility towards the monks of Canterbury, particularly over their administration of estates and revenues. Although a Benedictine monk himself, Theobald preferred the company of secular clerks, men of intellect rather than conspicuous piety. There can have been few more distinguished clerical households in the Middle Ages to compare with the men assembled by Theobald, and fewer still on whom the golden rewards of patronage and preferment were showered more lavishly. Roger of Pont l'Evêque became Archbishop of York (1154-81); John of Pagham, Bishop of Worcester (1151-7); John of Canterbury, Bishop of Poitiers (1162), Archbishop of Narbonne and finally Archbishop of Lyons (1182-93); Bartholomew, Bishop of Exeter (1161-84); Theobald's brother Walter, Bishop of Rochester (1148-82). Also attracted to Theobald's household were John of Salisbury, one of the leading European intellectuals of his generation, who wrote many of Theobald's official letters; Master Vacarius, a canon lawyer of international repute from Bologna; Jordan Fantosme, later master of the cathedral school at Winchester and author of a French verse account of the great rebellion of 1173-4; and Thomas Becket, the drama of whose career has tended to cast his old mentor in the shade. Yet it was Theobald who chose these men and, in many cases, provided their opportunity for public prominence.

Personally, Theobald presented an apparent contradiction. In private he was sharp tongued, garrulous and short tempered, but, according to Robert of Cricklade, trimmed his conversation when talking to powerful men. Patient, occasionally obsequious to superiors, Theobald could be aggressive, overbearing even violent towards inferiors. But, unlike his archdeacon and successor, Becket, he did not overreact to people or events. Publicly cautious and patient, he calculated his advantage with care, as when he arranged for Becket to become Henry II's chancellor in 1155 as the young, untried, foreign king's minder. Unglamorous; by no means a saint, even posthumously; a nepotist and a far from passionate monk, Theobald achieved much. He saw off the challenge of Henry of Blois to ecclesiastical dominance; he checked the business incompetence of the Canterbury monks; he firmly established the de facto primacy of Canterbury over York; he secured a reasonably smooth Angevin succession after a generation of civil war; he successfully promoted his protégés; he defined a semi-detached working relationship between the English church and the increasingly intrusive legalism of the papacy; he maintained the independence of the church without challenging its interdependence with the state. The measure of his achievement is perhaps to be found in the explosive chaos which followed his death: even that can be attributed in part to his success as a patron.

Further Reading
A. Saltman, *Theobald, Archbishop of Canterbury*, 1956.

THEODORE OF TARSUS, ST (602?-90) was Archbishop of Canterbury from 668 until 690 and a figure of major importance in the history of the English church. A native, like St Paul, of Tarsus in Cilicia, Theodore was born in or about 602. The first sixty-five years of his life – in the early Middle Ages a much longer than average lifespan – are almost a blank to us. We know only that he had studied at Athens at some period, and evidently become an extremely learned man; and that he was a monk. In 667 he was in Rome, though we do not know why. Not long before this the Archbishop-elect of Canterbury had come to Rome for consecration at the hands of Pope Vitalian but had died of the plague before he could receive it. Vitalian offered the vacant see to the African monk Hadrian, who declined it, suggesting Theodore's name instead. The offer was made, Theodore accepted, was consecrated (March 668) and journeyed to England in the company of Hadrian and Benedict Biscop. In the course of a leisurely journey through Gaul he spent some time with Agilbert at Paris who presumably briefed him on conditions in England. He reached Canterbury in May 669.

Theodore's appointment must on any showing be judged the most surprising in the whole history of the English church. An old man, he was taking up an office which was bound to be physically as well as mentally demanding. A Greek-speaking intellectual from the civilized Mediterranean, he was being sent to minister to barbarians barely converted to Christianity, whose language he could not speak, whose climate and food would almost certainly be uncongenial, whose social customs and political organization he would find unfamiliar and uncouth. The English church to which he was going was in a state of disarray. It had until recently been divided by the Paschal controversy, and the sores of that confict had not yet healed. It was lacking in structure and organization, and it was desperately short of manpower: at the time of Theodore's arrival there was only one properly constituted bishop in England, namely Wilfrid. Furthermore, England had recently been ravaged by plague, and it is likely that its inhabitants were frightened and demoralized. Part of the kingdom of Essex had reverted to paganism during the plague and the same could well have happened elsewhere.

The extraordinary thing is that despite these obstacles Theodore's archiepiscopate was a resounding success. He gave the English church an administrative shape that endured with little essential change for nearly 900 years. He introduced routines and disciplines for the day-to-day ordering of the church. As a teacher and patron of learning he built up a school at Canterbury which played an important part in introducing the Anglo-Saxons to the learning of Mediterranean Christendom. In short, he provided leadership, direction and inspiration. It was an astonishing achievement for a man in his seventies and eighties.

His first few years set the tone. Soon after his arrival he conducted a general visitation of all the English churches, a tour of inspection to acquaint himself with the country and its clergy. By 672 he had established a diocesan framework by appointing or confirming bishops in East Anglia, Northumbria, Mercia and Wessex. In 673 he held the first council of the whole English church, at Hertford. Its decrees were of the utmost significance in regulating the affairs of the church in England; for instance, in clarifying the relations between bishops by insisting that each had a distinct jurisdiction in his own diocese. Two of them were of special moment. The seventh decree laid down that annual ecclesiastical councils were to be held at a place named *Clovesho*. (This place has never satisfactorily been identified. It has been suggested that it might have been Brixworth in Northamptonshire, which is reasonably central and where there is an imposing Anglo-Saxon church which as it stands is probably of *c.*840 but which may overlie a building of Theodoran date.) What little evidence we have – for instance, casual references to councils in the letters of Aldhelm – suggests that Theodore's decree was not a dead letter and that regular church councils were indeed held. These councils were intended for the proper ordering of English church life but they had a further importance. The sense of unity and common purpose induced in those who attended them gradually served to wear down the barriers of tribe and region. The notion of 'the English church' slowly gained over the idea of a scatter of separate churches for the Kentishmen, or the Mercians, or the West Saxons, or the Northumbrians. And it was in some sense owing to Theodore's efforts that Bede could make a still more daring leap and give general currency to the idea – which he may have picked up from the writings of Pope Gregory – that the Anglo-Saxon inhabitants of Britain were all one *gens Anglorum*, one 'English people'.

The ninth decree at Hertford laid down 'that more bishops should be created as the number of believers increases', but the record continues darkly, 'however we passed over this matter for the present'. Theodore came from a Mediterranean world where dioceses were small. In England they were enormous: Wilfrid's bishopric of York embraced the whole area between the Humber and the Firth of Forth. Theodore was determined to reduce their size by multiplying the number of bishops, so that in a diocese of manageable size the diocesan could effectively discharge the pastoral duties which were his prime responsibility. His thinking was in line with that of Pope Gregory on this matter. The fact that the Hertford decree was not implemented shows us that Theodore had run into opposition. It presumably came from those bishops of big dioceses who were unwilling to submit to a reduction in their status, wealth and power. (There is plenty of evidence to suggest that English bishops were already rich and powerful. One of the reasons why Cuthbert was so reluctant to become a bishop in 685 was because he wished to shun these temptations.) Theodore was determined that this reform should take effect. He implemented it gradually by a tactic of prudent opportunism: whenever a bishopric fell vacant he moved in and divided it up. Theodore could usually rely on the co-operation of the local king; for example, it was at the request of King Ethelred that he divided the huge diocese of Mercia into five, probably in 679-80. In this Theodore showed tact. But he was also a tough man, perhaps not always altogether scrupulous, possibly not untouched by a streak of megalomania. He may too have been driven by the sense of urgency imparted by old age: an old man in a hurry. In trying to implement his plans he may vastly have extended the power of Canterbury over the English church beyond the limits laid down by Pope Gregory. This was how he was perceived at York. Theodore's most bitter opponent was York's Wilfrid. The quarrel between them is examined elsewhere. But we can note here that Theodore got his way. In 678 he divided the Northumbrian diocese into three and in 681 increased this to five. East Anglia was also divided (673) and Wessex followed a few years after Theodore's death (704-5). The diocesan structure created by Theodore survived with only small modifications, such as the twelfth-century creation of sees at Ely and Carlisle, until the 1540s.

The council of Hertford had also legislated on the subject of marriage. Theodore's teaching on moral and pastoral issues – the attempt to provide the basic essentials of Christian discipline for the laity – is preserved in a work known as his *Penitential*. (The book was put together in the form in which we have it by an anonymous editor after Theodore's death, but there is general agreement that the rulings it embodies do derive from his teaching.) A penitential is a kind of handbook for confessors, listing various sins and prescribing appropriate penances for them. Theodore's *Penitential* is of the greatest interest in showing what sort of pastoral problems he encountered among the Anglo-Saxons and what solutions he proposed to them. The claims made for the ecclesiastical guidance of daily life show Theodore's characteristically robust determination to christianize his barbarous new converts. But the *Penitential* also reveals a mind broad and humane. Within certain limits Theodore was prepared to adapt Christian moral teaching to meet the customs of the English. It was an important condition of the successful follow-up to the age of conversion that the English church should have been directed by a man so wisely liberal in outlook.

The anonymous compiler of the *Penitential* may have been educated in the school at Canterbury established by Theodore and Hadrian. Aldhelm allows us a glimpse of Theodore in class, 'hemmed in by a mass of Irish students like a savage wild boar checked by a snarling pack of hounds'. One can sense an atmosphere at once genial and boisterous. In the 1950s a German scholar identified some materials in an eleventh-century manuscript at Milan as fragments of biblical commentaries composed by Theodore. It thus became possible to characterize the method of scriptural exegesis practised at Canterbury, which was rather different from that employed by Bede at Jarrow; and to get a glance, in the surviving fragments, of Theodore expounding the flora and fauna of a middle-eastern holy book to a rapt audience on the shores of the North Sea. The curiosity about the Holy Places which we meet in such eighth-century travellers as Willibald of Eichstätt may have been stimulated directly or indirectly by Theodore's teaching. In the field of ecclesiastical law, Theodore's reputation stood high. This is attested not simply by the survival of his *Penitential* but also by the judgement of some of the most distinguished men of a slightly later date, such as Archbishop Egbert of York and Pope Zacharias in a letter to Boniface in 748. Theodore's intellectual attainments were evidently diverse: Bede tells a story which shows that he was regarded as an authority on medicine too.

Theodore died on 19 September 690 at the age of about eighty-eight. The sober judgement of a nineteenth-century scholar on his achievement is still the best epitaph to his career: 'It is difficult, if not impossible, to overstate the debt which England, Europe and Christian civilization owes to the work of Theodore.'

Further Reading
H. Mayr-Harting, *The Coming of Christianity to Anglo-Saxon England*, 1972.

THISTLEWOOD, ARTHUR (1770-1820) was a prime mover in a plot to murder the entire Cabinet. His origins are obscure. He is said to have been the illegitimate son of a Lincolnshire farmer. He had some pretensions to be a gentleman and in 1798 he was commissioned an ensign in the Militia. He had certainly visited America and France and, by one account, served with the French army. Jacobin ideas provide some clues to his career. From about 1797 it is evident that there was an element in the political underworld of London that put its hope in a violent coup which would rouse the mob to effective action. How great the power of that mob could be had been demonstrated by the Gordon riots of 1780. The turbulence of Westminster elections suggests that it could be roused again. The government took the threat seriously enough to watch suspects, penetrate tavern meetings with their spies, and arrest on mere suspicion. In 1799 most of the leaders of this school of extremists were in gaol. One of them, Despard, was to die on the scaffold in 1803 after being found guilty of high treason. After the death of his wife Thistlewood drifted from Lincoln to London and joined the Spencean Society: their plans for agrarian socialism were of seminal importance, but almost irrelevant in the short term. But among the Spenceans were men like Dr Watson and John Gale Jones, big men in the smoky, secret world of the London alehouses, where the talk was not only of principles but of revolutionary tactics.

In December 1816 a small Spencean committee including Watson and his crazy son, Preston, Hooper, Thistlewood – and Castle, the spy – called for a demonstration in Spa Fields. There had been a meeting the month before at which Henry Hunt had spoken, and secured signatures for a petition. He had not been allowed to present it to the prince regent and the second meeting was called ostensibly to protest against the government's attitude. But when Hunt arrived he found, in the wagon in the middle of the crowd, Dr Watson and Thistlewood. Young Watson, London's Camille Desmoulins, called for a march, behind the tricolour flag, to the Tower! One man, Preston or Thistlewood, managed to climb on to a wall of the Tower and summon the guard to surrender 'the Bastille'. With arms from a gunsmith's shop and some boisterous sailors at large, the mob could have been dangerous – but order was restored by nightfall. The physical force school, 'five fanatics hounded on by a spy', had made themselves ridiculous. Most of the crowd had stayed to hear Hunt. The government decided to proceed with a charge of treason against Thistlewood and his associates. Was treason the right charge? The sinister and farcical elements are equally balanced.

Moderate reformers were frightened away from the popular radical movement. Ministers meanwhile looked for another pretext to act against the reformers. As Cobbett saw it: 'They sigh for a PLOT ... they are absolutely pining and dying for a plot!' Thistlewood and his friends had already given them an excuse to discredit the popular movement. In 1819, they gave them their plot.

Thistlewood had been acquitted at his first trial, amidst general merriment. To such a man as Thistlewood, anguished by poverty, unstable and deluded, ridicule was hard to bear. In February 1818 he was imprisoned without trial for disturbing the peace: he had demanded 'satisfaction' from the Home Secretary. To keep him out of the way Sidmouth thought it worth paying his maintenance out of his own pocket! He came out after a year and joined Watson, Preston and Jones in the London 'Committee of Two Hundred'. The Committee planned the elaborate reception given to Hunt after Peterloo. Thistlewood and Hunt wrangled bitterly about tactics. Hunt feared with reason that Thistlewood's underground communications links were designed to provoke and control an open insurrection while Thistlewood believed that the radical leaders were throwing away the advantage afforded them by Peterloo; perhaps he was trying to prove to Hunt that he was not a spy. He counted on the workers of the slums. In the shoemakers' union there existed a revolutionary cell: the majority of his fellow conspirators were of this trade, radical by long tradition. Whatever his motives, whatever the nature of his support, his plan was a desperate one. It was suggested, as Thistlewood later alleged, by Edwards, brother to a former secretary of the Spenceans, who had first wanted to blow up the House of Commons. 'Edwards was ever at invention; and at length he proposed attacking them at a Cabinet-dinner.' Meetings were held in the loft at Cato Street. James Hugo, a butcher, planned a dramatic entrance: 'My Lords, I have got as good men here as the Manchester yeomanry – Enter, citizens, and do your duty.' The heads of Castlereagh and Sidmouth were to be placed on pikes and a provisional government was to be proclaimed.

The Cabinet dinner, announced by advertisement, was a hoax. Edwards, the spy, saw to it that the government knew all the details of the conspiracy he had helped to foment. The conspirators were seized, Thistlewood only after a struggle in which he killed a Bow Street runner. They were tried in April: five were sentenced to transportation, five to death. On the scaffold Thistlewood declared in his broad Lincolnshire vowels: 'I desire all here to remember, that I die in the cause of liberty'.

Further Reading
E. P. Thompson, *The Making of the English Working Class*, 1963.
John Stanhope, *Cato Street Conspiracy*, 1962.

THOMAS OF BAYEUX (Archbishop of York 1070-1100) was a member of a remarkable ecclesiastical dynasty: his brother Samson became Bishop of Worcester (1096-1112); one nephew, Thomas, was Archbishop of York (1109-14); another, Richard, was Bishop of Bayeux (1108-33). The family owed much to the patronage of Odo of Bayeux, whose influence almost certainly lay behind Thomas's appointment to York. The son of Osbert, a priest, and Muriel, he and his brother Samson were sent by Bishop Odo to Liège, presumably to complete their studies. Before his elevation to York he had been a canon and treasurer of Bayeux. By 1070 he seems to have become one of William I's chaplains. His had been the well trodden high road to ecclesiastical preferment. However, Thomas's tenure of the archdiocese was no sinecure. In particular, he had to cope with two intractable problems: externally the assertion of York's independence from the primacy of Canterbury; and internally the restoration of the church's finances and administration.

Although the status of York as a subservient archbishopric was anomalous in western Christendom, neither Lanfranc of Canterbury nor, even less, William I were prepared to concede the point. Politically, subjugation of York was one part of William's policy of subduing the north and reducing the prospects of local particularist support for any invader or rival claimant. For the same reason in the tenth century the Kings of England had attached York to the see of Worcester and entrusted both to loyal West Saxons. William's and Lanfranc's way was ostensibly more legalistic. Thomas waged a stern but unavailing campaign to establish the equality of York as a metropolitan see. After expressing reservations before his consecration by Lanfranc in 1070, he urged his claims to autonomy at Rome when he and Lanfranc went to collect their pallia in 1071. In 1072, a council at Winchester found in Canterbury's favour and Lanfranc had his primacy and right to York's profession of obedience upheld. The Archbishop of York was left with only Durham as a suffragan (Carlisle was not founded until 1133). Royal pressure not canon law or precedent determined the judgement; the papacy significantly failed to ratify the position. Indeed, the dispute rumbled on, occasionally flaring into spectacular, if often petty, rows, until the Reformation. The Archbishop of York still cannot wear his pontifical robes in the southern province, a lasting legacy of the Norman political and ecclesiastical settlement.

Within his province, Thomas met with more success. At York he organized a chapter of secular canons and introduced a system of prebends (i.e. lands and revenues owned by the cathedral but specifically attached to support individual canonries), no mean feat given the poverty and disruption of cathedral finances and personnel. The arrangement, although in tune with continental practice, contrasted with the monastic chapters of many southern cathedrals which Lanfranc, a monk, continued to support, not least at Canterbury itself. Indeed, the monk's customary disdain and suspicion of the secular priest may account for an edge in Lanfranc's relations with Thomas. It is possible, for instance, that Thomas, in common with many contemporary clerics, was married. The professional celibate would not approve. Yet as well as being a skilled administrator, Thomas was no philistine: a noted musician and patron of scholars, he was remembered by Hugh the Chantor a generation after his death as having rebuilt York Minster and restored the fortunes of a shattered diocese.

Further Reading
F. Barlow, *The English Church 1066-1154*, 1979.
G. Aylmer and R. Cant, *A History of York Minster*, 1977.

THOMAS OF LANCASTER (*c*.1278-1322), son of Edward I's brother Edmund and Queen Blanche, was a natural bulwark of the Crown. 'As each parent was of royal birth, he was clearly of nobler descent than the other earls.' Greatly favoured by Edward I, he had five earldoms: Lancaster, Leicester and Derby by inheritance; Lincoln and Salisbury by marriage to Alice Lacy. At £11,000 his income was twice that of the next greatest earl, his household cost half that of the king, and his lavishly feed retainers included two earls, nine bannerets, and fifty knights. His lands clustered thickly in Yorkshire, Lancashire and the north Midlands, a 'concentration over a wide area in contrast to those of other magnates which helped to make him the most powerful of the earls'. In 1308 he broke with the king and moved to permanent opposition and henceforth employed his power to frustrate effective government and the war against Scotland. Too strong to repress or coerce, he had to be conciliated: in 1317-18 the government negotiated with him like an independent state and contracted a formal treaty with him at Leake. He was indeed 'the supreme example of the overmighty subject' (McKisack).

Lancaster's misuse of his power reflects 'the repulsive nature of the man'. A generous almsgiver and pious benefactor, perhaps 'more than conventionally devout', he was also sexually immoral, quarrelsome, selfish and vindictive. He was rapacious to his tenants, maintained his retainers beyond the legitimate bounds of good lordship, and seized what he wanted in defiance of right and the law. He readily resorted to brutality, violence and private war in his Thorpe Waterville dispute with Pembroke, his suppression of Adam Banaster's rebellion, his feud with Warenne, Sir Gilbert Middleton's kidnapping of two cardinals, and when wasting Damory's lands. However justifiable, his hatred and distrust of the king soured national politics for years. Incompetent in office, petulantly critical when out, his support declined among the nobility, other northerners, and ultimately his own retainers. His wife left him in 1316. Having masterminded the Despenser War in 1321, it was his hatred for Badlesmere that enabled Edward to destroy him and his allies in 1322, when he was defeated at Boroughbridge and executed.

To Dr Phillips, Lancaster was a 'muddler and a messer, who nursed his hatred of the king and concealed his own ambitions and lack of constructive ideas behind the facade of the Ordinances and his claim to exercise authority as steward of England'. His claims were thus mere lip-service. Yet miracles were worked at his tomb and some saw him as a martyr, who died fighting a tyrannical government in the cause of reform. This was how Lancaster saw himself, modelling himself consciously on Simon Montfort, promoting the canonization of Cantelupe and Winchelsey. He repeatedly demanded implementation of the Ordinances, the resumption of grants, and the removal of evil councillors: in 1312-14; in power in 1314-16, when they were enforced; and as articles in the 1318 settlement. In 1312 'being of higher birth and more powerful than the rest, (he) took upon himself the peril of the business, and ordered Piers, after three terms of exile, as one disobedient to three lawful warnings, to be put to death'. At least some of his violence had behind it praiseworthy political aims. Lancaster was certainly consistent in his promotion of the Ordinances. If indeed 'his conduct in practice was inconsistent with his lofty claims', this reflects on his ability and character, not his intentions that are, perhaps, his only redeeming feature.

Further Reading
J. R. S. Phillips, *Aymer de Valence, Earl of Pembroke 1307-24: Baronial Politics in the Reign of Edward II*, 1972.
J. R. Maddicott, *Thomas of Lancaster 1307-1322: A Study in the Reign of Edward II*, 1970.

THOMAS OF WOODSTOCK, EARL OF BUCKINGHAM and DUKE OF GLOUCESTER (1355-97),

youngest son of Edward III, was a leading opponent of Richard II in 1386-9. His marriage to the heiress Eleanor Bohun, his creation as earl and duke, and his endowment by Richard II gave him the rank and wealth – perhaps £2,500 a year – commensurate with his royal birth. Hence the princely lifestyle represented by his armour, tapestries, jewels and books. Like his father and brothers, he jousted and fought abroad: at sea in 1377-8, as commander of the last great *chevauchée* from Calais to Brittany in 1380-1, in Scotland in 1385, and in Ireland in 1395. He took seriously his duties as Constable of England, presiding over several causes célèbres in the court of chivalry and codifying the law of arms. His veneration of St Thomas Becket, his foundation of Pleshey College, and his patronage of the Minoresses and other orders prove him a man of more than conventional piety. Both interests merge in his concern for the crusade: his own abortive campaign in Prussia in 1391 and his support for exiles from the middle east. He had been well educated and was perhaps unusually cultured. As a politician, he was positive and practical, assertive and decisive, frank and persuasive. His public outbursts of temper, sometimes a liability and sometimes assets, demonstrated how sincere and committed he always was to the cause at issue.

Thomas thus represented what contemporaries admired most in a great nobleman. Hence his popularity and the devotion he inspired in dependants. Yet compared with his brothers he should have been disappointed: 'a man of choleric temper and militant tastes whose misfortune it was to have been born too late' (McKisack). He was forced to share the Bohun inheritance and his royal endowment comprised annuities that were irregularly paid and scarcely converted into land. His hopes for an independent sphere of activity in Ireland were dashed and he failed to secure what military commands there were. In the mid 1380s he was offended by a king, who governed by a clique of intimates rather than his natural councillors – the princes of the blood and the nobility. The French war was prosecuted ineffectively: royal finances were mismanaged, so that his own annuities went unpaid; favours were heaped on unworthy favourites in preference to more deserving cases like his own; accusations of treason and murder plots were hatched against his brother Gaunt; and his honour was touched by the rejection of his niece Philippa Coucy by Robert Vere. Private and public grievances fused, so that he took the lead in the continuing criticisms of royal government by the House of Commons. In 1386 threats of deposition by Bishop Arundel and himself forced Richard II to attend parliament, dismiss his ministers, allow Suffolk's impeachment, and accept the appointment of a commission of reform. King Richard responded in 1387 by ignoring the commission and by securing judicial opinions that the acts of the Wonderful Parliament were invalid and indeed treasonable. Thomas and the Earls of Arundel, Warwick, Nottingham, and Derby – the five Lords Appellant – then accused the royal favourites of treason, defeated Vere at Radcot Bridge, and forced the king to comply. Richard *may* indeed have been temporarily deposed and Gloucester *may* have hoped briefly to succeed him. However that may be, the destruction of the king's favourites at the Merciless Parliament of 1388 was very largely Thomas's achievement. He it was who held together the disparate parts of the opposition and used the Commons to override the qualms of the Lords.

In 1386-9 Thomas restored what he saw as constitutional normality without ever departing from his obligation of allegiance to the Crown. Yet he paid a high price for his achievement. Once of age in 1389, Richard did not employ his uncle as his birth demanded and then, in 1397, destroyed him in revenge for 1388. He was murdered because Richard could not risk his public trial in parliament.

Further Reading
A. Tuck, *Richard II and the English Nobility*, 1973.
A. Goodman, *The Loyal Conspiracy. The Lords Appellant under Richard II*, 1971.

THOMSON, JAMES (1700-48), poet, was born at Ednam, where his father was minister, and spent his early life in the border country of Tweed and Jed. He went to the abbey school at Jedburgh and thence in 1715 to Edinburgh University. He was intended for the Presbyterian ministry, but was encouraged by friends to make a living as a tutor while he pursued his bent towards poetry. He came to London in 1725 and had his first important poem, *Winter*, ready for publication by March 1726. It was popular and was soon followed by *Summer* (1727) and *Spring* (1728). Completed by *Autumn*, the quartet was published under the title of *The Seasons* in 1730. The form of this poem was suggested by the *Georgics* of Virgil to whose themes and manner Thomson is clearly indebted. Johnson praised his originality: 'His numbers, his pauses, his diction are of his own growth, without transcription, without imitation.' But he owed much, for instance in his ornamental use of proper names, to Milton, and something also to another imitator of Milton, John Philips, author of *Cyder*.

Thomson's distinctive contribution was his choice of subject. At a time when most poets followed the pronouncement of Pope, that 'the proper study of mankind is man', he described the phenomena of nature. He is not properly to be called a forerunner of the Romantic Movement, for his skill was essentially descriptive and his language is as much restrained by the conventions of the time as by the limitations of his own outlook. He painted nature in fine and sometimes appropriate language; he did not write about himself under the form of writing about nature. His merits include, however, a patent delight in what he records, a felicity of phrase which evokes the image even in the most generalized of descriptions; and where he is more particular, an accurate and subtle sense of touch, smell and sound. His popularity with contemporaries owed much to the sentimental stories with which he pointed a moral and adorned the tale in a fashion suited to the season. A description of a thunderstorm, for instance, evokes the story of Celadon and Amelia, lovers parted by a thunderbolt. Nothing else that the poet touched had the same success as *The Seasons*. For the rest of his life the poet revised, improved, added to it.

Thomson enjoyed the support of patrons whom he rewarded with fulsome dedications and mention in his poems. Amongst the warmest of these was Lyttelton, himself a poet and better fitted for this than he was for politics; when he was Chancellor of the Exchequer, in 1744, he provided Thomson with the Surveyor-Generalship of the Leeward Islands, though it is unlikely that he knew where they were. Thomson thus became naturally the poet of the anti-Walpole faction, although he had dedicated one of his earlier poems to the minister. With his sinecures (he was also for a time Secretary of the Briefs of Chancery) and the profits of his poems, he was not obliged to toil for a living. Earlier in life he was tutor to the two boys of Lord Binning and later to the son of Lord Talbot, with whom he travelled to France and met Voltaire. Later he turned to tragedies such as *Sophonisba*, *Edward and Eleanore* and *Coriolanus*, of no special merit. Not all his poems deserve to be read; he was at his worst when engaged upon the lengthy discussion of an abstract theme. *Liberty*, in five books, tried the patience of a diminishing number of readers as it proceeded upon its prolix course. His last poem, the *Castle of Indolence*, which appeared in the year of his death, was, however, a success. In the course of this sustained allegory, the Knight of Art and Industry finds his home in Britain, guarded by Britannia and aided by Liberty. Thomson was, in his amiable and undemanding way, a 'patriot', as the Prince of Wales and his faction understood the term, and he wrote the words of *Rule Britannia* which appeared in a masque written for the Prince of Wales. It was upon the water, being rowed from Hammersmith to Richmond, where he lived for the last twelve years of his life, that he caught the chill from which he subsequently died.

Further Reading
G. C. Macauley, *James Thomson*, 1908.

THORESBY, JOHN (*c*.1295-1373), Archbishop of York, 'is a very interesting example of a great civil servant bishop, who took his episcopal duties seriously' (Pantin). Of gentle birth from Thoresby in Wensleydale and briefly a student at Oxford, he apparently served Thomas of Lancaster (*d*.1322) who presented him to his first living in 1320 and whose canonization he was seeking at the papal curia in 1330. He was receiver of the chamber and domestic chaplain to William Melton, the model royal minister and Archbishop of York, who collated him to at least three livings. He had become one of the Yorkshire group of royal clerks by 1330. The king's clerk and notary of chancery at £26 a year in 1336, he became master of the rolls in 1341, keeper of the privy seal in 1345, and Chancellor of England from 1349-56 – a crucial time to be principal royal minister. Inevitably he was also involved in diplomacy with the curia, France and Scotland. All his masters had rewarded him with livings, so that he became a notable pluralist: he was master of Gateshead Hospital (1333), Archdeacon of London (1339), Dean of Lichfield (1346), and held a string of positions in cathedrals and collegiate churches. A bishopric inevitably followed: the remote Welsh see of St David's in 1347, the bishopric of Worcester in 1349, and then, like his mentor Melton, the archbishopric of York in 1352. Edward III could hardly have placed a higher valuation on his services except Canterbury, which was offered to his successor as chancellor, William Edington.

Probably Thoresby never visited St David's and he certainly delayed his enthronement at Worcester for two years, but York was different. Yorkshire was his home country, he no longer held ministerial office after 1356, and he appears normally to have resided in his archdiocese. He involved himself in building works at York Minster, particularly the Lady Chapel, to which he contributed generously and where he established a chantry chapel. His reputation for peacemaking is best exemplified in the lasting settlement he reached in the struggle for precedence between York and Canterbury: each archbishop could henceforth carry his Cross in the other's province, the Archbishop of York would be entitled Primate of England and the Archbishop of Canterbury Primate of All England. He was also devout and of blameless private life.

Thoresby's main contribution to the spiritual life of the church was the *Lay Folks' Catechism* of 1357, which was designed to instil basic knowledge of the faith in the laity. Thoresby directed his parish clergy in Latin to teach their parishioners the fourteen articles of faith, ten commandments, the seven sacraments, seven works of mercy, seven cardinal virtues, and seven deadly sins.

Based on an earlier model of Archbishop Pecham and imitated later by Archbishop Islip at Canterbury, these instructions were original only in their comprehensiveness. What was novel was that Thoresby then commissioned from the Benedictine John Gaytrigg an English translation in verse, the *Lay Folks' Catechism*, which literate layfolk could read and all could learn, and encouraged them to do so by offering forty days' relief from suffering in purgatory to those who could recite it. The success of the English catechism as opposed to the relatively rare Latin instructions is indicated by the later issue of a pirate version by the Lollards containing unacknowledged heretical teachings. Thoresby thus contributed significantly to two important developments of his time: the growth of writings in English and the promotion of Christian knowledge among ordinary people.

Further Reading
W. A. Pantin, *The English Church in the Fourteenth Century*, 1955.
T. F. Simmons and H. E. Nolloth, *The Lay Folks' Catechism or the English and Latin versions of Archbishop Thoresby's Instruction for the People*, Early English Text Society 118, 1901.

THORKELL THE TALL (*d.* after 1023) was one of the Viking leaders prominent in English affairs late in the reign of Ethelred II and early in that of Canute. A native of Denmark, possibly connected with the Danish royal family, his early career is shrouded by legend. He emerges into the light of history as the leader of what a contemporary chronicler described as an 'immense raiding army' which landed in Kent in the summer of 1009. Between 1009 and 1012 Thorkell's forces ravaged and plundered much of midland and southern England. It was his men who murdered Archbishop Aelfheah of Canterbury at Greenwich in 1012, though Thorkell had tried in vain to prevent them. After the payment of Danegeld to them the Danish forces dispersed and Thorkell with a fleet of forty-five ships (indicating a manpower of about 3,500) entered the service of King Ethelred. He fought with Ethelred against Sweyn Forkbeard in 1013 and remained loyal to Ethelred throughout 1014. At some subsequent point he went over to Canute. It is assumed, though it cannot be proved, that Thorkell changed sides with Eadric Streona towards the end of 1015. At any rate, Canute had sufficient confidence in his loyalty to make him Earl of East Anglia in 1017. During Canute's absence in Denmark in 1019 Thorkell seems to have acted as the Regent of England. Then there came a sudden reversal in his fortunes. Towards the end of 1021 Thorkell was outlawed and banished by Canute; we know nothing certain about the background to this quarrel. Thorkell retired to Denmark but apparently remained powerful and a potential menace to

Canute. This brought the king back to Denmark in 1022. Thorkell was evidently strong enough to exact terms of reconciliation favourable to himself: Canute entrusted him with the government of Denmark. Nothing is heard of him subsequently and it is assumed that he died shortly after 1023.

THRING, EDWARD (1821-87), headmaster of Uppingham, had as much influence on the development of British public schools as Arnold. He took over a small grammar school of twenty-five boys and two masters in 1853, and transformed it into one of the leading English boarding schools, with 320 boys and thirty masters. He believed in small units, so boarding houses held a maximum of thirty boys and classes did not exceed twenty-five – this at a time when there were sometimes as many as sixty in a class at Rugby. He defeated the efforts of the trustees to run the school more economically by meeting the cost himself, running up an overdraft of £2,500. He aimed to educate the whole man, mind, body and spirit, by providing a curriculum, and extra-curricular activities, far broader than the traditional fare of classics and mathematics. French and German, the sciences, music, drawing, woodwork, gymnastics and natural history were all available to an Uppingham boy. In all this he was an innovator, as he was when he founded the first public school mission, started courses in the 'useful arts' such as cookery for the local community, and held the first meeting of what developed into the Headmasters Conference at Uppingham in 1869.

'Teddy' Thring, with bright blue eyes and a broad mouth, was made in the mould of the formidable head. He protected his school fiercely. When typhoid threatened it, he removed it for a year to the Welsh coast, thus forcing the parsimonious townsmen of Uppingham, deprived of their economic lifeblood, to dig up their drains to get it back again. When the Endowed Schools Commission tried to interfere with its foundation he stopped them in their tracks by planning to close it. Some argue that his success in publicizing the merits of the independent boarding school harmed British state-run education by keeping the upper and middle classes out of it. He died in harness.

Further Reading
Sir George Parkin, *Edward Thring: Headmaster of Uppingham School: Life, Diary and Letters*, 1900.

THROCKMORTON, FRANCIS (1554-84), conspirator, was a member of the large and well-known west Midland Catholic family, whose name sometimes appears as Throgmorton. The family seat was and is still at Coughton Court in Warwickshire. The Throckmortons intermarried with many of the leading, and especially Catholic, families, such as the Digbys and Catesbys, and their history is closely connected with that of the staunch

Roman Catholic families of the sixteenth and early seventeenth centuries. Although they were not directly involved in the Gunpowder Plot (Mr Thomas Throckmorton had prudently gone abroad), before going he had loaned Coughton Court to Digby, and it was there that the wives of the 1605 conspirators had waited for the news of the Gunpowder Plot. Long before that date, the family was directly and disastrously involved in what is known as the Throckmorton Plot, in the person of Francis Throckmorton, although he was no more than the agent carrying out other men's instructions.

Francis was the son of Sir John Throckmorton of Feckenham in Worcestershire, and Sir John was the seventh of eight sons of Sir George Throckmorton of Coughton Court, Warwickshire, and the brother of Sir Nicholas Throckmorton, the Elizabethan diplomatist. Francis, after matriculating at Oxford in 1572, in 1576 was entered as a student of the Inner Temple. In 1580 he went abroad with his brother Thomas: as an ardent Catholic he visited the English Catholic exiles on the continent and he heard plans for restoring the Catholic religion in England by means of a foreign invasion. He heard the story in France, he heard it in Madrid: in Paris he met Charles Paget and Thomas Morgan, the agents of Mary Stuart, and imbibed the same story. Put shortly, the plan was one devised by the Duke of Guise: his armies would invade Scotland and England at one and the same moment. He had originally intended to murder Elizabeth, but he gave up that idea. The English Catholics were to be roused against the government and Mary Stuart was to be put on the throne. The whole cost of the adventure was to be financed by the pope and the King of Spain. Guise himself was to lead the invasion on the south coast of England.

Walsingham was well aware that some such scheme was being planned, but he had no detailed information. He therefore set a spy to work in the French embassy, a Frenchman who signed himself Fagot. It was Fagot who gave Walsingham the clue that he needed, when he wrote to him, 'The chief agents of the Queen of Scots are Mr Throckmorton and Lord Henry Howard. They never come to the ambassador's house except at night' ... ' On the 29 April le Sieur Frocquemorton visited the ambassador's house.' At once Walsingham set spies to work on Throckmorton and early in November Throckmorton was arrested and his papers seized: these contained a list of Catholic noblemen, a plan of harbours suitable for landing military forces and a number of 'infamous pamphlets against her Majesty printed beyond the seas'. There is no doubt that Throckmorton had also organized communication between Morgan and Mary, Queen of Scots, and also the Spanish ambassador, Mendoza.

At his first examination Francis denied all knowledge of the papers: they had been 'foisted' upon him by the searchers of his house. Being urged to confess and being promised pardon if he would do so, he still refused to admit anything. He was then sent to the rack in the Tower, but he still refused to admit anything. Sent to the rack a second time, he collapsed and agreed to make a full confession. His confession did not in fact cover the whole conspiracy, but it probably covered all that Francis knew. The damning evidence against him was the confession that 'he had set down in his own hand certain special havens for the landing of forces' and had also 'noted the number of persons of power as he thought fit to be drawn to that action with the aptness of their dwellings to each port'. He also admitted that on this calculation the Duke of Guise had decided on Arundel in Sussex as his port of landing for the invasion of southern England.

In view of this confession and of the written evidence to support it, there could be no result but the execution of Throckmorton at Tyburn. One other result of this so-called Throckmorton Plot was the expulsion of the Spanish ambassador, Mendoza, from the kingdom, since he had known all the details and was deep in the whole design.

Further Reading
A. L. Rowse, *Ralegh and the Throckmortons*, 1962.

THURLOE, JOHN (1616-68), Cromwell's Secretary of State, was the son of an Essex rector, trained for the law at Lincoln's Inn, and rose in the world as steward and secretary of the parliamentarian leader, Oliver St John. In 1651 Thurloe accompanied St John to the Hague to take part in the abortive negotiations which preceded the First Dutch War, and in the following year he was appointed clerk to the Council of State. In effect he became the sole Secretary of State for nearly eight years, and all the principal civil business of the Commonwealth, foreign and domestic, passed through his hands. The volumes of his correspondence remain a major source for historians of the period. He developed a devoted loyalty to Cromwell and to the Protectorate as a system of government, and Cromwell clearly placed immense confidence in him. Yet Thurloe was in no sense an *éminence grise*. It is significant that the index of Firth's *Oliver Cromwell* contains only two references to Thurloe in some 470 pages. Unambitious, thorough, ceaselessly diligent and highly efficient, utterly reliable, Thurloe was the supreme servant of the Cromwellian state. As MP first for Ely and later for Cambridge University, he spoke in parliament in defence of the government's policy, yet there are few signs that he had any decisive influence in making it. His most celebrated, and most onerous, task was as the head of a wide-spread intelligence system whose function was to unearth the countless royalist plots to restore the monarchy and assassinate Cromwell. Thurloe's spies were to be found everywhere, in Madrid and the Hague, Dublin and the Scottish Highlands, in country houses and Leveller meetings, even in the royalist 'Sealed Knot' itself, and, aided by his censorship of the postal service, they were very successful. It is not so easy to assess the general achievement of Thurloe. There is some evidence that his office became something of a bottleneck, slowing down the dispatch of business. A small neat man, Thurloe was, of course, a Puritan, as the language in which he wrote to Henry Cromwell of his father's death indicates: 'the stroke is so sore, so stupendous … I can do nothing but put my mouth in the dust and say "It is the Lord"'. He was very much a Cromwellian. He had urged Oliver to take the Crown, and he did his best to stiffen Richard. With the end of the Protectorate he was dismissed; Monck recalled him, and he remained Secretary until just before the return of the king. His life was spared at the Restoration, in return for a detailed statement of the current diplomatic position. He remained in England under Charles II, but declined to enter his employment.

Further Reading
P. Aubrey, *Mr Secretary Thurloe*, 1989.
D. Underdown, *Royalist Conspiracy in England, 1649-1660*, 1960.
Edmund Baker, 'John Thurloe', *History Today*, August 1958, pp.548-55.

THURLOW, EDWARD, 1st BARON THURLOW (1731-1806) secured the highest legal places without ever showing himself to be a great lawyer. He benefited from the deference that politicians of his time paid to lawyers as interpreters of the constitution, but his long ascendancy was based upon force of personality. With a strong presence, a good mind and a cutting tongue, he had the hearty insensitiveness that can carry a man to the fore in politics. Coarse-grained, unsubtle, greedy for place, he was yet able to win the respect of better men, notably North and Pitt. To North he was a tower of strength; Pitt came to detest him, but valued his caustic common sense and his knowledge of men.

He was the son of a Norfolk clergyman, educated at Scarning School and at King's School, Canterbury. Perse Scholar at Caius College, Cambridge, he was sent down for insulting the dean. In a lawyer's office in Holborn he was a fellow pupil of Cowper. How different his career from that of the gentle poet who shrank and broke before responsibility! Thurlow soon made a name for skilful advocacy. In the celebrated Douglas case he secured a reversal of the decision of the Court of Session – and then fought a duel with the Duke of Hamilton's agent, Andrew Stuart. In 1770 he was appointed Solicitor-General, in 1771 Attorney-General. He overthrew Lord Mansfield's doctrine of perpetual copyright in *Donaldsons v. Becket* (1774) but opposed legislative settlement. By nature he was indolent and attachment to the status

quo is one of the two principles that can be discerned in his career. The other is a high view of royal prerogative. He won the approval of George III for his inflexible attitude towards the American colonies and became his trusted servant and confidant. Elevated to the woolsack in 1778, he remained there for fourteen years, with only one interval during the coalition of Fox and North in 1783. In the year before, he had been the one minister to survive the fall of North and take office under Rockingham.

'No-one,' said Fox, 'was ever so wise as Lord Thurlow looked.' Indeed he dominated the Lords as much by his appearance and manner as by what he said. He was also, however, skilful in debate, with a disconcerting memory, a genial sarcasm and a sharp eye for the weak points of his opponents. In his judicial capacity he was fair; in all his dealings there was a directness which inspired confidence. Dr Johnson enjoyed tilting with him: 'I honour Thurlow, sir: Thurlow is a fine fellow, he fairly puts his mind to yours.' But he might not have approved Thurlow's conduct of November 1788. The chancellor, who had before acted for the king in a matter so delicate as the notorious intervention to sway the Lords against Fox's India Bill, now, when George III was ill and a Regency was mooted, intrigued behind the backs of his colleagues with the Prince of Wales. George III recovered, Thurlow kept his place, but lost what remained of his reputation. He protested his loyalty in the most shameless way: 'If I forget my king, may God forget me', upon which Wilkes muttered, 'He will see you damned first', and Burke added 'The best thing that could happen to you'. Removed at last in 1792 he at once made his court with the Prince of Wales, but this did him little good. Before all else Thurlow was an authoritarian. He sympathized with Hastings, over whose trial he presided; less justifiably he defended the interests of the slave owners. With all his toughness and shrewdness he lacked the imagination and flexibility to be a great chancellor.

Further Reading
R. Gore-Brown, *Chancellor Thurlow, the Life and Times of an XVIIIth Century Lawyer*, 1953.

THURSTAN or THURSTIN OF YORK (*c.*1070-1140; Archbishop of York 1114-40), royal clerk, combative and independent prelate, patron of new religious orders, protector of hermits, and founder of a new diocese, embodied many of the distinctive features of the twelfth-century church, not least the capacity for controversy. His early career was conventional. Like so many Anglo-Norman bishops, he came from Bayeux, the son of a priest, Auger, who later became a canon of St Paul's. Either at Bayeux or at St Paul's Thurstan became the protégé of Ranulf Flambard, chief minister of William II and Bishop of Durham (1099-1128), joining a tight-knit group which dominated government of church and state. From the 1090s, Thurstan rose through the royal chapel, becoming a clerk of William II, chaplain and almoner of Henry I, and, like his father, a canon of St Paul's. In 1114, he followed many loyal servants of the Crown onto the episcopal bench as Archbishop of York. (His brother was made Bishop of Evreux at much the same time.) Presumably Henry I thought he had placed a dependable ally in the potentially troublesome northern province. If so, he was wrong. To all appearances one of the old school, Thurstan immediately displayed an obstinate legalism in refusing consecration or ordination from the Archbishop of Canterbury. From 1114 to 1121, with the support of Popes Paschal II (1099-1118) and Gelasius II (1118-19) and of Flambard (in exile at Bayeux, but technically his leading suffragan), he defied the king's attempts to force his submission to the primacy of Canterbury, spending much of that period in exile. After formally resigning his see in 1116, he was reconsecrated by Callistus II (1119-24) in 1119. Weakened by the rebellion of 1118-19 and the death of his son in the White Ship disaster, in 1120 Henry I agreed to Thurstan's return. The archbishop was enthroned at York in 1121 and was soon back in favour, conducting royal business. Compromise with Canterbury was reached in 1125, when Pope Honorius II (1124-30) gave the Archbishop of Canterbury legatine authority over the whole English church but did not insist on any formal submission by Thurstan.

Thurstan was notable for his personal piety. He protected and lent support to the hermits Godric of Finchale and Christina of Markyate against institutional jealousy and suspicion from the ecclesiastical hierarchy. A patron of the Augustinian canons who established their mission in the north-western counties of England, he was instrumental in the consequent establishment of the see of Carlisle whose first bishop he consecrated in 1133. A year before, Thurstan had sanctioned the exodus of monks from St Mary's, York to found the Cistercian monastery of Fountains on 200 acres the archbishop gave them in Skeldale, near Ripon. Thurstan, as few others, combined religious enthusiasm, political contacts and administrative efficiency. This ensured him an excellent press from contemporaries, particularly Cistercians. His extended contacts with what could be called the eremitic tendency within the church suggests a religious network of some complexity beyond the formal structures of dioceses, monasteries and parishes. A poweful patron, he seems to have possessed a share of the holiness of Anselm and the dogmatism of Becket, but with an eirenic quality all his own. His reputation was further enhanced by his organization of northern resistance to the Scottish invasion of 1138 which culminated in the English victory at the battle of the Standard. The chaotic divisions which afflicted the see of York after his death are perhaps the true measure of his skill in reconciling northern interests.

Further Reading
D. Nichols, *Thurstan of York*, 1964.

TIERNEY, GEORGE (1761-1830) was leader of the Whigs in the House of Commons from 1818 until his retirement from politics in 1828. The leaders of the several Whig factions that made up an opposition to Lord Liverpool's government sat in the House of Lords. It is surprising nonetheless to learn that the spokesman of these aristocratic politicians in the Commons was the son of a Spanish merchant. His early success in politics testifies to the impact of his personality. He began as the people's idol, another Burdett. His later career was a long anticlimax. It was generally held in the time of his leadership that he was lazy. He seems however to have had a clearer idea of the role of the opposition than his chief, Lord Grey. For failures of opposition Grey must take equal blame. Until they were presented with the reform movement in 1830 the opposition simply lacked a policy upon which they could unite.

Tierney was born in Gibraltar, but he had some Irish forbears and his firm dealt with English trade; he was educated at Eton and Peterhouse College, Cambridge. Although intended for the law, he enjoyed sufficient means after the deaths of his brothers to enter politics. In 1788 he boldly put himself forward as a candidate for Colchester, although that town was notorious for the length and expense of its elections: three recent candidates there had each become bankrupt. Tierney opposed the government candidate, George Jackson, but each candidate scored exactly the same number of votes and he was admitted to parliament only after a committee had investigated the election. He was nevertheless unseated in the following year. Some gentlemen in Southwark offered to put him forward as a candidate and pay his expenses. His opponent was George Thellerson, a director of the East India Company, a body that had been the subject of much pamphlet-attacking by Tierney. Thellerson was victorious, but Tierney, acting as his own counsel, petitioned against him and accused him of breaking a law of William III's day which forbade 'treating' – or offering free entertainment and drink to voters. The election was repeated, so was the 'treating' and so was Tierney's petition. Thellerson was finally unseated and Tierney elected in his place. Southwark later rejected him when he accepted an office under Addington in 1803.

He was an active opponent of William Pitt and in 1798 the two quarrelled violently in the Commons: Pitt asserted that Tierney's opposition to a bill 'for suspending seamen's protections' proceeded from 'a desire to obstruct the defence of the country', and Tierney demanded an apology, which Pitt refused, or a duel. It was no light matter, at a dark moment in the continental war, for the prime minister to risk his life in a duel on Putney Heath. As Pitt was thin and Tierney exceptionally corpulent, wits declared that Pitt's silhouette should be traced out on Tierney as the proper target area. Both parties missed with their first shots and Pitt fired into the air with his second. Honour satisfied, the duel was called off.

As England faced the danger of invasion Tierney was one of many who joined the Volunteer Movement. He was Lieutenant Colonel Commandant of the Somerset House volunteers, composed of clerks and government servants. He was Treasurer of the navy, 1803-4, and President of the Board of Control for India for a few months in 1806. At the end of his career he was made Master of the Mint, 1827-8, by Canning, as part of the alliance between the new prime minister and the Whigs. Between these two short episodes in office he was a prominent parliamentary opponent of the government and was considered leader of the opposition from 1818, after the death of Ponsonby. By then he was ineffective, though the repressive policy of the government gave opposition plenty to work on. During this period the Whigs, about 150, were a reasonably solid phalanx. But ministers like Peel and Huskisson took social and economic initiatives which disheartened Tierney and he did not live to see electoral reform become the issue which returned the Whigs to power. When Lord Goderich's ministry came to an end, in 1828, he retired from politics. He remained a cheerful man until the day of his death, despite the frustration of his dreams of office and asthmatic and dropsical complaints.

At his best Tierney had been a dreaded speaker in the House, noted for his sarcasm; Castlereagh suffered especially from his barbed wit. He was known to some of the younger members of the party as *Mother Cole*, after his habit of referring to himself as a plain, honest man, like the lady in Foote's farce who ran a brothel in Covent Garden, but protested stoutly that she was an honest woman.

Further Reading
Austin Mitchell, *The Whigs in Opposition*, 1967.
M. Roberts, *The Whig Party 1807-12*, 1939.
H. K. Olphin, *G. Tierney*, 1934.

TILLOTSON, JOHN (1630-94), Archbishop of Canterbury, was the son of a well-to-do Halifax clothworker who was at one time a prominent member of a Puritan congregation. Educated at Clare, Cambridge, where he was elected a Fellow in 1651, he departed from the Calvinism of his early years under the influence of the writings of Chillingworth. Appointed lecturer at the church of St Lawrence Jewry and preacher at Lincoln's Inn (1665), Tillotson won an immense reputation in Charles II's reign as a preacher, plain and direct in style, stressing man's moral duty and emphasizing the place of reason in religion. He was a vigorous opponent, in pamphlet and pulpit, of the claims of Rome, as for example in a famous sermon before the Commons on the anniversary of Gunpowder Plot in 1678. Dean of Canterbury from 1672, after the Revolution he was appointed Dean of St Paul's. Appropriately for a man who had appeared on the nonconforming side at the Savoy Conference, Tillotson was a supporter of the Toleration Act of 1689 and was energetic in promoting the abortive scheme of comprehension of the same year. In 1691, when Sancroft was deprived, Tillotson became Archbishop of Canterbury. His tenure was brief, for he died in 1694, yet the appointment of a churchman of latitudinarian views to the primacy was a significant milestone in the history of religion in England. His practical religion – reasonable, charitable, temperate, lacking the heat and passion of the previous generation but not yet sunk in the complacency of the next – represented the strongest element in the Anglicanism of his time.

TINDAL, MATTHEW (1657-1733) after a chequered career became one of the most influential of deists and the centre of warm controversy. He was at Exeter College, Oxford, and then a Fellow of All Souls. During James II's reign he turned Catholic. Later he avowed that he found its absurdities intolerable and rebounded into rationalism. As was proper in an Oxford don, he made no haste. Not until 1706 did he attract notice by his published sermon, *The Rights of the Christian Church established*. It was an attack upon the High Church position – and was ordered to be burnt, with Sacheverell's sermon, in 1710, by order of the House of Commons. He was an old man when he produced the first volume of *Christianity as Old as the Creation*, in 1730; the second volume never saw light as the manuscript came into the hands of Bishop Gibson, who decided that it would be unwise to add fuel to the flames. For Tindal, consolidating the position already reached by Tillotson, Hoadley and Clarke, argued that since God was good, wise and unchanging and since human nature was also constant in essentials, God's law was perfect, unalterable and available to all. He denied any exclusive claims to Christian revelation: why, he asked, should the American aborigine have been denied this special benefit by the Creator? It follows that he was dubious, too, of the value of specifically Christian observances.

In Tindal's book the great debate came to a climax. Other deists began to question the evidence for the stories of the Bible; miracles had already received rough treatment; now the Resurrection itself was questioned, notably by Woolston. Leland and Foster the Dissenters, tackled him; so did Law and, later, Warburton, amongst Anglicans. Tindal's conception was not ignoble for at the heart of it lies the idea that God must have dealt equally with all men; doctrines not universally revealed cannot be imposed upon all by God; reason alone is the faculty granted to all and reason must therefore be the sole judge. Its tendency to further the well-being of mankind is the only test of any creed. Obedience to nature is the one sufficient principle of the religious life, which consists 'in a constant disposition of mind to do all the good we can, and thereby render ourselves acceptable to God in answering the end of his creation'. Rules, dogmas and ways of worship must be judged by the degree to which they promote happiness. Asceticism has no more place than fanaticism in his system. We can see in his writing not only the lofty rationalism of Voltaire, who admired him as 'the intrepid defender of natural religion', but also the more mundane arguments of the utilitarians. An important result of his work, because it was superficially formidable, was to make theologians examine the evidence in a more critical spirit. Would Butler or Law, for instance, have written so well had it not been for the deist challenge?

Further Reading
R. N. Stromberg, *Religious Liberalism in Eighteenth-Century England*, 1954.
L. Stephen, *History of English Thought in the Eighteenth Century*, vol. 1, 1876.

TIPTOFT, JOHN, EARL OF WORCESTER (*c*.1427-70), 'Butcher of England', was 'the English nobleman of his age who came closest to the Italian prince of the Renaissance'. Although his father John (*d*.1443) was only the first Baron Tiptoft, he had established the estates and noble connections that enabled his son to advance himself to an earldom (1449) even before he displayed his outstanding ability. He was treasurer of England in 1452-4 and a royal councillor from 1453. Sent on embassy to Italy in 1458, Worcester delayed his return at least partly to avoid the Wars of the Roses until late in 1461, when it was safe to commit himself to the Yorkist cause. Edward IV advanced him at once. He became a councillor again, constable of England, chief justice of north Wales, constable of Portchester and the Tower, knight of the Garter (1462), treasurer of England again (1462-3), keeper of the seals (1463), diplomat and soldier. He sold his English offices in 1467 when sent as deputy to Ireland, where he unwisely (and perhaps unjustly) executed his predecessor the Earl of Desmond. Warwick's coup in 1469 caused Edward IV to recall Worcester and reappoint him as constable of England and (for the third time) lord treasurer. When Edward was deposed in 1470, Worcester was captured, and he alone was executed to great public rejoicing. He had exercised his responsibility as constable for trying traitors with great rigour. Minor offenders as well as ringleaders were executed and he impaled traitors as well as hanging, drawing and quartering them. At this

'the people of the land were greatly displeased and ever afterwards the Earl of Worcester was greatly hated among the people, for the disordinate death that he used'. He must die, they cried, 'for he had introduced the law of Padua' into England.

Whilst this claim was untrue, it shows how unusual Worcester was. He was fluent in Latin, studied at university – he was a lodger at University College, Oxford in 1440-2 – and developed a genuine understanding of Renaissance humanism. He sought to improve his Latin style even before 1458, when he studied at Padua, under the great Guarino da Verona at Ferrara, and then at Florence and Rome. His impressive library of classical and modern works showed a particular interest in Latin translations of Greek works. He patronized scholars, who dedicated their works to him, and even translated two Latin works into English himself. While he nearly purged his own Latin of barbarisms and errors, he cannot have penned the splendid oration that caused Pope Pius II to utter 'You alone of all the princes of this age are worthy to be compared in virtu and eloquence with the greatest Emperors of Greece and Rome.' His importance lay in his personal aspirations, in his patronage – only he and Bishop Grey genuinely assisted scholars – and in his wish to raise classical scholarship in England to Italian standards. Whilst the remedy he proposed to Oxford University may have been stillborn, he saw himself, not unjustly, as successor to Humphrey, Duke of Gloucester.

Worcester was highly complex. A conventional chivalric upbringing enabled him to draft ordinances for jousts and umpire tournaments. He went on pilgrimage to Palestine and asked to be beheaded with three blows in honour of the Trinity. Though proud of his lineage, he allowed seventeen years to elapse between the childless death of his second wife and his third marriage at fifty-two. His certainty in his own rightness accompanied a marked sense of humour and a talent for friendship. He cared little for English public opinion, yet wanted respect from humanists not for his rank but as a scholar. Even in England, he could be remembered as 'a man most learned in all the liberal arts and skilled in the knowledge of letters both sacred and secular'.

Further Reading
R. Weiss, *Humanism in England during the Fifteenth Century*, 1967.
R. J. Mitchell, *John Tiptoft 1427-70*, 1938.

TIREL III, WALTER (*fl*.1100), Lord of Poix, was notorious in the early twelfth century as the man who shot dead William II, King of England, during a deer hunt in the New Forest on 2 August 1100. His repeated and strenuous denials of responsibility made under oath to Abbot Suger of St Denis, chief minister of Louis VI of France, suggest that public infamy was as intrusive and tenacious as it is today. Castellan of Pontoise in the strategically important Vexin between Normandy and the lands of the King of France and related by marriage to the powerful Anglo-Norman Clare dynasty, Walter Tirel received lands from William I and was a close friend of William II. All contemporary accounts attribute William's death to a stray arrow, a hunting accident. Most, including William of Malmesbury, the Worcester chronicler, and Orderic Vitalis, name Walter Tirel as the unwitting culprit. It seems likely that he shot the arrow that missed a deer and killed the king. He certainly fled the scene immediately afterwards. Some modern conspiracy theorists have used this to support their reconstruction of a plot hatched by the Clares and William's brother, Henry. It is true that Henry was present on the fatal hunt and grasped the opportunity to sieze the throne. For him, the circumstances and timing of his brother's death were convenient, but probably fortuitous. William Rufus was not the first to die by accident in the New Forest. His brother, Richard, had been killed hunting there c.1070 and a nephew, also called Richard, had met a fate eerily similar to the king's in May 1100. Walter Tirel was not a scapegoat or a fall-guy. Subsequently, he neither suffered retribution nor enjoyed preferment. But to kill a king, even by accident, was an uncomfortable burden for a boon-companion to bear. As his confessions demonstrated, Walter Tirel was less concerned with the schemes of men than with the opinion of his peers and the designs of God.

TONE, THEOBALD WOLFE (1763-98), Irish revolutionary leader, was the son of Peter Tone, a Protestant coachmaker of Dublin. A clever but lazy boy who would have preferred to go into the army, Tone became a pensioner of Trinity College, Dublin, in 1781. He was nearly expelled for acting as second in a duel in which a man was killed, and he eloped with a girl of sixteen, Matilda Witherington. They were happy but penniless. After the birth of a daughter Tone went to London and enrolled as a student in the Middle Temple. He scarcely opened a law book, but with his younger brother, home from service in the East India Company, he devised a scheme for a military colony in a South Sea island: Pitt was not interested. Tone returned to Ireland after nearly two years (Christmas 1788) and was called to the Irish bar. Thomas Russell, the main founder of the United Irish Society, was an important influence on Tone at this time. Tone became a republican and avowed his aims: 'To break the connection with England, the never-failing source of all our political evils' and 'to substitute the common name of Irishman in place of the denominations'.

With Henry Flood he was elected an honorary member of the first company of Belfast Volunteers. He assisted Russell in the formation of the United Irishmen and devoted himself to bringing together the various interests in the patriotic movement. He played a major part in the great Catholic convention of December 1792 but he was disappointed by the failure of his leader, John Keogh, in negotiation with Lord Buckinghamshire. The Catholic convention voted Tone £1,500 and a gold medal, but he decided to try more extreme tactics.

Revolutionary France seemed to be Ireland's natural ally. A memorandum for the agent William Jackson, urging that the time was ripe for a French invasion, was betrayed to the government. By agreement with the government Tone took himself off to America in June 1795, a month after the United Irishmen had reorganized themselves on a rebellious basis. In Philadelphia he met the French ambassador, who approved his plan, worked out with Emmet and Russell, for securing French aid. In February 1796 Tone, alias James Smith, was in Paris, discussing invasion with Carnot and de la Croix.

He was given the commission of *chef de brigade*, but there were delays. Bad seamanship then spoiled the first attempt in December 1796. The French could have landed 12,000 men on an undefended shore; they delayed, a storm blew up, they cut their cables and ran. The death of Hoche, Tone's main ally, was a further setback (September 1797). Bonaparte was more interested in Egypt than in Ireland; later he was to regret it. When news came of the rising in Ireland (June 1798), he was on his way east and the Directory would only sanction small expeditions to different points along the coast. Humbert sailed in August with 1,000 men. In September Napper Tandy landed on Rutland Island with a band of Irish refugees. Tone himself sailed from Brest with General Hardy, the battleship *Hoche* and 3,000 men. Contrary winds delayed them and they did not arrive off Lough Swilly until 10 October. Before they could land they were attacked by an English squadron. The *Hoche* surrendered and Tone was taken prisoner. He was court-martialled: against the charge of treason he pleaded his duty as a French officer. He was only allowed to read portions of a prepared statement declaring his aims. He was found guilty; his request to be shot as a soldier was refused. To save himself from the gallows he cut his throat with a pen-knife. Meanwhile efforts had been made to transfer his case to the civil courts. The chief justice ordered the suspension of execution but a week later, 19 November, Tone died of his self-inflicted wound.

Tone's *Journals* present an entertaining picture of the man, but they were written mainly to amuse his wife and his friend Thomas Russell and should not be treated too seriously. His reputation in English history is that of a reckless rebel. He was indeed no lover of England or her rule. 'I hated her before my exile and I will hate her always.' By Irishmen, however, he can justly be seen as a patriot: optimistic, brave, an Irish Danton, open in his faults, a warm-hearted husband and father. His son William Tone served actively in the French and later in the American army, and subsequently wrote a life of his father. Today Irish exponents of violent revolution revere his name.

Further Reading
Marianne Elliot, *Wolfe Tone*, 1989.
T. Pakenham, *The Year of Liberty*, 1969.
W. T. W. Tone, *Life of Theobald Wolfe Tone*, 1826; edited and published as the *Autobiography of Wolfe Tone* by B. O'Brien, 1893.

TONSON, JACOB (1656?-1736), described in the *Dictionary of National Biography* as 'son of a London chirurgeon', was a successful publisher in a golden period of English literature, the Augustan Age when the greatest men of letters and the leading politicians were interlinked as never before or since. Apprenticed as a stationer in 1670, he started his own business at the Judge's Head in Chancery Lane in 1677; took a nephew into partnership in 1699; and retired about 1720 to an estate at Ledbury in Herefordshire. A genial yet shrewd businessman, he made substantial profits early in his career as a result of buying the copyright of *Paradise Lost*. Among the contemporaries whose work he published were Dryden, Addison, Steele and Pope. His relations with authors were not invariably happy, and Dryden has left a sour description of Tonson

> With leering looks, bull-faced and freckled-fair;
> With two left legs, and Judas-coloured hair,
> And frowsy pores that taint the ambient air.

Yet the gain was mutual: as the dramatist Wycherley put it to Pope, 'you will make Jacob's ladder raise you to immortality'. Contracts for state publishing added to Tonson's profits. Historians have reason to be grateful to him for reprinting Rymer's *Foedera*; so has the Cambridge University Press, whose first printed book (1698) was the opening volume, on *Horace*, of a series of quarto classics published by Tonson. Nor was his business flair confined to publishing: for he seems to have done well out of the investment in the South Sea Company, and even out of John Law's Mississippi Scheme.

Business, and literary men, provided one side of Jacob Tonson's career; the other – not separate from the first – came from politics. Towards the end of William III's reign a group of leading Whigs used to meet informally at an eating-house in Shire Lane near Temple Bar kept by one Christopher Cat, noted for his mutton pies. When Cat moved to the Fountain Tavern in the Strand (?1698), the 'Kit-Cat Club' moved with him, with Tonson in effect as its secretary. He was thus a central figure in the creation of perhaps the most famous political club in English history, whose members included Somers and Wharton and the young Robert Walpole, Addison and

Steele, Congreve and Vanbrugh. About 1703 they moved to the Kit-Cat room in Tonson's country house of Barn Elms, near Putney (which Vanbrugh had designed). The club is immortalized in the series of Kit-Cat portraits painted by Kneller for Tonson, now in the National Portrait Gallery. Thus Jacob Tonson the publisher – whom Pope, about 1731, described as 'full of matter, secret history and wit and spirit, at almost four-score' – played a role at once central and unusual in that critical generation of British history which followed the 'Glorious Revolution'.

Further Reading
John Carswell, *The Old Cause*, 1954 (especially Chapter VI).
Dictionary of National Biography, Jacob Tonson.

TOOKE, JOHN HORNE (1736-1812) was a radical clergyman with scholarly interests and a flair for publicity, who first made his name during the Wilkes affair and was still politically active in a somewhat anachronistic way at the turn of the century. He was the son of a well-to-do poulterer called Horne. (He later adopted the name of a friend, Tooke.) He seems to have been a clever, rather opinionated and argumentative boy. On one occasion he ran away from his tutor on the grounds that the tutor was 'bad at grammar'. He lost the sight of an eye in a fight with a schoolfellow. He distinguished himself at St John's College, Cambridge, and took orders, but without enthusiasm.

In 1760 he became the incumbent of a chapel of ease at Brentford. He preached good, practical sermons and studied medicine in order to set up a dispensary for parishioners. He grew increasingly casual, however, about their spiritual needs. In dress and conduct he was decidedly unclerical. He spent some time travelling abroad and fathered at least two illegitimate children. In 1766 he wrote a notorious letter in which he apologized for 'having the infectious hand of a bishop waved over me'. He made the acquaintance among others of Voltaire and Sterne and his ideas and style during this period show their influence. Rationalist and individualist, he was also a man who liked to make startling statements. 'I will have my black coat dyed red', he announced to the startled freemen of Middlesex. He seemed to enjoy a contest. He accused George Onslow of selling an office and was fined £400 after a celebrated libel case. He had the last word, however, since he appealed and secured a verdict against the great Mansfield in the Court of Common Pleas.

Wilkes's struggle against parliamentary privilege naturally appealed to Tooke and he supported him effectively at the Middlesex election of 1768. Along with some prominent and wealthy men he founded the Society of the Supporters of the Bill of Rights, in February 1769, to support 'Mr Wilkes and his cause'. He soon fell out with the people's champion, whom he suspected of marshalling support largely for his own benefit. In 1771 he formed the Constitutional Society. He was naturally regarded as a renegade by Wilkesites and he was burned in effigy by the mob during the election of sheriffs for the city in that year. He was indeed better suited to guerilla operations than to the more organized forms of political warfare. In 1774 he was summoned before the House of Commons to account for a violent attack on the Speaker, Norton. He escaped punishment on that occasion, but he was fined and imprisoned for a few months in 1778 for publishing a resolution to raise a subscription for the American colonists.

He was refused admission to the Bar by the Benchers of the Inner Temple. It was a cruel blow, as he had proven legal abilities and had already been offered some briefs. For a short time he set up as an agriculturalist with a farm at Witton in Huntingdonshire. It was hardly his métier and he soon gave up with an ague. Fortunately he inherited some money from his father and was enabled to live comfortably in Dean Street with his two daughters. He subsequently went to live at Purley. It was there that he wrote Επεα πτερο'εντα or *Diversions of Purley* (two volumes, 1786 and 1798) which established his reputation as a philologist. Philology, in his view, subserves philosophy: every word means a thing and reasoning is the art of putting words together. In his philosophical approach he influenced James Mill, amongst others, while in his emphasis upon the importance of studying Anglo-Saxon he has a significant place among early grammarians.

Dislike of Fox led him to contest Westminster against Fox in the election of 1790; he came bottom of the poll. Pitt allowed him to be tried for high treason in 1794, after a sham confession to being a spy. It may have been a foolish joke; it can hardly have deceived the ministers. He had Erskine to defend him; he enjoyed himself, mocking at the Attorney-General and clowning in the dock. He was very properly acquitted. He was no Jacobin and, if he occupied a position to the left of the parliamentary Whigs, it was only the position of an old-fashioned city tribune, who resented aristocratic privilege. His appearance suited the part. He was sturdy, keen-eyed and dressed like a prosperous tradesman. In 1796 he was again unsuccessful in a Westminster election, but in 1801 Lord Camelford brought the persistent old man in for Old Sarum. An act was subsequently passed declaring clergymen ineligible for parliament.

After 1792 he lived in a house on Wimbledon Common where he gardened and kept cows. He was greatly attached to his tom-cat. He was also celebrated for his Sunday dinners. He was formerly a great drinker of wine and is said to have left Porson and Boswell, two noted topers, under the table. In later life, however, he was abstemious. He claimed to have acquired his painful gout from drinking bad claret in prison. His friendships did not rely solely on his generous table. Men like Bentham, Paine, Thurlow and Erskine appreciated his mind and conversation. 'Your political principles,' Burdett once remarked, 'are as much out of fashion as your clothes!' 'I know it,' said Tooke, 'but the fashion must one day return or the nation be undone.'

Further Reading
G. S. Veitch, *Genesis of Parliamentary Reform*, 2nd edn, 1965.
A. Stephens, *Memoirs of John Horne Tooke*, 2 vols, 1813.

TOPCLIFFE, RICHARD (1532-1604), persecutor and torturer of Roman Catholics, came of a good county family, being the eldest son of Robert Topcliffe of Sowerby, in Lincolnshire, and his wife Margaret, daughter of Thomas, Lord Burgh, of Gainsborough. He entered parliament in 1572 as member for Beverley: in 1586 he was returned by Old Sarum, a constituency which he represented until shortly before his death in 1604.

He was taken into the service of Burghley in about 1573, and there is extant a letter from Topcliffe, in his execrable, even for those days, handwriting and spelling, in which he describes with relish the harsh treatment meted out to the Papists of Norwich.

From about 1586 and for the next twenty-five years Topcliffe became for his own contemporaries, Protestant or Catholic, what he has remained ever since, one of the most odious and detestable government officials in British history. 'Because the often exercise of the rack in the Tower was so odious and so much spoken of by the people, Topcliffe had authority to torment priests in his own house in such sort as he shall think good.' Topcliffe himself boasted that 'he had in his own home a machine, of his own invention, compared with which the ordinary rack was mere child's play' (*Dictionary of National Biography*). So loud were the complaints of both Protestant and Catholic that Burghley at one moment had Topcliffe arrested on the grounds that he had exceeded his instructions: but his imprisonment was short lived.

The most notorious cases in which Topcliffe played the part of the villain were those of Robert Southwell, the Bellamy family, Henry Walpole and Thomas Fitzherbert. The last proved such a scandal that Topcliffe found himself for a while in gaol, whence he wrote 'on Good or Evil Friday 1595' two letters to the queen – 'two more detestable compositions it would be difficult to find' (Dr A. Jessop, *One Generation of a Norfolk House*).

When Topcliffe tired of work and wanted to retire in peace, he obtained from the queen a grant of the Fitzherbert estates at Padley Manor in Derbyshire. Here he lived from 1603 until his death in 1604.

Further Reading
C. Devlin, 'Richard Topcliffe', *The Month*, 1951.
The Revd Sir John O'Connell, 'Richard Topcliffe', *Dublin Review*, 1934.

TOSTIG (*d.*1066) was Earl of Northumbria from 1055 to 1065. He was the third son of Earl Godwin and the younger brother of Harold. Tostig was probably born about 1025. We first hear of him in 1049 when he was active in naval operations against some Vikings from Ireland. In 1051 he married Judith, the sister of Count Baldwin V of Flanders; thereby becoming the brother-in-law of Duke William of Normandy. It was to Flanders that he accompanied his father when they were exiled in 1051-2. Three years after the family's restoration to the favour of King Edward Tostig was promoted to the earldom of Northumbria. This can be seen simply as part of the aggrandizement of the house of Godwin. It can also be interpreted as a daring political initiative on the part of the king. Northumbria had never been governed by a man from southern England. Tostig was brave, shrewd and hard. His appointment indicated Edward's intention of bringing a distant and unruly province under much firmer royal control.

Tostig tried hard for ten years but failed, and was ejected by a revolt which set in motion a train of events which were to be fatal not only to Tostig himself but also to the Anglo-Saxon kingdom of England. In the first place, he failed adequately to defend Northumbria from the Scots. In 1057 King Malcolm had finally rid himself of Macbeth and brought all of Scotland under his sway. Enabled thereby to turn his attention southward, he started raiding into England in 1058-9. In 1061, when Tostig was absent on a pilgrimage to Rome, Malcolm again attacked. A contemporary writer favourable to Tostig tells us that he riposted 'as much by cunning schemes as by martial courage and military campaigns'; another way of putting this would be to say that he did not fight back. We need not doubt Tostig's personal courage. There may have been good reasons for preferring diplomacy to force. The trouble was that the Northumbrians expected him to act with the martial heroism of an Uhtred or a Siward. Scottish raids caused destruction and suffering: captives, goods, livestock were being carried off; there may have been territorial losses too. By failing to meet force with force Tostig was falling short in one of his primary duties as Earl of Northumbria.

He failed, secondly, to get on with the people who mattered in the north. For example, in 1056 he was instrumental in the choice of a certain Ethelwine for the important bishopric of Durham. Ethelwine was a southerner like Tostig and he was not welcome to his cathedral community. Tostig and his wife were generous benefactors of Durham. (The quality of the works of art they had to offer can be gauged from the superlative manuscript known as the 'Gospels of Countess Judith', now in the Pierpont Morgan Library in New York, which she commissioned from a southern workshop, possibly Canterbury, between 1051 and 1065.) But generosity may not have outweighed the mishandling of ecclesiastical patronage. As far as the secular aristocracy was concerned, Tostig became involved – perhaps inevitably – in the violent feuds and faction-fighting of the sort that convulsed the families of Uhtred and Thurbrand. In 1063 he had two prominent Northumbrian noblemen murdered; another followed in 1064.

The rebels in 1065 had further grievances. Tostig had 'unjustly laid a heavy tribute on the whole of Northumbria'. It can be shown that Northumbrian tax-assessments were low in the eleventh century. It may be that Tostig simply tried to tax Northumbria as the remainder of the country was taxed. When King Edward was negotiating with the rebels in the autumn of 1065 they insisted that he 'renew the law of King Canute'. Is this an indication that Tostig had introduced new customs – West Saxon law to accompany West Saxon taxation – into his earldom? Possibly. It sounds very much the sort of thing the king may have had in mind in appointing Tostig.

In October 1065 rebellion broke out and Edward was compelled to sacrifice his minister. Tostig went into exile and spent the winter in Flanders. In the following year he attempted a military comeback, necessarily and tragically directed against his brother Harold, who had succeeded the old king in January. In May 1066 he appeared off the Isle of Wight with a fleet, raided the coastal parts of Sussex and occupied Sandwich for a time. Afterwards he made his way northwards, harrying in Norfolk on the way, until he landed in northern Lincolnshire. There he was defeated by the English defence forces, and fled to Scotland where he spent the summer. It is likely that he had already entered into negotiations with Harald Hardrada, King of Norway, with a view to joining his projected invasion of England.

The Norwegian fleet appeared in English waters towards the end of the summer, and Tostig joined it. The sequel is well known. After a hard-fought battle at Fulford on 20 September Harald of Norway and Tostig occupied the city of York. They then withdrew to Stamford Bridge to await hostages. There they were surprised by Harold of England on 25 September. The invaders were decisively defeated. Both Harald and Tostig were killed.

TOWNSHEND, CHARLES, 2nd VISCOUNT TOWNSHEND (1674-1738), statesman, inherited a considerable position in Norfolk. His father, Sir Horatio had been rewarded with a peerage for the part he played in the restoration of Charles II. After Eton and King's Charles entered politics an ardent Whig, like his neighbour Robert Walpole, whose sister Dorothy he married in 1713. He was given the task of conducting the negotiations of Gertrudenberg with the French and Dutch in 1709. The Anglo-Dutch treaty of that year, which provided for Dutch military help if the Hanoverian cause seemed in danger, greatly pleased the future George I. Townshend was marked for promotion and it came with his appointment in 1714 to be Secretary of State for the north. At first he was held to be the leading man in the administration, but the less experienced Stanhope soon emerged as the dominant influence. The aims of the two men did not differ widely; to undo any ill effects of the peace of Utrecht abroad and to consolidate the dynasty at home was their common purpose. In 1715 Townshend showed himself to be both zealous and thorough. His measures, the arrest for example of Sir William Wyndham, helped to keep the country calm. He never lacked moral courage nor shrank from decisions. His faults were rather over-hastiness at times and obstinacy. He lacked subtlety; once set on a course he would not easily be deflected.

Townshend shared in the achievement of the Triple Alliance, but delays in the completion of the treaty with France were the ostensible cause of his dismissal, in the polite form of preferment to Ireland, in December 1716. The breach was the predictable consequence of power shared between two men of strong will, before the notion of a prime minister had come to be accepted. It was exacerbated by the long absence of George I in Hanover and his inability to distinguish, as it seemed to Townshend and Walpole, between his duty as King of England and inclination as Elector of Hanover. Townshend was concerned about the rise of Russia and wanted the maritime powers and the emperor to agree on terms to end the protracted Northern War and re-establish a balance between Sweden and Russia. George was bent on securing Bremen and Verden and regarded Townshend's advice as unrealistic. The slowness of communications between Germany and London gave rise to misunderstandings on both sides. Townshend was only three months in Ireland before he joined Walpole in the stimulating business of opposition. This was effective enough, especially in the matter of the Peerage Bill, to convince Stanhope that there must be reconciliation. In 1720 the brothers-in-law returned to minor office, Townshend as President of the Council. Early in 1721 he took his former office as Secretary of State, vacated by the death of Stanhope. For the rest of the decade his was the guiding spirit in foreign affairs. Till 1724 he worked with Carteret, then virtually on his own.

During this period he had to deal with the stresses which arose, despite the existence of the Quadruple Alliance, over the claims of France, Spain and the emperor. Spain sought to recover Gibraltar and to assert her claims in Italy, the emperor to maintain himself in Italy and to promote the activities of the Ostend Company which was so unpopular with English merchants. After 1726, when Cardinal Fleury replaced Bourbon as first minister, Fleury sought *rapprochement* with Spain

and started to wriggle away from his commitments to England. Townshend stood firm on the French alliance and backed English trading and strategic interest wherever he saw them threatened. In 1725 the Spanish minister Ripperda came to terms with the emperor, Charles VI, in the Treaty of Vienna; secret clauses promised mutual support in the matter of the Ostend Company and Gibraltar. Townshend's principal concern was to destroy the former and keep the latter. By the Alliance of Hanover, Prussia was detached from the emperor and brought into line with England and France. In 1727 the Spanish embarked on the siege of Gibraltar. War was not declared but Townshend moved confidently towards it: parliament voted the taxes and Holland was sympathetic, attracted by Townshend's proposal for a partition of the Austrian Netherlands between Holland and France. Charles VI drew back and accepted a seven-year suspension of the Ostend Company. Negotiations for a permanent settlement began in 1728 at Soissons; while Townshend fretted at the formalities and delays, Walpole and Newcastle undermined his position. In 1729 the Treaty of Seville was signed. It was essentially Walpole's treaty, through the agency of Newcastle in his capacity as Secretary of State for the south. In return for support of Spain's claims in the Italian Duchies, the privileges of the *Asiento* were to be restored. The prospect of war receded but the rift between Walpole and Townshend had opened too wide. The land tax had risen to 4s. in the £. Walpole was alarmed by the cost of Townshend's subsidies, by Hessian troops and the mobilized fleets. He scented political danger at home; Townshend had become a liability. He could also see that Townshend was playing into the deceptively gentle hands of Fleury by his tough line with Austria. The disgruntled minister resigned in May 1730 when he found that the king preferred Newcastle's despatch to his. Significantly no colleague went with him. Walpole marked the change of direction by signing the second Treaty of Vienna with the emperor. So the Stanhope-Townshend policy of entente with France gave way to the older Whig conception of alliance with Austria and Holland.

To his credit Townshend left office no richer than he entered it. After his dismissal he had no further dealings with Walpole but left politics to return to his estates in Norfolk. His largeness of mind may seem admirable – but it has to be said that he had little choice. George II did not respect him as his father had done. He had neither taste nor patience for the political game; it is noteworthy that he had served no apprenticeship in the Commons. He had no party, little electoral interest. Newcastle had it in abundance and had used it to isolate Townshend. Walpole is open to the charge of ingratitude, but he had personal as well as political reasons for his actions. Dorothy's death in 1726 had removed the last personal tie between the two men. Walpole, relishing power, did not brook rivals easily. Townshend, who has still found no biographer, could be both peremptory and patronizing: Walpole was a squire, he a peer. Honest himself, restrained in his private life, he could not fail to disapprove of the blatant style of Walpole, whose great palace at Houghton, only a few miles away, outshone even his own stately Raynham. Ultimately however it came down to politics. There could be no real sharing of responsibility with Walpole. It was less surprising that the breach occurred than that it had not happened earlier.

'All Townshend's turnips and all Grosvenor's mines.' Pope's line recalls the source of Townshend's latter fame. Both the planting of turnips and the marling of light soils were established farming practices in the eastern counties and 'Turnip' Townshend's contribution to Norfolk agriculture was less as innovator than as advertisement for the four-course rotation of wheat, barley, clover and turnips. With so distinguished an advocate for the root crops that cleaned the ground and kept sheep and cattle in good winter condition, it can still be said that farming was improved by the enforced retirement of this energetic statesman.

Further Reading

J. Black, *British Foreign Policy in the Age of Walpole*, 1985.
Paul Langford, *Modern British Foreign Policy. The Eighteenth Century*, 1976.
L. B. Namier, *Charles Townshend*, 1964.
F. S. Oliver, *The Endless Adventure, 1710-35*, 3 vols, 1930-5.

TOWNSHEND, CHARLES (1725-67), son of the third Viscount Townshend and grandson of Walpole's able colleague, is as puzzling to historians as he was to his contemporaries. His career was throughout inconsistent, his character impetuous and unstable; his talents were formidable, his achievements meagre.

From his boyhood he suffered from some physical disability, hard to diagnose from his correspondence but very probably epilepsy. After adolescence he suffered bouts of malaise; under the sparkling guise of a buoyant personality there seems to have been much suffering from what he called his 'crazy constitution'. He lived uncertainly poised between sanity and disaster, between brilliance and breakdown. His parents were separated after he was fifteen, and he stayed thereafter with his father, an intelligent man but oppressive and demanding. Charles did not go to Eton, but later went to Clare College, Cambridge and subsequently to Leyden. He studied thereafter for the Bar at Lincoln's Inn, but in 1747 he was returned to parliament as MP for Great Yarmouth, where his family had influence. In 1755 he married Lady Dalkeith, eight years older than he, a lady of ample fortune. He was already, by then, a junior minister with a place on the Admiralty Board and soon became known as an expert in the affairs of the navy, the

colonies and especially America. The effects of this mastery of affairs were, however, diminished by his performances in parliament though, as Horace Walpole tells us, his speeches appealed to an assembly which relished fine phrases: 'Charles Townshend astonishes: but was far too severe to persuade, and too bold to convince … He only spoke to show how well he could adorn a bad cause, or demolish a good one,' he said of one characteristic effort. Nobody knew on what side of the House he would be at the end of the debate. He could speak with 'infinite rapidity, vehemence and parts' but his very brilliance aroused mistrust.

In October 1759 Newcastle, reshuffling his ministry, was tempted to make him Chancellor of the Exchequer 'but there is no depending on him, and his character will not go down in the city or anywhere else'. Yet his abil_ities were such that they compelled attention and in 1761 he was made Secretary at War. He resigned in December 1762, but was made President of the Board of Trade two months later. From now on his gyrations became more erratic, his disloyalty a by-word. He accepted a post under Grenville, attacked his measures, resigned and then, in the last year of Grenville's administration, accepted the post of Paymaster-General: he retained this office under Rockingham but it did not inhibit him from attacking him likewise. Meanwhile he was gravitating towards Chatham and was rewarded by the post of Chancellor of the Exchequer in his administration of 1766.

He may have commended himself to Chatham by his interest in American affairs – fatal irony as it was to turn out – but he was surely the most ill-fitting piece in the 'tesselated pavement' of Burke's famous description. Chatham soon fell ill and left the ministers virtually without guidance. Townshend, in 1767, produced a scheme to tax the colonies and mend the mother-country's finances, which was reasonable in theory but calamitous in practice. It is fair to him to emphasize that there was a problem. When critics of the government forced through a reduction in the Land Tax from 4s. to 3s. alternative revenue had to be found. A few weeks before, Townshend had boasted that he knew of a way to raise money from America; it seems that when pressed to disclose his plan he hastily worked out the idea of Customs duties on American imports. The colonists had said, during their resistance to the Stamp Act, that they would only accept taxes regulating trade; under this guise taxes that were obviously designed to raise revenue were concealed as duties on lead, glass, paper, painters' colours and tea imported from Britain. They could hardly have done more harm, for as taxes on British exports they raised protests at home, while across the Atlantic they symbolized Britain's determination to turn the Declaratory Act into hard cash. By asserting that the yield might help to pay executive officials in

America Townshend implied that he sought to make Americans more dependent upon the British government. 'Champagne Charlie', the handsome, reckless, bombastic minister, came to epitomize the arrogance of British government to Americans, who were already in a mood to question the whole relationship between their states and the mother-country. The Massachusetts circular drafted by Samuel Adams called upon all colonists to resist the duties. Having bequeathed this fruitful source of discord to the two great English-speaking peoples, Charles Townshend died suddenly on 4 September 1767, leaving his affairs in great disorder.

He was a lonely man; several of his closest intimates were disreputable men – like Theobald Taffe, professional gambler and swindler. He never gave himself a chance. Posturing and mimicry contributed to an impression of a man who was not to be relied on. The purpose of the statesman was lost in the turns of the clown. Paradoxically he was consistent in his most unfortunate act: the scheme of 1767 was that which he had first mooted as a junior minister in 1753. His last months were tragic in course and consequence; yet the comic image persists. Since he ridiculed his colleagues he was distrusted by them all. He could not have lasted much longer in office. To the end he joked about death, as naturally as he used to do about living. He was capable of tenderness as well as bravery, showed concern for the well-being of his children and he worked, without success, for legislation to improve the condition of the insane, whose fate, we may feel, his might so easily have been.

Further Reading
Sir Lewis Namier and John Brooke, *Charles Townshend*, 1964.

TRELAWNY, SIR JONATHAN, 3rd BARONET

(1650-1721), one of the Seven Bishops, was born at Pelynt, in Cornwall, son of a royalist who had suffered sequestration and imprisonment in the Civil War, and was educated at Westminster and Christ Church. In 1685 he was prominent in calling out the Cornish militia against Monmouth, and later in that year became Bishop of Bristol. A Tory churchman like Compton, he opposed both James II's Declarations of Indulgence and stood trial as one of the Seven in 1688. It seems likely that the famous refrain of his fellow Cornishmen,

> And shall Trelawny die?
> Then twenty thousand Cornishmen
> Will know the reason why

echoed what their grandfathers had sung sixty years before when the first Trelawny baronet was sent to the Tower by the Commons for opposing Sir John Eliot. When the Revolution came, Trelawny was one of the two bishops to oppose the Regency plan, and one of the only two of the Seven who swore allegiance to the new sovereigns. In 1689 he was translated to Exeter. Under William and Anne he was a prominent High Churchman, emphatic in stressing his power and dignity and hostile to the latitudinarian opinions of most of his fellow bishops. His importance was more political than ecclesiastical, for he had great electoral interests in Cornwall, claiming, for example, in 1702 to have returned eleven members for the government. In 1705 he deserted the 'High Tory' cause and lent his support to the Whig and moderate candidates pledged to support his fellow Cornishman Godolphin, and he was rewarded in 1707 by promotion to the see of Winchester. In 1713, after Godolphin's death, his electoral weight was exerted on behalf of Harley's followers, and he was a firm champion of the Hanoverian Succession. More convivial than spiritual, eminent by birth and territorial power rather than by learning, Trelawny represented a type of patriotic Anglicanism which played a significant role in the great decisions of 1688 and 1714.

TREVISA, MASTER JOHN (*d.*1402) is 'notable as an early translator of Latin works into English'. He was a Cornishman by birth and retained his Cornish contacts and interest in Cornwall whilst making his career elsewhere. He attended Oxford University, where he graduated as a Master of Arts. As a west-countryman he was a Fellow of Exeter College from about 1361 until 1369, when he became a Fellow of Queen's College, and was ordained in 1370. In 1379 he was expelled from Queen's College as unworthy with the provost and other Fellows. It was perhaps then that he entered the service of his patron Lord Berkeley, 'who may be called Thomas the Magnificent'. It was he, who by 1387 had made Trevisa vicar of Berkeley. About 1389 Trevisa also became a canon of the college of Westbury-upon-Trym. Although normally resident at Berkeley and the confidant of Lord Berkeley, whose castle was a stone's throw from his parish church, Trevisa was apparently absent for prolonged periods. He was presumably at Oxford in 1382-6 and 1394-6, when he rented rooms at Queen's College, probably to facilitate access to the works he was translating. Again about 1390 he travelled abroad, visiting Aachen and 'Ayges in Savoy', perhaps Aix-en-Provence.

Until the late fourteenth century Latin was the language of the church, learning and formal documents, and French was the language of the court and aristocracy. The first use of the English language in these contexts dates from the 1370s and 1380s and coincides with the poetic achievements of Chaucer, Langland, Gower and the Gawain poet. About 1385 Trevisa records that aristocrats were beginning to speak English to their children and that pupils at grammar schools were speaking English rather than French. These developments implied that educated people would be unable to read French in future and foreshadowed the enormous expansion of English usage in the next century. Encouraged and perhaps even persuaded by Lord Berkeley, Trevisa therefore set out to make 'famous works available to those who knew no Latin' (Gransden). His principal achievements were his translations of Higden's *Polychronicon* and Bartholomew Glanville's *De Proprietatibus Rerum*, 'the biggest encyclopaedia and the biggest history he could find'. The *Polychronicon* of Ranulph Higden, monk of Chester, was a vast universal chronicle from the Creation to 1360. Trevisa's continuation of it, though highly derivative and of little independent value, foreshadows 'the rise of the vernacular chronicle … the most remarkable historiographical development in the fifteenth century' (Gransden). These enormous projects were achievements enough for any translator, but Trevisa certainly tackled other works and yet more have been attributed to him. He did translate the apocryphal gospel of Nicodemus and was associated with the Lollard translation of the Bible at a time before Bible translation was condemned as heretical. He also favoured preaching in English and translated an anti-mendicant sermon by Archbishop FitzRalph, a choice which suggests a commitment to church reform that fell short of heresy.

Trevisa's original work was slight. His translations had no stylistic pretensions, but were clear, workmanlike and readable. They were also marred by frequent errors. His works were not widely read, far fewer copies surviving of his translation of the *Polychronicon* than of the Latin original, so his campaign of popularization achieved limited success. His significance does not rest however either in his popularity or the quality of his works, 'but in their interest as early examples of English prose' (Kingsford).

Further Reading
B. Cottle, *Triumph of English 1350-1400*, 1969.

TREVITHICK, RICHARD (1771-1833), engineer and inventor, designed the first efficient railway locomotive. Faults of temperament, shortage of capital and a run of bad luck combined to cheat him of the fame and fortune which he surely deserved. When he died, in relative poverty and obscurity, the 'railway age' had begun.

The son of a mining engineer who was himself a noted expert in pumping machinery, Trevithick was a wayward boy and a problem to his parents and teachers. He showed signs of the impulsiveness that was to mar his career. But he also displayed an inventive capacity that was perhaps all the stronger for his lack of formal education. His physical strength became a legend among the hardy miners of Illogan and Camborne. On one occasion he lifted a cast iron pump weighing nearly a ton; on another he threw a ball over Camborne's church tower, standing near enough, it was said, to touch the base with his foot! Equally impressive were his repairs and improvements to mining machinery. In this practical

school, where necessity was indeed mother of invention, and where there was fierce competition between designers for valuable orders of pumping and other machines, Trevithick learned to think boldly. He invented an improved stationary steam engine with the high pressure that James Watt had been afraid to use because of his fear of explosions, but which was necessary if locomotion were to be achieved.

Trevithick was only thirteen when Murdock set his tiny model locomotive chuffing along a footpath by Redruth church. Murdock became discouraged about the feasibility of steam traction but Trevithick realized that his own more powerful engine, running on rails, had a promising future. Claims are hard to disentangle, but most authorities accept that Trevithick's tramway travelling engine, at Penydarron in south Wales, was the true pioneer of railway engines. Trevithick went there to construct a forge engine, then he designed (about 1801) this engine for transporting metal from the furnace to the forge. Owing to the weakness of the lines and the breaking of tram plates it was eventually relegated to the role of a stationary engine; but not before its use had been justified beyond doubt.

Between 1804 and 1808 Trevithick was busy erecting high pressure stationary engines. In the latter year, however, he set up a circular railway in a field near the site of the future Euston station. Here, for a shilling, adventurous Londoners could travel behind 'Catch me who Can', a steam engine which regularly ran at twelve miles per hour. When a rail broke and the engine ploughed off into soft ground, Trevithick, who was already embarrassed by the failure of a scheme to construct a driftway under the Thames, abandoned his experiment. In 1812 we find him urging the merits of his steam engines for agricultural purposes. It seemed a wild idea at the time but his estimate of the use of steam for ploughing and threshing was both realistic and prophetic. In 1816 he went to Lima to work on the restoration of silver mines by using modern pumping machinery. Revolutionary disorders eventually destroyed Trevithick's machines and his brilliant prospects. Pressed into the army, he promptly invented a new gun! Between 1822 and 1826 he was engaged in mining operations in Costa Rica.

Trevithick was returning destitute to England when, by extraordinary chance, he met Robert Stephenson, in an inn at Cartagena. The younger man, whose father, George, was already establishing himself as a railway engineer, was destined to win fame and wealth in the 'railway age' that was to transform Britain's countryside, society and economy. Trevithick was to end in a pauper's grave at Dartford. His last years had been spent in typically bold schemes. Just before his death he designed a gilded cast-iron column, that was to be twice the height of the Great Pyramid, to celebrate the passing of the Great Reform Bill.

Further Reading
H. W. Dickinson and A. Titley, *Richard Trevithick*, 1934.

TROLLOPE, ANTHONY (1815-82) novelist, was the fourth son of Thomas Trollope, a barrister and Fellow of New College: a sound scholar, solemnly aware of being of good family, he cherished unrealistic expectations for his sons. An upright and conscientious man, but stiff, humourless and cross-tempered, Thomas made few friends – and received few briefs. Disillusioned, he turned to farming, for which he was scarcely qualified, on Lord Northwick's estate on Harrow Hill. Desperate, he would venture all on a plan to set up a commercial emporium in Cincinnati. Beside debts, his legacy was three forgotten numbers, with a pile of unfinished sheets, of the *Encyclopaedia Ecclesiastica*, his last venture. Anthony, author of forty-seven books, himself a generous, much disappointed father, recognized tragedy and was sparing in reproach. He attributed his unhappy boyhood to 'a mixture of poverty and gentle standing on the part of my father'. He would recall the recurring agony of his father's headaches: 'but he was never idle except when suffering.' Thomas reappears in *Ralph the Heir*, in the poignant figure of Sir Thomas Underwood, the reclusive chancery lawyer, aged sixty: it was Thomas Trollope's age at death.

'There ain't nowt a man can't bear if he only be dogged. It's dogged as does it. It ain't thinking about it.' So the author had Giles Hoggett say to Mr Crawley. The schoolboy had need of such philosophy. Sent to Harrow aged seven, he was still the youngest in the school when removed to a local private school. At twelve he went to Winchester, his father's school, to join his eldest brother Thomas; there he was bullied, and remained so unpromising a scholar that he had to come back, at fifteen, for another three years at Harrow. So far from moving along the expected path to a fellowship at New College, he was back where he had started – and worse, because his mother was in America and his father had moved to a tumble-down farmhouse at Wealdstone. Twice daily he had to tramp some three miles to Harrow Hill, and back, to be spurned at school for his dirty clothes and skulking manner. His *Autobiography* reveals how painful was the gap between his father's pretensions and the isolation of his days, framed by 'the horror of those dreadful walks': had he a right, 'a wretched farmer's boy, reeking from a dunghill, to sit next to the sons of peers …'? In 1827, influenced by her friend Fanny Wright, aflame with utopian idealism, his mother had gone to America. Her experience resembled, in the shock of disappointment, and exposure to the cruder kind of American, that of Dickens's *Martin Chuzzlewit*. Out of it came *The Domestic Manners of the Americans* (1832). It enjoyed a *succès d'estime*: 'Her volumes,' wrote her grateful son, 'were very bitter; but they were

very clever, and they saved the family from ruin.' Good-humoured, resourceful, a comfort and inspiration, Frances Trollope would sometimes be called vulgar. Like the worldly Dean Lovelace's in *Is he Popenjoy?*, there was 'trade' in her vicar father's family: Anthony was early taught to recognize the nuances of class distinction. Hers was a bracing example. Adversity taught her to act for herself.

Creditors closed in again after the family had moved back to their previous house on Harrow Hill. To evade the bailiffs, they decamped to Bruges. Fanny wrote romantic novels to sustain the forlorn household. Trollope's elder brother Henry died there of tuberculosis; there too, his father, 'broken-hearted', succumbed. His sister Emily would soon follow. Trollope saluted his mother's devotion and courage: he 'never saw equalled' the power by which she sustained, despite her nursing of three sick people, the flow of writing which paid the bills. She wrote novels, romantic or concerned with social problems, and books about her extensive travels. Eventually she settled with her son Thomas in Florence; there she died, aged eighty-four. Anthony did not follow her in the didactic vein but he had learned much from his mother. From her feud with the zealous Vicar of Harrow, Doctor Cunningham, surely came his distaste for the more inflexible kind of evangelical. Sensitive to religious feeling, respectful towards sound practice, the creator of Mr Slope had a keen eye for hypocrisy. From Frances's uncritical espousal of 'good causes', he derived, perhaps, his scorn for 'the shrieking sisterhood'. Mainly he learned that honesty, toil and generosity make for happiness: it is the wholesome, recurring theme of his novels.

When in Belgium, he was offered a commission in an Austrian cavalry regiment. Fortunately his was to be a more humdrum future. With a good fortune little appreciated at the time he secured a clerkship in the General Post Office in London: he served it from 1834 to 1867. He was frequently at odds with Sir Rowland Hill, author of the Penny Post which so enlarged its operations. Business brought out a tiresome side, a loud, blustering manner. He could however take pride in his work. He did more than any other official to create the country-wide network of collection and delivery. His travels, mainly on horseback, provided him with a unique chance to observe English society. First he had to escape from London and the lonely life of a bachelor living on £90 a year: it would reappear in *The Three Clerks*. The chance came with his posting to the south-west of Ireland as deputy postal surveyor.

Ireland was most important to Trollope. He had leisure to study the people and to appreciate their hospitality. He took to hunting. 'I have ever since been constant to the sport … I have written … on no subject with such delight as on that of hunting.' Reflecting on a favourite passage (perhaps that in *The American Senator*) where Trollope, heavy, short-sighted but possessed of 'good hands', is in the saddle again, evoking the scents and sounds of a winter's morning, many readers will feel grateful. He would fit his postal business to the local meets and turn up in post offices dressed for the chase. 'FREE TO HUNT': so he opened his diary for 1868, the year which saw his emancipation from the Post Office. Meanwhile Irish hunting introduced him to the lives both of the gentry and the ordinary people. He found his way to turn boyish daydreams to stories of real life. His first novel, *The Macdermots of Ballycloran*, with his later Irish novels, *The Kellys and the O'Kellys*, *Castle Richmond* and *The Landleaguers*, have but recently received their critical due: from the start Trollope showed himself to be a writer of rare skill and intuitive sympathy with different kinds of people. Now he found stability and happiness in marriage.

Rose Heseltine was the daughter of a Yorkshire bank manager, subsequently ruined after he had used bank funds to invest in a local railway. Behind the sorry episode loomed the figure of Hudson, the 'railway king': in generalized style he was to be Melmotte, the mysterious financier in *The Way We Live Now*. Rose would bear two sons and share staunchly in the difficult years before successful authorship and domestic plenty. Apart from an infatuation with the young American, Kate Field, who would provide a model for the attractive young women of his later novels, nothing would much disturb his emotional equilibrium. Rose remains an elusive figure, to be traced mainly in Trollope's appreciative references to the married state, woman's assumed goal; to bring doubt and hesitation, as to Clara in the *Belton Estate*; to be jealously competed for, as in Trollope's most disturbing essay in psychological analysis, *He Knew He Was Right* (1869). In his later novels Trollope could show that he was in advance of public feeling. He first became famous, however, by his success in creating an imagined world, Barchester, which was central to the interests of many readers and which 'revealed his complete appreciation of the usual' (Henry James).

Before returning to Ireland in 1855, Trollope spent two and a half years in the west of England. 'In this way I had an opportunity of seeing a considerable portion of Great Britain, with a minuteness which few have enjoyed.' One evening, in Salisbury he 'conceived the story of *The Warden*'. In Belfast, in 1856, he completed it. In 1867 *The Last Chronicle of Barset* was published, sixth and last in the series. By then, in *Can You Forgive Her?* (1864) he had introduced some of the cast of his political novels and, with the marriage of Plantagenet Palliser, future Duke of Omnium, to Lady Glencora, had laid the foundation for further stories centring upon two people, as wittily and as compassionately described as any in his repertoire. He had also written eight other

novels, notably *Orley Farm*, none without merit. He had settled to the discipline which he describes in the *Autobiography*. 'It was my practice to be at my table every morning at 5.30 a.m.; and it was also my practice to allow myself no mercy': there, with watch before him, he would read the previous day's production, then write his day's allowance, '250 words every quarter of an hour'. Published after his death, the *Autobiography* would harm his reputation because of his brisk treatment of the mechanics of writing. Meanwhile his reliability made him a prime choice for the editors of the literary magazines: *Framley Parsonage* grew from the proposal that he write for *Cornhill*.

He could command a high fee: £2,800 for example, for *The Claverings* (1866-7). Money was important. It enabled him to set up his sons as New Zealand sheep farmer and publisher respectively (neither venture prospered). We may believe him however when he asserts: 'though the money has been sweet, the respect, the friendships, and the mode of life which has been achieved, have been much sweeter.' There was a conscious moral purpose in Trollope's use of the term 'gentleman' to express his ideal. He delighted in his fictional worlds and in characters whom, like Archdeacon Grantly or Mary Thorne, he came to enjoy as if a member of the family. His likes are infectious, his dislikes compelling. What would we not give to meet Lady Glencora or to avoid Mr Scarborough? There is compassionate insight in his handling of characters whose plight he could understand: Mr Crawley, perpetual curate of Hogglestock, 'ruined' Carry Brattle. He could understand how people could be trapped by their history, like his first Irish characters, Thady and Feemy. Every experience provided grist to his mill. Convinced that to be in parliament would be the height of felicity (and mark of recognition?), he submitted himself, in 1867, to the electorate of Beverley, failed to secure enough of their venal votes – and erected a monument to the borough's infamy in the pages of *Ralph the Heir* (1871). In 1859, having left Ireland and been made superintendent of the eastern district, he settled at Waltham Cross. Travelling on special missions never dampened his enthusiasm: on a voyage to Egypt, in 1858, he wrote *Doctor Thorne*. The work completed, the next day he embarked on *The Bertrams*. He loved his work: 'There is no human bliss,' he wrote, 'equal to twelve hours of work with only six hours in which to do it.'

After his beloved Thackeray's death, Trollope held George Eliot to be first among contemporary novelists but he offered several self-revealing criticisms: 'Her imagination ... acts in analysing rather than creating.' In the later works: 'the philosopher so greatly overtops the portrait painter, that in the dissection of the mind, the outward signs seem to have been forgotten ... She struggles too hard to do work that shall be excellent.

She lacks ease.' Trollope did not lack ease and he knew his limitations. *La Vendée* was to be his first and last historical novel. His ease led sometimes into the commonplace. Several novels, like the serenely charming *Ayala's Angel*, are self-indulgent, slow-paced. Writing fluently, he corrected little. Yet few today would say that he wrote too much. Though his admirers included Newman, James and Tolstoy, his reputation was sinking during his last decade and it plummeted after his death. It began to revive with critical reassessment after the First World War. Modern times have brought yearning to rediscover the comforts and certainties of Barsetshire, the political world of a confident aristocracy. Of the great British novelists, he is among the most read. He set out to entertain and instruct. He succeeded.

Further Reading
Victoria Glendinning, *Anthony Trollope*, 1992.
N. J. Hall, *Anthony Trollope*, 1991.
A. Trollope, *Autobiography*, 1883.

TUDOR, JASPER, DUKE OF BEDFORD and EARL OF PEMBROKE (*c.*1431-95) outlasted the Yorkist dynasty that he had resisted for quarter of a century. Born at Hatfield in Hertfordshire, he was the second son of Katherine of France (*d.*1437), youngest daughter of Charles VI of France and dowager-queen of Henry V, by Owen (ap Maredudd ap) Tudor (*d.*1461), one of her Welsh servants. Their other children were Edmund, the eldest; Owen, who became a monk; and a daughter, who died in infancy. A statute of 1427-8 forbade the queen to marry, so her wedding was secret. Her children were discovered only on her premature death, when the Abbess of Barking took charge of them and their father was severely punished. They were half-brothers of King Henry VI, who had not many close relatives, and were abruptly called from obscurity in 1452, knighted, and created earls, Edmund, Earl of Richmond and Jasper, Earl of Pembroke. They were generously endowed with lands worth about £900 a year, which rose to £1,500 for Jasper when Edmund died in 1456. Edmund's child-bride, the great Lancastrian heiress Margaret Beaufort, bore him one posthumous son in 1457: Henry Tudor, the future Henry VII. Jasper remained a bachelor until after his nephew's accession.

Although their elevation was designed to buttress the ailing Lancastrian dynasty, the Tudor brothers did not equate their obligation of allegiance with support for the king's favourites and backed the Duke of York as Protector in 1454. Although Jasper took the king's side at the battle of St Albans in 1455, it was apparently on York's authority that Edmund was sent to restore order in Wales later that year. When York was dismissed as Protector in 1456, his retainers seized Edmund at Carmarthen and briefly imprisoned him before he died.

Jasper then took Edmund's place, restoring order and building up his own power in Wales, which he turned against the rebel Yorkists in 1459-61. His levies were defeated by the future Edward IV at Mortimer's Cross and he was still in Wales when the decisive battle of Towton was fought.

During the 1460s Jasper was a leading figure in Queen Margaret of Anjou's continued resistance. From Wales he proceeded to Scotland, to France to conclude a treaty, back to Scotland and the garrison of Bamburgh Castle, which capitulated on terms late in 1462. As he could not secure Henry VI's restoration, Jasper returned to Scotland, visited France and the north again, and was in Brittany in 1464 and France thereafter. In 1468 King Louis XI, his first cousin, backed an invasion of Wales, which reached Denbigh before it was defeated. Harlech Castle fell and the Lancastrian cause was hopelessly lost.

In 1470 Edward IV's erstwhile supporter Warwick the Kingmaker rebelled, was expelled from England, and agreed to restore Henry VI to his Crown. Jasper Tudor joined in the successful invasion, recovered his earldom and lands, and was recruiting in Wales in 1471, when the decisive battles were fought. Henry VI and his son were killed, Queen Margaret was a prisoner, and Jasper therefore resumed his interrupted exile, this time in Brittany and accompanied by his nephew Henry Tudor. The two Tudors represented unfinished business for Edward IV, who schemed for their return, but represented no real threat until Richard III usurped the throne and the princes in the Tower, his obvious rivals, disappeared. As in 1471, Henry VII's accession in 1485 owed more to the support of alienated Yorkists than erstwhile Lancastrians, among whom Jasper Tudor was pre-eminent. Now in his mid-fifties, the king's uncle and Duke of Bedford, Jasper stalwartly backed his nephew through his early crises. Married at last, he nevertheless failed to establish a dynasty of his own.

Further Reading
R. A. Griffiths and R. S. Thomas, *The Making of the Tudor Dynasty*, 1985.
R. A. Griffiths, *The Reign of King Henry VI 1422-61*, 1981.

TULL, JETHRO (1674-1741), writer and pioneer in agricultural matters, was an original and significant figure. Though it is no longer the fashion to see the agricultural revolution of the eighteenth century in terms of a few heroic leaders and developers, and though Tull's role remains controversial, his inventive career deserves notice. An Oxford man and a barrister who became a bencher of Gray's Inn in 1724, he became interested in seed drills when he was farming at Howberry near Wallingford. About 1701 he produced his horse-drawn drill, an improvement on the earlier model of Worlidge sixty years before. In his advocacy of sowing in drills rather than broadcast, and of hoeing regularly between the rows to produce a fine tilth and destroy weeds, he was rather a popularizer than an innovator. He was attacked for plagiarism. But he travelled extensively abroad, noting foreign methods and produced a series of treatises, notably *Horse-hoeing Husbandry* in 1733, which were influential. He could be quite wrong, as when he said that his pulverizing method would remove the need to practise crop rotation. But he was far from being a mere crank. The natural conservatism of farmers was leavened by inquiring spirits such as his. It remains to add, however, that he made more money by his books than by his husbandry at his own 'Prosperous Farm'.

Further Reading

G. E. Fussell, *Jethro Tull: his Influence on Mechanized Agriculture*, 1973.

TUNSTAL, CUTHBERT (1474-1559), Bishop of Durham, was born at Hackforth in Richmondshire (i.e. Yorkshire) in 1474. He was the son of Thomas Tunstal by his second wife, the daughter of Sir John Conyers, whom he did not marry until some years after the birth of the son. In 1491, at the age of seventeen, Cuthbert went to Oxford to Balliol College, but owing to an outbreak of the plague he left Oxford and migrated to Trinity College, Cambridge, where he stayed until 1499, when he travelled abroad to Padua. At Oxford he knew More, Grocyn, Linacre and Colet, and his chief academic interest was in mathematics. He became a Fellow of Trinity, and when he was at Padua he met some of the Renaissance leaders, such as the printer and publisher, Aldus Manutius. He was at Padua for six years and returned to England in 1505, after a visit to Rome.

By this time Tunstal certainly knew Greek and Hebrew; 'he was a very eloquent Rhetorician, a passing skilful mathematician (famous especially for Arithmetic, whereof he writ a work much esteemed), a great lawyer … and a profound divine' (Bishop Godwin). He was not ordained until 1509, but (as was quite usual) even before this preferments had been showered on him, so that he was both Prebendary of Lincoln and Archdeacon of Chester. In 1515 Warham made him his chancellor, and Tunstal's public life had begun. For the next seven years he was for the most part employed on diplomatic work. In 1521 he went on an embassy to the emperor, Charles V; the Lutheran movement was beginning, and Tunstal came away with a very bad impression of what he had seen of the Reformation in Germany. In 1522 Warham appointed him Bishop of London because 'he was a man of so good learning, virtue, and sadness, which shall be right meet and convenient to entertain ambassadors and other noble strangers at that notable and honorable city in the absence of the king's most noble grace'.

In 1522 he published his work on arithmetic, *De Arte Supputendi*, which he dedicated to his best friend, Sir Thomas More. This was the first work wholly on arithmetic to be printed in England, but it was never translated into English, and of its eight editions only the first was printed at home.

In 1523 Tunstal was made Keeper of the Privy Seal and he was now one of the most important civil and ecclesiastical servants of the Crown. But he did not neglect his diocese, where he set about dealing with a revival of Lollardy under the influence of the Lutherans. He had already in 1523 refused Tyndale's application to become one of his chaplains. Now in 1526 he prohibited various heretical books, including copies of Tyndale's New Testament. Three years later (1529), so determined was he to root out heresy, he bought up all the copies he could find of Tyndale's book in order to burn them. In fact, he only thereby increased the financial profits for Tyndale and enabled him to go ahead with more printings. Tunstal could never be called worldly-wise.

Tunstal remained Bishop of London until 1530: in that year he was translated to Durham by Papal Bull to succeed the fallen Wolsey. He was to hold this see from 1530 to 1552 and again from 1553 to 1559, being deprived in 1552 by Northumberland, reinstated by Mary, and deprived again by Elizabeth in 1559. He was essentially a conservative, in the true meaning of that word. Like nearly all the bishops of his time he accepted quite easily the abolition of the Papal jurisdiction in England: he could not at first accept the Royal Supremacy: but he was a loyal Englishman, and it needed only a tactful letter to bring him round to Henry VIII's point of view. Henry wrote to him that he had no intention of usurping spiritual jurisdiction, and Tunstal was satisfied (1536). In 1530 he had been made the President of the Council of the North. When the Pilgrimage of Grace broke out in 1536 – he described it as 'worse than the Turks' – he fled from Auckland. Tunstal was not a strong man and should never have been made President of the Council of the North, and indeed he lost the job in 1537.

When Edward VI came to the throne, Tunstal conformed to most of the ecclesiastical changes up to the time of Northumberland. But like many conscientious and generous-minded men, anxious to be reasonable, there was a point beyond which Tunstal could not be moved. He voted against the First Act of Uniformity and in 1552 he was deprived of his bishopric and imprisoned. It was also in part Northumberland's determination to secure the revenues of the see of Durham for himself and his friends which brought about the final breach between them.

On the accession of Mary I Tunstal was released and reappointed to the see of Durham. He went to Gravesend to welcome Reginald Pole to England, and he was at Mary's right hand at her coronation. When Elizabeth came to the throne (1558), Tunstal took no part in her coronation. In 1559 he refused the Oath of Supremacy and was deprived of his bishopric. He had also refused to take part in the consecration of Matthew Parker as Archbishop of Canterbury. He was inevitably deprived of his see and he was sent to live with Parker, who treated him with the greatest kindness. He died on 18 November 1559. Too often he was a man whose strength of character never quite matched his first-class abilities: but in general he preserved holiness in very unholy times.

Further Reading
L. Baldwin Smith, *Tudor Prelates and Politics*, 1953.
C. Sturge, *Cuthbert Tunstal*, 1934.
G. H. Ross-Lewin in *Typical English Churchmen*, 1909.

TURNER, JOSEPH MALLORD WILLIAM (1775-1851) would be named by many people as the greatest of English painters.

A visitor to the Royal Academy in the 1830s, if he went on one of the 'varnishing days' which preceded the annual exhibition, would have observed an elderly gentleman with a deep-weathered complexion and sharp, restless eyes under a tall, black hat; a black tail-coat, with the sleeves too long, surrounds his stubby body; his prominent nose is almost in contact with his canvas, so closely does he concentrate; and frequently he mutters to himself or makes an unintelligible joke. He has been here since breakfast and he will not leave before dark. He is in a state of constant activity, for he has learnt to rely on these three days in which to finish off his paintings which are to be exhibited. But he is not concerned only with himself: from time to time he will stump about the room, give oracular advice to a young Associate with a gruff 'Humph!' or 'What-r-doing?', and, if he spots a particularly delectable blob of colour on someone else's palette, he is quite likely to scoop it up and transfer it to his own.

The old man will die in the year of the Great Exhibition, leaving to the nation over 200 oil-paintings, no fewer than 19,000 watercolours and drawings, and a fortune which (but for the artifices of lawyers) would have gone to the support of needy artists.

His father was a barber; his mother went mad. Turner himself was born in Covent Garden, and died in Cheyne Walk; and, despite an extraordinary amount of travelling, he remained a Londoner at heart. Ruskin, who, with *Modern Painters* (1843-60) constituted himself Turner's champion at a time when people were finding it harder and harder to understand the master's work, compares in a famous passage (Vol. V) the youth of Giorgione, passed in the golden city of Venice, with that of Turner, spent in the slums of London. Perhaps it was Turner's acquaintance with the broad river, which he loved to frequent, on which he and his father went fishing from a small boat (it is, so far as we know, the only hobby he had), beside which he died, that first awoke in him an almost proprietary sense of the glory of nature.

Another life-long loyalty was to the Royal Academy. He was admitted a student at the Academy Schools in 1789, at the age of fourteen; he first exhibited in the following year; and was elected ARA only nine years later. He was RA in 1802, and Professor of Perspective there from 1808. For a man as solitary as Turner, who refused social ties and latterly lived secretly under an alias, the Academy was an essential anchor of stability and something like a home.

The secrecy in which he enveloped his activities has created special difficulties for his biographers; the earliest of whom (Walter Thornbury, 1861) preferred to give credit to a series of disreputable calumnies about Turner's private life than to believe what has emerged as the truth: that no modern artist has given such single-minded devotion to his work, and that his mysterious shifts were nothing else than an attempt to secure for himself conditions in which he could work with perfect concentration. Thus the story of his life – 'public' or 'private' – is the story of unremitting work. And, because he was capable of working on widely different compositions at the same time, attempts to classify his product, or to divide his life into stages of development, are bound to be imprecise. But certain generalizations can be made.

First, his oil-paintings form a small proportion of his total product. Because he was careless about technique and stored his paintings in alarming conditions of dirt and damp at his gallery in Queen Anne Street, many have lost their original brilliance. Yet their importance as a guide to his aspirations at all times of his maturity, and in particular in the last dazzling years, is indisputable. Watercolour, it is true, most naturally suited the impalpable nature of his imagery; so that, the more he sought to master the use of oils, the more he used them like watercolour. Yet it is the glory of oils that (if handled by a genius) they *can* be used like watercolour, and give an added depth and brilliance. Secondly, his procedure was to travel widely and light, making sketches (but no more) on the site. Scores of notebooks are filled with these precise notations of place and weather; but, perfect as many of them seem, none was intended to be a 'finished' picture. That came later, months or years later, when separate impressions were blended into a careful studio painting, in watercolour or in oils.

Many of his paintings passed to the engraver, or were engraved by Turner himself. The first to be so handled was the great *Shipwreck* of 1805 (Tate Gallery), an oil-painting which shows Turner's early mastery of the violence and depth of ocean. After that appeared by degrees the plates for the *Liber Studiorum* (a conscious imitation of Claude's *Liber Veritatis*), for *The Rivers of England, The Rivers of France*, the illustrations to Rogers's *Italy* and the Waverley Novels, and several other series. So popular were the engravings that copies found their way into the humblest homes. Here was the substance of his livelihood: it helps to explain why he was able to hoard his paintings and even buy them back into his own collection.

Next, it is said that Turner was unhappy in drawing the human figure. That is a just objection: in landscape he could group figures to advantage, but individually his figures are uninteresting and awkward. This can be explained in terms of his preoccupation with nature, or with the equally grand and mysterious impressions derived from the antiquity of buildings. His life shows that he was comparatively indifferent to human society. And Claude, who, along with Rembrandt, was his chief example, had equal difficulty in drawing the human figure.

This deficiency of Turner's work can also be explained in terms of his increasing impatience with mere detail. His artistic life can be seen as a progression from the scrupulous topographical drawing of his youth – when, in the company of Thomas Girtin, he toured the 'picturesque' buildings and scenery of England and Wales and attended that genial patron Dr Monro – to the bewildering, explosive visions of his last phase. These last paintings, although splendid in their breadth, are compounded of numberless stipplings and flakes of colour. So that it is not the case that he dispensed with detail, but rather that he dispensed with the traditional *furniture* of paintings, with detail which did not contribute to the overall effect of elemental mystery. Here was his point of greatest distance from the Pre-Raphaelites, who succeeded him in time; and it is not surprising to find that the human figure was part of the detail with which he desired to dispense.

In this progression there are certain milestones. The first oil-painting he exhibited was *Fishermen at Sea: off the Needles* (1796; on loan to the Tate Gallery). It is of special interest because in it Turner at once displays two themes which were to be characteristic: first, the Rembrandtian theme of local concentrations of light; secondly (and here Turner was attending to the normal facts of vision), the gathering of the interest of the picture into the central oval, leaving the edges undefined. *The Shipwreck* (1805: Tate Gallery) is an exaltation of the same themes.

His first visit to the Alps (in 1802, during the Peace of Amiens) aroused a hunger in him and revealed to him a realm in which he was to do some of his most original work. *The Falls of the Rhine at Schaffhausen* (1806: Boston) and *Snowstorm: Hannibal Crossing the Alps* (1812: Tate) were the mature fruits of the 400 drawings which he brought back – though it is true that the second-named, which in its violence looks forward to his last period, was also derived from a thunderstorm he witnessed on the Yorkshire moors, when he was staying with his friends the Fawkeses at Farnley Hall.

But meanwhile he continued to work in imitation of – or rather in competition with – the Dutch sea-painters and Claude. It was Walter Fawkes who bought *The Dort* (1818), one of the most perfect of Turner's water scenes in the Dutch style. And *Crossing the Brook* (1812: Tate) is a sublime recollection of Claude. But in the 1820s and 1830s Turner began to handle these traditions much more freely. His first visit to Venice (1819) gave him a new insight into the possibilities of water scenery, a view which was to emerge most splendidly in *The Burning of the Houses of Lords and Commons* (1835: Cleveland), *Norham Castle* (1840s: Tate), and the great Venetian watercolours; while his treatment of classical subjects – as *The Bay of Baiae* (1823: Tate) and *Ulysses Deriding Polyphemus* (1829: Tate) – was similarly enriched by his first-hand experience of the Italian landscape.

Another household at which Turner was welcome was that of Lord Egremont at Petworth. He began to paint there in 1809; it was there, in the winter of 1830, at the height of his success, that he filled a sketchbook (now in the British Museum) with the most astonishing series of impressions, high-speed records in watercolour of the Christmas visitors, of the rooms and decorations of the house, and of the winter skies; and it was there, in 1836 or so, that he painted in oils his *Interior at Petworth*, one of the earliest paintings of that final phase during which (in Kenneth Clark's words) 'the idea that the world is made up of solid objects with lines round them ceased to trouble him'.

For that is the characteristic of his final period – form gives place to atmosphere. *The Slave Ship* (1840: Boston) is transitional: the items of the picture, down to the manacled leg in the foreground, are recognizable, but they are used, not so much to tell a story, as to create an overall sense of horror so stark that Ruskin, whose father gave him the picture, could not live with it. In *Snow Storm: Steam Boat off a Harbour's Mouth* (1842: Tate), *Yachts Approaching the Coast* (1840s: Tate) and *Rain, Steam and Speed: the Great Western Railway* (1844: National Gallery) the form is minimal, yet not so that the meaning is lost. But they are paintings of pure weather, and they were done from personal observation. For, just as Turner had stood and sketched the night-sky made lurid by the burning Houses of Parliament, so now, at the age of nearly seventy, happening to be out in a small boat in a violent storm, he had himself tied to the mast, so that he could stay on deck for four hours and see into the heart of the storm. Shortly before his death, he was making studies of ice-bergs – 'Life piled on life were all too little'. He died on 19 December 1851, and was buried in the crypt of St Paul's, next to Sir Joshua Reynolds.

Further Reading
A. J. Finberg, *Life of J. M. W. Turner*, 1939.

TURPIN, RICHARD (1706-39), highwayman, is the subject of plentiful romance, but the facts of his life are sordid. The cult of the criminal, so strong then in England, as in France, made a hero out of unpromising material. Turpin was the son of an inn-keeper at Hempstead in Essex. He became a butcher who found meat for his shop by sheep-stealing. He then joined a gang of thieves who did not hesitate to treat their victims with violence: an old woman was put on a fire, a maid raped in the dairy where she hid. Turpin graduated a highwayman. Upon this lucrative trade the imagination of posterity has dwelt; even at the time, men like Duval and McLean were treated as heroes by sentimental ladies. In truth the insecurity of the roads was a social menace. Turpin's career did not last long. He shot, by accident, his partner Tom King. He was eventually arrested for horse-stealing, but not before he had shot one of his captors. He was cheered as he went to the gallows at York, dressed in a new frock coat and followed by five hired mourners. The *Newgate Calendar* records that the spectators 'seemed much affected by the fate of a man distinguished by the comeliness of his appearance'.

TYLER, WAT (*d.*1381), leader of the Peasants' Revolt, is one of the most famous and yet most obscure figures in late medieval England. He first appears as leader of the Kentish rebels. Contemporaries described him variously as a tiler, highwayman, or discharged soldier; from Kent or Essex; and a pseudonym for Jack Straw. None of these claims can be confirmed.

By drastically reducing English population the Black Death of 1348-9 should have improved the prospects of working people, who should have received more pay and paid less rents than before. Their lords, however, strove to maintain their incomes by fixing wages and by using serfdom to prevent free movement of labour and to keep up rents. To these underlying grievances should be added the appalling cost of the unsuccessful war against France. Ministers could not even protect the Kent coast and were denounced by the rebels as traitors. The final straw was the third poll tax, which was exceptionally heavy and touched even the poorest. These grievances were widely felt, so that the revolt was led by prosperous peasants and craftsmen, the leaders of their local communities.

Inquiries into tax evasion were rudely rebuffed at Fobbing in Essex and a judge sent to punish the culprits was even more roughly treated. The offenders appealed for support, provoking rebellion in Essex. Peasants and townsmen in Kent, East Anglia, and further afield followed suit. Tyler took command of the Kentish men at Maidstone about 7 June and led them to Canterbury and on 12 June to Blackheath, where he was recognized as overall leader of the uprising. His men entered the city of London, thus permitting attacks on John of Gaunt's palace of the Savoy and the Clerkenwell headquarters of the current treasurer of England. Tyler and Ball may have been principal draughtsmen of the peasants' manifesto, which made general demands much more radical than the freedom and pardons offered at Mile End by the king on 14 June. These offers satisfied the men of Essex, who went home, but not Tyler, who may not have been present. Later that day he seized the Tower, murdering the chancellor, Archbishop Sudbury, and the treasurer, and next day presented his own more extreme demands at Smithfield, where he was killed. The young King Richard memorably averted catastrophe, and the mob dispersed homewards, where they were pursued and punished.

Tyler lacked refinement. He drank 'villainously', swore frequently, and spoke coarsely. He was quick to anger, impulsive, violent, bloodthirsty, and vengeful. He was also a capable organizer. He determined the objectives, imposed his will on others, instilled them with urgency, and enforced discipline. It may have been to keep the disparate groups together that the manifesto was couched in general terms and that a distinction acceptable to all was made between the lawyers, royal ministers, leading nobles and bishops, who were to be killed, and the king, for whom they protested their loyalty. 'With whom hold you?' asked the peasants. 'With King Richard and with the true commons' was the password. Tyler negotiated in person, thrice rejecting draft charters, and refusing to be hurried: 'I will come when it pleases me so do', he said. He treated the king as a near equal. Maybe he became over-confident, vowing he would shave the heads (behead) of those who opposed him, declaring that in four months all law would come from his own mouth, and demanding the instant execution of an enemy at Smithfield. Perhaps, as the chronicler Walsingham says, he 'was beside himself in the insolent pride of success'. His meteoric political career ended in his death after one week.

Further Reading
T. H. Aston and R. H. Hilton, *The English Rising of 1381*, 1984.
R. B. Dobson, *The Peasants' Revolt of 1381*, 2nd edn, 1983.
E. B. Fryde, *The Great Revolt of 1381*, Historical Association Pamphlet, 1981.
R. H. Hilton, *Bond Men Made Free: Medieval Peasant Movements and the English Rising of 1381*, 1973.

TYNDALE, WILLIAM (the family also used the surname of Hutchyns) (*c.*1491/95-1536), translator of the Bible, was born almost certainly at Slimbridge in Gloucestershire, where is now established the Wildfowl Trust. It is possible that he was born on the west side of the Severn in Monmouthshire: certainly he was not born at North Nibley, where his monument now stands. The date of his birth is also uncertain, perhaps 1491, 1492, 1495. He was put to death at Vilvorde in the Netherlands in 1536. We know little of his early life and next to nothing of his family, which may possibly have tended towards Lollardy. Tyndale went to Magdalen Hall (later to be Hertford College), Oxford, in 1508 or 1510, under the name of Hychyns. He took his BA degree in 1512, his MA in 1515, and in 1518 he migrated probably to Cambridge to learn Greek, perhaps because Croke, the greatest teacher in Europe, had just returned to Cambridge and Tyndale wanted to read the New Testament in the original Greek. In 1522 he is found in the service of Sir John Walsh at Little Sodbury in Gloucestershire, probably as tutor to his children. He stayed there about two years and left at his own request. He had quarrelled with the local clergy and the visitors at Sir John's table, where he tactlessly aired his modern theological views, so much so, that he was arraigned before the Vicar-General of Gloucester as a dangerous heretic. (The Bishop of Gloucester was an Italian absentee, Giulio de' Medici, later Pope Clement VII.)

Tyndale was cleared of the charge of heresy, but it was better for all that he should leave the district. Sir John recommended him to Sir Henry Guildford who introduced him to Tunstal, Bishop of London. Tyndale had made up his mind that he must translate the New Testament into English as an antidote to the sickness from which he believed the church to be suffering. 'If God spare my life, ere many years I will cause a boy that driveth the plough shall know more of the scriptures than thou dost.' His plan now was to become chaplain to the Bishop of London, to live in his palace and there to translate the New Testament. But Tyndale was wholly unqualified for the post of chaplain and Tunstal told him that he had four chaplains already and had no room for any more.

Tyndale now fell in with a Gloucestershire man named Poyntz, a relation of Sir John Walsh, who arranged for him to preach at St Dunstan-in-the-West. Here he became acquainted with a rich cloth merchant, Henry Monmouth, who had him to live with him for the next six months. Tyndale soon grew weary of London: he was disgusted with the London 'praters', despised the pageantry of the church and was outraged by the magnificence of Wolsey. He made up his mind to go abroad, as 'there was no room in My Lord of London's house to translate the New Testament; but also that there was no place to do it in all England'.

It was while he was in London that Tyndale was first influenced by Lutheran ideas and it was here that he met and became friends with the future martyr, John Frith. When, therefore, he went abroad, he was already infected with heretical opinions. He set out with the intent to find some town where he could in peace translate the New Testament from the original Greek into vernacular English. The town he selected was Hamburg. Since he was destitute of money, somebody must have financed him. It must surely have been the Merchant Adventurers in London, of whom Henry Monmouth was one. They had agencies at Antwerp and Calais and were closely connected with Hamburg and Lübeck merchants in London. These wealthy merchants were much interested in Lutheranism, were strongly anti-clerical and hoped for a Lutheran reformation in England, partly in order to get rid of ecclesiastical laws which hampered their trade. They saw in Tyndale the right man for their purpose. They sent him to Germany where he could translate and have printed the New Testament in English, which they would arrange to smuggle into England.

At Hamburg Tyndale went to the house of a Protestant widow, Margaret von Emmersen, whose nephew was about to go to Wittenberg. Tyndale went with him, or as Sir Thomas More put it, 'gat him to Luther straight'. On 27 May 1524, there matriculated at the university a certain Gulielmus Daltin, who was in fact William Tyndale with the syllables reversed. He was probably the first Englishman to arrive at Wittenberg. He remained there from May to December 1524, when he returned to Hamburg to pick up a sum of money which had been sent to him by Henry Monmouth. In January 1525 he was back in Wittenberg, where he met a 'plausible but penniless' scoundrel named Roye, an apostate English friar, who now became Tyndale's amanuensis. In six weeks Tyndale's translation of the New Testament from Greek into English was copied out and the two of them went to Cologne to get the book printed (August 1525). Peter Quentel, a Catholic printer, was ready to print the book for the English market: a contract was made for a quarto volume with references, marginal notes and a prologue. It was a dangerous undertaking: Roye talked too much and the municipal authorities forbad any further printing. Only a fragment, less than half of the quarto as far as it had gone, is today in the British Museum, which is all that has survived of the gospels of St Matthew and St Mark which Quentel had printed before the work was stopped.

In September 1525 Tyndale and Roye went to Worms and started their work all over again. So rapidly did they work that the new complete version, printed by Schoeffer, in octavo, not quarto, was on sale in London early in March 1526. This edition was a plain text without glosses, references or prologue: the book was thus the less controversial, smaller and easier to smuggle, and cheaper to sell.

From 1526 to 1529 Tyndale was probably in Antwerp, where the Merchant Adventurers were strongly established, communications with England were easy and heretics escaping from persecution could foregather. In 1530 he went to Hamburg and on the way he was shipwrecked off the coast of Holland and lost all the manuscripts of his translation of the Old Testament. Once again he had to start afresh, this time helped by Miles

Coverdale. In 1530, hearing of the death of Wolsey, which made Antwerp a safer place, Tyndale returned thither and his translation of the Pentateuch from the original Hebrew text – Tyndale had taught himself Hebrew in two years – was issued from Hochstraten's press, although the imprint is of Lufft at Marburg. Unfortunately Tyndale rashly and unnecessarily added glosses to the text which laid him and his book open to the charge of heresy and alienated all orthodox people, especially the English bishops.

When the New Testament was distributed in 1528, Sir Thomas More wrote as a counterblast his *Dialogue Concerning Heresies and Matters of Religion*, a statement of Catholic doctrine running to some 170,000 words. Tyndale replied in 1530 in his *Answer unto Sir Thomas More's Dialogue*. This was an able piece of criticism, but it was spoiled by its intense bitterness and grossly unfair personal attacks on More. Unhappily More replied with his wearisome *Confutation* in which he sank to unaccustomed scurrility and abuse. 'This contest of Tyndale and More was the classic controversy of the English reformation. No other discussion was carried on between men of such pre-eminence and ability and with such clear apprehension of the points at issue. To More's assertion of the paramount authority of the church Tyndale replied by appealing to scripture, with an ultimate resort to individual judgement' (*Dictionary of National Biography*).

During this period Tyndale published four other works of importance. In 1528 there appeared *The Wicked Mammon*, a work which owed almost everything to Luther, and *The Obedience of a Christian Man*, again largely inspired by Luther, being a defence of despotic government and an attack on personal freedom. It is difficult not to feel that Tyndale allowed himself to be overwhelmed by Protestant influences, difficult to believe that these two books represent his real views and feelings. His *Practice of Prelates* (1530) was both a forthright attack on the Papacy and also on Wolsey and the divorce proceedings. Before this last book reached England, Cromwell had read the *Christian Obedience*, with the views of which both he and Henry VIII agreed so strongly that they tried to persuade Tyndale to return to England. The negotiations, which were carried out by Cromwell's friend, Stephen Vaughan, failed and Henry was so infuriated by one answer that Tyndale sent him that he tried to have Tyndale kidnapped (1531). Tyndale therefore left Antwerp for two years: when he returned in 1533 he went to live in the 'English House', a building set aside by the local authorities for the Merchant Adventurers in England.

Tyndale was now very near the end of his life. A handsome, unprincipled young man turned up in Antwerp and made friends with Tyndale. This was Henry Phillips, the son of a wealthy landowner in Dorset. Probably because he was desperately in need of money and hoped to recoup his fortunes by serving Charles V against the Protestants, Phillips, by means of the lowest forms of treachery, caused Tyndale to be arrested in Antwerp (1535). Tyndale was imprisoned in the state prison of Vilvorde, where he remained for eighteen months. In September Thomas Cromwell tried to get lenient treatment for him, but to no avail. In 1536 Tyndale was brought to trial, degraded from his ecclesiastical orders as a heretic and condemned to death. He was executed on 6 October 1536, being strangled before his body was given to the flames to be burnt. At the stake he is said to have cried out, 'Lord, open the King of England's eyes.' Years before he had written, 'If they shall burn me, they shall do no other thing than I look for.'

Tyndale ought to be looked upon as one of the great heroes in English history. He described himself as being 'evil favoured in this world and without grace in the sight of men'; it is true also that he was apt to attribute to his opponents the lowest motives, although they were honourable men like Sir Thomas More. But his life was one of 'utter disappointment and struggle – persecuted in one city, fleeing to another' (Chambers). Only a man of the toughest fibre and the most invincible faith could have achieved what Tyndale achieved. Fundamentally, he was a simple and reasonable man, never a very good judge of character (or he would never have taken up with Roye or been taken in by Phillips), a very remarkable linguist and a wonderful writer of English prose. He died a martyr and he had his reward, in the most ironical manner. Those who had persecuted him as a heretic for translating the New Testament at last came to the conclusion that an authorized version of the Bible must be made available to the people. In 1538 Henry VIII commanded that Matthew's Bible should be placed in every parish church. This book was a composite work 'truly and purely translated by Thomas Matthew'. Matthew was in fact Rogers, the first victim of the Marian persecutions. But who had made most of the translations? Part of the Old Testament was the work of Miles Coverdale: part of the Apocrypha was translated by Rogers; the Pentateuch, the Book of Jonah, almost certainly Joshua to II Chronicles, and the whole of the New Testament were the work of Tyndale. When the compilers of the Authorized Version in James I's reign came to do their work, it was to Tyndale that they turned, so that our Authorized Version today is mainly the work of Tyndale. Has any other one man given as great a gift to his own country, and as the centuries go by, to millions beyond his own country? Tyndale's Bible laid the foundations of the English literary language and his words and phrases have become part and parcel of the everyday speech of Englishmen.

Further Reading
C. H. Williams, *William Tyndale*, 1969.
J. H. Maclehose, *The Burnished Sword*, 1956.

C. Morris: *Political Thought in England, Tyndale to Hooker*, 1953.

W. E. Campbell, *Erasmus, Tyndale and More*, 1949.

H. Maynard Smith, *Henry VIII and the Reformation*, 1948.

R. W. Chambers, *Man's Unconquerable Mind*, 1939.

J. F. Mozley, *William Tyndale*, 1937.

TYRELL, SIR JAMES (1445-1502) is reputed to have murdered the princes in the Tower. Unlike most of Richard III's retainers, he was not a northerner, perhaps because his service to the then Duke of Gloucester dates back before Richard's acquisition of the Neville inheritance in 1471. James was the son of William Tyrell of Ipswich (Suff.). He was knighted at the battle of Tewkesbury and was certainly one of Richard's retainers in 1472. His activity as witness of ducal charters, trustee, deputy-chamberlain of the Exchequer, and under-constable marks him out as one of the duke's most trusted servants. Richard had few if any more important posts in his gift than those of sheriff of Glamorgan and constable of Cardiff, which made Tyrell the chief man in the region. Quite apart from his official fees of £110, he was able to attract a similar income from the Duke of Suffolk, Lord Dudley, and various ecclesiastics, besides his fee as steward of the duchy of Lancaster, lordship of Ogmore and the £100 a year profit he made as lessee of the lands of the Abbey of Tewkesbury in Glamorgan. He served in the Scottish war in 1482, when the duke made him a knight banneret, and in 1483 it was to him that Richard confided the custody of Archbishop Rotherham.

Tyrell was thus particularly well-placed to benefit from Richard's usurpation. He was appointed a knight of the body, master of the horse, master of the henxmen, chamberlain of the Exchequer, steward of the duchy of Cornwall, steward of lordships and constable of castles in Wales, and lieutenant of Guines by Calais. He was allowed to inherit his brother-in-law's lands in Cornwall – hence his appointment as JP for Cornwall – and was granted other confiscated lands. Such posts however carried duties and that Tyrell had incompatible responsibilities for defence in Cornwall, south Wales and Calais is a measure of Richard III's 'acute shortage of reliable manpower. Many tasks could only be given to men close to him and fully trusted by him'. When Tyrell was sent to take over Guines in 1485 after the commander's defection, he was nevertheless left in command in Glamorgan. Following Henry Tudor's landing, he was therefore unable to organize counter-measures in south Wales.

Clearly Tyrell was the sort of confidential servant that Richard would have trusted with such delicate and secret business as the murder of the princes in the Tower, if he indeed directed it. Sir Thomas More describes in detail the murder, which he places in the summer of 1483, when the princes probably did die, and Polydore Vergil also attributes the murder to Tyrell. Neither writer was an eye-witness and both were writing thirty years after the events described and indeed after the death of Tyrell himself. The source was allegedly a confession made by Tyrell before his death, which does not survive if indeed it ever existed. There is nothing inherently improbable in the story, but no part of it can be adequately corroborated and it must remain merely the most likely explanation of the princes' fate. There were obvious reasons for the crime to be concealed by the perpetrators before and after 1485.

Because Tyrell was at Guines at 1485, he missed the disaster of Bosworth and continued his career as trusted royal servant to Henry VII. He lost some offices and lands, yet retained his appointments as knight of the body, sheriff of Glamorgan and lieutenant of Guines. He was frequently at court, was employed on diplomatic and military missions, joined the royal council, and in 1495 was a trustee of the king's will. Almost unique in retaining his offices after Richard's fall, let alone securing further promotion, Tyrell was clearly a man whose remarkable ability demanded recognition. In 1501 however he was implicated in treason with Edmund de la Pole, Earl of Suffolk, the Yorkist pretender and a nobleman in his home area. He was condemned to death and executed in 1502. It is at this point that he is alleged to have made his notorious confession.

Further Reading

C. D. Ross, *Richard III*, 1981.

T. More, *History of King Richard III*, ed. R. S. Sylvester, 1963.

U

UDALL, NICHOLAS (1505-56), reformer, dramatist and schoolmaster was educated at Winchester and at Corpus Christi College, Oxford. While he was at Oxford he came strongly under the influence of the New Learning and in religion he favoured the Lutheran point of view. He came into prominence at court at the coronation of Anne Boleyn, when he was author, or part author, of the pageants and masques which formed a large part of the celebrations and which laid the foundations for his reputation as a literary man.

In 1534 he was appointed headmaster of Eton, soon after he had published a book entitled *Flowers for Latin Spekynge, selected and gathered out of Terence, and the same translated into Englysshe*. It was the custom at Eton for some of the boys to act the plays of Terence and Plautus under the direction of the headmaster 'about the feast of St Andrew', a custom very acceptable to Udall.

In 1541 his career as a schoolmaster came to an end – only temporarily, as it proved. A theft of silver images and other plate was committed by two of the scholars with the help of Udall's servant. Udall was examined on suspicion of having been aware of the theft, but although he appeared to be innocent of the theft, he confessed to being guilty of a moral offence with one of his pupils. He lost his mastership and was sent to the Marshalsea, but he was soon released and was once again in favour at court, and he also received several church preferments.

In 1549 he was employed by the government to write the answer to the demands of the west country rebels for the old religion to be restored. Udall's answer was a forceful and able reply to the Catholic arguments, and he defended with spirit the royal authority in matters of religion. On the accession of Mary, Udall was one of the few Protestants who were retained in favour and in employment, so much so that in 1554, in spite of his past record, he was made Master of Westminster School. This appointment is a proof of Mary's respect for learning and ability. He died in 1556 and was buried in St Margaret's, Westminster.

The importance of Udall lies in the fact that he combined in himself activities as a moderate Reformer, as a humanist and as an able dramatist. Only one of his plays remains to us, *Ralph Roister Doister*, which is generally regarded as the first genuine comedy in English literature. It was written almost certainly in 1553-4 and therefore must have been intended for the boys of Westminster School and not of Eton College. The play has close affinities with Plautus and Terence, but Udall has succeeded in making the characters recognizably English. There is only one early copy of the play in existence and it is in College Library at Eton.

Further Reading
Cambridge History of English Literature, 1967.
W. L. Edgerton, *Nicholas Udall*, 1965.
Maxwell Lyre, *History of Eton College*, 1911.
W. D. Cooper, Shakespeare Society's edition of *Ralph Roister Doister*, 1847.

UHTRED (*d.* 1016) was Earl of Northumbria from *c.*1006 until his murder, which gave rise to a celebrated feud, in 1016. Uhtred was descended from a family which had governed Bernicia, the northern half of Northumbria, in virtual independence of the Wessex-based Kings of England, from at least the last years of the ninth century. His vigorous defence of Northumbria from the Scots in about 1006 led King Elthelred II to add Deira, that is Yorkshire, to his earldom. Uhtred held the office of Earl of all Northumbria from then on. In 1013 he submitted to Sweyn Forkbeard but in the confused period following Sweyn's death in 1014 he went over to Edmund Ironside, with whom he was campaigning early in 1016 in the Midlands. Canute managed to slip into Uhtred's Yorkshire territories, forcing Uhtred to hasten back and submit to him. However, when the two men met, Uhtred was murdered at the instigation of Eadric Streona by another Northumbrian nobleman named Thurbrand. Both in its background and in its consequences there was more to this crime than meets the eye.

Uhtred had been thrice married. His first wife was a daughter of the Bishop of Durham; his second wife the daughter of a man prominent in Yorkshire; his third wife one of the many daughters of King Ethelred. (Uhtred was thus the brother-in-law of Eadric Streona who had him killed.) As a condition of his second marriage

Uhtred had promised his father-in-law that he would kill an enemy of his, Thurbrand. As we have seen, Thurbrand struck first. But Uhtred's blood had to be avenged. His son by his first marriage, Ealdred, became Earl of Northumbria in about 1019. At some date unknown Ealdred avenged his father by killing Thurbrand. The feud was inherited by Thurbrand's son Carl. For some time Carl and Ealdred sought to ambush one another, but friends intervened to reconcile the two families. Peace was patched up and Carl and Ealdred even pledged themselves to go on pilgrimage to Rome in brotherhood. But for reasons unknown the strife flared up again. In about 1038 Carl killed Ealdred at Rise, near Beverley. Ealdred left five daughters but no son. One of these girls married Siward, Earl of Northumbria, and their son Waltheof inherited the feud. He managed to corner Carl's sons and grandsons while they were feasting at Settrington, near Malton, and massacred all but two of them.

The story of this three-generation feud survives in a few paragraphs of a short tract composed at Durham about the year 1100. The author, whose main concern was with certain properties of the church of Durham transmitted through the bishop's daughter who was Uhtred's first wife, tells it casually, as though there was nothing specially unusual about it. It has been said that the story indicates how violent life was in a part of England which had experienced heavy Scandinavian influence. This is doubtful, for similar feuds can be traced in parts of early medieval Europe which received no Viking settlers. In any case, there is every likelihood that more than family honour was at stake. Uhtred's family was Bernician, Thurbrand's Deiran. It was a contest for local influence between rival networks of kinsmen and retainers. The chance survival of this document affords us a precious glimpse of the realities of regional power-struggles in later Anglo-Saxon England.

Further Reading
C. R. Hart, *The Early Charters of Northern England and the North Midlands*, 1975, contains a translation of the text.

USK, ADAM (*c*.1352-1430), the chronicler, was born in the Welsh Marcher lordship of Usk and was sent by its lord, Edmund, Earl of March (*d*.1381) to Oxford University. He became a notary public in 1381, Bachelor of Canon Law in 1387, principal of the civil law school, and by 1393 a Doctor of Civil Law. He held a succession of rectories from 1383 and was advocate at the court of Canterbury up to 1399, when his support for Henry IV transformed his fortunes. He visited Richard II in prison, advised on his deposition, was employed in royal diplomacy and legal business, and attracted the patronage of Archbishop Arundel. Perhaps because of the theft of a horse, perhaps because he wanted papal preferment, he left England for Rome in 1402, becoming a papal

chaplain and auditor of the sacred palace. His hopes of a bishopric were disappointed, but he was promoted to archdeaconries, canonries, and other livings that should have brought an income of about £250. This phase of his career ended with the pope's expulsion from Rome and Usk's humiliation by the Romans, which prompted him in 1406 to return home. Henry IV, however, refused him a pardon, so he languished abroad until 1411, when, now about sixty years of age, he proceeded secretly to Wales, briefly joined Glendower, and spent two years as a poor chantry priest at Pontypool. Pardoned at last, he resumed his legal practice and secured two rectories, which he occupied until 1428-9, when he was pensioned off.

Usk's *Chronicon* continues Higden's *Polychronicon*. Up to 1394 and from 1404 it is meagre, but in between it is full, detailed, and of primary importance for the exciting events of his turbulent life, especially the Lancastrian revolution, the papal Curia, and Glendower's rebellion. Usk was an acute eyewitness and his chronicle, although biased, is an independent account, which owes nothing to any other source.

Usk's *Chronicon* is also revealing about its author, who 'happily had enough vanity to think his personal experience not unworthy of a place among the general events of his time'. Personal reminiscences are interspersed with national and international events and indeed it is Usk's own career that shaped what he wrote. Inevitably he justified his own actions and condemned his opponents, but he supplies ample information for a more balanced – and not altogether favourable – judgement to be reached. His Welsh origins coloured his whole life: witness his riot against the northern scholars at Oxford in 1388-9, his repeated returns to Wales, his patronage of his home town, and his interest in the Mortimers and their relatives Archbishop Arundel and the Earl of Arundel. Whilst undoubtedly a learned man whose legal counsel was widely valued, he made excessive parade of his expertise – he 'certainly missed no opportunity for airing his knowledge' – and was once silenced by a bishop for an untimely display of learning. Vain and boastful, he probably exaggerated the eminence of his friends, the quality of his advice, and his influence on decisions and events, for he revealed himself to be a man without tact, sense of timing, discretion or judgement. Even by the standards of his time he was unduly credulous about signs and miracles and claimed to experience both visions and dreams, which he included as serious portents in his chronicle. Impulsive, passionate, and lacking a capacity for self-criticism, he blamed on others the misfortunes that he brought on himself. His naked pursuit of promotion and profit, which did not stop short at looting, accompanied generosity to friends and his native town. Whilst undoubtedly ill-suited for the bishopric he sought, he deserved more than the obscurity in which he died.

Further Reading

A. Gransden, *Historical Writing in England* ii, 1982.
E. M. Thompson, *Chronicon Adae de Usk AD1377-1421*, 1904.

UTHRED, JOHN (*c*.1320-97) of Boldon, 'the most distinguished of all the university monks' and the outstanding northern Benedictine of the fourteenth century, was never superior of a major monastery. Born at Boldon, a Durham estate, he went to Oxford as a secular clerk and entered Durham Cathedral Priory only in 1341. A brief term at the Durham cell at Stamford was followed by twenty years (1347-67) at another cell, Durham College at Oxford, where he became a doctor of theology in 1357 and was a distinguished teacher. He returned to Oxford only briefly in 1383-6. It was unusual to spend a lifetime in academic study like Walter Burley and still more unusual to remain a lifetime at university. Even when at Oxford in 1350-67 Uthred was Prior of Durham College. Subsequently he served three terms as prior of the cell of Finchale (1367-8, 1375-81, 1386-96) and two as subprior of the parent house at Durham (1368-75, 1381-3). Durham Priory sent him on visitations, to the convocation of the Church of York, and to General Chapters of the English Black Monks, for whom he also performed commissions. Once, uniquely for a monk who was not head of his house, the king sent him on embassy to Avignon. Such activities reveal Uthred as a busy administrator as well as a scholar and one moreover highly respected and trusted. His career demonstrates the concrete gains in prestige and administrative capacity that monasteries could make from their considerable financial sacrifice in sending inmates to university.

Uthred's reputation originated initially from his academic achievements and he never stopped writing. He was both a daring speculative theologian and a partisan controversialist. At his best he was an independent thinker, who grappled with problems directly and strove to find solutions. He could argue reasonably and persuasively. His best works, on the origins and essence of monasticism, reveal considerable capacity for research, a sense of the past, and 'remarkable serenity and rationality in their treatment'. On the other hand, unlike Adam Easton, he was capable of violent and scurrilous vituperation against his opponents and responded bitterly to criticism. His principal opponents were the friars and his younger Oxford contemporary John Wyclif. Uthred repeatedly defended monasticism against its enemies, attacking the mendicant ideal, defending monasticism and ecclesiastical endowments. Also, like Easton, he asserted the superiority of spiritual over temporal power. In his last years he wrote books of devotion. Before then, perhaps goaded by Wyclif, he defended traditional Catholic doctrines on holy communion and predestination, but his own views were not above criticism. Like many scholars of his time, who lived in an age of uncertainty, his theology was drawn from diverse sources including Ockham. It displayed some of the tendencies condemned by Bradwardine and it included his own doctrine of the clear vision. This asserted deathbed piety over lifetime religion and was condemned by the Benedictine Archbishop Langham in 1368. Uthred was upset, for he felt conventionally enough that academic speculation should be settled in the universities, but his condemnation – to be followed soon after by that of Wyclif – drew attention to the risks of free speculation and may have contributed to the loss of originality among English (and European) theologians. Obviously condemnation damaged Uthred's reputation as a theologian, but it had no apparent effect among Benedictines and he remained in responsible office until death.

Further Reading

D. Knowles, *The Religious Orders in England* ii, 1961.
W. A. Pantin, *The English Church in the Fourteenth Century*, 1955.

V

VALENCE, AYMER, EARL OF PEMBROKE
(*d*.1324) belonged to the international nobility. His maternal heritage comprised lands in England, Ireland and Wales, which provided an income of £3,000, second only to the Earls of Gloucester and Lancaster. He was briefly Lord of Bothwell in Scotland. From his father William, half-brother of Henry III, he inherited four French lordships, and other French property came with his second marriage. Both his wives were French noblewomen, daughters of the constable and butler of France respectively. He visited France almost every year, often on embassies in which his French connections were invaluable. Other missions took him to Scotland and the papal Curia. His military career commenced with Edward I's Flemish expedition of 1297. He served in Scotland each year from the Falkirk campaign of 1298 to 1303, latterly as lieutenant south of the Forth; in 1306-7, when he beat Bruce at Methven, but lost to him at Loudoun Hill; in the Bannockburn campaign of 1314; in 1315, 1319 and in 1323, when he was routed at Byland. In 1320 he was keeper of the realm. Like his older contemporary the Earl of Lincoln, Pembroke's career was spent in constant service to the Crown. Also like Lincoln, he died in harness, on embassy to France.

Historians have identified Pembroke as founder of a 'Middle Party', hostile both to the king's favourites and his enemies, which provided stable government in the years 1317-21. The 'Middle Party', however, is a myth and Pembroke was merely the most prominent of those of Edward II's advisers who owed nothing to their physical attractions. From Gaveston's death in 1312, Pembroke as royal councillor exercised his influence for moderation. That negotiations with opposing magnates in 1312-13 and 1317-18 ended in agreements rather than civil war is largely to his credit. Edward II valued his advice and often acted on it, but Pembroke's influence varied with that of others. In 1312-14, when he had no rivals, he was the king's chief councillor, but in 1314-16 he was supplanted by Warwick and Lancaster and in 1316-17 by a new court party. The famous indenture of 24 November 1317, traditionally the origin of the 'Middle Party', actually witnessed Pembroke and

Badlesmere as royal councillors restraining Damory (the current favourite) from exploiting the king's infatuation and securing Damory's support for their more sensible counsel. From 1318 on the rise of the Despensers progressively relegated Pembroke to secondary importance. Unlike the favourites, Pembroke never established a personal dominance over the king. Lack of authority, rather than moderation, explain why his rewards of office were so meagre and why Edward helped him so little with the ransom Pembroke incurred on royal embassy in 1317.

Like all noblemen, Pembroke preferred co-operation with the Crown to opposition. He may have considered Edward's weakness further cause for offering sound counsel. He certainly opposed the malign influence of successive favourites. Twice their dominance strained his allegiance. One such was Gaveston. Pembroke favoured his exile in 1308, was an Ordainer in 1310, and in 1312 fought against him. It was to Pembroke that Gaveston surrendered conditionally and Pembroke therefore who was dishonoured by his execution. Hence his reconciliation with the king, now without Gaveston, the cause of his original defection. Similarly in 1321 he sympathized with the Marchers and persuaded Edward to exile the Despensers. By supporting Edward against Badlesmere, he was committed against the Marchers and Lancaster, thus inadvertently assuring the Despensers of dominance. If indeed 'he was a man of moderate talents, whose ability was not up to the demands placed upon it in the crises of Edward II's reign', this was because the crises were insoluble without deposition of the king.

Further Reading
J. R. S. Phillips, *Aymer de Valence, Earl of Pembroke 1307-24: Baronial Politics in the Reign of Edward II*, 1972.

VANBRUGH, SIR JOHN (1664-1726), playwright and architect, was a Londoner, the son of a rich sugar-baker, with Flemish blood from his refugee grandfather. Brought up to be a gentleman, Vanbrugh was commissioned in the Earl of Huntingdon's regiment at twenty-two. From 1690 to 1692 he was imprisoned in France as a suspected spy, for some of the time in the Bastille, where he whiled away the hours writing plays. After a very short spell as a captain in the Marines, he devoted his considerable wit and his somewhat intermittent energies to writing for the theatre. He produced ten plays in all during his life. The first was *The Relapse* (1696), the best known *The Provok'd Wife* (1697), the most convincing *The Confederacy* (1705) which he adapted from the French. As a playwright Vanbrugh was fluent, readable, uneven and, by the standards of Restoration comedy, conventional in theme, tone and situation.

He became an architect quite suddenly, by designing the great Yorkshire mansion of Castle Howard for the Earl of Carlisle in 1699. He had had no sort of professional training, and therefore his appointment in 1702 as Comptroller of Works, involving the dismissal from that post of William Talman, the architect of Chatsworth, was a scandalous 'job' – though not quite as scandalous as Vanbrugh's further appointment, in 1704, as Clarencieux King of Arms, despite his complete contempt for heraldry. This succession of episodes, all contrived by his patron Carlisle, forms a curious beginning for a distinguished architectural career. He began building Castle Howard in 1701, and four years later he got an even more splendid commission, for Marlborough's palace of Blenheim. In 1705 also he built the Opera House in the Haymarket, and managed it for two years: it failed lamentably, partly at least because the acoustics were bad. In 1707 he began to remodel Kimbolton Castle, and in 1710 he designed King's Weston House near Bristol.

His later career was not without vicissitudes. Vanbrugh's politics were notoriously Whig. He was a founder-member of the Kit-Cat Club, and there were those, like Marlborough's Jacobite friend the Earl of Ailesbury, who believed that it was his Whig views that had made him architect of Blenheim. When the Whig ministers were turned out after 1710 Vanbrugh was in difficulty. Funds for Blenheim were cut off, and in 1712 he was dismissed from his comptrollership. But George I's accession in 1714 restored the Whigs. Vanbrugh not only recovered his office; he got a knighthood, and in 1716 took over from Wren as Surveyor at Greenwich, where he built an extraordinary dormitory block alongside his predecessor's hall. During the remaining years of his life he built three more mansions, Eastbury, Seaton Delaval and Grimsthorpe. Blenheim Palace itself was completed a year before his death in 1726, but not by Vanbrugh. He had become involved in a prolonged row with the Duchess of Marlborough, who eventually forbade him to appear at Blenheim at all and only paid her debts to him after Walpole had intervened.

Blenheim, at once castle and palace, was Vanbrugh's masterpiece, the most staggering achievement of the so-called 'English Baroque' style of which he was the most brilliant exponent. Yet Blenheim contains some of the work of Hawksmore, to whose professional expertise he owed much. Seaton Delaval, that unforgettable Northumbrian house, with its Tudor flavour and octagonal towers, its air of fantasy and impression of movement, is perhaps Vanbrugh's best memorial.

Further Reading
L. Whistler, *Sir John Vanbrugh, Architect and Dramatist*, 1938, and *The Imagination of Vanbrugh*, 1954.

VAN DYCK, SIR ANTHONY (1599-1641), painter, son of a prosperous Antwerp mercer, first came to England in 1620 and spent some months in the service of James I. From 1621 to 1632 he was on the continent, mostly in Italy and Flanders. Yet he kept in touch with England during this time, and in 1632 Charles I appointed him 'Principal Painter in ordinary to their Majesties', with a pension of £200 per annum, a knighthood, and a studio in Blackfriars. He spent almost all the remaining nine years of his life in England, producing his remarkable series of royal portraits and a large number of other masterpieces, many of them splendid portraits of the aristocracy. We know relatively little of the organization of the studio, save that he employed Flemish assistants who must have been responsible for the many replicas of his work which contemporaries demanded: its output was certainly very great. A man of distinguished bearing and courtly manners, an artist whose brilliant technique was established and international reputation secure before he settled in England, Van Dyck treated his patrons as his equals and shed a distinctive lustre upon the court of Charles I. A pupil of Rubens, deeply influenced by Titian and the Venetians, he owed nothing to England in his development as an artist. Yet his influence upon English history was immense in two ways. In the field of art itself, Van Dyck virtually created the pattern and the formulae within which English portrait-painting developed and functioned during the next two centuries. In that of historical understanding, he has exerted an imponderable influence upon our judgement of the Stuarts and of the Cavaliers. Certainly his portraits of the Stuarts flattered them as individuals. More significantly, he was, in the words of Ellis Waterhouse, used by Charles I 'as a propagandist in the cause of absolutism'. Over the centuries no man, except perhaps Charles I himself on the scaffold, has been a more successful champion of the Stuart cause than Van Dyck.

Further Reading
A. P. Oppé, 'Sir Anthony Van Dyck in England', *Burlington Magazine*, lxxix (1941), pp.186-90.

VANE THE YOUNGER, SIR HENRY (1613-62), Puritan politician, was born at Debden near Newport in Essex, the son of the elder Sir Henry who later became Comptroller and Treasurer of the royal household. Educated at Westminster and Magdalen Hall, Oxford, he had, in the words of his speech from the scaffold in

1662, 'been, till he was seventeen years old, a good fellow, but then it pleased God to lay a foundation of grace in his heart'. As his strange book, *The Retired Man's Meditations*, shows, there was something of the mystic in him. In 1635 he went to New England for conscience's sake, and for a year he was Governor of Massachusetts. Then he got involved in the controversy over saving grace provoked by Anne Hutchinson, and in 1637 he sailed back to England. Appointed joint Treasurer of the navy in 1639 and knighted in 1640, he nevertheless became a follower of Pym and sat in Long Parliament as member for Hull. He played a somewhat unsavoury role in the condemnation of Strafford; discovering in the papers of his father, now secretary to the Council, the records of the meeting in which Strafford had suggested bringing over the Irish army to reduce 'this kingdom', he had provided Pym with a copy which served as the basis for impeachment and attainder. Prominent in the war party from 1642, a lucid and persuasive speaker, Vane was the principal English negotiator of the Solemn League and Covenant and for a time a leader of the Commons after Pym's death in 1643. A champion of liberty of conscience, he fell out with the Presbyterian majority in the House. Yet he was no ardent supporter of the army and, although he was himself left in the Rump, he seems to have disapproved of Pride's Purge in 1648, and he played no part in the king's trial or in the events leading to it.

This did not stop him accepting the Republic. Vane believed in the sovereignty of the people, and saw the Rump as their remaining representative. So from 1649-53 he was a central figure in English government and in the project to perpetuate the power of the Rump. When Cromwell brought in his musketeers to dissolve it in 1653 Vane called out 'It is against morality and common honesty', to which Oliver replied, 'The Lord deliver me from Sir Henry Vane!' He declined to join Barebone's parliament, and in 1656 wrote the pamphlet *A Healing Question*, opposing secular control of religion and condemning the Protectorate. This led to a brief period of imprisonment. When Oliver died in 1658, Vane joined the soldiers in denouncing Richard and in destroying the Protectorate, and he enjoyed a further spell of power when the Rump was restored in 1659. But the swing to monarchy in 1660 left him, a convinced Republican, without friends. Arrested before the Restoration, he was excluded from the Act of Indemnity on the understanding that Charles would spare his life if he were attainted. Tried in 1662, he chose to defend himself by vindicating parliamentary sovereignty, and the king went back on his word. Pepys saw Vane executed, and noted the courage and the 'humility and gravity' with which he died.

Vane's end was in a sense a measure of the distrust he aroused. Lely's portrait reveals a man self-willed and fanatical, who, for all his wit and fine manners, made enemies too easily and too widely. Clarendon spoke of his 'very profound dissimulation', Richard Baxter of his 'Subtilty'. As J. H. Hexter has put it, Vane 'used men for his secret purposes and then tossed them aside'.* Nevertheless, he stood for two of the great liberal principles of modern English history, parliamentary sovereignty and religious freedom. There is no evidence that he championed either of them with anything but complete sincerity, and it is difficult to deny that he died because of his championship of them.

Further Reading
Violet A. Rowe, *Sir Henry Vane the Younger*, 1970.
Roger Howell, 'Henry Vane the Younger and the Politics of Religion', *History Today*, April 1963, pp.275-82.

VENNER, THOMAS (*d.*1661), Fifth Monarchist and rebel, was a master cooper who emigrated to Massachusetts in the 1630s. Back in England by 1651, he got employment as a cooper in the Tower of London but, it seems, was sacked because he tried to blow it up. In the later 1650s he was head of a Fifth Monarchist church in Swan Alley, Coleman Street. The Fifth Monarchists (who were probably never more than 10,000 all told) believed that with the coming of King Jesus the elect would rule over the ungodly. A minority among them were willing to accelerate this event by violence, the more since they were particularly hostile to the rule of Oliver Cromwell, whom they readily identified with the Beast of the Book of Revelation. Venner was one of these. Briefly imprisoned in 1656, after the breakdown of talks with the Protectorate government, he attempted an armed rising in 1657 and was gaoled again until 1659. Undaunted by the Restoration – an event which indeed was irrelevant to a man of his beliefs – he tried again in 1661. With about fifty supporters he proclaimed 'King Jesus and the heads upon the gate' in the streets of London. Life Guards and other troops crushed the rebels at once. Venner, wounded nineteen times, and twelve others were executed and their heads displayed on London Bridge. But London had been in confusion, and, in the words of David Ogg, 'unfortunately from the truth that the Fifth Monarchy men were extremists was deduced the unwarrantable opinion that all Dissenters were politically dangerous'.† For the main historical significance of Venner's Rising of 1661 and the panic it caused lies in the introduction of the Clarendon Code.

VERE, JOHN, EARL OF OXFORD (*c.*1443-1513) outlasted both the Yorkist dynasty he implacably opposed and the two kings whom he had helped to make. In 1462 his father and elder brother were executed for treason to Edward IV. John most likely succeeded because he married Warwick the Kingmaker's sister.

---

*J. H. Hexter, *The Reign of King Pym*, 1941, p.147.
†D. Ogg, *England in the Reign of Charles II*, 1956 edn, vol. I, p.208.

Probably the government misinterpreted his continued disaffection as Lancastrian when it arrested him in 1468. A rumour that he had confessed 'much thing' is unsubstantiated. Once released, he attended Clarence's forbidden wedding to Warwick's daughter at Calais in May 1469 and rebelled with them against King Edward and his favourites. Oxford wisely joined Warwick in exile in 1470 and returned with him to make Henry VI king again. The earl became steward of the household and executed his father's own executioner. In 1471 he repelled Edward IV at Cromer, clashed with him at Newark, and was defeated with Warwick at Barnet. Although he fled abroad, Oxford was irreconcilable. He continued to resist Edward even without an alternative king. With French backing in 1473, he raided St Osyth in Essex and seized St Michael's Mount, which he defended vigorously until his garrison accepted terms. Imprisoned at Hammes Castle near Calais, he failed to escape in 1477, but suborned his keeper in 1484. He joined Henry Tudor, fought for him at Bosworth in 1485, and became a bulwark of his régime. He recovered his inheritances, was appointed Great Chamberlain and Admiral of England and to many other offices. He held East Anglia, committing its levies to Henry's defence in 1487 and 1489. In 1499 as steward of England he even condemned Edward, Earl of Warwick, son of Clarence and grandson of Warwick the Kingmaker.

Oxford was a poor earl up to 1471 and his income of c.£1,900 in the mid-'90s did not rank with the richest nobles. His will and inventory suggest a plutocratic lifestyle, but contain cash and chattels worth only £8,206, not a vast sum. It was not great estates and wealth that enabled him to dominate East Anglia in 1470-1 and from 1485, but a combination of the eclipse of the de la Poles and Dukes of Norfolk and Oxford's own favour with the Crown, itself testimony to his ability. Like the Despensers in the 1320s, Suffolk in the 1450s and Hastings in the 1470s, Oxford's power was based on influence at court, not on the largest local estate. Norfolk possessed that, yet in 1470-1 he had to:

sue to him as humbly as ever I did to them. In so much that my Lord of Oxford shall have the rule of them and theirs by their own desires and great means. I [John Paston] trust we shall soon have other offices suitable for us, for my Master the Earl of Oxford bids me ask and have.

Backed with royal patronage, Oxford secured 'the faithful guiding and disposition of the country, to my great comfort and pleasure'. Again, from 1485, he dominated the region, arraying its forces against outside threats, sitting on commissions, and arbitrating disputes. He attracted many gentry to his service, rewarding fifty-six in his will 'for such true and faithful service as they have done to me'. Perhaps there is truth in the unsubstantiated legend of his fine by Henry VII for illegal retaining. He does not seem to have abused his power, as all medieval nobles were prone to do. As late as 1509 he hoped for a son, but none arrived. Future earls descended from his nephew. None achieved his political stature.

Further Reading
M. A. Hicks, 'The Last Days of Elizabeth, Countess of Oxford', *English Historical Review* ciii, 1988.
M. A. Hicks, *False, Fleeting, Perjur'd Clarence: George, Duke of Clarence 1449-78*, 1980.
R. Virgoe, 'The Recovery of the Howards in East Anglia, 1485-1529' in *Wealth and Power in Tudor England*, E. W. Ives, R. J. Knecht and J. J. Scarisbrick, eds, 1978.
C. L. Scofield, 'The Early Life of John de Vere, thirteenth Earl of Oxford', *English Historical Review* xxix, 1914.

VERE, ROBERT, EARL OF OXFORD (1362-92) (created Marquis of Dublin in 1385, and Duke of Ireland the following year) was the most important of Richard II's favourites. Succeeding as a child to his father's modest earldom, he became a royal kinsman by his marriage to Edward III's granddaughter Philippa Coucy and thus an intimate of his younger contemporary Richard II. Precisely what Richard saw in him is uncertain – although Vere was handsome, a homosexual relationship appears unlikely – but the king became quite besotted with him. Young though he was and indeed still technically a minor, Richard exercised considerable influence over policy in the early 1380s and distributed his own patronage, dismissing the veteran Lord Scrope of Bolton as chancellor, when he sought to restrain his generosity. Richard's favours were largely confined to a narrow group of courtiers headed by Vere. Whilst inevitably Vere channelled royal patronage to his dependants, he was himself the principal beneficiary of it, becoming among other things custodian of Colchester castle, sheriff of Rutland for life, Lord of Queenborough, guardian of Lord Roos, and the dominant figure in Cheshire and north Wales.

Such favours, however, pale beside Vere's remarkable promotion in rank. In 1386 the new rank of marquis was created for his benefit to give him precedence over the other earls and in 1386 he became Duke of Ireland, second only to John of Gaunt. He was allowed to quarter his arms with those of Edward the Confessor and was given palatine powers in Ireland, where Richard reserved only homage and gave him resources to undertake complete conquest. In fact, Vere never went to Ireland – probably he never intended to – and Richard even condoned his divorce from his royal wife and remarriage to his mistress Agnes Lancecrona, a German or Czech attendant of his queen, Anne of Bohemia.

Vere did not earn these favours by ability or good service. He was still only twenty-six years of age at his fall and had little experience to his credit. Indeed he seems to have been incompetent both as a soldier and administrator. He was arrogant, frivolous, immoral and empty-headed. His excessive promotion caused great offence, particularly as his birth and resources in no way surpassed those over whom he claimed precedence. His divorce offended the royal family and his grants often infringed the rights of others, notably the Duke of Gloucester and the king's half-brother John Holland. Hence his unpopularity at the time. Modern historians have been even more scathing. For Miss McKisack he was 'a man of neither talent nor judgement. Though not wanting in personal courage, Vere was foolish and irresponsible, rather than sinister and dangerous'. Certainly he seems to have had no distinctive policies to offer.

Opponents of the court did not accept that he was harmless. They wanted him destroyed. Suffolk's impeachment in 1386 had failed to curb Richard and his favourites and it was in anticipation of further trouble that Vere became justice of Chester and north Wales in September/October 1387. Later the same year Vere exploited their potential for military recruitment for the campaign that ended in his defeat at Radcot Bridge in Oxfordshire and confirmed the Lords Appellant in control. Vere himself swam the Thames to safety and fled abroad, thus escaping the sentence of death passed on him in his absence at the Merciless Parliament of 1388. Although the king wished to recall him, his magnates did not, and Vere died in poverty, still in exile, after a hunting accident in 1392. His formal reinterment at Earls Colne by the king in 1395 was poorly attended by the nobility, who remembered their ill-will towards him. Absence had not caused their hearts to grow fonder.

Further Reading
C. Given-Wilson, *The Royal Household and the King's Affinity: Service, Politics and Finance in England 1360-1413*, 1986.
J. A. Tuck, *Richard II and the English Nobility*, 1973.
A. B. Steel, *Richard II*, 1941.

VERGIL, POLYDORE (*c.*1470-1555), historian, was born at Urbino in Italy about 1470 and died there in 1555. He was educated at two universities, Padua and Bologna; he was for a time secretary to Guidobaldo, Duke of Urbino; and he was ordained at some date before 1496. His relation, Adriano Castelli, Cardinal of Corneto, became the official collector of Peter's Pence under Henry VII and was given the bishopric of Hereford. In 1502 Polydore came to England and joined Adriano: most of his life was thenceforward spent in England. He received the living of Church Langston in Leicestershire (1503), a prebend in Lincoln Cathedral and in Hereford Cathedral (1507); he was appointed Archdeacon of Wells (1508) and was given the prebend of Oxgate in St Paul's (1513), all owing to the influence of Adriano. In 1504 he was prosecuted for illegal speculation in foreign currency. In 1510 he secured a Papal bull for the foundation of St John's College, Cambridge.

In 1514 he went to Rome to try to get a cardinal's hat for Wolsey. On his return he was put in the Tower by Wolsey with Adriano, whom Wolsey blamed for his initial failure (1515), but when Wolsey was made cardinal that year, Polydore was released a few months later. The rest of his life was devoted to writing. He signed the denial of Papal supremacy, he accepted the Articles of 1536 and communion in both kinds in 1547. In 1553 he returned to Italy and died at Urbino in 1555.

In his own day Polydore's fame rested on his *De Inventoribus Rerum*, which was published in Venice in 1499. This book was written in three months and described the 'first begetters' of all human activities, e.g. the origin of the gods, language, religion, etc. In 1521 he greatly enlarged the book and dealt with the origins of Christianity, but because he traced some ceremonies back to pagan superstitions, the book was put on the Index. He had earlier written a small book, *Proverbiorum Libellus*, which brought about a quarrel with Erasmus. In 1525 Polydore edited the works of Gildas.

Today Polydore is chiefly remembered for his *Anglica Historia*. In 1506 Henry VII (or more probably Richard Fox, Bishop of Winchester) had suggested to him that he should write a history of England. The first printed edition appeared in 1534, a folio with illustrations by Holbein. The book was written in Latin and covered the history of England down to 1537. Down to 1450 the history is not much more than a compilation based on the old classical texts, such as Caesar, Polybius, Livy, Tacitus, etc., and on medieval histories such as Gildas and Bede, and on chroniclers such as William of Newburgh, William of Malmesbury, Geoffrey of Monmouth, etc. He also drew on manuscript sources, so that his book is in some respects a work of research. From 1450 down to 1537 Vergil's book becomes increasingly valuable as an original source, especially for the reign of Henry VII. His avowed purpose was twofold: to tell the truth and to justify the rise of the Tudor family. On the whole Polydore was an accurate historian, but now and again he allows his passions to colour his writing – for example, in Book xxvii, where his hatred for Wolsey undermines his respect for the truth.

Vergil was an exponent of the new methods of writing history: he tested his authorities and he based his judgements on rational commonsense. He was a bold writer and he did not hesitate to criticize some English customs, traditions and institutions, such as the universities, the monasteries and the lawyers, for which he incurred much odium.

> Maro and Polydore bore Vergil's name;
> One reaps a poet's, one a liar's fame.

He was even accused of destroying his original sources. He hated and deplored the growing nationalism, especially in France, which was causing such suffering to his own country of Italy through the Italian wars of Charles VIII and Louis XII.

Further Reading
Denys Hay, *Polydore Vergil, Renaissance Historian and Man of Letters*, 1952.
Polydore Vergil, *Anglica Historia, AD1485-1537*, ed. D. Hay, Camden Society, vol. lxxiv, 1950.

VERNON, EDWARD (1684-1757), admiral, was a greater man than the bare record of his life would suggest: it was his misfortune that most of his service was performed at a time when there was limited scope for distinction, but his humanity and practical sense contributed much to the well-being of the navy.

Edward Vernon's father was a Whig politician, Secretary of State from 1697 to 1700. He entered the navy in 1701, one of the earliest from his class to make a career at sea. He was also a more active politician than most naval officers, becoming a Member of Parliament in 1722, for Ipswich. Towards the end of the long peace of Walpole's administration, which was as irksome to the keen naval officer as it was to opposition politicians, Vernon stressed in speech after speech the weakness of the Spanish in the West Indies. He declared that he could take Porto Bello, haunt of the *gardacostas* who tried to stop the English trading in that area, with six ships. He was loud in his denunciation of the Convention of Pardo by which Walpole tried to patch up a settlement with Spain. When war came, in 1739, Vernon was promoted vice-admiral and dispatched to Porto Bello with eight ships. His orders were merely to burn the shipping in the harbour. Its defences looked formidable but Vernon prepared an assault worthy of Drake. After two days of fighting, on 22 November, he captured the place. The manner of the assault, besides the value of the place, particularly in the eyes of city and plantation men, made Vernon a public hero, as mugs and public houses bearing his effigy, roads and farmhouses named after him, testify to this day. But the early advantage was dissipated. Vernon believed that the ministry would be better to keep a large fleet in West Indian waters, 'by which means, let who will possess the country, our Royal Master may possess the wealth of it', than to mount expensive operations to capture the islands. Not only did they send out such an expedition but they delayed fatally in the process. Not until January 1741 did the fleet, thirty ships and 10,000 men, assemble; then the military commander, General Wentworth, carried out a pedantic assault by slow stages while his men were reduced by disease. In the end, Vernon had to re-embark the 2,500 survivors of the force. Similar attempts upon Santiago and Panama also failed dismally. At the end of 1742 Vernon was recalled to England, where the threat of French invasion and Jacobitism were causing alarm.

Vernon was a man of independent views and never afraid to speak his mind. He was bold enough to tell George II, in the year before the battle of Dettingen, that 'his Security lay in being master of the sea, and that when he ceased so to be, his land army could not preserve him'. He was a constant advocate of the seamen, whose conditions were indeed brutal and degrading. 'Our fleets,' he said, 'which are defrauded by injustice, are first manned by violence and maintained by cruelty.' They were, in effect, 'condemned to death, since they are never allowed again to set foot on shore, but turned over from ship to ship'. The abuse of the press gang was made worse by the vast expansion that became necessary when war was declared. Three times this occurred in this century – in 1739, 1755 and 1775, after years of peacetime neglect and contraction. It is surprising that battles could be won by raw crews lashed into subservience, that there was no serious general mutiny to the end of the century – and men could still feel devotion for their officers. One reason is that men such as Vernon understood their plight. Vernon is justly famous for his introduction of 'grog' (so called after his conspicuous grogram cloak), a quart of water mixed with a half-pint of rum, though this in itself was no cure for the plague of scurvy. But he was more remarkable in condemning in parliament the distribution of prize-money, 'the sailors' part having no proportion to that of the officers'. After he had been unjustly dismissed from the navy, Vernon displayed a characteristic interest in social problems. On similar lines to Fielding's *Proposal for the Poor*, he and other local landowners started a House of Industry at Nacton in Suffolk. It was far in advance of its time, with its separate apartments for married couples, single men and single women, and was copied elsewhere. His fine tomb at Nacton commemorates a man who cared for ordinary people more than seems to have been usual amongst the upper classes of his day.

Further Reading
Douglas Ford, *Admiral Vernon*, 1907.

VICTORIA, QUEEN (1819-1901). 'The thought of England without the queen is dreadful ... God help us all!' Princess May reflected the reaction of the country to the news of Victoria's death. It was not just its coincidence with the start of the new century and the shock of the Boer War which stunned her people, but her longevity and her strong identification with their instincts and beliefs. These made her the symbol and the rallying centre for the nation.

Throughout her life Victoria's was a robust and emphatic personality. Her father the Duke of Kent, one of George III's many eccentric sons, died eight months after her birth, and her mother, Victoria of Saxe-Coburg, devoted her life to her upbringing. So tight was her control that mother and daughter shared a bedroom in Kensington Palace until the day in 1837 when Victoria became queen. From that evening, however, the duchess found herself sleeping on her own, and her major-domo, Sir John Conroy, was precipitately removed from the new court. 'At 9 came Lord Melbourne,' wrote the new queen in her journal that day, 'whom I saw in my room, and of course quite ALONE, as I shall always do with all my Ministers.' Later she became closer again to her mother; and she remained devoted to 'dear Lehzen', her governess. Lehzen had coaxed her through her moods, and had seen to it that her charge acquired many accomplishments. Victoria was for the most part a ready learner. She had a good head for figures and a gift for languages; also a musical voice and a love of opera. Her artistic skill was shown in vivid line sketches and later in paintings, filling fifty albums. Many of her best were of people, especially of her children and grandchildren, and of Highland lassies: the last, in 1890, was of two of her Sikh soldiers. Her mind was quick and practical. The refinements of theological argument were not to her taste. 'That is what I call twaddle,' was her reaction to a bishop's attempt to comfort her after Albert's death by urging her to see herself as 'the Bride of Christ'. She believed in a Broad Church and good works: small daily tasks. 'I love to be employed: I hate to be idle.' Her serious sense of purpose showed itself early. 'I will be good', she said to Lehzen when she discovered, aged ten, that she would become queen when William IV died, and her journals are peppered with references to self-improvement. She also had in full measure those priceless gifts for public life: good health, energy and stamina. Everyone at her first Council was astonished at her poise and moved by her youth. It was a radiant start.

But her reputation was to swing violently. Her political education belonged at first to Melbourne. From this charming old Whig prime minister she accepted readily, with her mind, the limitations of a constitutional monarch; but her strong will and hot temper often took her over the brink of constitutional propriety. Both were in evidence in 1839. She refused to accept any changes amongst the Ladies of her Bedchamber when the Tories were to replace the Whigs in government. Peel abandoned his attempt to form a ministry because of her obstinacy over this, and political resentment was acute, made worse by Victoria giving credence to the rumour that one of her mother's (unmarried) Ladies from a Tory family, Flora Hastings, was pregnant, when she was actually suffering from a terminal stomach tumour. Two Tory ladies hissed the queen at Ascot; she wished she could have flogged them. Later she recorded that she had ridden in Rotten Row with Melbourne 'without one hiss'. There were to be other dark times, some much longer. At the start of the Crimean War crowds assembled near the Tower on a rumour that Albert and she were to be taken through the Traitors Gate. Things were to become still worse after Albert's death.

Much of her unpopularity was concentrated in the upper classes, and was focused on her Coburg relations. Her mother's brother Leopold had been close to the British throne, as the husband of George IV's only child and heir, Charlotte, who had died in childbirth. He worked hard and successfully to get alongside his niece, and to arrange a fresh Coburg marriage for her with young Albert, son of his elder brother. This plan might have backfired, for Victoria did not like being managed. But she fell in love as she looked down at the handsome twenty-year-old Albert from the top of the stairs at Windsor. She remained in love with him for the rest of her life, through twenty-one years of marriage and forty years of widowhood. Their relationship was sometimes stormy. He accused her of allowing their first baby to be starved: she purposefully emptied a cup of hot tea over his head. But his influence on her was deep. They worked with their desks alongside each other, they built their homes together at Osborne and at Balmoral, they were serious-minded parents who shared the upbringing of their many children. He even helped her choose her bonnets. For her he was the head of the family. When he was away she pined for him: when he died she kept him in the centre of her life. Anyone going round Osborne House or Frogmore Mausoleum can still see the shrines she made for him.

Victoria and Albert's family life set new standards in the British monarchy. She gave birth to nine children, five within seven years of her marriage. Although she found the physical aspects distasteful, and nicknamed a cow on the royal farm 'Princess Alice' when she heard that her daughter Alice was suckling her own child, royal life was domestic life. She and Albert normally lunched with their children, spent time with them in the evening and often visited their lessons. Victoria was quick to sell the Pavilion in Brighton which George IV had created, disliking the crowds as much as its garish style. In their search for privacy they went to the Isle of Wight, where Albert designed Osborne, and to Scotland, where they bought and developed Balmoral. There they lived as a family, with their jokes and their nicknames, their picnics and theatricals, even bathing expeditions at Osborne (though Victoria never learnt to swim and got a nasty shock when she put her head under water). They loved the Highlands of Scotland, which reminded Albert of his native Thuringia, and Victoria eventually published her *Leaves from a Highland Journal*, describing long expeditions on pony and foot. Back at Windsor, they bent their minds to the children's education. Vicky, the eldest, was bright: the boys less so, especially Bertie, the future Edward VII, who reacted against his sister and his tutors. Albert could coax him back to his books, but Victoria was impatient with him, and alarmed by his easy nature, and later by his love of pleasure. He was unworthy of his father, and she did not let him see state papers until he was over fifty. Victoria indeed became a formidable mother, especially after the death of Albert. 'They are in terror of the queen,' wrote her secretary of her sons: the Prince of Wales was described as perspiring in fear behind a pillar when arriving late for lunch. When Vicky went off to Berlin as a bride, she wrote to her as often as four times in one day; parcels included two pairs of stays with instructions on how to wear them. Later she liked to be called to the birth of each grandchild.

Albert's influence was strong on her approach to her task as queen. He encouraged her to focus on foreign policy, to insist on her right to see all despatches and to propose alterations. They travelled together. In 1843 she became the first English monarch to land in France since Henry VIII, when they visited Louis Philippe at Eu in their fine new paddle-steamer, the *Victoria and Albert*; and her journal bubbles with excitement and happiness, for his daughter Louise and his daughter-in-law Victoire were two of her closest friends. Albert, ever a Coburg, gave her a conservative pro-Austrian bias. They thus grew fiercely at odds with Palmerston, a Foreign Secretary who ran his own show and backed liberal and national uprisings. 'Pilgerstein' was his court nickname. They eventually persuaded the prime minister, Russell, to dismiss him, but when the electorate rejected Russell they had to accept its verdict. Throughout her reign the queen expressed strong views on European issues, and had close contacts with most courts. Her family network grew to proportions only previously reached by the Hapsburgs. Her daughter Vicky married Fritz, briefly kaiser, and their son was Kaiser William II. One granddaughter married Tsar Nicholas II; four others married kings. But there was no political power behind the letters and family gatherings: only when Victoria was in tune with the national mood could her influence be felt, and this was seldom the case while Albert was alive.

The trauma of his death in 1861 affected her for more than ten years. His portrait hung over the pillow of his empty bed, and his clothes were laid out each evening, with hot water and a clean towel. At first she would not attend the Privy Council, and communicated with it from another room through an intermediary. She did not appear in an open carriage until 1864. She first opened parliament again in 1866, crownless and clad entirely in black, and subsequently refused to do so for the first three years of Gladstone's ministry. By that time the physical depression had lifted, and warnings of impending insanity and threats of abdication were becoming unconvincing, especially as she was prepared to emerge whenever a parliamentary grant for one of her children was in the offing. Hidden from public view, she became known as 'The Widow of Windsor'.

Her reputation was also damaged by the arrival in England in 1864 of 'The Queen's Highland Servant', John Brown. Victoria was a woman who needed a man. Melbourne, Uncle Leopold, Wellington, Disraeli were all public figures to whom she could give her personal trust. In this time of private withdrawal she turned to Brown, one of the two ghillies who had looked after her and Albert, a handsome intelligent Scot with a blunt manner, a (well-managed) fondness for whisky, and a strong chin. He went everywhere with her, conspicuously dressed as a Highlander. He was 'handy', high praise in her vocabulary. 'He comes to my room after breakfast and after luncheon to get his orders, and everything is always *right*', she wrote to Vicky. His privileged status caused resentment in her household, and wild rumours were started that she had married him. But she refused to bow to this 'ill-natured gossip in the higher classes'. 1871 was her *annus horribilis*. She was seriously ill for the first time since childhood, had an abscess lanced and lost two stone. Criticisms of her absence came to a head with a pamphlet 'What Does She Do With It?' – 'It' being her Civil List, voted annually; and the radical MP Charles Dilke publicly proposed the end of the monarchy. In November the Prince of Wales went down with typhoid.

His recovery proved the turning point. There were deafening cheers when Victoria drove with him to the Thanksgiving Service at St Paul's. Dilke was booed in the House of Commons, and within three years she was back in the thick of politics. Where Gladstone's anxious strictures had failed, Disraeli's charm worked. Dizzy had backed the Albert Memorial project, had written to her during her illness, and greeted her as a fellow author after the publication of *The Highland Journal*. He sent her snowdrops, 'a Faery gift for Queen Titania herself', and, after buying the control of the Suez Canal, presented it to her: 'It is settled Ma'am, you have it!' She warmed to his style, and was soon pushing to have herself made Empress of India.

What would Albert have made of Disraeli, the Hebrew Conjuror? One fancies he would have preferred Gladstone, the disciple of his hero Peel. But this was a new Victoria, and much of Albert's schooling had faded. Her enthusiasm for science remained, but her intellectual and cultural interests waned. 'So much for Philosophy', she wrote when she heard that a Doctor of Philosophy had shot at the kaiser. From Albert's hopes for peace through Free Trade and the mutual respect of nations, she had moved far. She delighted in the 'high tone' of Disraeli's policy, and was soon to become a Jingoist, like her people. 'Giving up what one has is *always* a bad thing', she wrote to Salisbury when he arranged with Germany the exchange of Heligoland for Zanzibar. She felt a personal loyalty towards 'her' troops, and rejoiced in presenting the Victoria Cross to the heroes from Indian and African wars. The Empress of India was fascinated by the orient, and in 1887 she took on an Indian servant, 'the Munshi', who replaced John Brown as the man about court. Her Diamond Jubilee was a vast worldwide Imperial celebration.

At home, the unbiassed approach to Whig and Tory, towards which Albert had led her, disappeared completely. Her later years were dominated by her dislike of Gladstone. She disliked his policies; the disestablishment of the Church of Ireland and the reforms in the army, both areas of her personal prerogative. Home Rule for Ireland threatened the unity of her dominions. His 'tone' abroad was of the lowest, with shameful withdrawals in Afghanistan and Africa. When he allowed Gordon to die in Khartoum, she sent him an open telegram: '… to think that all this might have been prevented and many precious lives saved is too frightful.' She also disliked his style. He treated her to long lectures and tried to interfere, by suggesting inappropriate tasks for the Prince of Wales, and pushing her into more public appearances. In the country his public oratory seemed to threaten the constitutional balance, and to compete with her own relationship with her people: she wrote sarcastically of the 'Royal Progresses' of 'The People's William'. She came to see him as mad as well as bad, and her feelings became so intense that she went far beyond constitutional propriety. To frustrate his tactics over Home Rule in 1886, she wrote to Salisbury, leader of the Opposition: 'Pray advise me how to protest against such a fearful danger, and consult together HOW this contingency can be stopped.'

Long before her death this little old lady in black had become a legend. At the farthest reaches of her Empire on which the sun never set, some New Guinea tribes worshipped her as their Holy Mother. She continued to travel in Europe, and her annual visits to Nice during the 1890s give a flavour of her closing years. For her seven-coach train the lines were cleared. It slowed to 25 m.p.h. at night and stopped for an hour for her to dress. The Irish stew which she ate on it was kept luke-warm in red flannel cushions. But she stayed in a hotel, refusing to be restricted by buying her own villa, and she enjoyed trips out, including one to the Nice battle of flowers, where she was seen pelting French officers from her carriage. Back home, she was her people's queen. Her enthusiasm for progress caught their mood. So did her large family and domestic virtues. So did her robust patriotism. She had no doubts about the righteousness of the British cause in the Boer War: 'The Boers are horrid people, cruel and overbearing'; nor about a British victory. 'We are not interested in the possibilities of defeat,' she told Balfour during Black Week. 'They do not exist.' Small wonder that the British faced with apprehension a new century without her.

Further Reading
S. Weintraub, *Victoria, An Intimate Biography*, 1987.
Elizabeth Pakenham, *Victoria R.I.*, 1964.

Queen Victoria, *Leaves From the Journal of Our Life in the Highlands*, 1868.

VILLIERS, BARBARA, COUNTESS OF CASTLE-MAINE and DUCHESS OF CLEVELAND (1641-1709), mistress of Charles II, was the 'lady of youth and beauty, with whom the king had lived in great and notorious familiarity from the time of his coming into England', as Clarendon puts it. With auburn hair, wistful blue eyes and slim figure, she was very beautiful. She was also, in Burnet's words, 'enormously vicious and ravenous', and her lovers, besides Charles and her complaisant husband, Roger Palmer, whom she married in 1659 and who was created Earl of Castlemaine in 1661, included the Earl of Chesterfield, John Churchill, Ralph Montagu, the playwright William Wycherley, and Jacob Hall the rope-dancer. *Maîtresse en titre* for the first seven years of the reign, she was forced upon Catherine of Braganza as lady-in-waiting. In some ways her authority was great, as Henry Killigrew found when in 1666 he was banished from court, and she relished her part in the campaign which got rid of Clarendon in 1667. But her political influence was small, like that of all Charles's women except the Duchess of Portsmouth. For the king, as Clarendon observed, 'did not in his nature love a busy woman, and had an aversion from speaking with any woman, or hearing them speak, of any business but to that purpose he thought them all made for'. Financially as well as sexually greedy, Castlemaine did well out of her charms, with a grant in 1669 of £4,700 a year from the revenues of the post office, rents from Irish lands, the royal estate of Nonsuch, and sundry other items. She bore Charles at least five children. The hold of this 'lewd Imperial Whore' declined at the end of the 1660s, and her creation as Duchess of Cleveland in 1670 was a sign that she was pensioned off. Yet one later episode in her career was of political consequence. After living in Paris with Ralph Montagu, English ambassador to France, she complained to Charles in 1678 that he had seduced their daughter; Montagu was dismissed, and in revenge revealed to the Commons Danby's secret negotiations with Louis, action which led to the fall of Danby and the dissolution of the Cavalier parliament. She lived on until 1709. Her husband died in 1705, and the following year she diverted London society by marrying a former Major-General, 'Beau' Feilding. Before long he was in Newgate for maltreating her, and it was discovered that he already had a wife.

VILLIERS, GEORGE, 1st DUKE OF BUCKINGHAM (1592-1628), royal favourite, was the younger son by a second marriage of a knight from Brookesby in Leicestershire. Tall, well-proportioned, handsome, he was sent by his mother to France to master the courtly accomplishments of riding, dancing and duelling, and soon after his return he first met King James I, at Apethorpe in 1614. The king's passions were roused at once. He was beginning to tire of Carr, and a group of courtiers, notably Archbishop Abbot, deliberately backed the new young man. The appointment of Villiers as a Gentleman of the Bedchamber in the spring of 1615 began an ascent, which in Clarendon's phrase, 'was so quick, that it seemed rather a flight than a growth'. James showered titles and estates upon him, making him Master of the Horse and a viscount in 1616, an earl in 1617 and Master of the Wardrobe in 1617. With honours went political authority. Carr had been ruined in 1616 through the Overbury murder and the Howards were removed from power in 1618. Within four years of the Apethorpe meeting Buckingham, at twenty-six, had become the principal figure in the land, and for the next ten years he was the virtual ruler of England.

Buckingham had more than physical beauty and athletic skill to commend him. He had courage, charm and affability, he learned to dispatch business quickly, and his management of James and Charles showed both adroitness and a real loyalty. No doubt it was very much to his interest to suffer patiently James's petting and pawing of his 'Sweet Steenie', and the manner in which he pretended to return the king's love is as nauseating as it was skilful. In the circumstances his conquest, after an initial outburst of jealousy, of the friendship of the decorous Charles and the latter's deep devotion to him are remarkable phenomena. Not did he lack political talent. Whereas Carr had been a nincompoop dependent on Overbury's brains, Buckingham recognized both the need for financial reform and the ability of Cranfield to undertake it. Nevertheless, his rise and régime did irreparable damage to the relations between the Stuarts and their subjects. The roots of his greatness were tainted: he could never cease to be an upstart whose authority was founded upon his physical attractions for a drooling monarch, and he provides the classical example of 'the favourite' in modern English history. Moreover, the most obvious use he made of his power was to build up a network of nepotism and clientage, with his worthless relatives in high office. Fortified by the extension of monopolies and the sale of honours, such a system merely drove the country gentry away from sympathy with the Crown. As Christopher Hill has said, 'the monopolization of patronage by Buckingham did much to cause the division between court and country, the split in the ruling class, which made possible the Civil War'.* In the process he enriched himself on a gigantic scale, for his motive was as much profit as power. Buckingham was neither statesman nor competent administrator. Young, inexperienced, the spoiled darling of fortune, arrogantly confident of his ability to rule, he was – as

Clarendon points out in a distinctly generous assessment – unable through the very nature of his role to obtain the wise advice which he needed. The events of his years of power revealed that his 'policy' was merely an unhappy mixture of opportunism and selfishness. Above all, he proved hopelessly incapable of understanding and of managing the revolutionary force of his time, the opposition in the House of Commons.

The removal of the Howards and the employment of Cranfield as Lord Treasurer promised well. The realities emerged when the parliament of 1621, for which Buckingham had made no adequate preparation, attacked the monopolists, among whom the favourite's two brothers were prominent. The Lords were notably hostile to the upstart family, and Buckingham sacrificed the monopolists. He was happy to see Bacon become a scapegoat and happier still when James dissolved parliament in his fury at the 'Protestation' of the Commons. In foreign policy at this time Buckingham, gaining power as the king aged, warmly supported the Spanish marriage project and hobnobbed with the Spanish ambassador, Gondomar. When in 1623 Prince Charles produced his hare-brained scheme of going incognito to Madrid and returning with the Infanta as his bride, Buckingham helped persuade the reluctant James to let them go. He deeply offended the Spaniards by his careless manner and bad temper; yet he appears to have realized the folly of the whole enterprise more quickly than Charles. The two returned, as Tawney put it, 'in the mood of the disappointed suitor who demonstrates the depth of his devotion by cutting the ungrateful loved one's throat'.† Cashing in on the national joy over the fiasco in Madrid, he demanded war with Spain, in a short-lived agreement with the Commons. This entailed the sacrifice of Cranfield, who opposed the war and had already offended Buckingham by making it plain that his economies would not halt when they reached the Villiers family. When Cranfield was impeached, James, in a flash of wisdom from his dotage, cried out, 'By God, Steenie, you are a fool and will shortly repent this folly and will find that in this fit of popularity you are making a rod with which you will be scourged yourself'.

The old man died in March 1625. Buckingham's domination of the new king was complete, perhaps because he appealed to an underlying romanticism in Charles's complex personality. The results were two scandalously unsuccessful foreign wars and a gulf, never to be crossed, between Charles and the Commons. The war with Spain brought two disasters in 1625, both very largely the result of Buckingham's incompetent management. In March, Mansfeld's expedition withered away at Ostend, without ever encountering the enemy, and in October the attack on Cadiz collapsed in neglect,

---

*Christopher Hill, *The Century of Revolution*, 1961, p.71.

†R. H. Tawney, *Business and Politics under James I*, 1958, p.235.

cowardice and drunkenness. Parliament, meeting in the summer and denied an explanation of foreign policy, refused supply and was promptly dissolved when it showed signs of attacking Buckingham. Worse was to follow. Charles's French marriage (May 1625), itself a fatal fruit of Buckingham's policy, led first to the employment of English seamen against the Protestant stronghold of La Rochelle and then, through the breakdown of its terms, to a war with France. There were other and more important causes, notably mutual seizures of merchant shipping in the Channel and Buckingham's own behaviour in negotiations in Paris. Arrogantly offended that Richelieu declined to fall in with his plans for a joint attack upon Spain, he took revenge by making love to Louis XIII's queen, Anne of Austria. Meanwhile at home the second parliament of the reign (1626) had under Eliot's leadership launched an open attack upon Buckingham and demanded his impeachment. Charles saved his friend by dissolving the Houses, having again failed to get a grant.

Against this background of disunity and mismanagement the French war began in 1627. Buckingham in person led an expedition of 8,000 men to the Isle of Rhé to relieve the Huguenots besieged in La Rochelle. He showed bravery and energy, but the enterprise was a total failure. The troops were untrained and ill-provided, the naval planning was lamentably inefficient, and he returned to Portsmouth with half his force destroyed. A further expedition to Rhé later in the year under the Earl of Denbigh also achieved nothing, and Buckingham advised Charles to summon a third parliament in March 1628. The Commons, under the more moderate leadership of Coke and Wentworth, turned first to broader grievances and produced the Petition of Right, which Charles reluctantly accepted in June. But then, whipped up once more by Eliot, they drew up a remonstrance against the favourite, and Charles prorogued them at once. Buckingham went down to Portsmouth to prepare a third expedition to La Rochelle, and there in August he was assassinated by John Felton. The London crowds cheered the news. Certainly his murder removed an obstacle to good relations between Crown and parliament, for no man did more to misdirect the Stuarts. Yet the manner of his death, and the popular rejoicing, could not fail to sear the mind of a king whose politics were so much a matter of personal emotion.

Further Reading
Roger Lockyer, *Buckingham*, 1981.

VILLIERS, GEORGE, 2nd DUKE OF BUCKING-HAM (1628-87), member of the Cabal, in Dryden's words 'Chymist, Fidler, States-Man and Buffoon', was the second son of James I's favourite, his elder brother dying in infancy. Brought up as a boy with Charles II, he spent some of the Civil War years in Italy. In l647 he

recovered his sequestered estates, but lost them again when he rose with the royalists in the Second Civil War. Joining Charles II's court, he was with the king at Worcester and managed to escape to Rotterdam. At the exiled court he quarrelled incessantly with Hyde and began to intrigue with parliament for the return of his lands. In 1657 he slipped across to England to marry Fairfax's daughter Mary, and was imprisoned by the Protectorate government. Released, in 1660 he tried to join Fairfax when the latter raised the Yorkshire gentry, but the soldiers would not have so notorious a royalist with them.

Despite this equivocal background he returned to Charles's favour at the Restoration. He was admitted to the Privy Council in 1662; he was prominent in the period of the Cabal; and he was employed on missions to Louis XIV (1670) and William of Orange (1673). Yet he never held high office. Clarendon, to whom Buckingham led the opposition, kept him out in the early years of the reign. After Clarendon's fall in 1667 he did for a time exercise a considerable influence over the king, and, as frequent entries in Pepys's *Diary* for 1667-8 suggest, was widely rumoured to 'rule all'. But this is extremely doubtful and certainly whatever political influence he had over Charles declined from the time of the Treaty of Dover (1670); indeed, the bogus second treaty with France in that year was devised in order to throw dust in Buckingham's eyes. He quarrelled with Arlington and the Duke of York and moved into opposition to the Crown, setting himself up as a champion of the Dissenters and a patriotic Protestant, even though he was receiving large sums of money from Louis XIV. In 1677 he was imprisoned, with three other peers, for maintaining that the parliament which Charles had prorogued was automatically dissolved. He was released through the pleadings of Nell Gwyn. For a time he supported Shaftesbury's campaign for Exclusion, but he soon fell out with Shaftesbury and failed to support the bill in the Lords. He gradually cut adrift from the Country party and ceased by the early 1680s to take part in public life. Going to reside in Yorkshire, deeply in debt, he lived the life of a seedy country squire, and died as the result of a chill caught while digging out a fox.

Buckingham was a man of superb talents, good-looking, graceful, intelligent, witty, a musician and a playwright (his play *The Rehearsal*, a satire upon contemporary drama, was the prototype of Sheridan's *The Critic*). As Clarendon pointed out, he had the power to fascinate men: 'his quality and condescensions, the pleasantness of his humour and conversation, the extravagance and sharpness of his wit, unrestrained by any modesty or religion, drew persons of all affections and inclinations to like his company'. In view of his heredity and of his upbringing in civil war and exile, it is scarcely surprising that he had the fashionable vices of his age, and of his king; the Countess of Shrewsbury was his mistress, and he diverted Charles by mimicking Presbyterian preachers in obscene sermons. But Buckingham was too disreputable even for the Restoration. He was a bully as well as an adulterer: brutal to his wife, he murdered the Earl of Shrewsbury in a duel, relying upon the king's pardon. Too often his wit turned into a perverse quarrelsomeness, while his political opposition was never far from treason (as when he was put in the Tower in 1667 for 'caballing' against the king) because his politics were founded upon personal antipathies and momentary whims. Dryden's famous sketch of him as Zimri in *Absalom and Achitophel*, which portrays Buckingham's fickleness, is concerned, as the poet himself said, with his 'little extravagancies' and is therefore charitable. Burnet went deeper when he said that Buckingham 'had no principles of religion, virtue, or friendship'. Anthony à Wood, not surprisingly, condemned Buckingham as 'a great favourer of fanaticks and atheists'; yet it is difficult not to attribute even this, his support of toleration, merely to a dislike of Anglican respectability. Few men of such natural gifts in our history have squandered them so trivially.

Further Reading
Hester W. Chapman, *Great Villiers*, 1949.

VORTIGERN (*fl.c.*425-55?) was the name of a British ruler of the sub-Roman period, remembered in later Welsh legend as a scapegoat: the man who had invited the Saxons to Britain and thus precipitated their conquest of the island. We may suspect that the truth was a little more complicated than this. Our trouble is that we possess scarcely any reliable information about Vortigern. Gildas, who does not mention him by name, seems to refer to him as a 'proud tyrant'. Bede supplements the account of Gildas by naming Vortigern and referring to him as a king. By the time that Nennius was writing in the early ninth century many doubtful stories had gathered about Vortigern's doings. This is not much to go on, but it is very nearly all that there is.

Modern historians for the most part accept that Vortigern existed and that he exercised political authority over a part – perhaps a large part – of what had been Roman Britain. The period in which he ruled is perhaps most probably placed in the second quarter of the fifth century. It is entirely credible that he should have summoned Germanic mercenaries to Britain, settled them in bases 'in the eastern part of the island' (in the words of Gildas) and employed them to defend his territories from the attacks of other enemies, notably the Picts. Such a course of action was in line with standard late-Roman policy, well-attested in several areas of the late empire. Indeed, there is every likelihood that the Roman authorities had been following this practice in Britain in the latter part of the fourth century. These people were difficult to control. It is therefore equally credible that the mercenaries should have revolted against their paymaster, broken out from their bases, defeated Vortigern's forces and seized large tracts of British territory for themselves. Something like this may have happened, perhaps in the 440s: we shall never know for certain.

W

WADE, GEORGE (1673-1748), field marshal, was a good and steady soldier who is now best remembered as the builder of the military roads which helped to improve the economy of the Highlands and to subject the region to efficient government. He was first commissioned in the 'Tenth' in 1690, served in Flanders in William III's reign and at the start of the Spanish Succession War as adjutant-general in Galway's expedition to the peninsula; in 1707 he fought bravely at Almanza, where the English were defeated. He was present at the capture of Minorca in 1708 and in command of a brigade at Saragossa in 1710. In England in 1715 he was stationed in the west of England where the expected insurrection did not materialize. He captured Vigo in the short Spanish War of 1719.

In 1725, he was sent to Scotland with orders to execute, with Lord President Duncan Forbes, the provisions of the Act for Disarming the Highland Clans. He at once raised six companies of Highlanders, recruited from Whig clans, notably the Campbells; the number was later raised to ten and formed into the Black Watch, who were blooded on the field of Fontenoy. With this went the disarmament of Jacobite clans: easier to enact than to execute. Anyone who has tramped over General Wade's roads, that which crosses the Coryairack Pass for instance, reaching 2,500 feet and saving a journey of sixty miles, will appreciate Wade's achievement as road-builder. In 1731 one of the Macleods, who crossed the pass, saw six great fires at which six oxen were being roasted whole as a treat for the 500 soldiers who had just completed 'the great road for wheel-carriages between Fort Augustus and Ruthven, it being October 30th, His Majesty's Birthday'. Wade's roads were usually made fourteen or fifteen feet wide (many a modern Highland road is only ten!). Some of his bridges still stand; a particularly fine one is that which crosses the Spey beside the old barracks at Garvamore. By his work Perth was linked to Inverness, Fort Augustus and Fort William. In the '45, however, these places were so lightly garrisoned that improved communications were of more use to the Jacobites than to the defenders.

Wade was by then in Flanders. Promoted field marshal in 1743, he was made commander-in-chief in succession to Stair. His army being smaller than that of Marshal Saxe, a formidable man to oppose, the septuagenarian may be forgiven for slow and cautious tactics designed to avoid action. He was recalled to face the threat of invasion in England. His task was to concentrate what British regiments could be found in England or recalled from Flanders; he also called out the Militia. In the autumn of 1745 he moved slowly north-east to Newcastle, marched across in response to Murray's feint move only to find that the Jacobites had slipped past him, taken Carlisle and were apparently bound for London. The capital was covered, and Charles Edward turned back, but Wade made no attempt to intercept his return journey but stood on the border 'with his feet in the snow'. That was the end of a career in which he was respected by his troops for his personal qualities rather than for any genius for training or tactics. A strict disciplinarian, he seems also to have been a fair and considerate man.

Further Reading
J. B. Salmond, *Wade in Scotland*, 1934.

WAKE, WILLIAM (1657-1737) was an Archbishop of Canterbury whose ecumenical labours displayed a generous and scholarly spirit typical of the eighteenth-century church at its best. The son of a Dorset landowner of ancient family, he was educated at Blandford Grammar School and Christ Church, Oxford, before going to Paris as chaplain to the embassy in 1682. There he made friends among leading French churchmen at a time when the Gallican movement was at its height and when there was much talk of reunion. He acquired a sympathy with moderate church leaders such as Bossuet and a lasting interest in projects of reunion between the churches. He returned in 1685, the year in which the Revocation of the Edict of Nantes dealt a mortal blow to such projects and the accession of James II sharpened religious animosities in England. From 1688 to 1696 he was preacher at Gray's Inn. Another influential pulpit was opened to him when he became Rector of St James, Westminster, in 1693. He was already Doctor of Divinity and Canon of

Christ Church. In 1703 he became Dean of Exeter, in 1705 Bishop of Lincoln, where he was conscientious in his pastoral oversight of the huge diocese. In 1716, like Tenison before him, he was translated from Lincoln to Canterbury. His primacy is disappointing only by contrast with the high hopes that attended him, and with what he wanted to achieve.

In his reply to Bossuet's *Exposition* of the Roman Catholic faith, Wake established principles which he held to all his life: a distinction should be made between fundamental and secondary articles of faith, individual churches should enjoy a measure of liberty, churches might differ, even as much as the Anglican and Gallican churches, yet be in inter-communion. In a correspondence with du Pin (1717), a moderate French theologian with Jansenist leanings, Wake again displayed a reasonable eirenism and it was in this spirit that he took up the remains of a project for the unification of Reformed and Lutheran churches in Prussia, upon an episcopal basis, and the union of the resulting body with the Church of England. This scheme, promoted by Daniel Jablonski, a bishop of the Unitas Fratrum, the old reformed Church of Bohemia, was a promising one; there was a current of opinion in Germany, typified by Leibnitz, towards reunion; England's influence, because of her new connection with Hanover, was potentially great. In complexities as much political as theological the scheme faded away, and the only permanent result was the translation (1704), in German, of the *Book of Common Prayer*. Nor was any greater progress made with the Swiss churches, despite Wake's friendly contacts with prominent Swiss divines.

Wake believed ardently in episcopacy. He makes this clear in his picture of the Anglican church, 'Catholic in regimen, preserving the episcopal polity, duly moderated and divorced from all unjust dominion'. He encouraged foreign students to receive episcopal ordination before leaving the country. He defended the church at home alike against 'the new notions of libertinism' which he saw in Hoadly and others like him who wanted to minimize the authority of church and creed. He fell out of favour with the Whig ministers, as he did with some historians, because of his firm opposition to the Repeal of the Occasional Conformity Act. He wished the church to be comprehensive but not to the point of negation. He may more justly be criticized for his failure to reform those aspects of church government and life which mar the eighteenth-century church: the passive role of Convocation, pluralism and absenteeism of the clergy. But he could do little in the face of a deliberate policy of using church patronage for political ends.

The record at the end is a sound but modest one. His scholarship was preserved in many solid works of theology and history. He maintained a proper state; indeed, he is supposed to have been the last archbishop to have used his barge to travel in state from Lambeth to the Houses of Parliament. He married the daughter of a Norfolk knight, Etheldreda Hovell, produced a large family and left an ample fortune. He was also, however, a generous man who gave much to the restoration of buildings in his dioceses. He cannot be better summed up than in his own words: he hoped that when he came to judgement, 'tho' I have been an unprofitable servant, nevertheless I have ever sought, counselled, and with all my zeal and effort pursued those things which belong to the peace of Jerusalem'.

Further Reading
N. Sykes, *From Sheldon to Secker*, 1959.
N. Sykes, *William Wake*, 2 vols, 1957.

WAKEFIELD, EDWARD GIBBON (1798-1862), colonial planner, was a creative maverick, whose early escapades cast a long shadow over his career, but whose influence was felt, then and later, on the attitude of the British towards their colonies, and on the life of some of the largest and most important of these: Australia, New Zealand and Canada. He had to leave two schools, Westminster and Edinburgh High School. Aged twenty, he achieved a runaway marriage with an heiress. They were happy together, but she died before becoming entitled to her inheritance, and his second attempt to win a fortune was less successful and more disreputable. In 1828 he abducted another heiress (whom he had not met before) from school, married her in Gretna Green, and got as far as Calais. There – still a virgin – she was persuaded to return. Wakefield came back himself to face the music, and spent three years in Newgate Prison.

In Newgate, he wrote two books. One was on punishment, in which he argued that its deterrent effect depended less on its severity than on the likelihood of being caught. The other was on Australia, *A Letter from Sydney*, which purported to come from someone living out there. From then on, he developed and publicized ideas on the relationship of Britain with her colonies. He saw the potential of their empty spaces, but realized that many more labourers were needed to work the land. The flow of convicts, given their own properties when they arrived, inhibited efficient farming, and was creating a vicious society. Systematically planned emigration was needed, of people with appropriate skills, and with a healthy balance between men and women. Those arriving should be expected to work for a period before being allowed to buy land. The cost of this land should be enough to finance future emigration from Britain, but not so high as to deter purchasers: the 'Doctrine of Sufficient Price'. Such societies of responsible emigrants should be given the right to govern themselves in all domestic matters.

Wakefield's ideas appealed to a handful of vociferous Radicals, men such as Buller, Molesworth and Grote, and he put them into practice in south Australia (1834), and later in New Zealand, where he forced the government's hand: when his brother landed with a group of settlers (1839), over 6,000 emigrants followed in two years, and Captain Hobson proclaimed British sovereignty. The Treaty of Waitangi was signed in 1840, allocating land to the Maoris. Meanwhile, Wakefield had gone out to Canada with Lord Durham (1838), and his influence was strong, through Buller, in the drafting of the Durham Report, which united the Provinces of Upper and Lower Canada, and paved the way for self-government there. He often felt that he was swimming against the tide, for his ideas were deeply unfashionable. Most statesmen of the time saw colonies as an expensive encumbrance. Whig and Tory governments alike dragged their feet. Missionary societies tried to keep corrupting influences away from 'their' natives. Wakefield's own reputation prevented him from holding any Crown office. But he persevered through ill-health, acting as agent for existing New Zealand settlements, and encouraging new ones, including two (Deist though he was himself) which were specifically denominational; the Church of Scotland's around Dunedin, and the Church of England's around Canterbury. Through the Hungry Forties, emigration increased fast: in 1852, over 80,000 left Britain for Australasia. One of them, to New Zealand, was Gibbon Wakefield himself. By then, Wellington, where his brother had landed thirteen years earlier, had a Government House, a cricket pitch and a Royal Victoria Theatre. In that year, the settlements were bound together by a representative assembly, and before he died they had been granted responsible government. The links which tied the colonies of Wakefield's time to Britain were to prove more durable than those of later acquisitions.

WALERAN, LORD OF MEULAN, EARL OF WORCESTER (1104-66), for a few years at the beginning of Stephen's reign was possibly the most important man in England after the king. A descendant of Charlemagne, vain, rash, ambitious and proud, Waleran's career was one of brilliant failure. The elder of the twin sons of Robert of Meulan (d.1118), Henry I's chief adviser, Waleran and his brother Robert, later Earl of Leicester, were well educated, precocious and spoilt, not least by Henry I. After achieving majority in 1120, Waleran, having received the family lands in Normandy and France, experienced sharp changes of fortune. Eager for martial glory, Waleran rebelled against Henry I in 1123-4 on behalf of William Clito only to be crushingly defeated at the battle of Bourgtheroulde (March 1124). Imprisoned for five years, some of the time in chains, he was suddenly released and restored to high favour in 1129. One reason for this royal volte-face may have been Henry's desire to balance the court factions as part of his plans for the succession of his daughter Matilda. Another may have been the king's seduction of Waleran's sister, Elizabeth, who subsequently bore one of Henry's twenty or so illegitimate children. Whatever the cause, Waleran's restoration was complete. For the rest of Henry's reign, he and his brother were regularly at court and enjoyed extensive royal patronage. On Henry I's death in 1135, the twins, in return for large grants of land, supported Stephen. With his wide estates and political contacts in northern France, between 1136 and 1139 Waleran played a central role in trying to secure Norman allegiance to Stephen and repelling invasions by the rival Angevin claimants. Created Earl of Worcester late in 1138, between 1139 and 1141 Waleran was the leading adherent of the king's party in England, especially after he had engineered the fall of the justiciar, Roger of Salisbury, (in the words of one royal sympathizer, because of 'a furious blaze of envy') and Robert of Gloucester had defected to Matilda. It was probably Waleran who obtained the unexpected appointment of Theobald of Bec as Archbishop of Canterbury. In the early years of the civil war, Waleran was vigorous in the king's cause, especially in Worcestershire and Gloucestershire where the fighting was fiercest. 1141 brought disaster. Although fleeing in panic from the royalist defeat at Lincoln in February, Waleran remained loyal to Stephen and stood by Queen Matilda. However, the Angevin advances in Normandy put his French lands in jeopardy. In order to save them, in September 1141, under a truce negotiated by his brother, Waleran changed sides, accepted the claims of the Empress Matilda and left England, never to return. By virtue of his wealth and lineage, Waleran was welcomed by the Angevins, but as Henry FitzEmpress grew to maturity, his influence waned. Absent from France on pilgrimage (1144/5) and crusade (1146-9), after 1150 Waleran was gradually excluded from power in Normandy. His Worcester lands were confiscated in 1153 and, unlike his brother, there was no place for him at Henry II's court after 1154. Thereafter, his sympathies lay increasingly with French rather than Angevin interests. Waleran, an impulsive politician and notable intriguer, was unwilling to compromise self-interest to achieve power. He proved a destructive friend to Stephen by alienating other royal support and, ultimately, ruined himself, brought down by the circumstances of a divided Anglo-Norman state and his own pride. It is revealing that on at least three occasions he described himself as 'by Grace of God Count of Meulan', a typical insistence on his own importance and independence that proved fatal to his ambitions. There was another side. Waleran inspired personal devotion; he was loyal and generous; a patron of learning who himself dabbled in Latin verse. On the contemporary scale of values, such attributes commanded respect and gained applause.

Further Reading
D. Crouch, *The Beaumont Twins*, 1985.

WALKELIN OF WINCHESTER (*d*.1098; Bishop of Winchester 1070-98) was William Rufus's chief minister in the 1090s. Although not on the intimate terms of advisers such as Robert of Meulan, Walkelin was prominent in the king's council, often heading witness lists to charters and writs, and seems to have had charge of the king's financial affairs, in which he worked closely with Ranulf Flambard. It was said that Rufus's incessant demands for cash finally killed him. A Norman, royal clerk of William I and Canon of Rouen, whose brother became Abbot of Ely and nephew Bishop of Hereford and Archbishop of York, at Winchester Walkelin was typical of the new continental episcopate appointed by the Conqueror. Initially hostile to the local tradition of monastic chapters, his attempts to secularize Winchester were thwarted by Lanfranc and, despite the anomalous position of a secular clerk presiding over monks, came to be regarded with affection by them. In 1079, he began to rebuild his cathedral on a grand scale in monumental romanesque: austere, regular, massive, a statement as much about the new secular order as religion. Much of Walkelin's work survives, in the nave and transepts. As Bishop of Winchester, Walkelin was in a position to oversee the main royal treasury houses in the city's castle. Additionally, he acted as a royal commissioner in both secular and ecclesiastical matters: in 1089 he dealt with the restive monks of St Augustine's, Canterbury; in 1095 he investigated the rights of Herbert Losinga, Bishop of Thetford/Norwich; in 1096, he led a judicial circuit of the south-west to hear royal pleas. At court his authority grew in the early 1090s. After the death of Bishop William of Durham in January 1096, Walkelin was the dominant figure in the administration of England, organizing the geld of that year and acting as regent in Rufus's absence in France in 1097. Although he did not work alone, some historians have seen in Walkelin's activities the origins of the office of Chief Justiciar. This seems to be an exaggeration. Walkelin was the king's main administrative deputy, not his prime minister.

Further Reading
F. Barlow, *William Rufus*, 1983.

WALKER, GEORGE (1645?-90), the son of a Yorkshireman who became chancellor of the diocese of Armagh in Ireland, was educated at Glasgow University and later ordained. Parson at Donaghmore in Tyrone from 1674, he raised a Protestant force at Dungannon in the crisis of 1688 and became joint-Governor of Londonderry during its siege of 103 days in 1689, and the central figure in its resistance. He was hailed as a hero when he visited England afterwards. Returning to Ireland, he was killed at the Battle of the Boyne.

Further Reading
T. B. Macaulay, *History of England* (first pub. 1848, many eds), Chap. 12.

WALKER, OBADIAH (1616-99), a Yorkshireman from Darfield, near Barnsley, James II's chief agent in his attempt to Romanize Oxford, was a Fellow of University College who after his ejection by the parliamentarians in 1648 had travelled abroad and spent a good deal of time at Rome. Evelyn thought him 'a learned and most ingenious person' and advised a friend to put his two sons under his tuition: Walker later converted one of them to Catholicism. He was an influential figure in Oxford after his return there in 1665, and became a Master of his college in 1676. As early as 1678 an attempt was made to remove him as a suspected papist. In James's reign he came out openly in support of the king's schemes, obtaining a dispensation to keep his mastership, worshipping in a Roman chapel which he opened in the college, and encouraging the printing of propagandist books. According to Anthony à Wood, Walker, nicknamed 'Obadiah Ave-Maria', was very unpopular in Oxford: his chapel was fair game for those who wanted to cause a disturbance, like the gentleman-commoner of Christ Church 'who laughed and girn'd and shew'd a great deal of scorn', or the boy who hid a cat under his coat while mass was being sung which 'pulling by the tail, made her such an untunable noise that it put them to some disorder'. In 1688 he tried to flee abroad but was caught and put in the Tower until 1690. Deprived of his mastership, he died in London in 1699, having owed a good deal in his last years to the charity of one of his former pupils, Dr John Radcliffe, whom he had unsuccessfully tried to convert to Rome.

WALLACE, WILLIAM (1270-1305) was the leader of the guerrilla struggle which continued, even after the withdrawal of greater men, against the imposition of direct English rule upon Scotland in 1296.

Having enforced the abdication of John Balliol in July 1296, Edward removed to London the Stone of Destiny, the seat of Scottish kingship. These two acts were designed to symbolize the end of Scotland as an independent nation. Government north of the border was placed in the hands of Englishmen led by Hugh Cressingham and the Earl of Surrey. Many magnates came to accept a subordinate role in the administration of Scotland from Westminster. A brief military resistance was launched by Robert Bruce, James the Steward, William, Lord of Douglas and Bishop Wishart, but was quickly abandoned after a defeat at Irvine in July 1297. Lesser leaders remained in the field, and gained widespread support from even humbler people. There had already been disturbances directed against the government in

Ross, Argyll, Moray, Aberdeen, and elsewhere, when William Wallace killed the English sheriff of Lanark (May 1297). By June, there was widespread disorder in Scotland outside the eastern border country. Wallace was chiefly instrumental in pulling these outbreaks together into a rising. He seemed to be everywhere, nearly capturing Edward's justiciar Ormesby at Perth, yet in the same month encamped in Selkirk forest. In the north forces under de Moray captured Aberdeen and Inverness, and Montrose, Brechin and Forfar soon followed. In August Wallace and Andrew de Moray joined forces and soon controlled most of Scotland north of the Forth; by the year end the English administration was virtually bankrupt.

Edward did not believe the seriousness of situation as reported to him by Cressingham, and departed for Flanders in August, but his lieutenants mobilized a large army including heavy cavalry and Welsh archers. This was met by forces under Wallace and de Moray, which barred their way across the Forth at Stirling. The English could only traverse the bridge a few at a time, and the Scots were able to mount a timely attack which separated those who made it from those who had yet to cross. The English cavalry proved ineffective on the swampy ground on the north side of the river and the Welsh fled. Hugh Cressingham was killed at the battle, though the Earl of Surrey escaped to Berwick. The Scots were able to seize Stirling castle, besieging the other English garrisons, and by October were even mounting cross-border raids. The revolt was squashed by the disunity of the nobles, who could not agree on the royal Scottish house to be installed, and by brute force. In February, following his truce with France, Edward I returned to England. He crossed the Tweed on 3 July and at Falkirk on 22 July 1298, with the aid of the archers and heavy cavalry which the Scots (as yet) lacked, heavily defeated Wallace. Militarily, this was the end of his career. His movements afterwards are uncertain but there is some evidence that he went to France where King Philip furnished him with letters of recommendation to Pope Boniface VIII and King Hakon of Norway. Wallace returned to Scotland but was betrayed in Glasgow, captured, and in August 1305 tried for treason to a king he had never sworn an oath of loyalty to, nor even recognized, and executed in London. The charge of treason was especially ironic. Wallace gave his life in the cause of a free and independent Scotland under its legitimate king, John Balliol.

WALLER, SIR WILLIAM (1597-1668), parliamentarian commander, son of the Lieutenant of Dover and educated at Magdalen Hall, Oxford, fought as a professional soldier for the Venetian Republic and the Queen of Bohemia. He was knighted in 1622, but was later fined for brawling at court. When the Long Parliament met in 1640 Waller sat for Andover and soon became prominent in the opposition. As a commander in the war he took Portsmouth and was successful enough at first to be nicknamed 'William the Conqueror', but his later career was somewhat chequered. In 1643 he was soundly defeated by Hopton at Roundway Down, and although in 1644 he kept the royalists out of Sussex and recaptured Wiltshire and Hampshire by his victory at Cheriton, he was badly mauled by the king's army at Cropredy Bridge. In this winter of 1644-5 Waller, never a very effective disciplinarian, was one of the parliamentarian commanders most plagued by mutinies among his troops, and his military career ended with the Self-Denying Ordinance. Thereafter he was prominent as a Presbyterian leader in the Commons, becoming a bitter foe of the army commanders, who drove him into exile in 1647. After his return the following year he suffered at least two spells of imprisonment, and in the later 1650s he got in touch with the royalists. But he got no reward at the Restoration. Perhaps Waller, moderate, humane, typical of many responsible Englishmen on both sides in the Civil Wars, best deserves to be remembered for some phrases in a letter he wrote to Hopton, his former companion-in-arms in Germany and now commander of the opposing royalist forces, on the eve of the battle of Lansdown (1643): 'The great God, which is the searcher of my heart, knows with what a perfect hatred I detest this war without an enemy'.

Further Reading

J. Adair, *Roundhead General: a Military Biography of Sir William Waller*, 1969.
A. H. Burne and P. Young, *The Great Civil War*, 1959.

WALLIS, JOHN (1616-1703), mathematician and divine, son of a clergyman at Ashford in Kent, was educated at Felsted and at the notably Puritan college of Emmanuel, Cambridge, and was a pupil of the noted mathematician, William Oughtred. He put his mathematical ability to political use by deciphering code messages for the parliamentarians during the Civil War, and in the 1640s he held two London livings before being appointed to the Savilian Chair of Geometry at Oxford, when its royalist holder was ejected. During the Commonwealth he was one of the group of scientists whose meetings at Oxford foreshadowed the Royal Society, and his most celebrated work, the *Arithmetica Infinitorum*, which established his reputation, was published in 1657. A moderate in outlook and a trimmer in politics, he had no difficulty in making his peace with the monarchy in 1660 and was appointed a royal chaplain. For the next fifty years Wallis was one of the most distinguished intellectual figures in the country. Even Aubrey, who made him the subject of one of his less kind essays, calling him 'extremely greedy' of fame, said that Wallis 'to give him due praise, hath exceedingly well deserved of the commonwealth of learning'. His *Arithmetica*, the most significant mathematical work hitherto published in England, contained the germs of the calculus and directed Newton, who read it as an undergraduate, to the binomial theorem. Like so many of his contemporaries in the Royal Society, Wallis did not limit his creative activities to one field. In particular he was interested in the practical problems of speech, and carried out experiments in the training of the deaf and dumb.

Further Reading
J. F. Scott, *The Mathematical Work of John Wallis*, 1938.

WALPOLE, HORACE, 4th EARL OF ORFORD

(1717-91), diarist, was the third son of Robert Walpole by his first wife, Catherine Shorter; he was devoted to his mother and hurt by his father's indifference in the later years of the marriage. At Eton he exhibited precociously the wit and the somewhat rarefied literary tastes of his subsequent life; one of the set of aesthetes of which he was acknowledged leader was the poet Gray. He was at King's for four years, though he resided but irregularly. While still an undergraduate he was presented with the first of the sinecures which helped to make his life agreeable: at different times he was Usher of the Exchequer and Controller of the Pipe and Clerk of the Estreats. While out of England on a Grand Tour with Gray he was elected Member of Parliament. He enjoyed the advantages of being the son of a powerful minister and he was loyal to his father, but he was out of sympathy with his hearty way of life and did not attempt to emulate his career.

In 1742 Walpole made his maiden speech in the House which his father was just leaving: it was suitably filial and neatly phrased. He never entirely eschewed active politics. From 1757 until his retirement in 1768 he sat for King's Lynn, which occupied him more than the decayed boroughs of Callington and Castle Rising which he had represented before. He showed mettlesome spirit in his attempt, in 1757, to secure a stay of execution for Admiral Byng; but he preferred to exert influence through more indirect channels. For many years he championed the interests of his able relative, General Conway, whose comparative failure was a sharp disappointment to him. Meanwhile he recorded the political scenes of the age of the Pelhams and Pitt in letters, and in the memoirs (published after his death) which have provided rich material for historians, even where their inventive wit and biased views have disqualified them as serious evidence. His descriptions, amongst others, of the Duke of Newcastle at the funeral of George II, the trial of Lord Ferrers and the 'champagne' speech of Charles Townshend are rightly held to be classics of their kind. His letters, written to 150 different correspondents, a large number of them to his friends, Horace

Mann, minister in Italy, the Misses Berry and Mme du Deffant, friends of his old age, are self-conscious literary pieces intended for publication. The letters to Mann and Montagu, for instance, were returned by their recipients, edited and left to his executors in the shape of an historical chronicle. But Walpole wanted more than to be the Mme de Sévigné of his time: if he was a dilettante he was an active one. In 1747 he acquired Strawberry Hill, Twickenham, and set about creating there a Gothic house, modest in scale but unique in its fanciful antiquarianism. Sir Kenneth Clark has called it Gothic rococo; indeed it is far removed from the academic work of the professional architects of the nineteenth century, Butterfield, Street and Scott. Essentially it was a fancy, for, as he wrote of his 'small, capricious house', it was built 'to please my own taste and in some degree to realize my own visions'. His Gothic was that of an antiquarian and he always went to original Gothic work, nor did he invent new 'orders', like some later enthusiasts. There was of course something ridiculous about carefully imitated perpendicular framing the gold and crimson of eighteenth-century furnishing at its most sumptuous, and the tomb of Archbishop Bourchier reproduced in the gallery in gold network over looking-glass. Gothic was hardly evolved to make a frame for pictures, but the walls of Strawberry Hill were crowded with paintings in a medley of periods and styles, for Walpole was an avid collector.

His *Anecdotes of Painting* were based on the notebooks of George Vertue, a comprehensive collection of information about artists and architects. Walpole worked hard on these and performed valuable service in presenting information which might otherwise have been lost. His literary skill dressed up the material pleasantly, while his judgements, often sound, sometimes introduced the spice of the unexpected. Walpole has been pilloried for saying that Reynolds could not paint women and that Hardwick Hall was ugly, and for such passages of nonsense as that in which he praised Lady Lucan's water-colours. But many of his judgements stand the test of time, and if it is his weakness as a critic to slip into light-hearted discursions about inconsequential things, it is a large part of his attraction as a writer. He established his own printing press at Strawberry Hill; its output is now justly valued by bibliophiles. In 1757 Gray's *Odes* appeared, the first production, and never have author and publisher been more happily matched. Amongst other productions came his own essay in tragedy, *The Mysterious Mother*. The more interesting *Castle of Otranto* was published elsewhere; claimed by some critics as the first romantic novel, it is yet steeped in the atmosphere of Strawberry Hill.

Walpole was unfortunate in incurring odium for his part in the tragedy of Chatterton, when the most he could be accused of was failing to see straightaway through this elaborate deception. Although undoubtedly self-centred, he was not usually unkind; but he was prone to lapses of judgement that border upon absurdity. He lived usefully, in his own way, busily, elegantly. He appeared, however, for all his finesse, a trifle absurd to some of his contemporaries as to us, in his physical presence – he used, we are told, to enter a room as if he were stepping on a wet floor with his hat crushed between his knees – in his taste for melodrama in literature and architecture, in his febrile love of gossip, and in his last years, in an intense, exacting love for Mary Berry and her sister, less than half his age, but his 'twin wives', 'mes très chères Fraises'.

Further Reading
T. Howe, *Horace Walpole, the Great Outsider*, 1996.
W. S. Lewis, *Selected Letters of Horace Walpole*, 1973.
M. Hodgart, ed., *Memoirs and Portraits*, 1963.
R. W. Ketton-Cremer, *Horace Walpole*, 1940.

WALPOLE, SIR ROBERT, 1st EARL OF ORFORD

(1676-1745), principal minister of the Crown from 1721 to 1742, was born at the old manor house at Houghton in north Norfolk, the third son of nineteen children. His father had broken away from the cavalier tradition of this old county family and sat as a Whig in William III's parliaments. His early death in 1700 left Robert, because of the death of his elder brothers, to manage the family estates. He was educated at Eton, where he was a colleger, and at King's. He loved Eton and missed no opportunity later to advance the fortunes of his schoolfriends. But his intellectual interests did not last, for he became entirely absorbed in political business; relaxation he found in the talk of friends, in lavish entertainment and hunting. In 1700 he married Catherine Shorter, heiress to a timber merchant; her extravagance matched Walpole's own taste for good living and added to his debts.

He entered parliament for the pocket borough of Castle Rising in 1701 but, in the following year, he transferred to King's Lynn, in order to provide a safe seat for his uncle Horace. Lynn was then a thriving port and Walpole grew familiar with problems of trade. Within a few years he had come to be regarded as the leader of the Norfolk members. He lost no chance to cultivate the interests of friends and relations, notably his cousin and brother-in-law, Lord Townshend, and Charles Turner, a leading citizen of Lynn. From his earliest years Walpole exhibited a capacity for taking pains over people as well as over material concerns. In parliament he soon showed also that he could be formidable in debate. His friendship with Townshend provided an entry into Whig society, where he was valued for his direct manner and jovial temper. In the Commons he was fortunate in that most of the Whig leaders sat in the Upper House; in town, at the weekly meetings of the Kit-Cat Club, he learned about politics from such experienced hands as Somers, Halifax and Wharton.

In June 1705 Walpole was made a member of the naval council of Prince George, Lord High Admiral. In February 1708 he succeeded his Tory rival, St John, as Secretary at War: this gave him control, at the height of the war, of all aspects of military life in England and Scotland. In January 1710 he became Treasurer of the navy. Thus he was associated intimately with the conduct of the war – a Whig war since the Whigs had eased the Tories out of office and stood firm for the succession of the Archduke Charles to the Spanish throne. After the Tory victory of 1710 Walpole was marked for destruction, and in 1711 he was committed to the Tower after accusations of corruption in the negotiation of contracts. They were political charges, although evidence for them was not lacking, and Walpole's 'martyrdom', coming at the same time as Marlborough's disgrace, only enhanced his position with the Whigs.

The failure of Bolingbroke's plans for the accession of James Edward in 1714 found Walpole strongly placed amongst the Whigs who looked for places under George I. He was made first Paymaster, then, in 1715, First Lord of the Treasury and Chancellor of the Exchequer. Now he could indulge his love of building and display, and fortify himself by solid investment. Even by contemporary standards he was careless of the distinction between public and private money, as some remarked when they saw the great house of Orford rise in the grounds of Chelsea Hospital. The major part of the sums which passed through his hands in three years of office seems to have been the surplus which Paymasters were entitled to use for their own benefit; some may have been Chelsea Hospital funds which Walpole used to speculate with in transit. But the country benefited too from Walpole's financial sense. The measures which he took for the redemption of debt, the consolidation of rates of interest and the establishment of a sinking fund were models for subsequent work in this field. The precarious harmony of the Whig ministers was, however, destroyed by Townshend's misfortune in crossing the king in foreign affairs, and by the constitutional difficulties created by the king's absences in Germany. After Townshend was dismissed, Walpole followed his friend into opposition, along with a significant group, Pulteney, Methuen, Orford and his devoted friend, Devonshire. From April 1717 until June 1720, when he became Paymaster again, Walpole enjoyed the pleasures of faction. On at least one point, his opposition was far-sighted. He helped to destroy the Peerage Bill which, if it had been passed in 1719, would have turned the House of Lords into a closed oligarchy.

Walpole speculated rashly and lost heavily on the rise and fall of the South Sea Company stock in the summer of 1720. But his political gain was vast. He was not so closely involved as the principal ministers, Sunderland, Stanhope, Aislabie, and Craggs, father and son. The suicide of the elder Craggs, the disgrace of Aislabie and the younger Craggs and death by smallpox of the latter, the death of Stanhope in 1721 and of Sunderland the following year, cleared the way for his ascendancy. The way in which he set to work to re-establish public credit was typical of him: pragmatic and calm. What he did was less important than what he appeared to be doing. His scheme (proposed by his banker, Jacombe) for incorporating South Sea stock in that of the bank was not adopted, but it helped to restore confidence and persuade men to invest again. To contemporaries Walpole was not a financial wizard but the 'skreen-master general'. Defending directors and ministers against bitter attacks, he showed political courage; if he did not endear himself to the House, he made influential friends.

From 1721 to 1742 Walpole was First Lord of the Treasury. During this time he obtained a mastery over parliament and an initiative in the conduct of affairs which transformed the office he held. He was not the first to be called 'prime minister': Godolphin and Harley had enjoyed sufficient influence at Queen Anne's court, command of patronage and standing in parliament to earn the title, and the odium that went with it. After Walpole there were to be other First Lords who were not 'prime' ministers; the elder Pitt, who was, was a Secretary of State. In the government of the Pelhams there was no distinct head. Walpole's long tenure of office nevertheless proved decisive. The office of 'prime minister' evolved logically from the Crown's retreat from the active centre of government. It would not have been surprising in the emergencies of war; it was Walpole's special achievement that it happened during the 'pudding times' of a long peace. He was relentless in the pursuit of power, tenacious in his grasp. He was committed to no programme or timetable. It may be that principle was prominent only when wedded to political advantage. That does not mean however that there are no steady notions to be deducted from his acts and speeches.

Walpole held by the House of Hanover. His opposition to Toryism was as stern as it was shrewd. It was not his doing that Toryism was tainted with Jacobitism, but he made capital out of Bolingbroke's past errors and, till convinced, by 1726, that he was harmless, would not countenance his return from exile. Blooded in faction, he valued stability above all. He became supreme master of a system which 'was flexible enough to contain the competing demands of different interests and rival pressure groups' (Dickinson). At its heart was the parliamentary forum where the powerful and wealthy were sufficiently well represented to assume that they could work through the system: even when temporarily it did not favour them they could always hope to effect change. Parliament was open to external pressures through lobby,

petition and the voices, strident or seductive, of a free press. It also provided a well publicized arena for debate. Walpole there maintained his dominance by unremitting vigilance, by noting what would appeal to that impressionable assembly, not least the lucid presentation of facts and figures; above all by his handling of the Crown patronage. This gave rise to the complaint that he reduced corruption to a system but it must be remembered that he had to contend with a press persistently hostile, often scurrilous, which he did little to propitiate. More elevated writers might stand on principle; Grub Street noted the wealth that enabled him to play Maecenas – and employed its talents to denounce the means by which he apparently achieved it. Yet the judgement of a later master of the practice of politics should count for something: Burke wrote that 'he governed by party attachments. The charge of systematic corruption is less applicable to him, perhaps, than to any minister who ever served the Crown for so great a length of time'. Certainly the means of such 'corruption' did not increase during his ministry. Nor did Walpole monopolize patronage. Ecclesiastical preferment was only partly in his hands; both kings retained control over military and naval appointments.

Walpole had 'bottom', as contemporaries described those qualities of sound judgement and staying power, that even rivals had to recognize. One after another they were elbowed into eccentric corners, society's 'insiders' left to brood on the frustrations of being permanently 'out': Pulteney and Carteret, Wilmington after hopes briefly raised by the accession of George II, Chesterfield, and in 1730, his old ally Townshend. Memory of the Schism, the menace of Jacobitism, the cost of ambitious foreign policies and the violence of domestic mobs were all arguments which could weigh with king or parliament. In a country virtually unpoliced, when it was necessary to send for the troops when riot threatened, there was evidence to frighten the most fervent admirers of English liberty: the destruction of toll-gates in Herefordshire in 1734, attacks on Irish labourers in the Rag Fair riots of 1736, and most alarming, in the same year, the lynching of Captain Porteous in Edinburgh for acting against the ever popular trade of smuggling. Pleas for tough action were all the stronger for being presented in the bluff language of the country squire, sceptical of fine talk 'that buttered no parsnips'. Cultivated image or natural style, the lolling figure of the Commons chamber, stout and ruddy, munching his Norfolk russets, the dashing horseman who would hunt in Richmond Park if he could not get down to Houghton, provided cover for the shrewdest political mind of his generation. London laughed when it heard that Walpole had landed face down in the Richmond mud: in the political saddle he had a surer seat. In consideration of his managerial skills style must find a place; in the end however it was policies that counted. In parliament the squire predom-inated: many (though less than might be thought from their professions of disgust) spurned the places and jobs that would bind them to 'Robinocracy'. Alienated, these men of the 'country party' could endanger the dynasty. Walpole wooed them, supporting the stern Game Laws, notably the comprehensive 'Black Act' of 1723, further-ing private bills for enclosures and turnpikes. Above all he reduced the Land Tax which, when levied at 4*s*., placed a large share of the state's expenditure on the backs of the squirearchy. An essential part of the strategy behind his ill-fated Excise Bill of 1733, extending the duties already imposed on tea and coffee (1723) to wine and tobacco, was that it would enable him to perpetuate the low rate of 1*s*.

Clearly Walpole cannot be called a free trader; nor was he a rigid mercantilist. Always the pragmatist, he studied the needs and sentiment of city merchants and bankers. The lowest interest rates in Europe, down to three per cent by the late '30s, reflected their confidence in his financial management and consequent willingness to invest. His sinking fund was responsible for a significant reduction in the capital of the national debt. So far was he from being a purist in financial matters that he periodically raided it in order to keep expenditure down, and therefore taxation. In his revision of the customs rates, he removed all duties on the export of agricultural produce and on over 100 articles manufactured in Eng-land that found a market overseas. He abolished certain import duties in raw silk, flax and dyes. He laid down regulations of quality to maintain the standard of British products; to secure low wages, acts were passed requir-ing justices to fix wages. But to protect home industry Walpole retained high duties on the import of foreign goods which competed with English manufacturers. In his view of the colonies, Walpole was insular; inert, except when there was trouble. The colonies were looked on as a source of valuable raw materials, a market for English products, and they were forbidden, for the most part, to trade direct outside the mother-country. When the West Indian planters complained that the colonies were buying their sugar more cheaply from the French West Indies, Walpole produced the Molasses Act (1733), placing duties upon foreign sugar, placating the English planters – but alienating the colonists, though the duties were easily evaded. Ministerial action was for emergencies, or when there was an evident consensus.

Broadly speaking, two foreign policies were open to English statesmen in the eighteenth century: involve-ment in the dynastic wrangles of Europe with the commitments that this required, in the William-Marlborough-Stanhope tradition, or isolation, with some insurance in the shape of a close understanding with one country. The latter was the Tory idea as expressed in the peace of Utrecht and in essentials it was Walpole's. In 1730 he parted company with Townshend, who seemed to him to be precipitate in his engagements and to be endangering peace. After 1730 he was in control, with Newcastle and Harrington, Secretaries of State, at his service. In 1731 was signed the Treaty of Vienna: Eng-land guaranteed the Pragmatic Sanction while the emperor admitted Don Carlos to the Italian duchies that had been for so long a cause of strife. This treaty marked the end of the Stanhope-Townshend idea of co-operation with France and the return to the earlier system of alliance with the emperor. Unfortunately Walpole, an isolationist at heart, did not foster this alliance. Eng-land's influence was seen to dwindle when two years later, France and Spain made the first of the Family Compacts. When Fleury led France into the Polish Suc-cession war, Walpole refused to commit England to sup-port of the emperor; he rejoiced that he thus saved Eng-lish lives and shillings in a meaningless dispute, but he found too, as other English statesmen have found after him, that influence has to be paid for. He was edged out of the peace negotiations by Fleury. The Austrians were sore at what they regarded as his desertion. A year after another Treaty of Vienna of 1738, by which France gained Lorraine and the emperor nothing but a French guarantee of the Pragmatic Sanction, Walpole was driven into war with Spain without an ally in Europe.

Between the outbreak of war in 1739 and his fall from power in January 1742, Walpole fought to hold his pos-ition. His conduct of the war was uncertain, but he remained master of parliament to the end. His survival in these years indicates the strength of the position he had built for himself. The death of Queen Caroline, his friend and confidante, in 1737, was a blow to him, although the king remained loyal. An opposition had built up over the years composed of the hard core of Tories, the deprived Whigs led by men like Pulteney and Chesterfield whom Walpole had ousted, and those groups of aspiring polit-icians who saw the old minister as an obstacle to their advancement: the Leicester House faction who clustered round the Prince of Wales, embarrassing opponent of both king and minister; the Cobham cousinhood, amongst whom was the ardent young Pitt. The oppos-ition had already shown its teeth over the Excise Bill, withdrawn by Walpole after a country-wide campaign of unparalleled ferocity. It triumphed when it drove Walpole reluctantly into war with Spain in 1739, osten-sibly for the rights of Jenkins, the sailor who lost his ear, so he claimed, at the hands of *gardacostas* but really for freedom of trade in Spanish colonial waters. Walpole secured the Convention of Pardo and a small money compensation and urged that this be made the grounds of honourable treatment. But Pitt caught the mood of parliament and country when he championed the 'despairing merchants' and denounced the convention.

The war that followed was first popular but fruitless, after Admiral Vernon's seizure of Porto Bello. Walpole was unable to rise to the scale of the European war that this became when Frederick of Prussia seized Silesia from Austria in 1740. It would have mattered less had Newcastle been moderately competent. In the election of 1741 Walpole's majority was diminished, but he held on until February 1742; then he was defeated on an election petition – but he had already decided to resign. He had lost the support of the House of Commons without which no minister could long survive in the eighteenth century. He knew it. 'I have lived long enough in the world, Sir,' he said in debate in 1739, 'to know that the safety of a minister lies in his having the approbation of this House … I have always made it my first study to obtain it, and therefore I hope to stand.' When he met Pulteney in the House of Lords, soon after both men had accepted peerages, he is supposed to have remarked: 'You and I, my Lord, are now two as insignificant men as any in England.' This could not have been said in the reign of Queen Anne, when the Whig junto ruled the country from the House of Lords. Walpole had raised the House of Commons to a unique sense of authority. Even if, in his management of the House, he relied principally upon the 'old gang', the body of about 150 placemen who could be relied upon to support government in all weathers, he never became insensitive to the needs of the more independent members. He explained and defended his policies with clear reasoning and the plain words that won respect; he approached debate with an open mind and he could always be converted by good arguments. During the *Pax Walpoleana* there were few great public issues, but there was plenty of good debate.

He did not live long enough to enjoy his earldom or the treasures of his great house at Houghton. The king still consulted him 'in the closet' and the danger of impeachment in parliament for peculation receded after committees had sat to collect evidence against him. The pain of gout and the stone tormented his last years, but he was game to the end. It is hard to admire Walpole without reservation. His ministry was fairly called the Robinocracy, since his relatives and dependants enjoyed place at every level. He professed no idealism: 'I am no Saint, no Spartan, no reformer.' He was a man of coarse fibre. 'I have the right sow by the ear,' he said of his relationship with Queen Caroline. Even the pictures which form today the centre of the great Russian gallery of the Hermitage he bought with a sort of materialist gusto. Caricaturists dwelt upon the homely features and his vast bulk (he weighed twenty stone), historians have analysed the election lists, the petitions and his vast correspondence. The picture that emerges is a complex one, but certain qualities stand beyond dispute. He was endowed with a prodigious capacity for work and he devoted himself to the interests of his country as he saw

them. He was a man of great physical and moral courage. Finally there was a certain humanity about him; he worked, not in vain, for peace abroad and toleration at home.

Further Reading

J. H. Black, *Robert Walpole and the Nature of Politics in Early Eighteenth-Century England*, 1990.
J. H. Black, ed., *Britain in the Age of Walpole*, 1984.
H. T. Dickinson, *Walpole and the Whig Supremacy*, 1973.
J. H. Plumb, *Sir Robert Walpole*, vols I and II, 1956, 1960.

WALSINGHAM, SIR FRANCIS (1532-90), Secretary of State, was the only son among the six children of William Walsingham of Footscray in Kent and of his wife Joyce, daughter of Sir Edmund Denny of Cheshunt in Hertfordshire. His father died in 1533, and Joyce married Sir John Carey, uncle of the first Lord Hunsdon. Francis went up to King's, Cambridge, in 1548 and came down probably in 1550 without having taken a degree. The Denny family had strong Protestant leanings and King's was one of the most Protestant colleges in Cambridge, under its Provost Cheke: Francis must have been influenced by his surroundings, the more so since his tutor, Gardiner, was also a strong Protestant, and in 1549 Martin Bucer arrived in Cambridge and became Professor of Hebrew, being himself one of the greatest of the Protestant scholars. Francis was to be all his life an ardent and uncompromising Protestant.

Between 1550 and 1552 Walsingham was abroad learning the French and Italian languages. He was by nature a facile linguist, and this gift was to be the foundation of his political success when he entered the queen's service in 1568. He was entered as a member of Gray's Inn in 1552, but the next year the Catholic Mary Tudor succeeded to the throne and Walsingham left the country, ostensibly on the grounds of religion. Conyers Read suggests that possibly there were other reasons: that he might have been involved in the Protestant plots of Northumberland and Wyatt (*Sir Francis Walsingham*, i, p.22). During this exile he was at Padua University where he was appointed Consularius of the English Nation in the Faculty of Civil Law, a post he held from 1555 to the spring of 1556. During his sojourn in Italy he not only perfected his Italian, but he also learned much law and studied the political systems of continental countries. It is possible that before he returned home he visited Switzerland and had contacts with English Protestant exiles in Basle, Strasbourg and Frankfurt. He was certainly back in England in 1560, by which time Elizabeth I was on the throne.

In 1562 he was returned for the first time as MP for both Banbury and Lyme Regis: he chose to represent Lyme Regis. In that year he married a widow, Anne Carleill, who died in 1564 and gave him no children. Two years later he married the widow of Sir Richard

Worsley of the Isle of Wight, by whom he had one daughter, who married Sir Philip Sidney, and one who died early. In 1568 he entered the service of the queen, and he remained her most loyal servant for the next twenty-two years, up to the day of his death.

No doubt it was Walsingham's knowledge of foreign languages and the contacts which he maintained with friends abroad which first commended him to Burghley. In 1568 Walsingham supplied Cecil with a list of all persons arriving in Italy who might be dangerous to the queen and her government. In 1569 he was employed by the government's secret service in London and he played a part in unravelling the Ridolfi plot, although at one point he was completely hood-winked by Ridolfi.

From 1570 Walsingham was employed almost entirely on foreign affairs. In that year he was in France trying to secure toleration for the Huguenots. He was engaged in the matter of Elizabeth's projected marriage with Anjou. And in December of that year he supplanted Norris as ambassador in Paris. In conjunction with Sir Thomas Smith he negotiated the Treaty of Blois (1572), but friendship with France was disturbed by the Massacre of St Bartholomew (24 August 1572), which event left a lasting impression on Walsingham and much increased his Protestant fanaticism. In 1573 he left Paris and was made Secretary of State, a position he held until his death in 1590.

His administration of what we should now call the Foreign Office was shared to a large extent with Burghley, but it must be remembered that in foreign affairs the final decisions were Elizabeth's decisions. Broadly speaking, Burghley and the queen saw eye to eye in foreign affairs, and broadly speaking their policy was to play for time and to avoid committing themselves to one side or the other. This was diametrically opposed to Walsingham's views. He was not, like Burghley, a politician who was ready to trim his sails to suit the weather. Walsingham was an ardent Puritan and a man of inflexible principle. He had made up his mind that the one thing necessary for the safety of the country was the utter defeat of Spain and the removal of Mary, Queen of Scots. He was, therefore, uncompromisingly in favour of an alliance with Huguenot France and active intervention in the revolt of the Netherlands against Spain. James VI and Scotland must be made into friends. He was fully convinced that the struggle in Europe was not one between nation and nation, but between Catholicism and Protestantism. Walsingham was wrong in this belief. Elizabeth and Burghley had a juster understanding of the true state of affairs: that nationalism was a stronger force in Europe than religion. Walsingham was fearlessly outspoken to the queen in advocating his policy and trying to persuade her that hers was wrong, and Elizabeth was often driven to outbursts of fury against him. But she continued to use him in all her diplomatic business. At

first sight this is inexplicable, but probably the reasons are these: first and foremost, she knew that she could trust Walsingham to do his best to achieve her policy, however much he himself was personally opposed to it. She never doubted his abilities or his loyalty. In 1578 he was sent to the Low Countries to pursue a policy which Elizabeth knew well enough was exactly the opposite to what Walsingham approved. Walsingham bitterly resented the vacillations and procrastinations of the queen, yet he accepted, 'with never so ill a will', a mission to Scotland which might involve him in humiliation (1583). He must have had one moment of pleasure when in 1585 he was able to negotiate with the Dutch commissioner in London the terms on which the queen was ready to support the Netherlands against Spain. But even then by her vacillation and parsimony Walsingham was 'utterly discouraged'. From first to last Walsingham never had any success with the queen in advocating his policy and methods.

A second reason for using Walsingham was that he was always able to supply the fullest and most reliable information. His secret service was extraordinarily efficient. On it he spent the whole of his private fortune, so that he died in the utmost poverty. He had at times in his pay fifty-three agents in foreign courts and eighteen other spies. He would get the fullest information from thirteen towns in France, seven in the Low Countries, five in Spain, five in Italy, nine in Germany, three in the United Provinces, three in Turkey. He was both patient and ingenious in ferreting out the plots raised against Elizabeth, as, for example, the Parry and the Babington plots. Many of his agents were disreputable characters – he employed Christopher Marlowe – and Walsingham himself employed Machiavellian methods, but there is no conclusive evidence that he ever strained the law or justice against his victims. There was no cruelty in Walsingham: he regarded the Catholics as political dangers and as such they must be got out of the way, but he was strongly opposed to making them into martyrs: he preferred to have them detained or deported, and he once had an idea of founding an American colony for them. Only against Mary, Queen of Scots, 'that devilish woman', as he called her, was he determined to go to extremes, for he believed that she was the cause of all the trouble and that as long as she lived Elizabeth and the country were in the direst danger. After her execution he set about organizing the defences of the country against the Spanish invasion, which he clearly foresaw. Burghley told him 'you have fought more with your pen than many here in our English navy with their enemies'.

Ardent Protestant as Walsingham was, he was no fanatic. Camden called him 'a most sharp maintainer of the purer religion', but Walsingham himself understood that unity was essential, if English Protestantism was to survive. 'I would have all reformation done by public authority: it were very dangerous that every private man's zeal should carry sufficient authority of reforming things amiss.' He also held that men's consciences were 'not to be forced, but to be won and seduced by the force of truth, with the aid of time and the use of all good means of instruction and persuasion'. On the other hand, breaches of the law and peace and order he would have visited with the sternest measures.

Walsingham was a man who kept up with his times. He was a great supporter of all overseas adventures and he subscribed to Fenton's voyage in 1582-3: he took Richard Hakluyt into his pay, and Hakluyt dedicated the first edition of his *Voyages* to him; he corresponded with Lane, the explorer of Virginia, with Grenville and with Gilbert. He was greatly interested in the literature of his time and he was known to all the leading men of letters. All forms of learning earned his admiration and often his patronage – he founded a Divinity lecture at Oxford and he gave a polyglot Bible to King's College, Cambridge. Worldly honours did not much interest him, and Elizabeth was chary of rewarding her public servants – only Cecil was given a peerage. Walsingham's reward was a knighthood (1577). He was also made Chancellor of the Duchy of Lancaster (1587) and Chancellor of the Order of the Garter (1578).

Walsingham died on 6 April 1590. The news reached Philip II of Spain in a letter from a Spanish agent in England, who wrote: 'Secretary Walsingham has just expired, at the which there is much sorrow.' Philip scribbled in the margin: 'There, yes! But it is good news here.' That would have satisfied Walsingham as his epitaph.

Further Reading
Conyers Read, *Sir Francis Walsingham*, 1925.

WALSINGHAM, THOMAS (*c*.1345-1422) was 'the last of the great medieval chroniclers' (Emden). Presumably from Walsingham in Norfolk, he became a monk of St Albans – the premier English Benedictine house – about 1364. He was therefore already quite senior when he became precentor and head of the scriptorium about 1380 and started writing his chronicles. He was appointed prior of the cell of Wymondham (Norfolk) in 1394, but retired in 1396 at his own request, 'weary of worldly cares'. Thereafter he was a cloister monk at the mother-house without administrative responsibilities. While he continued to write history in his last years, he was no longer head of the scriptorium and devoted much attention to study of the classics. His commentary on Ovid's *Metamorphoses* and his works on the ancient gods, Trojan War and Alexander the Great probably took up more of his time than his chronicles.

Walsingham's early life was dominated by the great Abbot Thomas de la Mare, who built a new scriptorium, revived intellectual activity, and presumably encouraged Walsingham to restore St Albans's flagging tradition of historical writing. Starting apparently with modest intentions as historian of his own monastery and his own day from 1376, he ultimately produced a 'formidable body of writing and one unequalled by any other chronicler working in fourteenth-century England'. Like his predecessor and model Matthew Paris, he produced a *Great Chronicle* from 1272-1420, a *Short Chronicle*, and continued the *Deeds of the Abbots* to 1393. He also produced a *Book of Benefactors* and a history of Normandy (*Ypodigma Neustriae*). The relationship of these works is complex, partly because Walsingham treated the years before 1376 last, partly because he was no longer in charge of the scriptorium after 1394, and probably also because of successive revisions to rehabilitate John of Gaunt and take account of the Lancastrian succession to the English Crown. His works overlap in coverage and all have original contributions to make.

His principal achievement as historian was his full-scale coverage of English history of nearly half a century. Walsingham's great gift was as a reporter of current events. He was excellently informed and wrote close in time to the events he recorded – and thus reflects the opinions of at least some of his contemporaries. He often wrote in considerable detail in clear expressive prose.

He used a wide-range of oral and written sources and 'believed in stating even opponents' views'. On the debit side, like most medieval chroniclers, he loved prodigies and marvels and believed that History records God's rewards and punishments on good and evil. He was a Benedictine monk of St Albans, loyal to his house and order, and hence hostile to the Peasants Revolt, moral failings, and Wyclif, whom he denounced as 'angel of Satan and forerunner of Antichrist'. He was patriotic and anti-French, admired courage and chivalry, and feared that knightly standards were declining. Emotional, even hysterical and unrestrained in his denunciations, his early work virulently attacked John of Gaunt and was deservedly nicknamed the *Scandalous Chronicle*. Walsingham was not consistently anti-court or indeed politically or constitutionally principled in his stance, becoming increasingly pro-Lancastrian and praising Henry V in particular for his bravery and piety. He lacked the depth and range of Matthew Paris, 'operating entirely within the chronicle conventions of his time', but was nevertheless 'a not entirely unworthy successor'.

Further Reading
J. Taylor, *English Historical Literature in the Fourteenth Century*, 1987.
A. Gransden, *Historical Writing in England* ii, 1982.

WALTER, HUBERT (?*c*.1140/5-1205; Bishop of Salisbury 1189-93; Archbishop of Canterbury 1193-1205; justiciar 1193-8; chancellor 1199-1205) has been described as 'one of the greatest royal ministers of all time'. In organizing royal justice, finance, warfare or administration, he was supreme, his authority matched by his competence. For more than a decade, as chief minister, primate of England and papal legate, he dominated church and state with a thoroughness unmatched until Thomas Wolsey three centuries later. While his reputation among modern historians has been enhanced by his instituting efficient government record-keeping of lawsuits and official correspondence, of his achievement there is no doubt. Fifty years afterwards, the inventive Matthew Paris had King John exclaim on hearing of Hubert's death 'Now, for the first time am I truly King of England'. Although apocryphal, the sentiment was not inappropriate: if a litigant went over Justiciar Hubert's head directly to King Richard, he was liable to be punished; and in 1205, Chancellor Hubert effectively scuppered King John's projected invasion of France. Wherever he was active, Hubert, combining efficiency with ruthlessness, was a force to be reckoned with.

Born, probably at West Dereham, Norfolk, into the ranks of the lesser baronage, Hubert was educated in the household of his uncle, the powerful royal official Ranulf Glanvill (justiciar 1180-9), whose right-hand-man Hubert became in the 1180s. First appearing as a witness to royal charters in 1181/2, Hubert's rise was swift. A justice from 1184 and Dean of York in 1185, Hubert worked in the Exchequer and chancery. In 1189, Richard I elevated him to the bishopric of Salisbury, a move perhaps not uninfluenced by the presence at Salisbury of the depository of the Saladin Tithe. The Third Crusade was the making of Hubert. Accompanying his uncle Ranulf with the English advance-guard to Acre in 1190, the deaths of the other leaders left him in effective control of the beleaguered English force in the winter and spring of 1190-1. He rose to the challenge: he conducted the tortuous diplomacy with other contingents; administered a central fund to pay soldiers and provide for the provisioning of the destitute; and even led forays against the Muslims. On Richard's arrival in 1191, he became his close adviser, acting as his chief negotiator with Saladin and leading the first group of crusaders allowed to visit the Holy Sepulchre in Jerusalem under the terms of the treaty of 1192. Hearing of Richard's captivity on his way home, Hubert visited the king in Germany in 1193 and was sent to England to supervise the collection of the massive ransom. His reward was the archbishopric of Canterbury and the justiciarship, becoming, in effect, Richard's viceroy.

The justiciarship had elastic powers but two specific functions: the control of royal finances and the administration of justice. As a finance minister, Hubert was notoriously successful. The Ransom of 1193 raised 100,000 marks; scutages were extracted in 1195 and 1196; tallages on royal demesnes, including towns, in successive years from 1194; levies on wool were imposed on the sheep-ranches of the Gilbertines and Cistercians; and in 1194 a new land tax, the carucage, was instituted. According to the former royal justice Roger of Howden, Hubert raised 1,100,000 marks in two years 1194-6. Allowing for taxpayers' exaggeration, Hubert was collecting huge sums to pay for wars in Wales and France. Additional revenue came from feudal dues; miscellaneous, often large, debts to the Exchequer; and the profits of justice. These latter included fines (often levied as security for good behaviour), payments for writs and hearings, as well as innumerable douceurs from anxious litigants eager to ensure prompt and/or favourable judgements. Thus, Hubert's judicial role was linked to the financial. The general judicial eyres he organized in 1194 and 1198 were occasions to call in money owing as well as to dispense royal justice. Hubert also gained a reputation for his knowledge of legal custom. The permanent Curia Regis which sat at Westminster was attracting more business and the justices, inevitably, grew more professional than their predecessors whose activities had ranged more widely across royal business. Increasingly, *curiales* specialized in finance or law. A symptom of the increase in legal work may have been the introduction under Hubert of formal records of Curia Regis cases on rolls of parchment. With more business, the need to establish precedent and case law became more pressing. These rolls formed the basis of the first legal text-books in the following century. It is also true that Hubert had a tidy mind. The appearance of newly detailed evidence should not automatically persuade historians of significant developments in practice: Hubert's changes may have been motivated by considerations of bureaucratic efficiency, not more work. The same can be said of the enrollment of royal letters and patents during Hubert's period as chancellor under King John.

Away from Westminster, Hubert was involved in general royal policy. His major political achievement as justiciar was the pacification of the realm after the turmoil of Richard's absence, the opposition to Longchamp and the rebellion of Prince John. Involved in Richard's continental diplomacy, as well as providing for the king's wars, he also fought some of them. As at Acre in 1190-1, Hubert directed military operations at the sieges of Marlborough (1194); the Welsh campaigns of 1196 and 1197; and he helped raise the relief force for the siege of Painscastle shortly-before he retired from the justiciarship in 1198. Hubert was not a desk-bound bureaucrat: he was the king's chief agent, executive and minister.

Hubert was also archbishop and, from 1195 to 1198, papal legate. Most contemporaries were fairly sure where his priorities lay, especially those clergy whom he taxed. When secular circumstances demanded, Hubert ignored clerical privileges. But he worked with characteristic energy as an ecclesiastical judge; he conducted diocesan visitations; he chased up recalcitrant crusaders from Cornwall to Lincolnshire; he held a legatine council for the northern province in 1195, and a council for the south in 1200. In John's reign he protected monastic immunities and helped in the canonization of Wulfstan of Worcester and Gilbert of Sempringham (1203 and 1202 respectively). Unlike many, including perhaps Pope Innocent III (1198-1216), Hubert saw no contradiction in wielding the two swords of *regnum* and *sacerdotium*. He embodied the normal practice of twelfth-century Europe. In a sense, Hubert was what Henry II had hoped Becket would be. It was frankly hypocritical for Roger of Howden, a royal clerk who had spent years in government service instead of tending his flock in the East Riding, to condemn Hubert for preferring worldly office to spiritual ministry. Hubert was not a great religious leader and was no theologian, but he was efficient and thorough in church business, which is more than can be said of some other primates, more inspired, intelligent or passionate than he. At least in his ferocious conflict with the monks of Canterbury over his scheme to establish a college of secular canons at Lambeth, Hubert maintained the highest traditions of his office.

This is not to deny to Hubert a spiritual life. He embraced a variety of religious insurance policies. In 1193, he adopted the habit of an Augustinian canon at Merton Priory, a gesture which may or may not have been prompted by the new archbishop's desire to associate himself with his famous predecessor Thomas Becket who had gone to school there. In 1195, he became a *confrater* (i.e. an associate member) of the Cistercians, a connection which paid dividends when he persuaded the Cistercian abbots in England to write him a glowing testimonial to the pope. More intriguing was his reaction to a visit to the Carthusian house at Witham where he was so impressed by the sanctity of the monk Adam of Dryburgh that he insisted on receiving from him 'discipline with the rod'. What either party made of this scene where an obscure holy man beat the naked body of the most powerful man in England is not recorded.

Hubert's resignation as justiciar in 1198 scarcely interrupted his influence, if it lessened his load. His protégé Geoffrey FitzPeter succeeded him and he remained an intimate adviser of the king. In 1199, although initially reluctant, he decisively supported the accession of John, receiving the chancellorship as immediate reward. To consolidate his hold on England John, whose main interests were then continental, may have wished to recruit Hubert as an ally as much as a servant. Either way, it signalled that there would be little change in the tenor of English government which, in the long term, John may have regretted. Only after Hubert's death did John promote his own clients into posts of great influence.

Immediately, Hubert displayed his talents in the chancery. Within a month, a fixed schedule of fees for documents issued under the Great Seal was produced and chancery writs and charters began to be enrolled. His experience and relationship with other leading officials gave the new chancellor a brief far beyond his formal duties. He was active in diplomacy; in May 1202 he was sent to England to convey the king's commands to officials and to lead their counsels; in 1203, he was in charge of levying a seventh from the clergy; he continued to sit as a judge; he advised the king on all matters fiscal, political and administrative; he kept the church quiescent. The defeat in France in 1204 may have led to a cooling of relations with the king, but Hubert retained enough clout to dissuade John from his 1205 campaign. It may be that, at the end, within weeks of his own death, Hubert felt doubts or even remorse at the rapacity which was the inevitable accompaniment to war. Perhaps he saw that the administrative and political costs were proving too high. Perhaps he knew that John was no Richard, and that another French defeat could fatally compromise his position in England, especially as there was at the time no direct heir. Whatever the motive, the old minister prevailed; a familar circumstance.

If a definition of a great minister is that he fulfils his master's wishes, Hubert Walter was one of the greatest. Seemingly unencumbered by sophisticated education or lofty ideals, he was a practical genius who could organize anything, anywhere, anytime. Contemporaries noted his lack of learning: his Latin was apparently poor and he was an indifferent public speaker. But he had a clear mind and a huge capacity for work. His brilliance as an administrator, first prominently displayed in the unlikely surroundings of a disease-ridden army camp in Palestine, underpinned his success as a finance minister and judge. He knew how things and presumably people — worked; he knew what he and his masters wanted. In relations with his monarchs he showed conspicuous skill, unassuming and indispensible. He carefully built up a network of contacts in government service and, with equal care, and unlike his potential rival William Longchamp, did not dabble in politics on his own account. He made sure that his enemies were the king's. Despite his high ecclesiastical office, he espoused no political independence; not for him the mistakes of Henry of Blois or Stephen Langton. Loyalty, as he knew better than any, had its own reward.

His modus operandi was quietly and effectively self-interested. From the number of disseisins he had perpetrated which needed special investigation after his death, it is clear he used his judicial position for personal gain. In office, he had the use of large sums which passed through his hands for which rendering account could be delayed for years. He received money direct which normally went to the Exchequer. Although one modern apologist talks of Hubert's 'speculative investment' in royal wardships, corruption is a better word. In 1203, he paid 1,000 marks down, with a promise of a 3,000 more over three years for a rich royal wardship which netted 2,000 marks a year. In a sense, as justiciar and chancellor, he was dealing with himself, and so could make profits for all concerned, except the ward's family. Hubert used his public position to strike private deals as well. Thanks to his official intervention, the Abbot of Bury St Edmunds secured control of the wardship of Adam de Cokefield's granddaughter, which he then sold (freely?) to Hubert for 150 marks, although the going rate was 300. Hubert then sold the wardship on for 500 marks. Such manipulation of rank allowed Hubert to live lavishly and ostentatiously. He died a very wealthy man.

At its height, Hubert's power was awesome, but not invulnerable. When threatened, he showed his steel. In 1196, complaints that Hubert's régime was corrupt and rife with official peculation were directed at the king from two sources: William FitzOsbert, a prominent London citizen and rabblerouser, and Robert, Abbot of St Stephen's, Caen. The latter was sent by Richard to London to head an investigation into the conduct of the Exchequer and the honesty of the sheriffs rendering account there. The day before Abbot Robert arrived in London, FitzOsbert was hanged on the justiciar's orders for resisting arrest (by Hubert's men), causing an affray and manslaughter. At dinner with Hubert the following day, the newly arrived abbot was taken ill: he died five days later. William of Newburgh commented 'those who feared his coming, did not mourn his going'. The inquiry was cancelled.

Tall, handsome, diffident on the public stage, relentless behind it, Hubert Walter may appear the archetypal English mandarin. Yet he was a ruthless and effective politician too, not in the sense of competing with the baronial magnates in loud gestures of support or opposition to royal acts or in open, bitterly fought land disputes, but rather in council, on the bench and in administration. He provided the king with money and solutions to problems. Familiar with Exchequer, chancery, the court, the church, the siege and the battlefield, his versatility and command over the whole range of government business made him much more than a serviceable bureaucrat. It was Hubert's voice which was crucial in the acceptance of John as king in 1199. Hubert was formidable, unscrupulous but, it was said, sensitive to criticism. Many suffered at his régime's bullying, often vindictive pursuit of royal rights, fiscal exploitation and personal greed. Yet he set a standard of efficiency that his successors could but try to emulate. In his capacity for official business; administrative expertise and imagination; determined financial management; skill at handling kings, politicians and opponents; personal venality; political ruthlessness; and success,

Hubert Walter bears comparison with another Norfolk man – Robert Walpole.

Further Reading
C. R. Cheney, *Hubert Walter*, 1967.

WALTHEOF (*d.*1076) was the last of the Old English earls to survive under William I, his execution for treason in 1076 marking a significant stage in the aristocratic and tenurial revolution which followed 1066. Younger son of Earl Siward of Northumbria, Waltheof became Earl of Huntingdon probably in 1065. As one of the few English magnates not from the Godwin faction, he accepted and was accepted by William I, witnessing royal charters and remaining loyal to the new régime until in 1069 he joined with the Danes in their invasion of Northumbria. He was prominent in their capture of York, hoping, no doubt, to be restored to his father's position. This opportunism is perhaps more characteristic of English magnate reactions to the political turmoil of 1065-70 than any supposed national feeling. However, the revolt and invasion were defeated by William I's winter campaign of 1069-70. It is a measure of William's insecurity that when Waltheof submitted in 1070 he was restored to royal favour and, in 1072, added the earldom of Northumbria to his holdings. To bind him more tightly to the Norman dispensation, William gave him his niece Judith in marriage. But in 1075, Waltheof was implicated in the largely French revolt led by Ralph, Earl of Norfolk and Roger, Earl of Hereford. Despite his lack of military action, his confession, apparent contrition and the support of Archbishop Lanfranc, Waltheof was executed on 31 May 1076.

The king's motives are obscure. Waltheof was the only prominent Englishman to be executed in the reign. Perhaps his removal was part of William's justifiably nervous response to the problem of controlling Northumbria. It may have made sense to take the chance to remove a potential – and proven – focus of northern discontent. Yet Waltheof's heirs were not harried, one daughter marrying David I of Scotland (1142-53), another Ralph IV of Tosny, a leading Norman baron.

Waltheof is a significant reminder that the period around 1066 was transitional, with no necessarily definite beginnings or endings. Waltheof adapted to the new order, falling foul, it seems, of the ambitions and schemes of others, not least of parvenus Frenchmen. He married into the new élite, yet embodied the old. Heir to both English and Anglo-Danish traditions, it was he who completed one of the most celebrated of Anglo-Saxon blood-feuds. In 1016, Uhtred, Earl of Northumbria was murdered by a northern nobleman called Thurbrand. He was, in turn, killed by Uhtred's son and successor, Ealdred who was himself slain by Thurbrand's son, Carl. Waltheof's mother was Ealdred's daughter and he avenged his great-grandfather and grandfather by massacring a number of Carl's sons.

Waltheof himself was buried at Crowland Abbey where, as did many martyrs to royal policy in the Middle Ages, he found posthumous fame in a cult which, by the mid-twelfth century, was venerating him as a saint. Yet his career in the north shows that not far beneath the measured tones of Norman propagandists or the efficient gloss of English bureaucratic procedures simmered the violence of Dark Age epic.

Further Reading
F. Stenton, *Anglo-Saxon England*, 1943.

WALTON, IZAAK (1593-1683), biographer, was born at Stafford of yeoman stock, and after serving his apprenticeship in London became a prosperous iron-monger with a shop in Fleet Street. Royalist in his sympathies, he had the pattern of his life upset by the Civil Wars and gave up his business. When they were over he settled at Winchester, where after 1662 he lived in the palace of his friend Bishop Morley and where his daughter married a prebendary. Walton had two great gifts – a genius for friendship and an English style of natural, though not artless, simplicity. His five *Lives* were first published at intervals over nearly forty years: the first, that of Donne who had been his neighbour in London, came in 1640, and the last in 1678. His other celebrated work, the charming *Compleat Angler*, was written during the political troubles and published in 1653.

WALWYN, WILLIAM (1600-80) was born at Newland in the Malverns, second son of a prosperous landowner and a bishop's daughter, and like Lilburne was bound apprentice in London to a silk-dealer in Paternoster Row. He became a successful cloth-merchant, a member of the Merchant Adventurers, comfortably off, with a family even more numerous than that enjoyed by a radical tailor two centuries later, Francis Place: Walwyn is said to have had twenty children. He was widely read, unconventionally so for a man of his class, with Seneca, Lucian, Plutarch and Montaigne among his favourites. It is scarcely surprising that his religious opinions were somewhat heterodox, and he was an independent of an extreme kind, profoundly antinomian in his outlook. Walwyn's precise contribution to the Leveller movement is impossible to assess. Undoubtedly a wire-puller and perhaps an *éminence grise*, he had a clearer mind and one of finer texture than Lilburne, yet lacked the latter's zest for publicity. He was most celebrated as a pamphleteer, his first piece appearing in 1641, and it is perhaps significant that until 1646 he was mainly concerned to champion religious liberty, in such tracts as *The Power of Love* of 1643 and in his celebrated controversy with Thomas Edwards, the author of *Gangraena*. But after his meeting with

Lilburne in 1646 he became more involved in secular politics, and Joseph Frank has seen him as the 'guiding hand in the organization of radical propaganda and ... chief midwife at the birth of the Leveller party'. Certainly he was important in the Leveller pressure at the time of the Putney Debates, and in 1648 he wrote *The Bloody Project*, advocating a popular front against Presbyterians and royalists. The Republican government in its attack on the Levellers in 1649 arrested him along with Lilburne and Overton and sent him to the Tower. Thereafter little is heard of him, apart from a pamphlet defending trial by jury in 1651. It seems likely that he made his peace with the Commonwealth and turned his energies back into trade, for he appears to have been well-established and respected at the time of his death in 1680.

Further Reading
J. McMichael and B. Taft, eds, *Writings of William Walwyn*, 1989.
A. L. Morton, *The World of the Ranters*, 1970.
Joseph Frank, *The Levellers*, 1955.
W. Schenck, *The Concern for Social Justice in the Puritan Revolution*, 1948.

WARBECK, PERKIN (*c*.1474-99), impostor and pretender to the throne, first appeared on the political stage in the autumn of 1491 at Cork in Ireland. It was claimed at first that he was the Earl of Warwick, then that he was an illegitimate son of Richard III and finally, and for the rest of his career as an impostor, that he was Richard, Duke of York, the younger of the Princes in the Tower murdered by their uncle, Richard III. Henry VII immediately made great efforts to discover who this fraud was and eventually found that he was the son of a customs official from Tournai, a city in the Netherlands close to the French border. His name was Peter (or Perkin) Osbeck, sometimes spelt Werbecque, anglicized as Warbeck.

According to Warbeck's confession, made after he was captured, he assumed the role of Yorkist pretender largely by accident when acting as male model for a Breton merchant named Pregent Meno who called at Cork. The people of that town, impressed by his appearance, decked out in the imported finery of Meno, apparently took him for a nobleman and then began a rather Irish process of exaggeration. But this is surely too good to be true. There is some evidence that the French king, Charles VIII, who in 1491 was in conflict with Henry VII, was involved in the plot in some way before Warbeck arrived in Ireland. Warbeck's origins are also significant: Tournai was, for a time, the seat of the Duchess Margaret of Burgundy's court, and this fact suggests that the plot was hatched there, where Warbeck lived. A link with the Yorkist high command is provided by the fact that Warbeck was employed before 1491 as a servant of Sir Edward Brompton, a converted Portuguese Jew who had been a close adherent of the Yorkists and was made Governor of Guernsey by Edward IV.

Warbeck received little support in Ireland, perhaps understandably in view of Simnel's fate, and he went next to France. The war between Henry and Charles VIII, which broke out in 1492 ostensibly over Brittany, owed something to the presence of the pretender in the French court. Following his invasion of France, Henry secured a peace treaty with France, signed at Etaples in 1492, under the terms of which Warbeck was expelled. He turned up next in the Netherlands, under the protection of the duchess. Henry imposed an embargo on trade to the Low Countries to show his displeasure at this. In 1493, Warbeck appeared at the court of Maximilian Habsburg, head of the Holy Roman Empire, and was recognized as King Richard IV of England. Two years later, a conspiracy was revealed in England, implicating, among other important men, Sir William Stanley, the king's stepuncle. Stanley had been in communication with Warbeck and he was executed. In the same year (1495), Warbeck launched an abortive attack on the coast of Kent, at Deal, but his small force was easily repulsed. He attempted next to take Waterford in Ireland, but was sent packing by Sir Edward Poynings and so he fetched up finally in Scotland. James IV, who was at the time on bad terms with Henry, received him warmly and married him to a royal cousin, Lady Katherine Gordon. Henry was incensed at this recognition shown to the impostor and also at a raiding party which Warbeck accompanied a few miles over the border into northern England, and he prepared to lead an expedition into Scotland (1496). The threat of war made James IV treat for peace, and Warbeck left, via Ireland, for Cornwall (1497). He hoped to raise a rebellion among the troublesome Cornish who had only recently risen in rebellion against the king's taxes. Indeed, he did receive some support and led a force eastward, besieging Exeter and Taunton, both with no success. Warbeck's forces melted away as the king's army approached, and he fled to sanctuary at Beaulieu Abbey. Henry had decided at the beginning of his reign (and the pope had agreed) that sanctuary should not prevent arrest for treason, and Warbeck was captured. Henry spared his life, in an effort to make it appear that he had no fears of Warbeck, whereas, of course, the past six years of the reign had been dominated by the king's efforts to bring the pretender down. For a year, Warbeck lived as a courtier, but when he tried to escape he was placed in the Tower. In 1499 a plot was revealed, perhaps as the result of the activities of royal *agents provocateurs*, which involved Warbeck and the Earl of Warwick in a conspiracy to escape the Tower. Warbeck was hanged and Warwick beheaded. As for Lady Katherine Gordon, she was treated generously by the Tudors and married a further three times, finally dying in 1537.

WARBURTON, WILLIAM (1698-1779), theologian, a voluminous and controversial writer upon many topics, occupied a larger place in the view of his contemporaries than seems to be justified either by his scholarship or his personality. The son of George Warburton of Newark and of Elizabeth Holman, he was educated at Oakham School and articled to an attorney. He forsook law for Holy Orders, but never lost the lawyer's method and manner. He was presented in 1723, by the influence of a patron, with a Cambridge degree. Was there some element of inferiority complex in his assertive careerism? Whatever the cause, he was as earnest in his pursuit of influence as he was ruthless with men or ideas that he disagreed with. He passed from living to living; Greasely, Brant Broughton, Frisby all knew his name, but his energies were given to study and writing. He described his life as one of 'warfare on earth; that is to say with bigots and libertines'. He saw himself as animated by a desire for truth and regard for the Church of England, which might have been derived 'solely from the contemplation of nature and the unvariable reason of things'. His writing was intemperate, his arguments paradoxical to the point sometimes of absurdity, and his defence of the church, on the grounds of convenience and discipline, unspiritual and unconvincing. Formidable in learning, he yet lacked common sense and restraint. He attacked with relish deists, atheists, Methodists; most of his intelligent contemporaries were fools, knaves or 'cox-combs' – a favourite word. Johnson, Smollett, Garrick, Young, Priestley, all were damned in turn. The Moravian hymn book was 'a heap of blasphemous and beastly nonsense'. With *The Divine Legation of Moses Demonstrated* (first part 1737, second part 1741) and *The Alliance between Church and State* he established a name, however, for solid advocacy. Though he may have been to Bentley a man of 'monstrous appetite and bad digestion', Dr Johnson, pleased by his assault on Bolingbroke, dubbed him 'the last man who has written with a mind full of reading and reflection'. In 1738 he became chaplain to the Prince of Wales and prebends followed. The highest rewards were nevertheless slow to come. Not until 1757 did he become Dean of Bristol, in 1760 Bishop of Gloucester. He married an exceedingly lively girl, the daughter of Ralph Allen of Bath. Perhaps his closest friend was Bishop Hurd, the scholarly divine who was eccentric enough to refuse the primacy. It should be added that some of his targets were worthy ones: a famous sermon in 1766 denounced the slave trade.

Warburton seems to have been lukewarm in his own religious life. Was he also insincere in his theology, which often seems to be an academic exercise, devoid of feeling? For instance, the main argument of *The Divine Legation* was the paradoxical one that Mosaic laws must be divine in origin, since they did not contain a doctrine that was socially essential. Isaac Disraeli believed that he was inspired by 'the secret principle' of 'invention', a love of novelty for its own sake. He was an admirer of Bayle whom he resembles in erudition and liking for logical exercise. His failing was most in sensitiveness. He could accept no limitations to his sphere. He complacently put out the theory that Gothic architecture developed from the habit of 'this northern people having been accustomed to worship the Deity in groves' and he produced an unusually bad edition of Shakespeare (1747). When he became a friend of Pope and was left as his literary executor, he became involved in a savage quarrel with Bolingbroke. His gifts might have made him a splendid lawyer. As it was he served a God whom by his reasoning he reduced to the status of 'a mere heap of verbal formulae'.

Further Reading
A. W. Evans, *Warburton and the Warburtonians*, 1932.
Leslie Stephen, *History of English Thought in the Eighteenth Century*, 3rd edn, 1902. vol. I, chap. VII.

WARHAM, WILLIAM (1450?-1532), Archbishop of Canterbury, came of a Hampshire family and was educated at Winchester and at New College, Oxford, where he became a Fellow in 1475, a post which he held for thirteen years. He directed the school of Civil (Roman) Law in the university until he left Oxford in 1488 to practise as an advocate in London in the ecclesiastical Court of Arches. By 1490 he was one of the most considerable lawyers in the country, and in that year he travelled to Rome on business for the Bishop of Ely. In 1491 he was in Antwerp settling a dispute with the merchants of the Hanse: in 1493 he was again in Flanders, with Sir Edward Poynings, on an embassy to persuade the Dowager Duchess of Burgundy to abandon Perkin Warbeck. Although the mission failed, it is said that Warham's speech was an immense success. On 21 September 1493, Warham was ordained as sub-deacon at the age of forty-five and he now received many preferments. In 1494 he was made Master of the Rolls, in 1496 he negotiated the marriage of Arthur, Prince of Wales, with Catherine of Aragon, and from now onwards he was used in many important diplomatic cases by Henry VII, who trusted him completely. In 1502 he was consecrated Bishop of London, and in 1504 he became Archbishop of Canterbury and Lord Chancellor. The year 1506 saw him Chancellor of Oxford, and two years later he set about reforming some of the abuses in the Court of Audience. In 1509, he crowned Henry VIII and Catherine of Aragon and was appointed by the pope to present to Henry the Golden Rose.

The first part, the happiest and the most successful, of Warham's life was now finished. The accession of Henry VIII and the arrival of Wolsey marked the beginning of a new age in England. New men and new methods, new

policies also, were now to destroy the position of trust which Warham had enjoyed under Henry VII. By the time Wolsey became a cardinal in 1515 Warham's position both as a statesman and as archbishop was growing increasingly difficult. In that year Warham resigned from the chancellorship and he retired almost completely from the Council. For a while he still appeared on state occasions – in 1520 he was present at the Field of Cloth of Gold – but in ecclesiastical matters he represented an old and out-worn system. In 1512 he had quarrelled with Fox, Bishop of Winchester, over alleged encroachments by Canterbury on the jurisdictions of the suffragans. In 1523 he was to quarrel with the encroachments which Wolsey was making on the rights of Canterbury. And indeed Wolsey was totally ruthless and unreasonable. No doubt Warham was a stiff and upright man, who stood rigidly upon the old order, but Wolsey humiliated the archbishop in every sort of way. After 1515 no Cross was carried in front of the archbishop, even in his own diocese. At the ceremony when Wolsey received his cardinal's hat, Warham had to play a minor part, and the arrival of Campeggio further diminished his importance. It is difficult to say what were the real relations between Warham and Wolsey. In his letters Warham is always protesting how much he values Wolsey's kindnesses to him, but the language smacks strongly of the sycophantic style of the times. On the other hand, when Warham was once ill, Wolsey offered him quarters at Hampton Court.

There is no difficulty in judging the relations between Warham and the king. Once the divorce had been mooted and as soon as the Reformation Parliament met in 1529, Warham disliked most of Henry's policy. He declined to give a decision on the question of the validity of Henry's marriage: he was appointed one of the counsel for the queen, but Catherine had the lowest opinion of Warham's efforts on her behalf. Warham watched the development of the attacks on the church with consternation. It was he who suggested the addition to the title of Supreme Head of the Church at the time of the Pardon of the Clergy (1531). So far, Warham had not proved himself to be a very brave defender of the church: he had agreed to too many damaging compromises. He was an old man now: he had shirked advising Catherine on the plea that *Ira principis mors est*. But now at the last moment he roused himself to make a valiant stand. In February 1532 he gave notice at his last appearance in the House of Lords that he would in the next session move the repeal of all the statutes passed against the church since the beginning of that parliament. Henry's answer was to threaten Warham with a writ of praemunire. The archbishop saw clearly enough that a dangerous fate might now await him. The general weakness of the church in its resistance to Henry was symbolized when after much debate Convocation

1264 / WARHAM, WILLIAM

accepted the Submission of the Clergy (1532), by which the church in England surrendered its legislative independence to the king. Broken in health and too ill to leave his bed, he began to dictate the speech which he would make in the House of Lords: 'I intend to do only that I am bound to do by mine oath that I made at the time of my profession.' He refused to admit a royal claim which had brought about the martyrdom of Thomas Becket, 'which is the best death that can be ... I think it better for me to suffer the same, than in my conscience to confess this article to be praemunire for which St Thomas died.' Warham was always a better speaker of words than doer of actions. It was merciful that he should have died before any action was needed, on 23 August 1532.

Erasmus, whom Warham had more than once helped with generous gifts of money, has left a literary portrait of his friend in his *Ecclesiastes*. He tells us that Warham would give 'sumptuous entertainments, often to as many as 200 guests, he himself ate frugal meals and hardly tasted wine: he never prolonged the dinner above an hour, but yet was a most genial host: he never hunted or played at dice, but his chief recreation was reading'. His income was very large, but he spent £30,000 on repairs and building of new houses, so that when he died he was so poor that there was hardly enough money to pay for his funeral.

The fine portrait by Holbein at Lambeth, and perhaps even more the beautiful drawing for that portrait which is in the collection of drawings at Windsor, give a vivid picture of the archbishop in old age.

Further Reading
Hook, *Lives of the Archbishops of Canterbury*, New Series, vol. 1, 1868.

WARTON, THOMAS (1728-90) was the son of Thomas Warton, vicar of Basingstoke and Professor of Poetry at Oxford; an unconventional but much-loved Oxford figure, he became a better poet than his father, and also an historian of poetry, a biographer and an antiquarian.

He entered Trinity College, Oxford, in 1744, and was elected Fellow in 1751. The college, whose great gates ever stood shut until a Stuart should come to the throne again, was his home until his death. But he was no cloistered don. He attracted notice as a poet by a poem in praise of Oxford, *The Triumph of Isis*; he contributed to a series of Oxford collections of verse and edited two of them: *The Union* and *The Oxford Sausage*. From 1758 to 1768 he was Professor of Poetry. In 1785 he became Poet Laureate. His official odes were justly ridiculed. Some of his earlier verse is interesting, however, because, like his brother Joseph, the headmaster of Winchester, Warton revolted against the limitations of good sense and expressed himself with unfashionable feeling.

His criticism, too, expresses a romantic sensibility. His *Observations* on Spenser's *Faery Queen* appeared in 1754. The later years of his life were taken up mainly with the vast *History of English Poetry*. Only three volumes were finished by his death, taking the story up to the end of the Elizabethan age, but he also published a useful edition of Milton's poems. This is a Gothic work, rich, and various like his personality, reflecting his extensive reading of the classics as well as of early English texts.

Warton was a church-fancier and a lover of the picturesque. Tireless in his travels with pen and notebook, he liked to dwell upon old ruins and the 'flaunting ivy, that with mantle green invests some wasted tow'r'. His short essay of 1762 upon Gothic architecture was a scholarly, if inaccurate, prelude to the Gothic Revival. He was a friend of Dr Johnson, who relished his conversation and tapped his knowledge of the poets. 'I love the fellow dearly, for all I laugh at him,' he said, and a pleasant passage in Boswell describes their walks in the Oxfordshire countryside. Warton was too fond of acad_emic life to pay much attention to his duties as vicar of Kiddington but, characteristically, he wrote a history of the village. He cared little for social convention and liked to drink and smoke with the Oxford bargees. 'A little, squat, red-faced man' is a contemporary description of this engaging polymath who became Camden Professor of Ancient History in 1785, but might prefer to be known for the seven manuscript volumes of his archaeological tours which repose in Winchester College Library, for his skit on Oxford guide books *A Companion to the Guide*, or even for the lines he wrote on a blank leaf of Dugdale's *Monasticon* –

> Nor rough, nor barren are the winding ways
> Of hoar antiquity, but strown with flowers.

Further Reading
W. P. Ker, *Collected Essays*, vol. I, 1925.
C. Rinaker, *Thomas Warton*, 1916.

WATT, JAMES (1736-1819) is well described after an encounter with Sir Walter Scott in Edinburgh. He was over eighty, but 'the alert, kind, benevolent old man had his attention alive to every one's question, his information at every one's command'. Scott dilates upon the range of his interests; he talked with one man about the origin of the alphabet, with others of political economy and literature; he had read all the latest novels. 'This potent commander of the elements – this abridger of time and space – this magician, whose cloudy machinery has produced a change on the world, the effects of which, extraordinary as they are, are perhaps only now beginning to be felt – was not only the most profound man of science, the most successful combiner of powers and calculators of numbers as adapted to practical purposes – was not only one of the most generally well-informed – but one of the best and kindest of human beings.'

James Watt was the son of a merchant, baillie and elder of Greenock. He was not a robust boy, nor did he ever enjoy perfect health, though he lived long. From the burgh school he went to work first in London, then in Glasgow, as a maker of mathematical instruments; his father had some skill in this work himself. In 1764, when he was working for the university in this capacity, he was given one of Newcomen's steam engines to repair. At this time, Joseph Black, Professor of Medicine in Glasgow, was studying steam and enunciating his theory of latent heat. The subject was already one of some interest to Watt; indeed the old story that he had dreamed of the applications of steam while looking at his mother's kettle may be true. By the work of Newcomen and his successors, notably Smeaton, steam had been used for pumping machines since about 1720. The basic idea was simple: a piston at the top of a steam-filled cylinder was weighed down by air when the steam was condensed, and the pump was attached to the piston. By 1769 Smeaton was able to report that 100 such engines were at work on the northern coalfields alone. The biggest could lift 300 cwt. of water at one stroke, but were slow, making only some dozen strokes per minute and working only on the downward stroke of the piston. Watt's early experiments were only instrumental in saving heat and fuel; this was not of much interest to the coal-owners.

In 1769 Watt entered into partnership with Roebuck of the Carron ironworks and took out a patent for his improvements which proved hard and costly to enforce. These included the separate condenser, air pump, steam jacket for the cylinder, and the double-acting engine which utilized the piston in both strokes. After the failure of Roebuck, Matthew Boulton of the Soho works at Birmingham took Watt into a partnership which was to prove of the greatest importance, a classic alliance of inventor and manufacturer. The manufacture of the new steam engine was begun at Soho and it soon began to replace Newcomen's engines. In the next few years he got successive patents for the sun and planet motion, the expansion principle, the double engine, the parallel motion, a smokeless furnace and the governor. Boulton was a dynamic partner for Watt, but progress was relatively slow. Between 1775 and 1785 only sixty-six Watt engines were built, all small. Their use for the textile industry was not at first appreciated. Outside the mines and metal plants, Samuel Whitbread was one of the few to appreciate the use of steam; he had an engine installed in his brewery in 1786. In the '90s, however, the steam engine began to challenge water power's supremacy in the manufacturing industries. By 1800, when Watt's patent expired, the steam revolution was a fact. With cheap metal by then in good supply the way was clear

for the advance of the iron and textile industries, which were able to make most profitable use of steam. For this alone Watt would have a large place among the pioneers of the Industrial Revolution. But his fame should have a broader base.

Watt was an engineer of very adaptable skills. It was he who surveyed and planned the Monkland canal from Coatbridge to Glasgow, a money-spinner for the coal-owners and industrialists of Lanarkshire. He was also a scientist of distinction who could hold his own with men like Priestley, with whom he shared the discovery that water is a compound of the two elements, and with Lavoisier and Berthollet. He was a Fellow of the Royal Society and a corresponding member of the Institute of France. 'I saw a workman, and expected no more; but was surprised to find a philosopher': so a fellow member of the Lunar Society, John Robison recalled him. Watt invented the copying press and a way of recording weather in a systematic fashion. He built an organ and would, no doubt, if opportunity had come his way, have been an architect as well. But the heart of his busy life was Birmingham, where he lived until his death, and the happy partnership with Boulton, ended only by the latter's death in 1809. Here he continued to make improvements upon his steam engines, pistons, cylinders, connecting rods, indicators and boilers. He did not live to see the exciting application of steam engines to railway traction. If he had been born later we may be sure that he would have played a leading part in that advance.

Jeffries, a severe critic, spoke of Watt's 'kind of intellectual alchemy' by which he extracted from all subjects what was important and fastened upon it. Von Breder's portrait shows us an interesting sensitive face. Scientist, inventor, *philosophe*, Watt commands our admiration as much for what he was as for what he did.

Further Reading
L. T. C. Rolt, *James Watt*, 1964.
J. G. Crowther, *Scientist of the Industrial Revolution*, 1962.

WATTON, NUN OF (*fl.*late 1150s or 1160) was one of the victims of a monastic system which is more often remembered for its heroes. Although her name is unknown her story was recounted by Ailred of Rievaulx who was consulted over the case. Watton was a Gilbertine house in which nuns, canons, lay sisters and lay brothers lived, although rigidly segregated. The story reveals a darker side of the religious life, a world of tense closed communities in which a breakdown in discipline caused dislocation when spiritual harmony could be replaced by vengeance, cruelty, and barbarous violence; in which a social crisis released pent up forces of sexual jealousy or anxiety which, in turn, demanded harsh repression before an ordered norm could be recovered. There are elements of social ritual as well as religious extenuation in Ailred's account. The nun was caught in an affair with a lay brother. After she confessed, her fellow nuns beat her up; the younger nuns even wanted her burnt, flayed and branded. Although she avoided that, the nun was incarcerated in solitary confinement, her legs in chains, and fed on bread and water. When she was found to be pregnant, she was prevailed upon to disclose where her lover, who had fled the monastery, was living. By this time, the business had reached the ears of the founder of the order, Gilbert of Sempringham. On his orders, some other lay brothers caught and mugged the miscreant who was then handed over to the nuns. What happened next almost defies belief. The nuns 'wished to avenge the injury to their virginity'. While the man was held down by the other nuns, his mistress was forced to cut off his testicles, which were then thrust into her mouth 'just as they were, befouled with blood'. The man was returned to the lay brothers, and the nun to her prison. There, although this is concealed by a story of heavenly visitations, her baby was either aborted, still-born or disposed of, killed most likely, at birth. At this, the nun appeared 'virginal' again, and was released. God, as Ailred commented, had protected the nuns whose prayers throughout had been that He should be 'mindful of their virginal shame' and 'counteract the infamy and ward off danger'. As to the scenes of sadistic violence and sexual humiliation, Ailred expressed himself unhappy at the shedding of blood, although he commended the nuns' zeal in exacting revenge for what he, as they, saw as an insult to Christ. For Gilbert and Ailred, the matter was of discipline and upholding the sacred vows of the nuns, particularly in a new order which was bound to run risks of such liaisons. What they ignored were the dangers of admitting oblate nuns as young as four years old. The honour of the community is throughout seen as paramount over the individual: that, after all, was a central theme of rigorous monasticism. However, the problems of communal celibacy were heightened by an official imagery shot through with sublimated sexuality: Christ the bridegroom; the church his bride; the nun 'marrying' Christ etc. Even Ailred talks of nuns' 'ineffable raptures' at Mass. Above all, whatever the emotions and feelings of the actors in the drama, the events were seen, perhaps even by the participants, through a prism of absolute belief in a determining Divine Providence which stripped actions of temporal meaning by endowing them with spiritual significance. Ailred, making an edifying story out of the sordid scandal, was eager to avoid criticism of the community and, by implication, the monastic vocation. What is intriguing is that most educated contemporaries may have agreed with him.

Further Reading

G. Constable, 'Ailred of Rievaulx and the Nun of Watton', *Mediaeval Women*, ed. D. Baker, 1978.

WATTS, GEORGE FREDERIC (1817-1904), artist, was in his day regarded as the Grand Old Man of English Painting. Frederic Leighton called him 'England's Michelangelo': and there was certainly something in his high-mindedness, as well as in his choice of subject, that could momentarily sustain the comparison. Critics say that he curtailed his own originality by too much study of the sculptors of the Elgin Marbles (which were a kind of handbook for him) and of the great Renaissance masters. But his allegorical paintings *are* original, though now the least-admired of his work: his pencil-drawings are the best to come from his generation of artists; and his long series of portraits make the most complete record, and the most perceptive, of the leaders of that astonishing age.

He was the son of a piano maker and tuner who became more rather than less impoverished. He had no regular schooling, though he read a great deal. Somehow he grew up with a determination to use his art to raise the condition of mankind, by inspiring them to deeds of pity, self-sacrifice, purity and courage. In 1849, immediately after the Year of Revolutions, he showed *The People that Sat in Darkness* turning towards the growing dawn. In or around 1850, he painted *The Good Samaritan*, and a series of social-realist canvases which drew attention to conditions which disgraced society, and not least to the disgrace of the Irish Famine. Out of these earlier pictures grew his more philosophical allegories – *Mammon*, the *Love* trilogy, *The Dweller in the Innermost*, *Hope*, *Watchman, what of the Night?*, *For he had Great Possessions*, *The Court of Death* etc. He was typically Victorian in that he never forbore to preach, never lost the idea that men and women could be improved, and (though modest in himself) never doubted that his art might work some of that improvement. He himself said: 'My intention has not been so much to paint pictures that charm the eye, as to suggest great thoughts that will appeal to the imagination and the heart, and kindle all that is best and noblest in humanity.' And, on the negative side, the artist should busy himself with 'condemning in the most trenchant manner prevalent vices, and warning in deep tones against lapses from morals and duties'. Nothing could be further from Whistler's *The Red Rag*.

Although he did a great deal – by exhibiting his pictures in the East End, for example – to bring Art to the People, Watts blunted the force of his 'message' by an almost wilful obscurity – so that some of his allegories need verbal interpretation, like a joke which needs explaining. Also, with time, the prominence he gave to the educational purpose of a painting was given at some cost of careful technique. In any case, Allegory arouses a good deal of impatience today. The esteem in which such painters as Bacon and Freud are held, suggests that we prefer our 'truths' to be delivered straight from the shoulder. The popular verdict on Allegory is inclined to borrow Abraham Lincoln's words: 'Those who like this sort of thing will find this the sort of thing they like.' But we cannot ignore that the best known of Watts's allegorical paintings – *Hope* (1886, Tate Gallery), in which a blindfold girl, seated somewhere in the Universe, plays a broken lyre – inspired enormous affection; that it became a kind of vade mecum for desperate souls, evoked a splendid purple passage from G. K Chesterton in his study of Watts, and, more recently, was issued in reproduction to Egyptian troops after their defeat in the Six-Day War of 1967.

But the best of Watts's work – leaving aside his exquisite drawings – are his sculpture and his portraits. He came to sculpture only in the second half of his life. It was the same with his friend Leighton; and each of them produced a few, but distinguished, sculptures. Watts's remarkable *Physical Energy*, a huge equestrian statue which transposes one of the horsemen of the Parthenon into the twentieth century, was set up in the Matopos Hills of South Africa as a monument to Cecil Rhodes, but a replica can be seen in Kensington Gardens.

As for his portraits, Watts had always intended to make a gift to the nation of the most notable – to collect in a 'House of Fame' a generous sample of the genius of the Age. In 1895, the National Portrait Gallery accepted from him seventeen of his portraits. These were added to, and the Gallery now possesses nearly sixty. Of poets and artists alone, the collection includes portraits of Rossetti, Morris, Arnold, Browning, Tennyson, Swinburne, Leighton, Millais, Walter Crane, Julia Margaret Cameron, as well as self-portraits. There are politicians, ecclesiastics, a musician (Hallé), no captains of industry, but captains of war and Empire. And all or most of them are made to come alive by the vigour of one or two dominant characteristics insisted on above the others. Tennyson, for example, is the Seer. Cardinal Manning is all skin and bone – and ascetic spirituality. These portraits fairly crackle with the electricity of life. They also habitually dignify, even ennoble, the sitters. Watts has 'an overwhelming tendency to hero-worship' (Chesterton). Of course, there was a number of heroes to be worshipped, and Watts has found out many of them. But rather often (it seemed), 'The real men appear, if they present themselves afterwards, like mean and unsympathetic sketches from the Watts original' (Chesterton again). And this magnification of their best qualities has the effect (because such qualities are limited in variety) of giving them a 'family likeness' to each other, as if Watts were court-painter to a Victorian Mount Olympus.

Watts's own life was comparatively uneventful. In his early twenties, conscious that he was practically uneducated, he attended a 'crammer's' in Blackheath, run by a fanatically keen cricketer. It is strange to find Watts doing drawings for a book on Batting (the originals may be seen in the Pavilion at Lord's). But already he had attracted the first of his patrons, Alexander Constantine Ionides, the head of a Greek merchant-house. The Ionides family and connection were extensive; Watts painted five generations of them over the next half-century. The son of Alexander Constantine became famous as an art-collector, and bequeathed his collection, including many paintings by Watts, to the Victoria and Albert Museum. For Watts, the benefit cannot be overstated: the Ionides patronage gave him a staple of income which enabled him to become the breadwinner for his family, and to paint his more magniloquent pictures without always feeling that he had to sell them. Indeed, once he could afford to be so, he was consistently philanthropic.

In 1843, he won a £300 prize for his cartoon of *Caractacus*: an entry in the competition for the decoration of the Houses of Parliament, and a drawing which, though never executed, shows how far he had travelled as an artist. Now the prize-money enabled him to travel in reality: he spent the next four years mostly in Italy, delighting in the work of the Italian masters. He was 'taken up' by the British ambassador, Lord Holland, and his wife and circle; lived with them at their *palazzo* in Florence; and began a series of enormous canvases – e.g. *A Scene from Boccaccio*, half-Poussin in style, half-Raphael; thirty feet long; and on loan to Keble College, Oxford.

From then on his success proceeded almost without interruption – except in the case of his first marriage. In 1864, when he was forty-seven and she sixteen, he married Ellen Terry (already a promising actress); but the marriage went much the way of Ruskin's to Effie Gray, and they separated within a year.

It is clear, both from portraits and from the huge range of his acquaintance, that he was an attractive person: somewhat solemn and humourless certainly, but his grave solemnity with Mediterranean features – huge dark eyes when he was younger – won him much feminine adoration, and earned him the nickname 'Signor'. But it was his moral stature – or, rather, the unarguably moral tendency of his work – that, accommodating the mood of the time, gave him his unique prominence. His formidable second wife, Mary Fraser-Tytler of Inverness, did all she could to guard his health and aggrandize his reputation; but there is no reason to suppose that she had to conceal anything seriously discreditable to her idol. He twice declined a baronetcy, and was raised to the Order of Merit in 1902.

His old age he spent at Limnerslease, a house he had built (and named) at Compton in Surrey. Here he became an object of veneration as fulsome as that which Tennyson had attracted at Farringford (where Watts had lived for some years as the neighbour of the poet, who was probably his closest friend). In the last year of his life, at the instigation of Mary Watts, a picture gallery was added to the house at Compton. It was later enlarged, to include sculpture also. Two hundred of Watts's works are exhibited here. The crowds who leave the main road to visit the gallery today, are perpetuating the memory of a good man and a fine artist, who yet has been slower than his artist contemporaries to retrieve a portion of the celebrity which he enjoyed in the days when he and they were ranked with the greatest artists of the past.

Further Reading
Wilfrid Blunt, *'England's Michelangelo'*, 1975.

WATTS, ISAAC (1674-1748) has left a memorial in the shape of hymns which contain enough good poetry to ensure their survival, despite his strict Calvinist theology and natural archaisms of language. In the seventeenth century poets wrote for the accompaniment of some instrument, but their works were mostly intended for private use; there were some masterpieces, but only two attempts to compile a hymn book; neither Cosin nor Withers reached such a wide audience as Watts, with his *Hymns and Spiritual Songs in Three Books* (1707). With simple metres suitable for congregational singing, and poetry on nearly every page, Watts's collection had a large circulation from the start. 'Jesus shall reign where'er the sun', 'There is a land of pure delight' – such opening lines evoke at once the country congregation at evensong, candlelight reflective upon oak and deal, box pews and whitewashed walls, these enlivened perhaps by the texts and admonitions from scripture which he used to such good effect. Relevant, tidy, elevating but usually without the cloying sweetness, over-adorned or precious notes of many later hymn writers, Watts's hymns are springy and cheerful, even when he handles grave themes. In their restraint and grace they are as expressive of Augustan culture as the urbane work of Addison or the measured irony of Swift. The most famous of his hymns, 'O God, our help in ages past', has power still to emphasize the solemnity of a national occasion – or lend a reflective spirit to formal pomp.

Watts was a pioneer in his writing for children. In his preface to *Divine Songs attempted in Easy Language for the use of Children*, he addressed himself 'to all that are concerned in the Education of Children' in the hope that his songs, learned by heart, 'will be a constant furniture for the minds of children, that they may have something to think upon when alone, and sing over to themselves. This may sometimes give their thoughts a divine turn, and raise a young meditation.' His picture of the child may be over-sanguine but it lacked the overbearing and fussy character of some later 'edifying' works for children, and his lines reveal a tenderness and humour that contrast pleasantly with his stern beliefs. 'Let

dogs delight to bark and bite' and 'How doth the little busy bee' became household sayings in Watts's lifetime.

Watts lived a gentle, retiring life. For some thirty-five years he lived at Stoke Newington, with Sir Thomas and Lady Abney. (He had been at school at the notable academy there.) From Stoke Newington he would ride into London to preach at his dissenting chapel. He was not overworked for he had an assistant, and he was somewhat delicate. He found time to write doctrinal treatises, compile educational manuals, including *Logic* and *Scripture History*, both of which were successful. The admirable bust by Banks in Westminster Abbey shows an unusual face, sensitive, fine-drawn and keen; a man, one would guess, capable of spiritual concentration and insight.

Further Reading
E. G. Rupp, *Religion in England, 1688-1791*, 1986.

WAYNFLETE, WILLIAM (*c*.1394-1486), Bishop of Winchester from 1447 until his death, was the only schoolmaster to become a bishop in late medieval England. He was the son of Richard Patyn alias Barber of Wainfleet (Lincs.) by the daughter of a Cheshire knight. In 1416, when only an acolyte, he was already a Lincolnshire rector and was at a university, probably Oxford, graduating sometime as Bachelor of Theology. Experience in teaching, perhaps in Oxford, may have filled the period up to 1430, when he became headmaster of Winchester College, then the greatest English school. Twelve years later Henry VI poached him as second provost of Eton College. Waynflete probably moulded Henry's initial conception of a triple foundation of chantry, almshouse and school at Eton along the lines of Winchester College and modelled its link with King's College, Cambridge, Henry's other new venture, along the lines of Winchester College and New College, Oxford. That his inclination as well as his experience ran this way is suggested by his own subsequent foundations. His 'great discretion, high trust and fervent zeal' led in 1447 to appointment as Bishop of Winchester, the richest English see: a remarkable testimony to Henry's sense of priorities and his valuation of Waynflete's services. Waynflete was very close to the king. He was his confessor, baptized his son, and attended him both in 1455, when he recovered his sanity, and in 1470, when he recovered his throne. Hence perhaps the sacking of his palace in 1450, when other favoured bishops were murdered, and his term as Chancellor of England in 1456-60. His relations with Edward IV were generally good, but he was implicated in Cook's conspiracy in 1468 and supported the Readeption in 1470-1, when he escaped punishment for his misjudged loyalty.

Waynflete's long life enabled him to outlast rival claimants and to complete other people's projects, although not always as they wished: Eton and King's, Tattershall and Caister Colleges, and St Cross Hospital, Winchester. Many bishops patronized education, but none placed his stress on 'the practical side of teaching and schoolmastering' and none possessed the exceptional resources that made him 'the most prolific and influential founder in the fifteenth-century episcopate'. As early as 1448 he had founded Magdalen Hall, Oxford, later Magdalen College, whose seventy scholars ultimately matched Wykeham's New College and Henry VI's King's College. He lavishly endowed it with lands worth £675 a year. His feeder schools, Magdalen College and Wainfleet schools, were less grand than Winchester and Eton Colleges, but they were just as educationally innovative. Though no humanist himself, Waynflete was receptive to new ideas and new technology. Magdalen College School spear-headed a 'revolution in grammar teaching' along Renaissance lines, used new *printed* textbooks devised by its master John Anwykyll, and thus foreshadowed John Colet's more famous St Paul's School. Thus trained humanists went on to Magdalen College itself, where Waynflete's lectureships were a novelty copied in all future institutions. Such achievements explain the attribution to him of 'an outstanding role in the promotion of the educational revolution in England'.

Yet Waynflete was also a churchman. Though ordained late and non-resident as a rector, he was trained in theology and was an active and resident bishop. He wanted his students to become pastors and parsons, not lawyers and administrators. Hence his preference for theology as their course of study and his requirements that they should take out priest's orders within a year of their MA degree and that they should preach and say mass regularly. Moreover Magdalen College and Wainfleet School were chantries and a third one was founded in his cathedral. It was there among his fellow bishops that Waynflete chose burial.

Further Reading
V. Davis, 'William Waynflete and the Wars of the Roses', *Southern History* xi, 1989.
V. Davis, 'William Waynflete and the Educational Revolution of the Fifteenth Century' in *People, Politics and the Community in the Later Middle Ages*, J. Rosenthal and C. Richmond, eds, 1987.
R. A. Griffiths, *The Reign of King Henry VI 1422-61*, 1981.

WEBB, MATTHEW (1848-83), son of a Shropshire doctor, was the first man to swim the English Channel. He dived in off the Admiralty Pier at Dover at one o'clock on the afternoon of 24 August 1875, wearing a red silk costume, and touched ground at Cap Gris Nez at twenty to eleven on the morning of the 25th. It was his second attempt. The first, on 12 August, had failed when he drifted nine miles off course. This time, he was covered with porpoise grease and sustained by cod-liver

oil, beef tea, coffee, brandy and strong old ale. He used the breast stroke, at twenty strokes a minute. As he approached the French coast a wind got up, the water became choppy, and he made no progress for over an hour; so the triumph was all the greater. A handsome subscription was raised for him, and his presence at the London Stock Exchange brought business to a close. Jowett in Oxford could think of no rival feat in classical mythology, and it inspired a surge of interest in swimming.

Webb, a captain in the merchant navy, now decided to make his living as a swimming showman. But his capital dwindled, and in an effort to regain the acclaim of the public he attempted in 1883 a still more spectacular undertaking, and set out to swim from the USA to Canada across the rapids and whirlpools at the base of the Niagara Falls. Large sums were invested in the attempt, which caught the imagination of the press and the travel companies. Rowed to the edge of the rapids by a boatman, who had tried to dissuade him, he plunged in and battled his way through the rapids for eight minutes. But a whirlpool pulled him down. With his face towards Canada he was seen to throw up his arms and vanish. His body, recovered some days later, lies buried in the Oakwood Cemetery, close to the Falls.

WEBB, PHILIP SPEAKMAN (1831-1915), architect and designer, met William Morris when they were both working as young assistants in the Oxford office of the eminent church architect, George Edmund Street. It was the start of a lifelong friendship. Webb was serious and academic, very different in character from the ebullient Morris. But over the years they often collaborated. When Morris married, Webb built a house for him – the Red House at Bexleyheath. He also designed for him furniture, glass and metalwork, not only for this house but also for the firm of Morris & Co. Morris often asked for his help in drawing animals: Webb drew the birds in 'Trellis', a Morris wallpaper which is still well known today. He assisted Morris in the founding of the Society for the Protection of Ancient Buildings: both men campaigned hard for this cause.

In his lifetime Webb designed only about sixty buildings, almost entirely houses. In spite of his socialist beliefs, he was selective in his clients. He worked for intellectual, artistic and sometimes aristocratic patrons with whom he liked to build up a relationship over a lengthy period. Unlike many architects of his time, he worked with few assistants. His best known houses, such as Clouds in East Knoyle, Wiltshire, and Standen near East Grinstead in Sussex, took several years to complete.

Webb strove to design in a modern style. He wanted to create honest buildings, mixing elements from various periods. He made inventive use of traditional crafts and the local stone, flint and bricks. In the 1880s and 1890s he became a leading architect of the Arts and Crafts Movement, using vernacular features – gables, steep roofs, high chimneys and hung tiles – which have been copied in thousands of suburban houses ever since.

Further Reading
W. R. Lethaby, *Philip Webb and his work*, 1935.

WEDGWOOD, JOSIAH (1730-95) opened his first pottery in 1760 with a capital of about £20. When he died he had created a new artistic tradition and a large business. After a life of great generosity he left a private fortune of half a million pounds. He did not allow the loss of a leg by amputation to restrict him. He was an artist of industry, an entrepreneur of the most admirable sort; yet he was but the youngest of thirteen children of a Staffordshire potter and had little education beyond what he gave himself.

He first gained experience with the Staffordshire pioneer, Thomas Whieldon, one of the first to break away from the production of plain, serviceable ware and to make decorative china. From 1754 to 1759 Wedgwood worked with Whieldon and he began to envisage the commercial possibilities of good pottery when attention was paid to designs and decoration. Then he branched out himself with a factory at Ivy Burslem. Wedgwood was a founder of factory working; from the start he saw that art and profit must go together. Because raw materials were easy to obtain, the industry had previously been carried on by peasant craftsmen or small family businesses. The same man worked on several processes, and haphazard methods of glazing and firing led to accidents to men and to their wares. Marketing was local and little capital was accumulated to finance improvements. Wedgwood had the imagination to see that the products of Staffordshire might find favour in London, even abroad. Never before, and possibly never since, had so much money been allied to such cultivated taste in the upper classes of Europe. The time was ripe for the mass-production of beautiful objects.

Early in his career, Wedgwood employed his brother as a traveller in London. Later he had showrooms in London and Dublin and agents in countries abroad. The eighteenth century admired the patterns and figures of the ancient world. Their houses had classical facades, their halls were filled with sculptures of Greece and Rome. Wedgwood's vases went with the chimney-pieces of Robert Adam and the Renaissance paintings that were sent back in crates by the nobleman on his Grand Tour. He sought not only to please the fancy of the private collector but also to produce in quantity from standard designs. Upon the profitable base of ceramics from his large Etruria works (opened in 1769) he financed research into new methods and designs. His workmen exemplified the virtues of the division of labour before Adam Smith erected it into dogma: each worked at one

process. He employed the finest modellers, but they did not produce individual masterpieces; rather they acted as a team and the best designs were often the product of several minds. Among the artists who worked for him was John Flaxman; he specialized in copies of the antique, the best of which sold for £50. Wedgwood is, perhaps, best known for his Jasper ware made, after many experiments, from a compound of sulphite of baryta, clay, flint and carbonate of baryta which mixed into a smooth paste of exquisite texture. It would take a high polish and, when fired in the kiln with certain metallic oxides, could be stained or coloured in distinctive hues. Medallions and plaques, tea-sets, flower pots, bell-pulls, scent bottles and chessmen, especially ornamental vases, made the name of Wedgwood synonymous with restraint and elegance.

Wedgwood was a careful employer. He raised a village for the workers in Etruria, even instituted an insurance scheme. In 1783, however, when among other disturbances in the country there was a riot at Etruria and one of the ringleaders was hanged, he addressed a stern message to his workpeople, in the form of a pamphlet: 'I place my hopes, with some degree of confidence, in the rising generation, being persuaded that they will, by their better conduct, make atonement for this unhappy, this unwise slip of their fathers', he remarked, after observing how much prosperity had been brought into the region by well-directed industrialism.

His interest in selling his goods also stimulated the revolution in communications. Canals like the Grand Trunk Navigation cut the costs of inland transport and were kinder to his fragile goods than carts and rutted roads. Wedgwood could also secure clay by barge; besides the regular supply from Cornwall, he got it from America, and he even used clay from Sydney Cove, brought back by Joseph Banks and Cook. He could, however, be conservative where his industry's future was at stake. It was he who led the English merchants in successful opposition to the proposals of Pitt to admit the Irish to a greater share of English and colonial trade, fearing that cheap Irish labour would enable Irish manufacturers to undercut the English.

Wedgwood married a distant cousin; his eldest daughter, Susannah, married Robert Darwin, father of Charles Darwin. His third son was the first photographer (though he failed to discover a practical process). Over the last century no family has had a more notable record of intellectual achievement and public service.

Further Reading
R. Reilly, *Josiah Wedgwood*, 1992.
L. Weatherill, *The Pottery Trade and North Staffordshire 1660-1760*, 1971.
J. H. Plumb, 'Josiah Wedgwood', essay in *Men and Places*, 1963.
W. Burton, *Josiah Wedgwood and his Pottery*, 1922.

WELLESLEY, ARTHUR, 1st DUKE OF WELLINGTON (1769-1852) is one of the indisputably great figures of British history. Opinion may differ as to whether he was a finer soldier than Marlborough or Napoleon. Such questions will always be debated. It is enough to place his name alongside those masters of war. As a politician he had severe limitations. Like Coriolanus he was at different times the most popular and the most hated man in his country. He embodied some of the finest as well as some of the more insufferable traits of the aristocrat. He would always do what he believed to be right, regardless of party or public clamour.

He was the third son of the first Earl of Mornington and of Anne Hill-Trevor, the daughter of Lord Dungannon. Theirs was an old Anglo-Irish family: the name Wesley or Wellesley had only been added to that of Colley in 1728. Arthur spelled his name Wesley until 1798. He was most likely born in Dublin: the event did not seem important enough for an exact record. From his father, dilettante, musical and spendthrift, he inherited, no doubt, his love of music. He was a graceless, rather lonely boy; he was later stonily reticent about his boyhood. A portrait that survives shows a delicate face; the nose that was to be so famous already has a slight downward curve; the eyes were light blue, hair fair to brown. He was at the Diocesan School, Trim, then at Brown's preparatory school in Chelsea. He was not well prepared for Eton, nor did he flourish there. A schoolfellow describes him as 'quiet, dejected and observant'. Was this possibly a Churchillian reluctance to enter into activities in which he would not shine? He left Eton at fifteen, a dim figure after the brilliant school career of his eldest brother, Richard, to make way for the brighter younger brothers, Gerald and Henry. Neither at school nor afterwards was he a devoted Etonian. It seems, however, that he found his feet at Angers, where he attended the military school, learned some French and made the acquaintance of local nobles. Friends observed that it made a man of him; it also made him a soldier. At eighteen he was gazetted ensign in the 73rd Highland Regiment; his first action, reputedly, was to have one of his soldiers weighed in full kit.

In Ireland, where he served as an aide to the Duke of Buckingham, lord lieutenant, he hovered between the frivolous life of social Dublin and serious pursuits. He gambled heavily – but in his spare time he read Locke. Was he not struck by Locke's demonstration that all knowledge derived from experience? During his time in Ireland he met and wooed Kitty Pakenham, aged seventeen. His offer was rejected by her parents, since his prospects were uncertain. Yet he was making his way. In 1790 he had been elected member for Trim in the Dublin parliament. In 1793, the year of his proposal, he advanced by purchase to a lieutenant-colonelcy in the 33rd Foot. War was declared and the army expanding. In a serious mood he burned his violin; he would be a soldier without distractions.

His first active service was in the Low Countries under the Duke of York. When asked, forty-five years later, what he had learned there, he answered: 'Why, I learned what not to do, and that is always something'. He had seen the effects of divided command and a winter campaign undertaken without adequate preparation in food or clothing. The army was at its worst, after hurried recruitment following years of cheese-paring: there were casual, inexperienced officers, and men whom Fortescue was to call 'the offscouring of the nation'. Wellesley was blooded at Boxtel in September 1794, when his infantry beat off an enemy column. He might next have gone to the West Indies, but the squadron was turned back by a wild storm. The 33rd was ordered out to India. Wellesley sailed with a library of books: law, economics, military history, theology. Like Napoleon he was hungry for knowledge. Before he left he consulted Warren about his ailments. 'I have been attending a young man', said the doctor, 'whose conversation is the most extraordinary I have ever listened to … if this young man lives, he must one day be prime minister.'

India brought strenuous service in the best available school. In July 1797 Wellesley's eldest brother was appointed to be governor-general and began at once upon the forward policy which could only succeed if the army played its part. Arthur was presented with a unique chance of distinction. There was jealousy. Baird was upset when the younger man was appointed to the command of Seringapatam after Baird had led the assault. But he silenced his critics by his ability. After Tipu he dealt with Dhoonhiah Waugh. He was passed over in favour of Baird for an expedition to Mauritius (which was subsequently sent to Egypt to assist Abercromby). It turned out to be lucky that he did not go. In April 1802 he was promoted to major-general. At the end of that year Lord Wellesley made his alliance with the Peshwa of Poona, who had been driven out of his land by Holkar: this quarrel between the Maratha chiefs gave him the chance to deal with them separately, to humble their predatory power and to dispatch their able French advisers. Arthur wanted to harry them at once, before they could group. He began with the brilliant capture of Scindiah's great hill fortress, Ahmednuggur (August 1803). 'These English,' said a Maratha chief, 'are a strange people. They came here in the morning, surveyed the wall, walked over it, killed the garrison and returned to breakfast.'

At the battle of Assaye (24 September 1803) General Wellesley destroyed the military power of Scindiah. At odds of six to one, with troops who had already marched twenty-four hours, on ground that would not have favoured him had he not appreciated that he could outflank the enemy by crossing the River Kaitna, he won a classic victory. About his inspired guess at a ford that no-one could see, but the key to the battle, he declared: 'When one is strongly intent on an object, common sense will usually direct one to the right means.' Asked long afterwards what was 'the best thing' he ever did in the way of fighting, 'Assaye', he replied, without adding a word. In November he rubbed in his ascendancy with the smashing victory of Argaum. Then he captured the seemingly impregnable hill fortress of Gawilghur. He showed that guns and troops could move in precipitous mountains. He was to teach the French the same lesson.

He left India in March 1805 an experienced commander, and unbeaten. 'A sepoy general', Napoleon was to call him, but he understated the value of the Indian experience. He had learned to handle large forces in hot, dry country. He had learned to be firm with officers whose reckless drinking and quarrelling impaired efficiency. His Indian dispatches were meticulous in description. How did he find time for them? 'My rule was always to do the business of the day in the day.' He returned from India hard and fit.

He had remained single. Now he married Kitty Pakenham after proposing formally by letter before he had seen her again. The act was chivalrous, fatalistic, perhaps typical in its lack of understanding of the warmer, more spontaneous human feelings. From the start they were incompatible. He was imperious, easily irritated by disorder; she fluttery to the point of seeming feebleminded.

For about a year (1807-8) Wellesley was Chief Secretary of Ireland under the Duke of Richmond. In the middle of this period (August 1807) he left to command a brigade under Lord Cathcart in Canning's stroke against Copenhagen. This operation, boldly conceived, executed with brisk precision, registered his claims at the Horse Guards, where Indian experience counted for little. A greater chance came with the Spanish revolt of May 1808. In a Europe dominated by a single nation as never before, at last there was an opening to be exploited. Wellesley was busy assembling a force to invade Spanish America: now he was to take his 9,000 men to Portugal. His object was to eject the French from Lisbon; in the long term 'the absolute evacuation of the Peninsula by the troops of France'. In this task he was to succeed triumphantly. Vimiero, Busaco, Torres Vedras, Talavera, Badajoz, Fuentes de Onoro, the Arapiles, Vittoria and the battles of the Pyrenees – these names, so glorious in British military history, were but the greater landmarks in six years of campaigns; there were to be arduous trials and sharp setbacks, but no defeats. There was, however, a false beginning when, after winning the battles of Tolica and Vimiero, he was superseded in command, as arranged beforehand, by Burrard and Dalrymple. He put his name to the Convention of Cintra by which those cautious generals negotiated the evacuation

of Portugal by the French. Party venom and keen disappointment after victories which had led people to expect the destruction of the French army obscured the good sense of this treaty. Wellesley received an object lesson in the factiousness of politicians and the fickle sympathies of the mob. He returned briefly to Ireland after being exonerated by a court of inquiry. In the winter of 1808-9 Moore was forced to retreat through Spain to the sea. His force was evacuated from Corunna, but he died there. Against all objections Wellesley persisted in his belief that Portugal could be held. One politician believed in him: Castlereagh persuaded sceptical Cabinet colleagues that Wellesley should be sent to Portugal. So he left his plans for the draining of Irish bogs to establish a military presence in Portugal (April 1809). He did not return until his task was completed, five years afterwards.

Napoleon announced that he would drive the English 'leopards' into the sea but he did not supervise the operation in person. His contemptuous attitude encouraged his marshals to campaign recklessly. Wellington (to use the title he chose when he became a viscount after Talavera) demonstrated repeatedly the superiority of British fire-power in defensive positions. It is mistaken, however, to see him only as a defensive commander. This is to concentrate on the central campaign of the war, the defence of the lines of Torres Vedras to which he retired before Massena's invasion in 1810. His conception of defensive strategy was always dynamic, not a matter of waiting to be attacked; as he once wrote to a subordinate in India, 'You should attack any party that may come within … your reach.' Napoleon professed to believe that the British were brave but could not manoeuvre. Throughout, Wellington used the ground better than his opponents. Moreover, when he was sure of his ground, he could be swift and audacious. The brilliant crossing of the river Douro which discomfited Soult and won Oporto is a case in point. Another is the strategic surprise he secured by his two-pronged invasion of Spain in 1813, which led by way of great flanking movements to the battle of Vittoria and the final extrusion of the French. He was able to rely on sea power. There were only two practicable invasion routes and they were separated by mountain ranges and the River Tagus so that French forces operating on these lines of advance could not co-operate. He had adequate lateral roads, while the enemy were forced into cumbrous concentrations. Massena brought overwhelming force to bear in 1810. Then Wellington fell back on to his prepared lines and Massena starved before the redoubts and batteries of Torres Vedras.

Above all the Peninsular War depended upon supplies. Here was a subsistence economy with little left over for an army. His logistical planning rested upon the principle that 'Articles of provision are not to be trifled with or left to chance'. A flow of supplies came in from outside. Their distribution was the general's own concern. 'Minute and constant attendance to orders' is a regular theme. Delegation was not his strong point. He treated some of his officers as bumbling amateurs – but that is what they were. The difficulties of his army reflected an anarchic situation: overlapping jurisdictions at the top, purchase of commissions, and the gentlemanly approach to war which went with it. 'Nobody in the British army,' Wellington complained, 'ever reads a regulation or an order as if it were to be a guide for his conduct or in other manner than an amusing novel; and the consequence is that when complicated arrangements are to be carried into execution … every *gentleman* proceeds according to his fancy.' The men they commanded were attracted by drink and plunder, disciplined by the lash. How else would they accept the hardships of garrison duty in tropical climates – so much worse than the dangers of campaign – and the contempt of the civil population? Wellington had no illusions about his army. He saw it break into a hellish orgy after the capture of Badajoz, disintegrate in the retreat from Burgos. He was only being realistic when he declared that he had to rule with an iron hand. Deeply imbued as he was with the spirit of aristocracy, he was also a single-minded professional. He could rely upon two things: the bravery of the British soldier when he is well led, and a new seriousness of mind among many of his officers. His own aide-de-camp, Lord Fitzroy Somerset; the ever-dependable 'Daddy' Hill; John Colborne, colonel of the superbly efficient 52nd; Major Edward Somers-Cocks, Wellington's ideal of the officer and leader – these men may stand as representative of the best of his army.

Wellington was essentially an infantry soldier. He did not mass his guns, but sited them singly to support his line. Much of Spain and Portugal was unsuitable to cavalry. He had, indeed, little confidence in this arm, whose officers embodied some of the worst faults of the army. They relied too much on mere dash; nor did regimental officers control the advance. Where a charge was well conducted, as was that of le Marchant and his heavy dragoons at Salamanca, the effect was tremendous. The story of the cavalry is in the main, however, one of wasted opportunities, like Slade's futile action in 1812, which stung Wellington to words for which cavalrymen never forgave him. 'One would think that they cannot manoeuvre, excepting on Wimbledon Common.' The core of the army was therefore the infantry. Moore's Shorncliffe training had raised standards of fire-power and manoeuvrability. In the famous Brown Bess they had a better musket than their opponents. They were probably the most efficient troops in the world. Wellington believed that 'a disciplined infantry that keeps its order and reserves its fire has little to fear from cavalry'. Infantry attacks he met by adroit handling of the lines:

with flanks secured, the front sheltered if possible behind a crest from the enemy's artillery. Often, as at Busaco, the French columns would come through the fire of cannon and skirmishers only to encounter the main British line. Wellington would never commit himself beforehand to a rigid plan, but adapt his movements to those of the enemy.

Wellington's coolness under fire was proverbial. 'When I come myself, the soldiers think that what they have to do is the most important as I am there … and they will do for me what perhaps no-one else can make them do.' After the battle of Sorauren he wrote to his brother William: 'I escaped as usual unhurt, and I begin to believe that the finger of God is upon me.' He was everywhere in the thick of battle, reconnoitring, lying in a ditch with the infantry and directing their fire, rallying shaken troops. 'Never was courage so conspicuous; never was it so necessary' wrote a brigadier after Waterloo. In that battle Wellington exerted continuous tactical control. With his instinct for the crisis of the battle he recognized the attack of the Imperial Guard as such a moment, its repulse as the moment for decisive counter-attack. 'No cheering, my lads, but forward and complete your victory.' This was rhetoric indeed for the duke, famed for his laconic but clear orders.

Wellington stood on French soil on 7 October 1813, after the crossing of the Bidassoa. There ensued the battle of the Nivelle which showed Soult, as the Arapiles had shown Marmont, that he could be bold and imaginative in attack. The campaign that ensued was called by Oman 'the great game'. But the battle of Toulouse, on Easter Sunday, 1814, was 'a very severe affair'. In Toulouse Wellington heard that Napoleon had abdicated. He came home to a hero's welcome after a farewell order to his troops which was too spare and simple for his critics. The mischief lay not in the lack of high-flown phrases but in the dispersal of his army. His men believed that he could have held them together. When Napoleon returned to France and Wellington had to take to the field again, he had cause to bewail the lack of his seasoned troops. 'An infamous array' was his description of the allied force assembled in Belgium in March 1815. It was just good enough to resist Napoleon, aided by Napoleon's mistakes before and on the fatal day of Waterloo. The battle and the fighting that preceded it cannot be recounted in detail. He almost lost Quatre Bras, and Waterloo was a 'close-run thing'. For his outnumbered army it was a supreme test of endurance. Wellington had appeared not to doubt the outcome. 'Damn the fellow,' he remarked, as Napoleon launched charge after charge; 'he is a mere pounder after all.' Later, 'It was now to be seen which side has most bottom, and can withstand killing longest.' At 6.30 he was reported to have said: 'Night or the Prussians must come.' He had already won his battle before the

Prussians attacked, by the repulse of the Old Guard. The Prussians turned defeat into rout.

Wellington wrote the Waterloo dispatch in a state of emotional shock from the loss of so many friends. There was resentment at his failure to mention every regiment, every exploit. How could he have done so without a team of staff officers? We may marvel at the strength of this man who had been in the centre of battle all day: after a few hours' rest, having received reports of casualties which, as his doctor reported, made tears splash down, making furrows in the sweat and grime, writing a dispatch which covered four days of fighting from 15 to 18 June and filled four columns in *The Times*.

Wellington was made a duke in 1814. Chief of many foreign titles bestowed on him were those of Prince of Waterloo and Duke of Ciudad Rodrigo. In July 1814 he had to thank the House of Commons for a grant of £400,000 and the estate of Stratfield Saye in Hampshire was given to him by the nation. For three years he served as commander-in-chief of the army of occupation in Paris. It was he who induced Louis XVIII to accept Talleyrand and Fouché as advisers. He opposed resolutely, with Castlereagh's agreement, the dismemberment of France or reprisals. He also persuaded the House of Baring to advance a loan to the French government which enabled them to discharge their indemnity within three years. The recovery of France, so necessary to the equilibrium of Europe, owed much to his moderation; he despised meanness. He found that a French watch, with a map of Spain on the case, originally ordered for Joseph by Napoleon, had been withheld by the emperor after Joseph's defeat. 'A *gentleman*,' he said scornfully, 'would not have taken the moment when the poor devil had lost his *châteaux en Espagne*, to take away his watch also.'

He returned to England in 1818 and became Master of Ordnance in Lord Liverpool's Cabinet. He was not, of course, a simple soldier entering a political novitiate. He brought unique authority, in Europe no less than in England. With some historians as with some of his contemporaries, his military reputation has constituted an instant prejudice. 'The duke is a soldier,' wrote Scott in 1826; 'a bad education for a statesman in a free country.' 'A man educated in camps and ignorant of the British constitution,' wrote Lord Ellenborough in 1823. When Wellington formed his government in 1828 the Cabinet insisted upon his giving up command of the army. It was widely said that he would insist upon martial law and emergency measures, yet the evidence of his Cabinet career refutes the view that he was simply a dutiful soldier who sought military solutions.

From youth Wellington had been a politician as well as a soldier. It was then normal for a soldier or a sailor to have a parallel political career – and natural for the victor of Waterloo to wish to serve his country in the political sphere. He was authoritarian in political philosophy and practice, but he revered the constitution. During the last years of the Regency and the first years of his reign George IV harassed his ministers by insisting upon his divorce. Canning resigned, Liverpool wanted to; Wellington and Castlereagh remained firm. Wellington eventually got the king's permission to broaden the base of his administration and so averted the prospect of an 'ultra' ministry built around Sidmouth and Eldon. His moderate and practical outlook contributed, therefore, to the successes of Tory government in the more prosperous conditions of the early '20s. It was unfortunate that the unity for which he worked should have been marred by his quarrel with Canning. He had helped put Canning back into the Foreign Office after the death of Castlereagh, but he opposed Canning's most important decisions on foreign policy: recognition of the independence of the Spanish American colonies, for example. There was a strong personal antipathy, too. 'It was not what the duke said,' wrote Arbuthnot in 1825, 'but what he *looked* when Canning was mentioned.' He was sufficiently loyal to Liverpool and to his own ideal of government not to join with the 'ultra' peers to undermine Canning's position. But when Canning was chosen instead of him to succeed Liverpool as prime minister in 1827, Wellington had had enough. Supported by Peel, he refused to serve under him.

Ostensibly the reason was Catholic emancipation – but the real cause was personal. Uncharacteristically, Wellington had allowed himself to act in the spirit of faction. He was the only man at that juncture who could have preserved the unity of Toryism. It was, in Feiling's words, 'the end of a party'. Goderich succeeded Canning as head of the Canningite-Whig alliance. He proved too weak and in January 1828 the king sent for Wellington. He formed his Cabinet in such a way as to restore the balance of Liverpool's government. Huskisson and three other Canningites were included. They objected when he wished to adjust the new Corn Law to favour home-produced grain. He therefore manoeuvred them out of office, knowing that they could no longer turn to the Whigs and were therefore politically impotent.

He had rebuilt a sound position – but could he govern soundly? He wanted time – but Ireland would not wait. Wellington was faced by midsummer of 1828 with the choice: emancipation or civil war. He chose emancipation and stood firm, with Peel, against an emotional storm which would have overturned a lesser man. Not only at Oxford, where Peel lost his seat (or at Trollope's Ullathorne!) but among responsible Tories such as Winchelsea – with whom Wellington fought a duel! – there was a sense of betrayal. 'It is a bad business,' he told Sidmouth, 'but we are aground.' Conducting the measure through the Lords he showed familiarity not only with Ireland, but with the concordats of the

Catholic countries; he resisted the die-hards and wrested consent from the king. 'The people of England,' he once told a friend, 'must be governed by people who are not afraid.' Unfortunately more than firmness was required of a prime minister. He must be sensitive to other men's views; he must be prepared to delegate. Wellington tended to regard opposition as disloyalty and he took on too much himself. 'It can never be right,' said Mrs Arbuthnot, 'that the First Lord of the Treasury should be consulted as to who should be Colonel of the Life Guards.' His enormous strength was over-taxed. We see the strength of Lord Eldon's complaint that the duke was a man not of reason but of determination.

Slowly during 1829 Wellington won back the dissidents. George IV had been upset by Wellington, but he would not have Grey at any price. In 1830, the king died. The political battle was renewed upon new terms, but Wellington failed to adjust his position. He rejected the idea of taking Grey into his Cabinet. He could only hold off the Whig leader, no longer passive in opposition, if he had the solid support of the country gentlemen. Unfortunately they were alienated by his refusal to take steps to deal with the worsening condition of agriculture. Then he made his greatest blunder. When the new parliament met in the autumn of 1830, he declared unequivocally against reform. No ministry could survive if it did not make some change in that direction. At first he was moderate in opposition. In February the Belgian question troubled the government: the duke instructed his political lieutenants not to raise the matter in the Commons. He would not exploit a question of national security for party advantage. 'The duke thinks of nothing but the country,' wrote Ellenborough. But after the Whig success at the general election of April 1831, he was apparently saying 'The revolution is begun and nothing can save us.'

It was because of his unreasoning intransigence more than anything else that the Lords rejected the bill in the autumn. It is hard for us to recapture the fever of those months. Wellington was not alone in ascribing to the old constitution a sacred character. He had an instinctive understanding, we must remember, of the aristocratic ideal. As he later told Peel: 'It is not so easy to make men feel that they are of no consequence in the country, who had heretofore so much weight and still preserve their properties … and their seats in the House of Lords.' Privately he continued to be gloomy, even hysterically so. But in politics he regained his balance. In May 1832, when the king tried to rid himself of the Whigs, the duke prepared to take office, even to introduce a reform measure himself, to repeat his emancipation move. His colleague Peel did more than Place – or the mob who broke his windows at Apsley House on a night when his duchess lay dead in an upper room – to deter him from this hopeless attempt. Wellington resigned himself to the

Whig reform and saved his king from having to implement his promise to create new peers by persuading enough of the old ones to let the bill become law.

After the bill, Wellington handled the Tory peers with tact, complementing Peel's efforts to instruct the party in the Commons. A few months of power in 1834 and increased representation in the Commons bolstered Tory morale. Peel did not return to office until 1841. Meanwhile Wellington found himself on the defensive against a phalanx of peers who had found in Lyndhurst a capable 'ultra' leader. In the circumstances the duke did well to prevent the peers from using their majority to paralyse Whig government. Wellington affirmed his principle that the peers should not oppose the government on a major question, in 1846, when he persuaded the peers to pass the Corn Law repeal – though he did not personally approve of it. He held no departmental office in Peel's administration, though he was in the Cabinet. He was growing deaf and liable to seizures. He had made a great mistake when he resumed command of the army from his old subordinate Hill in 1842. (He had earlier succeeded the Duke of York in this capacity in 1819, relinquished it in pique when Canning became prime minister, resumed under Goderich, and then given it up reluctantly when he became prime minister.) For the greater part of the year he would with difficulty mount his horse and ride past admiring crowds to the Horse Guards: a painful dismounting was followed by irritable, sleepy hours at his desk. Officials at the ministry despaired. He obstructed necessary reforms. The army that fought and blundered in the Crimean War was essentially his army.

Wellington was as indifferent to adulation as to hatred. He hated pomp and heroics, flatterers and humbugs. He preferred to live simply in the midst of grandeur. The austerities he practised in war became second nature in peacetime. Creevey, invited to stay with him at his inn in France in 1818, was astonished by the wretched and dirty place, the scanty food – and the great man's apparent indifference to these shortcomings. His study in Apsley House had five doors – and five draughts. His mind was too keen to suffer fools gladly, he liked to express himself tersely and the impression we gain from his many recorded sayings is of sound horse-sense. How could they solve the problem of sparrows fouling the exhibits in the Crystal Palace? Queen Victoria sent for the duke. 'Sparrow-hawks, ma'am' was his answer.

Anybody who doubts his intellectual power should read his military dispatches; they are often masterpieces of economy and aptness of expression. De Quincey spoke of them as 'a monument raised to his reputation which will co-exist with our language'. His ability to clarify a complex problem, and to put his finger on the vital spot amounts sometimes to genius. The honesty of his judgements offended some. He did not shrink from hard truths – and undoubtedly liked to improve them sometimes by a caustic and ironic turn of phrase. 'The scum of the earth ... fellows who have all enlisted for drink', he said of British troops, comparing their recruitment with those of the French army. War had left him with few illusions. 'Take my word for it, if you had seen but one day of war you would pray the Almighty God that you might never see such a thing again.' Essentially he was not a hard man. He wept after the bloody storming of Badajoz. When his friend Arbuthnot was buried at Kensal Green, 'the hero of a hundred fights sat wrapped in his mourning cloak, with tears streaming down his cheeks'. Enriched by the nation, he felt he had an obligation to assist all who asked him. Arbuthnot found him one day stuffing banknotes into envelopes and asked him what he was doing. 'Doing? Doing what I am obliged to do every day. It would take the wealth of the Indies to meet all the demands that are made upon me.

It is easier, perhaps, to appreciate the Iron Duke than to warm to him. The Iron Duke's public virtues are well known. He stood for efficiency, honesty and dignity in the conduct of affairs. He always did his duty and rarely let personal considerations affect his choice of action. He ennobled the life of his time by what he was, as much as by what he did. Laden with honours and titles, familiar with courts and kings, uniquely trusted and revered, he remained entirely uncorrupted. Disraeli declared at the time of his death that he had left his country a great legacy: the contemplation of his character.

Further Reading

N. Gash, ed., *Studies in the Military and Political Career of the First Duke of Wellington*, 1990.
Elizabeth Longford, *Wellington*, 2 vols, 1969 and 1973.
M. Glover, *Wellington as Military Commander*, 1968.
A. Brett-James, ed., *Wellington at War, 1794-1815: A selection of his wartime letters*, 1961.

WELLESLEY, RICHARD COLLEY, MARQUIS WELLESLEY

WELLESLEY, RICHARD COLLEY, MARQUIS WELLESLEY (1760-1842), statesman, was the eldest son of Lord Mornington, and the elder brother of Arthur, Duke of Wellington. His career seems ultimately to have been disappointing only when measured against his pride and prospects. He might have become prime minister, and yet the qualities that made him a magnificent Governor-General of India would not have made him a good prime minister. The famous brothers were similar in appearance, in pride of family and will to serve. Richard was more imaginative, intellectually better endowed, but a man of caprice, a lover of gestures. His soldier brother was essentially a narrower person, whose sensitive and romantic feelings were subjected to the disciplines of a supremely purposeful life. If Arthur appears to be the greater man, it is mainly because of a directness, concentration and hard common sense which were perfectly suited to soldiering. They worked together in India and then their talents were perfectly complementary.

Lord Mornington was an Irish peer who flooded acres of land round his house at Dangan to improve the landscape, loved 'cool grots' and gratified his musical tastes by mustering his own orchestra. Richard was sent to Harrow and would no doubt have stayed there but for his part in a schoolboy demonstration against Dr Heath. He was removed to Eton, where he became a very fine scholar. He recited Lord Strafford's last speech before the royal family and the prime minister at the Speeches of 1778. He went to Christ Church and then took his seat in the Irish House of Lords. His horizons were enlarged in 1784 when he entered the British House of Commons – as an Irish peer was entitled to do (Castlereagh and Palmerston are two other notable examples). He always stood loose to political allegiance but, if anything, he was a Whig: a free-trader, an open-minded sympathizer with most sorts of reform and, like so many Irish gentlemen of the Ascendancy, an advocate of Catholic emancipation. He sat on the India board in 1793. In 1797 he was sent out as Governor-General with the English title of Baron Wellesley.

He came by himself, leaving behind the French lady, Hyacinthe Roland, his former mistress whom he had recently married. It was as though he had decided that women had no place in the exacting life of Indian government. He approached his task with dedicated seriousness. He saw India as a theatre in the world war with France. Dundas, who combined being minister of war with responsibility for India, was of his mind. Both men seem to have decided that they could sail on past the intentions of Pitt's India Act to an expansion of British rule and trade. Wellesley saw himself as responsible rather to the government than to the directors. From the start he was opposed by those who believed, like Charles Grant, later chairman of the company, then on the board of trade at Calcutta, that the limits had been reached. There were others, however, like David Scott of the directorate, who believed that the Indian princes were incapable of providing a balanced concert or sound administration. Wellesley believed that a forward policy was inevitable, if India were not to remain anarchic or be lost to the French. In practice the success of his first moves against the French led to his larger policy of British supremacy.

Wellesley presided over an informal ruling group in Government House, Calcutta. He evoked the loyalty of ambitious young men, who looked forward to carving their careers out of the conquest and administration of new lands. His magnificence did not escape comment. It was said that he wore his medals on his night shirt. The extravagance of viceregal ceremony no doubt shed a glow on those who participated. He looked the part: hawk-faced, with an air of command, repelling familiarity 'with a degree of vigour amounting to severity'. 'His great mind pervaded the whole,' wrote Malcolm, 'his spirit was infused into every agent he employed ... all sought his praise, all dreaded his censure.' Like Arthur Wellesley he was minutely careful of details. Like him, too, he concentrated power in his hands. He was, in Shawe's words, 'his own Secretary at War, his own minister of foreign relations, his own Master-General of Ordnance, and his own Chancellor of Exchequer ... there is no clashing of departments'. He achieved thereby the unity of purpose and action which is the hallmark of his governorship.

From the King of Oudh and the Nizam of Hyderabad, his chief allies, he demanded, in place of annual payments to maintain troops for their protection, the permanent cession of territory. The chosen land completed the encirclement of Oudh and shut off Hyderabad from the sea. Tipu of Mysore had been beaten but not subdued by Cornwallis. Wellesley had a pretext for action in some captured letters in which Tipu asked the French for military aid. Wellesley projected and his brother carried out an expedition to Seringapatam, strong in its island river site, but not strong enough to resist a brilliant assault (March 1799). Some rich areas of Mysore were kept for the company, another given to Hyderabad. A puppet ruler was placed over what was left. The ruler of the Carnatic was deposed, though his complicity in Tipu's schemes was vague. The company assumed in the Carnatic the full control which they had long enjoyed in Bengal. So the British were paramount beyond dispute in southern India. The Maratha confederacy of states embodied much of what was worst in India. The quarrels of the chiefs endangered the general peace. Wellesley's policy was to take advantage of these divisions. A prince in danger from his neighbours was encouraged to turn to the British for help. 'The princely fly was firmly enmeshed in the British web,' as V. A. Smith put it, and 'while most princes realized the strength of the British at the moment, few had much conception of the secret spring of power which would make the strength still greater.' So the British championed the cause of the Peshwa Baji Rao against Holkar, Sindia and the Rajah of Berar. In the wars that ensued Arthur Wellesley assumed over-all command. He defeated his enemies by swift, well-planned movements. At Assaye, in 1803, he destroyed the power of Sindia; in 1804 he attacked Holkar; in Trafalgar year the Grand Mogul accepted British protection. A great territorial empire was being carved out of decomposing native India.

A Governor-General's power was a heady potion for a man of Wellesley's temperament. The 'glorious little man' behaved at times like an impresario. For not sealing his letter in proper form the King of Oudh was addressed from a great height: 'Besides indicating a levity wholly unsuitable to the occasion,' he was 'Highly

deficient in the respect due to the first British Authority in India.' When crossed by a subordinate he could display a degree of affronted authority that bordered, to judge by letters, on the megalomaniac. Against such outbursts one must set the strains and ultimate loneliness of his position. The Directors were displeased by the expense of his administration. He did not obey the rules. He sent his brother Henry on a diplomatic mission, though he was not employed by the company. He built a palace in Calcutta and lived royally. His admirable suggestion for the setting up of a college at Calcutta to train civil servants was looked upon with suspicion by the directors who could hardly grasp that a commercial concern had become a vast territorial empire. In 1801 he had had the boldness to dispatch Baird, with an Indian force, to assist the campaign against the French in Egypt. He wished to use the British fleet to seize Mauritius from the French and Java from the Dutch. The directors could not deny great victories, nor overlook great risks. In 1804 Colonel Monson was defeated and Lake was repulsed at Bharatpur; two reverses to set against many victories, but enough for Wellesley's critics. He was recalled. The Maratha wars were left unfinished. His successor patched up a peace which benefited only the robber bands which flourished under Maratha protection.

Wellesley came home, in 1805, to threats of impeachment, but Fox (and no doubt with memories of Warren Hasting's futile ordeal) took no steps. Wellesley still felt that he had been ill-treated, that his Irish marquisate was scant recognition. His governorship had ended in frustration. How successful had he been? He had wielded a keen, sharp and purposeful blade in the jungle of Indian politics. It must be allowed that his judgement was mainly right; his methods, though high-handed, were effective. Against him it may be argued that he had broken what existed of authority in central India without putting anything in its place. He had pointed the way to British supremacy but in the short term he had overstrained her military and financial resources.

In 1809 Wellesley went to Spain to assist his brother as ambassador to the Junta. In December of that year he became Foreign Secretary. Prime Minister Perceval's intention was to create a government of national unity: Wellesley at the Foreign Office, Liverpool at the War Office, together represented the government's determination to pursue the Peninsular war. Unfortunately neither Wellesley nor his brother showed much confidence in Perceval. Wellesley was a troublesome colleague from the start. From the standpoint of men like Perceval and Liverpool his methods seemed unbusinesslike, his manner high-handed, his policy individualist to the point of disloyalty. He behaved as if he ought to be prime minister and was only serving in a subordinate capacity until the king and parliament recognized his claims.

Unfortunately for Wellesley, it was necessary to have some following or to find a formula to which men of different persuasions might adhere. This required a political skill which Wellesley lacked. He was not at home in domestic politics, where reticence and a willingness to compromise were prized. When, in the autumn of 1811, the anxiety of the regent to find a broad-bottomed ministry offered a chance at last, Wellesley found himself almost friendless. He had alienated influential Tories, while the Whigs, even Grenville, could not agree with him on his view of the war. The prince's attitude stiffened. The Whigs were given to understand that he preferred measures to men. Canning, Grey, Grenville and now Wellesley headed groups 'rich in debating points but poor in prospects' (Steven Watson). Before Spencer Perceval's death (1812) Wellesley had prepared a long attack on his handling of affairs. He was prevented by an indisposition from delivering it. After Perceval's death he published it and the world questioned his taste. Wellesley had one more chance then to form a government. Again, like Moira after him, he failed. The government prospered, not a little owing to his brother's victories. The rest of his political career was spent in opposition. When he denounced, with Grey, the breach with Napoleon in the Hundred Days, he fell out with his brother. Their relations henceforward were of mutual indifference, if not open antagonism.

In 1821 Wellesley became Lord Lieutenant of Ireland. Once more he found work which fitted him. In a period of difficulty, when 'oaths were of little obligation and human life of no value' (John Grattan), he fought against prejudice and conciliated where conciliation was possible. He suppressed Ribbonmen, Orangemen, Whiteboys and other terrorists, reorganized the police, reformed the magistracy and provided poor-relief. He resigned in 1828 when Wellington became prime minister. Ironically, therefore, he was not in office to see his brother, who had always opposed Catholic Emancipation, pass the measure which he had so long advocated. He did, however, briefly resume the lord lieutenancy under Grey.

The end of his life was contented. He cultivated the classics and enjoyed the friendships of like-minded men, notably Brougham. A second marriage in 1825 to Marianne Patterson, a young American widow, brought him great happiness. He left no legitimate children. By his own request he was buried in Eton College Chapel.

Further Reading
P. E. Roberts, *India under Wellesley*, 1929.
W. H. Hutton, *Marquis Wellesley*, 1897.

WENHAM, JANE (*d.*1730), of Hertfordshire, was the last woman to be convicted for witchcraft in England. At her trial (1712) the jury found her guilty despite the directions of the judge, Sir John Powell, who commented upon one of the charges that there was no law against flying. She was condemned to death but pardoned. The case provoked a number of pamphlets, on both sides. The Age of Reason brought the abolition of the death penalty for witchcraft in 1736.

WENTWORTH, CHARLES WATSON, EARL OF MALTON and 2nd MARQUIS OF ROCKINGHAM (1730-82) was an important figure in the politics of George III's reign. His large estates, his calm and disinterested approach and his common sense together placed him in the position of leading a distinct party for nearly twenty years. More brilliant men than he were willing to serve under him and the second at least of his two short administrations was rich in achievement.

He was indeed a characteristic product of the political conditions of the time. If he had not existed, one feels, someone else would have had a similar career, because of the need for a statesman with the personal gifts to form and lead a connection which would be close enough to provide a government. With party ties loose where they existed at all, with men counting before measures, much was asked of a political leader. He must either be conciliatory to the point of negation, like North, or he must be seen to stand for some principles which would be acceptable to the king as well as to the mass of independent members. The principles of the Rockingham Whigs, who were a more stable and coherent body than any other faction of the time, became increasingly unpalatable to the king as the American War proceeded; it was the failure of this war which gave them, at last, the chance to put their principles into action.

Rockingham's estates, principally in Yorkshire and Ireland, produced a rental estimated in 1761 at £24,000 a year. Arthur Young praised the management of his estates, saying that 'he never saw the advantages of a great fortune applied more nobly to the improvement of a country'. His early activities in parliament were concerned with promoting the interests of the Yorkshire woolgrowers. He was a keen racing man, a member of the newly formed Jockey Club and active in promoting the meetings at Doncaster and York. Upon such pursuits he might have been prepared to spend his life – but he inherited, too, a political tradition. His father, who had died in 1750, had owed his advancement in the peerage to the Pelhams. It was natural that Rockingham should succeed, in the years after Newcastle's resignation in 1762 and subsequent eclipse, to the leadership of the attenuated Newcastle interest. He was, however, a diffident politician and extraordinarily inexperienced when he succeeded Grenville as First Lord of the Treasury in July 1765. He had only been, for short periods, Lord Lieutenant of the West Riding and a Lord of the Bedchamber, and he seems, unlike Bute before him, to have had no illusions about his fitness for high office: 'Howsoever unsuitable I might be for that office from my health and inexperience in that sort of business, yet I thought it incumbent upon me to acquiesce in the attempting it'.

The ministry had certain assets. Rockingham was, in Burke's words, 'a man of honour and integrity'. He approached his task in a spirit of fairness. The ministry was a party one in that the main posts were filled by his candidates; but he tried, too, to rebuild the Pelham system upon a broad base and was always ready to receive recruits. The crucial figure here was Pitt, who made it plain that he would not serve in any but a dominant capacity. Grafton, who admired him, thus became disaffected, divided from the start. The choice of Grafton and Conway as Secretaries of State underlined the inexperience of this ministry. 'An administration of boys' George III called it. Grafton was indeed only thirty, while Conway, the principal spokesman in the Commons, was no match for Pitt or Grenville. After a promising start, the administration fell apart. The unpopular cider tax was abolished and the window tax modified; General Warrants were declared illegal and with them some of the debris of the Wilkes case. The question of American taxation, in which the government stood between the colonists' resentment and the reluctance of English squires to pay for American defence, was resolved by a supple manoeuvre: the repeal of the Stamp Act was preceded by a Declaratory Act affirming the right of parliament to tax the colonies. Commercial legislation included a treaty with Russia and the opening of certain ports in the West Indies to stimulate Caribbean trade. The administration drifted, however, towards crisis. The king seemed to regard it as a stop-gap, while the Duke of Cumberland, who was a useful patron and intermediary with the king, died a few months after it was formed. Grafton himself resigned in April 1766; Richmond, his successor, was thirty-one, virtually without political experience. Rockingham allowed his ministry to crumble. Conway was persuaded to stay on and serve under Chatham, whom the king summoned to form a government in July, when the pressure for a stronger head of affairs grew clamorous. Other members remained loyal to Rockingham and in their resignation from office together anticipated the party system of a later age.

Either because of the influence of the views of his secretary, Edmund Burke, upon the necessity of party, developed in his *Thoughts on the Present Discontents* (1770), or because he was anxious not to find himself again in the weak position of his first ministry, Rockingham insisted that, if he returned to office, it should be on his own terms. George was equally adamant for his right to select ministers. As the American war developed, and Rockingham and his associates continued to oppose it, even to the point of deploring British victories on the grounds that they postponed the independence which they regarded as both right and inevitable, George held more firmly to North. In these circumstances the opposition turned to the question of royal influence and planned to reduce it. When the movement for parliamentary reform swelled with county resolutions and petitions, Rockingham made certain contacts with it. His friend Savile was active in Yorkshire, where the freehold franchise was large, but Rockingham's main concern was to increase aristocratic independence, and a better means to this end was to attack the bloated establishment through which the Crown exercised its patronage: this was Burke's programme of 'oeconomical reform'. He was chary of popular excitements. As he wrote to a friend in February 1780, 'There are so many visionary schemes and expedients by way of reform on float that a general confusion and disagreement will ensue.' In that month he introduced his bill for 'the better regulation of His Majesty's civil establishments'. After keen debate and some success it was rejected, but Rockingham was encouraged to persist in this weapon of opposition, safer, as the Gordon Riots seemed to show, than direct appeal to the people, more damaging as an issue than Ireland.

In March 1782 North resigned and Rockingham took office with a strong hand of cards. He had held back to the point at which George III had virtually surrendered to him: as Richmond put it, 'all at your feet in the manner you would wish, and with the full means to do what is right'. The king had even considered abdication before accepting Rockingham's conditions, a free hand with regard to American independence, economical reform and the choice of ministers. In the latter, however, George had one compensation, for to offset Fox, whom he hated, there was Shelburne. Only Rockingham's tact prevented an open breach between the two Secretaries of State. Starting at a dark point of the war, lasting only four months, this was nonetheless a notable ministry. In Ireland he endeavoured to counter those critics who said that North's economic concessions were illusory by giving Ireland greater constitutional independence. Following the advice which Burke had expressed often in speeches, his government tried to build upon goodwill at the cost of formal ties. The right of the British parliament to legislate for Ireland was abrogated, as was the right of the Privy Council to alter Irish legislation. Indeed the constitutional links between Britain and Ireland became very slender. The Lord Lieutenant of Ireland was a member of the British Cabinet and Acts of Parliament required the Great Seal. Otherwise for a brief period Ireland enjoyed virtual independence. At home something was done to answer charges of corruption in public affairs: committees inquired into the methods whereby loans had been raised and contracts granted; salaries were introduced in certain grades of the civil service who had hitherto been paid, or had paid themselves, out of fees. Crewe's Act took away the vote from revenue officers who were supposed to be directly amenable to pressure from the state, their immediate employer. Clark's Act forced government contractors to choose between their contracts and their seats in parliament.

In the midst of this activity, on 1 July Rockingham, who had never been a robust man, died of influenza. If he had lived, the split which led to the brief administrations first of Shelburne, then of Fox and North, and subsequently the emergence of Pitt, might not have occurred and Fox, for one, might have had a more constructive career. Rockingham was not the last nor the least of those prime ministers whose task it has been to create a harmonious group in which more brilliant men can work. Langford writes of 'his instinct for compromise'. For all his limitations, the words of Burke's epitaph ring true: 'His virtues were his means'.

Further Reading

P. Langford, *The First Rockingham Administration 1765-6*, 1973.

R. Pares, *George III and the Politicians*, 1953.

WENTWORTH, PETER (*c.*1524-96), parliamentary critic of royal prerogative, was born about 1524 (not 1530, as in the *Dictionary of National Biography*). He was the elder son of Sir Nicholas Wentworth of Lillingstone Lovell, a village at that time in a piece of Oxfordshire surrounded by Buckinghamshire, but by the time Peter succeeded his father the village had been absorbed into Buckinghamshire. He was twice married; first, to Letitia Lane, whose mother was a cousin to Catherine Parr; secondly, to Elizabeth, sister of Sir Francis Walsingham. He entered Lincoln's Inn in 1542, but it was not until 1571, when he was just on forty-seven years of age, that he entered parliament as member for Barnstaple. He came into parliament, he said, because of his concern over the question of who was to succeed to the throne after Elizabeth: 'I was first stirred up to deal in it … by God's good motion, then by sundry grave and wise men unknown unto me, and also by lamentable messages sent unto me by men likewise unknown unto me.' He was to sit in six parliaments during the next twenty-two years, as member for Barnstaple, then Tregony, and lastly for Northampton. He was a man 'of a whet and vehement spirit', which got him into frequent and serious trouble with the queen for the attacks he made upon her, although he had a passionate love and reverence for her.

In his first parliament of 1571 he was a member of the committee which was formed in the House of Commons to submit a bill dealing with the Articles of Religion to the archbishop, Matthew Parker. Parker asked why the Articles for the Homilies and some other matters had been omitted. Wentworth's answer was, 'Surely sir, because we were so occupied in other matters that we had no time to examine them, how they agreed with the word of God.' 'What!' said Parker, 'Surely you mistook

the matter. You will refer yourselves wholly to us therein.' Wentworth retorted, 'No, by the faith I bear to God, we will pass nothing before we understand what it is, for that were but to make you popes. Make you popes who list, for we will make you none.' In this same parliament Sir Humphrey Gilbert made a speech defending the privileges of the Crown. Wentworth made a violent attack on Gilbert, noting 'his disposition to flatter or fawn on the prince, comparing him to the chameleon, which can change himself into all colours saving white'.

The discovery of the Ridolfi Plot in 1571 necessitated the calling of another parliament. Wentworth was returned for the seat of Tregony. Great pressure was put on the queen to execute Mary, Queen of Scots, or at least to attaint her: Elizabeth preferred to delay the attainder, but she sent for the committees of both Houses and treated them with such tact that the Commons moved a resolution that the thanks of the House be given to her. Wentworth opposed the resolution to return thanks, 'the which for my part I did not think her Majesty had deserved, so that my speech was to stay thanks'.

Parliament met again after an interval of three and a half years, in February 1576. During the interval Wentworth brooded on his experience in the Commons. He thought the House was too subservient to the queen. On the 8th Wentworth made a resolution on liberty of speech. He forthrightly attacked the queen for the 'great faults' she had committed. 'It is a dangerous thing in a prince unkindly to intreat and abuse his or her nobility and people, as her Majesty did the last parliament … ' Sir John Neale has called this 'the most remarkable speech hitherto conceived in the parliament of England … He was wrong, utterly wrong in his own generation; but the future hallowed his doctrine. He, indeed, as much as any of his colleagues, shaped that future' (*Elizabeth and her Parliaments, 1559-1581*, pp.318-25). The House stopped him, committed him to the serjeant's ward and appointed a committee to examine him 'for the extenuating of his fault'. As a result Wentworth was sent to the Tower, where he remained for rather more than a month: then the queen ordered his release and sent a very magnanimous message to the House of Commons. Wentworth was brought to the bar of the House, where he made a humble submission on his knees and was then allowed to take his seat again.

In 1579 Wentworth was in trouble with the Council. His bishop complained that many Puritans were resorting to his house at Lillingstone Lovell, where they received the Sacrament in Puritan fashion. Sir John Harington noted that Wentworth was 'a man of great accompt with all of that profession' in his neighbourhood.

Wentworth was not a member of the 1584/5 parliament, but he was returned for Northampton to the parliament of 1586/7, made necessary by the Babington

Plot. An attempt to reform the church along Presbyterian lines failed in the Commons, because the queen put a stop to it. Wentworth held that she thereby infringed the rights of the House. He therefore determined to make the Commons define their own rights to freedom of speech and no longer accept a definition laid down by the executive. He proposed to the House a series of questions, the answers to which would remain as the rulings of the House. Once more Wentworth, and four others, were sent to the Tower, not apparently for any speech made by them in the House, but for 'conferences in matters of religion' held outside the House where privilege did not arise. In fact, an organized campaign against the Elizabethan church settlement was being made, and the queen would have none of it. The Puritans had only narrowly failed to win their case in Convocation in the '60s. They were now fighting in parliament. Puritanism was also changing its character: in the past it had been a protest of Puritan clergy against religion being subordinated to politics. By Wentworth's time in the '80s it was beginning to be a protest of Puritan squires against control of the state by the bishops.

Up to this point Wentworth had been the champion of free speech, for he saw that the way for the Puritan cause to triumph was to make it a struggle for privilege in the House of Commons. If he could win freedom of speech there, the queen could no longer put a stop to the attacks on the church. From 1587, however, he ceased to think in terms of parliamentary privilege and became entirely taken up with the problem of the succession to the throne.

It is not known when Wentworth was released from the Tower. In 1587 he drafted *A Pithie Exhortation to her Majestie for establishing her succession to the crowne.* The tract urged the queen to nominate the heir to the throne: it drew a fearful picture of what would happen to England if she were to die without having established her successor: and it also warned her of the dreadful fate which would befall her own body and her own soul. Wentworth failed to win any sympathy for his course of action, and when the parliament ended, nothing had been done. In 1590 he tried to interest the Earl of Essex in his plan, but news of what was in his tract leaked out and he was summoned before the Council and put in the Gatehouse (August 1591). For a second time he tried to use Burghley to bring the queen over to his way of thinking, and of course failed. He was treated very leniently and was released on 21 November.

Ever an optimist, Wentworth was now convinced that the queen would call a parliament and declare the name of the heir to the throne. When she did call a parliament in 1593, he fully expected this to happen. He prepared a campaign for the House of Commons and called some friends together to discuss his speech, the bill he had drafted, a petition to the House of Lords, a thanksgiving if the queen agreed, and an attack on her if she refused. Few were ready to support Wentworth's scheme and then news of his intentions leaked out. He was summoned before the Council and once again found himself in the Tower. He never left that prison. He was not badly treated: he had considerable liberty and his wife was allowed to be with him. In 1594 he wrote his *Discourse containing the Author's opinion of the true and lawful successor to her Majesty* (published 1598). This was an answer to Father Parsons's *Conference about the Next Succession to the Crown of England*, in which the Jesuit repudiated the doctrine of divine hereditary right and implied that parliament could make null the hereditary right of James VI of Scotland to the English throne. Wentworth refuted Parsons's arguments and supported the right of James to succeed Elizabeth. He had previously been against the Scottish claim, perhaps because he was opposed to the succession of Mary, Queen of Scots. Her execution removed this stumbling block, but Wentworth found himself opposing Parsons for allegedly over-exalting parliament (Neale, *Elizabeth and her Parliaments, 1584-1601*, p.262). Efforts were made to secure his release, but these for unknown reasons failed. Wentworth died in the Tower in 1596.

The queen's policy on the succession problem was subtle, characteristic and successful: not to take action when no action was needed, to keep the succession uncertain, to dangle it in front of James VI, 'to be given or withheld according to his behaviour' (Neale, *Elizabeth and her Parliaments, 1584-1601*, pp.251-2). Wentworth wanted to wreck that policy: Elizabeth could only treat him as she did. He was wrong from first to last, but he was a man of passionate conviction, passionately devoted to the queen and to his country, but he totally lacked self-criticism. One of his contemporaries said of him that 'Mr Wentworth will never acknowledge himself to make a fault nor say that he is sorry for anything he doth speak'. The queen once said of him, 'Mr Wentworth has a good opinion of his own wit.' In his fight for freedom of speech he was far ahead of his own times: but he would not have extended freedom of speech to his opponents: it was lucky for the Stuarts that Wentworth was not in the House of Commons in days when he would have found much more support than he found in his own day: it was lucky for Wentworth that he was dealt with by a comparatively lenient sovereign, for he would have had shorter shrift from Charles I than he got from Elizabeth. Wentworth was a symbol of his own age – the fiery spirit of Essex and Ralegh burned as high in him; but he was also a pointer to the future, a forerunner of Pym and Hampden, but not a progenitor of the Earl of Strafford.

Further Reading
Sir John Neale, *English Historical Review*, 1924; *Elizabeth and her Parliaments*, 1953.

WENTWORTH, THOMAS, 1st EARL OF STRAFFORD

WENTWORTH, THOMAS, 1st EARL OF STRAFFORD (1593-1641), the most formidable of the ministers of the Stuarts, was born in London, the son of a wealthy Yorkshire landowner. He spent most of his youth in Yorkshire; his education was that customary to his class – the Inner Temple and St John's, Cambridge, to court at eighteen, a tour of France (1611-13). In 1614 his father died, leaving him the heir to considerable property around Gawthorp and Woodhouse in the West Riding, and to heavy responsibilities (there were nine younger children). Although the same year 1614 saw Wentworth's first election to the House of Commons, as member for Yorkshire in the Addled Parliament, he passed most of the next few years in administering his estates, increasing their profits and establishing his authority in the West Riding. But he was early ambitious to use his talents in national affairs, going often to London and winning useful friends at court like Archbishop Abbot, Sir George Calvert, the Secretary of State, and the rather shady financier, Sir Arthur Ingram. His opportunity came in the 1620s in the clashes of the Stuart kings and their parliaments – at first as an opponent of the court. He sat in four of the five parliaments of the 1620s, three times for Yorkshire and once (1624) for Pontefract. First prominent in 1621 as a moderate critic of royal policy, he was sufficiently important for the king deliberately to exclude him from the parliament of 1626 by picking him as Sheriff of Yorkshire. In 1627 he was one of those who refused to pay the Forced Loan, and he was briefly imprisoned in the Marshalsea; and for some weeks in 1628 he was the effective leader of opposition in the Commons, hoping that the Commons' grant of supply and the king's redress of grievances would 'go hand in hand as one joint and continued act'; and supporting Sir Edward Coke's project for the Petition of Right.

Then in the summer of 1628, he changed sides; he accepted a barony and became President of the Council of the North, the principal agent of the royal prerogative beyond the Trent. For this he was at his trial a few years later to be attacked as an apostate, and Macaulay would dub him 'the lost Archangel, the Satan of the Apostasy'. But in 1628 the gulf between court and Commons was not yet so deep. Wentworth had always been restrained in his opposition, far different in outlook from the extremer Eliot; and there were practical arguments, appealing strongly to a man of his cast of mind, for the view that the old Elizabethan harmony between Crown and parliament had now failed, and that until it could be restored only the Crown had the authority and the instruments to govern. Moreover, Wentworth was deeply ambitious, conscious of his powers and impatient to exercise them; and there was in him something of the harsh violence of the seventeenth-century north country in which he grew up. As Lord President he ruled the north in authoritarian fashion for some five years from the fine house at York, enforcing the Poor Law, upholding the prerogative powers of the Council, and humiliating northern magnates who resisted its edicts.

In 1633 he went to Ireland as Lord Deputy, drawn partly by 'the personal profit to be gained from the place', partly by the challenge that wretched and barbaric land offered to his own abilities and to the king's authority. Given full powers, and, on almost all occasions, full support from Whitehall, he 'ruled Ireland like a king', as one contemporary put it. In six years he reorganized the finances, the army and navy, the law courts; tackled the immensely complex land problem, brought new men and new vigour to the Protestant church; increased the revenue from the customs, began industrial projects, checked pirates; in all, he gave Ireland a brief spell of relative prosperity and more efficient administration. For the most part his policies were not novel. Plantations continued, he treated the Irish woollen industry as harshly as his predecessors had done, his vaunted linen project was a short-lived private monopoly which seems to have done more harm than good, the customs farm was on traditional lines. But he made himself felt as his predecessors had not, for he had more power and he used it more thoroughly and more brutally – thus creating a host of enemies throughout the land who were ready to turn upon him when he fell. There were two great changes. His financial policy was highly effective, so that no subsidy was needed from England; and he pursued among the Irish Protestants the Laudian policy of enforcing discipline upon the clergy and resuming ecclesiastical lands from the laity. His very success in these two directions, finance and religion, with its threats to the security of landed and mercantile property as well as to the beliefs of Puritan Ulstermen, aroused widespread discontent among the influential classes in Ireland – and contributed much to the fear which his name began to arouse in England. What made him the more hated was that he himself became 'monstrous' rich by such normal incidents of patronage as selling offices and taking over the bulk of the customs farm himself, while at the same time denouncing with a blend of harshness and moral superiority other men's financial intrigues. In 1639 his income from Irish sources was £13,000 a year, enough to make him one of the richest of Charles I's subjects. Finally, his rule in Ireland, intensely personal, left nothing permanent behind. By the middle of 1641, on the eve of the Ulster rising, his policies had utterly collapsed.

In 1629 he was appointed a member of the Privy Council; but he contributed little to the government of England in the 1630s. Partly this was through his absence in Ireland, yet mainly because he never had the entire trust of a king who was more than half afraid of the ruthlessness of Wentworth's methods. His main contact with English policy was indirect, through his correspondence with William Laud, appointed Archbishop of Canterbury in 1633. A deep friendship arose between the two, both by temperament authoritarian men of action, and from it emerged an attitude towards government to which they gave the name of 'Thorough' – an unsparing emphasis on loyalty to the Crown and on individual responsibility among the king's servants, combined with a relentless inquiry into abuses and a merciless crushing of opponents. Such an attitude was too far-reaching for Charles I and his courtiers. Yet when in 1638-9 the whole fabric of his government was threatened by the Scottish revolt against Laud's ecclesiastical policy, it was to Wentworth that the king turned for help, with the famous message ending, 'Come when you will, ye shall be welcome to your assured friend, Charles R'.

It was too late; the task was beyond the abilities and even the resolution of Wentworth – and it led straight to his own ruin. He came at once, to be given the earldom (of Strafford) he had long craved. He advised Charles to call a parliament, and when this, the Short Parliament (1640), declined to grant the supplies the king wanted until its accumulated grievances were dealt with, it was Strafford who took command of such forces as could be put in the field against the Scots. The position was hopeless; the king's army, in Strafford's own words, was 'altogether necessitous and unprovided of all necessaries'. The Scottish army occupied Northumberland and Durham, Charles was compelled to come to terms at Ripon, and to summon another parliament. Strafford, with high courage and perhaps believing even now in his ability to master the Commons, turned southward to continue serving his king – and to face the certain prospect of a demand for his own death; 'I am tomorrow to London with more danger beset, I believe, than ever man went with out of Yorkshire'. There had already been demonstrations against him by London mobs. Pym and the parliamentary leaders saw him as the greatest single peril to their cause. Clouds of witnesses, the accumulated enemies of eleven years of stern rule in the north and in Ireland, were ready to rise against him. So, when the Long Parliament met in November 1640, the first action of the Commons was the resolution to impeach Strafford of high treason. The trial before the Lords opened in March 1641. Strafford rebutted his accusers with great dexterity, and the impeachment, resting mainly on the charge that he had proposed to bring an Irish army to subdue England, seemed likely to break down. So a group of members in the Commons turned to the ruthless procedure of attainder, and carried a majority of their fellows with them in an atmosphere embittered by panic rumours of army plots against parliament. The Lords passed the attainder under pressure from violent crowds. Charles, who had but lately promised Strafford that he should not suffer in life, honour, or fortune – although Strafford had, in a letter of high nobility, absolved him from that promise – eventually yielded and signed the act for fear of an attack by the mob on his palace and his family. On 12 May a vast crowd, which some put as great as 200,000, saw Strafford beheaded on Tower Hill. No execution in English history has been greeted with greater public rejoicing.

Few Englishmen, even of the seventeenth century, have had a more ambiguous fame than Strafford; few, perhaps, have been so overrated both by their friends and by their enemies. Certainly, for all his courage and his idealistic devotion to the service of an unworthy king – for Strafford may be regarded as the most eminent of the many victims of Charles I – he had great faults and notable defects. 'Nature', said one contemporary, 'hath not given him generally a personal affability'; he was harsh, arrogant, domineering, vindictive, excessively sensitive both to praise and to criticism. He was highly strung and moody, frequently laid low by a variety of illnesses many of which must have been nervous in their origins; he desperately needed personal sympathy (he married three times, and the death of his second wife, Arabella Holles, in a premature confinement in 1631 was a shattering blow), and his intimate friends were few, though deeply loyal. In an age when politics were intensely personal he had a disastrous capacity for making enemies. This was the more serious in a man who tended to identify government with administration, and who so readily found the only solution to public problems in action by himself or by those loyal supporters whom he appointed to office, like his lifelong friends George Radcliffe and Christopher Wandesford, whom he made members of the Irish Council. His ambition was immense and plain. Nor was it for power only; he pursued energetically, and sometimes unscrupulously, the wealth in land and in cash which the seventeenth century saw as the necessary foundation and façade for political power and place. His Irish proconsulate yielded him a fortune as well as producing real, if temporary, benefits for many of his subjects. And his severity towards those who used government office to feather their own nests tended to blind him – though not his opponents – to his own not dissimilar activities. Strafford laid himself open to the charge that the laws he administered and the standards which he proclaimed did not always apply to himself; and this was an important element in the almost universal climate of hostility that brought about his fall.

Any assessment of Strafford's political career and of his place in English history is dominated by the fact that he chose what proved to be the losing side in the great political conflict of his age – in the central political conflict of modern British history. His belief in paternal government by the Crown was essentially Elizabethan. In so far as it rested upon a harmony between the Crown and a parliament representing the property-owning class it was out of date, disproved by the facts of political life in the 1620s and 1630s, by the personality of Charles I and by the revolutionary claims of the gentry who made up the House of Commons. At its highest Strafford's vision of government – like Strafford's character at its best – was a noble one, embracing justice as well as order and security, and extending these benefits to the community as a whole, to poor as well as rich, to the backward north as well as to the more settled south, to Irish as well as to English. Yet this is not the whole tale. The ideal could not be separated from the methods used to achieve it; Strafford was 'Black Tom Tyrant', the terrible exemplar of Stuart rule. It is Strafford's tragedy that he is perhaps the only great man in English history whose overwhelming impact on his fellow countrymen was simply to make them fear him. This was what lay behind the calculations of Pym and the hysteria of the mob in 1641; this was what inspired alike the terrible comment of Oliver St John, arguing the case for the attainder before the Lords, that 'it was never accounted either cruelty or foul play to knock foxes and wolves on the head … because they be beasts of prey', and the blunt phrase of Essex, 'stone dead hath no fellow.'

Further Reading
J. F. Merritt, *The Political World of Thomas Wentworth*, 1996.
C. V. Wedgwood, *Thomas Wentworth, First Earl of Strafford*, 1961.
H. F. Kearney, *Strafford in Ireland*, 1959.

WERFERTH (*d.*915) was Bishop of Worcester from about 872 until his death and one of the collaborators with King Alfred in the revival of English learning. Like Plegmund he was a native of Mercia and was appointed to his bishopric towards the end of the reign of King Burgred (852-74). In 874 he received an important grant of privileges from the succeeding king, Ceolwulf, the puppet ruler set up by the Danes. Perhaps he had to be enticed from Mercian loyalties by more than intellectual interests. He was later to refer to Alfred as 'his ring-giver … the greatest treasure-giver of all the kings he has ever heard tell of', and to be left a large sum of gold in Alfred's will. One suspects that Werferth may have found the service of Alfred as materially rewarding as did Asser.

We cannot be sure when he entered Alfred's entourage, though it was probably in the first half of the 880s. He had translated the *Dialogues* of Pope Gregory into English before 893, probably with a collaborator, at the king's command. We know that he received a copy of Alfred's translation of Gregory's *Pastoral Care*, for his own manuscript of it has survived: it is now in the Bodleian Library in Oxford. Like other associates of the king, Werferth was prominent in public affairs as well as in intellectual endeavour. He was instrumental in having the town of Worcester fortified by Ealdorman Ethelred

and his wife Ethelflaed in the 890s. He received a grant of land and privileges in London in 889 and a further grant in 898 when the replanning and fortification of the city were under discussion.

Over forty years a bishop, Werferth, like his fellow Mercian Plegmund, was a force for stability and continuity in anxious times and probably an important agent in the drawing together of Mercia and Wessex which preceded their more effective integration in the tenth century.

WESLEY, CHARLES (1707-88) was the younger brother of John and son of Samuel Wesley, the rector of Epworth. He became a sound scholar at Westminster and Christ Church and was ordained in 1735. In this year he went with John to Georgia as Oglethorpe's secretary. On his return he served for a spell as curate at Islington, but he soon became a regular itinerant preacher. From 1740 till he returned to London in 1771, he lived at Bristol. Less able than his famous brother and a less imposing personality, he was nonetheless an eloquent preacher. Though he mistrusted the raptures of the more fervent lay preachers he expresses in his hymns the force and faith of a sensitive, poetic soul. In the Wesleys' ministry of conversion hymns played a large part, and Charles was prolific in the art of representing simple faith in essential terms. The lyrical force of the best of these hymns can still be felt. What is Advent without the impressive thunder of 'Lo, he comes with clouds descending' or Christmas without 'Hark, the herald angels sing'? 'Love Divine, all loves excelling', and 'Soldiers of Christ, arise', to name only two more, are among the best-loved hymns of English churchpeople. He may have written as many as 7,000 hymns, for he had the inexhaustible vitality of his family. In the words of John's preface to the collection of 1780, which included also some from Watts and some translations from the German, the hymns formed 'a little body of experimental and practising Divinity'. Imperative, urgent, vivacious, less astringent than those of Donne and Herbert, but surer in sentiment than those of most of the nineteenth-century writers, Charles Wesley's hymns have played a large part in both Anglican and Nonconformist worship.

He married in 1749 a Welshwoman, Sarah Gwynne, whose beautiful singing voice led the singing in his congregation. Their two sons, Charles and Samuel, make their mark in turn as organists and composers. The latter entered the Roman Catholic faith in 1784. His father was no more distressed by this than he was by John's decision in the same year to ordain his own ministers; he was essentially a moderate, conservative man.

Further Reading
S. J. Royal, *John and Charles Wesley*, 1979.
M. F. Brailsford, *A Tale of Two Brothers*, 1954.

WESLEY, JOHN (1703-91), evangelist and founder of Methodism, by his fervent preaching and good organization, reawakened in thousands a sense of personal religion and created a movement of lasting social importance.

He was one of the youngest of nineteen children born to Susannah and Samuel Wesley at the rectory of Epworth. His father was a stern man who made it his life's work to minister to the primitive people of the north Lincolnshire marshlands. His own father and grandfather had been ejected from the church in the purge of 1662, but Samuel was a High Churchman, a supporter of Sacheverell and an irrepressible character; arrested once for debt, he had taken the opportunity to catechize his fellow prisoners in Lincoln jail. His wife came of good family and was proficient in Latin and Greek. She educated the children herself and inculcated in them her own intense faith in God. Concern for salvation and abhorrence of sin, a sense of living precariously between extremes, pervaded this household and affected the lives of all the children. The girls endured varying degrees of unhappiness in love and marriage, but two of the boys, John and his younger brother Charles, repaid their training by ardent evangelism. John was rescued at the age of six from a fire that destroyed the vicarage, 'a brand plucked from the burning' in his mother's phrase, and it is not fanciful to see a compelling sense of destiny even in his early years. From this isolated and self-supporting background he was sent to the Charterhouse and thence to Christ Church with an exhibition. Ordained deacon in 1725, he was made a Fellow of Lincoln College in 1726. Here the influences of George Whitefield, then at Pembroke College, and his brother Charles, his own careful reading of religious works and thoroughness in everything he undertook, with a habit of rigorous self-analysis, helped to turn him from the conventional course of scholar and tutor. From Jeremy Taylor's works he absorbed something of Christian life; from the mystic William Law he learned to think of a 'world sunk in sin' and to see the remedy in a change of spirit and in the deliberate cultivation of holiness that was needful 'if a man is to be in the favour of God'. Accepting the Bible as 'the one, the only standard of truth and the only model of pure religion' he tried at the same time to train himself by methodical devotion to the fasts and ceremonies of the church. The founder of Methodism was by instinct and design a High Churchman.

For two years he acted as curate for his father at the neighbouring hamlet of Wroot. In 1729 he returned to Lincoln and founded, with Charles and fourteen undergraduates, the 'Holy Club', whose austerities startled Oxford and killed one of its frailer members. They lay on the grass on frosty nights, fasted and denied themselves sleep, but they also visited sick people and prisoners.

Their 'methodism' had the approval of the Bishop of Oxford, but it was inward-looking for all its melodrama and challenge; it brought Wesley no sense of personal salvation and few of his companions went on with him to the next stage of development.

In 1735 he went with Charles to Georgia, General Oglethorpe's new colony, to bring the Gospel to the settlers and Indians. It was a disastrous venture into a more complicated society than he could have envisaged. John may have fallen in love with a Miss Hopkey whom he subsequently banned from Communion when she married someone else; in a claustrophobic and hysterical situation he seems to have behaved wilfully, and without much tact or self-control. So he was driven out amidst recriminations which dogged him for years. He had, however, met on the voyage out some Moravian brothers whose notions of personal salvation seemed to answer his need. To the question of their pastor Spangenburg, 'does the spirit of God bear witness with your spirit that you are a child of God?' he thought he saw a clue to his future course. He attended Moravian meetings in London and talked to the brethren in a mood of contrition. On 24 May 1738, at Aldersgate he experienced the mystical experience which brought him the sense and glow of certainty; 'I felt my heart strangely warmed. I felt that I did trust in Christ alone for salvation; and an assurance was given me that he had taken my sins, even mine, and saved me from the law of sin and death.' This revelation was a moment of release and commitment for a new work. From then, until his death, Wesley's efforts were directed towards his personal mission to the country. 'I look upon the world as my parish,' he said.

During the next fifty three years he travelled over 200,000 miles, preached over 40,000 sermons, read, wrote, edited, organized and prayed. No second of his day was left to chance – an uncomfortable regimen, as Dr Johnson found: 'John Wesley's conversation is good but he is never at leisure. He is always obliged to go at a certain hour. This is very disagreeable to a man who loves to fold his legs and have out his talk as I do.' We should not picture a wild fanatic. In his appearance he was small and neat, in manner calm. His directness of appeal, with the suggestion of pent-up force behind it, gained in emphasis by his restrained demeanour. He kept a journal which overflows with the spirit of missionary zeal but is free of the unctuousness which some of his followers displayed. It is a record of physical endurance and high courage; of the inspired and necessary egoism of the prophet. He wished to speak in churches and was reluctant to follow Whitefield's example and take to the fields. He was opposed, however, at all levels; not only by the prejudiced country parson but by the fair-minded Butler, then Bishop of Bristol, to whom the style and content of his sermons was uncongenial, too direct, too 'enthusiastic' and too liable to misinterpretation.

There was little space in the rational churchmanship of the eighteenth century for the personal appeal: are you saved? Moreover Wesley's gradual estrangement from the church was due to faults on both sides. Wesley thought nothing of infringing the cherished freehold of the vicar; his mission took no account of local circumstances; he displayed a spiritual pride and autocratic temper which justified his enemies' label 'Pope John'. Above all, his style of preaching caused hysteria and the instability of undirected religious feeling. For all that, Wesley's appeal was strong, because it supplied a need. The formal devotions of the church did not cater for the simple needs of the semi-literate and illiterate; its appointments and even its teaching reflected the class structure of the time. Large areas in the big towns and the new manufacturing and mining districts were missed out, because few adjustments were made to the traditional parishes. The need of these dispossessed folk drove Wesley to begin open-air preaching, beginning with a mass meeting of miners outside Bristol, and to start a new ministry outside the church. Step by step he moved toward schism, though he continued to profess membership of the church. In 1739 he opened his first chapel, in 1744 he set up a central organization at the Foundry in London. Lay preaching led to lay ordination, a decision forced upon him by the needs of the rapidly growing church in North America, in 1784. By then there were 356 chapels, served by preachers operating in circuits. The basic unit was the class, a group of about a dozen members from one district; above this was the band, subdivided according to sex and then again into unmarried and married. These groups reproduced the ideal of the Holy Club: communal confession of sins, prayer and giving. Even the poorest were expected to give something to the funds of the movement; the sense of responsibility this instilled, together with the puritan emphasis upon self-discipline, had an incalculable effect upon society in these years of accelerating industrial change.

Methodism, zealous, dynamic, co-ordinated, could have been a revolutionary force in a period ripe for revolution. That it was not was owing partly to the character of the founder. He was autocratic: the annual conference was simply a forum for his views and exhortations. He was also a profound conservative who denounced the American colonists as rebels and the French revolutionaries as children of Satan. He believed that society could be transformed only by individual and spiritual conversions. Salvation was not for him the end, nor preordained as Calvinists taught: it must be proved by good works, by practising the qualities of thrift and temperance. Wesley was intellectually curious (he was much impressed by a lecture of Benjamin Franklin's about electricity and embarked upon experiments of his

own), but he was also absurdly credulous. He believed in witches and, to find guidance in any problem he would open the Bible at random. With his absorption in his mission, it was inevitable that he should become narrow in his interests. He liked to sing but he was blind to beauty; the theatre he regarded as 'Satan's own ground'. He may have been no more than naive and insensitive but his conduct was exasperating enough to cause estrangement from his wife. His life was indeed too much swallowed up by his work for satisfactory personal relationships. He married Mrs Vazeille, a merchant's widow of forty-one, in 1751. She was a scold, he would not curtail his journeyings; they separated finally in 1776. His views about the upbringing of children would have been absurd if they had not been so influential. He believed that the rod was necessary to drive away the devil, that idle minutes were a danger to a child's soul and that a knowledge of the Bible and of the catechism was sufficient education. The movement for primary education was positively discouraged by Methodist parents at a time when there was an ever increasing demand for child labour in mine and mill. Irrational in a rational age, enthusiastic amongst men who abhorred enthusiasm, conservative in its teaching to the miserably poor, puritan in the midst of slums, the paradoxes of Methodism reflect the paradoxes in the life of John Wesley.

Further Reading
S. J. Rogal, *John and Charles Wesley*, 1979.
R. E. Davies and E. G. Rupp, *A History of the Methodist Church in Great Britain*, vol. 1, 1965.
B. Dobrée, *Three Eighteenth Century Figures*, 1962.
V. H. H. Green, *Young Mr Wesley*, 1961.
C. E. Vulliamy, *John Wesley*, 1931.
N. Curnock, ed., *Journal of John Wesley*, 8 vols, 1909-16. (Everyman edition in 3 vols.)

WESLEY, SAMUEL (1766-1837) was the greatest English musician of his time. He was the son of the hymn writer Charles Wesley and the nephew of the founder of Methodism. Both Samuel and his brother Charles were child prodigies – indeed there were two other musical prodigies in the late eighteenth century who fulfilled their early promise to some extent: Stephen Storace and William Crotch, but none so great as Samuel Wesley. At the age of eight he completed an oratorio, *Ruth*, which gained him the description 'the Mozart'. He studied the organ, violin and harpsichord and he and his brother gave concerts in their London house for seven years in the roles of boy composers and performers.

At the age of twenty-two, to the displeasure of his family, he became a Roman Catholic. In later life he returned to Anglicanism and denied having ever become a convert, saying that his interest in Catholicism had been limited to Gregorian music, but in fact a letter from Pope Pius VI exists which clearly indicates his conversion. This is an important aspect of his life; another, which may explain his curious denial, is that three years later, at the age of twenty-five, he fell into a deep excavation and damaged his brain, an injury which left him nervously ill and thereafter eccentric, illogical and confused.

Mrs Vincent Novello, the wife of the music publisher, wrote this to him: 'I knew him unfortunately too well. Pious Catholic, raving atheist; mad, reasonable; drunk and sober. The dread of all wives and regular families. A warm friend, a bitter foe; a satirical talker; a flatterer at times of those he cynically traduced at others; a blasphemer at times, a purling Methodist at others.' He was certainly well known in England as a conversationalist and a highly cultured, unconventional man, and as the greatest organist of his day. His main effort was devoted to spreading the works of J. S. Bach (whom he referred to as 'St Sebastian') by playing them up and down the country; perhaps it was therefore a just reward that his own compositions were more famous in Germany than in England. These were mainly for the Roman mass and other services, the most famous being an eight-part motet *In exitu Israel*. Others were *Exultate Deo* and *Dixit Dominus*. Later he wrote music for the Anglican mass and a great many glees and songs, symphonies, concerti, solos and chamber music, but never anything for the stage. His was original and vital music.

Because of recurring insanity he never became the permanent organist at a great church and instead spent his life from 1824 as organist of Camden Chapel (St Stephen's), Camden Town. That honour was left to his illegitimate son, Samuel Sebastian Wesley, who became a much appreciated and influential cathedral organist and composer of English church music.

WESLEY, SAMUEL SEBASTIAN (1810-76), organist and composer, was the illegitimate son of Samuel Wesley, who gave him his second name after his hero, Bach. This proved appropriate, for S. S. Wesley grew into the finest organist of his day. He was such a majestic performer that cathedrals went on bidding for his services long after his cantankerous behaviour had become known through all the closes of England. Wesley was a very difficult man to work with, and it was fortunate that the organ loft was a comparatively solitary arena for his talents. He managed to quarrel with the clergy in all the cathedrals in which he worked, Hereford, Exeter, Winchester and Gloucester, as well as those of Leeds Parish Church. Precentors were his particular targets. He had some grounds for complaint: the only adequate choir he performed with was at Leeds. At Hereford Cathedral he composed 'Blessed be the God and Father' for the group of trebles and the single bass voice, all that were available at Easter.

There were different reasons for his frequent moves.

He left Hereford after his runaway marriage to the dean's sister: took the post at Hampton Parish Church (when he was already organist at two other churches) before he was twenty for the fishing on the Thames: went to Winchester to get a free education at the college for his sons (and fish the Itchen?). But whenever he departed, he left angry enemies behind him. He seems to have been paranoiac about rivals, and he brooked no authority over him: so much so that he eventually published his own compositions rather than have to work with professional music publishers. He was cavalier in his use of deputies, even in cathedrals. Winchester College, to which, as well to the cathedral, he was contracted for daily services, was lucky if it saw him twice a week. Wesley had strong opinions on most matters. He disliked the Tractarians, and he deplored Beethoven. He composed many anthems. Some were on the grand scale – several sections in one big work, as in 'The Wilderness' and 'Blessed be the God and Father' – and powerfully dramatic. Others, like 'I Waited for the Lord', were short and simple. His techniques, especially his modulations, were in advance of his day, and contemporary church musicians dismissed them as improper distortions. Today they often seem old-fashioned, but choirs still love to sing them, and congregations to listen to them. In 1873, Gladstone, often a patron of musicians, awarded him a Civil List pension. It was the furthest anyone was prepared to go in honouring such an acerbic man.

WEST, BENJAMIN (1738-1820), history and portrait painter, was born in Pennsylvania of a Quaker family, and only came to London in 1763 after making the trip to Italy which was practically the *sine qua non* of ambitious artists. Here he very soon (and perhaps surprisingly for an American in those days) gained the king's patronage – to which in part he must have owed his being chosen a founder-member of the Academy (1768) and his election as President on the death of Reynolds (a position he held with generosity and great decorum for nearly thirty years). The public – as well as those who should have known better – applauded, even revered, his history paintings, of which it is sadly true that they are 'only great by the acre' as Hazlitt said. Although the introduction of modern costume and the commemoration of modern events gave them an immediacy which previous history paintings had lacked, there is little to be found in them beyond conventional expressions, sombre colours, and competent paintwork – one longs for something either to praise or to damn. The works of his contemporary John Singleton Copley, who was also a popular history painter of American birth – such works as *Charles I demanding the Surrender of the Five Members* or *The death of the Earl of Chatham* – have more verve in them and more truth. But of the two,

West was the public figure: only it was not sufficiently seen that his strong suit was not the heroic murals of Windsor and of Greenwich, not even the mere canvas-displays like *The Death of General Wolfe*, but an unassuming and agreeable series of portraits.

Further Reading
J. Galt, *Benjamin West*, 2 vols, 1850.

WESTON, RICHARD, 1st EARL OF PORTLAND

(1577-1635), came from an Essex family of Catholic traditions and was educated at Trinity College, Cambridge. As a courtier and holder of minor office he showed competence in business; James I made him Chancellor of the Exchequer in 1621, and Charles I, Lord High Treasurer in 1628. A crypto-Catholic and pro-Spanish in sympathy, he favoured the peace policy which enabled Charles I to dispense with parliament, and he was the main figure behind the fiscal devices adopted after 1629. For this as well as for personal reasons he was quite exceptionally unpopular. Clarendon praised the adroitness with which he 'did swim in these troubled and boisterous waters' in the days of Buckingham's supremacy, but for the rest denounced him in one of the most savage of all his studies as 'a man of big looks, and of a mean and abject spirit'. What angered men most was that while Portland demanded high taxes and economy from others, he engrossed lands and money for himself: twice the king paid his debts, amounting to £40,000, and also gave him Chute Forest in Hampshire into the bargain. Laud condemned him as 'Lady Mora', the very model of delay and sloth.

Further Reading
M. V. C. Alexander, *Charles I's Lord Treasurer*, 1975.

WESTON, RICHARD (1591-1651), agricultural

reformer, from Sutton in Surrey, Roman Catholic and royalist, fled to Flanders during the Civil War. He experimented with new rotations, including turnips and clover, and while in exile wrote a *Discourse of Husbandry used in Brabant and Flanders*, published in 1650. He also used locks to improve the navigation of the Rivery Wey between Guildford and Weybridge.

WHARTON, THOMAS, 1st MARQUIS OF WHARTON

(1648-1715), Whig politician, was the son of a wealthy Presbyterian Peer who had fought on the parliamentarian side in the Civil War and increased his wealth in the process. Brought up under a Puritan régime of discipline and hard work, he reacted full-bloodedly to the easier moral air of the Restoration, rapidly acquiring what Macaulay called 'the dissoluteness of the emancipated precisian'. A sceptic distinguished by the ribaldry of his conversation even in the reign of Charles II, a notorious rake and an unblushing liar, a jockey whose horses were remarkably successful at Newmarket, a brilliant swordsman who fought and won many duels, Thomas Wharton in his private life was scarcely a creditable – though by no means unique – offspring of the Puritan Revolution. But he drew his public principles also from that Revolution, and to these he adhered with a consistency unparalleled in his generation. Consequently, in the light of a career which began with Exclusion and finished with the Hanoverian Succession, he may be considered the most significant Whig politician between Shaftesbury and Walpole.

Entering the Commons in the year of the Test Act, he remained an MP until he inherited his father's title in 1696, sitting first for the Wharton borough of Wendover and then as one of the county members. Buckinghamshire was Hampden country and Nonconformist country too, and Tom Wharton was strongly for Exclusion. He kept clear of the Rye House Plot (though his house was searched) and of Monmouth's desperate venture; he was an intrepid duellist, but a cautious revolutionary who disliked backing losers. Outspoken in opposition to James's policy in the parliament of 1685, Wharton was one of the leading younger men in the conspiracy which prepared the way for William's invasion. He may even have drafted the famous invitation signed by the seven grandees, and certainly he was one of the first group of important Englishmen to join William at Exeter. And he made one other contribution to the enterprise of 1688. Wharton was the author of *Lilliburlero*, the Revolution song which was said to have 'whistled James out of three kingdoms'.

A member of the committee which drafted the Bill of Rights, Wharton was Comptroller of the Household from 1689 to 1702, a post which made him in practice the principal link between William and the Commons. Although his loyalty to the Revolution was complete and he never 'insured' at St Germain, his relations with William III were not easy, partly because his tough hard cynicism made little appeal to William, partly also because he did not share the king's readiness to find political virtue in men who were not Whigs. In these years, and to rather less extent in Anne's reign, Wharton's principal activity may be regarded as that of a party organizer. He seems to have arranged the meetings of the Whig Junto in each reign, and to have managed the Whig voting in the Commons while he was a member of the lower House. As for electioneering and borough-mongering, Wharton was at once a pioneer and an acknowledged expert, particularly, of course, on and near the Wharton properties in Buckinghamshire, Westmorland and Yorkshire.

Anne, who disapproved of his morals as well as of his partisan politics, dismissed him from office on her accession, and not until 1708, when he became Lord Lieutenant of Ireland, would she accept him again. In the interval he was involved in the franchise case of *Ashby v. White* (Ashby was a Whig cobbler in Wharton's own borough of Aylesbury), and, to greater national advantage, in promoting the Union with Scotland, which brought him an earldom. After the fall of the Whigs in 1710 Wharton was prominent in opposition to the Treaty of Utrecht and to such Tory measures as the Schism Act. He lived long enough to see the Hanoverians safely installed, and died a Marquis in 1715. By his persistent maintenance of the principles of the Glorious Revolution, 'Liberty and Property', 'Honest Tom' Wharton had prepared the way for the Whig supremacy of the eighteenth century.

Further Reading
John Carswell, *The Old Cause*, 1954, pp.25-127.

WHETEHAMSTEDE, JOHN (*c*.1390-1465), Abbot of St Albans (1420-40 and 1452-65), was one of the leading literary figures in fifteenth-century England. The son of Hugh and Margaret Bostock of Wheathampstead (Herts.), he followed an uncle into the great Benedictine abbey and was sent to Oxford University, where he became Prior of Gloucester College 1414-17 and doctor of divinity. He was abbot from 1420 until 1440, when he resigned from ill-health – apparently he was subject to uncontrollable blushing – but was re-elected in 1452 on the death of his allegedly laxer successor. As befitted the senior English Benedictine, he was on the English delegations to the General Councils of Pavia and Siena in 1423. In his last years his sight and hearing failed and he was crippled with arthritis.

Whetehamstede was shy and bashful in public, yet egotistical and boastful in his writings. He could be a harsh disciplinarian to his monks, yet could also be humane and win their affection. He placed a brass on his parents' tomb and sought fame for himself. He was utterly committed to his profession and to St Albans in particular. Like his predecessors he defended the abbey against its rivals and was therefore litigious; he sought extra privileges from Rome and adorned the buildings; he defended monasticism against attacks in General Council; and he sought to combat that 'ignorance of letters and neglect of study (that) relegates monks to obscurity'. He was himself a considerable scholar and patronized learning. He read extensively not just commonplace medieval texts, but Latin classics, Greek classics in translation, and even modern works by Italian humanists, many of which must have been in his own library. He contributed generously towards a library for Gloucester College and quadrupled the number of St Albans monks studying there. He gave his books to others, notably Humphrey, Duke of Gloucester, and included Italian humanists among his extensive scholarly correspondence. He was fascinated by the Renaissance and particularly admired the works of Boccaccio

and Petrarch. He wrote history, dictionaries of classical mythology, about heroes, etc., and was regarded in England as an outstanding Latin stylist. He is an important figure in the transmission of the Italian Renaissance to England, but his own humanism was merely a superficial veneer on an essentially medieval outlook. His historiography, encyclopaedism and Latin style all fit into medieval traditions and are not of high quality. His history is designed to present the most favourable view and consists mainly of anecdotes of purely local importance. His encyclopaedias display formidable learning without original thought. His flowery Latin is exuberantly stuffed with allusions of all kinds and is almost a caricature of late medieval finery. His sentences are inflated and contorted, his metaphors often so extravagant, that it is not easy to grasp the meanings he intended to convey.

No humanist could have written in this way, for Whetehamstede was quite unable to emulate the clarity and economy of their prose. Even his mastery of Latin grammar was not complete. He is thus 'one of the last English medieval polymaths rather than one of the early English humanists'. If his writings are thus less original and polished than he himself and many contemporaries supposed, he was nevertheless influential in his day and helped create conditions more propitious for the English humanists that followed.

Further Reading
A. Gransden, *Historical Writing in England* ii, 1982.
R. Weiss, *Humanism in England during the Fifteenth Century*, 3rd edn, 1967.
E. F. Jacob, 'Verborum Florida Venustas', *Essays in the Conciliar Epoch*, 3rd edn, 1963.

WHISTLER, JAMES ABBOTT McNEILL (1834-1903), painter and engraver, was the first American-born artist who was original enough, and sufficiently tenacious, to make a deep impression upon European art.

He was born in Lowell, Massachusetts. His mother was of Highland Scottish descent. His father, a railroad engineer, accepted an invitation from Tsar Nicholas I to drive a railway from St Petersburg to Moscow. His family followed; and it was found that the young James's drawings were already so promising that his parents sent him to the Imperial Academy of Fine Arts. Soon after completing the railway, the father died, and the family returned to New England. At sixteen, James entered West Point Military Academy, where his Commandant for a time was Robert E. Lee. Whistler's first engravings were in fact done for the US government's coastal survey. But he was not cut out for the military life; and in 1855, with the approval of his somewhat exigent mother, he left for Paris to study art.

He never returned to the States. His life was spent periodically in Paris, mostly in London. In Paris, he was accepted into the brilliant fraternity of artists which made the city the artistic capital of the world – and not only accepted, but honoured with medals and prizes. London he was fascinated by, but he was always an outsider there, scorned for many years by the artistic Establishment, and not least by the Royal Academy, which never made him a member, never even invited him to exhibit. It was as well that he had an irreducible assurance of his own genius.

He certainly appeared arrogant. His tongue was sharp; and the wit for which he was famous (and which is still quoted today) was often unbated, mordant, so that he made more enemies than friends. He said: 'My nature needs enemies.' And yet he was an engaging, attractive person, whose features, grinning or scowling or impudent, were more often portrayed than those of any contemporary artist. It helped, of course, that he wore a monocle, had a fine head of dark curls surmounted by a white plume of hair rising like a feather, was dressed extravagantly, and (though short in stature) had a commanding presence – an echo, perhaps, of West Point. Compared with British artists of the Victorian age, he appears more vivid, and more modern. And, unlike his great American predecessors – West, Copley, Stuart – he did not allow his innate originality to be deflected or absorbed by the impetus of the European tradition of painting.

And he was a great artist. For a long time after his death, it was his *etching* which was praised – the most brilliant etching done since Rembrandt's, it was said. To superlative draughtsmanship and composition, he added the gift of using the etching-needle to express delicate, closely-observed nuances of atmosphere and light. *The French Set* (published 1858) was followed by a set of sixteen etchings depicting the life of the Thames: the wharfs, cabins, taverns and warehouses, the multiple types of vessel, which were to be found on the great river 'below Bridge'. In all, he published about 300 engravings.

It was part of his creed to achieve the best artistic results by the simplest means. In etching, after all, there is not much room for affectation: and even there his strokes became more and more sparing. And, though he was a dandy in dress, the decoration of his house was extremely plain and uncluttered. Like many artists of the day, he had been captivated by the discovery of Japanese art and civilization (it was only in 1853 that Japan was 'opened' to the outside world). He and Rossetti were leaders of the fashion for collecting oriental china; but Whistler was also much interested in the flatness of perspective and the other 'breaking of rules' which he discovered in the Japanese wood-block artists, and the unfussiness of the domestic life which they portrayed. For a time, his own painting became almost a pastiche of the Japanese: e.g. *Variations in Flesh Colour and Green: The Balcony* (1865, Freer Gallery, Washington). But that

was only a step on the road to the formula of 'Art for Art's sake' – the theme of his *Ten o'Clock Lecture*, in which he set out some of the first principles of Modern Art. Chiefly, he believed that art should not be narrative, should not appeal to sentiment or idealism, should not even be morally uplifting. A sentence in his pugnacious volume, *The Gentle Art of Making Enemies*, states: 'Art should be independent of all clap-trap – should stand alone, and appeal to the artistic sense of eye or ear, without confounding this with emotions entirely foreign to it, as devotion, pity, love, patriotism and the like.' So he gave his paintings names borrowed from music: Nocturne, Symphony, Variations, Harmony, Arrangement. In 1877 the influential Walter Pater was to write: 'All art constantly aspires towards the condition of music.' A picture need not, then, represent a 'real' subject. Whistler agreed with his friend Baudelaire that, for the artist, 'It is not a matter of copying, but of interpreting in a simpler, more luminous language'.

In fact, he was never as abstract as Turner had become fifty years before. His Thames-side scenes express the essence of the river under certain conditions; and his portraits are, to the end, individual and vivid 'representations'. But all his work – portraits included – makes its effect by simplicity and the minimum of elaboration. In oils, he hated overpainting: if he was not satisfied, he scraped off, or simply scrapped the canvas, and began again. The result is that, in a lifetime of portrait-painting, he finished fewer than two dozen full-length portraits. Distinguished sitters were obliged to return time and time again – perhaps for scores of sittings – until they were exasperated or exhausted, and a 'stand-in' had to be found so that the work could be carried on. Cicely Alexander, a young girl, had to endure seventy sittings (often in tears) for the wonderful *Harmony in Grey and Green* (1872-3, Tate). Sickert said of Whistler: 'He wanted always to do the portrait at one sitting, either the first or the hundredth.' But the advantage of this fastidious method is that a 'good' Whistler is conspicuous for the economy of the paintwork, its translucency and apparent spontaneity, and for the freshness and assurance of the brush-strokes. The paint, Whistler said, should 'lie like breath on a pane of glass'. In this and other respects he can safely be compared with Velasquez and – his own favourite – Frans Hals. Yet his finest portraits: *Symphony in White No. 1: The White Girl* (1862, rejected by the Royal Academy, first exhibited at the famous Salon des Refusés of 1863, and now in the National Gallery of Art, Washington); *Symphony in White No. 2: The Little White Girl* (1864, Tate Gallery); *Arrangement in Grey and Black: The Artist's Mother* (1871, The Louvre, perhaps the best known portrait by an American artist); and *Arrangement in Grey and Black No. 2: Thomas Carlyle* (1872-3, Glasgow Art Gallery); all these have been so long cherished that their very familiarity makes it difficult for us to see that they are incomparable.

As for those curious titles: the musical borrowings are obvious; but we are also reminded that Whistler did not use brilliant colours. He boldly painted white on white, black on grey. He disliked the hard effects of bright sunshine, and much preferred the atmosphere of evening or night or misty dawn, when things became interesting because they had lost their sharpness and angularity, and were no longer distinct. Hence the *Nocturnes* or 'Night-Paintings', of which there are several in the Tate, and which come nearest to the abstract. They met with derision; and it was of one of them – *Nocturne in Black and Gold: The Falling Rocket* (1875, Detroit Institute of Art) – that Ruskin, still a respected critic, wrote: 'I never expected to hear a coxcomb ask 200 guineas for flinging a pot of paint in the public's face.' Whistler sued Ruskin for libel. During a series of exchanges which gave delight to the public, the Attorney General, appearing for Ruskin, asked: 'The labour of two days, then, is that for which you ask 200 guineas?' Whistler: 'No, I ask it for the knowledge of a lifetime.' The jury assessed damages at a farthing; but Whistler had won his verdict, and with it a victory for non-representational art.

There had been a curious interlude in 1866. Whistler's brother had volunteered for the southern side in the American Civil War. Whistler, perhaps feeling guilty that, as a West Point man, he had not returned to join the fighting, joined instead an expedition whose purpose was to assist the revolution of Chile and Peru against Spain. The party reached Valparaiso, achieved nothing – except some paintings by Whistler of the harbour, at evening, and at night, and veiled in mist. His other only 'trip abroad' was made in 1879. The expenses of the Ruskin trial had caused him to be declared bankrupt. He had to sell the White House (Tite Street, Chelsea), which had just been completed to his designs. The Fine Art Society came to his rescue: they gave him £600 and expenses to go to Venice and execute some etchings – which he did with his usual brilliance.

From the time that he returned to London a year later, his financial standing improved. His etchings always sold well. He was much sought after as a portrait-artist. He spent the winter of 1884 in Cornwall with Sickert, painting not landscapes but seascapes in watercolour (landscapes on the whole he disdained: 'There are too many trees in the country'). He finally married, in 1888; and his wife's illness and death by cancer eight years later caused him intense grief. He himself lived on into the new century, ill but dauntless. France, which had appointed him to the Legion of Honour, and had bought for the nation *The Artist's Mother*, honoured him again by the award of a double Grand Prix at the Exposition Universelle. Glasgow bought the *Thomas Carlyle*, and

gave Whistler a degree as well. London remained ambivalent. But by now, now that he was dying, there was no question of his stature as an artist – nor of the influence that he would continue to exert to the present day.

Although he had two illegitimate children, he preferred to make his wife's sister his sole heir. It is, therefore, her gift, to the Hunterian Art Gallery in the University of Glasgow, of Whistler's unsold pictures and prints, scrapbooks, correspondence, and even his paint-brushes and palette, that constitutes one of the two principal Whistler Collections. The other can be found in the gallery in Washington, DC, named after its founder, another great railroad man and Whistler's friend and patron, Charles L. Freer.

Further Reading
John Walker, *James McNeill Whistler*, 1987.
Tom Prideaux, *The World of Whistler*, 1970.

WHITBREAD, SAMUEL (1758-1815) was a wealthy brewer, a liberal-minded Whig Member of Parliament and a strong advocate of political and social reforms. His career is coloured by some of the virtues and values which we associate with the Victorians. But he is also a typical figure of the earnest, optimistic, industrious manufacturing class of the late eighteenth century. 'He felt himself an honest tradesman in an assembly of politicians' (Roberts). He was one of the early patrons of Watt, whose steam engine, which he installed in 1785 to drive the barley mills in place of twenty-four horses, was one of the sights of London. So was his curricle, built on the model of a modern bus: 'the body of it is near seven feet long; it will accommodate fourteen persons. It is in the form of a car, and made of wicker, painted yellow' (*Morning Chronicle*, August 1811). He was equally radical in his approach to politics.

He became member for Bedford in 1790. As the Eton friend and brother-in-law of Lord Grey he soon made his way into the charmed circle of Whig leadership. He was an effective orator in a somewhat bludgeoning manner and he showed a fine Foxite regard for principle. He moved the impeachment of Dundas in 1804. His speech upon the case of Mrs Clarke and the Duke of York filled eighty columns of *Hansard*. Ultimately, however, he failed to find fulfilment in politics. The limitations and prejudices of the Whig grandees, his own faults of personality, and political circumstances combined to thwart this man, whom Thomas Barnes, the radical editor of *The Times*, called 'England's greatest and most useful citizen'.

After the deaths of Fox and Pitt, on both sides of the house there ensued a chaos of personal groups. Grey and Grenville had sufficient experience in government of the ambition and duplicity of Napoleon to understand that England had to fight: their opposition was confined to methods of conducting the war. Whitbread and his friends of 'the Mountain' opposed the war from pacifist principles which appeared to their critics to be unpatriotic. He also went further than the official leadership in his support of reform. He wanted to draw the party into co-operation with the Burdett group and the extra-parliamentary movement. So the opposition became 'confoundedly embarrassed how to act with Whitbread and the *enragés*', as Lord Bulkeley observed. Whitbread's apparent irresponsibility was not due solely to his radical views. He was relentless in harrying ministers and uncovering scandals. He might justly claim to be more faithful to the tradition of Fox than Tierney, Petty or Ponsonby. Yet it was Ponsonby, a dull politician, who was chosen to lead the Whigs in the Commons. Whitbread was also passed over for ministerial office in the 'ministry of all talents'. From the fall of that administration until the assassination of Perceval (1807-12) he was the government's most persistent critic. When Castlereagh was the government's main representative in the Commons, the debate often resolved itself into a forensic duel between Whitbread and the foreign minister. And yet his liberalism and ambition made him as awkward to his own party as to the ministry. He was considered to be ill-mannered and he had a disconcerting temper. Whitbread lacked the tact and flexibility of the born politician. His dogmatic and outspoken manner was the opposite of Grey's reticence and patrician detachment. As the prospect of office receded, Whitbread's behaviour and pronouncements became more violent; the way in which he embraced the cause of the Princess of Wales disgusted many supporters. He could not recover the role which Brougham was later to assume – that of the educator of his party.

In 1806 Whitbread had brought forward, though without success, a bill for a rate-aided system of education. That the 'march of intellect' meant something more than a political slogan to him can be seen from the contents of his fine library, which contained a great range of pamphlets and books, the work of authors such as Bentham, Burke, Clarkson, Malthus, Paine, Priestley and Young, upon a variety of subjects, but especially the slave trade, Poor Law reform and the education of the working class. He put money and care into the management of the Drury Lane Theatre. He had his old house at Southill in Bedfordshire rebuilt by Henry Holland. Furniture and gardens were designed to fit the whole conception. The result was a complete and beautiful work of late Georgian art. But neither politics nor art brought serenity of mind to Whitbread. He suffered from periods of depression. In the end he cut his throat with a razor.

Further Reading
Roger Fulford, *Samuel Whitbread, 1764-1815*, 1967.
Michael Roberts, *The Whig Party: 1807-1812*, 1939.

WHITE, GILBERT (1720-93), author of *The Natural History and Antiquities of Selborne*, father of English naturalists and one of the best-loved of writers, was born at Selborne. He was educated at Basingstoke under Thomas Warton and at Oriel College, Oxford, where he became a Fellow. He returned after brief tenure of a curacy at Durley and the incumbency of Moreton Pinkney to the chalky hills and beech woods of his native Hampshire. We may be grateful that he did not become Provost of Oriel, as he hoped he might, but consoled himself with the curacy of Faringdon near Selborne (1758). His life was a quiet one; scarcely any details have survived even of his appearance, no portrait was painted of him and we know only that he was very short, upright in figure with stumpy legs. He was a model village parson, devoted to his people and interested in their ways, but fortunately his work left him ample time for observation, inquiry and writing. He started his natural history diary in 1751; in 1767 and 1769 respectively he began the irregular correspondence with Thomas Pennant and Daines Barrington, which forms the staple of the *Natural History*, eventually printed in 1788. The *Letters*, the *Naturalist's Calendars, Observations on Various Branches of Natural History and Antiquities*, together make only some 10,000 words, but they have been reprinted in over 150 editions.

Naturalists in the eighteenth century fall into distinct types, though the work of each was complementary. Most were preoccupied with classification, work that was made necessary by the opening up of new lands and observation of new species: among these were Buffon, Ray and Linnaeus who invented the binomial system of naming animals. Equally important, however, were the observers, concerned with their arrangement into species: of these Gilbert White was both typical and pre-eminent. Eventually, by the theory of organic evolution, in the middle of the nineteenth century the work of the classifiers and the observers was fused into a single science.

Gilbert White made some signal discoveries: the distinction between the English leaf warblers, chiff-chaff, willow-warbler and wood-warbler: the species of noctule bat, the harvest bat, the harvest mouse, the lesser whitethroat. He anticipated modern theories of bird-territory and also Darwin's conclusions about the origin of the domestic pigeon. His studies of the life-history of the nightjar, swallow, martin and swift are as accurate as they are pleasing. Sometimes he would shoot a bird to discover what would otherwise be out of reach, the anatomy of the cuckoo, for instance, to test the theory of an ingenious German about this bird's inability to hatch her own eggs. His work is redolent, however, of interest and sympathy for the creatures he observes; he was a gentle soul. Great naturalist as he was, he was no specialist. Everything comes under his eye – trees, fossils, local superstitions – and the result is a unique portrait of the countryside. A tiny corner of eastern Hampshire in the eighteenth century is preserved forever in his pages. An intellectual without sophistication, a scholar without pedantry, a humorous man and modest, his world is a pleasant one, with some of the calm that one sees about an eighteenth-century landscape. Politics, material cares, are remote; the phenomena of nature alone have power to disturb the serenity of woods and fields.

Further Reading
C. S. Emden, *Gilbert White in his Village*, 1956.
W. S. Scott, ed., *The Antiquities of Selborne*, 1950 (there have been numerous editions).
Johnson, ed., *Journals of Gilbert White*, 1931.

WHITEFIELD, GEORGE (1714-70), religious revivalist, was the son of an innkeeper, though of clerical family. Like Dr Johnson, he was a servitor at Pembroke College, Oxford, where he made the acquaintance of Charles Wesley. After his ordination in 1736 he began his life's work of preaching. He adopted the tactics already pioneered by Harris and Rowlands, who were engaged upon evangelical tours of Wales. When he was excluded from the pulpit by clergy who did not preach 'the true doctrine of Christ', he preached in the open air. An ugly man with a squint, not always dressed in his canonicals, unrestrained in his language by scholarly scruples, he used to gain an extraordinary command of his audience. His vivid style and his habitual themes of death, judgement and salvation had their greatest impact upon simple people. It was at a mass meeting of miners near Bristol, in 1739, that John Wesley became convinced that Whitefield's methods were justified, as a means of touching the people outside the parish system. His sincerity and passion also won more sophisticated minds. The diary of Lord Egmont, a devout churchman, records impressions of Whitefield after two sermons and a subsequent discussion. The service had begun with the singing of a psalm and 'a long pathetic prayer'. Then Whitefield 'preached by heart with much earnestness and spreading his arms very wide and was at no loss for words, and the people were very attentive'. Whitefield defended his methods: reprobates and dissenters, who would not normally go to church, might come from curiosity and go away edified. Egmont believed that he was sincere: 'he does indeed work a considerable reformation among the common people'. Less pious and more sceptical was Lord Chesterfield, who went to hear him from curiosity but was so caught up with Whitefield's account of the condition of the sinner trembling on the brink of the abyss as to exclaim: 'Good God! He's gone!'

Whitefield went with the Wesleys to Georgia in 1737 and made altogether seven visits to the New World; on the last, he died, in a small town in Massachusetts. At first he wished for a broad evangelical front, along with the other dissenting sects. Unlike the Wesleys, he was not institutionally minded, and the hold of the established church was never strong. Later his breach with them was widened by his adoption of Calvinist tenets, notably that salvation was preordained. In 1741 he opened his first tabernacle in London. In 1748 he became chaplain to Selina, Countess of Huntingdon, the pious founder of the old connection, who patronized with her money and interest a number of evangelical preachers and chapels. Whitefield was derided by those to whom any sort of enthusiasm was absurd. Horace Walpole wrote that 'he made more money than disturbances: his largest crops of proselytes lay among servant-maids; and his warmest devotees went to Bedlam without going to war' – allowing at least that the sermons were not inflammatory. His extravagances of language might cause hysteria but they also brought some colour, hope, perhaps, into drab and hopeless lives.

Further Reading
J. Downey, *The Eighteenth-Century Pulpit*, 1969.
J. D. Walsh, 'Origins of the Evangelical Revival' in G. V. Bennett and J. D. Walsh, *Essays in Modern Church History*, 1966.
L. Tyerman, *Life of Rev. George Whitefield*, 2 vols, 1876.

WHITGIFT, JOHN (1530-1604), Archbishop of Canterbury, was born at Grimsby in 1530. His father was a wealthy Grimsby merchant; his uncle Robert was Abbot of Wellow, near Grimsby, and it was his uncle who took him under his care and sent him to St Anthony's school in London, where had also been Sir Thomas More and Archbishop Heath. He lived with his aunt, but she threw him out because he refused to attend 'morrow mass', the first mass of the day, and would not be persuaded by some of the canons of St Paul's.

On the advice of his uncle, his father sent John to Queens' College, Cambridge, but the boy soon migrated to Pembroke (1550), where Nicholas Ridley was the non-resident Master and Grindal was President, and also Bradford, later the Marian martyr, was a Fellow, and became Whitgift's tutor. So promising a pupil did Whitgift prove that when his father's finances were affected by losses at sea, Ridley made the son a Bible Clerk, which enabled him to remain at Cambridge.

Whitgift justified the privilege. His success was swift and steady: 1553-4, BA; 1555, Fellow of Peterhouse; 1557, MA; 1560, ordained chaplain to Cox, the strongly anti-Roman Bishop of Ely and Rector of Teversham; 1563, BD and Lady Margaret Lecturer in Divinity; 1567, DD, Master of Pembroke, and immediately Master of Trinity. This last appointment was made in order to strengthen the Heads of Houses to deal with the growing trend in Cambridge towards Presbyterianism. In 1567 he became vice-chancellor and regius professor; in 1568, prebend of Ely. Being now far better off than ever before, he resigned the Regius Professorship and was succeeded by the holder of the Lady Margaret Chair: the latter was succeeded by Cartwright, and thus Whitgift had unwittingly provided Cartwright, later one of the leaders of Presbyterianism in England, with the chance which he wanted. In 1571 Whitgift became Dean of Lincoln and Parker gave him a dispensation to hold at one and the same time the deanery of Lincoln, the prebend of Ely, the mastership of Trinity and the Rectory of Teversham. In 1572 he became Prolocutor of the Lower House of Convocation (i.e. President). In this year there was published the very popular and successful *Admonition to the Parliament*, which advocated that the Church of England should be reformed on the Presbyterian model. Whitgift's *Answer* was the most learned and powerful defence of the Anglican settlement until Hooker's *Ecclesiastical Polity*.

In 1577 Whitgift was made Bishop of Worcester and soon after Vice-President of the Marches of Wales, while Sir Henry Sidney was away in Ireland. He proved himself a diligent, courageous and successful bishop, and a most able administrator in the difficult circumstances of the Welsh Marches.

In 1583 Grindal, Archbishop of Canterbury, died. He had been an unsuccessful archbishop, and when Whitgift was appointed to succeed him, he found a difficult and dangerous situation, in which ecclesiastical law was ignored, uniformity did not exist and the foundations of the Elizabethan settlement were being undermined. Between his appointment and his death he had restored peace and quiet to the church, at least for the time being. He had enforced the law, more often by tact than by violence, but he was never afraid to deal boldly with dangerous opponents, and he had made many improvements in the administration of the church. Both the queen and Burghley had complete confidence in him, as is shown by his being made a member of the Council, the first ecclesiastical member since the beginning of the reign.

He saw that the first thing to be done was to enforce the law, especially on the Puritans. He set about doing this by his Articles of 1583. The intention was to remove clergymen who would not agree with the doctrine, liturgy and constitution of the Church of England as by law established. Whitgift attempted to enforce conformity on Puritans through the Court of High Commission, using the ex officio oath to do so (an oath which bound them to give evidence of their opinions even if it might incriminate themselves). He was only partially successful, owing to the powerful support which the Puritans were able to mobilize against his inquisitorial methods. He saw also that there were genuine grievances against serious shortcomings in the church: he set about remedying these by his Articles of 1586 which had to do

with clerical education and preaching. He was determined to repress nonconformity, but he was also determined not to create Puritan martyrs as Mary Tudor had created Protestant martyrs. As time went on, he gradually reduced the severity of his rule and treated the Puritans with sympathy and kindness – he even welcomed Cartwright, when that extremist went to Warwick to Leicester's Hospital, now known as Lord Leycester's. But the Puritans never ceased to revile and calumniate him.

The variety of his work was enormous. He saw to it that the five vacant bishoprics were filled: he defended pluralism in order to improve the low standard of living and the penury of the clergy: he set about reforming the ecclesiastical courts, which were very unpopular owing to their dilatory ways, their expense and their extortions: he enforced orderliness at the two hospitals at Canterbury and also at All Souls College, of which he was Visitor. He realized that it was part of the church's duty to back up the social and economic policy of the government, so that in 1597-8 he instructed all the bishops to see that the laws against vagabonds and sturdy beggars were properly enforced. Being a bachelor and a wealthy pluralist, he had a good deal of money at his disposal, and this he spent lavishly, not only in entertaining on a scale worthy of his office, but on the relief of the poor, as when he founded the Hospital of the Holy Trinity at Croydon, and also on education, when he founded a free school at Croydon, still known as Whitgift School. He gave much attention to the training of young men both at Trinity, Cambridge, and at Lambeth: he founded a Bible Clerkship at Peterhouse.

Whitgift was essentially an administrator rather than a spiritual theologian. His work was to lay the foundations of a secure church on which others could build. The last ten years of his life saw the beginnings of this building which was later to develop according to the more theological, spiritual and Catholic conceptions of men like Lancelot Andrewes. It is to Whitgift's great credit that he recognized both the need and the opportunities for this beginning and encouraged the younger men to use them. The most notable example is the backing he gave to Hooker in writing the *Ecclesiastical Polity*.

One remarkable characteristic of Whitgift was his ability to subordinate his own instincts and inclinations to the general needs of the times. He was himself, if he could have had his own way theologically, a Calvinist, but he saw clearly that it was not right to try to inject Calvinism into the Anglican church as established in 1559. When the great attempt was made in 1595 by the Cambridge divines to get the archbishop to pronounce clearly in favour of Calvinistic doctrines, Whitgift summoned a conference to Lambeth and as a result he issued the Lambeth Articles which, while they conceded a good deal to the Calvinists, made some significant alterations in the original proposals and prevented the attempt to read a full Calvinistic doctrine into the old Thirty-Nine Articles.

When Elizabeth realized that she was dying, she sent for her 'little black husband' and Whitgift was with her to the end. He himself was now over seventy and worn out. He took some part in the Hampton Court Conference, but the immediate future lay with Bancroft, and Whitgift died on 29 February 1604. He was buried in the parish church at Croydon.

'He was of a middle stature, of a grave countenance and brown complexion, black hair and eyes; he wore his beard neither long nor thick.' He lived in splendour with a large army of retainers and he was on great occasions served 'upon the knee', 'for the upholding of the state that belonged unto his place'. Strype called him a 'man born for the benefit of his country and the good of his church'. His biographer, Sir George Paule, wrote, 'happy surely was it for that crazy state of the church (for so it was at this archbishop's first coming and long after) not to meet with too rough and boisterous a physician'. Queen Elizabeth, that shrewd and difficult lady, said, 'She pities him because she trusted him, and had thereby eased herself by laying the burthen of all her clergy-cares upon his shoulders; which he managed with prudence and piety.' Izaak Walton has drawn a characteristically friendly sketch of him – 'he was noted to be prudent and affable, and gentle by nature'. Characteristically, Macaulay has dismissed him in a few lines which reveal his misunderstanding of Whitgift, 'a narrow-minded, mean and tyrannical priest, who gained power by servility and adulation, and employed it in persecuting both those who agreed with Calvin about church government, and those who differed from Calvin touching the doctrine of Reprobation' (*Essay on Lord Bacon*). Perhaps those who knew him best may pass the final judgement. When about 1571 Whitgift had it in mind to leave Cambridge, the Heads of Houses wrote to Cecil, the chancellor, that should the vice-chancellor leave, 'the whole body of the university would lament', for he was 'wise, learned and wholly bent to the execution of good laws and statutes'. 'They could not want (i.e. do without) him'.

Further Reading

H. C. Porter, *Reformation and Reaction in Tudor Cambridge*, 1958.
V. J. K. Brook, *Whitgift and the English Church*, 1957.
P. M. Dawley, *John Whitgift and the Reformation*, 1955.
Izaak Walton, *Lives*.

WHITTINGHAM, WILLIAM (1524?-79), Dean of Durham, was born at Chester probably in 1524. He was educated at Brasenose College, Oxford. He became a BA and in 1545 a Fellow of All Souls, in 1548 Senior Student of Christ Church. At the age of twenty-six he was given leave by his college to travel in France, Germany and the Low Countries for three years. Most of that time was spent at Louvain University, where he married a strongly Protestant lady, and he became so proficient in the French language that he was often employed as an interpreter at the English embassy in Paris. There is no reason for accepting the idea that his wife was a sister of Calvin.

He returned to England just in time for the Nine Days' Reign of Lady Jane Grey. He was an extreme Protestant, and the accession of Mary to the throne made it dangerous for him to remain in England. With some difficulty he escaped overseas via Dover to France. On being questioned by the inn-keeper at Dover, Whittingham replied that he was going abroad 'because the Whore of Rome was again erected amongst them'. The inn-keeper was on the point of sending the party to a magistrate, but he was in some way cajoled into describing his female dog as 'one of the queen's kind', after which Whittingham was free to go on his travels.

He went to Frankfurt (June 1554), where he soon became involved in a violent dispute with other Protestants over the use of the Prayer Book. Most of the English exiles wanted to use Cranmer's Second Prayer Book, but Whittingham and John Knox wanted to start a new church with a prayer book of its own, much more extreme than their opponents cared for. So violent was Knox that he was expelled from the city. Whittingham soon followed him to Geneva (April 1555) with his party of twenty-seven supporters. Here was 'erected' the sort of church which Knox and Whittingham wanted. Whittingham was twice elected a 'Senior' or Elder of this church (1555 and 1556); he was then appointed Deacon (1558) and in 1559 he succeeded Knox as Minister.

During this time Whittingham was largely taken up with producing a new translation of the New Testament (1557), notable for its being the first English Bible to be divided into chapters and verses. His chief literary work was the 'Geneva Bible', known more vulgarly as the 'Breeches Bible', and closely connected with the name of Coverdale, but there is no doubt that Whittingham was responsible for most of the translation of the New Testament (1560). This book was the first to omit the Apocrypha and it became a popular Bible in English households, even after the Authorized Version of 1611.

The Prayer Book, known as the Genevan-English Order, published in 1556, was remarkable for the metrical versions of the Psalms which were included for congregational singing. This practice became very popular, and gradually there were introduced into the Book of Common Prayer metrical versions of passages from the Scriptures, such as those by Sternhold and Hopkins. Whittingham was the man who saved this practice from disappearing and who made it popular by his skill in selecting suitable tunes.

The accession of Elizabeth opened the way to a return to England. Whittingham was delayed by remaining in Geneva to complete the publishing of the Geneva Bible, but he was home in 1560 and attached himself to Ambrose Dudley, Earl of Warwick, and his brother Lord Robert Dudley, the future Earl of Leicester. In 1562 war broke out between England and France, and Warwick was sent to defend Havre: Whittingham went as his chaplain. It is said that his diligence in preaching was only equalled by his 'vigilance in discovering stratagems'. He preached always in armour and 'as the old captains and soldiers of Berwick would say, many years after, that – when any alarum came whilst he was preaching, he would be on the town walls as soon almost as any man'.

The reward for this service by the Church Militant was the deanery of Durham (1563). He proved in many ways to be an excellent choice: he paid strict attention to his religious activities, holding two services a day and giving three or four hours a day to teaching the children: he was socially a great success, living 'in the great love and liking of his neighbours, for his affability and bountiful hospitality'; and when he saw the Rebellion of the Northern Earls about to break out, he made every effort to persuade the bishop to take military measures in time, but he failed to move the timid Pilkington. He had better results at Newcastle, where by means of his efforts 'the rebels never dared attempt of the siege of that town'.

On the other hand, he ignored the Act of Uniformity and introduced into Durham Cathedral Genevan principles which he was compelled to abandon, when in 1566 Archbishop Parker published his 'Advertisements' to regulate such things as the out of doors dress of the clergy and the use of the surplice, as well as enforcing kneeling at the Communion. He also embarked on a policy of iconoclasm: he broke up the image of St Cuthbert in the cloisters, he removed grave-covers to use as paving-stones, stone coffins as cattle troughs and stoups for steeping 'their beef and salt fish in, having a conveyance in the bottoms for letting forth the water, as they had when they were in the church'. He lowered the frater roof and sold the lead for £20, while his wife burned the banner of St Cuthbert. These actions could be defended on the grounds that the queen had re-enacted the Injunction of 1547 for the removal of superstitious ornaments.

Whittingham was a difficult man and one not easily handled. He flatly refused to succeed to the office of Secretary of State in 1572. He boldly and successfully withstood his own bishop when Sandys, the new archbishop, ordered Barnes, Pilkington's successor, to visit the cathedral. Whittingham told the janitor to lock the door, the bishop tried to prevent him, the dean 'did a little interrupt him, taking hold of his gown', and kept the bishop out. Whittingham was then involved in other disputes: he was accused of adultery and of drunkenness, neither charge being well established; it was brought against him that he had never been properly ordained – nor in fact had he been ordained in the strict sense of the word, only 'ordered' as a minister at Geneva. Before any decision was arrived at on this point, Whittingham died at Durham in 1579.

He remains historically as an excellent example of that type of extreme Protestant who had little patience with the *via media* which Elizabeth wished to follow in matters ecclesiastical.

Further Reading

S. L. Greenslade, *Durham University Journal*, 1945-8.
James Wall, *The Church Quarterly*, 1936.
W. Whittingham, *The Troubles at Frankfurt*, ed. E. Arber, 1908.

WHITTINGTON, RICHARD (d.1423) was the outstanding London merchant of his day. He was the third son of Sir William Whittington of Pauntley (Gloucs.), an aristocrat of moderate means, and was apprenticed to a London mercer. He can never have been poor. Richard was already established in the city by 1379 and rapidly built up a successful business as a mercer dealing in bulk luxury fabrics, such as embroidered velvet, taffeta and cloth of gold. Particularly important customers were Richard II's favourite, the Earl of Oxford, the Earl of Derby (later Henry IV), and from 1389 Richard II himself, to whom Whittington supplied £3,474-worth in 1392-4, when he had five apprentices. This was the peak of Whittington's career as mercer: no new apprentices were enrolled after 1402, Henry IV proved a less valuable customer, and Whittington transferred his interest and capital to other areas. Trading with the Crown drew him into the speculative field of royal finance, which increasingly absorbed his energy and capital. Repayment of debts by the Crown was often by instalments from particular royal revenues (assignment), such as the customs, or by licences to ship wool free of custom, so Whittington was also involved in customs administration and the wool trade, in which he became a leading exporter. Finance and the wool trade were probably not particularly profitable, but they brought with them public office and status.

Whittington was three times master of the Mercer's Company, in 1395-6, 1401-2 and 1408-9, after which he abstained from company business. He was elected a common councillor of the City by 1384, sheriff in 1393, and alderman continuously from 1393. He was first appointed Lord Mayor in 1397 by Richard II, perhaps because the king wanted a compliant agent. It is striking that Whittington's nomination coincided with a large royal loan from the City and the repayment of royal debts due to Whittington himself. He was MP for the City in 1416. Two more terms as Lord Mayor in 1406 and 1419 singled Whittington out from his fellow aldermen, but he was never a knight, his knighthood – like his cat – being a later addition to his legend.

The legend of Whittington's stupendous wealth arises from the lavish charities established by his executors after his death and from his display of wealth during his life. In fact both employed the same resources. Whittington's lifetime loans ran into hundreds rather than thousands of pounds and his total capital was probably only about £6,000, an exceptional sum for a townsman, but not comparable with that of the nobility. The wealth of the aristocracy and most merchants was tied up in land or merchandise, but Whittington exceptionally kept his fortune in cash and thus had unusual liquid sums available for use at any time. The prior death of his wife, his lack of heirs, and the apparent absence of close friends or relatives meant that Whittington did not need to provide for any dependants in his will and could devote his whole fortune to the charities founded for the good of his soul. Such conduct conforms both to his cold egotism and to his conventionally orthodox piety. He left it to his executors to dispose of his wealth, often in ways of which he had no prior knowledge, and they did their work well: Whittington's almshouse, Whittington College, the foundation of the Guildhall Library, and the rebuilding of Newgate Prison earned him renown and indeed Whittington Hospital, Highgate remains today. Six thousand pounds for charity made a big splash in fifteenth-century London. Hence Whittington's fame and hence the development of his legend.

Further Reading
C. M. Barron, 'Richard Whittington: The Man behind the Myth', *Studies in London History*, ed. A. E. J. Hollaender and W. Kellaway, 1969

WHYMPER, EDWARD (1840-1911), mountaineer, was the first man to reach the summit of the Matterhorn, and, through the ensuing tragedy and the book he wrote afterwards, the best known of the pioneers of climbing. Mountaineering held much of the excitement for the Victorians that space travel was to have a century later, and was more accessible. The distaste and fear which eighteenth-century gentry had for crags and wilderness had given place to wonder, and a sense of the majesty of great hills, inspired by the Romantic movement in art and literature. Railways put the Alps within range of British climbers. The challenge of being the first to the top, the physical demands on strong young men, scientific research, and the instinct which drew religious people to the hills; all contributed to the opening up of this new sphere of adventure.

Whymper went to the Alps when he was twenty, because his skill as an engraver for his father had attracted the attention of the publishers, Longmans, who were producing a series on *Peaks, Passes and Glaciers*.

He was a natural climber, long-limbed and with exceptional stamina. By 1865 he had scaled many peaks hitherto unclimbed, and had made five unsuccessful attempts on the Matterhorn, on one occasion falling 200 feet. His sixth try was a spur-of-the-moment decision in Zermatt, when he met Lord Francis Douglas, the Rev. Charles Hudson and the nineteen-year-old Douglas Hadow, all of whom had the same aim. As Italians were known to be trying to be the first up, they set out next day. The route they chose, unattempted until then because it looked so daunting, proved surprisingly easy, and they reached the summit the following morning, looking down on the Italians far below. But as they descended Hadow slipped, and knocked the guide ahead from his perch. The rope above them snapped, and Whymper and two guides watched their four companions sliding on their backs, arms outstretched, down the smooth slabs of rock to the precipices, where they fell from sight onto the glaciers 4,000 feet below.

There was outrage at home. The Matterhorn is a sensational-looking peak, Hudson was a well-known climber, Douglas the brother of the Marquis of Queensberry. *The Times* thundered: 'What is the use of scaling precipitous rocks, and being for half an hour at the top of the terrestrial globe?' The queen wondered whether mountaineering could be banned. But when Whymper published *Scrambles amongst the Alps* in 1871, it proved a best-seller, despite its chunks of indigestible detail and occasional startlingly purple passages. His fame was assured.

Whymper was an amateur scientist who collected data wherever he went. In 1880 he spent thirty consecutive nights above 14,000 feet in the Andes (where he added the 20,498 feet Chimborazo to his collection of 'Firsts') to test the effects of high altitudes on the human body. He brought home fossils, plants and insects, as well as samples of volcanic dust from Cotopaxi. He studied the make-up and movement of glaciers, wrote a pamphlet on the aneroid barometer, became a skilful photographer. But this fine-looking man with a stern mouth grew increasingly dour. He lived apart from his guides even when sharing a tent with them. Though a member of the Alpine Club, he was a lonely and disputatious figure, shut up in a hard shell. The one woman who might have refreshed his life was nearly seventy when he met her, and died soon afterwards. His subsequent marriage, to a woman forty-five years younger than him, ended in separation four years later. When he was finally ill in Chamonix, he locked himself in his hotel room, to die without fuss, alone.

Further Reading
F. S. Smythe, *Edward Whymper*, 1940.
Edward Whymper, *Scrambles Amongst the Alps in the Years 1860-1869*, 6th edn, 1936.

WIGSTAN, ST or WYSTAN (*d.*849) was a prince of the royal family of Mercia who was murdered by a remote kinsman in a dynastic conflict in 849. After his death he was regarded as a saint and a local cult of him grew up at Repton where he was buried. Recent excavations at Repton have produced archaeological evidence of a flourishing cult in the pre-Conquest period, notably the construction of a system of passages giving access to the crypt where Wigstan's relics rested, apparently for the use of pilgrims coming to venerate them. Wigstan's relics were moved to the monastery of Evesham during the reign of Canute and the cult continued lively there during the remainder of the Middle Ages.

WIHTRED (*d.*725) ruled as King of Kent from 691 to 725. He was remembered in later Kentish tradition as 'the glorious king', and as with his contemporary Ine of Wessex one can sense that he was an imposing ruler. The early years of his reign were confused. More than one king claimed rule in Kent in the years 690-4, and it was probably not until after a settlement with Wessex in 694 to atone for the Kentish murder of Mul, the brother of Cadwalla, that Wihtred could feel secure. A charter of 694 records the stabilization of the frontiers of the kingdom along its earlier boundaries. In 695 Wihtred issued a code of laws: that one clause was identical to a clause in Ine's code suggests some co-operation between the two rulers.

Wihtred's law-code is chiefly remarkable for its evidence of the privileged position accorded to the church. Its first clause, for example, granted the church immunity from taxation. Royal authority was used to back up ecclesiastical precept on such matters as fasting, abstention from work on Sundays and the canonical rules governing marriage. It is surely permissible to see in this the influence of Kentish churchmen, most prominent among them Archbishop Brihtwold of Canterbury (693-731). Wihtred was a generous patron of monasteries: the houses at Canterbury, Minster-in-Thanet and Lyminge received grants of land from him.

The compensation paid to Ine of Wessex for Mul's death took the form of a very large sum of coin. Recent work by numismatists has demonstrated that Wihtred minted coin on a large and hitherto unsuspected scale. Trade with Franks and Frisians on the other side of the Channel played an important role in the economy of Kent. Wihtred's kingdom was wealthy and powerful. Kent had not yet declined into the status of a satellite of Mercia or Wessex.

WILBERFORCE, SAMUEL (1805-73), whose best work was done as Bishop of Oxford, has had a bad press. He got up against the future by defending the traditional doctrine of the Creation against Darwin's follower Huxley. Instinctively conservative, openly ambitious,

ready to jump in where angels feared to tread, he earned, through his eager courtesy, a reputation for being all things to all men. 'Sly Sam of Oxford', the diarist Greville called him. Sometimes dubbed 'Slippery Sam', he is often known as 'Soapy Sam'. Disraeli told the queen that he was 'a prelate who … is absolutely more odious in this country than Archbishop Laud'. Yet the daughter of one who worked with him wrote: 'No-one who recalls those days will ever forget the magical effect of his presence – like the coming of spring to a winter landscape', and he has more recently been described as one of the greatest bishops in the history of the Anglican church. The record needs further straightening.

To his father, the famous William Wilberforce, he seemed to have the gifts and the grace to fulfil God's purposes in the world in a special way. The family was a close one, brought up in Clapham, the power-house of the Evangelical Revival. Samuel and Robert wrote a five-volume life of their father. Later the clan of like-minded friends was extended, when three daughters of the clergyman John Sargent married Samuel, his brother Henry and Henry Manning. From this united, high-minded and happy base Samuel was ordained, and soon earned an exciting reputation for his eloquence, efficiency and stamina. He found time, while being a first-class parish priest, to travel widely and often, on speaking tours for missionary societies and as Archdeacon of Surrey. When he was taken up at court, where Victoria and Albert were his enthusiastic admirers, preferment soon followed. Briefly Dean of Westminster, he became Bishop of Oxford in 1845. Earlier he had written to Robert, in his open way, of 'my love of form – of cathedrals – of dignity'. He had his eye on greater dignity still. But his career came to a halt. He remained in Oxford for twenty-four years, and never became an archbishop, ending as Bishop of Winchester.

For this failure (for such it seemed to him and to others), his beliefs were as responsible as his character. He saw the Church of England as going back to early Christianity and providing the *via media* from it, between Protestant heresy and Roman corruption. This was an honourable Anglican stance, but in the ecclesiastical climate of his time it did not make him popular. Maintaining a central position, he appeared two-faced. 'I believe the Episcopal form of government is the appointment of God through his inspired apostles', he wrote, and he defended it robustly against attacks from every side. In so far as the Oxford Movement Tracts of Newman, Pusey and their allies defined the traditional Catholic nature of the Church of England and the importance of its sacraments, Wilberforce went with them, and he became a leading Tractarian. He was out of sympathy with the Evangelicals, and Low Churchmen did not like his episcopal purple. He opposed woolly liberals – the Broad Church – but alas, Prince Albert was a Broad Churchman. He also staunchly resisted Erastian attempts to assert state control over church doctrine, and made enemies of the Whigs, especially Russell and Palmerston. In 1847 Russell nominated as Bishop of Hereford Dr Hampden, already a controversial Regius Professor of Divinity at Oxford, who was suspected of unsound doctrine. Wilberforce led the church's attack on this choice before reading Hampden's lectures; then, on reading them, decided that they were not heretical after all, and retreated. His opponents crowed, but his faults were haste and honesty, not hypocrisy. However, Victoria, via Albert, never thought so well of him again. His only important political ally left was Gladstone.

On the other flank, he never wavered in his belief that Rome, with its idolizing of Saints and the Virgin Mary and its formularies for salvation, had corrupted Christ's truths. When Newman went over to Rome, Wilberforce called him 'the great pervert'. His grief was deeply felt when his brothers Henry and Robert, his sister, his brother-in-law the future Cardinal Manning, and eventually his daughter and her husband, all became Roman Catholics. He wrote as of a bereavement: 'The broken sleep, the heavy waking before the sorrow has shaped itself with returning consciousness, ... the clouding over of all the future.' It was the parting of friends. Yet his close connections with so many converts, at a time when the pope had re-established a Roman hierarchy in England, unjustly tainted him.

He became the leading spokesman for the church in the House of Lords, and as part of his drive to strengthen the church's control over its own doctrine he gradually had restored some of the old powers of Convocation, lost since the days of Walpole. As a diocesan bishop he set new standards. He was a workaholic, escaping from emptiness at the middle of his life after the early death of his wife: but he was much more than this, for he had a clear sense of direction. For the first time for more than two centuries the lead in the Church of England was to come from the top. He saw the bishop as 'the mainspring of all spiritual and religious agency in his diocese'. He worked to forge unity and mutual respect among his clergy, getting his rural deans to hold regular chapters for them. He brought the laity into the management of the church through diocesan societies, which raised over two million pounds for more and better-paid parish priests. He founded two colleges, Cuddesdon for training the clergy and Culham for training teachers. He lent his support and protection to new Anglican Sisterhoods, including St Mary's, Wantage, making them feel at home in the Church of England. His Lenten missions were famous, for he was no bureaucrat, but a front-line bishop who inspired and was loved.

It requires a leap of the imagination now to recapture the importance of an ecclesiastical statesman or the charm of a warm-hearted man. But when Samuel Wilberforce died, falling from his horse after a heart attack, the papers were full of little else, and special trains brought mourners to his funeral.

Further Reading
S. Meacham, *Lord Bishop: the life of Samuel Wilberforce, 1805-1873*, 1970.
D. Newsome, *The Parting of Friends: a study of the Wilberforces and Henry Manning*, 1966.

WILBERFORCE, WILLIAM (1759-1833), evangelical Christian, politician and social reformer, is best known for his part in the abolition of the slave trade, an act of unselfish policy which is among the best things done by an English parliament. His work and influence extended also to many causes less famous. No Englishman of his time did more for his fellow men.

His father, a wealthy Hull merchant, died when he was nine. From St John's College, Cambridge, he went into parliament; his first election at Hull in 1780 cost him £8,000. After 1784 he was one of the county members for Yorkshire. He had a good voice and was a fluent speaker, 'the nightingale of the House'. Pitt was devoted to him, but his friendships included also Fox and Sheridan. A delightfully open and humorous character made him popular in the House, but his unique position of moral authority came from his personal commitment to good causes. He was fearlessly independent: inclining always to pacifism he risked Pitt's anger in 1795 by speaking in favour of peace. Later he hurt Pitt deeply (and swayed the issue) by voting for the impeachment of Dundas. He seemed to be interested in political life only in so far as it gave him the opportunity to promote reform. In 1787 he wrote in his journal: 'God Almighty has placed before me two great objects, the suppression of the slave trade and the reformation of manners.'

Under the influence of Milner, Fellow and later President of Queens' College, Cambridge, and Newton, London vicar and former slaver, Wilberforce experienced 'a conversion' to evangelical Christianity. His conviction was fortified by the friendship of his aunt, Mrs Wilberforce of Wimbledon, her brother, John Thornton of Clapham, and his son Henry Thornton. With the latter he lived for two years; at about the same time John Venn became vicar of Clapham. With Lord Teignmouth, Zachary Macaulay and James Stephen these men formed a circle of devout, practical Christians who, because of their tendency to think and act together upon social and political questions, came to be called 'the Clapham Sect' or 'the Saints'. Single-minded, experts on their own chosen subjects and untied to any party or programme, they had an authority in parliament far larger than their voting strength might suggest. Wilberforce, regular in committee work and in attendance in the House, a competent and sometimes moving speaker, was their acknowledged leader. His life was grounded upon prayer and Bible-reading, and he conducted a steady offensive for the reform of the Church of England in the interests of 'vital religion'. But he was able to work with radicals, utilitarian or agnostic in their views, such as Bentham, Brougham, Romilly and Mackintosh. 'If to be an anti-slavist is to be a Saint' wrote Bentham, 'Saintship for me'. A few, notably Cobbett and Hazlitt, thought his religion pious cant because of his political conservatism. They marked his loyalty to traditional notions of class, his friendship with astute bankers. He was indeed orthodox in his view of society, but sensitive also to the conditions of the English poor.

He was one of the three founders of 'The Society for Bettering the Conditions and Increasing the Comforts of the Poor' which cared for the casualties of a raw industrial society. He supported Peel's Factory Bill of 1802 and asked that its benefits be extended to other industries. In 1812 he moved the promotion of 'An Association for the relief of the Manufacturing and Labouring Poor'. As member for Yorkshire he worked for the interests of the small farmer and manufacturer; in 1826 he directed a movement of private charity to relieve the suffering of the people. Two of the pioneers in the Factory Reform projects, Oastler and Wood, had been agents in the anti-slavery movement; a third, Sadleir, was Wilberforce's political agent in Yorkshire and a close friend. As Halévy wrote: 'The historian of the movement which produced the Factory Acts must not forget the many tributaries that swelled the main stream. But the source of the river was the piety and Christian sentiment of the Evangelicals'.

In an age when the state played a negative role, their initiatives were crucial. Wilberforce supported legislation to abolish the lottery, and duelling in the services. In tract and speech he attacked bull and bear baiting. He lent his weight to the campaign of Romilly for reform of 'our murderous laws'. He visited Newgate with Elizabeth Fry and he secured the passage of a bill (rejected by the Lords) to end the practice of employing 'climbing boys' as chimney sweeps. A strong believer in elementary education for all, he became a vice-president of the British and Foreign School Society. He encouraged Hannah More in her work for Sunday schools and wrote a book whose heavy title, *A practical view of the Prevailing Religious System of Professed Christians in the Higher and Middle Classes in this Country contrasted with Real Christianity*, did not prevent its running into five editions in six months. Its message is essentially that Christianity was the only remedy for the selfishness engendered by wealth, and the moral decline of England's expanding population in a time of revolution. Wilberforce contributed much to the growth of the spirit of moral earnestness which characterized the Victorians.

The Committee for the Abolition of the Slave Trade was formed in 1787. Its leaders wanted a spokesman in parliament. Neither Fox nor Pitt would take an initiative which might fatally divide their followings; Pitt did support Wilberforce and when, in 1788, the latter fell seriously ill, took charge of the first motion for an investigation, but the revolution and ensuing war damaged the cause of abolition. Pitt concentrated upon the war; public opinion was alarmed by the rebellion of black slaves in St Domingo; reform receded before the spectre of Jacobinism. Yet the movement grew, with Clarkson organizing corresponding committees, agents, public meetings, pamphlets, all rousing people to awareness. The methods adopted were important. According to G. M. Trevelyan, 'Public discussion and public agitation of every kind of question became the habit of the English people, very largely in imitation of Wilberforce's successful campaign'. The going was hard, and in 1800 he even dropped his annual motion for comprehensive abolition. In May 1804, however, his bill passed the Commons for the first time. After Pitt's death, Grenville, Grey and Fox put the weight of government behind the bill. In February 1807 both Houses passed it, and Wilberforce received a memorable ovation.

He laboured on, for the enforcement of the Act and towards its logical successor. At the end of the war Castlereagh insisted upon an anti-slave trade clause in the Treaty of Vienna: 'The nation is bent on this object. I believe there is hardly a village that has not met and petitioned upon it. Ministers must make it the basis of their policy.' Now the campaign for the abolition of slavery in the colonies passed to younger men. Wilberforce resigned from parliament in 1824 and died a few months before the Act was passed in 1833.

Coupland summarizes his achievement, after pointing out that the abolition came just in time, before the development of Africa could turn the continent into a vast slave plantation: 'More than any other man he had founded in the conscience of the British people a tradition of humanity and responsibility toward backward black people whose fate is in their hands.' Mackintosh 'never saw any one who touched life at so many points … When he was in the House of Commons he seemed to have the freshest mind of any man there'. Wilberforce had his critics; he had no enemies.

Further Reading
John Pollock, *Wilberforce*, 1977.
R. Coupland, *Wilberforce, A Narrative*, 1945.

WILD, JONATHAN (1683-1725), master-criminal, was more than any man responsible for the growth of crime in London at the start of the eighteenth century. A less attractive and less heroic figure than he appears in the largely fictitious pages of Fielding, he was perhaps more significant than even that student of the underworld may have realized. He realized that, in a big and crowded city, crime may be organized as a business; he has some claim, therefore, to be called the first of the racketeers.

His father was a poor carpenter of Wolverhampton, and he was apprenticed to a buckle-maker. While still an apprentice he married and had a son. Bored with making buckles after about ten years, he came to London. His career there followed a pattern on which the moralist may dwell. It was when he was in prison for debt that he met a prostitute, Mary Milliner, and became her ponce; soon he owned two brothels. He learned how to make money as a 'fence' – a receiver of stolen property – and by acting as broker for the return of such property. His arrangements benefited alike thieves who had easy money and victims who were otherwise unlikely to recover their goods. His career brought home to men like Fielding the pitiful inadequacy of law-enforcement. Wild actually set up an office in Cock Alley where those who had been robbed might apply to him. He grew rich, bought a country house, employed a manager and clerks. His private sloop conveyed stolen goods to a warehouse in Holland and brought back contraband. A special Act of Parliament made his reward technique a felony, but he merely changed his method. Eventually he was brought to trial when it emerged that he was organizing gangs over the whole country, some specializing in certain sorts of crime such as blackmail, others following the assizes or the country fairs. The evidence may have been exaggerated but, since Wild's life coincided with a great increase in robbery and violence and the roads, even in towns, were alarming to travellers, the charges were generally believed. The young attorney-general Yorke prosecuted for the Crown, Wild was found guilty of receiving reward for the return of stolen property and hanged at Tyburn. It may seem surprising that Wild escaped for so long the only remedy which Hanoverian England knew and applied to about 160 different offences, from murder to impersonating a Chelsea pensioner or damaging London Bridge – the rope. So it should be added that it was from the City Marshal himself, Charles Hitchen, that Wild received his first lessons in the business of receiving.

Further Reading
Henry Fielding, *Jonathan Wild* (a novel).

WILDE, OSCAR (1856-1900), wit, poet and dramatist, left rich material with which to celebrate his life: several exquisite comedies; stories variously enchanting or strange; some elegant epigrams; revealing letters: considerable literary production overall. The disaster that overcame him was commensurate: as if nothing but the grandest shipwreck were enough for so resplendent a craft.

Was sober respectability expected of this second son of the Irish surgeon, Sir William Wilde? His mother Jane was a poet and authority on Celtic folklore: he was christened Oscar Fingall O'Flahertie Wills. At Portora Royal School and Trinity College, Dublin he won prizes. At Magdalen College, Oxford (1874-8), he won the Newdigate Prize for poetry and a first class degree. He was devoted to Ruskin's ideal of the central importance of art in life. He needed no urging to follow Pater's way, to 'burn always with a hard gemlike flame'. His clothes were audacious, his talk affected. Oxford has seen other such peacocks. What set him apart, not the amiable buffoon of first impressions but a very prince of aesthetes, was that he was genuinely clever, an accomplished classical scholar, eloquent and, in his eccentric way, ambitious. He gave loving care to presenting his own personality. It was enough to be Oscar Wilde, a work of art, all wit and sensibility, a living challenge to puritans and philistines. Writing verse, he let meaning take second place to sound. *Poems* (1881) owed much to Keats, more, unfortunately, to Swinburne. In 1882 he went on a lecture tour in America. At the customs he announced that he had nothing to declare but his genius. Many were rapturous when he exhorted them to love beauty and art. Some thought him an arrogant puppy. He did not mind. Beyond his circle of devotees he expected, perhaps needed, rejection and scorn.

In 1884 he married Constance Lloyd, daughter of an Irish barrister. They had two sons. His need to make money drove his pen; his perfectionism ensured that he would not be content to live on other people's ideas – and phrases. 'I wish that I had said that,' he remarked, approving of some witticism. 'You will, Oscar, you will!' was the reply. From 1887 to 1889 Wilde was reduced to editing *Woman's World*. He reviewed books. He wrote *The Happy Prince and Other Tales* (1888), an allegory in the form of the fairy tale. Heavily handsome, typically attired in velvet, plum-coloured knickerbocker suit with black silk stockings, he was instantly recognizable. Among the like-minded he could be spell-binding. André Gide met him: 'Wilde did not converse – he told tales. During the whole meal he hardly stopped. He spoke in a slow, musical tone, and his very voice was wonderful.'

Stories like *Lord Arthur Savile's Crime*, colloquies like *The Decay of Living* and *The Critic as Artist* reveal Wilde's stretch of mind, his mastery of prose. But fame eluded him. To find it he ventured to test society's accepted bounds. In 1891 appeared *The Picture of Dorian Gray*. With the supernatural elements of the Gothic novel were mixed the sick fancies of French decadent fiction. Gray destroyed himself: an apparently moral ending. Wilde however insisted that art was amoral. His essays, published as *Intentions* (1891), promoted that view. He was influenced especially by the French poets Gautier and Baudelaire. Greece had been, France became, his spiritual home. It was the French effect that was appreciated by the audiences which flocked to *Lady Windermere's Fan* (1892). Within the conventions of the French comedy, he deployed his wit to dazzling effect.

Suddenly Wilde's name was everywhere. 'The man who can dominate a London dinner-table can dominate the world', he had said. Did the man who could so grasp, so define what was on the surface, see beneath it to its brittle foundations? The celebrant of what was most artificial and heartless in society would be its hero one day, its victim the next. Meanwhile he tasted fame, and held himself free to say, write and do what he wanted. *Salome*, written in French and designed to make the audience shudder by its depiction of unnatural passion, was censored. It appeared, however, in 1894, in English translation with illustrations by Aubrey Beardsley. Decadence now assumed a British look.

In 1893 *A Woman of No Importance* was produced; early in 1895, both *An Ideal Husband* and *The Importance of Being Earnest*. Lady Bracknell entered the select company of theatre's greatest characters. In his Oxford rooms he had once said that he wished he could 'live up to his blue china'. Now he was living up to the character described by Arthur Symons: 'not so much a person as an attitude.' Friends noticed a coarsening of looks and tone: one called him bloated. Self-indulgence was on an imperial scale, inviting hubris. His flaunted friendship with Lord Alfred Douglas enraged the latter's father, the Marquis of Queensberry, who accused Wilde of being a sodomite. Wilde was persuaded by Douglas, who detested his father, to sue Queensberry for criminal libel. His case collapsed. He was urged to flee to France. Bravely or foolishly Wilde refused. He was arrested, tried, retried after the first jury had failed to reach a verdict, and sentenced to two years' hard labour. At the time, shock, disgust, embarrassment were felt: least, perhaps, pity. Only a few friends remained loyal, Max Beerbohm and Robert Ross, later his literary executor, among them. Judgements have been different since: as much to do with his society as with him. His personal tragedy can be measured by the suddenness of fall and the contrasts: between fame, adulation, fleshpots; and the cold shoulders of 'friends', the scorn of the crowd, curious stares, prurience; the company of convicts, bitter sense of betrayal; the loneliness that he would describe in *The Ballad of Reading Gaol*; not least, the long humiliation of his wife.

In 1897 Wilde was released, a bankrupt. He went at once to France, under the name of 'Sebastian Melmoth', and settled near Dieppe. There he wrote the *Ballad*. Steady work was apparently beyond him. He travelled restlessly, then stayed in Paris. There, in November 1900, poor, pain-wracked, a penitent, in his last hours a Catholic, he died: an ear infection had brought on a sudden inflammation of the brain. In 1905 *De Profundis* was published. It was the severely cut version of the letter he had written, but never sent, to Lord Alfred. He accused him of distracting him and encouraging him in dissipation. It was the tragedy of this consummate artist, so deeply flawed, yet, as some wonderful letters reveal, gentle and innately good-natured, that he could so be distracted; that he could so destroy himself.

In 1909 his body was moved to the cemetery of Père Lachaise in Paris. Under Epstein's monument are his own words:

> And alien tears will fill for him
> Pity's long broken urn
> For his mourners will be outcast men,
> And outcasts always mourn.

Further Reading
Richard Ellman, *Oscar Wilde*, 1988.
Rupert Hart-Davis (ed), *The Letters of Oscar Wilde*, 1962.

WILDMAN, JOHN (1623-93), plotter, of whose origins we are ignorant, was educated at Cambridge and studied law in London. After 1655 he was usually known as 'Major Wildman', but his only recorded military activity took place in 1659, when with two other officers and 300 volunteers he persuaded the Governor of Windsor Castle to surrender it. His first appearance is as a Leveller in the Putney Debates of 1647, when he helped to draft *The Case of the Army Truly Stated* and *The Agreement of the People* and, although a civilian, acted as a 'mouth' of the common soldiers in the discussions with the officers. In 1648 the Commons, as alarmed as the army grandees by the Levellers, arrested Wildman and his friend Lilburne, and he spent six months in prison in the Fleet. In 1649 Wildman seems to have accepted the Republic and he gave most of his energies from 1650 to 1655 to a highly successful series of speculations, on his own behalf or as a commission agent, in the land market which resulted from the sales of royalist properties, emerging with a good deal of property and a comfortable fortune. But when he was elected for Scarborough in the first Protectorate Parliament (1654) and then excluded by the government, he turned to a course of plotting which, with intervals of imprisonment, lasted virtually for the remainder of his life. Involved in 1654 in the plot of the three colonels and in the scheme which led to the arrest of General Overton in Scotland, he devised a Republican plot of his own to raise an insurrection against the Protector in 1655, but was arrested while he was dictating a declaration of rebellion. Cromwell treated him extremely leniently; he was imprisoned for rather over a year and then released, very possibly in return for agreeing to act as a spy upon the royalists, with whom he was by now in touch. He bought himself the considerable estate of Becker in Berkshire and the Nonsuch Tavern in Covent Garden, and then plunged for the next three years into a weird tangle of conspiracies with Republicans, discontented clergymen, the Spanish rulers of the Netherlands and the exiled court of Charles II. The main aim of these proceedings was the assassination of Cromwell, and they came nearest to success in the 'Powder Plot' of 1657, when a box of gunpowder was smuggled into Whitehall Palace, at which point one of the gang betrayed the scheme. A succession of petty plots led to the arrest of a crop of royalists by the Protectorate intelligence service, and sharply diminished the confidence of Hyde and the wiser royalist chiefs in Wildman – who remained at large.

In 1659, after the fall of Richard Cromwell, Wildman was for a short time on the side of the government. A disciple of Harrington, he supported the petitions for a balanced republican scheme of government, acted as chairman of a 'Commonwealth' discussion club, and was one of a committee asked by Fleetwood to draft a new constitution. Even when the Restoration blew these gossamer projects away, Wildman contrived to remain near the centre of power, for he was for nearly a year and a half a principal figure in the government Post Office. It looks as though he set out to make it a nest of Republican intrigue; after various allegations against him, he was arrested – with Harrington and Praise-God Barebone among others – on a charge of being involved in a great conspiracy. Investigation did not produce the evidence to condemn him: Wildman was habitually cautious in speech. But in 1662 he was sent to the Scillies, beyond the reach of habeas corpus, and he did not leave prison until 1667. For the next twelve years, apart from a period abroad between 1670 and 1675, Wildman attached himself to Buckingham, for whom he acted as solicitor and trustee. In December 1667 Pepys recorded that someone told him that 'Wildman, the Fifth-Monarchy man, a great creature of the Duke of Buckingham's' had been nominated as one of a commission set up to examine the public accounts after the disasters of the Second Dutch War; but the Commons would not accept so notorious a character who was only two months out of gaol. Wildman was certainly not a Fifth Monarchist; his religious attitude was that of a sceptic. He supported Shaftesbury and sat for Great Bedwin in the Oxford Parliament of 1681, and during the next two years he was deeply – though as usual obscurely – involved in the events which brought the Whigs to ruin. He drafted manifestos and bought arms; it also appears that the idea of murdering the king, later worked up by the informers into the 'Rye House Plot', was originally Wildman's, though he later dropped it. Once more he was arrested (1683) and sent to the Tower. Although two small cannon were found in his cellar, there was again insufficient evidence, and he was set free.

When James II became king, Wildman was one of the small group of conspirators who prepared the way for Monmouth in England. Yet he did so reluctantly, for he thought little of Monmouth's character, and tried to stop him coming. When the revolt failed, Wildman fled overseas, first to Germany and then to Holland. He arrived at the Hague in 1688 in time to take part in propaganda for William's invasion, writing one influential pamphlet, the *Memorial of English Protestants*. He sailed with William to England, was a prominent member of the Convention Parliament, and was appointed Postmaster-General, holding the post until he was dismissed in 1691. By this time he had got involved in a Presbyterian plot against William's authority in Scotland. Yet he may have lost his office merely because the postal service did not function very efficiently in these years – for in 1692 William III knighted him, six months before he died. He reached the age of seventy, a remarkable achievement for so habitual and so unsuccessful a plotter.

Further Reading
Maurice Ashley, *John Wildman*, 1947.

WILFRID, ST (634-709) was a monk, Bishop of York, and the most prominent figure alongside Theodore in the history of the English church in the second half of the seventh century. Wilfrid's career can be known to us in unusual detail owing to the survival of a biography composed shortly after his death by his devoted chaplain Eddius at the request of Bishop Acca of Hexham. Eddius's *Life of Wilfrid* is full of detail, remarkably frank about the controversial aspects of a stormy career, and passionately partisan. Bede also has much to say about Wilfrid in his *Ecclesiastical History*. Bede had met Wilfrid, knew a good deal about him from friends such as Acca, and was probably familiar with Eddius's *Life*. His treatment of Wilfrid's career is much more discreet than that of Eddius. The resultant differences between our two major sources have given rise to much discussion and puzzlement. Wilfrid continues to be a controversial figure thirteen centuries after his lifetime.

Wilfrid was born into a Northumbrian family, almost certainly of noble rank, in 634. At the age of fourteen he experienced some kind of religious conversion and with the patronage of Eanflaed, the queen of King Oswy, he was placed in the monastery of Lindisfarne, then still under the rule of its Irish founder, Aidan. In about 652 he formed the ambition of going to Rome on pilgrimage. With the recommendation, once again, of Queen Eanflaed he went to Kent where he spent a year at the royal court. In 653 he set off for Rome in the company of Benedict Biscop. They travelled together as far as Lyons, where they parted company for reasons that remain unclear. Biscop went on to Rome while Wilfrid remained behind in Lyons where he had struck up a friendship with the bishop, Annemundus, and his brother Dalfinus, Count of Lyons. Annemundus indeed wanted to adopt Wilfrid as his son, offered him the hand of his niece in marriage and undertook to launch him upon a distinguished secular career in Gaul. Wilfrid resisted – though he may have been tempted: might this have been the occasion of his breach with Biscop? – and went on his way to Rome.

This first visit to Rome was of decisive importance in Wilfrid's life. He learned of Roman ecclesiastical usages, especially in the matter of the calculation of Easter, of which he was ignorant: this was to have important repercussions on his return to England. Perhaps even more significantly, in a Rome still mindful of Pope Gregory, Wilfrid was touched by a missionary impulse – as other visitors had been in the seventh century, notably the great Gallic missionary-bishop, Amandus, of whose evangelization of the Low Countries Wilfrid may already have heard something: this too was to bear fruit later on. Furthermore, Wilfrid had an audience with the pope. Pope Martin I was engaged at the time in a fierce theological dispute with the authorities in Constantinople. Towards the end of 654 he was to be kidnapped by emissaries of the Byzantine emperor and exiled to the Crimea. His death there in 655 was to be widely regarded as martyrdom. It is not fanciful to suppose that Wilfrid's witnessing of this unseemly conflict between church and state was to affect the stance he adopted in his later quarrels with successive Kings of Northumbria. Wilfrid's whole-hearted devotion to all things Roman never again wavered after the months he spent in Rome as an impressionable young man of twenty in the year 654.

After leaving Rome Wilfrid returned to Lyons where he spent the next three years with Bishop Annemundus. It was during this period that he received the monastic tonsure. Annemundus was murdered in 658. Wilfrid narrowly escaped the same fate and made his way back to England. Returning to Northumbria he attached himself to Alchfrith, son of Oswy, who was then ruling as a sub-king in Deira, the southern half of Northumbria. Alchfrith expelled the Irish monks whom he had recently established at Ripon and gave the monastery to Wilfrid instead. It was at Ripon that Wilfrid was ordained priest, probably early in 664, by Agilbert, the Frankish Bishop of Dorchester whom Wilfrid had probably already met in Wessex, who was visiting the Northumbrian royal court. Together Agilbert and Wilfrid attended the Synod of Whitby in 664. Wilfrid was the principal spokesman for the Roman party which carried the day in the question of the observance of Easter.

Shortly after the Synod Wilfrid was promoted to the bishopric of York. At this time the see of Canterbury was vacant, and since Wilfrid could not be consecrated by schismatic British or Irish bishops he went to Gaul. He received consecration at Compiègne at the hands of Agilbert, who was magnificently (and symbolically) assisted by eleven other bishops. Wilfrid tarried some

time in Gaul afterwards. During his absence from Northumbria, and in circumstances at which we can only guess – not improbably to be connected with a quarrel between King Oswy and his son Alchfrith – Oswy gave the bishopric of York to Chad. Wilfrid regarded this as illegal usurpation of his see. Moreover, Chad made matters worse by being consecrated by the simoniac Bishop Wine of Winchester and two of the schismatic British bishops. Wilfrid returned to Northumbria probably in 666, after shipwreck and battle with looters on the coast of still pagan Sussex. (It is some indication of the state he kept that he had a retinue of 120 men. The single ship in which they all travelled must therefore have been considerably larger than the forty-seater in which King Redwald had been buried at Sutton Hoo a generation earlier.) Finding Chad in possession of York, Wilfrid retired to his monastery of Ripon which formed his base for the next three years. During this period he occasionally discharged episcopal functions in Mercia and in Kent. Eddius also tells us that he founded more than one monastery in Mercia (one of them perhaps at Oundle) during this period, on the strength of landed endowments granted by King Wulfhere.

Archbishop Theodore reached England in May 669. In the course of the general visitation of the English churches which he conducted soon afterwards, Theodore removed Chad from York and replaced him with Wilfrid; Chad was soon afterwards compensated with a Mercian see at Lichfield. Wilfrid held the bishopric of York in peace from 669 until 678. These were busy years. Wilfrid rebuilt his cathedral church at York; he built a church at Ripon and another at his northernmost monastic foundation, Hexham. (The crypts which underlay the two latter churches still stand.) He was an active diocesan in the vast Northumbrian bishopric subject to him.

In 678 King Ecgfrith picked a quarrel with Wilfrid and enlisted the support of Archbishop Theodore. Grasping this opportunity to further his plans for the division of over-large dioceses, Theodore consecrated three new bishops for Northumbria. Wilfrid, incensed, set off for Rome to appeal to the pope. He spent the winter of 678-9 in Frisia preaching the gospel to the heathen, and then proceeded to Rome. His case was heard in a council presided over by Pope Agatho, and the decision went in his favour. So he returned to England in 680 armed with papal letters designed to effect his reinstatement in the see of York. But King Ecgfrith disregarded the papal decision, refused to reinstate Wilfrid and flung him into prison for nine months. In 681 he was released, but only on condition that he left Northumbria.

Wilfrid's exile lasted five years (681-6). Most of this period he spent in the kingdom of Sussex, preaching to the heathen under the patronage of its recently-converted king and founding a monastery at Selsey. He also spent some time in Wessex where he was active in the conversion of the inhabitants of the Isle of Wight, recently conquered by King Cadwalla. The king granted Wilfrid a quarter of the island and of the booty he had acquired by conquering it. Wilfrid gave these endowments to one of his nephews. It is an intriguing glimpse of the way in which from a certain aspect Wilfrid's operations were a kind of joint-stock enterprise bringing substantial benefits to his kin.

King Ecgfrith was killed in battle in 685. This marked a turning-point in Wilfrid's fortunes. He and Theodore were reconciled and the new King of Northumbria, Aldfrith, allowed Wilfrid to return as Bishop of York (late 686 or early 687). But he returned to a much diminished diocese. York was now the seat of the bishopric of Deira alone; Bernicia was divided between bishoprics at Lindisfarne, then under Cuthbert, and Hexham. Wilfrid administered the see of York for about five years. However, in 691 or 692 King Aldfrith quarrelled with him and he was again expelled. This time his exile was even longer, and we know less of it. We can trace him from time to time in Mercia, East Anglia and Kent. In 703 (probably) Aldfrith summoned Wilfrid to a council in Northumbria and made it clear that he intended to ruin him by depriving his churches and monasteries of all their endowments. Wilfrid, now in his seventieth year, at once set out for Rome to appeal against this treatment. Pope John VI upheld Wilfrid's case and in 705 he returned to England. Aldfrith of Northumbria died shortly afterwards and his successor Osred allowed Wilfrid back to Northumbria and to the custody of his monasteries. Wilfrid seems to have spent the last four years of his life in Northumbria, but it was at one of his Mercian monasteries, Oundle, that he died in 709.

It is customary to regard Wilfrid's career as turbulent. So indeed it was. But that we think of it thus is mainly because Eddius adopted the *tone* that he did in composing Wilfrid's biography. Other Anglo-Saxon bishops of this period may have had careers as stormy as Wilfrid's, but of which we know nothing. (It is salutary to consider what we might make of Wilfrid if we had only Bede's account of him.) We should resist the temptation – hallowed though it is by a long tradition of English, and especially Anglican historiography – to regard Wilfrid himself as touchy, self-centred and impetuous. When strong personalities come into conflict, hasty words will be uttered, violent actions ensue: of course they will. But the conflicts were not simply those of personality. The controversies in which Wilfrid engaged were genuine controversies. There were hard questions at issue. They had to be thrashed out. They would not just go away.

That conceded, it remains curiously difficult to be sure precisely what the successive controversies were actually about. (This may seem odd: but it arises from the divergences, already mentioned, between our two principal sources, Eddius and Bede.) The initial quarrel with

Ecgfrith of Northumbria was partly caused, we may suspect, by Wilfrid's encouragement of the queen in a vow of virginity. It was hardly calculated to endear him to a king who wanted an heir. The concentration of great landed wealth and ecclesiastical power in Wilfrid's hands aroused the envy of both Ecgfrith and Aldfrith; and behind this lurked knotty legal issues about the terms on which the church held its endowments. Wilfrid's friendship with successive rulers of Mercia was bound to cause apprehension to the rulers of Northumbria whose neighbours and rivals they were. And they were right to be apprehensive. Wilfrid was a kingmaker. In 676 he had supplied Dagobert II, then in exile in Ireland, with an army with which he won his way to the kingship of Austrasia (or East Francia). Wilfrid's chain of monasteries scattered from Hexham to Selsey, housing communities intensely loyal to their founder, constituted a following outside the control of kings whose authority was territorially circumscribed. Neither was it only kings who were envious and apprehensive. Eddius makes it clear that Wilfrid had enemies among the higher clergy of Northumbria, and behind these men (and women) we can sense the network of aristocratic clans from which they came. It was not that Wilfrid was a 'political' bishop; for that is what all bishops necessarily and usually unrepentantly were. But what we call 'politics' in the seventh century were compounded of family and feud, grievance and graft, and frequent violence. Wilfrid did not dictate the terms on which he lived. They were the common currency of a society of aristocratic warriors slowly adapting themselves to Christianity – and Christianity to themselves.

Important issues of principle lay behind Wilfrid's quarrels with two successive Archbishops of Canterbury, Theodore and Brihtwold. Pope Gregory had laid down a plan for the organization of the English church. Theodore's laudable desire to divide big bishoprics into more manageable units seemed, to a Bishop of York, to involve an assertion of the claims of Canterbury which went far beyond what Gregory had stipulated. This was offensive to a cleric of Wilfrid's Roman loyalties and Frankish experience; and when he appealed to Rome, Rome upheld him, though perhaps more hesitantly than he would have wished. Eddius saw these issues as clearcut. But they were not. This troubled Bede, and it has troubled many lesser historians of those conflicts ever since.

Conflict bulks large in contemporary accounts of Wilfrid. But to dwell on this facet of his career is to run the risk of laying insufficient stress on Wilfrid's other doings. He was perhaps the most important agent in the introduction of St Benedict's monastic Rule to England and in its diffusion here. His perception of its potential as an adjunct to evangelization, as for instance at Selsey, may not have gone unnoticed by the young Boniface. He was a patron of scholarship: it is Bede, not Eddius, who tells us that Wilfrid was 'very learned'. His missionary work in Frisia blazed a trail which others were soon to follow, notably his pupil Willibrord. He was the first prominent western churchman to make it his practice to appeal to the pope in the course of litigation; his example was to have very far-reaching effects upon the government of Latin Christendom. His building and embellishment of churches, at Ripon, York, Hexham and elsewhere – like Biscop's at Monkwearmouth and Jarrow – helped to familiarize the English with the dignified aesthetic of the Mediterranean world. The might and magnificence of his episcopal style, which he had learnt from his Frankish mentors Annemundus and Agilbert, may have occasioned anxiety to the stricter sort of churchman such as Bede; but it was an important element in the process of attracting the Anglo-Saxon élite into the church and thus furthering the christianization of the English.

At every point in his career Wilfrid touched the religious life of his countrymen with a current of creative vitality. This was how he was remembered at York. Some eighty years after his death Alcuin wrote that 'his fame shone far and wide by virtue of his achievements.' It was a just assessment.

After Wilfrid's death his body was carried by his grieving followers from Oundle to Ripon for burial. There his relics remained, the focus of a cult, for nearly two and a half centuries. Then, probably in 948, they were removed to Canterbury by Archbishop Oda and reinterred there. By one of history's ironies Wilfrid's mortal remains ended up as one of the most precious possessions of the cathedral church with whose archbishops he had spent so many years locked in conflict.

Further Reading
Eddius's biography of Wilfrid is available in two translations: one by B. Colgrave, *The Life of Bishop Wilfrid by Eddius Stephanus*, 1927, reprinted 1985, and the other by D. H. Farmer in a volume called *The Age of Bede*, 1983.

WILKES, JOHN (1727-97) was a man of no fixed principles who found himself engaged in a series of important constitutional conflicts. His career was active and vivid but historians dwell on it primarily because of the forces he aroused by his demagogic appeal. In the 1760s, when he was most active, English radicalism acquired a new impetus and direction.

He was the son of a wealthy distiller, educated at Leyden University and married, to please his parents, to the daughter of Dr Mead, a wealthy physician. She was ten years older than himself and they separated after she had borne him a daughter. He bought himself both a seat in parliament (Aylesbury) and the colonelcy of the Buckinghamshire Militia. Plausible and reckless, Wilkes lived giddily upon his wits. The devilment of the Hell Fire Club and the somewhat ludicrous blasphemies of the Monks of Medmenham can be evoked today by the curious visitor to the caves above West Wycombe. With Grafton, Dashwood and Sandwich amongst others, he set out to scandalize society, always going a little further, with cards and women, than the orthodox could approve. He had entered politics as the supporter of Pitt, but in 1761, encumbered with debts, he sought advancement from Bute. When Bute refused to make him either ambassador to Constantinople or governor of Quebec, Wilkes applied himself angrily to political journalism.

In the *North Briton*, whose title ostensibly referred to the sinister encroachment of Scotsmen upon English public life, he attacked the ministry in general and Bute and the Peace of 1763 in particular; he was helped by the raffish poet Churchill and more cautiously by Earl Temple, who used him as a political weapon against the ministry. Before the twenty-seventh number of this weekly journal appeared he was threatened with prosecution and had to fight a duel with Lord Talbot. In No. 45 he sailed too close to the wind of royal displeasure, when he described as a falsehood the passage in the king's speech referring to the peace as 'honourable to my crown and beneficial to my people'. The ministry, Grenville, Halifax and Egremont, issued a General Warrant ordering the arrest of all responsible for the *North Briton*'s publication. Halifax, acting as a magistrate, had Wilkes detained in the Tower and his papers searched. When Temple replied defiantly to the government's order to remove Colonel Wilkes from his post as High Sheriff of the county, he was dismissed from his lord lieutenancy. The government stood on treacherous ground. Wilkes, whose detention in the Tower enabled him to pose as a martyr while enjoying the attentions of his friends, secured his release on the grounds of parliamentary privilege. He then used his trial in the Court of Common Pleas in May 1763 to challenge the legality of the government's actions. The Chief Justice of Common Pleas, Pitt's friend, Pratt, put off decision about the legality of General Warrants, but declared that Wilkes was covered by parliamentary immunity since his offence was neither treason, felony, nor a breach of the peace. In his speech to the judge Wilkes said: 'The liberty of all peers and gentlemen and, what touches me more sensibly, that of all the middling and inferior set of people … is in my case this day to be finally decided upon.' He then accused the Secretaries of State of stealing his possessions and published their reply in the form of a pamphlet. In the Court of Common Pleas Pratt ruled against the legality of General Warrants and Wilkes recovered damages against the Under-Secretary of State, Robert Wood. Now he cut himself off from more respectable political associates by his crude appeal to the people.

In November 1763 the House of Commons voted

No. 45 a seditious libel and ordered it to be publicly burned. In the House of Lords Sandwich and Warburton, Bishop of Gloucester, brandished an obscene poem, the *Essay on Woman*, which Wilkes had been privately printing and which they had obtained by bribes, and the publication of pornography was added to the charges against him. Parliament was no longer disposed to allow him the protection of privilege and voted accordingly. Wilkes was wounded painfully in a duel with a Mr Martin, which gave him an excuse for not appearing in parliament. In December he departed for France, in January 1764 he was expelled from the House of Commons. Before the end of the year, as he did not appear to stand trial, he was outlawed. By his excesses Wilkes had contrived to spoil a good case. Nevertheless the opposition made a further issue of the General Warrants and the government won the division on the matter of their legality by only fourteen votes. The majority of members of the counties and the more open boroughs voted against them. The opposition turned to other game, but in the country Wilkes was not so quickly forgotten. The 'Crown and Anchor' clubs went on drinking their toasts to 'Wilkes and Liberty'. The wretch who had been bribed to hand over the *Essay on Woman* could find no-one to employ him, and committed suicide.

In 1768 Wilkes returned from exile and presented himself for election to parliament. He could not persuade the City of London to elect him: he secured 1,247 votes, but was bottom of the poll. The great politicians, the establishment of the city, were no longer prepared to take him seriously, so he looked for support in the restless, fringe-of-town population of Middlesex, where the freeholders were unruly and squires were weak. In the radical parson Horne Tooke, and Mr Serjeant Glynn, an antiquarian lawyer, Wilkes had two unorthodox men to work for his election. With a rowdy troupe of Spitalfields weavers behind him, amidst riots and drunkenness, Wilkes was returned with a majority of 465. He then had himself arrested, which had the desired result of arousing further excitement. On 10 May a man was killed when a crowd who had come to take him to parliament clashed with the troops defending the prison in St George's Fields. The jury at the inquest found a Scottish private guilty of murder (a grand jury at Guildford later found him not guilty) and Wilkes's letters made the most of the theme of 'Scottish butchers'. He escaped the charge of outlawry when Mansfield found an error in the phrasing of the writ. In June, however, he was fined and imprisoned on the original charges. Disorder continued, coming to a climax when his supporter Glynn was elected for the other seat in Middlesex. An ugly situation was developing in London, where strikes and stoppages brought workmen out of overcrowded tenements to roam the streets in protest against the ills of sweated labour. Grafton's ministry seems to have been virtually unanimous in its view that Wilkes should be expelled from parliament. Pratt, now Lord Camden and Lord Chancellor, thought so; as, outside the government, did Fox. In February 1769, on the motion of Barrington, he was expelled, but he aroused support amongst radical members, was elected as alderman for a city ward and then re-elected for Middlesex unopposed. The government could not now withdraw. As he was expelled, re-elected and expelled again, the case narrowed down to an issue of dangerous simplicity: the people versus the House of Commons.

The view of 'the people' in this case could not be mistaken, for when the ministry, in the fourth election, put up Colonel Luttrell against him, the latter was defeated by 1,143 to 296. The House pronounced however that Luttrell had been elected. The justification for this extreme statement of the rights of parliament was that it was necessary to defend its freedom of action in face of an illegal act of coercion – for so Wilkes's action appeared to his opponents. Others, however, saw his expulsion as a sign of the degenerate submission of the Commons to the executive and the court. On this Count Grafton, as the Junius letters show, was especially vulnerable. Wilkes himself could not wait upon the niceties of constitutional debate so, with Horne Tooke to aid him, he appealed again to the people. In February 1768 the Society for the Defence of the Bill of Rights had met for the first time, its object being to get Wilkes into parliament. It was largely middle-class and could raise £16,000 to pay his debts and expenses. A concerted attack of petitions assailed the ministry, none more aggressive than that of the city, which now recognized Wilkes's value as a stick with which to beat the 'corrupt' parliament.

By April 1770, when he came out of prison, Wilkes was representative of a programme, if not actually head of a party. Various opposition groups, Rockingham and Burke, Temple and Grenville, for their respective ends, roused public feeling. Apart from inquiries, for instance into the St George's Fields Massacre, two points may be specially noticed: improvement in the system of trial by jury so as to reduce the power of judges (especially in libel cases) and the right of the public to the whole revenue of India. The aims were too disparate, the organization too weak, for the movement to succeed. The Society of the Bill of Rights split when Wilkes declined to allow its money to be used to pay the expenses of a printer who was jailed for his defiance of Mansfield. Horne Tooke left the movement; Wilkes, who was more interested in his own cause than in radicalism, turned again to the mob. In 1771, when he was elected Sheriff of London, his platform was unabashedly demagogic. He advocated the abolition of the press gang and controlled bread prices. One more clash with the Commons came when they required three journalists to appear before them on the charge of reporting their proceedings. Again the issue was presented in the name of the people, but the real fight was between city and parliament; it was as a city magistrate that Wilkes was involved, when the city authorities refused to hand over Mr Miller of the *Evening Post*. When he, with the Lord Mayor and another city magistrate, was called to the House to answer for their conduct, he reopened his personal grievances. But the prime minister, now Lord North, saw to it that the summons to Wilkes was made out for a day when parliament would not be sitting; he was thus deprived of further opportunities of publicity.

In 1774 Wilkes was elected again for Middlesex and allowed to take his seat. He made little use of it, for now the poacher was turned game-keeper. In 1776 he introduced a bill for parliamentary reform but withdrew it without a division. The initiative passed to other men. Wilkes contented himself with campaigning for the formal expunging of the resolution of February 1769. This was done, and handsomely, in 1782, 'as being subversive of the Rights of the whole body of Electors of this Kingdom'. Meanwhile he had become Chamberlain of the City in 1774 and he had acted with resolution against the mob in 1780, directing the Guards outside the Bank of England. Wilkes had become a respectable and useful citizen, interesting himself in prison reform and religious toleration. To George III, who found him surprisingly civil, he admitted that he 'never was a Wilkite'. He had ever been the cool, sceptical, amused spectator of his own career. In scarlet coat and white-powdered wig, living contentedly with his last mistress, Polly, and several bastard children, he survived into an age which scarce remembered the significance of the phrase engraved on his coffin: 'The remains of John Wilkes, a Friend to Liberty'.

Further Reading

G. Rudé, *Wilkes and Liberty*, 1982.
J. Brewer, 'English Radicalism in the Age of George III' in J. G. A. Pocock, ed., *Three British Revolutions*, 1980.
I. R. Christie, *Wilkes, Wyvill and Reform*, 1962.
P. Quennell, *Four Portraits*, 1945.

WILKIE, SIR DAVID (1785-1841), painter, was one of the long line of 'sons of the manse' who have won fame south of the Border. His father was minister of the village of Cults, in Fife, and no doubt viewed with circumspection the hardening resolve of his third son to become an artist. But such was the boy's talent that eventually he was sent away to study art at the Trustees' Academy in Edinburgh. In 1804 he returned to Cults, and there painted his first important picture in the style which was to make him famous. It is a genre painting, a study of the neighbouring fair of Pitlessie, and, although wanting in colour-sense, it is a remarkably fresh and vigorous observation of village life. Its success led to

portrait-commissions in the neighbourhood, but that did not satisfy him; in the summer of 1805 he took ship for London, and entered the Academy Schools.

He made the most of the opportunity, which in those days only London offered, to study the old masters. As might be expected from *Pitlessie Fair*, he was profoundly impressed by Teniers, the Flemish genre painter of the seventeenth century; and it was on the strength of *Pitlessie Fair*, which the buyer had lent to Wilkie to show to would-be patrons, that he obtained from Lord Mansfield the order for *The Village Politicians*. He proceeded with other genre paintings in the Dutch and Flemish manner, with undertones of Hogarth: one of the best is *The Blind Fiddler*, commissioned by Sir George Beaumont, whose sensible and generous patronage of young artists is a feature of these years. Such paintings made a rapid success for Wilkie. The tall and ungainly youth, with his thatch of sandy hair, his east-coast intonation, and his truly Scottish incapacity for seeing a joke, was yet so well received that he was elected ARA in 1809, although eight days short of the minimum age, and RA two years later.

In 1810 his work was interrupted by the first serious onset of a type of neurasthenia which made him virtually incapable of working. Nevertheless in 1812 appeared *Village Festival* (for John Julius Angerstein, the connoisseur whose collection formed the basis of the National Gallery), and *Blindman's Buff*, a picture in which the energetic movement of a crowd of children is held in splendid balance. Soon after came *The Letter of Introduction*, where a dour bachelor, in dressing-gown and skull-cap, scrutinizes the references of a self-conscious young aspirant. Wilkie's reputation travelled abroad: in 1820 he finished, for the King of Bavaria, *The Reading of the Will* (Munich), perhaps the climax of his genre painting. The family has gathered round the lawyer in the parlour of the deceased, but what a family it is! – drawn in a crescent from the tender figure by the fire, patiently awaiting the best or the worst, to the florid lady of uncertain years, who has burst in on the proceedings, somewhat late, but claiming all for herself. It seems that he studied to express in a single picture the whole range of human emotion; and the picture is lovingly perfected to the last detail. About the same time he painted, for the Duke of Wellington, *Chelsea Pensioners Reading the Gazette of the Battle of Waterloo* (1822: Apsley House). When exhibited, it was phenomenally popular: people queued to see it.

In 1822, George IV paid the first royal visit to Scotland since the Union. Scott was master of ceremonies; Raeburn was knighted; Turner was there, filling his sketchbook as usual – and so was Wilkie. For him, the fruit of the expedition was two large commemorative paintings: a life-size full-length portrait of the kilted monarch, a little flattering, and the gorgeous *Entry of George IV into*

Holyrood House. By the time these were finished, the interest of Sir Robert Peel, and the personal knowledge of the king derived from the one or two sittings which he gave for the Scottish pictures, secured for Wilkie the position of King's Limner for Scotland, which fell vacant on Raeburn's death in 1823.

But in 1824 Wilkie had a recurrence of his nervous illness, induced by overwork and family troubles. He travelled abroad for three years and, while he gradually recovered his health, he imbibed ideas which were to alter fundamentally the character of his work. Especially he was influenced by the paintings of Velasquez which he saw in Madrid. On his return his technique becomes much looser and broader. He seems to have thought that his earlier works were too laboured, and to have attempted a more rapid execution. His figures are now no longer simply part of the pattern, but fill the canvas. These are fine pictures – the huge *Sir David Baird Finding the Body of Tippoo Sahib* (Edinburgh Castle) is one of the finest – but they are not unique, and there were many who regretted his deserting his familiar vein. In 1836 he was knighted, and in 1840 set out for the Holy Land in search of fresh material. He died at sea off Malta on his way back. There was a nationwide outburst of regret, but the most eloquent tribute was Turner's *Peace: Burial of Wilkie at Sea* (1842: Tate).

Wilkie's habit of working a species of bitumen even into his highlights, so as to avoid the 'chalkiness' which he abhorred, and to give more depth to his shadows, has caused many of his paintings to darken and crack. It is therefore all the harder for us to account for the enormous respect in which he was held by contemporary artists. John Martin placed Wilkie alongside Leonardo and Raphael and other imperishable giants in his *Last Judgement* of 1853. Nevertheless Wilkie brought English genre painting to its highest pitch since Hogarth; he had many followers in the nineteenth century; and it is a part of the simplicity of his character that, unlike Hogarth, he was innocent of social satire. Sir Robert Peel, as he lay dying, asked that Wilkie's *John Knox Preaching* (1832: Tate) should be placed within his sight.

Further Reading
A. Cunningham, *Life of Sir David Wilkie*, 1843.

WILKINS, JOHN (1614-72), scientist and divine, the son of an Oxford goldsmith, was born at Fawsley in Northamptonshire; his maternal grandfather was John 'Decalogue' Dod, joint-author with Robert Cleaver of the Puritan treatise on the Ten Commandments. Wilkins went to New Inn Hall and thence to Magdalen Hall, and after a short spell as Vicar of Fawsley became Chaplain to the Puritan peer Lord Saye and Sele and later to Charles Lewis, Elector Palatine. He sided with parliament and took the Covenant. Yet his real interests were

scientific. Evelyn calls him 'universally curious'. His first book – not very distinguished – was *Discovery of a New World, or Discourse On the World in the Moon* (1638), and Aubrey refers to 'Dr Wilkins his notion of an Umbrella-like invention for retarding a ship when she drives in a storm'. He was an energetic member of Robert Boyle's 'invisible college' in London from 1645 onwards. In 1648 he was appointed Warden of Wadham, a mark of his loyalty to the parliamentarian cause rather than of his learning. Yet it was a good appointment for the college and for Oxford. Wilkins, moderate and humane, in Burnet's startling tribute 'the wisest clergyman I ever knew', set firm academic standards and safeguarded the university both from the anti-intellectualism of the extremer Puritans and from the worst consequences of military rule. No doubt his marriage in 1656 to Robina, the widowed sister of Cromwell, made his task easier. Meanwhile the meetings of the London philosophers were continued at Wadham, with Wilkins at their centre. Out of them, after the Restoration, grew the Royal Society: Wilkins took the chair at the meeting held in 1660 to discuss this project, and was the first secretary after the society was chartered, so he has probably more claim than anyone else to be regarded as the principal figure in the foundation. He quickly made his peace with the Crown and with Anglicanism, and in 1668 was consecrated Bishop of Chester. That same year Pepys was busily reading Wilkins's *An Essay towards a Real Character and a Philosophical Language*, and next year he recorded – as 'foolish talk' – a rumour that Wilkins was to be made Lord Treasurer. Wilkins died in 1672. He was neither a distinguished scientist nor an outstanding scholar, but both the Royal Society and the University of Oxford owe him a great debt.

Further Reading
B. Shapiro, *John Wilkins: An Intellectual Biography*, 1969.
Margery Parver and E. J. Bowen, *The Beginning of the Royal Society*, 1960.

WILKINSON, JOHN (1728-1808), ironmaster, was one of the inventive and forceful personalities who helped to mould the industrial revolution. He grew up in the iron tradition, for his father, Isaac Wilkinson, was a resourceful ironmaster who took out patents for a number of inventions, the last being an iron blowing engine for coke-smelting iron ore. Other men grew rich on improvements on his ideas, but he died insolvent. His son, meanwhile, was sent to a dissenting academy at Kendal, typical of those schools which were such a valuable nursery of thoughtful and inventive minds.

Wilkinson married twice, in 1755 and 1763; both wives brought him the money which was a vital condition of success. Another was demand for his product: this was provided by the Seven Years' War and the expansion of armaments that went with it. In 1757 he set up the first furnace in the Black Country to produce coke-smelted iron, at Bradley. At the same time he became technical adviser to a consortium of Bristol merchants and Shropshire landowners who were building a foundry at Willey, on the opposite side of the river from the Darby works at Coalbrookdale. The pattern of the iron industry was changing fast, from small forges, charcoal-burning and scattered in forest areas, to the coal and iron-stone areas. East Shropshire, round the Severn, where now all is green or preserved in an admirable open-air museum, then provided the raw materials, and river transport as well. Wilkinson soon acquired complete control of Willey new furnace and directed the operations of his growing industrial empire from Broseley until, in 1779, he went to live in lonely state at Castlehead, Grange-over-Sands.

In 1762 he went into partnership with his father at Bersham, near Wrexham, producing naval cannon, piping of every sort and parts for the new steam engines. He perfected his father's blowing machine, and ousted him from active concern in the works. In 1774 he took out his patent for boring cannon from solid castings, by rotating the piece while keeping the boring bar steady. He also developed a cylinder-boring lathe on the opposite principle. These improvements gave England a vital lead in the production of arms. The French were concerned about the relative ineffectiveness of their cannon and secured the services of Wilkinson's brother William to build and equip a new ironworks. Technology then knew no frontiers. But there grew up later a damaging myth that John Wilkinson supplied the French with arms. In fact all he had done was to supply the Paris Waterworks Company with forty miles of iron piping – for which English travellers may have had cause to be grateful.

In the 1770s Bradley and Birmingham were linked by canal; by then Wilkinson was already supplying Boulton with castings. Now the success of the partnership of Boulton and Watt in the manufacture of steam engines owed much to the accurate castings and borings of Wilkinson's works. The American War brought great prosperity to the 'Iron Parliament', as it was called. Wilkinson spread out in other directions too, with interests in the copper industry of Cornwall, where he came to own six mines outright, and in the lead mines of north Wales. But as his concerns grew more extensive, troubles of every sort overtook him. He had no male heir and he could find no satisfactory lieutenant. Eventually he took a nephew, Thomas Jones, into his service. He quarrelled with his brother when he returned from France, and years were spent on wasteful disputes and an expensive suit in Chancery. He broke with Boulton and Watt when they found that he had been pirating their steam engine designs. They extracted large sums from him in compensation and then erected their own foundry.

In the 1790s Cort's new process of iron-making set an example of cheaper production which he was reluctant to follow. Technical difficulties were accompanied by a decline in his private life. He had always been a difficult man, wilful and imperious. When his only child married a Shropshire clergyman without his consent he 'vowed never to speak to her again'. While his second wife was still living at Castlehead, in about 1800, he took himself a mistress, Ann Lewis, who bore him three children. He later declared them legitimate, which led on his death to a further Chancery dispute instigated by Thomas Jones, who had hoped to succeed to his uncle.

When the old ironmaster died, he was already something of a legend. His iron bridge, iron barges, the iron pulpit, window sills and tombstones of Coalbrookdale Church, were daily reminders of the iron revolution which he had fostered. For all his coarseness he was a man of literate tastes. His interests were wide; he reclaimed land, founded banks, invested in canals. He minted his own copper coinage, for the convenient payment of workmen in his various concerns, and the profile of his strong features was familiar to many who never saw him in the flesh. He was painted by Gainsborough; his brother-in-law was Joseph Priestley. He touched the life of his time at many points. But at the end all was narrowed down to his ruling passion. At his own request he was buried in an iron coffin under an iron obelisk. It was said that, on the seventh anniversary of his death, he would revisit his blast furnaces on his grey horse – and on 14 July 1815, several thousand people assembled at Bradley to see the event. This was a substantial man indeed whose anticipated ghost could arouse such excitement.

Further Reading

W. H. Chaloner, *People and Industries*, 1963.
T. S. Ashton, *Iron and Steel in the Industrial Revolution*, 1924.

WILLEHAD, ST (*d.*789) was the first Bishop of Bremen in north Germany. He was educated in his native Northumbria, possibly at York with his contemporary Alcuin: the two men certainly knew one another in later life. Desiring to work as a missionary among the Frisians after the example of his fellow countryman Willibrord, Willehad was despatched across the North Sea with the blessing of a Northumbrian synod convoked by King Alchred (765-74), who was himself keenly interested in the progress of the Anglo-Saxon missions and a correspondent of Lul, the successor of Boniface in the see of Mainz: this would have been in about 770. He worked in Frisia for the next ten years.

In 780 he was sent by the Frankish King Charles (that is, Charles the Great or Charlemagne, 768-814) to work among the Saxons in the lower valleys of the rivers Elbe and Weser. Charles was at that time engaged in the gradual and ruthless conquest of Saxony and its incorporation into the Frankish kingdom. Two years later the Saxons rebelled under their leader Widukind against Frankish dominion. Willehad managed to escape from Saxony – several of his associates were killed – and after a pilgrimage to Rome settled at the monastery of Echternach, which had been founded by Willibrord and was at the time under the rule of an English abbot named Beornred, himself a relative of Willibrord and later to be Archbishop of Sens. Willehad spent two years there (783-5), engaged in teaching and writing. In 785 he returned to Saxony which Charles was engaged in pacifying, where he may have been responsible for the baptism of Widukind on his submission. In 787 he was consecrated Bishop of Bremen, the first episcopal see to be established in Saxony. But he did not live long enough to supervise the setting-up of the new Christian establishment. He died in 789 only a few days after the consecration of his new cathedral.

WILLIAM I, known as the Bastard or the Conqueror (*c*.1028-87; Duke of Normandy 1035-87; King of England 1066-87) exemplified with unsurpassed clarity a favoured theme of medieval writers, the unexpected turns of Fortune's wheel. He overcame adversities of birth, circumstances and opposition to seize the most glittering prize of the century and to die the most feared and respected ruler of his age. His deeds resounded through Europe and remain to this day a source of controversy and debate, of admiration and horror. If in no other respect, the accession of a Duke of Normandy and his heirs to the English throne fundamentally altered the perspective of English politics by opening an inescapably intimate continental dimension which formed a major theme of English history for the next few centuries and provided the chief distinctive feature of post-Conquest English history.

Born the illegitimate son of Robert the Devil, Duke of Normandy and Herleve, daughter of Fulbert of Falaise, allegedly a tanner, William was recognized in 1034 by the Norman magnates as heir to the duchy on the insistence of his father, who was about to embark on a pilgrimage to Jerusalem. Robert's death in Asia Minor on his return from the Holy Sepulchre in 1035 provoked a long and bitter struggle for power within and beyond the ducal dynasty during which ducal authority crumbled and from which William himself barely escaped with his life. It is said that his guardians were less fortunate: two were murdered; another poisoned and a fourth, the seneschal Osbern, killed in the very room in which the young duke was sleeping. William's survival largely depended on the assistance of Henry I, King of France, whose intervention culminated in the defeat of the anti-ducal rebels from Lower Normandy at Valès-Dunes in 1047. However, in the face of continued internal dissent, the rise of a hostile Anjou to the south

and a change in French policy, William's position was precarious until a French invasion was repulsed at Mortemer in 1054.

William's subsequent consolidation of control over both church and magnates depended crucially upon military success and his consequent ability to reward loyalty, attract support and punish opposition. Northern France, a patchwork of competing lordships and conflicting claims of allegiance, offered considerable scope for a vigorous and well-organized power. Between 1054 and 1064 William extended his influence and authority to Ponthieu, the Norman Vexin, Brittany and Maine. A Flemish alliance was achieved by his marriage (*c*.1051) to Matilda (*d*.1083) the diminutive but forceful daughter of Baldwin V, Count of Flanders. William also allied with the Counts of Boulogne. This network of alliances proved vital when William planned his invasion of England. Norman expansionism was considerably assisted by the chance of the deaths of Henry of France and Count Geoffrey Martel of Anjou in 1060. Both had been hostile to William's advances but were replaced respectively by a sympathetic minority government in France and a succession dispute in Anjou.

William, as all medieval rulers, relied for his success on co-operation with leading landholders and the church. The Norman military aristocracy was of recent creation and heavily dependent on ducal patronage. The church was dominated by prelates appointed either from the ducal and other noble families (such as William's uncle Mauger at Rouen or his half-brother Odo at Bayeux) or by ducal appointment (such as Lanfranc of Pavia at Bec and Caen). William's skill lay in identifying mutual self-interest: lands and military activity for the lay aristocracy; ducal patronage for ecclesiastical reform, endowments, buildings and the fashionable Truce of God movement for churchmen. The Truce of God movement, supported by William's government as early as 1042, required knights to swear to keep the peace for specified periods and to police that agreement, if necessary by taking arms against transgressors. For William this was a highly convenient combination of political control, social cohesion and ecclesiastical authority all under ducal protection.

The eleventh century saw acquisitive lords and knights from Normandy seek their fortunes far beyond the confines of the duchy, in the eastern Mediterranean, southern Italy and England. William's great-aunt, Emma, a daughter of Duke Richard I, married, in turn, Ethelred the Unready (King of England 978-1016) and Cnut (King of England 1016-35). Her son by Ethelred, Edward, spent his exile after 1016 at the Norman court and after becoming king himself in 1042 he introduced a number of Normans into England, notably his nephew Ralph the Timid as Earl of Hereford and Robert Champart of Jumièges successively as Bishop of London and, briefly, Archbishop of Canterbury. Whether the childless Edward offered William the inheritance of the throne in 1051-2, as Norman propagandists insisted after the Conquest, must remain speculation. Despite some evident falsehoods in the Norman version, it is possible that Edward took the opportunity of the disgrace of the powerful Godwins to cement an Anglo-Norman alliance and solve the chronic uncertainty over the succession. However, other sources, no less partisan and unreliable than the Norman chroniclers, tell different stories. Perhaps it is worth noting that in 1051-2 Edward had a number of male relatives closer in blood than William; that William was far from secure in Normandy; that it would have been gross political folly for Edward to close options so soon and so completely; and that, despite later Godwin special pleading and Westminster Abbey hagiography, Edward himself could have expected to have heirs, especially as he had just put aside his first wife presumably in the hope of a second, fruitful marriage. If an attempt is made to reconcile the various accounts, Norman, Scandinavian, Godwin and non-Godwin English, then Edward must appear the most eccentric, foolish and politically profligate and devious ruler in English history, promising his throne to anybody, indeed everybody, as whim and circumstance dictated. The fact is that there are no trustworthy sources for the period leading up to 1066. All are to some extent wise after the event and concerned to justify or explain or refute. Above all, the Norman writers, William of Poitiers and William of Jumièges are apologists determined to establish William's claim. But as they wrote after 1066, their interpretation cannot, as many modern historians have done, be taken at face or perhaps any value.

What can be suggested is that by 1064 William was interested in the succession to England as a natural further extension of his power, especially as he could – and did – assert a dynastic claim. Edward may actually have been trying to secure William's support for a non-Norman inheritance by sending to him Godwin hostages and then, in 1064, Harold Godwinson himself, the leading magnate in England. It is clear from Norman and English written sources, and the Bayeux Tapestry (perhaps devised under the patronage of Odo of Bayeux at Canterbury, a suggestion lent some support by its similarities to the account of 1066 by the Canterbury monk Eadmer) that the 1064 embassy of Harold was a diplomatic triumph for William. Eadmer even records Edward's sharp displeasure at the turn of events, an image perhaps preserved in the Bayeux Tapestry's cringing figure of Harold reporting back to an admonishing Edward. According to the Norman sources, Harold had sworn to be William's man and to help him secure the English succession. Whatever the truth, just as he confidently insisted on the legitimacy of his rights to overlordship in Brittany, the Vexin or Maine, William portrayed himself as believing in his absolute right to the English throne, a posture lent subsequent validity by friendly propagandists, supported by the verdict of events.

On hearing that Harold had been crowned King of England after Edward's death (January 1066), William began elaborate preparations. In a series of councils he attracted the support of his nobles. He publicized his claim at the Papal Curia, emphasizing the oath-breaking of Harold and the irregularities of the English church, which would be grist to the slow, sure-grinding mills of the holier-than-thou, purist élite then in control of the papacy. He received the blessing and a banner from Pope Alexander II, a signal, as he saw it, of the justice of his cause. Throughout, William laid claim to what modern historians call the moral high ground: at Hastings he wore a necklace of holy relics. His patronage of militant clerics and the Truce of God movement bore spectacular fruit.

William's wealth, reputation and carefully laid diplomacy attracted lords, knights and mercenaries from all over France and, it was said, beyond. Throughout the summer of 1066, ships were built and fitted in the Channel ports; equipment and horses were gathered. Modern assessments of the scale of William's enterprise tend to be conditioned by the weight of evidence. Yet, as we do not have much information about earlier amphibious operations, which, in English history, go back at least to Edwin of Northumbria's attack on the Isle of Man in the 620s, we should be wary of investing William's preparations with a uniqueness which may only be apparent because of the surviving evidence. Angles, Saxons, Jutes, Franks, Danes, Swedes and Norwegians, all had invasion fleets. Was William's so different?

William had not only isolated Harold diplomatically, but had also probably been in contact with Harold's brother Tostig and Harald Hadrada who were themselves planning an attack on England. A bloody crisis was inevitable, the tension being heightened by the appearance of Halley's Comet in the spring of 1066. In August William assembled his fleet in the River Dives, but contrary winds, and, perhaps, knowledge of English defences, delayed his sailing. The fleet was transferred to St Valéry on the Somme whence, at dusk on 27 September, it embarked for England, arriving, unopposed and intact, at Pevensey the next morning. The English defensive forces in the south had been disbanded on 8 September, as William probably knew, and Harold was in the north, having just defeated and killed Tostig and Hadrada at Stamford Bridge (25 September). The ensuing campaign showed William's skill and his luck in equal proportions. Establishing a fortified base at Hastings, William proceeded with the normal medieval tactic of concerted pillaging with the intention of drawing

Harold to precipitate action. It worked. Arriving with a hastily levied army, Harold offered battle immediately. The battle of Hastings, fought on Saturday, 14 October 1066, left Harold and his brothers dead, his army destroyed and the road to London and the Crown open. William had barely survived the battle himself, but he acquitted himself well as a field commander in what was his first pitched battle in sole charge (Henry I took the lead at Val-ès-Dunes and William was not at Mortemer). The rarity of set-piece battles is a feature of warfare in this period, some great warlords, for example Henry II of England (1154-89), never fighting any battles at all. Hastings reminds us why.

After a cleverly conceived and ruthlessly executed campaign of devastation, William forced the submission of the surviving English magnates, led by Aldred, Archbishop of York, the legitimist claimant, Edgar Atheling and the Earls Edwin and Morkere. The military *fait accompli* was sanctified on Christmas Day, 1066 when William was hallowed King of the English in Westminster Abbey, a scene of reconciliation and acceptance, William being attended not only by his French companions but also his English nobles and bishops. By adding an arc to the crown of Edward the Confessor, a sign of almost imperial pretensions, William indicated the grandeur of his designs in the British Isles.

The manner in which William held his kingdom was as impressive as the way in which it had been won. Between 1067 and 1075 a succession of rebellions were dealt with firmly. In one nine-month period in 1068 the new king subdued Exeter, parts of the west country and Midlands and York. The northern rising in 1069, when native earls allied with Scandinavian invaders, led to a winter campaign of deliberate cruelty. The so-called Harrying of the North lasted three months (January-March 1070), embraced parts of Wales, Lincolnshire, Yorkshire, Teesdale, Chester and Stafford, and left areas of Yorkshire wasted for a generation. Calculated violence was a noted and consistent instrument of William's policy. Twenty years earlier he had ordered that thirty-two citizens of Alençon have their hands and feet cut off, ostensibly because they had jeered at his illegitimacy, but more probably to encourage loyalty from this vital frontier town in southern Normandy. By the end of 1071, the Danish fleet had been paid off and Hereward the Wake flushed out of his base at Ely. William's régime fell heavily on French as well as English, but its effectiveness was not in doubt, as witnessed by the suppression of the 1075 revolt of the French Earls of Norfolk and Hereford in the king's absence.

Although there was little threat from Wales, the King of Scotland, Malcolm III (Canmore), eagerly fished in the troubled waters of English politics. In response, in 1072 in an effort to secure his northern frontier as he had his northern subjects, William launched one of his most remarkable campaigns. In a classic demonstration of the use of concentrated military aggression in pursuit of political advantage, William marched his army, shadowed by a fleet, up the east coast as far as the Tay where, at Abernethy, a cowed Malcolm was forced to come to terms. This, as all William's military success, was based on the employment of disciplined troops, mainly household knights and mercenaries, mobility and castles, such as those at Hastings, Exeter, Dover, London, Newcastle, Warwick and York built variously as part of aggressive military strategy, as focal points for controlling an occupied country and as centres of administration.

From 1072 William could concentrate on France, in particular his ambitions in Brittany, Maine and the Vexin. Defeats at Dol (1076) and Gerberoi (1079) at the hands of Norman rebels, and the disloyalty of his brother Odo and his eldest son Robert Curthose, placed William on the defensive in his later years, which makes his achievements in England the more remarkable.

With interests so far flung, William had to rely on a small group of faithful magnates, men such as his half-brother Robert of Mortain, William FitzOsbern, Roger of Beaumont, Bishop Geoffrey of Coutances and Archbishop Lanfranc. Their consistent support says much for William's ability to inspire loyalty. After the risings of the late 1060s and the execution of Earl Waltheof in 1076 for complicity in the 1075 rebellion, attempts to reconcile the surviving English lords were abandoned. By the end of his reign power and property had shifted wholesale from Englishmen to Frenchmen or Normans. The Domesday Survey of 1086 recorded only five per cent of the land held by members of the families of pre-Conquest owners, not all of them English, and only two Englishmen, Coleswein of Lincoln and Thorkell of Arden, held land directly from the king. The church presents the same picture. After 1070 many English bishops were dismissed and no new Englishmen were appointed. William and his archbishop, Lanfranc, introduced reforms in ecclesiastical law and diocesan organization based on continental models.

The tenurial, aristocratic and ecclesiastical revolution was sweeping and profound, but it was consequent on the replacement of English with French landlords and the new interests of the rulers rather than on any deliberate or accidental alterations of the structure of society, landholding or law. William did not introduce a new system of 'feudalism'. English thegns had held land in return for military service for centuries, their obligations becoming more regulated as the demands of central government became more effective. If William and his successors introduced a more precise method of assessing obligation, *servitium debitum*, and the so-called knights' fee, that was because of their need for defined resources to support their wars. The technology of war in pre-1066 England was not so very different from that in pre-1066

Normandy, as shown, for example, in the Bayeux Tapestry and descriptions of thegns' military equipment contained in Old English law codes. The new rulers were careful to assert that their land was held in all respects in the same way and with the same rights as those enjoyed by their English predecessors. Even the great Oath of Salisbury (1086), seen by some historians as demonstrating the feudalization of England, can be compared with the general oaths imposed by English kings over the previous century. What undoubtedly changed, not immediately but inexorably, was the idiom describing and defining tenurial relationships among the landed élite and, in a similar process, the language and articulation of the law. An early example of French management of an English system of rule is found in the record of the Penenden Heath inquiry (c.1072) into the rights in Kent of Archbishop Lanfranc and Odo of Bayeux. Although the case involved two leading tenants of the king, it was heard in the traditional English shire court. Although the presiding justice was the Norman Geoffrey of Coutances, he called upon the legal knowledge of the deposed English Bishop of Selsey, Aethelric: English law in a French context. What affected the French rulers was suitably rearticulated. What did not, namely the activities of the mass of the population, for example the manorial system, continued to develop as if Hastings had not been fought.

In 1066 England possessed a mature structure of government, administration and law, in most respects the superior to those of France and Normandy. William always insisted that he was a legitimate English king who respected English customs as surely as any of his predecessors. He wanted England to exploit not to change. Many historians have claimed that the Normans 'modernized' England. Recently, however, it has been observed how incompetently the new rulers managed traditional mechanisms of royal control, for instance the shire system and the coinage. Certainly, William's chief concern was less to understand the intricacies of English administrative habits than to obtain money in order to enhance and protect his position, especially in France. This desire attracted contemporary accusations of avarice and extortion. But, as the last crisis of his reign illustrates, William was no simple-minded thug.

At Christmas 1085, faced by the prospect of a huge Danish invasion and a fresh continental campaign, William and his advisers ordered the compilation of the Domesday Survey, which appears to have had the dual purpose of identifying the bases for innumerable disputes over possession of land and of reassessing income from property preliminary to a new, increased land tax. The resulting Domesday Book, although overtaken as an immediate administrative weapon by William's death, stands as a unique monument to English governmental tradition and Norman political initiative, and provides information unparalleled for any eleventh-century kingdom. At Salisbury, on 1 August 1086, William, about to depart for Normandy, extracted oaths of loyalty from his tenants-in-chief and their followers (one source says their knights; others their tenants).

Such harnessing of clear perceptions of political and fiscal needs with vigorous military and administrative action is typical of William's role. If not all his ambitions were achieved, if Maine and the French Vexin remained outside his grasp, if luck had played a vital role throughout his career, William's achievements remain stupendous. Determined, energetic, ruthless, William possessed a personality and practical intelligence which, more often than many rulers in history, allowed him to dominate his contemporaries and to control his destiny, from the precarious life of a hunted bastard to the most powerful position in western Europe. William's success transformed the political map of Europe and the course of English history. The Norman Conquest gave English politics a fresh context, English government and law a different language, English society a new ruling class, and English culture an additional perspective.

William himself was impressive in manner and, on the evidence of a surviving bone recovered after the desecration of his tomb during the French Revolution, tall (c.5ft 10ins). Contemporary physical descriptions are almost entirely formal, although he may have had a noticeably harsh voice, and, like so many medieval aristocrats, have run to fat. A man of at least conventional piety, he was an active and generous patron of the church. He died at St Gervais near Rouen on 9 September 1087, his final illness possibly resulting from a riding accident suffered during a characteristically vicious attack on Mantes. Active to the end in pursuit of his interests, William was a man who seized his opportunities with unrivalled vigour, and, as many contemporaries said, with unrivalled cruelty as well. Whatever judgement is made on the nature and extent of his influence on his time and his new kingdom, whether he is regarded as cypher or architect, William the Conqueror was and is one of the most notable figures in English history.

Further Reading
D. Bates, *William the Conqueror*, 1989.
D. C. Douglas, *William the Conqueror*, 1964.

WILLIAM II (c.1060-1100; King of England 1087-1100) has attracted more personal opprobrium than most English kings. His relatively brief reign has tended to be recalled for his morals, bad language, viciousness and dramatic death, not for his achievement in mastering the Anglo-Norman lands and, from inauspicious beginnings, becoming one of the most feared and respected rulers of his time.

William was the third, but second surviving, son of

William the Conqueror. His red face as much as his hair earned him the nickname Rufus. Unlike his eldest brother Robert Curthose, the younger William remained conspicuously loyal to his father during the family conflicts of the 1070s and 1080s: he was wounded at Gerberoi (1079) fighting against a rebellious coalition led by Curthose. His reward was designation as heir to England by the Conqueror on his deathbed in 1087, even though William had previously received no lands or titles. Seizing his opportunity with speed, William was crowned by Archbishop Lanfranc at Westminster on 26 September 1087, only seventeen days after his father's death at Rouen. Curthose, supported by his uncle Odo of Bayeux, refused to accept the division of the Anglo-Norman lands and disputed the succession in England. But after a short, vigorous campaign in 1088, Rufus suppressed opposition in England, in the process establishing his reputation as an effective warrior.

Between 1090 and 1096, Rufus bent his energy to consolidate his kingdom and reunite the Anglo-Norman dominions. He regularly invaded Normandy and, by vigorous military action and a skilful use of money, he managed to occupy or gain the allegiance of large parts of the duchy. In 1091, in alliance with Curthose, he ousted his younger brother Henry from the Cotentin in western Normandy, but from 1094 he and Henry co-operated against Robert. William's task was made easier by Curthose's failings as a ruler. An ineffectual politician, Curthose was unable to control his self-interested nobility. Instead, he fell back on a rootless charm and a name for bravery: he was no match for William. In 1096, the First Crusade provided unexpected relief for Robert and opportunity for William. In return for a mortgage of 10,000 marks to pay his brother's crusade expenses (raised in England by a heavy and unpopular tax of four shillings to the hide), William received the whole duchy for three years in pledge. From 1096 de facto Duke of Normandy, Rufus had reunited his father's possessions with much of the Conqueror's skill, determination and opportunism.

In England, apart from the civil war in 1088 and a revolt by the Mowbrays in 1095, Rufus's main concern was the protection of his frontiers. He campaigned against the Welsh (1095 and 1097) and Scots (1091) and in 1092 Cumbria was annexed. In 1097 Rufus was behind the establishment of Edgar as King of Scots who then acknowledged him as overlord. However, France continued to be Rufus's main concern as he attempted to make good his father's claims to the Vexin (1097-8) and Maine (1098 and 1099). Rufus's ambition ranged widely. With his bullish and seemingly limitless self-confidence, some even thought he aspired to the French Crown itself. He certainly cut a rather more impressive figure than the obese and lethargic King Philip. A characteristically bold plan to annexe Aquitaine in the same

manner as he had acquired Normandy, through a mortgage for the Count of Poitiers departing on crusade, was thwarted only by Rufus's death on 2 August 1100 when he was killed by a stray arrow while hunting deer in the New Forest.

The king's sudden death was a political sensation and a moralist's dream. No respecter of ecclesiastical privileges, William in death attracted the censure and hostile comment that few dared address to him in life. To die without time to confess or repent sins was seen as particularly awful in the Middle Ages, a judgement of God. Lurid stories filled with blood-curdling omens were soon embroidered around the fatal hunt. The reality was probably more chaotic than dramatic. Hunting accidents were commonplace: William's own brother, Richard, had been killed in the New Forest c.1070 and a nephew, a bastard of Curthose, had suffered an almost identical fate to William's only three months earlier. Some historians have smelt conspiracy rather than divine retribution in the king's death. Its timing was opportune for Henry, Rufus's younger brother, to seize the throne before Curthose had reached Normandy on return from his crusade. The man who most probably fired the deadly arrow, Walter Tirel of Poix, was a connection of the Clares who were close adherents of Henry. What we know of Henry suggests that he stopped at little that stood between him and his ambition. Cruel, violent, unsqueamish and unscrupulous, in fact just like Rufus, Henry, who happened to be one of the king's fellow hunters, certainly took full advantage of the situation. But beyond the circumstantial there is no evidence of premeditation: Henry's chance was fortuitous, not planned. Of that, contemporaries were more or less unanimous.

One cause of the suspicious, hostile, sanctimonious and scurrilous accounts in ecclesiastical chronicles of Rufus's life and death was his relationship with the church. Not only was his quarrel with Archbishop Anselm of Canterbury notorious, but his concerted exploitation of church land, especially during deliberately prolonged episcopal vacancies (during which time the king enjoyed the bishopric's revenues), earned him the posthumous dislike of clerical writers, ever fearful for their collective and corporate rights, privileges and, always, income. The confrontation with Anselm has received so much attention largely because of the work of Anselm's biographer and companion, Eadmer. It is worth noting, however, that despite the later clerical disapproval and condescension, Rufus never lost his grip on what he regarded as his church. Some writers, such as Orderic Vitalis, evidently preferred a vigorous if brusque ruler to the inept drift of a Curthose, even if strict canonical immunities suffered. The conflict with Anselm was unusual, if predictable. In 1088, Archbishop Lanfranc had sided with the king in deciding that the Bishop of

Durham, William of St Calais, a rebel sympathizer, should be answerable in the royal court as a tenant-in-chief and not be able to claim clerical immunity or appeal to the pope. This was Norman convention. Anselm himself was only too willing to co-operate with royal power: in 1096, for example, he and Rufus combined to prevent some monks of Cerne Abbas from illegally setting out on crusade. In principle, Anselm had little objection to working with the monarch. However, his over-precise academic intellect made him a tactless, over-fastidious and undiplomatic coadjutor of a king who suffered fools marginally better than those he deemed muddle-headed or obstructive. From William's point of view, Anselm was both. Their relations were fraught from the beginning, when, in 1093, a dangerously ill William had, in fear for his soul, forced a reluctant Anselm to become archbishop. Much of the antagonism was based on personal and local issues: the archbishop's military contribution; whether the archbishop or king had the right to decide which of two competing popes to recognize; and the right of the archbishop unilaterally to appeal to Rome. Although failing to oust Anselm at the Council of Rockingham (1095), Rufus managed to force the archbishop into exile in 1097 to the king's considerable financial and political benefit. It may be significant that none of Anselm's episcopal colleagues saw fit to share his exile: the dispute was between the king and archbishop, not state against church. Up to his death, Rufus was the clear winner.

The ineffective eccentricity of Anselm was the familiar consequence of the don in politics. Rufus relied, as had his father, on more practical sons of the church to effect his policies, men like Bishop Walkelin of Winchester and Ranulf Flambard, whom he elevated to the see of Durham in 1099 as reward for outstanding (some would say infamous) service in filling the king's coffers. But he was unafraid to destroy the unfaithful, as he showed when he broke his father's minister William of St Calais, Bishop of Durham, in 1088.

Rufus's reign was marked by heavy financial exactions commensurate with the scope of his political and military designs. National taxes, such as those of 1094 and 1096, were required to pay for constant war and the Normandy mortgage. It is possible that, in 1096 at least, the information gathered in Domesday Book (1086) was employed to increase revenue. Local justiciars extracted as much as they could from royal rights and dues in the counties. More notoriously, the profits of vacant bishoprics were ruthlessly exploited, although only two vacancies, Canterbury (1089-93) and Durham (1096-9) were in royal custody for more than a couple of years. His dealings with abbacies were equally a matter of profit and patronage. Yet, despite the injured hostility of ecclesiastical chroniclers, Rufus was no tyrant. He surrounded himself with a loyal group of administrators,

nobles and household companions. He consulted, as well as employed, his magnates, as over the 1096 tax, for it was on them that the king relied to fight his wars, to govern his country, secure his justice and collect his taxes. Testimony to his political as well as financial success is found in his achievements and his contemporary reputation. Abbot Suger of St Denis, writing a generation later, acutely described William as 'magnanimous', 'prodigal with the treasures of England, a brilliant recruiter and paymaster of soldiers'.

However, English chroniclers, from Eadmer to William of Malmesbury, Orderic Vitalis and Henry of Huntingdon, developed an increasingly unflattering portrait of a foul-mouthed, loutish homosexual; an almost demonic character for whom few good words could be found; an oppressor of the church whose death was a blessing and whose burial without ceremony or prayers just deserts. Of his bad language there are so many references as to be credible (his favourite oath being, somewhat obscurely, 'By the Face of Lucca' – a reference to a popular Italian icon of the time). All chroniclers note his blunt manner of talking, which matches a career driven by a practical intelligence as much as fierce energy. The earliest observer, Eadmer, noted that William's court in 1094 was crowded with effeminate young men, parading girlishly long hair, mincing walks and flirtatious glances. Predictably, Anselm, although interested, was unamused. William of Malmesbury added a quarter of a century later details of elaborate and garish shoes and tight-fitting clothes. Such stories were coupled with dark mutterings about the king's own sexual habits. When Anselm, in 1094, proposed holding a Church Council to condemn sodomy, William refused. But it was only many years after his death that explicit accusations of homosexuality were levelled against William himself. Much of the surrounding disapproval can be explained by an odd cultural barrier between France and England which amounted to little more than different fashions. As early as 1077, William of Poitiers had recorded the Norman astonishment at the English habit of men wearing their hair long, something only women did in macho Normandy. The association of long hair with degeneracy and moral turpitude was pursued by a Council at Rouen in 1096 which publically condemned long hair. This obsession has had a remarkably tenacious hold on the English aristocracy and their imitators by no means extinguished even today.

It is probable, therefore, that the chroniclers, uniformly monastic, were voicing prim, prudish, perhaps prurient dislike of a fashion they regarded as alien or out of date but which William and his courtiers had adopted rather ostentatiously: an English Conquest, perhaps. That Rufus was content if not eager to go his own way cannot surprise. After all, he is one of the very few whose first title was that of king: he had no previous claim to a lordship, earldom, county or principality. What is more remarkable was his failure to marry. Although his brothers left marriage until relatively late (Curthose at forty-seven; Henry I at thirty-two), for a monarch not to make provision for legitimate offspring is exceptional. The only clear parallel to Rufus's behaviour is remote: Aethelbald, King of Mercia and overlord of southern England (716-57). Otherwise the only adult monarch bachelors or spinsters since 1066 are Elizabeth I and Edward VIII, and he married as soon as he could after abdicating. It is possible that William was homosexual. Unusually for his family, no bastards are attributed to him. Given the manner of his death, the rumours of his life and the interests of his successor, it is understandable that writers coloured their accounts. William of Malmesbury depicts Rufus as a short, pot-bellied, red-faced braggart with long, combed fair hair who, despite these obvious physical disadvantages, nonetheless insisted on wearing the gaudiest of the latest male fashions.

Whatever the truth, William Rufus left few observers indifferent. Although it is impossible to be certain how, he made a powerful impression on those he encountered. His actions reveal him as a man of extraordinary, if occasionally undisciplined, energy, singular determination and exalted ambition. His career exudes self-confidence of a high order. But there was more to him than blustering activity. One July afternoon in 1099, while dining at Brockenhurst in the New Forest (another source has him hunting), he learnt that his garrison at Le Mans was under siege. He immediately set off towards the coast and, despite stormy weather and reluctant ferrymen, landed unscathed in Normandy at dawn the next day ready to raise an army. Such speed of reaction was, to say the least, unsettling to his opponents and cheering to his supporters.

Rufus effectively harnessed the resources of England to pursue deliberate policies of consolidation and aggression in France and the English Marches. If he was impatient and tolerated no opposition, he was also remarkably successful in achieving his designated ends. Much of the responsibility for the permanence of his father's conquests and the scope of his brother's dominance can be credited to Rufus. The anecdotes about him make him more vivid than either. Begun in 1097, Westminster Hall, which in spite of evidently hasty construction stands to this day, was, at 240' by 67' 6", by far the largest secular building in western Europe. It is typical of its builder that when he first saw it, William Rufus complained that it was too small.

Further Reading
F. Barlow, *William Rufus*, 1983.

WILLIAM III (1650-1702), 'The Deliverer' of 1688, was born at The Hague, the only child of William II of Orange and Mary, eldest daughter of Charles I. His father died before he was born and his mother when he was barely ten; his childhood was unhappy, disputed between his mother and his paternal grandmother; his future in the Netherlands uncertain, for Cromwell at the end of the First Dutch War (1652-4) compelled the Dutch Republican government to promise to exclude him from high office. In 1670 he paid his first visit to England shortly after his host Charles II had negotiated the Treaty of Dover which provided for the dismemberment of the United Provinces. Out of the war which followed came, when he was twenty-one, the leadership of his people and his life's work. The French invasion of the provinces in 1672 brought the downfall of the Republican government; William of Orange, called to be Stadtholder of Holland and Captain-General of the Dutch forces, led the nation in halting the French as his ancestor William the Silent had halted the Spaniards a century earlier. Henceforward he believed it his mission to prevent Louis XIV establishing hegemony over all Europe, a belief in destiny which fitted well with his Calvinism, as with the motto of the House of Orange, *Je maintiendrai*. It was a cold, hard passion, in a man who grew up taciturn, cautious, obstinate and occasionally ruthless. He wished above all to defeat the French on the battlefield, yet for all his personal bravery he was a mediocre general. The war continued until 1678, when the Dutch politicians against his wishes signed the Treaty of Nymegen, which William thought a defeat and which opened the way to a series of French diplomatic gains, notably in the Rhineland.

A year before the treaty William had taken the step which in the long run was to prove decisive in the conflict between Louis XIV and his foes. He married Mary, the eldest daughter of James II and heir-presumptive to the throne. Outwardly the marriage, blighted by lack of children, was not strikingly happy. William's behaviour was often surly, and he had his mistresses, yet they were neither so numerous nor so publicly flaunted as those of his two uncles. Nevertheless, Mary shared his resolution and responsibility, and his grief on her death in 1694 was intense and sincere. William's interest in events in Britain was profound during the years of uneasy peace with Louis which followed Nymegen; Whig refugees after the collapse of the Exclusion scheme kept him informed, and he took care to employ his own agents, especially during the growing crisis of James's reign. After the execution of Monmouth in 1685 he was the one hope of the English opposition, while for his part England was vital to all schemes against Louis, provided the mere threat of intervention there did not bring out France against the Dutch. William trod this tightrope delicately. Although he proceeded cautiously, from some time in 1687 he was preparing invasion, and when in 1688, following the birth of the Prince James Edward, Admiral

Herbert brought the famous invitation, he was ready to come as fast as circumstances would permit. Aided by James II's folly in refusing to ask for French help and by Louis's blunders in keeping his fleet in the Mediterranean and in marching his army to the upper Rhineland, he sailed in November, after a false start in October, and landed at Brixham on the anniversary of Gunpowder Plot, with the largest army that had ever invaded England. In the events that followed before James fled to France William showed great wisdom. He treated the invasion as a professional military operation until it was clear that there would be no armed resistance, he carefully refrained from taking any political decisions beyond such immediately practical ones as were needed to ensure law and order, and he took the calculated risk of allowing his father-in-law to escape.

By the end of 1688 he was in possession. But the Revolution had barely begun. He had been invited to save the Protestant religion, not to take the throne. To us today it seems inevitable that he should have become king, yet this was by no means apparent to contemporaries, especially to the Tories, and not until late February 1689, when he had made it clear that he would not be his 'wife's gentleman usher', did he and Mary accept the throne. Neither by temperament nor in view of the needs of the European situation (war with Louis broke out in 1689) did William want a throne whose powers were seriously restricted. Although the Revolution Settlement made possible the limited monarchy of later years, it left the prerogative in 1689 much what it had been since 1660. Use would be the test, and in domestic affairs at least William's use of the prerogative was astonishingly restrained. In some ways too he imposed his own character on the settlement. It was free from bloodshed and vindictiveness; there were few scapegoats, and those only for a short time; the mild treatment of Sunderland is the supreme example of this. The Toleration Act of 1689 reflected William's views and virtues as well as those of the Whigs. There were times when in the face of the disagreements among Englishmen and the obvious doubts many of them had about the durability of the settlement, he despaired, and as early as 1689 he threatened to return to Holland. Yet it was fundamentally clear that he was essential, and events drove the point home. His victory at the Boyne in 1690, with all its consequences in securing Ireland and sending James back to France, was decisive in confirming the events of 1688-9.

For William what mattered above all else was that England was committed to hostility to Louis XIV, to the War of the League of Augsburg (1689-97). It was not a successful war, apart from the Boyne and the naval battle of La Hogue (1692), which redeemed the defeat off Beachy Head (1690). William, whose generalship did not improve with time, was defeated at Steenkirk (1692) and Neerwinden (1693), and for most of the war the allied army in the Netherlands was tied down in endless sieges. The expedition to Brest (1694) failed in circumstances of treachery. Namur, indeed, was taken in 1695, but this simply offset its loss in 1692. When peace was made at Ryswick in 1697 its terms suggested that it was merely a truce – although Louis did indeed recognize William as King of England. Contemporaries thought it a disastrous war, and a costly one; and they would have been surprised to learn that later historians would acclaim its financial legacies, the Bank of England and the National Debt, as the greatest achievements of William's reign. Not the least of their grievances was William's readiness to employ foreign generals like Ginkel and Ruvigny. So in 1698 the Commons cut the army down to 7,000 men and sent home the Dutch Guards, the latter step being a deliberate insult which provoked William to the point of writing a speech of abdication.

The main reason why William employed Dutchmen was that he could not trust Englishmen. The fundamental problem of the reign, certainly of William's relationship with the English ruling class, was that of loyalty. Few politicians refrained from keeping in touch with James II at St Germain. The facts that this was inevitable in view of the insecurity of the Revolution settlement through most of William's reign and that William knew it to be inevitable did not reduce the tensions which resulted. From the circumstances of the Revolution, as well as from their earlier background, the Tories were less sympathetic to William than the Whigs, and, on the whole, more likely to take their Jacobitism seriously; the Whigs for their part were more interested in reducing the royal prerogative and therefore the less acceptable to any king on that account. Somers was the one orthodox Whig in whom William had much confidence. Of other politicians Shrewsbury and Sunderland, neither of them strong partisans, seem to have appealed to him most; but Shrewsbury was neurotic, Sunderland's record was too dark for even William to be able to give him high office, and Somers was extremely unpopular in the last years of the reign. What made the situation worse was William's prolonged absences abroad during the war years, and the unexpected death of Mary in 1694 added to the practical difficulties. Yet it also, on a longer view, compelled Englishmen to commit themselves more fully to William himself. The discovery of the Assassination Plot of 1696 stimulated loyalty, and led to the declaration of that year, that he was the 'rightful and lawful king'. Thereafter it was possible to regard his throne as secure – even though the problem of loyalty was never completely solved, and even though serious quarrels between William and his English subjects lay ahead.

For William of Orange had little flair for popularity, even if London crowds were ready enough at times to cheer him. Aloof, withdrawn, fiercely self-controlled, he suffered from asthma and thus escaped as much as he could from the smoke of London to the country air of Kensington or Hampton Court, or to the hunting which was his only pastime. His few intimate friends were Dutchmen like Bentinck and Keppel. He was never easy to get on with, for he expected his servants to practise the same selfless devotion to his cause as he himself showed. Tough in the way that only the man who is never wholly fit can be tough, he drove his ministers to the utmost, and few of them were equal to it. His qualities were austere ones for an age in which English courtiers had had little chance of experiencing them: he had no time for flatterers, he was loyal to his word, he was ready to take advice, he was a man of direct, not of deceitful, intelligence. Hence, as David Ogg has put it, 'he never aroused their contempt and eventually he won their respect'.

The last years of his reign, after Ryswick, were largely devoted to an attempt to solve the problem of the Spanish Succession on lines which did not allow Louis XIV to overturn the balance of power in Europe. The problem was little understood in England, and William conducted the diplomacy which led to the two Partition Treaties (1698 and 1699) in secret, not consulting English opinion until 1700. This brought an outcry. The Irish estates which he had so lavishly granted to his Dutch friends were taken away from them. The Act of Settlement (1701), made necessary by the death in 1700 of Princess Anne's only surviving child, the Duke of Gloucester, contained, as well as its provision for the Hanoverian Succession, clauses which were clearly shafts aimed at William, like those which prohibited future monarchs leaving the country without parliamentary permission or granting lands or office to foreigners. The gulf between William III and his English people seemed wider than ever it had been. But Louis XIV did much to close it, not so much by his acceptance of Charles II's will in November 1700 as by his blunders of 1701 – his invasion of the Spanish Netherlands and occupation of the Dutch Barrier fortresses, and his grant of the monopoly of Spanish-American trade to a French company. By the autumn much English opinion had swung round to support William's belief that war with Louis XIV must be renewed, and in September the Treaty of the Grand Alliance was signed. Within weeks Louis's final blunder, the recognition of the Old Pretender as James III, united the great mass of English opinion, Tory as well as Whig, squires and merchants alike, behind William in opposition to the arrogant attempt to dominate Europe and to place a Popish prince on the English throne. But by the time the actual fighting in the War of the Spanish Succession began in the spring of 1702, William III was dead; thrown when his horse stumbled, it is said over a molehill, in Hampton Court park, he was too frail and tired to recover from the shock.

'The little gentleman in black velvet' had, as G.M.Trevelyan observed, done his work too late to help either the Jacobites or Louis XIV. William had committed England to the final struggle with Louis XIV. Characteristically, he had overcome his deep distrust of Marlborough and nominated him as his successor in the conduct of the war; characteristically also he had, as his last piece of political advice to Englishmen, commended the project of a legislative union with Scotland. For William III, by far the ablest occupant of the English throne since the days of the Tudors, was distinguished by political judgement of a very high order. He was in some ways fortunate; both James II and Louis XIV aided him by crass blunders. But, as we have seen, he was ill served by English politicians, and his personal achievement, whether in retaining the throne or in carrying out the Revolution and in establishing the Settlement, was immense. His capacity for devotion to a cause no doubt contributed to this achievement. So did his profound belief in toleration and humanity, so too his essential and recognizable honesty of purpose. Yet the central element was a cautious, unhurried, wide-ranging judgement. He never won English hearts; as much perhaps because he was a European statesman as because he was a reserved and truculent man. To no one king does England owe so much, in constitutional evolution and international advance alike.

Further Reading
T. Claydon, *William III and the Godly Revolution*, 1996.
J. Miller, *The Glorious Revolution, 1688*, 1983.
J. R. Western, *Monarchy and Revolution*, 1972.
Stephen Baxter, *William III*, 1966.
D. Ogg, *William III*, 1956.

WILLIAM IV (1765-1837) was the third son of George III and Queen Charlotte. Since he was not thought of as a potential king he was allowed a normal upbringing and a chance to prove himself in a career. As a naval officer he was notable chiefly for his fussy approach to discipline. Criticism of his conduct was largely confined, however, to the navy. Such was the public contempt for George IV that his brother's accession in 1830 was hailed with joy. Ministers might be concerned about his impetuous temper and naive judgement. But Greville's private assessment (and he was no admirer of the family) probably represents what most politicians thought of their new sovereign, a fairly robust sixty-five-year-old: 'Altogether he seems a kind-hearted, well-meaning, not stupid, burlesque, bustling old fellow and, if he doesn't go mad, may make a very decent king, but he exhibits oddities.'

William Henry, Duke of Clarence, entered the navy at the age of thirteen and acquired a fair knowledge of seamanship. He served on the *Royal George* under Rodney in the Mediterranean, then under Hood on the West India station. He received his first command, a frigate, in April 1786, again in the West Indies. He had become friendly with Nelson and gave away the bride at Nelson's marriage at Nevis. In 1790 he commanded the *Valiant*, in the fleet sent to Vancouver to enforce English claims in the Nootka Sound dispute. His besetting fault as a commander was that he would quarrel with his subordinates. He was not so much harsh as irritatingly meticulous. He was promoted to rear-admiral in 1790 and did not serve again. He begged for a chance to serve in the war, but this was refused him. It would have been an embarrassment to the admiralty, since officers were reluctant to serve under him. So he settled down, disgruntled but not really bitter, to the life of a country gentleman at Bushey, with Mrs Jordan, an actress. Her new ménage was almost respectable by the standard of the royal dukes, though it aroused some derision; it seems to have been a happy one and she bore the duke no less than ten children. She also helped to support the extravagant household by continuing with her acting whenever she could. In 1811 William was reluctantly forced to give her up; he continued to be kind to her, and provided for their children, but she died abroad, and poor.

In 1817 the death of the Princess Charlotte brought him within two steps of the throne; he immediately took a wife, Adelaide of Saxe-Coburg-Meiningen; she was a tender and unselfish companion to him. When the death (1827) of his elder brother, the Duke of York, made him heir to the throne, Canning unwisely made him Lord High Admiral: the title was revived for him, an archaic and, as Canning no doubt assumed, empty distinction. But the duke was no less a Hanoverian for having been a naval officer – and he promptly took command of the Channel fleet. He began to promote his friends and assert his authority in the wildest manner and was made to resign. He was indignant but he got over it. There was a certain bluff honesty about the man which helped him to recognize his limitations.

His accession coincided with the Reform Bill crisis. Had he behaved as obstinately or rashly as some feared, he could have destroyed the monarchy. On the other hand a prolonged crisis of this sort gave the king a chance to prove the value of monarchy as the stable element in a changing world. It cannot be said that he was a model constitutional king. He understood too little and spoke his mind too freely for that. He believed, however, that it was his duty to support the prime minister, regardless of party: in this he was wisely tutored by his secretary, Taylor. He admired Wellington but was equally ready to accept Grey. He felt the strength of Tory opposition and argument, but he accepted, under pressure, what Lord Grey gave him to understand was necessary. He did not use his right of preliminary veto, as he was entitled to do. To prevent the threatened resignation of his Whig ministers in April 1831 he consented to dissolve parliament; when it became clear that it was essential to act quickly to forestall a motion against dissolution, he went at once. 'I'm always at single anchor,' he declared, sweeping aside officials' objections that the coachman and horse-guards were unready, the horses' manes unplaited! 'My Lord, I'll go, if I go in a hackney coach,' he told the apologetic Grey. He drove through cheering crowds to an angry chamber: as he ascended the steps of the throne it was seen that his crown, hastily donned, was balanced precariously on one side of his head. But his words were dignified: 'I have been induced to resort to this measure for the purpose of ascertaining the sense of my people.' When the election came he was disturbed by the violence of the mobs and 'out of spirits' at the prospect of a democratic future. But he maintained his trust in Grey, awarded him the Garter, resisted all Tory influences in court and family (Queen Adelaide favoured Wellington) and even consented at last to a new creation of peers, sufficient to secure the passage of the bill through the Lords. He later wrote a letter to the opposition peers advising them to give up their resistance. In the negative ways that were open to him he did right. The monarchy survived.

Think of William as king and he is odd, if not grotesque. Think of him as a retired naval gentleman of limited education, unused to contradiction and to sophisticated argument, and he becomes credible, even likeable. A fly sheet illustrating 'The Grey Horse and the Union Coach' showed a bystander asking the question: 'Pray, who drives the coach, neighbour?' The neighbour answers: 'Why, friend, she runs by steam now, but old Bill King, a sailor chap, drove her first.' The transition had to be made. William, 'true King of the Tories' though he might be in the eyes of a Grenville, helped to make it in a modest and honest way for which he deserves to be kindly remembered.

William was fond of his niece Victoria and bitterly disliked her mother, the Duchess of Kent, for keeping the girl away from his court. Indeed, one of his last public speeches contained such a rude attack upon her and so outspoken a wish that he should live long enough to prevent her being regent that some thought him quite mad. He had his wish. Queen Victoria acceded to the throne a month after she had come of age. How gratified he would have been, if he had foreseen how long and glorious her reign was to be.

Further Reading
P. Ziegler, *King William IV*, 1971.

WILLIAM (1103-20), the only legitimate son of Henry I, was more famous in death than in life. Through his mother, Matilda, descended from Ethelred the Unready, on him rested his father's dynastic ambition. To secure acceptance of his son's authority and succession, in 1115 and 1116 Henry made the barons of Normandy and

England swear homage and fealty to William. Although designation was not unknown in England, such a formal ceremony was unprecedented, a sign of Henry's own sense of vulnerability. In 1118-19, William acted as regent for his absent father before joining him in Normandy where, the following year, he married Matilda, daughter of the Count of Anjou and did homage to Louis VI for Normandy. But Henry's schemes came to nothing when, on the evening of 25 November, the White Ship, carrying William back to England, foundered off Barfleur. The prince had embarked late and so missed high tide; both passengers and crew were reported to have been drunk. As a result, the ship was driven hard into a rock in Barfleur harbour revealed by the ebb tide. In the ensuing panic, William was put into a lifeboat, but, seeing his half-sister still on board the stricken vessel, he ordered the boat to return to her rescue, only for it to be capsized by others desperate for rescue. Few if any on board that or any other Norman ship could swim. William, his sister, another illegitimate brother and many prominent courtiers and barons were drowned. Only Berold, a butcher from Rouen, survived to tell the tale – which he did, frequently. The disaster was so horrific in its political, let alone personal, implications, that none dared tell the king: they left it to a boy. By depriving Henry of a legitimate son, or the prospect of a grandson in the male line, the White Ship disaster changed the course of English history. The last fifteen years of Henry I's reign were spent trying, in the event unsuccessfully, to restore an ordered succession to his dominions. More immediately, the drama of the catastrophe was heightened by its unexpectedness. Between 1066 and 1144 there are no reports of any loss of life or even injuries as a result of a shipping accident in the English Channel, and only one reference to a vessel dragging its anchor in port. Small wonder contemporary monastic chroniclers had a field day in pointing the moral: man proposes; God disposes.

WILLIAM I (the Lion) (1143-1214) and Malcolm IV (the Maiden) each became King of Scotland following the early death of their father Henry, Earl of Northumbria, in 1152. Malcolm, the elder, designated heir to the throne by his grandfather, King David I, reigned from David's death in 1153 till his own in 1165, when William became king. It was one of the most enduring ambitions of William I to right a wrong which he felt had been done to himself and his brother. In 1157 at Chester, the young Malcolm IV had been forced by Henry II of England (r.1154-89) to cede the three counties of Northumbria gained for the Scottish Crown by David and, in compensation, allotted to William only the rump in Tynedale of the traditional earldom. Bellicose and impatient, William was determined to recover these losses.

In 1173, there erupted the rebellion against Henry II, fomented by his sons and backed by Louis VII of France. William allowed himself to be drawn into this dangerous quagmire, despite opposition to his policy from the barons of parliament. In July 1174, after some inconclusive engagements, he laid siege to Alnwick, and was captured with a small party nearby. Henry made the most of his luck. The Scottish king was escorted southwards into England, with feet bound together beneath the body of his horse, and imprisoned at Falaise in Normandy. Here, in December, he was forced to swear fealty to Henry, to relinquish his earldom of Huntingdon and to agree that the castles at Edinburgh, Stirling, Roxburgh, Jedburgh and Berwick should be garrisoned by English forces at Scottish expense. Such a disaster could not fail to undermine William's authority, if only because it enabled the English king to make good his claim to the homage of William's lords and bishops, who were forced to give hostages for their allegiance. Scotland's subordinacy was emphasized in 1185 by imposing upon its king a marriage with Ermengarde, the daughter of a mere Norman viscount, Robert Beaumont.

Opposition to the rule of the descendants of Malcolm III and Margaret continued during William's reign. Partly rooted in clan hostility to the Anglo-Normans and the process of feudalization, partly in dynastic jealousy, it was given impetus by the king's humiliation at the hands of the English. In Galloway, a decade of internecine bloodletting began in 1174. From 1179, Donald Macwilliam, a grandson of Duncan II (Malcolm's son by his first marriage to Ingibjorg) sought to further his own claim. After Donald's death in 1189, his son Guthred sought to continue the struggle until his capture and beheading in 1212. These challenges led in 1179, 1196-7 and 1202 to renewed efforts to establish royal authority in the far north-east, with the construction of castles at Dunskaith and Redcastle. For William's dynastic security depended not only on the elimination of pretenders but upon establishing feudal and kingly authority amongst the clansmen. In the north-east, he also needed to secure them from Norway and its earldom of Orkney, which then held Caithness and eastern Sutherland. About the turn of the century, Earl Harold and his family were subordinated, new and loyal feudal lords established, and William's royal authority extended in the far north-east, though little progress was made in the north-west Highlands; the Western Isles remained in Norwegian hands.

Many native magnates resented the alien French language and culture which William and his brother Malcolm had assimilated. Among them, there were leaders such as Somerled, who hoped to use nostalgia for the old Celtic religious observances to mobilize in the defence of his semi-independent lordship in Argyll; for completely symmetrical reasons, William was anxious to promote the new ways and removed from the jurisdiction of the traditionalist Iona its churches in Galloway. Here, as in most areas, the magnates had started to adopt feudal tenures, to forge links with Norman families and to extend earlier military obligations into such specifically feudal customs as providing knight-service and castle-guard for the king, to recognize the role of royal justiciars. From the late eighties, most of Scotland outside Argyll and the Western and Northern Isles were under William's control.

William's reign marked something of a breach with the pious style of the sons of Margaret, not the least in the king's reluctance to marry and his promiscuity. The early part of the reign was notable for the turbulence it brought to relations with Rome. At first, things had appeared to be set fair. In 1159, Pope Alexander III had signalled a repudiation of the jurisdictional rights of York in Scotland by appointing William, Bishop of Moray, as papal legate; soon, new bishops, of St Andrews and of Glasgow, were consecrated without reference to York. The shift had to do with the growing conflict between Henry II and Thomas Becket over the jurisdiction of the English church courts. Henry adopted an increasingly aggressive posture, and not only in the murder of Becket. For at Falaise, Scottish bishops and abbots, as well as barons, were forced to swear fealty to Henry and to acquiesce in the subordination of their church to that of England. Further demands for capitulation on this issue were placed upon William and the Scottish clergy at a council at Northampton in 1176, where the crudity of the English tactics was pointed up by an unedifying row between Canterbury and York. The Scots were helped in their resistance by the continued active support of Pope Alexander III who countermanded Henry's demands and, whilst promising an official investigation into the claims of York, instructed the Scottish clergy to obey only himself.

King William, however, was anxious to follow Henry's example by extending royal control of the church in Scotland, and his impatience and rigidity in this cause led him into a series of damaging confrontations. In 1178, the chapter of St Andrews elected John the Scot as bishop, and William countermanded the decision, intruding his chaplain Hugh into the post. John appealed to the pope, who sent a letter of protest to William. A papal legate arrived with instructions for the church council in Edinburgh (garrisoned, after Falaise, by the English); Hugh was deposed and John consecrated. Events now rapidly spiralled out of control. John was in turn deposed, and expelled by royal fiat. But Alexander raised the stakes again: reversing his policy on the vexed question of jurisdiction, he nominated Roger, Archbishop of York, as his legate in Scotland. Roger proceeded to excommunicate Hugh, and when King William sought to retaliate by banishing John's clerical

supporters, he himself was excommunicated. The damage caused took many years to undo. Eventually, after the death of Alexander, William secured the collation to St Andrews of his cousin and chancellor, Roger of Leicester, and agreed to John's election to Dunkeld. Relations with the papacy now improved. In 1192, Pope Celestine III confirmed that the Scottish church was to remain independent of York and Canterbury, though without an archbishop of its own and directly subordinate to Rome.

The death of Henry II and the departure of his successor Richard I for the crusades at the end of 1189 offered an opportunity for William to renegotiate some of the more humiliating conditions to which the English had subjected him in 1174. Richard had need of finance for his adventures, and in exchange for a promise of 10,000 merks released William from the treaty of Falaise. Later, William made much of a clause included in the quit-claim charter which hinted vaguely at the restoration of Northumberland. Both Richard and John repeatedly rejected this demand, even when tempted with a subsidy of 15,000 merks. Roxburgh and Berwick, were restored to Scottish hands in 1189, but John soon adopted a more aggressive policy than his brother. In 1209, across the river from Berwick, he constructed a new castle at Tweedmouth. When the Scots resisted, John marched a very large army to Norham. Thoroughly frightened, the ageing William provided fifteen hostages, including his daughters Margaret and Isabella, and paid 15,000 merks to the English king. The details of the peace are uncertain, but the gild merchants of Perth, summoned to the council in September 1209, seem to have won for their role in raising the money a royal charter, granting monopoly privileges. If, as is possible, John promised his sons Richard and Henry (later Henry III) to William's daughters, he broke his word: each endured a long-unmarried exile.

Other events of 1212 confirmed William's subordinate status. John sent troops to help in the suppression of Macwilliam and assumed the right to arrange the marriage of William's son, Alexander; Alexander II did marry Joan, sister of Henry III, in 1221. But these blessings reflected the reality of English overlordship in Scotland, as did John's ominous promise to support the rightful succession there. Whether from political weakness or gullibility, William accepted these terms. He may have set great store by the concession that English lands held by Scottish kings should pass to each successive heir before his accession. Perhaps he was taken in by verbal assurances that Northumbria might be included in this arrangement; if so, it might be remarked that John's promises were not worth the paper they were not written on.

William died at Stirling on 4 December 1214, and did not witness the imminent discomfiture of his old enemy,

WILLIAM AUGUSTUS, DUKE OF CUMBERLAND / 1323

John; his foreign policy failures proved to be of less lasting significance than his achievement in presiding over the triumph of feudalism in most parts of his kingdom.

WILLIAM AUGUSTUS, DUKE OF CUMBERLAND

WILLIAM AUGUSTUS, DUKE OF CUMBERLAND (1721-65) was included by Horace Walpole in his list of the great men whom he had known in his life. Since today he is remembered primarily as 'the butcher' of Culloden, and by the Scots as 'stinking Billy', it is right to recall that he was once admired for his courage and leadership.

The second surviving son of George II and Queen Caroline, he was born at Leicester House. At the age of four he was made first knight of the revived Order of the Garter. According to Lord King, then chancellor, the Prince of Wales, before his accession, planned to disinherit his detested elder son and make Cumberland heir to the throne. This came to nothing but, perhaps because he never stood first in line of succession, George II always enjoyed easy relations with his son. Originally intended for the navy, he chose the army and displayed courage and devotion to his service. He was first in action under his father at Dettingen, and was there wounded in the leg; the wound healed, but imperfectly, and gave him further trouble. In 1745, at the age of twenty-four, he was made Captain-General of the British forces attached to the allied army at Flanders, in place of the septuagenarian Wade. This appointment reflected the dearth of military talent in England after years of peace, but he distinguished himself nonetheless at Fontenoy, in April, where the English forces took the brunt of the French attacks before retreating in good order. One of his colonels, Joseph Yorke, wrote afterwards: 'I never saw or heard of such behaviour as the duke's: he rode every where, he encouraged the wavering, he complimented the bold, he threatened the cowards … Had the nation seen him they would have adored him.'

The nation soon had need of him, after Prince Charles Edward's landing in Scotland and his southward march. He was brought home in October to command the principal army at Lichfield, where he covered London during the prince's march to Derby. He then marched by slow stages towards the Highlands, on the tail of the retreating Jacobites; then Stirling, on 2 February, Aberdeen on 27 February, Nairn on 1 April. As he proceeded he took characteristic measures to ensure that his men would not run before the Highlanders, as had happened at Prestonpans and Falkirk. They were trained to fire with concentrated effect and to stand their ground. Cumberland's reputation, energy and thoroughness restored the morale of his men, and the battle of Culloden Moor was won before it started. The Highlanders who faced Cumberland's fresh troops and efficient artillery on 16 April, with the cold rain driving in their faces, were tired and starving, and the frenzied courage

of their attacks was useless in the face of accurate fire. Cumberland's victory was complete when he sent in his cavalry on the flanks, and with 2,000 dead or captured, the remnants of the Highlanders dispersed. Cumberland, who had but 300 casualties, was satisfied but, out of temper with the rebels whose rising had threatened his father's throne, he ordered their systematic extermination, the burning of their houses and the confiscation of their cattle. Cumberland stayed three months to see the operation launched, then returned to London to find that his heroic image was becoming tarnished by the stories of savagery assiduously circulated by his political opponents and by Jacobites. Dr Johnson once visited Bedlam and was struck by the sight of an inmate beating at his straw under the impression that he was punishing Cumberland for his cruelties in Scotland. The poor lunatic only expressed the popular view.

The story of the pacification of the Highlands is a distressing one; but Cumberland's conduct should be seen in perspective. The manners of the Highlanders were savage, their methods ferocious. Treason was an ugly word, and the cruelties of Cumberland's troops are paralleled by the grim reprisals of the law, which knew no distinction of birth or rank. Some of the worst atrocities were committed by Scottish Whigs, eager to pay off old scores. Cumberland's personal appearance told against him in the growth of the legend. He weighed eighteen stone and had porcine features and manners to match. Yet the responsibility for the policy remains his: he did nothing to mitigate the cruelties of Hawley's dragoons and showed no sign of regret. He was not a sensitive man.

He returned to Flanders in 1747 but did not add to his military reputation. At the battle of Laffeldt the allied army was again defeated. His dispositions were faulty and only the handling of the cavalry by Ligonier saved the army from disintegration. He was no more successful when he commanded again, at the start of the Seven Years' War. Defeated by the French at Hastenbeck in July 1757, he retreated northwards, was encircled by superior forces under Richelieu and signed the Convention of Klosterseven securing the neutrality of Hanover, in September. His orders had been inhibiting: George II was primarily anxious for the safety of Hanover and gave him full powers, as Pitt pointed out to him, to secure it. Cumberland was recalled and made to resign, while Pitt whom he had opposed and driven from office in April, promptly disavowed his convention. He consoled himself with his race-horses and with the pleasures of the table, for which he had a true Hanoverian appetite. He died, exhausted, at the early age of forty-four.

Cumberland's most important military contribution was in the unspectacular work of reform of discipline and training, and the inculcation of professional standards. It may be recalled that, when the garrison of

Minorca was attacked in 1756, almost all the officers were absent in London. Amateurism and slackness were Cumberland's targets; he attacked them with Germanic thoroughness. He was not able to end the purchase of commissions, but he insisted upon evidence of soldierly fitness. He attempted to limit the amount of leave that officers might take and the number of carriages they could take with them on campaigns. He might have attached less importance to the cut and colour of uniforms and spent more time on thinking about strategy, but he had an eye for merit in his subordinates and promoted forward and humane young officers such as Howe, Coote and Wolfe. It was the latter, the least conventional of soldiers, who said of Cumberland's dismissal that it was 'a public calamity'.

Further Reading

J. A. Houlding, *Fit for Service: the Training of the British Army, 1715-1795*, 1982.

Evan Charteris, *William Augustus, Duke of Cumberland, 1721-48*, 1913.

WILLIAM OF BRIOUZE or BRAOSE (d.1211) was at the centre of one of the most damaging causes célèbres of John's reign. After succeeding to his father's lands in Sussex, Devon and Wales in 1180, he proved himself a tough and ruthless fighter in the Angevin cause in the Welsh Marches and France. He was with Richard I at Chalus in 1199 and with John in Normandy 1202-3, when he captured Arthur of Brittany at Mirebeau in 1202. An arrogant and unpopular man, with a shrewish wife, William was showered with favour by John, receiving the extensive Irish lordship of Limerick in 1200-1, more castles in 1205 and lucrative marriages for his many children. For reasons not entirely clear, from 1205 John began to harry his former favourite, perhaps out of fear of his independent spirit or a desire to show that even those powerful by royal creation were subject to the king's will. It is certain that John determined to make an example of William and that William reacted with obstinacy, rashness and incompetence. The weapon William had placed in John's hands were his pledges of huge sums in return for royal grants (5,000 marks for Limerick in 1201; 800 marks for the castles in 1205) on which he subsequently defaulted. Not only did John undermine William's position in Ireland and deprive him of offices in England, he also had a legal case against him at the Exchequer. When the king demanded hostages in 1208, William initially blustered and his wife, Matilda, fatally for her, apparently excused her refusal to deliver her sons as hostages by accusing John of murdering his nephew Arthur. This was particularly provocative as William was probably one of the few who actually knew what had happened to Arthur and who could lend credence to the rumours that John himself had murdered his nephew in a drunken rage at Rouen in

April 1203. Whatever the personal edge, John proceeded vigorously. In 1209, William's chattels were distrained, castles surrendered, hostages promised and his English and Welsh lands pledged as security for repayment of his loan. To add pressure, John sent troops to attack William's Marcher lands. William and his family fled to Ireland, but returned in 1210 to avoid John's armies there. This was unavailing. Matilda and her eldest son were captured and taken to Windsor Castle where, despite offers of ransom, they were starved to death. William fled to France, where he died a broken man in 1211, his funeral being conducted by another exile from John's anger, Stephen Langton.

It was not William's harassment which shocked. As the king, supported by many leading barons, insisted in 1210, William was a contumacious debtor and rebel. It was the inexorable quality of the pursuit and the obscene cruelty of the treatment of Matilda and her son, attested by contemporaries, which made the case notorious. William could be said to have brought about his own ruin by failing to submit. There is little objective evidence that John was especially vindictive in the early stages of his attack. In the campaign to increase the effectiveness of the Exchequer's collection of revenue owing to the Crown, William's fate was to show other barons that none were immune from royal authority. Whether John's subsequent cruelty was informed by personal spite or misjudged sternness is impossible to say. However, the case of William and Matilda de Briouze showed an increasingly resentful baronage the lengths to which the king could go and, in time, would stand as a major indictment of John's policy, judgement and personality, a significant part of the myth of 'Bad King John'.

Further Reading

J. C. Holt, *The Northerners*, 1961.

W. L. Warren, *King John*, 1961.

WILLIAM OF CORBEIL (d.1136; Archbishop of Canterbury 1123-36) was the first post-Conquest Archbishop of Canterbury not to have been a monk. A scholar, who had studied under the influential Anselm of Laon; a close friend of Anselm of Canterbury; a clerk of Ranulf Flambard (apparently acting as tutor to Flambard's bastards); and Canon of Dover, in mid-career William sought a more rigorous religious life as an Augustinian canon, becoming prior of the new foundation of St Osyth's in Essex. After the death of Archbishop Ralf d'Escures in 1122, William's past as a well-connected secular clerk and his present as a canon regular (i.e. living under a rule) commended him as a candidate for Canterbury to Roger of Salisbury who, with royal backing, was eager to appoint someone who was not a monk. As archbishop William proved himself a vigorous reformer. At three councils at Westminster in

1125, 1127 and 1129, decrees were promulgated extending the definition of simony; limiting the number of fees permitted to be collected by clergy; outlawing clerical marriage and fornication; and prohibiting the inheritance of benefices. As most of these measures challenged traditions and appetites, they were widely ignored. William was more effective in resolving the long running dispute with York in Canterbury's favour, helped by some convenient forged documentary evidence. However, William was most notorious in the twelfth century for crowning King Stephen in 1135, in direct contravention of the oath he and the other bishops had sworn to Matilda in 1128. It was this act of perjury – or policy – which probably lay behind Henry of Huntingdon's damning verdict that William could not be praised 'because there is nothing to praise'. This was harsh, as William, although possibly avaricious, led an austere and blameless life, the priority he gave his spiritual and religious commitment being evinced in his Augustinian vocation. He must also have possessed some distinctive qualities of personality to be friends with both the saintly Anselm and worldly Flambard.

WILLIAM OF MALMESBURY (*c.*1095-*c.*1143) was one of the most distinguished English historians. The twelfth century witnessed a recrudescence of historical writing, stimulated by a general western European revival of learning and by events. On the continent, polemicists on both sides of the Investiture Contest between pope and emperor looked to the past to justify present policies. The First Crusade (1096-9) provoked an avalanche of contemporary narratives seeking to place this remarkable episode in a suitably providential frame as new, incontrovertible evidence of God's immanence. In England, although the unique vernacular tradition of historical narrative of the Anglo-Saxon Chronicle had become attenuated after 1066, the Norman Conquest provided a fresh spur to historical investigation. Monks had to justify their privileges; clerics were forced to reassess the insular Christian tradition in the new circumstances of largely foreign leadership; and scholars felt compelled to explain and judge the cataclysm which had overtaken Anglo-Saxon England. William of Malmesbury did all three.

Born of Anglo-Norman parents, William rose from a child oblate at Malmesbury to be the abbey's librarian and perhaps, in 1140, an unsuccessful candidate for the abbacy. As a historian he regarded himself as successor to Bede of Jarrow (672-735) whose *Ecclesiastical History of the English People* was the greatest and most influential historical work of early medieval England. Like Bede, William was a polymath whose scholarship found its basis in his monastic library. Through his reading, William mastered scripture, the classics, theology, hagiography, civil and canon law. But he did more.

A prominent feature of his writing is his use of topography and buildings as evidence. He appears to have travelled widely in England and his *Gesta Pontificum Anglorum* (1125) (*Deeds of the Bishops of the English*) has been described as an ecclesiastical gazetteer. Elsewhere, he points a wider political and moral argument by contrasting the meanness of Anglo-Saxon dwellings with the magnificence of new building by the Normans.

Such an eclectic approach to source material is paralleled by his extensive use of both past and contemporary literary narratives from Suetonius's *Lives of the Caesars*, Bede, and local historical traditions to eleventh- and twelfth-century authors such as William of Poitiers, William of Jumièges (for the Norman Conquest) and Fulcher of Chartres (on the First Crusade). Unafraid to flaunt his classical learning, his anthology of texts on Roman history, compiled in 1129, survives in a manuscript now in the Bodleian Library, Oxford. William's range embraced on the one hand archival documents (some, it must be said, forgeries, perhaps in the case of evidence on Malmesbury's antiquity concocted by William himself) and on the other a string of Rabelaisian anecdotes of debauchery and self-indulgence.

Part of William's posthumous reputation has depended on his leaving a substantial corpus of different literary works, the first English historian to do so since Bede. In 1125 he completed the first versions of his *Gesta Regum Anglorum*, a history of England from the arrival of the Saxons in the fifth century down to 1120, and the *Gesta Pontificum Anglorum*, a history of the English church to 1125. Between 1135 and 1143 he revised the *Gesta Regum* twice and the *Gesta Pontificum* once; he wrote a hagiographical Life of St Dunstan, in which he tried to demonstrate the ancient origins of Glastonbury, with the help of some dubious documentary material from Canterbury; and he completed his *De Antiquitate Glastoniensis Ecclesiae* on the origins of Glastonbury Abbey. In the last three years of his life William, by now an embittered and isolated figure at Malmesbury, compiled a *Historia Novella*, an account of recent events 1128-42, which was probably cut short by his own death.

Apart from local corporate pride, William's historical work was centrally concerned to reconcile the histories of pre- and post-Conquest England. His position is unusually ambivalent, which makes it more interesting. He wished to preserve the reputations of Anglo-Saxon saints; he called 14 October 1066 'a fatal day'; he stressed the continuity of English history. Yet he also sought to justify the Norman Conquest by condemning the English for sins of the flesh and casual religious observance. Harold II may have been personally brave, but his people were sinful and effeminate: William was always hot in disapproval of long hair and fancy clothes.

Of particular technical interest was William's development of a critical method in handling his sources. For example, he had little time for stories of Arthur, although this may have had as much to do with his dislike of the Welsh as his distrust of Geoffrey of Monmouth's fables. William laid claim to objectivity, although much of his account of 1066 is derived from Norman propaganda and his treatment of the early years of the civil war under Stephen is clearly that of a Matilda partisan. What is notable is that he admitted as much. Although happier in relating past events, his description of his own times in the *Historia Novella* is possibly the more intellectually remarkable, as he had no sources to guide him. Here his central interest in human affairs comes to the fore. More strongly than many medieval historians, William is prepared to speculate on human motive not just divine judgement. For example, he attributes Urban II's launching of the First Crusade to the pope's 'little known' desire to exploit any political disruption caused by the crusade to win back papal lands in central Italy. Among western writers, this secular analysis of the supreme sacred political event of the age is unique.

But there was another side to William of Malmesbury. Like many another apparently humane Benedictine scholar, he was snobbish; anti-semitic; a toady to patrons such as Robert of Gloucester, Matilda's chief supporter; a political time-server, as in his mealy-mouthed description of the distinctly unlikeable Henry I; and, for instance in his account of William Rufus, priggish to the point of prurience. But his achievement in restoring an English past to the Anglo-French élite of his day and subsequent generations remains one of the most impressive academic and intellectual feats in twelfth-century England.

Further Reading
R. Thomson, *William of Malmesbury*, 1987.
A. Gransden, *Historical Writing in England c.550-c.1307*, 1974.

WILLIAM OF NORWICH (1132/3-44) was an apprentice leather worker in Norwich whose unexplained murder provoked the first accusations of ritual killing of Christians by Jews and was the excuse for the creation of a cult which lasted until the Reformation. The charges against the Jews were not immediate on the discovery of William's body in a wood on the outskirts of Norwich, but his family, especially his uncle, a priest called Godwin, soon concocted a case for the cathedral authorities. Unnamed Jews were accused of kidnapping William and torturing him before crucifying the boy on Good Friday. The elements of blasphemy and ritual slaying, long part of medieval Christendom's myths about Judaism, were a potent mixture. There is not a shred of evidence to support the family's claims. The Jewish community in Norwich, there under the protection of the French authorities, was of very recent import. The growing prosperity of the third wealthiest town in England

may have increased their business in providing financial services. Resentment, and the initial popularity of the cult, seems to have come from those with modest means, urban artisans who, perhaps for the first time, were sufficiently well-off to get into debt. Whatever social or economic tensions the slanders concealed, the cult itself was manufactured by three people: Godwin; William Turbe, Prior of Norwich, then bishop 1146-74; and Thomas of Monmouth, who took over from Godwin as the cult's manager in 1150. Thomas supervised numerous translations of the pathetic corpse which, on one occasion, he relieved of some teeth for his private relic collection. In 1173, he composed the *Life and Miracles of St William*. The desire of the Norwich monks for an attractive cult of their own was as powerful as their anti-semitism. In the early years the pilgrims who received the saint's cures were very local, although by the time Thomas wrote the *Life*, the novelty had worn off in the immediate neighbourhood. The cult survived until the 1530s. The story of young William's killing was copied repeatedly, most famously in the events leading to the grisly pogrom surrounding the supposed martyrdom of nine-year-old Hugh of Lincoln in 1255. Chaucer's *Prioress's Tale* is very similar. The corruption of innocence made it an attractive literary device. More sinisterly, the cynical exploitation of an obscure tragedy set a pattern for self-righteous prejudice which increased as Jewish communities spread across Angevin England. The intolerance towards the Jews may have been fed by ignorance and a fear born of the endless repetition in words and images of the Passion and Crucifixion. But the outbreaks of anti-semitic violence, notably the massacres of Lent 1190 in Stamford, King's Lynn and York, were rarely spontaneous. Like the cult of St William, they were concerted expressions less of religious zeal than of secular antagonism for which horror stories such as the one invented by Godwin and his relations in Norwich in 1144 provided convenient fuel.

Further Reading
R. Finucane, *Miracles and Pilgrims*, 1977.

WILLIAM OF SENS (*d.*1180) has often been credited with introducing French Gothic style into English ecclesiastical architecture when he was placed in charge of the extensive remodelling of Canterbury Cathedral between 1174 and 1177. A fire had conveniently gutted the cathedral choir, giving the monks the opportunity to redesign it as a monument to Thomas Becket. To find the right mason, the monks held a medieval equivalent of an architects' competition. A number of master masons were interviewed before William of Sens was chosen. Our main source for the rebuilding, the eye-witness Gervase of Canterbury, described William as 'the most cunning craftsman in wood and stone'. One of his techniques was to make moulds which were then sent to the individual masons for cutting the stones. William oversaw the rebuilding for about three years before badly injuring his back in a fall of fifty feet from the wooden scaffolding. Crippled and bed-ridden, William struggled on for a short time giving instructions to a young monk (possibly Gervase himself) who supervised the work. This arrangement proved unsatisfactory. William soon relinquished his post to his namesake, William the Englishman, returning to France where he died on 11 August 1180.

While there are evident similarities between the new design of Canterbury in the 1170s and the Cathedral of Sens, begun in the 1140s and one of the earliest to be built in the new Gothic style, the most stylistically innovative parts of the rebuilding, for example the Trinity Chapel and Corona, date from after William of Sens had departed and must be credited to William the Englishman who completed the work in 1184. The latter was, according to Gervase, 'small in body, but in workmanship of many kinds acute and honest' and may have pursued a career as architect, engineer or carpenter at Canterbury and for the king until 1214. As for William of Sens, he was evidently widely travelled and experienced before 1174. It is possible he was attracted to Canterbury by the link between Sens and Becket, who had stayed there during his exile. It is as likely that he was on the look out for lucrative employment. William of Sens's appearance at Canterbury indicates a lively international traffic in masons and thus in artistic and architectural influences. However, the contribution of William the Englishman is a reminder of the equally significant role of local inspiration.

Further Reading
J. Harvey, *English Mediaeval Architects*, 1987.

WILLIAM OF ST CALAIS (*d*.1096; Bishop of Durham 1080-96) was trained under Bishop Odo at Bayeux, the Anglo-Norman administrative Sandhurst. Unlike many of his colleagues, William became a monk, his first offices being Prior of St Calais in Maine and Abbot of St Vincent-des-Près at Le Mans. He caught the eye of William I as a diplomat, but his experience of a frontier province may have influenced the king's decision to appoint him to the see of Durham in 1080 after the murder of Bishop Walcher. A conscientous and efficient diocesan, in 1083 he introduced monks to Durham Cathedral, thus founding a priory which remained a centre of scholarship and learning until the Reformation. If pious, William was also intelligent and ambitious. By the end of William I's reign he was a leading royal servant. Largely on manuscript evidence which associates the scribes of Domesday Book with the Durham scriptorium, it has been suggested that William was in overall administrative charge of the Domesday Survey. There are other references to William of St

Calais's concern with the details of which baron owned what, and it may be significant that every writ of William II referring to Domesday Book is witnessed by Bishop William. He was thus probably responsible for one of the most remarkable governmental achievements of the age. The absence of returns from north of the Tees, William's diocese, might also suggest his involvement as a relatively neutral organizer.

The Domesday Survey was conducted between Christmas 1085 and 1 August 1086. The kingdom was divided into seven circuits, each with its own commissioners, who were deliberately not drawn from local landowners. To reduce fraud, a second batch of commissioners was despatched shortly after the first to check the declarations. The material collected concerned the extent of holdings, ownership and revenues, calculated in terms of tangible assets such as mills, ploughs, ploughteams and labourers. The commissioners asked three further questions: what was the estate worth and whose was it: a) '*tempore regis Edwardi*' (i.e. in the time of Edward the-Confessor, 1066); b) when the present owner took possession; c) in 1086. The information was collated under counties, arranged by tenants-in-chief, i.e. those who held their lands directly from the king. Thus each county entry would begin by listing the holdings of the king, then the archbishop/bishop, then the leading barons and so on.

In fact Domesday Book is three separate texts:

1. The Exon Domesday, which covers the south-western counties, seems to be an early draft of material collected by one group of commissioners and is organized by tenants-in-chief and then by counties and not, as the others, vice versa;

2. Little Domesday, which contains a fair copy of returns from East Anglia;

3. Great Domesday, apparently a final, condensed text, covers all England south of the Tees except East Anglia and the City of London. The scale of the enterprise is only matched by its monumental result. Domesday was an apt nickname as the survey established, or sought to establish, title to land to which government officials referred for over a century after. Medieval rulers frequently surveyed their holdings, usually for fiscal reasons. In spirit, therefore, Domesday is not unique. But in size, detail and deliberation it stands alone as a towering monument to Anglo-Norman administrative skill. For it was a non-racial product. The main scribe of Great Domesday was, given his penchant for anglicizing place names, most likely English. But the guiding force, William I, and the executor, William of St Calais, were French.

One mystery surrounding Domesday is its purpose. It has variously been interpreted as a tax book preparatory to a new assessment of the land tax or a more efficient collection of the old; a schedule on which new feudal and military obligations could be calculated; a statement of ownership of land which confirmed title or provided the basis for the settlement of tenurial disputes; or an immediate reaction to a political crisis (the threatened Danish invasion) in which landowners co-operated in the assessment in order to curtail royal misuse of the right to billet troops. What can be said is that potentially Domesday Book had fiscal and tenurial application and must have had considerable magnate approval for the survey to be completed so quickly. It is intriguing, however, that for all its bureaucratic grandeur, Domesday was still-born. It existed, and exists, and was, and is, used as a mine of information. But it led to no obvious political or fiscal initiative. In part this may have been because its originator, William I, died in 1087. It may also have been because the minister most closely responsible, within fifteen months of the Conqueror's death, was on trial for treason.

On his accession, William II, says the *Anglo-Saxon Chronicle*, treated Bishop William 'so well that all England went by his counsel and did exactly as he wished'. This was hardly surprising if the bishop had the evidence of Domesday at his disposal: knowledge is power. However, during the civil war of 1087-8 between William II and his brother Robert Curthose and their uncle Odo of Bayeux, Bishop William deserted the king and refused to fight against the rebels. His reasons are obscure as he seemed to have got on well with Rufus, supplying smooth talk for a tongue-tied monarch. The king's reaction at what he saw as treachery was commensurately vigorous. The bishop was arraigned for treason at a royal court at Salisbury on 2 November 1088. The king, vocally supported by Archbishop Lanfranc, insisted that William was being tried as a secular lord: his ecclesiastical position and office were not in dispute. William, ever nimble in debate, adopted the mantle of Gregory VII, claiming canonical immunity from secular prosecution or trial, arguing that he could only be judged by fellow bishops or the pope. Lanfranc dismissed such posturing as irrelevant. William forfeited his temporalities and went into exile, possibly to the court of Robert Curthose. Lanfranc's rejection of William's arguments may have been prompted by disbelief at this royal clerk's sudden conversion to clerical immunity, which, ironically, William may have derived from Lanfranc's own collection of canon law. But this early example of the clash between royal and ecclesiastical jurisdiction reveals that the English clergy were traditionalists: unlike advanced Gregorians they continued to recognize the practical distinction between the spiritual and temporal spheres.

It is perhaps a sign of William's ability or Rufus's magnanimity that the bishop was restored to favour in 1091 and resumed his position as one of the king's closest advisers. In 1095, at the Council of Rockingham, he led the bishops in their repudiation of Archbishop Anselm, accusing the primate, unblushingly despite the events of 1088, of polluting his fealty to the king. William evidently chose arguments that would serve his immediate turn, and would, no doubt, have agreed with Winston Churchill that consistency is a mark of mediocrity. But the violence of his attack on Anselm lost William the support of the barons: he was, perhaps, too clever by half. He died on 2 January 1096, appropriately enough at the king's court at Windsor, for his career was crucially bound up with the government of the first two Norman kings. Yet he never neglected his diocese. Under his auspices, a new cathedral was begun in 1093. He thus lays claim to have been the begetter of two of the most impressive surviving monuments of his age: Domesday Book and Durham Cathedral.

Further Reading
J. C. Holt, *Domesday Studies*, 1987.

WILLIAM OF VALENCE (after 1225-96), the fourth son of Isabella of Angoulême, widow of King John and Hugh of Lusignan, Count of La Marche, was the most prominent and disliked of Henry III's Poitevin half-brothers who had their fortunes made in England after their arrival in 1247. William's brothers Guy and Geoffrey were richly rewarded with estates and pensions, while another brother, Aymer, received the richest see in England, Winchester (1250). For William himself was reserved the largest prize, a wealthy heiress, Joan of Munchesni, who brought with her property worth £700 a year, to which Henry added another £800 worth. For the next decade, William and his brothers continued to enjoy the king's largesse, despite the dwindling scope for royal patronage. By the mid-1250s, William was second only to Richard of Cornwall in preferment and prominence at court. This naturally caused resentment, especially among those like Simon de Montfort who thought they were insufficiently supported. Added insult was the king's explicit protection of his half-brothers from hostile legal action and their own rapacity and violence. They behaved, as indeed they were, above the law. One Norfolk chronicler wrote 'no Englishman could get his right or obtain a writ against them'. The Lusignans were not unique in this: in 1256, Henry included Richard of Cornwall, the Earl of Gloucester and his wife's uncle Peter of Savoy in this privilege. However, the Lusignans, through their aggressive exploitation of the king's friendship and immunity, were especially hated. Their apparent monopoly of royal favour turned jealousy into serious political opposition. It is striking that two of those associated in the protection against writs of 1256, Gloucester and Peter of Savoy, were among the first to attack Henry and the Lusignans in 1258. Simon de

Montfort's relations with William of Valance had been notoriously bad for years, the earl seeming to blame the Poitevin for much of his disappointment over patronage. However, the crisis of 1258-9 was lent its especially bitter edge by the collective vendetta against the Lusignan favourites who were the first casualties of their refusal to swear to the Provisions of Oxford, being forced into exile. The barons dressed up their factional rivalry by accusing the Lusignans of inciting the king to believe he was above the law. More significantly, the accident of their foreign birth allowed participants and observers alike to characterize the baronial reforms as in some sense a national reaction against malign alien influence. Thus, negatively, William and his brothers contributed to the emergence of national identity among the English political classes. Restored in 1261, William played a leading part in the royalist cause. Escaping after Lewes, he returned with an army in 1265 for the campaign which ended at Evesham. William's career remained attached to the monarchy. He went on crusade with the Lord Edward (1270-3) and continued assiduously to increase his landed holdings thereafter for the rest of his life. William, a lover of tournaments whose passion for his hobby extended to searching out the best horses in Europe, was vain and arrogant, with the love of those spoilt when young of throwing his weight about. That his power derived from no quality of his except the accident of birth was his blessing, but his patron's cross.

WILLIAM OF WARENNE (*d*.1088) was one of those followers of William of Normandy who made their fortunes by the conquest of England. The younger son of Rudulf of Varenne in Normandy (*d*.1074), he distinguished himself in ducal service as a very young man in the early 1050s. After the ducal victory at Mortemer (1054) he received estates in upper Normandy, but it was only after the English invasion that he attained the front rank. He fought at Hastings and was rewarded with lands which by 1086 extended into thirteen counties, most notably strategically important estates in Sussex centred round Lewes. By the end of William I's reign he was one of the dozen largest individual landowners in England. He repaid his debt with vigorous loyalty in both England and France. In 1075 he played a leading role in supressing the revolt of the Earls of Hereford and Norfolk. After the Conqueror's death, Warenne supported William Rufus in 1087-8 against Robert Curthose and Odo of Bayeux. Rufus encouraged his service by creating him Earl of Surrey in 1088. The same year Warenne was seriously wounded by an arrow in his leg at the siege of Pevensey and died at his foundation of Lewes Priory on 24 June 1088. Warenne's career was more than meteoric. A younger son of an obscure minor Norman nobleman, he had risen through conspicuous loyalty to his lord to

become not only one of the richest men in one of the richest kingdoms of Europe but also the founder of a dynasty which, powerful, wealthy and influential, survived as Earls of Surrey until 1347. Warenne's foundation at Lewes (1078/80) was the first Cluniac house in England, another sign of the Conquest's effect on establishing institutional as well as personal links across the Channel. Warenne's success depended on the traditional chivalric virtues of loyalty, bravery and prowess in arms. His life illustrates the stupendous prizes and the personal dangers on offer to those who joined the conquest of England. It was appropriate that Warenne's direct descendant, John de Warenne, Earl of Surrey (1231-1304), when challenged in 1278 by royal commissioners to produce title to his lands, produced an old rusty sword declaring 'Here, my Lord, is my warrant [*warrantus*: a pun which no doubt appealed to the somewhat intractable sense of honour of the time]. My ancestors came with William the Bastard and won their lands with the sword, and by the sword I will hold them against all comers.' Earl John won his case. William of Warenne would have approved.

WILLIAM OF YPRES (*d*.?1165), one of the leading mercenary captains of the mid-twelfth century, played a prominent role in support of King Stephen in the late 1130s and early 1140s. The illegitimate son of Philip of Loo and a wool-carder of Ypres, and a grandson of Count Robert I of Flanders (1071-93), he may have been involved in the plot to assassinate Count Charles the Good in 1127 and certainly was one of the competitors for the county in 1127-8. Expelled from Flanders in 1133, William found refuge in England. For a decade after 1135 he led Stephen's Flemish mercenaries, proving himself the king's most loyal and effective commander. In the process he acquired an evil reputation for ruthlessness and violence, beginning in Normandy on Stephen's ill-fated visit in 1137, when he and his troops antagonized and frightened the Norman aristocracy in equal measure. In 1141, he apparently abandoned Stephen to capture at the battle of Lincoln (February). But at least he and his soldiers lived to fight another day and in the following months when Stephen's cause hung in the balance he showed unswerving loyalty. It was William's tactical skill which led to the capture of Robert of Gloucester and the Rout of Winchester (September 1141) which restored the king's fortunes.

Later in the 1140s, as the general fighting died down, William appears to have mellowed, perhaps because he went blind. He turned his energies to ecclesiastical patronage, founding Boxley Abbey (1144-6), and political mediation, as in 1148 between Stephen and Archbishop Theobald. Stephen rewarded William with large estates and revenues in Kent which Henry II allowed him to keep, at least until 1156/7. As did many violent men of the time, William ended his days in the cloister, at St Peter's, Loo, in his native Flanders

Although the civil war highlighted his importance, it should be remembered that he was engaged by Stephen at the height of the king's power early in the reign. Mercenaries, i.e. paid soldiers, were not emergency expedients in the armies of the central Middle Ages, but a permanent and necessary presence. For instance, William II's reputation as a powerful warlord depended, according to Abbot Suger, on his being a 'brilliant recruiter and paymaster of knights'. William of Ypres's career presents a striking contradiction to the supposed norms of chivalric society. Against the topos of devoted martial valour of men serving their lords out of 'feudal' loyalty so carefully nurtured by predominantly clerical writers at least since the eighth century, William, who openly served for material profit, proved both more skilful and more loyal than his baronial colleagues. He, William Marshal and Richard I's mercenary commander Mercadier give the lie to the politically and socially comfortable conceit that trust could not be bought. Indeed, their activities suggest that it was not profit but the traditional bonds of aristocratic society that bred untrustworthiness. The barons who forced King John to sign Magna Carta in 1215 tacitly accepted this in their condemnation, by name, of the king's mercenary leaders in Clause 50. Gerard d'Athée, Engelard de Cigogné and the rest were dangerous precisely for the firmness of their devotion to the king: a marked contrast to their noble critics.

Further Reading
R. H. C. Davis, *King Stephen*, 1967.

WILLIAMS OF CONWAY, JOHN (1582-1650), Archbishop of York and the most distinguished Welshman of the seventeenth century, came from an ancient north Welsh family. Educated at Ruthin Grammar School and St John's College, Cambridge, of which he became a Fellow, Williams, an able scholar, fluent and witty in speech, politician rather than spiritual leader, accumulated a series of benefices, thanks largely to the patronage of Lord Ellesmere, before he hitched his wagon to Buckingham's star and became in 1620 Dean of Westminster, and in 1621 Bishop of Lincoln. Prudence rather than principle impelled him to decline consecration by Archbishop Abbot after the latter's unfortunate homicide. In 1621 also he was appointed Lord Keeper, and he held this office for the remainder of James I's reign. Shrewd and moderate in outlook even if he was an unblushing careerist, he gave Buckingham good advice, not always accepted; he told him to abandon the monopolists, and he was against the Spanish war. Characteristically, James I liked and appreciated Williams, just as he distrusted Laud.

Things were different after 1625. Neither the worldliness nor the moderation of Williams appealed to Charles I, and his opposition to war with Spain had lost him Buckingham's patronage. He was dismissed from the office of Lord Keeper, forbidden (even though he was Dean of Westminster) to take part in the coronation, and ordered to withdraw to his diocese. These were bitter blows, but Williams was neither broken nor abashed. In 1625 and 1628 he supported the policies of the Commons. Secure in his power in his great diocese, the largest in England, which he regarded almost as a feudal appanage; a pluralist who had amassed wealth by impropriations and who held rectories, prebends and the deanery of Westminster as well as Lincoln; he lived in high state in his palace at Buckden, building, planting and enclosing, patronizing scholars like Selden, entertaining and providing musical festivities at which he displayed his native gifts as a singer. From moderation, or independence, or perhaps lack of any real concern, Williams, in Professor Trevor-Roper's words, 'behaved throughout his career as if no differences in religious principles existed'.* Such an attitude may have had wisdom in it for the bishop of a diocese which in the 1630s contained a great many active Puritans, but it was anathema to Laud, a personal enemy since the days when they had clashed for Buckingham's patronage. There was a brush over Laud's effort to turn the communion table into an altar at the East End, and Williams licensed an anonymous book, really his own work, *The Holy Table, Name and Thing*, which took a moderate line. Yet Laud was clearly determined to crush Williams, and eventually he succeeded. From 1628 onwards a series of charges, ranging from revealing Privy Council secrets to favouring Puritans in his diocese, was brought in the Star Chamber. Williams, relying on friends at court, bribed witnesses to give false evidence and so played into Laud's hands. In 1637 he was fined £10,000, suspended from carrying out his episcopal functions, and sent to the Tower where he preferred to stay rather than accept exile to a Welsh or Irish bishopric. A second Star Chamber case, based on correspondence with the headmaster of Westminster School in which the latter called Laud 'a little meddling hocus-pocus', brought upon Williams a further fine of £8,000.

The coming of the Long Parliament reversed fortunes: Williams was released from the Tower in 1640, and Laud sent into it a few months later. Williams continued to take an independent line over religion, attempting to solve the problem of episcopacy by regulating the authority of bishops. Characteristically he advised the king to sign the attainder of Strafford in 1641 on the grounds that he must distinguish between his private conscience which told him to refuse and his public

*H. R. Trevor-Roper, *Archbishop Laud*, 1962 edn, p.54.

conscience which required him to sign in order to avert further bloodshed. Later the same year Charles made Williams, Archbishop of York, a barren gesture of moderation. Bishops were out of favour. In December, Williams and some of his brethren going to parliament had to be rescued from riotous apprentices, and when he and eleven other members of the bench formally protested that acts passed by the Lords in their absence were null and void, the Commons impeached them and the Lords sent them to the Tower.

When war broke out Williams went to York and joined Charles. Later he departed to north Wales and fortified Conway Castle for the king. There he quarrelled with the royalist military leaders, maintaining that their proceedings were damaging the interests of his people of north Wales. When in 1645 the royalist commander Sir John Owen dispossessed him of the castle, he came to terms with the parliamentarians and shortly before his death in 1646 assisted them in reducing it. This astute and resourceful Welshman blended calculating ambition and genuine moderation in a remarkable career. Playing the part of a prince of the church before both Laudian agents and Puritan sectaries, he spent £1,000 a year in charity in his diocese and left benefactions on a princely scale, including libraries to Westminster School, Lincoln College, Oxford, and St John's College, Cambridge, scholarships at Westminster and fellowships at St John's.

Further Reading
B. Dew Roberts, *Mitre and Musket*, 1938.

WILLIAMS, ROGER (1604?-83), champion of religious liberty, probably London-born, the protégé of Sir Edward Coke, was educated at Charterhouse and Pembroke College, Cambridge. He became a Puritan preacher and migrated to Massachusetts in 1630. There he quickly came into conflict with the Governor and the controlling body of freemen over the two beliefs which he was to champion for the remaining fifty years of his life – that the individual had the right to worship in whatever way he wished without any interference by the established church, and that the state had no right to interfere in matters of conscience. Expelled from Massachusetts, he moved into the Narrangansett country to the south and in 1636 founded the settlement of Providence. Rhode Island, the colony which developed round this nucleus, offered toleration to men and women of all faiths. In 1643-4 Williams visited England and secured from the parliamentarians a charter for the colonists. About the same time he wrote *The Bloudy Tenent of Persecution for Cause of Conscience*, a vigorous demand for religious liberty. The view that 'it is the will and command of God, that … the most Paganish, Jewish, Turkish or Antichristian consciences and worships' be permitted was acceptable to few in England in 1644, and the month after Williams set sail for Providence

again parliament ordered his book to be burned by the common hangman. He paid one more visit to England in 1651-4, and devoted the rest of his long life to the well-being of Rhode Island. Roger Williams, whose friends in England included Milton, Henry Vane the Younger and Hugh Peter, was in some ways a disputatious man, apt to provoke hostility. His historical achievement, in which he was a pioneer among Puritans, was to push the Puritan belief in the individual conscience to its logical conclusion of complete religious liberty, and to found in the tough yet favourable circumstances of seventeenth-century North America a colony based upon this.

Further Reading
S. H. Brockunier, *The Irrepressible Democrat, Roger Williams*, 1940.
J. Ernst, *Roger Williams*, 1932.

WILLIBALD, ST (*c.*700-86) was an English monk who travelled widely in the Mediterranean region as a pilgrim and ended up as Bishop of Eichstätt in Germany. A native of Wessex and a relative of Boniface, Willibald was brought up as a monk at Bishops Waltham in Hampshire. Touched by the impulse to undertake a pilgrimage to Rome – as King Cadwalla of Wessex had done and as King Ine was shortly to do – he set off accompanied by his brother Winnibald and his father in 720. But Rome was not enough for Willibald. While staying there he formed the intention of extending his pilgrimage to the Holy Land. In 722 he set out by way of Sicily, Greece, Cyprus and Syria and after various adventures, including imprisonment by the Muslim authorities in Homs, came safe to Jerusalem. After some considerable time spent in visiting the Holy Places of Palestine, Willibald travelled to Constantinople where he passed two years. In 729, after about seven years of travel, he returned to Italy and joined the monastic community at Monte Cassino. There he remained for about ten years. In about 739-40 he went to join his kinsman Boniface in Germany, and established a monastery at Eichstätt. In 741 Boniface consecrated him a bishop, probably intending him for the proposed new see at Erfurt. In the event, the establishment of Erfurt did not succeed, so a bishopric was created (by 745) for Willibald based on his own monastery at Eichstatt. He remained a missionary bishop in southern Germany for the rest of his life.

Willibald's brother Winnibald also gravitated to Germany. Together the brothers founded the monastery of Heidenheim. It was a double monastery for both monks and nuns on the Anglo-Saxon model. After Winnibald's death in 761 their sister Walburga became abbess: she has given her name, quite fortuitously, to the strange festivities of *Walpurgisnacht*. It was a nun of Heidenheim who took down from Willibald in his old age the story of his travels as a young man and recorded them in a work known as the *Hodoeporicon*.

Willibald was the earliest English traveller to the Middle East known to us. The *Hodoeporicon* reveals him as adventurous, inquisitive, observant, with a gift for vivid anecdote and a remarkable memory for detail. Many themes which have become familiar in English travel literature since his day were enunciated for the first time in Willibald's account. He was foolhardy and eccentric, climbing an active volcano in the Lipari Islands. He frequently fell ill. He did not always get on with foreign food: he refers to what seems to have been yoghourt with suspicion and distaste. Like many later English travellers he was irked by foreign officialdom. One of his most enjoyable stories, recounted with pride, tells how he ingeniously smuggled some precious balsam past customs officials in the Muslim city of Tyre. *Plus ça change.*

Further Reading

The *Hodoeporicon* is translated in C. H. Talbot, *The Anglo-Saxon Missionaries in Germany*, 1954.

WILLIBRORD, ST (658-739) was a Northumbrian monk who became a missionary to Frisia and Archbishop of Utrecht. He was educated under Wilfrid at Ripon, where he became a monk. In 677-8 he went to Ireland, where he remained for twelve years as a pupil of the Northumbrian exile Egbert. It was from Wilfrid and Egbert that he derived his vocation to work on the continent as a missionary. In 690, accompanied by eleven companions, he crossed to the mouth of the Rhine to begin preaching Christianity to the pagan Frisians. For this he needed the support of the secular authorities and turned to Pippin II, who was at that time the effective ruler, though not actually king, of the Franks. Frankish authority was being pushed gradually eastwards into Frisia and it is likely that Pippin saw Willibrord and his fellows as a potential adjunct of Frankish dominion. He willingly extended his protection to them. Willibrord took a further initiative which was to be very important for the future of the Frankish church. As might have been expected from a disciple of Wilfrid, he turned to Rome and obtained the sanction and encouragement of Pope Sergius I for the work he was intent on. A few years later, in 695, Willibrord paid a second visit to Rome at the insistence of Pippin, on which occasion Sergius consecrated him Archbishop of the Frisians. When he returned Pippin established him at Utrecht as his base of operations. It was Pippin and his family, again, who were the very generous patrons who helped Willibrord to establish a monastery further south, at Echternach in modern Luxembourg.

We know little in detail about the work which Willibrord accomplished during the long remainder of his life. Any correspondence which he kept – so illuminating in the case of his slightly younger contemporary Boniface – has not survived, and the biography composed about a generation after his death by his kinsman Alcuin is not very revealing about his missionary achievements. Bede, who was keenly interested in his work, tells us that Willibrord consecrated bishops, but we know nothing of them. Presumably Willibrord envisaged an ecclesiastical province based on Utrecht something along the lines of the province of Canterbury created by Augustine and Theodore. Whatever structure of ecclesiastical administration may have been set up, it did not long survive its founder: Utrecht was subsequently absorbed into the province of Cologne. However, the work of converting the Frisians did proceed, if slowly: much had been achieved, but much still remained to be done, by the time of Willibrord's death in 739.

It would seem that Willibrord had plans to extend his work beyond the mission field of Frisia. Echternach looks like a base for expansion into Thuringia and Hesse, the regions of central Germany south of Frisia where Boniface was to build on Willibrord's foundations in the 720s and 730s. Willibrord even tried to preach Christianity to the Danes, though with very little success.

The English missions to the continent, which were to have such momentous consequences for the development of European civilization, began remarkably quickly after the conversion of the English themselves. The last pagan kingdom of Anglo-Saxon England, the Isle of Wight, was nominally converted only three years before Willibrord set off for Frisia. Why were the English so eager to undertake missionary work abroad? There are several possible answers to this question. The Christian culture into which the English were growing was influenced by the evangelizing concerns of Pope Gregory I and by the ideal of 'pilgrimage for Christ' which, as in the case of Columba, merged imperceptibly into a missionary impulse. The two strands met in Wilfrid and Egbert, among others, and their pupil Willibrord. The Anglo-Saxons were conscious of the Germanic homeland from which they had once come and the more thoughtful churchmen among them felt a responsibility for the salvation of those who were, as Boniface put it in 738, 'of one blood and bone with us'. With Frisia in particular their connections were close. Frisians had settled in parts of eastern England. Anglo-Frisian trading connections of an intensity which we would not suspect from our few written references to them have been revealed by recent archaeological excavation. Above all, the Old English language of the seventh and eighth centuries was very close to the tongue of the Frisians: Anglo-Saxon missionaries were more intelligible to the Frisians than any others might have been.

The Frisians were gradually being conquered by the Franks. Frankish rulers such as Pippin II and his son

Charles Martel perceived that missionaries who were not Franks would be more acceptable to the subjugated peoples than those that were. This circumstance could present the missionaries with painful moral dilemmas. Boniface certainly felt them, as we know from his letters, and it is fair to suppose that Willibrord did too. It has always been a source of anxiety for Christian missionaries associated with an expanding imperial power. Exactly how intimate were these links with the Franks it is hard to say. Pippin and Charles Martel may have looked on Willibrord as in some sense 'their' man. But he may not have perceived the relationship in quite the same terms.

The problem thickens if we try to be aware of other missionaries, contemporaries of Willibrord's, in other regions of the Frankish eastern Marches. A patriotic tendency in English historiography has focussed attention too exclusively, if understandably, upon the Anglo-Saxon contribution to the conversion of Germany. There were other men at work, Irish, Aquitanian, Italian, Spanish, all of them to a greater or lesser degree dependent upon Frankish secular authority. Other men faced moral dilemmas, found different solutions to them. None of them, including Willibrord, was simply and cynically 'used' by Frankish power. The German mission field was both active and diverse in the eighth century. To emphasize this is not to belittle Willibrord's achievement. He was a big man. So was Boniface. Between them they exerted a more far-reaching influence upon European culture than any other Englishmen who have ever lived.

Further Reading
W. Levison, *England and the Continent in the Eighth Century*, 1946, remains the best account in English of Willibrord.

WILLOUGHBY, SIR HUGH (*d.*1554), navigator, was the son of Sir Henry Willoughby of Middleton, who was made a knight-banneret at the battle of Stoke in 1487 and died in 1528. The date of Hugh's birth is unknown. He first saw military service in Hertford's expedition to Scotland in 1544, when he was knighted at Leith on 11 May. From 1548-9 he was captain of Lowther Castle on the border. When Somerset fell from power, Willoughby lost a valuable patron: it may be either this or the suggestion of friends, among whom Sebastian Cabot would be one, which made him turn his thoughts to the sea.

By the middle of the sixteenth century the manufacture of woollen cloth in England had outstripped home consumption, and the continental markets, especially after the crash of Antwerp in 1551, were also shrinking. There was great need to find new markets, and the Far East seemed to be the most promising area. No doubt an additional, but subsidiary, attraction was the certainty of a valuable return cargo of pepper and spices (Foster, *England's Quest of Eastern Trade*, pp.5-6). The difficulty was how to get there without infringing the Spanish and Portuguese monopolies. In 1553 was formed in London a company of 200 shareholders with a capital of 240 shares of £25 each to open up trade with Cathay by sailing along the north-eastern shores of Europe by the so-called North-East Passage. The company was given a charter by Edward VI, and Sebastian Cabot became its first Governor.

The first expedition sent out by the company consisted of only three ships, of which the largest was the *Bona Esperanza*, 160 tons, commanded by Sir Hugh Willoughby as Captain-General, with Richard Chancellor in the *Edward Bonaventure* as Pilot-General. The third ship was the *Bona Confidentia*. The fleet set sail from Ratcliffe on 10 May 1553. In August, after passing the Lofoten Islands, Chancellor was separated from the other two ships by a storm and he therefore made straight for the rendezvous at Vardo. Willoughby and his ships never arrived there. For weeks they wandered about in ice and fog: they probably sighted the coast of Novaia Zemlia; in September they reached the bay of Arzina on the coast of Lapland. Here they spent the winter, but although they were provisioned for eighteen months, the arctic cold and possibly also scurvy caused them all to perish miserably (1554).

In the spring some Russian fishermen found the two ships and the frozen corpses, together with Willoughby's will and journal which prove that the party was alive in January 1554. The vessels were recovered and, manned with new crews, were brought home. The journal was printed by Hakluyt, and there is a manuscript copy of it in the Cottonian MSS (Otho E viii 10), but neither the original of it nor of the will can now be traced.

It was said that Willoughby's corpse was brought home for burial, but there is no proof of this at all. A tradition holds that his clothes were sent home and were used in painting the portrait preserved at Wollaton House as the only known authentic portrait of Willoughby: but this cannot be true, because the clothes belong to the seventeenth century (C. R. Beard, *Connoisseur*, July 1931).

Further Reading
W. Foster, *England's Quest of Eastern Trade*, 1933.
R. Hakluyt, *The Principal Navigations, Voyages, Trafiques and Discoveries of the English Nation*, Hakluyt Society, 1903-5.

WILSON, RICHARD (1714-82), landscape painter, was born on the Welsh border where his father held a living. In those days provincial artists of talent were practically obliged to go to London to complete their training and find a market; Wilson was no exception. For years he painted portraits of no particular excellence, and latterly was even engaged to paint the future George III and his brother, the Duke of York. Then, at the age of thirty-six, he travelled to Italy, where the artist Zuccarelli persuaded him to turn once and for all to landscape painting. Six years Wilson spent in Rome, and when he finally returned to England his head was full to bursting with the physical features – the noble ruins lit by the level southern light and the grander illumination of antiquity, the orderly sequence of plain, lake, grove and hill – which belonged to the Campagna; full too with the work of those European artists (particularly Claude, and Poussin) who had made the scenery of the Campagna their meat and drink. Those features Wilson proceeded to impress on the face of English landscape, so that even a *View on the Wye* breathes the air of the Appennines. But he painted some lovely pictures, the best of which (*Penn Ponds* and *The Thames at Twickenham*, for example) contain none of the Italian furniture and are pure England. Yet from the time of his return, few bought his pictures. Although he was a founder-member of the Royal Academy (1768) and exhibited there until 1780, only his appointment as librarian to the Academy saved him from the extremes of poverty. A small property at Llanberis fell to him by succession in time to allow him to die (1782) in his native country.

Wilson's landscapes were painted in the mould of Claude Poussin and Salvator Rosa at a time when those masters' works were the prey of the English lords and the quarry of their landscape-gardeners. But it was also the time when an English 'connoisseur' could say in public, 'You surely would not have me hang a modern English picture in my house, unless it were a portrait?' Wilson was not a foreigner, and that was a portion of his ill-success. He was also a gruff and unaccommodating man, ill-disposed to flattery, who could describe Gainsborough's foliage as 'fried parsley'. Most important, he was not the pure classicist which the patrons would have had him. In his love for the paintings of Cuyp and van Ruisdael and the other seventeenth-century Dutch landscape masters still then unappreciated in England, in his neglect of detailed representation in favour of a unified effect, in his imparting to nature in some of his landscapes – especially the Welsh ones, *Cader Idris* and *Snowdon from Llyn Ogwen* – qualities of solitude and grandeur and the true antiquity of geological time, he shows that he was mature enough to have intimations of the Romantic. Thus he was a prophet, and like most prophets, unpopular in his day and a little over-valued by posterity. To call him, for example, 'the father of English landscape' would be just, if George Lambert had not preceded him.

WINCHELSEY, ROBERT (*c*.1240-1313), Archbishop of Canterbury from 1294, was the greatest of the theologically-trained pastor-bishops in England at the turn of the thirteenth century. Born apparently at Old Winchelsea in Sussex, he was educated at the universities of Paris, where he headed the faculty of arts in 1267, and at Oxford, where he was a doctor of theology and chancellor of the university in 1288. He was a famous teacher, a supporter of student rights, and as a writer 'a model example of scholastic thought at its best'. A man of blameless personal life and utter integrity, the generous patron of learning and the poor, affable and good humoured at table, he was above all a man of principle, who resolved what was right and adhered to it regardless of consequences. He was, we are told, 'equitable in all things, severe in his censures and no respecter of persons, nor could many gifts turn him from justice'. 'Stern and determined', inflexible and uncompromising, he is recorded as acting in 'his rough way', with 'his accustomed ferocity', and with 'fury and obstinacy'.

Such a man was a worthy opponent for the equally self-righteous and unyielding Edward I. But Winchelsey was not an impractical idealist. He strove to take an independent line that gave the king and pope their dues and was yet in the best interests of the English church. He led from the front, fully accepting the consequences of his acts, but did not oblige others to proceed so far. In the early years of his archiepiscopate, from 1294-1303, assertion of ecclesiastical privilege brought Pope Boniface VIII into conflict with the Kings of France and England, both of whom wished to tax their clergy to finance their war over Gascony. Winchelsey recognized the justice of King Edward's appeal for financial support for defence of the realm and wanted to support him within reason, but Edward's demands were unreasonable and Winchelsey was forbidden to grant anything by Boniface VIII's bull *Clericis Laicos* (1296). Refusal of supply led to the outlawing of the clergy and their harrying, which included the seizure of Winchelsey's own horses. Although most clergy gave way, Winchelsey did not, and Edward was forced to recognize he had gone too far. Subsequently Winchelsey kept taxation to tenths levied only on clerical temporalities, not their spiritual income which he saw as sacred, granted freely by ecclesiastical assemblies, and administered by the clergy themselves.

The archbishop also sought to force royal clerks to reside and be ordained and he resisted deliberate attempts to extend royal patronage, for example in royal free chapels. Winchelsey was committed to the independence of church and clergy. His 'fight was against *all* lay encroachments upon ecclesiastical rights'. Hence his failure to make common cause with aristocratic opposition in and after 1297, which partly explains why clerical grievances were not satisfactorily resolved. In any case his battles with the Crown were not fought on equal terms: firstly, because such issues were settled in royal not church courts; secondly, because Boniface VIII progressively backed down on taxation, making it difficult for Winchelsey to maintain his independent stance; and thirdly and conclusively because Clement V, pope from 1305, placed good relations with his former master

Edward I ahead of ecclesiastical principles, conceding most of what the king wanted over Winchelsey's head and suspending the archbishop from office. Although Winchelsey was restored in 1307, the world had changed. Clement V deferred to Edward II's wishes and Winchelsey could not have continued his struggle even had he been physically fit enough to do so. The next archbishop, the non-graduate Walter Reynolds, was a devoted royal official like the unsuccessful Robert Burnell forty years earlier. What had disqualified Burnell was now what was required of an archbishop.

Further Reading

P. Heath, *Church and Realm 1272-1461*, 1988.

J. H. Denton, *Robert Winchelsey and the Crown 1294-1313: A study in the defence of ecclesiastical liberty*, 1980.

WINDHAM, WILLIAM (1750-1810) was war minister under Pitt and Dundas from 1794 to 1801, and later briefly in the 'ministry of all the talents'. He was one of the best parliamentary speakers of his day and an imaginative minister. In his ardent pursuit of new ideas and hasty, sometimes injudicious, efforts to execute them he recalls the youthful Churchill. He lacked the patient application of Castlereagh, who succeeded him in 1807, and he cannot be counted among great war ministers. As a politician he exposed himself to the charge of inconsistency. But the young man who became one of Dr Johnson's dearest friends, the middle-aged patriot who befriended Cobbett and sought to make that awkward individualist a good government man, the civilized Norfolk squire who was one of the earliest patrons of Humphrey Repton, cannot be judged as a politician alone. 'Weathercock Windham' was one of the most agreeable as well as one of the most capable men in public life.

The son of William Windham, a cavalry officer, and member of parliament, the author of a military manual and supporter of Chatham's militia scheme, he grew up at the family seat, Felbrigg, and went to Eton, Glasgow University, where he studied under the philosopher John Anderson, and University College, Oxford. His was a keen, ingenious mind. He was always fascinated by novelties: for a time he was much concerned with balloons. His friendship with Dr Johnson was a formative, inspiring experience. The old sage warmed to his enthusiasm and lively scholarship. 'Such conversation I shall not have again till I come back to the regions of literature; and there', said Johnson, 'Windham is *inter stellas luna minores*'. Windham tended his last illness and acted as a pallbearer at his funeral. For a time he carried on a hopeless, possibly platonic, affair with the wife of a Norfolk friend, John Byng. He was liable to bouts of melancholy and was happiest among his pictures and books at Felbrigg, or when he had important work to do. Reynolds's portrait of him in later life shows fine,

sensitive features, the face of a man of feeling – but one accustomed to thought.

He first tasted politics when he became secretary to the Lord Lieutenant of Ireland in 1783. 'Don't be afraid, sir,' said Johnson, when Windham consulted him upon a question of ethics, 'You will soon make a very pretty rascal.' But Windham was ever the most scrupulous of men, always threatening resignation on some point of principle when in office, happier when he was free to criticize. In 1784 he became member of parliament for Norwich. Like his Norfolk colleague, Coke of Holkham, he was a keen Whig. He assisted in the impeachment of Hastings. Later he followed Burke in opposition to the Revolution. Pitt recognized the value of this convert who was convinced of the necessity of war against France. In 1794 he made him Secretary at War with a seat in the Cabinet, but under Dundas, who had over-all powers of direction. Unfortunately Windham was, like Dundas, an amateur in strategy. His approach was coloured by his chivalrous sympathy for the émigrés, for whom he was made specially responsible. Lord Guilford once said that he could never see Windham without picturing Don Quixote with a barber's basin on his head. He never overcame his regret for the Bourbons. Veneration for Burke was his dominant political idea. The Breton fiasco of 1795 was a disillusioning reminder of the hazards of supporting a local rising in anything but overwhelming strength. British support was inadequate and the Vendéan rising was suppressed. If anything the British patronage of exiled nobles and Breton peasants strengthened the revolutionary government; it certainly contributed to the rise of Napoleon. Windham ought not to be blamed too severely for this or other failures of strategy. Pitt and Dundas allowed themselves the luxury of dispersal of effort when the army was too small and too badly trained for one successful expedition, let alone for a global war. Their policy was almost a caricature of the successful strategy pursued by the elder Pitt. Windham at least contributed a passionate will to win. He actually visited the campaign area during the Duke of York's operations in Flanders. And he perceived more plainly than others the need to improve conditions of pay and service. He understood the importance of propaganda and patronized Cobbett's *Porcupine*, then helped him found the *Political Register*. It is typical of the way in which Windham's schemes went awry that this paper, which began life as friend of church and state, became the most effective of radical journals, the scourge of governments.

He resigned with Pitt over the king's refusal to add Catholic Emancipation to Irish Union. He derided Addington and savaged the peace of Amiens; he was impatient with Pitt for not doing the same. His militant views lost him his seat at Norwich and, temporarily, his friendship with Coke. He could hardly be described now as a Whig. 'Who would repair their house during a hurricane?' was his rejoinder when men talked of reform. He returned to parliament as member for a Grenville borough. In 1804, however, he showed that he had his share of the spirit of party when he declined to enter Pitt's second administration. He was also convinced about the necessity for a settlement of the Irish question. In 1806 he became Secretary for War and Colonies in the 'ministry of all the talents' and put forward the scheme that embodied his thinking and experience, the General Training Act. The whole population was to be trained in batches of 200,000 at a time. Men were to be allowed to enlist for a short period and they were offered higher rates of pay if they chose to re-engage. The volunteer system was ended. The conception was sound, the execution poor. Windham should have given the business his whole time. Unfortunately he preferred to plan operations.

After the disastrous failure of Pitt's last coalition it seemed pointless to contest Napoleon's grip on the continent. The new world offered more scope; great trading interests were at stake. So ambitious operations were mounted. Popham captured Buenos Aires but it was subsequently lost. Whitelocke was sent to retrieve the situation and establish a permanent base. The idea was that the colonists would welcome the British as liberators. But Whitelocke failed to capture Buenos Aires after bloody assaults and sailed for home and court martial. Castlereagh inherited a bleak situation indeed. His first measures included a drastic reassessment of the role of the militia; he took 30,000 to be trained along with regulars. Windham naturally preferred his own scheme and attacked Castlereagh's. He opposed the assault on Copenhagen (1807) and the expedition to Walcheren (1809). He supported the Peninsular war, however, and it is sad that he did not live to see Wellington's final victories.

Further Reading

R. W. Ketton-Cremer, *The Early Life and Diaries of William Windham*, 1930.

WINSOR, FREDERICK ALBERT (1763-1830) was a pioneer of gas lighting and fuelling. In the early nineteenth century the demand for a new source of lighting came first from mill-owners who looked for something safer and cheaper than lamp oil for lighting their buildings at night. Napoleon's economic blockade interfered with the supply of whale oil and Russian tallow. In 1803 Winsor gave a demonstration of gas lighting at the Lyceum in the Strand. In 1807, on the king's birthday, he lit with gas the walls of Carlton House Gardens. If, however, sensational displays for specific occasions were to be turned into a regular source of energy, there must be a central generating plant, with mains leading from it. After giving evidence to parliament and the Privy Council, and appealing to the king, Winsor obtained a charter incorporating a 'National Light and Heat Company': it was subsequently renamed 'The Gas Light and Coke Company'.

In 1814 gas replaced oil in the lamps of the parish of St Margaret's, Westminster. The improvement in lighting made the streets safer against robbery. Insurance companies offered lower premiums for gas-lit mills. Gas lighting would affect workers by facilitating night work; it also enlarged the amenities of social life. Mechanics' Institutes, concert and meeting halls, could be lit by gas. A uniform, steady, clear light, where people had known only the flickering light of candles or the soft glow of oil lamps: here was the start of a profound social and cultural change. At first those who, like Sir Walter Scott, installed gas in a private house, were few and daring. But as a public amenity the innovation of wartime became the necessary work of peace. In 1815 Winsor went to instal gas lighting in Paris. On the continent, his patent privileges were flouted; in Britain rival companies exploited his achievements. He never made a great profit out of all his endeavours.

WINSTANLEY, GERRARD (1609?-after 1660), Digger and utopian writer, was born at Wigan, son of a cloth trader. We know little about his life and circumstances. Apprenticed in London, he went into trade but was hard hit by the economic troubles of the 1640s and retired into the country, living on the generosity of friends. He wrote his first pamphlet, a theological one, in 1648. In 1649-50 he was the main personality among the Diggers and wrote several pieces to justify them. The most remarkable of his writings, *The Law of Freedom*, was a utopian essay dedicated to Oliver Cromwell in 1652. We last hear of him in 1660, living in Cobham.* The Diggers, the group who dug up the commons in Surrey, at St George's Hill (near Walton-on-Thames) and Cobham, were few, humble and courageous. They saw their action as a symbol of the future, not as an attack on private property, and they did not touch the lands of the rich. Persecuted by the local squires and peasantry, haled before Fairfax, they survived rather over a year before being finally broken up. Winstanley deserves to be better known for his writing, for he was one of the most original thinkers among seventeenth-century radicals. A visionary, driven on like his contemporaries, the first Quakers, by a belief in an inner light, he appalled orthodox Calvinists by his universalist view that all men would be saved. He was a millenarian, though not one who foresaw a violent revolution. *The Law of Freedom* envisaged a community without private property, money and wage labour, and it takes its place in the pedigree of

---

*But see James Alsop, 'Gerrard Winstanley's later life', *Past and Present*, February 1979.

socialist thought. Its communism is the communism of the early Christians, and its classless society is closer to the dream of John Ball than to the doctrines of Karl Marx. Nevertheless, Winstanley, like Harrington, saw the origins of the upheavals of his day in social terms, and believed that political liberty must be accompanied by social equality.

Further Reading
C. Hill, ed., *Winstanley: The Law of Freedom and Other Writings*, 1973.
G. H. Sabine, ed., *The Works of Gerrard Winstanley*, 1941.

WINTHROP, JOHN (1588-1649), Puritan colonist, came from a mercantile and landed family in Suffolk, where he inherited the manor of Groton. Educated at Trinity College, Cambridge, Winthrop was a man of natural force of character and firmness of judgement who exemplified Puritan piety at its sternest. He was one of many, especially in East Anglia, who for religious reasons grew dissatisfied with Stuart rule in the 1620s, believing that 'evil times are coming when the church must fly to the wilderness', and in 1629 he made up his mind to sail to North America. Shrewd enough to take the lead in compelling the Massachusetts Bay Company to transfer in advance political authority to those who actually settled in the colony, he was one of the handful of its members who sailed with about 1,000 others of Puritan persuasion in 1630. As first Governor of the Massachusetts Bay Colony, Winthrop played the main role in its establishment in the area centred upon Charlestown and Boston. He was primarily responsible for the decision of 1631 whereby full citizenship – i.e. the right to be a freeman and to vote at meetings of the governing body of the colony – was to be limited to church members, and for the expulsion of Roger Williams and Anne Hutchinson, with their heretical opinions, from Massachusetts. Frequently re-elected to the governorship, Winthrop probably did more than any other single individual to give Massachusetts, and thereby New England as a whole, its peculiar pattern of narrow orthodoxy, by embodying Puritan beliefs in the laws and constitution of the colony. Like many of the early New Englanders, Winthrop was a good scholar with a strong belief in education. Harvard College was founded during his time, and he himself kept a journal which has been a valuable source for historians.

Further Reading
E. S. Morgan, *The Puritan Dilemma: The Story of John Winthrop*, 1958.

WISEMAN, CARDINAL (1802-65) was chosen by Pope Pius IX to spearhead the introduction of the Roman Catholic hierarchy into England: and a disastrous choice he proved. The son of Irish parents with Spanish connections, and a student in Rome from the age of twelve,

he was neither by background nor temperament well equipped for the task. He thought big and spoke even bigger, and he conned the pope, as well as himself, into believing that the Anglican church, which had so recently been the church of Newman and Manning, could eventually be brought back into the Catholic fold. When the pope made him Cardinal Archbishop of Westminster (1850), with twelve sees under him, he issued an exultant Pastoral Letter 'from out The Flaminian Gate of Rome'. 'Catholic England has been restored to its orbit in the ecclesiastical firmament.' This was 'the crowning day of long hopes and the opening day of bright prospects'. Protestant England was outraged, not least by the choice of Westminster. *The Times* thought it 'one of the grossest acts of folly and impertinence that the Court of Rome has ventured to commit since the people of England threw off its yoke', and the prime minister, Russell, pushed through an Act which made territorial titles illegal for Roman Catholic bishops.

Wiseman's standing amongst the old-fashioned English Catholics was damaged too. They disliked his Roman habits, and frustrated many of his efforts to work for the Catholic Irish labourers who had poured into England after the Famine. His administrative incompetence became notorious, and the trail of half-finished business was so thick that the bishops shunned his meetings. Diabetes had him in its grip for the last years of his life, and he ended a lonely man. But he never lost the backing of Rome, and he was succeeded by the man most likely to carry through his Romanizing policies, not an old English Catholic but the convert, Manning.

Further Reading
D. Gwynn, *Cardinal Wiseman*, 1950.

WOLFE, JAMES (1727-59), general, was the son of major-general Wolfe, an Irishman, and Henriette Thompson. He entered the army at fourteen; two years later he was adjutant of his regiment, the 12th, at Dettingen. He died at the head of his troops on the Heights of Abraham. The ensuing capture of Quebec was the beginning of the end of French rule in Canada; and Wolfe was only thirty-two years old. His daring exploit ensured his fame, but there is more to remember him by than this. Intelligent, ambitious, as scrupulous in training as bold in action, Wolfe had already established himself as an exceptional commander.

He was born at Westerham in Kent, and it is there that we meet him, 'the youngest lieutenant-colonel in the army', in Thackeray's novel *The Virginians*: 'Very lean and very pale; his hair was red, his nose and cheek-bones were high, but he had a fine courtesy towards his elders, a cordial greeting towards his friends and an animation in conversation which caused those who heard him to forget, even to admire, those homely looks.' The shock of hair, long upturned nose and receding chin lent themselves to caricature and Wolfe was physically fragile too. He was, however, both ardent and thorough; he sought active service and he learned from his experiences. After serving under Wade in Flanders, he missed Fontenoy, but was at Falkirk with Hawley and on the staff at Culloden. He was certainly no sentimentalist: of the British troops in Scotland he wrote: 'I knew their discipline to be bad and their valour precarious. They are easily put into disorder and hard to recover out of it.' He was proud, however, of the bayonet-work of his regiment at Culloden. He was not party to the brutalities that followed the battle. 'Pistol the rebel dog,' said Hawley of a young wounded Jacobite lying on the ground; but Wolfe refused, and offered his commission instead. Later, however, on garrison work at Inversnaid, he combed the area for fugitives. The Highlanders, he believed, were 'better governed by fear than favour'. Six years later he proposed a plan which, had it been carried out, would have involved a deliberate massacre of the Clan Macpherson. 'Would you believe I am so bloody?' he wrote. ''Twas my real intention.' Yet it was to be the Highlanders who, kilted in the government's black tartan, scrambled up the Heights of Abraham.

The British army has always had a few officers who have not been content with the routines of regimental soldiering in peacetime. Like Wolfe, they have usually been derided by their fellow officers. He was sharply critical of ignorance and inertia. He studied Latin and mathematics. In the winter of 1752 he got leave to go to Paris to perfect his French, but he was not allowed to study the French or other continental armies. In the invasion of 1755 he practised his men in tactics specially devised to repel landings. He saw this problem from the other side when he took part in the abortive expedition to Rochefort in 1757. His conspicuous gallantry there was recognized by Pitt, who appointed him to serve under Amherst in Canada. In the attack upon Louisburg in May 1758 he led his part of the landing party to success through angry surf and fierce fire. He went home to recover his health for he was 'in very bad condition both with the gravel and rheumatism'. In the same letter he said: 'I have signified to Mr Pitt that he may dispose of my slight carcase as he pleases.' Pitt chose him to command the expedition being fitted out against Quebec. Newcastle demurred to George II, on the grounds that Wolfe was mad. 'Mad, is he?' replied the old king; 'Then I hope he will bite some of my other generals.'

Wolfe meanwhile became engaged to Miss Katherine Lowther, of the great northern family. He was in love, but he did not hesitate before the call to glory. He found Quebec well prepared, apparently impregnable. Montcalm had ample warning and 16,000 men in a natural fortress. Wolfe was attacked by fireships: spectacular affray but harmless. In an attack upon Montcalm's lines in July he suffered a costly repulse. He was fertile in expedients, his troops learned to adapt themselves and the fleet under Saunders was effective. But the operations of Amherst on the Lakes did not cause any significant diversion and Wolfe was faced by failure. Under strain he ordered the wholesale burning of outlying settlements. In August he grew ill, but recovered enough to project an audacious attack. The plan to land at the Anse du Foulon and climb the Heights of Abraham seems to have emanated from his brigadiers, Monckton, Townshend and Murray; but Wolfe made it his responsibility. His soldiers had come to love their narrow-shouldered commander, feverishly bright-eyed but pale and worn. He was too much a professional soldier to under-estimate the risks, but he faced them with stoicism. He used the fleet, drifting up and down the river, to keep the French guessing. On 12 September Wolfe issued his last orders, and ended: 'The officers and men will remember what their country expects from them, and what a determined body of soldiers inured to war is capable of doing against five weak French battalions mingled with a disorderly peasantry.' What they had to do was to climb the Heights of Abraham, 4,800 strong, in the teeth of twice that number.

Admiral Saunders made a noisy diversion ten miles away while preparations were made aboard Holmes's squadron anchored off Cap Rouge. On the night of the 12th, Wolfe told Jervis, commander of the *Porcupine* and his schoolfellow, that he expected to die the next day, and gave him his miniature of Miss Lowther to return to her. At about 2 a.m. the small boats cast off with the current and bore their infantrymen silently down the St Lawrence. In later life, John Robison, Professor of Natural History at Edinburgh, but then a young midshipman, would tell how Wolfe recited Gray's *Elegy* to the other officers in his boat. 'Gentlemen,' he said, 'I would rather have written those lines than take Quebec.' They came up to a cliff wall of rock and forest. Sentries were answered by a French-speaking officer. From the landing-place volunteers scaled the Heights and secured an outpost, then somehow the troops scrambled up and formed squares on the plateau above. There at dawn the choice was victory or ruin: there was no retreat. Montcalm attacked him before his best regiments were ready and the French, white-coated regulars, colonial militia and war-painted Indians, assaulted Wolfe's scarlet lines in vain. Wolfe was three times wounded as he led the counter-charge on the English right, but he lived long enough to know that the day was won. His last words were an order to cut off the French retreat at the bridge over Charles River; then: 'Now, God be praised, I will die in peace.' Montcalm, too, was taken into the city to die. 'Never was rout more complete than that of our army,' said a French official. Quebec itself need not have fallen, but it was abandoned almost at once. In England the news was received with acclaim. Walpole wrote:

'They triumphed and they wept; for Wolfe had fallen in the hour of victory.' Wolfe's 'path of glory' had seized the imagination of people who yet could scarcely have measured the significance of the capture of Quebec.

Further Reading
R. Reilley, *Wolfe of Quebec*, 1973.
C. P. Stacey, *Quebec*, 1959.
W. T. Waugh, *James Wolfe, Man and Soldier*, 1928.

WOLLSTONECRAFT, MARY (1759-97), or Mrs Godwin as she became, was ahead of her time in her courageous championship of the rights of women. She was the child of an unhappy marriage. Her father was a gentleman-farmer who squandered his inheritance. Besides her mother, one of her two sisters and her close friend Fanny Blood (the first unhappily married, the second apparently kept on a string by a man who professed love but would not commit himself to marriage) exemplified for her the cruel lot of women under the man-made laws and conventions of society. Mary herself had to take work as a governess after trying to run a school at Newington Green with her married sister Eliza (Mrs Bishop, who had eventually run away from her husband). Her experience as governess of Lady Kingsborough's children in County Cork opened her eyes to Irish extremes of wealth and poverty. She visited peasants in their cabins, brooded upon her dependent status, read Rousseau and wrote an autobiographical novel, *Mary*. Joseph Johnson, the progressive publisher, who had already given her £10 for *Thoughts on the Education of Daughters*, accepted the novel and urged her to come to London and a literary life.

Miss Wollstonecraft reviewed books, translated, wrote articles, and sharpened her mind in Johnson's salon in St Paul's Churchyard. With Paine, Godwin and the artist Fuscli for friends, she became an agnostic and a radical. Fuseli she loved in a demanding but Platonic fashion. 'If I thought my passion criminal,' she wrote 'I would conquer it or die in the attempt.' Intellectual power and passionate feeling could find no synthesis in her hectic but essentially lonely life. In 1788 she wrote *Original Stories from Real Life*. In 1792, in response to Burke's *Reflections* and as a sequel to her own *Rights of Man*, came an immediate success, *Vindication of the Rights of Women*. The book is long, its reasoning often cogent, but marred by an incoherent style, as if she were overcome by the strength of her feelings. Democracy was astir and events in America and France excited this sensitive, spirited woman, who craved independence, and male companionship on equal terms.

She wanted a proper education for women, believing that they would no longer 'degrade their characters with littleness, if they were led to respect themselves, if political and moral subjects were opened to them'. She advocated a freedom in morality which shocked people

who were ready, nonetheless, to accept fashionable liaisons. She went to Paris, where she saw Louis XVI going to his execution, met revolutionary leaders, the Rolands, Brissot, and 'Citizen' Paine, and lived with an American, Gilbert Imlay, by whom she had a child, Fanny (May 1794). When he was unfaithful, she tried to drown herself. She found a brief happiness, however, with William Godwin, author of *Political Justice*, an admirer and suitable soul-mate. In Godwin's words, 'Friendship melted into love'. She married him in March 1797, but died in September of the same year at the birth of their daughter Mary, who was to be the second wife of the poet Shelley.

Further Reading
Claire Tomalin, *The Life and Death of Mary Wollstonecraft*, 1974.
W. Godwin, *Memoirs of the Author of A Vindication of the Rights of Women*, ed. W. Clark Durant, 1927.

WOLSELEY, GARNET JOSEPH, 1st VISCOUNT (1833-1913), 'Our only general', as Disraeli called him, made his way up the army from a modest Irish background by gallantry, intelligence and the power of his pen. Burma, the Crimea, India during the Mutiny, China and Canada; he had fought in them all before he was thirty, sustaining wounds including the loss of an eye, and becoming a lieutenant colonel. In 1873 he led a successful expedition inland from the Gold Coast against King Kofi of the Ashantis, which earned him £25,000 from parliament, degrees from Oxford and Cambridge, and a KCB. George Grossmith donned his huge moustaches to play the 'very model of a modern Major General' in *The Pirates of Penzance*. The climax of his career in the field was his storming of the fortified lines of Arabi Pasha outside Cairo at Tel-el-Kebir in 1882, achieved by surprise after a long night march. Subsequently, he led the expedition to Khartoum to rescue Gordon.

Back home, he was one of the few officers to support Cardwell's army reforms, and after the abolition of the purchase of commissions he collected round him professional officers of talent. These became known as Wolseley's African Ring, and officers in the Indian army, backed by 'our only other general' Roberts, found promotion hard when Wolseley became Adjutant General. He made enemies with his sharp tongue, and the letters to his wife give an uncensored flavour of his style: Roberts was 'a scheming little Indian', the Duke of Cambridge 'The Great German Sausage'. He worked hard at the War Office to get the army to train for war instead of parading at peace. He became Commander-in-Chief in 1895, but by then his memory had already started to fail. He prepared a mobilization plan which worked smoothly when the Boer War started, and he organized an intelligence report showing how dangerously underprepared we were for a Boer attack. But he was on bad terms with the Secretary of State for War, Lord Lansdowne, an old friend of Roberts, and when the war came he was sidelined, not even being consulted when Roberts replaced Buller in command there. Eventually Roberts, though a year his senior, succeeded him. It was a sad end to the career of the first fully professional field marshal of the reign.

Further Reading
Viscount Wolseley, *The Story of a Soldier's Life*, 2 vols, 1903.

WOLSEY, THOMAS (*c*.1473-1530), Cardinal Archbishop of York, Lord Chancellor and Henry VIII's chief minister from 1515 to 1529, was born about 1473 and died in 1530. Rumour held it that he was the son of a butcher in Ipswich: Cavendish, his gentleman usher and eventual biographer, says that he was 'an honest poor man's son'. He went up to Magdalen, Oxford, where he became famous as the 'boy-bachelor' who took his BA degree at the age of fifteen. He became a Fellow of his college, was ordained priest in 1498 and became bursar of the college in 1499, an office which he was compelled to resign allegedly for applying moneys to the completion of Magdalen Tower without the sanction of the college authorities. He became chaplain to Archbishop Deane of Canterbury and on his death chaplain to Sir Richard Nanfan, the Deputy of Calais. Nanfan died in 1507, but he had recommended Wolsey to Henry VII, whose chaplain he now became. Two years later Henry died and probably owing to the influence of the Lady Margaret Beaufort, who had small opinion of Wolsey, it was some months before Henry VIII gave him any office (1509).

1512 marks the first moment when Wolsey took a major part in deciding governmental policy. He supported the war against France to aid Pope Julius II. The expedition of 1513 was the work of Wolsey, who took into his own hands the entire organization of the war. He was triumphantly successful, and the campaign which brought to the English armies the victories at Thérouanne and Tournai and at the battle of the Spurs convinced Henry that Wolsey was indispensable.

As he rose in royal service, so Wolsey amassed offices in church and state. He became Dean of Lincoln in 1509, of Hereford in 1512, Bishop of Tournai in 1513, Bishop of Lincoln in 1514, the see of which he relinquished on becoming Archbishop of York in the same year. In 1515 Pope Leo X made him a cardinal and in 1515, when Warham resigned from the chancellorship, Wolsey was made Lord Chancellor in his place. In 1518 he achieved his great ambition when he was created *legatus a latere*. He also possessed at various times the Abbey of St Albans, the richest abbey in England: the bishopric of Bath and Wells (1518), exchanged for that of Durham (1524), exchanged for that of Winchester (1529), the

richest see in England. Between 1515 and 1529 Wolsey, although he was always ultimately dependent on the will of the king, was to all intents and purposes the chief minister of England. He governed the state through the chancellorship, the church through his legateship. In these fourteen years he became one of the most powerful men England has ever known. At the height of his power he received £35,000 a year (perhaps equal to a quarter of the royal income) and he conducted himself with a pomp and pride which galled the nobility. He built Hampton Court Palace, and travelled accompanied by literally hundreds of his servants.

Wolsey has suffered badly at the hands of historians who have taken at face value the criticism of those who wrote immediately after his fall from power or who were the great cardinal's enemies. If he was rich, it is only fair to say that as a churchman he created no great dynasty at the nation's expense (unlike the Cecils and Howards, for example) and that he enriched himself largely at the cost of the church in the true medieval fashion of a royal minister. He also spent lavishly in the royal service, financing his diplomatic missions out of his own pocket. He built, but he also gave Hampton Court to the king. It was not in the sixteenth century expected that a great royal servant should conduct his affairs with more than a pretence of modesty, especially when he went to meet foreigners. If Wolsey was 'vulgar', at least he had the excuse of his birth, which others – like Henry himself – could not plead.

Wolsey's great interest, like that of his king, was in foreign affairs. Here he has been badly misunderstood. It used to be claimed that he used English foreign policy to serve the interests of the Papacy, at first to achieve his legateship, then to make himself pope. This view has now been demolished by detailed research, which has shown that Wolsey himself never actively sought to be pope, although Henry VIII himself toyed with the idea. If English foreign policy did follow the papal line it was due in part to the simple fact that both England and the papacy were anti-French during most of this period. The governing factor in the foreign policy of England while Wolsey held sway was Henry VIII's desire for glory and honour, which Wolsey sought to implement as best he might. If this policy failed, or was expensive, the fault lay not with Wolsey but with the king. It has been argued that Wolsey in fact used his talents to restrain the king's appetite for war. This was partly to save money, but also because Wolsey had accepted the pacifist case argued by the humanists like Colet and Erasmus. Such a view of Wolsey as a peacemonger has been criticized in its turn, but there would seem to be something in it, if we accept that this was as much Henry's policy perhaps as Wolsey's, and that on occasion the rhetoric of peace provided a good smokescreen for warlike preparations (as in 1520). Wolsey was able to develop such a peace policy – if such it was – in the years between 1514 and 1522. The summit of his achievement here was reached in 1518 when the great Peace of London was signed by twenty-four nations: a treaty of universal, perpetual peace, which placed London at the centre of the diplomatic world. Of course, the peace lasted only for a few months, and Wolsey's pride and egotism shines through the whole episode. As the Venetian ambassador said: 'Nothing pleases him more than to be called the arbiter of the affairs of Christendom.' Nevertheless, such great international treaties also redounded greatly to the credit and glory of the king. In the end, peace could not last for ever, since Wolsey must serve the king and if the king wanted war, Wolsey had to serve him loyally: he sighed as a peacemaker, but obeyed as a careerist.

In his government of England, in his domestic policy, Wolsey continued the policy of Henry VII. He was not a great innovator in the field of administration like Thomas Cromwell, but worked with the materials already at hand. He maintained firm control over the nobility; punishing those who stepped out of line with a strong hand. The execution of the Duke of Buckingham in 1521 on a charge of treason was a measure taken very much in the tradition of the first Tudor, to defend the dynasty from possible threats – however remote – of subversion, and to frighten the rest of the nobility into obedience. This hardly made Wolsey popular with the upper classes, but it was clearly the best policy for the monarch and nation as a whole. Wolsey was likewise unpopular with parliament, perhaps for rather similar reasons. Between 1515 and 1529, parliament met only once (in 1523) and on that occasion some of its members were critical of foreign policy. This, it has been argued, was a demonstration of opposition to a policy of war organized by Wolsey himself in order to persuade the king to make peace. But there seems to be little real evidence to support such a view, and it seems likely that parliament in 1523 was as much opposed to Wolsey as to war. Wolsey's failure to call parliament frequently contrasts markedly with the great use made at other times in Henry VIII's reign of that institution, but it is very similar to the attitude to parliament of Henry VII and Edward IV.

Wolsey taxed heavily during his reign, but this was largely to satisfy the needs of royal foreign policy. Between 1513 and 1527 England paid the king £413,000 in taxes and £250,000 in forced loans. This compares with taxation in the years 1485-97 of only £258,000. These figures show Wolsey's considerable success as a tax-collector. Wolsey also ordered a major new assessment of the nation's wealth and military resources in 1522 in order to tax more fairly, and on this he based his demands for 'loans' in 1522 and 1523. Wolsey's attempts to gain money to pay for Henry's

wars finally came unstuck in 1525 when his request for an 'Amicable Grant' met with flat refusal in the country and the threat of a rebellion. Faced with this crisis Henry VIII called a Great Council and announced his intention to excuse payment of the grant, pardoning those who had already opposed the tax and in effect blaming Wolsey for the whole episode. This illustrates another way in which Wolsey was useful to the king: as a scapegoat in case anything went wrong.

Wolsey may have been unpopular with the people as a result of taxation, but he sought to protect the commons from the more greedy of the 'caterpillars of the commonwealth', the enclosers of land. He instituted a great commission in 1517 to inquire into enclosure, and followed this up with over 260 prosecutions in Chancery. He continued to show an interest in this great social problem by issuing proclamations in 1526, 1528 and 1529 against enclosure. It is reasonable to doubt how much success these policies had in the long term, but anything which protected the peasantry from the pressure of 'market forces', even slightly, must have been welcome relief in what one historian sees as an 'Age of Plunder'.

Wolsey was an enthusiastic and able judge. As chancellor, he presided in Chancery and played a dominant role in the court of the council in Star Chamber and in the court of requests. To all these courts he encouraged men to come with their suits, speeding up the process of justice and seeking to protect the weak from the mighty. He can in some ways be seen as the founder of the court of Star Chamber; at least he transformed it into an institution of state with fixed rules of procedure. Wolsey used his legal power to threaten the unruly upper classes: as he put it, 'to learn them the law of the Star Chamber'. He boasted to the king in 1518 that: 'For your realm our Lord be thanked it was never in such peace nor tranquillity. For all this summer I have heard neither of riot, felony nor forcible entry, but that your laws be in every place indifferently ministered without leaning of any manner.'

Wolsey was head of the church of England as legate. He established a degree of independence from Rome in this capacity which paved the way perhaps for the royal supremacy established in 1534. He practised little ecclesiastical reform, although there was some, especially of the friars. He projected a major reorganization of small monasteries and the creation of thirteen new sees but failed to bring this to pass. His greatest work as a churchman was to found a new college at Oxford, Cardinal College, later called Christ Church, endowed by dissolving a number of small abbeys. He also founded a new school in his home town, Ipswich, although Henry VIII destroyed it when Wolsey fell.

Wolsey lost the king's favour when he failed in the years 1527-9 to secure an annulment of Henry's marriage to Catherine of Aragon. While it may be true that he disliked the idea that the king should divorce the queen, he nevertheless threw himself into the project with gusto. In the end what defeated him was the power of Charles V in Italy and the pope's consequent inability to grant the divorce. On 24 June 1529, he lamented that 'the pope has refused all the concessions which, relying on him, I had promised the king … and that will be my ruin'.

Having failed to win for Henry the divorce, Wolsey was no longer of any use to Henry. Between August and October 1529 it was clear that Wolsey was rapidly losing favour. On 9 October he was indicted for praemunire. On 18 October he gave up the great seal. On 22 October he confessed his guilt. The king had for fourteen years given Wolsey his unstinted confidence and now at his fall Henry dealt generously with him. When the new parliament on 3 November launched a grand attack on Wolsey and arraigned him on forty-four charges, Henry refused to take any action and saved him from being imprisoned. Wolsey was allowed to retain some of his benefices and property and to retire to his archbishopric of York. It is a comment on Wolsey's views of an ecclesiastic's duties that he had never visited York since he was appointed archbishop fifteen years before. Nor did he in fact ever reach York. He moved northwards at a snail's pace and got no farther than Cawood. During this time he entered into most indiscreet correspondence with Rome, and this became known to the government. Wolsey had taken with him on his journey northwards 600 horsemen in his train, intending to make his enthronement at York a splendid spectacle. The government was determined to prevent him. On Friday 4 November 1530, he was arrested and ordered to London. On the 24th at Leicester he died.

Wolsey had served Henry VIII well and was shabbily treated by him, as so many others were. His former protégé, Sir Thomas More, denounced him in parliament as 'the great wether', or ewe, who had infected the rest of the flock with disease and who was now turned out by the shepherd. Only Thomas Cromwell, to his great credit, stood by his old master, defending him in parliament and working to save his Oxford college. In the end, any comparison between Cromwell and Wolsey inevitably redounds to the credit of the former. Wolsey worked with the enthusiasm and drive of ten men, but he was flawed in many ways. By his ostentatious flaunting of wealth and power, he exposed the clergy as a whole to dangerous attack and contributed to the fall of the medieval church. He left few lasting monuments to his work. He was the last of the great ecclesiastical statesmen who had flourished in the Middle Ages and he had been content to work in a system which had long existed unreformed. In this capacity he may be held to have served his master and his country tolerably well, and to

have continued to build on the stability and peace first established in 1485.

Further Reading
P. Gwyn, *Historical Journal*, 1980.
D. S. Chambers, *Bulletin of the Institute for Historical Research*, 1965.
G. Cavendish, *The Life and Death of Cardinal Wolsey*, ed. Sylvester, 1959.
A. F. Pollard, *Wolsey*, 1919.

WOOD, ANTHONY À (1632-95), the Oxford antiquary, was born in a house opposite Merton College, the house where he lived all his days. Educated at New College School, Thame Grammar School, and Merton, where he was admitted as an undergraduate in 1647, Wood inherited a modest independent income, sufficient to enable him to devote his life to the collection of materials for the history of Oxford and, in particular, of the university and its members. Two volumes were published in his lifetime – the *Historia et Antiquitates Universitatis Oxoniensis* (*History and Antiquities of Oxford*) (1691-2). He left also at his death many other papers, including a good deal of autobiographical material; and the whole collection has been of great value to historians, not least in providing a view of Oxford during the revolutionary years of the seventeenth century. Wood was an unattractive character – peevish, spiteful and quarrelsome, living alone in a couple of attics, growing more bitter as the years increased his deafness, morbidly interested in mortality and illness. His dealings with the kindly Aubrey, who supplied him with an immense quantity of information, do him little credit. He was extremely unpopular in Oxford and was at one time suspected of being a Papist. In 1693 he was at the instance of the second Earl of Clarendon accused of libelling the first earl, Charles II's minister, in *Athenae Oxonienses*, and the book was publicly burned. Yet the savagery which made his contemporaries hate him gives a tang to his account of Restoration Oxford and a sharp individuality to his comments on events and persons. A gossip and an abusive one, educated, shrewd, utterly reactionary, Wood had the diarist's eye for detail and flair for the pithy phrase. He died in 1695, having set his papers in order and supervised the digging of his grave in Merton.

Further Reading
Llewelyn Powis, ed., *The Life and Times of Anthony à Wood*, 1961, is an abridgement of the five volumes edited by Andrew Clark, 1891-1900.

WOODFORDE, JAMES (1740-1803), country parson and diarist, made but small stir in his day; when, however, his diary was published in five volumes between 1924 and 1931 he was hailed as a diarist worthy to stand with Pepys and Evelyn. His special claim to distinction is that he was an ordinary man, writing about ordinary country folk. Besides being uncommonly entertaining, Woodforde's placid chronicle is a rich mine for those who want to dig into the unchronicled past. What Gilbert White did for the natural history of Hampshire, Woodforde did for the people of the Norfolk countryside: farmer and labourer, shopkeeper and servant; blacksmith, bishop, parson and squire – we see them through his observant eye. Nothing was too small for him, so we know what he ate, who came to his church, how his dogs fared, how he suffered from toothache.

The great world impinged upon Woodforde: he dined at Oxford, where he was a Fellow of New College, he visited the great houses of Norfolk, recorded the event with satisfaction when Mr Pitt was delayed at an inn with him for shortage of horses, and registered the victories and crises of successive wars. But the appeal of the diary lies most in its glimpses of rustic life. Woodforde was a curate in Somerset for some years. But the longest part of his diary deals with his life as rector of Weston Longueville in Norfolk from 1776 to his death. He was of his age, no enthusiast; services were unadorned, Communions rare and solemn. His piety was nonetheless constant and unaffected. After being jilted by a girl when he was thirty-four he did not marry, and his life was devoted to the well-being of his parishioners. He did not neglect his own comfort: we see him tucking in with relish to his favourite 'plumb pudding', working through meals that would floor most men today. The reader who wants to know about the domestic life of the period, in cottage as well as parsonage, about smallpox and smuggling, country medicine and country churches, prices, partridges and pigs, should turn to Woodforde. There he will enter into a vanished world: for all its poverty, disease and toil an Arcadian scene amongst the elms and oaks, the high hedgerows and flint church towers of inland Norfolk. His account is plain, clear and light, like the sky of his adopted county, and as full of pleasant surprises as his favourite river Wensum was full of trout and pike.

Further Reading
J. Beresford, ed., *The Diary of a Country Parson*, 5 vols, 1924-31.

WOOLER, THOMAS (1786-1853) was a Yorkshire-born printer who had served his apprenticeship in Shoreditch and learned about politics in the small debating societies which met at the Mermaid, Hackney. In 1808 he became printer and editor of *The Reasoner*. In 1815 he founded *The Stage*, in which rather laboured satire and high-flying rhetoric anticipated the style of *The Black Dwarf*. This latter paper, published each Sunday morning in Sun Street, Finsbury, commanded for a time the largest radical audience after the *Political Register*. The post-war years were the heyday of radical journalism, a time when Lord Eldon could speak of

'wagons filled with seditious papers in order to be distributed through every village, to be scattered over the highways, to be introduced into cottages', when there was 'scarcely a village in the kingdom that had not its little shop in which nothing was sold but blasphemy and sedition'.

From its foundation in 1817 until its demise in 1824 *The Black Dwarf* was influential; during Cobbett's absence in America it led the field. *The Examiner* held aloof from the plebeian struggle: the Hunts wrote for the intelligentsia. Sherwin's *Register* and Wade's *Gorgon* were perhaps the *Dwarf*'s closest rivals. Wade's fortnightly *Black Book* was deadly in its documentation of sinecures, nepotism and corruption in church and state. *The Black Dwarf* excelled in vivid presentation of radical themes. Wooler used to set up his articles in type direct, without manuscript. His style was grandiloquent. He believed in organization upon the open and constitutionalist pattern. 'Let us look at and emulate the patient resolution of the Quakers. They have conquered *without arms* – without *violence* – without threats. They conquered by union.' He was also ready to go further, if constitutional means should fail. 'The *right* of the people to resist *oppression always exists*, and ... the *requisite power* to do this always resides in the *general will* of the people.' But how was the 'general will' to be interpreted, made effective? He was bitter against Cobbett for renouncing the clubs in 1817. How else, he asked, was the public voice to be given body and direction? 'The man who would *divide* the public, in effect *destroys* the public mind.'

In June 1817 Wooler was put on trial before Mr Justice Abbot and a special jury for some passages in an April issue in which he had denounced ministers for 'infamous duplicity and dreadful treachery' (they had suspended the Habeas Corpus Act in the previous month) and for sacrificing 'that constitution which France had never thought of assailing, and which she never wished to injure'. Wooler undertook his own defence and 'won the applause of a great part of the audience, which the sheriffs found it difficult to repress' (*Annual Register*). A verdict of 'guilty' was recorded. During his subsequent trial on a second charge, that of having derided the right of petitioning, it was revealed that three of the jurors had dissented from the original verdict. The second trial ended with a verdict of 'Not Guilty'. The Crown had hoped to muzzle *The Black Dwarf* before it gained too strong a hold. They would have been wiser to accept Wooler's contention that the finding of the first jury constituted an acquittal. They presented him with valuable advertisement for his journal and his cause. And they had exposed themselves to a further attack upon the way in which London special juries were named. After Wooler, the pamphlet-publisher Hone was tried on three counts and found 'Not Guilty'.

In 1819 Wooler took part in the election of Sir Charles Wolseley to be 'legislatory attorney' for Birmingham – and, like Wolseley, he was imprisoned for eighteen months, in Warwick gaol. Searching for other means of employment he had sought to become a barrister, but the Benchers of Lincoln's Inn refused to take him as a student. So he became a prisoner's advocate at the police courts, being employed in this capacity by the well-known Old Bailey lawyer, Samuel Harmer. After the Reform Act of 1832 he declared that he was finished with politics for 'these damned Whigs have taken all the sedition out of my hands'. He had contributed to their success. He has an important place in the long struggle for the freedom of the press.

Further Reading
W. D. Wickwar, *The Struggle for the Freedom of the Press*, 1928.

WORCESTER, WILLIAM alias BOTONER (1415-c.1483), the antiquary, was one of the new gentlemen-bureaucrats of late medieval England. He was born in Bristol and was educated at Oxford University in 1432-8. He was financed there by the distinguished soldier Sir John Fastolf, whom he served from 1439-59 in many different capacities. His only official office was steward of Castle Combe (Wilts.), but he wrote Fastolf's letters and was sometimes called his secretary; he organized his extensive land-purchases, researching titles and defending them in the courts; he supervised his building operations; he toured his estates; and he was his doctor in his last years. As Fastolf's executor he realized his assets, lobbied the great, and litigated in church and secular courts. Prevented from fulfilling Fastolf's wishes, he compromised in 1472 with Bishop Waynflete, who diverted endowments from Caister College to Magdalen College, Oxford. Fastolf's affairs were finally settled about 1477. Worcester was thus one of the expert administrators so indispensable in late medieval England. A century earlier he would have been a cleric, but Worcester, though pious enough, remained a layman and married. His service did not make his fortune, for Fastolf was a particularly mean employer. Only in the 1470s did Worcester achieve financial security and time for the leisure interests crowded out by his professional career.

Worcester's inquiries were wide-ranging and miscellaneous. He was interested in zoology and botany, medicine, geography and topography, heraldry and genealogy, architecture and antiquities, history and legend, classical literature, the Greek and Hebrew languages. He used them in his work, for example when valuing properties and tracing titles, and his work informed his studies with expert knowledge of land law, surveying and building costs. Manuscript books, documents, buildings and monuments, and oral history were all grist to his mill. He recorded his discoveries and sources in notebooks organized thematically with a view to eventual publication. Some have been published as they stand. Of his finished works, we have his *Survey of Bristol*, his *Book of Noblesse*, and his translation of Cicero's *Of Old Age*, and the works of others that he corrected. Much more has been lost.

Worcester was an indefatigable researcher, who consulted his sources for the information they contained. He was untouched by Renaissance notions of style or history. His Latin was pedestrian and workaday; he did not discriminate between history and legend, oral history and folklore; and his historical work was rough and incoherent. Such criticisms, however, are misdirected. Worcester did not aspire to be a humanist and even those fifteenth-century Englishmen who did shared his emphasis on matter over manner. We should appreciate his documentary expertise, his criticism of modern stories, and his awareness of historical change. What we have are not finished histories, but his notes.

Few of us would care to be judged posthumously by the evidence of our notebooks alone, let alone our prose style. If all he had done was to fill a handful of notebooks, that would still be remarkable on more than one count, of which the least weighty perhaps is the value of their contents to us; yet that is great indeed.

He was instead an antiquary, founder of a great tradition, and the anticipator of many later developments. His *Itineraries* precede by fifty years those of Leland and are inferior only in quantity, not quality; his *Survey of Bristol* foreshadows those of Stow and Hooker on London and Exeter a century later; his lost *Ancient Families of Norfolk* was the first county history; and his lost *Acts of Sir John Fastolf* was a pioneering biography. We should regret what is lost, not what remains.

Further Reading
A. Gransden, *Historical Writing in England* ii, 1982.
K. B. McFarlane, 'William Worcester: A Preliminary Survey' in *England in the Fifteenth Century*, G. L. Harriss, ed., 1981.

WORDSWORTH, WILLIAM (1770-1850), poet, was born at Cockermouth in Cumberland where the Derwent runs out into the sea. His father, John Wordsworth, was an attorney and agent to the Lowther family. His mother, Ann, was the daughter of William Cookson, a linen-draper of Penrith, and of Dorothy Crackanthorpe; the Crackanthorpes were an old county family. William was the second son. His mother died when he was eight and the family was dispersed. The four boys were sent in turn to Hawkshead grammar school, coming home only for the holidays. After the death of his father in 1783, home was that of an uncle, Christopher Cookson, at Penrith, or Richard Wordsworth at Whitehaven. His headmaster from 1781 to 1786 was William Taylor, lover of poetry and a scholar, who lent William his books. William lodged with a 'dame' and escaped the more rigorous discipline of Taylor's school house. Outside school hours the boys roamed freely. William's father had taught him to learn large portions of poetry and he plunged avidly into Fielding, Swift and Cervantes. He listened intently to the ballads and border-lore of the country 'back of Skiddaw', and he was always fascinated by the lonely travellers who were later recreated in his poems: the Pedlar, the Discharged Soldier and the Leech-gatherer. Certain things moved him overwhelmingly: a drowned man, a rotting gibbet; or the running water of a stream, the music of a wren, a solitary flute; or wind in fir trees. His youth was marked by 'spots of time', incidents or sights transformed by a capacity for intense emotion, memory pictures to which he 'often would repair and thence drink as at a fountain'.

We can follow in his autobiographical poems the stages of his emotional development. The disciplines of mathematics and classics were balanced by solitary walks, fishing, bird's-nesting, skating and other country sports. Chasing lapwings, playing ducks-and-drakes or coursing with his friends, Wordsworth was not a lonely boy. But he had a gift for solitude. On a country walk, he might come suddenly into contact with an experience of 'dream-like vividness and splendour'. So he was 'often unable to think of external things as having external existence'. He went on: 'I communed with all I saw as something set apart from but inherent in my own immaterial nature. Many times while going to school have I grasped at a wall or tree to recall myself from this abyss of idealism to the reality'. From his early observations of natural beauty came the imagery of his greatest poetry. He ascribed to his sister his habit of minute observation 'She gave me eyes, she gave me ears' – but it was also born in him, a natural poet's gift. Dorothy's influence was important: theirs were complementary natures. Her delicate insights and tenderness softened William's 'stiff, violent and moody temper' which had so worried his mother. Her companionship, resumed after 1787, was to him 'a joy above all joys'. Together they explored the fells and vales of Eamont and Eden, read the poems of Burns and 'saw into the life of things'. Thus was established a relationship of trust and sympathy which was to be for both the most important of their lives.

In the same year William went to Cambridge, to St John's College, where he spent four years 'joyous as a lark'. Finding that he knew much of what was required, he eschewed the prescribed courses and read for pleasure. He learned Italian, read widely and shed conventional religious beliefs. He despised the dons, 'some elderly men unscoured, grotesque in character, tricked out like aged trees', and deplored the 'frantic and dissolute' undergraduate life. Early poems reveal little originality. Crabbe, Beattie, Cowper and Collins were the strongest influences on his style. In 1790, with his Welsh friend Robert Jones, he went on a walking tour in the Alps and whetted his appetite for 'mighty forms'. Other gentlemen sought the picturesque, but not usually on foot with but £20 in pocket! So far were William's feelings at this time from being exclusively poetical that he thought seriously about becoming a soldier. He certainly did not intend to be ordained. A short stay in London in 1791 brought him no nearer to choice of career. In the autumn, still in wayward mood, he went back to France. He visited the National Assembly, became imbued with the spirit of liberty, unsullied as it was then by terror, and met, among others, Beaupuy, a chivalrous revolutionary, and Annette Vallon.

She was twenty-five, the daughter of a surgeon, and lived in Orleans where Wordsworth had gone to learn French. They lived together; but two months before she was due to give birth to his child Wordsworth returned to Paris. There in December 1792 he heard of the birth of a daughter and hurriedly left for England. These facts were unknown for a century because Wordsworth suppressed them; the secret remained with the family and a few discreet friends. Why did he desert a girl whom he seems to have loved passionately and to have meant to marry? Did he intend to return? Was he warned of the forthcoming war with England and of his own danger? Possibly his slender funds had run out. Wordsworth had responded joyously to the sense of liberation and to Beaupuy's love of humanity, when 'to be young was very heaven'. In his months with Annette his ecstasy was concentrated in a more personal way: he was capable of intense, worshipping love. When Wordsworth returned to England his life had been shaken, and his poetic nature roused, not only perhaps by love but by the abrupt end, and long suppression, of the affair. Herbert Read, dwelling on this latter aspect, held that the affair ' transformed his being'. It was the 'deepest experience of Wordsworth's life – the emotional complex from which all his subsequent career flows in its intricacy and uncertainty'.

Wordsworth secured the publication of *The Evening Walk* and *Descriptive Sketches* by Joseph Johnson, friend of Blake and Priestley. He was anxious about the violent trend in France. A hasty visit to France – the evidence for it is uncertain – would only have confirmed these misgivings. He did not meet William Godwin until 1795 but he read *Political Justice* soon after his return from France. Godwin condemned revolutions because they 'confound the process of nature and reason'. Journalistic efforts, like his *Letter to the Bishop of Llandaff*, an analysis of the causes of poverty, which even Johnson refused to publish, pointed Wordsworth to a new means of livelihood. He had good friends: Raisley Calvert bequeathed him a small legacy before he died in January 1795. Racedown Lodge, in the Dorset hills, was made available to him, and there he settled down with Dorothy.

At a time when he could have remained in mental chaos, brooding over the past, Dorothy's faith 'preserved him still a poet'. Their ménage puzzled the country people. From his habit of wandering round with a small telescope and a notebook, Wordsworth was thought to be bewitching the cattle and later was reported as a spy! Here he rewrote 'Salisbury Plain', composed *The Borderers*, a play on a didactic principle, then some works in a calmer mood, notably 'The Ruined Cottage'. In this poem poverty is still a preoccupation, but Margaret, the humble heroine, emerges as an individual. Wordsworth the social reformer, isolated in his sense of personal suffering, is becoming the poet of the heart and of nature.

In 1796 Samuel Taylor Coleridge fell under Wordsworth's spell. As he described it, Wordsworth's poem 'The Female Vagrant' made a sudden effect on his mind: 'It was the union of deep feeling with profound thought ... and above all the original gift of spreading the tone, the atmosphere ... of the ideal world around forms, incidents and situations of which custom had bedimmed all the lustre'. When the Wordsworths went to stay with Coleridge at Nether Stowey in midsummer 1797, an association of mutual admiration was born. The Wordsworths moved to Alfoxden House near Stowey. They made free with one another's houses, talked endlessly, 'wantoned in wild poesy'. 'Kubla Khan', 'The Ancient Mariner' and 'Christabel' were the result. 'Three people, but one soul' was Coleridge's description of the unusual trio. Dorothy helped turn Coleridge's philosophic mind towards outward things; Wordsworth gave Coleridge understanding; Coleridge gave Wordsworth 'praise and the courage to be himself'. They walked together in November 1797 around the Quantocks and along the coast, and planned 'The Ancient Mariner'.

William settled to writing poetry in the purposeful way that characterized his periodic creative spells. Whole passages that later formed part of *The Excursion* and *The Prelude*, fragments of blank verse, were written at this time, often incorporating Dorothy's observations as recorded in her journal. Two characteristics of Wordsworth's poetry can be seen already: he looks back upon his youth and its discoveries; and he tries to express the mental states which were produced by his communing with nature. Between February and May 1798 he composed most of the poems which he published in September in *Lyrical Ballads* – and 'Peter Bell'; and the beginnings of *The Recluse*, later to be found in *The Excursion*. The *Lyrical Ballads* contained 'The Ancient Mariner' and three other poems by Coleridge, but the bulk was provided by Wordsworth's ballads and lyrics; characters of rustic life are the subject of poems like 'Simon Lee' and 'Goody Blake', while other pieces such as 'Lines written in Early Spring' express ideas which Coleridge described as 'semi-atheism'.

'Lines Written a few miles above Tintern Abbey' was added to *Lyrical Ballads* while the volume was in the press: in form an autobiographical sketch and a rhapsody upon his experiences. With Dorothy in July 1798 he toured the Wye valley rediscovering the delectable country through which he had wandered in 1793. He began the poem 'upon leaving Tintern ... and concluded it just as I was entering Bristol in the evening, after a ramble of four or five days ... Not a line of it was altered and not any part of it was written down till I reached Bristol.' Wordsworth describes in 'Tintern Abbey' the change in outlook since he first saw the 'steep woods and lofty banks' of the Wye. Then he consumed the sights of nature with sensuous violence: 'the sounding cataract haunted me like a passion', the forms of nature were 'then to me an appetite'. Now he had learned to listen more calmly to 'the still, sad music of humanity' and he had a clearer sense of the existence all around him of 'a motion and a spirit', universal, vague but immeasurably grand. The intuitions of boyhood are confirmed, nature and humanity reconciled. The poem concludes with a tribute to his sister, who had been the agent of this restoration. With her, and through her eyes, he could relive the past.

In June 1798 the young Hazlitt met Wordsworth and found him more 'gaunt and Don Quixote-like' than he expected. 'He was quaintly dressed ... in a brown fustian jacket and striped pantaloons ... There was a severe, worn pressure of thought about his temples, a fire in his eye (as if he saw more in objects than the outward appearance), an intense, high, narrow forehead, a Roman nose, cheeks furrowed by strong purpose and feeling, and a convulsive inclination to laughter about the mouth'. He talked 'very naturally and freely, with a mixture of clear, gushing accents in his voice, a deep, guttural intonation, and a strong tincture of the northern burr, like the crust on wine'. De Quincey noticed especially the poet's eyes: 'An appearance the most solemn and spiritual that it is possible for a human eye to wear'.

In September 1798 the Wordsworths and Coleridge went to Germany. They divided, the Wordsworths going to Goslar, where they were virtually imprisoned by frost and lack of funds. Wordsworth made slow progress with German, but began what was to be *The Prelude*, besides writing 'Lucy Gray' and 'Ruth'. In May they came back to live at Sockburn-on-Tees, with the Hutchinson family. Mary Hutchinson the Wordsworths had known since their Penrith days. Wordsworth had always been fond of her; she had stayed with them at Racedown. He finally married her in October 1802. She would be the domestic, childbearing partner in the household of poetry. In the months before the marriage it was Dorothy who wrote most of the letters as if she were the intermediary between William and his intended bride. Before the wedding Wordsworth spent a month at Calais with Dorothy, Annette and his daughter Caroline; perhaps it was to see his daughter, perhaps to convince Annette, who had been living resigned as 'the widow Williams', that marriage was no longer feasible. This encounter seems oddly insensitive. Wordsworth's private relationships were made to fit into the pattern of his work. Dorothy Wordsworth may have loved Coleridge: there are hints of this in her journals. She undoubtedly loved William enough to accept her special position in the *ménage à trois* which was established after the marriage. She was sustained by her admiration for William's genius: she served at his altar. Mary made William a good wife; she seems to have lived contentedly in a household that was surprisingly free of jealousy.

In December 1799 the Wordsworths decided to go and live at Grasmere. They took a cottage at Town End (now Dove Cottage) with an orchard above it whence they could see 'the lake, the church, Helm Crag, and two-thirds of the vale'. The life they lived is recreated in Dorothy's journal, an intimate, evocative account. They felt they had come home after many wanderings. Their life was austere, for they were as poor as the 'statesmen', farmers of that infertile district. The family was steadily enlarged by the birth of children – five in all – and they were seldom without visitors and guests, notable among them Coleridge, who took a nearby house, Greta Hall.

While much of the poetry of the early Grasmere period was of the sort that his critics thought worthless, poetry of the 'light of common day', Wordsworth was also anxious to respond to Coleridge's insistence upon a philosophical scheme. Coleridge could never accept Wordsworth's choice of 'simple and unelaborated expressions', his concern with the 'low and rustic life' in which condition 'the passions of men are incorporated with the beautiful and permanent forms of nature'. *Lyrical Ballads*, from whose preface these words are taken, was an odd match between different kinds of poems, though linked by two agreed principles: 'faithful adherence to the truth of nature' and 'the power of giving interests to novelty by the modifying powers of imagination'. Coleridge could not make Wordsworth a philosopher. But Wordsworth did, in his preface to the second edition of *Lyrical Ballads*, develop his distinctive view of poetry. 'Poetry takes its origins from emotion recollected in tranquillity: the tranquillity gradually disappears, and an emotion, kindred to that which was before the subject of contemplation, is gradually produced, and does itself actually exist in the mind.' No-one before had so exactly analysed the process of creation. As for his methods of working – Dorothy described his ardour once by the word 'kindled' – especially his habit

of composing out of doors, walking fast between two fixed points, chanting his poetry.

Wordsworth himself preferred to group his poems according to their subject, as for example 'Poems of the Imagination', 'Poems of Fancy', rather than chronologically. His output was enormous though irregular. Critics tend to treat him as a spent force after *The Excursion* (1814). He was capable, however, almost to the end, of rising above the pedestrian: *The Power of Sound* was written in 1828, *Yarrow Revisited* in 1831. He had acquired a bank of imagery upon which, when he was stirred, he could draw for verse which could still please. It is not, however, upon the years of hack-work and homilies that one should dwell, when the mystical power had waned and, as Hazlitt put it, 'the power of his mind preys on itself' – or, as another said, he was 'an owl in the daylight'. The best idea of the poet can be gained from an account of the spring of 1802, Wordsworth's second great time of lyrical creation.

Writing almost every day, in a white heat of inspiration, he got into his stride with a series of poems, like 'Alice Fell' in his simplest style; then the first of the three butterfly poems; on 23 March, 'a mild morning, William worked at the Cuckow poem'. The cuckoo's call was heard in imagination, a herald from a spiritual world: what Wordsworth did to the cuckoo, 'a wandering voice', as he said, dispossesses the bird almost of a corporeal existence. So the poem perfectly represents Wordsworth's imagination, gazing at the world of sense until it 'revealed the invisible world'. 'The Rainbow' and the first lines of 'Intimations of Immortality' followed. 'The Tinker' and several poems about wild flowers were written at this time; so was the first of the skylark poems, whose freedom of metre matches the bird's joyous flight. Finally, on 3-4 May, was written 'The Leech-gatherer or Resolution and Independence', a recreation of an earlier encounter and a detailed illustration of the way in which the poet could still be moved to the point of entering a visionary state. He was just thirty-two and at the mature point of his poetic development. 'William worked at the *Leech Gatherer* almost incessantly from morning till tea time ... and was oppressed and sick at heart, for he wearied himself to death. After tea he wrote two stanzas in the manner of Thomson's *Castle of Indolence* and was tired out'. These stanzas reveal what he thought of himself, the alternating elation and depression, and the way he was mastered by his muse. 'I wandered lonely as a cloud' was to come later; he had seen, this April, the daffodils beside Ullswater and stored the memory away to be recalled at a later date. 'The Solitary Reaper', the rest of 'The Ode' and of *The Prelude* were not yet written. But he was never again to achieve such an outpouring of genius.

In Wordsworth's move towards the conservatism of his later years certain landmarks may be distinguished. In

1803 Sir George Beaumont, the artist, gave him some land. He became a freeholder of Westmorland, a voter and an active force in local politics. The Wordsworth family had been meanly treated by the first Earl Lowther. The second earl made amends and helped the poet: in March 1813 Wordsworth was made Distributor of Stamps for Westmorland. The duties were not nominal, sometimes vexatious, and always a tie. His gains were not unreasonable for he had to support a growing family and he made pitifully little from his poems. When he flung himself into the celebrated election of 1818, defending the Lowther interest against the Whig Brougham with two 'addresses to the freeholders of Westmorland', his critics were quick to point the moral. To men like Hazlitt and Shelley he was simply an apostate. Like so many of his generation Wordsworth had sickened of the Jacobinism that had destroyed the generous revolution of his youth. He had not approved the first war. But after 1803 he responded heartily to the patriotic mood. He became a volunteer at Grasmere. When he ceased to be a revolutionary, he continued to be a puritan: 'plain living and high thinking' was his creed to the end. He clung to his hope of being a prophet of nature, that 'what we have loved, others will love'. He was more sensitive than most of his generation to the wretchedness of industrial towns. His conservatism acquired querulous notes in old age but it was never ignoble or merely defensive. He came to see in the church the natural guardian of good order and morality. In education, under the control of the church, he saw the best cure for moral ills: the ninth book of *The Excursion* pleads for Anglican primary education for all. If he despised 'the rabble' he also appealed for an early reform of the Poor Laws.

As Wordsworth grew older he had recurring eye trouble, though he never went blind. Domestic calamities pressed hard. A terrible blow was the death by shipwreck in 1805 of his brother John, a good-natured sea-captain, whose ambition was to make enough money to settle down (perhaps marry Sara Hutchinson, Mary's sister) and help the penurious Wordsworths. In 1812 two children (Catherine and Thomas) died. Dorothy had a total breakdown in health in 1829; her mind partially gave way and she became a demanding and trying invalid. Wordsworth has seemed sometimes to be too self-absorbed; if this were true, he made amends in the way in which he accepted the burden of his sister's dotage. Age had not diminished his own capacity for feeling. He had always been prone to tears; when his daughter Dora died in 1847 he was terribly stricken. He died in loneliness. As a poet too he had been essentially a lonely figure. Some young Victorians proclaimed themselves 'Wordsworthians'. In his best work he speaks to every generation. The poet of nature was also the poet of mind which he elevates in a way that leaves little room for a greater being, for the mind 'keeps her own inviolate retirement, subject there to conscience only'. This was a height on which no man could stay for long. The descent may seem that of an egotist, wrapped in self-contemplation. But it was a height that few other English poets achieved.

Further Reading

Dorothy Moorman, *Wordsworth*, 2 vols, 1957, 1965.
E. de Selincourt, ed., *Letters of William and Dorothy Wordsworth*, 6 vols, 1935-9.

WORTLEY MONTAGU, LADY MARY (1689-1762) was the daughter of Evelyn Pierrepont, afterwards Duke of Kingston, and of Mary Fielding, daughter of Lord Denbigh. She was largely self-educated which, as so often in the case of well-bred girls brought up amid beautiful objects and good libraries, produced the happiest effect. She later studied Latin surreptitiously, but she thought scholarship was for professional men and advised women to conceal their learning as they would a physical defect. So much for her name as a 'bluestocking'. Her critical intelligence and sensibility made an impact upon Mr Wortley Montagu; the letters which Mary addressed to his sister were undoubtedly intended for his eye, the answers dictated by him. When her father planned marriage for her with another man, in 1712, she eloped with Montagu.

The grandson of Pepys's friend the Earl of Sandwich, and some years her elder, he was a man of ability and a scholar, the confidant of the Whig leaders and a Lord of the Treasury under George I. From 1716 to 1718 he was ambassador in Constantinople. Her letters from Vienna and Constantinople were the basis of her reputation in her own age. Indeed they are fascinating and no less so because they seem to be largely accurate. If she drew upon her imagination for her celebrated account of her visit to the bagnio, she also seems to have been well informed. These letters seem to have been prepared later for publication, from entries in her diaries. In Constantinople she learned of the smallpox inoculation which had been introduced by the Circassians and, when she returned, she had her children inoculated against the disease which had marred her own looks; she convinced some fashionable doctors of the utility of this treatment – and even the royal family, after she had induced George II to order the inoculation of three men and three women, convicts in Newgate gaol.

For some years she was prominent in society. Her husband was a hot opponent of Walpole, which accounts for Horace Walpole's dislike of her, but she was always a controversial figure. At first the close friend of Alexander Pope, and his neighbour at Twickenham, she quarrelled with him in 1721; thereafter there was mutual recrimination and abuse, venomous on his side. In 1739 she separated from her husband; he was growing notoriously mean and her fashionable activities may have irritated him, but some affection seems to have survived. She did not return from her self-imposed exile in Italy until after his death in 1761, and soon followed him to the grave. From Italy her letters continued to delight her friends. She was conscious of her powers and once compared her letters to those of Mme de Sévigné: 'very pretty they are, but I assert without the least vanity that mine will be full as entertaining forty years hence. I advise you therefore to put none of them to the use of waste paper'. Her style was easy and unforced. But she was less feminine, less sentimental, less naive than Mme de Sévigné. She admired Fielding and scoffed at Richardson; the latter is quite demolished in one caustic letter. With the interest of her sex in engagements, 'conquests', and tattle of the fashionable world went intellectual interests as broad as they were unpretentious. Emancipated as she was in her views and comments, she was seldom coarse, and her comments on places, people and books are often shrewd. From the letters of this unusual person we learn much, and most pleasantly, about the author and the century in which she lived.

Further Reading
R. Halsband, ed., *The Letters of Lady Mary Wortley Montagu*, 3 vols, 1965-7.

WREN, SIR CHRISTOPHER (1632-1723), architect, was born at East Knoyle, in Wiltshire, the son of the rector and the nephew of Matthew Wren, the Laudian bishop. When Christopher was little more than a year old his father was appointed Dean of Windsor. The Civil Wars disrupted the household, and Wren, according to Aubrey, 'a youth of prodigious inventive wit', got 'his first Instructions in Geometry and Arithmetic' from his brother-in-law, William Holder, rector of Bletchington, in Oxfordshire, in whose house the family took refuge. He was sent to Busby at Westminster, and went on to Wadham College, Oxford, when he was seventeen. Already Wren's interests were clearly scientific: he had made astronomical models and a water-clock, and assisted the eminent anatomist Charles Scarburgh in dissecting, and he quickly proved himself a brilliant young addition to the group – including Wallis, Goddard, Petty and Wilkins, the last of whom was the Warden of Wren's college – who were making Oxford a centre of the new scientific spirit during the Commonwealth period. Wren became a Fellow of All Souls in 1653 and gave his main attention to astronomy, investigating the rings of Saturn. The following year Evelyn dined at All Souls and met 'that miracle of a youth, Mr Christopher Wren'; and later he visited Dr Wilkins who showed him 'Shadows, Dials, Perspectives, places to introduce the Species, and many other artificial, mathematical, Magical curiosities: A Way-Wiser, a Thermometer; a monstrous Magnes, Conic and other Sections, a Balance on a demie Circle, most of

them of his own and that prodigious young scholar, Mr Chr: Wren'.

In 1657 his brilliance was recognized by election at twenty-five as Professor of Anatomy at Gresham College. Four years later he returned to Oxford as Savilian Professor of Astronomy, a chair which he retained until 1673. Naturally he was one of the promoters of the Royal Society, and he wrote the preamble to its charter. We find him in the 1660s taking an original and leading part in scientific investigation, whether in his own research or in the experimental activities of the Society. He continued to work at the rings of Saturn (where Huygens forestalled him) and the satellites of Jupiter; devised a geometrical method of determining a comet's path; constructed an apparatus of suspended balls, to which Newton later referred in the *Principia*, in order to 'determine the rules of the collision and mutual rebound of hard bodies'; demanded the keeping of records of the weather and of agricultural prices; and invented an improved weather-clock and a method of grinding hyperbolical lenses. In 1662 Evelyn saw him display 'his ingenious thermometer' to the Royal Society, and in 1664 he found Wren, Boyle and Wallis at Oxford 'observing the Discus of the Sun for the passing of Mercury that day'. It was characteristic of the age as well as a tribute to his mathematical qualifications that Wren was offered early in Charles II's reign a commission to survey and direct the establishment of Tangier as a naval base. He declined the offer on the plea of health. The true reason may have been that he had already committed himself to the first of his architectural enterprises.

Wren the scientist in his early thirties was already celebrated. Wren the man, at this or any time in his life, is not easy to delineate. Both Evelyn and Aubrey knew him well, yet they tell us surprisingly little about what sort of man he was. Evelyn offers little more than the refrain which he used, for example, in 1664, 'that incomparable genius, and my worthy friend'. Aubrey reported to Anthony à Wood an instance of what sounds like characteristic kindness, saying that 'Dr Christopher Wren, my dear friend, without my knowledge contrived an employment for me'; it was work for Ogilby the publisher, at a time when Aubrey was in great need. Wren himself left little evidence, for he seems to have disliked writing. The most valuable material comes from Hooke, who worked closely with Wren on the rebuilding of London in the 1670s and was clearly devoted to him. His celebrated tribute, 'that since the time of Archimedes there scarce ever has met in one man, in so great perfection, such a mechanical hand and so philosophical a mind' has a lapidary ring, yet in the light of Hooke's comments in his diary it was genuine. Wren was slight of build, courteous and kindly, equable in temper, reticent and hating fuss, something of a precisian, dedicated to his work, quietly yet profoundly ambitious. He was twice married – the first time at the age of thirty-seven – and twice widowed, and this may have added sadness to his gravity. He was President of the Royal Society from 1681 to 1683. Although he was thrice elected to parliament (1685, 1689, 1701), Wren seems to have been as unpolitical as any public man could be in the second half of the seventeenth century, holding an important state appointment for fifty years during the reigns of five sovereigns. Neither Popish Plot nor Revolution, nor even the partisan feuds of Anne's reign, uprooted him. It is a tribute to his genius, perhaps also to a sense of national pride.

The career as an architect which revealed this genius began when Gilbert Sheldon, promoted to the see of London from the Wardenship of All Souls, decided to present to the University of Oxford a building to be used for the conferment of degrees and other ceremonial purposes, and invited the brilliant Fellow of his college to design it. The assumptions and the technical qualifications which have since come to divide the 'professions' into separate and rigid specialisms did not exist in the seventeenth century. Christopher Wren was a distinguished experimental scientist, deeply interested in geometry, and a fine draughtsman with a flair for constructing models. It is not in the least surprising that Sheldon invited him, nor, given that Wren was naturally ambitious and willing to undertake responsibility, that he accepted. He designed a model of the new Sheldonian Theatre and displayed it in 1663, and by 1669 the building was finished. A highly original piece of work, of a type hitherto unknown in England, it stands today as one of the most compelling buildings in a city of much fine architecture, and it created something of a sensation in the 1660s. At about the same time as the Sheldonian, too, Wren designed for Pembroke College, Cambridge, the first wholly classical college chapel in England. Meanwhile, in the interval between the design and the completion of the Sheldonian, two things had happened which confirmed Wren in his turn to architecture and settled the pattern of his life. First, he had visited Paris (1665-6), then in the early stages of the architectural transformation wrought by Louis XIV's reign. Wren had studied new mansions within the city and country houses outside, watched the changes which were being made in the Louvre and the Tuileries, met the great Italian architect Bernini, made drawings, bought engravings, and come home deeply impressed. Secondly, the Great Fire of 1666 had gutted much of the City of London and provided an opportunity for reconstruction at once urgent and unparalleled.

Wren had in fact already been consulted by Sheldon and Sancroft about the rehabilitation of old St Paul's, and had put forward his views in the form of a design. The matter had been discussed at a meeting held only a few days before the Fire, where John Evelyn joined Wren in proposing a new foundation 'with a noble Cupola, a form of church building not as yet known in England, but of wonderful grace'. Within a week after the Fire, Wren submitted to the authorities a plan for the reconstruction of the entire city area. Perhaps inevitably – because of the complex problem of property rights and the desperate need for speed in the rehousing – it was rejected. There was no comprehensive plan, and Wren had relatively little direct responsibility for London's new secular buildings, although he shared with Hooke the engineering work on the Fleet Canal. His opportunity lay in ecclesiastical building. Between the London Rebuilding Act of 1670 and the end of the century he built a great group of new churches in the capital – and the new St Paul's Cathedral.

By the time Wren began this task he had been appointed (1669) Surveyor of the Royal Works, over the head of Inigo Jones's assistant, John Webb, a far more experienced man. This post, with its office and residence in Scotland Yard, carried with it the responsibility for all Crown building, and later was to enable Wren to do some of his finest work. For the present it brought him status, and was followed in 1673 by a knighthood. London's needs for materials and labour were paramount, and Wren turned first to the London churches. He provided designs for fifty-one, and fifteen were actually under construction by 1670. The detailed supervision of the work was often undertaken by the three City Surveyors, of whom Hooke was one. Although in general Wren's churches were on a 'central' pattern, emphasizing the role of the congregation in Protestant worship, their plans were remarkably varied. Many, particularly of the earlier ones, were later destroyed, especially in the Second World War; among those that have survived, or that have been faithfully restored, St Stephen, Walbrook, and St James, Piccadilly, provide interesting and contrasting examples. Broadly, by 1685 Wren had completed his work on the city churches, except that he later added to the London skyline a number of delightful classical steeples of a kind unique in western Europe (e.g. that of St Bride, Fleet Street). By this date he had already begun several other buildings whose varied purposes enabled him to experiment and to show the variety of his genius. For example, in 1676-84 he built the superbly proportioned and dignified Library of Trinity College, Cambridge, and in 1681-2 he completed Wolsey's gateway at Christ Church, Oxford, by building the upper part of Tom Tower in his own version of Gothic. These were 'private' buildings – and Trinity Library he did for nothing, out of friendship for Isaac Barrow. As Surveyor he designed in these middle years of his career the austere Chelsea Hospital (1682-92) and a palace at Winchester for Charles II, almost finished when the king died in 1685 but never continued.

St Paul's Cathedral, the most celebrated of Wren's

triumphs, was begun in 1675. Wren had produced his first designs for old St Paul's in his early thirties. The lines along which his new building was constructed were a compromise: he could not persuade the chapter to accept the sumptuously classical 'Great Model' (still to be seen in the Trophy Room at St Paul's), but neither did he follow the basically Gothic 'Warrant' design to which royal approval was given in 1675. Instead, by his famous, and much-criticized, screen walls he gave the building the unity of classical design. The most splendid achievement of all, the great dome, a magnificent extension of the circular pattern of the classical temple, was not started until 1697, the year in which the first service was held in the new cathedral. The western towers, based fairly closely on those of Borromini at S. Agnese in Rome, followed in the early years of the new century. By 1709 the building was structurally complete. To its making other artists of distinction had contributed much. Among the masons there had been Edward Pierce, the sculptor of the bust of Wren at Oxford; among the carvers in wood and stone, Grinling Gibbons, the brilliant young Dutchman whom Evelyn had discovered working 'in a poor solitary thatched house' and had commended to Wren. Yet the central glory of the design and of the incomparable achievement belongs unquestionably to Wren.

He was seventy-seven when St Paul's was finished. In the reigns of James II and William III he had, as Royal Surveyor, designed other fine buildings. His Whitehall extensions of 1685-8 were, unhappily, burned down in 1698. His additions to Hampton Court, begun in 1689, were only a modest part of a great design which would have destroyed the Tudor palace but which was never completed. He did the charming south front of William's palace at Kensington. Above all in this group, he designed the lovely Painted Hall of the Royal Naval Hospital, at Greenwich, begun in 1695 and completed by 1702. Apart from the finishing of St Paul's, this was Wren's last notable building. There are indications in the 1690s, scarcely surprising in view of his age and of the prodigious range of his work since the 1660s, that his vitality and resource were diminishing. He clearly began to rely heavily upon his protégé Nicholas Hawksmore. A new generation was arising, symbolized by the appointment in 1702 to the post next below Wren's, the Comptrollership of Works, of John Vanbrugh, who both as architect and as man was of very different style from Wren, who nevertheless seems to have got on well with him. Castle Howard and Blenheim were massive demonstrations that 'the age of Wren' was over. There were occasional fusses about St Paul's. In 1697 his salary was cut by half until six months after the building should be complete, as an inducement to speed up the pace. After it was finished there was a row about the railings round the churchyard, in which Wren was overruled, as he was

over the far more serious question of the appointment of James Thornhill to paint the interior of the dome. In 1717 he objected in vain to the proposal to put a stone balustrade round the cathedral, making the savage comment 'ladies' think nothing well without an edging'. In 1719 he was dismissed from the Surveyorship: the 'job' was outrageous, organized by the man who succeeded him. Wren accepted it with dignity. He lived on until he was over ninety, dying in his sleep after dinner one day in 1723.

Further Reading
Kerry Downes, *The Architecture of Wren*, 1982.
Margaret Whinney, *Wren*, 1971.
Sir J. Summerson, *Christopher Wren*, 1953.

WRIGHT, JOSEPH (1734-97), painter, is known as 'Wright of Derby' because he was one of the few painters of this period to follow his career in the industrial Midlands. He was trained as a portrait painter in London under Thomas Hudson (who had earlier taken Reynolds as a pupil); made the customary journey to Italy; tried to establish himself as a fashionable portrait painter in Bath; exhibited for a time at the Royal Academy. But Derby his birthplace, and the delicious valleys of Dore and Derwent, always drew him back. It was here that he mainly lived and worked; here also that he made his friends – scientists, engineers, and industrialists, presiding over the infancy of the Industrial Revolution. Among his finest portraits are those of Sir Richard Arkwright of the spinning frame, Samuel Crompton of the spinning mule, Jedediah Strutt, John Whitehurst and Erasmus Darwin (who became Wright's own physician).

But he was more than a good portrait painter of the second rank. All his life he was fascinated by the illustrative effects of light shining in darkness – a domain explored by names as distinguished as Caravaggio and Honthorst (and of course Rembrandt) but yielding to Wright nonetheless a rich crop of moonlit, candlelit and firelit scenes. What is unique about him is that he harnessed this formula to his own mechanical bent, to create a series of tableaux which are the first pictorial records of the dawn of the Industrial Revolution. *A Philosopher lecturing on the Orrery* (Derby) and *An Experiment on a Bird in the Air Pump* (Tate Gallery) are only the two best known: paintings of scientific exercises, dramatized by the centrifugal glow illuminating the bodies of the watchers. As industry quickly took root in Derbyshire Wright's imagination was haunted by the incandescence of furnaces, by the blaze of foundries. The paintings which followed are more truly history paintings than most of what passed under that name.

He used the same principle of 'light shining in darkness' to make paintings of the eruption of Vesuvius (which he had witnessed), of a sombre landscape slashed by a rainbow, of dazzling sunsets, cottages on fire, of

The Earthstopper on the Banks of the Derwent (Derby) and *An Academy by Lamplight* (Mellon Collection), which are highly dramatic in themselves, and give a foretaste of Romanticism.

It is rare to find a provincial artist who has so many arrows to his bow. Often in a gallery one is startled into saying, 'Can that really be by Wright, and was he so various?'

Further Reading
Judy Egerton, *Catalogue of Wright of Derby Exhibition*, Tate Gallery Publications, 1990.
Benedict Nicholson, *Joseph Wright of Derby*, 2 vols, 1968.

WULFRIC (*d.c.*1004) was the founder of the monastery of Burton-on-Trent, the northernmost house established in the course of the English monastic revival of the tenth century. Wulfric was a nobleman of the northern region of Mercia, rich, devout and loyal to the house of Wessex – a significant combination of qualities. His loyalty is attested by his subscriptions to royal charters between *c.*970 and 1002. (Such subscriptions usually indicate that the witness in question was in attendance at the royal court and among the king's counsellors or witan, 'wise men'.) We have in addition the evidence of a grant of land to him by King Ethelred II in 995 made 'on account of the most faithful obedience with which he has served me'. Wulfric was a reliable king's man.

His loyalty was worth having, for he was a man of enormous landed wealth and therefore influence and power. We can gauge the extent of his territorial resources owing to the fortunate survival of his will, drawn up between 1002 and 1004. He disposed of about eighty separate landed estates scattered over a dozen counties ranging from Yorkshire in the north to Gloucestershire in the south and from the Wirral peninsula in Cheshire to the west across to the Lincolnshire Wolds in the east. The greatest concentration lay in Derbyshire, Staffordshire and Leicestershire. Some of these estates were of modest size, but others were huge, such for example as the estate of Conisbrough in Yorkshire. Conisbrough means 'king's fortress'. The magnificent twelfth-century castle keep which still stands there serves as a reminder of the strategic importance of the place, commanding the crossing of the river Don on the main route from south to north. It must have been an important strongpoint in the fighting between the West Saxon kings and the Danes of Northumbria in the second quarter of the tenth century. It is likely, though we cannot prove it, that Conisbrough had been granted to Wulfric's family by one of the Kings of Wessex. Some of Wulfric's estates were certainly acquired by royal grant. But the bulk of them seem to have been inherited from his father (whose name is unknown) and his mother Wulfrun.

Wulfric had no son. His only child, a daughter who may perhaps have been an invalid, received a few small bequests. His brother Aelfhelm, Ealdorman of southern Northumbria from *c.*993 to 1006, received much, and so did Aelfhelm's sons. So too did his sister's family. But in the main his generosity was directed at his monastic foundation at Burton-on-Trent, which received no less than forty-eight estates together with much livestock and movable goods. Burton was the most notable, though not the only, manifestation of Wulfric's piety. Its first abbot was a monk of Winchester. This is significant. Winchester was the home of the reformed monasticism established by Bishop Ethelwold and King Edgar. Wulfric's foundation was not simply an act of personal piety designed to secure the salvation of his soul: it was also a means by which West Saxon cultural, and indeed political, influence seeped into a region hitherto largely immune from it. In this context it is noteworthy that Wulfric made it clear in his will that he looked to the king and the Archbishop of Canterbury, as well as to his brother, to be the patrons of his monastery after his death.

Wulfric's career and connections, in so far as we can make them out from his will and other records, have something to tell us about the process by which West Saxon authority was made effective over the Danelaw and a unified kingdom of England emerged in the tenth century. These documents also reveal something of the sheer wealth of the aristocracy, and that not just in land: the amount of gold that Wulfric disposed of is remarkable. The Danes who systematically plundered England during Ethelred II's reign were correct in their assessment of it as an extremely rich country. Documents of a slightly later date have another lesson to teach. For reasons unknown, Wulfric's family fell foul of the king not long after his death. His brother Aelfhelm was killed in 1006 and his two sons blinded. Morcar, the husband of Wulfric's niece, was killed in 1015 and his brother with him. Much of the family property was confiscated by the king. The family monastery at Burton also suffered. Its endowments as recorded in Domesday Book (1086) were less than half those listed in Wulfric's will of eighty years earlier. The history of the family and of the monastery in the eleventh century illustrate the fragility of landed power at that period and the fluidity of late Anglo-Saxon society.

Further Reading
P. H. Sawyer has edited *The Charters of Burton Abbey*, 1979, with an important introduction on Wulfric and his family.

WULFRIC OF HASELBURY (*c.*1090-1155), a parish priest in Wiltshire turned anchorite, lived in a small cell attached to the parish church of Haselbury Plucknett (Wiltshire) for thirty years from 1125 until his death. In the 1180s Prior John of the Cistercian house at Ford wrote an admiring biography which allows sharp insights into the function of a holy man in twelfth-century society. The central feature was the most obvious. By virtue of being restricted to his cell or the adjacent parish church and his extreme religious exercises, such as praying all night in the church or even in a tub of cold water, Wulfric was dissociated from the world. He was thought of as neutral in the social tensions of an economically prosperous and expanding locality, but powerful through his personal relationship with God. In fact, Wulfric had an unrivalled network of local information and gossip and a keen self-interest which showed itself in his lethal habit of cursing his enemies – from mice to men – who tended to drop dead on demand. A combination of a one-man Citizen's Advice Bureau, consultant psychologist and local ombudsman, Wulfric established his credentials as social arbiter, prophet and healer by results, for which he was financially rewarded by grateful clients. He amassed wealth, which he used to distribute alms and endow monasteries. Although his food came from the Cluniac house of Montacute, Wulfric was particularly close to the Cistercians for whom he conducted recruitment interviews. It was this connection which probably explains John of Ford's enthusiasm. Wulfric's education and knowledge of French allowed him to upstage the parish priest in dealings with the aristocracy, and thus provided an important and seemingly dispassionate link between social groups. Having apparently opted out of the secular and ecclesiastical rat race, Wulfric acquired considerable power, certainly more than if he had remained a parish priest. With his wide contacts, energetic servant, full-time scribe and full treasure chest, Wulfric was running a profitable business under the guise – genuine or not – of simplicity and self-abnegation. His wealth included livestock, gold, silver and expensive textiles. His advice, especially medical, was often common sense, but it was authoritative and acceptable from a man uniquely placed to resolve local disputes and negotiate with external forces such as landlords, other villages and God. Wulfric's curses and manipulation of gossip reveal a nastily vindictive, neurotic personality for whom less restricted or contrived contact with the outside world might have proved disastrous. His proclaimed purpose was moral improvement of his fellow men. To this end he acted as a relief agency. An unusual entrepreneur in an age of opportunism, his career demonstrates that holiness can be materially significant but that holy men are not necessarily nice people.

Further Reading
H. Mayr-Harting, 'The Functions of a Twelfth-Century Recluse', *History* lx, 1975.

WULFSTAN (*d*.1023), Archbishop of York 1002-23, was the most distinguished intellectual figure of the late Anglo-Saxon church and a statesman of the first rank under Ethelred II and Canute. He was probably a native of the eastern Danelaw and received his early training as a monk, perhaps at Ely where he was later buried. He became Bishop of London in 996 and was promoted to York in 1002. Like several other tenth- and eleventh-century Archbishops of York he held the see of Worcester in plurality with York for part of his archiepiscopate (until 1016).

Wulfstan was a prolific writer. He and his friend Aelfric were the most commanding figures of the intellectual revival that grew out of the movement of ecclesiastical reform initiated by Dunstan, Ethelwold and Oswald. But while these three churchmen had been mainly concerned with the regular religious life of monastic communities, Wulfstan's concerns were wider. He addressed himself to the proper ordering of Christian society as a whole, secular as well as ecclesiastical, and in particular to the conduct and obligations of bishops and kings. This preoccupation was given intensity by the troubled times in which he lived. Wulfstan interpreted the Danish attacks on England during the reign of Ethelred as a punishment inflicted by God upon an erring people. The point was made vehemently in his best-known work, the *Sermo Lupi ad Anglos* ('The sermon of the Wolf to the English'), composed probably in 1014. (*Lupus*, 'the wolf', was a literary alias used by Wulfstan in a play upon the first syllable of his name.)

Understand well also that now for many years the devil has led astray this people too greatly and there has been little loyalty among men … If we are to experience any improvement we must then deserve better of God than we have previously done. For with great deserts have we merited the miseries which oppress us, and with great deserts must we obtain relief from God if henceforward things are to start to improve. For lo! we know full well that a great breach will require much repair, and a great fire no little water if the fire is to be quenched at all; and great is the necessity for every man that he keep henceforward God's laws eagerly.

Wulfstan's message was bleak. Like Gildas, whom he quoted, he indulged to the full what Gibbon once unforgettably described as 'the natural pessimism of sacred oratory'.

Wulfstan's works were for the most part written in the vernacular, rather than Latin, in order to reach as wide an audience as possible. His prose style, of which the above is a sample, was distinctive. By using stylistic criteria scholars have been able to identify a large number of works as his. They may be roughly classified into two groups, the legal and the homiletic. But these are not rigid categories, for the two genres overlap and interpenetrate. The legal writings possess to a striking degree the character of homilies, while the sermons are much concerned with the legal and customary obligations of Christian people. The two strands come together in Wulfstan's most ambitious work, the *Institutes of Polity, Civil and Ecclesiastical*, on which he was working towards the end of his life. It embodies his mature reflections on the duties of the different groups of people who together constitute the society of Christians. As such, the *Institutes of Polity* is heir to a long tradition of political and social thought which reaches ultimately back to St Paul. But its more immediate ancestry is to be sought in the writings of the Carolingian period, and it has analogies with the works of his continental contemporaries, especially the bishops of Germany and northern France.

Wulfstan was a man of wide intellectual cultivation who was steeped in the works of the leading thinkers of the Carolingian age, such as Alcuin and Bishop Theodulf of Orléans (*d*.821). That age had been remarkable for the definitive articulation by churchmen of a body of theory designed to guide secular rulers such as Charlemagne, Louis the Pious and Charles the Bald along what they called 'the royal road' to *sapientia*, 'wisdom'. Wisdom was regarded not as an abstract intellectual quality but as a disposition and a technique for the right guidance of a community in harmonious accord with God-given standards of public and private morality. For Wulfstan such guidance was a task at once urgent and sombre. The kings he served left much to be desired. Ethelred was an unjust as well as an ineffective ruler who needed correction. Canute was a barbarian conqueror who needed schooling in the basic disciplines of Christian rulership. Wulfstan's concerns find vivid expression in the legal texts which he drew up for these kings. He was responsible for at least three of the legislative enactments of Ethelred's later years, in 1008, 1009 and 1014. In 1018 he drafted legislation for Canute and in 1020-2 was responsible for drawing up Canute's definitive law-code, the most comprehensive piece of legislation issued by any ruler of the Anglo-Saxon period.

The clergy also needed guidance. Wulfstan composed tracts on the duties of bishops. Some of his sermons are pastoral letters to the clergy of his diocese, and he also commissioned two pastoral letters from Aelfric. Another sermon is devoted to the conduct of communities of canons, largely drawn from the Carolingian author Amalarius of Metz. He composed a tract on the examination of candidates for ordination to the priesthood. The so-called 'Northumbrian Priests' Law' is a set of directives to the clergy of the diocese of York.

Wulfstan was not just a theorist who told kings and clergy what they ought to be doing. He was an active diocesan bishop as well. He restored monastic life at Gloucester. He was vigilant in his care for the well-being of his churches: surveys of the archiepiscopal estates of York and annotations in his own hand in a register of Worcester documents testify to this. A collection of penitential letters shows him imposing the disciplinary procedures of the church upon erring members of his flock at both London and York. He enlarged the libraries at York and Worcester.

Wulfstan was not an original thinker. He looked mainly to the past, and his overriding concern was to proclaim and enforce the law of God as it had come down to him. It was a concern shared by other English bishops among his contemporaries, but because they have left no body of writings behind them their thoughts and aspirations are not accessible to us as Wulfstan's are. The readiness of the leading English clergy to shoulder the burden of proclaiming moral and legal norms during a time of trouble was a tribute to their training, their corporate spirit and their courage. It was also an important condition for the stability of English social and political institutions.

WULFSTAN, ST (*c*.1010-95; Bishop of Worcester 1062-95) was the last surviving pre-Conquest bishop who, while revering the traditions of Anglo-Saxon episcopal monasticism, actively supported the Norman régime. Unlike some contemporaries and modern historians, Wulfstan saw no contradiction in this. A patron and preserver of English learning, he sent a favoured pupil, Nicholas, to study under the rigorous Lanfranc at Canterbury. Wulfstan was son of one of the Bishop of Worcester's servants. After education at Evesham and Peterborough Abbeys, he returned to Worcester where he spent most of the rest of his career. Ordained when a member of the household of Bishop Brihtheah (1033-8), he soon abandoned his secular living at Hawkesbury and returned to Worcester to become a monk. In the cathedral priory he rose to become prior. When the pluralist Aldred of York was induced to give up the diocese of Worcester in 1062, Wulfstan was the unexpected choice as his successor. Perhaps his appointment was not so surprising: steeped in Worcester tradition, Wulfstan continued to fight for its privileges long after 1066. As a diocesan bishop, he was conscientious and efficient, seeing his role as extending beyond the focal points of monasteries. Capitalizing on the recent extension of the parochial system, Wulfstan perambulated his diocese, preaching and personally supervising baptisms and confessions. In this, he was in step with continental practices and his episcopate suggests that the well publicized discrepancy between England and the rest of the western church was somewhat exaggerated. With his colleague Aethelwig, Abbot of Evesham, he not only accepted the new dispensation after 1066, but convinced William I of his loyalty. Probably it was this as much as any apparent holiness or efficiency which enabled him to survive the purge of Anglo-Saxon bishops in 1070-2. A trusted associate of Lanfranc, he repaid the Anglo-Norman state with energetic service. In 1075 and 1088 he supported the king against rebels and rivals. His posthumous reputation depended heavily on his legacy at Worcester, which produced at least two considerable historians in the following century, Florence and John, and his biography written in English by Coleman, Wulfstan's chaplain. Coleman's *Life* was given wider circulation on being translated into Latin by William of Malmesbury for whom Wulfstan was an emblematic figure: a holy Englishman, noted for piety and simplicity, who recognized and embraced the virtues of the French conquerors without disclaiming his inheritance. Of Wulfstan's local status there was no doubt. A cult sprang up at Worcester soon after his death and he was canonized in 1203. In 1216, King John, *in extremis*, chose to be buried at Wulfstan's shrine in Worcester Cathedral. John may have wished to be identified with a national, English interest against the rebels who had sought assistance from Prince Louis of France. After Edward the Confessor, whose shrine at Westminster was inaccessible to royalists in 1216, Wulfstan represented the best known and most respected example of English sanctity. But Wulfstan was more. He was no solitary monk yearning for escape from his episcopal duties. While remaining true to his self-denying vocation, he cared not just for the laity but as keenly as any twelfth-century legist Wulfstan was determined to secure the rights and privileges of Worcester. In pursuit of this policy he commissioned a cartulary from Hemming, a Worcester monk, of documents crucial to the defence of Worcester property and estates. In this Wulfstan was a link between the fierce corporate ecclesiastical identities of the tenth and twelfth centuries.

Further Reading
E. Mason, *St Wulfstan of Worcester*, 1990.

WYATT, JAMES (1746-1813), architect, came of a family which spawned architects. He rose quickly to a position of unbounded regard, in which he was officially confirmed when he succeeded on Chambers's death (1796) to the Surveyor-Generalship.

He was an artist of astonishing versatility and a genius for borrowing other people's styles. Thus he confessed that 'when he came from Italy he found the public taste corrupted by the Adams, and he was obliged to comply with it'. But his first adventure was in winning the competition (in 1770) for rebuilding the Pantheon in Oxford Street, a temple of concerts and masquerades. Wyatt's Pantheon was burnt down in 1792, but it caused a furore on its erection. The great domed interior was an amalgam of Santa Sophia and the Roman Pantheon – though, as the upper part was entirely of wood, the technical achievement was hardly comparable. But Wyatt's name was made. He had drawn on the Adam brothers for some of the ornament of the Pantheon; the brothers had complained of his plagiarism. He proceeded to build Heaton and to complete Heveningham in a style which must have confirmed their worst fears – and they were right to regret his competition, for the things were brilliantly done and in perfect taste: somehow he seemed to make decoration *mean* more. He then built mausoleums based

on designs in Chambers's *Treatise*; and the severer classicism of Chambers is seen again in the interior of Wyatt's Dodington and at the Oriel College Library. But he seemed to have little to say entirely of his own in the tale of classical architecture.

Meanwhile, however, he had taken up Gothic. Perhaps his interest was aroused when he was employed to do some restoration at Salisbury Cathedral. His first essay proper was the house of Lee Priory, which, though it clearly harks back to Horace Walpole's Strawberry Hill, shows, as perhaps no other neo-Gothic building had shown, that the architect knew what Gothic was really about. Then came Fonthill, which, until its destruction, must have been the most sensational house in England. Built in the pattern of a huge cross, with an octagonal tower in the manner of Ely Cathedral which soared to three-quarters the height of the spire of Salisbury, it was the expression in stone of the fantastic nature of its founder, William Beckford. Beckford hurried on the work; Wyatt (of whom Beckford said 'if he can get near a big fire and have a bottle by him, he cares for nothing else') was characteristically indolent in supervising the supporting arches; and the great tower collapsed a score of years later. After Fonthill, the Gothic Ashridge, built for the Earl of Bridgewater in 1806-13, must, despite its huge central hall, have seemed a mild conception.

Other architects took fire at Wyatt's Gothic, but he was the acknowledged leader of the revival, who prepared the way for Barrie and Pugin. He perished in a carriage accident in 1813.

Further Reading
J. M. Robinson, *The Wyatts, An architectural dynasty*, 1979.

WYCLIF, MASTER JOHN (*c*.1330-84), the 'evangelical doctor', was a heretic and the inspiration of England's only late medieval heretical sect: Lollardy. Except that he was a Yorkshireman, almost nothing is known of his early life, and he first occurs in 1356 as a bachelor of arts and Fellow of Merton College. From there he moved to be Master of Balliol in 1360-1 and Warden of Canterbury College from 1365, whence he was ousted, when it became a monastic college in 1371. He entered royal service, but even moderate preferment obstinately refused to come. Thwarted ambition may have contributed to his increasing radicalism and ultimately heresy, although these were also logical extensions of his more orthodox beliefs. Although some of his doctrines were condemned, Wyclif himself never was – his friends were too powerful – and he was allowed to live out his last years in peace and to die naturally at his Leicestershire rectory, where he continued to write to the last and to reject the authority of the church establishment. He did not found the Lollard movement, which was the work of his pupils.

Wyclif has been called the 'Morning Star of the

Reformation', but those conclusions he shared with the sixteenth-century Protestant reformers were reached from quite a different direction. Where Luther condemned medieval scholasticism, Wyclif was a scholastic theologian – a product of the medieval academic system. He was a speculative philosopher before he was a theologian and his theology arose from his philosophy. Whereas Ockham had argued that only things that could be observed or experienced were real, Wyclif thought concepts – such as predestination – were just as real. From this emerged his belief that all being, all ideas and all matter were eternal. They came of God and were indestructible and unchanging. Hence he believed that all the Bible, even contradictions within it, were literally true. Hence too his doctrine of predestination: what God knew now must always have been. It was the pursuit of such theories to their logical extremes that made Wyclif's thought so dangerous.

Wyclif was always an extremist: an extremist philosopher before he became an extremist theologian. Utterly self-confident and convinced of his own rightness, he argued vigorously and at great length in treatises and disputations alike, sweeping aside the tentative replies of contemporaries, who were uncertain and intellectually less distinguished. Such qualities were valued by the Crown, which wanted him to frighten the clergy into paying more taxes for fear of losing their endowments. Wyclif's *On Civil Dominion* (*c*.1376) extended FitzRalph's argument that sinners could not exercise authority to argue that sinful clergy could be deprived of their lands. This theory was later applied by Lollards to tithes and to rents due to lay lords. About 1379, like Bradwardine, he claimed that God had settled in advance who was saved and who was damned. The Church of God, wrote Wyclif, thus consisted only of the saved, who were known only to God: the clergy and church establishment, even the pope, did not know if they were saved or 'the limb of the fiend'. They deserved respect only if saved and their functions, such as celebrating mass, were strictly useless as salvation had been settled beforehand. That was in theory: in practice Wyclif continued to write about the mass and died hearing it. His thought did not constitute a coherent system, but a series of interlocking and mutually contradictory ideas developed in the last decade of his life. All of it, however, threatened the church as it was and carried dangerous implications for state and society as well.

Further Reading

J. Robson, *John Wyclif and the Oxford Schools*, 1961.

K. B. McFarlane, *John Wycliffe and the Beginnings of English Nonconformity*, 1952.

WYDEVILLE, ANTHONY (*c*.1442-83), Lord Scales (1460) and Earl Rivers (1469), was a man of many talents and enthusiasms. Like his father he was a proficient soldier and distinguished jouster. He served repeatedly on land and sea from 1459 and fought at Towton and Barnet, where he was wounded. His most famous tournament against the Bastard of Burgundy reveals not just skill at arms (and perhaps also his gamesmanship), but a knowledge of the chivalric code and courtly love conventions worthy of his Burgundian relatives. His pilgrimages to Santiago, Rome and Bury St Edmunds were conventional enough, but his proposed crusade against the Saracens of Portugal had become unusual by the fifteenth century and his hair shirt and religious reading mark him as a man of highly individual piety. Devotional and moral works were not just read, they were translated from the French, and they were published. That his *Dictes and Sayings of the Philosophers* (1477) was the first book printed in England marks him out as receptive to new ideas. The *Moral Proverbs* (1478) and *Cordyale* (1479) followed. It was his unique combination of military, moral, and literary qualities as much as his birth and connections that made him the obvious choice to be governor of Edward, Prince of Wales, the future Edward V. His literary interests above all may explain Mancini's unusual enconium: Rivers was, he wrote, 'a kind, serious and just man, and one tested by every vicissitude of life; whatever his prosperity, he had injured nobody, though benefiting many'. Mancini's tribute captures a certain lack of drive, that prompted him to go on pilgrimage or crusade, when administrative and military tasks remained undone. It infuriated Edward IV and perhaps explains why he deprived his brother-in-law so quickly of such frontline political appointments as constable of England and captain of Calais, for which Rivers seems otherwise so well-fitted. It may explain why Rivers failed to perceive Gloucester as his enemy in 1483. It has certainly caused modern historians to label him a dilettante and to ask 'what is the point' of his career. Such attitudes make the underlying assumption that competitive self-aggrandizement is normal. Those satisfied with what they have and without incentives to seek more may have been more common than we suppose.

Rivers, after all, had risen rapidly and effortlessly in the world. Raised to the baronage by his own marriage in 1460, his sister's marriage brought him to the limelight and made him rapidly governor of the Isle of Wight, Lord of Jersey, keeper of Portchester, and in 1469 an earl. He had no children, took his time in remarrying, and divided his property between his two unmarried brothers. If conscious of kinship, they were not dynasts. But his correspondence reveals a good grasp of affairs and awareness of financial implications, legal title, and government procedures. Royal favour, dubious titles, technicalities, speculation on forfeitures, and force if necessary all had their place. He was an effective diplomat and administrator. As governor of the Prince of

Wales, he used the principality and duchy of Cornwall as a source of money, patronage and manpower, moulding them into a power-base for himself and his family much more important than his own estates. He fixed parliamentary elections and negotiated his way into control of the Tower. In short, Rivers was as adept and formidable a politician as any other, but politics was not an obsession pursued to the exclusion of everything else. Had it been, had he distrusted even friends and put naked self-interest first, he would not have placed himself at Gloucester's mercy in 1483 and might therefore have survived.

Further Reading
C. D. Ross, *Richard III*, 1981.
M. A. Hicks, 'The Changing Role of the Wydevilles in Yorkist Politics' in *Patronage, Pedigree and Power in Later Medieval England*, C. D. Ross, ed., 1979.
J. R. Lander, *Crown and Nobility 1450-1509*, 1976.
C. D. Ross, *Edward IV*, 1974.
E. W. Ives, 'Andrew Dymmock and the Papers of Antony, Earl Rivers, 1482-3', *Bulletin of the Institute of Historical Research* xli, 1968.

WYDEVILLE, ELIZABETH (*c.*1440-92), consort of Edward IV, was highly exceptional among English queens and hence highly controversial. She was the first English queen since King John's Isabella of Gloucester to be native born, she was of relatively humble rank, and she was already widowed with children when she married the king. Her marriage was clandestine, brought no diplomatic advantages, and was based purely on sex appeal. Unlike the foreign princesses who normally became queens, Elizabeth had both parents, two sons, five brothers, five sisters, and many cousins already living in England. King Edward felt obliged to provide generously for them all, mainly by marrying them into the peerage, and thus created a powerful political faction around the queen. All these circumstances were criticized at the time and contributed to those animosities within the government that contributed to the collapse of the Yorkist dynasty.

Elizabeth was the daughter of Jacquetta of Luxemberg, Dowager-Duchess of Bedford, by Richard Wydeville, created Lord Rivers in 1448. Whilst she was one of the European nobility on her mother's side, she belonged only to the county gentry through her father. Her first marriage was to Sir John Grey, heir to the Midlands barony of Ferrers of Groby. Following his death, her mother-in-law withheld her jointure, and it was to secure royal support that Elizabeth heavily bribed Lord Hastings for access to the king. Susceptible to her feminine wiles, Edward wanted to seduce her, but she virtuously declined any terms short of marriage. They married on May Day 1464. This romantic story of virtue rewarded rapidly attracted European renown. Three sons and eight daughters were its fruit.

Understandably the Wydevilles stressed their international connections, notably in the famous tournament with the Bastard of Burgundy in 1467. They encouraged Edward to ally with Burgundy. This and the Wydeville-Herbert stranglehold on patronage precipitated Warwick's coup of 1469 and the death of the queen's father and brother. It was in sanctuary in 1471 that the queen bore the future Edward V, around whom the family built their hopes during Edward IV's second reign. Her brother Earl Rivers dominated the prince's household, supervised his education, and made his resources into a power-base for the family in preparation for when the prince would reign. The great Exeter and Norfolk inheritances were secured for her sons Prince Richard, Thomas Grey, Marquis of Dorset, and Lord Richard Grey. A potential threat, the king's elder brother Clarence, was eliminated in 1478. At court the queen's son Dorset and brother Sir Edward Wydeville competed for influence with Lord Hastings. Once Edward IV was dead, the queen intervened decisively to take control at Westminster and to organize the immediate majority of Edward V. This device was designed to prevent a protectorate and to move to Wydeville rule based on their influence of the king. It frightened too many people, however, generated opposition and unpopularity, and thus facilitated the succession of Richard III. Rivers and Lord Richard Grey were executed, the princes disappeared, and Elizabeth and her daughters took sanctuary.

Only when sure that the princes were dead and that Richard III had won did Elizabeth agree to a pension and a guaranteed future for her now bastardized daughters. She had miscalculated again, for Henry Tudor became Henry VII and married her eldest daughter Elizabeth of York. Elizabeth Wydeville was not rehabilitated. Alleged dabbling in treason enabled her to be deprived of her dower, to considerable royal profit, in 1487. She was almost without property at her death in Bermondsey Abbey.

Further Reading
C. D. Ross, *Richard III*, 1981.
M. A. Hicks, 'The Changing Role of the Wydevilles in Yorkist Politics' in *Patronage, Pedigree and Power in Later Medieval England*, C. D. Ross, ed., 1979.
J. R. Lander, *Crown and Nobility 1450-1509*, 1976.
C. D. Ross, *Edward IV*, 1974.
C. Fahy, 'The Marriage of Edward IV and Elizabeth Woodville: A New Italian Source', *English Historical Review* lxxvi, 1961.
D. MacGibbon, *Elizabeth Woodville*, 1938.
G. Smith, *The Coronation of Elizabeth Woodville*, 1935.

WYDEVILLE, RICHARD, EARL RIVERS (*c.*1410-69) made his fortune from two remarkable marriages. The Wydevilles of Grafton Regis were a minor Northamptonshire family with minimal estates. Richard's father distinguished himself in France in the service of Henry V and the Regent Bedford. Richard's career appeared likely to follow a similar course. Knighted in 1426, he too served in France, and like his sons was a successful jouster. Young, athletic, chivalric and French-speaking, he was presumably also handsome and charming in 1436, when he married Bedford's widow Jacquetta of Luxemberg (d.1472). Herself a member of the European nobility, daughter of the Count of St Pol and descendant of Charlemagne, she was also Henry VI's aunt by marriage. As a mésalliance it ranks second only to Queen Katherine's marriage to Owen Tudor. With her connections and wealth, Richard's military and administrative career took off. He was created Lord Rivers in 1448, became a knight of the Garter and royal councillor in 1450, seneschal of Aquitaine and lieutenant of Calais. He married his three eldest children into the baronage. But he failed significantly to extend his estates to compensate for the loss of Jacquetta's dower on her death. Neither was he accepted as an equal by all the established nobility, such as Warwick the Kingmaker, who firmly reminded him in 1460 that:

his father was but a squire and brought up with King Henry V and since himself made by marriage and also made lord and that it was not his part to have language of lords, being of the king's blood.

Perhaps, therefore, Rivers was fortunate that Edward IV accepted his submission after his usurpation and restored him to his council. He was not sufficiently in favour to intercede with Edward for his widowed daughter Elizabeth. She, however, secretly married the king: a mésalliance if anything more shocking than that of Rivers himself and even more profitable. Edward was obliged to endow his queen, who patronized her kinsmen, but he was certainly not obliged to provide for the whole family, still less on the scale that he did. Rivers himself was created an earl and was appointed treasurer and constable of England, posts that carried the massive income of £1,586 and offered further scope for patronage. Several of the grants to him and his sons were bought back for them by the king. Five heirs to peerages were bought to marry Elizabeth's sisters and another for her son by promotion in rank, grants of land, and gifts of cash from King Edward. Apparently fathers stated their terms to Rivers, who extracted the concessions from the king, who clearly considered that no sister-in-law should be less than a countess. The family also used its favour to extort concessions from third parties. The greed of the Wydevilles and especially Rivers became a byword – 'The Rivers are so high that I could hardly escape through them,' it was joked – and they became extremely unpopular. Their rise was too great and too rapid.

More important, they made the king unpopular and were obvious targets as evil councillors in Warwick's manifesto in 1469. His rebellion demonstrated conclusively that the Wydevilles were merely courtiers, without the land or military resources to help the king through the crisis. Rivers was executed and the Duchess Jacquetta was charged with sorcery. High favour returned after 1471, but so too did the political penalties. Rivers's five sons died childless, three violently, and the marriages produced unity of interest for only a decade. The Wydevilles were a transient phenomenon in English politics.

Further Reading

M. A. Hicks, 'The Changing Role of the Wydevilles in Yorkist Politics' in *Patronage, Pedigree and Power in Later Medieval England*, ed. C. D. Ross, 1979.
J. R. Lander, *Crown and Nobility 1450-1509*, 1976.
C. D. Ross, *Edward IV*, 1974.

WYKEHAM, WILLIAM (*c*.1324-1404), Bishop of Winchester, was the greatest patron of education in late medieval England. Of humble birth, he was born at Wickham in Hampshire and educated at Winchester. He had entered royal service by 1347 and was employed by Edward III to supervise his building projects, especially at Windsor and Queenborough Castles, rising to be clerk of works. His buildings were close to King Edward's heart and brought Wykeham to his attention and favour. From clerk of works he rose in 1363 to be keeper of the privy seal, one of the three great officers of state, and in 1367 he became Chancellor of England. It was a 'pre-episcopal career unique among Edward's hierarchy' (Highfield). Inevitably the king rewarded him with ecclesiastical benefices, so he became the greatest pluralist of his day: in 1365 his total income from this source was £873 and in 1367 he became Bishop of Winchester. To secure this last promotion Edward III engaged in a remarkable trial of strength with a hostile pope. Wykeham lacked the university education increasingly expected of bishops, but he was nevertheless literate in English, French and Latin.

Unlike most 'civil-servant bishops', Wykeham did not rise through the great departments of state, but came to ministerial office as an outsider, promoted by the personal favour of an ailing king. In the 1360s, we are told, 'everything was done by him and without him nothing was done'. He was twice chancellor, in 1367-71 and in 1389-91; he sat frequently on commissions of reform in the 1380s; and he was an assiduous member of the royal council, attending on 270 days in the year 1378-9. He had been dismissed as chancellor in 1371 and he joined in the assault on the king's favourites in 1376. This excited the wrath of John of Gaunt and led to accusations against himself for mismanagement of the French war. Fortunately the other bishops united in Wykeham's support. During the political crises of 1386-8 he was a committed supporter of the Lords Appellant and was lucky to escape Richard II's revenge in 1397. It was a political career of exceptional length and importance. 'For long periods Wykeham belonged to a small circle of courtiers whose inside knowledge and influence allowed them to obtain many things by royal grant or licence and to buy cheap what they could get free.' Such opportunities were essential to finance his foundations and to raise his kin into the ranks of the gentry. Even forty years' tenure of the richest bishopric in England was scarcely sufficient for such lavish expenditure.

Wykeham's chantry in Winchester Cathedral and his two colleges secured prayers for his soul and testify to his piety. His colleges and Winchester Cathedral nave, the work of the architects Yevele and Wynford, mark him as a great builder and a great patron of the arts. Only an 'indefatigable man of business' could have financed them and legally secured the necessary endowments. His educational foundations were unique in their conception. Winchester College was the first English collegiate school. It offered free places for the exceptional number of seventy scholars. New College, Oxford was the first college to cater primarily for undergraduates and its seventy students made it the largest college at either university. Together they formed a dual foundation: pupils of Winchester College progressed naturally to New College. These features were imitated before 1500 only by Henry VI's colleges of Eton and King's, Cambridge, which were not on the scale of Wykeham's foundations. Wykeham was thus the outstanding late medieval benefactor of education.

Further Reading
P. Partner, 'William of Wykeham and the Historians', *Winchester College: Sixth-Century Essays*, ed. R. Custance, 1982.
N. Orme, *English Schools in the Middle Ages*, 1978.

WYNDHAM, SIR WILLIAM, 3rd BARONET (1687-1740), Tory politician, was born at Orchard Wyndham in Somerset. His family cherished a tradition of stubborn loyalty to the Crown and his father had opposed the election of William of Orange and Mary. Wyndham was educated at Eton and Christ Church and entered parliament in 1710 as member for Somerset. He became Master of the Queen's Buckhounds and, in 1712, Secretary at War. He was a member of the right-wing October Club and a founder of the Brothers Club of which Swift was a member. He introduced the Schism Bill which made reception of the sacrament the test of teaching in a school, a measure which, though it passed the House by a majority of 100, reflected an old-fashioned view of the relationship of church and state and was repealed soon after the accession of George I.

When Bolingbroke left the country in 1715, Wyndham stayed. At the start of the Jacobite risings his father-in-law, the Duke of Somerset, secured the king's promise that Wyndham would not be arrested; but the ministry did not think that he could be trusted. A thousand pounds was put on his head, he surrendered himself and was put in the Tower, and the Duke of Somerset resigned all his offices in a fury. When he was a boy, Wyndham had been warned by two different fortune-tellers to 'beware of the white horse'; as he passed beneath the gate of the Tower a painter was busy adding the arms of the Elector of Hanover to the royal crest: the White Horse. He spent eight months in the Tower before release, but he was never brought to trial. Gradually Wyndham came to accept the new dynasty, recognizing like Bolingbroke that loyalty to James Edward Stuart was futile. He was devoted to Bolingbroke, but to us Wyndham may appear the better man; less brilliant but more constant. His perspectives were broader than those of Shippen, leader of the Jacobite Tories. His group, supported by the admirable Lord Gower, a bye-word for integrity, made up in constancy what it lacked in numbers. Wyndham may have lacked the ruthlessness of a successful party leader but he was a fine speaker. He had a slight stammer, but a presence and a power of developing argument that compelled attention. Walpole respected him as a man who spoke a language above that of mere party interest. From his impartial place Speaker Onslow was well-qualified to judge him and in his opinion he was 'the most made for a great man of any that I have known in this age'. Pope wrote, admittedly with a Tory bias, of

> Wyndham, just to freedom and the throne,
> The master of our passions, and his own.

Thanks partly to Wyndham the Tory party kept their ideological character and their ability to act in concert. It cannot, however be said that the Tories were able to make much impact upon Walpole's administration. There was a divergence of policy between Wyndham and Shippen, and despite Bolingbroke's hard work and *The Craftsman*'s propaganda, no strong base for action in the alliance of Wyndham and Pulteney, 'the two consuls'. At heart Wyndham was more the country squire than the dedicated leader of party. Aided, perhaps, by his second marriage to the Whiggish Lady Blandford, he gravitated towards a philosophical central position. The incapacity of the Tories was revealed when they solemnly seceded from parliament in 1739. Yet Walpole feared him and was mightily relieved by his death. Wyndham was out hunting and was thrown when jumping a ditch. He was riding a white horse.

Further Reading
Linda Colley, *In Defiance of Oligarchy*, 1982.

WYNFORD, WILLIAM (*c.*1340-1405), master mason, was the great architect who remodelled the Norman nave of Winchester Cathedral into one of the masterpieces of English Perpendicular Gothic. He was apparently a west countryman, probably from the Somerset village of Winford near Bristol and possibly of gentle birth. He first appears in 1360 as one of the master masons working for the king at Windsor Castle and was promoted next year to joint direction of building there. He was appointed a royal esquire in 1369, feed at £10 a year from 1372, and worked not just at Windsor but also at Orwell and elsewhere. His superior at Windsor was the king's clerk of works, William Wykeham, then provost of Wells Cathedral and subsequently Bishop of Winchester. It was probably therefore Wykeham who secured his appointment as master mason at Wells Cathedral in 1365 and he certainly employed Wynford later on his own building operations. Among his other clients were Abingdon Abbey (1375-6), Southampton corporation in 1378-9, and Queen's College at Oxford (1400-2). Work at Wardour Castle, Yeovil Church, and Arundel College have also been attributed to him on stylistic grounds, for he is one of the first architects with a personal style quite distinct from those of his fellows. As one of the leaders of his profession, he should have made a good living, certainly married, and fathered a son, probably at Windsor, whom he educated at Wykeham's foundations of Winchester College and New College, Oxford. Perhaps William Wynford's wife was dead by 1399, when he was granted a corrody by Winchester Cathedral Priory entitling him to free meals for life – not much of a risk for a sexagenarian – but he lived off the premises and possessed a private oratory in 1402.

Wynford's two principal employers were Wells Cathedral Chapter and William Wykeham. It was also his buildings for them that have survived best. He was architect of Wells Cathedral from 1365 until death, a period which coincided with substantial remodelling of the existing church, for example by inserting tracery in the early English nave windows, and perhaps also the construction of the Chain Gate and Vicars Close. His most important project there, however, was undoubtedly the great south tower of the west front, which set a model for spireless square-topped towers imitated in the north-west tower of the cathedral and by the many splendid towers of Somerset's parish churches erected during the remainder of the Middle Ages. Some, indeed, may have been his work. For Wykeham he was probably the designer of New College, begun in 1379, certainly the architect at Winchester College, commenced in 1387, and worked also on his castle at Farnham in Surrey. He must have co-operated on some of these operations with his great contemporary Henry Yevele. Wynford liaised closely with Wykeham, dining with him thirteen times in July, August and September 1393, rather more frequently than Yevele, and was depicted in glass by his grateful employer at Winchester College. Wykeham had inherited the project of rebuilding Winchester Cathedral

nave from his predecessor Edington, who had completed little more than the west front at his death in 1366. When Wykeham resumed work on the nave in 1394 it was presumably Wynford, as master mason, who devised the more economical approach of recasting the original by enclosing the Norman pillars within Perpendicular mouldings rather than demolishing the existing structure and starting anew. This device was cheaper than total rebuilding and much quicker. Presumably it explains how operations could be completed within the lifetime of the now aged Wykeham. Despite cutting corners the result was also one of the great Perpendicular naves, comparable to, yet quite different from, Prior Chillenden's splendid nave at Canterbury Cathedral, which is normally attributed to Henry Yevele. Work on the Winchester nave was completed only shortly before the deaths of both patron and architect.

WYVILL, CHRISTOPHER (1740-1822) was an ordained country gentleman of strong personality and original views who led and organized radical opinion in his county, created a short-lived but important instrument of political pressure and furthered the movement for parliamentary reform.

He came of an old Yorkshire family; after the death of his baronet cousin and brother-in-law in 1774 he came into the family estate of Constable Burton and a rent roll of £4,000 a year. From Queens' College, Cambridge, Wyvill had entered a family living, Black Otley in Essex, which he kept after he went to reside in Yorkshire; he was interested in ecclesiastical affairs but he handed over work and emoluments to a curate. As a clergyman he had qualms over the Thirty-Nine Articles and leaning towards Unitarianism. As a landowner he was not content to grumble about the corruption of court and government but used his influence to make the 'county interest' mean something more than a few individual votes against the ministry. In 1779 there was discontent about Lord North's conduct of affairs. High taxation brought only stalemate in America but public funds and places served, it seemed, to keep Lord North in power with a tame majority and a partisan king: Members of Parliament were for sale. One solution, urged by Dr Jebb, was to extend the popular side of the old constitution, notably the Westminster and Middlesex seats, and Wyvill was later to demand more representation for 'those great unrepresented towns and districts of the metropolis'. At first, however, he sought to exploit the grievances of the freeholders and to increase the number of county seats so as to balance the minions of the boroughs. In this he was supported by Sir George Savile, a Yorkshire county member. Wyvill was content at first to ride with the county magnates. The Yorkshire Association, mooted in his circular of November 1779, aired at a meeting of Yorkshire freeholders in December and formed in the following spring, had the support of the Rockingham faction.

There was an impressive show of unanimity from the largest county. Grievances and solutions were alike plainly expressed: taxes were too high, executive power too large; the number of independent men of standing in the House of Commons should be increased. The Yorkshire Association, and others like it, should be instruments of reform 'by legal and constitutional means'. At the next general election a concerted opposition to opponents of reform would secure a House of Commons well disposed to reform. The movement grew rapidly. Petitions were sent in, Committees of Action formed in a number of counties; soon an informal central committee was sitting in London. In all this Wyvill led, organized and inspired. In his private character and public behaviour he epitomized the qualities of the independent politician, in whom, he believed, lay the salvation of the country: single-minded and energetic, cautious in tactics but assured and direct in all his dealings. Later in life he avowed that he only took part in politics from 'a detestation of corruption, that execrable principle of government; from indignation at direct and open invasion of our rights; and from an honest zeal to defend public liberty'.

The words make stirring reading in our century. They were also, however, the stock phrases of those politicians who had less altruistic motives for talking the language of reform. Though Wyvill and Granville Sharp wished their general assembly to be free from party ties and even individual Members of Parliament, the latter were admitted; furthermore only twelve counties and four cities were represented. The movement never became truly national; in London, its authority was compromised by the parallel activities of the Westminster Committee, closely linked to parliament through the

patronage of Fox. Inevitably there was a discrepancy of aims: Wyvill was not a doctrinaire radical like Jebb, nor a demagogue like Charles James Fox. His ideas and the lobbying power of his followers lent power to the elbow of Rockingham and Burke and their projects of Oeconomical Reform; they were not interested, however, in franchise reform. Meanwhile the extremism of men like Cartwright, who demanded 'equal, annual and universal representation', alarmed moderates. Wyvill toiled strenuously with petitions, plans and debates in committees but he found the going slow. In 1782-3, after the minor revolution of the Oeconomical Reform measures, the movement reached a climax. He found an intelligent champion in William Pitt, through their mutual friend Lord Mahon. Wyvill's object was to produce a nation-wide demonstration in favour of reform in the constituencies. Despite Yorkshire's firm lead, this never gathered enough force to convince Pitt that he must go beyond modest proposals (Wyvill wanted to abolish fifty boroughs). Neither in opposition nor in office did Pitt manage to secure a majority: there was indifference in the country; in parliament, where two-thirds voted against his second Reform Bill, a stone wall.

Wyvill was active again when the French Revolution aroused popular feeling. He found Jacobinism 'wild work' and he deplored the emergence of 'a lawless and furious rabble' but he did not lose faith in reform. In 1811 he joined in a Reform Society which contained such varied names as Burdett, Cobbett and Henry Hunt. He died ten years before the Reform Bill which embodied his ideals. He had done more than any man to educate and prepare public opinion for constitutional reform.

Further Reading
I. R. Christie, *Wilkes, Wyvill and Reform*, 1961.

Y

YEVELE, HENRY (*c*.1320-1400), master mason of London, has been described as perhaps 'the greatest English architect'. He came from Derbyshire, perhaps from Uttoxeter or nearby Yeaveley, and may have already qualified as a master mason before coming to London, where he became a freeman in 1353 and was an acknowledged leader of his craft in 1355-6. By 1357 he was working for St Albans Abbey and probably also at Kennington for the Black Prince. By 1360 he was in royal service and directing works both at the palace of Westminster and the Tower of London. Yevele was somewhat older than his great contemporary Wynford and earlier in royal service, which may explain why he was more extensively employed by the Crown. However that may be, he worked at several other royal places – Eltham, Sheen, Baynard's Castle in London – and undertook building at half a dozen royal castles. He also tackled tombs with effigies, certainly contracting for those of Richard II, his consort, and Cardinal Langham in Westminster Abbey. He may also have made those of Edward III there and the Black Prince in Canterbury Cathedral. He had an extensive practice with many other clients. Among the more eminent were the city of London, for whom he maintained old London bridge for thirty years from 1365; John of Gaunt, Duke of Lancaster, for whom he worked on the Savoy and the tomb of the Duchess Blanche in 1374-5 and on Hertford Castle somewhat later; William Wykeham, Bishop of Winchester, for whom he worked on New College, Oxford with William Wynford and perhaps on other projects in Winchester itself; Lord Cobham, for whom he designed Cooling Castle in Kent (1380-2) and worked on the parish church of St Dunstans-in-the-East in London; and Westminster Abbey and the chapter of St Paul's Cathedral. He probably undertook many other private commissions in London's 100 medieval churches, which have now largely disappeared. Yet other projects have been attributed to him on the basis of his distinctive style, which, however, was quickly imitated by others. The most important of these is the nave of Canterbury Cathedral, one of the masterpieces of English Perpendicular, which was built at the same time as Wynford's nave at Winchester Cathedral and yet is stylistically quite different.

Yevele became a Londoner, marrying into a family of London tradesmen and playing a full part in city life. His decision to practise from the capital may explain why he was apparently more extensively employed than Wynford and certainly accounts for his many London commissions. Some at least of his monuments were prepared in London, packed, and despatched for reassembly locally. He kept a large stock of materials, comprising stone, alabaster, tiles, lead, and latten, some of which were supplied to other London workshops. He has been taken as the model of a skilled London craftsman, albeit an outstandingly able and successful one. He should have made a good living, for he was a royal esquire from 1369, feed by the city from 1365, and doubtless by other clients. Certainly he dealt extensively in city property; on his death he possessed several tenements and quays in the parish of St Magnus. His own house there contained a private chapel, in which he was licensed to hold divine service in 1400, and he could afford to establish a chantry of two priests in St Magnus's church, where he belonged to the fraternity of Salve Regina. He also held lands in Southwark. Like his friend Wynford, he remained in harness until the end.

Further Reading

E. M. Veale, 'Craftsmen and the Economy of London in the Fourteenth Century', *Studies in London History presented to Philip Edmund Jones*, ed. A. E. J. Hollaender and W. Kellaway, 1969.

J. H. Harvey, *Henry Yevele*, 2nd edn, 1946.

YORK, HENRY BENEDICT (1725-1807), cardinal, last of the Stuarts, 'Henry IX, King of Great Britain' as the few remaining devotees of the family preferred to call him, was the younger son of James Edward Stuart and of Maria-Clementina Sobieski. Since his mother retired to a convent and his father was of a melancholy disposition, his boyhood lacked excitement. He was devoted to his more active elder brother Charles Edward, but was not let in to the secret of the '45 and took no part in that adventure. Devout and gentle as his father, he became ordained and was provided with three Italian bishoprics and made cardinal: nothing could be imagined better calculated to kill any hope of a legitimist restoration to the British throne. By the time 'James III' died, the Papacy had concluded that the Stuarts had no political future and refused to recognize Charles Edward as king. When Charles Edward died, however, in 1788, Henry styled himself king, in the words of his medal, 'Not by the will of men, but by the Grace of God': last sad formula of the Stuarts. When the French invaded Italy his palace at Frascati was sacked. George III, hearing of his plight, sent him, as one gentleman to another, a pension to ensure his comfort. Jacobitism was dead, laid into the earth with fitting gesture of chivalry and generosity. Henry bequeathed his remaining Crown jewels to the Prince of Wales.

YORKE, PHILIP, EARL OF HARDWICKE (1690-1764)

was a great Lord Chancellor at a time when the law and its high officers enjoyed more esteem and power than at any other time. The church and its affairs had retreated from their dominant position in politics, the bishops were appointed on political grounds and behaved, in their political capacity, as puppets; even the High Church Dr Johnson declared that he would rather be a judge than a bishop. The mystique of the law replaced that of the church, a natural consequence of 1688 which had been, in spirit and terminology, a lawyers' revolution; the work largely of the great Somers. Its acts enshrined the notions to be found in the pages of Locke, for whom the chief end of civil society was the preservation of property and of the rights of the individual. Law was the guardian of the people, but 'the people' narrowly conceived, as by Sidney Smith in 1830, as 'the great mass of those who have opinions worth hearing, and property worth defending'. In practice the law was the expression of a minority, disinterestedly firm in defence of the constitution but conservative in its view of society. There were 160 felonies punishable by death by the end of George II's reign and no significant movement for reform of the criminal law. At the same time, the subject enjoyed a measure of protection under the law which was unique in Europe. At the apex of this brutal but majestic system was the Lord Chancellor. For nineteen years this supreme office was occupied by Lord Hardwicke.

Like many great lawyers of the time, his origins were humble; he was the son of a country attorney, but a brilliant career at Westminster and the patronage of Lord Macclesfield provided him with an opening in parliament: he sat for the Pelhams's borough of Seaford. When he was asked by his prospective father-in-law what property he possessed, he had, he replied, a perch of ground in Westminster Hall. He was loyal to his patrons and richly rewarded for it. In 1720, aged only thirty, he became Solicitor-General, three years later Attorney-General. In this capacity he prosecuted for the Crown, amongst others, the notorious criminals Jonathan Wild and Jack Sheppard. In 1734 he became Lord Chief Justice and Baron Hardwicke. In 1737 he succeeded Talbot on the Woolsack. From 1742 to 1756 he played an important political role, as the partner of the Pelhams. The best head among the ministers, he provided a conciliatory influence amidst the intrigues of the various groups; he was efficient and cool, notably in the flutter of the '45. His handsome presence and unfailing lucidity dominated the House of Lords. On occasions he could be devastating. When Henry Fox tried to ingratiate himself after opposing Hardwicke's Marriage Bill and describing its author as a giant spider, he replied: 'I despise the scurrility and reject the adulation.' In 1754 he was entrusted with the reconstruction of the Cabinet and rewarded with an earldom. He had already acquired a fortune to hand on to his sons. He did not underrate his own abilities: his pomposity is understandable but not endearing. He was an influential if cautious politician, but it was as a lawyer that his work was of lasting significance.

He had the advantage of being as familiar with the common law as with equity and he completed the work of previous chancellors in harmonizing the two systems. *Aequitas sequitur legem*, as he said in one of his judgements: equity existed to supplement and not to replace the common law. Over 100 years were to pass before the equity and common law jurisdictions came to be administered in the same courts, but his work prepared the way for this partial fusion. As Holdsworth said of him: 'Hardwicke laid the foundations and erected a large part of the edifice of modern equity.' He saw in rules the safeguard of liberty and Chancery's intricate rules were stabilized under him. There was danger in this as we are reminded by the later condition of Chancery that Dickens exposed. It was to Hardwicke's credit, however, that at a time when politics were venal, the law courts were respected for impartiality. The importance of this lay partly in the fact that England was changing rapidly in his time, while the union with Scotland created new problems because of the differences between the two legal systems. In 1708, the House of Lords held that its jurisdiction extended to appeals from the Scottish courts, though no comparable appellate jurisdiction had been known in Scotland before. In 1719 the same was extended by statute to Ireland. He had wide powers and he used them to establish a general code of precedents by which his successors might be guided. In Scotland he had specially to legislate for the clans after the rising of '45: aiming at a unified government in Scotland, he curbed the rights of the clans, abolished their private jurisdiction and proscribed their peculiar dress.

At home he drew upon his large experience of runaway

marriage cases to draw up the Marriage Act of 1753, which is still the basis of modern marriage law: provisions were made for the consent of guardians in the case of minors, and for the calling of banns, and licences were required for any departure from the general rule. Hardwicke was attacked for promoting this measure by conservative or romantic-minded politicians, like Charles Townshend, on the grounds that it was indelicate, or an infringement upon personal liberty. Normally he aimed at clarification rather than radical alteration of laws: 'Certainty is the mother of repose, and therefore the law aims at certainty' was his favourite maxim. He believed that all important legislation should be initiated in the House of Lords, and it was on this ground, as much as on the poor drafting of the measure, that he opposed Pitt's urgently required Militia Act of 1756. He clashed with Pitt too over the interpretation of habeas corpus. Pitt framed a bill to provide for the gap in the Act of 1679 which had become evident when a man was seized by the press-gang, applied for a writ of habeas corpus and been refused on the grounds that it only applied to criminal cases. Hardwicke secured the rejection of the bill, on the grounds that it took away the judges' discretionary power. Pitt was precipitate and he should have consulted legal advisers before rushing into the technical field of writs, but Hardwicke was taking a narrow view: an Act extending the operation of the writ was passed later, in 1816.

Hardwicke was convinced that the law must be adamant in an age of licence; characteristically he disliked the freedom of the press, and it was on his advice that his son, then Attorney-General, advised Grenville's ministry in its proceedings against Wilkes. He was a conservative, who believed that England had 'by far the best body of laws that human wisdom can claim', but he was no blind reactionary. In a century when the continental monarchies were all exploiting the principle that the will of the monarch is the supreme law of the state, England owed much to Hardwicke's conception of the supremacy of law.

Hardwicke was a handsome man, a good story-teller, impressive in society, but thought to be mean. The counterpane of his bed, people said, was made by sewing together the bags in which the Great Seal was delivered to him. He set out to create a great family: it was after his death that his son, thrust too precipitately into the office of Lord Chancellor, committed suicide.

Further Reading
P. C. Yorke, *The Life of Lord Chancellor Hardwicke*, 3 vols, 1913.

YOUNG, ARTHUR (1741-1820) was the most prolific of the eighteenth-century writers about agriculture. If not the soundest upon technical questions (where most would prefer William Marshall), he is certainly the most

colourful, while as an historical source he is in a class of his own. For students of the French Revolution, for instance, his survey of the French countryside (*Travels in France and Italy, 1787-90*) provides invaluable evidence. In the course of his varied career he was pamphleteer and author, parliamentary reporter, farmer, estate steward and secretary to the Board of Agriculture. An unkind critic labelled him as the failed farmer who preached what he had found difficulty in practising. But his failures came when he was young. When later he inherited the family property in Suffolk he managed it successfully – at least in the intervals between periods of travel and government business.

He was the son of Arthur Young, squire and rector of Bradfield in Suffolk. His mother was Anna Coussmaker. While still at school at Lavenham he began to write a history of England. Apprenticed to a counting house at King's Lynn he found time to write political pamphlets and four novels. In 1759 his father died, heavily indebted; Young gave up the idea of a business career and went to London, where he started a monthly magazine, *The Universal Museum*, whose reception was as depressing as its title. Young retired to the country and began working a small farm on the Bradfield estate, now his mother's. In 1765 he married Martha Allen. She bore him several children but he complained of her temper. Justifiably or not he was a neglectful husband. On the odd, cold memorial tablet he set up after her death in 1815 he simply records that she was 'the great granddaughter of John Allen esq., of Lyng house in the county of Norfolk, the first person, according to the Comte de Boulainvilliers, who there used marl'.

In 1767 Young wrote the *Farmer's Letters to the People*, a premature effort as he later recognized. At the same time he was experiencing the practical difficulties of farming. He took 'a very fine farm' of 300 acres in Essex, experimented, lost money, and paid £100 to a farmer to take it over. Setting out to view other farms he collected observations for *A Six Weeks Tour through the Southern Counties of England and Wales*. For nine years he farmed 100 acres at North Mimms in Hertfordshire. 'A hungry, vitriolic gravel,' he said, 'I occupied for nine years the jaw of a wolf.' From this infertile base however he sallied out on further tours (in 1770 appeared his northern *Tour*, in 1771, the eastern). He wrote pamphlets as diverse as *The State of the French Nation* and *The Management of Hogs*. 'No cart horse,' he declared, 'ever laboured as I did at this period [1770], spending like an idiot, always in debt, in spite of what I earned with the sweat of my brow.' In 1772 he thought of emigrating – but instead he undertook the reporting of parliamentary debates for the *Morning Post*, walking home seventeen miles to North Mimms every Saturday and back on Monday morning. In 1774 came *Political Arithmetic*, an immediate success, and election to the Royal Society.

In 1776 he went to Ireland; a servant stole his trunk on the way back and his journal and soil specimens were lost. He was for a time (1777-9) an agent in County Cork for Lord Kingsborough's estates (where Mary Wollstonecroft was soon to record, from her viewpoint as governess to the landlord's children, the degraded poverty of the people). He returned to take another farm. In 1784 he began his *Annals of Agriculture*, a monthly publication which was to last till 1809 and provide a forum for progressive views and news of experiments. Among his contributors were George III (under the name of his shepherd Ralph Robinson), Bentham and Coke of Holkham. From Bradfield, which he had inherited in 1785 on his mother's death, he visited Bakewell, the great breeder of Leicestershire. He had already been influential in securing the abolition of the bounty on land carriage of corn to Dublin. Now Pitt consulted Young on further measures. In 1787 he accompanied the comte de la Rochefoucauld on a journey across France; he had been introduced by the count's tutor who had 'given some attention to agriculture' and sought out the now famous writer. Out of this journey and those which followed came the celebrated *Travels*. After travelling for 100 miles on his second journey his mare fell blind; but he finished his journey and brought her safely back to Bradfield – with, amongst other things, some chicory seed which he sowed successfully. In 1789 he took a post-chaise to bring back interesting soils and manufactures and extended his travels to Italy. He was an eye witness at Paris and Versailles of some of the first scenes of the Revolution. An illness, in 1790, brought him near to death. With recovery came sober reflection and a somewhat introverted and depressing account of his past life in the *Annals*. Like Cobbett, another prodigious worker, Young took himself very seriously.

In 1793 Pitt made him secretary of the new Board of Agriculture. He was soon at loggerheads with the President, Sinclair, criticizing him for an amateurish approach and inept appointments. Of the important series of reports on counties Young wrote the *General View of the Agriculture of the County of Suffolk*; his son Arthur did the same for Sussex. He continued to be active in pamphlet writing. Pitt was pleased by their patriotic tone (Young proposed a 'horse militia corps' as early as 1789; in 1793 he enrolled in the yeomanry at Bury) but rejected his plan for 'regulation by parliament of the price of labour'.

In 1791 Young's youngest daughter, Martha Ann, or 'Bobbin' as he called her, died, aged fourteen. He seems to have been quite broken by the tragedy. Something of his sadness can be imagined when we read their letters – for he wrote to her the most detailed accounts of his French travels when she was only six! – and from his instructions for her burial, 'in my pew, fixing the coffin so that when I kneel it will be between her head and her

dear heart'. The pessimistic strains, the over-wrought moods now grew into a settled despondency. For the last years of his life he was blind. In 1811 he was operated on for cataract. Wilberforce visited him and spoke so movingly of the loss sustained to agriculture by the death of the Duke of Grafton that Young wept; the last chance of saving his eyesight was therefore lost.

With his enthusiasm for improvements of all kinds, his somewhat haphazard method of working and his reliance upon personal contacts with farmers and landowners rather than upon analytical or statistical approach, Young lays himself open to the charge of inconsistency. He took advanced positions upon such topics as leases, tithes and open fields which he was later forced to modify. In particular he came to revise his early opinion concerning enclosures, though it was of the methods rather than the principle that he disapproved. He was dismayed by the actual deterioration of labourers' conditions in some enclosed villages. He was confronted of course with a trend outside the control of legislators – a soaring population. But he was sensibly constructive in his proposals. He believed that the cheapest way of providing for the poor would be to put labouring families on the areas of waste that still remained uncultivated on the fringe of enclosed villages, with a cottage and three acres apiece which they should be allowed to keep for as long as they did not apply for parish relief. Property, he held, gave the poor the incentive to work hard, live frugally and save, not only their own pride, but the parish rates as well. In some counties there was no wasteland. That fact inspired a justly famous passage: 'Go to an alehouse kitchen of an old-enclosed country, and there you will see the origin of poverty and the poor rates. For whom are they to be sober? For whom are they to save? For the parish? If I am diligent shall I have leave to build a cottage? If I am sober, shall I have land to buy a cow? If I am frugal, shall I have half an acre of potatoes? You offer no motives, you have nothing but a parish officer and a workhouse. Bring me another pot.' Young did not of course lose his faith in the efficacy of enclosures. The following passage from his *General View of Oxfordshire* (1809) is eloquent with the scorn of the improver for the 'goths and vandals of farmers' who would not change their ways: 'liberal communication, the result of enlarged ideas', such as he might expect from the modern farmer, 'was contrasted with a dark ignorance under the covert of wise suspicion; a sullen reserve lest landlords should be rendered too knowing ... The old openfield school must die off before new ideas can become generally rooted.'

Further Reading

J. D. Chambers and G. E. Mingay, *The Agricultural Revolution 1750-1880*, 1966.
Matilda Betham-Edwards, ed., *The Autobiography of Arthur Young*, 1898.

Z

ZOFFANY, JOHANN (1733-1810), a German-born painter, studied in Italy and came to England in the 1750s when Arthur Devis was painting conversation pieces so still as to seem timeless. The conversation piece was an eighteenth-century confection, hit upon first by Hogarth and designed to relieve family groups of the apparatus of shepherds' crooks, clouds, harps and fillets with which they had been encumbered, and to depict them as they were in their life of every day. This was Zoffany's métier: whether he paints *Lord Willoughby de Broke and his Family*, grouped on a rich carpet round the coffee urn while the fire crackles happily in the background, or *The Garricks with Dr Johnson taking tea on the lawn in front of their villa at Twickenham*, he is perfectly at home among the respectable bourgeois comforts which were the lot of so many families of the time – of which indeed his scrupulously faithful renderings must be borne in mind when Hogarth conducts us down Gin Lane or Gillray introduces us to the Union Club.

Elsewhere he paints his friend Garrick in theatrical roles, and depicts the equally theatrical milieu of *The Tribune at the Uffizi* or the Academy schools. He was in fact a founder-member of the Academy, at the king's direction.

INDEX

ACKNOWLEDGEMENTS

The authors of the individual volumes in the *Who's Who in British History* series:

Who's Who in Roman Britain and Anglo-Saxon England
Richard Fletcher

Who's Who in Early Medieval England
Christopher Tyerman

Who's Who in Late Medieval England
Michael Hicks

Who's Who in Tudor England
C. R. N. Routh revised Peter Holmes

Who's Who in Stuart Britain
Peter Hill

Who's Who in Early Hanoverian Britain
Geoffrey Treasure

Who's Who in Late Hanoverian Britain
Geoffrey Treasure

Who's Who in Victorian Britain
Roger Ellis

Series Editor
Geoffrey Treasure